EX LIBRIS

Henry 'Chips' Channon

The Diaries: 1938–43

Edited by
Simon Heffer

HUTCHINSON
LONDON

1 3 5 7 9 10 8 6 4 2

Hutchinson
20 Vauxhall Bridge Road
London SW1V 2SA

Hutchinson is part of the Penguin Random House group of companies
whose addresses can be found at global.penguinrandomhouse.com.

Penguin
Random House
UK

First published by Hutchinson in 2021

*This book contains some language that is outdated and offensive. Such language does not
reflect our beliefs or values either as individuals or as a company, but at Penguin Random House
we believe it is important to maintain these books as an accurate historical record. In most cases,
our readers want to read the original text and we trust them to recognise historical and
literary context.*

www.penguin.co.uk

A CIP catalogue record for this book is available from the British Library.

ISBN 9781786331823

Typeset in 11/13.5 pt Minion MM Roman
by Integra Software Services Pvt. Ltd, Pondicherry

Printed and bound in Latvia by Livonia Print Ltd.

The authorised representative in the EEA is Penguin Random House Ireland,
Morrison Chambers, 32 Nassau Street, Dublin D02 YH68.

Penguin Random House is committed to a sustainable future for
our business, our readers and our planet. This book is made from
Forest Stewardship Council® certified paper.

Contents

Foreword to Volume 2

We are very pleased now to be able to publish this second volume of our grandfather's diaries and with this volume we have again had help and advice from Robin Howard, our co-trustee; Georgina Capel, our literary agent; Nigel Wilcockson, associate publisher at our publishers, Penguin Random House; and Hugo Vickers. However, as with the first volume, our greatest debt of gratitude goes to Professor Simon Heffer, who has continued to bring to the task of editing this volume the same outstanding skills, knowledge, dedication and great enthusiasm he brought to editing the first volume.

We would also like to acknowledge again the contribution made by Helen Howard in preparing copies of the manuscripts and then helping to check their transcription, and to offer our thanks to the transcribers who worked on this volume: Consuela Barker, Fergus Burnand, Alex Colville, Domenica Dunne, Ned Dunne and Luke Regan.

We have asked the publishers to reproduce after this foreword our foreword to Volume 1, so that readers of this second volume can fully understand the background to the publication of what will ultimately be a three-volume version of our grandfather's diaries. We would also like to bring to readers' attention the two important points we made in the last paragraph which equally apply to this volume.

Georgia Fanshawe and Henry Channon

General Foreword

Our grandfather's diaries have been part of our lives since we have been old enough to be aware of them. During the lifetime of our father, Paul Channon, Lord Kelvedon, we knew he was approached a number of times over the years about publishing them in full. However, we were also aware of the dilemma he faced, given the initial negative reaction to the heavily abridged edition that was published in 1967, and the fact that many people mentioned in the diaries – members of the wider family, friends and acquaintances – were still alive.

The last time our father gave serious consideration to publishing a full version was in 2004, when he asked Kenneth Rose to review those diaries that had not been represented in the published abridgement (1918 and 1923–28, and also the diaries for the years 1954 and 1958 which had turned up in a car boot sale a few years earlier). He also discussed the matter, and Kenneth's review, with us and with Robin Howard, who is our co-trustee for the diaries, and who has acted as an adviser to the Guinness family for many years. He told Robin that he was still in two minds about what to do, but urged that if he had not arranged publication of the full diaries during his lifetime, Robin should encourage us to do so. The fact that a clause in our grandfather's will expressed the hope that the full diaries would be published sixty years after his death – in other words, in 2018 – added to the expectation that a full version would eventually see the light of day.

We are therefore very pleased that we have been able to realise our grandfather's and our father's ambition. This would not have been possible, however, without the considerable help and advice of Robin, who, after we had held some abortive discussions with another editor in 2012, offered in late 2016 to take on the task of arranging the full transcription of the diaries. He has gone on to help us agree the appointment of our literary agent, editor and publisher.

The other person we are greatly indebted to is Professor Simon Heffer, who has brought to the task of editing the diaries his outstanding skills and knowledge, as well as great enthusiasm and application. It has been an enormous pleasure working with him.

We would also like to acknowledge the help we have received from Dr Oliver Cox and David Howell of Oxford University, who gave us advice on the handling of the manuscript diaries and other archive material; Alan Williams, who gave us advice on various legal agreements; our literary agent, Georgina Capel; Nigel Wilcockson, publishing director at our publishers, Penguin Random House; and Hugo Vickers, who kindly agreed to read the text of Volume 1 and who made some very helpful comments. In addition, we would like to acknowledge the contribution made by Helen Howard, who has assisted Robin by preparing copies of the manuscript diaries for use by the transcribers and Simon and then checking and correcting the transcriptions, and we offer our thanks to the transcribers who worked on Volume 1: Ralph Lopes, Isabella Darby, Haseeb Iqbal and Gabriella Dawson.

Finally, we would like to mention two important points about this new edition. Firstly, given the historical value of the diaries, we felt it vital that Simon should have full editorial control over what to include. Secondly, as Simon discusses more fully in his Introduction, we wish to stress that because the diaries inevitably reflect the attitudes of the time they were written, they include some language and opinions that are now rightly considered to be outdated and offensive. They also contain sometimes critical or disparaging comments and disclosures about the parents and relatives of members of our wider family and friends. We want to make it clear that such material has been retained solely to ensure the editorial integrity of the diaries, and that its inclusion does not mean that we in any way condone it, or wish to cause embarrassment or offence.

Georgia Fanshawe and Henry Channon

Editor's Introduction

This second of the three volumes of the unexpurgated diaries of Henry 'Chips' Channon (1897–1958) covers a period of just under five years; five of the most dramatic and tumultuous years in British history. The diaries open in October 1938, just as Neville Chamberlain, the Prime Minister of the National Government that has ruled since 1931, has returned from Munich, and his meeting with Hitler at which the Sudetenland was carved out of Czechoslovakia and given to the Nazi Reich. Channon, as an appeaser and a deeply loyal devotee of Chamberlain, is relieved and delighted, describing Chamberlain in the entry for 1 October 1938 as 'the man of the age'. The volume ends in late July 1943, as Mussolini is toppled and the Allies, having forced the Germans out of North Africa, are fighting their way through Sicily. By that stage Channon has witnessed the fall of Chamberlain, the rise of Churchill, the Battle of Britain and the Blitz. There have been massive changes in the world, and in Channon's life and character.

When the volume opens Channon is about to complete three years as Conservative MP for Southend, in Essex, a seat he inherited from his mother-in-law, the Countess of Iveagh. He had since the previous March been parliamentary private secretary to R. A. 'Rab' Butler, Under-Secretary of State at the Foreign Office and Conservative MP for Saffron Walden, in the corner of Essex diagonally opposite Southend. Butler was more significant than most ministers of his rank because the Foreign Secretary, Lord Halifax (Channon's uncle by marriage), was in the House of Lords, which meant Butler answered for the department in the Commons. Although the post gave Butler, who was only 35, experience far ahead of his years, it also had the misfortune of linking him specifically to Chamberlain's and Halifax's appeasement policy. This would affect perceptions of him for the rest of his career, and twice – in 1957 and 1963 – prevent him from becoming leader and Prime Minister.

Never in his own political career would Channon be so close to the heart of politics as in this period. However, in 1941 Butler was promoted to the presidency of the Board of Education, where he set about designing his revolutionary 1944 Education Act. There was never any question of Channon accompanying Butler to his new billet: the two men's relations were perfectly good, but the next step for Channon would either have been to move to a junior ministerial post or to revert to the back benches. Churchill did not regard him as suitable for promotion. Their social interactions had been somewhat artificial. Channon hated Churchill's son Randolph – 'he ought to be hamstrung . . . . he has no redeeming qualities and his . . . . heart beats with jealousy of me particularly. I will do him in eventually,' wrote Channon on 12 April 1939. But above all Channon's ultra-Chamberlainite, pro-appeasement history would have created the greatest mistrust, and Channon did not have the intellectual rigour and record of administrative competence that made Butler useful to Churchill.

In this volume we see Channon first of all disillusioned by the eventual adoption of the path to war that he thought Chamberlain had avoided; and then by the failure of Chamberlain (who was, by early 1940, in any case mortally ill) to manage his party through the uneasy period of the Phoney War. He is slow to be reconciled to Churchill ('that angry bullfrog, slave of a prejudice' as he calls him on 3 October 1938), not least because of his continuing animosity towards Randolph, but also because of his distaste for many of the people with whom Churchill surrounds himself; and he is not slow to criticise him, or them, in the diaries. For example Duff Cooper, also on 3 October 1938, is 'plump, conceited, tiresome . . . . a little strutting cunt-struck bantam cock'. Channon favoured appeasement partly because he felt Hitler's Germany was the only hope of keeping Stalin and Bolshevism at bay, something about which he regarded Britain as being too pusillanimous; and partly because, like many of his generation, the thought of another war horrified him.

Once Channon has ceased to be a PPS and has left the Foreign Office, politics becomes less important in his life, and he reverts more to the personality he exhibited before he went into the Commons, in which his social life becomes central to his existence. While the likes of Lady Cunard and Mrs Corrigan and their salons never left his orbit, they and others like them become more central to Channon's life once it is clear to him that he has gone as far in politics as he is likely to. And, indeed, it is the fact that Channon was, in political terms, to be something of an outsider in perpetuity that caused his diaries to be so candid and revealing as they are. It is hard to imagine his having the time to keep them had he held a demanding office of state, or to have taken the risk of stating what he really felt about his colleagues and the officials with whom he worked.

After 1941, and before his partner Peter Coats (see below) returns from the war, Channon is a somewhat lonely figure, searching for and finding friendship and companionship mainly in his political colleagues, notably his brother-in-law Alan Lennox-Boyd, but also Harold Balfour. Once he and his wife split up he is also left to contemplate the full effect of the absence of his son Paul, to whom he was unaffectedly devoted – 'my delectable dauphin' as he refers to him on 18 July 1939 – and who was evacuated to America in 1940. On 27 September 1942, a month after his friend and neighbour the Duke of Kent was killed on active service and with Channon still reeling from this, the diarist notes that 'Almost everything that I loved has disappeared in under three years'. But he is defiant nonetheless, his spirit to survive and will to live evident as ever. 'I have only my adorable dauphin, Peter [Coats], and a few other friends, my money and, as Cyrano put it, "mon panache"!'

His loyalty to those friends, though, is striking, and it persists through good times and bad. He stands by Prince Fritzi of Prussia, in exile in England by the Second World War, even though such a friendship is politically inexpedient. He anxiously follows the fate of Prince Paul of Yugoslavia, to whom he has been devoted since Oxford days, after the Prince is ousted from power. When Paul Latham, MP for Scarborough and Whitby, is imprisoned over a homosexual scandal, Channon is among the very few not to forsake him. Friendships can also modify prejudices. Though, for example, the diaries betray an anti-Semitic attitude sadly not untypical of his time and class, Channon is devoted to Leslie Hore-Belisha and he slowly comes round to the Amery family, forging a relationship with them that will become more obvious in Volume 3. Ultimately, when confronted with the wicked actions of the Nazis against the Jews, he concedes how appalling this is. On 17 December 1942, when Eden shared with the Commons details about the Nazi death camps, Channon has, at last, a *moment révélateur*:

> Yesterday one despaired of democracy, it behaved so querulously; today it was sublime. Anthony read out a statement in regard to the extermination of Jews in East Europe; whereupon Jimmie de Rothschild rose and with immense dignity and his voice vibrating with emotion, spoke for five minutes in moving terms on the plight of these peoples. There were tears in his eyes and I feared that he might break down; the House caught the spirit and was deeply moved. Somebody suggested that we stand to pay our respects to those suffering peoples; and the House as a whole rose and stood for a few frozen seconds in silence. My back tingled – it was a fine moment . . . .

II

The key changes in Channon's private life in these years are the break-up of his marriage and his forming of a close attachment with another man. Channon met Peter Coats (1910–90) at a ball given by Lord Kemsley at Chandos House on 3 July 1939, two months before war broke out. Four days later they met again at Blenheim, and Channon was immediately, and powerfully, attracted to him, finding him 'a … Pierrot of charm and Aryan good looks'. Channon showed his regard in the way that came most naturally to him: he notes on 3 January 1940, six months after they had met, that he has spent £1,000 on him: equivalent to around £55,000 in 2021 prices.

Coats was an Old Etonian from a Scottish textile family, who had grown up in Ayrshire. Before the war he became popular in London society as an invaluable spare man, not only with the necessary looks and manners but also no threat to any of the young women who might meet him. He wrote for *House and Garden* in the 1930s; he was an officer in the Territorial Army and as such was mobilised on the eve of war; and he spent that war in the Middle East, North Africa and India. He was recruited to the staff of General Sir Archibald Wavell (later Field Marshal Earl Wavell) and served as his aide-de-camp when he was Commander-in-Chief, Middle East and as his Comptroller when he was Viceroy of India. When Coats was demobilised in 1946 he went to live with Channon in Belgrave Square, served on *Vogue*'s editorial staff and worked in interior decoration and garden design; he survived Channon by more than thirty years. Never as well regarded in London society as Channon, and seen by some of Channon's friends as rather leeching off him, Coats was known as 'Petticoats', or by the most waspish as 'Mrs Chips'. However, Coats cannot be faulted in his efforts to protect Channon's posthumous reputation, and his loyalty to him was not in question.

In the highly abridged first published version of these diaries, prepared by Coats, edited by Robert Rhodes James and published in 1967, the end of the Channons' marriage is presented as a vague matter of fact, with an almost complete absence of detail. In the unexpurgated diaries, the realities of the disintegration of the Channon marriage are laid out long before Coats enters Channon's life. On 3 October 1938 Channon writes of his wife that 'she is in a highly inflammable state, and I try my very utmost to do everything not only to soothe her, but to make her happier. *Que faire?*' Three weeks later, on 25 October, he writes: 'Honor in a depressing, gloomy mood which cuts my heart and drenches my hopes.' On 29 October he says that 'for Honor, I would do anything', and his sincerity is not to be doubted. But Lady Honor, who was 29 and twelve years his junior, was bored with him and had already, as recounted in Volume 1, had adventures with a priapic Hungarian count and a ski-instructor. A month later he is close to admitting defeat: 'She is eccentric, undemonstrative, yet I love her still. I don't think she loves me now.' After a miserable Christmas spent with the Guinnesses, Channon records (27 December 1938) that 'she wants to go skiing again to Switzerland at once and spend three months there. She will end badly: there is something rather brutal about it, so crude and fierce and she is *mal-entourée* there. I am convinced of that …' On 8 January 1939 he notes: 'Honor in an endocrine mood, hard, selfish, uninterested, tonight. Said she would never have more children: I must look elsewhere for them. Evening ended on an unpleasant note.' Six months later, days after he met Coats and with Lady Honor away on a July skiing expedition, he records (13 July 1939): 'A very curt, cold, brief little letter from Honor. I am sad and apprehensive about her: but *quoi faire*? I fear trouble ultimately.'

As I mentioned in the introduction to Volume 1, Rhodes James never saw Channon's original manuscript, but worked on his edition using a document prepared over several years, after Channon's death in October 1958, that Coats distilled from the manuscript. That document was heavily abridged and sanitised, not least because of the laws of libel and assertions Channon had made about many people who, at the time of publication in 1967, were very much still alive and holding serious public or social positions. In addition to these prolific acts of sanitisation there were two major ones. Coats went to pains to conceal the truth about the end of Channon's marriage and about his relationship with him, and for two very good reasons. First, Lady Honor Svejdar (as she had become after her second marriage) was still alive, and indeed was sent the proofs to read and to amend where she felt necessary; second, Coats (who hardly features in the Rhodes James edition, despite having been central to Channon's life for its last nineteen years) appears not to have desired the recognition he was due for the part he played in that life. Channon is never explicit about his relationship with Coats, whether in this volume or in the subsequent one, but it is highly probable that it was at times an actively homosexual one: though in the period covered in this volume the two men were largely separated by Coats's absence overseas on military service. However, the relationship between them was for its duration stigmatised by its illegality, illegality that ended only in the year Rhodes James's edition was published. Coats, who was a fastidious man, was certainly not ready to reveal that relationship to a wider world, even had Channon's family wanted him to.

It was generally supposed, before the publication of this volume, that Coats's arrival in Channon's life was what broke up his marriage. The diaries show this was not true. Lady Honor's various infidelities began to be catalogued in Volume 1; in this volume she finally leaves Channon for a horse dealer, or horse-coper, from a neighbouring village in Essex. There were hints in Volume 1 of Channon's romantic interest in some men, notably Viscount Gage and Prince Paul of Yugoslavia. He never made it clear in Volume 1 whether these relationships went beyond a romantic dream, and whether any sexual activity took place. Once he meets Coats he seems to become explicitly bisexual; Channon describes without any inhibition his feelings for Coats, and how important Coats is in his life, but he also writes sometimes of how alluring he finds some of the women he meets. As will become clear in the third and final volume, his sexual journey still had some way to go.

III

It may be helpful if I say a little about my editorial methods. I have attempted to give everyone who appears in the diaries a footnote: this has not been possible in some cases for those who did not have a public life and who are not easily traceable. I have, for the most part, repeated footnotes from Volume 1 for those whose biographical details also appear there, and for the most significant characters there is a dramatis personae at the start of this volume. Footnotes ending in an asterisk (*) are concise versions of longer footnotes to be found in Volume 1. In deciding what to leave out, I have sought to leave in everything of historical significance, and anything that illustrates important developments in

Channon's character or the characters of his close associates and family. I have usually left out repetitions, lists of those attending social events, and so on: this volume contains around 440,000 words of Channon's texts, representing over three-quarters of what he recorded in that period. These early years of the war were the years in which he wrote most. Some of the ellipses in the diaries are for a series of words that are indecipherable; where an individual word is illegible, this is specified in parentheses. Sometimes Channon uses ellipses himself, and these are presented by three dots. Where I have eliminated material I have indicated this with an ellipsis of four dots. Channon's spelling was good, and I have silently corrected his rare errors. My correction of his very occasional grammatical mistakes is usually silent too.

As with Volume 1, it is important to remind readers that this is a historical document, and must be treated as such. Homosexuality, divorce and promiscuity, all of which feature in the diaries, offended and outraged many of Channon's generation. Casual racism, to which few paid close attention until after the Second World War, is expressed with less restraint. Channon sometimes uses deeply offensive terms about, for example, black and Jewish people that are rightly condemned today, and would indeed have been distasteful to many when he wrote them; some of his remarks about Jews, deeply unpleasant in any context, are all the more so given the horrors being executed in Germany and the countries it had conquered at the very time Channon was writing. As with such incidences in Volume 1, the Trustees, editor and publisher deliberated at length whether to include or exclude such passages from this edition. After careful consideration, it was decided to leave them in, while seeking, through the footnotes, to contextualise them. The diaries are a valuable historical document, and it was felt the text should not be falsified to create a sanitised and therefore unhistorical and anachronistic picture not just of how Channon wrote and spoke, but of how many others in the society in which he lived also wrote and spoke.

I have censored nothing except one detail that adds nothing to historical knowledge but would cause distress to people who are still alive. Where Channon has made a disobliging reference to or claim about someone or something that is known to be wrong, this is pointed out in a footnote. It has not been the intention or desire of the editor, Trustees or publishers to offend or misrepresent anyone, dead or alive, but to try to achieve that often elusive aim of history, to search for and establish the truth – which, the Bible tells us, is great and shall prevail. One can only hope that sharing Chips Channon's account of these five years, like the rest of his diaries, makes some contribution to that truth, as well as entertaining those who read him, and greatly illuminating the age in which he lived and the people he knew.

Editor's Acknowledgements

My first debt is to the Trustees of the literary estate of Sir Henry Channon – his grandchildren Georgia Fanshawe and Henry Channon, and Robin Howard – for asking me to edit these *Diaries*. I could not have wanted to work with more considerate, helpful and understanding people, and they, and Katie Channon, have made the entire project a huge pleasure for me. To edit a complete edition had been a much sought-after task by generations of writers and historians ever since the heavily abridged and redacted *Diaries* appeared in 1967, and I am sensible of the honour done me in inviting me to take up this highly enjoyable and fascinating challenge.

I am also deeply grateful to Hugo Vickers, who generously made available to me his enormous expertise in the social and royal history of the period to help me avoid either lacunae or egregious errors in the footnotes, for reading the proofs with great care and being available on many occasions to answer enquiries I made of him. Such errors as remain are entirely mine. Sue Brealey also read the proofs to great effect with her customary meticulousness. Emily Ward made a crucial introduction and Shannon Mullen suggested an important refinement to the presentation of the work. The Trustees employed a team of painstaking transcribers who made a digital version of a manuscript, over the three volumes, of around two million words, which made my task as Editor infinitely easier than it would otherwise have been, and I thank them sincerely. At the publisher's, Amy Musgrave was responsible for the superb design of the cover and Peter Ward designed the text; David Milner copy-edited the manuscript with exemplary skill, and Jonathan Wadman's proof reading was of the same calibre. Alex Bell created a superb index.

My thanks, too, to my editor and publisher, Nigel Wilcockson, for seeing this project through. My agent, Georgina Capel, who also acted for the Trustees, was tireless in her support of us and as always she has my profound gratitude. Above all, my work in editing the *Diaries* was eased and supported from beginning to end by my wife Diana, and I valued too the constant contribution to my morale by my sons, Fred and Johnnie. And Chips – with whom I feel on sobriquet terms after all we have been through together – has been an enriching presence in my life for the last three years. I salute his memory for having the wit to write his magnificent *Diaries*, and to write them so well. I hope he would find the finished product, to use one of his favourite terms, *réussi*.

Simon Heffer
Great Leighs
15 April 2021

Dramatis Personae

Names are given first in the form most commonly adopted in the diaries.

Family

Lady Honor Channon (1909–76). Honor Dorothy Mary Guinness, Channon's wife from 1933 and eldest daughter of the 2nd Earl of Iveagh.

Paul Channon (1935–2007). Henry Paul Guinness Channon, Channon's son. Educated at Eton and, like his father, Christ Church, Oxford. While still a second-year undergraduate he succeeded his father as Conservative MP for Southend West, a seat he held from 1959 (when he was Baby of the House) until raised to the peerage as Baron Kelvedon (life peer) in 1997. Like his father, he acted as parliamentary private secretary to R. A. Butler and served in junior ministerial jobs in Edward Heath's administration. Under Mrs Thatcher he served as Minister of State for the Civil Service, the Arts and then for Trade and Industry before joining the Cabinet as Secretary of State for Trade in 1986. He became Transport Secretary in 1987 and served until 1989. He married, in 1963, Ingrid Olivia Georgia Wyndham, who had been married to his cousin Jonathan Guinness, 3rd Baron Moyne.

Lord Iveagh (1874–1967). Rupert Edward Cecil Lee Guinness, 2nd Earl of Iveagh, Channon's father-in-law. He succeeded his own father as Chairman of the Guinness brewery, holding the post for thirty-five years and overseeing a period of great expansion and success in the business. He was also a distinguished agriculturalist who greatly improved his estate at Elveden in Suffolk; part of his extensive philanthropy (in both Britain and Ireland) was to fund agricultural research. He was awarded the Garter in 1955 and made a fellow of the Royal Society in 1964.

Lady Iveagh (1881–1966). Lady Gwendolen Florence Mary Onslow, wife of the 2nd Earl of Iveagh, and Channon's mother-in-law. Daughter of the 4th Earl of Onslow, she succeeded her husband as MP for Southend from 1927 until 1935.

Patsy Guinness (1918–2001). Lady Patricia Florence Susan Guinness, second daughter of the 2nd Earl of Iveagh and Channon's sister-in-law.

Brigid Guinness (1920–95). Lady Brigid Katharine Rachel Guinness, third and youngest daughter of the 2nd Earl of Iveagh, and Channon's sister-in-law.

Close friends, associates and political colleagues

Attlee, Clement Richard (1883–1967). Led the Labour Party from 1935 to 1955, was Lord Privy Seal in Churchill's coalition administration from 1940 to 1942, Deputy Prime Minister from 1942 to 1945 and Prime Minister from 1945 to 1951.

Balfour, Harold Harington (1897–1988). A regular officer in the RAF, and before that a fighter ace in the Royal Flying Corps, in which he reached the rank of major and won the Military Cross, and Bar. He was Conservative MP for the Isle of Thanet from 1929 to 1945, and Under-Secretary of State for Air from 1938 to 1944. He was raised to the peerage as 1st Baron Balfour of Inchrye in 1945.

Buccleuch, Mollie (1872–1954). Margaret Alice 'Mollie' Bridgeman, daughter of the 4th Earl of Bradford, married in 1893 John Charles Montagu Douglas Scott (1864–1935), by courtesy Earl of Dalkeith from 1884 to 1914, when he succeeded his father as 7th Duke of Buccleuch and 9th Duke of Queensberry. Although Chips calls her Mollie she spelt her name Molly and is thus indexed in Volume 1.

Buccleuch, Walter (1894–1973). Walter John Montagu Douglas Scott, by courtesy Earl of Dalkeith from 1914 to 1935, when he succeeded his father as 8th Duke of Buccleuch and 10th Duke of Queensberry. He married, in 1921, Vreda Esther Mary Lascelles (1900–93), daughter of Major William Lascelles and granddaughter of the 10th Duke of St Albans.

Butler, Richard Austen ('Rab') (1902–82). One of the most influential politicians of the mid-twentieth century, though his support for appeasement and unbridled quick wit helped ensure he never became leader of the Conservative Party, despite being in the frame in 1957 to succeed Anthony Eden, and in 1963 to succeed Macmillan. MP for Saffron Walden from 1929 to 1965, he would, as under-secretary at the Foreign Office at the time of Munich, play a significant part in Channon's political career. He went on to be a great reforming Minister of Education from 1941 to 1945. He married, firstly, in 1926, Sydney Elizabeth Courtauld (1902–54), and, secondly, in 1959, Mollie Courtauld (née Montgomerie) (1908–2009), widow of his first wife's cousin.

Chamberlain, (Arthur) Neville (1869–1940). Son of Joseph Chamberlain and half-brother of Sir Austen, he was Conservative MP for Birmingham Ladywood from 1918 to 1929 and for Birmingham Edgbaston from 1929 to 1940. From 1922 onwards he held various Cabinet posts, notably as Minister for Health from 1924 to 1929 and Chancellor of the Exchequer from 1931 to 1937. He succeeded Stanley Baldwin as Prime Minister in 1937, serving until 1940. He led the country into the Second World War, his policy of appeasing Hitler – exemplified by the Munich Agreement – having failed, but resigned in May 1940. He remained leader of the Conservative Party during Churchill's premiership, until his death in November 1940. Channon admired him enormously.

Churchill, Winston Leonard Spencer (1874–1965). Elected as a Conservative MP for Oldham in 1900, he crossed the floor in 1904 to become a Liberal, before rejoining the Conservatives as MP for Epping from 1924 to 1945 and for Woodford from 1945 to 1964. He held numerous Cabinet posts from 1908 to 1929, and was a vigorous opponent of appeasement during the 1930s (hence, in part, Channon's hostility to him). After Neville Chamberlain's resignation in 1940, Churchill became Prime Minister, serving in this role until 1945 and from 1951 to 1955. He married in 1908 Clementine Ogilvy Hozier (1885–1977).

Coats, Peter (1910–90). A garden writer, photographer and designer, he met Channon in 1939 and became an intimate friend. During the Second World War, he served as aide-de-camp to General Wavell.

Cooper, Lady Diana (1892–1986). Diana Olivia Winifred Maud Manners, by courtesy Lady Diana Manners, the youngest daughter of the 8th Duke of Rutland, though probably the daughter of Harry Cust, one of the Souls, editor of the *Pall Mall Gazette* and Conservative MP. Celebrated as one of the most beautiful women in England, she was a member of the Coterie, her generation's equivalent of the Souls, where she met Duff Cooper, whom she married much against the wishes of her family. She appeared in some silent films and was asked to play the Madonna in Karl Vollmöller's wordless stage spectacle *The Miracle*, directed by Max Reinhardt, to huge acclaim: she toured the production for twelve years. The money she made allowed Cooper to enter politics and her many absences facilitated his womanising, which she tolerated. When he was ennobled as Viscount Norwich she continued to be known as Lady Diana Cooper, on the grounds that 'Norwich' sounded to her like 'porridge'.

Cooper, (Alfred) Duff (1890–1954). Joined the Diplomatic Service in 1913 and served in the Grenadier Guards for the last eighteen months of the First World War, being awarded the DSO. He married Lady Diana Manners in 1919 but was a career womaniser. He became Conservative MP for Oldham in 1924 but lost in 1929, returning to Parliament having won the Westminster St George's by-election in 1931, holding the seat until 1945. He quickly attained junior office and in 1935 became Secretary of State for War. In 1937 he became First Lord of the Admiralty but resigned in 1938 over the Munich agreement. Churchill deployed him in various roles between 1940 and 1944, when he became Ambassador to Paris, a post he held until 1948. He was knighted in 1948 and raised to the peerage as 1st Viscount Norwich in 1952.

Cripps, (Richard) Stafford (1889–1952). Labour MP for Bristol East from 1931 to 1950. He briefly served as Solicitor-General in the 1931 Labour government, and was knighted. He held several posts in the coalition Cabinet from 1942 to 1945 and in the Attlee government, and was Chancellor of the Exchequer from 1947 to 1950. He was a nephew of Beatrice Webb and made a reputation as one of the party's foremost intellectuals.

Cunard, Emerald (1872–1948). Maud Alice Burke, born in San Francisco, married in 1895 Sir Bache Cunard, 3rd Bt (1851–1925), grandson of the shipping line's founder. They lived largely apart from 1911, Cunard basing himself in Leicestershire where he enjoyed field sports. In London with their daughter Nancy Clara (1896–1965), Lady Cunard – who after her husband's death became known as 'Emerald' – established one of the leading salons of the era, which thrived until the Second World War. After separating from her husband she became the mistress of Sir Thomas Beecham, the conductor, and funded many of his musical projects.

Dufferin, Basil (1909–45). Basil Sheridan Hamilton-Temple-Blackwood, by courtesy Earl of Ava, until he succeeded his father as 4th Marquess of Dufferin and Ava in 1930. Perpetuating the family curse of premature death (his father died in a plane crash; one uncle perished in the Second Boer War and another in the First World War), he was killed when a Japanese shell landed on him in Burma in March 1945.

Dufferin, Maureen (1907–98). Maureen Constance Guinness, a cousin of Channon's wife Honor, married Basil Dufferin in 1930.

Dunglass, Alec (1903–95). Alexander Frederick Douglas-Home, by courtesy Lord Dunglass from 1918 to 1951, when he succeeded his father as 14th Earl of Home. He renounced his hereditary peerage in 1963 to become leader of the Conservative Party and Prime Minister, serving until 1964. He was Conservative MP for Lanark from 1931 to 1945 and from 1950 to 1951, and for Kinross and Western Perthshire from 1963 to 1974. He was Commonwealth Secretary from 1955 to 1960 and Foreign Secretary from 1960 to 1963 and from 1970 to 1974. He became Chamberlain's PPS in 1936 and served until 1940. He was created Baron Home of the Hirsel (life peerage) in 1974.

Eden, (Robert) Anthony (1897–1977). Son of Sir William Eden, Bt, of County Durham. He won the Military Cross in the Great War and became in 1918 the youngest brigade major in the Army. He was MP for Warwick and Leamington from 1923 to 1957 and became Lord Privy Seal in 1933. Later in 1935 he became Foreign Secretary, until resigning over appeasement in 1938 (hence, in part, Channon's hostility to him). Churchill appointed him Secretary of State for War in 1940 and, later that year, Foreign Secretary. He returned to that post in 1951 and was Prime Minister from 1955 to 1957. He became a Knight of the Garter in 1954 and was raised to the peerage as 1st Earl of Avon in 1961.

Halifax, Lord (1881–1959). Edward Frederick Lindley Wood, son of the 2nd Viscount Halifax. He was a fellow of All Souls from 1903 to 1910, then MP for Ripon from 1910 to 1925, becoming a Cabinet minister as President of the Board of Education in 1922 and, from 1924, Minister of Agriculture. He was raised to the peerage as Baron Irwin in 1925 on accepting the Viceroyalty of India, which he held from 1926 until 1931, and succeeded his father as 3rd Viscount Halifax in 1934. He became a Knight of the Garter in 1931. He served again at Education from 1932 to 1935, then as Secretary of State for War from 1935 and as Foreign Secretary in 1938, when he became closely identified with appeasement. He almost became Prime Minister in 1940; but instead went as Ambassador to the United States from 1941 to 1946. He married, in 1908, Lady Dorothy Evelyn Augusta Onslow (1885–1976), daughter of the 4th Earl of Onslow, and later Channon's aunt by marriage. Halifax was advanced to an earldom in 1944. For many years Alexandra 'Baba' Curzon was his mistress.

Henderson, Nevile (1882–1942). Joined the Foreign Office in 1905 and served as Minister Plenipotentiary to Yugoslavia from 1929 to 1935, as Ambassador to Argentina from 1935 to 1937, and as Ambassador to Germany from 1937 to 1939. He was knighted in 1932. A firm believer in appeasement, and highly sympathetic to German nationalism, he played a significant role in persuading Chamberlain not to provoke Hitler into a war. Against the advice of the Foreign Office and to the fury of Robert Vansittart, Henderson attended the Nuremberg Rally in September 1937; and after attending the next one, in September 1938, strongly advised Chamberlain to enter into the Munich Agreement, and took Germany's part in arguments with the Foreign Office up to the declaration of war.

Hoare, Samuel John Gurney ('Sam') (1880–1959). Succeeded his father as 2nd Bt in 1915. He was Conservative MP for Chelsea from 1910 to 1944 and successively Secretary of State for Air (three times), Secretary of State for India, Foreign Secretary, First Lord of the Admiralty, Home Secretary and Lord Privy Seal. An appeaser, he was sent to Madrid by Churchill as Ambassador to Spain in 1940. He was raised to the peerage as Viscount Templewood in 1944.

Hore-Belisha, (Isaac) Leslie (1893–1957). Son of Jacob Isaac Belisha, he came from a Sephardic Jewish family that had settled in Manchester in the eighteenth century. Elected Liberal MP for Plymouth Devonport in 1923, he aligned himself with Sir John Simon at the time of the formation of the National Government in 1931, and in 1932 became Financial Secretary to the Treasury. Appointed Minister of Transport in 1934, he invented the Belisha beacon to highlight the existence of zebra crossings, and took trunk roads under the control of central government to help develop an improved national road network. He was Secretary of State for War from 1937 to 1940, when he was sacked because of his poor relations with senior officers. One of Channon's closest friends.

Kent, Duchess of (1906–68). Princess Marina of Greece and Denmark, daughter of Prince Nicholas of Greece. She married the Duke of Kent in 1934.

Kent, Duke of (1902–42). Prince George Edward Alexander Edmund, fourth son of King George V and Queen Mary, created Duke of Kent 1934; married in 1934 Princess Marina of Greece and Denmark. Although known before his marriage to have had a number of mistresses he was also believed to be bisexual, and became one of Channon's closest friends. He was killed on active service with the RAF in 1942 when his flying boat crashed into a hillside in Caithness.

Lennox-Boyd, Alan (1904–83). Conservative MP for Mid-Bedfordshire from 1931 to 1960, he served as Minister of Transport from 1952 to 1954 and Colonial Secretary from 1954 to 1959. He then became managing director of Arthur Guinness and Sons, a post he held until 1967. He was raised to the peerage as 1st Viscount Boyd of Merton in 1960. Married to Channon's sister-in-law, Patricia Florence Susan Guinness (1918–2001), he was one of Channon's most intimate friends.

Llewellin, John Jestyn ('Jay') (1893–1957). MP for Uxbridge from 1929 to 1945; he held several posts in the wartime coalition government and was raised to the peerage as 1st Baron Llewellin in 1945. A good friend of Channon's.

Lloyd George, David (1863–1945). Liberal MP for Caernarvon Boroughs from 1890 to 1945, Prime Minister of Great Britain from 1916 to 1922, and of Ireland from 1916 to 1921, and leader of the Liberal Party from 1926 to 1931. Largely a spent force by the later 1930s, he was raised to an earldom in 1945 but died before he could take his seat in the House of Lords.

Londonderry, Lady (1878–1959). Edith Helen 'Circe' Chaplin, daughter of the 1st Viscount Chaplin, married Viscount Castlereagh (later 7th Marquess of Londonderry) in 1899. There was much talk in society about her friendship with James Ramsay MacDonald, the widowed leader of the Labour Party; and she was a passionate gardener.

Londonderry, Lord (1878–1949). Charles Stewart Henry Vane-Tempest-Stewart, 7th Marquess of Londonderry. He was appointed a Knight of the Garter in 1919 and served as Secretary of State for Air from 1931 to 1935. He went out of favour because of his close links with, and apparent regard for, the Nazis in Germany.

Margesson, (Henry) David Reginald (1890–1965). Conservative MP from 1922 to 1942. From 1931 to 1940 he was government Chief Whip, renowned for his occasionally menacing and bullying approach, and from 1940 to 1942 was Secretary of State for

War. He was raised to the peerage as 1st Viscount Margesson in 1942, having been sacked from the Cabinet and replaced by his Permanent Secretary.

Morrison, Herbert Stanley (1888–1965). A local Labour politician in London before being elected to Parliament in 1923 for Hackney South, he lost his seat in 1924 but returned in 1929, serving as Minister of Transport. He lost his seat in 1931 and resumed a career in London politics, becoming leader of the London County Council in 1934. His legacy was substantial: he created London Transport, established the Green Belt and oversaw the building of numerous housing estates in the inner London suburbs. Returned to Parliament in 1935, he sat for Hackney South until 1945 and then for Lewisham East from 1945 to 1950 and Lewisham South from 1950 to 1959. He was briefly Minister of Supply in Churchill's wartime coalition, then Home Secretary from 1940 to 1945. He was deputy leader of the Labour Party from 1945 to 1956, and served as Leader of the House of Commons and Lord President of the Council from 1945 to 1951, then briefly Foreign Secretary. He was raised to the peerage as Baron Morrison of Lambeth (life peer) in 1959. For all his success, he was widely disliked by both opponents and colleagues.

Morrison, William Shepherd ('Shakes') (1893–1961). A Scotsman, he was educated in Edinburgh, and was MP for Cirencester and Tewkesbury from 1929 to 1959, as a Conservative until 1951 and then as Speaker of the House of Commons. He was raised to the peerage as 1st Viscount Dunrossil in 1959, and served as Governor-General of Australia from 1960 until his sudden death a year later. He held several ministerial posts, culminating in the Postmaster-Generalship from 1940 to 1942, but lacked the trust of Churchill and so failed to achieve the high expectations Channon and others had of him. He was known as 'Shakes' because of his fondness for quoting Shakespeare in his speeches. He married, in 1924, Catherine Allison Swan (1898–1983).

Prince Paul of Yugoslavia (1893–1976). Prince Regent of Yugoslavia (the Kingdom of the Serbs, Croats and Slovenes) from 1934 to 1941 during the minority of Peter II. He and Channon met at Oxford and become close friends. He was the nephew of King Peter I and married Princess Olga of Greece and Denmark (1903–97), sister-in-law of another of Channon's close friends, the Duke of Kent. After treating with the Germans in 1941 Paul was forced from Yugoslavia and forbidden ever to return; the post-war Communist regime stripped him of his property and proclaimed him an enemy of the state. Until 1945 the British authorities held him in Kenya under house arrest. Serbia rehabilitated him posthumously in 2011, after which he was reburied with Princess Olga and their son Nicholas.

Simon, John Allsebrook (1873–1954). Son of a Manchester Congregationalist minister, he was a remarkable survivor: Liberal MP for Walthamstow from 1906 to 1918 and for Spen Valley from 1922 to 1940. He was Solicitor-General, Attorney-General, Home Secretary twice, Foreign Secretary (at the time of the visit to Hitler), Chancellor of the Exchequer and Lord Chancellor. He was remarkably unpopular with parliamentary colleagues. He was raised to the peerage as 1st Viscount Simon in 1940.

Thomas, James Henry ('Jim') (1874–1949). General Secretary of the National Union of Railwaymen from 1916 to 1931 and Labour MP for Derby from 1910 to 1936. He served as Colonial Secretary in the first Labour government, as Lord Privy Seal from 1929 to 1930, Dominions Secretary from 1930 to 1935, and Colonial Secretary again from 1935 to 1936. Much liked by King George V, Thomas was forced to resign from the government and Parliament in 1936 after being accused of giving inside information on proposed tax changes to stock-market investors.

Wavell, Archibald Percival (1883–1950). A career soldier, who, at the beginning of the Second World War, was General Officer Commanding in Palestine, before briefly being given Southern Command in Britain and, in February 1940, becoming Commander-in-Chief Middle East. In 1941 he became C-in-C in India, and was promoted to field marshal in 1943. Peter Coats served as his aide-de-camp, and he became good friends with Channon.

Wedderburn, Jim (1902–83). Henry James Scrymgeour-Wedderburn, Unionist MP for West Renfrewshire from 1931 to 1945. He held junior ministerial office in the Chamberlain, Churchill and Macmillan administrations. In 1952 the House of Lords upheld his claim to the dormant viscountcy of Dudhope and Scrymgeour in the peerage of Scotland and, the following year, to the dormant earldom of Dundee and Inverkeithing, when he became 11th Earl of Dundee.

Wood, (Howard) Kingsley (1881–1943). Son of a Methodist minister, he was an insurance lawyer – of such eminence that he was knighted for his work in 1918 – and was Conservative MP for Woolwich West from 1918 to 1943. A close confidant of Neville Chamberlain, he held office from 1931 to 1943 as, successively, Postmaster-General, Minister of Health, Secretary of State for Air, Lord Privy Seal and Chancellor of the Exchequer.

1938

This volume of the diary opens on the day after Neville Chamberlain's return from his meeting with Hitler at Munich, at which he believed he had secured 'peace in our time'.

SATURDAY 1ST OCTOBER

Chamberlain has had more ovations. He is the man of the age ... Duff [Cooper] has resigned in a well-written letter. The PM immediately accepted the resignation. All this hinted to him in very plain language that his services were no longer required. We shall hear more of this ... personally my reactions are mixed. I am sorry for Diana [Cooper]: they give up £5,000 per annum, and a lovely house – and for what? Duff thinks he will make money at literature? How? His Haig was a failure and his much-heralded Talleyrand, while highly readable, was really only a condensed cut from the famous four-vol. life of Talleyrand.[1]

The House of Stanley is unfortunate; poor Edward[2] is slowly dying of a malignant disease; Lord Derby[3] is ill from anxiety and last night Portia[4] (drunk, as usual, I am told) fell and broke some of her joints. The great fortune, complicatedly divided, will suffer enormously if either Lord Derby, or dear red-nosed Edward, should die.

Emerald [Cunard] had a heart attack and nearly died a fortnight ago. She is better now and rang me up to gossip.

SUNDAY 2ND OCTOBER   KELVEDON[5]

A miserable wet day: now that there is no war one feels *désoeuvré*,[6] and weak. A big week before me. I fear the poor divine PM will have to face a battery of critics

---

1 Cooper's book on Field Marshal Earl Haig had been published in 1935. The *Spectator* review described it as 'a model of elegant biography, though it did not go very deep'. The life of Talleyrand to which Channon refers is presumably that by the duc de Broglie, published in 1891. He later says it had three volumes.

2 Edward Montagu Cavendish Stanley (1894–1938), by courtesy Lord Stanley, eldest son of the 17th Earl of Derby (*vide infra*). He had been appointed Dominions Secretary five months previously.*

3 Edward George Villiers Stanley (1865–1948), 17th Earl of Derby, Conservative politician and diplomat.*

4 Sibyl Louise Beatrix 'Portia' Cadogan (1893–1969), wife of Lord Stanley.*

5 Kelvedon Hall, the Channons' country house in Essex.

6 At a loose end.

in the House of Commons next week. The Iveaghs plus Brigid[1] came to dine *en route* from Elveden[2] to London. All very charming. Much political talk. I asked them to warn 'Master' (as we call Lord Halifax) that there is still an attempt, or rather a wish, in the FO to sabotage him and the PM.

MONDAY 3RD OCTOBER   *5 BELGRAVE SQUARE*[3]

Honor[4] and I motored up and I rushed to the Foreign Office. The storm breaks over the government this afternoon for having preserved peace!

I was out of sorts and unsuccessful. With great difficulty I obtained a ticket for the Commons for my mother-in-law, who wanted to hear the PM. As I was waiting for her I ran into Eric Duncannon,[5] who wanted something to eat. I took him to the Strangers' dining room, and in the course of our talk he admitted that he hoped for Chichester, to succeed Jack Courtauld.[6] A gorgeous seat, better even than Southend. One day, but not at the present rate, Eric and I may be the only Tories left in the H of C. When my mother-in-law arrived there was no ticket. In a frenzy I rushed about and at last found her one.

The big debate began: I could scarcely control my rage against the wicked insurgents who from ambition, stupidity and hatred of Chamberlain, would now upset the govt. They are led by Winston Churchill, that angry bullfrog, slave of a prejudice, and, of course, that ass Anthony Eden who is one of the most unaware, ill-informed people I have ever known. It is a sad reflection on democracy that he is still popular with a certain section. Actually he is being used by the communists – communism working upwards!

The crowded House was restless, and when the PM took his seat directly in front of me, there was cheering, but not the hysterical enthusiasm of last Wednesday. Duff Cooper rose from the seat traditionally kept for retiring, resigning ministers, the third corner seat immediately below the gangway . . . my plump, conceited, tiresome Duff. He did not impress the House; his arguments were flat, inconclusive, although he had marshalled them, by committing them to memory. Only once he paused. The House took the speech as a dignified farewell from a man whom they are tired of. Duff is not a parliamentarian: he is a little

1 Lady Brigid Katharine Rachel Guinness (1920–95), third and youngest daughter of the 2nd Earl of Iveagh, sister of Channon's wife Honor (qv).
2 The Iveaghs' estate in Suffolk.
3 The Channons' London house.
4 Lady Honor Dorothy Mary Guinness (1909–76), eldest daughter of the 2nd Earl of Iveagh (qv). She and Channon married in 1933.
5 Frederick Edward Neuflize 'Eric' Ponsonby (1913–93), by courtesy Viscount Duncannon from 1920 to 1956, when he succeeded his father as 10th Earl of Bessborough. He was a diplomat and a banker.
6 John Sewell Courtauld (1880–1942) won the MC in the Great War and sat as Conservative MP for Chichester from 1924 until his death. Duncannon did not succeed him.

strutting cunt-struck bantam cock, outrageously conceited and bad-mannered. I have tried unsuccessfully (and at times with fleeting success) to like him now for twenty years. He has qualities, a wonderfully retentive memory for passages in literature, and he is quick to see the point. But he is charmless, unkind even to Diana, and a bore. His real defect is a lack of imagination, and thus he is a poor writer, although his English is distinguished. Diana was in the Weeping Gallery, Mrs FitzRoy's[1] enclosure, as were the Kents.[2] He was over the clock. I met the Duchess of Kent coming out of Mrs FitzRoy's enclosure and we had a chat. She was looking radiantly sad, as she often does.

The PM followed Duff's rather contradictory personal explanation; the PM was calm, and parliamentary; but he was tired and Wednesday's glow had gone. We settled down to an endless debate – the greatest man of all time will hear himself abused; but Attlee who answered him was mild and unconvincing. The Opposition fear a general election which would wipe them out of existence. Eden followed; he was charmless, looked old, and almost wicked. His glamour has gone, and he now shares the St Helena[3] bench (third below the gangway) with his old enemy Duff Cooper. There was always jealousy and antipathy between them, and I have cleverly and unsuspiciously played on it, succeeding in pitting Diana C against Eden, which, as he is so impersonal, so humanless [*sic*], was not difficult. Will they now sink their differences? Anthony made a platitudinous address, which was neither violent or interesting. Jim Thomas, Anthony's jackal, watched and listened with rapt admiration. Jim T is now the Chief Whip of the Shadow government, of which Winston is the Prime Minister and Arch Intriguer. I met Winston in the lavatory behind the Rialto[4] and forced him to talk to me, making a few remarks praising his nephew, Johnny Churchill's work here at Kelvedon. Winston, who for a great man confuses his personal relations with his politics to a surprising degree, was half-nettled, half-disarmed, and we chatted with amiability. That ass Ronnie Cartland,[5] whom I personally like, I overheard say to Grenfell,[6] the Labour member, that the Con govt had not gone to war because we feared our dividends would suffer!! He is a sex-starved, intense, honest, narrow, dangerous little boy whose only enjoyment is voting against the govt.

1 Muriel Douglas-Pennant (1869–1962), married in 1928 the Speaker of the House of Commons, Edward FitzRoy (qv).
2 Prince George, Duke of Kent (1902–42), and Princess Marina of Greece and Denmark, Duchess of Kent (1906–68).*
3 Napoleon's place of exile.
4 Slang for the Commons' Members' Lobby.
5 John Ronald Hamilton Cartland (1907–40), Conservative MP, anti-appeaser and brother of the romantic novelist Barbara Cartland (qv). He was killed at the Battle of Dunkirk.
6 David Rhys 'Dai' Grenfell (1881–1968) was Labour MP for Gower from 1922 to 1959. He had become a coal miner at the age of 12 but put himself through night school to obtain the qualifications needed to join the management of a mine. He served as Secretary for Mines at the Board of Trade from 1940 to 1945.

I rang up Honor at dinner time, we are staying in London tonight, and was horrified to hear that Dr Law[1] had prescribed a three-months' trip abroad. He wants her to leave immediately; otherwise he will not be responsible for her nervous consequences. Certainly she is in a highly inflammable state, and I try my very utmost to do everything not only to soothe her, but to make her happier. *Que faire?*[2] ... I had no dinner, sat on the bench, and worried about my wife. The House buzzed with intrigue, but I bet that there would not be a serious revolt against the govt, at least not a revolt which would be reflected in the division lobbies ... Yet already one hears the pattering footsteps of the Francophiles, who wanted a war – even when France did not. Most of these people come from the same group, London society; they are brought up in the Quai d'Orsay[3] traditions, and are enraged that they are no longer the ruling group in the H of C. They will blow their foolish heads off this week for their collapse ... Sam Hoare wound up for the govt in the best speech he has made in the present parliament.

TUESDAY 4TH OCTOBER

Life is too full, too nervous. In the rush of the FO work there is my poor wife who is ill, nervous, worn out (from doing nothing). Today she went to Holker[4] to stay with the Cavendishes, as Diana Cavendish,[5] ex-Boothby, who has made a mess of her own life, is now trying to make a mess of Honor's. I saw my mother-in-law at the H of C and we had a confidential talk; she, too, is upset about Honor. Perhaps she had better go away and ski – but there is no snow. I then led Lady Iveagh to the Lords; in the lobby we met Lady Halifax, very chic and gay, walking with George Gage.[6] I followed them into the Chamber and heard Lord Baldwin[7] make his maiden speech. He spoke from the front bench below the gangway; wearing a grey suit, leaning on his hickory stick, he looked the country gentleman and his

---

1 Their general practitioner.
2 What's to be done?
3 The French Foreign Ministry.
4 A property of the Cavendish family near Grange-over-Sands in Cumbria.
5 Diana Cavendish (1909–92), daughter of Lord Richard Cavendish and niece of the 9th Duke of Devonshire, married in 1935 Robert Boothby (qv), whose mistress, Lady Dorothy Macmillan, was her first cousin. In 1971 she would become the third wife of Viscount Gage (*vide infra*).
6 Henry Rainald 'George' Gage (1895–1982) had succeeded his father as 6th Viscount Gage in 1912. He had fought in the Coldstream Guards during the Great War, reaching the rank of captain, and became an active peer for the Conservative Party, and a courtier. In 1931 he married Imogen Grenfell*, daughter of Lord and Lady Desborough*. Channon and he had been very close, especially in Channon's immediate post-Oxford years.
7 Stanley Baldwin (1867–1947), Worcestershire ironmaster, was Conservative MP for Bewdley from 1908 to 1937. He became leader of his party in 1923 and was Prime Minister of Great Britain and Northern Ireland from 1923 to 1924, 1924 to 1929, and 1935 to 1937. On his retirement he was raised to the peerage as 1st Earl Baldwin of Bewdley and Viscount Corvedale.

speech was a House of Commons one, and it was a tribute to the Prime Minister. The Lords lapped it up: I hurried back to our Chamber and passed a note to the PM letting him know of 'SB's' speech. He turned and gave one of his intoxicating smiles, a touch tired, but his dark eyes flashed appreciation. He is so curiously susceptible to attention and flattery from the young. So long as the Chamberlain reign continues, and nothing goes amiss, I am on the fairway.

Tom Inskip,[1] big, burly, immense, made an impressive speech, winding up. He was in good form. 'Worth the crisis,' was my verdict which re-echoed down the lobbies. Chamberlain is tired today; the debate has gone against us, and all the people who a week ago were in a funk, are now belittling their saviour . . . I am disgusted by the lack of gratitude.

I dined with Euan Wallace,[2] David Margesson, Walter Elliot[3] and Rob Bernays[4] . . . Rab [Butler] didn't come but remained on the bench. John Simon to my surprise asked me to dine with him: he has these sudden flashes of geniality. Diana was to have been with us, but at the last moment she deserted us to join Winston . . . is it part of the Insurgents Party policy? Already the Coopers regret their forced retirement. I don't really know whether Diana knows the full truth: or whether she is genuinely convinced that Duff has resigned because of his high principles. She must know her little ex-Sea Lord too well. David Margesson at dinner was divine but distant; is he on the wing? Will he be First Lord? Does he hear the lapping of the waves? I don't think that Chamberlain will let him go now.

WEDNESDAY 5TH OCTOBER

A scramble this morning at the FO with a huge batch of Questions; and on top of it the whips rang me at 11.30 to say that the PM wanted Rab to wind up tonight. I helped Rab all day with his speech etc. The dreary debate continued: Winston's contribution enlivened the House, discomfited the front bench but did not [illegible] weaken the govt's excellent case. Winston went on *ad nauseam*

---

1 Thomas Inskip (1876–1947) was a lawyer and Conservative MP whose career culminated in his being first Lord Chancellor, and then, from 1940 to 1946, Lord Chief Justice of England.
2 David Euan Wallace (1892–1941) was a Conservative MP from 1922 to 1923 and from 1924 to 1941. He held several ministerial appointments. Both his sons by his first marriage and one from his second were killed in action in the Second World War, and another died while on active service.
3 Walter Elliot Elliot (1888–1958) was educated in Glasgow, where he qualified as a doctor. Apart from breaks in 1923–4 and 1945–6 he sat for Scottish seats as a Conservative from 1915 until 1958. He was Secretary of State for Scotland from 1936 to 1938, and Minister of Health from 1938 to 1940.
4 Robert Hamilton Bernays (1902–45) was National Liberal MP for Bristol North from 1931 to 1945. He held junior office in the Chamberlain government in the ministries of Health and Transport from 1937 to 1940. He was a close friend of Harold Nicolson (qv), and may have had a homosexual affair with him. He was killed in a plane crash while flying to visit British troops overseas in 1945.

deploring that we had not taken stronger action against the dictators. However much he twists his words, he was really saying – as Duff has said privately to anyone who would listen for years – 'Why not war in my time?' (and with the natural corollary, with me in office?). Simon made a magnificent speech, quoting Shelley's great lines about 'Hope'.[1] Anthony Eden, his dignity gone, is seen shuffling along corridors fraternising with the Labour Party and his own little band of sycophants.

THURSDAY 6TH OCTOBER

We met at eleven and for some anxious hours we listened to the dwindling debate. Would the PM do well? Would the Eden–Cooper conclave actually vote against us and persuade many others to do so? At 3.13 the PM rose: he was quietly magnificent (and I looked up at Mrs Chamberlain in the Speaker's Gallery where she has sat for four long days) and made so moving an appeal, so devoid of resentment or bitterness, that I should have thought he would have led a unanimous House behind him into the division lobby. He even had time to make a gay reference to Winston Churchill, with whom he had crossed swords earlier in the day, when he called his utterances 'unworthy' of him, and Winston was howled down, unable for a minute or two to get a hearing. This was the reception given to the Arch Intriguer who saw himself as the new PM. It was the second time in my brief career that I have heard him howled down, the former occasion was at the time of the abdication. I was sitting just behind the PM throughout the debate, and early on, when he snubbed Winston, there was a flash of rage in his dark eyes, they actually sparkled with anger. The House was with him and he was aware of the strength of his following. All day the political atmosphere was clearing and even the St Vitus antics of the Conservative Opposition were powerless to stem the Chamberlain tide, which swelled and swelled until he rose to speak: there was then a hush and his speech was magnificent. At length he sat down, and the fateful divisions began, the first was the Socialist Amendment and the figures were 369 for the govt, 130 against peace and the govt.

I was almost the first to congratulate the PM. I followed him to the Rialto and after murmuring a few bromides I whispered to him my message from the Prince Regent[2] to the effect that Yugoslavia would always be on our side, as much as ever she dared during Paul's regime, and I added that the Regent thought him the greatest man in history. The PM, who had first made one of the most remarkable speeches in the whole history of the House, put out his hand and tapped my arm,

1 From the end of his verse drama *Prometheus Unbound* – 'to hope till Hope creates / from its own wreck the thing it contemplates; / Neither to change, nor falter, nor repent; / This, like thy glory, Titan, is to be / Good, great and joyous, beautiful and free; / This is alone Life, Joy, Empire, and Victory.'
2 Prince Paul of Yugoslavia.

and beamed with pleasure. There were two red spots on his cheeks, he looked positively jubilant. I left him to vote. The figures were received with cheers, but the Churchillian Group conspicuous for their disloyalty sat glum, sullen and wrong. Old Winston looked like an angry Buddha. The figures for the next division, which was the main Question, were better still: 366 for us, 144 for war.

As they were read out it was obvious that while some of our members abstained, a few Labour people had done likewise, Thurtle[1] for one. Cheers greeted the result, we shouted, we waved our handkerchiefs, there were deafening roars of 'Hear! Hear!' There was pandemonium and the PM quietly, with his usual gentle dignity, walked out followed, or rather shepherded, by Alec Dunglass, whom he adores. Alec is the ideal PPS, and there is a curious quiet sympathy between them. We had won; but it might have been a better victory. The French were about unanimous (only 73 against, and of these 71 were communists) in their support of Daladier[2] in the Chamber yesterday.

I motored back to the beauty and peace of Kelvedon.

FRIDAY 7TH OCTOBER

Honor is crossing today in an appalling gale to be at Clandeboye[3] for the christening of the Dufferins' daughter.[4] I woke early to peruse Hansard and try and detect the Glamour Boys[5] who either voted against us, or abstained. They were not so numerous: Winston; Anthony Eden; Cranborne[6] who is particularly irritating and mad at the moment; Sidney Herbert;[7] Duff Cooper; Jim Thomas; that ass, who is a joke in the House because of his stupidity, Derrick Gunston;[8] and

1 Ernest Thurtle (1884–1954) was Labour MP for Shoreditch from 1923 to 1931 and from 1935 to 1954. He had fought with distinction in the Great War and been badly wounded at Cambrai.

2 Édouard Daladier (1884–1970), Prime Minister of France in 1933, 1934, and from 1938–40.

3 The seat of the Marquess of Dufferin and Ava, in Co. Down.

4 He means son; the Dufferins' only son Sheridan Frederick Terence Hamilton-Temple-Blackwood (1938–88) had been born the previous July. He was Earl of Ava by courtesy until he succeeded his father as 5th Marquess in 1945.

5 The name Neville Chamberlain gave to the group of anti-appeasers, largely followers of Eden, who increasingly spoke out against Hitler and the threat they perceived he posed.

6 Robert Arthur James Gascoyne-Cecil (1893–1972), by courtesy Viscount Cranborne from 1903 to 1947, when he succeeded his father as 5th Marquess of Salisbury. Known as 'Bobbety', he was Conservative MP for South Dorset from 1929 to 1941, when he was summoned to the House of Lords by a writ of acceleration in the Barony of Cecil of Essendon, one of his father's titles. He was Under-Secretary of State for Foreign Affairs from 1935 to 1938, when he resigned over appeasement; and served in several Cabinet posts during the post-war coalition, leading the Conservative Party in the House of Lords from 1942 to 1957.

7 Sir Sidney Herbert (1890–1939), 1st Bt.

8 Derrick Wellesley Gunston (1891–1985) was awarded the Military Cross in the Great War and was Unionist MP for Thornbury from 1924 until 1945. He was created 1st Bt in 1938.

Hubert Duggan.[1] I cannot ever forgive him our old friendship which I deliberately killed (and I have qualms of conscience about my action) and is now buried. The little ass; I have always had a contempt for him; of recent years we have tried to keep up the appearances of friendship, and nothing is so unsatisfactory. I shall stop him getting financial assistance from Central Office at the next election.

They say that Edward Stanley has resigned as he is so ill: he need not have bothered. He will die, I have always said so. His illness is so mysterious. It will kill Portia not being Lady Derby.

I had a banquet in Southend; but I could not concentrate on preparing a speech, and so went, as it were, empty-handed. The result was one of the best speeches I have ever made, it was a fascinating defence of the PM and I was greeted with thunderous applause. He is King of the World now. I was self-confident, and a little drunk.

SUNDAY 9TH OCTOBER

As I dressed, Patsy[2] sat with me and said she was seeing too much of Alan [Lennox-Boyd], and that she was going to break with him . . . As I was going to bed – I had been sick – and it was 1 a.m. – Alan burst into my room. He had had a scene with Patsy, a quarrel, and he had proposed marriage and been refused. All very upsetting and he much upset.

My little boy is 3 today.

MONDAY 10TH OCTOBER   *KELVEDON*

Before I was properly awake Patsy Guinness, with the eyes of one who has not slept, burst into my room. Yes, she had told Alan she would see him no more – except as a friend on formal occasions – for some time. He had been upset, pounced upon her, kissed her and asked her to marry him! They had been wandering about in the moonlight by the pavilion and then came into the drawing room and talked half the night. She vowed she was furious – but I doubted it. To prove her point she waved a note from him to the effect that he was returning here tomorrow to fetch her . . . She called him Henlein,[3] says she feels like Czechoslovakia. Later she and I drove to Southend and all the way I praised Alan, pleaded his suit, assuming that she had or would accept him. She was obdurate: at the General Hospital I

---

1 Hubert John Duggan (1904–43) was Conservative MP for Acton from 1931 to 1943. He was the son of Lady Curzon (qv) by her first marriage to Alfredo Huberto Duggan (1875–1915), a wealthy Irish Argentinian.

2 Lady Patricia Florence Susan Guinness (1918–2001), second daughter of the 2nd Earl of Iveagh. She was Channon's sister-in-law.

3 Konrad Henlein (1898–1945) was the Nazi Gauleiter of the Sudetenland territories of Czechoslovakia, annexed by Germany at this time.

stayed half an hour seeing the staff, making arrangements for the royal visit on Wednesday. When I came out I noticed a difference in Patsy. Why not accept him? she said. All afternoon she was in a very different mood and came round more and more to the prospect. The difference in age – he is fourteen years older – she does not mind. She would have a nice long widowhood in which to recover![1]

TUESDAY 11TH OCTOBER

Honor came back this morning from Clandeboye . . . . I sent H a note to the station to prepare her for the patrician developments. Of course she was thrilled and urged Patsy to accept him.

We had a little tea party in the dining room with a cake to celebrate Paul's third birthday. Alan gave him an impressive tricycle. Sunday was really Paul's birthday, but Honor was not here. I put it out of my mind and only today are we celebrating. He is an affectionate, most loving, loveable mite, highly sensitive and intelligent, with a determined will of his own (mine!) plus some good Guinness obstinacy. I love him deeply, and he loves me first, although he is becoming more fond of Honor, and she of him, lately.

Patsy was nervous and fidgeting and refused to greet Alan in public after their row on Sunday night – they had not communicated since. Honor and I contrived to be out of the way when they met. The meeting must have been a success, for they went away smiling. The engagement, I prophesy, will be public within a week!

WEDNESDAY 12TH OCTOBER   *KELVEDON*

I did not sleep, flushed with last night's success. There are moments when I am self-confident, triumphant, and this very feeling of success seems to beget new success.

Up early, as we had the royal visit. The lodges were furnished, or at least nearly so, and the front drive was used. At eleven o'clock the Iveaghs arrived, and I cheered them with an optimistic account of Patsy's intentions and a telegram in code came to me to prepare them for an engagement. The Duchess of Kent accompanied by Marjorie Brecknock[2] arrived ten minutes early. I presented the party and we went into lunch, which was excellent and well served and done. Confidential talk with the Duchess: she is very pro-Chamberlain, rabid against Eden. I begged her to influence the King and Queen against Eden; she replied that she had done so; the King was sound; the Queen less so, as she quite liked Anthony. The Duchess added shrewdly that she herself was so violently pro-Chamberlain

---

1 She in fact survived him by eighteen years.
2 Marjorie Minna Jenkins (1900–89) married in 1920 John Charles Henry Pratt (1899–1983), by courtesy Earl of Brecknock. She was lady-in-waiting to the Duchess of Kent (qv).

that she did her case harm. She was lovely, glowing with aristocratic beauty, but her hair was a bit scrawny at the back. She wore four ropes of pearls and a vast clip. After luncheon we showed her over the house and then left, preceding her by five minutes.

Hock and royalty were too much for Victor Raikes[1] and he tried to kiss Honor in the car – with me present! Our car was cheered all along the route to Rochford as it was mistaken for the royal one. There were two ceremonies (and as I had invited the Duchess, I had to arrange them, soothing the ruffled and jealous feelings of the rival authorities); and Rochford being the more official passed off with clock-like precision. The Duchess was beautiful, gracious, dignified, superb . . . Honor and I and the others left before her so as to be at the Southend Hospital in time to receive her. Much enthusiasm and confusion at Southend, excited nurses, pandemonic [sic] matron etc. . . . . all passed off successfully, but the Mayor's feelings were ruffled. Luckily, but only at the last second, I remembered to include the Mayoress in the private ladies' tea party . . . . [which also included] the matron whose one ambition seemed to be that the HRH should use her lavatory seat, which she had had especially painted. She whispered her difficulties to Honor, who intimated to Princess Marina, and the Duchess did go. Home at six, exhausted. The Iveaghs stayed the night and we again discussed Patsy's matrimonial plans. Honor rang her up, and it now seems certain that she will marry Alan! I am overjoyed. This engagement is my creation and my dream: I hope I shall not be let down. Honor is feeling better, but tired; however she is more normal.

SUNDAY 16TH OCTOBER   KELVEDON

Edward Stanley died this afternoon from his mysterious long-drawn-out illness. He has been kept alive by morphia for weeks now . . . He was only 44, always seemed older. He was courteous, almost handsome, gentle, genial, gay, simple and loyal. He enjoyed fun and society, but was quite unmalicious, and good, stolid, rather German (all Lord Derby's three children are German, and show strongly the inheritance of their grandmother, the old 'Double Duchess' *alten geboren* – a Hanoverian family).[2] The past few months Edward had lost his spirits and gaiety and looked morose and miserable. He was often in our house, always accepted our every invitation; fundamentally I wonder whether he was not unhappy? His growing deafness disturbed him and threatened to restrict his political career, but

---

1 Henry Victor Alpin MacKinnon Raikes (1901–86) was Conservative MP for South East Essex, a neighbouring constituency to Channon's.

2 Channon refers to Luise Friederike Auguste, Countess von Alten (1832–1911), who married in 1852 the 7th Duke of Manchester and, after his death in 1890, married in 1892 the 8th Duke of Devonshire, hence her sobriquet. Stanley's mother – the 17th Earl of Derby's wife – was Lady Alice Montagu (1862–1957), the Double Duchess's daughter by Manchester. '*Geboren*' means 'born'.

it was Portia, his half-mad, always drunk, yet amusing, gay, loyal, curious wife, who upset him. He was anxious about her, terrified of her, ashamed of her . . . at times. Her biting tongue and bullying character eclipsed and frightened him. Oddly enough neither Portia nor Edward cared much for their two eldest boys, John and Richard, who are both charming. They both worshipped the youngest, Hughie, who is rather spoilt. John is now Lord Stanley, soon[1] to be Lord Derby; but owing to the unfortunate ramifications of death duties, settlements to avoid them, and the tricky three-year clause, I fear that the great Derby wealth is now a closed chapter.

MONDAY 17TH OCTOBER

A long, long but highly successful day at Southend with meetings, and interviews etc. I am more rested; but this morning an appalling scene took place. Paul was maddeningly disobedient, and finally in a rage I shook him and scolded him – he was frightened, poor darling mite and lay on the floor sobbing out his little heart, screaming 'Naughty Daddy,' and wanting his Nannie. I thought I should die of remorse: for half an hour I begged him to play with me again, and suddenly he leapt up, put his tear-stained little face against my unshaven one, and told me he loved me. I felt a great wave of tenderness for him rising within me. I love him to a point of folly.

Tassilo Fürstenberg[2] is today marrying Clara Agnelli,[3] that wild darkey girl whom he will never be able to hold for long. Still she wanted him; and he was willing. I introduced them, and at her mother's urgent request bullied him into marrying her. Two marriages I have made.

The Iveaghs wrote that they were very grateful for what we had done about Patsy and Alan. That engagement was formally announced this morning. What will Jim Thomas think in his jealous black heart?[4] How many will detect my hand?

TUESDAY 18TH OCTOBER

The great question now is: who will get govt jobs?[5] Will there be a major reshuffle? My candidate for the Admiralty is Ivor Plymouth:[6] I have taken steps but probably

1 He would not succeed his grandfather until 1948.
2 Prince Tassilo zu Fürstenberg (1903–87).*
3 Clara Jeanne Agnelli (1920–2016) was the granddaughter of Giovanni Agnelli, the founder of Fiat.
4 Channon was clearly under the impression, perhaps correctly, that Thomas and Lennox-Boyd had had a sexual relationship.
5 Following Cooper's resignation from the Admiralty and Stanley's death: the latter had been Dominions Secretary.
6 Ivor Miles Windsor-Clive (1889–1943) succeeded his father as 2nd Earl of Plymouth in 1923. He was Under-Secretary of State at the Foreign Office from 1936 to 1939.*

too late. I have an appalling premonition that Rab Butler will be promoted from the Foreign Office. I should have to go too: and no other job would sort of please me so much. What if he were made Minister of Agriculture? I should accept a whipship. I cannot stir up much enthusiasm, however, as I should, at least for a little, infinitely prefer to remain at the Foreign Office.

THURSDAY 20TH OCTOBER

A long day: Victor Raikes and I motored to London; I looked in at the Foreign Office where the atmosphere, as usual, in that Garden of Anthony Eden, is distinctly chilly towards Chamberlain. Rab hard at work with a committee . . . . including Wogan Philipps,[1] once a handsome playboy, who whilst about to be engaged to Daphne Vivian (now Weymouth)[2] fell on a fence and was impaled. For some years he was impotent, and later, recovering, married Rosamond Lehmann[3] the novelist. Since then he has become increasingly left wing, and his shabby clothes today revealed his leanings.

Thence to the Abbey to attend Edward Stanley's magnificent memorial service. It was crowded out: a more fashionable congregation, although heavily in black, was never before in the Abbey . . . . Mr Attlee sat with the Edens and Anthony's hair looked bleached. Just before the choir entered, the Chamberlains arrived and he took his seat in the first stall, and prayed a long time. I watched him throughout the ceremony, he looked very alive and sad, and when a sunbeam fell on him he seemed, what he is, a saint!! He seemed profoundly moved, and I wonder whether he could be only thinking of Edward, whom he liked but could not have loved: I suspected his thoughts were further away, in Munich and to the calamity he had averted. Leslie Belisha also in a stall, looked gay and debonair: he is being less hideous, the procession of clergy, all looked older than the man in whose memory the service was. I joined Patsy and Alan L[ennox]-B[oyd] . . . they looked positively beaming, Alan very handsome indeed. I drove them to the Carlton Club, and in the members' yard whilst waiting for the car Mr Attlee came up and congratulated the engaged couple. His eyes were red with weeping: the service, he said simply, had got him down. No wonder: the 'Last

1 Wogan Philipps (1902–93) succeeded his father as 2nd Baron Milford in 1962. He married, first, in 1928 Rosamond Lehmann (*vide infra*). He became an ambulance driver on the Republican side in the Spanish Civil War, joined the Communist Party of Great Britain shortly after his return, and was the first and so far only member of the CPGB to sit in the House of Lords.

2 Daphne Winifred Louise Vivian (1904–97), daughter of the 4th Baron Vivian, married in 1927 Henry Frederick Thynne, Viscount Weymouth (qv).*

3 Rosamond Nina Lehmann (1901–90) married as her second husband Wogan Philipps in 1928 and bore him two children; she had an affair with Cecil Day-Lewis and she and Philipps divorced in 1944. Following the success of her first novel, *Dusty Answer*, in 1927 she made a success as a novelist, and also as a vociferous anti-fascist.

Post' followed by Chopin was immensely moving. I never liked Mr Attlee so much before. I lunched alone with Patsy: she is madly in love with Alan now. Later we adjourned to Cartier's where I bought her a gold cigarette case as an engagement present, and diamond buttons for him. And I selected a dressing case for him as a present from Patsy. A rush and change at Belgrave Square, and I caught the 5.30 train for Clacton with Sam Hoare and Rab, and Mrs Rab. At Clacton there was an enormous pro-government rally and Sam and Rab, who spoke (none too well, I thought; just adequate) were much cheered. I drove back to Kelvedon in a thick fog, a typical Essex night – two hours' drive, dangerous and cold.

FRIDAY 21ST OCTOBER

I presided at a Trafalgar dinner[1] in Southend and attended several other functions. The sands are running out: I am exhausted. I shall die young, and while it will be consoling to be buried in little Kelvedon church, I shall hate to leave Paul . . . and this lovely place, and my dear, not always happy, wife.

SATURDAY 22ND OCTOBER

Honor came back [from Holker], seemingly better. Alan and Patsy also here: he and I drove to Southend, where we were professionally charming at three functions and spoke. One of my ex-opponents in Southend, a puce-faced man, Victor Tattersall,[2] who so resembles Ribbentrop,[3] asked me if I was 'on the Square', and wanted me to join a Lodge. I am rather intrigued by the idea: I should enjoy the masochistic initiation ceremonies I think!

MONDAY 24TH OCTOBER

I am dreading Rab's possible appointment to the Ministry of Agriculture.

TUESDAY 25TH OCTOBER

Honor in a depressing, gloomy mood which cuts my heart and drenches my hopes. I spent the whole day with her and arranged for her to ride. We walked home from Kelvedon Hatch,[4] a cold, wet-ish gloomy night. It was *Wuthering*

---

1 It was the 133rd anniversary of the battle in 1805.
2 Victor Tattersall (1899–1959) was Mayor of Southend in 1931–2. He never opposed Channon in an election, so in describing him as an opponent Channon must be indicating that Tattersall was a member of the Liberal Party.
3 Joachim von Ribbentrop (1893–1946) was Foreign Minister of Nazi Germany from 1938 to 1945 and was hanged at Nuremberg the following year.*
4 The nearby village.

Heights – once back Honor's mood changed. Perhaps it is exercise she needs most. I don't understand the delay over the appointments, or rather of the Cabinet reshuffle.

WEDNESDAY 26TH OCTOBER

Honor still in the dumps: at luncheon my poor worn-out tummy turned and I could not eat. Thus I was not at my best in Southend at a bazaar and a meeting. Later I recovered and was warmed and touched by a riotous reception I received at the Leigh Conservative Club where I addressed 500 people.

A long confidential talk with Alderman Tweedy-Smith,[1] the head of the local Liberals, confirmed my impression that the man is an opinionated ass, light metal, no danger to us, and personally well disposed towards me. He believes in birching boys, 'a well-tanned bottom', he said, 'is often the foundation of a great career'. Birching is back, coming in again.[2] Personally I am in favour of it, so long as it is neither cruel, too severe or administered in a spirit of revenge. I never respected my father in the least; had he had the courage to give me a couple of well-deserved whippings, I should not have had all my life the greatest contempt for him.

At midnight I heard the news: 'Lucky Jim' Stanhope[3] has been given the Admiralty and Buck De La Warr,[4] the great opportunist of modern times, has been transferred from the Privy [Council] to the Board of Education. A very uninspiring and probably only preliminary change.

---

1 Robert Tweedy-Smith (1864–1948) was a Justice of the Peace and had been Mayor of Southend-on-Sea in 1932–3.

2 Judicial corporal punishment had not been abolished, but had since the Great War fallen out of favour with some more progressive magistrates and judges. It was removed from the statute book for criminal offences in 1948.

3 James Richard Stanhope (1880–1967), by courtesy Viscount Mahon until 1905, when he succeeded his father as 7th Earl Stanhope. He held junior ministerial office under Lloyd George and Baldwin and in the National Government, joining the Cabinet as First Commissioner of Works in 1936, becoming Leader of the Lords in February 1938. He was replaced at the Admiralty by Churchill in 1939, and, regarded as an arch appeaser, did not serve in the Churchill administration after 1940. He became a Knight of the Garter in 1934. In 1952 he succeeded a kinsman as 13th Earl of Chesterfield, though never used the title. He left Chevening, in Kent, to the nation and it is used as a grace-and-favour weekend house for holders of great offices of state.

4 Herbrand Edward Dundonald Brassey Sackville, known as 'Buck' or 'Buckie' (1900–76), by courtesy Lord Buckhurst until 1915, when he succeeded his father as 9th Earl De La Warr. He was the first hereditary peer to join the Labour Party, and became a Lord in Waiting, or whip in the House of Lords, in Ramsay MacDonald's first administration in 1924. He later joined the Conservative Party and was Postmaster-General in Churchill's administration between 1951 and 1955.

THURSDAY 27TH OCTOBER

Honor very well, and we are happy together again. She rode again today and enjoyed herself. Quintin Hogg[1] has won the Oxford by-election; he had only [blank] votes less than did his predecessor Bob Bourne;[2] and he was subjected to the most fierce and wicked by-election fought for years. It is a govt triumph.

FRIDAY 28TH OCTOBER

We went up to London, lunched at the Belgian Embassy to meet the Crown Princess of Italy.[3] She is like Honor, fair, good-looking, rather grandiose in manner, hates society, and loves mountaineering, and all forms of violent exercise. Of course she is unhappily married: wives of Glamour Boys usually are .... The Princess had been at school[4] in Brentwood – four miles from here [Kelvedon] – and only a few days ago had been to see the venerable Mother Superior aged over 80, whom she had known, loved and feared as a child. The Princess remembered me quite well; I danced with her twelve years ago at Eileen Sutherland's[5] ball, and played tennis with her, too, in Belgrave Square! She has not been to England since. She is a restless, under-served sexually woman. Lunch was too drawn out – the Athlones,[6] both very amiable, and annoyed at the prospect of King Carol's[7] visit. Princess Alice was vituperative

1 Quintin McGarel Hogg (1907–2001) succeeded his father (qv) as 2nd Viscount Hailsham in 1950. He held various ministerial and Cabinet posts in the Conservative governments between 1951 and 1964, being Leader of the Lords from 1960 to 1963, when he renounced his peerage in order to contest the leadership of his party. He was unsuccessful. In 1970 he was raised again to the peerage as Baron Hailsham of St Marylebone and served as Lord Chancellor until 1974, resuming the office between 1979 and 1987. He became a Knight of the Garter in 1988. The Oxford by-election became a micro-referendum on Munich; Patrick Gordon Walker, the Labour candidate, withdrew, as did the Liberal, and both parties supported Alexander Dunlop 'Sandie' Lindsay (1879–1952), the Master of Balliol, who stood as an Independent Progressive. Hogg – whose opponents used the slogan 'a vote for Hogg is a vote for Hitler' – won by 15,797 votes to 12,363, the Tory vote down by just 6.7 per cent on the 1935 election. Lindsay, who was Professor of Moral Philosophy in the university, was supported by Churchill and Harold Macmillan; in 1945 he was raised to the peerage as 1st Baron Lindsay of Birker.
2 Robert Croft Bourne (1888–1938) was a former Olympic oarsman who sat for Oxford as a Conservative from 1924 to 1938, and was Deputy Speaker of the Commons from 1931 until his sudden death.
3 Formerly Princess Marie-José of Belgium.*
4 At the Ursuline Convent School there: she and her family were evacuated to England during the Great War.
5 Eileen Gwladys Butler (1891–1943), daughter of the 7th Earl of Lanesborough and wife of the 5th Duke of Sutherland.*
6 The Earl and Countess of Athlone – Prince Alexander of Teck (1874–1957), Queen Mary's brother, and Princess Alice (1883–1981).*
7 King Carol II of Romania.*

about him. I happened to say that he had bought the *Nahlin*,[1] the Duke of Windsor's old yacht. 'He would!' Princess Alice retorted. Much kissing between the royalties . . . The Princess of Piedmont[2] stayed until 3.30, and by then Honor was in despair. At last we got away. Pompous royal functions can be very exhausting. Honor went to see Anne Feversham and her baby daughter Clarissa – or Marina.[3] Honor and the Duchess of Kent are to be godmothers! Those poor Kents – three years in Australia.[4] I am glad for her sake. She will get him back, make a man of him. He will not be able to shop on a grand scale, nor drink so much, nor sit up all night with Glamour Boys! I shall miss them however . . .

SATURDAY 29TH OCTOBER

Honor rode. We are recovering from yesterday! We have a mad plan of dashing suddenly and now to the USA for three weeks, taking Paul with us. Honor could go on to Ketchum in Idaho to ski whilst I would take Paul to see my mother. I wonder whether I can get away. Of course I don't want to leave the FO, Rab, Kelvedon and all. It would be an uncomfortable and expensive uprooting. Still . . . for Honor, I would do anything.

SUNDAY 30TH OCTOBER

Va-et-vient[5] at Kelvedon. Prince Fritzi[6] of Prussia came here for the day: he is first back from Germany via Doorn, where he stayed with the Kaiser[7] whom he loves. Fritzi looks bronzed and strong and the weeks of work in the army have improved him. He had been terrified of war; all Germany had feared it. The army and the Potsdam Group are averse to it and are growing increasingly

---

1 The yacht had been lent to the then King in the summer of 1936, and he had taken Mrs Simpson, the Duff Coopers and others with him on a cruise that confirmed his determination to marry his mistress.
2 Another title of the Crown Princess.
3 Anne Feversham (1910–95) was the daughter of the 1st Earl of Halifax* and in 1936 married 'Sim' Duncombe, 3rd Earl of Feversham*. She was first cousin to Lady Honor Channon: their mothers were sisters. The child, born on 11 October 1938, was Lady Clarissa Duncombe.
4 It had just been announced that the Duke of Kent would take up the post of Governor-General of Australia in November 1939. Shortly after the outbreak of war the following September it was announced that the appointment had been postponed.
5 Comings and goings.
6 Prince Friedrich Georg Wilhelm Christoph of Prussia (1911–66) was a grandson of Kaiser Wilhelm II. He would marry, in 1945 after a war spent in internment camps, Lady Brigid Guinness (qv).
7 Kaiser Wilhelm II, in exile there since his abdication in November 1918.

hostile to the Hitler[1] regime – the regime more than the man. Himmler and Ribbentrop are the dangers ... Fritzi is laying siege, a slow-waiting siege to the throne. We shall live to see him emperor. I have always said so, and have worked for the restoration of the Hohenzollern dynasty . . . Fritzi thinks the Nazi leaders will eventually devour one another and then there will be a *coup d'état* by the army, which while not breaking with the Nazis completely, will restore the dynasty and the old Junker regime.[2] Fritzi had to rush back to London to have tea with Queen Mary, who dotes on him. He has been working, and at last succeeded, in once more establishing good relations between her and his grandfather. The exile at Doorn now writes regularly to Queen Mary, and to his old uncle, the Duke of Connaught.[3] They are in the twilight of their lives and it is pleasant that between them at least there is no more war bitterness. The Kaiser told Fritzi only last week that he is still haunted by the fate which befell the Tsar and his family. He had sent the Tsar a telegram offering him a free and protected passage through Germany, or an escort of battleships, had he wished to escape by sea. This was at the moment when the Tsar had tried to get to England. It was Lloyd George who spoilt and stopped everything and the late King had been weak with him thinking the danger not immediate.[4] Their responsibility in the matter has been like a millstone hanging on the necks of both Queen Mary and King George. Their failure to help their poor Russian relations in the hour of danger is the one blot on their lives. Of late, Queen Mary has been sorely conscience-stricken.

1 Adolf Hitler (1889–1945) was born in Austria but moved to Germany in 1913. He had a conception of German history embodied in his idea of a Reich of German-speaking Teutons that included German and Austrian lands but expressly excluded Jews, Slavs and non-white races. A racially motivated nationalist, he led the Nazi party from 1921 to 1945, was Chancellor of Germany from 1933 and *Führer*, or leader, of the German people from 1934. His decision to invade Poland in 1939 started the Second World War; his decision to invade Russia in 1941 ensured he lost it. Having narrowly avoided assassination in 1944, he committed suicide in April 1945.

2 Channon refers to the situation in Imperial Germany from 1871 to 1918 when the Kaiser ruled, as his forebears the kings of Prussia had done, with the assistance of the old Prussian aristocracy.

3 Prince Arthur William Patrick Albert (1850–1942), 1st Duke of Connaught and Strathearn, was the third son of Queen Victoria, younger brother of the late Kaiserin (mother of Wilhelm II), and uncle of King George V.

4 This is not true. Lloyd George had been happy to grant asylum to the Tsar and his family, as the head of state of a major British ally in the fight against Germany. The King was willing at first to take his Prime Minister's advice but was talked out of doing so by Lord Stamfordham, his private secretary, who feared it would spark a workers' revolt in Britain to have a man the labour movement regarded as a despot given a haven among them. King George V and Queen Mary did, indeed, regret the fate of the Romanovs, but there is no evidence they regretted the decision.

MONDAY 31ST OCTOBER   *KELVEDON*

My last day here in peace and I am not ready for Parliament, nor London life. I feel old, run-down, and my heart occasionally thumps. I don't want to die until I am a peer, and Kelvedon has been made perfection, a paradise for Paul. It is nearly so now. I love the [illegible] furniture, the details, the old brewery now used as our Austrian room. Alan and Patsy came here for the night. Patsy talking of nothing but her babies to come, and her husband-to-be was much shocked, but secretly pleased, as any man would be. I wish I could look forward to more.

TUESDAY 1ST NOVEMBER

I drove up to London with Alan L-B, and rushed to the Foreign Office. We are inundated with work and today the Opposition raise Munich and what has happened since the Adjournment. Lunched with Harold [Balfour] at the Savoy and Helen Fitzgerald[1] came too. They are much in love and Harold's prestige amongst the boys had consequently soared, but an *amour* means a great expense in time and money and in H's case is certainly not worth it!! Harold delightful. Thence to the H of C, and was pleased to see everyone again certainly. Much rushing about, and I caught the Opposition plotting. By Opposition nowadays, I mean, of course, that little group of Glamour Boys who, drenched in stupidity, tinged with sedition, are attempting to torpedo the Prime Minister. He is too lenient with them.

    The debate proceeded, and the PM, sitting directly in front of me, looked somewhat aged and his hair needed cutting. He is greyer than before Munich. He still mutters little asides to David Margesson, to Rab, or whoever is next to him. It was a desultory debate. Vyvyan Adams,[2] who is much opposed to us, complained to me that he had not been called by the Speaker[3] for nine months. I went to the Speaker and after a little preliminary flattery suggested that he call Adams. He promised that he would, and later he did. Adams attacked us violently! Thus are things done in democratic England. Later Bill Astor[4] spoke well of his recent experiences in Sudeten Land [*sic*] and impressed the House. He is so sound, so sensible, and so shrewd, although he lacks grace and charm. As [Oliver] Stanley

1 Helen Gascoigne Drury (1896–1957), daughter of Major General Charles Drury, of Nova Scotia, and sister of Lady Beaverbrook, had married in 1923 Evelyn Charles Fitzgerald (qv). They remained married at this time.
2 Samuel Vyvyan Trerice Adams (1900–51) was Conservative MP for Leeds West from 1931 to 1945.
3 Edward Algernon FitzRoy (1869–1943), second son of the 3rd Baron Southampton, was a Conservative MP from 1900 to 1928, when he was elected Speaker of the House of Commons.
4 William Waldorf Astor (1907–66) succeeded his father as 3rd Viscount Astor in 1952. He was Conservative MP for Fulham East from 1935 to 1945 and for Wycombe from 1951 to 1952. From 1936 to 1937 he was PPS to Samuel Hoare (qv).

was winding-up,[1] Bill, Harold and I slipped away to the Savoy, where exhausted and sleepy, we drank much champagne and flitted from table to table and found each group more maddening than the others – a lot of pro-Jewish, irresponsible people[2] – Noël Coward[3] was with Venetia Montagu[4] and they had been dining at the Admiralty with the Coopers [who] are limpet-like in their determination not to evacuate their lovely house (apparently Lady Stanhope[5] shows no desire to move in); Sibyl Colefax[6] was with Oliver Messel[7] – two anti-Chamberlain tables, and then another Jim Thomas and Ronnie Cartland, 'little people', there. Home – too tired to drive the great Rolls well, I bumped the mudguard. Alan not in yet: Honor at Kelvedon. We are still toying with the idea of going to the USA next week. Quintin Hogg took his seat today; he looked grim but gay. Lord Hailsham[8] watched from the gallery. I thought of my poor Edward Marjoribanks[9] and his sad life.

WEDNESDAY 2ND NOVEMBER

The long-proposed debate on the Italian agreement came at last today. The PM, who is becoming increasingly dictatorial (and fortunately always right) wants to

1   Left blank in the text, as presumably Channon could not recall who wound up for the government, and forgot to fill in the name later. Hansard records it was Oliver Frederick George Stanley (1896–1950), second son of the 17th Earl of Derby and younger brother of Edward, Lord Stanley, who had died two weeks earlier (qqv). Oliver sat in the Cabinet as President of the Board of Trade from 1937 to 1940.
2   Channon only occasionally challenges his own casual anti-Semitism – sadly not untypical of people of his class – in the late 1930s and early 1940s, though he comes to be shocked by revelations of the extremes of the Nazi persecution of the Jews. See his diary entries for 21 November 1938 (following Kristallnacht) and 17 December 1942 (following a speech by Rothschild in the Commons about the fate of Eastern European Jews). On this latter occasion, Channon is among the MPs who rises in silent tribute.
3   Noël Peirce Coward (1889–1973), writer, director and actor.*
4   Beatrice Venetia Stanley (1887–1948), daughter of the 4th Baron Sheffield and 4th Baron Stanley of Alderley, had been the love-object of H. H. Asquith in the years before 1915. Asquith was unhinged when, that May, she announced her engagement to his junior ministerial colleague, Edwin Montagu, whom she married that summer.
5   Lady Eileen Agatha Browne (1889–1940), daughter of the 6th Marquess of Sligo, married the 7th Earl Stanhope in 1921.
6   Lady Colefax, the celebrated interior designer.*
7   Oliver Messel was a leading stage, ballet and film-set designer.
8   Douglas McGarel Hogg KC (1872–1950) had been Attorney-General in Bonar Law's administration and then in Baldwin's, became Lord Chancellor in March 1928 and served until the following June, then again from 1935 until 1938. He was Leader of the House of Lords and Secretary of State for War in the National Government from 1931 to 1935. He was raised to the peerage as Baron Hailsham in 1928 and advanced to a viscountcy in 1929.
9   Edward Marjoribanks (1900–32) was 1st Viscount Hailsham's stepson; he committed suicide by shooting himself in Hailsham's billiard room after having been jilted for a second time.

reward Signor Mussolini for his help at Munich, and it is the ratification of this agreement which the Duce wants, as it will confer recognition on the King of Italy as Emperor of Abyssinia. I helped Rab at the FO in the morning and we talked about the idea of Chamberlain and Halifax going to Paris on an official visit. Lunched with Harold, young Giovanni Agnelli,[1] Alan and Patsy. All the afternoon I was on the bench taking notes, running errands, fagging. The PM made a brilliant speech . . . But the debate was singularly lifeless, dull and foregone. The official Opposition are madly pro-war – with anybody. Towards the end of the afternoon Anthony Eden got up and he filled the House. He made a bitter but polite attack on the govt. How wicked he can look! There is a left leer in his eye, even his clothes lack the patrician suavity of old.

As the division had approached I found myself alone on the second bench, with Ernest Brown[2] the sole occupant of the front bench. Suddenly a hand was placed on my shoulder and looking up I saw that my friend was Anthony Eden. We had an easy, friendly, whispered even affectionate talk. Then he murmured 'Come out a moment,' and I followed him into the Aye lobby[3] and we went into the lavatory and we p----d together. He was charm itself; he had not seen much of me all these years, he had been so busy; did I love the Foreign Office, I was, he had heard it said, a great success there. Were we in our Essex house yet? We must meet soon; it was 'lovely' to dine out in peace; he was really enjoying his freedom (if so, why his frantic efforts to get back into power by any possible means, honest or otherwise?); he would never again raise his voice about foreign affairs in the House. We had a surprisingly warm reconciliation and I left him aglow with appeasement; I have always liked him, always thought him 'simple', and do still. Why he should have selected this moment to want to make an advance I don't know. Possibly he thought I would intimate to high grandees his determination never to refer again to foreign affairs. If he thought so, he was, for once in his disastrous career, right; for I rushed to the Prime Minister's room and told him! He smiled, murmured 'I am glad to hear it.' I returned to the bench and when one of the Opposition began to clamour for a member of the government I scanned all the ministers' rooms. Sam Hoare was charming but refused to come to the rescue as he had a conference. Eventually I found both Oliver Stanley and Walter Elliot, who resumed their places on the bench. The debate was desultory,

---

1 Giovanni 'Gianni' Agnelli (1921–2003) was the grandson of the founder of Fiat, the motor company of which he assumed control in 1966. He was at this stage studying law at the University of Turin. In the war he was wounded twice on the Eastern Front, and once in a bar in North Africa in a fight with a German officer over a woman.

2 Alfred Ernest Brown (1881–1962) was Liberal MP for Rugby from 1923 to 1924 and for Leith from 1927 to 1945. He was Minister of Labour from 1935 to 1940 and held a succession of ministerial appointments in the Churchill coalition from 1940 to 1945. He sat as a Liberal National from 1931 and led the Liberal National Party from 1940 to 1945.

3 The passage through which, when a division is held, MPs walk to register support of the motion.

nobody was much interested; everyone wants friendships with Italy, that is all save a few frenzied enemies of Mussolini, and of course, the Labour Party. Rab wound up and very bad he was, too; but the Opposition were in a noisy, rather drunken, hilarious mood and gave him a rough passage.

At 11.30 I looked in at Sibyl Colefax's, where she had a small supper party. Very Red atmosphere: soon we shall have a certain section of London society, café society and the intelligentsia leading the Communist Party or leading the self-same doctrines! This is what happened in Russia, in France, in Spain before the revolutions. It is dangerous – except that in England everything passes eventually. I drove Duff and Diana back to the Admiralty, where they are <u>still</u> living. Duff voted with the govt tonight. He could hardly do otherwise, as he was a member of the govt when the Italian agreement was negotiated. The figures were high and now the Italian episode is ended – what a triumph for Sam Hoare!! He is vindicated at long last. Dropping the Coopers, I forlornly returned to Sibyl Colefax's and I soon found myself arguing with Noël Coward, who has set himself up as a political hostess!! He is violently anti-German, anti-Italian, anti-Franco and *ipso facto* neo-Russian. He is bitten by communism – he has tried almost everything else! It is the last adventure of the emotionally bankrupt – one should never argue with the irresponsible . . . I left rather than continue the argument.

The recent government changes please nobody, and augur for an early election.

Thursday 3rd November

Morning at the FO. I did not have the courage to tell Rab that he had spoken badly. The debate was on air-raid precautions and took the form of a vote of censure. At twelve noon came a message that the PM had a tummy upset as he had eaten rich food last night. It was given out to the newspapers that he had a slight chill. I think he is tired and couldn't face the long debate today, which began with a speech by Herbert Morrison which lasted one hour forty minutes. I hate him; he is so cocksure, so rude, and unattractive. Certainly he is quick and able. I went back to No. 5 [Belgrave Square] to see Fritzi of Prussia who entrusted to me a secret letter from his father the Crown Prince for the PM. I promised to deliver it and did.

Diana Cooper rang me up and later got her agent to do so trying to find out who is standing against Duff in the next election. I played her. It is, of course, Kenneth de Courcy,[1] who might well get in. The Coopers are terrified. It will do them good. But I cannot interfere, as I don't choose to lose the Coopers' friendship – yet! But I am tired to death of them.

---

1 Kenneth Hugh de Courcy (1909–99) was a Galway-born businessman who edited *Intelligence Digest*. A committed appeaser, he was active in the Imperial Policy Group, whose membership included a number of right-wing Tory MPs, and so close a supporter of King Edward VIII that he was associated with plots to restore him to the throne. He was imprisoned for fraud in the 1960s, though there was some doubt about the safety of his conviction.

I dined with the Euan Wallaces. Euan is in a sulk because he has not been put into the Cabinet. (I happen to know that Neville C dislikes him, or at least has the lowest opinion of his qualifications.) Probably it is not desirable to have another Edenite in the Cabinet now. Barbie Wallace[1] is frankly Edenite and had spent the afternoon with all the Glamour Boys buzzing about talking at Noël Coward's studio, where he had a cocktail party for the 'Opposition'; it is v undignified for this group to revolve around Noël and betrays their silliness. He is about the best they can produce. There is a cleavage in London society about Chamberlain; but the ranks may come together again when we are faced with an election. Barbie said that the Eden–Cranborne–Thomas–Churchill group were jubilant today because the govt had had a bad day, as Herbert Morrison's speech was v damning to us. What loyalty! What judgement! Her sympathies all lie in that direction and no doubt she does Euan harm. I drove back to Kelvedon arriving here just after midnight.

I looked into the Lords; Lord Crewe[2] was speaking and told the House that he remembered the fuss when Queen Victoria assumed the Imperial dignity of India. He is old,[3] Lord Crewe, v handsome and distinguished, with his cheeks so red we wondered if they were painted. He nearly bought Kelvedon five years ago.

MONDAY 7TH NOVEMBER   KELVEDON

Lord Camrose's[4] long illness explains the recent opposition of the *Telegraph* to peace, Chamberlain and the govt. Perhaps his recovery will bring about a change of policy. Seymour,[5] snobbish and capitalistic, is very Red, or rather, pro-Winston. More he had been influenced by Virginia Cowles,[6] that female journalist whom I suspect of being a communist agent. She seduces the youth of England: sleeps with them and infects them with Eden-itis. She ought to be deported. It is curious that over the crisis the rival houses, the Astors and the Berrys,[7] who often see

---

1 Barbara Lutyens (1898–1981), daughter of Sir Edwin Lutyens, married Euan Wallace (qv) in 1920.

2 Robert Offley Ashburton Crewe-Milnes (1858–1945) succeeded his father as 2nd Baron Houghton in 1885 and was advanced to the earldom of Crewe in 1895.*

3 Crewe was 80.

4 William Ewart Berry (1879–1954) was born in Merthyr Tydfil and set up his own local newspaper in 1901. He became proprietor of the *Sunday Times* in 1915, the *Financial Times* in 1919 and of the *Daily Telegraph* in 1927, which he amalgamated with the *Morning Post* when he bought the latter in 1937. He was a strong financial supporter of Churchill. He was created 1st Bt in 1921 and raised to the peerage as 1st Baron Camrose in 1929; and was advanced to a viscountcy in 1941. He married, in 1905, Mary Agnes Corns, with whom he had eight children.

5 John Seymour Berry (1909–95) was Deputy Chairman of the *Daily Telegraph* from 1939 to 1987. He succeeded his father as 2nd Viscount Camrose in 1954. He married in 1986 Joan Yarde-Buller*, whose previous two husbands were Loel Guinness and Prince Ali Khan*.

6 Harriet Virginia Spencer Cowles (1910–83), of Vermont, made her name as a correspondent covering the Spanish Civil War, and went on to write a number of acclaimed novels.

7 John Jacob Astor V (1886–1971) had bought *The Times* in 1922. The *Daily Telegraph*, owned by Lord Camrose (qv) and the Berry family, was its great commercial rival.

eye to eye, have disagreed. And it is the Astors who have won. They were united over the abdication, and largely engineered it. But as I say, the Berrys have been handicapped over the crisis by their chief's illness. They are a dreadful family: I regret having made friends with them. Their crudeness, metallic unaristocratic point of view reminds one of not quite first-rate yet accepted Americans.

I have made elaborate arrangements for my papers, put them in a safe in the basement, in a special room.

Brigid Guinness came to see us for a moment *en route* from Elveden to Paris. She was wearing a blue belt marked '*Vive* Chamberlain'.

There is still so much to do here at Kelvedon that I despair of the outside, of the grounds, ever being lovely.

TUESDAY 8TH NOVEMBER

The fourth session of this most fateful, eventful parliament opened today. I wonder what it will unfold for us? A war? An election? In the past three years we have had everything else, scandals, political strife, resignations, abdication and coronation . . .

I motored up early, and came directly to the House. The usual hum, the usual top hats; and I took my place in the East Gallery of the Lords. Already the peeresses were pouring in, and Grace Curzon[1] on the marchionesses' bench looked like a great meringue, vast, sugary and imposing. Lady Baldwin is thinner; since she became a countess, perhaps she wears tighter stays. The duchesses with few exceptions looked drab: the Somerset[2] looked like a housekeeper, the little Richmond[3] of no account, but the chic duchesses, Eileen and Mollie[4] were ablaze. Kakoo Rutland[5] wore scarlet and was a touch cheap: the honours were all Moucher Devonshire's,[6] who sat there for the first time. She looked extraordinarily imposing in black with the Devonshire tiara . . . On the whole the display was less than usual, the peeresses more obscure . . . Margot Oxford[7] looked like a Spectre

---

1 Grace Elvina Hinds (1885–1958), from Alabama, married in 1917 as her second husband Earl (later 1st Marquess) Curzon of Kedleston (qv).*

2 Edith Mary Parker (1883–1962), married in 1906 Evelyn Francis Edward Seymour (1882– 1954), Lord Seymour by courtesy from 1923 to 1931, when he succeeded his father as 17th Duke of Somerset.

3 Elizabeth Grace Hudson (1900–92), married in 1927 Frederick Charles Gordon-Lennox (1904–89), Lord Settrington by courtesy until 1928 and Earl of March by courtesy from then until 1935 when he succeeded his father as 9th Duke of Richmond, 9th Duke of Lennox and 4th Duke of Gordon.

4 The Duchess of Sutherland and the Dowager Duchess of Buccleuch (widow of the 7th Duke) respectively.

5 Kathleen 'Kakoo' Tennant (1894–1989), wife of the 9th Duke of Rutland*.

6 Mary Alice 'Moucher' Gascoyne-Cecil (1895–1988), wife of the 10th Duke of Devonshire*.

7 Emma Alice Margaret 'Margot' Tennant (1864–1945), wife of H. H. Asquith; with his elevation to an earldom in 1925 she became Countess of Oxford and Asquith.

of Death, and she moved animatedly about. The Sovereigns[1] were a little late, and Queen Elizabeth[2] was obviously nervous and ill at ease, but she looked well, if more solemn than usual. The King, after the first appalling pause when in an agony one wonders whether he will ever get the words out, read the speech in a clear voice with barely any trace of effort. The words are especially selected for him, as some consonants he cannot cope with. It was all quickly over and the Sovereigns bowed and departed in a blaze of red and jewels. There was not last year's splendour, nor any of the sad fey atmosphere of the time when Edward VIII looking like a beautiful child, was the cynosure of every admiring eye . . . Today that dreadful old Archbishop was still prancing about.

Alan [Lennox-Boyd] seems happy, not mad. He is a Will O' the Wisp, and scatters his forces. He knows nothing of the opposite sex and is quite uninterested in it. A queer augury for marital life.

I thought about the Opening of Parliament tonight and the curious way in which the English (who are certainly mad at the moment) cling to their traditions. It was, as ever, an Alice in Wonderland scene.

WEDNESDAY 9TH NOVEMBER

The wave of anti-Chamberlain feeling, largely confined to London society, seems to be growing. Honor, 'nervy', motored back to Kelvedon after dinner. My father would have been 70 today were he alive.

THURSDAY 10TH NOVEMBER

H of C all day. I am the supreme attender. I am tired, though: I sense the sands running out. Perhaps I shall die young.

MONDAY 14TH NOVEMBER

Up to London and to the FO. Many Questions. Rab went to Bridgwater to speak in the by-election and I secretly wanted to accompany him.[3] It was in Bridgwater that my Channon grandfather, the first Henry, was born, although his family

---

1 Channon occasionally uses this solecism to describe the King and Queen. The King was the Sovereign; the Queen his consort.
2 Lady Elizabeth Angela Marguerite Bowes-Lyon (1900–2002), daughter of the 14th and 1st Earl of Strathmore and Kinghorne, married in 1923 Prince Albert, Duke of York, who in 1936 became King George VI.
3 The Bridgwater by-election, in Somerset, caused by the appointment of the sitting Conservative MP as a High Court judge, took place on 17 November, and proved a disaster for the government. Vernon Bartlett (1894–1983), a well-known journalist, stood as an Independent Progressive candidate on an anti-appeasement ticket with the support of the Labour and Liberal parties. On an 82 per cent turnout Bartlett won by 2,332 votes.

came from Ottery St Mary. This evening Arthur Henderson[1] warned me that he was raising Winterton's[2] recent indiscretions over Russia in the House. I hurried to the telephone, warned the FO and asked for a brief for the Prime Minister. He came to the H of C at 9.30, read the memo prepared by the FO and asked me, 'What do I do now?' with that strange little smile which makes me love him. I then tackled Arthur Henderson and by means of cajolery and clumsy flattery, he showed me the notes for his speech and told me all that he was going to say. I walked slowly away, but once out of his sight, dashed to the PM's room. He was alone, and smiled as I walked in. I reported, rather flurriedly [sic], all that Arthur Henderson (he is an amiable lightweight) had told me and the PM beamed. He was thus able to draw up his case and he thoroughly trounced poor Arthur, who squirmed uncomfortably all unconscious of my Judas action.

TUESDAY 15TH NOVEMBER

The pogroms in Germany[3] and the persecutions there have roused much indignation everywhere. Hitler never helps us and always makes Chamberlain's task more difficult. One cannot say so, but the sympathies of many people are not altogether with the unfortunate Jews. Indeed, many important members of their race do not attempt to deny their disappointment that there was not a world war in September, which would have crushed Nazidom.

WEDNESDAY 16TH NOVEMBER

Honor and I dined in her room: she was in excellent spirits. We dressed afterwards and went on to Buckingham Palace. Honor looked magnificent, ablaze with many sapphires and diamonds. The reception was very mixed: a third list, I fear: hardly any of our friends. We stood about with the Butlers (Rab looking

---

1 Arthur Henderson (1893–1968), the son of Arthur Henderson, former leader of the Labour Party, was a Labour MP. After holding junior office in the coalition and Attlee governments he was Secretary of State for Air from 1947 to 1951. He was raised to a life peerage in 1966 as Baron Rowley.

2 Edward Turnour (1883–1962) succeeded his father as 6th Earl Winterton in 1907. As Chancellor of the Duchy of Lancaster, he had embarrassed the government by suggesting Russia had been no help at all during the Munich crisis.*

3 Channon refers to Kristallnacht, when in Germany on the night of 9–10 November thugs led by Sturmabteilung paramilitaries wrecked synagogues and shops, businesses and houses owned by Jews, without any interference from the authorities. The alleged provocation for the pogrom was the assassination in Paris on 9 November of Ernst vom Rath (1909–38), a German diplomat, by Herschel Grynszpan, a 17-year-old Jewish boy who had just heard of the deportation of his parents from Germany to Poland, where they were placed in a refugee camp on the border. Even appeasers of the Nazis, including *The Times*, registered their horror at what had happened.

tired, Sydney[1] very underdressed) for half an hour. The young Norfolks joined us. About eleven the Household Officers began wandering about and presently, very slowly, with no fuss, the King and Queen appeared. She looked well in a crinoline and he was grinning and looked very young as all his family do. I saw him gossiping with Gerry Wellesley[2] and I looked away, as I know it would give Gerry too much pleasure if he knew I had seen them together. The King and Queen advanced, talked to the Norfolks and went the length of the long room, stopping now and then to chat with friends. Queen Mary entered from the opposite door and was much more dignified. She glittered with five diamond necklaces about her throat and neck. Pamela Berry[3] whispered to me 'She has bagged all the best jewels.' She has. Walter Buccleuch joked with Honor as he waited. The little Queen looked well, and gave me a dazzling blue smile with her wide lapis eyes. The King continued to grin. At last they disappeared into another room, and George Gage entered piloting the King of Romania[4] who is gross, flashy, gay and rather fun. Honor and I were presented. Then the Kents came in and walked up to us: she outshone everyone as usual: she was glamorously lovely, slender and glittering, with that distinction and glow of her own. She asked us to luncheon on Wednesday next, said that Paul and Olga[5] would arrive on Monday and we had a long gossip. Rab and Mrs Rab were immediately opposite and commented on our royal favour. Princess Marina introduced me to Crown Prince Michael,[6] an extraordinarily handsome tall youth. He is shy and bored; but when he smiles two dimples appear. He has some of his mother's charm, and little of his father's flashiness. The Duchess of Gloucester looked sweet and demure and elegant in a crinoline dress not unlike the Queen's. Queen Mary advanced upon us, and beside her all royalties except the Kents look second-rate. She shook hands with Honor and me and joked with Mr Kennedy,[7] the American Ambassador, who was immediately behind us. He presented two of his daughters – entranced they looked – to her. She was in blue with mountains of jewels . . . The royalties moved into the gallery and Honor began to get tired and we soon left. Below we

---

1 Sydney Elizabeth Courtauld (1902–54) married Butler in 1926. She was the daughter of Samuel Courtauld*, founder of the Courtauld Institute of Art.
2 Gerald Wellesley (1885–1972), by courtesy Lord Gerald until 1943 when he succeeded his nephew as 7th Duke of Wellington.
3 Lady Pamela Margaret Elizabeth Smith (1915–82), daughter of the 1st Earl of Birkenhead, married in 1936 William Berry, younger brother of Seymour Berry (qqv).
4 King Carol II (1893–1953).*
5 Prince and Princess Paul of Yugoslavia, the latter the Duchess of Kent's (qv) sister.
6 King Michael I (1921–2017).*
7 Joseph Patrick Kennedy (1888–1969), father of the future American President John F. Kennedy (qv).*

found the Pembrokes[1] and the Anthony Edens waiting for their cars. 'The worst of being sacked is, you can never find your car,' Anthony laughed. I introduced him to Honor. Lady Pembroke wore the tiara with the huge sapphire. We were back at Belgrave Square at 12.30 and H left immediately for Kelvedon.

THURSDAY 17TH NOVEMBER

Diana Cooper rang me early to hear all about the BP party, to which they had not been invited. Was it, she wondered, because Duff had resigned, or because she had curtsied to the Duchess of Windsor in Paris? ... the Coopers – *enfin*[2] – are leaving the Admiralty today, and will stay for a time with Emerald [Cunard] ...

A long day at the House: it was the day when the Glamour Boys hoped to damage us, and Winston Churchill made a terrific attack on the govt, and he begged fifty Conservatives to follow him into the lobby.[3] Actually only Messrs Macmillan[4] and Bob Boothby[5] did go, the figures, a majority of 196 for the govt, were satisfactory. The PM spoke for one hour one minute, very well, clearly, and amusingly, answering his critics, defending his Defence fears and refusing to create a Ministry of Supply. He retorted to Winston, and the House laughed. But the surprise of the day was Duff Cooper's sycophantic speech in which he praised the Prime Minister, and generally did a sugary suck-up to the govt, which he seemed so eager to leave a few weeks ago. Is he alarmed by the alliance of his constituents, or does he regret his harsh and rude words to the PM which resulted in his downfall? Everyone, says the proverb, pushes over a falling fence, and maybe he is humiliated by his recent snub. He refused to follow Winston, much to the latter's disappointment; on the other hand I am

1 Reginald Herbert (1880–1960), by courtesy Lord Herbert from 1895 to 1913, when he succeeded his father as 15th Earl of Pembroke and 12th Earl of Montgomery, married, in 1904, Lady Beatrice Eleanor Paget (1883–1973), daughter of Lord Alexander Victor Paget and sister of the 6th Marquess of Anglesey.

2 At last.

3 It was the debate on the King's Speech, in which anti-appeasers strove to draw attention to how underpowered Britain's defences were.

4 Maurice Harold Macmillan (1894–1986) was Conservative MP for Stockton-on-Tees from 1924 to 1929 and from 1931 to 1945, and for Bromley from 1945 to 1964. He became a fierce critic of Neville Chamberlain and was given office by Winston Churchill in 1940. He ended up as Minister of Defence, Foreign Secretary, Chancellor of the Exchequer and, from 1957 to 1963, Prime Minister. He was awarded the Order of Merit and, in 1984, raised to the peerage as 1st Earl of Stockton.

5 Robert John Graham Boothby (1900–86) was a Conservative MP in Aberdeenshire from 1924 to 1958. He married, in 1935, Diana Cavendish (qv); they were divorced in 1937. He was created a life peer in 1958 by Harold Macmillan, whose wife, Lady Dorothy, had been Boothby's mistress since 1930.

not sure that the govt, more especially the PM, was pleased at the unexpected support. Tired, I let myself be taken to Jim Wedderburn's house to drink with him and Bill Astor.

FRIDAY 18TH NOVEMBER

Alan's 34th birthday . . . Wayward, weak, intoxicating Alan . . .

I returned to the H of C and was dumbfounded by the news of the Bridgwater election. Vernon Bartlett, standing as an Independent, had a great victory over the govt candidate. This is the worst blow the govt has had since 1935. Of course there are extenuating explanations, but these are meagre comfort. The Central Office machine is cumbersome, inefficient, and wants overhauling. Otherwise we shall lose the election; but poor comfort for the Socialists . . .

SATURDAY 19TH NOVEMBER

We are appalled by Alan's off-hand manner, indeed his neglect of Patsy. He has not gone to Elveden this weekend to the royal party and she is there alone . . . too cavalier of him.

That gawky good-tongued absurd hoyden Viola Tree[1] has followed her husband to the grave. She was young, immense, funny and kindly. I have never liked Trees of any description. And Lord Beauchamp[2] died in New York, aged only 66. What a turbulent life. Rank, riches, arrogance, intelligence, achievement, high office, seven children, the god's gifts at his feet, and he *gaspillé*-ed[3] them all for the most sterile of all vices – footmen!! There has never been such a scandal in England, and yet people, on the whole, minded very little. The whole story very Roman, classic. That large, pompous, humourless Lord Beauchamp, a deep radical who flaunted his garter and his privileges, who adored his adoring, doting, silly, sentimental, gushing wife, fathered her seven children, and suddenly unmasked! The Duke of Westminster, his vindictive brother-in-law, pursued him, hounded him out of the country – he was allowed to go. But King George V, when told, remarked 'I thought those sort of people shot themselves.' The cruelty, the hypocrisy of the whole drama is a long book. At last he was allowed to return, had a ball, and left again. Now it is over! Lady Beauchamp, I hope punished by her Maker, is languishing in Purgatory,[4] and fat

---

1 Viola Tree (1884–1938), a noted Edwardian beauty, actress and singer, was a daughter of Herbert Beerbohm Tree, the celebrated actor-manager. Her husband, Alan Parsons, a drama critic, had died in 1933 at the age of 44.
2 William Lygon (1872–1938) had succeeded his father as 7th Earl Beauchamp in 1891.*
3 *Gaspiller* is a French verb meaning to squander.
4 Lady Beauchamp had died in 1936.

Elmley[1] becomes an earl and funnier still his Dutch flamboyant childless wife a countess. *Finis* can be written at the end of the declension of one of England's most patrician houses. But their sensuality, their beauty, their misfortunes will be long remembered. All sensuous and oversexed, all Lygons homosexual.

MONDAY 21ST NOVEMBER

I drove up in the fog, and we are now resuming residence in London. I was quite miserable to leave my hauntingly lovely schloss. The glorious weather has changed. I gave old Josh Wedgwood[2] a small present of a plaque I found in an antique shop: it is of his ancestor, the original potter. He was enchanted. Foreign Office much the same, except that now that Rex Leeper[3] has had the sack as the result of a long intrigue on my part, I have much more power and can influence the press. The newspapers splash the arrival of the Regent, my dearly beloved Paul who comes this evening!

Rab was tired today. Queen Maud of Norway died last night aged 69, the last child of King Edward's. The race is not long-lived, the ones I mean of the Danish strain.[4] Seven years have taken the Princess Royal, Princess Victoria, George V and now the Queen who was the youngest of all. She was the least dull of the three sisters, which is saying much. She had no friends, but liked dancing, and was thin, gaunt, dull but good. We have a month's Court mourning. I seem to wear a black tie for such queer unexpected people. Queen Victoria's grandchildren do not show the same stamina as characterised the older generation. I wonder whether the prophecy made to me by a fortune-teller years ago will come true, 'You will survive all Queen Victoria's grandchildren by seven years, seven weeks and seven days.' There were dozens of them, but now I am becoming rather

1 William Lygon (1903–79), by courtesy Viscount Elmley until he succeeded his father as 8th Earl Beauchamp. He married, in 1936, Else 'Mona' Schiwe (1895–1989), the daughter of a Danish, not Dutch, actor. Their marriage remained childless and the Beauchamp peerages became extinct with the 8th Earl's death.

2 Josiah 'Josh' Clement Wedgwood (1872–1943) was the Labour MP for Newcastle-under-Lyme, for which constituency he had also sat as a Liberal and Independent Labour MP. He was created 1st Baron Wedgwood in 1942. The potter Josiah Wedgwood was his great-great-grandfather.

3 Reginald Wildig Allen 'Rex' Leeper (1888–1968), a counsellor in the Foreign Office, later Ambassador to Greece and to the Argentine Republic. He was also responsible for founding the British Council. Channon had long disapproved of him because of his anti-appeasement sympathies.

4 The 'Danish strain' had little to do with it. The mother of Edward VII's children, Queen Alexandra, died just before her 81st birthday; the King, undermined by nicotine and gluttony, died at 68, younger even than his daughter, but at least not so young as his father, Prince Albert, who died at 42.

alarmed. I suppose the Queen of Spain and Drino Carisbrooke[1] are my best hopes of longevity.

No one ever accused me of being anti-German; but really I can no longer cope with the present regime, which seems to have lost all sense and reason. Are they mad? The Jewish persecutions carried to such a fiendish degree are short-sighted, cruel and unnecessary, and now, so newspapers tell us, we shall have Roman Catholic persecutions. The secret telegrams, too, do not give a very roseate account of Hitler's present attitude. He is becoming increasingly morose, and anti-English generally. He quite likes Chamberlain but thinks we are an effete, finished race. He is right, of course. We shall be a second Holland – in time. But the Dominions are still full of vigour.

The PM is in excellent fettle, not at all downcast by the Bridgwater result.

We dined altogether at the House of C, Patsy, Alan, Honor and I, and our guests, Peter Loxley,[2] Rab Butler, and Ernest Brown, that great frog of a man with a booming voice, fine blue eyes and a warm heart. He is teetotal and a non-smoker and gaily pleasant and full of repartee. Rab told Honor that I had great gifts, the chief being my writing: that he feared he was preventing me from writing, and was afraid my pen would become rusty. Honor was very pleased; neither knew that I pen you, Diary, depository of my secrets.

TUESDAY 22ND NOVEMBER

I woke worn out. Morning at the FO, lunched with Honor, and after Questions at the House of Commons, I went to Cartier's to meet the Prince Regent:[3] he was with the Duke of Kent who looked played out, worn and not as exquisite as usual. He cannot afford not to look exquisite. I bought a Victorian emerald brooch, a sort of spray for Alan L-B to give to Patsy as a wedding present.

Diana Cavendish . . . . came up to see me: Duff Cooper, she tells me, is becoming very obstreperous; last week he actually attacked George Herbert,[4] tried to throttle him, and on Sunday he had a violent quarrel with Daisy

---

1 The Queen of Spain (Victoria Eugenie of Battenberg)* survived Channon by eleven years. Prince Alexander 'Drino' of Battenberg (1886–1960), 1st Marquess of Carisbrooke, died less than eighteen months after Channon, but was nonetheless Queen Victoria's last surviving grandson. Her last surviving granddaughter, Princess Alice, Countess of Athlone (qv), died in her 98th year in 1981. Had Channon survived to the age of 91 the prophecy would have been true.

2 Peter Noel Loxley (1905–45) was a career diplomat who, while a First Secretary in the Foreign Office, was killed in a plane crash in Malta on the way to the Yalta 'Big Three' conference in 1945.

3 Prince Paul of Yugoslavia.

4 Anthony Edward George Herbert (1911–71), younger brother of Sidney Herbert (qv) and youngest son of the 15th Earl of Pembroke.

Fellowes[1] at Crichel. He is a very second-rate fellow is Master Cooper: I have always known it. Others weren't so sure.

My mother is rather on my mind lately: usually I rarely give her a thought. She is the most exasperating human being, without a redeeming quality, that I have ever met. But she is persistent, and will always sacrifice all to an end that is not worthwhile. I am sorry for her: at times I have actively hated her. With the years any antipathy has cooled, now I pity her, and want never to see her, but my conscience tells me that I must go to the USA once again before she dies. She will be 70 next July 19th.

WEDNESDAY 23RD NOVEMBER

I only feel well and fit with an empty stomach: I was magnificent this morning, and gaily drove to the FO, thus missing the Prince Regent's visit to No. 5 [Belgrave Square], where he waited for some time. There I lunched with Honor and ever since I am *congestionné*,[2] ill, absurdly stale. Is it exercise I need, or a jolly thorough fornication, or what?

The PM and Lord Halifax and their consorts crossed the Channel in an appalling gale. The visit to the French government will lack *Stimmung*[3] and success: everyone is against it. The Germans are annoyed, and France at the threshold or rather at the crossroads is not eager for it. France now must either perish with an unpredictable future or rally further around Daladier and his govt. I fear for France's future, and sometimes for our own.

They are beginning to fear me now at the FO, and Rex Leeper actually asked me to do him a favour! I miss Kelvedon.

I talked to the Prince Regent on the telephone: the whole royal family at the unearthly hour of 9 a.m. had attended a memorial service for Queen Maud in the Marlborough House Chapel. Royalties love obsequies, anything to do with Court mourning.

I am trying to do a favour for every MP, and building up a position here of considerable popularity. Why? Rab is shrewd, calculating, and his [illegible] mind, while never flashy or meretricious, is alert and far-sighted. He treats everyone as an oriental and is playing with us all. He sometimes looks, acts and appears as most ingenuous, even naif, but he would be a fool who was deceived. If he had more outward gifts he might be PM. Yesterday he talked to me about his wife, her brutal frankness, blunt honesty which often caused him heart burnings. His

---

1 Marguerite Séverine Philippine Decazes de Glücksberg (1890–1962) married in 1919 as her second husband. Reginald Allwyn Fellowes (1884–1953), after which she was known as Daisy Fellowes. A *grande horizontale*, she had had an affair with Duff Cooper and tried to seduce Winston Churchill, whose cousin her second husband was.

2 Congested, or flushed.

3 Mood, atmosphere or tone.

brother is soon to be married to a dull girl from the Isle of Man, and the wedding is to take place there. Sydney Butler not only refuses to go, but worse, she won't hear of Rab going. Yesterday I met his parents, his father, the [blank], is a fat, little fellow of 60, but Lady Butler I thought a grand old girl, rather overdressed, grey, and not a day over 58.[1] She is tall, jingles when she walks, worships Rab, who – and this is the most charming incident I have observed of him – could not resist showing off his impressed parents. They sat alone in our room, 21 D, and after Questions Rab, followed by the faithful Peter Loxley and me, joined them. He gave us all orders, quickly, rather Napoleonically interviewed three MPs who were brusquely dismissed, business was dispatched, documents were signed . . . and the parents sat gasping with pleasure.

Shall I give a banquet for the Prince Regent? Diana Cooper complained to me on the telephone that I had dropped her: they are feeling the adverse wind. It is so difficult (I find at least) to be easy, gay, affectionate and above all natural with people when one violently disapproves of actions they have taken, or even disagrees on an important issue. Worse for me: I know the truth and have a contempt for Duff in consequence. He lost his temper in the Cabinet, flew in a rage at several ministers, insulted Chamberlain, and later . . . . he observed Chamberlain's very manner towards him immediately after his return from Munich; and so Duff resigned, pretending to the world, the House, to Diana, possibly to himself, that he resigned on an issue, 'to hold up his head', etc., all that nonsense. He resigned simply because in an hour or so he would have been dismissed. The hint to go was plain enough. Duff himself has referred to the evident relief of everyone at his departure. There he was right, I will move heaven and earth to prevent his return to High Politics. It would be dangerous for this country. Above all he wanted 'war in my time'[2] when he was Sec of State for War or 1st Lord of the Admiralty. We might have won, and he would have been a hero; we might have lost and he would have gone down to history in either case. Now he is a rather second-rate journalist who has an overpaid contract with the *Evening Standard*, and his articles are dull and unread.

I dined with Emerald, and what in theory sounds an entrancing party, was incredibly tiring: Leslie Hore-Belisha, the Abdys,[3] the Coopers, Naps Alington,[4]

---

1 Butler's father, Montagu Sherard Dawes Butler (1873–1952), had been a provincial Indian governor from 1925 to 1933 and until 1937 Lieutenant Governor of the Isle of Man, when he became Master of Pembroke College, Cambridge. He was knighted in 1924. He married, in 1901, Ann Gertrude Smith (1876–1954). When Channon met them they were 65 and 62 respectively.

2 A parody of Chamberlain's 'peace in our time' slogan.

3 Robert Henry Edward Abdy (1896–1976), who had succeeded his father as 5th Bt in 1921, married in 1930 as his second wife Helen Diana Bridgeman (1907–67), daughter of the 5th Earl of Bradford, and by courtesy Lady Diana.

4 Napier George Henry Sturt (1896–1940), who in 1919 succeeded his father as 3rd Baron Alington of Crichel.

Venetia Montagu, old Placci,[1] Lady Ribblesdale,[2] eleven in all: mostly anti-Chamberlain, anti-government, pro-Red, pro-Barcelona . . . I kept my temper and my silence and left immediately I could decently do so. The atmosphere was too civilised, the flickering candles, the anti-German diatribes. But blows were avoided: they are not always. Duff, I hear, assaulted George Herbert about a fortnight ago,[3] after a political argument, and throttled him. They made it up officially but George Herbert, that tall courtier and Slavic Conservative, has still a stiff neck.

THURSDAY 24TH NOVEMBER

I rose exhausted and rushed to Buck's Club to await the Prince Regent: we shopped together at Cartier's etc., walked up and down Bond Street, had oysters at Prunier's, and gossiped to our heart's content. At one o'clock we drove in my car to Buckingham Palace to the private Belgian door, and Paul showed me the so-called 'Belgian suite' where he and Olga are living. It is hideously Edwardian, but comfortable, with Buhl furniture from Kensington Palace etc. but actually wallpaper on the walls. It is nearly period, and in twenty years such decor will be thought the *dernier cri*.[4] Princess Olga has new emeralds, some reset. We drove to the Kents' where we lunched, a large party, the Duchess lovely and affectionate; the Duke playful and pleasant; Hannah Gubbay,[5] the Regent and Olga; Emerald Cunard; 'Teenie' Cazalet;[6] Malcolm Bullock;[7] Sir Kenneth and Lady Clark (a most irritating bogus couple);[8] Alice Hofmannsthal[9] . . . Food excellent, party *gemütlich*,[10] atmosphere gay. After luncheon I stood in the window with the Duke and he gossiped. I told him that his Australian governorship would save him £500,000, or more, the money he would have spent in shops. Melbourne, nor Sydney, has no Cartier, or Rochelle Thomas or a Moss Harris[11] – none of the

---

1   Carlo Placci (1861–1941) was a London-born Italian man of letters.
2   Ava Lowie Willing (1868–1958), who married in 1919 the 4th Baron Ribblesdale. Her first husband had been John Jacob Astor IV (1864–1912), who went down with the *Titanic*.
3   This clearly fascinated Channon so much he mentions it for a second time.
4   The height of fashion.
5   Hannah Gubbay was a close friend of Sir Philip Sassoon (qv) and the main beneficiary of his will.
6   Victor Alexander 'Teenie' Cazalet MC (1896–1943) had sat on the Supreme War Council at Versailles after the Great War. He was Conservative MP for Chippenham from 1924 to 1943.
7   Harold Malcolm Bullock (1889–1966), Conservative MP.
8   Kenneth Mackenzie Clark (1903–83) was from 1934 to 1946 Director of the National Gallery. He became a famous broadcaster presenting the BBC television series *Civilisation* in 1969. He married, in 1927, Elizabeth Winifred 'Jane' Martin (1902–76). He was knighted in 1938 and raised to the peerage as Baron Clark (life peer) in 1969.*
9   Ava Alice Muriel Astor (1902–56), who in 1933 had married as her second husband Raimund von Hofmannsthal (qv).*
10 Cheerful and pleasant.
11 J. Rochelle Thomas and Moss Harris & Sons were leading antique dealers whose main showrooms in the 1930s were in St James's.

shops where he spends hours and thousands. He laughed. The royal children came in: Edward has a pretty but sulky face, and he told me that he has kissed my Paul this morning on his return. Alexandra is a Meissen Miss, a dream of doll-like beauty, and she smiles, smiles, shows her teeth and smiles again. They both have lovely golden curly hair. Edward is not so large, so lively, so intelligent or so conversational as my Paul, but he has an older face, perhaps more bred. Rather a Nattier[1] expression. After luncheon there was a tea party for children at Mrs Cazalet's for the Prime Minister's grandchildren. Paul went and was the success of the afternoon; but he spent most of his time kissing Prince Edward. They are too sweet together. And Edward, so pleased is he at Paul returning, has told the policeman!!

David Margesson at lunch announced that the Duchess of Atholl has applied for the Chiltern Hundreds,[2] thereby cleverly forcing a by-election. It is a shrewd move which she is entitled to take, and I hear she will win a by-election. She is mad, unbalanced and quite cracked; but she is no fool, and she may embarrass us . . .

The Regent has aged a little, not much: he is more charming than ever, but a touch more serious.

Friday 25th November

Telephoned to the Regent and went with him to Buckingham Palace. Home for luncheon with Honor and later drove her to Victoria where I said 'goodbye'. We were both, I think, moved and certainly embarrassed. I could think of nothing to say, and dreaded the long wait before the train slipped out. At last I kissed her 'goodbye'. 'Take good care of Paul,' she smiled coldly. 'You need have no fear of that,' I assured and walked away. Now she is alone and *en route* for Innsbruck on a dreary expedition. She is eccentric, undemonstrative, yet I love her still. I don't think she loves me now.

I was in a rage with Alice Hofmannsthal, who promised to be here at 7.50. I waited until 8.10 and then drove off without her to Buckingham Palace to pick up Paul and Olga and we went to a most fatiguing revue with Leslie Henson.[3] Alice joined us there very late, but looked distinguished and was very chic. She is amazingly well-bred always. Afterwards we went to the Savoy to supper. The royals

---

1 Jean-Marc Nattier (1685–1766) was a French portrait painter.

2 An office of profit under the Crown, for which a Member of Parliament who wishes to retire other than after a dissolution of Parliament applies in order to disqualify him or herself from staying in the House of Commons.

3 Leslie Lincoln Henson (1891–1957) had enjoyed a long career as a music-hall turn before branching out into acting and film and theatre production. He would be one of the founders of the Entertainments National Service Association (ENSA), which entertained troops during the Second World War. His second wife, Gladys Henson (*née* Gunn) (1897–1982), was a stalwart of Ealing Studios' films.

are enjoying their semi-mourning which while it precludes society, allows them to dine out with intimates. Long conversation and one of the happiest evenings I have ever had, although we were up until 2 a.m. Alice so sweet, as was Olga who gave her an ikon from 'Mamma and me' to bring her happiness. Poor Alice, her matrimonial affairs again crashed, she so soon to divorce her flashy, *cabotin*,[1] semi-servile husband[2] so that he can legalise his liaisons with lovely Liz Paget.[3]

I drove the royals back to Buckingham Palace and went in for a moment of affectionate chat, into the Belgian suite, and thereon home.

SUNDAY 27TH NOVEMBER   *KELVEDON*

After a night of wet dreams (really at my age it is surprising and perhaps reassuring) I woke weak: Paul climbed into my bed; he is always asking questions about spanking – does he want one? Then breakfast and the newspapers. That Red ass, bore, and tiresome woman the Duchess of Atholl is to be opposed after all by a local Chamberlain Conservative! She will win, thanks to her local backing and the election will be considered an anti-Chamberlain victory.

I came here for the day, it is cold, but lovely. Batsi, I think, is pregnant, but will they have two puppies? She is more affectionate than my adored Bundi.

Emerald rang me up; she was offended because I said that she was surrounded by 'Bolshies' meaning the Coopers and others. She is anti-Duff, although he is living there. She thinks him foolish to have resigned, and tried to pretend that he resigned over the League of Nations. He hasn't struck anyone lately, the wild little turkey-cock. All my dislike of him for fifteen years is now showing itself.

Kelvedon looks lovely, but it is cold. The estate is smaller in the winter with the leaves gone. Only the sheldrake remain.

Wolkoff[4] saw Anthony Eden go into the Red Embassy on Friday: what has Maisky[5] to say to Eden?

Emerald says that Noël Coward is so old-fashioned, and out of date. She is right.

MONDAY 28TH NOVEMBER

A full-ish grand day. Early to the Foreign Office, and then a luncheon party at Lord Halifax's. He had been with Prince Paul for an hour at Buck House this

---

1 Poseur.
2 Raimund von Hofmannsthal (1906–74).*
3 Lady Elizabeth Paget (1916–80), daughter of the 6th Marquess of Anglesey.
4 Admiral Nikolai Wolkoff (1870–1954) was Imperial Russia's last naval attaché in London. He stayed in London after the revolution and became a British subject in 1935. He and his daughter were organisers of the London community of White Russians but both came under suspicion as Nazi sympathisers.
5 Ivan Maisky (1884–1975), the Soviet Ambassador to London.

morning and both told me afterwards how very much he liked the other. At lunch there were: Londonderrys, Willingdons,[1] Birkenheads,[2] and the Portuguese Ambassador;[3] I was between the Ambassadress and Sheila Birkenhead. Atrocious food, hideous but still rather grandiose and musty house . . . Lord H has more charm than any worldly man: she is amiable, a touch whimsical, which my mother-in-law[4] is not. She is a lighter metal, more glittering, less solid . . . . I rushed back for Questions, but I am not somehow taking the House as seriously as usual this week. Everything must go by the board when the Regent is here.

I came home about five o'clock as I had a cocktail party. I feared that no one would turn up: it was, however, a riotous success, only a touch too grand. Emerald arrived an hour early, and was followed by the Yugoslav Minister[5] and Mme Kassidolatz, and Sheila Milbanke,[6] an appalling mixture. Then appeared Charles Peake,[7] my bonnie Charlie of the Foreign Office, Lady Oxford,[8] looking like a death mask but Emerald greeted her, 'Look at little Margot. Isn't she looking refreshing?' Then the Yugoslav, Paul and Princess Olga, dignified, royal and amiable. After that about fifty people came, including the King of Greece who stayed for an hour, as did the Buccleuchs. Walter Buccleuch very gay and fun. Paul had first a long *entretien*[9] with Charles Peake, then with Margot, and lastly with Rab, who was impressed by meeting so many royalties and duchesses. First I introduced him to the King of Greece; and afterwards he sat down with Paul on a sofa and had a political crack. People wandered about – Mary Herbert[10] very pregnant, the Hambledens[11] charming, etc. Naps Alington; Diana C underdressed in a tweed; Fritzi of Prussia too stimulating and exciting for words (Rab had a talk with him too) . . . many others. None of the MPs came, but I had only asked three

---

1 Freeman Freeman-Thomas (1866–1941), 1st Marquess of Willingdon, had been Viceroy of India from 1931 to 1936. In 1892 he married Marie Adelaide Brassey (1875–1960).*

2 Frederick Winston Furneaux Smith (1907–75), by courtesy Viscount Furneaux from 1922 to 1930, when he succeeded his father* as 2nd Earl Birkenhead. He married in 1935 Sheila Berry (1913–92), daughter of the 1st Viscount Camrose (qv).

3 Dr Armindo Rodrigues de Sttau Monteiro (1896–1955) was a university professor who became Portuguese Ambassador to the United Kingdom in 1936 and served until 1943. He married, in 1925, Lúcia Rebelo Cancela Infante de Lacerda (1903–80).

4 Lady Iveagh was the sister of Lady Halifax (qv).

5 Dragomir Kassidolatz.

6 Margaret Sheila Mackellar Chisholm (1895–1969), from New South Wales, had been pursued by the Duke of York before his marriage, despite being married herself at the time to Lord Loughborough. Her second marriage was to Sir John 'Buffles' Milbanke (qv).

7 Charles Brinsley Pemberton Peake (1897–1958) was a senior diplomat, later becoming Ambassador to Yugoslavia (1946–51) and to Greece (1951–7).

8 Formerly Mrs Asquith.

9 Interview.

10 Mary Dorothea Hope (1903–95), by courtesy Lady Mary Hope, married in 1936 Sidney Herbert, by courtesy Lord Herbert (qv).

11 William Henry Smith and the former Lady Patricia Herbert.

or four. Alan, I kept away, as his brother Francis[1] has come down with scarlet fever. If Alan gets it the wedding will be off or postponed. As it is he nearly drives poor Patsy insane with his rushings about, goings and comings . . .

It was eight o'clock (and by then I was drunk) before the royalties left. Paul rang me immediately from Buckingham Palace to thank me: they had enjoyed themselves. The rooms look lovely, particularly the dining room heavy with Meissen and food in the candlelight. I refused to give Diana C dinner and joined Harold [Balfour] at the H of Commons and we dined together. Diana meanwhile had picked up Euan [Wallace] and David Margesson and were embarrassingly near at the next table. Tommy Dugdale[2] was with them.

A word about Tommy Dugdale: he is the govt spy. He was Baldwin's PPS and now is being groomed for the future Chief Whip, of that I am convinced. He is good, good-natured, good-hearted, but treacherous all right. He reports every conversation to the PM or to David and his role is to pump people. Poor Jim Thomas is his pawn, or dupe. Previous to the abdication he listened in to all the ex-King's telephone conversations and reported them. I was shocked when I discovered that: how did the govt dare to do such a thing? . . . Of course we are living in a semi-fascist era.

After dinner I went home and changed and joined Prince Paul, Princess Olga, Teenie Cazalet, the two Buccleuchs and the Jock Balfours[3] at the Savoy where we had an enjoyable supper party. I am quite dizzy with the success of my cocktail party, if so royal a function could be so frivolously described. Only Mrs Chamberlain didn't come.

WEDNESDAY 30TH NOVEMBER

A Southend party to see the H of C. Shopped with the Regent; we idled in Bond Street, we went to shops, we laughed like our ancient selves, sauntered in a rakish manner, evading the detectives. He loves me, deeply, I think. Not as much as I love him. We went to Spink's,[4] Cartier's, Rochelle Thomas, elsewhere. I have ordered a [illegible] inkstand for his Christmas present from Spink's.

---

1 Francis Gordon Lennox-Boyd (1909–44). He was the second of Alan Lennox-Boyd's brothers to die in the war, being killed on D-Day while commanding the 22nd Independent Parachute Company, and the third to die prematurely.

2 Thomas Lionel Dugdale (1897–1977) was Conservative MP for Richmond from 1929 to 1959. He was Stanley Baldwin's parliamentary private secretary; and was Minister of Agriculture from 1951 to 1954, when he resigned over his technical responsibility for the Crichel Down affair, where the government was forced to hand back land acquired from the Alington family. He was created 1st Bt in 1945 and raised to the peerage as 1st Baron Crathorne in 1959.

3 John Balfour (1894–1983) was a diplomat who, despite his antipathy to the Franco regime, served as British Ambassador to Spain from 1951 to 1954. He married, in 1933, Frances van Millingen (1904–99), daughter of Prof. Alexander van Millingen.

4 The celebrated coin and medal dealer, then in St James's.

THURSDAY 1ST DECEMBER

A long time at the House. In the evening, I dined at home by myself and then dressed and joined the Regent, Princess Olga, Prince Fritzi of Prussia, Mollie Buccleuch, the Hambledens . . . . at Ciro's. A gay evening in this place where so much of our youth, the Regent's and mine, has been spent. Mollie Buccleuch is very Chamberlain, very against Betty Cranborne[1] and her other Cavendish cousins who are too Red for her. Both Betty Cranborne and Beatrice Eden[2] go about saying that they are ashamed to be English that we are not at war! The whole Cecil family has behaved outrageously, even dishonestly over the crisis! Mollie Buccleuch told me that she knows that Joe Kennedy, that [illegible] charlatan the American Ambassador, has been disloyal to Halifax and Chamberlain. He is an Edenite.[3] Anthony told Mollie so when she met him at Eton at St Andrew's Day. We stayed late at Ciro's and I drove everyone home late. Princess Olga had sat last night at dinner at BP next to Lord Halifax and had been much under his spell. Luckily I had run into Lord H this afternoon coming out of the Foreign Office and had walked with him for a little – he gave me an envoy to him from someone connected with the King of Greece. I asked him if his 'flirtation' with the Regent continued – they had been together for an hour on Monday, and he replied that he had another conversation with him last night at Buckingham Palace, and also that he had found Princess Paul absolutely charming . . . so tonight I was able to repeat to her his praises and she was pleased . . . The Queen arranged a small dinner for them in the absence of the King who is shooting duck at Sandringham. She didn't ask me I notice!!!

Drank too much and home too late – royalty is a heady wine.

FRIDAY 2ND DECEMBER

Anthony Eden was to have sailed tomorrow in the *Nomadic* accompanied by [his wife] Beatrice, her brother and Ronnie Tree,[4] and the Hinchingbrookes,[5] but –

---

1 Elizabeth Vere Cavendish (1897–1982) married in 1915 Robert 'Bobbety' Gascoyne-Cecil, Viscount Cranborne, later 5th Marquess of Salisbury*.

2 Beatrice Helen Beckett (1905–57), daughter of Sir William Beckett, banker, married in 1923 Anthony Eden (qv). They divorced in 1950.

3 This observation was not well informed. Kennedy was pro-Hitler and pro-appeasement, and was ultimately removed by Roosevelt partly because of his disloyalty to a president whom he hoped to succeed, and partly because of his increasingly loud defeatism.

4 Arthur Ronald Lambert Field Tree (1897–1976) was Conservative MP for Harborough from 1933 to 1945. A strong anti-appeaser, he would become a close associate of Churchill in the later 1930s. He later developed the Sandy Lane resort in Barbados.

5 Alexander Victor Edward Paulet Montagu (1906–95) was by courtesy Viscount Hinchingbrooke from 1916 to 1962, when he succeeded his father as 10th Earl of Sandwich; he disclaimed his peerages in 1964. He was Conservative MP for South Dorset from 1941 to 1962. He married, in 1934, Maud Rosemary Peto (1916–98); they were divorced in 1958, and he remarried. Despite this, and having fathered seven children with his first wife, he was predominantly homosexual, and accused by his youngest son of being a serial paedophile.

owing to the very troubled conditions in France – the great democracy Anthony admires so much was unable to man her finest ship, and he has had to transfer to the *Aquitania*! Much amused comment – why couldn't he sail in a British ship in the first place? The Insurgents' cause is abating: they are all sixes and sevens – Chamberlain reigns almost supreme.

SATURDAY 3RD DECEMBER

I found on my return late last night a message to ring the Regent but it was too late to do so. However he rang me early this morning and I met him at Spink's at 11 a.m. He made several purchases – often he looks at everything, buys nothing and goes away. It is only when he is shopping, appraising, that he becomes like an *antiquaire*. I drove back with him to Buckingham Palace and talked of the Windsors, whom no one remembers now, or wouldn't if Barbie Wallace and Diana Cooper had not taken it in their heads to curtsey to her when they were last in Paris! Diana has changed since her fall from power. A quiet evening . . . Paul and Olga left for Coppins[1] about six. I arranged to join them tomorrow.

SUNDAY 4TH DECEMBER

Channon visits Eton to see Prince Paul's son Alexander, who was studying there, then returns to Coppins.

I left for London to attend to my dinner party. The hour before a dinner is always confusing, and until 8 p.m. I didn't know whether or not to expect Basil Dufferin[2] who is notoriously slack about his social engagements. I tried to persuade the royals to come, but they refused.

A most gay, *réussi*[3] evening. The Chief Whip was in wine and freely announced, in answer to a question from Lady Cunard, that he was backing Lord Halifax to be Prime Minister should Chamberlain suddenly die, be shot, or resign. We discussed all the Cabinet, the possibility of reshuffle etc. He and Emerald and Loelia Westminster[4] left at 2.05! Poppy Thursby[5] had had too much to drink, quite obviously, and she became lachrymose, and then made the most amazing, and wicked confidence, which shows that people are gossiping about Honor and me, as I have sometimes feared. Poppy said that the Eden people in London went about last year saying that Honor neglected her child, did not care for it, and that I had attempted to turn the Iveaghs against her! A monstrous *potin*.[6] I only want

---

1 The Buckinghamshire country house of the Duke and Duchess of Kent.
2 Basil Sheridan Hamilton-Temple-Blackwood (1909–45), 4th Marquess of Dufferin and Ava.*
3 Successful.
4 Loelia Mary Ponsonby (1902–93), wife of the 2nd Duke of Westminster.
5 Helen Azalea 'Poppy' Baring (1901–80) married in 1928 William Piers 'Peter' Thursby (1904–77)*.
6 Piece of gossip.

them to help to prevent my wife doing anything foolish, for decidedly she is not normal now. And I never once mentioned her to her parents until last October, and then only gently in reference to her going abroad for three months, as she was ordered to do – and didn't – by our Dr Law, who looks like a German U-boat commander . . . these remarks of Poppy's rather poisoned my party. I loathe criticism and it upsets me always.

MONDAY 5TH DECEMBER

This afternoon the Regent rang me, and I arranged for Sir Alex Cadogan[1] to call on him at Buckingham Palace at six o'clock. It was a flattering coup at the Foreign Office for me, and frankly I enjoyed it. Later I met him for a second and he was very polite. I shopped with the Regent – that is I rushed away directly Questions were over, and picked him up at his dentist's. Long talks. He is now definitely very pro-Bertie and Elizabeth,[2] with whom he is still staying. He is bored by them secretly, thinks them dull-ish and a touch bourgeois, but realises that they have done their job well and saved the monarchy. He feels that he has behaved shabbily to the Windsors and doesn't know what to do. Royalties are curious in their personal relations with one another . . .

Last night we all discussed Duff and I asked Helen Fitzgerald, who had been staying at Lavington with the Wallaces, and only motored up in time to dine, whether there had been any incidents, as I knew the Coopers were also weekending there (there had been a shoot). Helen laughingly retorted that no one had been even struck, that Duff was as quiet as a lamb, apparently on his good behaviour since fighting so many people, and striking at least two . . . I would have forgotten this conversation had today not brought the news of a full-dress row last night at Lavington after dinner. Lady Pembroke made some deprecatory remark about Diana and Barbie Wallace dropping curtsies to the Windsors; whereupon Duff flew into a rage and insulted Lady Pembroke, called her a snob, and a bloody bitch etc. etc. Buffles[3] had wanted to restrain him and had to be held back. The evening practically ended in a *mêlée* and Barbie Wallace, the distraught but innocent hostess, retired to bed in indignant self-defence.

TUESDAY 6TH DECEMBER

A full day. London with its complications. I rushed to the Foreign Office, thence to Victoria to take leave of the Regent, who arrived smiling and debonair, with

---

1 Alexander Montagu George Cadogan (1884–1968) was Permanent Under-Secretary of State for Foreign Affairs from 1938 to 1946. Channon often refers to him using the diminutive 'Alec' *.
2 The King and Queen.
3 John Charles Peniston 'Buffles' Milbanke (1902–47) succeeded as 11th Bt in 1915 after his father's death on active service in the Dardanelles.

Princess Olga, very royal. The royal waiting room was full of diplomats, Corbin[1] the Frenchman, and the large staff of blacks from the Yugoslav Legation! We were all greeted ceremoniously and there was first the hint of a twinkle in the Regent's eye . . . Then he got into the train. There were at least fifty policemen, more than usual, I noticed. He stood in the doorway of the carriage chatting to us all, and, as usual, I had the sinking feeling which I always had when he leaves – for the day he will go away and never return, the victim of some fanatic's aim. The train pulled out, 'Goodbye Chips,' he half whispered and I turned away . . . then I drove Jock Balfour, who is really very rich, back to the Foreign Office.

When I got back to the FO I heard that there was a report that Croat desperadoes were arriving here in order to shoot my beloved Prince Paul, my alter ego, the human being with whom I feel the most in tune in the whole world . . . and my heart sank. Luckily he is gone . . .

I dined with Emerald and picked up Loelia Westminster to escort there. She was resplendent in furs and jewels . . . Portia Stanley in a fiendish temper. She is so dazed and unhappy, and she still limps . . . her life came to a full-stop with Edward's death but she will recover . . . I drove Loelia home eventually; it was nearly one o'clock and she suggested, or rather hinted, that I take her to the Embassy Club to supper and dance. How queer I am: I pretended to misunderstand and having left her, as it was 'cold', I suddenly told the chauffeur to drive me to Jim Thomas's around the corner. He was in and charming. We talked late, and I pumped him, and got much Eden news.

WEDNESDAY 7TH DECEMBER

I lunched with Jim Wedderburn, who adores me now, is my slave. He rings me up constantly, makes scenes of jealousy, and he is becoming increasingly complicated and a problem. He asked the Tommy Dugdales and John Colville[2] to meet me, at my request. Tommy Dugdale is the mystery man of the govt. He has no opinions, he is not an intriguer, is a good sort and yet he is the arch informer. He listens, listens, offends no one and reports all . . . It was he, I have since found out, who listened in, who tapped all the late King's private telephone calls at the time of the abdication, and, of course, reported them all to Baldwin. Tommy is square, short, smiling and shrewd. He has merry brown eyes, white teeth, black shining hair, and always wears a double-breasted pinhead grey suiting. He is married to

---

1 Charles Corbin (1881–1970) was French Ambassador to the United Kingdom from 1933 to 1940.
2 David John Colville (1894–1954) was a Scottish ironmaster who sat as a National Liberal MP for Midlothian and Peebles Northern from 1929 to 1943, when he was appointed Governor of Bombay. He was Secretary of State for Scotland from 1938 to 1940 and was raised to the peerage as 1st Baron Clydesmuir in 1948.

Nancy Tennant[1] ... half-sister of Lady Oxford. She is a good, dull, plain female. I quite liked her. Tommy's great dupe is Jim Thomas, my poor friend, who trusts him and tells him everything. John Colville, the Sec of State for Scotland, has an enormous bottom, is friendly and quite able; but he is unexciting.

FRIDAY 9TH DECEMBER

I drove to Southend to attend the West Country Dance. I was late, bad-tempered and worn out. The Patsy–Alan romance wears me, and worries me; he rushes about so, isn't in love with her, and she hysterically half-suspects his indifference.

MONDAY 12TH DECEMBER

I lunched with the Butlers at 2 Smith Square. Rab now knows that he is to be a Privy Counsellor and he is delighted. So is she. They give me some of the credit for it ... The PM was very in the 'dumps': I have never known him so tired and depressed. He seemed quite miserable and the smile he gave ... The spirits of the Edenites and Churchillians rose, and Dunglass[2] looked miserable. Later he (Dunglass) cornered Rab and Geoffrey Lloyd[3] for an hour and asked their help and advice.

TUESDAY 13TH DECEMBER

A full day again. It began by Rab telling me that he feared, indeed, almost prophesied an immediate general election, that is directly after the Rome visit,[4] or more probably still early in February. The PM is toying with the idea of meeting the House and then dissolving it ... it seems that when Rob Hudson[5] went to him and threatened to resign if Belisha were not sacked from the War Office, he said that four other under-secretaries would go with him; the PM retorted that if Hudson persisted in his threats he would have an election now. Hudson backed down somewhat ... Rab told me this (I had already picked it up, but wanting details, pretended to know nothing, as that is the best policy to adopt when

1 Nancy Tennant (1904–69) was the daughter of Sir Charles Tennant, 1st Bt, and married Dugdale (qv) in 1936 as her second husband.
2 Lord Dunglass was Chamberlain's parliamentary private secretary.
3 Geoffrey William Lloyd (1902–84) was a Conservative MP for seats in Birmingham from 1931 to 1945 and from 1950 to 1974. He had been private secretary and then parliamentary private secretary to Stanley Baldwin. He held junior office throughout the period from 1935 to 1945, was Minister of Fuel and Power from 1951 to 1955 and Minister of Education from 1957 to 1959. He was raised to the peerage as Baron Geoffrey-Lloyd (life peer) in 1974.
4 Chamberlain would visit Mussolini in Rome from 11 to 14 January 1939.
5 Robert Spear Hudson (1886–1957) was at this time Secretary for Overseas Trade. He was increasingly anti-appeasement and had expressed reservations to Chamberlain in the preceding days about the government's level of preparedness for war, reservations shared by several others. He did not resign, but his actions were noted and he had sufficient of Churchill's confidence to serve in the wartime coalition.

one wants to paste together bits of a story, particularly when one's informant is longing to confide in one); I listened and promised to say nothing. It was the day of my biggest propaganda luncheon party, eighteen or nineteen men ... I walked across to 10 Downing Street ostensibly to ask Dunglass to luncheon, but also to pick up any stray bits ... I ran into Mrs Chamberlain who looked rather *affairée*;[1] she smiled and rushed by, very well dressed. Alec Dunglass put me on a sofa under the staircase and we had a confidential chat: he asked me what I thought *re* any immediate election etc. I canvassed the cause of agriculture. I feel it is foolish to jeopardise the agricultural seats, which is to play the Socialist game, and I told him so. He agreed ... He could not lunch and asked who was coming. He smiled when I said 'Rob Hudson' – and I knew!! When I got back to Belgrave Square I found a note from Hudson to the effect that he had gastric flu and couldn't come!! He doesn't want to identify himself apparently with the propaganda of the govt of which he is a member!!

In the evening I changed and went to the Wallaces' party. It was given by Barbie and Helen Fitzgerald, an impromptu affair, but all London – all my old London that once I loved, feared, envied and moved about in. The only newcomers are the Butlers, who looked out of place ... I saw Lady Pembroke nod slightly to Duff Cooper, who reddened and returned the bow. Very *grande dame* of her. She now says that she had fully expected Duff to strike her. The story got out by Diana letting Randolph [Churchill] know,[2] who instantly published it in the *Standard*.

Channon then includes the following passage, which seems to have been gestating for some time:

Random reflections:
Over the Czech crisis and its sensible solution the Astor dynasty not only had its way but led the movement: the Rothermere[3] and Beaverbrook[4]

1 Busy, preoccupied.
2 Randolph Frederick Edward Spencer-Churchill (1911–68), son of Sir Winston Churchill, spent his life in his father's shadow, and with few of his qualities and little of his talent. He mostly earned his living by writing and from 1940 to 1945 was a Conservative Member of Parliament, before being defeated in the Labour landslide. In 1939 he married Pamela Digby (qv).
3 Harold Sidney Harmsworth (1868–1940), younger brother of Alfred Harmsworth, 1st Viscount Northcliffe, was co-founder with him of the *Daily Mail* and various other newspapers and periodicals, in which he acquired a controlling interest on Northcliffe's death in 1922. He became 1st Bt in 1910, was raised to the peerage as 1st Baron Rothermere in 1914, and advanced to a viscountcy in 1919. He and his newspapers would become strong advocates of appeasement and he was a fervent admirer of Hitler.
4 William Maxwell Aitken (1879–1964), from Ontario, Canada, had through his business dealings and friendships with Andrew Bonar Law and David Lloyd George acquired astonishing political influence. A Unionist MP from 1911 to 1916, he was raised to the peerage as 1st Baron Beaverbrook in 1917 very much against the wishes of King George V, and served in Lloyd George's War Cabinet – and, from 1940 to 1945, in Churchill's. He became proprietor of the *Daily Express* in 1916.

press followed suit enthusiastically – the powerful Berry clan and Press were, however, opposed to Munich, critical of Chamberlain, and have continued so, although K(?), a realist, is giving in; and Camrose, in all justice, has been very ill. Nevertheless over this crisis the Astors have won, and the Berrys have lost. The Rothermere and Beaverbrook press have merely joined and supported the winning side. Over the abdication the Astors and Berrys vied with each other in traducing Edward VIII and intrigued against him for months: he had, however (and still has at heart), both the Rothermere and Beaverbrook factions. The Astors and Berrys are fundamentally strait-laced, and puritanical: there they converge. But the Astors want peace with Germany thank God. I think it is largely Lothian's[1] influence on Lady Astor.[2] In any case the Jewish blood, and origin of the Astors is much more remote than in the Berrys where, I suppose, it is fairly recent.

Again over the abdication and the Czech crisis, one cannot help but be struck by the fact that we had in each case the right man for the job. I doubt whether Chamberlain would have been equally successful with the abdication problem – Baldwin's touch was masterly, whatever one's sympathies!! Certainly Baldwin as Prime Minister during these recent weeks would not have behaved in the superhuman way that Chamberlain did. He could not have flown to Berchtesgaden – not he! He wouldn't have known where it was!

In the MS Channon has ended this passage with 'MORE TO COME'.
There are two entries for the next day.

WEDNESDAY 14TH DECEMBER

Day began with an early message that my beloved Batsi, my Bundarch bitch, had one puppy in the night, born dead – as so often happens with only one. The vet has been sent for, and she has been taken by him to Chelmsford to be watched in case there are more, and for complications. She is supposed to be all right. Naturally I am disappointed, as we had wanted to breed this intoxicating breed in Essex. Perhaps next time I shall be luckier. I believe Lady Halifax's bitch also produced a dead puppy, and next time had ten healthy ones.

---

1 Philip Henry Kerr (1882–1940) succeeded his cousin as 11th Marquess of Lothian in 1930. He had been a member of Lord Milner's 'kindergarten' in South Africa and became Lloyd George's private secretary in 1916. In the 1930s he was a prominent appeaser; and was appointed as the United Kingdom Ambassador to America in 1939.
2 Nancy Witcher Langhorne (1879–1964), of Danville, Virginia, married in 1906 as her second husband Waldorf Astor (1879–1952). When he succeeded in 1919 to his father's viscountcy she succeeded him as Conservative MP for Plymouth Sutton, which she represented until 1945.

WEDNESDAY 14TH DECEMBER

Very early a.m.

Very foolishly I stayed at the Wallaces' party last night until 4 a.m., and drank too much champagne – as, indeed, did everyone else. The Butlers were there, he in his black waistcoat, as befitted a minister in mourning, had come on from the foreign-press banquet where Chamberlain had made a very great speech in which he gently castigated the German press. The German Ambassador and the German press correspondents stayed away, boycotted the banquet at the last moment, thus creating a bad impression. They are too tactless always: yet I sympathise with their point of view; we constantly attack Germany so why should she not attack our statesmen? The PM's stock rose tonight perhaps enough to prevent or postpone an election. The Wallace collection[1] was a riotous, smart affair, all one's friends, all the companions of my youth. I sat with the Butlers for a bit as they were fish out of water and knew no one. Maureen Stanley[2] was tipsy as usual. All the flight, the gay, the careless . . . I danced with Sheila Milbanke, Mary Herbert, others . . . They played 'The Lambeth Walk' . . . . Diana Cooper told me that people were trying to make trouble between her and me that I had spread stories about Duff etc. I denied it, as I had tried to be careful not to become entangled in this business.

Home at four. Alan L-B already asleep.

A message came this morning that the Duchess of Kent wanted me to take her to the theatre tonight, but I couldn't, as I must attend a Law Society banquet in Southend, and do not dare 'chuck' so near an election.

Later

Many Questions, and Rab is exhausted. However I spoke to David Margesson again and he assures me that following his promise to me, he has arranged for Rab to be made a Privy Counsellor in the New Year's Honours. I came home early, but was upset to hear that the Duchess of Kent wanted supper, and I had no time in which to arrange it: hurriedly I ordered blinis etc., and sent off half a dozen messages and then dressing in a white tie I left for Southend at 5.20. Soon I was caught in a thick fog near Epping, and for the rest of the way we crawled, feeling our way, inch by inch. By the Fortune of War, a pub, fourteen miles this side of Southend, I got out, seeing a light, and walked to it. It was the pub: and from there I telephoned to Southend to say that I could not get there.

1 A pun on the London gallery and museum of the same name.
2 Maureen Helen Vane-Tempest-Stewart (1900–42), eldest daughter of the 7th Marquess of Londonderry, and from 1915 Lady Maureen by courtesy, married in 1920 the Conservative MP Oliver Stanley, younger brother of Edward, Lord Stanley (qqv).*

Once again I have had to 'chuck' the Law Society. In the warmth of the pub I drank, parleyed with the locals, and began to glow with port and relief. After a pause, we started back and I was at Belgrave Square by ten, but *sans* banquet, *sans* dinner, *sans* anything. At eleven the Duchess, accompanied by Princess Olga and Mme Ralli[1] arrived, soon to be followed by David Herbert[2] and Michael Duff[3] and we were a friendly gay sextette [*sic*]. The Duchess was . . . delicious, warm-hearted, chic and sensible. We discussed Lady Pembroke's recent row with Duff Cooper, and the Duchess said that both Diana Cooper and Barbie Wallace were '*des crétines*':[4] it is all over this curtseying business to the Duchess of Windsor. Everyone deplores the incident: I think she should be made an HRH and that would be an end to the matter. They left me at 1.30 after caviar, champagne and chatter, and I immediately went on to the Londonderry House ball, which was still in progress. Diana Cooper, looking now like a frail small Bernhardt,[5] again accused me of intriguing against Duff. Of course I strongly denied the charge and she can have no real knowledge of how far I did plot against him. He is a third-rate little fellow, a peppery parakeet. Gage admitted to me that he had let out to Diana things, that he had been trapped into betraying me. I am tired of Diana: I get bored with people always after seven years; and our great friendship has lasted just seven and a half years.

I sat with Leslie Hore-Belisha drinking sweet champagne and at length drove him home to Stratford Place where he lives: I went in with him and we were both drunk, confidential and intimate. We confessed to each other that we had both slept with Isabelle Clow[6] years ago, and others. He showed me over his eccentric house with [illegible] medallions, plaques and portraits of his mother. It is smug, luxurious, *boîte*[7] of a well-kept tart! And it is a touch Jewish. He is getting fat and gross, but very nice, warm, friendly and brilliant . . . he doesn't allow himself to become too self-assured. Home at 5.45 with a headache and exhausted. What an evening! Six hours lost in the fog on the arterial road! Two hours with the glowing, glamorous Duchess of Kent, *un mauvais quart d'heure*[8] at Londonderry House, and then the dawn hours on a sofa drinking hot Ovaltine with the Minister of War.

1 Julie Marie 'Lilia' Pringo (1901–78), who married in 1921 Jean Ralli, was a lifelong friend of the Duchess of Kent and Princess Olga, and became close to Cecil Beaton. Channon usually calls her 'Lelia'.
2 David Alexander Reginald Herbert (1908–95), second son of the 15th Earl of Pembroke. After Eton he had stints as an actor and cabaret performer. He lived for half a century in Tangier, being nicknamed 'The Queen of Tangier' by Ian Fleming (qv).
3 Charles Michael Robert Vivian Duff (1907–80), succeeded his father as 3rd Bt in 1914.
4 Fools.
5 He alludes to the French actress Sarah Bernhardt (1844–1923).
6 Isabelle Patchin Mann (1887–1939), wife of William Clow Jr.
7 Usually used to mean a nightclub, here a boudoir.
8 An unpleasant, but brief, experience.

THURSDAY 15TH DECEMBER

A less insane day, but I woke with a head of lead, ill, old and hunched . . . lazily I loafed *au lit* until ten, and then to the FO, where I had a confidential chat with Rab, who thinks Shakespeare Morrison[1] a v poor fellow . . . In the afternoon I looked in at 11 Downing Street to an 'At Home' given by Lady Simon,[2] a simple *Hausfrau* who is obsessed by slavery and has campaigned against it all her life. 'Hasn't my wife made this house charming?' the Chancellor asked of me. And the guests were requested to file out through his study so that they might look at his mother's portrait by Gerald Kelly.[3] A remarkable old lady, she looks like Simon's twin, with a touch of Sargent's[4] mother about this striking picture. Simon worshipped her; he is as mother-mad as Belisha.

FRIDAY 16TH DECEMBER

I am a little perturbed by Alan who is so obviously not in love with Patsy and yet likes her. She is mad about him, insanely, devouringly, possessively, licentiously, tactlessly in love with him. *Que faire?* I hope he will be sweet to her.

SUNDAY 18TH DECEMBER   *LEEDS CASTLE*[5]

Leeds all day, morning in bed, conversations with Geoffrey Lloyd, who as usual, has a Brazilian lady in tow – he can never resist the darkly romantic dago type. He finds them dashing but Kay Norton[6] tells me that he doesn't go to bed with them or anyone else – that he is in fact: a virgin. I have my private doubts. Pauline Winn,[7] who

1 William Shepherd Morrison (1893–1961) was a senior Conservative MP who later became Speaker of the House of Commons and Governor-General of Australia. His nickname 'Shakes' came from his fondness for quoting Shakespeare.*

2 Kathleen Rochard Harvey (1869–1955) had been governess to the children of the widowed Sir John Simon, and they married in 1917.

3 Gerald Festus Kelly (1879–1972) was an acclaimed British portraitist. He painted Somerset Maugham (qv) eighteen times, and also did notable portraits of T. S. Eliot (qv) and Ralph Vaughan Williams. He was knighted in 1945 and served as President of the Royal Academy from 1949 to 1954.

4 Coats appears to have crossed this out and written 'Whistler's' instead; which was as Rhodes James published it.

5 Near Maidstone in Kent.

6 Katharine 'Kay' Edith Carlotta Norton (1883–1961) was the daughter of the 5th Baron Grantley.

7 Her mother Olive, Lady Baillie (qv), was the daughter of Almeric Paget, 1st Baron Queenborough (qv), and had been married to Charles Winn until their divorce in 1925. Her aunt Dorothy Wyndham Paget (1905–60) owned racehorses and was a prodigious gambler, and also sponsored the Bentley motor racing team in the late 1920s. Because of her nocturnal existence her bookmaker employed someone to take her telephone calls during the night, often for her to put money on horses in races that had already happened. She gave her word she did not know the result and, on the grounds that many horses she backed had already lost, her bookmakers believed her and paid out when she won.

is already just like her mother, was amusing about her mother's mad sister, Dorothy Paget, who is a famous eccentric. The woman lives alone in Balfour Place, eats like a horse, gets up at 7 p.m., dines at 6 a.m., keeps a double staff of servants to administer to her eccentricities. Occasionally she goes to a play, takes a large box, sits alone, and is always accompanied by a hamper of food which she munches during the play.

Alan, Patsy and Brigid, marvellously beautiful, dined with me. Afterwards an unpleasant half-joking *scène de jalousie*[1] on Patsy's part. She is so *unsoignée*[2] and very much on Alan's nerves. He is on the point of breaking off the engagement. She, poor darling, is so in love. It is that. I pleaded with him to follow her home to St James's Square, and he did – and is there now as I write . . .

MONDAY 19TH DECEMBER

A parliamentary day, fireworks and fun, but a governmental triumph. All the morning we prepared fifty Questions which is a record for any dept. I walked over to the House at one o'clock and received fifty Indians and showed them over the Palace of Westminster; a boring chore, to please Lord Halifax.

I took the Questions into the PM's room and found the little man as usual alone. (His secretaries are second-rate and slack in my opinion.) 'May I give you your Questions, sir?' 'Yes, come in,' he smiled and I followed him. We had a few words and I left . . . The debate, a vote of censure moved by the Opposition,[3] began with a diatribe by Dalton.[4] The PM followed and was at his very best, tolerant, easy, smiling but important. He has now learned all the rhetorical tricks and used them all. But it is a very personal government . . . very one man! He held and thrilled the House . . . He was followed by Archie Sinclair,[5] who always

1 Jealous tiff.
2 Ungroomed.
3 The motion was that 'this House has no confidence in the Foreign Policy of His Majesty's Government'.
4 Edward Hugh John Neale Dalton (1887–1962), known as Hugh, was the son of Queen Victoria's chaplain, who also acted as tutor to King George V when the latter was a boy. Educated at Eton and King's College, Cambridge, Dalton was a socialist from his adolescence and was elected Labour MP for Peckham in 1924, and sat for Bishop Auckland from 1929 to 1931. He lost the seat that year but regained it in 1935, holding it until 1959. He held a junior Foreign Office post in the 1929–31 Labour government, and in the Churchill coalition was Minister for Economic Warfare from 1940 to 1942 and President of the Board of Trade from 1942 to 1945. He was Chancellor of the Exchequer from 1945 to 1947, when he had to resign after a Budget leak. He returned to the Cabinet six months later as Chancellor of the Duchy of Lancaster. He was raised to the peerage as Baron Dalton (life peer) in 1960.
5 Archibald Henry Macdonald Sinclair (1890–1970) succeeded his grandfather as 4th Bt in 1912. He had been Churchill's second-in-command on the Western Front in 1916 and his military secretary when Churchill was Secretary of State for War. He was Liberal MP for Caithness and Sutherland from 1922 to 1945, Scottish Secretary from 1931 to 1932 and Secretary of State for Air from 1940 to 1945. He led the Liberal Party from 1935 to 1945 and was raised to the peerage as 1st Viscount Thurso in 1952.

provides a pleasant interval during which one can go out for a drink or a cup of tea ... then by young Quintin Hogg who made his second speech since his recent election. It was soon stiff, oratorical, and debating, but the House, whilst recognising its obvious merits, was not altogether pleased that so new and young a member should be so self-assured. He stood behind me, and swayed as he spoke but betrayed no modesty, no nervousness. Lloyd George, who followed, was frankly funny, and he convulsed the House, as he twitted the Prime Minister, but he said little of value. The PM roared with genuine laughter as the arrows hit him.

Cranborne, as usual, disingenuous, wordy, and I think, foolish, made a non-committal speech. I am very anti-Cecil, a dreadful race of clerics with tepid water diluting their indigo blood ... I had stolen out to dine with Jim Wedderburn and Shakes Morrison. We ate oysters and drank stout in the Strangers' Room, and Shakes, with his beautiful sensitive mouth, recited poetry. He had always recited poetry, he told us, and that was why at school he was nicknamed 'Shakes'. He talked of his four sons: it is the second he loves, the cleverest; the elder, he described as a nice laddie but 'dull and stupid'. I went back to the bench and found that Rab had had no dinner and was consequently irritable. He had been closeted with [Sir John] Simon for an hour or more preparing the wind-up. I made him get out and have oysters and a drink ... All day I did errands and chores and flitted about amongst the Great.

The late edition of the *Evening Standard* devoted the whole front page to the alleged govt revolt, led by Rob Hudson against Leslie Belisha. I tore off the page and passed it to the PM, who was on the front bench. He read it, took off his spectacles, sniffed, and smiled quietly. Later I ran into Rob Hudson in the lavatory. 'I see the *Standard* has spilt the beans,' he said. He is guilty!! On my way to our room I saw Leslie Belisha who took my arm, and I led him aside and told him of the article, which he had not yet seen. Then he told me the whole story: it was apparently true. It seems that Rob Hudson and Donald Strathcona,[1] supported by Basil Dufferin, had lodged a protest through Rob Hudson on Monday the 12th, to the effect that unless Belisha went, they turned. Such treachery on the part of Strathcona, who is a decent fellow, is surprising ... The PM had parried Rob's remarks with the threat of an immediate election ... This was the day that the PM was so depressed, although he knew of the revolt – as did we all – a few days before, for he resented such tactics. Hudson, who is a shit, and a time-server and personal enemy of David Margesson's, was at last mortified. How the story got out now after ten days, is, of course, due to

---

1 Donald Sterling Palmer Howard (1891–1959) was elected Conservative MP for Cumberland North in 1922, holding the seat until he succeeded his mother in 1926 as 3rd Baron Strathcona and Mount Royal. He was Under-Secretary of State for War from 1934 to 1939, latterly serving under Belisha.

Randolph Churchill who causes most of the trouble, or rather reveals it, political and social in London. Belisha was summoned to see the PM in his room at 9.30 and took the hearty line that it was outrageous for subordinates to blackmail the PM etc. The Prime Minister, who never relishes disloyalty, was impressed and decided to stand by him. David Margesson, who was dining with his three children, is anxious.

TUESDAY 20TH DECEMBER

The whole story of the revolt by young ministers is now out: it seems that Rob Hudson, Strathcona and Basil Dufferin – who is now in danger of losing his wife, his money and his job all at one fell swoop – took an oath of secrecy and determined to get rid of Belisha. It is particularly caddish of Strathcona, who is Belisha's chief,[1] and he had never once complained to him direct. Hudson was the prime mover and he went to the PM last week, threatened him with these resignations, and this was the day when the PM was so depressed and dismayed. The PM counter-attacked with the threat of an immediate election. The secret was fairly well kept until on Sunday night Basil in his cups confided in Randolph, who rang Beaverbrook in Paris. Beaverbrook said 'publish', and so last night we had the story in full. It has made a most unfortunate impression. Belisha is cheerful, however. I went along to the Lords' Library with Gage for a drink and there I found huddled together my lords Dufferin and Strathcona on a sofa splitting a whisky and soda! We caught them red-handed and they looked sheepish, indeed, like naughty schoolboys.

I dined with Pamela Berry, a party for some ball which she is organising, which I did not attend. I was between Venetia [Montagu] and Maureen [Dufferin[2]]; the latter left the dining room to talk to Eddie Devonshire[3] with whom she is having a hot affair! Venetia very anti-Chamberlain: it is a revolting exhibition of religious and racial prejudice! I hate her for it.

I returned to the House for an Adjournment [debate] on Spain. Rab, who wound up skilfully, bamboozled the Opposition.

WEDNESDAY 21ST DECEMBER

A miserable day of waiting. The weather is appalling, trains delayed.

Snow everywhere . . . Honor was due back at 3.20, and the car waited, whilst I telephoned frantically. At eight o'clock she had not yet come and I went to dine

---

1 It was the other way round: Strathcona answered to Belisha.
2 Maureen Constance Guinness (1907–98), a cousin of Channon's wife Honor, married in 1930 the 4th Marquess of Dufferin and Ava*.
3 Edward William Spencer Cavendish (1895–1950), by courtesy Marquess of Hartington from 1908 to 1938, when he succeeded his father as 10th Duke of Devonshire.*

with Alfred Beit[1] without her! A large dinner, but scarcely people one would invite to meet the Kents!! Princess Paul and Princess Marina both looking dreams of loveliness, arrived punctually. I was between the Duchess of Kent and Winnie Portarlington.[2] The house is fantastic, I like it. It is a touch vulgar, but blatantly foreign . . . The lights change during dinner and light up the Murillos[3] . . . Bad food . . . Duchess divine. Honor rang me during dinner and I got up to talk to her. Later I came back to Belgrave Square to see her. She was already half asleep, and no better. That I saw at once, and was consequently miserable.

I joined the Kents (he had come on), and we went to Ciro's, where we stayed for all hours of the night!! Home at 4.30, sharing a taxi with them.

The Kents gave me a fine pair of Dresden vases with links for a Christmas present. We are taking them to Kelvedon. Prince and Princess Paul have sent an enamel box, pink and *dix-huitième*,[4] a dream of beauty.

Thursday 22nd December

All day at the H of C, and at the Foreign Office, intriguing and setting up. I fear in my bones that today may be my last one at the Foreign Office! So does Rab. Or almost the last. I dined there, too . . . an enchanting evening. I was most amusing and gay, and adored it. Happier than I have been for months.

Honor shopped and is already worn out with London.

It has now transpired that the Dufferins spent last weekend with the Elvedens at the Old Rectory, Elveden. They left there by car too late to have dined with Randolph. Basil either had supper with him on Sunday night or revealed the plot to him on Monday before lunch. I think the former theory is true. I must find out.

Friday 23rd December

A nervous irritation [*sic*] day, everything went wrong: weather, stupid servants . . . At length Honor left for Elveden, she is far from well, and looks worn out, after three weeks' holiday skiing. I fear there is something organically wrong with her.

Saturday 24th December

I left at noon for Elveden. Alan, the flighty bridegroom, jumps about, runs in and out, like a lunatic . . . he went to Henlow[5] for the night to spend Christmas Eve with his mother.

---

1 Alfred Lane Beit (1903–94) succeeded his father as 2nd Bt in 1930. From 1931 to 1945 he was Conservative MP for St Pancras South East, and served in Bomber Command in the Second World War. He was a noted philanthropist.
2 Winnifreda Yuill (1886–1975) married in 1907 the 6th Earl of Portarlington*.
3 Bartolomé Esteban Murillo (1617–82) was a leading painter of the Spanish baroque.
4 Eighteenth century.
5 A Bedfordshire village and location of the Lennox-Boyd family house.

Here there are Lord and Lady Iveagh, pleased as Punch about the wedding and the arrangements, the people, the fuss . . .

I sent the Duchess of Kent an exquisite Fabergé reading-glass, which I was lucky enough to find. I wanted it so much myself . . .

SUNDAY 25TH DECEMBER

I went with the family and the Elvedens to church. Honor stayed behind in a bad temper. She is always sulky and surly now . . . Patsy came down in her green Salzburg clothes which she has been wearing for weeks, with a deplorable lack of vanity. They irritate Alan, and I begged Honor to get her into something else, which she did.

Arthur Elveden,[1] enormous again, read the lessons and later we went to the Old Rectory for family Christmas luncheon. They have made the old Suffolk house charming: it is gay, liveable, pleasant and rather American. Delicious food, and we stuffed.

Breakfast was a function and a feature. Even Honor came down and there was a big present distribution. I gave Honor three Fabergé cigarette cases, and had them marked and arranged. One I had given her years ago I had converted by Cartier into a vanity case. She has now two complete sets, a white one, and a blue one of great value and beauty. She gave me a pair of emerald links which I am to return to have made into ruby ones, which I want . . . Lady Iveagh gave me a watch that had belonged to the Sultan; whilst Patsy and Alan gave me a beautiful blue watch with a fountain on it, a real *bibelot*.[2] Paul had many presents from Princess Olga, the Kents, his godmothers, others . . .

More food, crackers and fun. Appalling weather: we are snowed up. And what of the wedding?

TUESDAY 27TH DECEMBER   *ELVEDEN*

Risking the treacherous roads Honor and I drove here in the snow after luncheon, and arranged the house for the honeymooners[3] who are to come here on Thursday. H in a gay, delicious mood . . . and I wonder . . . I wondered then . . . but it passed, as I saw I was being got round; she wants to go skiing again to Switzerland at once and spend three months there. She will end badly: there is

---

1 Arthur Onslow Edward Guinness (1912–45), by courtesy from 1927 Viscount Elveden, the younger brother of Channon's wife, Honor. He served as a major in the 55th Anti-Tank Regiment and was killed in action in the Netherlands when a V2 rocket hit the officers' mess.

2 An ornament or trinket.

3 Lennox-Boyd and Lady Patricia Guinness were due to marry on 29 December.

something rather brutal about it, so crude and fierce and she is *mal-entourée*[1] there. I am convinced of that . . .

WEDNESDAY 28TH DECEMBER   *ELVEDEN*

We came back here, after I had chucked the Old People's Dinner at Southend. There was really too much to do . . . Elveden *en fête*, the whole house open. And we are thirty-seven to dine. Mrs Lennox-Boyd,[2] the domineering mother who looks like a crumpet, [and] the eldest son, George[3] who is a rotter and a poseur, I think are staying in the house. Alan and Donald[4] are with the Elvedens as is Jim Wedderburn – much to his annoyance as he is in love with Brigid now . . . Ernest Brown, who booms with his great preacher's voice, has taken charge of the celebrations. He has been given the King's room. Then there are Freya Stark,[5] who is the Lady Hester Stanhope[6] of the age, and wears bizarre square clothes; Lord and Lady Brocket,[7] overdressed and young and fresh – she is called 'Lilac Time'; dear Mr Bland;[8] Lady Halifax; Harold Balfour, [and] many more . . . Dinner was fantastic. Lady Halifax and I had a most confidential talk and I told her of the treacheries in the FO. She was non-committal but not surprised. At the end of dinner Ernest Brown rose and in a bombastic speech proposed the health of the bride and bridegroom. He called Patsy 'Pat', and welcomed her to the

1 Surrounded by bad people or influences. It is clear from Channon's musings earlier in the entry that he again suspects Lady Honor of conducting an affair.
2 Florence Annie Warburton Begbie (1871–1949), married in 1901 as his second wife Alan Walter Boyd (1855–1934), who changed his surname by deed poll to Lennox-Boyd in 1925.
3 George 'Geordie' Lennox-Boyd (1902–43) was the first of two of Alan Lennox-Boyd's brothers to die in the Second World War. He served in the Highland Light Infantry and was repatriated in November 1943 to a military hospital in Scotland, suffering from pneumonia, of which he died.
4 Donald Breay Hague Lennox-Boyd (1906–39) was visiting Germany in April 1939 with his brother George when the Nazis arrested them in Stuttgart. He died in custody. He was arrested during a raid on a homosexual bar, having gone off on an assignation with a storm trooper (see entries for 4–8 April 1939). His death notice in *The Times* said simply 'suddenly, when abroad'.
5 Freya Madeline Stark (1893–1993) gained a reputation as an intrepid traveller and travel writer, undertaking dangerous expeditions to the Middle East and Afghanistan. She was a close friend of Donald Lennox-Boyd and of the family, and had a circle of mainly homosexual male friends. She served with distinction in the Ministry of Information during the Second World War and was awarded the DBE in 1972.
6 Lady Hester Lucy Stanhope (1776–1839), daughter of the 3rd Earl Stanhope, was a prodigious archaeologist and traveller.
7 Arthur Ronald Nall Nall-Cain (1904–67) was Conservative MP for Wavertree from 1931 to 1934, when he succeeded his father as 2nd Baron Brocket. He was a Nazi sympathiser, a friend of Ribbentrop (qv), an occasional go-between for the British and German governments, and a notorious absentee landlord in regard to his Scottish estates. He married in 1927 Angela Beatrix Pennyman (1906–75).
8 Christopher Harry Bland (1867–1947), the Guinness family's man of affairs.

Ministry. He was good, if perhaps embarrassing. Alan followed him and was his usual charming self, and he made affectionate references to me, which touched me. Patsy, blushing, was forced to her feet, and she was adequately facetious – said that when Alan reached Downing Street she would ask us all to tea!! Then we all filed into the library to see the presents: there were an impressive lot, except for presents given by the constituents.

Patsy [had] from her mother a diamond tiara much refurbished. This tiara .... was Lady Iveagh's third, and was given to her by her father, old Lord Onslow, when she married. There is now a large diamond on the top which Bland had found in an envelope amongst the papers of the late Lord Iveagh years after he died. It was so carefully put away, and separate from his many jewels, that it may have some history.

Jim Wedderburn nearly tearful at dinner. He regrets now that he didn't marry Patsy himself. The usual remorse of the left-behind. Poor Jim. And Brigid won't have him.

And so at last to bed – the disjointed party separated. The evening went with a swing. I felt an emotion of power: I had brought it about; I had brought Alan into our lives, and encouraged him to marry Patsy, made it possible, brought them together at the fatal weekend at Kelvedon in October. May I never regret it.

THURSDAY 29TH DECEMBER

The great wedding day began with a message from Jim Wedderburn that he must see me and soon he arrived from the other house. We paced the snow-covered drive and he expressed himself clumsily: he is unhappy; he wanted to marry Patsy ... then he became attracted by Brigid, and now has lost both. Also he loves me more than any man. All this he told me, as I shivered coatless outside Elveden ... then we went in, and I advised him to take a holiday and try and forget his troubles. He is too introspective, probably, like any Scottish young laird, he is a virgin.

As Jim and I were talking inside there was very nearly a serious accident, as a car suddenly started, the door flew open, struck Lady Iveagh and crushed her against the pillar of the *porte-cochère*.[1] She was bruised somewhat and badly shaken. Only a fraction of an inch and a second saved her from being crushed to death. It is too horrible to think about . . . I walked with Jim in the icy cold to the Old Rectory to call on Alan. We found him still in bed talking to his rather amiable but zany feckless brother Donald. (Alan loves Francis . . . the best, but he is a victim of scarlet fever and so unable to come to the wedding.) I ordered two bottles of champagne, the bridegroom, Harold, Jim, Donald and I all drank

---

1 The porch extending outwards from a great house, wide enough for a carriage or coach to be driven underneath it.

... Alan lay back in white pyjamas unshaved and excited. At last we left him to change and returned to Elveden. An early lunch at twelve o'clock, and soon afterwards MPs and others began to arrive in spite of the Russian weather. At 1.30 I went over to the church and already it was crowded with tenants of the Iveaghs and constituents of Alan's. These came in eight charabancs, out for a treat. The wedding passed off well enough ... Paul was an enchanting page, but he had trouble with his top hat at the door and a friendly policeman helped him. We waited for a little as the special train from London was delayed. Eventually the church was crammed and Patsy, dignified and handsome, arrived on the arm of her father. Alan, meanwhile, had arrived with his brother George, who was his best man, and the service began. Benjamin Guinness, Arthur's altogether delectable child, who is only nineteen months, was restless and eventually sat on my knees. Then a *sauve qui peut*[1] to the house and a queue of hundreds to congratulate the pair – the very fortunate, very rich pair!! .... I looked after the MPs etc. and eventually led everyone up to the room (Lady Iveagh's sitting room) where Alan was changing. We were about a dozen ... We all drank more champagne from the loving cup he had [been] given. Soon Honor, too, joined us. (She can rarely bring herself nowadays to be civil to ordinary mortals, but one must be gentle and tolerant, as she is not yet well.) Brigid was very attracted to Patrick Buchan-Hepburn,[2] Alan now wants to pull that off!! At last they left in a rain of rice and confetti and rose petals – for Kelvedon where I have made elaborate arrangements for the bridal pair. Patsy, who has been nervous lately, and overtired and overstrung, looked radiant. The other guests lingered on ...

Dinner was small and we discussed the wedding: parents happy. Lady Iveagh, to the amusement of all, busy making plans for Brigid's marriage!

FRIDAY 30TH DECEMBER

I awoke with a splitting head after too much champagne and excitement. Honor wanted to go to London in spite of the filthy road and I fear I was ungracious, even bad-tempered. It seemed madness to go up to London for no reason, and sulkily I refused. H didn't seem to mind, and went alone. She rang me about six o'clock in good temper, and she has selected the car she wants.

I slept long and am almost recovered. I was literally 'out' for four hours this afternoon.

---

1 Every man for himself.
2 Patrick George Thomas Buchan-Hepburn (1901–74) was Conservative MP for East Toxteth from 1931 to 1950 and for Beckenham from 1950 to 1957. He was the party's Chief Whip from 1948 to 1955, and from 1958 to 1962 was the first and only Governor of the West Indies Federation. He was raised to the peerage in 1957 as 1st Baron Hailes.

SATURDAY 31ST DECEMBER   *KELVEDON*

We all assembled here, Arthur and Elizabeth Elveden from London; Honor from London; the Iveaghs, Brigid and I from Elveden; the honeymooners were here – or rather had been up to London and came in soon after we did, both looking well. The honeymoon so far has been a success. Patsy told Honor that Alan was in a state . . . . After a time he . . . . went back to his bed both nights. They occupy the Empire suite. I deplore such tactics, the double bed is the secret of marriage and all my troubles began from the date that I deserted it. Alan confided to me that all had been well! He is still overexcited . . .

A pleasant dinner and how happy and satisfied the Iveaghs must have been, surrounded by all their four children and their new in-laws whom they like – only the mites, the tiny grandsons, are absent and they are not far away at Elveden . . . We drank much, had claret cup, and again rum punch at midnight. All very happy and a touch tipsy, I thought.

This formidable year is dead.

1939

The first weeks of the 1939 diary were recorded on loose pages torn from a writing book, and as a result some pages have been lost. Thus there are a few gaps in the diary for this month. Channon started a new bound writing book on 31 January 1939.

SUNDAY 1ST JANUARY

I woke with the traditional New Year's headache, and Alan Lennox-Boyd barged into my bedroom, a rather radiant, exuberant bridegroom. He and Patsy left here at 10 a.m. to catch the Paris plane, and it was a great send-off they had, with lots of luggage, excitement, and cheering relatives. It was lovely for the Iveaghs to be surrounded by their four children and three-in-laws, all of whom they luckily like. Only the tiny grandsons were absent from the family reunion, and they are snugly at Elveden not far away. None of us had slept and the house was too hot. The Elvedens, impressed by the beauty of our house, left in the evening . . . . Honor bought a new car, a blue Packard for skiing.

MONDAY 2ND JANUARY

The Channons leave for Elveden, where there is a house party in honour of the Prime Minister.

The Iveaghs left early, and Honor and I and Brigid followed in the afternoon. Bad weather. Much talk on the now all-engrossing problem: who is Brigid to marry? She is such a dazzling girl, so lovely, so classic, so unspoilt, Greek and intelligent.

I am quite schoolgirlish in my hysterical, almost fanatical worship of the PM; and was enchanted when Lord Iveagh asked me to meet him at the front door and escort him to his room. I did with glee. I paced the front hall restlessly until at last his car, very late, arrived. He had come from Ely. He said 'Hello, Chips!' as he got out, and stumbled on the steps, without hurting himself. He refused a drink, and I led him to the King's beds and sitting room . . . . We waited for a clumsy footman to unpack and he and I talked for twenty dazzling minutes!! I was intoxicated with his charm. He was so pleased about the Duchess of Atholl,[1]

---

1 The Duchess claimed to have been deselected by her constituency Unionist party in Kinross and West Perthshire over her profound opposition to appeasement, and in November 1938 she resigned the seat. A by-election was called for 21 December in which she stood as an independent; she lost.

so looking forward to his Rome visit. He is quite unperturbed about the future, is calm, self-assured and very amusing. I told him that Jim Wedderburn had sent off twelve Chamberlain dolls to some recalcitrant MPs and he was amused when I quoted the replies. At 9.30 I led him into the Big Hall where the party was assembled. Everyone twitted me with having drawn his bath and perhaps rubbed him down! My passion for Neville is well known. I was next to bad Maud Hoare[1] at dinner; when the men left Lord Iveagh moved across the table and sat between the PM and Sam Hoare. I made George Herbert tell the story of how Duff Cooper had recently assaulted him, throttled him and got on his chest all because he had defended the PM. The scene occurred a few weekends ago staying with Sidney Herbert.[2] The PM was much amused and proceeded to abuse Duff rather violently, and said that he was 'no man for teamwork'. Sam Hoare chipped in that he could not write: '*Haig* was unreadable and *Talleyrand* a good, indeed, an adequate abridgement of a three-volume work on Talleyrand in French . . . .' The PM scoffingly told us that Duff had written to him on New Year's Day wishing him health and happiness and apologising for anything that he may have written which could have given him offence; it was not his fault, Duff had explained, it was his constitution. The PM obviously dislikes him . . . The PM was most affectionate to me.

Sam Hoare told Honor a riveting secret story: he was in Italy in charge of our propaganda during the war, and after the defeat at Caporetto[3] where half Italy wished to retire from the war, he struggled to keep her in. He was told that there was a powerful Socialist, a fellow called Mussolini in Milan, who owned a newspaper there. He might be able to keep Italy in the war, at least he would be able to guarantee Milan and the North if sufficiently bribed. Sam Hoare 'for a very considerable sum, indeed' did buy the newspaper, Mussolini kept his bargain, and arranged for processions of beaten-up gangsters and thugs to process the streets in Milan with placards [reading] '*Mutilati della Guerra*'.[4] Already a brilliant showman, he skilfully arranged war propaganda. The money was used to form the Fascist party and to finance the March on Rome.[5] Thus English government cash created in an important way the Fascist revolution. This is very secret, and Mussolini when he meets Sam Hoare now is inclined to

---

1 Lady Maud Lygon (1882–1962), daughter of the 6th Earl Beauchamp, had married in 1909 Sir Samuel Hoare*.

2 Sidney Herbert (1906–69), by courtesy Lord Herbert, succeeded his father as 16th Earl of Pembroke and 13th Earl of Montgomery in 1960. He became equerry to the Duke of Kent in 1935 and, after the Duke's death in 1942, private secretary to the Duchess.

3 Now in Slovenia (and called Kobarid), the scene of the Central Powers' rout of the Italian army in October–November 1917.

4 War-wounded.

5 In October 1922, the prelude to Mussolini's taking power.

gloss over the former meeting. 'Yes, we once met,' he said. Sam Hoare still has in his private possession documents relating to this curious transaction.

His [Chamberlain's] dislike of Duff is obvious, his contempt for Anthony Eden rather more concealed, but still quite apparent. What fools are these two young men not to appreciate the greatest man of all time. Sam Hoare obsequious to Honor and wants her [illegible] on his side in his plot and plan to become PM, to succeed Neville. I think he will fail for we shall back Halifax in the saddle and I am working to that end.

Rab was, this morning, made a Privy Counsellor. It was in the honours list along with the same distinction for Harry Crookshank.[1] I knew, of course, and had David [Margesson]'s promise long ago. Yes I am delighted, for his is a well-deserved honour. No one has worked so hard. When I hinted to Sam Hoare that I hoped that Rab would not be moved to the Ministry of Agriculture or elsewhere, he replied to my intense relief that Rab would remain at the FO during the lifetime of the present parliament as he had become so necessary to the PM.

TUESDAY 3RD JANUARY

I was up at eight, down at nine; the excitement of proximity to my god prevented me from sleeping. He is in the room opposite my own. He was gay at breakfast, talked of the House, of MPs, etc. At 10.30 we went out shooting, a lovely but cold Norfolk day, and the flat bleak country and woods looked lovely and still. The PM shot well, indeed with amazing accuracy, but was excelled by Sam Hoare. I stood with them for two drives: and I was able to drop a little poison against [Rex] Leeper to both. Sam Hoare agrees and says so, he admitted him to be a danger but added that Halifax did not realise nor recognise the importance of loyal underlings. The PM smiled understandingly but said nothing. He did say, however, that he hoped Franco would not win too quickly. What did he mean by that, in the midst of Franco's greatest, and, we hope, decisive advance?[2] We discussed Rome, and he asked me what was the atmosphere there, and did I like Mussolini?

We came back to the house for luncheon, and fearing lest I had been a touch pushing with Neville I avoided him: it was unnecessary as he went out of the

---

1 Harry Frederick Comfort Crookshank (1893–1961) had been badly wounded in the Great War, being castrated by a shrapnel blast in 1916. After serving in the Foreign Office he was elected Conservative MP for Gainsborough in 1924, holding the seat until 1956 when he was raised to the peerage as 1st Viscount Crookshank. At the time of his appointment to the Privy Council he was Secretary for Mines; he served as Financial Secretary to the Treasury from 1939 to 1943 and as Postmaster-General from 1943 to 1945. In Churchill's peacetime administration he was Minister of Health, Lord Privy Seal and Leader of the House of Commons.

2 Franco was in the process of conquering Catalonia. On 27 February the British government, and the French, would recognise his regime.

way to be charming to me. The day was a great success, a bag of 818 without the 'pick-up'. The head keeper, Turner, who is a martinet and no respecter of persons, as usual, rode his pony and conducted the manoeuvres in a Napoleonic manner. He gave the order to shoot everything except English partridges. Many French ones were consequently shot, and someone slipped up somewhere as one English one was shot and it was placed surreptitiously with the PM's 'bag'. He [Chamberlain] pointed this out and with mock indignation declared that his Home Secretary was under suspicion.

THURSDAY 5TH JANUARY   KELVEDON

All day in Southend, and came back to dine with Honor, who had been in London all day. She was morose and uncommunicative.

I hope Hitler won't take too much this year: 1938 gave him both Austria and Czechoslovakia. Roosevelt in a wild diatribe[1] last night harangued Congress in a speech of shocking taste: all my sympathies were with the people he attacked so crudely; nevertheless his sermon may serve as a useful warning to the dictators, and perhaps we shall have peace throughout 1939.

SATURDAY 7TH JANUARY

Franco is making rapid advances, his offensive being cleverly timed to impress Chamberlain, and to strengthen Mussolini's hand next week: he may be able to claim that the war is practically over.

SUNDAY 8TH JANUARY

Honor and I motored to Stanstead Hall, Halstead, to lunch with the Butlers. He is so pleased at being a PC [Privy Counsellor], which he said he owed largely to me. She was gay, and pleasant and I am glad to relate on better terms with Honor, who really detests her appalling food in a dreadful house – but I smiled when I met their three little boys, particularly the youngest James, a fat apple of two, who at first bellowed when he saw us, and later made friends. I had sent him a Chamberlain [doll] for Christmas – Rab remarked to his wife: 'He is the first of your children, Sydney.' He quite obviously likes his youngest best.

Home for tea, and played with my own adorable little boy, who came back yesterday from Elveden. He is ever so beguiling, so affectionate. This morning he cried because he could not find me. Honor read to him. She teases him at times! My God, how I ache for more like him . . .

1 His State of the Union address, in which he warned that the world was at danger from war.

Honor in an endocrine mood, hard, selfish, uninterested, tonight. Said she would never have more children: I must look elsewhere for them. Evening ended on an unpleasant note.

Monday 9th January

When H is so disgruntled and unappreciative, I, in consequence, become uneasy, nervous. I long now for next Monday when I shall be alone for a fortnight. How salutary is solitude. Sleepy tonight. Honor read H. A. L. Fisher's brilliant history of Europe.[1] She was in a better mood ... still far from satisfactory.

Tuesday 10th January

I dreamt that I was married to Rachel Howard[2] and had, by her, many unattractive wall-eyed Catholic brats: that I was a tyrant in the home, feared and adored by all. Is this suppression?

I drove up to London, called at the Foreign Office, and was in rage with a note which I found permitted by Orme Sargent.[3] He is one of the *worst* of the Foreign Office mandarins, Red and Edenite, traitorous ... I reported him to Butler: what good will that do? Rab is weak with them as is Halifax. Lunched alone at the Carlton Club. Still feel frustrated.

Dined with Sir Patrick Hannon,[4] a large dinner of men, and talked to Nevile Henderson, whom I found changed. He has had cancer of the throat and seems very ill indeed. He seemed fragile, but charming, and very distinguished. He told the assembled gleefully that he was going to Sandringham for a week to recuperate. He thinks my Paul, the Regent, the cleverest diplomat in Europe ... At dinner there were several conversations on Germany and questions were just to Henderson. Rob Hudson was caddish, as usual, and said that only 25 per cent of the country were behind Chamberlain – this from a member of the government!! Henderson was scathing and suggested that there ought to be concentration camps in this country to get rid of the govt's enemies!! Henderson gave vivid pictures of Germany, and said how he once lost his temper last year

---

1 Probably Fisher's *The Republican Tradition in Europe*, published in 1911.
2 Mary Rachel Fitzalan-Howard (1905–92), Lady Rachel by courtesy, daughter of the Duke and Duchess of Norfolk.*
3 Harold Orme Garton Sargent (1884–1962) joined the Foreign Office in 1906 and served at the Paris Peace Conference in 1919. He was a strong anti-appeaser and was Permanent Under-Secretary for Foreign Affairs from 1946 to 1949. It is not clear what note he permitted to be circulated, but it seems to have challenged the appeasement orthodoxy to which Butler and Channon subscribed. His nickname was 'Moley'.
4 Patrick Joseph Henry Hannon (1874–1963) had been an Irish agriculturalist before sitting as Unionist MP for Birmingham Moseley from 1921 to 1950. He had been a supporter of the British Fascists in the 1920s. He was knighted in 1935.

with Ribbentrop in front of Hitler, and told Ribbentrop that he knew nothing of England, nothing at all. When he recovered he was surprised to see Hitler roaring with laughter: the Führer had evidently enjoyed hearing his jackal attacked! Henderson went on, praised Goebbels[1] slightly; but remains true to Göring[2] whom he definitely likes.

Someone asked what would have happened had Chamberlain not made the Munich Agreement: Germany would have marched immediately into Prague, and there would have been general war directly the French marched – there was always the possibility that the French would not have marched! Hitler's stock, while high, very high, is probably declining, and definitely less than last year for all his territorial and diplomatic successes. The cheers are less. Chamberlain gets the cheers in Germany today. Henderson thinks that Winston Churchill and Duff Cooper are a menace to world peace. He asked Göring recently what the field marshal thought would happen had there been a war, and Göring replied 'We should have been beaten, of course; but there would not have been a Czech left!!' All Henderson's arguments reinforce and commend Chamberlain's attitude . . . how foolish he makes Duff Cooper look . . . Duff has an article in tonight's *Evening Standard* in which he throws bouquets at Neville and Halifax – he is trying to worm himself back into Cabinet circles again. And he will not succeed.

The PM and Halifax . . . . left for Rome this morning. There was an unfortunate demonstration at Victoria, where a gang of the unemployed appeared with a coffin bearing a placard 'Appease the unemployed, not Mussolini'. This unimportant but unfortunate incident will create a bad impression abroad. Sir Herbert Smith,[3] also a Birmingham bigwig, was next to me, and he attacked Ronnie Cartland

---

1 Paul Joseph Goebbels (1897–1945) was Hitler's Minister of Propaganda from 1933 to 1945, and one of the main drivers of the campaign against the Jews. He exerted an iron control over the German press and radio, and exploited the relatively new medium of film. He had taken a PhD in nineteenth-century drama from Heidelberg in 1921; he was also an insatiable womaniser, and an exhaustive diarist; he nearly became a Catholic priest. He married, in 1931, Johanna Maria Magdalena 'Magda' Quandt, *née* Ritschel (1901–45), a devoted Nazi and close friend of Hitler. Together they poisoned their six children in May 1945 before killing themselves as the Russians advanced on Berlin.

2 Hermann Wilhelm Göring (1893–1946) had been a fighter pilot of distinction in the Great War. He was an early Nazi party member, wounded in the Munich Beer Hall Putsch of 1923, and became a morphine addict to manage the pain of his injuries. He joined Hitler's government after the latter's victory in 1933 and as one of his first acts organised the creation of the Gestapo, the Nazi secret police. He was an economic minister after 1936 and in charge of the Luftwaffe, the German air force. Hitler nominated him in 1941 as his heir. He became notorious for looting art treasures from murdered Jews and conquered nations. Sentenced to death at Nuremberg, he managed to commit suicide using a concealed cyanide pill the night before he was to be hanged.

3 Herbert Smith (1872–1943) was a Kidderminster carpet manufacturer. One of Lloyd George's 'new men', he served on various industry bodies during the Great War and was created 1st Bt in 1920.

with violence. He told me that Ronnie has been severely dressed-down by his constituents, that he had arranged a general meeting and asked for a vote of confidence; instead the meeting passed a resolution in favour of Chamberlain. He is unpopular in King's Norton and may not get in again. I was secretly pleased, as Ronnie has been so stupidly anti-Chamberlain. He gets a sexual kick by voting against the government.

FRIDAY 13TH JANUARY

I went to the Foreign Office to see Rab. They were without real news of the Rome visit; but the general impression is that it has not exactly come off, although it improved our relations with that fascinating and important power . . . . I lunched alone with Rab off pork and port at Smith Square. He repeats himself, is very sly and subtle, but not meretricious . . . reserve-reserve, all the way is his motto. Today he was more expansive: he never takes a bachelor seriously, he is an incomplete man; Rob Hudson is a shit, a second-rater; Shakes Morrison . . . an amiable individual who isn't 'up to it'; Shakes will never go far . . . these were his confidences to me . . . there will be no major reshuffle in the immediate prospect. Tommy Dugdale rang him on the telephone from Yorkshire to tell him so. Rab thinks Anthony Eden is played out, has fallen flat . . . Halifax is really too cynical . . . these are his reflections. The PM, he knows, was furious at going to see the Pope today. His Unitarian conscience is offended: and he fears a loss of votes!!

I drove Rab to the station, and parted with the 'Rt Hon. Gentleman' at Victoria, where joined by Peter Loxley and others of the press, they left for Geneva. I am glad I am not going. I want to be alone. I am exhausted today.

Rab and I both secretly fear that the Germans have designs on Holland; we shall hear more from that quarter, always they have 'trumped up' a silly incident.

SATURDAY 14TH JANUARY

All day at Southend, as I was moved by the poor children playing at the Estuary Club.[1] I talked to the one mute, scarcely older than Paul, a little girl called Mary Collet – I wonder what will happen to her? She tried to lisp her full name and address, and had I been able to understand her, I should have sent her a present tomorrow. She was one of eight children of an unemployed house-painter. Honor doesn't realise how other people live. She is fundamentally warped. I almost envied that unemployed house-painter with eight children and the dole – I, with my dauphin[2] and our millions. Home about eight, and a peaceful evening.

1 A social club in Leigh-on-Sea, founded in 1932.
2 His 3-year-old son, Paul.

SUNDAY 15TH JANUARY

All day by myself. I thought about me, my past, amazing; my future doubtful . . .
I feel that 1939 may not be a lucky year for me. I seem to have lost my grasp, and
my luck. The day began badly as the chef gave me notice as he cannot get on with
Nannie. No news of Honor[1] . . . Franco is forging ahead towards Barcelona . . . .

Old Brolly [Chamberlain] got back from Rome, his status enhanced, his
prestige increased. He is winning through and will probably be Premier for years
to come. He was well received in London.

MONDAY 16TH JANUARY

Franco took Zaragoza last evening, thank God!

TUESDAY 17TH JANUARY

At ten I left in the green chariot[2] for London. At the Foreign Office I found
myself alone in our office, and I enjoyed myself hugely. I opened boxes, read
'most secret' dispatches, wrote letters and did chores. My friend Harold Caccia[3]
was also alone in the Permanent Under-Secretary's room as Lord Halifax is *en
route* for Geneva, and returns only tonight. Caccia and I signed the letters. He is
a charmer, looks like an inflated cherub, speaks Chinese to his cook, and was best
man to Peter Loxley. He has gay blue eyes and is friendly to all . . . looked in at
the Carlton Club in search of news and found none . . . . lunched with Emerald,
who was fantastic, gay, whimsical, absurd, she danced about in her conversation
trying to keep it off anything controversial as the Coopers were there. Duff was
quite pleasant and didn't strike anyone . . . . He was ill at ease with the Duke of
Alba,[4] as he has recently said that a Franco victory would be a disaster. Alba was
very *grand seigneur* and asked him if he had written any new books lately – 'You
ought to write,' he smiled. Duff gulped taking the remark to mean that the Duke
had not read his really twaddleish articles in the *Evening Standard*. Diana, just
back from Montgenèvre, looked lovely and lithe, really remarkably beautiful.
Like Emerald and Lady Curzon she likes a ridiculously small hat.

Grace Curzon was fat, ample, lavishly dressed like an over-ripe Tiepolo.[5]
She lied a lot: said that the Argentine government had just paid her £3,000 for

---

1 She had gone two days earlier to Gstaad to ski.
2 Channon's Rolls-Royce.
3 Harold Anthony Caccia (1905–90) was a career diplomat who became Ambassador to
   Austria in 1951, serving until 1954, and then Ambassador to the United States from 1956 to
   1961. He was knighted in 1950 and raised to the peerage as Baron Caccia (life peer) in 1965.*
4 Jacobo Fitz-James Stuart y Falcó (1878–1953), 17th Duke of Alba, since 1936 Franco's man in
   London.*
5 The Venetian painter.

a portrait of Canning by Lawrence. I remember it well, first at Montacute and later at Hackwood.[1] She has a similar portrait of Pitt attributed to Hoppner:[2] these were purchases of Lord Curzon.[3] Shall I try to buy the Pitt? How well it would look in the drawing room. We managed to keep off France and Munich as luncheon proceeded.

Charming and humorous letter from Honor written on Saturday.

WEDNESDAY 18TH JANUARY

To the Foreign Office in the morning, and I saw a smallish crowd assembled outside No. 10 waiting to watch the Cabinet ministers go in. I wished. How pleasant is the office when the masters are away. Walked to the Carlton Club where I went down alone to lunch, but was quickly joined by Shakes Morrison, with his charming gay manner. He talked all during luncheon, gay, flowing charm, and we were soon joined by Walter Elliot: I thus had two Cabinet ministers as my companions, and as they had just left the Cabinet I tried to pump them. I was not successful, except I gathered they were in good spirits, and that Brolly was boisterously happy. Thus no election. There is gloom, however, at the Foreign Office. This is the year, they keep on saying just as they did last year – as it so nearly was.

FRIDAY 20TH JANUARY

Esmond Harmsworth,[4] handsome, simple, a touch dull, but charming, a little deaf . . . arrived here for the weekend bringing his lady love, Ann O'Neill.[5] The charming Charteris sisters are practically 'tarts' but distinguished ones.

Went to Southend to see the Mayor, and I have started an appeal to help the local unemployed.

1 Montacute House in Somerset, and Hackwood Park in Hampshire, residences of the Curzon family.
2 John Hoppner (1758–1810), English portraitist.
3 George Nathaniel Curzon (1859–1925) was one of the great proconsuls and statesmen of his age. He was Conservative MP for Southport from 1886 to 1898, when he was raised to the peerage as 1st Baron Curzon of Kedleston (in the Irish peerage, so he could sit again in the House of Commons) on his appointment as Viceroy of India; he was advanced to an earldom as Earl Curzon of Kedleston in 1911; and finally to a marquessate as Marquess Curzon of Kedleston in 1921.*
4 Esmond Cecil Harmsworth (1898–1978) succeeded his father as 2nd Viscount Rothermere in 1940. He was Chairman of the Daily Mail and General Trust Ltd from 1938 until his death.
5 Ann Geraldine Mary Charteris (1913–81) married in 1932 Shane Edward Robert O'Neill (1907–44), 3rd Baron O'Neill. After he was killed in action, in 1945 she married Esmond Harmsworth, 2nd Viscount Rothermere (*vide supra*), and after their divorce in 1952, Ian Fleming (qv).

SUNDAY 22ND JANUARY

I rang Honor . . . and she sounded gay, well and happy. I love her.

MONDAY 23RD JANUARY

At the Foreign Office most of the day, and helped Rab to receive a deputation of angry ladies who we feared, at one moment, would clock him. They are the pro-Red fanatics, Violet Bonham Carter,[1] Miss Sylvia Pankhurst[2] – a desperate left-wing individual, angry, short-haired and lesbian, Jennie Lee,[3] Rosamond Lehmann in bright red, many more communistical-inclined females . . . Rab told me that at Geneva last week Lord Halifax once more raised the question of whether Anthony Eden should be allowed 'back'. He is in favour of his restoration, but the PM is against it. Rab convinced him that it would be a mistake.

SATURDAY 28TH JANUARY   *KELVEDON*

Harold [Balfour] and Rob Bernays arrived to stay, ministers both, but not friends. They are getting on better. Bernays is very vicious sexually I have discovered. His secret is well-kept.[4]

SUNDAY 29TH JANUARY

The new Cabinet changes were announced: Reggie Dorman-Smith[5] is to be Minister of Agriculture in place of Shakes Morrison: it will be a popular, although surprising appointment. Reggie at 39 in the Cabinet and a Right Honourable. It is an astonishing risk (he has never done anything in the House) which may

---

1 Helen Violet Asquith (1887–1969) married in 1915 Maurice Bonham Carter (1880–1960) who was H. H. Asquith's private secretary when Asquith was Prime Minister. From 1925 she was by courtesy Lady Violet Bonham Carter, after her father was created an earl.

2 Estelle Sylvia Pankhurst (1882–1960) had like her mother Emmeline and sister Christabel been a leading suffragette, but unlike them was a committed supporter of the labour movement. An early member of the Communist Party of Great Britain, she was expelled over doctrinal differences. In the late 1930s she was a militant opponent of Italian policy in Abyssinia, and her activities were monitored by MI5.

3 Janet 'Jennie' Lee (1904–88) was Labour MP for North Lanarkshire from 1929 to 1931 and for Cannock from 1945 to 1970. She was Minister for the Arts from 1964 to 1970, when she was raised to the peerage as Baroness Lee of Asheridge (life peerage). She married Aneurin Bevan (1897–1960) in 1934.

4 He was a flagellomaniac.

5 Reginald Hugh Dorman-Smith (1899–1977) had been a professional soldier before becoming a farmer, and was president of the National Farmers Union by the age of 32. His popularity among his fellow farmers was a key reason for his appointment. He was Conservative MP for Petersfield from 1935 to 1941, when he became the Governor of Burma, a post he held until 1946. He was knighted in 1937.

placate the farmers and the whole agricultural vote! Chatfield[1] becomes Minister for the Co-ordination of Defence in lieu [of] Inskip,[2] who refusing the Woolsack goes to the Dominions Office. [Earl] Winterton dropped almost altogether, dismissed from the Cabinet and fobbed off with Paymaster-Generalship, an unpaid sinecure. Shakes becomes Chancellor of the Duchy, where he will do defence work. Master Munster[3] succeeds Strathcona, who has got the sack for his recent disloyalty. Quite sensational change.

Very late with Rob Bernays discussing his vices and unsatisfied lusts. He is perfectly hideous, yet has an attractive smile and his sensitive face lights up with intelligence.

MONDAY 30TH JANUARY

I thought of my wife the whole evening. Bless her. I wish she were here, I wish she were happier.

I am sad to leave Kelvedon in the morning, sorry to leave my dear dogs, so trusting and attractive and miserable at leaving this lovely house smelling of hyacinths . . . it is midnight, and for the third time I felt a slightly uncanny atmosphere . . . but I don't credit the tales of headless nuns, and queer elementals . . . Kelvedon has much atmosphere, but it is never unpleasant – it is dignified and distinguished.

Hitler's great speech[4] has proved not to be so alarming as the pessimists warned us . . .

TUESDAY 31ST JANUARY

I left Kelvedon reluctantly this morning, and sat, bored and overdressed in a stuffy businessmen's train from Brentwood . . . the Foreign Office were in two

1 Alfred Ernle Montacute Chatfield (1873–1967) had a distinguished naval career that culminated in his becoming First Sea Lord in 1933 and serving until 1938. He was raised to the peerage as 1st Baron Chatfield in 1937. As Admiral Beatty's flag captain at the Battle of Jutland in 1916 it was he to whom Beatty made his famous remark that 'there seems to be something wrong with our bloody ships today'.
2 Thomas Inskip.* He would not be able to avoid the Woolsack for long, being moved there the day war broke out in September 1939.
3 Geoffrey William Richard Hugh FitzClarence (1906–75) succeeded his uncle as 5th Earl of Munster in 1928. Prior to becoming Under-Secretary of State for War in this reshuffle, he had been Paymaster-General since the previous June. He served in both of Churchill's administrations, and in Eden's.
4 Hitler addressed the Reichstag on 30 January 1939, the sixth anniversary of his coming to power, making what has become known as his 'prophecy' speech, in which he forecast that if a war broke out it would portend the annihilation of European Jewry. As much of his speech was devoted to a tedious account of the glorious history of the Nazi Party, the threat to Europe's Jews was less noted than it might otherwise have been.

moods, relief at Hitler's really reasonable and quieting speech last night, and on some sides, regret and resentful at being proved fake prophets ... the same people who went about warning us [of] Hitler's dastardly intentions, now complain that his speech was too mild. The English are definitely mad, and in their decadence it becomes more transparent.

[In the Commons] The PM had first read out a statement about his Rome visit. His speech was modulated, and the Speaker was weak with the ill-mannered and noisy Opposition. Archie Sinclair was ridiculous for over an hour. Anthony Eden lounged about, looking old, tired and disqualified and hideous ...

Winston Churchill came in only for a moment, late ... Lloyd George sat fumbling with his notes, and at last scenting that the occasion was not sufficiently important for him to speak, left ... I sat all day and evening on the PPS's bench, darting about with messages. Rab rose at 10.25 and spoke well but was too friendly to the Spanish 'Reds' – it was a gesture to the man who was down, and rather [illegible] as he is in sympathy with Franco. The PM is cockahoop, and sat chuckling immediately in front of me. He is so pleased with the recent turn of events that there is danger now of an election. His new optimism is dangerous ...

There was an attack on Duff in the Smoking Room: one of his sillier and more ill-timed articles appeared in this evening's *Standard*. Communists demonstrated outside the House demanding 'Arms for Spain'. Poor Shakes Morrison is down and discouraged but he will revive soon enough ...

Home late and very tired. Of course I forgot to eat all day. I talked to Honor on the telephone at Mürren and she seemed well, but less amiable than last time.

WEDNESDAY 1ST FEBRUARY

I walked to the Foreign Office and later escorted Rab to the Privy Council, where he rehearsed tomorrow's ceremony where he is to be introduced. As I left him I ran into Reggie Dorman-Smith, who was extraordinarily social and pleased with himself – he was, too, on the way to the rehearsal. As he is not yet a Privy Counsellor until tomorrow he could not attend this morning's Cabinet meeting as the Cabinet is technically a committee of the Privy Council. He can scarcely credit his meteoric rise to dizzy eminence, but it will not alter him.

I went into Charles Peake's room and there I found grey, bilious Leeper who, to my rage and surprise called me 'Chips'. He is a deplorable creature and I cannot get the Foreign Office to oust these pink traitors, all of them still infatuated with Eden. Oh! Eden, what crimes are committed in thy name.

The Foreign Office wants a purge and a reorganisation. Bill Astor is to withdraw, he says, from the St George's Conservative Association so strongly does he disapprove of Duff Cooper and his inflammatory articles ... The annual ward meeting of the Con. Assoc. was arranged for next Wednesday, as usual at Lord Hambleden's house. In the past the member, Duff, has been either too busy, or has not bothered to attend. However, he recently announced that he would appear on Wednesday whereupon Billy Hambleden withdrew his invitation to the ward, as he will not have Duff in his house. It is partly political, and partly because of Duff's insulting behaviour to Lady Pembroke … he is a tactless fellow, our inflated conceited turkey-cock of a Cooper. I am very against him and fan every flame.

Thursday 2nd February

Gage proposed himself to luncheon and we had a long intimate talk. He has long since lost any charm for me, yet I have a sneaking sort of protective affection for him; but I'm not devoid of an itch to tease and prick him. Today I dealt him a masterly blow, and have been chuckling with delight all day. He asked me in the autumn to use my powers of intrigue, and my persuasion with the Prime Minister and Lord Halifax, to get him a job – he has been Lord in Waiting now since 1924, with one short Labour interval, and not unnaturally he thinks he ought to be given an under-secretaryship since he is as able probably as Sim Feversham.[1] I had promised to do what I could, which I didn't for a variety of reasons: (a) that I should probably fail; (b) that it suits me better for him to remain at Court; (c) why should I break my neck, everything considered for him? … but I told him none of these things just hinted rather crudely that he had been passed over because he was suspected of 'Eden-itis'! He has been seen often with Eden, and has played with Ronnie Tree off and on for years. My prick was a thunderbolt and he was indignant but impressed. I prophesy that he will now drop Ronnie Tree, who irritates me more and more … I drove him to the Houses of Parliament. This afternoon I slept for two hours in the library and my own snores awoke me … . and I found that we had reached the fantastic Pension scheme, a plan to provide indigent MPs over 60, or their widows, with an income of £150 per annum. In other words we are asked to dock members £12 per annum for the benefit of others, as it is inconceivable that many of us should not have at least £130 a year to live on. Still we never know!! Like almost everyone on our side I was resolved to vote against the measures, which in any case, were clumsily drafted, and a half-baked sentimental bit of legislation. The PM rose, and made a brilliant cunning contribution supporting the measure, whilst insisting that it was a free vote. He was humorous, and then made a Baldwinian effort to placate the Labour Party – and succeeded. They were stunned by his logic, his humour and sympathy and, I think, liked him for the first time. He swayed some votes undoubtedly, and I then decided to abstain. Then Duff rose,

---

1 Charles William Slingsby 'Sim' Duncombe (1906–63), Viscount Helmsley from 1915 to 1916, when he succeeded his father as 3rd Earl of Feversham, was Halifax's son-in-law. He had been Parliamentary Secretary to the Ministry of Agriculture and Fisheries since 1936.*

staging a 'comeback' and in a pompous absurd little declaration, which showed that he had not read his brief, he harangued against the scheme, thus at once offending both the Labour people and the PM. He was shouted at by various indignant members, 'NO! NO! Read the bill!' The speech was so maddening that I promptly went into the division lobby and voted for the bill. I was glad I did; my action pleased the Labour Party, and also it ill behoves the very rich to vote against the measure. I saw Oliver Stanley and Euan Wallace with me. The very rich behaved well.

Then I rushed home, and dressed in a rush, with the result that I cut myself shaving, and went to dine with the Duke of Kent . . . just off.

Friday 3rd February

I sat up so late last night that I could neither face my diary nor do my daily exercises this morning – both of which so contribute to my well-being for the rest of the day.

I arrived at No. 3 [Belgrave Square] with the Duke of Kent for dinner and found a most ill-assorted party of fourteen people, social waifs and strays evidently, collected by the Duke to amuse himself during the Duchess's absence – she is in Athens. The most surprising guest (and the most delighted to be there) was Mr Rootes,[1] the motor magnate millionaire, ex-lover of Lady Castlerosse. Bad food, but glorious china for the usual *bibelots*. We went on to a private cinema performance in Wardour Street and at 1.30 as it ended my old enemy (but recently reconciled), Freda Casa Maury,[2] asked me back to her house for a drink and foolishly I went. A modern affair, is this freshly constructed villa in modest Hamilton Terrace.[3] There is one huge room, white with much glass, and modern things. It is gay and attractive but no atmosphere, no *bibelots* . . . Freda is happily married to . . . Bobby Casa Maury; and although she is a grandmother she doesn't look 40, and is still languorously in love – I am told that passion is not all spent yet in that *ménage*. *Qui sait?*[4] There was champagne, and an Augustus John-looking [illegible] who sang and played badly for two hours . . . I left at 5.30,

---

1 William Edward Rootes (1894–1964) was trained as an apprentice by Singer cars and in 1913 set up his own car dealership; he also helped with the maintenance of aero engines during the Great War. In the Second World War he oversaw production of aircraft and their engines, and helped supply military vehicles. He was knighted in 1942 and created 1st Baron Rootes in 1959.

2 Winifred May 'Freda' Birkin (1894–1983) married in 1913 William Dudley Ward MP; she was mistress of the Prince of Wales from 1918 until supplanted by Mrs Simpson in 1934. She married in 1937 Pedro Jose Isidro Manuel Ricardo Mones (1895–1968), Marqués de Casa Maury.

3 Between Maida Vale and St John's Wood.

4 Who knows?

the Duke remaining still. Edwina Mountbatten[1] eclipsed the other professional beauties as she always does. Dickie Mountbatten[2] has lost his looks, charm and glamour, but is still pleasant.

Today I feel weak. I am too old a bird for these late nights. I went to the Foreign Office, then the House of Commons, and in a daze lunched with Mike Wardell[3] at the *Evening Standard* offices. I tried to do some pro-Chamberlain, anti-Cooper, anti-Churchill work, but am not sure that Mike was responsive. He is like a child, so excited with his new building which has cost a packet and will not be ready for some months yet. The *Standard* is doing well, very well. Beaverbrook is ill, has had a slight operation. Then I drove to the House of Commons, picked up Ronnie Cartland and we went shopping. He is an amiable gossip and I gave him a second-rate sauce boat. He said that that bald-headed ass, Paul Emrys-Evans,[4] had attacked him for staying with me – 'one of the enemy', he called me, because I am anti-Eden. It is really too silly. Ronnie, who is one of them, agrees that such a faction can never go far.

Bed at 6.30 and I had hope to sleep for twelve hours or more.

There have been serious explosions, bombs found in the Underground; a reign of terror has gone on for weeks now. It is alleged to be the work of Irish extremists.[5]

S ATURDAY 4 TH F EBRUARY

I drove to the House of Commons, and found it heavily guarded, with a policeman before every door, so great is the fear of explosions. I talked to Honor on the telephone. I wonder whether she and Diana [Cavendish] are not for the first time a touch bored? They come back on February 18th.

1   Edwina Cynthia Annette Ashley (1901–60) married in 1922 Lord Louis Mountbatten (*vide infra*).
2   Louis Francis Albert Victor Nicholas Mountbatten (1900–79), son of Prince Louis Alexander of Battenberg, and from 1917 Lord Louis Mountbatten by courtesy. His family nickname was 'Dickie'. He was raised to the peerage as 1st Viscount Mountbatten of Burma in 1946, and advanced to an earldom the following year on his resignation as Viceroy of India. He also became an admiral of the fleet, First Sea Lord and Chief of the Defence Staff. He was assassinated by the IRA.*
3   A senior lieutenant of Lord Beaverbrook*.
4   Paul Vychan Emrys-Evans (1894–1967) was Conservative MP for South Derbyshire from 1931 to 1945, and was Under-Secretary of State for Dominion Affairs from 1942 to 1945.
5   It was the work of the Irish Republican Army, and was known as the S-Plan, or Sabotage Plan. The IRA had declared war on Britain on 12 January 1939, justifying its action by deeming Britain the occupying power of Northern Ireland, and a bombing campaign on the mainland started on 16 January. The two bombs on the Underground to which Channon refers were at Tottenham Court Road and Leicester Square stations and were triggered on 4 February, the day after the date of this diary entry. Two people were injured. The campaign continued until the late winter of 1940 and two IRA men were hanged in February 1940 for the murder of a 21-year-old woman in an attack on Coventry in August 1939.

SUNDAY 5TH FEBRUARY

Up late, did exercise, had a massage and none of these things relieved my acute indigestion and blown-out feeling. What can I do?

Harold Balfour to luncheon and we gossiped just about politics and then his love affairs – the last two both began in this house, first with Virginia Agnelli, with whom he had a sharp quick affair, terminated by absence and distance, and then just a year ago he met Helen Fitzgerald in this house and very soon it was a liaison, which now, after a year, it still is. His family know nothing. Of course he is very attractive, and handsome and a touch dashing . . . he works too hard.

The government had a good press today. It is Chamberlain Sunday. All is well in Paradise. Anyone who opposes him comes a cropper. Look at that supreme ass Derrick Gunston, his former PPS, who has had the impudence and temerity to oppose him – he has broken his back skating or tobogganing, and now I read that Ronnie Tree, of whom curiously enough I dreamt last night, was badly hurt out hunting yesterday . . . Life for the moment is lovely.

MONDAY 6TH FEBRUARY

The Iveaghs to lunch, very affectionate and friendly, and I went to the House of Commons. As I was standing at the Bar of the House Anthony Eden came up to me and said angrily, 'I hear, Chips, you say that my American trip was a failure and that I am a disaster.'[1] Surprised, I weakly retorted 'That's news to me.' 'Well thank you for your tribute,' he announced and walked away. I am sorry, really sorry to have offended him; but I consider him a menace to the future of the world, but a diminishing menace. I wrote him a cool little note and later when we met he smiled. I came home here at 6.30 and am going to bed, as I feel ill.

SUNDAY 12TH FEBRUARY

I have been ill since last Monday with flu, high temperatures and depression. Today I got up. Alan and Patsy, Harold, and Rob Bernays all came to see me. Honor telephoned that she has gone to Kitzbühel. The Iveaghs very kind and loving and both rang me every day on the telephone to inquire. I love them.

MONDAY 13TH FEBRUARY

I went for a while to my two Paradises, the Foreign Office, and the House of Commons – but weak and dejected I returned to my bed.

---

1 Eden had visited America in December 1938 at the invitation of the National Association of Manufacturers, and had delivered a keynote speech in New York to an audience of 4,000 people on the subject of 'the gathering storm' – a phrase Churchill purloined for his volume on the build-up to war. His trip was widely deemed a great diplomatic success, and he had private talks with Roosevelt while there.

THURSDAY 16TH FEBRUARY

A hectic afternoon. I took [illegible] constituents to Mrs Chamberlain's for tea and then rushed back to the House of Commons to hear Lord Halifax address the Foreign Office Committee. He was brilliant, beguiled them, led them up the garden path, played them, impressed them with his charm, sincerity and high ideals. He fascinates and bamboozles everyone. Is he saint turned worldling, or worldling become saint?

FRIDAY 17TH FEBRUARY

Too down all the week to record my thoughts; flu leaves one working at half-cock. Today I had twenty-one men to luncheon, the lobby journalists who have been amiable to me, and as guests of honour, Alec Cadogan – correct, suave, Edwardian – and Rab. I put the two Under-Secretaries of State one at each end of the table.[1] It was a great success.

Jim Thomas dined with me and spilt his animal spirit and charm. He is a weakling without judgement, without honour, but somehow loveable. I am always, alas, attracted by weakness. He stayed very, very late, and we talked until we were hungry; then went to the kitchen and cooked eggs . . . Bed at four. Foolishly. How Jim loathes Alan; and how jealous he is of him.

SATURDAY 18TH FEBRUARY

I was a hopeless case all day. Honor rang me from Paris, and later arrived with Diana Cavendish by air at Croydon. Honor is amazing, good looks, quite lovely and gay. I am sad and disappointed to be down and lifeless and listless. I am ageing: I must write my will; and meanwhile recover my spirits.

SUNDAY 19TH FEBRUARY

Honor and I drove to Kelvedon which looked lovely. We walked about the gardens . . .

We had a dinner party for 21; it was successful. I was between Loelia Westminster and Sheila Birkenhead. Duff amiable and on his best behaviour drinking only red wine . . . Everyone stayed until 1.30, and I persuaded Loelia to agree to dispose of her house to the Lennox-Boyds – 1 Little College Street,[2] a house I have always loved. I knew it well in the Stanleys' regime and at various

---

1 Sir Alexander Cadogan was a Permanent Under-Secretary; Butler was Parliamentary Under-Secretary.
2 Elsewhere he writes No 8, which was correct.

times it was let to Spears,[1] and to the Dufferins – they were living there when he was killed[2] . . . now Alan and Patsy are installed there luxuriously.

Honor looked a vision of beauty. She has got her looks back, and her health and spirits.

MONDAY 20TH FEBRUARY

Again I felt ill and had to come home to recover. Perhaps it was a hangover? About eight I took my temperature and it was 99.4; but too late to chuck our royal dinner party at the Kents. I nearly fainted at dinner; but luckily I had taken the precaution of having a footman ring up to say that I must return immediately to the H of C. I got the message, bore it bravely, with cold sweat pouring down my body, counting the minutes. At last I could bear it no more, and apologised to the Duke, saying I was going back to the House of Commons – I rushed home and was violently sick. Then I rang up the doctor who came at once. I foresaw a bad bout of flu, or a recurrence . . . but he said it was only an upset of the tummy, and so it proved to be. Too much champagne last night.

I watch the PM and others in their full vigour at 70,[3] and I weak and tired at 40. It is deplorable.

THURSDAY 23RD FEBRUARY

Honor and I dined at the House of Commons. We were to have gone to see [the] Chamberlains 'At Home', but there was a comedy at the House of Commons which kept me busy, and I could not get away. The Socialists lost their temper and kept us late. Home at 2.30, worn out. I don't like late nights at the House anymore. It gets so cold. All-night sittings have at least some *Stimmung*! But just to be kept up because the Socialists are in a bad temper, or because one has been fool enough not to leave, is boring.

FRIDAY 24TH FEBRUARY

What a flop, Anthony Eden. We were discussing his declension today. And it is a year and nearly a week since we manoeuvred to get him out. I cannot take the credit – I wish I could – for his fall. He engineered that himself; but certainly my campaign against him bore fruit and helped prepare the ground. For six months not a day passed that I did not drop poison into ministerial ears about the lies of

---

1 Edward Louis Spears had been a senior liaison officer between the British and French armies in the Great War, and was now Conservative MP for Carlisle.*

2 The 3rd Marquess, who was killed in a plane crash on 21 July 1930.

3 Chamberlain would be dead by the end of 1940.

the Eden influence ... I am not as able as Anthony, but am more resolute, subtler, and cleverer.

Honor and I lunched with Grace Curzon of Kedleston in a private suite at the Dorchester, a luxurious meal ... We waited some time for the Duke of Alba who did not arrive. Perhaps he is being recognised; we all laughed. (We have decided to recognise Franco next Monday simultaneously with the French – two years too late!)

MONDAY 27TH FEBRUARY

Alan, rushing about like an inspired lunatic, had a nasty accident yesterday at Henlow: he fell sixteen feet, fractured his foot, bruised his ribs, and was knocked for a second unconscious. Poor Patsy she has indeed taken on a career in marrying him ...

We dined *en famille*, the Iveaghs, us, all at 8 Little College Street with Patsy and Alan. My mother-in-law was charm itself, gentle, affectionate, understanding, and a touch distant to Honor whose long absences she deplores. I returned to the House after dinner as there was the threat of an adjournment. I had to gauge the situation: at 10.15 I concluded that there might be trouble, and I rang up the Ritz where Rab was dining with the Arabs, got him to the telephone and warned him. He returned just in time ... and I also produced two people from the Foreign Office. Promptly at 11.06 Arthur Henderson rose and we had our Libyan debate. The Italians ... I hate saying it ... are letting us down in the spirit, if not in the letter of Anglo-Italian agreement by sending reinforcements to Libya. So we were on a bad wicket ... came home but Honor was already asleep.

TUESDAY 28TH FEBRUARY

A big day. Honor, accompanied by Diana and Sibyl Cavendish[1] (she supports them both now), left at 2 p.m. for Mürren. She seemed pleased to go, which is always worrying; but she was gentle and sweet and the visit has been a success. I was cold, cold as only I can be, to Lady Moyra Cavendish[2] who came to Victoria to see them off. She is a rabid anti-Chamberlain critic, a pro-Cranborne fanatic. He, by the way, has jaundice. I think he is having a change of life.

---

1 Sibyl Moyra Cavendish (1915–2004), fifth daughter of Lord Richard Cavendish (*vide infra*) and younger sister of Diana Cavendish (qv). She married, in 1941, Revd Lawrence Gregson Fell Dykes (1906–93).
2 Lady Moyra de Vere Beauclerk (1876–1942), daughter of the 10th Duke of St Albans, married in 1895 Lord Richard Cavendish (1871–1946), younger brother of the 9th Duke of Devonshire.

After I left Victoria I was sad, melancholy and wished things were not as they are . . . soon I was plunged into the activities of the big debate. For yesterday – two years too late – we recognised Franco, and the Socialists had their last snarl today. Attlee opened the debate, which took the form of a vote of censure. He renewed his pusillanimous attack on the Prime Minister, in so doing that he lost the respect of the House, for he said little about the subject before the House. The PM rose, and never have I so admired him, for at first, I feared he would retaliate as he looked annoyed. Instead with almost sublime restraint he coolly remarked that he would resist the temptation to castigate the Leader of the Opposition, and he then proceeded to state the government's case for the recognition of the Spanish Nationalists as the legitimate government of Spain. He was devastatingly clear, and made an iron-clad case which our opponents found difficult, indeed impossible to answer. Their only reply was rage and abuse. When Anthony Eden got up, they looked more hopeful; but he made a calm, conciliatory speech (dull and platitudinous like everything he says) in favour of the govt, so that there was little kick left in the Opposition. I had prepared Rab to wind up and he was busy preparing his speech when about 3.15 David Margesson sent for him to say that after all he was going to put up old Inskip, since the Labour Party demanded a Cabinet minister to wind up. I hurriedly informed Rab that he would not be required. He had complained of overwork, and now when relieved he seemed disappointed as people always are. I am rather sorry he did not wind up as the House was easy and good-humoured; I had thought it would be otherwise. All day I was at the bench, running errands . . . fagging, occasionally rewarded by one of those intoxicating careless smiles from the PM. I sat, as always, immediately behind him. No lunch: no tea: no dinner: only excited snacks in the lobby Bar. The hours passed and it became increasingly clear that the House was sick unto death of Spain, that it recognised the necessity, indeed the urgency, of establishing friendly relations with Franco – the sooner the better. When fat, funny Inskip rose to wind up he had an easy passage; and he was both firm and humorous. At last we went home after a huge government majority and even the Edenites all voted for us, a troupe of middle-aged ballerinas. How foolish they must now look. What a fool is Jim Thomas: I must thrust him out of my life, but somehow cannot bring myself to do so.

Home – worn out – late. *Viva Franco! Viva España.*

WEDNESDAY 1ST MARCH

I woke dreaming still of our amazing little god, the PM, so courageous, humorous, sound, and amiable. Not even England has ever produced such a man.

I felt ill, worn out with emotions and work and late nights. I must sometimes be alone, and I am that never.

SUNDAY 5TH MARCH

My strength is really failing me. I am so tired sometimes. Yet I must be attractive still as never before have I had so much sexual success as during the past few weeks. I haven't the time to follow it up.

TUESDAY 7TH MARCH

My birthday. No presents except Honor's picture of the House of Commons, the Hogarth one, a satin reading-stand from Alan and Patsy, and a bloodstone *bibelot* from my *belle-mère*.[1]

We had Foreign Office estimates, which meant a long day at the House with an unbearable amount of fagging . . . I was run off my feet. Luckily they came to an end at eight, and I was able to dine with a select party of the MPs – the 1936 Club – who entertained the Prime Minister. He was jolly, enjoying himself and amazingly open and confiding. Members plied him with questions. He smiled, sometimes roared with laughter, answered each one with humorous precision. Someone asked him if it was true that Hitler disliked him, and he retorted that he had heard many contradictory reports on this subject, his last interview with Hitler was very friendly. The PM foresees no crisis on the horizon, all is well; he thinks the Russian peril receding, and the dangers of a German war are less every day, as our rearmament expands. An intoxicating evening.

THURSDAY 9TH MARCH

Lunching with the Cazalets. They have a remarkable collection of glorious Augustus Johns. Mrs Cazalet[2] is indignant, as indeed we all are, at the treachery of that charming, gay, low-born fellow Louis Bromfield,[3] whom we have all cosseted, taken up, spoilt, slept with, and launched in London. He has, in his recent return to the States, published an infamous pamphlet attacking this country, in which he insults Lord Halifax and the PM and others. He thinks England is dead and beat. He is right, of course; it is the swan song of this enchanted island but it is bad taste, indeed unpardonable to say so. I am apprehensive of the future, very. Appeasement cannot last indefinitely. The Boche or the Italians will surely let us down. The situation in Palestine is grave.[4]

1 Mother-in-law.
2 Maud Lucia Heron-Maxwell (1868–1952). Her husband had died in 1932, so Channon's reference to 'the Cazalets' is presumably to her and her son Victor and possibly her daughter Thelma (qqv).*
3 Louis Bromfield (1896–1956), born Brumfield, was a novelist and agriculturalist from Ohio.
4 Palestine had been ruled by a British mandate since 1920; there had been an Arab revolt there since 1936. Since 7 February, a conference had been taking place at St James's Palace to discuss how the territory could be ruled once the mandate ended.

Jim Thomas came home with me for a drink and chat. He is so amiable now and rather 'sucking up'.

SATURDAY 11TH MARCH

A rest: a Turkish bath, a visit to the American Consulate – to sign a power-of-attorney, as I gather, there is an excellent chance of my American property improving. Higher rentals.

The Coopers dined as did the Abdys, Emerald and Harold Balfour: I made the mistake of including Georg Federer,[1] the Second Secretary of the German Embassy, who had been recommended to me . . . as a handsome *charmeur*.[2] He is neither, but quite adequate. The Coopers were rude to him.

MONDAY 13TH MARCH

Very big dinner party. I wanted to enjoy it in peace and also to keep Rab free, so I manoeuvred to have the business of the House instead – at least I had not that to worry about. All yesterday I telephoned frantically to get men, and now this morning early Portia Stanley chucked me, and was two women short. I . . . . sent an SOS to Jean Norton[3] and Kitty Brownlow[4] who both came. I felt ill all day, which was a disadvantage.

Having finally adjusted my dinner party by 4.30, I went to the Bath Club for a 'Turker' in fear and trembling that perhaps a man might chuck me. Luckily none did and the house looked a vista of beauty, flowers, candlelight and general loveliness. The Duke of Alba arrived first and I introduced him as the Spanish Ambassador. It was the first party he had attended in his new official capacity. Rab was next to the Duchess of Kent and they liked each other, for each partly to please me, and partly from mutual curiosity turned their full charms on the others. Mollie Buccleuch was bored: there is always the guest bored at every party. The Duke of Kent was happy and both Shakespeare Morrison and Alba 'over the port' monopolised him. Dinner was excellent; the dining room was a dream of rococo beauty, and all went well. Afterwards there was a slight *gêne*[5] until I got the bridge four consisting of the Duke of Kent, Jean Norton, Loelia

1 Georg Federer (1905–84) was a German career diplomat. He had served in Riga before joining the London Embassy in 1938, and spent much of the war in Switzerland. His career continued after the war in America and Egypt.

2 Charmer.

3 Jean Mary Kinloch (1898–1945) was married to Richard Henry Brinsley Norton (1892–1954), who succeeded his father in 1943 as 6th Baron Grantley. She was Lord Beaverbrook's mistress for twenty years, though shared that role with numerous others. Their affair is believed to have precipitated the early death of Lady Beaverbrook in 1927.

4 Katherine Harriet Kinloch (1906–52) married in 1927 the 6th Baron Brownlow (qv).

5 Moment of embarrassment.

Westminster and Teenie Cazalet settled. Even then, a pause until I could get people seated. I led different men to talk to the Duchess of K. Shakes was clumsy, to my surprise he treated her like a public meeting. Then Alba and he went off together and liked each other. And I put Duncannon there. Emerald, looking like Mme de Pompadour, joined us at midnight. She had been dining with the Lytteltons.[1] She was in a bad temper and would not do 'her stuff'. I think Rab, who by now was a touch tipsy . . . . (I had arranged the dinner to divert him, as he has been far too hard-working of late, leading a double life with his Foreign Office work and the Palestine Conference on his shoulders as well), alarmed her. He was very gay and we heard his famous pheasant cackle, which means that he is amused . . . he has so little fun; but he doesn't like it. The social side of his scheme of life are [sic] amateurishly arranged and [his wife] Sydney is without social sense: and his secretariat is unskilled. These few details may prevent his rise to the heights. Otherwise his course to No. 10 is a straight one. The Kents . . . . enjoyed themselves. They did not leave until 1.30, nor did anyone else. The Duke remarked after winning 30 shillings 'they can't play at all'. All the women – yes, even the government's wives – were well dressed, but I insisted that the men wear black ties, since the Duke prefers it. There is no halfway house with royalties really: it is either black ties, or tails and decorations. The Duchess of Kent did not go to 'the ladies' – how does she manage? All royalties have amazing bladders. The last few minutes are a haze: I had drunk too much champagne and was tired, but the evening, a mixture of society and the government, was a success. I must repeat it soon. But it is such a complicated business ensuring that we are not needed at the House of Commons. Today I was lucky, or rather far-sighted as I managed to arrange the business of the House.

TUESDAY 14TH MARCH

There were rumblings at the Foreign Office of renewed trouble in Czechoslovakia. We did not at first take them v seriously; but learned that the Czech government had resigned and that Hitler had summoned the President to Berlin. It looks as if he is going to break the Munich Agreement, and throw Chamberlain over, and become an international gangster.

---

1 Oliver Lyttelton (1893–1972) became Managing Director of the British Metals Corporation and from 1940 to 1954 was Conservative MP for Aldershot. He was one of the businessmen brought into the government by Churchill, and served as President of the Board of Trade from 1940 to 1941 and in the 'caretaker' government of 1945. He was resident minister in the Middle East from 1941 to 1942 and Minister of Production from 1942 to 1945. From 1951 to 1954 he was Colonial Secretary and in the latter year was raised to the peerage as 1st Viscount Chandos. In 1920 he married Lady Moira Godolphin Osborne, daughter of the 10th Duke of Leeds.

At Question Time there were questions about the Czech situation and news came via the tape that German soldiers had invaded Czechoslovakia; that Ruthenia was proclaimed independent. We have another crisis. Beware of the Ides of March! It is just a year today since German troops entered and took poor languid, helpless, prostrate Austria. Hitler is never helpful – to his friends!

WEDNESDAY 15TH MARCH

Hitler has entered Prague apparently, and Czechoslovakia has ceased to exist.[1] No balder, bolder defiance of the written bond has ever been committed in History. I don't mind what he did; but the manner of it surpasses comprehension, and his callous desertion of the Prime Minister is stupefying. I can never forgive him for making his enemies become both prophets and right. It is a great day for the Socialists and for the Edenites. The PM is discouraged, horrified. He acceded to the demand of the Opposition for a debate, and the business of the House was altered. The PM rose and calmly, but with a broken heart, made a frank statement of the facts as he knew them. The reports were largely unconfirmed, and based on press reports; consequently the PM was obliged to be cool and so was accused of being unmoved by events. Whenever he is aloof, he is said to be heartless when he is only being cautious. I thought he looked miserable. His whole policy of appeasement is in ruins. Munich is a torn-up episode; yet never has he been proved more abundantly right, for he gave us six months of peace in which we rearmed; so he was right to try appeasement, rather than the warlike policy. I was relieved at how little personal criticism there was of the Apostle of Peace, and Grenfell,[2] who opened for the Opposition, was more impressive than Attlee; he was saner, more manly, more eloquent and he held the attention and regard of the House.

Later I came home here with Jim Thomas and we had a cold supper, brilliantly prepared, together and talked late.

Rab was irritable and worn out. My dinner party, although it was a change and amused him, fatigued him. Rab is in a rage, too, with recent events, indignant at Hitler's methods, rather than with his accomplishments. And he said rightly enough that the *Drang nach Osten*[3] which his new policy seemed to indicate was a relief, a disguised blessing to the Empire. Hitler was going towards the East instead of snarling at us. I agreed, and deplore the senseless hysteria. The Cabinet sat and I am told they were like a lot of angry frustrated hens. Simon in an appalling

---

1 The previous day the Slovak state, a client of Germany, had been proclaimed. On 15 March the Wehrmacht occupied the rest of the former Czechoslovakia and the Germans proclaimed the Protectorate of Bohemia and Moravia.
2 David 'Dai' Grenfell. *
3 Drive to the East, a term first used in the nineteenth century about the most likely nature of German expansionism.

winding-up speech which was ill-prepared and badly received, seemed to pour water on any return to collective security which our 'left-wingers' are clamouring for. The country is stirred to its depths ... the rage against Germany is rising. Few realise that for all his aggressions he has acquired nothing new, nothing that was not – not an inch, not an acre – within the compass of the old Germanic empires before the war. But he has broken his solemn pledges, and recanted his great theory of self-determination, and his social theories of only wanting Germans. Rab and I alone are hopeful that the situation may be sound, at least for some time longer.

My poor dearly beloved little Neville. He looked borne down [upon] today.

Jim Thomas, that political weathercock, already was a little less obsequious tonight for his hopes soar once more. He dined and fagged Anthony, who by the way, was not hostile to the government and he took me by the arm at one moment.

A day of shattered hopes.

THURSDAY 16TH MARCH

No one can now prophesy what will happen: of course there are the usual wild rumours of mobilisation, calling-up and of leave stopped. People are shuddering lest London be bombed this weekend. Why?

In the course of the Navy estimates this afternoon Duff lost his temper and called Hitler 'a thrice-mouthed perjurer, a breaker of oaths' etc. Therein will be more trouble.

The Foreign Affairs Committee meeting passed off peacefully enough and there was no criticism of the Prime Minister. On the contrary, I rang up No. 10 and left a message for him saying that all was well. I wanted to cheer him as he is depressed – almost broken-hearted today. No wonder. He had, however, to attend the Court tonight. His energy is staggering.

FRIDAY 17TH MARCH

After lunching with Emerald – David Margesson; Loelia Westminster; Grace Curzon, who tried to sell me everything she still possesses – I drove to the H of C. The lobby was in a turmoil as a rumour had reached it that there was serious difference of opinion between Neville and Edward.[1] It is lunchtime: they are as one, although there have been recent indications that Edward H is becoming mildly influenced by the Foreign Office mandarins.

The crisis news seemed somewhat better. At least not worse. I don't believe in the approaching war. I drove to Southend, telephoning before to arrange for the

1 Lord Halifax.

PM's great Birmingham speech to be relayed. My big meeting at Southend went well and we were all well received. Proceedings opened with the relaying of the PM's speech which lasted forty minutes. It was strong meat, it was magnificent and held us spellbound. He told in polite but decisive language the whole story of his negotiations with Hitler and his treachery. The PM hinted at a new policy, or rather of a return to an old faded friend, Collective Security. Lady Iveagh and I spoke well; as I was leaving, having been professionally gracious for an hour, the Mayor sent me a message to come to the Cricket Ball. I went, was gay, and intelligent and no doubt made a good impression.

Back to the hotel worn out at 1.35 a.m. What a day. The country is solidly behind Chamberlain now: criticism is temporarily stilled.

SATURDAY 18TH MARCH

I drove, after a Southend meeting, to Kelvedon, and *en route*, I thought about the PM's magnificent speech of last night in which he was not too proud to reveal his disappointment, his hopes so hugely shattered by Hitler. All he said was a heady wine. I trust somehow policy will not go too far the other way.

Kelvedon disappointed me – I find it lovely perhaps, but small and not sufficiently splendid. And the work seems so slow. Will the gardens and planting ever be finished? Then I came up to London, rather reluctant to leave my white Bundi behind. London, I found, was in a fever of excitement. The Cabinet was sitting still: the newspapers talked of a German ultimatum to Romania. I rang various ministers and now know the strange truth. Rob Bernays, an excitable, pleasant youth, sensitive and Semitic, left-wing and intensely anti-German, had yesterday to make a big speech. *En route* to the station he dropped in at the Ritz to have tea with Princess Marthe Bibesco,[1] a famous *mondaine*,[2] exotic, writer and *amoureuse*[3] – she was the mistress of Lord Thomson,[4] and later wrote his biography after he was killed in the R101 disaster. One can picture the scene, the reclining, luxurious lady in a tea-gown and pearls, surrounded by roses, and the impressed young under-secretary dazzled by the *mise en scène*. She coyly trapped him and told him that she knew that King Carol had had an ultimatum from the

---

1 Marthe Lahovary.*
2 Socialite.
3 A romantic.
4 Christopher Birdwood Thomson (1875–1930) came from a distinguished military family and had been a soldier himself, reaching the rank of lieutenant colonel. He joined the Labour Party and twice failed to be elected as an MP, but was raised to the peerage in 1924 when becoming Secretary of State for Air in Ramsay MacDonald's first administration. When MacDonald returned to power in 1929 Thomson was restored to the same office and, as Channon correctly says, was killed in the R101 disaster of October 1930, which led to the cancellation of the British airship programme. He had met Princess Bibesco in 1915 when serving as British military attaché to Romania.

German government, saying that they would invade Romania etc. etc. How could she get the news to the English government? She knew no one . . . Bernays believed her, not realising that the ordinary channels existed for carrying such information, were it true. He rushed to a call box and frantically poured out the tale to Walter Elliot, who immediately rang up Oliver Stanley at the Foreign Office. Stanley knowing nothing sent for Tilea,[1] the Romanian Minister, who is Marthe Bibesco's tool, her appointee, and probably, although not certainly, her lover. Tilea, perhaps in the plot, was guarded, and thinking that the FO either knew too much, or too little, led them to believe the Bibesco's [sic] romance: he seemed to acquiesce, at least not to deny her fabrication. No. 10 was informed, Cabinet ministers cancelled their weekend plans and this evening there was a Cabinet called to consider the emergency situation which had arisen. Were we to guarantee the Romanian oil fields, her frontiers against German aggression?? Meanwhile, late this afternoon a message came from Sir R. Hoare,[2] our Minister at Bucharest, saying nothing was known in Romania of such an ultimatum. This is the bald truth: but it is midnight now and this country believes what it has read in the evening newspaper and has gone to bed hating Germany more than ever, and resigned to the inevitability of war. It has taken me all evening to piece this tale together. I have rung the Foreign Office, I have talked with both Loxley and the resident clerks, and I have had three telephone conversations with Bernays who himself confessed and admitted the whole tale. He defends himself by saying it was his duty to warn the government. Perhaps it was, but he has made us ridiculous in the eyes of Europe, I fear. I shall send in a secret report to the PM of this shady story.

Now we have begun to flirt with Russia. We must be in very low water indeed to have to do that.

I might add that Tilea, very recently sent here by King Carol, is a crony of Harold Nicolson,[3] and rather 'suspect'.[4]

SUNDAY 19TH MARCH

Whilst the Chancelleries of Europe had hummed with diplomatic activity, whilst HMG has been struggling to create an anti-German bloc, I had been touring Bedfordshire. At Silsoe I met the Lennox-Boyds by arrangement and we went

1 Viorel Virgil Tilea (1896–1972) was Romania's Ambassador to Britain from 1938 to 1940.
2 Reginald Henry Hoare (1882–1954) was British Minister at Teheran from 1931 to 1934 and then at Bucharest until 1941. He was knighted in 1933.
3 Harold George Nicolson (1886–1968), son of the 1st Baron Carnock, worked in the Foreign Office from 1909 to 1929, before becoming a full-time writer and journalist. He joined the New Party of Oswald Mosley (qv) but left when Mosley became a fascist; he sat as National Labour MP for Leicester West from 1935 to 1945 and was an early anti-appeaser. After Channon he is probably the most renowned diarist of the era; and like him was bisexual."
4 Tilea has come to be regarded by history as the architect of this scare. By 'suspect' Channon indicates that he considered the Ambassador an anti-appeaser, thanks not least to the company he kept.

first to inspect Wrest Park, the ancient home of the dukes of Kent – non-royal ones.[1] I fell in love with the place: its bogus rococo, its grandeur, its water and temples, its avenues of Portuguese laurels, its statues and splendid suite of rooms all make me dissatisfied with Kelvedon which I was beginning to love. Never have I wanted a house so much as Wrest . . . And never will [it] be mine. Alan wants Wrest; but Patsy, cautious and unimaginative, does not. Never in all England have I been so captivated by a place, and to think we might have had it; it would have been unpractical, far from Southend and too expensive to keep up . . . . we went on to Ampthill House,[2] where Loelia Westminster joined us, to lunch with an absurd old walrus, Sir Anthony Wingfield,[3] who is an octogenarian vulgarian in love, although a widower with a family, with Alan! He was enchanted to entertain a Duchess: we sat through a pompous meal of eight courses. There were stray Russell relations impressed that we were Woburn-bound.

At three o'clock the Lennox-Boyds, Loelia and I in three grand cars arrived at Woburn Abbey, and one was immediately stuck by the well-kept-up splendour . . . We were shown in and received by the Duke, aged 84![4] He wore grey trousers and a white satin tie, and seemed ageless but aged, withered, colourless, but *grand seigneur*. Lady Ampthill[5] was acting as hostess and the pair of them showed us over the palace, room after room, with fires in each. Many were very fine, very famous pictures; but the general effect is spoilt by having too many. Eighteen full-length Sir Joshuas[6] in one room! Forty Canalettos in another! One room entirely painted by Van Dyck.[7] One clearly looked impressed but the general effect is not beautiful nor pleasing. But the long views from the windows of the lakes and ducks are. I was disappointed but conscious, too, of the atmosphere, of the feudal magnificence and ceremonial that is maintained. There were thirty cars and chauffeurs, none are ever used; there are fires in all the twenty or more drawing rooms where no one ever sits. The Duke is silent, dull, and is interested only in his staggering possessions. There was a pompous tea party, which, alas!

1 The present house was built to designs of its then owner, 2nd Earl de Grey, in the 1830s. The park was laid out for the 1st Duke of Kent (1671–1740), who was raised to a dukedom having succeeded his father as 12th Earl of Kent, and who served in several high offices at the court of Queen Anne.

2 A house of the 1680s in a Capability Brown park, now divided up into flats.

3 Sir Anthony Wingfield (1857–1952) was a Bedfordshire landowner and sometime High Sheriff of the county.

4 The Duke was in fact 81: Herbrand Arthur Russell (1858–1940), Lord Herbrand Russell from 1872 until 1893, when he succeeded his brother as 11th Duke of Bedford. He was married, in 1888, to Mary du Caurroy Tribe (1865–1937).

5 Margaret Lygon (1874–1957), Lady Margaret by courtesy, was the daughter of the 6th Earl Beauchamp. She married the 2nd Baron Ampthill (1869–1935) in 1894.

6 Sir Joshua Reynolds (1723–92) was an English painter and first President of the Royal Academy.

7 Sir Anthony Van Dyck (1599–1641), a Flemish painter famous for his portraits of the English Court.

took too much time and we did not see the famous Chinese dairy which interested me more than the fish. His wealth is incalculable, I suppose. He must be nearly as rich as my father-in-law!

Home at 2 a.m. London was not being bombed. That, I suppose, is something.

MONDAY 20TH MARCH

Nevile Henderson was recalled yesterday from Berlin, and Herr Dirksen,[1] the German Ambassador, left London. The situation is grave. We must restrain our right-wingers or they may go too far the other way.

TUESDAY 21ST MARCH

Frog Week[2] began this weekend . . . I walked back [from St James's] to the House of Commons and we arrived just in time to watch the procession arrive. The Lebruns looked well, and Mme [Lebrun] was dressed like the Queen, in clinging grey and furs. Much cheering from the crowds. Hitler has guaranteed the success of this week.

I was worn out, and went to bed for three hours. Rob Bernays came to dine with me, and at considerable cost. I was able to get the whole Tilea tale out of him again. It is all too true, desperately true. What I didn't tell him is that Alec Cadogan has sent for Tilea and rebuked him for giving false information. What an extraordinary situation and incident.

The Lebruns are dining at Buckingham Palace at a great banquet to which my Rab and his humourless Frau were not invited.

Thanks to Hitler Frog Week will be a tremendous success. Rob Bernays is really the earnest political creature that walks – or rather talks. I didn't even think I liked him: he is so Jewish in his outlook, appearance, and shuffling manner. But he has charm and a sudden smile and a sharp brain if an unbalanced one. Rab has the greatest contempt for him.

Sidney Herbert[3] has died in the south of France. No loss to me: little to anyone else. He has been ill for years. Self-indulgent, intolerant, a bore, common, he has too long been overrated and conceited, like all of his gay pre-war group who survived. He was violently hostile to Chamberlain and resented the new regime.

WEDNESDAY 22ND MARCH

Our attention is now riveted on foreign affairs again. An absurd round robin is being hawked around Europe asking Poland (who was cautious in her reply),

---

1 Eduard von Dirksen.*
2 The state visit to Britain of Albert Lebrun, the President of France, and Mme Lebrun.
3 Sir Sidney Herbert the Conservative MP, not Sidney Herbert who would become the 16th Earl of Pembroke (qqv).

Yugoslavia, Romania and perhaps others to join in a non-aggression pact. We shall enormously enlarge our commitments and reap little advantage, except possibly prestige and strategic value. The smaller nations are chary, particularly my Paul's regime in remote Belgrade.

The Iveaghs to lunch and I talked to my wife on the telephone. She is still philandering mysteriously at Breuil.[1]

Memel was today ceded to Germany by the Lithuanian government under threats of invasion and aerial bombardment. Tactless of Hitler to force us into a general holy alliance against him. A few unconverted people are hoping even until now, since the Czech excitement after a week has somewhat abated, to avoid such a course. But Memel, not in itself very important, is the camel-breaking straw and the Cabinet is now unanimous that 'something must be done'. The PM has been pressed in the House to be more explicit – so far he has refused to be drawn since his heart is not in it. At Birmingham when he made his magnificent speech he was still smarting with rage and resentment against the German Chancellor, and moreover he wanted to consolidate Conservative opinion. Now this mood is passing ... but Halifax, a touch influenced by the mandarins in the Forbidden City, i.e., the Foreign Office, is beginning to hate the Devil more than his works; and clever people at the FO knowing his religious tendencies have been stressing tales of Church persecution in Germany. I had tried to offset them.

Tonight was the grand Great Gala at Covent Garden for the Frogs. I wore my court dress – I am only happy in velvet really – and escorted Loelia Westminster to Emerald's, where we all dined. I had taken a box @ £26 and invited Loelia and the Lennox-Boyds as my guests. Emerald's dinner was a good sight – about ten *faubourg*[2] Frogs ... our beauties, literally covered with jewels made a much better show. The first person I saw was my v old friend Achille Murat,[3] the boon companion of my youth – it is twenty years since I last saw him and he has not changed an iota. The same singularity of manner which reminds one of his maternal grandmother that remarkable old duchesse de Rohan; the same quiet sly smile which suggests his mother, the annoying Marie Murat of my youth (now comtesse de Chambrun): and he looks young. He recognised me immediately, fell on my neck, and we talked of old days. I asked him what had happened to

---

1 A ski resort on the Italian–French border.
2 The '*faubourg*' was a synonym for the French nobility, and the highest echelon of Parisian society. It began as shorthand for the Faubourg Saint-Germain, in what is now the 7th arrondissement of the city, on the *rive gauche*. It is the location of the French National Assembly, many government offices and embassies, and since the time of Louis XIV has been the home of the aristocracy in the capital, usually in spectacular *hôtels particuliers*, or grand town houses.
3 Achille Alain Joachim Napoléon Murat (1898–1987), nephew by marriage of Princesse Eugène Murat, who had befriended Channon in Paris.

him: 'I fell out of a balloon, married, had had six children, and two "misses"':[1] thus he summed up his career. I was genuinely delighted to see him: his wife is a gay *poseur*,[2] and like his mother, *une jolie laide*.[3] I was between two French women at dinner: one Princesse Galitzine (*née* Gramont)[4] wore fine jewels which could not possibly have been cleaned since the French Revolution, and as she turned I saw the blue rim on her bosom made by the dirty gold! How shabby Frenchwomen are, at least aristocratic ones, when compared with our English ones. A distinguished dinner, Circe Londonderry[5] draped in diamonds and turquoises, Belgian Ambassador, Loelia Westminster, Diana Cooper – looking a touch Sadler's Wells, and not grand enough for the occasion. She rarely wears grand *tenue*[6] and gold does not suit her; and, of course, the Frogs. We went on to the Opera in our finery, and the roads were well policed so we arrived easily. Covent Garden was breathtaking in its magnificence. There was a vast Royal Box in the centre, designed by Rex Whistler[7] . . . It was light, gay, pretty but a touch [illegible][8] and nightclubbish. I didn't approve of it. To the left was the government box; to the right the diplomatic one, we were next but one, only the Camroses between us. Slowly the whole spectacle opened before us; and we had the greatest fun watching the arrivals. HMG was fantastic, they arrived swiftly in pairs, the little drab Attlees sitting in the far corner in dull evening clothes . . . Lady Maugham[9] with a curl on her wrinkled forehead, Simon separated from his wife by a gangway. Bernays escorted Mrs Walter Elliot[10] in Walter's absence: . . . Diana De La Warr,[11] ever the gushing governess, made a point of going to talk to the Attlees to make them feel at home, and in so doing stripped their isolation . . .

---

1 Thus in the MS; perhaps Murat was alluding to his wife having twice miscarried.

2 Channon's French is usually better than this: he means *poseuse*.

3 A French expression describing a woman who is apparently plain but can appear attractive.

4 Antonie Claude Corisande de Gramont (1885–1942), married in 1918 Prince Augustin Petrovich Galitzine.

5 Edith Helen 'Circe' Chaplin (1878–1959), daughter of the 1st Viscount Chaplin, married in 1899 the 7th Marquess of Londonderry.

6 Clothes.

7 Reginald John 'Rex' Whistler (1905–44) was hugely in demand as a designer of stage sets, posters and books, and also of murals and *trompe l'oeil*. He was killed in the Battle of Normandy in 1944.

8 Rhodes James (p. 188) has 'tinselly', which it certainly is not: the much shorter illegible word looks more like 'filthy' or 'dirty'.

9 Helen Mary Romer (1872–1950) married in 1896 Frederic Herbert Maugham (1866–1958), who was Lord Chancellor from 1938 to 1939. He was raised to the peerage as Baron Maugham (life peer) in 1935 and advanced to a viscountcy in 1939. He was the elder brother of Somerset Maugham*.

10 Katharine Tennant (1903–94), daughter of Sir Charles Tennant, 1st Bt, and half-sister of Margot Asquith, Countess of Oxford and Asquith (qv), married Walter Elliot (qv) as his second wife in 1934. Active herself in charitable and political work she was elevated to the peerage as Baroness Elliot of Harwood in 1958, one of the first women life peers.

11 Formerly Diana Leigh.*

At last the Prime Minister and Mrs Chamberlain, who looked like a Gunther's cake in pale pink with a pink boa, arrived. Alan [Lennox-Boyd] and I applauded, cheered, and the grand well-bred audience took up the cheers, and he had a rousing reception which pleased him and we had his now famous smile. The Halifaxes were the last to come: they had been at the French Embassy banquet. These functions do not tire him, and he is fundamentally social, but they are an added strain to the poor PM, already overworked. He looked worn out this morning. Meantime the ambassadors filed in. Of course, the German is away – Alba was much the handsomest. Firstly at ten o'clock arrived the royal family with the Lebruns. They filled the large box and were given a reception almost as rousing as the Chamberlains. The Queen looked lovely and distinguished. Queen Mary grey and hard. I watched her for a long time. She is ageing. Lebrun sat between the two queens, his wife between the King and the Duke of Kent. They all looked well, even glamorous, but of course Princess Marina extinguished them all, with her shimmering slimness and glowing looks. Mme Lebrun behaved with a simple dignity which was warmly commended. Her clothes had been made by Worth and a jeweller in the rue de la Paix lent her a few ornaments to wear. She looked all right. Below the box was the public and a few people whom the K and Q had invited as their guests, Edens, Baldwins, and surprisingly enough the Weymouths – why? – Grace Curzon and others. It was very foolish of them not to include the Butlers, to whom I offered the good stalls, but they somewhat indignantly spurned them.

Almost everyone in the Opera House was in levee dress or uniform; half the women wore tiaras; it was a brave sight, enough to impress the Frogs and excite the envy of the Germans. Shall we ever see so grand a gala again? I think so . . . the Kents smilingly waved to us . . . . Anthony Eden, I am told, was cheered by the crowd outside, which if true, is a pity, and their foolish ovations incite him to make more platitudinous speeches and intrigue clumsily against the government. He is the architect of all our misfortunes . . . at last the curtain went up, and we had the first interminable act of *The Sleeping Princess*.[1] Well done, but infinitely boring. Then a long interval when Thomas Beecham[2] conducted a too long piece[3] which bored the restless, snobbish audience. I enjoyed it as I could watch the 'Sleeping Government' opposite. The Chamberlains stepped unobviously away . . . there was now conversation, staring at the royalties, flashing of tiaras. Then the third act of the same ballet. It would save so much hassle and money had there been no programme at all. People only wanted to stare at one another.

---

1 Better known as *The Sleeping Beauty*, by Tchaikovsky.
2 Thomas Beecham (1879–1961) succeeded his father as 2nd Bt in 1916. He used his inherited fortune, from the family business making laxative pills, to promote concerts that he conducted, and became one of the most celebrated conductors in the world. Lady Cunard was his mistress for many years.
3 Debussy's *Ibéria*.

There was appalling traffic trouble finding our cars. Literally hundreds of people wandered about on the coldest night of the week looking and waiting for footmen. What the local people must have thought, much display and ostentation I don't know, except that English crowds always like a grand show. Home at 1 a.m. A grand day. The *ancien régime* dies hard in England – and we are not dead yet.

THURSDAY 23RD MARCH

I am glutted with the great. An early start, as I had invited Mrs Gaterhill, a constituent,[1] to Westminster Hall to see the Big Frogs. The little woman gurgled with Gallic glee, as we drove up to the great doors in my green Rolls. All the great of England filed in, and at the top of the steps sat the Cabinet, the Speaker, the Lord Chancellor and others. At eleven o'clock bugles blew, the North doors were opened and the Lebruns entered escorted by Lord Ancaster,[2] as Great Chamberlain of the Palace of Westminster. We rose, and there were probably 1,500 of us, as the little party passed. Mme Lebrun, who looked self-possessed and amiable, indeed even chic and having considerable *chien*[3] for an old bourgeoise, smiled, and conducted herself with dignity. The President (who, I am assured calls her 'Pom-Pom') was immaculately dressed. One of the overenthusiastic MPs shouted out '*Vive le Président!*' There was much hand-clapping and cheering. Hitler is responsible for the success of this rally, certainly. The Lord Chamberlain made a slightly fatuous speech of welcome and was followed by the Speaker who was quite excellent. He so rarely speaks, it is always a surprise to hear him do it so well! But the President in rousing oratorical French eclipsed them both. He 'orated' his thanks in French and all the well-known words and clichés came tumbling out . . . '*chaleureuse*',[4] '*bon accueil*'[5] etc. etc. After the 'Marseillaise' and 'God Save the King' had been played the presidential party proceeded into the Houses of Parliament. I and very shy Mrs Gaterhill followed and we met then the Lebruns, being escorted by the Chamberlains and David Margesson from out of the Chamber itself. It is absurd to look as French as President Lebrun! I caught his brown eye! From here they left for Windsor Castle to lunch with the Monarchs![6] They are having such a success with our Royal Family that he is certain to be

1 In another hand, presumably Peter Coats's, the word 'French' has been inserted before 'constituent'.
2 Gilbert Heathcote-Drummond-Willoughby (1867–1951), by courtesy Lord Willoughby de Eresby until 1910, when he succeeded his father as 2nd Earl of Ancaster.
3 *Avoir du chien* is a French idiom meaning 'has some allure'.
4 Warm.
5 A good, or warm, welcome.
6 *Sic.* As so often, Channon forgets there is only one monarch, who has a consort.

re-elected President. The French are already beginning to say that if the Lebruns are good enough for Queen Mary, then they are good enough for them!

I walked home via the Foreign Office – still in a state of somewhat foolish alarm – and as I waited for Loelia Westminster, who was to pick me up as we were both lunching with the Kents, the Duke of Alba was announced. After I had given him some sherry, he asked me whether I knew that Grandi,[1] my dear bearded adorable Grandi, is to succeed Ciano[2] as the head of Foreign Affairs in Rome? He, the Ambassador, had heard it from General Franco, and he gave me permission to pass on the information, which I later did. He, Loelia Westminster, and I then walked to the Kents, where there was a pleasant party, Emerald, David Margesson, etc. . . . . we played afterwards with the children, who are now very pretty. The infant Princess[3] smiles, shows tiny teeth and looks provocative. Edward scowls. They didn't remember me until the Duke said 'This is Chips, Paul's father.' Later the children sat up to a piano and pummelled it. I repeated to David Margesson what Alba had told me, and he passed it on later to the Prime Minister, who was greatly pleased.

I had an extraordinary passage with Neville Chamberlain today! I arrived back at the House late and flushed after my royal lunch. The box with the Questions was still on the table in my room (21D). I opened it and saw the draft of an answer to a Private Notice Question in regard to an 'attitude to recent events'. All the morning the FO had been working on the draft reply and Rab had taken it on to No. 10 for the PM to 'vet', as is done daily. The PM in consultation with Rab modified it – the original draft had been drawn up by Alec Cadogan. I now took it along to the PM who was alone in his room . . . 'I am sorry, I am late,' I said. He smiled and I told him the Alba and Grandi tale (which later David Margesson repeated to him). Then handing him the flimsy,[4] I said 'It's pretty stiff. I suppose it has got to be?' He agreed. With a pencil I altered a few stinging lines. I encouraged him: he needed it not. 'I can type,' I said. He altered it still more, and I rushed back to 21D, and showed the alterations which were more in tone and manner than in actual fact to Rab, who in my absence had arrived. He agreed – and I hastily typed out two copies of the amended statement which may prevent or postpone war rather than precipitate it. It does not actually attack Germany, and now throws the grammar into the subjunctive. I rushed back to the bench in

---

1 Dino Grandi (1895–1988), 1st Count of Mordano, was a Fascist lawyer who had become close to Mussolini and was Italian Foreign Minister from 1929 to 1932, when he became Italian Ambassador to London,.

2 Gian Galeazzo Ciano (1903–44), 2nd Count of Cortellazzo and Buccari, was Mussolini's son-in-law and his Foreign Minister from 1936 to 1943. To appease the Nazis, he was shot on Mussolini's orders.

3 Princess Alexandra.

4 A carbon copy on very thin paper.

the House and handed him our final corrected version – 'Give a copy to Steward,'[1] or 'Warn Steward,' I forget which the PM said. I rushed out again and found him just as he was about to give out the earlier draft to the press. The PM read out my clumsily typed copy which I later managed to extricate from his papers – he always hands them to me with a gracious smile . . . . the actual typescript of what he read out and I typed.[2] He had been tired this morning after the long strain of his disappointments and the Frog functions and had given in to Cadogan and Horace Wilson,[3] although wanting to change it. I had needed only a tiny push to influence him: and that I had given him. Perhaps I have made History . . . or prevented it, which is often more important.

Dined again in levee dress, this time at the Bessboroughs.[4] About fifty people, tiara-ed, and decorated . . . We went on to the Foreign Office [for a theatrical performance] . . . the guests filed in below us, the government and wives, many of whom had been omitted and only asked because I sent in a memo to the effect that they must! Alan and I in our resplendent clothes (actually his green ministerial uniform is rather drab), walked up and down between the rows of Life Guards. They looked magnificent. Suddenly we met Queen Elizabeth and President Lebrun face to face. I did a 'bunk', and half-faded, half-fell into a doorway, with Alan in front of me. She saw me and smiled non-committally with a touch of a twinkle which she keeps for her old friends. The rest of the dinner party followed . . . Anthony, Winston all the pro-Frogs, anti-peace, anti-German people, and the procession wound its way below where it was joined by minor members of the royal family, and they took up their places opposite the improvised stage. I watched them. Queen Mary was looking more rested and handsome than last night. The audience was superb – the room glittered with jewels. The Duke of Portland looked like a Xmas tree, as did Circe Londonderry and Mollie Buccleuch and others. The French must have been impressed by our bejewelled aristocracy.

Bed at about 2 a.m. – my eyes tired of gazing on such jewels, my tongue fed up with prattling musty French. It has been a dazzling week of splendour. Shall we ever see the like again?

---

1 George Steward, a former Foreign Office official, was the Prime Minister's press officer, and the first holder of that post, serving from 1930 to 1940.

2 See Hansard, 23 March 1939, Vol. 345, Col. 1462.

3 Horace John Wilson (1882–1972) was a senior civil servant and Chamberlain's *de facto* Chief of Staff.

4 Vere Brabazon Ponsonby (1880–1956), by courtesy Viscount Duncannon from 1906 to 1920, when he succeeded his father as 9th Earl of Bessborough. He was a Conservative MP from 1910 to 1920 and Governor-General of Canada from 1931 to 1935. He married, in 1912, Roberte Poupart de Neuflize (1892–1979).

FRIDAY 24TH MARCH

Chamberlain's note of warning in his statement yesterday has been well received, even in Germany. Thank God I helped to modify it.

There was the patter of 'glamorous' feet today; and meetings in Philip Sassoon's[1] room of the unofficial and glamorous Opposition. Jim Thomas rushes about like a lunatic with some anti-Chamberlain petition.

SATURDAY 25TH MARCH

There is war fun, perpetual jitters: at first I naturally believed that the majority of these rumours were just put about by people of that persuasion which seems to hate Germany more than it loves England and would embroil us in war with her. They think, like Duff and Winston, that Germany must be punished. But now I had reason to think that probably some of these rumours are actually put about by the Nazis with the definite intention of alarming us. They think that as we are so silly as to believe these wild tales, well, they will invent more and keep us nervously 'on the hop' for months to come. Germany is furious about the Anglo-Polish agreement. Possibly she is impressed.

My friend Federer from the German Embassy rang up, and I promptly asked him to luncheon. He came and stayed until 4.30, and I gave him a thorough mental spanking, told him of our disappointment with Hitler etc., and of English determination now to withstand further aggression.

SUNDAY 26TH MARCH

I am not sure that the Polish guarantee is wise. It may stiffen the resistance of the Poles, as we did unintentionally stiffen the Czechs last year.

TUESDAY 28TH MARCH

Jim Thomas canvassed half the House of Commons in his insane efforts to get them to sign an ill-phrased petition which while ostensibly calling for compulsory [military] training, really tries to drives a wedge between Neville and Halifax. He had it in his hand outside the Smoking Room; half in jest I snatched it, and rushed to my room – his old one – and made two typewritten copies . . . one I gave to the PM who thanked me gravely, and the other to David Margesson.

Usual feverish fuss. There was excitement in the lobbies before the 1922 Committee banquet to the Prime Minister and Jim Thomas and one or two

---

1 Philip Albert Gustave David Sassoon (1888–1939) succeeded his father as 3rd Bt in 1912. He was the cousin of Siegfried Sassoon (qv). From 1912 until his death he was Conservative MP for Hythe.*

other asses hesitated whether to go. Only one did, old Somerville,[1] who was placed next to the Prime Minister! who had not yet read the list of signatures to the 'glamorous' petition.[2] If he had he would have read Somerville's. The old gentleman thought that he was urging conscription but the document, drafted by Duff Cooper on Thursday night last at 17 Little College Street in Jim Thomas's house, meant more than that: it aimed at sabotaging Neville. It has had the inevitable result of rallying the Chamberlain forces around him more solidly than ever, and of delaying conscription. I am in favour of conscription on other grounds than military ones: I think it will spread conservatism, break down class hatred, increase the physical well-being and happiness of the nation and reduce unemployment: I had always refused to take the war seriously . . .

The PM had a riotous reception and was cheered and cheered; and he was so much moved, and made no attempt to conceal his emotion . . . He proceeded to give us (over a hundred members) a frank, firm talk: he referred to his betrayal by Hitler, was scathing and yet humorous about him . . . and then touched on conscription. He had decided against it for the moment as he did not wish to divide the nation. (It will take another dictator's coup to bring that it in here, as I remarked to Alec Dunglass, and he agreed.) But he had made sweeping plans for the reorganisation and expansion of the territorials. The plans will be announced tomorrow . . . . I felt warm within as he talked, the way I do when I play with Paul, and I know now that I love the PM with mixed feelings of hero-worship and admiration . . . . and more. I want to embrace him: I trust I shall never be so foolish as to do so!! At the end of the banquet, which was a very great success, we walked through the tunnel from the St Stephen's Club to the PM's room, where he had preceded us. He smiled and was gay and asked me if I had noticed (by then he had been told!)

I rushed home. Changed and went on to Jean Norton's little party for her daughter Sarah. It was very young, very gay, much champagne. All the *jeunesse dorée*[3] . . . . I very gradually became intoxicated and more garrulous. The Kents arrived late and, seeing the Gloucesters, they soon left. They are not on intimate terms with them, although there is little or no hostility between them; but the Kents resent the very great glamour being shared by the older, and more important technically, couple.

THURSDAY 30TH MARCH

There was yet another Cabinet meeting this morning to discuss the international situation. They sat long . . . the Iveaghs came to lunch . . . at five o'clock the Cabinet

---

1 Annesley Ashworth Somerville (1858–1942) had been a master at Eton. He was Conservative MP for Windsor from 1922 until his death.
2 Named presumably after the 'Glamour Boys', the Edenites.
3 Gilded youth.

Foreign Policy Subcommittee met and took a definite stand against aggression. Rab has been invited informally by the PM on several occasions to attend these meetings of the special committee. More and more the PM depends on him: I suspect that Halifax is slightly annoyed. This afternoon the meeting took place in the House of Commons, in the PM's private room. Rab was not summoned to attend: I hung about the little passage, invented pretexts to talk to Dunglass, but Rab was not mentioned. Either he was forgotten or deliberately left out. Peter Loxley and I drove away and discussed the ominous omission. I then stopped the car by a nearby call box (the one in Stafford Place off Buckingham Palace Road, and directly opposite Leslie Belisha's house). There I rang up Oscar Cleverly[1] in the PM's Secretaries' Room at the H of C, and knowing that Rab was not there, I asked for him. Cleverly, rather embarrassed and unhelpful, replied that 'Butler isn't here. He isn't expected.' But I made my point by appearing surprised; and also I decided there and then that Cleverly must go. He is weak, and if not exactly against us, he is not sufficiently for us.

FRIDAY 31ST MARCH

A typed copy of the statement below is clipped into diary immediately before 31st March entry and there is written on it '(March 31st) Friday's statement. Actual copy read out 4 p.m.'

Question – *to ask the Prime Minister whether he can now make a statement as to the European situation.*

Answer – *as I said this morning His Majesty's Government have no official confirmation of the rumours of any projected attack on Poland and they must not therefore be taken as accepting them as true.*

I am glad to take this opportunity of stating again the general policy of His Majesty's Government. They have constantly advocated the adjustment, by way of free negotiation between the parties concerned, of any differences that may arise between them. They consider that this is the natural and proper course where differences exist. In their opinion there should be no question incapable of solution by peaceful means and they would see no justification for the substitution of force or threats of force for the method of negotiation.

As the House is aware, certain consultations are now proceeding with other governments. In order to make perfectly clear the position of His Majesty's Government in the meantime before those consultations are concluded, I now have to inform the House that during that period in the event of any action which clearly threatened Polish independence, and which the Polish government accordingly

---

1 Osmund Somers Cleverly (1891–1966), known as Oscar, was principal private secretary to the Prime Minister (both Baldwin and Chamberlain) from 1936 to 1939. He was knighted in 1951.

considered it vital to resist with their national forces, His Majesty's Government would feel themselves bound at once to lend the Polish government all support in their power. They have given the Polish government an assurance to this effect.

I may add that the French government have authorised me to make it plain that they stand in the same position in this matter as do His Majesty's Government.

Neville made a great and historic statement in the House; it went extremely well.

There was a meeting of the Cabinet Foreign Policy Subcommittee this morning which Rab attended. And I arranged last night with Dunglass that he is no more to await a special summons but to be present automatically. It was known too late to alter the decision to make an unconditional written guarantee to Poland and that the PM announced to a cheering house. Alone almost Rab and I are dubious as to the wisdom of such a course.

SATURDAY 1ST APRIL   *CAMFIELD PLACE, ESSENDON*[1]

I drove to Kelvedon, hung pictures, saw gardeners; the house looked pleasant but disappointingly small. Then on here to stay with Lord Queenborough,[2] an amiable *grand seigneur* who at the age of 77[3] entertains the *jeunesse politique*. Alan, who is here, is his blue rose. Alan is a gerontophile . . . for he is surrounded always by doting old gentlemen who patronise him – Sir Anthony Wingfield, the Duke of Bedford . . . etc. The house is well arranged and beautifully run and luxurious and the quite excellent food is served with Edwardian splendour. The old gentleman is alert and keenly interested in politics. Only his memory is a touch enfeebled. He has taken a fancy to me and has induced me today to become a member of the society of St George and St Stephen's Club!! He told us many stories at dinner, and one of a conversation he had years and years ago with Joe Chamberlain whom he congratulated on the successes of Austen Chamberlain.[4] The old man was obviously pleased, but added 'Wait until you see my Neville!'

Hitler spoke, and was calm. We could not listen in as the broadcast was turned off. Queenborough also told me that Queen Mary had said to him, in reply to a question as to when the Duke of Windsor would return to this country, 'not until he comes to my funeral'. She is a hard-hearted woman.

---

1 In Hertfordshire, near Hatfield; at various times the home of Beatrix Potter and Dame Barbara Cartland.

2 Almeric Hugh Paget (1861–1949), Conservative MP for Cambridge 1910–17, was raised to the peerage as 1st Baron Queenborough in 1918. He was an admirer of Hitler.

3 He had turned 78 a fortnight earlier.

4 Joseph Austen Chamberlain (1863–1937), statesman son of Joseph Chamberlain and elder half-brother of Neville Chamberlain.*

SUNDAY 2ND APRIL

All day at Camfield . . . We motored up to London tonight. Everyone seems happy about our guarantee of Poland; I think it is madness.

MONDAY 3RD APRIL

A long debate at the House . . .

I was awakened at 7.45 by Lady Oxford asking me to get her a ticket; I did. I lunched at the Lennox-Boyds. All except Mr Bland were pro-Polish. Rab is not; he is opposed to our present foreign policy, and deplores our statement on Friday which he was able to tone down, fortunately. He wants to resign over it.

The debate was a star one. It was opened by Greenwood,[1] who has behaved with dignity and helpfulness during the crisis. Like most drunks he is really rather decent at heart. Neville followed and although he pleased the House, I was not so enthusiastic as usual. And I felt, too, that his heart was not in his new policy which has been forced upon him by Hitler. He was followed by Winston, who did not harangue the government, but praised it – is he bidding once again for power? And will he again be disappointed? I think so. His speech was not damaging, but, of course, rude to Germany. Lloyd George followed, and I was immediately opposite him, as I sat in my usual place directly back of the PM. Lloyd George seemed old, garrulous and mischievous. He made a series of outrageous statements which must have hurt the Empire and imperilled peace. So indiscreet he was – yet there was logic in what he said – that Paddy Hannon[2] rose and asked him if he realised how much harm he was doing.[3] Ll G replied that he would follow up his remarks with constructive statements. He did not, not one. The House was shocked and intimidated. Anthony Eden, looking ill and old, and shockingly shabby, made a platitudinous speech. He meant well and he conferred with Rab, in the lobby beforehand . . . speeches followed one another until nearly 11 p.m. Cripps,[4] although expelled from the Labour Party, delivered a diatribe from the Labour front bench. The House watched, saw that there would be no opposition, and was soon bored after the big battalions had done their roaring. At eight Jim Thomas fetched me to say that Fritzi of Prussia was still there (I had put him with the gallery) and was waiting for me. I gave

---

1 Arthur Greenwood (1880–1954), deputy leader of the Labour Party from 1935 to 1945.
2 Sir Patrick Hannon; see entry for 10 January 1939 and footnote.
3 Lloyd George began by congratulating the government on adopting a policy of 'no cowardly surrender to aggressors' (Hansard, 3 April 1939, Vol. 345, Col. 2505). He then said that if Britain gave its word to defend Poland against Hitler, it would have to do so. He annoyed some MPs by pointing out that Britain was weaker than it should be and its potential enemy stronger than it realised.
4 Sir Stafford Cripps. He had been expelled by his party for advocating a popular front with the communists, but would rejoin in 1945, having served in the War Cabinet.

him dinner along with Peter Loxley and Kirkpatrick[1] of the Foreign Office. Jim later, who is usually anti-Nazi, talked fluent German to Fritzi, who asked me to promise that I would look after him in case of a war, as he intended to stay here and be interned in this country throughout the duration of hostilities. He has his eye on the Potsdam throne in twenty years' time. He doesn't think that Hitler will dare to risk a war now. Perhaps, however Lloyd George's speech will drive him into one. I hated that Old Father Christmas tonight, with his haggard face, too blue suit and white locks, and unscrupulous attack. Simon wound up with one of his typical barrister orations, sly, insinuating and suddenly pointful. The House rose, without a division, before 11 p.m. I led Fritzi to the Strangers' Smoking Room and found Winston, Lloyd George, Boothby, Randolph Churchill all in a triumphant huddle surrounding Maisky![2] Maisky, the Ambassador of torture, murder and every crime in the calendar. To these depths have the Churchill–Eden group descended.

Drove Prince Fritzi home. Before we left, we walked along to my room, and I saw the PM leaving behind the glass windows. He looked up and smiled. I then walked towards his room and seeing Cleverly called out, 'Well, that went very well!' – meaning the debate – and the PM announced from the stairs, thinking I was addressing him, 'Yes, Chips it did. Goodnight.' I didn't reply, embarrassed.

The delegation including the Polish arrived today. I am apprehensive lest we go too far with the Poles; they may land us in either a war, or at best difficulties over Danzig.[3]

TUESDAY 4TH APRIL

I am apprehensive about our new policy. We have made a pledge we cannot implement and will look both treacherous and ridiculous in the event of German invasion of Poland.

This morning I wandered into the Private Secretary's room where I found Nevile Henderson, debonair and elegant, sitting on a desk. We had a few words, Hitler, he thinks, is partly mad and is under the domination of his more violent followers, the companions of his Munich days. They, and Ribbentrop (ever a 'yes man'), are urging him on to new adventures. Hitler is in a rage against us, and our governessy interference. First it was the communists, then the Jews and now it is

1 Ivone Augustine Kirkpatrick (1897–1964) had been wounded in the Great War before serving in military intelligence and controlling a group of spies. He joined the Foreign Office in 1919 and was First Secretary at the British Embassy in Berlin from 1933 to 1938 and held key diplomatic and intelligence posts during the Second World War, was knighted in 1948, and became High Commissioner for Germany in 1950. From 1953 to 1957 he was Permanent Under-Secretary at the Foreign Office.
2 The Soviet Ambassador.
3 Danzig, after the Treaty of Versailles, had been separated from Germany by a land corridor that gave Poland access to the Baltic Sea.

the British Empire!! He loathes us. At any moment he might commit a *coup de tête*.[1] Yet the man, Nevile H went on, is not altogether bad. He ought to negotiate an arrangement for the rectification of the Polish corridor and Danzig, which would be quite legitimate, and then at the Nuremberg Conference announce to the German people that he had lifted them from the position of the world's doormat to their present proud position, and how he was going to retire to live in his mountain fortress!! Germany could choose, Göring, or the Hohenzollerns, or whomsoever she liked . . . Nevile H doesn't pretend that he thinks Hitler will follow such a course, but more surprising things have happened.

I am disgruntled and liverish today – and fat . . . I kept out of the Prime Minister's way today, as I am embarrassed by last evening's incident. He must have thought me very pushing.

The Household Appointments were announced today, Waterhouse,[2] Charles Kerr,[3] and Jimmie Edmondson[4] as I thought. This arrangement leaves the post of assistant whip vacant. I walked deliberately past David [Margesson] tonight but he did not offer it to me. Perhaps he thinks I am valuable where I am, or thinks I am too identified with the Chamberlain Group to be promoted. Will he make a gesture towards the Edenites? I avoided Jim Thomas. I hate him at times.

Later

I was awakened by an urgent telephone message that Alan was *en route* to see me. He arrived distraught and as he sat on my bed he babbled an incredible story which sounded too melodramatic and unlikely to be true. It seems that last Wednesday, a week tomorrow, his two brothers, George and Donald, arrived in the evening from Cologne at Stuttgart. Donald, the mad attractive one, had parted from his brother at the station saying he would join him at their hotel about midnight. George watched him go off with an ugly storm trooper. About 10.30 George, having dined alone, was just getting into bed when the dreaded Gestapo arrived and arrested him. He was taken to prison, stripped and questioned, and told that Donald had been arrested for spying, and also for homosexuality: at least for consorting with soldiers. For nearly a week, that is until yesterday he was detained and never once saw Donald, although he fears he heard him shrieking. The German gaolers were kind to George in spite of the fact that he says he had

1 Impulsive act.
2 Charles Waterhouse MC (1895–1975) was Conservative MP for Leicester South from 1924 to 1945. He spent much of his political career in the Whips' Office.*
3 Charles Iain Kerr (1874–1968) was National Liberal MP for Montrose Burghs from 1932 to 1940, when he was raised to the peerage as 1st Baron Teviot. He served as Comptroller of the Household in the National Government's Whips' Office from 1939 to 1940.
4 Albert James Edmondson (1887–1959) was Conservative MP for Banbury from 1922 to 1945, when he was raised to the peerage as 1st Baron Sandford, having been knighted in 1934. He served in the Whips' Office from 1939 to 1945.

only bread and water and shared a cell with a murderer. All this he told me on the telephone from Henlow. I realised at once that we are faced with a major scandal! He only arrived at 11.30 tonight from Stuttgart and had first a word with Alan who, contrite, came to me for help.

King Ghazi of Iraq[1] was killed by a motor car. He is unlucky with motoring since his chauffeur gave him [the] clap only recently!

WEDNESDAY 5TH APRIL

When I woke this morning I could scarcely believe in Alan's nocturnal visit. However he rang me and implored my help; but George Lennox-Boyd rang up from Henlow Grange advising me to do nothing as he is convinced that his brother will be shortly released, as the Gestapo officers promised. Alan eventually agreed to leave matters to my judgement . . . . I walked to the Foreign Office, and wondered what to do, thought of the unfortunate fellow languishing in gaol. About 11 a.m. I decided to tell Rab, who immediately dictated a memo for Kirkpatrick, whom I next consulted. He telephoned to Smallbones,[2] our Consul-General at Frankfurt am Main, who promised us a report. An hour later Smallbones rang up excitedly saying that the charge against Donald was not one of spying but of homosexuality, and that his trial is to be held tomorrow. The Gestapo officials assured him that the evidence was overwhelming. I had to break this news to Alan, who is convinced that Donald will be released tomorrow, as is likely? [*sic*]

Honor got back from Breuil at 6.30, and I found her refreshed, charming and almost her old self. Has the nightmare lifted, the clashing of nerves and love faded?

I picked up Rab at 3 Smith Square, his poky, tasteless dwelling, and drove him to the Polish Embassy where there was a very grand dinner for Col. Beck.[3] . . . Half the great of England were present . . . . Halifax, resplendent in his orders, and I told him that Honor reports all well in Italy, and that the Italians are becoming

---

1 Ghazi bin Faisal (1912–39) succeeded his father, Faisal I, as King of the Hashemite Kingdom of Iraq in 1933. It was believed he was killed deliberately on the orders of the Iraqi Prime Minister, Nuri al-Said (1888–1958), who disagreed with Ghazi's plan to unify Iraq and Kuwait.

2 Robert Smallbones (1884–1976) joined the Foreign Office in 1910 serving in Africa, Norway, Slovakia and Croatia before becoming Consul-General at Frankfurt am Main in 1932. He had acquired a reputation for pursuing what would now be called human rights causes throughout his service and issued visas to numerous Jews seeking to leave Germany after Kristallnacht in 1938; it is estimated he managed to evacuate 48,000 Jews from Germany and was in the process of arranging for the evacuation of 50,000 more when he was forced from Germany by the declaration of war. He was posthumously declared a British Hero of the Holocaust in 2013. He served in Brazil from 1940 to 1945 and spent his retirement there.

3 Józef Beck (1894–1944) was Foreign Minister of Poland from 1932 to 1939. He was leading a Polish delegation to Britain at the time. After the German conquest of Poland he spent the war interned in Romania, where he died of tuberculosis.

anti-German. Vansittart[1] and I had a long talk and he was as charming as only he can be. Anthony Eden put his arm in mine . . . Rab was shy, out of it as he sometimes is in very grand circles. That slippery slime, Alec Hardinge[2] was the other side of the leper Leeper!, who is the most objectionable man in the whole Foreign Office, the most dangerous mandarin in that Forbidden City. I will get him out of the FO if it takes me twenty years . . . Rab is annoyed that he is not more consulted by Halifax, who in spite of demands to the contrary is veering away from the Prime Minister, [and] tends to keep Rab in the background. I always wondered whether Halifax would succeed in getting the FO down; but I was not prepared for them getting him down, which is, I hear, what has happened . . . . Back at 3 Smith Square, Rab and I gossiped until Rob Hudson, whose voice I heard outside, called. He had come on from the dinner. He is enjoying a certain vogue now since his successful trip to Moscow and the Baltic capitals. Then I came home. Honor was already asleep.

Last night during the Foreign Office banquet word was bought to the PM that 'Lucky Jim' Stanhope had made an indiscreet speech, something about men being on duty to man anti-aircraft guns. The PM to prevent the alarm spreading gave orders that the speech should be treated as D.[3] There was a rumpus in the House today. The PM's intention, as he humorously pointed out, was meant to get the remarks denied publicity. The anti-Stanhope faction will now grow.

THURSDAY 6TH APRIL

The House met early. I went first to the Foreign Office, and we had rather a scramble to get the Questions ready in time. I looked in on Roger Makins[4] for a moment and persuaded him to ring up Frankfurt a/m, and he told the Consul to spare no [illegible] of money, if need be, to rescue Donald Lennox-Boyd from the Gestapo's clutches. The Consul, Mr Smallbones, promised to let us know the result of the trial by telephone this evening. If he is acquitted he is to go to The Hague as Alan and Patsy were crossing over tonight!!

I drove Rab and Peter Foxley to Downing Street. They followed the PM out of No. 10. He was cheered by the waiting crowds . . . at the House he announced our agreement with Poland[5] and was well received. As I walked out of the Chamber I was given a message to ring up the Foreign Office immediately. I did so, and

1 Robert Gilbert Vansittart (1881–1957) was Permanent Under-Secretary at the Foreign Office from 1930 to 1938, and would be raised to the peerage in 1941 as 1st Baron Vansittart.
2 Alexander Henry Louis Hardinge (1894–1960) was the former private secretary to King Edward VIII, whom Channon unfairly blamed for causing the abdication.
3 A D-Notice is a means by which the press is advised that to publish something could impair national security.
4 Foreign Office official.
5 A military alliance, the details pending further negotiation, promising British and French support in the event of a threat to Polish independence.

Roger Makins begged me to come back at once. I looked for Alan and was told he was in Ernest Brown's room closeted with him. I barged in, 'Come to the FO at once with me!' I said. 'I'll follow on,' Alan replied. I hurried across Whitehall, apprehensive. So Donald has been sentenced I first thought, but by Roger's face I knew it was worse! The Consul has reported that Donald had hanged himself last night in his cell! I went away to my room in order to ring up Alan not to come to the Foreign Office, but I found him already there sitting anxiously at my desk. I led him into Rab's room, as he was still lunching at the House of Commons. Then I broke it to Alan as gently as I could. He broke down, clasped my knees in his arms, moaned and sobbed and I feared he would foam at the mouth. I got him a glass of water. Presently he recovered a little of his colour, and I saw he would not faint. I comforted him as best I could, and led him out of the building. We walked in a daze along Princes Street and at a pub I led him in and forced him to drink two glasses of neat brandy. Flushed and hysterical we got to 8 Little College St and there we found Patsy and told her. Alan again collapsed, and we left him for a moment. I tried to organise . . . to impress upon them both the absolute necessity for silence, for discretion; otherwise the scandal would engulf us all. Alan wildly shouted, and left the house to fetch Dr Plesch,[1] the Hungarian-Jewish quack doctor who tends Mrs Lennox-Boyd. At that moment Honor arrived very gay in red velvet and sparkling with rubies. We told her and she, too, became glum and serious. We spent the afternoon trying to arrange matters but Alan was hopeless from the first. The secret can well be kept. We telephoned madly, made arrangements for Francis Lennox-Boyd to fly to Stuttgart on Monday to fetch the body . . . at last we left, and I went back with Honor to the Foreign Office. I introduced the staff to her; and we told Rab the truth about Donald, but he thinks it is foul play. He knows nothing of homosexuality.

We all drove, Honor, Patsy and I, to Kelvedon, which is looking lovely. Alan has gone down to Henlow to try and break the news to his old mother. All Lennox-Boyds had a mother-worship, sexual fascination complex. I fear a scandal and that Alan, if he doesn't break down completely, will at least fail at his work. I am sorry for Donald; but what a selfish action. Why not wait at least until tomorrow when the trial came up, as he might have been acquitted? A certain homosexual baronet was recently allowed to hop his bail in Germany after a

---

1 János Oscar Plesch (1878–1957) was a Hungarian academic pathologist, physiologist and physician with an international reputation for his research on blood circulation, and he invented a device to measure blood pressure. He was Einstein's doctor for twenty-five years. His reputation as a quack, which was widely shared, seems to have been prompted by his being required to requalify as a doctor in order to practise when he came to Britain.

similar charge had been preferred against him . . . or was he beaten to death by angry Nazis?[1]

GOOD FRIDAY, 7TH APRIL   KELVEDON

Honor and I and Patsy arrived here last night, and the house looks a dream of spring loveliness. It is hot, the garden is looking tidier and there are early blossomings. Much telephoning to Henlow. Alan has told his mother that Donald L-B died for his country, that he was in the secret service (and there is just enough suspicion to make the latter plausible). Alan has had what amounts to a breakdown; so has his surviving brother, but the old lady is magnificent. She has been bullied by her sons – who misguidedly imagine they are being kind – into leaving comfortable Henlow for a Northern motor-trip to distract her. Alan seems to have lost all reason and sense; it has been a bitter blow. I fear the scandal must leak out.

This morning early John Coulson,[2] who is the gargoyle-looking, but very charming and intelligent Resident Clerk, was awakened at 5.30 by a message to say that Italians are occupying Albania. The report proved to be only too true; King Zog[3] has fled, whilst Queen Geraldine[4] (a semi-American, semi-tart *née* Apponyi) and her two day old baby son have fled to Greece. There is unrest; international disturbance. I don't know whether to cable the Iveaghs to return from Asolo. A terrible inevitability of war has descended on us. '*Et tu Benito?*' Mussolini has only recently assured us that she had no territorial claims on Albania and her invasion or really annexation of the little land, however explained away as perhaps necessary, is nevertheless a violation of the Anglo-Italian agreement.

1 Channon, perhaps at Butler's prompting, may get nearer the truth than the official version of events. Donald Lennox-Boyd had done intelligence work in the army and there were rumours he had spied for Britain on his visit to Germany. He was well known by family and close friends to be homosexual. Before his body could be repatriated it was cremated, perhaps to destroy evidence of physical injury beyond what a hanging would have caused.
2 John Eltringham Coulson (1909–97) joined the Diplomatic Service in 1932 and from 1960 to 1963 was British Ambassador to Sweden. He served as Secretary-General of the European Free Trade Association from 1965 to 1972.
3 Ahmet Muhtar bey Zogolli (1895–1961), who from 1922 took the surname Zogu, came from a family of Albanian landowners, and became a provincial governor after the Great War, before joining the government. He served as Prime Minister from 1922 to 1924, President from 1925 to 1928, and then was declared Albania's first and last King, as Zog I, in September 1928. He allegedly survived over fifty assassination attempts, and as a *soi-disant* king was regarded as an upstart by other European royal families. The feeble Albanian regime became entirely dependent on Italy during the 1930s, and on the birth of Zog's heir apparent Mussolini invaded and declared a protectorate.
4 Géraldine Margit Virginia Olga Mária Apponyi de Nagy-Appony (1915–2002) was the daughter of a Hungarian count and an American mother. She married Zog in 1938. Their son, Crown Prince Leka Zogu (1939–2011), was born two days before the Italian invasion of Albania.

War seems nearer now that the dictators are drawing together, and that their methods show stark and brutal similarity. We listened into the radio and were depressed indeed.

Alan has rung Patsy. He is coming up to London tomorrow, and Honor is going to meet him in London, instead of Patsy who is worn out and possibly pregnant.[1]

SATURDAY 8TH APRIL

The statesmen are in London, and the PM will return from Scotland. The FO is in a fever of excitement and Parliament may be recalled. The extremists and left-wingers generally of the Nicolson[2] School want to renounce the Anglo-Italian agreement.

Alan rushed to London from Edinburgh, where the mad Lennox-Boyds had transported their ailing bereaved mother. They are all behaving like Bedlamites and of course refuse to accept the official version of Donald's dramatic death. They picture fantastic incidents, work up theories and are generally convinced that he was beaten up by Nazis. Alan was surprised to find Honor instead of Patsy waiting for him; she tried to reason with him but he was tired, demented, foolish. He went to the H of Commons and stole a piece of War Office notepaper from the Secretary of State's room and he wrote his mother a letter of consolation full of dark hints and forged it 'Leslie Hore-Belisha'; the old lady, who isn't half the fool Alan thinks, is to be deluded into believing that her son was a hero instead of a homosexual. Alan will not go to Germany; someone ought to fetch the ashes . . . Francis, the languid youngest, who was to have gone on Monday, has been prevented by Alan from doing so.

Honor never mentions Diana Cavendish and I wonder whether they had either a row or is she tired of her? Honor gets tired of people, drops them and never thinks of them again . . .

EASTER SUNDAY, 9TH APRIL

The Pope ticked off the dictators when he delivered his Easter sermon. This country is in an acute state of 'jitters'. I do not understand why. Why shouldn't Italy take Albania, a bandit-infested little country anyway? I am sorry for the Regent;[3] he is a nut in a nutcracker with enemies on all sides of him, and Italy on two fronts. I have written to him offering him Kelvedon as an asylum should Yugoslavia, too, be invaded, as is possible.

1 She was. Their first son, Simon, would be born on 7 December.
2 Harold Nicolson was a leading anti-appeaser.
3 Prince Paul of Yugoslavia.

We had the wireless turned on during dinner; everyone depressed. The PM has returned to London, abandoning his fishing. Halifax saw Signor Crolla, chargé d'affaires,[1] three times today. I was all day on the telephone to the FO.

MONDAY 10TH APRIL

Glorious weather. We lunched out of doors, basked in the sun, and Honor and I and two guests actually plunged into the water. Kelvedon a dream of fruit blossom and spring loveliness. War is unthinkable . . . I played with my Paul and we caught frogs together.

The Cabinet sat for the first time on a Bank Holiday since the war. I rang up Rab, who was not alarmist. I gather that Neville will not consider renouncing the Anglo-Italian agreement as we shall have a parliamentary storm.

TUESDAY 11TH APRIL

I went up to London and left Honor and our party basking in the heat of the pool. I found the FO depressed. There is a general malaise in the telegrams and I am convinced that alarmist rumours are actively put about by dictator propaganda agents with an attempt to frighten us; thereby showing an ignorance of Anglo-Saxon nature, which is steeled by opposition. Nevertheless I have long been convinced that the heyday of this great Empire is over; this is decadence, the 'kill'; we are soft, degenerate; there are few great men. No one really cares constructively; only hate (and that is a prerogative of the Labour Party) is left.

What is so annoying is that the Churchills and Coopers are being proved half right! The atmosphere grows tense: there are signs of war in Holland, in Yugoslavia and elsewhere, and Greece, although Italy has practically guaranteed the latter's frontiers. There are rumours of Corfu being attacked. Alone Rab is calm but Halifax, who I am beginning to admire less, is wobbly and intriguing.

Back to Kelvedon, which is lovely and hot. Serge Obolensky,[2] my old, very old friend, whom I still love, although he bores me, is rather to my relief for Paris to stay with Laura Corrigan,[3] who is laying million-franc bets that there will be no major war . . . but I am distrustful of our new 'friends'; of our flirtation with Russia.

---

1 Guido Crolla (1897–?) had served in the Secretariat of the League of Nations, as a member of the political section, before being posted to London as counsellor.
2 Prince Sergei ('Serge') Platonovich Obolensky Neledinsky-Meletsky (1890–1978) had been educated at Oxford and became part of the Russian diaspora after the revolution. He emigrated to America and became a successful businessman.*
3 Laura Mae Whitlock (1879–1948), daughter of a handyman from Wisconsin, married in 1916 as her second husband James William Corrigan (1880–1928), a steel magnate from Cleveland, Ohio. She was a noted philanthropist as well as a society hostess.

The Lennox-Boyds, Alan and Patsy . . . . (why take her?) flew this morning to Frankfurt to identify Donald's body, order the cremation and bring back the ashes.[1]

Conscription is coming before May 1st.

WEDNESDAY 12TH APRIL

Alan has behaved with almost incredible cowardness [*sic*], and caddishness. He flew with Patsy yesterday to Frankfurt a/m, refused to go on to Stuttgart or to see his brother's body and left immediately for Ostend where he this morning chartered an aeroplane for Scotland to join his mother. I talked to him tonight. His conduct in leaving his 21-year-old bride behind in a strange city to bring back the ashes is beyond belief. She should not have become involved in the scandal at all. The newspapers had now got hold of it and Diana Cooper tells me it is the talk of London that he was beaten up by Nazis. I rang up Alan and fear my voice betrayed how shocked I was by his cowardly abandonment of his child wife . . . she is being looked after by Consul, Mr Smallbone. I also warned him that the newspapers have heard the tale, and that Randolph[2] is hot on the scent to ferret it out. I feel I can never count on Alan again.

I am exhausted.

Albania has offered the crown to King Victor Emmanuel; and Winston Churchill's stock is rising again. Randolph Churchill is now the menace of London: he ought to be hamstrung . . . . he has no redeeming qualities and his [illegible] heart beats with jealousy of me particularly. I will do him in eventually.

Mike Wardell has told Alan that there is a rumour from Germany that Donald's eyes were gouged out by the Nazis.

THURSDAY 13TH APRIL

Up to London early as we are faced with a big debate. Rab walked out to No. 10 with Halifax who remarked 'I suppose you are coming to give the PM moral support.' Halifax is weaned away from Neville now on many points but Rab, as Alec Dunglass told me, sees eye to eye with him. He feels at home with Rab, more than with anyone . . . there was a Foreign Affairs Committee meeting and Rab, who attended it, assured me that there would be no guarantee to Romania, only to Greece. There was, however, a last-moment change, due to pressure from the French.

Patsy is still in Frankfurt, abandoned by her husband, whilst he has flown to his mother at North Berwick. The press refer to the strange death of a minister's

---

1 Unknown to them, the Nazi authorities had already ordered the cremation.
2 Churchill, then a gossip writer for the *Evening Standard*.

brother and say that he was arrested and later 'beaten up'. Actually the Nazis are not really responsible: George Lennox-Boyd, who is a pusillanimous cad, rushed back to save his own skin without trying to help his brother. Donald was a queer fish, sly, gay, puckish, attractive. I wish now I had known him better. I did not think he would commit suicide because of homosexual charges.

The debate was perhaps disappointing. The Prime Minister was modulated, calm, and not as inspiring as usual. He is not happy in his new role of the protagonist of diluted collective security. Not at all. The sooner we get him back on appeasement the better. To my surprise he added to the guarantee to Greece one for Romania. This was a last moment decision taken after luncheon at the urgent request of the French. It does not really matter as we should have to come in in any case were Romania attacked.

I had a long and unpleasant interview with George Lennox-Boyd who is an ass, a silly one. It was prior to one of the many memorial services to Donald Lennox-Boyd, who as he committed suicide is not entitled to any.

SATURDAY 15TH APRIL   *KELVEDON*

There were two services for Donald Lennox-Boyd, one at Henlow, one at Bournemouth. Poor Patsy flew back yesterday clutching his ashes in a parcel. Alan has behaved shabbily in this matter. Honor and I are in a rage with him.

The Dufferins are here re-honeymooning: also here [is] Fritzi of Prussia . . . Much talk: mostly anti-Hitler. Of course Fritzi is careful, but he told me that Hitler had dined quietly some years ago at Cecilienhof with his parents. There had been only the Crown Prince and Princess and one of their sons present, Hitler had sat on a sofa after dinner and had solemnly declared that it was his intention of restoring the monarchy directly he could. The Imperial family believed him. Perhaps he meant it at the time. Perhaps he meant it altogether!

President Roosevelt has made an impassioned appeal to the dictators asking for an assurance of their non-aggressive intentions. It is a courageous move on Roosevelt's part, but I cannot join in the general fulsome praise. I think it is rather ill-timed; but it may rally the States around him.

SUNDAY 16TH APRIL

Lazy day. The 'Boche boys'[1] played golf; the Dufferins fornicated; the clocks were put on an hour to conform with summer time . . . . Fritzi played his accordion. I promised to put him up here throughout the war, when he can be interned.[2]

---

1 Prince 'Fritzi' and an unnamed German friend who had accompanied him.
2 He was in fact sent to an internment camp in Canada, though stayed with Channon in 1939–40 before he was arrested as an enemy alien. He returned to England in 1941 and did agricultural work.

He won't fight for the Nazis, whose regime he thinks repugnant and doomed. Internal dissent will blow it sky high soon, and Hitler of necessity [will] be shot. These are his predictions.

Diana Cooper sent me a message from Breccles to ring her urgently. I did; she thinks that there will be war by Tuesday: the Jewish groups, who long for war so to punish Germany, are delighted. They work on poor Diana's nerves. I told her not to be such as ass. Basil Dufferin is very delightful, but I fear he is a Winstonian and boasts of it.

MONDAY 17TH APRIL

I drove to Southend, received an idiotic Peace Deputation, and later . . . . returned exhilarated to Kelvedon to find Alan Lennox-Boyd and Patsy just off to bed. Patsy is all day in tears and not so pleased by her pregnancy. Alan is nearly a lunatic. I have had two rows with him today. It is not my fault that his brother died, or rather hanged himself in homosexual circumstances in a Stuttgart gaol.

Back to Kelvedon late. I talked to the Duchess of Kent; they are leaving in semi-secrecy to spend four days in Paris, as the Windsors are away in the South it is an opportune moment.

Hitler has summoned the Reichstag for April 28th when it is supposed he will reply to President Roosevelt's well-intentioned but misguided speech.

TUESDAY 18TH APRIL

The House met again. Walter [Buccleuch] whispered to me that he had only today returned from Berlin where he had twice seen Ribbentrop, who he was convinced did not want a war; nor did other German officials. Walter thinks we are on the wrong tack politically: that we are foolish to think war inevitable, etc. . . . . I begged him to see the Prime Minister and offered to arrange a meeting. Walter looked surprised . . .

Alec Dunglass, with whom I am becoming increasingly intimate, and I had a long confidential chat. I saw at once that I was being sounded and I gave an anti-Winston tirade. By all means he must be kept out of the Cabinet! I was aware that there is a movement afoot to give him the Admiralty and I have warned Rab.

WEDNESDAY 19TH APRIL

I thought on my brief conversation with Walter Buccleuch and rang him up and begged him to come at once to the Foreign Office. He did, and I ushered him into Rab, and they had forty minutes' confidential talk. Rab later wrote out a memo of their conversation and showed one copy to the PM and gave the other to Halifax. The PM then sent for Walter via Mrs Chamberlain – who talked to Mollie on the telephone. The PM kept Walter for an hour this evening, and seized upon his report, which coincides with his own news. We are back now on appeasement. Walter's visit has a great effect on Halifax (I gave him in the Lords a letter written by Walter). The Russian policy is now off, and we are trying to seek a way out of it. Back to appeasement.

My warning last evening to Rab about the project to include Winston in the Cabinet, by sacking Stanhope and replacing him with Winston, was only just in time; as Rab was sitting in his Smith Square study last night for a moment before going to bed he heard a knock at the door and opened it to Tommy Dugdale (who more than anyone nowadays has his finger in the political pots and plots – he, Alec and David [Margesson]). He asked for Rab's advice re Winston. Should the PM, or should he not, offer him a seat in the Cabinet? Rab, primed by me, said emphatically 'No'!

THURSDAY 20TH APRIL

I took Alan, charming and less mad than usual, to dine at Buck's Club, and we went to the Gate Review [sic] which I saw for the second consecutive time. He laughed uproariously and I think the evening did him good. He rang Patsy at Kelvedon to say that he would not be back tonight, and like a bourgeois wife she flew into a rage. She is very unreasonable and does nothing to save Alan's strength and energy; on the other hand she is justified for she is deeply jealous of his matriarch of a mother, and of Alan's insane passion for her. Patsy thinks rightly that if Alan can and does motor many miles about going to see the old harridan, why shouldn't he equally motor to see her? Alan's devotion to his mother is supreme selfishness: he thinks it fine; it is really rather ridiculous.

The PM played with the House today. In answer to a question he announced that a Ministry of Supply would be set up and that the name of the Right Honourable Member who would be appointed to the post was ... and he paused as the temperature of the House rose ... 'Burgin'![1] The House, expecting, half-hoping, half-fearing that it would be Winston, was amazed.

The usual excitement in the House and on all calculations there must be a move up for someone. And there is also the post of assistant whip going. I went to Alec Dunglass and he gave me the new appointments which will be announced tomorrow.

Euan [Wallace] goes to the Transport Ministry (and all day there has been a fuss as to whether or not he would be included in the Cabinet). The PM was against including him as he doesn't like Euan, but he gave way to David Margesson who has magnificently rewarded Euan now for his friendship. It is

---

1 Edward Leslie Burgin (1887–1945) was Liberal MP for Luton and, since 1937, Minister of Transport. As an arch appeaser, he was sacked by Churchill in 1940.*

thought that Euan will remain in the Cabinet until after the election and then be shelved with a peerage. A sane and serious award for his long service.

Geoffrey Lloyd to become Minister of Mines, but when I told him this he did not know it, and was half-pleased, half-disappointed as he was hoping, in the event of a reshuffle, to get FST,[1] which has gone to Harry Crookshank, who is now on the threshold of the Cabinet. (I thought he wanted to be Speaker.) He has been an excellent Minister of Mines, and even his extraordinary appearance, his faultless clothes, inevitable top hat, and exaggerated manners have impressed the miners. He has no balls; they were cut off after the war and Diana Cooper, serving as a nurse, was present at the operation – she told me so herself.

These appointments leave a vacancy at the Home Office, and the Under-Secretaryship has been given to Osbert Peake,[2] a popular, but not very great appointment. I should have preferred Ralph Assheton[3] or Victor Raikes; their chances were both considered and ultimately they will both get jobs. Both are abler than Osbert, whom I have known since Oxford days when for a time we were intimate. I never really liked him, and don't like him now, but I admit he has improved or his face has become sad. Jock McEwen[4] has been appointed assistant whip. I do not take this as a snub to me, nor even as a 'passover'. The Whips' Room are taking him in to succeed James Stuart,[5] who because of domestic difficulties must soon leave the government. Probably he will stay on until after the election, and then Jock will take his place. If anything this appointment improves my chances and doesn't put anyone senior to me whom I would mind. Jock is older, been in the House longer and is generally quite suitable. I am delighted. I am sorry for both Victor Raikes and Ralph Assheton, whose claims have been considered and passed over – temporarily at least – in favour of Osbert.

It was today decided in view of Walter Buccleuch's information to send back Nevile Henderson to Berlin. He is leaving at once. It was a mistake to have had him here so long. Conscription has been decided upon.

---

1 Financial Secretary to the Treasury, then regarded as the most senior non-Cabinet post.

2 Osbert Peake (1897–1966) was a Tory MP for Leeds North from 1929 to 1955, and for Leeds North East from 1955 to 1956. He was Minister of Pensions from 1951 to 1955, and was raised to the peerage as 1st Viscount Ingleby in 1956.

3 Ralph Assheton (1901–84), Conservative MP for Rushcliffe, succeeded Crookshank as Financial Secretary to the Treasury in 1943.*

4 John Helias Finnie McEwen (1894–1962) was Conservative MP for Berwick and Haddington from 1931 to 1945, and was Under-Secretary of State for Scotland from 1939 to 1940. He was created 1st Bt in 1953.

5 James Gray Stuart (1897–1971) was Conservative MP for Moray and Nairn from 1923 to 1959 and, having served as a whip and then Chief Whip, was Secretary of State for Scotland from 1951 to 1957. He was raised to the peerage as 1st Viscount Stuart of Findhorn in 1959.

FRIDAY 21ST APRIL

Drove to Kelvedon. Honor, Brigid and I went to dine at Langleys,[1] leaving the *ménage* Lennox-Boyd behind, both in a fiendish temper. The Donald tragedy is wrecking Alan: he cannot reconcile himself to it and thinks, or tries to think, that the Nazis tortured him. He has written a second note on War Office paper to Mrs Lennox-Boyd, and the poor old lady who is far from being a complete fool, now believes her son died a hero's death . . . Walter Buccleuch was told by Ribbentrop the truth.

Langleys was an adventure: I had expected a lovely house and it is, William and Mary with earlier rooms with stucco work and Jacobean ceilings; many amazing pictures and interesting attractive things not very well but most painstakingly arranged by 'Bill' Tufnell,[2] the *Schlossherr*.[3] For three centuries the Tufnells have lived a gentry life at Langleys [illegible] the Chelmsford countryside. He continues and lives a semi-feudal life. He is younger, handsomer, more affectionate than I had supposed. He is fussy, finicky, and totally humourless, yet he has a certain charm and is obviously impressed by us beyond measure. He fawned on Honor, whom he liked better than me. We were shown over the house including the Maple Victorian Suite which he occupied. Brigid and I nudged each other and I pointed to the bridal bed! Not for her, however, as she is too attractive, and really too rich for him. An enjoyable evening. I was definitely out to charm him and fear I failed, but he leapt at my invitation to dine tomorrow.

The ministerial changes were announced and were as I was told.

SUNDAY 23RD APRIL

Wet weather. We all passed the afternoon at Langleys where Bill Tufnell provided us with an elaborate tea and we saw the house. We are leaving obsessed by him. Shall I get him?

I am distressed about an alleged rapprochement with Russia. It is madness. I have worked tooth and nail against it; I am not yet defeated. I have definite hopes of averting any such shame alliance. Already our flirtation has caused us to lose caste in Yugoslavia – almost driven Paul into the anti-Comintern pact, in Spain, in Portugal, in Poland and elsewhere. People in this country are mad. I think this whole race is mad now. Definitely mad on the subject of Hitler. Many people believe that war will break out after Hitler's speech next Friday.

---

1 A house at Great Waltham, just north of Chelmsford, about twenty miles from Kelvedon Hall.
2 John Jolliffe Tufnell (1900–90), landowner.
3 Master of the house.

TUESDAY 25TH APRIL

Momentous day, [the] death, or perhaps only [the] unconsciousness of our class
...I spent the morning at the Foreign Office...I drove Rab to lunch at Buckingham
Palace, where he arrived punctually. He admires the Queen but thinks her
snobbish...Then to the House of Commons...Dull Budget performance: I could
not get interested. Simon was dull, academic and his voice sounded monotonous.
Towards the end he delivered a series of knockout blows – our income will be
seriously curtailed. 20 per cent on the upper grades of the Surtax. We now pay
fourteen shillings in the pound![1]

I am depressed about the Budget and feel that our whole civilisation hangs
by such a hair now: without Chamberlain we should have gone under long ago.
The Cabinet met here at 5 p.m. and decided definitively on conscription. It will
be announced tomorrow. I am heavily in favour of it.

WEDNESDAY 26TH APRIL

The newspapers print 'Conscription' in large letters. There will be a parliamentary
storm and a government victory! I rang up Alec Dunglass and urged him to induce
the PM to broadcast an appeal to the nation if not tonight, then on Saturday. He
promised to give the PM my message.

The Budget is more alarming than I had understood. It will mean drastic
curtailment of our personal expenditure. The country has 'taken' the Budget in
its stride, will it also take conscription? Much intriguing . . . and I had several
long intimate conferences with Alec Dunglass who is a miracle of tact, humour
and sound sense. He adores Neville so much that he has even begun to look like
him. He has a tiny room of his own, a sort of dungeon, on the ground floor where
he concocts arrangements. He thinks that there may well be an election should
the Socialists overdo their opposition to conscription. When it was announced,
Attlee was shaking with rage and the PM had a rough passage. There were rude
interruptions and shouts of 'Resign', 'Hitler', and other offensive remarks.
Wisely the Speaker didn't interfere. Immediately it was over I walked away to the
PM's room and as we chatted, the secretaries and I, he appeared smiling. There
was even colour in his pale cheeks and his dark eyes shone. He patted me on the
shoulder . . . 'It went well, I thought.' We immediately lied and I referred to the
Socialists' silences when he hinted at an election. He seemed amused. The whole
country is behind him. His amazing physique, his rather enigmatic personality,
his steadiness of purpose have captivated the country – and infuriated London
society.

---

1 The tax increases were required to fund what was now a massive rearmament programme.

THURSDAY 27TH APRIL

Blum[1] has telephoned an urgent appeal to Attlee to modify the violently anti-Conscription attitude of our socialists. Apparently Blum was persuaded by Bullitt,[2] the rampageous and deplorable US Ambassador in Paris, to take this line . . . it has had an effect.

The PM gave a calm review of the conscription problem[3] and he was neither barracked nor interrupted. Archie Sinclair was singularly, even for him, bombastically inept. Throughout his long speech I watched the PM write copious notes on House of Commons writing paper. I wondered what could so interest him in Archie's diatribe!! It was notes on salmon fishing which he wrote out and passed to Anthony Crossley who is writing a book on the subject!!!![4] What a commentary on Chamberlain, especially as AC has been one of the disloyal band! Nothing has been too bad for him to say against the PM, who now with his infinite patience helps him with his book!! I hope the Crossleys keep the notes in their family archives. I would!! The speech of the afternoon was Winston's, a magnificent effort. Duff Cooper speaking without notes was excellent too. The Conservative Party is a love club again . . . no election now. No split either. The debate dragged on and at the final vote, the three-line whip, we had a majority of 243. The figures were excellent. The most important decision since the war has passed off peacefully. The Labour people were uncomfortable and in a false position!

Jim Thomas rang with offensive tone, 'I am glad you came around to my opinions.' 'I didn't know you ever had any,' I retorted. I hate him.

Home at 12.30 after listening to Leslie Belisha. who wound up for the government in an impassioned inspired emotional speech. Honor rang up from Kelvedon and we gossiped.

I had a little talk with Lloyd George, whom I met coming out of my room. He said that he would speak next Thursday. How hale and healthy he looks in his

1 André Léon Blum (1872–1950) was three times Prime Minister of France. A committed anti-appeaser and then anti-Pétainiste, he was sent to Buchenwald concentration camp and, being Jewish, was lucky to survive. He resumed his political career after the war and his third premiership lasted just five weeks in 1946–7.
2 William Christian Bullitt Jr (1891–1967) was an American journalist and novelist who became a diplomat. From 1933 to 1936 he was the United States' first ambassador to the Soviet Union, and then until 1940 was the ambassador to France. His decision to remain in Paris after the Germans invaded rather than go with the French government to Bordeaux cost him his intimate friendship with Roosevelt, who considered he was grandstanding, and derailed a potential political career.
3 In a Commons debate on compulsory military training.
4 One of the two Conservative MPs for Oldham (the other being Hamilton Kerr*). Although killed in a plane crash less than four months later, Crossley completed the book, and it was published as *The Floating Line for Salmon and Sea Trout*.

powder blue suiting, his bronzed complexion. He has a gay walk – almost as gay a gait as Neville's!

FRIDAY 28TH APRIL

I have unearthed a plot at the Foreign Office: Oliver Harvey,[1] Vansittart, Collier[2] and Leeper are determined to get Chamberlain out, and probably Winston in. They are capable of anything.

At 12.30 a copy of Hitler's speech[3] was delivered to us. It is good stuff, and I fear that all my sympathies are with him in what he says. He complains of the usual injustices . . . he is conciliatory about England. In tone the speech is moderate.

The House rose early and I am off to Kelvedon, relieved by the tone and tenor of Hitler's speech; but depressed by a chance remark of Rab's. He thinks the speech skilful and statesmanlike, even conciliatory; but he wishes he had resigned at the time of the Polish Guarantee, which he considers highly dangerous and possibly fatal to England. 'Towards the middle of May will be the difficult time. I think there will be trouble then,' he said.

SUNDAY 30TH APRIL

So we are still at peace. I consider that the press has been unfair in its reception of Hitler's speech in particular to his friendly references to England. It is hopeless in England: give a dog a bad name and he can never recover.

MONDAY 1ST MAY

The House is dull. Long conference again with Alec Dunglass and we are agreed that something must be done almost immediately to soften the resistance of the Poles, to make them more reasonable towards the Germans' just demands on Danzig; and also to make some overture, however slight, towards Germany. I promised to confer with Rab along these lines and later did so. He immediately

---

1 Oliver Charles Harvey (1893–1968) served as British Ambassador to France from 1948 to 1954.*

2 Laurence Collier (1890–1976) headed the Northern Section of the Foreign Office. He would be Ambassador to Norway (including to its government-in-exile during the war) from 1939 to 1950.

3 Ostensibly his reply to Roosevelt's recent message to him, but also an announcement that he was ending the Anglo-German naval agreement, and a demand to Poland to allow the Germans untrammelled access through the corridor to Danzig, with Danzig being formally incorporated into Germany. He also lectured Roosevelt on the question of *Lebensraum* – the need for space for Germany's people. Channon's belief that the speech was 'conciliatory', and Butler's, if Channon interpreted him correctly, was naive to say the least.

asked for an interview with Halifax which later he had. The PM wrote out a longish letter in his own flowing hand for Halifax and gave it to me. 'Please get this letter to Edward immediately,' he said. I personally carried it from the House of Commons (in the rain sharing my umbrella with Rab, who always carries a stick and doesn't possess an umbrella) to the Foreign Office, where I gave it to Harold Caccia who carried it to the adjoining room to hand to Halifax, who, for once, was behind time with his appointments . . . . The delay kept Corbin impatiently waiting in the Ambassadors' Room.

Honor and I went on to a small dance given jointly by Pamela Berry and Sheila Birkenhead at 44 Cadogan Place. The tiny house was skilfully transformed into a ballroom – an enjoyable evening; I had a long dance with Eileen Sutherland who is chaperoning Elizabeth Leveson-Gower[1] whose resemblance to her dead mother[2] is uncanny; sat a whole dance with Bill Tufnell, talked with the Duchess of Kent who looked a dream of beauty and was dressed *à la Grecque*. The evening, however, was nearly spoilt by my Honor's eccentric behaviour. At 1 a.m., I noticed that she was very drunk: fearing a scene I tactfully got near to her, and eventually led her home . . . as we got into our car we met Emerald, radiantly cheerful, arriving on the arm of Sir Thomas Beecham from the opening night at the opera. Only Duff, unluckily, and Jim Thomas saw how drunk Honor was, as we met them on the stairs. Honor later said that she had been feeling unwell all day, had eaten nothing, and when she called to see Anne Feversham had drunk three cocktails foolishly. I gave her four aspirins, two tumblers of cold water, Brand Seltzer and put her to bed. She gradually sobered. I don't know what Tufnell must have thought of her.

TUESDAY 2ND MAY

A late luncheon at Emerald's for the Brazilian and French ambassadors . . . . I was next to Lady Chamberlain[3] and we had an hour's talk: I subtly praised the PM. Lady Chamberlain has just come back from Greece via Rome and she gave me Mussolini news. The Duce is about to become a father again! The mother is the *petite bourgeoise* with whom he has been consorting for two years or more – the husband was sent to Abyssinia but didn't die! Mussolini is enchanted with himself: at the same time he is cohabiting with the fair South German girl sent to Rome by the Nazis. Given up to the practices of love, he is losing reality and depending more and more on Ciano,[4] who has become impossible, and probably

---

1 Elizabeth Millicent Sutherland Leveson-Gower (1921–2019) succeeded her uncle, 5th Duke of Sutherland, in one of his subsidiary earldoms as Countess of Sutherland in her own right, in 1963.
2 Elizabeth Demarest (1892–1931) of New York City.
3 Ivy Muriel Dundas, widow of Sir Austen.*
4 Count Ciano, his son-in-law.

almost certainly in the pay of Germans. Ciano is an erotic too, and the whole Italian government has now become a sort of brothel and is losing touch rapidly with the population which is pro-English . . . . all this from Lady Chamberlain!! She thinks the Italians had meant to attack Corfu but were frightened by our fleet. She was in Greece at the time and lunched with King George and Mrs James!![1] . . . Lady Chamberlain is very pro-Italian, all her policy and influences have been directed to improving our relations with Italy, so her remarks are probably true. She is disappointed with Mussolini, and made no attempt to see him during her twenty-four-hour stay in Rome. Ciano, however, sent someone from the Palazzo Office to call on her . . . she was interesting, too, about the Chamberlains. 'Annie'[2] she lightly dismissed as knowing nothing of foreign affairs. The PM gets all his mental stimulus and confidence from his two maiden sisters, with whom he corresponds constantly. Neither he nor Mrs Chamberlain cares much for their children. They had always been absorbed in themselves to the exclusion of their children, who are, in any case, dull . . . She told me much of the Chamberlain home life, of old Joe and his first two wives who both died in childbirth, one in giving birth to Austen, the second in giving birth to her third daughter, now also dead . . .

WEDNESDAY 3RD MAY

I attended the Brewery meeting and once again heard the doleful account of how our fortunes are diminishing . . . . All breweries are doing badly. I lunched there and then came on to the House of Commons . . . then Walter Buccleuch sent me an SOS and I spent an hour with him in the House of Lords. He is deeply concerned by our foreign policy, and rather committed to the pro-German view, or policy of appeasement. Like me he sees the press, the Churchills, the Coopers and others driving us to war.

Earlier in the day he had been seriously 'ticked off', by Alec Hardinge for his 'intervention'. He had been 'sent for': they nearly came to blows. I widened the wedge between them. Evidently Alec Hardinge is not as popular or as omnipotent as I thought. The royal brothers mistrust him. He is an avowed Edenite, a Churchillian . . . I know this and laid it on with a trowel. Walter is happy about the King, but fears the Queen's views are not now sound whatever they may have been before. She leans slightly towards Eden. I knew it; she is surrounded by those sort of people, Philip Sassoon, Hannah [Gubbay] . . . etc.

---

1 Mary Venetia Cavendish-Bentinck (1861–1948) was related to the dukes of Portland and the Bowes-Lyon family, and therefore to Queen Elizabeth, whose godmother she was. She married, in 1885, John Arthur James (1853–1917), a highly successful breeder of racehorses.
2 Anne de Vere Cole (1883–1967) married Neville Chamberlain in 1911. She was instrumental in encouraging him to go into politics.

Jim PL Thomas[1] warned me that he is resigning the whip if anything savouring of appeasement is begun again. I see a political battle raging for next week once it's known that Russia is to be snubbed, or rather let down gently. I returned: 'Let's get this straight, you say I am for appeasement, are you then for war?' And he laughably replied 'Yes.'

I have no doubt that Duff, Anthony, Bobbety Cranborne . . . . and above all Winston are plotting to overthrow us. They see themselves as an alternative government, and waging and winning a war against Nazidom.

After an hour with Walter I saw how indignant he was that Alec Hardinge should dare to tick him off because he had been useful. He wonders at whose instigation his rebuke had been administered: I tried to convince him that it was Alec's own idea since he alone, except the King, saw the telegrams . . . Walter is distressed as he realises his influence is greater whilst he can remain unobtrusive. I begged him to go to Belgrade at once, and he is calling the Regent. But there is barely time before Paul pays his official visit to Rome on the 10th.

I felt antisocial tonight, and continued to dine like a Labour MP in the tea room off a scrambled egg and tea. No wines! I darted down the lobby avoiding people I could have joined. I warned Tommy Dugdale that the Glamour Boys are becoming restive again. I foresee trouble ahead when the news of the breakdown with Soviet Russia gets out! I had a confidential talk, too, with Ernest Brown who told me that one member of Cabinet (Oliver? Euan?) betrays its decisions to the Glamour Boys, as he is secretly one of them at heart. I don't think it can be Euan as he has not been there long enough. Perhaps it is Buck De La Warr, that ingenious gay play-Labour boy.

As I was writing these very lines a journalist rang me up to say that the news has just come that Litvinov[2] has resigned and has been replaced by Molotov.[3] Will he be shot? I certainly hope so. I rang up both Rab and Halifax and told them.

There was some consternation in the lobbies and David Margesson sent for me, as he wanted a line to give the boys. I rang Smith Square but the Butlers' butler refused to be disturbed, and there was no reply . . . there rarely is. I then walked on and although I threw pennies at the window, was unable to raise anyone in 3

---

1 The Conservative MP for Hereford.*

2 Meir Henoch Wallach-Finkelstein, who later took the *nom de guerre* Maxim Maximovich Litvinov (1876–1951), was the Soviet Union's People's Commissar for Foreign Affairs from 1930 to 1939. Far from being shot, he became Soviet Ambassador to the United States in 1941.

3 Vyacheslav Mikhailovich Skryabin (1890–1986) took the *nom de guerre* Molotov, related to the Russian word for a hammer, when still a teenager. A protégé of Stalin, he chaired the Council of People's Commissars from 1930 to 1941, in which post he ruthlessly forced through Stalin's policy of collectivisation, and was Minister of Foreign Affairs from 1939 to 1949 and from 1953 to 1956. In August 1939 he concluded the pact with Ribbentrop that opened the way for Germany to invade Poland.

Smith Square. It was 11.15. Rab retires early and so looks so old. The lobbies were still humming on my return and silly Jim Thomas rushed up and said 'If you let Russia slip through your fingers I will never forgive you.' The ass.

Excited, I walked home with Bartle Bull,[1] enchanted by this Litvinov development.

THURSDAY 4TH MAY

A House day, with four committees all meeting at 5 p.m., I somehow managed to attend them all. And we had the Prime Minister's speech on conscription: suave, even-tempered, it demolished the embarrassed Opposition. There is little life left in the Labour leaders.

Fearing a 'glamorous movement' I packed the Foreign Affairs Committee with sound Chamberlain chaps and we elected Sir John Wardlaw-Milne,[2] a semi-die-hard as chairman in the room of Jock McEwen, recently made a whip. The new chairman will be fair and will tolerate no nonsense from the glamour group, who are being tiresome today.

I was dining with Diana Cooper at the Dorchester where she had collected sixty chums in aid of a charity function. She is the past mistress of using other people; but she is so charming that one doesn't mind. (I must say I resent not being repaid the £10 I lent her in Geneva.)

The international news is almost the same, but there is a gradual, general lessening of tension.

FRIDAY 5TH MAY

The PM decided to make a statement in regards to Russia this morning, so we all assembled at the Foreign Office promptly at ten o'clock, and later drove to the House of Commons. At eleven the PM rose, and in fine fighting fettle he delivered a series of deadly blows to Attlee and others. He was scathing and revealed both his dislike of the 'Bollos'[3] and of Russia. The Edenites had intended to join forces over this issue, i.e., the entering into a pact with Russia, but none of them turned up. Rab and I were talking with David Margesson in our room and I made some slight remarks – 'the trouble with the Glamour Boys is that they can never get up. They are all (__)[4] at the 400 Club.' 'Or in bed together!' David Margesson

---

1 Bartle Brennan Bull (1902–50) was a Canadian-born barrister who sat as Conservative MP for Enfield from 1935 to 1945.
2 John Sydney Wardlaw-Milne (1879–1967) was Conservative MP for Kidderminster from 1922 to 1945. He was knighted in 1932. In July 1942 he was one of those who forced a vote of confidence in Churchill's premiership; it failed by 475 votes to 25.
3 Bolsheviks.
4 Thus in MS.

retorted. We all roared and he begged me not to repeat his remark. What does he know of such goings-on? I could tell him that his suspicions are partly justified.

There has been a swan tragedy. Elsa has sat for nearly six weeks on a large nest with her nine eggs! Last Wednesday she was disturbed; the eggs disappeared and she either ate them or they were stolen. Today they seem very dejected. How unlucky we are with our breeding at Kelvedon – the dog's puppies born dead, and now the swans are frustrated . . . and I, privately aching for more children.

This morning Walter Buccleuch rang me up and we had a long talk. He is still disturbed with our policy and implores us to go carefully with Russia, and not to plunge into an unnecessary war with Germany over Danzig. He regrets slightly recent expulsions of Germans from London. Yesterday he was commanded to Buck House and again shortly 'ticked off' by Alec Hardinge, who said that the King wanted to see him for five minutes. He was ushered into the presence and realised that the audience had been arranged by Alec Hardinge so that the King could rebuke Walter for his amateur diplomacy etc. Instead the King kept him for thirty-five minutes and listened intently to all Walter said and was impressed thereby, so sucks to that shit Hardinge. Walter now hates him and proposes to say so to the Kents, with whom he is lunching.

SATURDAY 6TH MAY

An unbelievable day, glorious weather, tulips and first blossom, a summery haze . . . England at its best. Loxleys, Friedrich [Fritzi] of Prussia, Brigid (and wouldn't it be divine if I could marry them off), John Coulson and Sheila Milbanke, annoyingly young and attractive are here.

I reread Colonel Beck's long-awaited reply to Hitler. It was made yesterday at Warsaw, and taking the cue from our advisers he was firm but conciliatory. Possibly after all there may be a peaceful solution of the Danzig question. 'God'[1] was in a rage yesterday and in the morning whilst he was going over Questions with Rab and Peter Loxley he delivered himself of an angry tirade against the Glamour Boys, more particularly Bobbety Cranborne, who is the most dangerous of the lot! Beware of rampant idealists. All Cecils are that.

The K and Q have sailed amongst much publicity for Canada and the States!

TUESDAY 9TH MAY

I took Rab at luncheon time to the Bath Club where we swam together. He has so little pleasure and complains constantly of the dullness of his life and his uninteresting background. No wonder: Sydney is a determined bore. Rab has little social sense, no lightness of touch; is not a man of the world: and he

---

1 Chamberlain.

is unpunctual; very rude, but has great charm which lends colour to his high intelligence. His capacity for work is immense; slowly he has become the PM's blue-eyed boy.

I had a long talk with Bill Astor in my room. He doesn't resent my rudeness to his mother[1] who was referred to yesterday in the debate as 'the member for Berlin'. She is giving a ball tonight to which we were uninvited. I shall never cross her threshold again. She is loathed in the House nowadays by all parties.

The Duke of Windsor is never well advised. His broadcast speech[2] last night was a fine performance but it was ill-timed. It was extraordinarily tactless of him to broadcast to the States on the eve of the King's arrival there. Naturally the gesture will be misconstrued. How else? I feel it is the Duchess of Windsor who, whilst clever, has never been a psychologist. Sheila Milbanke, who has been there recently, reported well of them; said they were both happy and charming.

The BBC did not relay the Duke's speech, which is a pity, but what else could it do?

WEDNESDAY 10TH MAY

All morning at the Foreign Office, intriguing and arranging matters. The hours pass in a confusion of secret telephone calls and conversations. The really only startling thing about my intrigues is that they always come off – all except my plot to get rid of Rex Leeper, who is the end. There was excitement this morning about our Russian negotiations, which I deplore. Halifax is unhappy about them. At one o'clock Rab and Peter Loxley crossed over to No. 10 to see the Prime Minister, but without the answer to the Private Notice Question by Attlee. I was sent to Halifax's room to fetch it; it was being hurriedly typed out, after revision. At length it came and Halifax cursorily glanced at it, and then tucked it under his right arm [and] remarked 'I'll take it over myself.' I went with him to No. 10 and for the first time in my life I noticed that he was [illegible] and irritable: his famous urbanity had deserted him. Indeed he was so petulant that I wondered whether I had annoyed him; but later Rab reassured me by remarking how 'on edge' the 'S of S' had been. The strain is getting him down somewhat: and I am told that the PM is showing signs of strain. That is the danger of the present government: it is almost a one-man show; thus should Neville collapse or die or resign the whole National Government would cave in; for regarding Edward Halifax, he is surrounded by comparative nonentities. I should find myself in the political wildness [sic], and I couldn't bear it. I should resign and write books . . . .

---

1 Lady Astor.
2 The Duke had made a broadcast from Verdun appealing for world peace.

The Russian statement was firstly read out at the end of Questions as an answer to Attlee: it was well received. The PM's heart however is Hitler's, as much as he may deplore the Führer's methods and resent his treachery.

At five o'clock I left in my grand green Rolls for Southend where I picked up Honor at the Grand Hotel. She had been there, poor darling, since 3 p.m., when she had escorted Lady Halifax to the Kursaal.[1] Lady Halifax, at my request, had opened the annual Hospital bazaar, and had been warmly received. We dined with the Mayor at Porter's Green, and contrary to my expectations, I rather liked the Bishop of Chelmsford,[2] who is a solid 'leftie'. He was amiable and undistinguished and it was obvious that he was unaware of my hostility to him (nor does he know that I sent 300 pamphlets attacking him anonymously to my constituents). I hope to get him translated, and Archdeacon Gowing[3] elevated to the see. The Bishop preached a good conventional sermon at St Mary's Church later: we all attended in company with the Corporation. It was the twenty-fifth anniversary of the founding of the diocese.

Honor was sweet and patient and after eight hours in Southend, we drove back to Kelvedon where Fritzi was awaiting us. He is living at Kelvedon now: he was gay and charming and very funny about his step-grandmother, the Kaiser's second wife,[4] whom he describes as a 'plumpish purplish woman' . . . Bed by 11.30. Kelvedon, as ever, a miracle of beauty – Lady Halifax was much impressed.

THURSDAY 11TH MAY

Honor, Prince Fritzi and I motored up to London early. We had a gay conversation about Bill Tufnell and his dinner party at Langleys on Tuesday, and how completely humourless he is . . . and about the Prince of Wales, I mean, Duke of Windsor, and his really annoying ignorance. Fritzi told us how he had been to Berlin during the Republic, and had been taken to Potsdam where he was conducted through the Neues Palais and driven through their private park. Yet he did not call at Cecilienhof to pay his respects to Fritzi's parents, who, after all, were closely related to our royal house. It is typical of the Duke of Windsor and explains his fall. He never knew anyone until a few months before the abdication!

Lord Perth,[5] somewhat to my surprise, called on me this morning and we had an hour's conversation. He was riveting about Italian policy; said that originally Italy (much as Yugoslavia is doing now) had decided it was preferable to have a

---

1 Southend-on-Sea's great amusement park.
2 Henry Albert Wilson (1876–1961) was Bishop of Chelmsford from 1929 to 1950. One of his main causes was opposition to a relaxation of the divorce laws.
3 Ellis Norman Gowing (1883–1960), an Australian by birth, was Archdeacon of Southend from 1938 to 1953. Channon never secured him his bishopric.
4 Princess Hermine Reuss of Greiz (1887–1947) married Kaiser Wilhelm II in 1922.
5 7th Earl of Perth, Ambassador to Rome since 1933.*

friendly Germany on the Brenner[1] to a hostile one; and Mussolini had not wanted to fight her alone. This was the beginning of the axis which Anthony's disastrous policy consolidated. At Stresa[2] we had not once mentioned Abyssinia, and by Simon's silence and MacDonald's aloofness, Mussolini had concluded that he was free to proceed in Abyssinia . . . more interesting still, probably as it's fresh news, was Perth's impressions of the Albanian adventure. He was not shocked by it; it had long been understood that Italy had a claim over Albania, and had even at one moment been given it at Versailles! For many years now Italy had exercised a sort of semi-suzerainty over Albania and had paid large subsidies for the development of the country to King Zog, who latterly became both ungrateful and insubordinate. On April 4th, Tuesday, Ciano had sent him an ultimatum, which he was convinced that King Zog would accept, to the effect that Italy meant business and that he was to become a sort of puppet, like Farouk[3] in Egypt. Zog procrastinated, began to take defensive measures; and on Good Friday the 7th the Italians walked in. Had they waited until after the Easter festival, say on Easter Tuesday, they would have lost more lives, and killed more Albanians. Perth thinks the whole affair regrettable, but inevitable and exaggerated.

Rab and I walking back to the Foreign Office met Kingsley Wood[4] who confided us his fears that 'God' is becoming really fagged out and shows increasing signs of serious strains. Later in the afternoon he, God, made his great speech to a mass meeting of Women Conservatives in the Albert Hall. The speech was written, all except the personal touches, by Rab, and the PM had an unprecedented reception. Never in England has there been such enthusiasm shown and he was much touched, and apparently it did him good. He came here (House of Commons) for a moment and returned to No. 10 Downing Street to be massaged at 7 p.m.

It was decided to make a statement of our agreement with Turkey[5] tomorrow, and a Private Notice Question was drafted. I tried to find Mr Attlee to give it to him, and at length found him drinking in the Smoking Room with Ronnie Tree, and three lords! Titchfield,[6] James Willoughby de Eresby,[7] and

---

1 The Brenner Pass is the border between Italy and Austria, so since the *Anschluss* of March 1938 Italy's border with the Third Reich.
2 The conference of 1935 between the United Kingdom, France and Italy that reaffirmed the Treaty of Locarno and made common cause to contain Nazi Germany.
3 His Sultanic Highness Farouk bin Fuad, Hereditary Prince of Egypt and Sudan (1920–65), succeeded his father as King Farouk of Egypt and the Sudan in 1936.
4 Then Secretary of State for Air.
5 That the two countries should co-operate in the event of war breaking out in the Mediterranean.
6 William Arthur Henry Cavendish-Bentinck (1893–1977), by courtesy Marquess of Titchfield until 1943, when he succeeded his father as 7th Duke of Portland. He was Conservative MP for Newark from 1922 until 1943.
7 Gilbert James Heathcote-Drummond-Willoughby (1907–83), by courtesy Lord Willoughby de Eresby from 1910 to 1951, when he succeeded his father (qv) as 3rd Earl of Ancaster. He was Conservative MP for Rutland and Stamford from 1933 to 1950.

Bobbety Cranborne. Such is Socialism in England! I wondered which was the more pleased, Attlee or Ronnie Tree. I walked along the lobby with Attlee and he was surprisingly amiable, as he always is in private. He took the Question but doesn't know the answer: nor do we yet. There is still doubt as to whether it will be Bipartite, the Turks and us, or Tripartite, [illegible, but indicating the UK], Turkey and France. The Turkeys mistrust the Frogs, and rightly . . .

Walter Buccleuch rang up and wanted to see me urgently: I smuggled him in our room at the House of Commons, as we don't wish to awake the suspicion of 'the Glamour group'. I told him to drive direct to the Speaker's Yard. He did: even so he narrowly missed running into Bobbety Cranborne who in a priest-like gait sauntered, if saunter a Cecil can!, across the Members' Yard. He sang out to me just as Walter appeared, but the latter slid into a doorway. Long talk with Walter in our room as we waited for Rab, who was late – as he always is – to arrive. Between us, Buccleuch and us, we have stopped this rot of expelling further Germans from this country. He says that at no time in all history has a foreign statesman gone out of his way to be so complimentary about England as was the Führer in his great Reichstag speech: and yet he has had not a word of thanks, nor acknowledgement either from the press or the government. He is right. We talked, too, of the Regent, who is today in Rome on an official visit being received by Mussolini, and entertained by King Victor Emmanuel etc. Rab came in, and surprised to see us, kept Walter in conversation for an hour. Meanwhile I had taken steps and no further expulsions will now take place.

Blum is in London: he is the real architect of many of our woes and it is revolting to see the Churchill gang kowtowing to this Jewish agitator who has done infinite harm.

I saw an unexpected letter at the Foreign Office. Halifax has arranged for Queen Mary to have copies of all confidential telegrams sent abroad. A box will be dispatched to Marlborough House – a quite unorthodox, but excellent procedure. Possibly this is a temporary measure to last during the visit of the K and Q to America. But more and more we are being ruled by a small group of thirty to forty people – including myself! Alec Dunglass and I have woven a net around the PM whom we love, admire, worship and would protect from interfering, unimportant noodles. Both he and Halifax are oligarchic in mind and method.

FRIDAY 12TH MAY

The Turkish agreement was read out today. Attlee asked the PM the question I had given him but ten minutes before he decided to postpone giving the answer until just before the House rose as we had secret hopes that the Turks would by then complete arrangements with France and the agreement could have been Tripartite instead of Bipartite. However no such news arrived; and when we telephoned to the Embassy in Paris, we learned that there had been a hitch. 'Turkeys don't like Frogs.' The French, as usual, are so uncompromising, and refuse to give an inch and so lose miles all around.

SUNDAY 14TH MAY

Honor rang up cheerfully from Paris.

The publicity about the royal progress across the Atlantic is nauseating:[1] one would think no one had ever crossed the ocean before.

MONDAY 15TH MAY

Rab prophesies trouble over Danzig during the next few days; all along he has dreaded the middle of May and advised his wife to curtail her American trip. She got back tonight.

The Russian reply[2] has come: it is a refusal of our terms. We are playing, of course, for time as both Halifax and the PM are reluctant to embrace the Russian bear!

To avoid offending Diana [Cooper] I answered her SOS and went to 34 Chapel Street to her cocktail party to meet a Finnish woman: by so doing I missed a brace of divisions, and was rudely treated by Lady Colefax who accused me of having a 'swollen head'; of being important; of being grand, etc. I could have throttled her; instead, in offering a lift to Rob Bernays, she insisted on coming, and thus used my car. I was civil as I am sorry for her. How all this little group resent my attitude, and more, my boredom with them! They all seem so trivial and uninteresting, even Diana. I am sick unto death of the lot – Diana has made her house attractive and the library will be charming indeed. Randolph Churchill looked 30,[3] he must weigh sixteen stone.

The division bell seemed never to stop tonight. The PM sent for Rab but I explained . . . that he had gone to Waterloo to fetch his wife on her return from the States. More and more the PM relies on Rab's judgement. Both regret the Polish guarantee: both deplored it at the time. Both are determined to prevent an Anglo-Russian alliance which is the pet scheme of the left-pink clique in the Foreign Office. The Foreign Office really needs a purge.

1　It may have been: but the long-term effect of the King and Queen's visit did no harm when it came to consolidating Anglo-American relations both before and after America's entry to the war in December 1941.

2　To suggestions of co-operation against the Nazi threat. The Russians, at the time, were seeking to make a non-aggression pact with the Nazis, not to fight them.

3　He was almost 28, so this was not too appalling.

TUESDAY 16TH MAY

I had lobbied all the ministers I could catch as against a Russian alliance. Sam Hoare was affectionate, friendly and sensible: so was Ernest Brown, who told me how pleased he is with Alan . . .

Nevile Henderson's dispatch for the year 1938 in which he describes the whole terrifying history of Germany for that year makes memorable reading. I would do anything to get hold of a copy for sake-keeping; but it is not allowed outside the Foreign Office. It is a brilliant résumé, and paints the Führer as a mystical, vague bad-tempered ogre.

The PM was humorous at Question Time, and later smiled as he walked slowly by me. Reggie Dorman-Smith pinched my bottom during the division. It seems we shall have our 'hols' curtailed. Harold Balfour, whom I drove home last night, says we shall sit in September. He is still sorely smitten with Helen's[1] charms. It is a hot affair at full heat.

I gather it has been now decided not to embrace the Russian bear, but to hold out a hand and accept its clammy paw. No more. The worst of both worlds; the traditional Baldwin policy. The people in this country are either mad or blind or both on the subject of Germany. I think it is an illness of the spirit: so much hate is engendered in concentration camps and elsewhere, and being in the atmosphere its germs affect the most unexpected people. One can almost tell now at a glance who and who has not been caught by the virus. Certainly a moment's conversation is sufficient. And those suffering for this mental malady loathe the healthy-minded and pursue us with their malice.

Honor got back from Paris by aeroplane tonight: we talked on the telephone but she was already asleep when I came in.

WEDNESDAY 17TH MAY

Embrace the Bear, or not to embrace? Every day there is a change and I am plotting hard to prevent a Russian alliance unless there are sufficient safeguards. Dunglass is helping me. The chances are about even, but I fear we may give in and thus imperil our dignity, and our future.

FRIDAY 19TH MAY

A supreme, superb parliamentary day in which I revelled. It was the Debate on Foreign Affairs, and Russia, was, of course, the *clou*.[2] Arrived at the Foreign Office at ten, and at three minutes to eleven we jumped into my green Rolls, and arrived in the very nick of time. The PM looked tired and a touch rattled. I doubted

1 Helen Fitzgerald.
2 The main attraction.

whether he would make a good speech. The debate . . . opened by Lloyd George who spoke for fifty-eight minutes. I was immediately facing him and more than once caught his blue eye. There were flashes of fun, extraordinary vivacity for a man of his age, but his speech moved no one and lacked his usual brilliance. The House was patient but bored; the Gallery, of course strained every ear, whilst the old wizard poured out his ineffectual, untrue, irrelevant criticisms. I wondered, was he at the beginning of his dotage? Or merely the decline of his great powers? He challenged us again and again on Russia: why didn't we come out into the open and embrace her? I looked up at Maisky, the smirking cat, who leant over the railing of the ambassadorial gallery and sat so sinister and smug. (Are we to place our honour, our safety into those bloodstained hands?) . . . I carried in messages, papers and telegrams for the Foreign Office. The PM was courteous and smiling. Once or twice he snorted as he does when disgruntled. He loathes LG[1] . . . then we had Attlee, and his speech was less vehement than usual. Indeed it was, as the PM later described it, a somewhat thoughtful speech. He is a bee without a sting, and today there was merely a buzz. He is much more effective when mild. He even held the House, no easy task for the dull little man, who apart from his 'Spanish influenza'[2] is not a bad fellow. Socially he is pleasant. The Bloomsbury intellectual.

The PM rose without enthusiasm and I think the House expected an indifferent speech. So at first it seemed; but after a sly snub for Maisky, whom in veiled language the PM accused of betraying our negotiations to the press (true!), he warmed to his brief. The PM went on; after touching on Turkey he proceeded to expand on a general theory of present-day foreign policy and he became magnificent, calm, spacious, and added comic relief by several playful shafts aimed at Lloyd George. The PM referred to Russia and the difficulties we encountered with other countries apropos of our Russian negotiations, not mentioning any country, particularly Poland by name. To go back: there hangs a tale about this: Winston Churchill had in his pocket a letter from the President of Poland saying that he has no objection to a Russian alliance; Winston intended to interject and read out the letter, thus sabotaging the PM's remarks. He told several people, and I heard it from Jim Thomas, who stupidly taunted me with Winston's triumph-to-be. I was in the Aye lobby at the time and hurriedly scribbled a pencil line repeating what I had heard. I passed it to the PM, who smilingly acknowledged it. Luckily this was done – as at the end of the PM's speech he was hard-pressed by the House, and by LG in particular, to say 'what countries' the PM had in mind. Old Winston not three yards away, and looking like an enraged bull, sat

1 A loathing that went back almost a quarter of a century, when Lloyd George asked
   Chamberlain to be Director of National Service during the Great War, and then refused to
   support his initiatives.
2 His failure to support Franco. Ironically, when Attlee became Prime Minister, good relations with Franco's Spain were very much a priority.

fuming and fumbling his notes . . . with the Polish letter probably amongst them. His disappointment was obvious and later (he spoke next) he referred to 'the cool and deft parliamentary reply' which the PM had made. How he and Neville loathe each other! A deep hatred: more than a psychological antipathy.[1]

The PM had successfully demolished Lloyd George and the really absurd arguments he used. By then we, the govt, were winning. Winston, however, was unhelpful, pro-Russian and I must say, funny. J. J. Davidson,[2] the uncouth Labour member for Maryhill, followed with a surprisingly foolish protest against the presence of our Ambassador at the Victory March in Madrid today. I had arranged with the Speaker to get the creature called so that we might head off an adjournment debate on the subject next week. Victor Raikes, aside from one surprising slip about Yugoslavia, made a most sensible contribution; probably the wisest speech of the day. He was followed by that platitudinous dull, Anthony Eden, who said nothing new. He is a puppet of the extremists in the Foreign Office. Those mandarins have too long exercised a sinister power, and Anthony has ever been their mouthpiece. He is the ventriloquist's doll of old Leeper . . . . it was a sad and snubbing experience for Anthony, since at one moment there were only fourteen members in the Chamber. A few filtered in to hear him, but at no time, although he spoke for half an hour, was the House crowded or even interested . . . Butler had sensed what was coming, and whispered to me to fetch a Cabinet minister at once from somewhere as it looked discourteous to Anthony, and he feared trouble. I got up and went to the lobbies, but I took my time about it. I saw no one: and I deliberately waited for about five minutes, lit a cigarette went into the lavatory etc., and at last went to the dining room. I wanted to draw attention to the poor attendance in the Chamber but for the opposite motive. I found old Walter Elliot finishing off a ripe Camembert and persuaded him to come and sit on the bench. As he was getting up the division bell rang – progress was being reported!! Anthony's humiliation was complete; but the Glamour Boys registered their support of him by abstaining in the voting, all except [Ronald] Cartland who actually voted against us! . . . Archie Sinclair, dull, monotonous, and flamboyant, wound up for the Opposition. Then came Rab who summed up adequately, indeed with more brilliance than usual. He even taunted Winston C. I sat immediately behind him, interested and proud. At length we divided 96 to 220. Those Glamorous friends, most of them, abstained.

Alec Dunglass says that we had not lost yet: we are not yet married to the Russian bear.

---

1 Channon misjudged the relationship between Chamberlain and Churchill, which was one
   of more respect than he seems to have realised.
2 John James Davidson (1898–1976) was MP for Glasgow Maryhill from 1935 to 1945.

MONDAY 22ND MAY

I was rushed and also sleepy, as I never sleep at Kelvedon, and so after three nights I could not keep awake. So I stole into the library and dozed for an hour whilst I ought to have been on duty on the PPS bench. I went home to dress and took Honor to dine at 17 Grosvenor Place, the Guinnesses' London house which they had lent to the Dufferins. It was a big, boring dinner. Honor was next to Lord Astor who was charming to her, and to me: I escorted Lady Astor, who looked well. Evidently my stinging remarks hurt her as I hope they did, for she complained to Honor that she had only praised our enchanting child and I had turned on her 'like a lunatic'. I don't know why she should alone be privileged to be rude, insulting and interfering with people. If more people had the courage to answer her, she wouldn't be so wild in her remarks . . . Lady Baldwin in black velvet and a bogus tiara was next to Basil. She looked quaint, indeed. Bad food: grand house but old-fashioned and many of the family pictures need cleaning . . . Honor looked like a grand duchess with her emeralds, and was in great good looks. She went on to a charity film show, was 'presented' to the Duchess of Gloucester. I returned to the House in time to do yeoman service, and Rab later wound up for the first day of the big debate, which on the whole has not done too badly for the government. Rab made one of his typical stonewalling speeches; it meant little or nothing, and was deliberately dull. It is his gift to conceal his personality and personal opinions and convictions, which are often strong, with a cloak of what seems bureaucratic neutrality. Then the House is unaware of his strong right views.

This evening a telephone message came from Geneva from Lord Halifax that he wanted Rab to go out there tomorrow to take his place at the council. I am not altogether unsuspicious that such a summons at this particular juncture in *Weltpolitik*[1] is not without motive, as Halifax on Wednesday at the coming Cabinet will advocate a Russian alliance; for having jumped that way, he has now jumped further than anyone, and, knowing Rab's violent dislike of any such association and his influence over the Prime Minister, he may want him out of the way. I am opposed to Rab going, and notably against the Russian pact. If one lies down with dogs one gets covered with fleas . . .

TUESDAY 23RD MAY

At 8.30 Harold Balfour picked me up and I whisked him in my green Rolls to Northolt Aerodrome for the giant air display attended by members of both Houses of Parliament. The hoi polloi of guests drove down in charabancs. It was a great day for Harold and he enjoyed his hour of glory, playing host to the great and the little. It was brilliantly arranged, a hitchless programme . . . hot weather,

---

1 Literally, world politics: international relations.

impressive display, good lunch for 500 people, fighting planes . . . Harold was most engaging. He had my car drawn up outside the tent and we both enjoyed our little moment of triumph as we drove off together.

Back at the Foreign Office by 3.15, just in time to see Rab before he left for Geneva. I sent him to Croydon in my car accompanied by his doting, boring wife. I went to the House of Commons, and listened to Winston's tirade against the White Paper.[1] The government had a bad day, and when the actual question was put our majority was only 89, a shockingly low number for a three-line whip. David Margesson was furious and the government was visibly shaken. Several ministers abstained or [illegible] excuses for non-voting, that silly old maid, Walter Elliot, amongst them. But I saw Rob Bernays, who always protests . . . . troop into the govt lobby. There was a shock of surprise.

I fear the worst about Russia tomorrow. Tonight Rab takes the train from Paris and arrives at 5 a.m. at Geneva; Lord Halifax is coming back, their trains will cross, like their policies. Someone asked in India, 'What is the Viceroy thinking?' 'Whom did he see last?' was the retort.

WEDNESDAY 24TH MAY

With Rab in Geneva there was more work to be done at the Foreign Office in preparing Questions; and the sitting of the Cabinet delayed us. About one o'clock the news came through: the bear is in the bag. We are tied to Russia: we have embraced the monster. At least, so they seem to think. But Halifax has been shrewder than one thought: after prolonged consultation with Maisky in Geneva they worked out a formula for mutual co-operation against aggression, based on the Covenant of the League.[2] Thus really our new obligations mean everything and yet nothing. A military alliance might have been the signal for an immediate war, 'blown the gaffe'; but a Geneva alliance is so flimsy, so idealistic and unpractical that it can only cause the Nazis to poke fun at us. Halifax has really done well.

I lunched with Emerald; and was next to David Margesson; but I am so tired that I was stupid and a bore . . . . I left before the end of lunch to rush to the Foreign Office to pick up the red box, and the typed statement about Russia which the PM later read out. It was a colourless affair, merely said in hopeful terms that it was now believed that an agreement would shortly be reached. The House was enchanted; but the terms are still unagreed upon and I wonder whether the Russians will not run out: they are principally determined to get Chamberlain out . . . at all costs. Until now they had been outmanoeuvred; but I feel they are

1 The White Paper was about the future governance of Palestine, for which Britain held a League of Nations mandate.
2 The 1920 Covenant of the League of Nations attempted to prevent countries going to war, and arose out of the Versailles Peace Conference of 1919.

not yet defeated. I met Alec Cadogan in the lavatory and told him I thought it was outrageous of us to embrace the foul bear. Necessity makes for unpleasant bedfellows, he remarked. He went on that it was better to be allied to Russia than to be eaten alive.

We are now faced with another ticklish problem: the *de facto* recognition of the Czechoslovakian conquest. The Germans announce that they will no longer recognise extra-territorial rights of diplomatic representations at Prague: thus we must ask for a new exequatur.[1] We have, in fact, decided to do so. The Foreign Office waited to announce that fact today, whether from commonsense motives, or to deal the poor PM another deft blow, I am not decided. Peter Loxley crossed over to No. 10 and had twenty minutes alone with the PM who was in high spirits, and seemingly not too depressed by our Russian entanglements. He remarked however that he wished to send 'the boys away happy' for Whitsuntide and did not propose to make any statement in regard to Czechoslovakia. At lunch David Margesson told me that the PM had consulted him earlier in the morning on the subject, and that it was David who objected to a public discussion. David is down: angry about the low Palestinian majority, discouraged by recent by-elections.[2]

Queen Mary's accident[3] seems to have been more serious than it at first seemed. Her Essex visit is cancelled; so she will not come to Kelvedon after all. Perhaps she will never come now!!

I sat in my room working and writing. At eight I rang up Rab in Geneva and at the same time talked to Sydney in Smith Square on another line: thus acting as liaison between husband and wife. I conveyed to him the story of how Halifax had completely dominated the Cabinet this morning over Russia. In the midst of our triangular conversation the division bell rang faintly; I could not vote. Later I reported to the whips that the bell was broken and I had not heard it.

Worn out, I had a snack in the tea room. Dick Law,[4] the silent, boring, friendless son of Bonar Law sat, interpretative and unhappy. He is the world's greatest bore: only Ronnie Cartland likes him; but the German boys had recently

1   This legal term describes the authority one sovereign state gives to the diplomatic representation of another to operate officially in their country.

2   The Tories had not lost any recent by-elections but their vote was down. That day, the party lost a by-election in Kennington, London, to the Labour Party.

3   Queen Mary's car was in a collision with a lorry in Putney on 23 May, as she returned to Marlborough House from a visit to the Royal Horticultural Society's gardens at Wisley in Surrey. Her car overturned leaving her with 'bruising and shock' according to her doctors' bulletin.

4   Richard Kidston Law (1901–80) was the youngest son of Andrew Bonar Law (1858–1923), Prime Minister 1922–3. He sat as Conservative MP for Hull South West from 1931 to 1945, when he lost his seat; he sat for Kensington South from November 1945 to 1950, and then for Haltemprice until 1954, when he was raised to the peerage as 1st Baron Coleraine. He held a succession of middle-ranking ministerial posts in Churchill's wartime administration.

taken him up slightly because of his disloyalty to the PM that in their eyes is virtue enough . . . The PM is almost cockahoop as he is going to Scotland tonight and will not again darken the House until June 5th – to his infinite joy.

Seeing Tommy Dugdale speeding by the door, I seized such an opportune moment for a private chat. I suggested that Rab be made Lord Privy Seal, yet kept in his present job: such an arrangement might well be arranged and it would not only give Rab a seat in the Cabinet but would strengthen the PM's hand. Tommy's black dancing mischievous eyes lit up – it was an idea after his own heart. He asked me for a few days to 'nose about' and advised me not 'to run it' – yet. But I saw that I had made an impression.

THURSDAY 25TH MAY

John Simon is taking the foreign affairs debate tomorrow raised by the Opposition on the adjournment; it was a struggle to induce him to agree, and he insisted that Rab be present 'to hold his hand' – a monstrous stipulation. Peter Loxley and I had hoped to get him off this added chore and I paid several frantic visits to the Whips' Office, but to no avail. He must come back, Simon insisted. He was adamant. He is always bloody-minded, and poor Conant,[1] his abject long-suffering PPS, too was played out. We rang up Geneva from the Private Secretaries' Room . . . We told Rab that he must return; so he is leaving Geneva tonight by humble train for Paris.

FRIDAY 26TH MAY

Peter Loxley – ever dignified and calm – and I drove to Croydon to meet the Paris plane, which was late. Rab descended dressed in his House of Commons clothes. Short coat: striped trousers. We rushed him to the House of Commons, but that ass Smale[2] lost his way and we seemed headed for Brighton. A moment of panic: perhaps we shouldn't get back in time at all! Confusion, nerves; we turned back and after racing for miles arrived at Battersea Park. We were saved; but only barely so. Rab read out the typed answers to his Questions which Peter had prepared. We reached the House of Commons at 11.02, and luckily they were still at prayers. We had one brief moment, at then the Questions were called. He answered them very well, and no one was aware of the flurry we had been in.

A morning like this takes days off one's life . . . I was nervous, irritable and unattractive – but so handsomely dressed that I felt self-confident although Dennis

---

1 Roger John Edward Conant (1899–1973) was Conservative MP for Chesterfield from 1931 to 1935; for Bewdley from 1937 to 1950; and for Rutland and Stamford from 1950 to 1959. He was Comptroller of the Household – a senior whip – from 1951 to 1954, when he was created 1st Bt.
2 Channon's chauffeur.

Herbert[1] asked me where my carnation was! The Chair notices everything!! I read the telegrams as I sat on the bench, and seeing that Princess Irene of Greece[2] is to announce her engagement shortly to the Duke of Spoleto,[3] I rang through to 3 Belgrave Square to talk to the Duchess of Kent about it. She was out, and later rang me to the excitement of the staff. I told her the news, and I was amazed that she had not heard of it. She was rather piqued. Spoleto, she told me, had been on the verge of marrying her nearly fourteen years ago, but had run out. Since then he has cavorted himself 'to the left and right': now, less attractive, he is prepared to settle down … Half an hour's talk with Princess Marina. Spoleto, I have always liked: he is gay, inconsequent, wonderful-looking. He rather flirted with Honor on our honeymoon, but she prefers Aosta.[4] Princess Irene is a fine Nordic female of charm, beauty and successes. For a brief moment it was whispered that if possibly King Edward VIII would be induced to look at her …! – but he wouldn't. She has not the character, personality nor charm of her eldest sister, Princess Helen of Romania! Still it is a good match and ought to dispel rumours of an Italian occupation of Greece.

Rab and I, a brace of crocks, drove to Kelvedon in the heat, and he changed into his car.[5] I was grateful for the gossip and drive down. He was more affectionate and captivating than ever before and he startled me by saying that a vast reshuffle, reorganisation of the Foreign Office is about to take place. All my prayers, all my intrigue are coming to bear fruit! The whole affair is in hand. Rab asked my advice and we agreed on the following appointments, if they could be brought about:

Sir Ronald Campbell,[6] now Minister at Belgrade to be Ambassador in Paris.

Ronald Campbell,[7] Minister in Paris to be Minister in Belgrade (a curious [illegible], the two men with the same name, more or less swapping posts).

Oliver Harvey (the dangerous, sly 'rapier') to be Minister in Paris.

1 Dennis Henry Herbert (1869–1947) was Conservative MP for Watford from 1918 to 1943, and Deputy Speaker – Chairman of Ways and Means – from 1931 to 1943. He was raised to the peerage as 1st Baron Hemingford in 1943.
2 Princess Irene of Greece and Denmark (1904–74) was daughter of King Constantine I of Greece. She would in 1941 become Queen Consort of Croatia.
3 Prince Aimone (1900–48), Duke of Spoleto. In 1942 he became the 4th Duke of Aosta on the death of his elder brother (*vide infra*).
4 Amedeo Umberto Isabella Luigi Filippo Maria Giuseppe Giovanni di Savoia-Aosta (1898– 1942) succeeded his father as 3rd Duke of Aosta in 1931. From 1937 to 1941 he was Viceroy of Italian East Africa. He was captured by the British and interned in Kenya, where he died of malaria and tuberculosis.
5 That is, picked up his car, which he had left at Kelvedon.
6 Ronald Hugh Campbell (1883–1953) had joined the Diplomatic Service in 1906, had been in Belgrade since 1935, and moved to Paris where he was in post until the fall of France. Evacuated by the Royal Navy, he served as Ambassador to Portugal from 1940 to 1945. He was knighted in 1936.
7 Ronald Ian Campbell (1890–1983) served in Belgrade as Envoy Extraordinary and Minister Plenipotentiary from 1939 to 1941. He held the same post in Washington DC from 1941 to 1944, and was Ambassador to Egypt from 1946 to 1950. He was knighted in 1941.

Nevile Butler[1] to become 1st Private Secretary to Lord Halifax in Harvey's place.

And a grand clean sweep of the major three criminals, or mandarins par excellence; Sir Orme Sargent, Laurence Collier, and Rex Leeper. They will be swept away. This is our plan, our great purge: I can think of little else. But how to wait until September? It is a risk: a war, an election, Neville might die or resign . . . all of this should have happened a year ago. The PM is slow but sure. What, I wonder, will happen to Vansittart in this first-class Palace-revolution-to-be?

Rab roamed about the garden; we were friendly and affectionate together; more than ever before. Kelvedon looked its best and the green, and the flaming azaleas were balm to our tired eyes and overworked and overstretched nerves. He left for Stanstead [Hall]. Honor and I had a quiet evening.

SATURDAY 27TH MAY

No sleep last night. But a glorious supreme day of sun and water-bathing. I am too tired to read, to write, to concentrate, or even to decide . . . and deciding is what I like best.

No party, thank the Lord and no war now. The Martian[2] clouds seem to be receding. I think we are safe until August, or, more probably September. Hitler is fuming, sulking at Berchtesgaden. We are all having a much more pleasant holiday than at Easter!

Rab in the car yesterday gave me a full and dramatic account of a recent meeting which he arranged at 3 Smith Square: there were present only the German Ambassador, Dirksen; Halifax and himself. It was a quiet, civil meeting lasting nearly two hours – but Dirksen was unable to reassure Halifax sufficiently to torpedo our negotiations with the Bear.

TUESDAY 30TH MAY

Rab rang up and wanted to come to luncheon, but as Honor went to London for the day, I Houdini-ed out of it! Lazed alone all day, lunched with my divine child whom I could eat. I love him so much.

WEDNESDAY 31ST MAY

I drove to London early, dictated letters, had my hair cut by my usual Figaro,[3] who on Sunday shaved poor Philip Sassoon. He is dying: there is just a ray of

---

1 Nevile Montagu Butler (1893–1973) was Minister at the British Embassy in Washington DC from 1940 to 1941, and then headed the Foreign Office's North American Department from 1941 to 1944. He was Ambassador to Brazil from 1947 to 1951 and to the Netherlands from 1952 to 1954. He was knighted in 1947.

2 *Sic*: he means 'martial'.

3 The eponymous barber in Rossini's *The Barber of Seville* is called Figaro.

hope, as he still wants to live. Went to the Foreign Office where there is no news at all: everyone, including Halifax, is away. There were some disturbing telegrams, particularly a long report sent from Percy Loraine[1] of his recent interview with Mussolini, who was grim and glum. He asked Percy Loraine whether it was still in Italy's interests, in view of an encirclement policy, to adhere to the Anglo-Italian agreement. He said that he was thinking of renouncing it; did not say that he would do so. Percy Loraine took a firm line with him, and the meeting while scarcely cordial, passed off well enough. The termination of the Anglo-Italian agreement is thus in the air. I don't think it will occur: but if it did, it would be a smashing blow to poor Neville.

I lunched with the Kents, and probably talked too much. The house was gay with flowers and very magnificent. They are entertaining heavily and had had the Kingsley Woods etc. to dine last evening, and tonight *inter alia* the Shakespeare Morrisons. Princess Marina looked lovely but thin and tired. That lunatic Mrs Corey[2] was next to me, and she kept repeating tactless observations, 'Mr Bullitt – you know, Chips – the American Ambassador in Paris – is madly in love with the Duchess of Windsor.' Twice she said this, and Princess Marina on my left, turned away . . . Emerald was gay and amusing but she is never at her best with royalty and becomes a touch reserved and restrained. Good food. Princess Marina and I had long talks about Hitler and the approaching visit of the Regent to him. She also said that on Friday after I had told her of Princess Irene's engagement she had happened to speak to Princess Olga on the telephone from Belgrade. She, too, had heard nothing; and so she put through a call to Athens to Irene! Princess Marina . . . dripped with sapphires. She was scathing about Geoffrey Lloyd whose unbred manners offend her.

I had an hour with our financial secretary, Captain Verschoyle,[3] trying to get our bills down. The household accounts etc. come to about £1000 per month and I can never succeed in reducing them substantially.

I, too, had an interview with our doctor, Law, who examined me. He says my heart is tired and sluggish, my nerves worn out, and my feet so flat that I may need an operation. He wanted me to go away for a holiday for two months but I refused to leave the House of Commons, and the Foreign Office. He says I am naturally strong, but I am killing myself.

---

1 Percy Lyham Loraine (1880–1961) had joined the Diplomatic Service in 1904 and was Ambassador to Italy from 1939 to 1940.*

2 Mabelle Gilman (1874–1960) was an American actress who retired from the stage in 1907 when she married the industrialist William Ellis Corey. He bought her, among other things, a chateau in France, where she was captured by the invading Germans in 1940 and interned until 1942. She and Corey divorced in 1923.

3 Frederick Hildyard Hawkins Stuart Verschoyle (1894–1961), who served in the Great War in the Royal Inniskilling Fusiliers and retired in the rank of captain. He was an employee of the Guinness family.

I returned to Kelvedon depressed and worn out, but cheered up somewhat after champagne. Honor was sympathetic: she is looking very lovely now. Very lovely indeed. But she goes up to London mysteriously (I think to see a doctor), and comes back. It is always in the morning. She went yesterday and goes again tomorrow.

THURSDAY 1ST JUNE

Honor left at 9.30 on one of her mysterious London jaunts. Paul was very naughty and obstreperous: I left after.

We decided not to go to Maimie Lygon's[1] operatic wedding this afternoon. She is marrying Prince Vsevolod of Russia[2] in the Greek Church. He is dull, grave and nice, and resembles his uncle King Alexander[3] who was both good and intelligent. Maimie may become, in some senses at least, another Catherine the Great. Yet another chapter in the great Lygon saga.

Bill Tufnell came over from Langleys. What a charming bore he is. I am tempted to make him fashionable.

SATURDAY 3RD JUNE

The Iveaghs had chucked us for the West End as my brilliant (and adored and adorable) *belle-mère* has one of her attacks of nervous indigestion which come to her when she is tired. She has been exhausted by her late nights and taking out Brigid to debutante balls!

Philip Sassoon died today. He will be a loss to the London pageant as no one infused so much colour and personality. He was sleek, clever, amiable, but treacherous and snobbish; but he was kindly yet fickle, gay yet moody and entertained with oriental lavishness in his three rather fatiguing palaces of which Trent[4] is the loveliest. Philip exerted an enormous and unfortunate influence on a section of London society, and on the Air Force. He was invidious, cloying, vicious, yet most pleasant and witty and talked with an accent all his own – it has been much imitated! 'His teeth rattled like dice in a box' – 'it was so quiet at Lympne[5] one could hear the dogs barking at Beauvais' – typical of his clichés! He was a homosexual; but there was never an open scandal, although much

---

1 Lady Mary 'Maimie' Lygon (1910–82), third daughter of the 7th Earl Beauchamp. She and Prince Vsevolod had been married in a civil ceremony the previous day.
2 Prince Vsevolod Ivanovich of Russia (1914–73) was a distant cousin of Tsar Nicholas II who escaped being murdered with other Romanovs in 1918 when, aged 4, he was taken to Sweden by his grandmother. He was educated at Eton and Oxford and spent the rest of his life in Britain. His marriage to Lady Mary broke up in 1956 and he married twice more.
3 King Alexander I of Yugoslavia (1888–1934).*
4 Trent Park in north London.
5 Port Lympne, Sassoon's house in Kent.

amused speculation on the subject. His favourites were usually young pilots in the Force. He was Under-Secretary of State of Air for eleven years,[1] and was an adequate if uninspired administrator. More than the air, he loved the arts and collected with a flair and lavishness unequalled in London society or elsewhere. He had a prolonged and hazardous friendship with the Prince of Wales, whom he worshipped for years: their quarrels were famous. He also was on intimate terms with the King and Queen Mary. He had the homosexual's gift for getting on with royalties and they haunted his house. He was loyal to them if to no one else. Politicians he dropped immediately and blatantly the moment they fell from office or power. The Eden reign was the longest, but of late he was inclined to drop him too, much to Anthony's amused resentment. Philip was never in on the Chamberlain racket and his power waned with Baldwin's retirement; he then despaired ... but his thirst for life, youth, glamour, colour and royalties was never quashed. He was sly, invidious, unreliable, insinuating, oily, eely, feminine. His sympathies were all with the Glamour Boys; yet he hated and was ashamed of Jews.[2] He really loved jewelled elephants, contrasting colours, the bizarre, the beautiful and the bad.

SUNDAY 4TH JUNE

An old neighbour, Major Capel Cure[3] of Blake Hall, called. He was born in 1853, and used to come to Kelvedon in the 90s. He had been up to the House of Commons once when Gladstone was Prime Minister! The old gentleman referred to an MP as a 'conceited young puppy', I think he meant Macnamara.[4] I gently agreed! But I soon discovered it was Winston he meant. Winston, who is twenty-two[5] years younger than he! He told me much of Kelvedon and the Wrights and of early days in Essex. One Wright who married Lord Petre's[6] daughter lived with his cook at Kelvedon, and was worshipped by his Petre brother-in-law – all a long time ago. He is remarkably hale and drove his own car in a rickety fashion.

---

1 Not all in one stint: from 1924 to 1929 and from 1931 to 1937.
2 He was from one of the grandest Jewish families in the country, and his mother was a Rothschild.
3 George Edward Capel Cure (1853–1943) was a member of a family who had lived at Blake Hall, Bobbingworth – about five miles from Kelvedon – since the late eighteenth century. The house, which was an RAF operations' centre during the Second World War, remains in the family.
4 John Robert Jermain Macnamara (1905–1944) was elected as Conservative MP for Chelmsford in 1935. He was part of the Anglo-German Fellowship and for a time had as his personal assistant Guy Burgess, later exposed as a Soviet spy. A colonel in the infantry, he was killed in action in Italy.
5 Actually twenty-one years younger.
6 The Petres are another old Essex family, from Ingatestone, about seven miles from Kelvedon.

MONDAY 5TH JUNE

In the great heat I returned reluctantly to London: Honor followed. I was glad to see everyone again and my improved appearance was much commented upon. I looked dazzling brown . . . No excitement at the Office. Poor Mussolini is very angry at our so-called encirclement policy. He may renounce the Anglo-Italian agreement.

The PM was 'sparky', Rab said, after, he had seen him. He did not seem so at Question Time, when a disaster nearly occurred, as the statement in regard to the appalling submarine disaster[1] did not arrive . . . I anxiously watched the clock. Jay Llewellin,[2] ever calm, was unruffled, but Geoffrey Shakespeare fidgeted and looked highly nervous and worn out by the anxieties of the past few days. David Margesson fumed – and the news got about that we must delay matters for a few moments; so silly supplementaries were asked until the long-waited-for statement appeared. His voice betraying his emotion, he read it out: to the satisfaction of the House, he proposed a full inquiry. There is now a suspicion of sabotage . . . the accident may well be another IRA act of terrorism organised by either Jewish or communist agents. It was diabolically cunning.[3]

Honor and I dined at home and our dining room looked lovely indeed. Honor was like a goddess and wore white, which contrasted with her brown skin and huge emeralds. We joined Emerald at the opera for a fine performance of *Tristan*.[4] In the foyer we came across Norman Gwatkin[5] talking to Alba and I joined them. Gwatkin was charming, but a touch disappointing . . . shall I pursue him further? I left as King Mark[6] ranted and returned to the House in time to hear Alan wind up for the government at the Ministry of Labour vote. He did well. He suggested going to Pratt's for supper, but hearing that Randolph Churchill, Bob

1 HMS *Thetis*, a Group 1 T-Class submarine launched the previous June, had begun sea trials in March 1939. On 1 June while diving in Liverpool Bay a problem with a torpedo tube caused the vessel to hit the seabed at a depth of 150 feet. Of the 103 men aboard, 99 died, including shipbuilders on the test run. With war imminent the vessel was salvaged, being beached on the day war was declared. It was recommissioned in 1940 as HMS *Thunderbolt*, but was lost with all hands in March 1943, sunk off Sicily by an Italian corvette.
2 John Jestyn Llewellin (1893–1957) was Conservative MP for Uxbridge, and served in several posts in the wartime coalition government.
3 It was cock-up rather than conspiracy: a combination of a design fault and human error sank the *Thetis*.
4 Wagner's *Tristan und Isolde*.
5 Norman Wilmshurst Gwatkin (1899–1971) was a professional soldier and courtier, at this point Assistant Comptroller of the Lord Chamberlain's office. He commanded the 5th Guards Armoured Brigade during the invasion of Normandy in 1944 and was awarded the Distinguished Service Order. He served at court as an extra equerry to the Sovereign from 1950 until his death, was Secretary and Registrar of the Order of Merit from 1963, and was knighted in the same year.
6 A character in the opera.

Boothby and co were going there, I lured him to the Savoy, where Harold Balfour dropped us.

I sat alone with Alan and we discussed love and hate and matrimony and money. Patsy is not being easy with her baby and irritates him. They had just come back from a most unfortunate trip to the South of France which they both hated. Alan is in better spirits, and as he is much thinner he looks handsome again. We had an imperial pint of champagne and then walked home. In the Strand we saw placards 'Duchess of Kent shot at!'; and, shocked, I bought the newspaper. It seems someone shot at her as she was driving away from Belgrave Square at about 8.40 this evening.[1] She was untouched . . . When I got back to Belgrave Square a small crowd had gathered, although it was 1.40 a.m. I gossiped with my policeman friend and he told me that the Duchess was unaware of the incident when it occurred but is now shocked and resentful, naturally. The man has been detained. It is about two years ago that Mahon[2] made an attempt on the Duke of Windsor – and unluckily missed him. Had he died he would have gone down in history as one of the greatest of our kings . . . instead . . . Honor was still awake . . . I told her of the attempt.

Tuesday 6th June

I woke after only five hours' sleep, in a fiendish temper. Massage did not help: I am worn out, but don't look it. To the Foreign Office where the Queen of Spain's secretary rang up to offer me three alternative dates as HM is anxious to lunch or dine with us at 5 Belgrave Square. I decided on June 22nd. Prince Fritzi came to call on us before luncheon as he was lunching next door with the Kents. We drank tomato juice and gossiped and he showed me a cable he had had this morning from his grandfather, the old Kaiser at Doorn, expressing his horror and sorrow at the *Thetis* disaster. I asked to be allowed to keep it, and show it to the Prime Minister which I did later during a division. 'The Germans have behaved very well about it,' the PM said. He was pleased . . . I sent a note in to the Duchess of Kent to say how horrified I was[3] and she replied by a telegram within a few hours. Honor, looking really magnificent, and I walked to the Belgian Embassy to lunch. There we found a large party of the fashionables, and semi-political. All the guests were punctual, as we were talking to the Dowager Duchess of

---

1 The would-be assassin was Ledwedge Vincent Lawlor, a 45-year-old welder's assistant, who fired a sawn-off shotgun at the Duchess's car as she was being driven from 3 Belgrave Square to a cinema to see *Wuthering Heights*. He was immediately arrested by two policemen waiting to hold up the traffic for the Duchess's car. Lawlor was an Australian, and was sent back there for trial.

2 *Sic*: this attempt was made by a man called McMahon, on 16 July 1936 – so almost three years earlier.

3 By the incident the previous night (*vide supra*).

Norfolk[1] (whom I had always thought an extraordinarily nice woman, as friendly as she is plain), the Chamberlains were announced, and there fell that hush one associates with the arrival of royalty. Mrs C – gracious and well dressed – was followed by the PM, who looked remarkably handsome, even debonair in his pearl-grey morning coat. They did *le cercle*[2] like reigning sovereigns! One was tempted to curtsey to them. I happened to stand between Ronnie Tree and Robin Castlereagh:[3] to them the PM nodded his head coldly, to Robin he said 'Good d'ye do [sic],' but to me he smiled and said 'Hello Chips!' – to my intense delight as that [illegible] Tree was infuriated.

Then to the House of Commons, leaving Honor, magnificently dressed in the grey number she had worn at Arthur Elveden's wedding and many sapphires behind ... all evening here at the House of Commons, and had tea on the terrace to people's surprise with Mathers,[4] a Labour whip .... didn't dine ... slept, fussed and sat about until 2.30 a.m. when the House rose at last. Everyone here was on edge, irritable, and both Alan and the Astor shrew were attacked, the former most unjustly. Old Astor is now the most hated member at the House of Commons. People see through her at last: she has become a bore and out-of-date! The heat contributed to the general acerbity! ....

As I was sitting in our room a cable came announcing the death of Isabelle Clow, and my thoughts were jolted back to long ago days when she loved me. The liaison with her lasted from October 1924 to Feb 1925 when I sailed for Europe. I was in Chicago from October until February, for the longest period in my adult life; and then it was that I became reconciled to my father, gathered the material for *Joan Kennedy*[5] and in general the long fallow months were not unprofitable. My affair with Isabelle began quietly and continued for the whole period – nights ... in a smaller house which the Clows owned, near the golf club, furtive meetings in Chicago at various hotels ... even had breakfast and quick flurried fornications after her dental-working husband departed for his office. I learned much ... she was a fragile woman with a frail spirit, she had fastidious taste, an exotic point of view, cultured sense of humour, and more fantastic clinging clothes ... she reminded one of pearl lying on grey velvet ... and she was wasted in her provincial life. With the tubercular woman's avid craving for love, she was

1 Gwendolen Constable-Maxwell, widow of the 15th Duke.*
2 Went round the room.
3 Robin Vane-Tempest-Stewart (1902–55), Unionist MP for County Down, and by courtesy Viscount Castlereagh until 1949 when he succeeded his father as 8th Marquess of Londonderry.
4 George Mathers (1886–1965) was Labour MP for Edinburgh West from 1929 to 1931, for Linlithgowshire from 1935 to 1945 and for West Lothian from 1945 to 1951. He was a Labour whip from 1935 to 1946, serving from 1944 to 1945 in the coalition government and under Attlee from 1945 to 1946. He was raised to the peerage as 1st Baron Mathers in 1952.
5 Channon's novel, published in 1929.

passionate, and perhaps even a lonely bisexual. In Chicago at least she was the queen of local fashion and everything she did was in the grand manner. She gave me handsome presents, entertained me, and was desperately in love with me, then a fairly handsome fellow ten years younger than herself. Her husband, who is a nice creature, desperately American, worshipped her, and at first tolerated me. Later he liked me, although we had nothing in common. Possibly he had suspicions about her sex life (she had later an affair with Leslie Hore-Belisha at Biarritz). Her taste was impeccable and only when she arrived in New York did she seem a touch provincial. In London she made a better impression: her two Nordic daughters are uninteresting, the younger one has something of her mother in her. I feel now that my last link with Chicago is severed now . . . We are all ageing and I mind dreadfully.

Raimund von Hofmannsthal, a gay, brilliant, Jew, son of the poet[1] . . . was this morning married to lovely Liz Paget, much to the annoyance of the Angleseys who are nevertheless resigned to the match. Alice, his wife, has gone off sulking to Paris, whilst her admirer, a Mr Hamish Hamilton,[2] refuses to marry her – he has run out, as he cannot face the complications. And never was a man more sane! John Rutland[3] sent a letter of condolences to Charlie Anglesey,[4] an act in doubtful taste. I always prophesied that the Hof-marriage would crack, and now I foresee disaster in this new alliance – the boy is charming enough but half a Jew and half a cad.

THURSDAY 8TH JUNE

I dressed slowly in my Fauntleroy number[5] (which I was wearing for the tenth time)
    Kent wedding
    2 hunt balls
    2 speaker's parties
    2 speeches – Covent Garden, Foreign Office
    2 birthday banquets at Foreign Office
    1 Coronation itself
    (and once lent to Bill Mabane),[6]

1 He was the son of the Austrian author Hugo von Hofmannsthal (1874–1929).
2 James 'Jamie' Hamish Hamilton (1900–88) founded in 1931 the publishing house that bore his name. He rowed for Britain in the 1928 Olympic Games.
3 John Henry Montagu Manners (1886–1940), 9th Duke of Rutland.*
4 Charles Henry Alexander Paget (1885–1947), 6th Marquess of Anglesey, father of the bride.*
5 Court dress.
6 William Mabane (1895–1969) was Liberal MP for Huddersfield from 1931 to 1945. He held several junior offices in the Chamberlain and Churchill governments.*

drove to 12 Chester Street where I picked up Freddie Birkenhead[1] and we went in together. We ran into Halifax who smiled his welcome. The scene was very splendid, grander far than last year. The ambassadors milled about, and old Cartier[2] was the most gorgeous (and probably the shrewdest). Alba was slim and handsome and a touch deaf; Corbin dull and steely ... only Joë Kennedy, the smiling American who is so like a dentist, Dirksen the bald Silesian, and Maisky were in ordinary evening clothes – almost everyone else was splendid, and glittered with orders. The PM looked extraordinarily young and slender. We sat at a horseshoe table and I was between the Italian and Paraguayan chargés d'affaires,[3] with the former, Signor Crolla, I had a riveting conversation. He is despairing about Anglo-Italian relations; he regrets the turn things have taken, and deplores our short-sightedness, blames Eden for the mess we are all in: he forged the axis; he made Hitler's rise so easy ... everything always is traceable to Anthony's pig-headedness. Crolla is not optimistic: he fears a war, Ciano is not afraid of one. I tried to soothe the man; he said he wished to have an Anglo-Italian alliance, instead of just an agreement ... much wine, food, flowers, splendour ... the chandeliers recently brought from an old Embassy in Vienna and cleaned by Philip Sassoon, sparkled ... [at] The end of dinner Lord Halifax grandly proposed the traditional two toasts ... a string band played; there was *conversazione* as we moved uneasily about. The Yugoslav chargé d'affaires[4] was sycophantic because of the Regent: the man is firmly pro-ally and anti-axis ... the Nepalese Minister's[5] religion forbids them to drive, but he came in later to pay his respects to Lord Halifax; and his plumed hat hung with gorgeous emeralds. I went about urging the Cabinet to go back and vote and did whip up a few. I drove back to the House with Malcolm MacDonald,[6] who was flushed and friendly. I like him. Once at the House I slipped ordinary trousers over my velvet breeches, and put on a short coat and black tie and voted in the division: I forgot however to change my buckled pumps and they were noticed.

Halifax is almost indefatigable as the PM. I heard him in the Lords today make his famous statement which is in the nature of a bombshell – a new bid for

1 2nd Earl Birkenhead. See entry for 28 November 1938 and footnote.
2 Baron Émile-Ernest de Cartier de Marchienne (1871–1946), the Belgian Ambassador.*
3 Dr Don Rogelio Espinoza had been Paraguayan chargé d'affaires since 1933.
4 Dragomir Kassidolatz.
5 Lieutenant General Krishna Shamsher Jang Bahadur Rana (1900–77) had been the Nepalese Minister in London since 1935, and was a son of a prime minister of Nepal.
6 Malcolm John MacDonald (1901–81), son of Ramsay MacDonald, was Labour MP for Bassetlaw from 1929 to 1935 (National Labour after 1931) and National Labour MP for Ross and Cromarty from 1936 to 1945. He was Secretary of State for the Dominions and Colonies between 1935 and 1940 and Minister of Health from 1940 to 1941. He was High Commissioner to Canada from 1941 to 1946 and to India from 1955 to 1960; and Governor-General of Kenya from 1963 to 1964.

appeasement! He opened the door to Germany for further negotiations; it is an astute move which will frighten Moscow and possibly placate Berlin.

FRIDAY 9TH JUNE   *KELVEDON*

I drove here with Harold Balfour and Fritzi of Prussia has joined us. We are all worn out: Kelvedon looks a dream . . . there are many tiny ducklings on the lake . . . the blue borders of azaleas are the colour of the sky . . . my baby boy was waiting for me.

Honor has confessed to me that she has been painted by Ian Campbell-Gray[1] and her mysterious meetings and trips to London were really only sittings. The portrait of her in ski-clothes is now finished and is my anniversary present. I had not seen it; but I am much pleased and touched and relieved: One should never think the worst; it so often doesn't occur.

I met Halifax and Jack Herbert[2] in the Park. They often work together in the morning and Jack passes on to him the atmosphere of the House of Commons. Halifax is over-inclined to listen to the Glamour Boys, or at least to attach too much importance to this noisy minority.

SATURDAY 10TH JUNE

A day of sunbathing and rest: I am intoxicated with the beauty of Kelvedon. There was another accoutrement – a black Muscovy duck produced fifteen tiny balls of fluff. We found them much to my Paul's delight. Batsi, the dog, too, is pregnant. I itch for more children . . . more of a heat haze.

Helen Fitzgerald arrived, accompanied by her husband Evelyn (to the disappointment of Harold who loves her), and also Laura Corrigan who is a dynamo of energy and conversation. She even talks of royalties when standing on her head!

SUNDAY 11TH JUNE

Fritzi of Prussia is really an adorable gay man, and so unspoilt and attractive. Unfortunately he hates Laura Corrigan who bores him with long tales of his relations. She is in tremendous form, liberating energy . . . but she talks too much of death: she says she has left a sapphire ring to Honor . . . . She gives

---

1 Ian Douglas Campbell-Gray (1901–46) would marry, as her second husband, Diana Cavendish (qv) in 1942. He fenced for Britain in the 1936 Olympics and fought in the Second World War, reaching the rank of lieutenant colonel.

2 John Arthur Herbert (1895–1943) was Conservative MP for Monmouth from 1934 to 1939 and Governor of Bengal from 1939 to 1943. He has been held partly responsible for the Bengal famine of 1943.

everything away, and has first presented all her silver to Sheila Milbanke. Laura is an astounding woman, a very tremendous personality, and a colossal bore. I felt attracted towards her today ... poor old Evelyn, all his friends are dying, and he too, feels his age. He is an executor of Philip Sassoon's will. Old black Hannah Gubbay gets Lympne outright and Trent for life. Trent reverts at her death to the Cholmondeley children.[1] The fortune is considerable.

Evelyn wandered about and spent the day feeding the ducks ...

MONDAY 12TH JUNE

I met Halifax going into No. 10 this morning. He has lost a little of his bonhomie: I think he is worn out. Long conversations with Rab. Rex Leeper is going apparently, and soon. The Foreign Office purge looks like a reality.

Tea at the House with Ronnie Cartland and I twitted him about his unexpected friendship with Tony Muirhead,[2] that ponderous Under-Secretary who looks like a tortoise and lives in medieval discomfort at Staffordshire. He is mad about Ronnie who is some twenty years his junior.

No social engagements this week – a relief: I had a glass of milk instead of dining and feel well.

TUESDAY 13TH JUNE

I slept ten hours and then was pummelled by my sadistic Swedish masseur, I feel well. I sleep so badly in the country, particularly at Kelvedon where the air is so stimulating that everyone complains of insomnia. Back in Belgrave Square I sleep marvellously.

WEDNESDAY 14TH JUNE

It is Ascot week but that festival is now out of date and more unfashionable than ever! This year there is not even a Windsor Party or royal procession to lend a touch of colour.

We lunched at Hanover Lodge with Alice Hofmannsthal and I saw her various children. Evidently she is not going to marry Hamish Hamilton, who I am told, has refused her. He is wise: it would be too much to take on. Honor,

---

1 The three children of Sir Philip Sassoon's younger sister, Sybil (1894–1989), by marriage the Marchioness of Cholmondeley.*

2 Anthony John Muirhead (1890–1939) won the Military Cross and Bar in the Great War and served between the wars in the Territorial Army, reaching the rank of lieutenant colonel. He was Conservative MP for Wells from 1929 to 1939 and an under-secretary, first for Air and then for Burma, from 1937 until his death. He committed suicide in October 1939, allegedly because he feared a leg injury rendered him unfit for active service in the war.

whose good looks and chic have been the talk of London, looked untidy and unwell today. She left afterwards for Kelvedon.

From ten until 11.30 we had 'Spanish Trouble', an absurd meaningless debate, the point at issue being the Italian war materiel left behind in Spain. Rab answered well, and 'stonewalled' with success; but his English is inelegant and his sentences undistinguished. Surprising in one so intelligent. It was an empty House, David Margesson remarked that his whips were so hopeless that they could scarcely 'pump shit'[1] unless he undid their flies for them!

THURSDAY 15TH JUNE

I dined at the House with the 1936 Club, at which Lord Chatfield was the guest of honour. He spoke bluntly and frankly of our defence – he is the Minister for the Co-ordination of Defence. Every day, he said, that war is averted or postponed, is valuable: we are not rearming at a terrific pace ... He is a clean-cut sailor with a sailor's clear eye and charm. Everyone was charming to me .... I am suddenly popular again: why?

SATURDAY 17TH JUNE

An Essex day. Honor and I drove to the other Kelvedon, bought some pharmaceutical jars at the local *antiquaire*, and lunched with the Boultons[2] at Braxted Park.[3] It is a lovely house, romantic in the midst of a fine park with fine trees. It could be made a glorious place. At the moment it is dark, down-at-heel, shabby, and dull. Boulton is an attractive man, but a touch fraudulent; she looks like a cook. Two dark genetic sons were present.[4] Honor and I both half envious of the house – Kelvedon is prettier and gayer and more accessible to London, so perhaps better for us.

Honor and I separated at Chelmsford and I slept for an hour in a lane, and went on to the Lawns at Rochford where a Conservative fête organised by Victor Raikes was being held. Reggie Dorman-Smith spoke well and with charm and self-assurance. I like him immensely: he is a first-rate Cabinet minister at his job. He drove back to Kelvedon with me and is staying here: he seems lonely and all his boyish spirits and charm ... I am told his marriage doesn't run well – and nothing is so crippling to a man as that unless he has great gifts. Victor Raikes

---

1 Channon mishears a naval expression: 'to pump ship' means 'to urinate'.

2 William Whytehead Boulton (1873–1949) was Conservative MP for Sheffield Central from 1931 to 1945. He served as a whip in the Churchill coalition from 1940 to 1944. He was created 1st Bt in 1944. He married, in 1903, Rosalind Mary Milburn (1881–1969).

3 Off the main London to Colchester road between Witham and the town of Kelvedon, about twenty-seven miles from Kelvedon Hall.

4 The Boultons had four sons: it is not clear which two these were.

is also here, untidy and brilliant, and he has brought his old father.[1] The old gentleman is nearly 76 and has great charm and wit, and suggests old sherry, the Senior Common Room and Dr Johnson. He is still active and very humorous. We drank much . . . and when Alan Lennox-Boyd arrived the atmosphere was electrified. He has so much charm and personality. We drank a magnum of champagne and attacked Anthony Eden until he had not a shred left. Old Raikes was contemptuous about him: Alan, Victor and I joined in the chorus and so impressed Reggie D-S, who was riveted. We had been unaware that Eden's unpopularity had reached such a pitch.

MONDAY 19TH JUNE

We moved to London. All day I have been popular (and perhaps powerful): I held almost a court in the lobby. Sam Hoare affectionate, the PM gave me one of his dazzling smiles; Jay Llewellin asked me to dine; Harold Balfour gave me a drink; Jim Wedderburn sat with me for an hour; we are asked everywhere . . . on the wave again . . .

As I was writing these lines in our room, 21D, in popped Sir Horace Wilson to confer with Rab. I fear they guessed it was a diary. He is a subtle old fish is Horace Wilson . . . and certainly the *éminence grise* of 10 Downing Street.

I am alone at the House tonight as Honor has gone to dine with Max Beaverbrook at Stornoway House. He rang her up at Kelvedon himself to invite her. There is a Channon boom on . . . He always pretends to love her – a mock flirtation.

TUESDAY 20TH JUNE

Honor sat up last night until 3.30 at Stornoway House where she dined with Max Beaverbrook who was in a Bacchic mood. Rothermere was also there and Kitty Brownlow. Max kept saying 'if only Honor would divorce Chips and marry me . . .' The old Silenus[2] drank too much 1906 champagne and eventually removed his trousers. Diana Cooper, who arrived with Duff about two, said that she had never seen people so drunk. This week will kill Honor. We dined together late at home and went on to Londonderry House where there was an old-fashioned collation. Flowers, bouquets, paper hats . . . the figures were led by foreigners. People were embarrassed at first but eventually entered the fray with *entrain*.[3] I watched the young: the three gay men *en vue*[4] for different reasons are young

---

1 Henry St John Digby Raikes (1863–1943) was both the son and father of Conservative Members of Parliament; his father, Henry Cecil Raikes (1838–91), held various seats in the Commons from 1868 to 1891 and was Postmaster-General from 1886 to 1891.
2 The Greek god of drunkenness, tutor of Dionysus.
3 Spirit.
4 Prominent.

Lord Townshend[1] who is tall, handsome, Nordic and masculine: I think the Londonderrys would like him for the sophisticated Mairi;[2] young Lord Wilton[3] (who is of course, Sam Ashton's natural child and his sister who is engaged to marry a jockey), who unlike Townshend is not a debutante's delight: quite on the contrary. He is, I am told, the new male tart. He gets his weariness and looks from his mother Brenda,[4] that lovely Swede who died of drugs . . . both are rather common but attractive. Then there is Granby[5] once a merry lad; but now he looks old and played-out. Honor thought he was like a Neapolitan . . . but he isn't.

There is a great Channon wave at the moment: we are popular, *répandus*,[6] indeed run after: we are asked to every lighted candle, to every dinner and everyone is charming. Is it social? Is it political? A combination? Or what? Even Honor is aware of it and says it is overwhelmingly obvious. Lord Londonderry rose when we arrived and kissed Honor warmly. There were no royalties except Fritzi and the Infanta[7] in the crowded ballroom. We stayed until 1.30 and then went to supper below, where we joined Lady Crewe[8] – even she was agreeable and talked of Kelvedon. She was, as ever, with Napier [Alington] and she looked well with her rubies. Well, as mutton dressed as lamb ever does . . .

WEDNESDAY 21ST JUNE

We lunched with Laura – for it is High-Corrigan season now – to meet the Queen of Spain.[9] Both Honor and I were highly placed: I was between comtesse Charles

---

1 George John Patrick Dominic Townshend (1916–2010), Viscount Raynham by courtesy until 1921 when he succeeded his father as 7th Marquess Townshend. On 2 March 2009 he broke the record for holding a peerage longer than anyone else in history – passing the 87 years, 104 days of the 13th Lord Sinclair. He married that autumn, but not Lady Mairi.

2 Lady Mairi Elizabeth Vane-Tempest-Stewart (1921–2009), daughter of the Londonderrys.

3 Seymour William Arthur John Egerton (1921–99), Viscount Grey de Wilton by courtesy until 1927 when he succeeded his father as 7th Earl of Wilton.

4 Brenda Petersen (1896–1930), daughter of Sir William Petersen, married the 6th Earl of Wilton in 1917.

5 Charles John Robert Manners (1919–99), Marquess of Granby, who the following year would succeed his father as 10th Duke of Rutland.*

6 Literally 'widespread', in this context 'ubiquitous'.

7 Infanta María Cristina of Spain (Doña María Cristina Teresa Alejandra María de Guadalupe María de la Concepción Ildefonsa Victoria Eugenia de Borbón y Battenberg) (1911–96) was the fifth child and younger daughter of the exiled King Alfonso of Spain, and with her family resident in Italy. In 1940 she renounced her right of succession and married, morganatically, Enrico Eugenio Marone-Cinzano (1895–1968), 1st Count of Marone.

8 Margaret Etienne Hannah 'Peggy' Primrose (1881–1967), daughter of the 5th Earl of Rosebery, in 1899 married as his second wife the 1st Marquess of Crewe*. Their daughter was Mary, Duchess of Roxburghe*.

9 Victoria Eugenie ('Ena') of Battenberg (1887–1969), married in 1906 King Alfonso XIII of Spain.*

de Polignac;[1] a woman still beautiful with great wide passionate eyes, she has had scores of lovers and as Mme de Jaunez she was the toast of Paris before the war; and Lady Willingdon, as funny and gossipy and dictatorial as ever. I had always got on with her. She misses her old glory and is relegated now to living at Walmer Castle in comparative simplicity. The Queen was one off me, and she was jolly, handsome, imposing and almost plump. She was next to Honor . . . . who talked to her until 2.30, when I became fidgety as we had early Foreign Office questions. When the ladies got up David Margesson, Hore-Belisha and I slipped out behind the dining room and rushed to the House of Commons. I brought Leslie H-B back to the House of Commons, rather flushed after a too full and fashionable function . . .

I am distressed as David will be leaving us soon[2] and for me much of the light, fun and point of the House of Commons will go. His successor, Tommy Dugdale, is subtler, possibly slyer, certainly more suave but he lacks David's firmness, his contact with society and his boisterous bonhomie which makes Margesson the supreme Chief Whip of all time.

I dined at the annual banquet of the 1900 Club; a large dreary well-attended function . . . . The guest of honour was Halifax and he had all the applause: his personal reception was almost enthusiastic. Winston Churchill, who proposed his health, was coolly, almost embarrassingly, coldly received. His speech was not up to his usual standard: he must have sensed the hostility in the atmosphere. His references to Soviet Russia were hissed . . . . A dull affair; and too much platitudinous complimenting on the high table . . . . I left quickly, having sat next to Charles Taylor,[3] the pretty calf-like MP for Eastbourne and went to the Elvedens to pick up Honor. There I found a young people's dinner party, all tiresomely hostile to the Prime Minister, and these young men who owe their lives to him were being amusing at his expense!

I am sick of society.

THURSDAY 22ND JUNE

Tonight we had our great dinner party, which was to celebrate Franco's victory, do homage to Queen Ena and plot the restoration of the Spanish throne to her son. It was a risky business, mixing high society with so many obscure, or more accurately, socially unknown, MPs! – but it came off beyond our wildest hopes.

---

1 Jeanne de Montagnac (1882–1966), married in 1925 as her second husband comte Charles de Polignac.
2 Margesson in fact remained Chief Whip until December 1940, when he became Secretary of State for War.
3 Charles Stuart Taylor (1910–89) was the youngest MP in the House of Commons when elected for Eastbourne in 1935, and sat as a Conservative until 1974. He was a major in the Royal Artillery during the Second World War and was knighted in 1954.

The house looked a vision of loveliness, banked with flowers from Kelvedon and Pyrford,[1] and Honor dripped with emeralds and wore her tiara. The guests were punctual, and the first to arrive was Henry Page Croft,[2] the pompous MP for Bournemouth. In ten minutes' time the room was full of buzzing, be-tiara-ed women, and men in decorations lapping up cocktails . . . . The Queen was punctual and magnificent in black with many pearls and an imposing diadem and emerald tiara. Honor and I met her at the door, escorted her and the Infanta Maria Cristina into the morning room. The guests did not stop their chatter as is usual and thus Honor's task was made more clumsy but she did it well. Dinner was announced punctually enough, and we walked into dinner: the dining room took one's breath away: the beauty of the candlelight, and the Dresden pieces each one surrounded by small roses . . . the Queen was instantly amiable and praised the room. Then followed the most appalling ten minutes of my life: due to some hitch in the domestic arrangements the blinis, the first course, were delayed. No one noticed for a moment or two, but gradually there was a *gêne* which lashings of champagne eased. Honor sitting opposite between Drino Carisbrooke[3] and Leslie Hore-Belisha looked miserable. When at long last they arrived, the uneasiness passed and the dinner became almost a riotous success. The Infanta talked to Michael Duff, so I was free for nearly an hour to talk to the Queen who was very agreeable, very charming and intelligent. She is bitter about the past, bitter about King Alfonso and confided in me that at one moment the Spanish people had offered to make her Regent and she had refused . . . . she had been brought to Spain by Alfonso and would go with him – she is very anti-Semitic and thinks that the Jews are responsible for the Revolution in Spain. The Jews and the left-wing doctrinarians murdered 2 million people. She does not think that Franco will join the axis unless our foolish extremists push him into so doing. She said that letters to Negrin,[4] including one from Winston Churchill, had been found in Madrid. She loathes him and Eden and Duff Cooper . . . we gossiped, too, and when I suggested that we marry Alba to Lady Curzon the Queen replied: 'I admit it is a long way back, but Jimmie is too Scotch for that!'[5] A brilliant retort!

Dinner was really excellent, and the champagne magnificent. When the ladies left, I sat with Norman Gwatkin whom I rather fancy. He is Assistant to

---

1 Pyrford Court, the Guinnesses' country house near Woking in Surrey.
2 Henry Page Croft (1881–1947) was Conservative MP for Christchurch and then for Bournemouth from 1910 to 1940, when he was raised to the peerage as 1st Baron Croft and served as Under-Secretary of State for War from 1940 to 1945. He worked closely with Churchill during the late 1930s as a committed anti-appeaser.
3 1st Marquess of Carisbrooke. See entry for 21 November 1938 and footnote.
4 Juan Negrín y López, the Socialist Prime Minister of Spain from 1937 to 1939.
5 The Duke of Alba was the descendant of a bastard son of King James II and VII of England and Scotland.

the Lord Chamberlain; he looks Edwardian in appearance and manner; he was adjutant for the Coldstreams and so has all their manners and tricks of mind and speech – possibly he is a touch climbing . . . we went to the library, where I found the Queen seated with Honor and Eileen Sutherland on a sofa before the fire (luckily it was a cool evening). Soon a circle of Franco sympathisers was formed around the Queen and I led different MPs up to her. She was expansive, frank, friendly and very *grande dame*. Hours passed and I began to fear that she would never go . . . The Infanta, Loelia Westminster, Lord Kemsley[1] and Jim Wedderburn played bridge in the morning room below. Little groups formed themselves and I fear that Eileen Sutherland was bored and anxious to go on to the Kennedys'[2] ball. About 1 a.m. she rose and somehow it seemed a signal as the Queen glanced at the clock. Luckily she had had half an hour with Rab who with his wife had come in from the Dutch Legation where they had been dining. Again and again I heard his famous cackle which is unique and so pleasant to hear for it means that he is amused. Really it is like laying down coveys of pheasants but Sydney, who has no sense of humour, is always embarrassed by it . . . tonight she kissed Honor who in her surprise did not take it too well and behaved as if she had been hit by a cricket bat! At length I showed the Queen to her car, as she left graciously and reluctantly. The evening was a fantastic success, for some of the guests remained behind. Lord Kemsley by now was very tight and had difficulty with his syllables, as did Victor Raikes, who was exaggeratedly polite as he always is when he has drunk too much. Eileen Sutherland, who broke three wine glasses, looked very ducal with her fine diamonds and her orders: she was even more imposing than the Queen. Irene Carisbrooke[3] is a gentle, delightful creature: he a boring pompous semi-caddish demi-royalty.

After the Butlers left us, he still cackling, and Sydney praising Bill Tufnell whom they had never met before, curiously enough; Honor and I went on to . . . a gloomy supper party given to meet Mrs Clare Boothe Brokaw Luce,[4] a cynical

---

1 James Gomer Berry (1883–1968) was co-proprietor of the *Daily Telegraph* with his brother Lord Camrose (qv) and Lord Burnham. He founded Kemsley Newspapers, owners of the *Sunday Times* and the *Daily Sketch*. He was awarded a baronetcy in 1928, raised to the peerage as 1st Baron Kemsley in 1936 and advanced to a viscountcy in 1945.
2 Joseph Kennedy (qv), United States Ambassador to London.
3 Irene Frances Adza Denison (1890–1956) married in 1917 Prince Alexander of Battenberg, 1st Marquess of Carisbrooke (qv).
4 Ann Clare Boothe (1903–87) had originally intended to be an actress, but married in 1923 the clothing magnate George Tuttle Brokaw; the marriage was dissolved in 1929. In 1935 she married Henry Luce, the publisher of *Time*, *Life* and *Fortune* magazines. She made a name as a writer and journalist, and sat in the House of Representatives from 1943 to 1947. President Eisenhower, for whom she campaigned in 1952, appointed her US Ambassador to Italy the following year, and she served until 1956. Eisenhower appointed her Ambassador to Brazil in 1959, but she resigned after just four days because of opposition from Democrats to her appointment.

and chic American whom I had always loathed! Randolph Churchill was there, and Edward Stanley of Alderley,[1] and the atmosphere was unfriendly. Not so the Kents who were both extremely charming: he had grumbles with Lord Forbes,[2] whom he snubbed for having attacked the Duchess in the *Sunday Express*. It is surprising and undignified of Forbes to become a second-rate society gossip writer. What can the Granards think of such a scion? I was annoyed by now, and with difficulty led Honor home – four late nights she has had. She hates parties in theory but in practice will never leave them; and whilst always very sweet, is inconsiderate. She never thinks about others and is indifferent, or seemingly so, as to how tired I may be!

The evening was fantastic. I hope we restore the Bourbons! And also that my sister-in-law will not become Brigid Belisha. Leslie 'Mars'[3] never left her tonight ...

FRIDAY 23RD JUNE

I could not sleep: my head spun ... I kept thinking of our flamboyantly successful royal party and of all the comic incidents and the unexpected people who found themselves thrown together.

I ran into poor old Jim Thomas[4] in the House of Commons; he was behind the Chair in the Ministers' Lobby: I don't know him, but watched several of the Cabinet pass, Walter Elliot, Shakes Morrison, and others. All were civil, even gushing; but Oliver Stanley who of late has been quite extraordinarily charming to me, carried the meeting off better than the others. 'How are you? Have you seen my father lately?' I heard him say, and old JH flushed with obvious pleasure.

MONDAY 26TH JUNE

Honor and I came up this morning and at one o'clock she left by car for Croydon where she flies to Berne on a skiing expedition. It is an eccentric scheme and only Honor would find snow in July! Possibly there is something behind it, but I doubt it. I think she genuinely likes skiing and gets bored in London. I was sad

---

1 Edward John Stanley (1907–71) succeeded his father as 6th Baron Stanley of Alderley in 1931.

2 Arthur Patrick Hastings Forbes (1915–92), Viscount Forbes by courtesy until 1915 when he succeeded his father as 9th Earl of Granard. His career as a gossip columnist did not survive the declaration of war.

3 The god of war: Hore-Belisha was Secretary of State for War.

4 James Henry Thomas (1874–1949) had served as Colonial Secretary in the first Labour government, as Lord Privy Seal from 1929 to 1930, Dominions Secretary from 1930 to 1935, and Colonial Secretary again from 1935 to 1936. Much liked by King George V, Thomas had been forced to resign from the government and Parliament in 1936 after being accused of giving inside information on proposed tax changes to stock-market investors.

and sorry to see her go off, and Paul, too, seemed to mind. But he never really minds anything much.

TUESDAY 27TH JUNE

Honor arrived safely at Rome. I lunched with the Sitwells,[1] Loelia Westminster flamboyantly dressed, Ian Fleming[2] and others. We all discussed Laura Corrigan, who says she is going to die, or at any rate stop entertaining. She dined at the House of Commons tonight with Harold Balfour and me . . . Home late and tired. There were many divisions. As Jack Herbert is now to be Governor of Bengal I am wondering whether I shall be moved up into the Whips' Room? I am almost dreading the wrench it would involve; yet I feel a far-sighted policy would be to get a whipship. I fear I shall never really get it with such an enemy as James Stuart there to thwart me. I should dread leaving the Foreign Office, but Rab cannot be there forever. And it is many years before he will be PM. Perhaps I had better get the wheels in motion now for promotion.

Rab entertained the Prime Minister and Mrs C to luncheon at Smith Square. Tommy Dugdale was also present and I wonder what conspiracy was hatched.

WEDNESDAY 28TH JUNE

Dined at Laura Corrigan's, a gigantic party of above 150 covers. I was given an exceptionally good place at the Duchess of Kent's table.

Laura changed her game; she has been waking up to this alteration for some years. Tonight there were no naked Japanese wrestlers, no gilded jugglers flung into the air, no apache dancers – the only cabaret was the German Ambassador and Frau von Dirksen, who waited forty minutes for us to come out of the dining room! There were many tiaras and much splendour: it was almost Derby House . . . I dined with Mollie Buccleuch (who is now known as 'Midnight Moll' as she fetches young men . . . and goes to nightclubs . . . and . . .), Eileen Sutherland, Laura herself and many more. There was an atmosphere of almost pre-war splendour which even the unfortunate fusing of the lights in the picture gallery could not dim. I remember many balls there with Queen Mary present in the past: tonight was about as grand as any of its predecessors. I am sure the Edwardian brigade, Buckingham Palace, will be annoyed at Laura's great success. Gwatkin came in late but I hadn't a chance to talk to him: the champagne was indifferent. I left about 2.30. Poor Laura, like Hitler, thinks that she will die

---

1 Sacheverell Reresby 'Sachie' Sitwell (1897–1988) married in 1925 Georgia Doble (1905–80).*
2 Ian Lancaster Fleming (1908–64) was working unsatisfactorily in the City, but became an officer in Naval intelligence during the war, a role to which he had been covertly recruited the month before this meeting with Channon. After the war he became a newspaper executive, and in 1952 began to write the James Bond novels.

next year: this season is her swansong. She believes in astrology. I don't know her age: but her passport, obviously faked, made her out to be 42 in 1932 when we yachted with her, for I saw it. Probably she took ten years off. Then she is 59.[1] Her hands are old; but she seems as young as the Prime Minister and her energy equals his. This morning I went into No. 10 about Questions: the Cabinet had just risen and all the red boxes lay on the long table in the vestibule. John Simon passed into No. 11 by the communication door opened for him. The PM was most friendly and even funny: but [some] meaty decisions had been taken. We are going to warn Germany in no uncertain terms that any nonsense about Danzig means war. I personally think our policy mad; but I am powerless to alter it. All we can do is to restrain the firebrands somewhat – as I waited for Rab and the PM Mrs Chamberlain swept past me. She stopped and was as silly as ever. She is delightful, whimsical and really a bit mad, I think. 'God' worships her . . . and she adores him. They are determined to stay in Downing Street for another ten years!

THURSDAY 29TH JUNE

Lunched with the Kents, who both looked tired after their spate of late nights. Her sleepy eyes are the loveliest in the world . . . pleasant party. After luncheon the royal children were brought in beautifully dressed. They are both like 'Papa' as they call him. Princess Alexandra is flirtatious and smiling and she rushed to the piano and thumped it as did little Edward who is so pretty, so sultry, so silent. He is a dream child, an indignant Hoppner.[2] She is lavish in her pretty ways and coquettish manners. David Margesson, unusually driving, offered me a lift to the House but I remained behind to talk with the Duchess of Kent. I looked fat, and I fear, foolish in my over-smart clothes which I sometimes effect. Napier Alington, that catarrhal 'charmer', came home with me and we chatted for an hour as in old days: I can never resist his fascinating tired velvety manner; his Pierrot[3] looks and sad stag eyes. What a waste, for his intelligence is acute, his reading considerable, and his seductive power unsurpassed and yet he has been willing to sacrifice all of that, and his health and handsome vitality, on the altars of pleasure.

When I got back to the House I fetched Rab, with whom I am becoming increasingly intimate, and I escorted him to the Foreign Affairs Committee, which he addressed for forty minutes, exerting a calming effect. He was cool, balanced and unalarming – the boys went away soothed and reassured. The alarms and rumours he discounted.

1 She had been 60 the previous 2 January.
2 The painter.*
3 Clown-like.

I contrived to dine almost alone; but I sat with Charles Wood[1] as he ate. He is a pillar of society, cautious, conservative, and chic: eldest sons cannot afford to be foolish these days and he isn't .... Charles and I went out to his car at 9.15 and listened to the broadcasting of his father's great speech: Lord Halifax was addressing the Institute of Foreign Affairs at Chatham House and 'the speech' carefully prepared by the whole Cabinet or at least approved by it and even passed by the Labour Opposition, was read slowly. I listened intently for a bit: Charles's car was parked in the Members' Yard, and it thrilled him to hear his father's voice so distinctly. It was the only radio as there is none that I know of in the House of Commons ... but at last, although I knew I was listening to the most important speech made by an English statesman since the war, I fell asleep and only awoke when Charles stirred beside me. We went back into the House and the news of the speech was soon brought in and everywhere met with approval. It was too anti-German for me, and humanless [sic]. People are really remarkably hysterical about Danzig, a city that is 99 per cent German, and is 'free against its will' – a ludicrous situation. The whole outlook is appalling, Hitler's a bandit, we all mad; Russia slyly waiting and waiting ...

FRIDAY 30TH JUNE

Dressed in a little Friday, blue flannel number, I lunched with Emerald where I found the Spanish and Belgian ambassadors, Sir Robert and Lady Vansittart,[2] Lady Londonderry, Laura Corrigan, Sir George Clark,[3] and Brendan Bracken[4] – a distinguished party; but Emerald, irritated by Grace Curzon chucking at 1.40, refused to be amusing. No fireworks, no fun. I was next to Lady Vansittart, a dreamy fool: I slyly pumped her and I am sorry to record that she fell into my lap and attacked the Prime Minister wholeheartedly. She even called him 'a fool'. I knew of the Vansittarts' disloyalty and of their real tendencies ... but I doubted somewhat that she would be silly enough to say those sort of things to me. The Foreign Office is a dreadful place and responsible for much of the world's misery

---

1 Charles Ingram Courtenay Wood (1912–80), by courtesy Lord Irwin until 1959, when he succeeded his father as 2nd Earl of Halifax. He was Conservative MP for the City of York from 1937 to 1945. He was Channon's cousin by marriage.
2 Sarita Enriqueta Ward (1891–1985), married in 1931 as his second wife Robert Vansittart*.
3 George Ernest Clark (1882–1950) succeeded his father as 2nd Bt in 1935. He had been Chairman of the Great Northern Railway.
4 Brendan Rendall Bracken (1901–58) was an Irish adventurer and fantasist who nonetheless became a successful newspaper publisher and, after becoming close to Winston Churchill, a politician and Cabinet minister. He was a Conservative MP from 1929 to 1952. He founded the *Banker* and merged the *Financial News* into the *Financial Times*. From 1941 to 1945 he was Minister of Information. He was raised to the peerage as 1st Viscount Bracken in 1952.

. . . . I rushed back to the House of Commons in time to vote, where on the Ministry of Labour Supply day, an important division after all, we could only muster a majority of 18!! This morning David Margesson had oiled[1] Rab, praised him, and praised me very much, too. Rab repeated it all: he also said that at the Halifax luncheon party yesterday I was mentioned and lauded.

Perhaps it is part of the general charm wave which has not yet abated.

I was lucky tonight as the *Evening Standard* has got hold of Geyr's[2] secret visit to Ronnie Brocket's[3] house where Walter Buccleuch and I met last Friday – today week. Brocket and Buccleuch are both mentioned – but not me. This is a piece of luck on which Walter complimented me tonight at the Ball. I fear it will come out later.

I drove to Pyrford, Fritzi of Prussia . . . following in a small car. Fritzi went to dine at Sutton with the Sutherlands for their vast party. We all followed: (Hugh) Euston,[4] the mild, Nordic-looking heir of the Graftons. A nice boy whom I should like for my brother-in-law but I am beginning to believe that Brigid prefers David Astor[5] – that would be an interesting alliance!! Lorna Harmsworth,[6] Esmond's elder daughter, a plump and exceedingly sexy bosomy bacchante[7] of 19 . . . The House was floodlit and not crowded altogether there were at least 600 people present. Eileen [Sutherland] in white and wearing many jewels looked magnificent: she stood at the top of the gallery stairs receiving with Elizabeth Leveson-Gower and Geordie Sutherland[8] helping her. All London was present: everyone we had ever heard of. I was immediately led up to the Queen of Spain who was in white and wearing many pearls. We had a long gossip and she sent George Cholmondeley[9] away as we continued our political discussions.

---

1 That is, flattered him.

2 Leo Dietrich Franz Geyr von Schweppenburg (1886–1974) was a member of the Prussian aristocracy and a general in the Wehrmacht. In September 1939 he would command a Panzer division in the invasion of Poland and in 1944 would command an armoured division in Normandy. He had been German Military Attaché in London from 1933 to 1937 and retained numerous high-society contacts there. He appears to have been in London to renew those contacts and to gather information about British attitudes to further German aggression.

3 Lord Brocket, a well-known Nazi sympathiser; see entry for 28 December 1938 and footnote.

4 Hugh Denis Charles FitzRoy (1919–2011), Earl of Euston until 1970 when he succeeded his father as 11th Duke of Grafton.

5 Francis David Langhorne Astor (1912–2001) was the third child of Lord and Lady Astor*. He was editor of *The Observer*, which his father had owned, from 1948 to 1975.

6 Lorna Peggy Vyvyan Harmsworth (1920–2014), daughter of the 2nd Viscount Rothermere (qv).

7 A votary of Bacchus, the god of wine.

8 George Granville 'Geordie' Sutherland-Leveson-Gower (1888–1963), 5th Duke of Sutherland.*

9 George Horatio Charles Cholmondeley (1883–1968), 5th Marquess of Cholmondeley. He married, in 1913, Sybil Sassoon (1894–1989), sister of Sir Philip Sassoon (qv).*

She was enraptured with our dinner party and said so a dozen times. Her face is a libidinous one and for a second I wondered was she flirtatious? She almost excited me: it would be fun to have an affair with a queen. Shall I pursue it? Her conversation is lecherous enough . . . then I had a talk with the old Duchess of Norfolk who told me how surprised she had been by [her daughter] Rachel's engagement to Colin Davidson, whom she has known all his life . . . then I danced at random with everyone, drank a little too much, sat out with Irene Carisbrooke, chatted with many, had an interesting conversation with Jack Herbert whose governorship of Bengal will be announced tomorrow. On all sides he was being congratulated: he will be an excellent proconsul, tall, dignified, solid and solemn, he has every qualification including a high sense of duty. He is pleased, but Mary, his wife, is less so . . . He told me that I should be made a whip 'before long', but when I attempted to draw him out, he became whip-like again; but he said enough to make me realise that my name is in the tapes: and has probably been turned down either because I am doing so well where I am, as David had told Rab, or because he thinks the moment inappropriate, or possibly on account of James Stuart's opposition. He was at the ball tonight dancing with Mollie Buccleuch . . . She, by the way, danced every dance except one with young Granby.

I hope I was not too foolish tonight: certainly I could not get away, and Lady Londonderry asked me to dance. She was wild and incoherent and although she looked impressive she spat at me. She has a way of blowing saliva at me: also she bumped me with her tiara. We drank much champagne together and she told me startling things about her children, particularly Maureen Stanley[1] whom she dislikes. She only cares for the youngest, the sophisticated Mairi. Romaine Castlereagh[2] she pulled in pieces, and said that Robin was weak and worthless. What a curious habit she has of always running down her children.

At last, it was 4.40, I collected Laura Harmsworth and Fritzi of Prussia and we drove back to Pyrford. It was already daylight; I had seen all London, and sat up until the dawn although I had thought to go to bed at eleven. Perhaps I am not so old or so tired as I thought.

Seymour Berry was both drunk and mysterious: he hinted at a dark plot which 'would be the greatest defeat the PM and David Margesson had had yet'. I am not sure what he means. He is very Red in foreign politics and a violent supporter of Winston: it must have something to do with him.

---

1 Wife of Oliver Stanley (qv).
2 Violet Gwladys Romaine Combe (1904–51) married in 1931 Robin Vane-Tempest-Stewart, Viscount Castlereagh*, who would succeed his father in 1949 as 8th Marquess of Londonderry.

SATURDAY 1ST JULY

There has been more alarming news about Danzig, later of a 'putsch', of occupation etc.[1] Everyone is most gloomy.

SUNDAY 2ND JULY

I have been thinking over Seymour's ominous words: is he aiming at the overthrow of the government, or the inclusion of Winston? For a week now the Glamour Boys have been strangely quiet, and absent from the House of Commons. I know that there is a semi-secret [illegible] going on now at Crichel where Naps, an ardent Edenite, is entertaining *inter alia* Anthony and Winston.

MONDAY 3RD JULY

The Berry cat is out of the bag: the *Daily Telegraph* today produces a full leader of a column and a half demanding the inclusion of Winston Churchill in the government. It is a threatening 'leader'. I made up my mind to wake Margesson and I drove to the Foreign Office. I crossed over to the Whips' Office and after discovering that he had not yet arrived, I waited for him by the steps. At length he arrived, debonair, bare-headed, swaggeringly handsome. I spilt the beans. He was annoyed and had heard nothing, nothing at all. He had not even read the *Telegraph*, as he had rushed up from the country. He rushed into the Whips' Office to read it before going to consult the PM. Later David told me that he had repeated Seymour's sinister remarks to him. The PM was taken aback. All day David kept sending for me and by the afternoon it was clear that a huge conspiracy had been hatched. The press lords were to combine in an attempt to force the Prime Minister into inviting Winston into the government: the plot had been engineered by Randolph and Seymour etc. It may fail. I hope it will. The Edenites had foolishly joined with them hoping to get a Cabinet seat for Anthony.

I lunched with Sibyl Colefax, a party for Rachel and Colin Davidson: pleasant, but much talk of Churchill. Later at Question Time 'God' gave me a pertinent warm smile: it was his gentle way of thanking me. The whips wondered whether Lord Kemsley was of the plot, so I decided to go to their ball tonight and 'pump' him. Walking in the lobby I overheard Jim Thomas say to Anthony 'We cannot

---

1 On 28 June millions of Poles swore an oath that they would never allow themselves to be cut off from the Baltic Sea, and told Germany they were prepared to fight for Danzig to remain a free city. On 3 July Chamberlain would tell the Commons that 'extensive measures of a military character are being carried out in the Free City' and that 'a large and increasing number of German nationals have recently arrived . . . ostensibly as tourists, and a local defence corps is being formed under the name of the Heimwehr'. Chamberlain refused to say whether or not these acts were illegal.

count on the *Evening Standard*. They will let us down.' What a clumsy group of plotters they are, actuated by an almost childish love of intrigue. Winston would mean certain war. His supporters pretend that an invitation to him to join the Cabinet would be a stern warning to Hitler that we mean business. I think and repeat that this country is mad – utterly mad – to wish to risk a war for something that doesn't concern us ...

I dined at Emerald's, a large *décousu*[1] party without reason or plot, and boring really. Grace Curzon in pale blue looked magnificent: she was next to the Duke of Argyll .... We had a long talk about poor Portia Stanley who is healing up:[2] she is half mad with herbs, drugs, sleeping draughts, money and misery. She is desperate and misses Edward more every day: she is tormented by his loss and the cruel fact that she will never be Lady Derby after all. She has always been selfish but a loyal friend and I am sorry for her, and fond of her.

The Kemsleys' ball at Chandos House was overcrowded. The luminous, ample, colourful Lady Kemsley[3] tried to combine two things, a great ball and a debutantes' party, and in so doing failed in both. It was very hot ... I was sent for by Lord Kemsley and told to look after the Queen of Spain. I did: I had supper with HM and we talked for an hour or more. She was wearing glorious diamonds. She told me of Spanish Court life, how she had gone always to La Granja[4] in June for six weeks, to Santander for August, San Sebastian for September and to Barcelona for the autumn weeks to the modern palace built for them by the people. The rest of the year, except for a visit to England, was always passed in Madrid. She is having great social success now and is much sought after. She loathes Vansittart and snubbed him at Windsor when he hoped that France would be lenient with the (Red) criminals! Winston Churchill and Anthony Eden are her other *bêtes noires*. When Lord Kemsley returned to her I skilfully drew him into the conversation, and 'sounded' him. I was relieved to discover that he is anti-Anthony, anti-Churchill and angered by the great plot for their reinstatement.

I looked for Norman Gwatkin everywhere but he could not be found. I thought of Peter Coats,[5] whom I met for the first time at dinner tonight, charming and gay. I talked to Princess Marina who never in the many years that I had

---

1 Disjointed, literally 'unstitched'.
2 After the death of her husband Edward, Lord Stanley (qv), which had occurred the previous October.
3 Marie Edith Dresselhuys (*née* Merandon du Plessis) (1888–1976), married as her second husband James Gomer Berry, Lord Kemsley*, in 1931.
4 Palacio Real de La Granja de San Ildefonso is near Segovia, about fifty miles north of Madrid, and has been a royal palace since the eighteenth century and was a summer residence for the Spanish royal family. It is now a museum.
5 For more details about Peter Coats, see the introduction.

known her looked so lonely. She was in white satin and diamonds. The Duke was charming and funny.

TUESDAY 4TH JULY

I repeated my conversation with Lord Kemsley to David Margesson, who immediately communicated it to the Prime Minister, for whom I am this week acting as PPS in Dunglass's absence. I had a luncheon party, a lot of bores, people to whom I was indebted. At 1.30 I had a message that Maureen Dufferin had 'chucked'; that would have made me thirteen, so I bullied both her and Jim Wedderburn by means of SOS messages to come. And they both did. Luncheon was a fair success, but I had the feeling that everyone expected to meet grander people than they did, and were disappointed.

The Churchill plot continues, but I am told that God has dug his toes in about it, luckily.

Dined with a group of Oxford chaps, a club called 'The Cloister' as Peter Loxley's guest. Later at the House of Commons I picked up Jim Thomas and brought him back here to gossip. He is annoyed by the Churchill plot, to which he originally subscribed, as Winston is stealing all Anthony's thunder. There is thus division in Tuscany. I must repeat all this in the morning.

The negotiations with Russia are going very badly. Perhaps they will break down.

WEDNESDAY 5TH JULY

The news I picked up from Jim Thomas was warmly welcomed by the whips, and has made Winston's inclusion even more unlikely and remote. I have frustrated him: he little guessed when he antagonised me what a powerful enemy I should become. I have learnt a lesson: beware of the humble; they can do one in as I have done him in, at least, temporarily.

Much conversation with Rab, who increasingly consults me. He begged Halifax not to go too far with the Russian reptilians.

Churchill plot is a wet squib. I came home and saw my baby boy. I rang up Honor who is adoring her ski-trip at the Jungfraujoch[1] where there is glorious snow. Then I wrote my diary and did work. How pleasant it is to be here.

I hear my sister-in-law Brigid fancies Lord Haig.[2] That would be all right. He is mild and *mièvre*,[3] but I shall encourage the match.

---

1 In Switzerland, in the Bernese Alps.
2 George Alexander Eugene Douglas Haig (1918–2009) was by courtesy Viscount Dawick from 1919 to 1928 when he succeeded his father as 2nd Earl Haig. He did not marry until 1956.
3 Soppy.

THURSDAY 6TH JULY

From what I could gather of David Margesson's recent communication with Rab I am not to be made a whip just now for several reasons, primarily because I am thought to be indispensable to Rab. Thus I am punished for being successful: I am not disappointed, indeed I dreaded promotion as it would entail leaving the Foreign Office which I love: I revel in the diplomatic atmosphere.

The plot to include Winston is dying down. One can never defeat the Berrys combined with the Astors: they were united over the abdication, the Astors were pro-Munich and defeated the Berrys who are against it: but on this issue of including Churchill, and possibly Eden, in the Cabinet, the Berrys are themselves divided, Camrose being pro-Churchill, but Kemsley mercifully being against the scheme. The Astors, surprisingly enough, take a strong pro-Churchill line. Lady Astor, who is a bitch at heart, and a really worthless self-seeking adventurer has made a volte-face, and frightened by anonymous letters and gossip about the so-called 'Cliveden Set' has thrown over her principle and is urging Chamberlain against his better judgement to take this plunge . . . . he won't, David assures me. I am sure that old Garvin[1] will produce a bombastic leader in next Sunday's *Observer*.

I went to Dover House, the Scottish Office, for a cocktail: there I found the government, pipers and many Scottish people. There was an aroma of mothballs. How badly dressed is the Scottish aristocracy! I told old Lady Airlie,[2] whom I met in the room where once her ancestor (by marriage) Lady Caroline Lamb had reigned, that she must be made Secretary of State for Scotland. She laughed . . . but when I repeated the joke to Mrs Neville Chamberlain, who daily becomes madder and more whimsical, she didn't smile. She hardly registers to reality these days! Then on to Warwick House where there was a mammoth cocktail party given by Esmond Harmsworth. He told me in confidence that he is anti-Churchill really, but he nevertheless believes that his inclusion in the Cabinet is inevitable. I tried to dissuade him.[3]

Dinner at Michael Duff's in Charles Street. He is a curious Pierrot, an inspired child, secretive and shrewd and not altogether normal. He loves old ladies, dowagers, royalties and tiaras. Dinner of twenty-six, but the room was

---

1 James Louis Garvin (1868–1947) edited *The Observer* from 1908 until 1942, when he fell out with the Astor family – who owned the paper – over his support for Churchill. He wrote a massive biography of Joseph Chamberlain, which remained unfinished at Garvin's death and was completed by Julian Amery (qv).

2 Mabell Frances Elizabeth Gore (1866–1956), daughter of Viscount Sudley, widow of the 11th Earl of Airlie.

3 Harmsworth was also influenced by the active support that his father, Lord Rothermere, gave the appeasement lobby; and indeed had over the preceding years given the Nazi regime itself.

unfriendly and charged with hate for me as that old dragon, the she-Desborough[1] was present: she is eternal, looks not a day older than she did twenty years ago. She is a serpent ever ready to strike, and always stinging. There is no devilry she is incapable of, and it was a mistake making her so resolute an enemy. She was civil, I was cold, but we chatted in a banal, freezing manner and daughter Mogs[2] was opposite me at dinner. On to Holland House . . . There were no AA men, or special police, just [traffic] congestion – at last we arrived but by then the party spirit had already died. Immediately we were in a jam, pink debutantes, be-tiaraed dowagers, ambassadors, royalties, all in a crowd such as we had never seen . . . The ballroom was like a cup final, and I thought that Emerald Cunard would faint . . . . One could not dance, one could not move . . . eventually I found the Infanta Maria Cristina and Princess Cecilie of Prussia[3] and I piloted them to the supper room on the first floor where we had some champagne. All London was present; Lady Haddington,[4] whom I dislike, stood out: she wore a large crown, the finest at the ball. I escorted the exhausted Infanta to a private room to join her mother. There I found the Queen of Spain on a sofa . . . The Queen of England was with Lord Rochester.[5] Both the queens smiled at me and I bowed. Then I joined Irene Carisbrooke just inside the royal room, and we waited on the stairways for the royal family to leave. I thought the Queen would never move, and no one could leave as the royal cars blocked the way. I had asked for the Queen of Spain's car and was told it could not approach until the King had left. Queen Elizabeth, in her attempt to help him, has become too prominent and steals his thunder. She was in white and wore a crown, and generally looked like Lady Haddington, who spends her life imitating her. The Queen emerged from the royal room, everyone bowed, she smiled and stopped to chat with Lionel Portarlington.[6] The King followed showing his teeth, as he often does. He looked young. The Kents I did not see.

Still in a foul temper I asked for my car, and waited for forty minutes for it: the arrangements had been left to the gardeners, I hear. Home at 3.30, bored and angry, and unimpressed by the romance of Holland House, which usually impressed me. Still I suppose there was a certain Disraelian splendour: the duchesses looked well, and the atmosphere must be much as it was a century ago

---

1 Ethel 'Ettie' Fane (1867–1952) married in 1887 William Henry Grenfell (1855–1945), 1st Baron Desborough. She had been a lady-in-waiting to Queen Mary. In the 1920s, she and Channon had developed a feud.*
2 Alexandra Imogen Clair Grenfell (1905–69) married in 1931 Viscount Gage*.
3 Daughter of the Crown Prince of Prussia and sister of 'Fritzi'.*
4 Sarah Cook (1903–95), married in 1923 the 12th Earl of Haddington.
5 Ernest Henry Lamb (1876–1955) was Liberal MP for Rochester from 1910 to 1918. He joined the Labour Party in 1929 and was raised to the peerage in 1931, serving in the National Government as Paymaster-General from then until 1935.
6 Lionel Arthur Henry Seymour Dawson-Damer (1883–1959), 6th Earl of Portarlington.*

when queens did not go to Holland House . . . I tried to find Norman Gwatkin to give him a lift, but he was busy piloting the royalties, finding detectives etc. Perhaps he can't [be] very attractive after all. I had a conversation with David Margesson, who had come on from the House: he was charm itself but never mentioned the whips. I am out of the running, I think. I should like to be appointed before Geneva and so not be obliged to go there.

FRIDAY 7TH JULY

Twenty-four hours of splendour, of old-world magnificence, of England that is supposed to be dead and isn't.

I woke tired after a late night, and went to the Foreign Office. The news is rather better abroad and on the home front we have won, at least, temporarily. Churchill and Eden are out, and will stay out for the time being. Then I slept and at 5 p.m. left for Weston[1] to stay with the Sitwells, a lovely fast drive. We dined gaily and I was funny and felt well. The Ali Khans[2] are here, bubbling with happiness, and love and riches. She has enormously improved in looks and charm. There is also Peter Coats, a well-meaning pierrot of charm and Aryan good looks. I like him: it was mutual. We shall be friends, as he is [illegible] and companionable, gentle and friendly. He, Sachie and I drove in my car to Blenheim, the others following. Blenheim was stupendous: I have seen much, travelled far, and am accustomed to splendour but there has never been anything like tonight. The Palace was floodlit, and its great baroque beauty could be seen for miles. The lakes were floodlit and better still the famous terraces. They were blue and green, and Tyroleans walked about singing – and although there were 700 people or even more, it was never in the least crowded. It was gay, young, brilliant and perfection. Silly Bill Tufnell said that his mind was at ease for the first time in his life! I danced with everyone, a long bit with Mary Herbert, so soon to go to Australia with Sheila, with Joan Khan, and Georgia [Sitwell] my hostess, and many, many more. The great hall was lined with a buffet where people congregated whilst below in the Chinese suite there was supper and there I saw Winston Churchill, Anthony Eden with Daphne Weymouth,[3] who never left Anthony the whole evening . . . what was all that about!! Seymour Berry was particularly pleasant, and Sheila sincerely insincere . . . I had several breakfasts, one in the great dining room and I thought of other dinners there long ago, with the late Duke[4] as a divorcé, and later when married

---

1 Weston Hall, near Towcester.
2 Prince Ali Khan (1911–60) and Joan Yarde-Buller (1908–97). They had married in 1936 after Yarde-Buller's divorce from her first husband, Loel Guinness. In 1986 she married her third husband, Seymour Berry (qv).
3 See entry for 20 October 1938 and footnote.
4 Charles Richard John Spencer-Churchill (1871–1934), 9th Duke of Marlborough.*

to Gladys[1] – no one knows where she is but there is a rumour that she lives in the village nearly half-mad and half-incognito. Madame Balsan,[2] distinguished but deaf, was tonight the heroine and she wondered about the Palace where once she reigned, holding again a court almost Proustian. The whole world was there, but I thought the Duchess of Kent, who had motored from Himley[3] after a day of ceremonies, looked tired. She overdoes it. I was loath to leave but did so about 4.30, and took one last look at the baroque terraces with the lake below, at the gold statues, at the Great Palace. Shall we ever see the like again? Is such a function not out of date? There were rivers of champagne, an adequate supper …I drove back with Sachie and Peter Coats, and got to sleep early at 7 a.m.

SATURDAY 8TH JULY

I dozed a little: Peter Coats dressed in khaki came in to say 'goodbye' as he was leaving to drill his Territorials; charming he looked, and half asleep I thought he was the Prince of Wales fifteen years ago. We lunched sleepily at 2 p.m. and then I motored across England. Kelvedon lovely, and baby Paul was feeding the ducks. He gave a whoop of delight at seeing me: and we played together until he was sick – he gets excited.

Dined at Langleys: Bill Tufnell very curious, and I left early because of the blackout and drove myself home and lost the way outside Chelmsford. Back at midnight. Life seems a dream, these past forty-eight hours.

Patrick Buchan-Hepburn has been made a whip, a stupid appointment which will offend and please no one. He is fundamentally stupid. I should have been better at it.

What a week of balls, Sutton, Holland House and Blenheim. Such a triptych of splendour, of the old order is hardly to be imagined as happening in these days.

MONDAY 10TH JULY

Little Princess Cecilie of Prussia is staying with me at 5 Belgrave Square, and she has brought a dark, engaging damsel, a Miss Cynthia Elliot.[4] They lunched in

---

1 Gladys Marie Deacon (1881–1977) married the 9th Duke in 1921, after having been his mistress for many years. She was becoming a recluse and was living at Chacombe, near Banbury, not at Woodstock or anywhere else adjoining Blenheim Palace.
2 Consuelo Vanderbilt (1877–1964) was the wife of the 9th Duke of Marlborough from 1895 to 1921, when they divorced. The marriage was later annulled. She married the same year, as her second husband, Lieutenant Colonel Louis Jacques Balsan (1868–1956), a famous aviator, balloonist and socialite, who according to Hugo Vickers' book *The Sphinx: The Life of Gladys Deacon* benefited greatly from injections of monkey gland.
3 Himley Hall in Staffordshire, seat of the earls of Dudley.
4 Cynthia Sophie Elliot (1916–91) married in 1944 Leslie Hore-Belisha (qv), who was twenty-three years her senior. She served as a Red Cross nurse in a German prisoner-of-war camp from 1940 to 1944.

and I collected Masters Coats, Tony Loughborough,[1] and young Jack Kennedy[2] to amuse them. A hilarious little party and later I took them all here to the House as they wanted to see the PM .... I was in attendance on God, and my young friends were impressed. Cecilie is attractive, but not so pretty or so charming as Fritzi. She is small, snobbish and pleasing. Once I had thought to marry her to the Prince of Wales. If only he had ... Norman Gwatkin dined with me, and is empty and Edwardian with an ease of manner and considerable charm. He is a very old-fashioned chap, with an out-of-date face: many of the old courtiers, typified by the Keppels,[3] are like that. I brought him here,[4] and he was surrounded by friends. Almost an ovation. Later he and I went back to drink with Alan at Little College Street.

Home at 1.30 for no real reason and worn out. The Halifaxes entertained the King and Queen at dinner last night: I wonder why they did not invite me?

TUESDAY 11TH JULY

The war seems a little remote: perhaps it will never come: it seems less a reality and there is no news ....

I lunched with Alan and Patsy to meet the Queen of Spain. They had collected a pleasant party, Ernest Brown; and the Yeats-Browns[5] of *Bengal Lancer* fame – (I was disappointed in him, a thin, crisp, studious creature, and not the *beau sabreur*[6] I had expected); Halifaxes, so gracious both ... Loelia Westminster in her own house; Father D'Arcy,[7] the Jesuit Priest and the real head of the Jesuit movement in England; Lord Queenborough, and others. I lent plate, footmen, and my *savoir faire*. Both Alan and Patsy a touch flustered. The Queen arrived punctually, not so Loelia who kept us waiting for ten minutes. Halifax was next to the Queen and listened to her propaganda with his grave smile ...

1 Anthony Hugh Francis Harry St Clair-Erskine (1917–77), Viscount Loughborough. He would soon succeed his grandfather as 6th Earl of Rosslyn.*

2 John Fitzgerald Kennedy (1917–63) became 35th President of the United States of America, serving from 1961 until his assassination in Dallas in November 1963.

3 Alice Frederica Edmonstone (1868–1947) married in 1891 George Keppel (1865–1947). She was a noted society beauty and hostess before and after the Great War, best known for having been the mistress of King Edward VII from 1898 until his death in 1910.

4 The House of Commons.

5 Francis Charles Claypon Yeats-Brown (1886–1944) was a former army officer who became a journalist and achieved fame with his memoir *The Lives of a Bengal Lancer*, published in 1930; it was made into a Hollywood film starring Gary Cooper in 1935. He married, as his second wife, Olga Phillips (1909–82) in 1938.

6 Dashing swordsman, or hero.

7 Martin Cyril D'Arcy (1888–1976) entered the Society of Jesus in 1907, after Stonyhurst. He was ordained priest in 1921 and wrote works of religious philosophy. He was a close spiritual adviser of Eric Gill, Edwin Lutyens and Evelyn Waugh.

I went home for a moment and found Nannie, or rather an ex-Nannie, in tears.[1] She had arrived back today from the hospital and I could not conceal the fact of how unwelcome she was. Suddenly I was sorry for her and realised that she had always been kind to my little boy whom I love so deeply, so desperately. Is this a strain of sadism in me? Am I cruel to those who love me? I tire of people, turn against them after years; and now I am against Nannie who has been a deplorable influence on Paul ...

Dinner at Laura Corrigan's. I fetched the Infanta at 34 Porchester Terrace and escorted her to the dinner dance. The Queen of Spain lives in a smallish house, chosen probably both because of its cheapness and proximity to Kensington Palace. The Infanta talked of her mother: what was she to do? Live in a palace with an aged lady-in-waiting, after the Restoration? The Queen is 52, remarkably handsome and gay; the role of a dowager queen would not suit her ... and she will not be reconciled with King Alfonso. Even if she did, rows would soon begin again ... the Infanta is unhappy about her mother. When we arrived at Laura's, our hostess surrounded by a bevy of beauties, who were acting as co-hostesses ... They were Elizabeth Scott[2] (Mollie Buccleuch's very pink, very pretty Dresden-china daughter); Mairi Stewart, so gay and sophisticated and much the best, as her parents make it clear, of the Londonderry children; Sarah Churchill,[3] blue-eyed and polite, Elizabeth Leveson-Gower, dark and full of unexpected fire ... these are the daughters of our great houses, and an attractive lot they are. I wish my Brigid were there ... There were about 160 people at dinner and I found myself at Laura's table: I am always at the top table at Laura's and tonight I have the American Ambassadress on my left ... Mrs Kennedy[4] is an uninteresting little body, pleasant and extraordinarily young-looking to be the mother of nine. She has an unpleasant voice, says nothing of interest and keeps a diary. I like people who keep diaries: they are not as others, at least not quite (I feel my character and capabilities developing these recent weeks at an alarming rate) ...

The ball proceeded and I enjoyed it hugely; so much so that I did not go on to Lord Beaverbrook's ball. I hear it was an orgy; but I am tired of that over-clever, over-magnetic collection of positive people with too much personality ... I stayed at Laura's, philandered with the young, danced with the Ambassadress ... at 3.30 Peter Coats and I drove the Infanta to Porchester Terrace and then went to Belgrave Square for a drink and talk.

---

1 Channon had sacked Paul's nanny, who had discovered her fate after returning from a spell in hospital.

2 Lady Elizabeth Diana Montagu Douglas Scott (1922–2012): she married, in 1946, Hugh Algernon Percy, 10th Duke of Northumberland (1914–88).

3 Lady Sarah Consuelo Spencer-Churchill (1921–2000) was the eldest child of the 10th Duke of Marlborough.

4 Rose Elizabeth Fitzgerald (1890–1995) married Joseph Patrick Kennedy (qv), of whom her father, the Mayor of Boston, deeply disapproved, in 1914.

WEDNESDAY 12TH JULY

Brendan Bracken had some American guests to tea on the terrace yesterday: they had come over in 'The Clipper'.[1] That is all one hears nowadays, 'Clipper'. Talks of people breakfasting in Marseilles and dining in New York, all too Jules Verne and deplorable for words. America is quite near enough . . .

Lunched (I slept for one and a half hours), at the Brazilian Embassy, a dullish party to meet the German Ambassador. I had a talk with him and found him agreeable and not rattled. I was next to old Julia Maguire,[2] who was dressed in cherry red. She had smothered rouge anyhow all over her pantomime face. Could this Peel harridan have been such a charmer, as she is alleged to have been? She was Cecil Rhodes's *grande amie*.[3]

I dined with Emerald: a boring party . . . . I had claustrophobia only slightly relieved by watching poor old Mrs [Ronnie] Greville (old, ill, enormous, and panting under the weight of her emeralds).[4] Winston Churchill was next to her. How they dislike each other, and for all his gimmicks, genius, and amazing versatility, she is the shrewder of the two. I left directly I could, having hated my evening.

THURSDAY 13TH JULY

A very curt, cold, brief little letter from Honor. I am sad and apprehensive about her: but *que faire*? I fear trouble ultimately. I lunched with Lord Halifax at the Carlton Hotel, a party to meet the Spanish journalists. I hate Spaniards. Halifax presided with his usual ecclesiastic charm. I was amazed to see Wilfrid Roberts,[5] that arch shit, and most violent of all the pro-Red-Barcelona MPs, stand and drink Franco's health.

I was in a frenzy this afternoon as Rab asked me to arrange a banquet next Thursday for M. Moshanov,[6] the Bulgarian Speaker. I telephoned frantically,

---

1   The Boeing 314 Clipper, a flying boat, had flown for the first time the previous year and had just been introduced into passenger service, the first transatlantic flight between Port Washington and Southampton having happened on 24 June.

2   Julia Beatrice Peel (1864–1949), daughter of the 1st Viscount Peel, Speaker of the House of Commons from 1884 to 1895; she married in 1895 James Rochfort Maguire, who had been at Oxford with Cecil Rhodes and became his close associate.

3   Great ladyfriend, with an innuendo of 'mistress', though that allegation is unproven.

4   Margaret 'Maggie' Helen Anderson (1863–1942), daughter of William McEwan, Scottish brewing magnate. She married in 1891 Ronald Henry Fulke Greville (1864–1908), who became a Conservative MP; a close friend of Queen Mary, she was one of London's leading hostesses before and after the Great War. Although always referred to as Mrs Ronnie Greville, she had become Dame Margaret Greville in 1922.

5   Wilfrid Roberts (1900–91) was Liberal MP for North Cumberland from 1935 to 1950. He had been a strong supporter of the Republican cause in the Spanish Civil War.

6   Stoycho Moshanov (1892–1975) was Chairman of the Bulgarian National Assembly from May 1938 to October 1939.

tried to engage a room in vain, and rather dreaded the necessary arrangements. At last I hit upon the happy idea of persuading the Speaker to invite him and his wife. It is quite unprecedented; but he liked it, and even seemed pleased. It is a most tactful courtesy and Rab was impressed and grateful. I went to see Subbotić[1] at the Yugoslav Legation at 5 p.m. and spent an hour giving him social and political advice as to how to make his legation a success. It was on the tip of my tongue to remark that the last two ministers had died too quickly . . . . he [is] a stocky Balkan with a teethy [*sic*] grin – how can I tell him that he smells of garlic and that the English don't like it.

I left him to go and see Mrs Cornelius Vanderbilt,[2] my old crony, the white-haired Queen of New York. She is unchanged, gushing, grey-haired, affectionate and blessed (like me!) by royalty. I have not seen her for three years and found her the same good firm friend . . . she is very pro-Chamberlain! I then rushed to Smith Square to dress my Rab. He didn't bathe, shave or do any of the one hundred toilet tasks which twice daily I perform. I then drove him to the Pilgrims' Dinner, and returned eventually to the House as the Members' Pensions Bill was being discussed. Chamberlain was suave, gay and showed a certain understanding: he pleased the Labour Party mainly. After a somewhat needlessly heated debate, during which Duff Cooper made an absurd contribution which offended both the Opposition and the front bench (and he wants to placate both), we divided. There was an overwhelming majority, on a 'free vote' which the whips removed, in favour. We have signed away £12 per annum for the rest of our parliamentary days as it is unlikely that any of us shall ever be in quite such low financial states as to require the pension. Still I voted for the measure, and Alan, much to my annoyance, did not. He was quite obstinate about it and showed his limitations. He is injudicious in the extreme. He has offended the Labour people, who will now guy him more than ever. I suddenly hated him in a flash. Once I loved him: I am fond of him still, but money is corroding him quickly – only six months married. What will he be in a year's time? I went home cross and disappointed: but I should have been more so had I not chanced on the PM, who gave me one of his smiles of such dazzling warmth that I felt warm and glowed for a moment.

I was told today that it has been definitely decided not to give the Garter to Paul[3] when he arrives, as it is never given to non-reigning sovereigns! I retorted

---

1 Ivan Subbotić (1893–1973) was the Yugoslav Minister in London from 1939 to 1941. He was regarded as one of his country's foremost diplomats and had been his country's representative to the League of Nations from 1935 until 1939. He later became Yugoslavia's representative to the Red Cross, and settled in the United States after the war, practising as a lawyer in New York.

2 Grace Graham Wilson (1870–1953), who in 1896 had married (greatly against his father's wishes) Cornelius Vanderbilt III (qv).

3 The Regent of Yugoslavia.

that this was nonsense and when I went home I did a bit of research work amongst the old Garters, and found to my delight some fourteen non-reigning 'Chevaliers de la Jarretière': I made out the list and gave it to Lord Halifax.

FRIDAY 14TH JULY

Six years married today. I am sorry my marriage is not more of a success. Perhaps I am to blame . . . but H has a most complicated aloof mysterious nature. I sent her a telegram to thank her for her portrait given me by her as an anniversary present. It is by Ian Campbell-Gray. I like it. She did not reply. She is still . . . . skiing dangerously with Brigid. I don't envy them. It is a sort of madness.

Princess Cecilie of Prussia has been staying with me in London for a few days. Last evening and again this morning I found the Grand Duke Vladimir,[1] a large youth, sharing a sofa with her. It looked like an engagement to me. When Rab arrived for luncheon I presented him. Vladimir (future Tsar of all the Russians?) is working under an assumed name in a factory in the North. I took to him, but he is heavy. The Russians and the Prussians . . . Rab and Esmond Harmsworth lunched with me privately and we had a long and interesting political discussion. Rab drew him out brilliantly . . . we sat until nearly four and then I went to see old Mr Bland, our [Guinness] trustee.

At four a royal tea party again with Vladimir, Princess Cecilie and others: Peter Coats and I left them and motored to Kelvedon, stopping *en route* at Brentwood to see Batsi and her seven pups. She seemed a happy and good mother, but was not particularly pleased to see me. The puppies, four bitches, three dogs, are the size of rats and their eyes, of course, still closed.

A peaceful heavenly evening at Kelvedon which looks lovely. Peter Coats is most delightful, knowledgeable and gay . . .

The Regent arrives, rather to my annoyance as I am so busy and tired, on Monday.

MONDAY 17TH JULY

Somewhat eagerly I waited for the post this morning: there was no invitation to the Court ball[2] . . . . Only because of it being for Paul do I really mind . . . He

---

1 Prince Vladimir Kirillovich (1917–92) was born in Finland, where his father, Grand Duke Cyril Vladimirovich, had fled after the revolution. He studied at the University of London and worked for a time in Blackstone agricultural equipment factory in Lincolnshire. When his father died in October 1938 he assumed the headship of the Romanov family, and became claimant to the Russian imperial throne. Interned by the Germans in 1942 for refusing to encourage Russians to support Hitler and help overthrow communism, he managed to evade Soviet capture in 1945 and spent the rest of his days between Spain and Brittany.

2 To be held in the Regent's honour.

arrived this evening with Olga and from Munich. It is very exciting and I long to see him.

I dined with the Queen of Spain at 34 Porchester Terrace. She keeps up mild state[1] well-blended with simplicity. I was on her left . . . Patsy had called for me wearing a tiara, which we sent home by my chauffeur. The Queen wore many pearls. Conversation was easy, fluent and very anti-Semite. I have never heard such tales and revelations as to their intrigues. Can they be even half true? The Queen of Spain, and others all prophesy revolution here eventually. Already there are symptoms of it, just as there were in Spain before 1931. On the sofa after dinner the Queen and I had a long talk, and I grew sleepy . . . she told me that Hore-Belisha on that very sofa had attempted to make love to her!!

Home at 12.30.

TUESDAY 18TH JULY

I woke bad-tempered and sulky: I was rude to my masseur and generally fiendish to the servants, but divine to my delectable dauphin.[2] I rang the Regent at Buckingham Palace and he asked me to lunch with him very sweetly. At 1.15 I went into the Kents' house (taking my baby son and the Nannie): there I found Princess Marina a vision of glamorous beauty, Princess Olga thin and distinguished, and my Regent youthful in grey flannels. They immediately seized my child, kissed and made much of him. He behaved very well. Then I drove with the royalties to Luigi's, a restaurant in Jermyn Street where we were received with some pother. We all drank cider, and ate vegetables. All were worn out.

Princess Olga said that Hitler had really been charming to her, that . . . . she liked him: he been much impressed by her cool distinction and her jewels, and told everyone she was what he had always pictured a great lady and beautiful princess to be. Their visit to Berlin was a huge success, but I gathered Paul made no commitments, no promises. After lunch the princesses left us and he and I walked down Piccadilly and to the National Gallery where we wandered about, gossiping and looking at the pictures . . . After some happy minutes I left him at three o'clock at 3 Belgrave Square and I went off to the House of Commons to vote . . . .

In the morning early I called on the Duke of Buccleuch and he received me *en négligé*[3] as he was going to a levee. We discussed the political situation, and I assured him that there was to be no war this year. Such, too, is his impression. I told him (after all Walter is the Lord Steward) that I had not been invited to the ball tomorrow: he was surprised, or pretended to be. Then I went to see David

---

1 That is, a level of pomp commensurate with being in exile, but still a Queen.
2 His son.
3 Literally untidy, in this sense as not yet dressed.

Margesson and told him: he was annoyed and rang up Alec Hardinge about me. I doubt whether there will be any developments. I am really rather annoyed by this oversight, or deliberate snub. Of course the King and Queen can ask whom they like to Buck House, but 700 people have been commanded to meet my greatest friend.

I slept this afternoon, exhausted and irritable . . . I have suddenly lost my high spirits and even Paul's visit doesn't exhilarate me as it should. He is down too, depressed and perhaps poor. He thinks war ultimately inevitable. I talked to Honor on the telephone: she, too, was low and depressing although she is enjoying herself . . . .

The Regent has been given the Garter!: my handiwork. For months I have been plotting and working for that.

WEDNESDAY 19TH JULY

I woke after a very [illegible] and short night, still depressed. I was in a rage when I remembered an invitation had not come for tonight's ball: I think it was remiss of the Regent to do nothing about it, particularly as he and Olga dined alone last night with the King and Queen and went to a revue with them. I rang him up: he was dozing and we had a gentle but unsatisfactory conversation. I felt dashed . . .

Today is my poor frustrated mother's birthday. She is 70, looks 100; and is lonely, sad, and self-centred and miserable. I don't suppose I should even see her alive again. I had never cared for her at all since I was about 12.

I lunched with the Kents, the Duchess dazzling, beautiful, radiant with the famous alabaster glow; yet she looks tired and depressed. Life is too full for her and she never rests or reads . . . the royal children are sulky Hoppners. Edward said to our new Nannie 'What's your name?' 'Nannie Waite,' she replied. 'You must be very heavy if you are a Weight,' he retorted. He is a savvy child, and very like his spoilt father. Paul lunched with the Prime Minister with whom he had a long talk at the Buckingham Palace banquet on Monday night.

All day I felt depressed not going to Buckingham Palace and really I looked foolish. It is monstrous: I had not discovered who my enemy at Court is but I suspect both Alec Hardinge and Arthur Penn,[1] although it is ordinarily that [illegible] fool, Sir Smith Child,[2] who as Master of the Household arranges the

---

1 Arthur Horace Penn (1886–1960) trained as a barrister but became a professional soldier and won the Military Cross while serving with the Grenadier Guards in the Great War. He joined the Royal Household in 1937 and became private secretary and Treasurer to Queen Elizabeth, whose close friend he had been before her marriage. He was also Groom-in-Waiting to King George VI and to Queen Elizabeth II. He was knighted in 1949.

2 Smith Hill Child (1880–1958) was a professional soldier who left the Army in 1924 in the rank of brigadier general. He was Conservative MP for Stone from 1918 to 1922. He joined the Royal Household in 1927, becoming Deputy Master in 1929 and was appointed Master in 1936, retiring in 1941. He succeeded his grandfather as 2nd Bt in 1896.

entertaining. I foolishly played a practical joke on him when I was young and irresponsible.

Dinner at the Sutherlands ... Eileen S is really one of the sweetest of women and one of my great friends. I was on her right. Geordie looked distinguished and handsome in his knee breeches. Luckily none of the others were going to the ball, so I was less embarrassed. I walked home feeling like Cinderella: a few cars with tiara-ed women passed *en route* for the ball. Nearly 800 people have been invited. I shall not forget this slight – sometimes I dislike the Queen of England! And I know her fundamentally treacherous character. She is not ambitious; not in the least, but as the only other hand she is remarkably snobbish *qua* birth. It is a Victorian kind of snobbery.

I went to bed in a rage: these setbacks occur every few years, and are quickly forgotten.

Peter [Coats] rang me in the night. He is remarkably devoted.

Geoffrey Lloyd was at lunch at the Kents: so that row has been made up. The Queen of Spain v affable: I think she slightly fancies me.

THURSDAY 20TH JULY

Fritzi rang me up and gave me an account of the ball. He had asked Queen Mary to waltz but she had replied that her figure now was no longer right for dancing; but she thanked him saying that no one else had asked her! The ball, I hear, was a success. Diana Cooper was resplendent in Honor's tiara.

Luncheon at Mrs Corrigan's was on the grand scale. Forty covers for the Kennedys, dukes, duchesses, and Mrs Vanderbilt who was most impressed. I was next to Lady Vansittart, who is really an ass. After luncheon I had a gust of popularity, Eileen Sutherland and Mary Marlborough[1] surrounding and teasing me. They ring me up at dressing time and after hearing my voice say 'Goodbye Mr Chips'[2] and hang up. No one had mentioned the ball. Grace Curzon asked me whether I could induce the Regent to buy Lord Curzon's garter, his diamond star. She had once mentioned the sum of £250, but today said she would take £265 for it. I promised her to see what I could do.

The Regent rang up but seemed very rushed. I went to Buckingham Palace to see him for a moment: they have 'their' usual Belgian suite which is really only moderately comfortable! Full of Empire pieces and some of Elizabeth's finely bound books.

Tonight was my Speaker's party! The famous dinner which I induced him to give. I fetched the Moshanovs, Monsieur et Madame, from the Rembrandt Hotel.

---

1 Alexandra Mary Cadogan (1900–61), wife of the 10th Duke.
2 The film of James Hilton's eponymous novel (published in 1934), starring Robert Donat and Greer Garson, was one of the great box-office successes of that summer.

He is a garrulous Bulgar, and is the Speaker of their local Parliament. I escorted them to the Speaker's House, and presented them to him and Mrs FitzRoy. A gloomy little party slightly leavened by the presence of the Jebbs[1] whom I had suggested to Sir Ralph Verney, the Speaker's secretary. Dinner mediocre with quails, but the drink was excellent. After dinner Mrs FitzRoy and I escorted the party over to the House of Commons, showed the Moshanovs the most interesting places, and returned to the Speaker's House by the private door. An ingenious very English evening. The Speaker's atrocious French shocked me; yet he was charming and caustic in English. He is 70. The Moshanovs left at 10.10, a few minutes before my car arrived, which cast a slight *gêne*. I returned to the House to vote and went home early.

Peter [Coats] dropped in for drinks. The Kents had a large dinner party for Queen Mary and Mrs Vanderbilt and the Regent. The royal Garden Party was cancelled owing to a downpour; but it gave me a chance to wear my grey morning coat at luncheon.

FRIDAY 21ST JULY

I decided not to ring the Regent but by 9.30 he had telephoned to me twice and so I relented and went to Buckingham Palace. The idiotic Serbian servants beckoned me into Princess Olga's room and there she stood only in her shift! She screamed and I left. Then Paul came to me, charming, affectionate, divine and I realised once again that I love him really more than anyone after my child. I sat in his bathroom as he finished dressing and he showed me a model of garter star submitted to him by Garrard's: they are asking £800 for it. It gave me an idea, and later whilst he talked to Subbotić, his minister, in the sitting room, I stepped in to have a word with Princess Olga and asked her whether he wanted a diamond star. He most decisively did, she said. He and I went out shopping: he loves looking at modern pictures which he never buys. Cézannes, Renoirs are his favourites, and as he was sitting in ecstasy before a Cézanne at [blank] Gallery in Bond Street I stepped away and rang up Grace Curzon asking her to fetch the star. She repeated that it would be £265. I decided to give it to the Regent: after all I obtained the Garter for him by first suggesting it to Lord Halifax and to the Prime Minister, and harassing them for months past. Now I bought the diamond star which Lord Curzon had often worn: it was a bit of history. He loved both Paul and me. He had got it from the Cadogan family – Earl Cadogan had it, and it had formerly belonged to the Duke of Somerset, now the stones are old, and the setting very fine . . . Paul was much touched and insisted on paying for it but I flatly refused. The whole episode

---

1 Hubert Miles Gladwyn Jebb (1900–96) was a career diplomat. In the Second World War he became chief executive of the Special Operations Executive. He was Britain's Ambassador to the United Nations from 1950 to 1954 and to Paris from 1954 to 1960. He was raised to the peerage as 1st Baron Gladwyn in 1960. He married in 1929 Cynthia Noble (1898–1990).*

is my handiwork and is a gesture for all his kindness to me. (By the way, he said he did something about me and the Court ball, and it was an oversight.) He was telling the truth.

The Regent fears that war is ultimately inevitable but not necessarily over Danzig: he thinks we are mad always to oppose Germany and never ever try to understand the German point of view. They are all gangsters, however, all except Göring, who has some redeeming traits. And Hitler himself '*c'est un très grand homme*'.[1] Reluctantly I left the Regent, as I had promised to lunch with the Kemsleys, where I found a grand party. I was next to Lady Ribblesdale, and although cold at first, we parted friends. So that frost has melted. There were about 30 people including the Oliveiras.[2] Lady Kemsley entertains constantly, and well, she is an avid hostess. During luncheon a message came in that the Prince Regent was expecting me to tea at Buckingham Palace and also to go to the play with them tonight, which is difficult as I had people staying at Kelvedon. After luncheon I hurriedly made some arrangements, and went home to fetch the star which Grace had sent around. It is magnificent. I rushed to the House to vote and then took it to Buckingham Palace. The Regent was touched beyond words, and very sweet. He pinned it to his day clothes and we had a cosy, gay hour. I told him all about Peter and everything else. Then I left him to dress, and I went to see Grace Curzon in her dingy little Eaton Square house, which is really her old mother's. It is dark, horrible and tasteless. I cannot imagine why she doesn't do it up. I gave her £265 in a sealed envelope. She said that she had given Lord Curzon the Garter after she married and she gave me the receipts from Garrard's etc.

At 8.45 I picked up the Regent and Princess Olga and we went to the Gate Revue where we were joined by Alice Hofmannsthal and Rex Whistler. The royalties did not enjoy the show: it is too local, the joke routines too intimate for them. Bill Mabane, a rather common nice fellow in the House, MP for Huddersfield, was sitting behind me, and was much impressed, as the royal party was cheered and we were much photographed.

We went on to the Savoy for supper, and there sitting in sullen silence were James Stuart and Colin Davidson. I avoided them. Mollie Buccleuch, whom James so loves, was with a large party of Indians etc. A supper party was enlivened by a film showing the arrival of Paul and Olga at Victoria: they enjoyed it, and relished the enthusiastic clapping of the crowd. Unfortunately King Zog and Queen Geraldine, when they appeared on the screen, had an ovation which was semi-satirical. The Kents joined us, having come on from a Chamber of Commerce reception. Both looked radiant but cross and tired. She soothes him and panders to his whims: they all do. I danced with the Duchess and she was sweet indeed and affectionate and tired.

---

1 'He's a very great man'.
2 The Brazilian Ambassador and his wife.

The royal party broke up about 1.30, and I said a sad farewell to the Kents, and drove down to Kelvedon where I arrived at 3 a.m. Bundi was waiting for me; but my guests were asleep.

SATURDAY 22ND JULY

I awoke late: a grey-ish day: we have not seen the sun since before Whitsuntide. Poppy Thursby is here and in Honor's Chapel bedroom suite she has neither husband nor lover here. The Milbankes, whom I love (but they bore me), are in the Empire suite: they all arrived last night whilst I was philandering with the royalties. Sheila Milbanke is one of the most remarkable personalities in London, youthful to a point that is incredible (sons of 23 and 21) . . . chic, and sweet and gentle yet a 'tough baby', loyal, loving and generally divine, she manages her life beautifully. I purposely did not invite Seymour Berry, ever her faithful lover, but he rang me and so I weakly gave in. He arrived before dinner, was charming, and never once mentioned politics which was a blessing as he is the spearhead of the Churchill movement, and very boring, unreasonable and violent about it. He must have Jewish blood to be so anti-Chamberlain![1] David Margesson, manly, firm, affectionate, handsome, loyal and fine, is here: I love him. And in the afternoon Helen Fitzgerald and her paramour, Harold Balfour, arrived together. A perfect party. Many jokes, mostly about Mrs Corrigan who has deluged us all with expensive and useless presents. Sheila has a silver dinner service, worth £5,000; Poppy a medallioned dressing service worth even more: and to me she has given, or rather has offered, a crocodile desk set costing £224 at Asprey's. I hate it . . . we drank much, lazed, gossiped, and then at 8.30 Lady Cunard and Mrs Corrigan arrived together! A very hilarious evening, as both the old girls were funny, high-spirited and slightly antagonistic to each other. A most successful party; all arranged really to please David who is not any Chief Whip (and that he will not be much longer) but one of my loves.

MONDAY 24TH JULY

Fritzi of Prussia rang me up at 2.30pm just as I was about to go bed [for an afternoon nap], and I took him to the House of Commons to dine. A most pleasant dinner; but we were interrupted by an urgent message to ring the Regent. When I did I was told he was with the Queen, so we didn't make contact with him: which was just as well as after I dropped Fritzi at the International Sportsmen's Club, where he has lived all these years, Peter came to see me and tired as I was, we gossiped late again.

I felt liverish and unattractive today: too much Kelvedon food and champagne. And I so want to be well and vigorous tomorrow.

---

1 He did not. He was Welsh. He had no Jewish ancestry.

TUESDAY 25TH JULY

I woke well and refreshed. It is curious that PC[1] never tires me, but makes me happy, and stimulates me. He is an attractive Pierrot, cosy and gay and well informed. He reminds me of coral: he is pink and gold like an Assam cherub and companionable and gentle and amazingly well dressed.

All this morning I feared I would get a 'chuck' for my grand luncheon party, and I did. The Kents rang up about eleven to say that they were lunching with the King and Queen at Buckingham Palace to say 'goodbye' to them as they were leaving England tomorrow. Thus I was fourteen and terrified that someone would run out; so I rushed to the Foreign Office and picked up Gladwyn Jebb, who was flattered to be asked .... The Butlers arrived early and looked bourgeois indeed, he in a drab blue suiting, she [with] no pearls or chic. The others drifted in, Princess Olga [and] the Regent soon followed, and pressed in my hand a set of diamond and ruby buttons the splendour of which almost blinded me. Eight buttons, and three studs, of five diamonds with an impressive ruby bar crossing them! They are really for baby Paul, but I was to wear them until he was 21. They must have cost £400. I was speechless and *ébloui*.[2] The Queen of Spain, heavy, Germanic but delightful, followed ... Just as we walked into luncheon Vansittart arrived, late as usual – but in the very nick of time. We swept into luncheon which was excellent and well served: it was all a great success, except that there were no duchesses, which always makes a party. The Kents would have over-weighed it and I am glad they chucked and also the seating would have been extremely difficult. As we left the dining room baby Paul appeared and behaved well. I left the Regent closeted with Rab Butler and David Margesson in the Smoking Room whilst the other guests went up to the library where we all sat about until 3.30.

Bed fairly early, and all in.

WEDNESDAY 26TH JULY

Although I am in glorious health due to large doses of glucose, I tire easily and am forced to sleep in the afternoons, either in the library at the House, with the recently married Alfred Beit snoring by my side, or I go home and collapse. This morning I picked up the Regent at Buckingham Palace at eleven and we shopped for two hours. He said he adored my child more than any after his own younger ones (he has never cared for Alexander, the elder boy, who is and has become perfectly charming). He laughingly added that baby Paul was the nearest thing we could do together after all these years, it was the nearest thing to our having a baby together. I reminded him that had such a phenomenon been possible that

1 Peter Coats, with whom Channon was clearly spending much time since their meeting earlier that month.
2 Dazzled.

'it' would have been 18 just going to Oxford, or he retorted 'a debutante going to parties with Mollie Buccleuch's and Mary Marlborough's girls'![1] We roared with laughter so loudly that the detective sitting in the front of my Rolls turned around to look at us. After he left, I rushed to the Foreign Office where I found that Peter C had rung me already several times. I got on to him and we lunched together at the House of Commons. He looked very handsome, like a Fragonard.[2]

About five o'clock I went home to receive Sir George Sitwell,[3] Sachie's eccentric Renaissance father who is a *cinquecento*[4] character. An old man of over 70,[5] he is capricious, cold, cruel, vindictive and cuttingly witty: yet he adores his grandchildren, although he has been tyrannical to his own children and even allowed that gaunt wife of his, Lady Ida,[6] to go to prison for debt on some trivial charge to do with a cheque. Sachie said that he would like to show him our famous dining room. I had it lighted up by the candles for them, and Emerald and Poppy Thursby, Peter Coats and others drifted in to have a glimpse of the famous man who suggests Barbarossa[7] or Malatesta.[8] He seemed mild, good-mannered and cheerful, but I bet his thin lips and tapping hands could say and do cruel things .... after they all left – Peter to do his drills (he is an officer in the Middlesex Yeomanry) – I rang up the Regent but was answered by Princess Olga who was cold, stiff and inexpressive. I was chilled, but a few moments later she rang me back and explained that she was sitting alone with the Queen and I had interrupted a personal conversation – she was apologetic and sweet and begged me to accompany them to the Palladium tonight, which I did. They, or rather she, adored the coarse slapstick comedy, and like all royalties hooted over the lavatory jokes. The Regent was quiet and silent, and during the interval said that we must go and dine. Our cars were not yet returned, so we drove in a humble taxi to the Savoy, and had a riotous supper *à trois*. About midnight they left to

1 The inference one can draw from this is that Channon and the Regent had had a homo-sexual liaison as undergraduates.
2 There were several French painters by this name in the eighteenth and nineteenth centuries, and also a sculptor: Channon could be referring to any of them.
3 George Reresby Sitwell (1860–1943) was Conservative MP for Scarborough from 1885 to 1886 and from 1892 to 1895. He succeeded his father as 4th Bt in 1862, holding the baron-etcy for eighty-one years. Red-headed in his youth and middle age, his family called him 'Ginger' or 'the Red Death'.
4 Sixteenth century.
5 He was 79.
6 Ida Emily Augusta Denison (1869–1937), by courtesy Lady Ida from 1887, daughter of the 1st Earl of Londesborough, married Sir George Sitwell (*vide supra*) in 1886. In 1915, having acquired a drink problem, she had accumulated such vast debts that Sir George refused to pay them off and she was sent to Holloway prison for three months.
7 Meaning 'red beard' in Italian, it was the sobriquet of Frederick I, Holy Roman Emperor from 1155 to 1190.
8 The Malatestas were a dynasty of military leaders, landowners and magnates in Renaissance Italy.

go on to the Allendales'[1] ball, which has a small party for the King and Queen. Princess Olga complained that she must wear a tiara, which she adores doing.

I slept alone and well.

I 'chucked' Emerald's big dinner party tonight and in so doing fear I offended Bill Tufnell, who came up from Langleys to go at my instigation. He sounded annoyed on the telephone.

THURSDAY 27TH JULY

Today is the Mayor's garden party in Southend; but I had rather lost interest in the constituency, which is foolish with an election impending. Directly I am rested I will take it up with new zest. I sent, however, a telegram saying that I could not attend today. I lunched with Alice Hof[2] at Hanover Lodge, a pleasant party of the Regent's cronies, Norah Lindsay,[3] Lady Ribblesdale, two Buccleuchs, Malcolm Bullock, Victor Cazalet and self. I arrived a touch early and was shown into the drawing room where I found Norah Lindsay alone. We have been *en froid*[4] for two years ever since Honor refused to employ her to do the garden at Kelvedon. I had only once seen her since at the Savoy when she was arctic. Today she was charming, and we were almost on easy, intimate terms again. I quite enjoyed meeting her ... she looked well, and was in a good mood. Perhaps she realised it was not the moment to be cold whilst the Pauls are here. Luncheon was excellent and I was between Mollie Buccleuch and old Lady Ribblesdale, a great beauty that she is, is growing old fast now: she is a bit deaf and a bit 'gaga'; told me the same stories as she did last week when I met her at the Kemsleys!! After luncheon there was a terrific conversation led by Teenie Cazalet, who always lacks finesse and tact. He made many well-intentioned but foolish statements which infuriated the Regent, who ultimately flew at him angrily. Teenie, whose hide is made of rhinoceros leather, was unmoved. At 4.30 we broke up and I drove the Regent and Walter Buccleuch to 2 Grosvenor Place, where we passed an hour nearly mooching about the half-closed house admiring the glorious pictures and miniatures. Walter, or perhaps Mollie, has enormously livened up the house: it was so gloomy and ill-arranged in the old Duchess's reign. New treasures have come to light, and a picture recently cleaned has proved to be an El Greco. There can be no private individual on earth with such splendid possessions as Walter Buccleuch. Eight houses full of them ...

I left them to rush home to receive Lord Chatfield, the Minister for the Co-ordination of Defence. The Regent had requested me to get hold of him privately so that they might have a confidential and secret talk. Lord Chatfield,

---

1 2nd Viscount and Viscountess Allendale.*
2 Alice Astor, ex-wife of Raimund von Hofmannsthal.
3 Norah Mary Madeline Bourke (1873–1948), garden designer, married in 1895 Harry Lindsay (1866–1939).*
4 Having cool relations.

very much the busy business sort, arrived punctually at six followed by his Finnish son-in-law, Patrick Donner,[1] the MP for Basingstoke. Paul soon arrived and having introduced them I took Patrick Donner up to the library and left the great to their secret military conversation undisturbed. I learnt later that they discussed military measures in case of war, for the Regent is more pro-English than many of our own people. (But he doesn't believe in promoting a conflict!) At 7.10 Lord Chatfield left, and by then I had gone up to dress as I was dining with Mrs Vansittart and the Queen of Spain at 7.30. The Regent came up and watched me as I dressed, and seemed pleased that I was wearing the gorgeous diamond and ruby links and buttons which he has given to my son. He had found Chatfield helpful; charming and satisfactory . . . .

Friday 28th July

An early rush to the Office as we had our supplementary estimates today. Not a difficult debate, but much fetching of messages and fagging generally. Rab wound up well in a humorous speech which amused everyone. I was directly behind him all day, and did not eat or leave his side.

I was home by five o'clock, and rang Lord Carnarvon's[2] Nursing Home for news of Prince Paul as he had a most difficult wisdom tooth extraction today. I was told that he was resting peacefully now, but that the operation had been most difficult, even dangerous and that he was one hour twenty-five minutes under the anaesthetic. Relieved that it was over I left for Kelvedon accompanied by Eric Duncannon and Peter Coats, who did not take to each other. *Jalousie du métier?*[3] Peter is so distinguished but of common origin, Eric is like a footman *in excelsis*, beautiful but boring and already a little dried up!

Saturday 29th July

Awoke late, refreshed and happy; I sang in my bath and felt all day the cheeriness of contentment. Eric, Peter and I slept all the afternoon in the sun and we bathed. Towards teatime Emerald arrived like a whirlwind, and she was escorted by Sir Thomas Beecham, who was in a benign mood, gay, teasing, satisfied . . . . and watched Emerald, and entered into her moods. She was captivating, chatted,

---

1 Patrick William Donner (1904–88) was Conservative MP for Islington West from 1931 to 1935 and for Basingstoke from 1935 to 1955. Born in Finland of a Finnish father, he had a Scottish mother. Although associated with Mosleyite and anti-Semitic groups he fought in the RAF during the Second World War and was knighted in 1953.

2 Henry George Alfred Marius Victor Francis Herbert (1898–1987), by courtesy Lord Porchester until 1923, when he succeeded his father as 6th Earl of Carnarvon.

3 Professional jealousy. Coats at this stage worked in advertising; Lord Duncannon, heir to the 9th Earl of Bessborough (qv), was a junior diplomat.

talked of music . . . and society and Mrs Vanderbilt . . . a most successful evening: but I drank too much champagne.

Peter very pleasant and companionable, quite remarkably so. Georgia Sitwell a touch long-winded; Sachie gay and charming. Bed at 1.20, when Emerald left. She always slightly spoils her visits by staying too long.

SUNDAY 30TH JULY

I motored Peter to London early: he was in khaki and looked like the Prince of Wales ages ago. Dropping him at Waterloo where he joined his territorial unit, I remembered old days when Jeffrey Holmesdale[1] looking like him, used to go back to the front from Paris. It was the Gare du Nord all over again, only twenty years later. One doesn't change . . . . I then drove to Belgrave Square, collected fruit and flowers and went to call upon the Regent at Lady Carnarvon's[2] home. I was only allowed in for ten minutes: he was so wan, pale and emaciated and I realised what an appalling time he had had. His most hot hands held mine affectionately and never had I felt more intimate with him, nor loved him more. I stole away sadly, loath to leave him. The dental surgeon intercepted me at the stairs and told me how desperately alarmed he had been. The operation was severe: twice he had had to change his coat, so covered was he with blood. And he fully appreciated his responsibility – the very peace of Europe being on his patient. Twice he feared he would not be successful . . . the man was obviously much moved by what he and the Regent had been through.

A pleasant afternoon at Kelvedon! Honor misses all the fun always.

MONDAY 31ST JULY

The great Foreign Office debate. The house was crowded and we arrived armed with briefs. First there were many questions, and then Archie Sinclair, in a singularly irrelevant vapid speech, proceeded to attack Neville; he was followed by that able but unattractive renegade, Hugh Dalton. The PM sat through it with his good-honoured dignity: when his time came he lashed at them both with vigour and skill in what was probably his most brilliant speech. He seemed to enjoy himself and his quiver was full of arrows, which he shot with deadly aim. Both Sinclair and Dalton were demolished. The PM walked, talked like a debutante:

---

1 Jeffrey John Archer Amherst (1896–1993), Viscount Holmesdale by courtesy from 1910 to 1927, when he succeeded his father as 5th Earl Amherst. He never married. He was awarded the Military Cross in the Great War and had met Channon in Paris while on leave from the Army. He is briefly mentioned in the diary entry for 31 December 1918, but one might conclude from this recollection of him that he and Channon had some sort of relationship, and Channon is feeling similar feelings for Coats.
2 Anne Catherine Tredick Wendell (1900–77), of New York, was the former wife of the 6th Earl of Carnarvon*. They divorced in 1936.

this remarkable old man, surely the most miraculous human alive, shows no signs of fatigue, of age, of exhaustion, even of irritation. His steely intelligence, his alert, his piercing shafts, his amused contempt for fools . . . he is an inspiration, a god . . . But today he surpassed himself. Rab wound up but neither he nor Eden won laurels: the House was left gasping by the splendid performance of its leader: even those whose violent hostility he arouses are nevertheless proud of him.

I sent ice cream made of blackcurrants, which the Regent so loves, to him to the Nursing Home: but I could not go near him, being detained all the day on the bench. How I shall hate it when my job terminates, as it must.

TUESDAY 1ST AUGUST

The Regent, still tired and ill, came to luncheon, and brought Nicky his second son, an alert but conceited little monkey, and dear Alexander the elder boy. Princess Olga was late and charming. We had a pleasant family luncheon: Princess Olga said that she had dined alone with the King and Queen and they talked only of the Windsors. 'Were they sorry for him?' I asked. '*Non. Il l'embête et comment!*'[1] I had heard before that the King has become rather violent against his predecessor: they are a violent, disloyal family, always argue about one another. After the Yugoslavs left I went to the House: I had rather neglected Parliament since the arrival of the Regent; and moreover it has been such a successful, satisfactory season enjoyed by everyone from old to the babies – my duty is finished at leaving London – that I threw myself into it. And who knows whether we shall soon have another? Certainly not so spectacular a one . . .

I invited Mrs Vanderbilt, Lady Cunard, Leslie Hore-Belisha, Harold Balfour to dine at the House of Commons for our last dinner of the session. The Lennox-Boyds proposed themselves, and I collected Jim Wedderburn who was alone. The Regent rang me up about 7.30 to say that he really felt too ill to come: the doctor had forbidden him to go out and talk. I was disappointed, as the others would have been so thrilled to meet him and Princess Olga; but actually I was relieved as there would have been much fuss and bother . . . as royalties don't often come to the Strangers' dining room. Mrs Vanderbilt and Emerald kept me waiting forty-five minutes and we were all in a rage and showed our annoyance. However, our irritation was soon drowned in champagne. Leslie Belisha was very tiddly, affectionate, very loveable. I am very fond of him; certainly he likes me enormously . . . A successful, expensive and unnecessary evening.

A letter from Peter and many postcards and snapshots from Honor who is adoring her curious, cold, isolated holiday halfway up to heaven on the Jungfrau.

The Regent was reminiscing at luncheon: our blue rococo banqueting hall always makes him think of our famous Edward VIII dinner party a few days before

---

1 'No. He doesn't half bother them!'

the abdication trouble began.[1] He retold the story today of how the then King sent for his brother, the Duke of Kent, on that famous Thursday. He had himself only just come back from his triumphant tour in Wales; he began by saying that he wanted his brother to know – before they met that evening at 'Chips's Dinner Party', that he was going to marry Wallis! The Duke of Kent gasped, 'What will she call herself?' 'Call herself,' the King echoed, 'what do you think? Queen of England of course.' 'She is going to be Queen?' 'Yes, and Empress of India, the whole bag of tricks.' The King was cockahoop, gay, happy, confident. This was on Thursday evening, November the 19th about 7.30 p.m. The Duke, flabbergasted, rushed home to dress and to tell his wife. He found the Duchess of Kent and Princess Olga in floods of tears – they had only just heard of the death of Prince Alfonso of Spain who had been killed in the Spanish war – and miserable for their cousin 'Bee'[2] whom they rushed to console. They could scarcely take in the staggering news of their other cousin, 'David' England's[3] dramatic and fatal intention. Looking back upon it, no wonder Princess Olga was late. Honor and I were surprisingly unconscious of the hidden drama being behind our dinner party. The Duke of Kent irritated, fuming, had not known whether to congratulate Wallis when he saw her. The *gêne* that evening was [so] great that it became dramatic.

WEDNESDAY 2ND AUGUST

A crowded day. Sapping one's strength and teasing one's nerves . . . . first to the Foreign Office, then rushed to Waterloo (where I always seem to be going these days) to say farewell of Mrs Vanderbilt who is off to New York. Only little Mary Roxburghe[4] and I were there to see her off. I like Mary Roxburghe – she will be a remarkable Duchess. I always flirt with her slightly and wish it might lead to other things. She attracts me, with her gay, arrogant smile, her white teeth and dark hair; even her Jewish swarthiness is attractive. The only thing about her I dislike is her mother, Peggy Crewe,[5] known as 'Lady Screw'! . . . . then I attended the Guinness Directors meeting. It was a depressing meeting; I was reminded of a Frans Hals[6] canvas: gloomy old men lacking vision and imagination. Of

1 See Vol. I, entry for 19 November 1936.
2 Princess Beatrice.
3 That is, the Duke of Windsor.
4 Mary Evelyn Hungerford Crewe-Milnes (1915–2014), daughter of the 1st Marquess of Crewe (qv). She married, in October 1935, George Victor Robert John Innes-Ker (1903–74), who had succeeded his father as 9th Duke of Roxburghe in 1932. They divorced in 1953. Channon's remarks about her Jewishness stem from her descent, through her mother and grandmother (Lady Rosebery), from Baron Nathan Mayer Rothschild, founder of the investment bank NM Rothschild and Sons.
5 Lady Crewe, wife of the 1st Marquess. See entry for 20 June 1939 and footnote.
6 Franz Hals the Elder (1582–1666), a Dutch portrait painter, best known for *The Laughing Cavalier.*

course the profits are down again: it is clumsily handled, and the great company is living on the past already. Watney Combe have shot ahead of us. I am alarmed, seriously alarmed, and fear that ours is a declining industry. Still, the reserves are so enormous (about £10 million), and I was out of sympathy with the Board's decision to cut the bonus from 3 per cent to 2 per cent, making a distribution of 26 per cent rather than 29 per cent.

At Victoria Station in the Royal Waiting Room I found a large gathering of top-hatted people come to take farewell of the Regent. There were nearly a hundred policemen and much confusion. The Minister, Subbotić, who smells horribly of garlic . . . . and many others present. At last they came, Princess Olga, very affectionate to me, the two boys, Miss Fox, the famous governess of the family, and my Prince Paul who whispered to me 'You have made my visit to London – I love you so much dear Chips,' and I felt rewarded for all the great trouble I had taken with them. They are angels. I escorted them to the train: there were cheers from the waiting crowds separated from us by a cordon of police, and they boarded the train. The Regent squeezed my fingers, and slowly it moved out: I felt a gulp of misery as I always do when they leave. Perhaps this time more than ever before, as he looked old, haggard and ill. And who knows what war will intervene? In what altered circumstances shall we meet next time? And worse, we may never meet again! Some assassin's bullet may cut short that valuable life. We are both over 40 . . . it was a wrench . . . I felt sick with misery as we drove back to Belgrave Square where I joined my mother-in-law who was happily playing with baby Paul. I found that the Regent's last action in London had been to send a huge panda to the baby: I am so happy that he loves him. It is an added bit of happiness; sometimes life gives us that . . .

Then to the House of Commons for Foreign Office Questions. I was in a mellow mood and little prepared for the astonishing debate which followed. It was on the question of adjourning the House until October 3rd, which is too soon to meet again. The Opposition tabled an Amendment that we should come back on August 21st, the usual political manoeuvre which means little. But this time things did not work out quite like that: it was made an occasion by the Glamour group to attack the Prime Minister personally; it was an organised demonstration held by Winston Churchill who in a funny but bad speech said we must come back on the 21st, and gave many reasons including his theme song that the dictators help themselves to countries whilst we are on holiday! Speech after speech followed along these lines, but except Sir Herbert Williams[1] and Victor Raikes, who made a commonsense defence of the government in vigorous terms, all were against the PM. He grinned and bore it. I left the Chamber for a

---

1 Herbert Geraint Williams (1884–1954) was Conservative MP for Reading from 1924 to 1929; for Croydon South from 1932 to 1950; and for Croydon East from 1950 to 1954. He was knighted in 1939 and created 1st Bt in 1953.

little, made a small investigation: Austria was taken on the night of March 11th–
12th, Friday night, whilst the House was sitting but away for the weekend; Prague
was raped on March 15th and all that day, Wednesday, we debated the matter in the
House; we talked but were powerless. Albania was taken by Mussolini on Good
Friday a few hours after the House rose – I made notes of the dates and handed
them to the PM who put on his glasses, read them, and smiled his approval at me.
All were points either in favour of the House sitting permanently, or of adjourning
normally; since to go away for seventeen days will be the worst of both worlds.
The PM used these notes with devastating effect when he rose for the second time
about seven. He had had enough: for three hours he had heard himself abused,
insulted by all the hawks in the House. Such a lack of hope, of clear thinking, could
hardly be imagined. It was enough to make one despair of democracy altogether:
if the House was to behave like that it had better be abolished!! I am becoming
increasingly anti-democratic: England was all right when she was ruled by the
aristocracy, but these democratic demagogues will be her undoing . . . . at seven
the PM rose, bored [illegible] and angry and in a ruthless, devastating speech
castigated the Opposition and was merciless to his over-rebellious followers!
They glowered with rage. I feared (or rather hoped) that Winston would have a
fatal attack of apoplexy. He had no armour, no weapons against the PM's cool and
cutting logic. None at all, especially as he had admitted that 'we cannot sit all the
time'. But the PM by the very brilliance of his performance – and it was his third
in one week – infuriated the House. Everyone hates the truth about himself. When
he sat down there were roars of delight, approval and also of rage. He had kept
his followers roaring with laughter, for half an hour. That self-opinionated ass,
Ronnie Cartland, rose and in a violent, crude, tactless, ungentlemanlike speech
he attacked the PM and entered into an undignified duel with Paddy Hannon.
The House will not forget Ronnie's gaffe, and the Birmingham members[1] will
never forgive him. I know him well: he is conceited, narrow, able; with no 'give'
in his character, he is a bigot, a hypocrite, the worst sort of Englishman who is
perpetually asking himself, if he is doing right? . . . superficially he is agreeable, but
he is pernickety, small-minded and old-maidish. The effect was deplorable – but,
fortunately for him, David M was out of the Chamber at the moment and only
rushed back when the outbreak was over. No one who was not present can believe
the bitterness and bad taste of the attack . . .

The hours passed, and dinner was waiting at Belgrave Square, ordered at
8.30. As the PM said that he regarded the division as a vote of confidence no one
could leave and it was nearly ten before we filed twice into the lobby. There were
nineteen glamorous abstentions; but Anthony Eden found it convenient to have
a cold and was not present: thus one cannot stigmatise him as an abstainer. But
the Glamour Boys did not dare, not even Cartland, to go into the Opposite lobby.

---

1 Cartland's constituency was King's Norton in Birmingham.

I have never known so acrimonious an atmosphere, such hate and foolishness. MPs are sorely in need of a holiday, judging by their speeches, as the PM was not slow to tell them!

Alan and I, angry, hungry, nervously bankrupt, emotionally exhausted, rushed to Belgrave Square. It was ten o'clock, dinner had been waiting for over an hour; the house looked lovely in the candlelight but Patsy was in tears, hysterical and unreasonable, and asked why no one had rung her up? Alan ought really to have done so; I had sent one message. I was rather sharp with her, thinking she was unreasonable, and she flounced out of the room into the street, Alan following and I was left with a sumptuous banquet and no one to eat it. I followed them to the Square but the Kents' policeman said that they walked into Wilton Crescent, and I was damned if I would follow them further . . . . I dined alone in a rage, and drank a whole bottle of Krug 1920. Alan rang up to leave a message that they were not returning . . . . Later I telephoned to him at the House, and we both caddishly blamed Patsy, whom he had dropped dinner-less at St James's Square. An unpleasant end to a too-full day, and the only row, last row of the summer. I am tired.

I wonder when Honor will come back? I am beginning to be apprehensive about her, probably wrongly. I am furious and lonely tonight: my wife in Switzerland, my baby dauphin asleep; my best friend racing across Europe in his royal train; my boy-friend[1] in camp . . . life is dark and I am worn out. The weather is foul and for the first time I am beginning to mind it.

THURSDAY 3RD AUGUST

A less difficult day: the baby left for Kelvedon, complaining that he preferred London; and with the Regent gone I was able to go earlier to the Foreign Office. Rab is exhausted mentally and physically and looks untidy and is going bald; but he is sweet, considerate and equable.

Lunched with Emerald, a small party . . . . I left for the Bath Club where I slept for three hours. I am shocked by my increased weight: it is 12 stone 7 lb. Deplorable. So tonight I didn't drink at all, but am writing these lines instead.

Thelma Cazalet,[2] who looks like a governess and is one of the greatest bores on earth, was married in the Crypt[3] to David Keir, a dark and handsome journalist who cannot be in love with her. How I pity him having to sleep with her!![4] Both

---

1 Coats.
2 Thelma Cazalet (1899–1989) served as Conservative MP for Islington East from 1931 to 1945. She was a prominent feminist. After her marriage she became Thelma Cazalet-Kier.
3 The crypt of St Stephen's Chapel in the Palace of Westminster, known as St Mary Undercroft.
4 Their marriage lasted until his death in 1969. There were no children.

the PM and Lloyd George were present at the distinguished service – the first time a woman MP has ever been married in the Crypt.

Yesterday nearly killed me with all its expenditure of energy. This morning I rang up Patsy and we made up our little dust-up! No news of Honor.

FRIDAY 4TH AUGUST

Yet another Foreign Office debate, but a minor one from our point of view as the Prime Minister was in charge and spoke firmly and well. He pleased the House and we went away happy; he was anxious to conciliate everyone, and did so by his warnings to Japan that it might be necessary to send our fleet to the Pacific. Both Winston and Lloyd George (Tweedledum and Tweedledee) sat glaring at the PM from their opposite corners; but pleased, or at least satisfied by his remarks, they tore up their notes and went away. They never come to the House except to speak. They have outlived their usefulness and welcome; although Winston has still some following, Lloyd George has none . . . . I left about four o'clock, looked in at the Foreign Office and dragged Rab along to the Secretaries' Room where the famous tea party was in progress. The shabby pot, the biscuit tin, the Woolworth cups . . . all this is the holy of holies to the young diplomats, and the best of their era. We all parted on good terms, and the hols began.

I drove in the rain to Polesden Lacey[1] where I have not been for fifteen years! That is a long time. The gardens are glorious, the grounds magnificently green and well kept. There is a silence, a spaciousness that comes from great wealth long established; but the house, whilst Edwardian to a degree and comfortable and full of rare china and expensive treasures, is really a monster. I was told that Mrs Greville would see me at 7.30, and I went for a walk meanwhile and got caught *sans* my missing mackintosh in a shower. I returned dripping and was shown up to her little boudoir and found her changed, older, thinner, and gentler with her grey hair. We gossiped; she was awful about Mrs Vanderbilt whom she professes to love, and kind about Mrs Corrigan whom she hates. The rising star as against the fading ones? There is no one on earth quite as skilfully malicious as old Maggie. Mrs Vanderbilt told her that she wanted to live in England. 'No, Grace, there are enough queens here now,' she had retorted. She was vituperative about almost everyone for forty minutes, and it was a scramble to get dressed. As it was I was the last down, and walked into the Hall as the gong was sounded. Alas! The Queen of Spain and the others were already down, as was my hostess. I fear I got a bad mark . . . . I was next to the Queen of Spain and we had an amazing dinner: she told us licentious tales (she is very bawdy in her conversation) about King Alfonso's relatives, the different Infantes and Infantas of the past. Delicious

---

1 Seat of Mrs Ronnie Greville, bought for her in 1906 by her father, William McEwan, a brewer.

food, but Edwardian; and the dining room heavy with pictures .... after dinner we adjourned into the Italian drawing room and Mrs Greville held a little court! The Queen sat on a stool before the fire, warmed her hands, played with her pearls and told us interesting stories of the Empress Eugenie,[1] who was her godmother. During the conversation a message came from the Duke of Connaught asking the Queen to luncheon on Sunday. Mrs Greville frowned slightly and, taking the hint, HM sent word that Wednesday next would be more convenient; the old butler presently to say that His Royal Highness would expect Her Majesty to luncheon on Wednesday next. At 10.30 the Queen rose and sent her aged and ailing hostess to bed: she was wheeled out. Then we sat down and the Queen taught us a boring card game called pinochle which is the rage in Rome. Very boring but slightly funny. I suspect that the Queen secretly fancies me, but she would never admit it, or succumb, even if I were to make up to her, which I have neither the time nor inclination to do: but I like her .... Bed about twelve. I am not sure that I was a great success. The atmosphere was heavy, and I tired, tired, worn out and stale, but happy.

SATURDAY 5TH AUGUST

I drove Sir Ronald Graham[2] to London: he was the most successful Ambassador since the war and is still on terms of the warmest friendship and intimacy both with the Italian royal family, with whom he stays every year for the trout fishing in the North of Italy above Turin, and with the Duce whom he admires immensely. Graham is now relieved; he is very anti-Anthony and would, he told me, have resigned his Embassy in Rome rather than pursue Anthony's policy of sanctions. Actually he left before they were put into operation. He thinks this country mad; it seems as if it were bent on self-destruction: such always is the folly of the left-wing doctrinaires.

In London I repacked, and collected all my diaries from my locker at the House of Commons and drove down to Kelvedon arriving about seven. Paul and Bundi both pleased to see me. My little boy has enormously improved since the arrival of the new Nannie .... Bed early.

The war declared a quarter of a century ago today.

To my surprise the radio had a long, detailed piece about the arrival of the Duke and Duchess of Windsor at a prize fight at Monte Carlo. Descriptions of her clothes and coiffure were given: I had never heard her name on the BBC before. Is this a departure, a decision, or an accident?

1 María Eugenia Ignacia Agustina de Palafox y Kirkpatrick (Eugénie de Montijo, 1826–1920) was Empress of the French from 1853 after her marriage in that year to the Emperor Napoleon III. Born in Granada, she was the daughter of the Grandee Don Cipriano de Palafox y Portocarrero, 15th Duke of Peñaranda de Duero.
2 Ronald William Graham (1870–1949) joined the Diplomatic Service in 1892, and served as Ambassador to Italy from 1921 to 1933.*

MONDAY 7TH AUGUST

The sun has not shone for seven weeks, and one is consequently depressed . . . . up at eight o'clock, wrote, played with Paul whose charm increases daily, but he is obstinate about learning French. He lunched with me.

Honor comes back tonight! I am thrilled to see her again.

Later

Honor arrived about six, looking extremely well, thin, clear-eyed, happy and handsome, but looked a touch fantastic in her skiing boots which, she said, she was unable to pack. We had a happy evening together making future and holiday plans. Paul, too, was intoxicating, and I was happy, all of us, united.

TUESDAY 8TH AUGUST

I woke at six, got up and went for a long walk in the woods with Bundi. There were yokels working, cleaning debris. The Essex sun shone through the trees; the noise of chopping, and of boughs dragged over turf: it was like a Grimm fairy story . . . back at 7.30 and astonished the household by asking for breakfast.

My child to lunch with us; atrocious weather: appalling complications with our ex-Nannie who is semi-insane as a result of having her festering uterus removed. Honor calm and very sweet and very bored: I don't wonder really. She is not domestic: she only likes wild expeditions and uncouth creatures.

WEDNESDAY 9TH AUGUST

Honor went to London for the day to her coiffeurs etc. I had the secretary down for the day and did an exhausting amount of work. Worn out, I went for an hour's trudge in the rain. Such depressing weather. Paul is very intelligent, alarmingly so; but, like me, he hates the French and won't learn their lingo from Mlle Laurent, the gay girl who is here for that purpose.

I am down, depressed, perhaps my pressure is too low again. *Que faire?* I should like to go out and get drunk with Peter Coats, who, infuriatingly, is under canvas (and hating it) in Dorset.

I am rereading *Northanger Abbey*. Having always been foolishly extravagant, I now have economy mania and go about putting out lights etc.

THURSDAY 10TH AUGUST

I am sad to be *en froid* with the Coopers, but they are so anti-Chamberlain, and worse, so pro-Jew, that I cannot see them in intimacy, lest we have a row, and that I am anxious to avoid. Duff is such a choleric little cock bantam, no one is safe.

The threatened war has not taken place, nor do I see it on the immediate horizon. Nor can I settle down to campaigning in Southend; perhaps I shan't do anything there and trust to fate.

SATURDAY 12TH AUGUST

Great treat: I lay all day in the sun; we lunched at the pavilion. I look a different creature after only twelve days of sunlight. Peter rang up from Weymouth.

SUNDAY 13TH AUGUST

Intense heat again. Honor and I lay naked all day in the garden until teatime when Federer[1] of the German Embassy arrived to stay, a pleasant fellow, he takes a most gloomy view of the international situation; thinks there may well be war this actual summer. In any case it is inevitable: Germany and England shout from opposite windows and neither hears the other, nor wants to hear . . . . He is staying the night.

MONDAY 14TH AUGUST

I went to London in a gay, pagan mood – but spent an anxious hour trying to find out whether or not Honor was coming with me. Curiously enough I am shy of my new intimacy with Peter. I met him at Buck's. We shopped, and I bought him a suit at Keogh's, and bought him gay trifles. We drank at Buck's, saw too many people . . . then, Peter and I lunched at Luigi's in Jermyn Street and went back to No. 5 Belgrave Square, where we gossiped gaily and cosily and dangerously for two hours . . . I love him really. He is like a Fragonard, amber and pink . . . .
I dictated a new will.

WEDNESDAY 16TH AUGUST

I went to London by train, visited the dentist, the Foreign Office, shopped, and met Peter who looked like an Edwardian Pierrot, or dandy. We lunched together in Hyde Park at an open-air restaurant and pretended we were at Longchamp. Later we went to the [illegible] where he has a flat. I gave him some ruby links; I was sad to leave him, and arranged to meet him at Saint-Malo on Monday [Saturday] morning the 3rd of September on my way to Geneva. We might motor for a day or so.
Honor met me at six o'clock and drove back to Kelvedon happily.
I am worn out again, but look well.

1 Georg Federer.

FRIDAY 18TH AUGUST

No news of Peter: he is shockingly silent.

Our puppies were brought back from the Brentwood Kennels – seven powder-puffs, they are wildly attractive, white, woolly and unplayful.

SATURDAY 19TH AUGUST

Basil Dufferin arrived in a fiendish temper and [with] a red rose; he is surly, rude to his wife, silent and does not eat: he drinks, drinks – soaks in whisky, port and gin all day and lays up Kümmel after dinner. He is in a highly nervous and difficult mood and chafes at his harness; he wants to get away from Maureen, who bores and irritates him but he realises the disadvantages of leaving her; and what a divorce would do to him; finish him politically and financially. Maureen, of course, would, or could marry Eddie Devonshire[1] who is longing for her; he is quite willing to get a divorce etc. The whole situation is bad . . . unhealthy. My sympathies are really with Maureen, as Basil D and A is too intolerably rude, malevolent, selfish . . . . he never makes the least effort to be agreeable to anyone. He is only saved by his intelligence.

Maureen was in tears and confessed to Honor, after the others had gone to bed, that she wished to leave Basil but didn't see how it could be arranged.

Peter Coats is crossing to Saint-Malo tonight . . .

SUNDAY 20TH AUGUST

Kelvedon is looking a dream of vernal[2] lush beauty. We lazed all day, lay about in the garden . . . . the political atmosphere, or rather the international one is worsening. I am genuinely apprehensive.

MONDAY 21ST AUGUST

Our guests left us, and I went to Southend to see my agent and make some preparations for the autumn election. I do not see it yet . . . and feel that, if it does take place, I may be unopposed.

TUESDAY 22ND AUGUST

I begin a new volume[3] on a day that seems historic; I feel that a new era, perhaps the last, has opened for England, and incidentally for me. It began this

1 10th Duke of Devonshire.
2 Not an adjective one would normally apply to Essex in August, as it means 'springlike'.
3 A new exercise book, in which he kept the diary.

morning, when sleepily I opened the newspaper and read emblazoned across the ever-sensational *Express*: German–Russian pact.[1] Then I realised that the Russians have double-crossed us, as I always believed they would. They have been coquetting secretly with Germany even as our negotiations proceeded: they are the foulest people on earth. They are nice to their fiendish type. Now it looks like a war, and a possible partition of Poland. The Russians have not unnaturally decided that the Germans are the best bet, and even as our conversations continue, Ribbentrop is flying to Moscow to conclude their death pact. Even so I refuse to be too pessimistic . . . but it seems like the end of our world, that is if Russia and Germany really get together. But we shall regain Japan, and possibly Italy . . . oh! Anthony Eden, may you be forgiven . . .

Brigid Guinness looking like a Greek damsel of beauty arrived from Elveden, and we played tennis and talked in the heat. The roses, the scented garden, the puppies, the loveliness of life; could it really all be ending? . . . I sent a cablegram to Rab, urging his immediate return. The Cabinet sat all day, and it is announced tonight that the House will meet again on Thursday to pass emergency legislation.

Perhaps we have a few more days, even weeks of peace; but a partition of Poland seems inevitable, and if Poland resists we automatically go to war, a busybody's interfering war, and march resolutely to the doom of England and the Empire . . . Wireless news was depressing.

WEDNESDAY 23RD AUGUST

Lay about all day, feeling that we are perhaps headed for ruin: the news is disturbing. We had a depressing family dinner; they are dejected. Plans made for sending Paul and the Elvedens' child to Clandeboye in case of hostilities.

I cannot bear to think that our world is crumbling to ruins. I refuse to admit it.

THURSDAY 24TH AUGUST

I went up to London by an early train: the Iveaghs followed by car later. I had found crowds in Downing Street waiting to cheer the PM (later I saw him come in from Buckingham Palace and he had his usual ovation, which always pleases

---

1 The pact concluded between Ribbentrop as German Foreign Minister and Molotov, his Soviet counterpart, would be concluded in Moscow the following day. It was a non-aggression pact and promised that neither party would ally itself with an enemy of the other. It paved the way for the carving up of Poland and, thus, for the Second World War. Hitler unilaterally repudiated it when ordering the invasion of the Soviet Union in June 1941. The anti-capitalism of both countries provided one of the bases for the negotiations that preceded the pact.

him). The Foreign Office is depressed, fully aware of the seriousness of the situation. There seems no way out. Either:

Hitler must climb down
Poland must give in
Or negotiations must take place
otherwise conflict.

Worked all the morning and then walked to the House of Commons, where masses of people were gathered to watch the arrival of the MPs . . . I had a hurried lunch with Rob Bernays, and we watched the other ministers come in and meet one another; all looked well, many were bronzed. Harold Balfour was tawny and his face blistered from a motoring mishap. At 2.45 the House met, and after the Speaker had made the usual remarks about the recent deaths of Anthony Crossley and another member the Prime Minister rose. He was cheered, as was Mr Attlee, who made his first appearance since his long illness. The Prime Minister spoke in well-modulated phrases; he was moderate, clear, and admirable, but there was little passion or emotion. And I thought of the crisis last September and the excitement then. There was little resemblance to that hectic day. This afternoon; the House was calm, bored, even irritated at having its holiday cut short by Hitler. I looked about me; Lloyd George opposite me, and Winston Churchill a little to the right below me, those twin apostles of Russian friendship, looked old, foolish, and dejected. Winston held his face in his hands, and occasionally he nodded his old porcine head in agreement with the PM. I was directly behind Neville and admired him immensely as he unfolded his story of Russian perfidy and German aspirations so coolly. He satisfied but did not thrill the House; there is a wave of hypocrisy in the country which finds its expression in the Commons: everyone, the newspapers, one's friends, keeps on repeating that we are a united nation, that we are solidly behind Poland etc. in the belief that the constant repetition will cause it to become true. Actually everyone, secretly, or openly, hopes that the Poles will climb down . . . Chamberlain was followed by Arthur Greenwood, in a most mediocre speech in which he pledged the support of the Socialists to the government. Archibald Sinclair was then almost ludicrous and the dreary debate dragged on. Democracy at its dullest! The Emergency Powers Act was quickly passed and we the House adjourned temporarily whilst the measure went to the House of Lords. I rushed home and had a long telephone talk with the Prince Regent, and I told him that we had secret high hopes of Mussolini renouncing his German friend! He did not quite believe it. Alan and I gave our in-laws an excellent dinner and they dropped me at Belgrave Square, and I go early to bed after an exhausting and nervous day. The whole House expects war: only I (who deplored the Polish Pact) do not. Even Rab, who came back from the

South of France, is pessimistic. Halifax made two indifferent speeches, one in the Lords, and the other on the radio.

I suppose it is like getting married; the second time it is impossible to work up the same excitement. Certainly London is calm, almost indifferent to what may happen. A frightening calm.

The cause of the whole trouble is very largely the negative, intransigent attitude of our rulers, men like Euan Wallace who gets all his ideas from that firebrand, bantam cock Duff Cooper.

Anthony Eden contributed a few bromide remarks to the debate. He is very much a back number! Last time he spoke he advocated relations with Russia. The Glamour Boys were conspicuously down today.

FRIDAY 25TH AUGUST

All day at the Foreign Office wondering whether there would be war. Every few minutes the barometer rose and fell. Halifax is worn out and shows it. The Polish guarantee is his pet scheme, his favourite godchild, and look where it has landed us now.

I lunched with Alan Lennox-Boyd at the Marlborough, where we met the Duke of Alba, who is delighted naturally by the turn of events. 'Now we know where we are,' he said. 'The decent people all on one side, the "voyeur" on the other.' I also saw Brocket and put him up to calling at the German Embassy this afternoon: he is *persona grata* there. Later I returned to the Marlborough Club for his report; he had had an hour with Dr Kordt,[1] who is acting chargé d'affaires and K was confidential (they are friends!). I made a 'memo' of this important conversation and gave it to Rab who will pass it on to the Cabinet.

The Italian telegrams are very thrilling: it looks as if Ciano and Mussolini will climb down; they are searching for a way out of the axis; they would like to *lâché*[2] Hitler. We must make it easy for them. Evidently they had heard that the [Russo-German] alliance is definitely unpopular in Italy.

Paul rang up from Yugoslavia again and in guarded words I gave him the news.

Honor fetched me at 5.30 and we drove to Kelvedon in the heat; both exhausted and nervous. We had not been long back when Harold Balfour rang me from the Air Ministry today that news – good news – had come through from Berlin: that Hitler had sent for Nevile Henderson, who was to return to London

---

1 Theodor Kordt (1893–1962) had been part of the Oster Conspiracy in September 1938, named after its leader, Oberstleutnant Hans Oster, which had planned to assassinate Hitler had he started a war with Czechoslovakia over the Sudetenland. His younger brother Erich, also a diplomat, had been part of the conspiracy too, and had urged Britain through various channels to stand up to Hitler: their advice was ignored.
2 Drop or break with.

tomorrow to report the conversation to Chamberlain. I rang up the Foreign Office and was told that the telegram, a long one, from Henderson, was being decoded.

News of the Henderson–Hitler meeting had been telephoned to the office from Berlin a few minutes after Honor and I left London.

We listened at the radio: the real news. I went to bed, and at 11.45 Harold again rang me, this time from the Savoy, to say that he had just spoken to Kingsley Wood who told him that the weather was improving! Good news. I don't believe in the war; nor does an Italian chef, who today visited his Embassy and was definitely told that there would be no war as far as the Italians are concerned. That is something.

Bundi has fallen in love with the gardener's bitch, a mongrel terrier, and he has become restless and impossible, like all people in love.

SATURDAY 26TH AUGUST

The newspapers this morning are far from reassuring: but I still think we are on the verge of a diplomatic arrangement which may prevent the outbreak.

I drove up to London, signed my will (the third I have made in my life: in this one I left everything to my baby Paul whose charm, beauty, and boisterous sweetness surpasses anything I had ever known). Then to the Foreign Office, which I found in a turmoil. Sir Nevile Henderson was due back from Berlin by air at two o'clock. He was a bit late as the car broke down from Croydon. He came to the office for a moment before crossing over to No. 10, where he lunched with the Prime Minister *en petit comité*[1] with Rab, Halifax and Alec Cadogan. When I arrived Rab was at No. 10, conferring with the PM. Rab was more cheerful early in the day as thinking that the [illegible] act of Hitler in offering to negotiate was a healthy supposition. But the offer was so stiff and the government's reaction so negative, both Rab and I fear the door is almost slammed again. Whilst he was at No. 10 Arthur Henderson called to see Rab and I interviewed him instead: he was disappointed, expecting higher fry. He reported to me that Admiral Horthy[2] and the Prime Minister of Hungary[3] had confided in him that they would never allow German troops to violate their frontiers; only a change of government as the result of a Nazi coup would bring in Hungary on the German side.

1 In a select group.
2 Miklós Horthy de Nagybánya (1868–1957) was a naval officer who rose to be commander-in-chief of the Austro-Hungarian Navy by the end of the Great War. After the collapse of the Habsburg Empire he led an army to Budapest and was invited to become Regent of Hungary in 1920, a post he held until 1944. Such reluctant support as he gave to Nazi Germany was bred by his profound opposition to communism.
3 Count Pál János Ede Teleki de Szék (1879–1941) was Prime Minister of the Kingdom of Hungary from 1920 to 1921 and from 1939 to 1941. When he failed to keep Hungary non-aligned in 1941 he committed suicide.

About one o'clock, after much ringing-up to Peter Coats, Honor and others, Peter Loxley and I walked to the Travellers Club to lunch. In the park we ran into Leslie Hore-Belisha walking with Lord Gort.[1] I deserted Peter and joined the War Office. Leslie is pessimistic, and is almost looking forward to a war – he thinks we have the Germans[2] cornered. I fear, and deplore this attitude in the government; and later, twice, I came across it in David Margesson.

It was five before we left, Peter Coats and I, for Kelvedon where we found Honor and Brigid still basking by the pool. It looked lovely in the gloaming. Later Peter and I went for a walk in the recently cleaned woods, and talked of our future, fun, and other youthful plans. I feel that Honor instinctively dislikes him and I much regret it, but fear it is inevitable. But he is so gay, so cosy, and so infinitely pleasant to have about me.

SUNDAY 27TH AUGUST

A lovely day at Kelvedon with Honor, my Paul, my Peter, my puppies . . . Honor looked lovely. We sunbathed; Brigid, whom I had hoped to marry to Peter Coats, disliked him. The sisters said he 'jaggered'[3] me.

The war news is not good: rumours, counter-rumours.

MONDAY 28TH AUGUST

Motored to London with Peter Coats. Exhausted: the 'War of Nerves' is beginning to get one down, and every day one thinks is the crucial one . . . If only we can get through tonight . . . Peter Coats, on his arrival, found that he was called up and has been sent to a vicarage at Paddington Green with his territorials.

Honor rang up: she wanted to be in the movement, so I collected Harold, Charles Peake, Peter Loxley and we all dined together at Quaglino's, a dinner which

---

1 John Standish Surtees Prendergast Vereker (1886–1946) succeeded his father as 6th Viscount Gort in 1902. He joined the Army in 1904 and enjoyed a distinguished career, winning the Victoria Cross in the closing weeks of the Great War, also winning the DSO and Bar and being eight times mentioned in dispatches, earning the nickname 'Tiger' Gort. He became a full general in 1937, having been Belisha's Military Secretary, and was promoted to Chief of the Imperial General Staff. He would command the British Expeditionary Force in September 1939. Belisha disliked Gort, thinking him stupid, but Belisha lost the argument and was dismissed from the War Office amidst claims of anti-Semitism. Gort ordered the retreat to Dunkirk, thereby saving a considerable portion of the BEF, though opening himself up to accusations of defeatism. Churchill assigned him to non-martial roles for the rest of the war, as Governor of Gibraltar and then of Malta, during which time he was promoted to field marshal.
2 Thus in the MS. Rhodes James has 'Russians'.
3 A verb Channon uses to suggest someone who sucks up to, leeches off or ingratiates himself with somebody else.

cost £15! Much champagne, and *Homard à la Neville Chamberlain*,[1] and grouse. It was an electric night; all London seemed to be there . . . . A most stimulating and successful evening which Honor much enjoyed. There was news, some of it secret, some of it semi-secret . . . . The Foreign Office had made arrangements to go to Cheltenham; the Ministry of Labour to Leamington Spa; the Air Ministry to Worcester and the King and Queen have taken in the name of the French Ambassador a country house near Worcester. The West Country will come into its own.

The whole secret story (which we didn't discuss tonight, needless to say) of 'the Walrus',[2] as one of the individuals has come to be known, is so extraordinary. A Balt, named Mr D—, and a Mr Spencer of mid-Beds have been negotiating secretly here and pretend to come from General Göring, who hints that he is anxious to dethrone Hitler, and set himself up, perhaps as a General Monck,[3] and restore the Hohenzollerns etc. I doubt the validity of the Walrus's credentials, but he is taken seriously by Halifax. A secret plane transported the two emissaries clandestinely here; the news got out, at least the arrival but not the identity of the men. This foolish and melodramatic story is known to about ten people: special facilities were accorded them at the airport.

None of us here completely lost hope that peace may be saved.

All night, mostly, at the Foreign Office.

TUESDAY 29TH AUGUST

Things are looking up: for there are accounts of the Hitler regime cracking, of the Nazi leaders quarrelling amongst themselves: of food shortages etc. . . . . . UK is up, and perhaps Neville will triumph! *Viva* Chamberlain!

I drove Jim Wedderburn to Kelvedon, and found it lovely as ever. It was a glorious lovely evening, and as we walked about, I thanked God for one more day of peace and beauty here . . . . will the sun set on peace tomorrow? I came here because I thought there must be a *détente*,[4] our reply has been sent to Germany and it is not thought likely the answer will come through tonight. Certainly it had not been even received by Nevile Henderson at 6 p.m., when we telephoned to Berlin to inquire.

---

1 It is not clear of what this lobster dish consisted.
2 *Nom de guerre* of Johann Birger Essen Dahlerus (1891–1957), a Swedish businessman and friend of Göring, who tried with the help of several British business contacts to avert the war.
3 George Monck (1608–70) was a captain general in the New Model Army but played a leading role in Charles II's restoration in 1660, for which he was created 1st Duke of Albemarle.
4 Literally, 'relaxation'; in the diplomatic sense, an easing of relations.

WEDNESDAY 30TH AUGUST

Of course all the excitement happened in my short absence. The long answer from the German government came and was thought to be unsatisfactory by most. The Cabinet met to consider it: we are still urging Germany and Poland to negotiate, but the Germans seem determined to have their war and are as unaccommodating as possible. All day we were on a see-saw, peace–war–peace. The Italian news is distinctly encouraging, and Ciano has now definitely promised that Italy will be neutral, that she has veered around to us etc. He is trying to induce Mussolini to come around to us . . . but Leger[1] of the French Foreign Office has sent a telegram warning us not to believe these tales, that Italy is playing a double game etc. And his gloomy report corroborates Paul of Yugoslavia's impressions who warned me by telephone not to trust 'The Macaronis'.

Peter Coats came to the Bath Club and I was enchanted. We had a swim together and then he went rushing off; Honor, Brigid and I dined at Prunier's and had nine oysters each. The meal was gloomy at first but we cheered up . . . . Honor was interested in watching Ian Campbell-Gray who recently painted her portrait, dining with some bohemian beauty.

. . . . Tentative evacuation has been ordered for tomorrow. Peace is in the balance, see-sawing.

THURSDAY 31ST AUGUST

All the morning on the telephone arranging with Honor, who had luckily returned to Kelvedon, to transport Paul. At last she decided to send him and arranged for him to sleep tonight at Rockingham Castle, and tomorrow he goes to Holker for a night and crosses via Heysham to Belfast, where he will be met by the Dufferins' car and remain at Clandeboye 'for the duration': it is the hardest part of war for me to be separated from my adorable mite.

Just before luncheon a most encouraging telegram came, hinting that the Germans would climb down. I thought it was all over; Rab was most hopeful, and I waltzed out to lunch, meeting Lady Halifax and the Iveaghs at the Park entrance. I told them the good news, and jubilantly we separated. Then I walked to the Air Ministry and told Harold [Balfour], who was incredulous at first; and on the way to lunch at the Carlton Grill we ran into little Kingsley Wood (who is the only real Conservative except Neville in the Cabinet) and he nodded approvingly. 'I always said there would be no war,' he said. Harold and I had a riotous luncheon; but when I went back to the Foreign Office the news was again

---

1 Alexis Leger (1887–1975) was a French diplomat from 1914 to 1940, but also a renowned poet who won the Nobel Prize in Literature in 1960. He was dismissed from the Diplomatic Service after the fall of France in 1940 because of his anti-Nazi beliefs, and went into exile in Washington DC. He wrote under the name of Saint-John Perse.

dark. It oscillates . . . . Really both the Nevilles,[1] Chamberlain and Henderson, should be made dukes!!

FRIDAY 1ST SEPTEMBER

The household returned to London. Alan and Harold came to lunch with Honor and me. We faced the facts – we are on the very verge of war, as Poland was this morning invaded by German troops, they will carve up the country with the help of the Russians. There were 'goodbyes'; Honor went to Kelvedon. We had a blackout in the evening: the streets in utter disbelief and all day the servants have been frantically hanging black curtains . . .

Evening with Peter Coats who wears like a Fabergé cigarette case [*sic*].

SATURDAY 2ND SEPTEMBER

It is really tomorrow, and it is 1.25 a.m., that dejected, despondent, despairing I sit down in my bedroom (for the last time?) to chronicle today's events. They are appalling, and any faith I had left in Democracy is gone, any glimmer of hope that the English were not mad has faded. Mad. More than mad . . . This morning began with nervous fusses here at home with hysterical and foolish servants, then I walked to the Foreign Office, and I talked at length with Rab, who was strangely cheerful; but he seemed disappointed when I told him that he is not to be made Minister of Economic Warfare but to remain on at the Foreign Office when war breaks out . . . The morning passed in reading telegrams, waiting about; outside all seemed natural, possibly fewer cars, but there is no sign of evacuation in this part of London. At 12.30 Alec Dunglass crossed over from No. 10 and we talked secretly with Rab. Alec still thinks that the brand might be snatched from the burning, some sort of *démarche*[2] might be made through an intermediary, which would induce the Germans to retire from Poland, where the tempo of this half-hearted war increases slightly. Both the offensive and defensive are mild . . .[3]

I had no luncheon, walked with Rab to the House of Commons, and rushed out forgetting it was Saturday, to buy him a hat. By 2.30 I was back in my room at the House of Commons, and I rang the private secretaries asking where the box was with the Statement which the Chancellor was to make. It had been delayed. At last it arrived, but only two minutes before the Speaker took the Chair. Rab and I walked along and I caught sight of John Simon's bald white head (he has

---

1 Nevile Henderson spelled his Christian name with one 'l'.
2 A political initiative.
3 This was nonsense: the fighting was ferocious, the first use of 'Blitzkrieg', or lightning war. If this was the information coming into the Foreign Office on 2 September, it was wrong.

been the Judas of the Day[1] – may God forgive him!). We caught him up, and he whispered to Rab that he had only just received an urgent message not to make the statement as important news had come from Italy. The moment prayers were over he made a brief announcement to the House that the Prime Minister would make a statement later. I rushed out, found Rab in deep conference, although a peripatetic one, with Halifax. They walked to the Lords together, and I followed, trying to listen. When we reached the Prince's Chamber, which was full of eager peers, my father-in-law seized me and delayed me. When I broke away, Rab told me that the Italians had offered to negotiate, to call together a five-power conference etc. Halifax rose, looking like a stained-glass figure, and told their Lordships to come back at six. Then he went, followed by Rab to No. 10. The PM considered Ciano's message of sufficient importance to call together an immediate Cabinet at 4.30 at No. 10. There was a *sauve qui peut* from the front bench, and the House at once sensed that there was something afoot. I remained in our room so as not to be trapped into saying anything indiscreet . . . Rab rang me about six, the Cabinet had just risen; it had been, he said, stormy, and only a very stiff reply was forthcoming to Ciano: but it would be as reasonable as Chamberlain could make it under the circumstances. There was then a long, and most unfortunate wait, and very likely the final cause of tomorrow's war[2] – for it must be tomorrow now, since we have had our miracle today and did not profit by it; for during the long time which it ensued the nervous House, chafing under delay, and genuinely distressed, some of them, by our guarantee to Poland having been immediately operative, quenched their thirst in the Smoking Room, and when they returned to hear the PM's statement, many of them were full of 'Dutch Courage'; one noticed their flushed faces . . . meantime the Cabinet had risen and retired. The PM was left behind with Halifax to draft his statement, and a clumsy or rather inartistic document it was, too. At the same time they had to ring up Paris and convey to them Ciano's offer (at the time I understood this to be so, but later tonight I had reason to believe that the French were already aware of it this morning). In any case the French Cabinet met immediately and began to discuss it. They demanded more time: and it was first suggested that the Germans should be told that unless they evacuated Poland within a week we should declare war jointly with the French (this proposal is supposed to have originated with Bonnet,[3] who is anti-war). There were long telephonic conversations and the time limit

---

1 It is unclear what this refers to. Simon had, as a member of Asquith's administration in 1914, threatened to resign rather than support the declaration of war; was talked out of it, but resigned in January 1916 after the introduction of conscription. If Channon was attacking him for changing sides in his attitude to a war against Hitler, it was deeply unrealistic, as events were about to prove.

2 Coats, in the text he gave to Rhodes James, has garbled this and has it as 'the final course of tomorrow's war'. It is not thus in the MS.

3 Georges-Étienne Bonnet (1889–1973), the French Foreign Minister.

was whittled down to forty-eight hours! The PM arrived at last, and I instantly told Rab, who had had ten minutes' sleep, and I woke him, handed him a very icy martini which exhilarated him, and together we walked into the PM's room where we found Alec Dunglass, Rucker[1] and David Margesson. Arthur Greenwood and Archie Sinclair had just been summoned into the inner room and the PM told them the news about the French evasive delays (they are not so prepared as we are, nor is their evacuation so well advanced). We waited outside and someone said something funny about Horace Wilson which threw us all into fits of laughter. I supposed it was nerves – the first laugh for weeks, but when Rab gave us his famous cackle, David Margesson and I doubled up, roared until the tears came... David remarked 'I'd give a hundred quid to be present when Winston is told that there is to be no war.' Suddenly the PM's bell rang, and David was summoned into the presence. By now our spirits were soared, peace might be saved, by a miracle, by Mussolini's intervention ... We followed the PM into the House, which was crowded and grim. The long wait had irritated everyone, and it would have been longer still had I not reminded the secretaries that Halifax had probably already made his identical statement in the Lords...

The PM rose, was cheered, but not over-much, and then he read out his statement, which was ill-conceived. It began by saying that as yet no answer had come to our warning to Berlin, and the House, thus prepared to unsheathe the sword, was aghast when it was hinted that peace might yet be saved. I have never seen such an ugly exhibition: there were roars of disapproval; Duff Cooper, I hoped, would have an epileptic fit, as his cheeks, like an angry frog's, began to swell. Amery[2] hissed (in both cases *Cherchez le Juif*[3]). Decidedly the PM had not a very good reception, but Greenwood who followed him attempted to soothe

1 Arthur Nevil Rucker (1895–1991), who had worked for Chamberlain as a junior official in the 1920s, when he was Minister of Health, had recently become his principal private secretary. Assigned to Cairo for special duties during the war, he was knighted in 1942. He was a driving force behind the creation of the National Health Service after returning to the Ministry of Health in 1943, then became Deputy Director of the United Nations' refugee organisation, and between 1956 and 1966 served as Deputy Chairman and then Chairman of the Stevenage New Town Corporation.

2 Leopold Charles Maurice Stennett Amery (1873–1955) sat as a Birmingham Conservative MP from 1911 to 1945. A staunch imperialist, he was First Lord of the Admiralty under Bonar Law and Baldwin, and Colonial and Dominions Secretary in Baldwin's 1924–9 administration. He would be Secretary of State for India from 1940 to 1945. One of his sons was hanged for treason and the other became a Cabinet minister. In this Commons debate of 2 September 1939 he famously called out to Arthur Greenwood 'Speak for England, Arthur!'

3 'Look for the Jew'. Channon, clearly in the grip of some degree of paranoia in the tension of the moment, is unpleasantly hinting that Amery, with whom Channon would soon become good friends, and Cooper wanted war because of some Jewish heritage. Amery's mother was from a Jewish family from Budapest that had largely converted to Protestantism. There is no evidence that Cooper had any Jewish blood.

the House whilst maintaining his own dignity. Maxton[1] made an impassioned appeal to the PM to continue his good work, not to be rushed, but he was almost shouted down. All the old Munich rage all over again; all the resentment against Chamberlain: all those who want to die abused Caesar. John McGovern[2] leant over to strike Kirby[3] (Labour member for Everton) but the Speaker pretended not to see . . . there were a few other short speeches and the House, after Chamberlain rose for the second time and promised a definite answer by noon tomorrow when the House will meet again – for the first time on a Sunday in all its history.

The Cabinet and the appeasers, Rab included, were discouraged by the reception the insane House of Commons gave to the glimmer of peace: they began to say, [Walter] Elliot etc., that the PM was not accurate in reporting to the House the findings of the Cabinet.

All evening at the Foreign Office, which was in a state of funk lest they should not have their pet war: Butler and I struggled hard . . . . there were countless telephone calls to Paris and we were told that the French, led by Bonnet, would not shorten their ultimatum to Germany: it would be for a whole week! We knew that we could not hold the House of Commons for so long, then a compromise of forty-eight hours from tomorrow morning was offered as a compromise [sic] – the Frogs, at first, would not agree. And here the War Party, suddenly strengthened by John Simon, who, I suppose, saw his chance of becoming PM, began to argue for shorter ultimatum still – the Cabinet sat long. Terrific excitement; wild talk of the French ratting altogether, of our fighting them and 'the whole world' . . . . Peter Loxley and I crossed over to No. 10 Downing Street, after the private secretaries had rung us to come and join the fun. There came on to rain a storm, terrific, ominous – 'When the rains came'.[4] I saw Alec Dunglass. 'Are we all mad?' I asked him, 'You are not the only one who thinks so,' he retorted. The PM came out of a side room followed by Horace Wilson and Rab. He looked well, almost relieved that the dread decision was taken and the appalling battle over – we would give Germany only two hours' ultimatum (this was an answer to the French to make them ashamed). The Cabinet had insisted; the War Party was led by Simon, Oliver Stanley, Walter Elliot, and, I believe Shakespeare Morrison: the Peace Party were the PM, Kingsley Wood, but they were overruled. I sat on Rucker's (the most amiable, able Chief Private Secretary) desk. The door opened

1 James Maxton (1885–1946) was a veteran of 'Red Clydeside' and led the Independent Labour Party after breaking with MacDonald. He was MP for Glasgow Bridgeton from 1922 to 1946. Admired for his oratory, he was an ardent pacifist.

2 John McGovern (1887–1968) was Labour (and for some years Independent Labour) MP for Glasgow Shettleston from 1930 to 1959.

3 Bertie Kirby (1887–1953) was Labour MP for Liverpool Everton (not 'Euston', as Rhodes James has it) from 1935 to 1950. He was a former policeman and had been decorated for his service as a battery sergeant major during the Great War.

4 The Rains Came, the title of a popular Hollywood film that year, starring Myrna Loy and Tyrone Power.

into the Cabinet Room; and I saw Sam Hoare, alone in a dinner jacket. The various chiefs of staff were wandering about in uniform: and Corbin, the steely, grey, Frog Ambassador slunk into another room and was soon in conference with the PM. He was told our decision: we had already instructed Nevile Henderson to ask for an interview tomorrow morning at 9 a.m. and to inform the German government that unless news came by 11 a.m. that the German government had ordered the withdrawal of their forces from Poland that we should be at war . . . This message was sent, I think, about 11 p.m. . . . The French immediately climbed down and it was understood from Corbin that the French Ambassador [to Berlin], M. Coulondre,[1] should ask for an interview tomorrow at noon, and give the German government seventeen hours, that is until 5 a.m. on Monday morning, to withdraw. The French government have not sufficiently completed their mobilisation and evacuation and all day they had been pressing us to hold back a few more hours . . . Broken-hearted I begged David Margesson to do something; but he was determined. 'It must be war, Chips, old boy,' he said, 'there's no other way out.' Then I pleaded that Anthony Eden must not be in the War Cabinet: his inclusion would so infuriate Italy. I was eloquent, and made some impression: David told me that he must be given something: the country demanded it, but it would be a minor post . . . I decided to go home: there were no cars; it was a blinding rain . . . Peter Loxley trudged out into it . . . Cabinet ministers, chiefs of staff, all wandered hopelessly about. We left Rab with the PM who was about to go to bed, for his last night of peace. Wet typists trotted in the downpour: only people emerging from No. 10 knew the facts . . . Peter and I left: I wanted to walk, as it cleared a little: he would not. It was dark, a precaution against air raids. We found a taxi. Peter dropped me. I am home. I shall not sleep; in a few hours we shall be at war and the PM will have lost his great battle for peace – but he may triumph yet.

I rang Harold Balfour: he had seen Lord Halifax at the Savoy with Geoffrey Dawson, editor of *The Times*; at the next table were Duff and Diana with those 'Glamorous' Knights, Ronnie Tree and Jim Thomas.

Nous sommes en guerre.[2]

I was annoyed with Oliver Stanley; I whispered to him details of Mussolini's plan, we were standing behind the Chair – he looked cheated, annoyed; he is one of the pro-war people. Later he came up to me. 'You were wrong. It is only a manoeuvre on Ciano's part,' he said. He is so German himself, like a neurotic Heidelberg professor. A dreadful couple, the Oliver Stanleys, selfish, hostile to their children. She licentious and drunken, both cheap and conceited. He and Euan Wallace all along have led the War Party in the Cabinet, egged on by Duff out-of-it!

---

1 Robert Coulondre (1885–1959) joined the Quai d'Orsay (the French Foreign Ministry) in 1909. He was Ambassador to Moscow from 1936 to 1938 and to Berlin from 1938 to 1939. He was briefly Ambassador to Switzerland in 1940.
2 We are at war.

My baby arrived safely at Clandeboye: Honor has about twenty evacuees, some with impetigo, at Kelvedon.

In the MS of the diary immediately following the entry for 2 September 1939 is the entry for 25 September, and this is the order in one of the typed transcripts, made by Coats for Rhodes James's edition. However, there is another version of the typed transcript that has entries for some of the intervening days, most of which are included in the Rhodes James edition. What follows until 25 September is therefore a copy of the typed transcript with those entries. The original MS for these days is missing, so cannot be checked for accuracy or to see what may have been edited out.

SUNDAY 3RD SEPTEMBER

10.57 a.m. The PM is to broadcast at 11.15 and in a few moments a state of war will be declared. The method, while to my mind precipitate and brusque, is undoubtedly popular. Everyone is smiling, the weather is glorious but I feel that our world or all that remains of it, is committing suicide, whilst Stalin laughs and the Kremlin triumphs. If only we can win a quick war, and dislodge the Nazi regime. That would mean a Neville victory, a November election, and triumph. The mandarins at the Foreign Office are sad, but not altogether displeased, for their long hatred, their spleen at the Teuton is to be assuaged. And Jewry the world over triumphs . . .[1] In London the church bells are ringing, people draw more closely together, everyone is kind and considerate, and all are quietly appreciative of what the government has done. The arrangements have been smooth, swift and skilful, but it is nevertheless a tragedy that the War Party have won. I went up with Victor Perowne[2] to the FO wireless station and listened to the PM. He was dignified and moving, brief and sad. He had barely finished when the sirens announced an air raid (and later Rab told me that he had been with him in the room at No. 10 whilst the actual broadcast was being done, that the PM had not been warned of the air-raid rehearsal and was visibly shaken when the sirens blew). Though we thought it was a rehearsal we all went to our assigned rooms. Ours is 172 and nearest the garden door, a commodious but comfortless suite. There I found several typists and we were soon joined by Rab and others. The wailing noise continued, and finally the heavy doors were shut. 'It's like the *Thetis*,'[3] I remarked. Soon, however, the all-clear sounded.

Afterwards Rab and I, accompanying Lord Halifax, walked to Westminster stared at by a silent crowd. The House was crowded. There were perhaps half a dozen uniforms. I took my place just behind where the PM sits. He came in looking

---

1 This foolish remark does not appear in Rhodes James, for obvious reasons.
2 John Victor Thomas Woolrych Tait Perowne (1897–1951) had been a minor war poet and joined the Diplomatic Service after the Great War. He became Envoy Extraordinary to the Holy See in 1947, dying in office. He was knighted in 1950.
3 The submarine recently lost at sea.

smiling and well and we all rose and cheered; but the Opposition who yesterday growled at him for not declaring war, today were too churlish to cheer him for having done so. There was a pause, and a feeling of unreality, while the clerks read out their mumbo-jumbo to do with party procedure. Then he rose, more cheers . . . and he spoke feelingly of the collapse of all his hopes. I was wet-eyed, but indignant with the Opposition for their bad manners. Old Josh Wedgwood, who is more than a little mad, was disgustingly jubilant. Duff Cooper grinned, Anthony Eden was expressionless, and when Greenwood began speaking, I looked up at the Ambassadors' Gallery, and there in a distinguished huddle were the Duke of Alba, Joe Kennedy and the Belgian,[1] sitting with the French and Polish ambassadors, who both looked worn out. A little later Maisky dared to appear, and he beamed his Cheshire-cat smile. No wonder. It is the moment he has long intrigued and hoped for . . . The other speakers did not hold me, though Winston spoke well. It was McGovern, the extreme left-winger, the ILP member for Shettleston, who made, to me at least, the best speech and certainly the most sensible. He said that the mood of the country will certainly change, that the people will not forgive this senseless war, which God knows was more nearly averted than even McGovern knew. Even this morning the mysterious 'Walrus' rang up again from Berlin; his role has never been explained. He is the mystery of the whole crisis, urging us always to be firm with Hitler, pretending to come at Göring's request, and consulted by the Cabinet, by Halifax, by everyone. In the evening I dined with Peter Loxley and Harold Balfour at the Savoy, in semi-darkness. The restaurant was almost empty and the streets completely black. In the night there was another air-raid alarm but I did not awake until called by the butler. Then I joined the servants in the cellar, where I found everyone good-tempered and funny. The Duke of Kent sent me a message asking me to go to his shelter next door, but I was too sleepy and declined.

MONDAY 4TH SEPTEMBER

I woke after my short and disturbed night to read that we had lost a ship, the *Athenia*,[2] with about 1,400 people abroad, all probably drowned; then I walked to the Foreign Office; all the major new appointments have been announced;

---

1 Baron Émile-Ernest de Cartier de Marchienne.*
2 The SS *Athenia*, built in 1922, left Glasgow for Montreal via Belfast on 1 September. She carried 1,103 passengers (including around 500 Jewish refugees) and 315 crew. A U-boat spotted her on the evening of 3 September and after a pursuit of three hours fired two torpedoes at her, between Rockall and Tory Island off the north-west coast of Ireland. She remained afloat for fourteen hours. Many of the ninety-eight passengers and nineteen crew who died were near where the torpedoes hit; and a lifeboat was crushed by a rescue ship. The U-boat commander, branded a war criminal, claimed he thought the *Athenia* was a troopship. Some of those killed were Americans, and the Germans feared it would provoke America to join the war against them.

Winston is back at the Admiralty and in the War Cabinet of nine. Anthony Eden is at the Dominions Office with access to the War Cabinet, a fact much commented on by the Italian wireless. I talked with Rab about our personal futures; I am in some doubt as to what to do. Remain here? Or break out and take some semi-military occupation ... I, with my flat feet, my stomach, my inefficiency and loathing of drill exercise, discipline and danger? Rab is worried too, and somewhat disappointed at having been refused the new Ministry of Economic Warfare. But really, as both David Margesson and Alec Dunglass told me, he is far more needed at the FO as both the PM and the S[ecretary] of S[tate] so depended upon him. Indeed he is the PM's 'blue-eyed boy'. He (I have positive information on this point) was considered both for the Ministry of Information and for Economic Warfare, but in each case the PM refused to release him from his present important duties. Rab is pleased but disappointed. Later he will be rewarded.[1]

TUESDAY 5TH SEPTEMBER

I was grateful for an uninterrupted night's sleep, and today I feel like a lion. How enjoyable it would all be if it were not for the war. In fact, I am almost ashamed of my high spirits and rude return to health and energy.

The Belgian Ambassador, that dear bewhiskered *grand seigneur*, is indignant with us for being so stupid as to send our planes over Belgium yesterday, and he called just now to protest. I tried to soothe him, which was not difficult as he is so very pro-British. His Excellency took on a new lease of life when his termagant of an American wife died recently and is thoroughly enjoying his unexpected widowerhood.

I had tea with the Duchess of Kent, who looked sadly lovely with her amber eyes, and I wondered once whether they were tear-stained? We sat in what was once her little private sitting room, but today there were two chairs only and a tea tray. The house had been completely dismantled and there were only a few packing cases and dust sheets about, and few traces of its former gaiety and happiness. All the Duke's expensive toys, his lovely *bibelots*, his books, his Panninis,[2] his Meissen, all had been removed, mostly to the Pantechnicon.[3] They now have no London home at all. We had a sad conversation about poor Prince Paul struggling and hoping for peace in his mountain fastness of Brdo, and of her

---

1 Butler, with his strong record as an appeaser, only survived into the Churchill government because the new Prime Minister recognised his considerable ability. He was promoted to the Cabinet as President of the Board of Education in 1941, and prepared and piloted through the landmark Education Act of 1944.

2 Giovanni Paolo Pannini (1691–1765) was famous for painting vistas of Rome.

3 The storage facility used by the removals company of the same name. The Kents were due to leave for Australia, where he was to be Governor-General.

sister Princess 'Woolly',[1] now in Germany and overnight an 'enemy', but with all her heart with us. The position of people like the Toerrings is terrible, anti-Nazi, pro-English, but obliged to fight for the Nazi regime and perhaps die for it. It was a sad little talk and I think we both felt a touch like Ruth amid the alien corn,[2] aliens in this incredibly lovely and loveable England. Princess Marina, more than me, for I have never known any other life really, except for my youthful Parisian flash.

I later dined with Harold Balfour at the Aperitif. He promised to make me a wing commander whenever I liked or felt impelled, but he advised 'not yet'. Meanwhile I am useful, happy and busy and in the know, if not very glamorous, in my present job.

WEDNESDAY 6TH SEPTEMBER

Awakened at 6.40 by the siren's sad song. I took to the cellars but shall not do so again. Two dreary hours wasted.

A typical Anthony Eden story. He asked his new secretary at the Dominions Office to ask for his map of Europe back. It would be hardly recognisable now. How like him to be so devoid of all reality. There is little reality either at the House of Commons, which at the moment has ceased to interest me, though of course it is there that ultimately everything is decided. Today I watched Winston whispering to the PM (I am immediately behind them). He is behaving well, but their deep mutual antagonism must sooner or later flare up and make co-operation impossible. Winston will surely be *frondeur*[3] and attempt and probably succeed in ousting the PM. Then we shall all be sacked, and there will be a 'glamorous' central government, reinforced by extreme-left Conservatives and some Socialists who are already saying that while they have refused to serve under Neville they would agree to under Winston. I see it coming.

THURSDAY 7TH SEPTEMBER

It was a lovely English lush morning, and I walked all the way to the House with Ralph Assheton, whose appointment as Parliamentary Secretary to the Ministry of Labour was announced this morning. What a warm-hearted charmer, and so good and honest. He will do well, and I have long urged his claims to office. *En*

---

1 Princess Elizabeth of Greece and Denmark (1904–55). She was married to Count Carl Theodor of Toerring-Jettenbach*. Because of her thick hair her family nicknamed her 'Woolly'.

2 A biblical reference: Ruth 2:2–3. Keats, in his 'Ode to a Nightingale', alluded to 'the self-same song that found a path / Through the sad heart of Ruth, when, sick for home, / She stood in tears amid the alien corn.'

3 A rebel.

route, we met the Neville Chamberlains, followed by two detectives, who gave us dazzling smiles. The Chamberlains, not the detectives.

There is now a whip's vacancy again, though it may well not be filled as the H of C work will be minimised. However, my hopes rose when this afternoon Harris,[1] the *éminence grise* of the Whips' Room, told me that the Chief Whip was looking everywhere for me. My heart beat fast, then half sank; a whip at last, and yet not quite when I want to be. Excitedly, I sought out the Chief Whip, but all he wanted was help in getting the Queensberrys[2] out of France, where they have foolishly got themselves stranded. I was at once disappointed and relieved. Yet I feel my present Foreign Office job cannot continue indefinitely. I must get fixed before the Churchill group bring off their plot to oust the PM, and Winston, who sees himself as the Lloyd George of this war, packs the government with his henchmen; but I do not think the plot can ripen for some months yet.

Warsaw is in serious danger, and Hitler no doubt will make a peace offer next week, asking us to accept the *fait accompli*, a proposal which will certainly be scornfully refused.

Friday 8th September

I met Nevile Henderson who looked worn, but brown, and as usual, faultlessly dressed. He told me that he and his staff took four days to get back from Berlin, though the German Foreign Office were most polite, and indeed almost cried when they left.

Saturday 9th September

Emerald is completely discouraged, indeed demoralised by the war and I heard today at the Foreign Office that the French fear that it will last at least until the spring of 1941; here we are more optimistic, though the news from Poland continues appalling, and, amongst many other places, Łańcut,[3] the Potockis' operatic castle, has been taken. It was twice occupied during the Great War.

---

1 Charles Joseph William Harris (1901–86) was the son of a stud groom and a lady's maid. As a boy scout helping out at a naval base during the Great War he impressed Dudley Ward, who became a Liberal whip, and who found him clerical work in the Whips' Office. He rose meteorically, and was private secretary to the Chief Whip from 1919 to 1961, except during the Labour governments of 1924 and 1929–31, when he fulfilled the same function for the Conservative Chief Whip in Opposition. He was knighted in 1952.

2 Francis Archibald Kelhead Douglas (1896–1954), by courtesy Viscount Drumlanrig from 1900 until 1920, when he succeeded his father as 11th Marquess of Queensberry. He married in 1926, as his second wife, Catherine Sabine Mann.

3 Łańcut is in what is now south-eastern Poland, near the borders with present-day Ukraine and Slovakia. Channon's friends the Potockis lived in Łańcut Castle, which survived the war, and is now a designated historical monument open to the public.

Since then it has stood, like an isolated rock, forgotten by fate and much enjoyed by the privileged few who were asked to stay there, though I personally always felt a sense of doom under its roof.

SUNDAY 10TH SEPTEMBER

I went to Kelvedon on Saturday afternoon in lovely weather in the hope of a peaceful perfect Sunday, but it was not to be. There were endless decisions to be made; papers to be stored; fuss and confusion; irritated servants; neglected dogs; plate room and cellar complications. We packed up all our jewelled toys, the Fabergé *bibelots* and gold watches, etc., and counted the wine, then we welcomed 150 refugees, all nice East End people, but Honor was depressed and worn out, and our Sunday not as happy as I had hoped.

On my way I looked in at Buck's and saw several swaggering officers with highly polished belts stuffing themselves with oysters, and I met Victor Warrender[1] talking to Strathcona and others.

Then I shopped and bought some books for Fritzi, now interned happily at Kelburn, where he is Lord Glasgow's[2] 'prisoner'. All morning I went about carrying an absurd gas mask in a canvas bag, which I found a bore.

Peter Loxley has now left us definitely and was this morning replaced by Geoffrey Harrison,[3] who returned only on Friday from Berlin. He is pleasant, very much of a Wykehamist, but alert, able and probably adequate; but I shall always prefer Peter Loxley who charms everyone.

The PM has the lowest opinion of the FO, who are largely responsible for this war, with their insensate hatred of Germany, their pro-Russian feelings and their mandarin Chauvinistic leanings; now some are aghast, some delighted at having their own way. It is mostly Leeper; it took me months of intrigue to get him out of here, and his appointment as Minister to Bucharest was a godsend. But it came too late for him to go, and now he is at the Ministry of Information trying to thwart the PM at every turn. He is a nefarious influence.

---

1 Victor Alexander George Anthony Warrender (1899–1993) succeeded his father as 8th Bt in 1917. He was Conservative MP for Grantham from 1923 to 1942. He went on to hold several junior ministerial and Whips' Office posts and was raised to the peerage in 1942 as 1st Lord Bruntisfield.

2 Patrick James Boyle (1874–1963), Viscount Kelburn by courtesy from 1890 until 1915, when he succeeded his father as 8th Earl of Glasgow. A virulent anti-communist, he was associated with various neo-fascist groups in the 1920s and 1930s, and was a member of the Anglo-German Fellowship. His seat was Kelburn in Ayrshire, a county of which he was Vice Lord Lieutenant from 1942 to 1945. 'Fritzi' survived in these genial surroundings, and as a house guest of the Channons at Kelvedon, until being arrested as an enemy alien in May 1940.

3 Geoffrey Wedgwood Harrison (1908–1990) joined the Foreign Office in 1932 and eventually became Ambassador to, successively, Brazil, Iran and the Soviet Union, whence he was recalled after an affair with a chambermaid at his embassy. He was knighted in 1955.

WEDNESDAY 13TH SEPTEMBER

The Windsors arrived back last night, and are staying with the Metcalfes[1] near Ashdown. The journey over was arranged with the utmost secrecy; it is dramatic, the ex-king returning after nearly three years' exile, with the woman he loves on his arm, uncertain of their reception. I must find out. It would be much better to be big and broad-minded about it now. I hear that the two queens discussed the matter yesterday. But the Fort[2] has not yet been made ready for their reception and it seems that the present arrangements are purely temporary. I wonder who will be the first to see them?

THURSDAY 14TH SEPTEMBER

Diana Cooper rang me this morning for the first time since the war. She is in a terrible state, nervous and apprehensive. Yet she and Duff have done more than any other couple to bring the war about. Duff, at the moment, is out of a job, unhappy and resentful. He knows that Chamberlain will never forgive him. Diana asked me why Duff was not included in the new government? I had infinite pleasure in blandly replying that I had never heard his name mentioned either way; he was simply not considered.[3] This afternoon I saw Duff having a long heart-to-heart with Winston at the House of Commons. I am told that Winston is already driving the Admiralty to distraction by his interference and energy.

SUNDAY 17TH SEPTEMBER

A glorious September day at Kelvedon, where I bathed in the pool, and then in a bath towel rang up the FO to be told the grim news that the Russians had definitely invaded Poland. Now the Nazis and the Bolsheviks have combined to destroy civilisation, and the outlook for the world looks ghastly.

MONDAY 18TH SEPTEMBER

I drove up to London, and lunched with Emerald where I sat next to old Margot Oxford, crisp, rude but as affectionate as ever.
    She is very pro-Chamberlain and angry with her stepchildren, who are not. She is against the blackout, deprecates any danger from air raids, and thinks gas

---

1 Edward Dudley 'Fruity' Metcalfe (1887–1957), and his wife Lady Alexandra Naldera 'Baba' Curzon (1904–95).* Lord Louis Mountbatten had brought the Windsors back to Britain on a destroyer: the ex-king was given the rank of major general (even though he was technically a field marshal) and was attached to the British Military Mission in France.
2 Fort Belvedere in Windsor Great Park, the Duke's former residence which had been empty since the abdication.
3 Churchill would make him Minister of Information in May 1940.

masks unnecessary. I agree up to a point, though I rather enjoy the blackouts. She said one would have disliked Lord Kitchener[1] intensely if one had not happened to like him, whereupon Emerald said that she had found him 'alarmingly dull'. Once, in desperation, she asked him who was his favourite author and after long hesitation he replied 'Stanley Weyman'.[2] We wondered who would be the Kitchener of this war: 'Certainly not Hore-Belisha,' Margot volunteered. How she dislikes him.

There is now a tendency to say that the Russian intervention in Poland is not so serious as we originally feared. Dalton, who called at the Foreign Office this morning, looking evil and sardonic, takes that line.

TUESDAY 19TH SEPTEMBER

What I have always half foreseen, half feared as a nightmare, is now a possibility, that is an entire alteration in the European system, with the power of Russia enormously strengthened. There will be, indeed, some sort of Bolshevik regime over most of our continent; but not quite yet; the USA may save us, but our days of power are over for a long time to come. Meanwhile, the war in Poland is drawing to a close, and another few days will see the end. Then activities will be transferred to the Western Front, and we shall begin to have a bad time, to put it mildly.

I had a secret conference with Dunglass, who shares my ideas. He is pro-peace, as I am, now that the Russian devils have come in. But we both realise that there are insuperable difficulties: Hitler's first conditions for peace would take the form of revenging himself on the Empire, which would be followed by political disturbances here anyway. The country is not yet ready for peace. I think that Neville made a mistake in not resigning after Prague; it would have been better for this war to have been declared by the left, or by the Churchill centre.

WEDNESDAY 20TH SEPTEMBER

We shall see great developments during the next three months, though only I seem apprehensive as to the ultimate outcome of the war. Unless of course the USA comes in.

I forgot to say yesterday that as I left the FO by the ambassadors' entrance I caught a glimpse of the Duke of Windsor, who was driving away in an ordinary blue car. He had just been received by Lord Halifax, and looked tired, I thought.

---

1 Horatio Herbert Kitchener (1850–1916), 1st Earl Kitchener and Field Marshal, Secretary of State for War 1914–16, died when the ship carrying him on a mission to Russia hit a mine off the Orkney Islands.
2 Stanley Weyman (1855–1928) wrote romances set in sixteenth- and seventeenth-century France. He was highly acclaimed, counting Oscar Wilde and Graham Greene among his admirers, so any ridicule of Kitchener (*vide supra*) for liking him may be misplaced.

I raised my hat but it was too late, and he did not see me. Their visit has been a flop; due I fear to the hardness of the old Queen, who is quite unforgiving. Later I mentioned having seen the Duke to Princess Marina, whose only comment was 'I haven't and don't want to.' She added she had not seen him since our famous dinner party here nearly three years ago.

I think that Kingsley Wood might easily become our next PM and that is now the PM's intention. He purposely put Inskip on the Woolsack in order to clear the way for Kingsley Wood. The PM thinks that Halifax would only be a stopgap. I am nervous and discouraged; my world has collapsed; I should like to bury myself in Devonshire. I came with a war, perhaps I shall go with one.

The fact is I am just the wrong age for this war. 42: old enough not to have to do anything, yet occasionally embarrassed, and envious of people in uniform. Perhaps unfortunately, I look much younger than I am.

FRIDAY 22ND SEPTEMBER

Honor came up yesterday and I took her, Brigid and Harold Balfour to luncheon at the Ritz, which has become fantastically fashionable; all the great, the gay, the government; we knew 95 per cent of everyone there. But Ritzes always thrive in wartime, as we are all cookless. Also in wartime the herd instinct rises. Charlie Londonderry,[1] in a tweed suit, came and talked to us. He had just issued a rather undignified denial that he has been interned as a German spy.

SATURDAY 23RD SEPTEMBER

I lunched at the Spanish Embassy and talked at great length to Eddie Devonshire, who is always kindly, though deaf. But he is obdurate about his son Billy Hartington's[2] engagement to Miss Kennedy; he will not budge; the Kennedy alliance is not to his liking; he has an anti-Catholic mania and has forbidden the match.

I heard it confirmed at lunch that the Potockis are still living at Łańcut; they seem to be above reality, and never touched by events. But the new Bolshevik line included Lemberg,[3] which is dangerously near. Poor Poland! The Belgian Ambassador remarked the other day that the eighteenth century had at least rid the world of two evils, religious oppression and Poland, but that the twentieth century had brought both back.

---

1 The man known as 'the Londonderry Herr' might have thought himself lucky not to be interned, given his overt sympathies towards Hitler.
2 William John Robert Cavendish (1917–44), Earl of Burlington by courtesy until 1938 and then Marquess of Hartington, married Kathleen Agnes 'Kick' Kennedy (1920–48), daughter of Joseph Kennedy (qv), shortly before being killed in action in September 1944.
3 Now Lviv.

SUNDAY 24TH SEPTEMBER

'Musso' has made his long-waited 'peace' speech[1] at Bologna, and it was temperate, as if he knew in advance that such a *démarche* would fall on deaf, determined ears. We are resolved to fight this grim war to the end, as it had to come sometime. That seems to be the prevailing spirit.

MONDAY 25TH SEPTEMBER

A most exhausting day at the Foreign Office . . . . All day ambassadors poured in; I had a brief word with Halifax, who looks more than ever like a saint.

I flopped into my bed worn out – no new developments: Warsaw still holds out.

This morning on my arrival I very nearly knocked over the PM. Already I cannot use the Park as my morning constitutional for fear of meeting him; now I cannot drive for fear of running over him. 'What did you do during the Great War?'[2] – the answer 'Ran over the Prime Minister' would not be too good!

TUESDAY 26TH SEPTEMBER

The Duchess of Kent rang me very early, and later came to lunch. She looked lovely and was very sweet. We had long talks – only her and Peter Coats, who looks young and handsome in uniform. I opened the big dining room and it looked lovely . . . happy little party. Queen Mary sent me a message via the Duchess to ask for Fritzi's address. She was enchanted to see Peter Coats, but I think it is Garrett Moore[3] she likes most at the moment. She originally liked Peter because he looks and acts like the Duke of Kent, but is much nicer and more attractive.

The House of Commons was crowded, and the PM made his usual dignified statement: unfortunately he was followed by Winston, who executed a *tour de force*, a brilliant bit of acting and exposition in describing in detail the work of the Admiralty. He amused, and I fear, impressed the House . . . . He must have taken endless trouble with his speech, and it was a contrast, which was noticed, to the PM's colourless statement. I am sure Winston is angling for the Premiership, convinced of it: the moment is not yet ripe, but already today I noticed signs of the Glamour Boys beginning to intrigue again. I met Dunglass in the lavatory and he agreed. We must watch out.

---

1 Mussolini said Italy would remain neutral, but that the Polish problem had been 'liquidated' and that the French and the British should simply accept the *fait accompli*.

2 Channon calls it thus: 'The Second World War' was not then current.

3 Charles Garrett Ponsonby Moore (1910–89), by courtesy Viscount Moore until 1957, when he succeeded his father* as 11th Earl of Drogheda. He was Managing Director of the *Financial Times* from 1946 to 1972, in which year he became a Knight of the Garter.

In the manuscript diary after the entry for 26 September 1939 is the entry for
3 October, and this order follows that of one of the typed transcripts. Another
typed transcript, however, has entries for some of the intervening days, and
much of this material is included in Rhodes James. What follows is a copy of
the typed transcript: the editor has not had the original text, which is missing,
against which to check it.

WEDNESDAY 27TH SEPTEMBER

The first war Budget. At 3.45. Simon rose (he was directly in front of me) and in
unctuous tones, not unlike the Archbishop of Canterbury, opened his staggering
Budget. He warned the House of its impending severity, yet there was a gasp
when he said that income tax would be 7/6d in the £. The crowded House was
dumbfounded, yet took it good-naturedly enough. Simon went on, and with
many a deft blow practically demolished the edifice of capitalism. One felt like
an Aunt Sally under his attacks (the poor old Guinness trustee, Mr Bland, could
stand it no more, and I saw him leave the gallery) blow after blow; increased
surtax; lower allowances; raised duties on wine, cigarettes and sugar; substantially
increased death duties. It is all so bad that one can only make the best of it, and
reorganise one's life accordingly.

THURSDAY 28TH SEPTEMBER

Our first important visitor was the Polish Ambassador,[1] who is so angry with
Lloyd George that he has almost forgotten the plight of Warsaw and the loss of his
palace there. 'A dishonest old man,' he ranted. And he is.

Both Rab and I dislike the presence of the Turk in Moscow. Shall the Crescent
join the Swastika? Is all anti-Christendom to be anti-us too?

Very secret. The 'Walrus' is in London. He arrived today by plane and this
time his visit is known to Hitler. Halifax and others are seeing him this afternoon.
No one knows of this. What nefarious message does he bring?

FRIDAY 29TH SEPTEMBER

The now fabulously mysterious 'Walrus', i.e. Mr Lazarus,[2] was interviewed
secretly yesterday. He arrived by boat[3] via Holland and so caused no comment.
His other trips were all made by air. This morning he walked about the Foreign

---

1 Count Edward Bernard Raczyński (1891–1993) was Polish Ambassador to the United
   Kingdom from 1934 to 1945; he also served as Foreign Minister of the government-in-exile
   from 1941 to 1943, and as President-in-Exile from 1979 to 1986.
2 Dahlerus.
3 Presumably Channon's earlier information had been corrected.

Office openly and was seen by Geoffrey Harris in the passage. Also Cadogan had a talk with him and a report of their conversation was given to Lord Halifax, who read it, I believe, at the War Cabinet.

It is the usual personal plea for peace, and again hints at making Göring head of the German state. Ribbentrop and Molotov have today signed their treaty for the final partition of Poland and for their future joint action. They now say that all responsibility for the future of the war must fall on the Democratic Western Powers. Reactions to the theory are as expected, and the French, always realistic, say 'we had better make peace, as we can never restore Poland to its old frontiers, and how indeed should we ever dislodge the Russians from Poland even if we succeeded in ousting the Germans?'

Sunday 1st October

I had a secret rendezvous at, of all places, Madame Tussaud's.[1] Afterwards I looked at the exhibits. Princess Marina is unrecognisable, though Queen Mary is brilliant. Hitler has been removed, perhaps to the Chamber of Horrors, and I was surprised to see Euan Wallace immortalised in wax, but they have no figure of Rab. I must see to that. In the afternoon the House was calm and uninteresting. Rab described a certain official at the much-libelled Ministry of Information as being like a nonconformist accountant in a disorderly house which was extending credit. He is enchanting sometimes.

Friday 6th October

Hitler made his big, but disappointing speech[2] to the Reichstag this afternoon: it was delivered in the Opera House where Honor and I once attended a sumptuous – almost beyond belief – banquet given by Göring in 1936 . . . the speech was relayed slowly, and we went home without actually knowing its full content. Rab is unimpressed by it, and he agrees with me that we are probably committing suicide, perhaps sacrificing the Empire, even wishing defeat, unless we accept, or negotiate better terms; that is not the popular view: almost everyone is pro-war.

Saturday 7th October

Channon goes to Cheltenham, possible evacuation centre for the Foreign Office, to undertake reconnaissance.

---

1 It is unclear with whom.
2 An entirely dishonest account of the campaign in Poland preceded, for over an hour, a plea to Britain and France to agree to peace terms, and an attack on Churchill.

Gaily I drove here, with 'sixpence in my pocket'. Didn't like the Bellevue Hotel, and moved to another. Dined at the Plaza, which already has much atmosphere: it is almost like Amiens in wartime, spies, uniforms, wine, girls, blackout . . . very happy and gay and *gemütlich*.

SUNDAY 8TH OCTOBER

Drove about KA,[1] which will be the future capital of England, if the raids become too bad. The town has a Jane Austen air, promenades and parade and colonnades: the aimless statues, the spa . . . . accompanied by an inefficient, indeed, congenial billeting-officer, we drove about searching for a suitable house and at length decided on Prestbury House which is ideally suitable being commodious and only 1½ [miles] to KA. Rab and I will set up housekeeping together there . . . . The *antiquaires* were shut. I drove back to London, giving no lifts to drunken old ladies . . . I wanted to stay *en route*, but finally went to Belgrave Square, arriving in time to see a huge fire at the Pantechnicon. Thirty-five fire engines unable to cope with it. I am glad nothing of ours was in there: I removed it all last year including my tins of diaries etc. We watched the flames and the crowds. How angry[2] the Duke of Kent will be, as he has only just sent his things there, all his *bibelots* and his books, his Meissen and his Fabergé . . . .
     Alan, Peter and I all dined gaily and happily.

TUESDAY 10TH OCTOBER

Russia helps herself to a new country every day, and no one minds[3] . . . it is only German crimes which raise indignation in the minds of the English.
     My mornings are madly busy, my afternoons exhausting at the House, although I always try for twenty minutes' siesta in the silence room. Today I walked home to luncheon with my in-laws, and was nearly run over in The Mall by a royal car. I jumped to avoid it and saw Queen Mary swathed in grey, very erect, dignified and painted. There was an amethyst brooch in her grey toque. The car passed into Buckingham Palace, where she was lunching. My in-laws very charming and gay. Pyrford is half-shut and they are picnicking there: they are looking forward to the two new babies, Patsy's and Elizabeth's.[4] Will Honor never

---

1 The government code for Cheltenham.
2 Channon has crossed this out and substituted 'querulous'.
3 The Soviet Union was forcing 'mutual assistance' treaties on the Lithuanians, Latvians and Estonians. It would invade the following summer and, after a short and brutal oppression, be driven out by the Germans in 1941, only to occupy the region again in 1944.
4 Lady Elizabeth Hare (1914–90), wife of Arthur Guinness, Viscount Elveden (qv). Their daughter Elizabeth Maria (qv) would be born on 31 October.

have another? Lord Iveagh is depressed, sees his vast fortune slipping from him; his world crashing.

I dined alone, exhausted: Alan had a friend to stay, a gay constituent, Major Miller, aged 27.[1] When Peter came in, they sniffed at each other, and Peter whispered to me 'I see every minister has his bit of khaki!'

I listened to Kingsley Wood's great statement about the air situation. It was a broad, rich statement but badly delivered, and the House slept . . . he read it as if he was dictating to a typist. I fear that in spite of its definite worth, he did not stake his claim to the future Premiership. There are so many 'Crown Princes' about . . .

I drove Rab home and he is in despair: the intransigent attitude of the Cabinet seems hopeless.[2] We are in for a long war now . . . Alec Dunglass, Rab and I have lost another round, for which our youth and the Empire will have to pay. There were rows in the Cabinet yesterday and today; but I fear they resulted in stiffening the PM's attitude. Unexpectedly enough there was disagreement between Winston and Eden, the latter put forward the Dominions point of view. I quickly made hay whilst this happy sun shone and conveyed to silly Jim Thomas that Winston was intriguing against Anthony. We must play them off against one another.

WEDNESDAY 11TH OCTOBER

The Duchess of Kent rang up and 'chucked' luncheon: she came instead for drinks about 6 p.m. I had Loelia Westminster, Alan, and Peter to lunch. Much conversation about the bogus Thames, the camouflaged artificial one a few miles away . . . .[3]

This morning Rab was sent for by the Secretary of State and Cadogan and told by them that they had carefully considered his view; that they were obliged, but reluctant, to overrule it; and that the statement to be made tomorrow was almost, but not quite, a definite refusal of Hitler's terms . . . Rab has, however, succeeded at keeping the door slightly ajar. He is depressed as he fears he might have done more. He is right: they are wrong, wrong as they were over the absurdity of the Polish Guarantee which he and I fought so strongly and so vainly against at the time.

1 Unidentified.
2 Butler was keen that the supposed olive branch Hitler had held out to Britain and France during his speech should be grasped; the Cabinet, aware of Hitler's record as a liar, had more sense.
3 A possible decoy river to divert enemy aircraft away from the capital. The idea appears to have come to nothing.

Mrs Rosemary Cresswell, the Queen of Yugoslavia's[1] mysterious girlfriend[2] sent me another large packet for HM. I put it into the bag.[3] Only lesbians write such long letters.

Both Winston and Anthony agreeable to me in the lobby; but both know I am their enemy. Harold B stoutly insists that Anthony is 'wet' and 'congenial'.

Shall we be bombed on Friday night?

I had another talk with the Duchess of Kent about the Windsors: no one 'of the family' saw him, only the King who received him as Sovereign. Queen Mary cries and cries because her eldest son did not call upon her; but he refused to go unless accompanied by his wife: impasse. The Royal Family behaved shabbily, like true Hanoverians; and I have heard them criticised.

THURSDAY 12TH OCTOBER

An unreal day, and now in the gloaming I sit, with my fountain pen in the Chamber and scribble ... The front bench is nearly deserted, only Anthony Eden in a flashy suit with some still remnants of his fading good looks, Miss Horsbrugh,[4] able and alert: and a brace of dim whips .... Opposite is Stafford Cripps, who has just spoken: I have arranged for him to see Halifax tomorrow. Charles Emmott[5] is speaking, dribbling intolerable platitudes. The House is bored and dimly lit. Mr Amery has just begun his habitual hymn of hate against Hitler .... Rab is disgruntled with democracy and has gone out for a brief respite ... and today might have been so glorious had there been either spirit or sense left in England ....

Got up late, shared breakfast about nine o'clock with Alan; who is inconsolable at being appointed to the Ministry of Food. The PM sent for him last evening and so charmingly asked him to agree to the Ministry that a refusal, or even a lack of grace, was impossible. The PM insisted that the Food Ministry is the weak link in our defensive chain. (I happen to think that he has no confidence, although he likes him, in Shakes Morrison)[6] ... I walked to the Foreign Office, talked twice to the Duchess of Kent who gave me parcels for the bag to send on to Princess Olga.

1　Marie of Hohenzollern-Sigmaringen, former Queen Consort of Yugoslavia (1900–61), wife of King Alexander (1888–1934) until his assassination. She was a cousin by marriage of Prince Paul of Yugoslavia (qv).

2　Violet Rosemary Cresswell (1903–83). Technically Mrs Cresswell was Queen Marie of Yugoslavia's lady-in-waiting; the Queen had lived in England since 1937.

3　His Majesty's post or dispatch bags.

4　Florence Gertrude Horsbrugh (1889–1969) was a Conservative MP who held junior ministerial office from 1939 and throughout the wartime coalition, and from 1951 to 1954 was Minister of Education, the first Conservative woman and only the third woman to sit in the Cabinet. She was raised to the peerage as Baroness Horsbrugh (life peer) in 1959.

5　Charles Ernest George Campbell Emmott (1898–1953), Conservative MP for East Surrey.

6　Morrison had just been moved from the Ministry of Agriculture to head the Ministry of Food; he would be replaced by Lord Woolton (qv) in April 1940.

Then I consulted a solicitor and made arrangements for the letting of Prestbury House in case of a general evacuation. Home to lunch . . . . Honor had come up from Kelvedon: she was tired and nervous, dejected and discouraging, and I was unhappy. Her nervous structure, like her mother's, is weak. But she has got her mother's wonderfully firm and fine character to help her surmount her illnesses, and misfortunes. She drove me to the House, and as we left Belgrave Square we saw the Duchess of Kent come to call on her, but we were late and did not go back.

The House was crowded and inattentive, half hoping for peace, but determined really on war – which equals Empire-suicide? I flitted about and found a ticket for Nevile Henderson, who is somewhat recovered. He was, as usual, smartly dressed, and he has as ever, no matter how fatigued, a fashionable air. I introduced him to the Duke of Alba, the Belgian Ambassador, and others . . . . Maisky was over the clock, smirking. There were no royalties . . . the PM came in early, calm, icy, charming. I sat immediately behind him. Questions were interminable, and he rose at 3.50 and slowly and deliberately made his famous statement,[1] which we have read and had a finger in. I have his actual copy and will preserve it. It was messed about by so many people that I feared it would sound stale, but it had a facile parliamentary triumph. The House liked it, and Neville's stock rose (correspondingly, Churchill shares declined). But it was a barren triumph really, devoid of hope, [illegible] of any practical purpose.

Nevertheless he was much cheered and I was glad. Even fat wicked old Winston, sitting opposite (there was no room on the government bench for his baroque bottom), joined in the cheering. I felt, however, that Neville's heart was not in his brief and his personal hatred of Hitler helped him through it. He might have come to the House today, as he did last year, like a Prince of Peace, and announced the end of this utterly senseless war, which has lost its meaning or object . . . . Rab agrees with me, and he has worked bravely and feverishly for four days to modify the statement, and even succeeded slightly. He had nearly an hour alone with the PM, and several conversations with Halifax and Alec Cadogan, with whom he made his position clear, and his views had been filed at the Foreign Office. History will show that he was right.[2] He thinks the war a huge mistake, first as the guarantee to Poland was foolish, and fateful. He fears we are risking defeat – all this we are sacrificing for what? For a Poland that can never be reconstructed . . . Madness . . . This morning as Rab and I were walking towards the Russian Legation we ran into Harold Nicolson, who accompanied us for a

1 His reply to Hitler's attempt at peace proposals. Chamberlain said that 'it would be impossible for Great Britain to accept any such basis without forfeiting her honour and abandoning her claim that international disputes should be settled by discussion and not by force.' (Hansard, 12 October 1939, Vol. 352, Col. 565.)

2 Sadly for Butler, history would do nothing of the sort. It was not least his conduct during this period that helped ensure he was twice passed over for the leadership of his party, in 1957 and 1963, the folk memory in the Conservative Party being a long one.

while. He is singing a very different tune now from what he preached before: he wants peace now, or at least we must consider proposals. What a volte-face our ex-warmongers are making: they are on the run, and after decrying the PM for months for not going to war, they are now attacking him for continuing it when they all got it. Their reactions to Hitler were sexual I think.

The Polish Ambassador called at the Foreign Office, and he introduced M. Zaleski,[1] the new Polish Foreign Secretary of the non-existent Polish government. I ushered them into Rab's presence – he is [illegible] unimpressed by ambassadors. Zaleski is a distinguished gentleman, or so he feels. The Poles all behave better than did those infernal Czechs!

The House of Commons is deplorably unreal; a bomb would change the atmosphere. Today's session reminded one of a third-rate debating society. I left at 8.30 to dine with Loelia Westminster at 8 Little College Street: an excellent dinner, but only one footman. I was on her right, and Rachel Davidson[2] the other side. She is a handsome Holbein,[3] looks like a Habsburg empress, and is much improved since her marriage. She is obviously mad about Colin and will steady him and make him an excellent wife.

Honor went back to Kelvedon, still down and deflated.

FRIDAY 13TH OCTOBER

Nevile Henderson sat in my room all the morning making notes: he is distressed and says that Göring will now attack England, and probably London with all his might, and his famous suicide squadron will bomb us out of existence.

Honor rang up from Kelvedon and seemed in better spirits. Duff and Diana slipped away yesterday to New York, where he will do infinite harm. Still it is well to have him out of the country. He flatters himself that the Germans will make a special attempt to blow him up.

I went to Euston to take farewell of Harold Balfour who is going on a mission to Canada via the *Duchess of York*. 'I am sure she will be safe,' I said to Harold, who smiled. I gave him a flask of brandy and a case of champagne. And he left – I was miserable. What if he is sunk by a U-Boat? I should not mind, as my parliamentary career would be much affected; for of late I care less for it – I only want a Palladian villa with Peter [Coats] in some restful Paradise and there to write – I am weary of wealth, bored by politics.

Peter dined, we both got drunk; it was so enjoyable.

---

1 August Zaleski (1883–1972) had studied in London before the Great War and had been unable to return home once it broke out. He joined Poland's Diplomatic Service in 1918 and served abroad in various capacities before twice being Minister of Foreign Affairs. He became President of Poland's government-in-exile in 1947, serving until his death in 1972.
2 Formerly Lady Rachel Fitzalan-Howard (qv).
3 Hans Holbein the Younger (1497–1543) was a major German portrait painter.

SUNDAY 15TH OCTOBER

Jay Llewellin came to lunch and stayed the night. He is so good, so British, slow, but sure. I feel ill, and was offended with Honor for attacking Peter Coats rather savagely. She must have some feminine intuition about him.

MONDAY 16TH OCTOBER

I went to the Foreign Office depressed and cold. I think I have a chill. Peter's gay insouciant voice cheered me. I am fed up with this irritating and ridiculous war . . . I went home, half in anger, half in chill and went to bed: later I got up as Peter was dining: then Alan telephoned that he was bringing 'Tupps' Ramsbotham,[1] an amiable, intelligent, white-haired Commissioner of Works. He is charming, looks older than he is; but he has little cultural flair and was uninterested in our famous dining room. We attacked both Anthony Eden and Winston Churchill all during dinner: Peter was bored but charming.

The Germans raided Edinburgh this afternoon.[2]

TUESDAY 17TH OCTOBER

Rab rang up, told me to remain in bed, which I did all day. I had a temperature, and feel lousy. But I read, and revelled in my being alone. Alan came in at dressing-time; he had sat next to Lady Astor at the Yugoslavia Legation and she had attacked me. The virago is obsessed by me: there is no doubt. She is also afraid of my vitriolic tongue.

WEDNESDAY 18TH OCTOBER

In bed all day, weak . . . . Peter rang up a few times and I thought about him . . . . he is tall, extremely well built, graceful and gaily gracious; his features are soft, his face flushed with exercise, and his large blue eyes look wonderingly at me; his hair recedes on both sides of his head, leaving a centre mane of auburn which is shot with red, gold and brown. He is 'like Ariel' . . . and he moves rapidly with insouciance: his hands and feet are strong and virile, and the one suggestion of effeminacy is perhaps in his very beardless chin, and in the way he tosses his head to the right, and in his full warm mouth. There is a determination about this Cupidon,[3] as well as wit, light erudition and a most plausible social manner which knows no failures. He is like an Elizabethan physically, but his mind . . . . is Edwardian.

1 Herwald 'Tupps' Ramsbotham (1887–1971) was Conservative MP for Lancaster from 1929 to 1941. He was in the Cabinet from 1940 to 1941 as President of the Board of Education.
2 It was an attempted attack on the Forth Bridge.
3 The French name for Cupid.

There were air raids, or alarms, along the east coast yesterday: but Honor at Kelvedon heard nothing, although Brigid, happening to be at Ongar, had the yellow warning.

Life is meaningless: we are drifting, all of us, to disaster.

The U-boat campaign is proving too successful; and Winston, I am told, had a cold reception in the House. The PM was cheered. I listened to the parliamentary news on the radio and it filled me with nostalgia to be away: and then I knew how I should miss it, were I ever to leave the House for the Upper Chamber.

THURSDAY 19TH OCTOBER

I am getting up and going out: my 'fire' restored. Honor rang up cheerfully and sweetly from Kelvedon.

The war is still a mess: but the Turks are playing up and have evidently broken off with the Russians. I am glad we have one triumph.

I got up late and went to the Foreign Office which I found in a turmoil. There was 'a flap on' as our young typist said: there were strong rumours that the Turks would sign the treaty at 4.30 Greenwich time, which meant 5.30 here. The PM, goaded by the discouraged whips, wished to announce the conclusion of the treaty in order to score a point, to offset the deplorable effect of the *Royal Oak*[1] sinking; to send the boys away happy; to use the Chief Whip's usual phrase. But how to arrange matters? A cable from Ankara, where the treaty was to be signed, would take five hours in wartime. We rang the Admiralty; they wanted to help but could not guarantee 'a flash' in so short a time. Then the head of the wireless department was consulted, and by very secret means he promised to get the news through quickly. A mysterious individual, it was arranged, would ring our room at the Foreign Office, and ask for me and give me the news of the confirmation of the treaty, directly it was humanly possible. The news could not come before 5.30 . . . . I waited apprehensively and excitedly. The PM was in his [room], presiding over a War Cabinet. He was anxious for news from Ankara. For an hour I waited, [word missing] every frivolous and unimportant tremble of the bell.

In the diary MS there are no more entries after 19 October, and all the pages are blank. The next volume of the MS starts on 25 December 1939, but a number of pages have been torn out of this diary before the first entry. Coats made a schedule that lists the diaries' contents, and according to this he had access to an MS for November and December 1939. This has gone missing, but was edited and had been typed. There are two versions of this typed transcript with entries for some of the missing days, some of which were included in Rhodes James's

---

1 On 14 October, the battleship HMS *Royal Oak* had been sunk by a U-boat while at anchor at Scapa Flow in Orkney. Out of a complement of 1,234 crew, 835 died.

edition. The editor has taken material from both versions for what follows until
25 December, but has not been able to check it against an original MS.

SUNDAY 22ND OCTOBER

The country, perhaps falsely, is much encouraged by the successful outcome of
the Turkish treaty and today I met Fellowes,[1] the House Clerk, in the park, and
we arranged between us that the treaty with the Turks should not lie on the table
for three weeks as is usual. It is only custom, not the law. I will see the Opposition
about it tomorrow.

TUESDAY 24TH OCTOBER

I had an hour with Alec Dunglass and we plotted for Rab to go to the India
Office as Secretary of State in the spring; and Alec took kindly to my plea that
Nevile Henderson be given a peerage immediately. Then we fell into wishful talk.
I said if only 'The Reaper' would cast his eye on the Admiralty. Alec retorted
that he feared the Reaper's right hand had lost its cunning if he could leave both
Hitler and Winston alive. Then I tried to wangle the Admiralty for Rab, but Alec
thought that Winston would only leave it either in a hearse, or to go to No. 10. He
preferred the former alternative.

I arranged with the Whips and the PM for him to have a word with Mr Attlee,
so that our treaty with Turkey might be immediately ratified.

THURSDAY 26TH OCTOBER

A long day both at the FO and the House of Commons. My life is a Congress
of Vienna one. Ministers here, ministers there, ambassadors on the telephone,
indeed I now call everyone, servants included, 'Excellency'. Today the Yugoslav
called, a gauche, genial Balkan, who smells of garlic and always treats me as one of
the Yugoslav royal family.

THURSDAY 2ND NOVEMBER

I lunched at the Ritz with Eileen Sutherland, whom I had not seen since the far
away summer, that feverish season when night after night we went to balls and fêtes,
each one more splendid and sumptuous than the others; it was a sort of sunset
glow before the storm. We sat and drank cocktails, the dukes of Marlborough

---

1 Edward Abdy Fellowes (1895–1970) became a junior clerk in the House of Commons after
   demobilisation from the Army in 1919, having won the Military Cross on active service
   with the Royal West Surrey Regiment. He served as Chief Clerk from 1954 to 1961 and was
   knighted in 1955.

(who calls his wife, who is in uniform, the General),[1] Northumberland[2] and Leeds,[3] more like a Pekinese than ever. It was 'The Dukeries' *in excelsis*. Eileen told me rather sadly that they have shut up Hampden House.[4] I dined there in the summer, her last dinner party as it worked out. Londonderry House, too, has been shut, and also Holland House, where there will surely never be another ball . . . again I was at the 'house cooling'. It is sad that the houses of the great will never again open their hospitable doors. Emerald, too, is trying to sell her house. It would indeed be the end of a chapter, were that to go. However, I have had twenty years of splendour, fun and life, the Twilight of the Gods, it was worth it and nothing matters now . . . I have Gibbonian apprehensions.[5]

FRIDAY 3RD NOVEMBER

I tried to sell 5 Belgrave Square to the Brazilians for their embassy. The new man is apparently anxious to buy a house as soon as he arrives.

SATURDAY 4TH NOVEMBER

There is no real war, just as there was no real reason for one. Hitler is indeed shrewd. Is he trying to bore us into peace?

MONDAY 13TH NOVEMBER

As I walked rather late and lazily to the Foreign Office, I came on a little troop of soldiers marching down Constitution Hill, led by an officer who was unrecognisable, under his tin helmet and strap. Suddenly be gave an order in a rasping voice, and I knew it was my old friend Hubert Duggan. I hung back and he did not see me. I felt shy in my civilian clothes, but much more ashamed of my shabby treatment of him; I deliberately tried to kill his friendship, which was once very deep and real and loyal for me. And I have succeeded. In fact, we are now almost enemies. He says it is because he is poor now and unimportant. I fear it is really because he bores me, and I am tired of him.

---

1 The Duchess was Commandant of the Auxiliary Territorial Service.
2 Henry George Alan Percy (1912–40), by courtesy Lord Lovaine until 1918 and then Earl Percy until he succeeded his father as 9th Duke of Northumberland in 1930. He was killed in May 1940 during the retreat to Dunkirk.
3 John Francis Godolphin Osborne (1901–63), by courtesy Marquess of Carmarthen, succeeded his father as 11th Duke of Leeds in 1927.
4 In Mayfair, the Sutherlands' London house.
5 He alludes to the author of *The History of the Decline and Fall of the Roman Empire*, Edward Gibbon.

THURSDAY 16TH NOVEMBER

I lunched with Circe Londonderry and her daughter Mairi at the Dorchester. The only other guest was Harold Macmillan, who for all his intelligence, is lacking in judgement and is a too facile critic of the government and the PM.

FRIDAY 24TH NOVEMBER

The war at sea intensifies and we have had a series of maritime knocks, though none sufficiently serious to be alarming. I trust that Joe Kennedy, the jaunty American Ambassador, is wrong, for he prophesies the end of everything, and goes about saying that England is committing suicide. My reason tells me he is wrong, that everything is on our side, but my intuition warns me that he may have something.

TUESDAY 28TH NOVEMBER

At the Opening of Parliament the King was in naval uniform, and the Queen wore trailing black velvet, furs and pearls, and I have never seen her so regal and beautiful. She was dressed to perfection. Everyone remarked on it. I have so often watched this ceremony in the days of peace with King George and Queen Mary floodlit with splendour; with the Royal Commission, in 1935, because Princess Victoria had died that morning; in 1936 when King Edward VIII opened Parliament looking more curiously boyish than ever in his robes. It was a wistful ceremony, and his last public appearance ... since then the present Sovereigns [*sic*] have done it, and there has always been the fear, as there was today, that the King would stammer, in fact, it is always a relief when he finishes his speech. I could not help contrasting this morning's quiet solemnity with all the Nazi fanfare, though there was a Merovingian[1] touch about the King today. The company rose as the King and Queen bowed and slowly left the Chamber, the King holding the Queen's hand. Back in the Commons lobby, several old members who should have known better smoked, and were stopped as the House was suspended, not adjourned.

Rab asked me whether Maisky and he could lunch alone at Belgrave Square today for a secret meeting, as he did not want to be seen with him in public. The lunch apparently was a success: I never thought that the Russian Ambassador would ever cross my threshold; I checked up on the snuffboxes on my return but did not notice anything missing. Rab said that His Excellency is an agreeable scoundrel.

---

1 The Merovingians ruled almost all of what is now France and Belgium, and much of what is now Germany, from the fifth to the eighth centuries.

THURSDAY 30TH NOVEMBER

When I arrived at the FO this morning at about 10.30, I heard that Russia had begun to attack Finland by land, sea and air, and that Helsinki was even then being bombed. Is this the beginning of the real war?[1]

FRIDAY 1ST DECEMBER

The debate yesterday dragged drearily to its close when Malcolm MacDonald wound up for the government. His speech, which was irrelevant and bored the House, was designed for a wider audience and will have a good effect on the colonies and abroad. The whole show, however, was jam for Goebbels. I have always said that it was sufficient to take some Socialists to the House, force them to listen to their leaders' speeches to make them vote Conservative. Today I go further. It would be almost enough to make any sane individual turn towards a totalitarian form of government.

MONDAY 4TH DECEMBER

Princess Louise, Duchess of Argyll,[2] is dead aged 91. She was the great-aunt of the King and eldest surviving child of Queen Victoria. She was born in 1848, the Year of Revolution, married during the Franco-Prussian War, and in fact was a link with time. I never met her, but I saw her on several occasions and was always told that she was the most amiable and intelligent of Queen Victoria's children; she was even a beauty, dressed well, and was something of an artist. The Duke of Kent always sucked up to her in hopes of inheriting her fortune, which must be considerable. She married a member of the House of Commons[3] and is the first princess to marry outside the royal circle for generations. Curiously enough, I knew her stepmother-in-law,[4] and once stayed in the same house with her, Blythe Hall, the Lathoms'[5] Lancashire seat.

---

1 It was the beginning of the Winter War, which lasted until 12 March 1940, and was ended by an agreement by the Finns to cede 11 per cent of their territory to the Soviet Union. The Russians attempted to justify this act of naked aggression by claiming it was essential for the security of Leningrad.

2 Princess Louisa Caroline Alberta (1848–1939) was the sixth child of Queen Victoria and Prince Albert; she married the 9th Duke of Argyll in 1871.

3 Her husband, John Campbell (1845–1914), by courtesy the Marquess of Lorne until 1900 when he succeeded his father as 9th Duke of Argyll, sat in the Commons from 1868 to 1875 as Liberal MP for Argyllshire, and from 1895 to 1900 as Liberal Unionist MP for Manchester South. For part of the interim he was Governor-General of Canada.

4 Ina McNeill (1843–1925). She married, in 1895 as his third wife, the 8th Duke of Argyll. She was an Extra Woman of the Bedchamber to Queen Victoria.

5 The earls of Lathom – the village in Lancashire where Blythe Hall is situated – occupied the house from 1826 to 1933, when it became a Catholic seminary. Later, it became a hotel.

THURSDAY 7TH DECEMBER

The *Te Deums* of the unreal League of Nations must be sung next week, and my Rab will be the principal delegate. Should I accompany or stay behind and 'run' the Foreign Office? Which? I am torn with doubt. I don't want to go; but fear it would be *occasion manquée*[1] not to; but I suggested this morning that Eddie Devonshire be appointed as second delegate under Rab. An under-secretary who is a duke would be perfect. The Cabinet jumped at the suggestion and charged Anthony Eden with a message to Eddie asking him to go.

Later – Rab has definitely asked me to go with him to Geneva tomorrow, but I cannot face the flying, the cold and the rush. I suggested, as a compromise, that I should follow him on Monday, but Eddie is definitely going, and will leave on Saturday.

In the middle of all the fuss over the Geneva excursion Miss Fox,[2] the famous old Royal Governess, rang me up and asked to see me. She duly appeared, very upset, the old noddle, that Alexander of Yugoslavia[3] has been 'reported' by his Housemaster, Roe, to the Headmaster, and has probably been beaten. I like Alexander, and think him a charming boy, but only hope that the Headmaster dealt severely enough with him. A severe whipping would do him the world of good. In fact I hinted as much to Roe when I was last at Eton two Sundays ago. Alexander ought to be whipped weekly. It might instil some sense into him. I agree with Halifax, and am on the side of the birch for boys, frequently and sternly administered, the more exalted the bottom the more necessary it usually is.

Emerald and Jock Colville[4] lunched. Jock is now Neville's secretary, and Emerald quite startled him by suddenly asking him whether he thought Queen Mary had any tact?

SUNDAY 10TH DECEMBER

An intoxicating day spent with someone I have hardly seen alone since January, i.e. myself. There is no such blissful companionship, no such satisfactory or stimulating friendship. I got up late, wrote many letters, tidied up and telephoned.

---

1 A missed opportunity.
2 Kate Fox, who trained as a 'lady nurse' at the Norland Institute, had worked for the Greek royal family since 1903. She had been the governess of Princess Marina and Princess Olga (qqv), and was now watching over Princess Olga's son.
3 Prince Alexander (1924–2016), son of Prince Paul and Princess Olga. He was 15 at the time.
4 John Rupert 'Jock' Colville (1915–87) joined the Diplomatic Service in 1937 and in 1939 was seconded to be Chamberlain's private secretary. For much of the war he worked for Churchill, whom initially he disliked but to whom he became devoted, and returned to his side during the 1951–5 government. He left public service after 1955 and built a successful career as a banker and as a writer. He was knighted in 1974.

The war is one hundred days old, and a damned bore it is, though no one seems to talk about it now. It might be somewhere very remote, and I feel that there is a definite danger in such detachment.

WEDNESDAY 13TH DECEMBER

Mr Bland, dear old boy, came to lunch and told us how he had once taken the Iveagh jewels to Russia for Lady Iveagh (Honor's grandmother) to wear at the coronation of the Tsar and how she had outshone all the grand duchesses. I am not surprised, her great collection is now scattered amongst her grandchildren, and daughters-in-law. However Honor has one of the tiaras.

There was a secret session, and Questions proceeded in a normal way. At the end of them I went out for a moment and ran into the Duke of Kent, who was in naval uniform, and we chatted. He was amiable enough, and I came back to the Chamber just in time to hear the PM move that 'strangers be ordered to retire', and the galleries were emptied. Peers remained. Quintin Hogg, foolishly and youthfully, rose to protest against the presence of Gallacher,[1] the communist. It was a mistake, as Gallacher is being carefully watched. Hogg protested with dignity, but he raised the temperature of the House, always an undesirable thing to do. Then the debate began.

THURSDAY 14TH DECEMBER

As each session closes, the PM seems to be in even better form and fettle – though I secretly feel he hates the House of Commons: certainly he has a deep contempt for parliamentary interference and fussiness; and who can blame him?

FRIDAY 15TH DECEMBER

All morning I waited for news of Rab, who is supposed to be descending from the skies from Geneva via Paris. It was he who insisted on the expulsion of Germany from the League [of Nations] yesterday, a magnificent piece of diplomacy.

SATURDAY 16TH DECEMBER

I hear that an important French delegate arrived somewhere the other day a little late for luncheon and found the other guests seated; he was next to an English general and was impressed by his neighbour's good looks and military bearing. He was surprised however when towards the end of luncheon the General produced a lipstick and used it. The Frenchman was amazed until he discovered that he had

---

1 William Gallacher (1881–1965) was a veteran of 'Red Clydeside', a founder of the Communist Party of Great Britain and the Communist MP for West Fife from 1935 to 1950.

been sitting next to the Duchess of Marlborough in uniform, and it is true that Mary looks surprisingly manly and martial.

There is excitement over the great naval battle in progress off Montevideo.[1]

SUNDAY 17TH DECEMBER

The whole world is waiting for news of the *Graf Spee*, which has taken refuge from our fleet in Montevideo. In a few hours' time the much-vaunted German pocket battleship will have to decide to be interned, to scuttle herself or to fight her way out. Fritzi, the Kaiser's grandchild, who is staying secretly at Kelvedon, and I listened to the news together. We afterwards talked of the so-called Russian Grand Duchess Anastasia.[2] Fritzi told me his mother, the Crown Princess, once interviewed the impostor who claimed to be a daughter of the Tsar. Princess Cecilie said that it was quite impossible that the woman could be what she claimed, as there was no family resemblance whatever. The poor thing seemed half-demented, and was obviously the tool of a designing[3] clique.

MONDAY 18TH DECEMBER

The scuttling of the *Graf Spee* off Montevideo is a welcome tonic, and will give a fillip to the Navy and to the world in general. Already our sailors are being referred to as Nelson's grandsons.

The meet of the hounds took place at Kelvedon for the first time for forty years – and was a lovely sight. Honor and I dispensed hospitality in the hall where a long table had been set up, laden with cherry brandy and other drinks: the meet and the *Graf Spee* have revived my faith in Old England. Poor German Fritzi, tactfully, kept in the background.

In the afternoon I came up to the FO to receive Gripenberg,[4] the Finnish Minister, who is amazingly cheerful and even confident: perhaps, after all, Finland will not be conquered.

Now the manuscript diary resumes, at Kelvedon.

1 The Battle of the River Plate, which resulted in the scuttling of the German heavy cruiser *Graf Spee*.
2 The Grand Duchess Anastasia Nikolaevna of Russia (1901–18), Tsar Nicholas II's youngest daughter, was murdered with the rest of her immediate family in Yekaterinburg by Bolsheviks. A number of impostors emerged in the years after her death, the most notorious – and the one to whom Channon refers – being Anna Anderson (1896–1984), whose real name was Franziska Schanzkowska, a Prussian, and after whose death DNA tests proved to be no relation of the Romanovs.
3 Plotting: he alludes to a conspiracy.
4 Georg Achates Gripenberg (1890–1975) was the Finnish Minister to the United Kingdom from 1933 to 1941, to Sweden from 1943 to 1956 and Ambassador to the United Nations from 1956 to 1958.

MONDAY 25TH DECEMBER

Essex is wrapt [*sic*] in fog: it is like a winding sheet. Catarrhal, and half-suffocated, I came down to breakfast after sending a sheaf of telegrams and telephoning to poor Peter at the Olde Bell Hotel; but Peter Pan had fled, gone philandering somewhere no doubt. I was relieved, yet subdued, too . . .

Breakfast *en famille* with Honor, Brigid and Fritzi who must be thinking of Potsdam and of other happier holidays. We had a plethora of presents, and quite forgot about the war in the excitement of opening them. From Honor I had a magnificent pair of Dresden apostles, St Thomas and St Peter; from the Iveaghs a set of Saint-Simon;[1] and from the Duke and Duchess of Kent a satin Fabergé-esque cigarette case; from Alan, a real gold Fabergé case with a ruby – very grand; from the Prince Regent a pair of gold links with his *chiffre*[2] surrounding the garter; etc., etc. From my baby boy a diary; from Peter his photograph framed and books; after breakfast I rang up Clandeboye and had a word with little Paul who seemed pleased and we talked for a moment. And I also rang Alexander of Yugoslavia who is staying with Miss Fox and a tutor at 13 Grange Road, Cambridge. Then we dressed, went for a walk and the day passed pleasantly enough. My war was forgotten in the land of plenty of Kelvedon, where there is always too much to eat and drink. Rab rang me from Stanstead after lunch, and we had a good gossip; he loathes holidays, rest and country life . . . . Yesterday we had a tree, presents and party for the gardeners and staff – about thirty in all, and Honor distributed presents and I made a speech. All very feudal. Kelvedon looks a dream of beauty . . . . I went for a walk and in the woods came on many pigs – it was almost classical.

I reread *Paradise City*[3] today and thought how excellent and really underrated it is. Peter liked it: and I wondered, too, to what lengths will my fecund friendship with him take me? . . . And I read *Caroline of England*, an excellent and highly readable book by Peter Quennell.[4] Harold Balfour, who was here, left us yesterday: he wants me to go to France to visit the front this weekend. And such an expedition would recall adventures [*sic*] paid in 1918 to the then front.

Fritzi at dinner was very charming and he told me of the revolution in Germany,[5] and how his grandfather, living in his special train near Spa, had

---

1 Louis de Rouvroy, duc de Saint-Simon (1675–1755) was a sometime courtier of Louis XIV but better known as a diplomat, and better known still as a memoirist of multiple volumes.

2 *Chiffre* literally means figure, but in this instance it refers to the Regent's royal cipher.

3 Channon's own second novel, published in 1931, about American capitalism.

4 Peter Courtney Quennell (1905–93) was a man of letters who specialised in literary biography and essays. *Caroline of England* is a life of Caroline of Ansbach, Queen Consort of King George II. Married five times, Quennell was knighted the year before his death.

5 The events of the autumn of 1918 when Germany capitulated and the Hohenzollern dynasty fell.

refused to abdicate; after a strong interview with Hindenburg[1] he had gone to bed. It was Hindenburg, so Fritzi assures me, who gave the order for the train to move on, and the Kaiser was astonished and enraged to find himself over the Dutch frontier. It was then too late. The Imperial children with the Crown Princess had gone to the Neues Palais from nearby Cecilienhof to spend a few days with their grandmother, the Kaiserin, who was alone. When they heard that the Kaiser had fled, or been abducted into Holland, they sat up all night wondering what to do. The guards were thought to be rather revolutionary, and the children were ordered not to look out – but they climbed up in one of the ballrooms, peered out and saw nothing.

The Kaiserin, ever the faithful wife, decided to join her husband and left next day. She was quite unmolested. The Crown Princess, however, said that they had to deal with Germans, not Russians, and she refused to leave Potsdam. Instead she removed her six children to Cecilienhof, where they remained. The first few weeks were anxious, and there were occasional alarms. Fears of reds who might want to assassinate or perhaps assault them. But nothing even happened and they survived the storm in increasing safety . . .

London is deserted: the Cabinet has flown; half the army is on leave; luckily a heavy fog envelops England and there will be no air raids tonight!!

TUESDAY 26TH DECEMBER

Intense cold, but beauty, too, and this place is a dream of loveliness, and like a beautiful woman who flowers under attention; all our care is now having an effect. Honor in happier mood, too. A pleasant day *sans* letters, *sans* newspapers. I wonder where Peter is . . . I am too cold almost to care.

Despairing letters from Walter Buccleuch who writes by almost every post urging peace. He is our defeatist Duke, and perhaps he is right.

I feel low: in a mood that I would not wish away; yet it is hardly ecstasy.

WEDNESDAY 27TH DECEMBER

The war seems so remote; but the newspapers keep us up to it: it is a half-hearted affair; only three killed of the British forces in France after nearly four months. Incredible . . . Fritzi went to London: Honor hunted . . . . Fritzi of Prussia is an angel of sweetness, good breeding and charm – I really only like royalties, and Peter, whom I rang up tonight.

---

1 Paul Ludwig Hans Anton von Beneckendorff und von Hindenburg (1847–1934) was a Prussian aristocrat who commanded the Imperial German army in the Great War, becoming effectively military dictator by the end of it, and was President of Germany from 1925 to 1934.

THURSDAY 28TH DECEMBER

I went to London by train – and Honor spent a somewhat exhausting and mysterious day seeing houses – I went first to the Foreign Office, where there is gossip of Göring trying to sell the pass; he sees himself as a General Monck and is allegedly to be plotting against Hitler.[1] Their regime must soon crack . . . Lunched at home, and entertained Emerald; Charles Somerset[2] – too tall and boring; Shakespeare Morrison who bristled with charm, and after an extremely good luncheon (he was unimpressed by Fritzi) he went off and announced a lot of tiresome restrictions.[3] His Raeburn[4] beauty is very great, and his vivacious manner, the burr in his voice, and voluptuous mouth are fascinating, indeed.

Fritzi and I travelled back to Kelvedon by a late train; Liverpool Street was hell let loose in the cold, fog and the crowds. At Brentwood we found snow and darkness and the Packard, which had been bumped. It is the second accident our cars have had, and when we got back to Kelvedon Honor had not yet returned. I was cold, and alarmed about her; but she soon arrived.

FRIDAY 29TH DECEMBER

An icy day! I wrote letters and slept and overate. Bill Tufnell shot with the Butlers, near Stanstead, and rang up to say how much he disliked them.

SATURDAY 30TH DECEMBER

Miss Fox, the ageing, dull but worthy duenna of the Nicholas family,[5] rang up from Cambridge to ask whether young Alexander could come here for the weekend. He took a train from Bishop's Stortford and neglected to get out. Appalling muddles about meeting him; the day seemed to go wrong altogether: some poltergeist was playing impish tricks. At length the boy, almost a young man, arrived and I liked him very much. He will do, probably, for the role of the future Prince Consort.[6] I must arrange that – he is handsome, strong, and throneless. He in no way resembles his father and I look in vain for a trait or a gesture which suggests the Regent: but there is none. He is rather Romanov.

---

1   Channon, doubtless encouraged by 'Fritzi', continued to harbour fantasies that the Germans would realise Hitler's ghastliness and remove him, and restore the Hohenzollerns.

2   Charles Alexander Somerset (1901–81), a descendant of the 5th Duke of Beaufort.

3   In his role as Food Minister.

4   Sir Henry Raeburn (1756–1823), portrait artist.

5   He refers to the Nicholas family because Princess Olga's (and Princess Marina, the Duchess of Kent's) father was Prince Nicholas of Greece and Denmark, and Miss Fox had been their governess.

6   That is, that he ought to marry the future Queen Elizabeth II.

Alan has written to Honor asking her to take him to dine with Max Beaverbrook so that he can make peace between the Beaver and Shakes Morrison... Honor reluctantly agrees to do this...

Gay evening, our little princelings have formed an axis and seem intimate. They talk in English. Fritzi played the harmonica-accordion, his strongest instrument. Alexander thoroughly enjoys himself.

Sunday 31st December

The last day of the year: what will the new one bring to us in the way of political, social, and financial changes? Will the war be won, and we, as a class, done? And me personally? I fled from the dining room after Honor and Brigid had left, and rang up Peter .... and we had an affectionate talk ... he has written to me every day for a week. Honor worn out, went to bed early; but Bill Tufnell, Alexander of Yugoslavia, Fritzi, Brigid and I saw the New Year in, and drank hot punch. Bill left for Langleys, but hardly was I in bed before I heard him at the door: the cold and fog were so intense that he came back asking for a bed. He is very dull, very handsome, very nice.

1940

MONDAY 1ST JANUARY

Alexander returned to Cambridge . . . The Iveaghs arrived for the night; and I attempted in a confidential conversation to warn her that the . . . . brewery is not doing as well as we should like . . . I was not at my best, feeling liverish and dejected – and apprehensive about the coming year and its complications.

TUESDAY 2ND JANUARY

I was relieved and happy to be back once more in Belgrave Square.

Honor and Fritzi followed me to London later. H arranged to dine with Beaverbrook and she took Alan and Fritzi. I dined alone, read and worked.

There is a plot afoot to get rid of Leslie Hore-Belisha.[1] Rab had it from Horace Wilson this morning. The generals are restive; his methods are too drastic and he has accelerated the pace more than perhaps was wise.

WEDNESDAY 3RD JANUARY

A dreadful night. H came in about 1 a.m. in hysterics; she shouted, woke me, was sick and in tears: it was partly 'nerves' and possibly a bit of drink combined. The dinner at Stornoway House had been too successful, with Beaverbrook at his most charming. Winston Churchill joined them and they had a gay, champagne evening. The others remained on and I hear that they came in at 3.30. What a sitter-up Max is.

---

1 Belisha had indeed fallen out with members of the General Staff, notably Lord Gort (qv); but some Tory MPs had been after his blood since Munich, since they felt his strategy at the War Office was based on Britain being able to avoid involvement in any European war. Gort was especially irate that the expansion of the Territorial Army, announced the previous March, happened without his being consulted. Blatant anti-Semitism unquestionably also played a role in the problem; General Sir Henry Pownall, the BEF's Chief of Staff and highly decorated in the Great War, observed that two men as different as Gort and Belisha – 'a great gentleman and an obscure, shallow-brained, charlatan, political Jewboy' – could not be expected to see eye to eye. (Quoted in A. J. Trythall, *Journal of Contemporary History*, Vol. 16, No. 3, p. 400.)

I was all day at the FO .... we went over the MS of Nevile Henderson's book[1] about the war. It would be disastrous if it were published as it reveals our vacillating policy and our offer of colonies etc. and it praises both Hitler and Göring. We decided to prune it severely before it is published.

Three letters from Peter, and one from the Duke of Kent.

Honor was ill all the day: we lunched together in her room and she returned to Kelvedon. I dined alone. I ordered a handsome dressing-case for Peter at Asprey's. I have now spent about £1,000 on him so far ....

The anti-Belisha plot has assumed alarming dimensions and the poor PM is in a dilemma, either Leslie goes, or many of the Staff. Leslie isn't aware, so far, of the projected *coup de main*.[2] So I wrote him a private word of warning, and as he is surrounded by traitors at the War Office I sent it to Miss Sloane,[3] his personal private devoted secretary who is half a nannie, half a mistress to him. She worships him but he looks on her only as an efficient woman. She will pass it directly on. I am dining alone which is bliss.

THURSDAY 4TH JANUARY

The plot against Belisha is growing, and I am told today that David Margesson has been offered the War Office and if he will accept poor Leslie is for it – but every effort will be made to find him some other job, as unlike Eden and Duff Cooper he is liked by the PM, and has been a definite success.

I ran into Arthur Hope,[4] who this morning sent me £50 as first repayment of my lunatic[5] loan of £200 to him last year. He is temporarily at the War Office before he goes to India in March as Governor of Madras. We chatted, and he thinks Leslie will not survive the weekend; then I ran into Victor Warrender who, as F[inancial] S[ecretary] to the War Office is in a delicate position. Victor is loyal to his chief, is a gentleman, but dislikes him really. He hinted to me that the gong had sounded. Now I know.

Lunched and dined with Alan, lunch at the Marlborough Club. We dined *en pajama* and talked late. When I rang Peter at the Olde Bell, Barnby Moor,[6] he had already gone to bed 'with a cold', I was told. I was disappointed, naturally.

---

1 Published later in 1940 as *Failure of a Mission: Berlin 1937–39*. Its posthumous reputation, like Henderson's, is not good.
2 Surprise attack.
3 Hilde Sloane (1892–1983) was Belisha's private secretary throughout his career in public life, and became the legatee of his private archive when he died in 1957, despite his having married by then.
4 Arthur James Hope (1897–1958) was Conservative MP for Nuneaton from 1924 to 1929 and for Aston from 1931 to 1939; a senior government whip from 1937 to 1939; and Governor of Madras from 1940 to 1946. He succeeded his father as 2nd Baron Rankeillour in 1949.
5 The word 'mad' is crossed out.
6 In Nottinghamshire, near East Retford, where Coats was billeted.

FRIDAY 5TH JANUARY

I selfishly hope that David Margesson will not accept the War Office, as that would mean James Stuart as Chief Whip.[1] He has not the necessary qualities, insight, popularity, nor tact for the job. I will work against that. I hoped last night that the storm might blow over but this morning Rab saw Horace Wilson get into a taxi and say 'to the Ministry of Information'. Later Rucker told Rab that the 'changes had been made'. We don't know yet what they are.

Emerald Cunard lunched, as did Sir Joseph Addison,[2] a long-winded witty bore who was outrageously treated by the Foreign Office and by Anthony Eden, when he was Minister in Prague. He was sacked. But now he is a man with a grievance, which is always a danger and a bore. Rab went to the country . . . his curiosity is aroused by the impending re-shuffle.

I came home . . . . [and] went up to the study to telephone to Peter, a long and satisfying conversation except that he told me his regiment leaves for Palestine on January 18th, which is cruel. There is something so doom-like about a date. Alan, who was motoring to Pyrford to see Patsy, let himself be persuaded not to go because of the fog; but when he rang up Patsy, she was, as always, hysterical and unreasonable. She is v difficult and spoilt and I am glad not to be married to her. Honor and Brigid are both infinitely more intelligent and easier to live with.

SATURDAY 6TH JANUARY

I woke with a dreadful head, and felt discouraged and sick – and the newspapers lying at my side caught my eye – 'Belisha resigns'. It is a sensation, and seems to have caught both the press and the public unawares and unprepared. I think it is a calamity especially as he is replaced by Oliver Stanley, a very dry stick, and to me a dull and deplorable figure . . . . Sir John Reith,[3] whom I dislike and disapprove

---

1 Stuart would indeed succeed Margesson, but not for almost another year. Oliver Stanley was about to succeed Belisha.

2 Joseph Addison (1879–1953) was a career diplomat who had been Minister to the Baltic States from 1927 to 1930 and to Czechoslovakia from 1930 to 1936. Eden (and Vansittart) may have disliked him because of the lengths to which he went in dispatches to disparage the Czechoslovak government and particularly Edvard Beneš, the Foreign Minister who later became the country's President.

3 John Charles Walsham Reith (1889–1971) was one of the titanic figures of the inter-war years, having become general manager of the British Broadcasting Company in 1922 and the first Director-General of the British Broadcasting Corporation in 1927, when he was knighted. Feeling he had done all he could at the BBC he left in 1938 to become Chairman of Imperial Airways. In 1940 he held three government posts in quick succession, as Minister of Information, Minister of Transport and then until 1942 as Minister of Works. He was briefly National MP for Southampton before being raised to the peerage as 1st Baron Reith in 1940. He left the government in Churchill's reshuffle after the fall of Singapore in 1942, having never been able to cohabit successfully with the Civil Service; and nor did he get on with Churchill. He took a commission in the Royal Naval Volunteer Reserve and ended the war in the rank of captain.

of, becomes Minister of Information (probably he is the man for the job) and Sir Andrew Duncan[1] succeeds Oliver at the Board of Trade, a post Leslie, with dignity, refused. He is now out in the cold – but only temporarily, and I foresee a great political future for him.[2] It is a pity he isn't a Conservative (he is at heart).

History will prove that he was right in his reforms, and also that Chamberlain was right in letting him go, since the war must be won and a divided and dissatisfied War Office would never lead us to victory. Leslie's methods were too democratic, too startling – but he had the youth of the nation behind him. Of course all the anti-Jews are enchanted.

I went to the FO and later walked to Grosvenor Square to lunch with Emerald ... The Belisha bombshell was the only subject mentioned. It is first-class political sensation.

The truth: I have not yet discovered all the facts, but so much is true: there has been an anti-Belisha faction in the House, at the War Office and in the Army for some time. His mania for publicity, his courting of public favour and his democratic methods of reorganising the Army have all made him many enemies. Every peace-seeker disappointed in his hopes, anyone refused a commission and large sections of the aristocracy who saw their sons serving in the ranks, turned against him and he went blandly, blindly on with his reforms etc. Then a cabal was formed headed by people on the General Staff – still they could not oust him, until they hit on the brilliant idea of roping in the Duke of Gloucester,[3] professional soldier that he is. He took up the cause and told his brother the King. The Crown decided to intervene dramatically and sent for the PM, told him to get rid of Leslie (whom they have long disliked for private reasons; i.e.: because he was loyal to the Windsors and was the one minister who liked and fought for them).[4] The PM, startled by the King's complaint, gave in: it turned the scales. The PM had long been aware of the movement but had firmly supported Leslie ... on Thursday he was sent for to come to No. 10 and, suspecting nothing, he

1 Andrew Rae Duncan (1884–1952) was Chairman of the British Iron and Steel Federation, and had been Chairman of the Central Electricity Board; he was also a director of the Bank of England and of Imperial Chemical Industries. He was knighted in 1921. A by-election was created for him so he could join the government, and he was National MP for the City of London from 1940 to 1950. After serving briefly at the Board of Trade he served as Minister of Supply from 1940 to 1941; then returned to Trade until 1942, before returning to Supply, where he remained until 1945.

2 This was the end of Belisha's ministerial career: the Conservative Party, who apart from Channon and like most senior Army officers regarded him as flashy and vulgar, was strongly opposed to his return to government.

3 Prince Henry William Frederick Albert (1900–74) was the third son of King George V and Queen Mary, created Duke of Gloucester in 1928; he married in 1935 Lady Alice Christabel Montagu Douglas Scott (1901–2004), daughter of the 7th Duke of Buccleuch.

4 This version of events must be treated with caution. If George VI had felt he had the power to order the sacking of ministers who had supported his brother, Churchill would never have been restored to office the previous September.

and the PM had a conversation during which the PM asked him to accept the Board of Trade. Belisha was startled and asked why (evidently he didn't believe my mildly worded warning). He was told he must go; but the PM was as gentle as he could be. Leslie demanded an hour in which to consider his position, and went out for a walk in St James's Park . . . he could hardly believe his ears (he knows nothing of the royal intervention): later he returned to No. 10, saw the PM again and reported to him that he would not accept the Board of Trade, that he would never serve under Chamberlain again, that he mistrusted him; that the PM who had long supported him had thrown him over; how could he, Belisha, be assured that the PM would not do so again? There was some bitterness but no scene, and Belisha agreed not to make a statement, not to attack the govt. Dazed, fallen from power and grandeur he left, an unhappy man.

There is no MS traceable for 7–10 January 1940; what follows until 11 January is from Coats's typed transcript.

MONDAY 8TH JANUARY

London is agog with Belisha tales and it is certain that the Court is deeply implicated, as it has now leaked out that the King himself insisted on Leslie's resignation, and that he was egged on by both the Queen and the Duke of Gloucester, neither of whom have [sic] forgotten Belisha's loyalty to his then Sovereign at the time of the abdication, when, indeed, he was the only Cabinet minister who had the courage to stand up for Edward VIII. Ever since, the Court minions – headed by Alec Hardinge – have been intriguing [to cause] his downfall. Alec Hardinge completely rules the King, and is very anti-Chamberlain: and Maureen Stanley, who will surely benefit from the change, has also been at work – dropping poison into the Queen's ear. One of the Foreign Office junta had the inspiration to drag in the Duke of Gloucester, who has never yet meddled in politics; and when the King went to France the stage was set to turn him against Belisha. All this will do the monarchy harm, as they should not intrigue or dabble in politics: though I must admit that when the King has done so in the past, he has usually been right: but George VI is not George V and Hardinge is certainly not Lord Stamfordham.[1] Alone of Leslie's former colleagues Kingsley Wood tried to save him, and urged him at least to consider the offer of the Board of Trade: but, after consulting Beverley Baxter,[2] Leslie decided against it, and moreover, told the Prime Minister that he would in no circumstances ever serve under him again.

1 George V's private secretary.
2 Arthur Beverley Baxter (1891–1964) was Canadian by birth who in 1920 started a career in journalism in London, working for his fellow countryman Lord Beaverbrook (qv). He was editor-in-chief of the *Daily Express* from 1929 to 1933. He was Conservative MP for Wood Green (1935–50) and Southgate (1950–64). In his later years he was a part-time theatre critic. He was knighted in 1954.

Throughout the crisis David Margesson's stature has increased: he has strengthened his influence over the Prime Minister, he has shown tact with the Palace and has now appointed a great friend to the War Office: *en plus*[1] he has succeeded in not offending Belisha personally. He shot at Lavington on Saturday and Euan Wallace and Harold Balfour discussed the situation, and while on the subject of intrigues and cabals, went on to declare that they would not serve under Winston Churchill if he became Prime Minister as a result of a plot against Neville: people say that so glibly.[2]

Harold blames the Court for this blasted Belisha business, though he admits that there are many who will not regret his departure. Now the King has begun to interfere with the Air Ministry appointments, to the annoyance of the General Staff and of Kingsley Wood: of course the Monarch is put up to everything by Alec Hardinge and the Queen. I have for some time suspected that she is trying to exert too great an influence; she is a snob at heart, much more than any real royalty would be. When I discussed this today with Rab, he agreed and added, unless they are more careful we shall get the Windsors back.

Meanwhile the Prime Minister is put in a difficult position, and is blamed by everyone for what is really the King's high-handed action; and it seems that both the government and the Palace are astonished by the fuss that has been caused by the publicity and headlines and are a bit shaken. Alec Hardinge spent the morning at No. 10 with David Margesson.

THURSDAY 11TH JANUARY

I am appalled by the Churchillian-cum-Stanley plots to send an expeditionary force immediately to Sweden, and perhaps to Norway; the same brain that was responsible for the Dardanelles campaign[3] has conceived this wild enterprise.

To Churchill thousands of lives are nothing; but the old ruffian will be defeated this time, I think. Rab is aghast not only by the folly of the plan but by the Secretary of State's[4] curious weakness in allowing it to go so far. For so

---

1 Moreover.
2 Wallace did not serve under Churchill; Balfour did.
3 The attempt to attack the Dardanelles in the spring of 1915, conceived by Churchill as First Lord of the Admiralty, was one of the leading military disasters of the Great War. It caused the resignation of Admiral Lord ('Jacky') Fisher, the First Sea Lord; the fall of the Asquith administration and its replacement by the coalition he led until December 1916; and Churchill's removal from that office. He spent much of the rest of his life seeking to vindicate himself, largely unsuccessfully. The 1940 plan for a naval attack in the Baltic, known as Operation Catherine and designed to stop Swedish iron ore reaching Germany, was abandoned on 20 January after stringent objections by Admiral Sir Dudley Pound, the First Sea Lord (qv).
4 Halifax.

high-principled a man, he can be very dishonest; to him the means never matter – it is only the end.

FRIDAY 12TH JANUARY

Awoke after only a few hours' sleep wanting to feel well and gay but I was exhausted. I went to the office and discovered that the War Cabinet are discussing Sweden this morning. Ismay,[1] bizarrely, is backing Rab. Home to luncheon where I had collected Emerald, Winnie Portarlington, Lady Juliet Duff,[2] Georgia Sitwell, Rob Bernays, Peter Hesketh,[3] Hector Bolitho[4] . . . . all to meet my Peter who arrived from Retford by train and late. He swept into lunch, looking like Ariel, and was immediately captivating . . . he was excited, intoxicated by his luncheon party, for people, parties, personalities go to his pretty head . . . later we shopped together until 6 p.m. when Victor Mallet[5] looked in for a drink and remained an hour, entranced by Peter's fluency about Stockholm . . . . Peter and I had an egg, then collected Georgia Sitwell, and joined by Emerald and Rob Bernays we went to *The Importance of Being Earnest*, a very finished production and highly amusing. Lady Bracknell talks just like Emerald. We had supper at the Savoy where Loelia Westminster, her admirer, Sir Kenneth Clark, Victor Mallet and Zita James[6] also joined us; all v pleasant . . .

---

1 Hastings Lionel 'Pug' Ismay (1887–1965) joined the Army in 1904 and went initially to serve in India, where he had been born: his father, Sir Stanley Ismay, had been a member of the Viceroy's Legislative Council. He became Secretary of the Committee of Imperial Defence in 1938 and was promoted to major general in 1939, working closely with Chamberlain once the CID was absorbed into the workings of the War Cabinet. He would become Churchill's chief staff officer shortly before Churchill became Prime Minister, and remained his main military adviser throughout the war, and his main channel of liaison to service chiefs. He was knighted in 1940. After the war he was raised to the peerage as 1st Baron Ismay, and served as Chief of Staff to Mountbatten (qv) during his short Viceroyalty. When Churchill returned to power in 1951 he appointed Ismay Secretary of State for Commonwealth Relations, and from 1952 to 1957 he was Secretary-General of NATO. He became a Knight of the Garter in 1957.

2 Gladys Mary Juliet Lowther (1881–1965), by courtesy Lady Juliet, married Sir Robert George Vivian Duff, 2nd Bt, in 1903. She was the mother of Sir Michael Duff*. After her first husband was killed in action in 1914 she married, in 1919, Major Keith Trevor, whom she divorced in 1926. She then reverted to the surname of Lowther, though Channon calls her by her original married name, Duff.

3 Charles Peter Fleetwood Hesketh (1905–85) was an author and illustrator, and architectural correspondent of the *Daily Telegraph* from 1964 to 1967.

4 Henry Hector Bolitho (1897–1974), born in New Zealand, settled in Britain in the 1920s and became a prodigious author of biographies, novels, travelogues, topography, histories and books on royalty.

5 Victor Alexander Louis Mallet (1893–1969) was a career diplomat who joined the Diplomatic Service in 1919. Among his many postings abroad, he was Envoy Extraordinary to Sweden from 1940 to 1945. He was knighted in 1944.

6 Zita Jungman (1903–2006) had in the 1920s been one of the 'bright young things'. She had married, in 1929, Arthur James, but they divorced in 1932.

SATURDAY 13TH JANUARY

The War Cabinet has <u>scotched</u> the plans for the invasion of Sweden. Rab's succinct and excellent minute played some role.

 P and I shopped and I bought him a plethora of presents . . . .

SUNDAY 14TH JANUARY

. . . . Peter and I breakfasted and then I took him to King's Cross – a v sad farewell, cold, dramatic and sick at heart and in the tummy. It was like the old war . . . and the train pulled out. I shall perhaps never see him again; not like this. In any case circumstances will have changed . . . in a daze I walked in the fog to the FO where I discovered considerable excitement over rumours of an impending German invasion of Belgium. I rang Rab at Stanstead where he is weekending, to warn him that there was a meeting of the Cabinet this morning, and that Halifax would soon return. Later I rang the Duchess of Kent to tell her and we had a talk.

 Alan v charming, indeed, I love him; he is one of the most loveable of men.

 I was ill, sick at heart, down all day; couldn't face Kelvedon in the cold and fog . . . rested.

MONDAY 15TH JANUARY

I wrote seven letters to P today: I must try to put him from my thoughts.

 Sydney Butler sent a message from Stanstead that Rab has flu with a temperature of 102 and will not be returning to the office for ten days or more. He looked ill all last week: he has long overworked and I have often feared a breakdown was in store for him. He is so clever, so shrewd and far-sighted about everything except his health, and his social arrangements and engagements.

TUESDAY 16TH JANUARY

I woke ill and exceedingly depressed; long talks with Honor and wrote my letters and then went into the FO. I am broken-hearted and realise how foolish I am: it doesn't help . . . . Questions were soon over . . . . the House was very crowded; the galleries were full; for the world and particularly Whitehall loves a victim and a show; a relic of the spirit which applauded the arena. Questions were rushed through and Belisha did not appear until just in time to be called. He looked ill, old and grey and I was sorry for him. He sat in Winston's old seat, the corner one in the front row below the gangway. He rose and with some dignity and little bitterness (he seemed more broken than bitter) he quietly made his apologies. There was only one Belisha touch and that was when he referred to the democratisation of the Army which was to fight for Democracy – this brought a cheap cheer from the Opposition. I looked about the crowded House; no royal dukes, no dukes at all, but many peers, including Munster,[1] who is largely responsible for his fall. Kemsley, Walter Moyne,[2] others . . . .

The House decidedly did not give him a good reception. He seemed to infer[3] that his relations with the PM remained excellent: at the v end of his short speech, he became eloquent (a practised effect) about the prosecution of the war . . . . The ministers in front of me were obviously embarrassed; but I was sorry for him. How far he has fallen; a fortnight ago he was surrounded, flattered by MPs soliciting favours – today he is pariah, almost a political outcast. But he will return unless there is something shady as yet unrevealed to me . . . . I recalled the other resigning speeches; Sam Hoare's magnificent *mea culpa*, which was Cato-like in its eloquence, and as it so proved in its cold common sense;[4] and then Duff's fantastic nonsense after Munich[5] – he had memorised his piece, and impressed parts of the House with what they thought his sincerity – which was overpowering. Anthony's farewell, stinging and reproachful, I missed, as Harold Balfour and I were in the train on our way back from Sestriere[6] . . . .

Of all these Belisha's in a way was the best as it was not dramatic nor rude; but he had his cheap jibe about Democracy, and he hinted weakly why he refused the Board of Trade.

He sat down: few cheers. The PM on the other hand had a warm reception, but he was not at his best, and he seemed to be (for the first time to me) aged and colourless. He emphasised his good relations with Belisha, but firmly declined to give all his reasons for Belisha's resignation. He toned it down, behaved splendidly (it was really Buckingham Palace which he could not refer to). Then he continued his statement, his review of the war; but it all fell flat on a disappointed House. Attlee supported the government and hundreds of MPs dispersed. I came home, tired – in heart and head, and wretched. A miasma has fallen on my mind, clouded my spirits and wrecked my present life. I am desperately unhappy, apprehensive and bilious. Everything goes wrong. *Que faire?* I must try to pull myself together and recover, or all is lost. I am sending for my baby boy: he alone can cheer me, and dissipate my gloom . . . .

1 5th Earl of Munster.
2 Walter Edward Guinness (1880–1944), son of the 1st Earl of Iveagh, had a distinguished military career, and sat as a Conservative MP for Bury St Edmunds from 1907 to 1931, serving under Winston Churchill as Financial Secretary to the Treasury from 1924 to 1925, when he became Minister of Agriculture, a post he held until 1929. He was raised to the peerage as 1st Baron Moyne in 1932. Churchill appointed him Colonial Secretary and Leader of the House of Lords in 1941 and from 1942 to 1944 he was Minister Resident in the Middle East. He was assassinated in Palestine in 1944 by members of Lehi, a Jewish militant group. As Lord Iveagh's brother he was Channon's uncle by marriage.
3 Channon of course means 'imply'.
4 See Vol. I, entry for 19 December 1935.
5 See entry for 3 October 1938.
6 A ski resort in the western Italian alps.

Rab Butler is better tonight: I rang up Stanstead and talked to Sydney.

The Finns are continuing their fantastic success against the Bolsheviks. There is potentially a *détente* re the supposed invasion of the Low Countries by Germany.

Judging by Leslie's remarks today he knows who are the architects of his downfall, and his clear digs – and there were only two – whilst to the uninitiated would be taken as slurs upon the PM, were obviously slurs and sly allusions to the Sovereign!

A long farewell conversation with Peter who leaves tomorrow: he was not in his most intoxicating mood, distant and flustered and tired and unhappy . . . .

WEDNESDAY 17TH JANUARY

The dull day began well with an hour's telephone conversation with Honor, and a letter from the D[uke] of Kent. But an indifferent one from Peter sent a chilly blast through my heart: is he only a light-hearted Ariel? Now that conditions have so altered, and he is leaving, perhaps for years in Palestine, has he done with me? Have I now pledged my happiness into his keeping, bartered my [illegible] and content . . . what strange malady is this? What virus? What miasma of the mind?

I am no one's boon companion now: I am too dull, too interested in one person . . . . I can scarcely agree to a fixture with anyone, and lunched not, dined not, but snacked. The House of C was dull and empty; it lacked yesterday's *Stimmung*. But I had a pee with Leslie who was affectionate; and gay, seemingly recovered from his shock . . . . I admired his debonair courage and I suspect he knows now the whole story (which I wrote in glamorous detail to the Regent today). Alan dined last evening with Max Beaverbrook where there were Sam Hoare and Terence O'Connor[1] and they openly hinted at the truth . . . . The monarchy has dealt itself a severe blow, although it has won the round as it always does in England.

THURSDAY 18TH JANUARY

A long, mixed day. I woke miserable, and Alan came to cheer me with his breezy charm . . . . It is icily cold and I was reluctant to get up, as nothing matters now. Talked to my wife, who is never intuitive or tactful and is uninterested in others' moods . . . . The Duchess of Kent rang me and invited me to lunch with them at Claridge's, and I 'chucked' Emerald and accepted. I walked to the office where I was soon involved in a turmoil of complications – a fat envelope arrived from Belgrade addressed to me in Princess Elizabeth Toerring's handwriting – but not a line to me. An enemy! The most charming of mortals[2] . . . . And as I was

---

1 Sir Terence James O'Connor MP (1891–1940), Solicitor-General since 1936.
2 Channon is distressed that someone to whom he had felt so close is now, as a German, an enemy.

talking later to Queen Marie [of Yugoslavia] on the telephone Nevile Henderson called on me. For the first time I didn't really like him: he looked old, fragile and frazzled and abused Emerald ... he is *à côté*[1] in England I fear. Then a most ticklish situation arose as to the proposed publication of the Blue Book describing our negotiations with Russia. It had been particularly decided to publish and much work and time have been lavished on its preparation; suddenly there is a volte-face in policy and as we do not come out of it too well the Cabinet want to withhold printing. The technical point rose as to whether we could withdraw the dummy cover laid before Christmas. It was 11.10 and the Cabinet had to know by 11.30. I rang up Sir Gilbert Campion[2] frantically and he gave me the desired and complicated information which I passed to Halifax in a minute. He took it to the Cabinet...

I .... was telephoned by David Margesson to come and see him .... I was ushered into the Chief's presence, felt like a schoolboy. He told me that Nancy Astor, that busybody bitch, was campaigning against me for harbouring poor Fritzi at Kelvedon. She was saying that we must be pro-German. David thinks that the story might do me harm politically.

I came home despondent to find a note from Peter, a business note, car details; it stabbed me with his coldness; but I think it was [a] rush at the bell,[3] as he said on the telephone. Perhaps I shall hear again. I am ill with emotion, frustration .... tonight poor Peter is rushing across France. Is he devoted or heartless, and out, as Paul Latham[4] warned me, for what he can get? No ...

FRIDAY 19TH JANUARY

I have had four great friendships (and one or two lesser ones); three of them were cerebral, the Prince Regent first and foremost; George Gage and Hubert Duggan – those last two both move me now; and lastly, less exhausting, Serge Obolensky. To this quartet I now add [illegible] Peter; none has given me more; none has taken more out of me.

A pleasant enough day, and I was so beautifully dressed that I felt quite cheered up: I went to the FO and in Rab's absence I threw my weight about.

1 This literally and usually means 'close by', but Channon seems to be using it to mean 'to one side' or 'sidelined'.
2 Gilbert Francis Montriou Campion (1882–1958) was Clerk of the House of Commons from 1937 to 1950. He was knighted in 1938 and raised to the peerage as 1st Baron Campion in 1950.
3 In other words, Coats was in too much of a hurry to engage in pleasantries.
4 Herbert Paul Latham (1905–55) succeeded his father as 2nd Bt in 1931. He married, in 1933, Lady Patricia Doreen Moore (1912–47), daughter of the 10th Earl of Drogheda (qv). Latham was Conservative MP for Scarborough and Whitby from 1931 to 1941. An officer in the Royal Artillery, he was court-martialled in 1941 for committing homosexual acts and tried to commit suicide (see entry for 26 June 1941 and footnote).*

Went to lunch with darling Alice[1] at Hanover Lodge where I found the Kents . . . .
Lovely food which one notices in wartime; I drank hock, felt sleepy, and was
enchanted when the D of Kent suggested a walk. We drove in his Bentley for a
bit, then parked the car by Regent's Park and went for a long hike for nearly an
hour in the intense cold. He was enchanting, and so handsome and treacherous,
but sweet. Then he drove me to the Foreign Office . . . . At the FO (I had tea with
the grandees as usual) there was still some doubt as to whether the Blue Book,
containing the Russian proposals, should or should not be published; in any case
the Cabinet have not definitely decided . . . . And Attlee is for publication.

There has been a big scandal half hushed up at the Foreign Office: an old-timer
in the Deciphering Room has been sentenced to ten years for betraying secrets to
the Russians over a long period: he was sentenced under the Official Secrets Act,
and not for treason.

SATURDAY 20TH JANUARY

A most unsatisfactory day. Breakfasted with Alan, drove to the FO and back, felt
liverish and petulant – train-ed to Kelvedon; the train was twenty-five minutes
late; it is colder than poor Finland. Honor irritated and irritating, but without
realising it was I who was to blame, I yet did nothing. Black thoughts: snarled at
people, particularly Brigid and compared them all unfavourably to Peter. Snapped
at Honor; was ashamed, and later she came to my room as I dressed and I feel
cheered and remorseful and was gay at dinner . . . .

Bed at last . . . . H drinks too much and is rarely, if ever, completely sober after
dinner. Bed at last, bored, beastly and frozen.

SUNDAY 21ST JANUARY

A wretched Sunday of intense cold. I complained all day: everything got on my
nerves and I showed it. Suddenly I decided to go to London after dinner – a
long trek in the cold and snow. An absolutely dazzling young officer about 6 ft
tall, probably in the Grenadiers, shared my compartment . . . . Back blissful [to
Belgrave Square] (and warm again – how I loathe the country in the wintertime).
I find Alan philandering with Michael Rose,[2] who fascinate each other. I call them
'the Herricks' – (gather ye rosebuds while ye may). I know, and cannot admit
what is my ailment: but I have lost 7 lb since a week.[3]

Alan's sudden happiness adds to my dull despair. And I ache for my child.

---

1 Von Hofmannsthal.
2 Edward Michael Rose (1913–86) joined the Foreign Office in 1937. He would be Ambassador
   to the Congo from 1963 to 1965. Lennox-Boyd had been pursuing him for some weeks.
3 He means 'in a week'.

MONDAY 22ND JANUARY

It was a joy to wake up in London and I went to the office, after shopping with Alan – he bought a Cartier wristwatch for Michael Rose for £59.

Fritzi looked in: he gave me further news to the effect that a German military coup will take place in the spring: Hitler and Göring will be deposed and shot, and a Potsdam Regency will take their place. He has been secretly informed that the Nazis, Göring in particular, are using my Regent's name, and forging papers over his signature . . . .

Jock Colville is indignant about the Duke of Windsor who did not even inform the King of his impending arrival.[1] He just turned up mysteriously!

TUESDAY 23RD JANUARY

I was told that Ralph Stevenson[2] wanted to see me urgently at the FO and so I returned there from the House; but he was attending a meeting. As I sat waiting for him I spied on his desk an envelope addressed in Fritzi's handwriting to the Queen of Denmark. I had put the letter in the bag about a week ago! So I was involved in communications with the enemy! Could anything be more ridiculous! Discouraged I left without waiting for Ralph.

WEDNESDAY 24TH JANUARY

I was right, but forewarned, Ralph Stevenson met me in the passage and very gently, very charmingly returned to me the letter I had sent to the Queen of Denmark: it contained enclosures to the Crown Princess Cecilie[3] and Princess Cecilie[4] from Fritzi. Ralph tipped me not to use the bag there: it would damage me and my career. Fritzi's was an obvious 'plant'; he must be more careful. And moreover that bitch Lady Astor had approached Alec Cadogan and complained to him Honor was harbouring Fritzi at Kelvedon. She is an interfering lunatic, an over-busy bitch devoid of balance, charm, fixity of purpose and common sense or kindness. She hates me because I see through her and was courageous enough to be rude to her.

I lunched with Emerald, Kakoo Rutland, Sibyl Colefax (very cold because I have dropped her) and others. Little Roger Manners[5] aged 14 was next to me.

---

1 The ex-King had just returned to England.
2 Ralph Clarmont Skrine Stevenson (1895–1977) fought in the Rifle Brigade in the Great War, reaching the rank of captain, and joined the Foreign Office in 1919. From 1939 to 1941 he was Lord Halifax's principal private secretary, and between 1943 and 1955 was Ambassador, successively, to Yugoslavia, China and Egypt. He was knighted in 1946.
3 Cecilie of Mecklenburg-Schwerin, Fritzi's mother.
4 Cecilie of Prussia, Fritzi's sister.
5 Lord Roger Manners (1925–2017) was the youngest son of the 9th Duke of Rutland (qv).

He returns to Eton this afternoon. He is a dark, gay child and I remember years ago writing to George Gage, who happened to be abroad, telling him of Roger's arrival!! Now he is an Eton boy, and a very engaging one. Emerald amused him and he was not in the least terrified of a large and fashionable luncheon party. I asked him if he liked his tutor (Reggie Colquhoun)[1] and he startled me by replying 'I think he is inept and inconsequential.' I left the party to rush to the House to be present for Questions.

The visit of the Duke of Windsor remains a mystery: we think it was to see his solicitor (or dentist?).

THURSDAY 25TH JANUARY

To the House: the PM has been in a fiendish temper all day and cursed poor Jock Colville twice. He complained too of being badly briefed by the Foreign Office – he was. He glared angrily at everyone: he becomes impatient at implied criticism. I had nearly an hour's conversation with David Margesson and as we left the tea room and came into the Chamber we found that Lloyd George was speaking. For forty minutes he ranted, made a political harangue which helped no one. He is an old devil. Much that he said was inaccurate and rambling; but he still held the House with his stagey tricks. He contradicted himself; he lowered his voice; his white mane looked thicker than ever – he continued to abuse us, and I noticed Gwilym Lloyd George,[2] who was sitting immediately in front of me, stir uneasily and a little ashamedly.

Honor rang up to say that she was going to Clacton for two days' rest and escape. I hope it is so. And where, oh where, is my perfect Peter? Approaching Palestine? On whom he is turning his charm, and those grey eyes, who is looking at them in admiration.

FRIDAY 26TH JANUARY

Life is improving: I went to bed early last night and woke refreshed, almost radiant; and lying on my tray was a longish letter from Peter, posted, I suppose, at Marseilles. A vivid graphic description of his journey from Retford to Southampton and across France. He has a gripping style and he will be a great writer. All so far has gone well.

---

1 William Reginald Colquhoun (1899–1971) was a housemaster at Eton from 1935 to 1940, when he rejoined the Scots Guards, in which he had briefly served in the Great War.

2 Gwilym Lloyd George (1894–1967), younger son of David Lloyd George (qv), was Liberal MP for Pembrokeshire from 1922 to 1924 and from 1929 to 1950, and Liberal and Conservative MP for Newcastle upon Tyne North from 1951 to 1957. He was Minister of Fuel and Power from 1942 to 1945, Minister of Food from 1951 to 1954 and Home Secretary from 1954 to 1957. He was raised to the peerage as 1st Viscount Tenby in 1957.

The Regent writes that we should watch Russia; he seems to have an instinct or intuition based on some illusory information that a Romanov restoration in Russia if not imminent is not now impossible. Of all the unexpected whirligigs of fortunes such a development would be the most fantastic.

Shakes Morrison proposed himself to dine here and was magnificently gay and charming. I slyly inferred[1] that Lady Astor campaigns against him. There is a plot afoot to turn him out of the Food Ministry: Alan, embarrassed and ever loyal, is aware of it.[2]

SATURDAY 27TH JANUARY

Infinitely relieved to get a telegram last night announcing Paul's arrival – no U-boat has waylaid him. His train was two hours late and I waited feverishly for the little lad. He has developed; is taller, even more friendly and gracious – almost royal in his manner; he asked the new servants their names, and solemnly shook them by the hand: he was gay, gentle, and good-mannered. He and the Nannie lunched with me in the Amalienburg[3] and then they left for Kelvedon in the Rolls. I followed in Peter's little car which he has given me. But it smells of him: there is an undefinable Proustian association; I seem to visualise him, as I sit where he used to, and hold the steering wheel . . . . Waves of him come over me . . . and pass. What an insidious, subtle creature he is.

Honor came back to Kelvedon this afternoon from her 'rest' at Clacton – so she says; but her conduct of late is so increasingly curious that I now believe nothing, and care less – yet I was half convinced of her fairy story of the seaside hotel. She was pleased to see Paul but remarked with much truth that the child is wholly mine, and in no way resembles her physically or mentally. 'Paul hasn't a single trait of mine,' she sighed. It is truth, although I regret it. I played with him, read to him . . . . and he seemed so happy and affectionate that perhaps he is pleased to be back at Kelvedon.

Kelvedon is icy; but it is more *gemütlich* when H and I are alone. The lovely moody house looked its most beautiful as it lay brooding in the snow; at times it is more lovely than at others . . . . And the dirty grey dogs, like a flock of inspired sheep, are gambolling in the snow . . . . Much happier than last week.

I told H of the political complications and consequences of having Fritzi to stay: how that viperish vixen[4] complained to Alec Cadogan and to David Margesson. Honor was in a rage, and very loyal: we decided to go tomorrow to

1 He means implied.
2 The plot would not unfold until early April.
3 The Channons' lavish dining room at 5 Belgrave Square, inspired by the rococo Amalienburg hunting lodge in Munich. See Vol. I, entry for 17 June 1935 and footnote.
4 Lady Astor.

see him at the Normans' house,[1] near Much Hadham, and proposed ourselves to lunch.

Drogo Montagu[2] has been killed: he was so gay, so very handsome, so unscrupulous; it is all very sad. Everyone fell in love with him; he married two rich wives i.e. Tanis Guinness, and then Janet Campbell. He spent all the money he could mulch from their fathers and then left them . . . . He was a cad, of course, but such a charming, genial, open one that no one cared.

SUNDAY 28TH JANUARY

A day of adventures: first I played with my dauphin who, for all his charm, sometimes reminds me of my mother, who has less charm than any human I ever met, and yet has a compelling personality. His eyes, although brown – and hers are pale lapis – are like hers. I pray to heaven that he will be unlike her, and have a happier fate.

H and I set out in the extreme cold and snow for Much Hadham. All was well until we arrived at the Normans' gate: it was impossible to drive up to the house because of the ice and sleet; we then attempted to get in by the back drive and in so doing were twice caught in snowdrifts. The first time, we were luckily pushed out; the second time we abandoned the car and walked up to the house both frozen and up to our waists in snow: we arrived at what must have once been a beautiful Georgian house, now ruined by tasteless additions: the inside was deplorable: Burne-Joneses on the walls, crude discomfort and decoration. Mr R. C. Norman, the v handsome widower of a Bridgeman,[3] is a brother of Montagu Norman, the mysterious Governor of the Bank of England. He is tall and young-looking and distinguished . . . . Luncheon proceeded. Fritzi most affectionate and pleased to see us. We told him a vague story of the necessity of having our boiler at Kelvedon repaired in order to gain time. This handsome, sweet and very honest boy must not even suspect that he is unwanted anywhere. Next week we

1   Moor Place, at Much Hadham in Hertfordshire, had been left to Montagu Collet Norman (1871–1950), the Governor of the Bank of England from 1920 to 1944, by his father in 1916; but he passed it to his brother Ronald Collet Norman (1873–1963), who became Chairman both of the BBC Board of Governors (1935–9) and the London County Council (1918–19). They had offered Prince Friedrich sanctuary while he awaited news of his fate as an enemy alien, albeit one opposed to Hitler.
2   William Drogo Sturges Montagu (1908–40) was the son of the 9th Earl of Sandwich. He married firstly, in 1931, Tanis Eva Bulkeley Guinness (1908–93), and they divorced in 1935; and secondly, as her second husband, Janet Gladys Campbell (*née* Aitken) (1908–88), daughter of the 1st Baron Beaverbrook (qv). He was killed in a flying accident while serving with the Royal Auxiliary Air Force.
3   His wife was Lady Florence Sibell Bridgeman (1877–1959), daughter of the 4th Earl of Bradford, and she was not dead.

shall adjust matters so that we may return . . . . Then H and I returned to Kelvedon in safety, cold and bored. Paul was waiting to be played with; he is an angel.

The war will wreck marriages, institutions and habits: even I, a dyed-in-the-wool Conservative, am restless.

MONDAY 29TH JANUARY

I drove up to London and was hopelessly delayed by snowdrifts: the trip took me four hours from Kelvedon but I stupidly bumped the Coats car and it had to be taken to the Ford Company.

. . . . There were two dazzling letters from Peter on the hall table, both written in his vivid graphic style and posted from his port of embarkation (Marseilles, I supposed). I was enchanted . . . relieved.

Rab is back, recovered from flu; I was glad to see him again but I enjoyed the independence and kudos of running the Office in his absence.

TUESDAY 30TH JANUARY

Arctic cold and everything is horrible . . . . I told David Margesson of Honor's successful visit to Lady Astor,[1] so now Fritzi can return to us in safety.

Alan and I rushed to see Michael Rose, ill in Eccleston Square; he lives in squalor in a dingy flat, but was so delightful one forgot the poverty of his surroundings. Standing sentinel was John Fowler,[2] a tiresome knave who is an interior decorator connected with Sibyl Colefax's firm; he is his ex-Pollux, and rather resents, although is flattered by being succeeded by Alan. I rang up Buck's Club and ordered oysters and champagne sent around immediately in the blackout to soothe Michael. He was impressed and enchanted. Alan, half-crazed with love and overwork, was infuriating. At last I got him back to Belgrave Square . . . .

WEDNESDAY 31ST JANUARY

Another month draws to a close, and I, at least, have not been uncomfortable or made to make great sacrifices: of course my money is gone to the Exchequer and my happiness has gone to Palestine.

Honor and I lunched with the Yugoslavs, an 'important' party overorganised: Winston and Clemmie Churchill, both very charming to me – he markedly so, and later in the House went out of the way to be agreeable (what does it mean? Is he courting his enemies, blazing the trail to the Premiership?). I admit to being much mollified, but I trust him not . . . .

---

1 The details of this visit are not given in the diaries, but plainly Lady Honor talked Lady
   Astor out of her fears about Fritzi.
2 John Beresford Fowler (1906–77), co-founder of the firm Colefax & Fowler.

Intense depression when I came home. I miss Hephaestion.[1] Alan sees Michael Rose all day; hurried assignations; presents; furtive meetings; notes; declarations. How feverish friendships can be, if one lets oneself go . . . .

THURSDAY 1ST FEBRUARY

Four years ago tonight I slept in this house for the first time: I remember the Regent coming to see me in the morning and we sat on packing cases in the unlived-in house. What full years. I am aghast where they have led me. I wish I had them over again to live a bit differently: a few major mistakes made in my white room[2] here – if only I could undo them, I should be happier, indeed.

I hear that Alec Hardinge attacked the Prime Minister at lunch today.

Sheila Milbanke looking young and pretty came to lunch, and she brought Tony Rosslyn,[3] her divine boy. He has been desperately ill, owing to the appalling conditions which he has been subjected to as a private. He came in battledress. No one knows who he is or where he is serving; he gets on well with his colleagues but the discomforts are shocking. Sheila and I discussed poor Peter's death. She was bathing a baby at Lavington when she was told that Buffles, her husband, was on the telephone. She thought it was only his intention to wish her a happy birthday; and he told her that her second son had been killed. She was very dazed, went in a trance to Scotland to the funeral and only broke down later, a case of delayed reactions. She worshipped him. She is very frail, very sweet; and everyone has been touched and wretched about it, even the King and Queen who sent for her to come to Buckingham Palace to say how sorry they were. She cried; I almost did; and we parted on most affectionate and sad terms . . . . I to the House.

The PM made an excellent speech: it is remarkable how he can make one a day. John Simon wound up amusingly; as he was speaking (I stood behind the Chair), Winston came in, and asked me several questions, before sitting at the end of the bench.

A blow, perhaps providential, has fallen: Michael Rose rushed into my room at the FO, looking flustered and miserable. I followed him into the passage and

---

1 A Macedonian general in the fourth century BC who was Alexander the Great's closest friend and shared all his secrets.

2 One of the rooms at 5 Belgrave Square: possibly his drawing room, or his bedroom.

3 Lady Milbanke's first husband, Lord Loughborough, had been the heir apparent to the 5th Earl of Rosslyn, whom he predeceased when falling out of a window in 1929. The earldom passed to their son, Anthony (qv), who succeeded his grandfather as 6th Earl of Rosslyn in 1939 (see entry for 10 July 1939 and footnote). His brother Peter George Alexander St Clair-Erskine (1918–39), of 111 Squadron Royal Air Force, had been killed in a flying accident on 8 September 1939.

he told me that an hour before he had been summonsed by that shit Ivo Mallet,[1] rebuked for being 'uppish', and told that he had been appointed to Oslo. He must leave within fourteen days. He is wretched, and talks of 'chucking everything'. Alan is worse, desperately distraught; but I think it is for the best in the end, as so intense a friendship could not continue without debacle, tragedy or explosions, possibly scandal. It is never any use telling people that! But I tried to console them both! Alan and he met five times today furtively and rang for a few minutes each time ....

FRIDAY 2ND FEBRUARY

Michael Duff has made an ass of himself in Paris by going about saying that he was on an important mission, which of course he was not. The French government complained of his chatter and feverish activities: his journey there was taken on behalf of the Imperial Policy Group, but even so he was self-appointed. It was an artful but transparent dodge to evade military service! I wonder what will now happen to him, as he has been recently refused a visa to go abroad again. It is the *embusqué de luxe.*[2]

Emerald Cunard has left 7 Grosvenor Square, and has taken refuge at the Ritz: it is the end of an epoch, and I wonder whether she will have the wit and energy, and luck to begin again her great career in another house – No. 7 where the great met, the gay, where statesmen consorted with society and writers with the rich – and where for one and a half years the Edwardian drama of love and abdication was enacted. It had a rococo atmosphere, the conversation in the candlelight, the elegance, the *bibelots* and the books; more it was a rallying point for most of London society; and they too stupid to amuse the hostess who refused to invite them, were disdainful. But the Court, and one cannot overlook their stupidity, always frowned on so brilliant a salon; indeed Emerald's only failure (and her failures were always her enemies) were both the queens, and Lady Astor and Lady Derby – everyone else flocked. To some it was the most supreme bliss to cross her threshold. Her kindness equals her wit; above all it is her curious mind, and the lilt of wonder in her voice as she says something calculatedly and fantastically absurd. One must rally around her now; and who knows, perhaps the salon is not yet dead because the *salonière* has taken herself to an hotel for a time. I love her deeply.

SUNDAY 4TH FEBRUARY

The great thaw has set in and there is nothing but slush where there was snow: it is much warmer.

---

1 William Ivo Mallet (1900–88) had joined the Diplomatic Service in 1925 and was Halifax's assistant private secretary between 1938 and 1941.*
2 The ultimate cushy wartime job.

Alan rushed up to London where he spent most of the day with Sir John Simon, lunching with him and explaining the food situation (which, I fear, Shakes Morrison, the responsible and irresponsible Minister, seems to ignore). Alan stayed on at 11 Downing Street to tea. As he left he struck a personal note, and inquired for the very ill Lady Simon. 'My wife combines courage with fidelity, the two greatest qualities I know,' the Chancellor replied. And he went on to say that once in Hong Kong with great difficulty he and his wife had visited an opium den where the only visitor was an English sailor busily puffing at his pipe. 'Aren't you ashamed of yourself, my man, you an Englishman! What would your wife and children think of you, if they knew? Get up and go away at once.' 'Very well ma'am,' and the loutish fellow shuffled off. Alan was impressed – 'The story is entirely apocryphal but typical of the way in which Lady Simon would have behaved in such circumstances,' the Chancellor added. What an extraordinary and brilliant man, unloved, even disliked by most people, because he is always inconsiderate although occasionally charming, and often caddish.

I came up to London by train and tube and rather enjoyed it; here I found Alan, dressed like a bridegroom, just off to take out Michael Rose, that handsome, but coarse, Foreign Office Ganymede.

Monday 5th February

The Lennox-Boyd *ménage* left here today to take up their residence at the Dorchester Hotel which Alan loathes; it is all because Patsy wants to have him alone to herself. I think that they will soon return to me here, but I don't know, nor much care.

How can I get £650 out of Arthur Hope, which he owes me?[1]

Honor has sent me up Buda, a divine white and woolly bitch, the prettiest of Bundi's children; but I love him best. I don't know that I can ever love a bitch.

It is a week or more since I have seen the Kents: can it mean anything? They have taken all the steps of late in seeking me out; must I entertain for them? And the Duchess told Natasha Bagration[2] only a few days ago that she loved me.

The house is mysteriously quiet, with the quiet which one knows will not be broken . . . . the Lennox-Boyds I miss not yet, at all; but he rushed to the Foreign Office this evening at 7.30 in the blackout to see me.

---

1 This has risen from a stated loan of £200 last month.
2 Princess Natalia 'Natasha' Bagration (1914–84) was the daughter of Prince Constantine Bagration of Mukhrani, a Georgian nobleman. Her mother was a Romanov, Princess Tatiana Constantinovna of Russia, and through her Russian family she was a cousin of the Duchess of Kent.

TUESDAY 6TH FEBRUARY

Woke feeling well and vigorous: one should never go out at night, or see people too late, if one wants to be at one's best on the following day. Lunched with Barbie and Euan Wallace at 47 Park Street where they have taken a temporary flat: Euan shares it with Tupps Ramsbotham and Shakes Morrison and they are known as the Three Mayfair Musketeers: Euan is Porthos obviously; Shakes is Aramis, and Tuppy Athos, I suppose. A worldly little household. Much talk at luncheon of the recent row between young 'Ed' Stanley of Alderley[1] who in a fit of rage struck Valentine Castlerosse[2] at the 400 Club where they were supping. Castlerosse quite unjustifiably had accused the young lord of being an *embusqué*.[3] The incident has been reported to the Admiralty and it is feared that Edward will be cashiered. People must not really strike one another in public; only Duff Cooper does that.

Dined in the evening with Alan and Patsy in their new splendour at the Dorchester, and I took Mr Tufnell with me; but not before he had unburdened himself about Brigid (who by the way is staying here but I have not seen her: she is being as mysterious and eccentric as Honor). He wants to marry her; and I discouraged him, knowing that she would never look at him; he told me he never told the truth about his age (like me!). He is fundamentally the stupidest man I have ever known yet he is unconsciously funny and so doesn't bore me.

The two new ministers, Sir John Reith (whom I have nicknamed 'Dracula') and Sir Andrew Duncan were introduced in the House today; both were shy and Reith, towering above me, was the more embarrassed and conspicuous of the two. He is too Lowland Scotch, too humourless for me . . . . To go out with him would be like dining with Gibraltar.

WEDNESDAY 7TH FEBRUARY

Sir John Reith answered his first Question today and he was put off his stride by the usual cheek which welcomes a new minister. And the new President of the Board of Trade, [Sir Andrew] Duncan, to whom I chatted, actually called me 'sir'. Am I so old and obese, or he so middle class?

I had a reply to my cable from Peter: he is staying at the Hotel Pavelshad at Haifa. H is on one of her mysterious jaunts – out all day from Kelvedon since 10 a.m. and not back until late at night. What can she be doing? Once before I was suspicious and uneasy and later discovered that she was having her portrait

---

1 6th Baron Stanley of Alderley. See entry for 22 June 1939 and footnote.
2 Valentine Edward Charles Browne (1891–1943), by courtesy Viscount Castlerosse from 1905 to 1941, when he succeeded his father as 6th Earl of Kenmare. He was at this time a gossip writer.
3 A shirker.

painted which she later gave me. Would to God that this mysterious behaviour is equally innocent. I feel it is NOT.

THURSDAY 8TH FEBRUARY

. . . . To make matters less sweet and smooth I was snapping at and tactless to Honor on the telephone this morning; that spoilt my day. I am so unhappy, and a great malady eats into my soul, and nothing matters except what I cannot have, and perhaps shall never know again . . . .

A long, discursive letter from Peter written in the Haifa Bay, as he lay in his bunk: he is angling for the job of ADC to Sir Archibald P. Wavell,[1] General Commander-in-Chief of the Southern Command, hence the v grandest of all in Palestine. Peter is so damnably agreeable that he will wangle it: perhaps someone can help him.

Harold Balfour rang me and I rushed into the Air Ministry to say 'goodbye' to him as he is leaving tonight secretly for Poole, and tomorrow in the dawn he leaves by flying boat for Cairo and Baghdad. He will be a whole day in Palestine, and my heart thumped so. I longed to go with him and he would have preferred me to Anthony Eden, whom he dislikes and disapproves of. Anthony . . . . is going to welcome the New Zealand troops on behalf of the King. The whole expedition is very hush-hush; and they expect to be back in England by Saturday week. Harold was v gay and in his most adventuresome mood; he is never frightened of anything . . . .

I left the Air Ministry feeling wasted, aimless with my wings cut; for I could have recommended Harold to take me with him – or more easily have sent messages or a letter to P; I had to decide quickly, I thought better not for a variety of reasons. But in a few days he will be flying over Haifa . . . .

I slept for an hour, had a hot bath, dined alone, drank a bit of port and recovered my health and energies. About 10 p.m. Honor rang up from Kelvedon

---

1 Archibald Percival Wavell (1883–1950) joined the Army in 1901 and saw action in the Second Boer War. He won the Military Cross, but lost his left eye, in the second battle of Ypres. He held senior staff appointments throughout the 1920s but in 1930 was given command of an infantry brigade and in 1932 was made ADC to the King. He later became General Officer Commanding in Palestine, before briefly being given Southern Command in Britain and, in February 1940, becoming Commander-in-Chief Middle East. In 1941 he became C-in-C in India; and was promoted to field marshal in 1943. Later that year he became the penultimate Viceroy, serving until 1947. He was knighted in 1939 and raised to the peerage as 1st Viscount Wavell in 1943, being advanced to an earldom in 1947. He was a considerable scholar, and among his many books was his celebrated anthology of poetry, *Other Men's Flowers*, published in 1944. He had a difficult relationship with Churchill but survived, being transferred from direct military command to the Viceroyalty not least in Churchill's hope that he would cause him less trouble.

and was sweetness itself, even affectionate and we chatted gaily and happily for half an hour. How extraordinary marriage is with its ups and downs.

A quiet evening of uninterrupted bliss.

FRIDAY 9TH FEBRUARY

Walter Buccleuch called at the FO in the morning: he is slow, shy, but sure and I am devoted to him. He says that the King is inclined to avoid him: he often writes to him but fears that Alec Hardinge, that green-eyed monster of treachery, holds up the letters. He and Alec are at loggerheads, and Walter assured me that AH though still all-powerful at the Palace, is not really liked or trusted by the Sovereigns [*sic*].

Honor arrived about one o'clock, really inadequately dressed for a very grand luncheon party: we walked to the Romanian Legation and found a terrific party, the French, Belgian and Italian[1] ambassadors...And punctually, wearing a tailcoat, appeared the Prime Minister and Mrs Chamberlain; he was amiable, smiling, gay and gracious and said 'Hello Chips' with his little laugh. Mrs C – rather gruff and vague as she is always. Honor was next to Bastianini who is canine, attractive, young and dark and provocative: but he has not Grandi's distinction, elegance, and bland bonhomie: he is even a wee bit common, but *plein de chien*.[2] I hope that Peter never meets him .... Luncheon proceeded pleasantly enough, but it was after the ladies left that the real business began. The PM was seated over his coffee with the Italian and the Romanian[3] and they fell into a deep conversation which lasted until 3.40. I have never seen the PM stay so long anywhere, and seem to enjoy himself so much. Tilea was all out to flatter and cajole him and I must say succeeded. When we at length joined the ladies I found that Honor had fled, as she had an appointment with Nevile Henderson as they are organising a fund for the relief of English nationals returned from Germany and elsewhere. I walked to the office; from what I can pick up, I gather that there may well be a war development next week, or, perhaps and, political ones. Will Shakespeare Morrison stay the course? There is an undercurrent of feeling, gaining clarity, that he is weak, unfitted for the job and unlucky; I don't know; but Alan, his loyal and devoted henchman, admits that Morrison is unsuited to a future at Food.

Honor went back to Kelvedon so as to avoid going to Pyrford for the christening[4] tomorrow: it suffices for a thing, or ceremony to be faintly an

---

1 Giuseppe Bastianini (1899–1961) had been involved in Fascist politics in Italy since the early 1920s. In the 1930s he served as Italian Ambassador to Poland, and was instrumental in persuading Mussolini to delay Italy's entry to the war on the grounds that many Italians felt sympathy with Catholic Poland. He served as Ambassador to the United Kingdom from late 1939 until Italy entered the war on 10 June 1940. He then became a highly controversial Governor of Dalmatia, whence he oversaw the deportation of the Jews.

2 Full of allure.

3 Viorel Tilea.

4 Of the Lennox-Boyds' first son, Simon Donald Rupert Neville, born 7 December 1939.

obligation, for her to refuse blankly to be interested in it. Curious woman, my farouche and independent wife.

Rab could not make up his mind whether or not to go to Stanstead for the night and eventually didn't. He is bad about time, and talks too much with his visitors. Yet the fact that we are at peace, and not at war, with Japan is probably due to his efforts alone. It is his greatest achievement and which he has been working on for two years; he has always believed in appeasing the Japanese.

Alan rushed in to Belgrave Square where he is staying the night, as did Michael Rose, who is v handsome with his wonderful lapis eyes. They both dined with me, very *épris*[1] with each other, and I left them to their own vices . . . . and went reluctantly, sadly and alone to bed.

TUESDAY 13TH FEBRUARY

A cable came tonight from Cairo from P that he has the plum job in the whole army, ADC to the General of the Eastern[2] Command, Sir Archibald Wavell. Peter is extremely *bienveillant*[3] and will always land on his faery feet: I am enchanted, only fear that he may be weaned from me: he will become increasingly military and important and wedded to Egypt. Personally I think it is the best job in HM's whole forces.

WEDNESDAY 14TH FEBRUARY

Valentine's Day – and how far away is my Valentine –

I am worn out and sadly in need of a rest . . . . I had short chats with both Winston Churchill and Lloyd George: these old Tweedledee and Tweedledum have rooms along our end of the corridor. Indeed we are sandwiched in between them; LG seemed the more alert and hale of the two, in his usual too-blue suit, blue tie and flowing mane: he doesn't really know me. Winston, a fountain of energy, dislikes me intensely and shows it, although he tries not to. He sidles away from me, looks down as he talks, that is if he thinks one is not his political follower. And I am known as an irreconcilable Chamberlain man.

Dined with *les beaux-parents*[4] at the Dorchester, which with the war has become the centre of London. Dozens of people who have abandoned their homes have moved there including the Halifaxes. The Iveaghs both delightful, but vituperative about poor Alan whom they do not like or trust, I fear; they say he is mother-mad, entirely under the sway and influence of that old harridan, which is unfortunately true. Lady Iveagh said she had thought and hoped that

1 In love.
2 Actually, Middle East Command.
3 Kindly, well-meaning.
4 His parents-in-law.

Alan would have been 'another Chips' but he wasn't at all. I tried to defend him, but I failed. It is his flightiness and strange Oedipus complex which disturb them, and they realise that Patsy, whilst madly, overwhelmingly in love with him, is not happy, nor satisfied. I am not sure that the marriage can last[1] . . . .

The Iveaghs inveighed against the Ministry of Food and insist that poor Shakes Morrison is responsible for the chaos that reigns there – which he is; and they warned me that the confusion and muddle in that important ministry would result in bringing down the government. I was impressed by all that they said, and when I left them I returned to the House of Commons and immediately sought out Dunglass who was alone, as it happened, in the PM's room. I unfolded my story and he promised to take up the matter at once: I fear now that if I have not unseated poor Shakes then at least I have put him on trial.

THURSDAY 15TH FEBRUARY

I bungled today badly. I drove instead of walking, and felt congested, liverish and oh! so tired out . . . . W. W. Boulton[2] of Braxted Park, a very attractive house in Essex, has been made a Lord of the Treasury; I wonder why I was not appointed? I think it is because I am supposed to be doing so well where I am, and I should hate to be moved from the Foreign Office . . . . Apropos of whips, they were all singularly inept today and Patrick Buchan-Hepburn was really too rude and foolish. He infuriated Rab, to whom he was rude. We had the Agricultural Bill which was to be followed by the India Orders and a Rating Bill. I was 'on duty' to let Rab know: but tired, my touch atrophied, I definitely 'muffed it', although even David Margesson gave me false advice. At nine o'clock I rang up Rab and told him to leave his dinner (he was at 12 North Audley Street) and return to the H of Commons. He did, and arrived at 9.15. Two anxious hours passed, there were the usual parliamentary delays and the Report stage of our estimates was only reached at 11.35. There was not one member of the Opposition present and so our Estimates were passed on 'the nod'. Rab was petulant: he is so regular in his habits and loathes his meals or sleep to be disturbed. He is really extraordinarily regular.

Fritzi of Prussia came to breakfast (he is living again at Kelvedon with Honor, but is up for the day) and we walked to the Office. He wrote Xmas cards to almost all of his English relations who had been so charming and affectionate to him – and only the Kents (who sent him a silver box and a card) replied! The royalties are really untrustworthy; but I am shocked that they could have behaved so badly to their pet protégé and cousin; particularly is it narrow and cowardly of Queen Mary and Princess Alice of Athlone, although Queen Mary did send him a message via me and the Colvilles – but only after I had asked for it.

---

1 It did, until death them did part when he was killed while crossing the road in 1983.
2 William Whytehead Boulton. See entry for 17 June 1939.

FRIDAY 16TH FEBRUARY

Honor rang up and said that she would be arriving in time to dine; later I discovered that she left Kelvedon early in the morning and she reached Belgrave Square handsome but a bit intoxicated at 8 p.m. Her life is most mysterious at the moment and I pray that she will not make a complete fool of herself . . . . Can it be Richard Temple?[1] I don't know who else. She must be guilty or why should she make a mystery of it?

Michael Duff came to lunch with me as I wished to pump him about his foolish adventures in Paris. (Vansittart told Rab that Michael is an incurable homosexual!) Michael began by attacking Chamberlain and I almost turned him out of the house. I was so angry and shouting that he was terrified. It was typical of the very foolish youth who blamed the PM for not having war earlier, and yet, when it comes, does nothing to join in any public service. It is scandalous.

I dropped Rab at the Russian Embassy where he was to have a tête-à-tête with Maisky. I personally would not darken that man's doors; it is degrading to accept Soviet hospitality, yet I suppose Rab was right really, as he may have learned much. He stayed so long that I wondered whether he had been the victim of foul play. At four o'clock, however, he rang up to say that he was going direct to Paddington, and would I meet him there with his bag and papers. I did: unfortunately he was travelling to Oxford, where he is speaking at a Union banquet in honour of the Polish Ambassador, in the company of Ronnie and Mrs Tree whom I cannot bear, although I speak to him now in the House. My dislike of him has almost been surpassed by my hatred of his noisy, neurotic noodle of a wife, who is spoilt, intense, sexy and generally insufferable. I didn't speak to her.

Honor arrived and was pleasant (but deceitful) and we dined gaily in the Amalienburg here and then went to *Heil Cinderella*[2] the Cecil Beaton[3] revue; an amateurish effort which is hugely foolish and fun. It is always agreeable to see one's friends making fools of themselves . . . . I am beginning to hate women, although this is a new phase; they are untrustworthy usually, too emotional, and not very pleasant or constructive characters . . . . I shouldn't mind if I never saw one again . . . .

---

1 Richard Durand Temple (1880–1962) succeeded his father as 3rd Bt in 1931. He fought in the Boer War and Great War, in which he won the DSO. He retired in the rank of lieutenant colonel. Channon suspected he and Lady Honor were having an affair.

2 A pantomime written by Beaton (*vide infra*) and John Sutro and designed by Beaton, who also played an ugly sister. It mocked Nazism and all profits went to war charities.

3 Cecil Walter Hardy Beaton (1904–80) was a photographer, designer, painter and diarist who worked extensively for *Vogue* and photographed many of the 'bright young things'. He made a reputation as a war photographer during the Second World War and, thanks to the patronage of Queen Elizabeth, as a renowned royal photographer. He was knighted in 1972. His diaries have been published.

We came out in the rain, avoiding the Kents: the rather *outré* audience lingered under the portico. I fetched a taxi and we came home and chatted by the fire in the morning room. Honor drank four whiskies and sodas and two Guinnesses and, beyond a slight hint in her voice, betrayed no sign of intoxication. She was cheerful. I should have passed out after so much to drink.

Saturday 17th February

It is a month today[1] that Peter and I chatted rather unsatisfactorily on the telephone an hour or so before he left for Palestine; and it is five weeks today that we sallied forth for our last expedition together: we dined at Scott's, I was dull . . . . and I was dejected, disagreeable and drunk; later we had a mild reconciliation and farewell – a fraction of our separation is over; and judging by his letters he minds it as much as I. Perhaps he is really fond of me?

Honor . . . . left for Kelvedon, insisting rather tactlessly that she wished to be independent. So I seized the chance to remain in London for a quiet weekend of recuperation.

I am happiest alone, but miss my child; and fitfully wish I had gone to Kelvedon to see him. Instead I went over our finances which are in a parlous, but not desperate, condition.

The Rabs are spending the weekend at Ditchley;[2] I was annoyed and fear the Trees[3] will make propaganda against me. And I am also amused by the Trees' siege of Rab, whom they have spotted as being the coming man; he has no rival. Britain is bereft of talent; the old nation is sagging . . . .

As I write these lines H rang up from Kelvedon and was very sweet and affectionate. Perhaps I am only a green-eyed imaginative monster.

An exploit reminiscent of Drake and the Elizabethan days has recurred in Norwegian territorial waters; on v doubtful legal ground we heavily stormed a German vessel the *Altmark* by a *coup de main* and rescued 299 of our men who have been held prisoner for months, and had been intolerably treated.[4] The Norwegian government is embarrassed and enraged and in minutes called this

---

1 Channon in fact records the conversation a month and a day earlier.
2 Ditchley Park, the country house in Oxfordshire where Churchill often stayed in lieu of Chequers, for security reasons, during the first years of the war. It was owned by the Trees (*vide infra*).
3 Ronald Tree* had married in 1920 as her second husband Nancy Keene Perkins (1897–1994), who in 1944 became the owner of Colefax & Fowler.
4 The men had been captured when their ship was sunk by the *Graf Spee* in the South Atlantic. It was disabled by RAF aircraft, boarded by men from HMS *Cossack*, and the prisoners liberated. The legal question arose from its being in Norwegian waters, the act of attack and boarding being a breach of neutrality. The Norwegians were furious, but the British argued that the ship had no right to seek immunity from attack by being in neutral waters. The point remains unresolved to this day.

afternoon to protest to Halifax: but the whole country is delighted. It is a typically Winstonian action, but actually it is the result of joint War Cabinet action. Everyone will approve, although there may be repercussions later.

SUNDAY 18TH FEBRUARY

It is snowing and I am enchanted not to be in the country. H just rang up: she is alone at Kelvedon, which I call 'Helsinki Hall', it is so cold, with Fritzi. Perhaps I was foolish not to go to the country.[1]

 .... I called on Mrs Greville who received me in her luxurious little boudoir, still full of *bibelots* and rich *objets de vertu*[2] and pictures at the back of 16 Charles Street. She was full of social and political gossip, having lunched today with [John] Simon and Sam Hoare. She looked well and was in tremendous spirits. Lady Crewe, *cassante*,[3] but much more friendly came, and was almost polite to me. Suddenly I felt that even the old hostility between us had died. There was never any reason for it that I knew of: only Naps [Alington] with whom she suspected that I was once too intimate. But all that was v long ago. Louis Greig[4] also came in and was pleasant. We discussed the war, which Mrs G has always opposed: she thinks it ridiculous, and is not afraid of saying so. She asked kindly of Fritzi. She sat, like a great jewelled-toad, in a golden bowl exuding amusing poison about everyone, particularly Lady Oxford, who pesters her with begging letters. Lady Oxford has a curious and not very amiable habit of writing frank letters asking for a little money now and then; but she lives well with a butler and a footman and plays continuous and atrocious bridge. 'Mrs Ronnie' is a terrific character, a 'leftover' from a vanishing age; but in spite of her infirmities and her 73[5] years she is full of life, venom and agility. She has always been good to me ... she says she is ruined, and must live on her capital. Tea was served by four menservants in the 'grand manner'. The old regime will see her out.

 Dined alone, resisting several temptations; in fact everyone except Peter bores me now. Alan rang up that he was entertaining for Michael Rose, a farewell party; the dazzling creature leaves tomorrow and a good thing too.

---

1 He contradicts himself.
2 Antique objects of especially fine workmanship.
3 Brittle.
4 Louis Leisler Greig (1880–1953) joined the Royal Navy after qualifying as a doctor at Glasgow University and practising in the Gorbals. He befriended the future King George VI – then Prince Albert, who was fifteen years his junior – at Osborne Naval College, acted as his mentor and served with him in HMS *Cumberland*. He was appointed equerry to the Prince in 1918 and partnered him at tennis at Wimbledon. He became a stockbroker, was knighted in 1932, and in 1937 was appointed Extra Gentleman Usher to the King. He joined the RAF as a liaison officer in 1939 and reached the rank of group captain.
5 Mrs Ronnie Greville was 76.

MONDAY 19TH FEBRUARY

Ordered masses of clothes at luncheon time; and dined in with Honor in her lovely Empire bedroom. We had oysters and champagne and she was charming, if a bit mysterious. She is most definitely 'up to something'; but I am now resolved, resigned to ignore it. And rightly.

I set the wheels in motion today to sack Vansittart: he must be made a peer,[1] but cashiered. Too long has his baneful influence exerted an evil sway over our foreign policy.

I sent Michael Rose a pack of small pearl studs to wear when he dines with Prince Olaf [sic].[2] He left, with a little chorus of worshippers to see him off at Liverpool Street for Perth. Alan is suicidal; really quite unbalanced.

There has been another Belisha bombshell: he wrote an article for last Sunday's News of the World: it was stopped at the last minute by the censor, and certain portions were deleted, but not until after he had been rung up by Halifax on Saturday night. Even the Prime Minister was brought into it; it was decided that Leslie had been too recently in the government for him to make certain statements, as his words were of necessity inspired by recent knowledge which he had shared with the Cabinet. The PM actually believed that Belisha was acting injudiciously but not deliberately. He now knows, after Leslie wrote him a tactless and whining letter, that he behaved caddishly. I am surprised and disappointed. Belisha has fallen very far; and people are prophesying that he will go very 'left'; perhaps form a centre party later.

No letter from Peter and it is some days since I have heard from him; but I feel that he doesn't want to alter anything.

TUESDAY 20TH FEBRUARY

All day Alan was like a lunatic and talks of doing a Gretna Green; of rushing to Perth in pursuit of his Fair Friend ...

I 'loafed' about the House, picking up news, intriguing against Vansittart. In the lobby I ran into Lady Astor and puckishly turned my charm onto her and surprised, bewildered she fell into my trap. She is dynamic, unbalanced, foolish

---

1 Thus in the MS. Rhodes James's version, presumably written by Coats, has 'who I have decided to have made a peer'; which was precisely the sort of misrepresentation of Channon's idea of himself that attracted such criticism of his personality when the diaries were published in 1967. Channon knew very well he could decide nothing of the sort and had he said so would have looked foolish. Vansittart would not leave his post as the government's Chief Diplomatic Adviser until 1941, when he would go to the Lords.

2 Prince Alexander Edward Christian Frederik of Glücksberg (1903–91) was given the Norwegian name Olav when his father, Prince Carl of Denmark, was elected (as Haakon VII) King of Norway in 1905. His mother was Princess Maud, daughter of King Edward VII. Olav succeeded his father as King of Norway, with the regnal name Olav V, in 1957.

but warm-hearted so long as she can patronise. Her blue eyes are beautiful still; we chatted almost amiably and she said that my child was the most remarkable little boy she had ever seen – a shortcut of course, to my heart.

WEDNESDAY 21ST FEBRUARY

Alan sent me a cryptic message that he had rushed to Scotland: he is joining Michael Rose at Perth for another feverish farewell. It is a charming but dangerously strange interlude.

It was a big day in the House: there was a storm over the coal shortage, followed by a barracking of poor Shakes Morrison at Question Time – and Alan, philandering in Scotland, was not present to help him . . . . Paul Latham, looking rabbity, with nicotine-stained moustache and fingers, came to my room to gossip. He has had a lonely war on the south coast, divorced from his friends, his two houses, Herstmonceux and Hyde Park Gardens, shut, separated from his wife, he is a pathetic creature, lonely, whining and a bore. He has traces still of his former good looks. He complained of poverty, and once he had £100,000 per annum; he says that Mayfair will soon became a devastated area. With the foolish frenzy of the very rich when they attempt to economise he smokes only Virginia cigarettes and tries to live on his Army pay. He asked my advice about Scarborough;[1] should he stay on? I am in two minds and reserved my counsel. I like talking to him as alone he talks of Peter and their long ago friendship which was disastrous for them both.

After the divisions I was sitting with Jim Wedderburn and Terence O'Connor in the Smoking Room where we were joined by Sir John Simon, who was whimsical and discursive. He told us tales of the splendid response that has been made by all sorts of people to his appeal for funds and loans. And a few days ago he found a large box with his personal letters next to his bed when he was called. He pushed it, and it seemed to rattle; he rang for his servant and gingerly they carried it to his study where they placed it in a bucket of water, lest it was an IRA bomb. Very cautiously, the Chancellor still in his dressing gown, they opened the parcel with a pair of scissors – it contained a note, a gold watch-chain and a few other trinkets, which were some poor widow's contribution towards the war! The Iron Chancellor is a shrewd man, who always gives the impression that he wants to ingratiate himself with his companions and yet always says or does something which prevents him from pleasing. He is handling the finances of the country in a masterly manner and may save us all yet from bankruptcy and ruin!

Patrick Buchan-Hepburn made me peace overtures and I accepted them: we discussed Alan's mad expedition to join his Fair Maid at Perth. It is madness, but perhaps understandable for in these uncertain days risks are worthwhile and

---

1 Latham's constituency.

friendships take on new values . . . and snatched happiness, however illicit, is enviable and excusable.

THURSDAY 22ND FEBRUARY

A crowded diplomatic day. *D'abord*[1] I went to the Abbey to attend a memorial service for Lord Tweedsmuir:[2] it was crowded with Canadian troops who gaped at the great; the government occupied the stalls, and the P Minister sat in his usual seat, the highest stall. I was opposite him as I was at Edward Stanley's memorial service, and I watched his sad, lean face: he looked like some medieval saint for his features, when relaxed, have a mystical quality. Next to him was Simon, looking a worldly prelate, and then Halifax, who could have graced the pontifical throne. The service was dull, and I was disgusted to see that wicked Archbishop[3] in the procession. His face is hard, horrible, inhuman, bereft of any of the kindlier virtues; the wonderful Abbey was crowded, and I thought of John Tweedsmuir's kindness, and his carbuncle and how he helped me over *Joan Kennedy* and had corrected the MSS. As he must have done for half a hundred other young writers, for he adored youth, most particularly gilded or high-born youth . . . the organ droned out the anthems, the Archbishop's cold, calculating voice answered . . . and as I came away in the cloister I met the Bessboroughs chatting with Lady Astor who even in church must make a clown of herself; with them were Lord and Lady Baldwin with that female jackal, Jim Thomas.

Dispirited, somehow, I returned to the Foreign Office where I picked up Rab and we went to lunch at the Japanese Embassy, where there was a little celebration to commemorate our improved relations with Japan. The intention was unexpressed but it was obvious and Rab, who is responsible for the improved relations, was the guest of honour, although he yielded in precedence to both Sir John Reith and Sir Dudley Pound.[4] I was next to the latter. Reith, now universally known as 'Dracula', I am beginning to like. He has unexpected amiability, a good

---

1 First of all.
2 John Buchan (1875–1940) had been a member of Lord Milner's Kindergarten of brilliant young men (see Vol. I, entry for 13 May 1925 and footnote). He played an important role in the dissemination of British propaganda during the Great War: and was celebrated as an adventure novelist, renowned for *The Thirty-Nine Steps* and *Greenmantle*. He would become a Conservative MP in 1927, serve as Governor-General of Canada from 1935 to 1940, and was elevated to the peerage as 1st Baron Tweedsmuir in 1935.
3 William Cosmo Gordon Lang (1864–1945), Archbishop of Canterbury, against whom Channon bore a grudge over the abdication. See Vol. I, entries for 14 December 1936 and succeeding days.*
4 Alfred Dudley Pickman Rogers Pound (1877–1943) joined the Royal Navy in 1891 and commanded HMS *Colossus* at the Battle of Jutland. He was knighted in 1930, and appointed First Sea Lord and admiral of the fleet in 1939. He had been largely responsible for thwarting Churchill's plan to send a naval expedition to the Baltic.

smile, and surprisingly fashionable clothes. He towers above me and I asked him what he thought of *The Times*'s leader which castigated poor Belisha so cruelly this morning? But Dracula had not yet read it .... Luncheon proceeded and there was the usual shy silence one must bridge with Orientals. Two Japanese attachés at my end of the table told me that rice is no use as an aphrodisiac: it must be largely supplemented by fish. The Japanese owe their high birth rate to heavy consumption of fish ...

Dudley Pound, a common old boy, was funny at Winston's expense; but I gather that they have reached a modus vivendi of not too uneasy a nature ...

To the House in the afternoon, and there I slept soundly for an hour. I also arranged with Jim Thomas to come to B Square to sup with me later; but he didn't turn up and I was in a liverish rage with him.

As I was about to leave the Foreign Office – about 7 p.m. – Rab rushed into my room to tell of his amazing hour with that Antichrist, Monsieur Maisky, who had just left him. The Soviet Embassy had brought offers of peace: Russia would like an immediate armistice with Finland, and suggested that England in the person, if possible, of R. A. Butler should mediate. It is a monstrous and diabolically clever scheme: his dove is only a vulture and I hope will be so considered. Rab will report his interview to the Cabinet and presumably to the Finns.

I went to bed in a temper, too, with Arthur Hope, who has now left for Madras – stolen away like a thief in the night without making the least attempt to repay me my money. I shouldn't sit down under such treatment: I will give him one more week, and then write him a snorter to India. The future Lord Rankeillour will be my inveterate enemy, but his fragile friendship is not worth £650. How foolish it is to lend: in almost any instance friendship is flung to the winds.

Poor Prince Fritzi: for some days he has been depressed and half-ill. Today he went up to London to see his doctor who told him that he has German measles ... I hope that neither Paul nor I get the complaint: Honor had it two years ago and is more or less immune.

FRIDAY 23RD FEBRUARY

Jim Thomas rang up to apologise and I snapped his head off: I am done with that feline, silly creature.

To the Foreign Office, but not to work, as there was a review being held on the Parade of the officers and men of the *Exeter* and *Ajax*.[1] An Admiralty show engineered by Mr Churchill: one of his attempts to work up popularity

---

1 Both ships had taken part in the Battle of the River Plate, forcing the *Graf Spee* to be scuttled. HMS *Exeter* was sunk in March 1942 in the Second Battle of the Java Sea. Of the 652 men rescued 152 died in Japanese captivity. HMS *Ajax* was disabled by a bomb in 1943 but returned to service the following year and survived the war.

for himself. (He is determined to reach No. 10, but even if he does, which I still doubt, it would be but for a brief reign.) As I turned into Downing Street I met the Chamberlain car: crowds cheered him, and removed their hats as if for royalty. I watched the ceremony, but was too far away to see well. I made out the King and Queen as they walked from group to group, closely followed by Chamberlain with his famous umbrella, and Winston carrying a stick. Bored, I rushed out shopping; and left for Kelvedon.

I had a letter from Peter asking me to send his car out to Cairo, a complicated proceeding; instead I called him offering him £200 for it, which would enable him to buy a car locally, and I could keep his. A more simple matter, and incidentally a present for him. He writes glowing accounts of *la vie mondaine du Caire*.[1]

SATURDAY 24TH FEBRUARY   *KELVEDON*

A warm blue English day, the first since nine weeks . . . . Honor hunted. Alice von Hofmannsthal came down to tea looking like a weary Winterhalter.[2]

I played with my baby in bed: he seized the house telephone, which he adores, and after pushing the buttons, had imaginary conversations with both Hitler and Neville Chamberlain. The change in his little voice as he talked to each, was amusing. Hitler, he told him, was a horrible man; of Mr Chamberlain he asked 'How is Mrs Chamberlain?'

SUNDAY 25TH FEBRUARY

A long tramp over our muddy fields: it is refreshing to feel life once more pulsating; one's interests in the garden and trees is revived. And it is pleasant, too, being alone with H and Paul – for the first time for ages, as poor Fritzi is in London suffering with German measles which has swept the country, particularly the army.

MONDAY 26TH FEBRUARY

I had two long political *causeries*[3] behind closed walls, the first with David Margesson, and I confided in him the story of Arthur Hope. He was horrified but not surprised and he advised me to write Arthur a 'snorter' which I have now done. David will go to Zetland[4] about him and have him recalled. We discussed other things – nothing is too much trouble for my David who is a marvellous

---

1 Fashionable life in Cairo.
2 Franz Xaver Winterhalter (1805–73) was a German artist best known as a Court portraitist.
3 Discussions.
4 Lawrence John Lumley Dundas (1876–1961) succeeded his father as 2nd Marquess of Zetland in 1929. He was Secretary of State for India from 1935 to 1940. He wrote an authoritative three-volume life of Lord Curzon.*

friend, loyal, operative, painstaking, powerful. Then I went along to the PM's room and had an hour with Alec Dunglass, whom I like and envy and admire more every day. He tells me that the PM is jubilant; the worldwide praise which has hailed his Saturday speech[1] has been a tonic to him. Yesterday he took Mrs Chamberlain to Kew Gardens: he is cockahoop, as indeed I thought he looked when I ran into him in the lobby. He had more colour in his face.

Dined with Alan and Patsy at the House; Hector Bolitho, a plump eunuch, and another airman, were with us. Alan was rather tipsy and we had a tipsy conversation afterwards which alarmed me. At times he is definitely mad: he railed against the marriage state and Patsy's surliness – she can be very boring! I tremble for their marriage. Then he rang up his mother and had the usual nauseating conversation: he makes violent sugary love to the old girl (who is a sort of silvery fiend) over the telephone and she persuaded him to go down to Henlow tomorrow morning at 6 a.m. to say 'goodbye' to her although he only left her yesterday, as both he and Patsy are leaving for Palestine on Wednesday, mad. Mad.

TUESDAY 27TH FEBRUARY

Dictated most of the morning; then drove to 3 Pembroke Walk to have the first sitting for my portrait. James Gunn[2] is attractive and he kept up a flow of political conversation for one and a half hours. He told me that never once in the fourteen or fifteen times that the Prime Minister sat to him, was he ever late, interrupted, nor did he alter an appointment. He is a Chamberlain fan . . . . As Gunn chatted away my picture began to take shape and I was amazed by the result in so short a time. The charcoal lines were already like me! It will be a brilliant portrait . . . On easels were unfinished portraits of Helen Fitzgerald, which I didn't much like; and one only just begun but already excellent and lifelike of Tony Loughborough. There was a huge canvas of Hilaire Belloc[3] . . . . I enjoyed my sitting and munched sandwiches, talked and smoked. Next week I shall take baby Paul who is to be put in the picture . . .

Emerald tells me that Kingsley Wood is for the high-jump next since Shakes Morrison has weathered the storm. Shakes was, I thought, a touch cold to me:

1 Outlining Britain's war aims, notably the liberation and independence of the Poles and the Czechs.
2 Herbert James Gunn (1893–1964) was a portrait and landscape painter. Glaswegian by birth, he trained at the School of Art there and at the Edinburgh College of Art. He was knighted in 1963.
3 Joseph Hilaire Pierre René Belloc (1870–1953) was a satirist, comic poet, polemicist and historian. He had a French father and an English mother, was born in France, but became a British subject in 1902. He collaborated extensively with G. K. Chesterton, and from 1906 to 1910 was Liberal MP for Salford.

and I wondered whether he had heard that I had been intriguing against him. Later, however he was very charming.

There has been an unfortunate paragraph in the *Evening Standard*, saying that Fritzi was our guest at Kelvedon: it was inevitable, and the wonder is that we should so long have kept it out – as he is in London perhaps it is a fortunate moment for it to come out.

WEDNESDAY 28TH FEBRUARY

More Fritzi fuss: it is disgusting, cruel and worse, stupid, the way people persecute this poor boy, probably because he is a princeling. I feel uneasy in the Commons today, the way one does when one is out of favour with one's fellows. A charming cablegram from Peter cheered me.

Alan rang me from the airport very early: he and Patsy left for Palestine via Paris and Rome. They fly part of the way: it is all part of Alan's mad family worship; he has not seen his brother Francis since before Christmas and cannot bear the separation any longer. It is really monstrous that his personal emotions should so triumph over his governmental and [illegible] duties. Still it is not my business, and it is Alan's. Yesterday morning, Tuesday, he left London at 6 a.m. to drive particularly to Henlow to take leave of his mother, whom he had only quitted the day before. There has never been such a vampire, such a tyrant as that saccharine-y old bore who seems so simple and dull on the surface. At least three of her four sons are in love with her. And now she has managed to get her grandson, Simon, there to stay with her indefinitely. The Iveaghs are in a rage about it – possibly unjustifiably, as they themselves are in Italy.

Harold [Balfour] gave me a long account of an extraordinary luncheon he had had at Bordeaux with Anthony Eden, on their way back from Cairo last week: he is a determined anti-Edenite, and thinks him foolish, frivolous and fatuous. However, chance threw them together on their dramatic 'trek' and apparently they fraternised over their *vins*.[1] Anthony attacked me with animosity, but, Harold added, with a regretful tinge, as we had once been great friends. Now I was 'hopeless', he insisted, and he criticised my friendship with Prince Paul, Regent of Yugoslavia; he added that it was disgraceful we should be so intimate and I in the Foreign Office! What an extraordinary reflexion as both Paul and I are his oldest friends almost: Paul is the greatest friend England has ever had. No wonder is it that Eden is such a famous flop; then he continued that he had written a letter of protest to Halifax, after my appointment to the Foreign Office, and Halifax had replied that he was unaware, completely unaware, of my appointment. Now who is lying? Harold? If so, why? Anthony (who is more cunning than most people suggest, but cunning only when on the defensive) or Halifax? Dishonest, fundamentally, as

1 Wines.

Halifax is, he couldn't lie to that extent, since he encouraged Rab to appoint me, and Honor had rung up Dorothy H[1] and persuaded her to help my candidature, which she did.... The whole story reveals Anthony in an unpleasant light; and he added that he had never met Alan L-B. Such a nincompoop can never rise higher: Rab says that he feels physically sick whenever he must talk to him.

THURSDAY 29TH FEBRUARY

Rab and I went together to the lobby lunch at the Victoria Hotel; it was in honour of Winston Churchill and he made a most amusing if somewhat over-personal speech which lasted forty minutes, and never once did he mention anything other than himself. Nevertheless he was brilliant. He was to the right of the chairman, the Prime Minister, jovial, a little flushed, to his right. All seemed peaceful between them and at the close of his remarks Winston pledged himself to serve loyally the 'Captain' for the duration of the voyage; and Chamberlain, sweetly, shyly, bowed his thanks. There were 250 people present, the annual kowtow of the politicians to the press, a rather sickening exhibition of sycophancy. 'The Black Rat' bowed coldly to me (Alec Hardinge who is the narrowest and wrongest man I know – a definite danger to the dynasty, with his mincing manners, his Jewish prefect mentality).[2] I heard him say to Oliver Stanley, patronisingly, 'You are dining with us (!) at the Palace on Monday. Black tie. It's a man's party,' and Oliver obsequiously nodded. What a clique; and they are all suspicious of me for they know that I see through them. They, too, wanted the war – helped to lure us into this catastrophe from which we shall never recover. The age is dying; a new era may perhaps dawn; but never the same; both Rab and I fear that we shall not win; at best it will be an unsatisfactory stalemate.

Back to the House, where I was horrified to hear that Seymour Cocks[3] has put down a question about poor Fritzi for Thursday March 7th, my birthday, too. I saw him, and tried to persuade him to withdraw, as he and I have always been friendly. He half-refused. The House was perplexed by the Fritzi story.

FRIDAY 1ST MARCH

Every day this week I had some communication, either cable or missive, from Monsieur Manteaux![4] Our intimacy bridges the thousands of miles and fills HM's bags! Most of the day at the House; drove Rab to the Romanian Legation where

---

1 Dorothy Evelyn Augusta Onslow (1885–1976), daughter of the 4th Earl of Onslow, who in 1908 had married Lord Halifax (qv). She was Channon's aunt by marriage.*
2 An absurd insult, not least because Hardinge had not a drop of Jewish blood.
3 Frederick Seymour Cocks (1882–1953), by trade a journalist, was Labour MP for Broxtowe from 1929 to 1953.
4 *Un manteau* is French for a coat; *manteaux* is the plural.

he lunched secretly, and later fetched him. He had also seen Horace Wilson privately this morning.

Considerable excitement about Fritzi; so much so that I went to see him at 11 Wilton Crescent where he is staying . . . . I told him frankly that he cannot come back to Kelvedon for a little; but it almost broke my heart to do so. He understood and was very sweet. Possibly he must have his tonsils out next week; in any case the decision is deferred for a week, and he has agreed not to come back until Thursday. Poor dear boy; he is so honest, so fine, so high-principled. That dreadful Louis Spears[1] complained to Alec Dunglass that we were harbouring a violent Nazi in our midst. Such cruelty! I am in a rage about it . . . .

Dined alone and revelled in the peace. Am I suddenly unpopular? If so, why? Because of Prince Fritzi, of Peter? I don't understand and don't much care; but my stock this week seems to be down. One imagines these things: next week I must make some social effort.

SATURDAY 2ND MARCH

I went around to 11 Wilton Crescent . . . . and there saw poor Fritzi in bed; he is depressed by the newspaper fuss, and also he is to be operated on for tonsils next week. I consoled him; people are such cowards and so unjust. When I came home to pick up my little car, I found a most abusive letter from a stranger, an individual named Charles Goff, who insults me because I have harboured Fritzi, 'the grandson of the filthy Kaiser'. Then I went to the Foreign Office, wrote to Peter, and sent off the letters plus some trivial presents to him via the War Office bag which leaves on Monday. We are now in constant communications and his friendship is a solace to me, certainly.

MONDAY 4TH MARCH

I had a tepid letter from Peter: he is engulfed in his new life. It is a job of tremendous importance and I am happy for him although I fear he may slip from my clutches.

TUESDAY 5TH MARCH

A frenzied day. The Duchess of Kent, radiantly lovely and gay, and even spicy in her conversation, came to lunch, as did Princess Natasha Bagration . . . . Ralph Stevenson of the Foreign Office, and Prince Fritzi: poor boy – he goes to a nursing home under the incognito of Count Luges tonight and in the morning will have his tonsils out. He is unhappy, poor boy, and disturbed by the questions down[2] tomorrow. Luncheon was riotous . . . afterwards I drove my son to the studio of James Gunn

---

1 Conservative MP for Carlisle; a close friend of Churchill and a committed anti-appeaser.
2 In the House of Commons, about him, but not to be answered until 7 March.

and he worked on our portrait. Paul harped on his boy jokes – 'Will Mr Gunn shoot? Will he go off?' A pleasant hour, and Paul impressed Gunn by his precociousness and character. When the Duchess of Kent at lunch spoke to him, he said, 'Wait until I have finished my bow!' His charm is immense and his wild energy terrific.

Honor rang me several times . . . . We chatted and I came home to ring her again. She was very sweet; and I wondered why. Then she talked of going away secretly for a few days, and I could not but suspect 'on-goings': I don't know what to say.

WEDNESDAY 6TH MARCH

I had a long talk with Paul Latham about Peter; he prophesied that he would not leave me; it would be the other way! Said he clung, is a luscious limpet. I hope so.

Poor Maxine Elliott is dead, aged (officially) 69.[1] She was a great character; an immense bulk of a woman with dark eyes – probably the most amazing eyes one has ever seen. She became first a courtesan, then a *grande dame* via the stage, and collected a huge fortune. Old Pierpont Morgan;[2] Lord Rosebery[3] – up to a point; Lord Cholmondeley; Lord Curzon; Edward VII; and many others have shared her tempestuous bed. She was loveable, fat – oh! so fat, witty and gracious. She ate too much, huge wads of butter . . . . Life becomes more and more precious. I am 100 years old tomorrow but no longer liable for military service.[4] That is something!

THURSDAY 7TH MARCH

A dreary birthday: how I hate them; no presents but an offer of one from my wife, who, however, neglected to send me a telegram or message – she is on one of her mysterious absences. She is definitely odd, and her eccentricity and deceptions make me unhappy; but I must be philosophic.

To the office: Rab gives me much more work, and trusts me more. I walked to lunch with Margot Oxford at 44 Bedford Square, arriving a moment or two early I went into a Bloomsbury lodging house and pretended I wanted a room, which was shown me. Oh! The horror of the poverty; but the excitements of the *Gemütlichkeit*[5] atmosphere of a double room – with a person unknown? The

---

1   Jessie Dermott (1868–1940) was an American actress under the name Maxine Elliott. She was helped to become rich by J. P. Morgan (*vide infra*) and opened her own theatre in New York. She made a few silent films but retired from acting in 1920. She was 72 at her death having, like Channon, taken two years off her age.

2   John Pierpont Morgan (1837–1918), American financier and founder of the eponymous banking firm.

3   Albert Edward Harry Meyer Archibald Primrose (1882–1974), by courtesy Lord Dalmeny until 1929, when he succeeded his father as 6th Earl of Rosebery.

4   The maximum call-up age was 41. He was 43 the next day, but, as usual, was deceiving even himself that he was about to be 41.

5   Channon uses the word as an adjective; it is a noun, meaning 'comfort' or 'cosiness'.

slatternly landlady asked me 25s per head. As she pointed to the brass double bed, she said 'Is your friend a lady or gentleman?' – and I thought of the *luxe* of Belgrave Square and half-smiled – then I walked on to lunch. Margot rose and kissed me. She looked like an antique skeleton: in black satin with a bright red coat. She whispered a few words of thanks for my present (recent cheque)[1] which helped her over her bridge .... she received us in her ground-floor library, books, photographs, *bibelots* . . . A German arrived, a Dr Sherints,[2] a German refugee, an iron manufacturer, and ex-supporter of Hitler's. A gay young man, friendly, pleasant. Conversation at luncheon rather good; Sherints talked of the Führer, said he could, at times, be normal; then suddenly 'it', as he called it, a form of beast, or inner monster, would take possession of Hitler, and he would rage and rant, and become another creature; then the mood would pass, and gradually he would re-become himself . . . he is a homosexual. Papen[3] told him that he had looked up Hitler's military record in 1931; found out that Hitler had never risen above the rank of corporal, although he had been a brave soldier; and his failure to rise was due to his very pronounced homosexuality; in later years he reformed; and in his famous purge[4] he deliberately tried to eliminate all homosexuals from his Nazi Party which had become and still is riddled with it [homosexuality]. After the purge (it appears)[5] sadism became the fashionable Nazi vice . . . of course all this may be propaganda . . . .

When I arrived at the House, I went up to the Members' Gallery and hid behind the grill. I waited nervously for the question about poor Fritzi which has given me so much anxiety. But when it came, due to my machinations and personal popularity in the House, there were no supplementaries, only the question put by Seymour Cocks and John Anderson's[6] calm reply that the Aliens' Permit was granted at Glasgow . . . . I was infinitely relieved and became as air.

1 This is added to the MS in pencil.
2 I have been unable to trace Sherints or to determine who he was. Channon may have miswritten his name.
3 Franz Joseph Hermann Michael Maria von Papen (1879–1969) was Chancellor of Germany in 1932 and Vice Chancellor under Hitler, whose ascent to power he had assisted, in 1933–4. He was German Ambassador to Austria from 1934 to 1938 and to Turkey from 1939 to 1944. Arraigned at Nuremberg, he was acquitted.
4 The Röhm purge, or 'Night of the Long Knives' in June 1934.
5 The parenthetical matter is added in pencil in the MS.
6 John Anderson (1882–1958) had come top in the Civil Service examination and joined the Colonial Office in 1905. He became an under-secretary at the Ministry of Shipping in 1917, at an unusually early age, and was knighted in 1919. He headed the Home Office from 1922 to 1932 and in that year was appointed Governor of Bengal, serving until 1937. He sat as National Independent MP for the Combined Scottish Universities from 1938 to 1950 and served in the Cabinet from 1938 to 1945 as Lord Privy Seal, Home Secretary, Lord President of the Council and, from 1943 to 1945, Chancellor of the Exchequer. He was raised to the peerage as 1st Viscount Waverley in 1952 and became a member of the Order of Merit in 1956.

FRIDAY 8TH MARCH

A very exhausting day with much to and fro from the Foreign Office. I slipped into Lord Halifax's room; he was alone; looked tired and ecclesiastic – I asked him whether I should go to Belgrade for Easter and he warmly approved of the project and encouraged me to go . . . . Rab left for Stanstead and was piqued that he had not been invited to meet Mr Sumner Welles[1] who arrives on Sunday on his much-publicised mission.

To entertain Leslie Hore-Belisha whom I love, I gave him, Emerald Cunard and Barbie Wallace dinner. He arrived thirty-five minutes late, as he always is. He was gay and happy, and although there were frequent references to his recent 'fall' he did not mind. Said he had had many explanations of it, but the real one was not forthcoming. (I know of course.)

We went on to *The Beggar's Opera* which is always enjoyable – a new production . . . . Leslie and I paraded about the foyer and he was instantly recognised, and soon an admiring crowd gathered around him and he was asked for his autograph several times. Very graciously he complied . . . I had a chance to attack Anthony Eden to him and did!!

We went to the Savoy Grill for supper . . . . Leslie held forth about the war: he is arguing for a campaign against Russia – we must attack her now and save Finland: we must take action etc. I felt ill but nevertheless supper was fun. He told us how he had behaved at a weekend at Chequers. Mrs Chamberlain said to him at dinner, 'Is it true you never get up until 12.30?' Leslie, nettled, replied, 'Never before 3.30 or four in the afternoon.' Mrs C, always gullible and humourless, was shocked. On Sunday morning he came down at 6.30, rang the bell which was answered by sleepy servants. 'What, no breakfast yet?' he demanded. He stayed about: at 8.15 the PM appeared and Leslie said to him: 'Does no one ever get up in this house?' The PM was amused and saw through the little plot – this was last summer before the war. He will go far, Leslie: he is much too ebullient and intelligent to be held down for long. He half-attacked Winston for agreeing to return to the government without insisting as a *sine qua non*[2] that Duff Cooper, too, should be reinstated. Winston had let Duff down (*Dieu merci!*[3]) . . . . Leslie has the greatest admiration for Duff which is due, I think, because Duff got him into White's Club (with some little difficulty).[4] Leslie always grateful for a good turn has never forgotten this action. And he admires Duff for his picturesque

---

1 Benjamin Sumner Welles (1892–1961) had entered the United States foreign service in 1914 on the advice of Franklin D. Roosevelt, a family friend; and became Roosevelt's chief foreign affairs adviser for much of his presidency. He was Under-Secretary of State from 1937 to 1943. He visited Italy, Germany, France and Britain in March 1940 to help broker peace, but had no success.
2 An essential condition.
3 Thank God.
4 White's had a reputation then not just for being a club only for those from the most elite public schools, but also for virulent anti-Semitism.

personality, his love of literature, the ladies, wine and pleasure. Secs him as a most colourful personality, instead of the little common *foulain*[1] cad, which he is.

Leslie tells me that Gerry Wellesley is now known on the [Army] staff as 'the Iron Duchess'.

Sunday 10th March

I hogged it in bed until eleven, telephoned to Honor and others; then got up, still feeling congested and odd, dressed luxuriantly and went to call upon poor Fritzi, who looks wan and pale and ill, still. He is unhappy, too; feels that he is wanted nowhere. I am so sorry for him; but the publicity is of his own making, a Russian friend gave him away.

Then to drinks with Alice at Hanover Lodge which always looks shabby: she has no gaiety in her schemes of decoration and now with sandbags etc., it looks gloomier than ever. A lovely day enlivened us a little .... and soon the Kents arrived separately, both cheerful, charming and easy. Much gossip at lunch, some historical. She dripped with gorgeous gadgets [*sic*]. He covers her with new jewels. He said that the Duke of Windsor always pretended not to remember Queen Victoria, who had adored him; it was a trick of his to irritate his relations. He twitted Princess Marina about some shady relation of hers, and she retorted, 'What about the Duchess of Windsor – she's your relation, not mine.' I have almost decided to go to Yugoslavia for Easter, secretly and by air. It may be the last time that there is a Yugoslavia to go to.

I saw Sumner Welles, but only in the distance. He was going into the Embassy in Grosvenor Square accompanied by Joe Kennedy and another, just as I passed.

Long conversation about links at lunch; both Alice and I had met the Empress Eugenie. The Duke of Kent remembers the old very old Duchess of Mecklenburg, Queen Mary's aunt, who died at the age of 93.[2] The Kent children had sat on the Duke of Connaught's knee, but will not remember it. My Paul, I said, perhaps tactlessly, had pulled Queen Mary's nose, when she came here to tea.

Monday 11th March

Refreshed, reinvigorated by my peaceful weekend I walked gaily to the Foreign Office unaware of the complications I should find there. A dinner party had been sprung on Rab for tonight to entertain, as it were, 'the second eleven', the suite of Mr Sumner Welles, that is Mr Jay Pierrepont Moffat,[3] and Mr Hartwell

---

1 Thus in the MS; Channon has coined this French adjective, derived from *foule*, a crowd, insinuating that Cooper was one of the common herd.
2 Actually 94.
3 Jay Pierrepont Moffat (1896–1943) was a lifelong diplomat and the deputy head of Welles's European mission. He served as United States Ambassador to Canada from 1940 to 1943. He died aged only 47 after complications arising from surgery.

Johnson.[1] No steps had been taken: it was eleven o'clock and Rab merely remarked, 'Organise a party' – and I did. Frantic telephoning, refusals, rebuffs, absences, previous engagements all complicated: but at long last I assembled fifteen people together at Claridge's; a very distinguished little banquet, with the heads, really, of the three fighting services. The party was highly successful. Lord Halifax meanwhile was entertaining Sumner Welles at the Dorchester and foolishly put Anthony Eden next to Welles. I don't understand Halifax's *tendresse* for that nincompoop. He is the wet type which infuriates serious Americans. My opinion of Halifax sinks every day; will he be known as the man who failed, the sublime failure? I wonder . . . . of course his character and charm are unparalleled . . . . .

The Americans are shrewdly sizing up the situation; perhaps they think, as I do, that we are doomed. They were famously impressed by Göring, but loathed Ribbentrop and Hitler.

TUESDAY 12TH MARCH

Walked to the Office and was horrified by the news. The govt have arranged to send a large expeditionary force immediately to Finland to help in the war if the present peace negotiations break down. Either way we are in a hopeless jam: if Finland capitulates the Russians will be released to fight elsewhere; if she fights on we must assist her and all transports and convoys, some of them at least, will be sunk: the whole expedition may end in disaster. Rab is deeply perturbed and wants to resign in protest; I persuaded him not to do so, and I think he will not. But he was right about Poland, said that the giving of the guarantee would lead to Poland's dismemberment, which it did. The sending of a force to Finland, he thinks, will pull down the govt, and not save the Finns. Halifax has been pushed into this by Winston. He is so weak. And only a few weeks ago Winston was campaigning for an alliance with Russia! How can a man be such a turncoat? The French, too are pushing us . . . . Came home about 7.30 but my Paul had already gone to bed. I was feeling quite gay until H rang up; she was depressing and carping and left me with a vacuum feeling in my tummy, as she often does. She is so destructive, idle, bored and complaining.

WEDNESDAY 13TH MARCH

The newspapers announced the tragic capitulation of the Finns to the harsh Russian terms and the epic struggle ended at 11 a.m. There can be no worse case of flagrant blackmail in history, than this hold-up of the heroic republic. The

---

1 Hartwell Johnson (1898–1974) was the third most senior member of Welles's mission and would later serve in Peru, France and Egypt and act as special assistant to Welles.

Foreign Office was in a frenzy, but really relieved as our expeditionary force, ready to sail, would have had a hazardous task; they should have been bombed by the Berlin boys *en route*, and excited much opposition, at least passive, possibly active, in the Scandinavian countries. Sweden has behaved badly; each country thinks she may be the last to be thrown to the wolves, and so continues . . . luckily Rab's foresight (and more) prevented another Munich, and had we entertained Maisky's proposals, we should have been accused of another Munich. That is certainly not the case this time: our consciences are clear. But more and more it becomes evident that civilisation is threatened. The PM made a short, terse statement to the House, and he was well received except by Leslie Hore-Belisha who has always advocated an invasion of Russia. The PM's statement, corrected by him, Rab and others, I have kept, with his comments and changes. I was obliged to run to the Lords at the very last second to correct Halifax's statement so that the two would be identical.

I had a 'snorter' back from Gerry [Wellesley]: without beginning or end; rude, brutal, and now we are declared enemies. I answered him subtly but stingingly. Never will I speak to him again now. He is so tactless, crude, rude, harsh and brutal. I have always known that he was not a gentleman, with hard hands, and peasant physique. He half-hinted as much long ago; but I have forgiven him much; been tolerant of his petty snobberies, etc., given him employment, etc. And helped him considerably over his matrimonial difficulties long ago. Now I hate him: he had only to write back a polite note – all would have been well. But I always doubt the real efficacy of reconciliations – they rarely work out.

Harold Nicolson has penned a vituperative, silly, ill-informed and dangerous attack in *The Spectator* on Joe Kennedy. Poor Harold is bitter that he has been such a failure in the House; he is mad, is having a change of life, I fear, all old women do.

THURSDAY 14TH MARCH

I drove Honor to the new Dolphin Square buildings . . . . which are a vast tenement of doubtful reputations and New York atmosphere; she refused to tell me – but banteringly – why she was going there. H – very sweet and bejewelled. She looked ill. Then to the H of Commons where there is consternation mixed with relief at the Finnish capitulation. We have suffered a diplomatic reverse, but are saved from a most embarrassing situation.

Dined alone in peace. I am almost decided to go to Belgrade next week.

FRIDAY 15TH MARCH

Spent the day arranging for my trip to Belgrade next Friday; I am overexcited about it.

Alan saw six of my letters to P in the rack of the hotel in Haifa last week – no wonder P has complained of no news – Al forwarded them on to him in Cairo. He couldn't get to Cairo. Alan is v mad . . . .

Rab thinks we shall have a negotiated peace thanks to Welles's visit; probably in the summer. There will follow a political crisis and possibly a Socialist govt. The Socialists want 'to rat' on the war; but will attack us for doing so.

SATURDAY 16TH MARCH

I went to Southend, driving the little Ford. I attended my General Meeting: my interest in the constituency, now that there may be no election for years to come, is waning. I had to justify the govt action on Finland – of course all my sympathies are with that nation, but I realise how lucky we are to have escaped sending an expeditionary force to help them.

The meeting was a success. Kelvedon looked lovely! Honor and I had a peaceful evening together; but, as usual, she drank too much. What I cannot stop, I need not decry.

SUNDAY 17TH MARCH

Although I am going away for a fortnight, and have scarcely seen Honor for weeks, she chooses today to stay away all day in order (she says) to see a horse! There must be more in it than that.

Home for tea: the Lennox-Boyds came. Alan, very mad; and his eyes furtive and his face hardened – he is losing a little of his gentle sweetness. We intended to drive up to London, but an appalling argument ensued over Finland. Honor was hostile to Alan, sparks flew: at last I went to bed – Alan and Patsy remained for the night in a sullen mood.

A big German raid over Scapa Flow. Hitler and Mussolini are meeting at Bremen.

MONDAY 18TH MARCH

Came up to London in the morning; still nervous and aggrieved with Alan. Later he rang me up and we lunched together at the House. I warned him that his marriage was likely to crack – his selfishness is colossal and his insane worship of that vampire, his mother, will lead him to disaster. He cannot see it: I should like him to profit by my mistakes – but he won't.

TUESDAY 19TH MARCH

All my plans for my dash to Belgrade are now made: visas; diplomatic *laissez-passers*; tickets, all is in order . . .

A big Finnish debate in the House. The PM, scenting a note of challenge in the Commons, made the speech of his life really, and completely demolished the Finnish case against him. It was a magnificent effort for a man of 71.... He skilfully hinted to the House that there might be Cabinet changes (they will come soon now, and Winston will be Minister of Co-ordination: Chatfield and Hankey[1] will be dropped, I think). The House cheered.... I went along to his secretary's room with the papers, and suddenly met the PM as he left for home. This supreme, lonely old man smiled, stopped. 'Well, Chips, what did you think of the debate? How did it go?' 'You were magnificent, sir,' I answered, and he hesitated, smiled again, put his hand on my arm and went away. I felt a wave of sentiment for him, then thought of Peter, then of my child .... and soon I left for home. It was a glorious night, and London never looked so beautiful in the clear moonlight. I thought of our great raid over Sylt[2] even now, perhaps continuing. It is the return visit for the Scapa Flow raid.

Those pirouetting, effeminate, foolish, frivolous Glamour Boys rushed about excitedly today, giggling and girlish. They imagined that Neville would have a bad day – instead he triumphed. They were more out to damn Neville than to win the war.

WEDNESDAY 20TH MARCH

Shall I return from Yugoslavia? Shall dire disaster trip me up?

The air raid last night at Sylt was repeated early this morning: I fear that we may expect reprisals although its success makes anything endurable. The country is encouraged, heartened by this daring raid. I went to see Fritzi of P later .... He knows Sylt well, he told me. I offered to pay for his operation: the poor boy has only £400 in the world, and if the war lasts long he will be penniless ...

Anthony Eden glared at me: I must try and conciliate him as he may rise to some eminence one day – but it would be a disaster for this country if he did.

I am alone, arranging for my departure. I am almost anxious already to be back again.

---

1 Maurice Pascal Alers Hankey (1877–1963) was commissioned into the Royal Marine Artillery but soon showed high administrative gifts, and in 1908 became Naval Assistant Secretary to the Committee of Imperial Defence. From then on he worked in Whitehall, becoming Secretary of the Committee in 1912 (a post he held until 1938) and, from December 1916, the first Secretary of the Cabinet, a post he also held until his retirement. He was knighted in 1916. In 1939 he was raised to the peerage as 1st Baron Hankey and Chamberlain appointed him Minister without Portfolio once war broke out, aware as he was of Hankey's key role in organising Whitehall during the previous conflict. He served Churchill as Chancellor of the Duchy of Lancaster from 1940 to 1941.

2 An island in the far north of Germany, on the North Sea and near the Danish border, which the Germans were rapidly turning into a fortress.

Probably I shall not write again before I leave for Yugoslavia, and one is not allowed by the Censorship to take too many papers about with one ...

THURSDAY 21ST MARCH

Lunched with Alan at the House: the lobbies were alive with rumours of possible Cabinet reshuffle (which will take place on Wednesday), and speculation .... On my return to the Office I was summoned by Lord Halifax, who received me in his great room. He looked older and tired. We discussed the Balkan situation and he sent many messages to the Prince Regent ... He seems cheerful still: the great raid over Sylt has cheered everyone ...

GOOD FRIDAY, 22ND MARCH   *WAGON-LIT*

I flew to Paris, easily and comfortably .... There were delays and queues at Heston and Le Bourget. A smooth easy passage. In Paris, which looked gay and cheerful, I rushed to the Ritz where Laura [Corrigan] had put her suite at my disposal. The Lorelei, I call it. It is most of the front of the first floor. Laura Corrigan is an amazing woman: all her great energies are now no longer lavished on society, but on the war. She has organised a great relief fund known as the Bienvenue and has sent literally thousands of pounds to a French regiment which she has adopted. Associated with her are the *faubourg* ladies.[1] She was very affectionate and pleased to see me .... She told me that she had invited the Coopers in to meet me at six o'clock. Now my expedition is a semi-mission and it is important that few people should know of it. The Coopers above all – the gossiping Churchillian, anti-Chamberlainites. I crept out and hid in Laura's dining room as they were announced. I heard Diana ask, 'How is Chips? Still praising that awful old Chamberlain?' Laura answered tactfully, and I dined in solitary state unbeknown to the Coopers who were only a few feet away from me. It is monstrous of them to attack the Prime Minister and I was furious ..... Laura did her best to get rid of them, but Duff sat drinking and chatting. At last she rose – joined me for supper, turning them out. Then Laura drove me to the Gare de Lyon and I am now embarked on my Balkan adventure. Unfortunately, my door opens into the compartment of Beith,[2] who is in the Foreign Office. He is *en route* to take up his post at Athens. More unwanted companionship.

1 Women of Parisian high society.
2 John Greville Stanley Beith (1914–2000) joined the Diplomatic Service in 1937; Athens was his first overseas posting, but he was evacuated from there to Buenos Aires as the Germans invaded in 1941. He was British Ambassador to Israel from 1963 to 1965 and to Belgium from 1969 to 1974. He was knighted in 1969.

S A T U R D A Y 2 3 R D M A R C H

All day in the train; I slept late . . . . I dined with Beith and unsuccessfully scrutinised him.

A quarter of an hour at Venice was nostalgic . . . . And I thought of all my past fun there.

E A S T E R S U N D A Y , 2 4 T H M A R C H   *B E L I D V O R*[1] – *B E L G R A D E*

I arrived at dawn and was driven to this lovely, Janssen white[2] palace seven kilometres from Belgrade. It is *grand luxe*, glorious food, and everywhere silent, sullen bowing Serbs; sentries, heel-clicking ADCs . . . . glorious long view over the Sava valley. I changed luxuriously in my very grandiose suite; and then the Regent, plump and pretty as a partridge came to me. We embraced warmly. Here also the Toerring couple – (Germans??!!) – Princess Elizabeth, sweeter, simpler than ever; he, 'Toto',[3] silent, reserved, very like King Leopold, his cousin. They are absent from Munich for a few days. She is openly anti-Nazi; he, I suspect, secretly so. She adores him; I am attracted by him, but he is a Boche for all his Wittelsbach blood. That creates a wall between us. The country and particularly its rulers are very pro-English; and will, one day, join the Allies – when they are ready and they dare.

It is lovely to overeat again; to read in bed with the light on. And how soothing is splendour, how luscious the food. The good pictures have been sent away; but like the other palace is full of treasures and arranged in excellent taste, there were many traces of me – four silver candlesticks – Adam design – on the dining-room table; a . . . . coffee pot and Empire vermeil salt arrangement – the twin to one I have at Kelvedon: I bought them both at Vevey in 1938; a rich Georgian ink-stand on the Regent's writing table; box, a lapis one and one in the dining room, these and other of my presents were dotted about . . . The Regent has reconstructed the old library from Chesterfield House (which I well remember) and it is there he passes his life ruling the country with great skill and daring cunning . . . . He has fine books including a set of the first published edition of Goethe which Hitler gave him! How he hates the Huns.

I almost wept I was so warmly received: how charming they all are . . . . And it is warm, and lovely. The Danube and the Sava are both overflowing – and the Danube, alas, is unfreezing which will help Germany.

The Regent drives me about Belgrade in his fast Mercedes given him by General Göring. The capital is an amusing mixture of Munich and Hoboken.

Three people curtsied to me today! They think I am a Greek prince!

---

1 The White Palace.
2 The name of a breed of white pigeon.
3 Count Carl Theodor of Toerring-Jettenbach (1900–67).*

MONDAY 25TH MARCH

Toto Toerring, my enemy, drove me into Belgrade and we walked about the town, saw the fortress etc. The people are rather Turkish-looking. The fringe of the East.

Later we all drove – again at breakneck speed with police cars following – to Paula, the huge, granite monument to the war dead erected at vast expense by the late King Alexander. It is a high, high impressive monument with panoramic views of Belgrade, and the distant Danube.

The Regent and I tried to get in touch with Peter Coats, who is flying back from [illegible]¹ to Cairo today; and if possible, to bring him here for a few idyllic days.

TUESDAY 26TH MARCH

We drove, the Regent and I, to Topola, the mosaic-ed mausoleum of the Karageorgeviches and eighty kilometres from Belgrade.² It is a vast edifice, high and icy: within are the tombs, and [in] one of them, I suppose, in the course of time my beloved Paul will lie. King Alexander is in one. They are slabs of marble over-simply inscribed. The walls are riotous rivals of Ravenna; too bright still. It was a warm day, but a breath of the cold air of death blew through the church where we were officially received. I am a little surprised by the lack of graciousness displayed by both the Regent and his consort towards their people .... On the way he talked of Queen Marie, whom we all call 'the local one', and of her intrigues, her stupid lies, her laziness and appetite .... And he told me too, more of his famous fascinating visit to Berlin; and how Princess Olga sat next to Hitler for seven evenings at dinner .... Etc., etc. Paul refused a German decoration. Never have the Germans taken more trouble; never has it borne less fruit .... Paul's instinct has been unerring, faultless: he is one of the most astute diplomatists and statesmen of our time.³

As we came out of the church we ran into the little King;⁴ a slim, slender stripling of 16; he has developed since I saw him last. He speaks broad American,

1 Presumably somewhere in Yugoslavia, within easy reach of Belgrade.
2 St George's church, a substantial building with five domes, also known as Openlac, on top of the hill of the same name and the burial place of the Karageorgeviches since the early nineteenth century.
3 Prince Paul, instinctively hostile to Hitler, had felt cornered when the Ribbentrop–Molotov Pact had been concluded the previous August. Strategically weak, he refused to join with the Allies for fear of invasion and declared neutrality when Poland was attacked. In March 1941 he was pressed to sign the Tripartite Treaty with the Axis, and was removed in favour of King Peter two days later. The Allies considered he had treated with the Germans and had him put under house arrest in Africa for the rest of the war.
4 Prince Peter of Yugoslavia (1923–70) succeeded his father as King of Yugoslavia in 1934 and was proclaimed King Peter II in 1941, aged 17, after Prince Paul was removed as Regent in a coup d'état. He was deposed in November 1945, went into exile in Chicago and drank himself to death.

is alert, aware, intelligent. He lives surrounded by a coterie of carefully selected contemporaries and is a happy Prince, well-mannered and educated. He owes his pleasant existence to Paul. Will he be able to control the country when he succeeds in eighteen months' time? He gave us a heavy tea in the small mountain villa where he and his companions are spending a few days.

This morning the Regent took me to see the little King's palace, Beli Dedinje, which shares the same park as Beli Dvor. It is a Californian hacienda which might well house a Geisha, or Santa Barbara Vanderbilt; it is a touch theatrical (a legacy of the Romanian family); and the star turns were the subterranean apartments copied from the Kremlin, hideous vaulted chambers of bright mosaic and painted stone which include King Alexander's private theatre. The young King is equally interested in films, film actresses pouting, and motor cars . . . . Tea with the little King.

WEDNESDAY 27TH MARCH

I went to Belgrade, shopped, bought an Empire cup each for Princess Woolly,[1] and for Princess Olga, visited the Prince Paul museum – which he has put in his old town-palace. The King's adjoining palace is still sometimes used on official occasions. Then I lunched at our Legation with Ronnie Campbell,[2] our rather silent bachelor Minister . . . . [also there] was a Mr Andres,[3] the Yugoslav Minister of Commerce, a lively loquacious self-important Balkan who is ardently pro-Ally. He had, however, just returned from Berlin where he had spent some hours closeted alone with General Göring. He is convinced of Germany's ultimate defeat (I wish I was!); so is the Regent who says he is Britain's Ambassador to Belgrade.

The little King dined; very sweet in his tuxedo, as he calls it. He has taken to me. His mother is still philandering in England with Mrs Cresswell. Much royal conversation. I missed the comte de Paris[4] who has just left. He has now telegraphed that his wife at distant Petropolis has presented him with a sixth child.

The Regent very affectionate; we recalled that our ancient affectionate 'axis' lacks only a few months before coming of age – twenty-one years next November.

1 Princess Elizabeth of Greece and Denmark. See entry for 5 September 1939 and footnote.
2 Ronald Ian Campbell, not to be confused with Sir Ronald Hugh Campbell (qv), whom he succeeded at Belgrade.
3 Dr Ivan Andres (1883–1959) served Prince Paul as Minister for Trade and Industry from 1939 to 1941.
4 Henri Robert Ferdinand Marie d'Orléans (1908–99), from birth until 1929 Prince Henri d'Orléans and from 1929 comte de Paris, was from 1940 the Orléaniste pretender to the throne of France. His wife, Princess Isabelle of Orléans-Braganza (1911–2003), eventually presented him with eleven children.

Thursday 28th March

We lunched with the King in the grand downstairs dining room; excellent food
and I immediately had indigestion. We stayed on and he showed us films he had
taken. He adores films and one of the upstairs rooms he has converted into a sort
of film club, called Toso; there he compiles a monthly magazine of film news in
Serbian and it is printed. He gave me a copy. He calls me 'Chips'. And I don't know
whether since I have always known him, to call him 'Peter' or 'sir'. He is angular,
self-assured.

A dinner party at the Palace; considerable state .... White ties – a film followed.
At 10.30 the royals rose rather brusquely and after winking at me, left; I followed them
up to the little sitting room which Princess Olga uses. Everything is very well done.

German economic penetration in this country is considerable; but as a
race they are loathed. Sooner or later Yugoslavia will enter the war on our side:
meanwhile the railway sidings are blocked with oil being shipped to Germany,
which comes from Bulgaria and Turkey, from Russia.

Friday 29th March

A sad day, really. I was loath to leave, but it seemed misguided to alter all my
plans, although both the Regent and Princess Olga begged me to stay on.
Mornings are a bore, as he is engrossed in affairs of state; the two Toerrings
however came to my rooms. How eagerly would my English enemies seize upon
this friendship, if they knew it. Toto Toerring took me this morning to the royal
stables. Beautifully kept, there are many horses including the famous Lipizzaner
white ones which come from the Spanish Riding School in Vienna. They are
literally snow-white. The Simmental cattle are well housed. There is much waste
in the royal households here and so many hundreds of suave, sullen flunkeys and
courtiers ....

We lunched alone in the little apartments. The afternoon I spent with the
Regent: he gave me carved amethyst links which look like scarabs, they belonged
formerly to his father; and also a three-volume set of Lord Chesterfield's letters;
and finally he made me a Chevalier of the Order of the White Eagle, a handsome
decoration – the first I have ever had! I am proud and delighted. After dinner we
were shown a film of their state visit to Berlin, marvellously done, the arrivals,
fêtes, reviews, parties, interviews. Frequent close-ups of Hitler at his most
amiable – he was polite, ingratiating the whole time; the arrangements made
to seduce and impress the Regent and Princess Olga were terrific. Eight days of
them! And a failure, for Paul returned more pro-Ally than ever.

I almost wept as I took leave of them all. I was rather tipsy. Paul came to the
door, pressed my hand, and watched me drive away .... into the night. Shall I
ever see him again, so well, so powerful, or will the Nazis swoop down upon him
and destroy his haven and his people – *qui sait?*

I was miserable to leave; he has been one of the great emotional influences in my life. He; my friendship with him; George; Honor: my marriage; and lately Peter – but the last Pierrot has not influenced my mode of living or outlook – yet! At 10.20 the train pulled out of Belgrade and my Balkan adventure had ended.

SATURDAY 30TH MARCH

All day resting in the train: how I adore a day apart from the world. There was snow in Yugoslavia; but Italy was warm and blossoming. Venice looked ideally Canaletto-esque;[1] Padua, Vicenza, Brescia, all friends, whizzed past. I spoke to no one but read about the Bonapartes.

SUNDAY 31ST MARCH

Arrived at ten in Paris where Laura's car met me and whisked me first to the Ritz, where I changed. So much of my life has been spent in this hotel . . . then I drove to the Embassy, left letters and went on to Versailles, where Laura has taken a . . . . charmingly arranged cottage-de-luxe, a perfect *nid d'amour*.[2]

Laura and I drove into Paris and dined *à deux* at the crowded Scheherazade. Paris is gayer and more lit up by night than is London.

MONDAY 1ST APRIL

I had a lovely day alone but suffered from indigestion and lecherous thoughts, which I was able later to dissipate by judicious treatment of a punitive character . . . . I wandered about Paris, so beautiful, so tantalising: the shops are more fascinating than ever and there is little sign of war except the absence of buses. There are fewer uniforms than in London, and no English on leave like last time. There are 4½ million men mobilised but one doesn't see them. I behaved like a lecherous lunatic this afternoon: my sexual powers and appetites have increased during the past year. I am really a tiger now . . . .

I had a cocktail with Elsie Mendl,[3] who was at the Ritz; she received on a chaise longue, talked volubly and was full of life and quips. She shows no sign of age as yet, and she must be nearly 90. She sees much of the Windsors, but Laura won't meet them, says that 'their company is too mixed'.

Although I suffered internally today from indigestion or illness, nevertheless, I am much better – in good looks and spirits. My trip has done me a world of good.

---

1 Giovanni Antonio Canal (1697–1768) was a Venetian painter of the Rococo period famous for his land and seascapes of the city.
2 Love nest.
3 Elsie de Wolfe (1865–1950), credited with inventing the profession of interior design, was a New Yorker by birth. She married Sir Charles Mendl in 1926. She was 74, not 90.

TUESDAY 2ND APRIL

I idled, shopped, but spent little, and then lunched at the Embassy. I was alone except for Hugo Baring,[1] with the ambassadorial couple.[2] I liked them both; they were interested in Belgrade and wanted to know every detail of life at Beli Dvor and clamoured for news of the Regent and Princess Olga with whom they were on fairly intimate terms. The Ambassador is alive, overdressed, and pleasant; she is a touch grey and simple but adequate.

The afternoon flashed past, as it always does, when one drinks white wine for lunch. I sat with Laura for a little and was then rung on the telephone by Leslie Hore-Belisha, and I went to have a drink with him after he returned from the Chambre[3] where he had been conferring with Herriot.[4] He does not seem depressed but I fear his political stock is at a low ebb. He should have been made Minister of Information, but when I broached the matter he declared emphatically that he would not accept that or any other post in the present govt. He wants and needs a long rest.

I had a manicure: I only bite two fingers now: the other eight are beautiful.

WEDNESDAY 3RD APRIL   *BELGRAVE SQUARE*

Flew over in bumpy weather and it took two hours. I am always apprehensive – rushed home to change into more political garb, and found H, very sweet indeed, and a large luncheon party going on given by Alan. Honor gave me a handsome gold and turquoise Easter egg.

I went to the House, to join Rab. He whispered to me that the reshuffle would take place tonight. I did some rapid ferreting and got all the changes within twenty minutes. Poor Shakes Morrison has had a setback, and an obscure business peer, Lord Woolton,[5] has been made Minister of Food: that and the return to the Air

---

1 Hugo Baring (1876–1949) was the sixth son of the 1st Baron Revelstoke.

2 Sir Ronald Campbell and Lady Campbell, *née* Helen Graham.

3 The lower house of the French legislature.

4 Édouard Marie Herriot (1872–1957) was a prominent radical politician in the Third Republic, and three times Prime Minister between 1924 and 1932. From 1905 until his death he was Mayor of Lyon, except between 1940 and 1945 when he was interned in Germany.

5 Frederick James Marquis (1883–1964) would not remain obscure for long, as his name became associated with the food rationing of the Second World War and with the eponymous 'Woolton Pie', comprising root vegetables in oatmeal. He was a successful retail executive, working for the Lewis group in Liverpool, and was raised to the peerage as 1st Baron Woolton in 1939. He was deemed a highly successful Minister of Food, serving until 1943, when he joined the War Cabinet as Minister of Reconstruction. After Churchill lost the 1945 general election Woolton became the party Chairman, and between 1951 and 1955 served as Lord President of the Council and Chancellor of the Duchy of Lancaster while remaining Chairman of the party. He was advanced to a viscountcy in 1953 and to an earldom, as 1st Earl of Woolton and Viscount Walberton, in 1956.

Ministry by Sam Hoare are the sensational changes; the others are only moves across the chessboard. Harold Balfour is furious as he is devoted to Kingsley Wood and almost refused to work under Hoare. Rab was offered Food definitely and half-offered any change that he might wish. Wisely he chose to stay where he is. The House was excited, as it always is, when there is a reshuffle in the atmosphere, as everyone half-hopes that he will be included. But this time, by leaving the Under-Secretaryship of Information vacant, no new blood is absorbed.

THURSDAY 4TH APRIL

The press announced the reshuffle: no excitements, no sensations and very little enthusiasm anywhere. Poor Sam Hoare is not popular; and I am told that Winston is furious – that is always something.

I had a friendly (forced on my part) conversation with Duff, whom I had not seen since July. He mentioned 'hearing of me' in Paris and I suppressed a smile, remembering how I had eavesdropped throughout his call upon Laura. He made only £1,800 from his fiasco-ed lecture tour in America, so he told us.

FRIDAY 5TH APRIL

Shakes Morrison had a secret meeting here where he entertained Lord Perry[1] to lunch, all most mysterious and hush-hush. He is very dejected by his seemed failure. He must now lie low.

Nevile Henderson called on me at the FO. Whilst he looked a little better, he nonetheless is fading; even looks untidy and deranged, this once so debonair figure.

Dined in: the mass of work, the morass of complications, financial, political and domestic overpowers me. I need a long holiday.

I read a frightening telegram from Paris – a long angry dinner took place last night between Winston C and Monsieur Reynaud,[2] the third being the host, Sir Ronald Campbell.

Winston spent three hours trying unsuccessfully to persuade Reynaud to agree to violent and immediate (and perhaps foolish) naval actions. Daladier[3] is against it. But I fear Winston will win this time and disaster will follow in his wake.

---

1 Percival Lea Dewhurst Perry (1878–1956) was a car manufacturer and from 1928 to 1948 was Chairman of the Ford Motor Company in Britain. He was knighted in 1918 and raised to the peerage as 1st Baron Perry in 1938.
2 Paul Reynaud (1878–1966) had become Prime Minister and Minister of Foreign Affairs of France on 21 March following Daladier's resignation. He would leave the government on 16 June for refusing to consider an armistice with Germany.
3 Daladier continued as Defence Minister.

SATURDAY 6TH APRIL   *KELVEDON*

I drove here: the house is hauntingly beautiful; there are swans nesting on the lake; the blossom trees are about to burst into colour; Honor very sweet and, I think, rather apologetic for having collected so boring a party for my first weekend – it is Brigid's really . . . . I could hardly be civil to them, so exhausted was I.

SUNDAY 7TH APRIL

My grandmother's birthday – how she hated the anniversary, yet liked the fuss and follies of birthday parcels. She was very like me.

All day at Kelvedon, about seven I got bored and came up to London, dined alone. Later Alan L-B came to see me and we had a deeply intimate conversation here and then I drove with him to the Ministry of Food. He is intoxicated with his new powers, and he is to all intents and purposes the Minister since his chief, Lord Woolton, is in the Lords.

Alan is still deeply disturbed by his great friendship with Michael Rose. He wrote long letters to Michael and to Prince Olaf of Norway to bring them together and tomorrow I put them in the Oslo bag.

MONDAY 8TH APRIL

The FO was very hectic today with Norwegian notes and fears lest Norway break off her relations with us . . . .

TUESDAY 9TH APRIL

I was rung up by Alan and Honor before eight; both had heard rumours of an invasion of Denmark. I rang the FO; they had heard nothing, of course. Then I got onto Reuters and the news was confirmed; it seems the Germans walked into Denmark at 4.30 a.m. this morning;[1] and later we heard the agonising news that Norway, too, had been taken! This comes from too precipitate action; where was our fleet?[2] Why had not Winston done something? When we embarked on such a foolhardy adventure, why had not we foreseen such action? All day worse news came in of crashing countries. Sweden is mobilising, against us? This is the darkest day of the war. I am really terrified now of the result.

I was later in-waiting on the Prime Minister, and he seemed calm and thanked me affectionately for nothing. But his hands twitched his papers (which

---

1 The Nazi line was that the invasion would protect Denmark from Franco-British attack. The invasion of Norway, to secure its ore supplies, occurred simultaneously.
2 Channon refers to Royal Naval activity off the coast of Norway, notably Operation Wilfred, a mine-laying operation that coincidentally happened just as the Germans were launching their invasion; the latter was not retaliation for the former.

I afterwards took from him) as he waited to make his statement. He was calm, courageous and impressed the House who gave him an ovation. I think that someone has blundered and suspect old Winston . . . . the FO was in a flurry all day. I . . . . came home emotionally exhausted and anxious to be alone. Naval action is supposed to be in progress.

An ultimatum has been made to Sweden by the Germans; the Bernadottes[1] are in a state . . . . More Marseilles trouble. And no news of the Danish royal family, nor of the Norwegians . . . .

I rang Honor at 9.20 and the butler announced 'that her Ladyship had not come in yet'. What can she be doing? And who is behind her vagaries? My darling wife has no worldly sense whatever and allows herself to be 'got hold of' by adventurers etc.

WEDNESDAY 10TH APRIL

No country has crashed, no throne has tottered today – but there are such disturbing rumours. We have fears for Holland; and there are fears that Sweden will be invaded by Russia and probably the invasion of Salonika by Italy will follow. What a world. Everything is crumbling; and shall we emerge victorious? Will life be worth it? Will not Halifax go down in history as the sublime failure? I waited upon him this morning along with Colonel Nathan[2] at a vast political banquet at the Dorchester. There were 520 guests, a fairly distinguished gathering. Nathan who is a plump, genial Jew of ability and social aspirations, organised the function. Halifax spoke well – but I left in the middle of it to rush to the House because of our Questions . . . . The PM spoke dramatically at the end of Questions as he described the naval battle off Narvik,[3] a battle which might never have been necessary. Where was our fleet, why was not Narvik watched and the invasion of Norway allowed? . . . . There has been no news of the Danish royal family, nor of the Norwegian King – except that his government fled to Hamar[4] followed by our Legation.

---

1 The Swedish royal family, descended from Napoleon's general of the same name.
2 Harry Nathan, Labour MP for Wandsworth. He would soon be ennobled, to create a parliamentary seat for Ernest Bevin (qv).*
3 Narvik was an ice-free harbour in northern Norway used for shipments of iron ore from
   Sweden and therefore of huge strategic interest to both sides. The Royal Navy had the best of
   two sea battles there on 10 and 13 April, but there was no means of driving the Germans, who
   had invaded on 9 April, out of the port. After the Allies' initial success they were later driven
   out of Norway, and the Allied failures there in early May were pivotal in Chamberlain's
   surrender of office. It was ironic that he should make way for Churchill, at whose feet as First
   Lord of the Admiralty the shortcomings of the Norway campaign could mostly be laid.
4 Hamar is a small city eighty miles north of Oslo. The government and the King, Haakon
   VII, then moved on to Elverum, twenty miles east, which was heavily bombed by the
   Germans after a failed attempt to capture the King and his ministers.

I am extremely anxious about the picture. Poor Fritzi: he will have no more news about his aunt, the Queen of Denmark: she is probably a politely treated prisoner.

I drove Rab home from the FO. He is not happy about the situation and all his fears have been justified. He has the lowest opinion of Winston's character, judgement and intelligence. Even added that he was not even sorry for Halifax and the PM, who had been foolish enough to listen to him. Whenever the PM allows himself to be over-persuaded by Winston or others – goes against his own inner judgement – disaster follows for the nation.

Will Italy land at Corfu, the Russians invade Sweden, and the Germans take Holland? All these are quite possible.

THURSDAY 11TH APRIL

I am increasingly disappointed in Halifax; he is magnificent, almost sublime, but weak, too easily swayed. He has been weak with Winston and hence the muddle we are in: all day conflicting news came in of supposed naval battles and victories off the Norwegian coast; little was substantiated . . . .

Honor and I went to the Ritz for a cocktail and then to the Italian Embassy for lunch; a longish function. Bastianini's charm is overpowering, and she is a pleasant woman . . . . Sir John Reith drove Honor and me to the House of C. She adored him, and I am coming around to Dracula. He has immense charm and height . . . . At the end of Questions Winston Churchill arrived and took his place on the front bench. He was greeted with perfunctory cheers and his long-winded, dull statement pleased no one. He looked tired and ill and made little attempt to touch the real point – why did we allow Narvik to be captured? Where was the fleet? Wouldn't it have been wiser to have stopped the Germans, especially if this invasion had been so long and elaborately planned, why hadn't we been aware of it? Is our naval intelligence so weak – and Narvik above all, where our attentions ought to have been focused? He spoke for an hour and a flop it was. He, too, is too facetious when a grave manner would be more appropriate. To make heavy jokes when hundreds are drowning and dying for their country is unseemly for the head of the Navy.[1] I made as much anti-Churchill propaganda as possible – but it was unnecessary. The House was hostile to him and he knew it. He sat down in an almost ominous silence . . . . Then I went back to the Office. Rab is chairman of the Balkan Committee and also of the Italian Committee. His power increases. I drove him to the Chinese Embassy where he dined. We talked of Chatfield and I suggested that he go to Japan as Ambassador and thus relieve

---

1   The First Lord of the Admiralty was not the head of the Navy, merely the minister respon-
    sible for it.

the chargé [d'affaires][1] who I suspect of not being clever. Our Diplomatic Service is not what it was.

Companionship, when one is obsessed by one person, is often intolerable. A great passion, as has been said, afterwards turns to acid in the stomach.

FRIDAY 12TH APRIL

No tragic news except that we had not yet had a resounding sea victory nor yet defeated the Germans, nor ousted them from Norway. But Sweden and Holland are threatened and there are rumours of an Italo-Spanish coup against Gibraltar, rumours of an Italian occupation of Corfu. Holland and Belgium may be invaded at any moment. Yet such is the vitality and confidence of this country that seemingly only I am dubious as to the final result: defeat seems inadmissible to the English mind. But I can envisage it, as we are fighting such powerful enemies . . .

The in-laws to lunch: and I tried to wheedle £30,000 out of them to pay off our overdraft – but I fear I was unsuccessful. Perhaps he hasn't it! For it means a similar sum to all the daughters . . . . Our financial situation is gloomy indeed: we shall have only £8,000 or £9,000 a year net with these crushing taxes.[2]

Dined alone . . . . Alan rings me every few moments so anxious is he about Michael Rose, who like poor King Haakon is being harried about by bombs in Norway!!

I stayed at the Foreign Office until eight in order to drive Rab home; about 7.30 I looked out of the window and in the evening light I saw the PM and Mrs Chamberlain both wearing hats and overcoats, pacing their little garden. Around and around they went – poor Neville – will he be proved wrong about Italy?[3] Will he have to eat his hat? We must have a resounding victory to convince the world of our supremacy.

Mrs Patrick Campbell is dead aged 75, and her husband Cornwallis-West is engaged to be married for the third time.[4] At 24 he married Lady Randolph Churchill – he liked old ladies, and she young men. Years later he married 'Mrs Pat'.

1 Robert Leslie Craigie (1883–1959) was British Ambassador to Japan from 1937 to 1941. He was knighted in 1936. He served as UK representative to the United Nations War Crimes Commission from 1945 to 1948.

2 £1,000 in 1940 would be worth around £56,400 today, so Channon was contemplating having to survive on a post-tax income of about £450,000–£500,000 a year in 2021 terms.

3 Chamberlain continued to hope that Italy would not ally with the Axis; however, on 10 June once it was clear France would fall, Mussolini did.

4 Beatrice Rose Stella Tanner (1865–1940) was a doyenne of the late Victorian and Edwardian stage. Her first husband, from whom she derived her professional name, had died in the Second Boer War and she later married George Frederick Cornwallis-West (1874–1951), who had been Winston Churchill's stepfather.

I was present at a party when they met; I was coming down Ned Lathom's[1] narrow staircase (it was at his house, 47 Gt Cumberland Place, where he lived in foolish splendour) accompanying Lady Randolph, 'Aunt Jennie' as I called her, to the door when we met the married couple, 'Mrs Pat' and her husband face to face. It must have been about 1920. There was a tense moment and we passed on; no word of greeting was exchanged. Soon afterwards Cornwallis-West – who was known as 'Old Wives' Tale' – left her. Then I often saw Mrs Pat, who was immense, with a deep voice and a heavy dark manner. She lived in Pont Street in near poverty; but she was always faithful to Ned Lathom and helped and consoled him when he fell upon evil days – one of his few friends who was loyal to him in his adversity. She became poorer and poorer and one day I went to see her and asked her to give [George] Gage elocution lessons as he spoke so indistinctly in the Lords. He had, and it was a secret, almost twelve lessons from her, and grumbled about her fee. In those days she would come to luncheon at Buckingham Street; always dramatic and *un peu à la pose*,[2] she would thunder at one. Later she went to Hollywood and I never saw her again.

The war news is distressing – we must do something soon to impress Italy.

SATURDAY 13TH APRIL

Rab fears that we might well lose the initial phase of the war; the Admiralty and General Staff have been late and remiss, while Hitler conquers countries.

I sat to James Gunn at his studio; but I am a bad sitter as I always fall asleep. Then I drove to Pyrford and found my *beaux-parents* alone – a pleasant place, the gardens still well kept, and there are symptoms of spring; rhodos aflame; blossom bursting; we ate peacock for dinner, and excellent it was, more succulent than pheasant. After dinner a long conversation *à trois*, mostly about finances, and they are very mysterious. I gather we are still *malgré*[3] taxation very rich. Our difficulties are to be smoothed . . . . They are both ducks, very loveable, reliable, good and so reliable [*sic*]. I am devoted to them. She is very nice. As we went to bed the butler, the famous Pallant, announced that there had been a naval victory at Narvik.

SUNDAY 14TH APRIL

The day with my in-laws. It began well; I was called at 8.30 and my father-in-law had sent up the radio to which I listened in bed as I drank my coffee. The news is

---

1 Edward William Bootle-Wilbraham (1895–1930), by courtesy Lord Skelmersdale from 1898 to 1910, when he succeeded his father as 3rd Earl of Lathom and 4th Baron Skelmersdale. A lover and crucial financial backer of Noël Coward (qv), he was a failed playwright and squandered his modest family fortune on theatrical ventures, lavish parties and presents for his boyfriends. He died, penniless, of tuberculosis.
2 Not strictly idiomatic in French, this phrase is used by Channon to mean 'striking a pose'.
3 In spite of.

reassuring: seven German ships sunk, which means that nearly half the German Navy is at the bottom of the sea;[1] and almost more important we have laid minefields across the Baltic; Germany is hemmed in now; a brilliant strategic act. What will Hitler do to retaliate? I fear the Russians will now intervene . . . . Brilliant as this action is, it doesn't excuse our Admiralty allowing the landing at Narvik, and the invasion of Norway, where there are reported to be nearly two divisions. They are now cut off, or about so. Probably the whole Scandinavian adventure is a Hitlerian feint and he will presently launch a surprise attack elsewhere . . . .

Donald Lennox-Boyd died a year ago yesterday[2] and the mystery of his murder or suicide remains still unexplained. Alan took his brother to Bournemouth to visit his grave yesterday; today they are back.

MONDAY 15TH APRIL

My in-laws lunched; I adore them.

The news is increasingly bad; an Italian coup is clearly imminent – but somehow I think it will not come just yet, if at all. The Duce is an expert sabre-rattler. But we must make preparations: Italy, possibly followed by Spain, might go to war against us; communications would be difficult; we should be heavily bombed; the Maginot Line would be stormed; the Empire would be threatened. Civilisation would be ablaze.

I didn't dine but joined Emerald at the Gate Theatre to see *The Jersey Lily*, a little play about Mrs Langtry[3] by Basil Bartlett, who married her granddaughter, Lady Malcolm's girl. A pleasant trivial little play interesting because it portrays King Edward VII on the stage; the theme is the love affair between Prince Louis of Battenberg and Mrs Langtry (the offspring of this romance is Lady Malcolm, who was only told who her father was when she was 20, by the then Mrs Asquith). I remember Mrs Langtry: she came to Chicago in early 1917 and I attended the huge Allied Bazaar and I danced with her several times. She was an old tart of a

---

1 A wild exaggeration, as are most of the assertions here. The Kriegsmarine had at this point only two modern battleships, but half a dozen heavy cruisers, half a dozen light cruisers, nearly thirty destroyers and eleven auxiliary cruisers; plus torpedo boats, numerous other surface vessels, and a huge submarine fleet.

2 Donald Lennox-Boyd died on 5 April 1939, not 13 April as Channon states.

3 Emilie Charlotte Le Breton (1853–1929) was daughter of the Rector and Dean of Jersey. She married, in 1874, Edward Langtry, an Irish landowner; but in 1877 met the Prince of Wales and soon became his mistress. She had an affair with Prince Louis of Battenberg, father of Lord Louis Mountbatten (qv), in 1879; their daughter Jeanne Marie (1881–1964) was passed off as Langtry's child; and she married, in 1902, Sir Ian Malcolm. Mrs Langtry's lifestyle bankrupted her husband; she became an actress and the most renowned *grande horizontale*. It has been suggested that the father of the child was in fact Arthur Jones, himself fathered illegitimately by 7th Viscount Ranelagh, who was also a friend of Mrs Langtry.

girl with, I seem to remember, reddish hair and a flamboyant manner. She was then very old.[1]

I went back with Emerald to the Ritz and we had soup together at midnight. She leaves for abroad, accompanied by Sir Thomas [Beecham], on Wednesday. She was quite coy about this often-repeated honeymoon.

A very charming letter from Peter.

TUESDAY 16TH APRIL

The Norwegian news is so slow: why cannot we take more violent action? The General Staff have let us down; and now I am told that they are all to be replaced. Dill[2] will succeed Ironside[3] who has proved slow and ineffectual. Although 70 per cent of the whole German fleet is sunk, neutrals will only be impressed by a decisive Scandinavian victory.

The news from Yugoslavia is grave and my poor beloved Paul is distraught: however I know his plans, and he will fight any invader, and he himself has made elaborate preparations for the safety of little Peter and himself.

I came home in the hope of a quiet evening with my letters and my diary but both Alan and Harold B[alfour] had rung up suggesting themselves and they came to interrupt my loneliness; each was disappointed to find the other. Harold had wanted to discuss the situation, the impending changes and his liaison with Helen Fitz[gerald]; Alan wanted to talk about Michael Rose, and he eventually did, as Harold left us. We all drank much champagne and ate the caviar which Tilea[4] had sent me. There is no news of our 'lost' Legation in Norway; fugitives they are, following King Haakon. Alan is distraught.

There has been a political kite – to send Malcolm MacDonald to the Foreign Office as a sort of Deputy Foreign Secretary. There were later remarks of Anthony Eden returning. *The Times* this morning published a ridiculous leader about tired ministers which infuriated the Prime Minister. He complains that he is surrounded by 'old men' who get fatigued – they are all a lot younger than he.

---

1 In 1917 Mrs Langtry was 64.
2 John Greer Dill (1881–1944) became Chief of the Imperial General Staff in May 1940, having commanded I Corps in France since the previous September. In April he became Ironside's Vice Chief, before replacing him. He and Churchill got on poorly and in November 1941 Dill was promoted to field marshal and sent to Washington as Churchill's personal military representative. He was knighted in 1937.
3 William Edmund Ironside (1880–1959) was appointed Chief of the Imperial General Staff in 1939 but replaced in 1940 by Dill (*vide supra*). He commanded Home Forces for two months before being promoted to field marshal, and raised to the peerage as 1st Baron Ironside, at which point he retired; he had been knighted in 1919 after distinguished service in the Great War.
4 The Romanian Ambassador.

Ironside has delayed the sailing of 17,000 Chasseurs Alpins[1] for Norway in the most incomprehensible manner.

WEDNESDAY 17TH APRIL

An exhausting day. Princess Olga rang me at 10.30 that she would like to lunch: I quickly said 'Ritz' to save myself trouble; she said she would ring the Kents. I immediately rang up Lady Halifax, and he answered the telephone at the Dorchester. I invited them to come, and rather to my surprise and delight they both accepted, and we lunched *à six* in a quiet corner table. The restaurant was agog and everyone stared at us, which I was second-rate enough to half enjoy. I put Princess Olga opposite me, with the Duke of Kent on her right and Halifax on her left. He had just come from the War Cabinet. He was charming, gay, and v pleased with his little party as he is susceptible to both beauty and royalty: the combination he finds irresistible. He began by having a quiet confidential talk with Princess Olga, and later towards the end of a very good lunch, which I had ordered, he was amusing about his interview yesterday with Dr Marie Stopes,[2] who came to the Foreign Office and said that she had had affairs with 500 Germans at Munich, then with 500 Chinamen[3] – so she knew men better than any other woman. She was prepared, she told Lord Halifax, to accept Cabinet office, and would he pass on her request to the Prime Minister? Princess Olga then amused us with tales of General Göring and his vanities, his lotions, his bottles from Elizabeth Arden and other beauty specialists – a most successful luncheon party; but Halifax sometimes makes me shy. Back to the Office: Rab was impressed by my luncheon, to which I had invited him, but he was already engaged, unfortunately, to go to Maureen Stanley's.

. . . . All the time I could not throw off the sadness which fell over me from reading the telegrams about the dangers to Yugoslavia . . . . Then on to the Savoy: I went to the telephone as Princess Marina rang up her maid at Buckingham Palace and told her that she had decided to sleep at the Dorchester with Princess Olga, and to take her things there. The Duke is at Coppins for the night so did not come with us . . . . I talked at length with the Duchess about Peter Coats: she is aware that he adores her. We sat there until nearly one in the Savoy restaurant, and then the royal sisters left. Tremendous fuss about their departure . . . . At midnight Ivor Churchill[4] left us for a moment to find out whether there was any

---

1 Soldiers trained for Arctic conditions.
2 Marie Charlotte Carmichael Stopes (1880–1958) was a botanist by training who campaigned for women's reproductive rights and opened the first contraception clinic in Britain; she also wrote the sex manual *Married Love*, and was a committed eugenicist.
3 Thus in the MS. Rhodes James has 'over 100 Germans and then with at least 100 Americans'.
4 Lord Ivor Charles Spencer-Churchill (1898–1956), younger son of the 9th Duke of Marlborough and cousin of Winston Churchill.

news. He came back announcing that Yugoslavia had commercial *pourparlers*[1] with Russia! Will miracles never stop happening! Olga was angered.

Rab was distressed with the Downing Street plan to nominate Malcolm MacDonald to the FO. I determined to take steps, and after my luncheon party I caught David Margesson in the lobby and he led me to his private sanctum. I told him that Rab was distressed, even angry, and also that he had an appointment with the Prime Minister at 4.30. David was instantly sympathetic – I always manage him easily – said that he must speak to the PM before he saw Rab. And he went at once to the PM's room and I watched him go in, as Rab, unaware of my swift action, waited in the Secretaries' Room. David told the PM that I had confided in him Rab's reaction. The PM agreed not to betray me and when a moment later, he received Rab, he was particularly gushing and said that he hoped that Rab could carry on alone at the FO, even if Halifax took a holiday. Rab, infinitely relieved, agreed. No mention was made of MacDonald. Rab was jubilant, and when I met the PM coming out of his room he sweetly and simply thanked me for my intervention.

Thanks to Rab's intervention, goaded by me, the Chasseurs Alpins have sailed for Norway.

Thursday 18th April

I wrote a long, fulsome, rather beautiful letter to Peter; and I had a sad one from Paul in Belgrade who hourly suspects an invasion from probably both Italy and Germany. His position is terrible; but at least he will be safe, I pray almighty God! I love and like him probably more than anyone in the world. He is even, he said, jealous of Peter.

All day we waited about wondering when news would come; and no news came. The Italians, although they are still sabre-rattling, have made as yet no move . . . . Rab and I dined, along with sixty other MPs, at the House of Commons at a banquet to honour Signor Bastianini. There was some atmosphere, but on the whole the evening passed off well. The Ambassador was genial, pleasing, and very attractive and friendly – he was especially nice to me. Mostly we wore white ties, but Rab arrived in day clothes having been kept at the office . . . . Rab followed and he was subtle and firm and pleased the Ambassador and everyone else. Amery sailed near the wind with his remarks but avoided a scene or embarrassment. One MP at my table, J. P. Morris,[2] Con member for Salford, was rather drunk and kept murmuring 'Bloody wops!' At the end of dinner I drew a sort of cordon around him and thus prevented him approaching our guests or creating a scene . . . . .

---

1 Talks.
2 John Patrick Morris (1894–1962) was a stockbroker who sat as Conservative MP for Salford North from 1931 to 1945.

Fritzi left Kelvedon yesterday for Cambridge to take up residence there as he is to study at Corpus [Christi] as an undergraduate. I cleverly contrived to get Vansittart to vouch for him. Van is obviously mad; he wrote two fantastic memos about nothing at all. I persuaded Rab to write 'they are round and they bounce' on one of them. I expect trouble over this . . . . We are on the evening tide and must take action against the anti-Chamberlain men still in the Office.

We are still too slow over Norway: why cannot we recapture it?

FRIDAY 19TH APRIL

Princess Olga rang up early to say that Paul had telephoned to her last night, that he had already sent his daughter 'Pixie'[1] to Switzerland. She ought to have arrived there today; he was taking no chances for her safety . . .

A quiet day: indigestion; a visit to my dentist, and tea with Princess Olga who leaves tonight for Drumlanrig.[2] She is much worried and distressed at leaving Paul alone to face his problems.

SUNDAY 21ST APRIL

A gloriously lovely day that was half-spoilt for me by the presence of these unnecessary children[3] who use Kelvedon as a hotel – have they nowhere to go? Or Honor no one else to invite? She took me to see the farm she has bought. Cow Farm, a collection of fields near Doddinghurst, for which she had paid £4,000. A foolish and rash experiment, I think . . . . H and I went home to luncheon, and Harold Balfour came down to spend the day. He was charming; all the 'children' are like so many puppies, they litter the house with their paraphernalia, use my racquet, clothes and generally bore me. Honor said she wouldn't invite them again.

Hours passed and still no bad news: possibly there will be none. But my thoughts are with Paul, alone, reigning, remote and beset on all sides by greedy enemies. Life is drab: but Kelvedon looks lovely: there are swans breeding in the lake; white dogs sit lazily on the drive; blossom is bursting; there are [illegible] tulips . . . . Honor and I had a very long and satisfactory talk which soothed and relieved me. We also discussed our money matters which, extraordinarily enough, are better than most people's . . . .

MONDAY 22ND APRIL

Long letters from Peter, delightful creature. I adore him still and probably forever.

---

1 Princess Elizabeth of Yugoslavia (b.1936).
2 Drumlanrig Castle in Dumfries and Galloway, ancestral home of the Buccleuchs.
3 Young friends of Lady Honor and her sisters.

The news on the whole is reassuring: Italy is piping down and although my poor Paul is far from safe . . . . I don't think Mussolini will risk it. Ciano[1] is back, recovered from his influenza, and will hold the fort.

TUESDAY 23RD APRIL

The Budget: it lacked seasoning, and the House was not exceptionally crowded. No one expected fireworks: instead we had two hours from Sir John Simon. It was a remarkably dull speech full of minor irritating taxes, but we have not been seriously hit. The penny on beer will be offset by the heavy whisky tax, as more people presumably will drink Guinness . . . .

WEDNESDAY 24TH APRIL

What an extraordinary race! People are complaining that the Budget is not sufficiently stiff. What do people want?

I lunched at the Yugoslav Legation, a little party given by Princess Olga. There: the Halifaxes (I was next to her); the Kenneth Clarks – he is an ambitious, artistic arriviste, and she a silly governess; Maureen Stanley – sober for once, etc. Princess Olga was very sweet, very dignified. Halifax loves her! '*Il l'aime*,'[2] Rab laughed. 'It's his war aim,' I retorted. I went back to the House where I was soon surrounded. I am a sort of Susannah doing countless favours for old gentlemen. Gage, who came to see me, was impressed, as I held a little court in the Members' Lobby. I love the 'racket' and would not be out of it. Nearly every day I write either to the Regent or Peter – Peter or Paul. And they give me *un objet*, a *but*[3] in life.

THURSDAY 25TH APRIL

The House was overcrowded and pleasant and I was surrounded by people all day, which always stimulates me. Dunglass pumped me; did I think that Winston, the man who has never been right, should be deflated, was the moment ripe to begin to sell him? Ought he to leave the Admiralty? Evidently these thoughts are in Neville's head. Of course he ought to go from the Admiralty . . . . Of course he might go, but who could we replace him with? I could think of no one . . . but the country is definitely beginning to tire of Winston, and I am alarmed for a country, which could have made him an idol and for ministers, who could be influenced by this brilliant, puffing old charlatan. The news from Norway is not satisfactory; and he is responsible . . . his crash, or semi-crash, is one of this consolations of the war.

1 Mussolini's son-in-law and Italian Foreign Minister.
2 'He loves her'.
3 End, or aim.

The PM looked well. Lady Halifax said yesterday to me that whenever she sees him, he looks smaller; he is shrivelling before our eyes. Perhaps this is true – physically!

Princess Olga talked to Paul in Belgrade: he seemed more cheerful. The clouds are lifting slightly.

I heard today that Winston Churchill, the man who has never been right, has been intriguing again. Chagrined by his failure at the Admiralty, he is now throwing off his mask and plotting against 'Nugger',[1] under whom up to now he has loyally served for nearly eight months. He envisages running the show himself: all this was inevitable and I am surprised it did not come before. He has had secret conversations and meetings with Archie Sinclair, A. V. Alexander[2] and Mr Attlee and they are drawing up an alternative government with the idea of succeeding 'God' or if he lives too long – indeed at the first favourable moment. Eden is on the fringe of the plot, watches and waits for his chance. Our failure in Norway is attributable to Winston and yet he would profit by it. I am appalled. I passed on this news to the right quarters . . . .

I forgot to record the death of the Duke of Rutland, which has caused no stir and certainly occasioned no regrets. He was a *poseur*, artistic, theatrical, like all his family; and, I always suspected, not quite a gentleman. He had a pseudo grand-manner, knew few people; was steely and amorous – he had been having a violent affair with Hilda Lezard, ex-Wardell[3] . . . who is a tigress in bed. I dare say she indirectly killed him. He gave himself great airs, insisted on white ties at Belvoir and Haddon. He was always pleasant to me; he was bored by life; and cared for dreary medieval tiles and quaint relics and customs of the past. He was unpopular and rather rejoiced that he was. He was 53, I think.

FRIDAY 26TH APRIL

The plot spreads. Last night Harold Balfour and Kingsley Wood took David M out to dine at the Mirabelle restaurant and warned him of the 'glamorous' developments of which he was already half-aware. It was decided to send Kingsley to No. 10 at ten o'clock and he was to warn the PM and consult with him. He did: the PM was angry and shaken and indignant. We are 'in' for a first-class political struggle between the Chamberlain men and the 'glamorous' elements: possibly not now. We may weather this storm but there is trouble ahead, which

1 Apparently a term for Chamberlain.
2 Albert Victor Alexander (1885–1965) was Labour MP for Sheffield Hillsborough. He was three times First Lord of the Admiralty, including throughout the wartime coalition, and Minister of Defence from 1946 to 1950.*
3 Hilda Susan Ellen Cooper (1891–1977) married in 1918 as her third husband John Michael Stewart Wardell, and in 1929 as her fourth husband Julien Lezard (1902–58).*

is of course *confiture pour les boches*.[1] Oh, why cannot Churchill die or break up – he is, by the way, showing signs of doing the latter. Failure, strain and criticism is getting him down and making him disloyal. We must watch out.

This morning I consulted Rab, who seemed half-aware of this development but urged me to confer with Dunglass; so I crossed to No. 10. The War Cabinet was sitting but I found Alec in the outer room and I passed on to him all I knew, had heard and surmised. He was riveted and said that the PM after his talk with Kingsley last night had decided to do little: he would give Winston more rope in the hope and conviction that soon he would hang himself. The PM wants him deflated; but thinks the moment has not yet come when it would be advisable to 'sack' him, which he has decided to do ultimately. Winston C has not fully made up his mind to try to sabotage the PM. He still hesitates, and we shall consolidate our forces. Meanwhile the position in Norway is terrible, desperate, far worse than the public realises, and Winston, who refused to allow the fleet to move on the 9th, is primarily to blame. Nor has the War Office done well. Winston and Oliver Stanley have a private feud; all is *à tort et à travers*.[2] God help the country. Only Chamberlain can save us . . .

I had Fraulein Wagner,[3] the huge 22-year-old granddaughter of the composer, and Mrs [*sic*] Geissmar[4] to luncheon, also Nicholas Lawford[5] and Harold B. The Valkyrie has been brought up practically by Hitler who looks upon the Wagner children as a race, sacred and apart. Now she has turned against him and is publishing shortly a book which reveals him in a most unpleasant light. She and her friend, the woman doctor, who is Thomas Beecham's private secretary, are almost authorities on the sexual activities of the Nazis.

Rab complained to me that he had no youth, no gaiety or frivolity. I am convinced that he married Sydney for her ducats. No one could love such a

---

1 Literally, 'jam for the Germans'.

2 The French idiom is used to mean 'wildly'. Here, it means 'all over the place'.

3 Friedelind Wagner (1918–91), daughter of Siegfried Wagner, granddaughter of Richard Wagner and great-granddaughter of Franz Liszt, had arrived in England, via Switzerland, Paris and Calais, on 2 March 1940. She was interned from 27 May 1940 to 15 February 1941, then became an anti-Nazi newspaper columnist before leaving for America. Her mother, Winifred Williams, a Welshwoman, was one of Hitler's most devoted admirers. Fraulein Wagner was reconciled with the family after the war.

4 Berta Geissmar (1892–1949), who had been secretary to Wilhelm Furtwängler, the composer and foremost interpreter of the works of Richard Wagner. Because she was Jewish she had had to leave Germany in 1934, but was employed by Sir Thomas Beecham (qv) on reaching London. She was unmarried and although described by Channon as a 'woman doctor', her PhD had been rejected when she submitted it at Heidelberg during the Great War. She was unmarried.

5 Valentine George Nicholas Lawford (1911–91) was private secretary successively to three Foreign Secretaries – Lord Halifax, Anthony Eden and Ernest Bevin – between 1939 and 1946. He regularly acted as Churchill's interpreter during the war. From 1938 until his death he was the partner of the fashion photographer Horst P. Horst.

charmless female, not possibly. He is so charming, so clever, so balanced. His weaknesses are his inability to terminate an interview, his unpunctuality and his indecisions in trivial personal matters!

Micky Renshaw[1] came to say 'goodbye' to me; tomorrow he joins up in the RASC.[2] I gave him a wireless set. He warned me that Peter has made powerful enemies in Cairo who are jealous of his *succès*; he refused to name his informant, but I suspect Lady Crewe, who always makes trouble wherever and whenever she can; she is a desperate Jewess; unfortunately intelligent, scheming, cold and important. I wrote off at once to tell him. Dear boy.

H is busy all day at her farm: how long will this mania last? It is an expensive one and will lead to trouble.

I drove Rab around the Park and wondered at the vernal beauty, and pledged hostility to Winston.

SATURDAY 27TH APRIL

This morning I sat to James Gunn in his Pembroke Walk studio; he is not without charm, but is a bore, humourless, and an amateur Foreign Secretary – there are some 2,000,000 of them about. Thence to the FO, where the news is depressing. Very. We are about to retire from Norway, or at least, the southern part of it and there will be a secret meeting of the Supreme War Council this afternoon. Already the Frogs have arrived. They are keener than we are, more eager to help the Norwegians – and it was us, or rather Winston, who let us in for the whole debacle. The delay in sending the fleet on the fatal 10th of April may cost us the war. Rab was tired, affectionate, charming, wistful and I left him at 1.20 with regret, as I had to rush to the Dorchester Hotel where I lunched with 'the sisterhood': Olga, thin, solemn and imposing; Duchess of Kent, smiling, bejewelled apricot; and Johnny Lucinge,[3] quiet, correct and superficial. Pleasant party, but I was depressed by the news; the disturbing rumours of an Italo-Germanic invasion of Yugoslavia on the 2nd or 3rd! . . . . Princess Olga was subdued and talked of getting 'Bertie'[4] to send a battleship to fetch her baby from France – it is still in Switzerland, and so I didn't point out that perhaps our Navy had other things to do . . . . Royalties are occasionally wildly impractical. But it takes more than a war or threats of impending disaster to depress the Duchess. She was in rollicking spirits and

---

1 Michael Oliver Wenman Renshaw (1908–78), son of Arthur and Lady Winifred Renshaw, worked from 1932 in the advertising department of the *Sunday Times*. He became advertising director in 1953. Ian Fleming (qv), with whom Renshaw was at Eton, described him as 'psychologically unable to say anything but to old foreign duchesses'.
2 Royal Army Service Corps.
3 Prince Jean-Louis de Faucigny-Lucinge (1904–92), a descendant of Louis IX of France. He married, in 1923, Mary Liliane-Matilde 'Baba' d'Erlanger (1901–45), a celebrated model for Cecil Beaton.
4 King George VI.

looked a vision . . . . I left them reluctantly at 3.30, left a letter at the War Office for the Middle East bag for Peter. I came here. Kelvedon is a dream – swans, blossom, white dogs, and my baby boy.[1] He had tea with us. Honor very well and sweet, but she drank five whiskies and sodas, and what is alarming is that they had no effect whatever. Then she read to the child, and I walked about the garden and thought about doom, and how precarious everything is – all was green and luscious and there was that subtle gauzy haze which one finds in Essex.

A peaceful evening: no real news has leaked out from Norway but the people are beginning to know that all is not well.

Honor is obsessed by her farm; she always plunges so wholeheartedly into experiments and experiences. How long will this one last?

MONDAY 29TH APRIL

Drove to London, my little car, Peter's little car, full of flowers. Here no news yet. I am not in contact today. Rab seemed *distrait*[2] and discouraged. He hinted that the Supreme War Council had definitely and wrongly decided to abandon Norway, all except Narvik. It will be a blow, perhaps a decisive one, to our prestige and may well be the deciding factor in the war.

I came home, depressed by an airy epistle from Peter C: now immersed in his Cairo life, he is losing interest in London and me. It is understandable: he writes vivid descriptions of his new life and he adds that 'we' are hopeful about Maud, as he calls Norway. Little does he know of the tragic situation; of our ignominious retreat; of Italy's treachery and Yugoslavian alarms.

Alan, typically vague, selfish, charming, and unpunctual ruined my evening. He rang up to say that he would be here, at Belgrave Square at 6.15. He arrived after 7 . . . . then Alan insisted that I dine with him and Patsy (I wanted to be alone) and weakly I consented. She has so little defence against his persuasive powers and his immense charm – later they fetched me and I discovered that I was not the only guest, but an unfortunate creature, John Fowler, an employee in the Colefax Company and a slave of Michael Rose's, had come too. I was quite gay, and we dined off Italian food, for the last time – at Isola Bella. Then I came home to bed. Alan, later, followed me here. Patsy is frenziedly in love with him still, but torments him with her constant attentions. She dropped him at the Ministry of Food tonight and then rang him three different times to see when he was returning . . . . he, at times, is desperately bored.

---

1 Just as many evacuated children had returned to London from the country during the Phoney War, Paul, aged four and a half, had been brought back from Clandeboye. The situation would change again after the invasion of the Low Countries.
2 Absent-minded, distracted.

Tuesday 30th April

I am angry with the War Office, with their dilatoriness, their time lag . . . I have never been able to get anything done since Leslie Belisha left. Victor Warrender, now happily transferred, was hopeless, and Oliver Stanley is an unsympathetic machine. I saw Belisha: bronzed and gay, and affectionate, he has a loveable side . . . . There is more talk in the House of a cabal against poor Neville. 'They' are saying it is 1915 all over again; that Winston had more vigour and the country behind him, that he should supplant him. I think we are in for a big political battle, but will survive the first round, and shall have a respite. Then Winston will be thrown over and eventually he may return triumphant. I don't know. It is a race between him and the Prime Minister: health is the decisive factor. The PM will not relinquish his office easily, nor without a struggle . . . .

The afternoon at the House . . . . I sat with that *papier mâché* man, Jim Thomas, for an hour, and decided that he knew nothing of any plot: when there is one, I always get it out of him: evidently the Eden group are staying their hand.

I had a shock when I arrived this morning to find Rab and others wondering whether to declare war on Italy at once – directly she violated Yugoslavian neutrality! Surely madness, and yet I want help rushed to help the Regent. Everyone seems to think it now a foregone conclusion that Italy will walk into Belgrade before May 15th. I don't. This evening as I came back I met Lord Halifax getting into his car and we had a brief chat; he said that the *Rex*[1] had sailed today for New York, which is always an indication that Italy has no immediate intentions of going to war with us; and also Marshal Badoglio[2] is still the Italian Generalissimo – he is a friend of the Allies! Perhaps there is, after all, a respite for a little. Another month joins its predecessors: we can live only in the moment now. The future is too precarious.

Wednesday 1st May

Oh! The excitements, the thrills, the atmosphere of ill-concealed nervousness and self-interest which comes over the H of C when there is a political crisis on, or rumours of a reshuffle. Such it is now . . . Winston, who is the villain of the piece, is being lauded by both the Socialist and Liberal Opposition, and being tempted to

---

1 The SS *Rex* was a luxury Italian ocean liner, launched in 1931. It would shortly be withdrawn from passenger service; RAF bombers sank it in September 1944.

2 Pietro Badoglio (1871–1956) was commissioned into the Italian Army in 1890 and by the time of Italy's catastrophic Great War defeat at Caporetto in 1917, for which he was largely responsible, he was a lieutenant general. In 1926 he was promoted to the rank of marshal. After the war he used his authority to cover up his part in the catastrophe, and began a political career that culminated in his becoming Prime Minister after Mussolini's fall in 1943. He was Chief of Staff of the Army from 1925 to 1940 and completed the invasion of Abyssinia, using highly controversial methods such as mustard gas, and was created Duke of Addis Abeba [*sic*] in recognition of his triumph.

lead a revolt against the PM, who unfazed, and full of fight still, is playing a deep game. He has given Winston more rope, made him what amounts to Director of Operations. He sat smoking and drinking in the Smoking Room tonight, the wicked old hypocrite, and he was surrounded by his scheming sycophants, A. V. Alexander and Archie Sinclair – the new 'Shadow Cabinet'. I think Neville will outmanoeuvre him: I was sitting with Alan and Victor Raikes, who confided in me that he will expose him on Tuesday in the big debate.[1] He hopes to unmask Winston: there is growing feeling against him, and Raikes in his project will find unexpected allies.

I woke early and heard of an aeroplane crashing on an Essex town; fearing that it might be Brentwood or Southend, I rang up Harold Balfour who said it was Clacton. Six people have been killed and over a hundred wounded: our first internal casualty. I think the Germans will attempt an invasion, and personally I think Newcastle, which lies nearest to Norway, may be their objective.

The country is gradually realising that we are abandoning Norway, or at best, the southern parts of it. Such a defeat, or rather retreat, is a severe blow to our pride.

Talked with Alec Dunglass; with David Margesson, with his faithful *suivant*,[2] Harris;[3] with Harold, Alan, Rab and others: I found them all anti-Winston, but alarmed by his popularity in the country. A Westminster war added to a German one is really too much. I read with pleasure a leader in the *News* attacking Archie Sinclair; I gave it to Alec, who rushed it into the PM, who smilingly kept it.

Long talk with Jock Colville, whom I like enormously: we are going out together tomorrow. He has immense charm, is simpatico and altogether a friend worth making. He likes me. I am having a *succès* suddenly. I like new friends; old ones exhaust and bore me – it is the same. The edge goes.

THURSDAY 2ND MAY

The Westminster squall threatens to become a war: it is monstrous that the PM and Halifax should be subjected to this additional anxiety and strain when all their energies should be devoted to winning the war. I am reluctantly realising that Neville's days are, after all, numbered. A few months more and we shall have a different, but not so very different cast.

1 The debate scheduled to begin on 7 May, and to be concluded on the following day, was on the conduct of the war. It is known to history as 'The Norway Debate', and when the government's majority was cut to 81, Chamberlain realised he had no choice but to resign.
2 Follower.
3 Percy Alfred Harris (1876–1952) was Liberal MP for Harborough from 1916 to 1918 and for Bethnal Green South West from 1922 to 1945. He was Liberal Chief Whip from 1935 to 1945 and deputy leader of his party from 1940 to 1945. He was created 1st Bt in 1932.

The Duchess of Kent, Princess Olga and Walter Buccleuch lunched with me here .... Princess Olga is still alarmed about Belgrade and the Italian intentions. I think that Paul has secretly slipped to the frontier and met King Carol at his hunting-box. No letters came today in the Belgrade bag.

I walked with Walter to Westminster: he is dull, deafish, but a dear; but I fear he has been sadly duped by the Nazis. Even now he is for a negotiated peace ... When I arrived we were already half-through Questions ... [Chamberlain] looked infinitely small, but vibrant and vital. He rose, amidst cheers and made what he called an interim statement: it was a brilliant effort and the House agreed to suspend judgement. Definitely the PM got away with it – a few days more of power before we are threatened.

I gossiped in the House, made anti-Churchill propaganda, praised the PM, flitted from group to group and even sat with Jim Thomas for half an hour. Then I went back to the Office where Jock Colville fetched me and we went to see *King Lear* at the Old Vic. A brilliant performance with John Gielgud.[1]

FRIDAY 3RD MAY

Winston C is in a corner: the fiasco in Norway is due altogether to his unsound advice; and benefiting by the storm he hoped to supplant the PM. He has been definitely disloyal, and certainly tempted by the crisis; but the PM has outmanoeuvred him and he is not too deeply committed to turn traitor. He will be in the uncomfortable position of having to defend his policy, his mistakes against his own supporters and followers who would like him to reign. We shall have two very remarkable days. David M says we are in the very eve of the greatest political crisis since August 1931. We have been nine years in power, a long time.

SATURDAY 4TH MAY   KELVEDON

Tired and irritable I came here, after a visit from Alan. I played with my baby: Honor was out – at her farm, I suppose. She has no moderation in her enthusiasms. I was a touch affronted as she did not come in until seven.

We talked – she drank five whiskies – and dined, and I went early to bed.

SUNDAY 5TH MAY

Honor went out at nine, and came in only at 1 p.m. Again I felt slighted and showed it: I passed the afternoon in the garden asleep by way of revenge. Honor looked unhappy – she never gives a thought to another human being, yet is well-meaning. I am profoundly sorry for her and the harm I am half-responsible for

1 Arthur John Gielgud (1904–2000), a leading stage and, later, film actor.

having done her; but with a touch of give or understanding or tenderness in her complicated character all would have been well.

There is a storm of abuse at the PM in the Sunday press. He is in for a bad time but I prophesy that he will weather this storm, but it may be his last victory.

MONDAY 6TH MAY

Drove up this morning after a most disappointing weekend. This intolerable tension cannot last; I try to steel myself for the sake of my very remarkable child – he is all I care about really.

Alan rang me in a frenzy and I met him at the Carlton Club: he is disturbed by the Cabinet decision to call up the 1904 class[1] which will include him.

On my way back to the Office I met first Harris who is confident of victory, and then Alec Dunglass who tells me the PM is down and depressed. We must cheer and encourage him: I sent Rab over to No. 10 to do so, and he did, meeting Margesson as he went in. Rothermere has come out against the govt; Kemsley is pro-it; the *Telegraph* and Beaverbrook are mildly critical but stay their hand. Herbert Morrison rang up to ask for an appointment with Halifax – is he to offer him the throne? He wouldn't take it from Neville.

Long talks with Harold B, who has an excellent political nose: he thinks the game is up – but not just yet. Perhaps by July. Rab thinks that the PM will eventually retire, but is too cautious to hazard a date. Political life for me will lose most of its fascination when Neville goes: no longer shall I be in the inner counsels of the racket.

I am told that Stafford Cripps drew up the astonishingly feeble Cabinet forecast which appeared in the *Daily Mail* today. Luckily he includes Rab; moves him to the India Office. Shall I be there too? Would I go? I also hear that the King is much disturbed. He has been 'got at' by Alec Hardinge who is an active, violent anti-Chamberlain man. The 'Black Rat' is increasingly dangerous and sees himself as ruling the country.

Arthur Hope's cheque, dated May 2nd, for the remaining £650 which he owes me, was returned to me by the Bank today. He has behaved <u>abominably</u> to me; he puts me off from month to month with plausible letters, sometimes doesn't even answer me, pretends to send cheques which never arrive and finally sends me a 'dud' cheque for £650. Harold says I have the govt by 'the short hairs'. I wonder!! I am bewildered and will take no violent inoperable action for several days, probably not until this political crisis has passed, as I want David Margesson's all-valuable, always-wise advice.

I am down; dejected and dispirited and I am on the eve of a storm.

---

1 The decision to conscript those born in 1904 – Lennox-Boyd was born on 18 November that year.

Tuesday 7th May

A dreadful day: the political crisis overshadows everything; one cannot eat, sleep nor concentrate. Usual raillery at the FO . . . I walked over to the House, and full it was already buzzing. The Glamour Boys are smacking their lips and intriguing; their full strength is not yet known. After Questions I went into the lavatory behind the Chair, and a moment later the Prime Minister came in smiling: we chatted for a moment, but it was he who made the conversation, as I was suddenly stilled and shy by my affection for him. 'It is very crowded,' I said. 'Yes,' he smiled. 'Is your wife here, Chips?' But she wasn't. She never is. Five minutes later he was on his feet and was given a warm welcome. He spoke haltingly and did not make a good case; he fumbled his words and seemed tired and embarrassed. No wonder he is exhausted: who would not be? All day and all night he works, whilst the small fry criticise. I realised at once that the House was not with him; he warmed up a little towards the middle of his speech; but the very crowded House . . . . was restive. The PM sat down at last, but the opening attack was a half-hearted affair, almost a failure. Opposition members were offensive and acrimonious – how they hate him and how unjustly. He was followed by Attlee and then by Archie Sinclair, neither were effective. Long dreary speeches followed, almost all were attacks on the govt and one gradually realised that there was treachery in the ranks. Roger Keyes,[1] an ex-hero, but a man with a grievance, was damning; and he had come to the House in the uniform of an Admiral of the Fleet with three rows of medals – questionable taste but it lent him dignity. The atmosphere was intense, and everywhere were heard the whispers, 'What will Winston do? Will he be loyal?' . . . Dined with Alan and Patsy and we were joined for a bit by David Margesson who seemed confident; but he has been powerful so long, been so aloof that possibly he is, as his enemies are always asserting, losing touch?

Oliver Stanley wound up for the govt, and it was a shocking performance, lukewarm and ineffectual. Thus our two big speeches so far have misfired and I am more uneasy now about tomorrow especially as it is rumoured that the Opposition will challenge the govt with a division.[2] We have scarcely time to collect our household troops, as so many of them are scattered, and serving abroad . . . . Archie Southby[3] had a row with Anthony Eden who is becoming increasingly

---

1 Roger John Brownlow Keyes (1872–1945) was a naval officer who had led the Zeebrugge Raid on German submarine pens in 1918. He commanded both the Atlantic and Mediterranean fleets and attained the rank of admiral of the fleet. He was Conservative MP for Portsmouth North from 1934 to 1943. He was raised to the peerage as 1st Baron Keyes in 1943.

2 They did.

3 Archibald Richard James Southby (1886–1969) was Conservative MP for Epsom from 1928 until 1947. He had hitherto been a career Royal Navy officer. He was created 1st Bt in 1937. He had spoken in the debate that day after Leo Amery's (qv) hostile speech about the government, in which Amery had quoted Cromwell: Southby's appeal for calm fell on deaf ears.

haughty and touchy: he resents any criticism and his vanity develops daily. God help Britain if he and his Namby Pamby followers ever come to power.

I was in and out of the Dixième Bureau[1] all day, collecting shrapnel and gossip for the PM's devoted entourage. His mighty throne rocks tonight . . .

Alan and I went to have a drink at 9 Little Chester Street where Hector Bolitho and Rodney Wilkinson[2] share a house – a rather attractive *nid d'amour* . . . . Rodney has a glow of attraction with his warm velvety face and rich luscious lips . . . But he is dull, I fear. Then Alan and I came home and a Rabelaisian scene followed which I cannot bring myself to describe – I was not so much shocked as disgusted.

WEDNESDAY 8TH MAY

The cataclysmic day has drawn to a welcome close: I am worn out, revolted by the ingratitude of my fellow beings, nauseated by the insanity of the House of Commons which might, I have long thought it, although I love it, be abolished.

When I arrived I heard that Terence O'Connor[3] had died at the age of 49. I always disliked him: he was common, clever, and a climber: he loved Helen Fitzgerald, who prefers Harold.

The atmosphere of the House was definitely excited and it intensified as the long hours passed. Herbert Morrison opened the debate with vituperation and announced that the Opposition would challenge the govt with a division. The PM, angry and worn out, intervened to say that the govt accepted the challenge and called upon his friends to rally around and support him. Possibly he was tactless, but I don't quite see what other course he could have adopted. We then knew that it was to be war. Samuel Hoare, the pet aversion of the Labour Party (because he tried to avert war between us and Italy in 1935) made a boring contribution as a defence of the govt. He did not help, it only exacerbated [*sic*]. Atmosphere rose, hearts hardened, tempers sharpened and I realised that there is nothing so revolting as the House of Commons on an ugly night. Little Neville seemed heartbroken, shrivelled, but courteous and patient: I sat behind him for a long time hoping to surround him with an aura of affection. I looked up into Mrs FitzRoy's Gallery and always I caught the eye of poor Mrs Chamberlain who has been there for two days. She is an unhappy, loyal good woman, although an absurd ass, whom one cannot resist. She was in black, black hat and gloves, black everything with a bunch of violets pinned to her coat. She looked infinitely sad as she peered down in the mad arena in which wolves had got loose, wolves out for

1 10 Downing Street.
2 Rodney Levett Wilkinson (1910–40) was a career RAF officer. Commanding 266 Squadron, he would be killed in the Battle of Britain on 16 August 1940 when his Spitfire collided with an Me109 over Deal on the Kent coast.
3 The Solicitor-General. He was actually still only 48 when he died.

Chamberlain's blood. Lady [Austen] Chamberlain, hatless, with long earrings was in the next aperture and they reminded me of nuns at a grill . . . .

For hours the issue was in doubt: Duff Cooper made a damaging speech in which he said that he hoped we should get on more actively with the war etc., curious advice from someone who has been away for four months lecturing in the USA . . . but all the nincompoops to whom Neville has refused office, all the affronted, all the intellectual pansies and Eden-hangers-on are jubilant and out for a holiday – this when the Empire is on the brink of destruction. I hated them all and longed to get up and say that if Neville was harmed it would be England that would suffer . . . . the whispering in the lobbies was unbearable. Ham Kerr[1] offered to bet that a hundred govt supporters would vote against the regime; I scoffed. Mrs Tate[2] offered to bet me £5-5-0 that over fifty would do so, but refused to take up the challenge when I agreed although she did lay an even 'fiver' with Alan. Lady Astor rushed about intriguing, enjoying the fray and smell of blood; she has joined hands with the Insurgents, probably because she is an unbalanced hoyden, but also must be in the limelight – and also she was seriously rattled by 'the Cliveden Set' allegations which were made against her before the war. Now at all costs she wants to live them down. Never in my long life have I ever come in contact with a more altogether foolish and unbearable character. She is only a cheap sensation-seeker and artist. There is no prostitute so desperate as the puritanical one. My hatred and contempt for her are limitless.

At last the atmosphere became so horrible that I decided I must leave for a little and I ran into Paul Latham who asked me to dine at the Savoy: in Palace Yard we met Brabner,[3] a stocky, handsome youth and member for Hythe who succeeded Philip Sassoon. He came along with us: he had been summoned by telephone by the whips who, however, seemed to feel that they had the situation well in hand. It reached my ears from many sources that Winston was advising his followers to vote against the govt. He, of course, must defend it, being of it . . . . but many backbenchers were independent. It is a cunning game but a

---

1 Hamilton William Kerr (1903–74) was a journalist before being elected as one of the two Conservative MPs for Oldham in 1931 (the other being Anthony Crossley, qv), holding the seat until 1945.

2 Maybird Hogg (1893–1947) was Conservative MP for Willesden West from 1931 to 1935 and for Frome from 1935 to 1945. She married in 1925, as her second husband, Henry Tate, and adopted the Christian names Mavis Constance. She had a nervous breakdown in 1940 and killed herself by gas in 1947, having been ill since visiting Buchenwald concentration camp in 1945.

3 Rupert Arnold Brabner (1911–45) was Conservative MP for Hythe from 1939 to 1945 and served as Under-Secretary of State for Air between 1944 and 1945. He served in the Fleet Air Arm during the war and reached the rank of commander; he was a fighter ace, with five and a half kills to his credit and one more probable, and was awarded the DSO and the DSC. He died when an aircraft taking him to Canada was lost off the Azores shortly before the end of the war.

transparent one; and he wins either way. If the govt were defeated he might become PM; if he weathers the storm his powers will be increased. A most dishonest procedure, but that hearty ruffian will do anything to get to No. 10 – possibly, when the goal is his, he may become more scrupulous ... At the Savoy were the Trees with their boss, that old lighthouse, Sir John Reith; and at another table the Dashwoods[1] with Alec Hardinge – the Black Rat. For the past fortnight his name has kept cropping up and there is no doubt he wants to upset Neville just as he did Belisha. But the Black Rat joining forces with Winston, who so stoutly opposed the abdication, is surprising. The Black Rat's mother-in-law is a most dangerous, domineering old harridan.[2] Oh! England you are in a mess .... Brabner, who lives in Epping Forest and seems rather middle class but pleasant, left us and Paul and I were left to gossip about Peter, in whom Paul is still mildly interested; but always says he is snobbish, adores royalties and ambassadors, and that we were made for each other ...

We went back to the pandemonium. Alexander was speaking, winding up for the Opposition: the real issue of the debate, Norway, had long since been lost sight of, and speakers attacked on any possible ground ... and the murmuring doubt was in everyone's mind, would Winston be loyal? He rose, and one saw at once that he was in a bellicose mood, alive and enjoying himself, realising the unusual position in which he found himself, i.e. that of defending his enemies, and a cause in which he did not believe. He made a slashing vigorous speech, a magnificent piece of oratory. I was in the gallery, behind him with Rab, who was several times convulsed with laughter. Winston told the story of the Norwegian campaign, justified it, trounced the Opposition, demolished Roger Keyes, etc. How much of the fire was real, how much ersatz we shall never know; but he amused everyone, dazzled them by his virtuosity – and, as was later revealed by the division results – influenced no one. He taunted the Opposition, accused Shinwell[3] of 'skulking'; a Labour MP, worse for drink, had never heard the word and thought Winston had said skunk .... The House resembled Bedlam and at one moment the Labour Party were really angry, although I suspected a private arrangement had been made between the 'Glamours' and the Opposition ...

1 John Lindsay Dashwood (1896–1966) succeeded his father as 10th Bt in 1908. He married, in 1922, Helen Moira Eaton (1899–1989), a Canadian.

2 Violet Georgina Maxse (1872–1958) married first in 1894 Lord Edward Cecil, and after his death married second, in 1921, 1st Viscount Milner. She was editor of the political monthly *National Review*.

3 Emanuel Shinwell (1884–1986) was born in the East End of London but moved to Glasgow as a child and was an activist on 'Red Clydeside'. He sat in the Commons as a Labour MP from 1922 to 1924, 1928 to 1931, and 1935 to 1970. He had held junior office in MacDonald's Labour governments but bitterly opposed the National Government. He was Minister of Fuel and then Secretary of State for War and then Defence in the Attlee government of 1945–51. Overcoming his detestation of the aristocracy, he agreed to be raised to the peerage as Baron Shinwell (life peer) in 1970.

When I asked Roy Wise[1] how many rats would vote against the govt, he retorted he was one: it was the only way to shock us out of our complacency, he said. I told him he was playing with dynamite. Charles Taylor, pretty calf, came up to me. 'We're going to get your government out tonight,' he said. Feeling grew: people seemed to get a sensation out of being treacherous. Still we thought we should survive. At last the Speaker called a division, which Winston nearly talked out. I went to the Aye lobby, which seemed thin for a three-line whip. We watched the Insurgents file out of the Opposition lobby – Teenie Cazalet could not make up his mind and abstained – 'Quislings' we shouted at them, 'Rats', 'Yes-men', they retorted and I saw all the expected ones, and many others. As Hubert [Duggan] emerged my heart snapped against him forever. Someone spied Ronnie Tree: 'Quisling Tree' they called out! The name stuck. For a PPS who has been actively associated with the govt to do such a shabby trick is unforgivable. Then I voted – as usual everyone wondered how many had 'dared' to vote against us – so many people threatened to and funked it at the last moment. Lurking about in our lobby were Anthony Eden and Jim Thomas, who looked triumphant; Winston and his PPS Brendan Bracken, but another Churchillian or Edenite. They had done their subterranean work well and Winston's fiery oration had influenced no one . . . . I went back to the Chamber, took my usual seat behind Neville. 'We are all right,' I heard someone say, and so it seemed as David came in and went to the right, the winning side, of the table, followed by the other tellers. '281 to 200',[2] he read, and the Speaker repeated the very ominous figures. There were shouts of 'Resign! Resign!' And that old ape, Josh Wedgwood, began waving arms and singing 'Rule, Britannia'. Harold Macmillan, sitting next to him, joined him but they were howled down.

Neville appeared bowled over by the figures and was the first to rise. He looked grave and thoughtful, and sad. He walked calmly to the door and his supporters rose and cheered him lustily, and he disappeared to join Mrs Chamberlain. There were no great crowds to cheer him as there were before and after Munich, only a solitary little man who has done his best for England . . . . I seized Harold and Alan, and longing to get away from the scene of treachery and human fallibility, we drove to the Mirabelle to 'celebrate' the victory, if victory it is. We drank champagne, drank Chamberlain's health and speculated on the future. Neville can do nothing; he can reconstruct his government; he can resign. No one knows. Harold thinks he will take the vote as one of insufficient confidence; I thought he would take it as a warning, as a red light. He ought to have resigned on Monday last – the whole affair has been mishandled: we had all

---

1 Alfred Roy Wise (1901–74) was Conservative MP for Smethwick from 1931 to 1945 and for Rugby from 1959 to 1966.
2 281 for the government; 200 against. Chamberlain had expected a much greater majority, given the National Government's notional support in the House. He knew the game was up.

the cards, the power of possession, and allowed this to happen. Now the govt is seriously jarred and confidence is gone. Hitler will be quick to take advantage of our divided counsels, perhaps even tonight.

Then I walked home, uneasy, unhappy! What changes does this fatal division portend? I am disgusted by politics and human nature and long to live, like Walpole,[1] a semi-social, semi-literary life in a Strawberry Hill – only not Gothic – of my own. Perhaps I shall. And I should like Peter there to share it.

Meanwhile what will dear wily old Neville do? He may swim but not for long: oh! The cruelty of a pack in pursuit, the blindness of politicians, the selfishness of office-seekers . . . . Shall I crash in the crumble of the Chamberlain edifice?

Thursday 9th May

I woke as if emerging from a long nightmare: all was well on earth and Chamberlain reigned on high. But the telephone soon brought me to face reality; first Harold Balfour, who said that the PM would really resign after last night's vote; then Alan, whose intelligence is far superior to Harold's, but whose judgement is nil, flighty, irresponsible and over-loyal and emotional: he said a majority of 81 was sufficient. Neville could make minor changes and remain. Rab rang, too: he was non-committal, hopes that Chamberlain will ride this very bad storm. Then I went to the H of C, which met at eleven. It was curiously calm after the roar of last night; 'the Glamour' element tiptoes about, excited, but disappointed for it seems that they had expected a still greater number of defections. The PM entered the Chamber, calmly; cautiously he gave an answer to a question. I had a talk with him behind the Chair, said it had been 'terrific' yesterday and murmured a few banalities which, while nothing in themselves, revealed to him my loyalty and affection. He was geniality itself and did not even look tired. He has already been conferring with several people about what course to take – probably the resignation and reconstruction of his whole govt. But rumours of his retirement are rife. The whips are dismayed. No one is happy, and personally I think Herr Hitler will attempt one of his great coups now that we are practically without a government. Duff Cooper and Co. will have been the shoehorn.

The House was full of rumour, intrigue, plot and counter-plot and I rushed about, talked too much and made myself both conspicuous and a nuisance. Dunglass asked me to find out the attitude of the Labour Party to serving under Neville. I did: I approached Colonel Nathan, a plump Jew, ex-Liberal who is an enterprising neighbour and almost a gentleman: at first something might be arranged, but after several conferences he reported to me that the position was hopeless, that even if the Labour leaders would serve under Chamberlain, their

---

1 Horatio 'Horace' Walpole (1717–97), Whig politician, man of letters and 4th Earl of Orford. He built Strawberry Hill House in Twickenham.

backbenchers would never allow it. I passed on all these fluctuations to the Dixième Bureau where Dunglass, Arthur Rucker,[1] Jock Colville sat in hopeless idleness snatching at any shard of hope, whereas almost any vigorous action might have been more useful.

Occasionally David Margesson would rush in, and then for a time the doors were barred, as the War Cabinet met. Alone the PM remained imperturbable.

. . . . There is anger, too, with Lady Astor, who voted against us not because she is in sympathy with the traitors, but because she nurses a grievance that Lord Astor was not made a Food Comptroller. Such are politics in a Democracy! I wish Parliament could be abolished: it deserves to be after last night's shocking performance.

Rab had an adjournment;[2] and I sat behind him until I was asked to help find Herbert Williams and three other powerful Tory MPs who were ushered into the PM's room at three o'clock. They explained that they would continue to support him but demanded drastic changes in the govt. Everyone agrees, they, I, the Socialists, that Walter Elliot, and Sam Hoare, must be discarded and perhaps others . . . . The PM received them courteously. Earlier he had sent for Victor Cazalet and asked why he had abstained: Victor took the line (as did Roy Wise) that he did not want Neville to go; but that he wanted to jolt[3] the government out of its complacency.

Earlier, on the motion for the adjournment, Richard Law,[4] a humourless horror, continued the attack on the govt, and Lloyd George, stung into fury by an attack made on him by Beverley Baxter,[5] made a fiery defence of his attitude in a deplorable speech which will obviously be of immense value to the German propagandists. He practically said that the Allies were responsible for the war; this is very likely true, but why say so now? He is full of fire and beans and his bronzed skin, white locks, and cheap blue suitings, make him a doughty figure . . . . I stayed in the Chamber until it rose, and it behaved as if it had a hangover; people were ashamed of their behaviour and of other people's disloyalties. The 'Treachery Bench', or 'Traitor's Gate' was deserted, and Ronnie Tree has been forced to resign. We are still in power, but for how long?

I went back to the office, and went over to No. 10, where a long conversation has been held between Winston, Lord Halifax and Neville, each saying to the other two, 'You must be PM' – and each one, no doubt, secretly wanting it for himself. Different statesmen were sent for, Sam Hoare, Kingsley Wood and others . . . . It was decided at last to invite the Labour leaders to call at No. 10, and Attlee and [Arthur] Greenwood soon arrived and spent three-quarters of

1 Chamberlain's principal private secretary.
2 That is, he had to speak for the government in a debate on the adjournment.
3 It is probably thus, but the word is obscured by an inkblot in the MS.
4 Conservative MP for Hull South West (qv).
5 Conservative MP for Wood Green (qv).

an hour with Neville, who tried to persuade them to join the govt and then form a real coalition. They went away promising to let the PM know their decision tomorrow. I left the FO at about eight o'clock; Neville still reigns, and I go, exhausted to bed. But I am apprehensive as I hear disquieting rumours that the Glamour Boys had been egging on old Lord Salisbury,[1] who is nearly 'gaga', to intrigue with the Labour Party and this put their price up. Neville has already agreed, under pressure, to sacrifice both Simon and Sam Hoare.

I am worn out nervously and have a pain in the neck. I am glad I am not dancing all night with the Kents' party.

I suddenly remembered that I have not heard from Peter since last Saturday.

FRIDAY 10TH MAY

Perhaps the darkest day in English history. I was still asleep, recovering from the emotions of the past few days, when my private telephone tinkled and it was Harold speaking from the Air Ministry. Holland and Belgium invaded; bombs falling on Brussels, parachutists landing at The Hague etc. Another of Hitler's brilliantly conceived coups done with lightning precision. Of course he seized upon the psychological moment when England is politically divided and the ruling caste is seething with dissension and anger. I suppose he heard of Wednesday's debate and fatal division yesterday morning and immediately acted upon it.[2] It took only a few hours to prepare this further crime and all day Holland and Belgium have been invaded. I rang up Alan who curiously enough never knows anything, nor did Rodney Wilkinson – who for all his really invidious charm has a middle-class mind – then I dressed and went to the FO. Princess Olga rang up asking for news and suggested going out tonight! I telephoned about frantically to find a free young man and could only get Rodney. At the Office all was in confusion, and the mandarins, some of them, seemed more downhearted that the invasion of the Low Countries had probably saved Chamberlain, than depressed by the invasion itself. It was the popular view this morning that Neville was saved, for after all his policy had been vindicated swiftly, surely, suddenly in the last twenty-four hours. Had he sent immense numbers of troops to Norway, where should we be now? This latest coup is probably the prelude to a concentrated attack on England with all imaginable horrors.

Telegrams poured in, and messages from the House. Harold rang me up, he thinks Neville may be saved. The War Cabinet met at 8 a.m. and again

1 James Edward Hubert Gascoyne-Cecil (1861–1947), by courtesy Viscount Cranborne from 1868 to 1903, when he succeeded his father as 4th Marquess of Salisbury. He held several government offices, and was Leader of the House of Lords from 1925 to 1929.
2 He did nothing of the sort. Hitler had ordered plans for the invasion to be drawn up the previous October and had resolved to do it once matters were settled in Denmark and Norway.

at eleven. One would think that the PM would be glad to divest himself of his grave responsibilities. Evidence accumulated during the day that the whole story of the past few days was the result of deliberate treachery. It is even whispered that Winston gave orders to his followers and fans in the House to vote against the govt, which he, on the surface, defended so vigorously. It is significant that when one analyses the figures not one follower of Winston's, except Brendan Bracken, his PPS, came into the govt lobby. We have witnessed a filthy political intrigue. And the country when it becomes aware of it will be horrified . . . . Their glamorous young men sold the pass. Duff Cooper is English for Quisling. All the morning support for Neville seemed to gain ground. Roy Wise went to see him and apologised for voting against him: others did likewise. No one knew yet which way the cat would jump . . . .

I rang up Princess Olga who had lunched with the Halifaxes (they didn't invite us, I notice) at the Dorchester. She had sat between Halifax and Dill, the rising military star; and she had had a talk with the PM who was calm and charming and showed little effect of the battle that has been waging about him. He did say, however, that Lloyd George's personal attack on him surpassed anything he had ever heard in Parliament.

Now the drama begins: the Chamberlains returned to No. 10, and sometime during the afternoon a message came from the Labour people that they would join a govt, but refused to serve under Chamberlain. Action had to be taken immediately: Neville hesitated for half an hour, and meanwhile Dunglass rang me – couldn't Rab do anything with Halifax, plead with him to take it on? Rab was doubtful as he had already this morning and yesterday had such conversations with 'the Pope' who was firm – he would not be Prime Minister. I don't understand why, since a more ambitious man never lived, nor one with, in a way, a higher sense of duty and *noblesse oblige*. Nevertheless I persuaded Rab to go along to Halifax's room for one last final try: he found H closed with Alba,[1] and waited. Three minutes later H had slipped out to go to the dentist's without Rab seeing him and Nicholas Valentine Lawford,[2] the rather Third Empire secretary, who neglected to tell Halifax that Rab was waiting, may well have played a decisive negative role in history. Rab came back to our room, angry and discouraged, and we rang No. 10; but Alec Dunglass said that already the die had been cast: it seems that Winston had half thrown away his mask and was pressing the PM to resign and at once. Winston feared that the Dutch invasions would bring about a reaction in Neville's favour. A message was sent to the Palace and an audience arranged for six o'clock – it seemed now that only a miracle could save Chamberlain, and perhaps England.

---

1 The Duke of Alba, the Spanish Ambassador (qv).
2 Channon has reversed Lawford's Christian names, though he was known as Nicholas.

I sat numb with misery and mused on this fantastic day .... And on my lunch with Harold at Belgrave Square and our drive along the Strand with startling placards everywhere: 'Paris Raided' – 'Brussels Bombed' – 'Lille Bombed' – 'Many killed at Lyon' and finally 'Bombs in Kent'. We had stopped, bought the newspapers and read of the rain of horrors falling everywhere. Harold told me that elaborate plans had been made for retaliation tonight along the Ruhr ... From five until 6.30 or afterwards I was miserable and rushed from room to room, and incidentally had tea in the Secretaries' Room with the Dutch Foreign Minister, M. van Kleffens,[1] a tall thin, youngish man with a nose rivalling Cyrano's, and the Dutch Minister of Colonies, Mr Welter,[2] an older man. These 'Flying Dutchmen' had had a day indeed; they were both awakened about 3.30 a.m. by the noise of gunfire over The Hague, and had quickly dressed. A Cabinet meeting was called for 4.30 and all presided over by Queen Wilhelmina[3] – in tweeds! She was in a high rage against the Germans and full of fight. A decision was taken to dispatch the members of the govt at once to England. And these two left The Hague at 8 a.m. in a Dutch seaplane. Over Scheveningen their plane was hit by German gunfire, and somewhat crippled they got as far as Brighton, where they came down in the sea and after being rescued were almost arrested! Then they came to London and found themselves arriving in the midst of a colossal crisis. They pleaded for help for the Netherlands, but it was already dispatched. They are to remain here for a bit to keep contact: all this they told me in broken English but I think I understood it correctly ...

At 6.30 I rang up No. 10 and the loyal Miss Watson[4] told me that the PM would broadcast at 9 p.m. and, her voice breaking, she hung up the receiver. Shortly afterwards Alec Dunglass and Jock Colville arrived in our rooms and told us the terrible tale. The PM had just come back from the Palace, Winston had kissed hands and was now Premier. Alec thought that the King had been a bit too precipitate; he is always led by the apron strings of Alec Hardinge who now has a third major victory to his credit, first the abdication, then the fall of Belisha, and now that of Neville .... We were all sad, angry and felt cheated and outwitted. England in her darkest hour had surrendered her destiny to the

---

1 Eelco Nicolaas van Kleffens (1894–1983) was a diplomat and international lawyer who served as Dutch Foreign Minister from 1939 to 1946, after which he was the country's permanent representative to the United Nations until 1956 and its Ambassador to the United States.

2 Charles Joseph Ignace Marie Welter (1880–1972) was Dutch Minister of Colonial Affairs three times between 1926 and 1941, and leader of the Catholic National Party from 1948 to 1956.

3 Wilhelmina Helena Pauline Marie (1880–1962) succeeded William III as Queen of the Netherlands in 1890, and reigned until her abdication in 1948.*

4 Edith Margaret Watson (1879–1953) was private secretary to Bonar Law, Ramsay MacDonald, Stanley Baldwin, Chamberlain and Churchill, serving in Downing Street from 1922 to 1945. She was awarded the CBE in 1919 and the CVO in 1937.

greatest opportunist and political adventurer alive!! Rab was cold, and added that if Halifax and Chamberlain allowed themselves to be duped and bamboozled by Winston, that arch scoundrel, they deserved to be. Alec who more than any other, has been with the Prime Minister these past few weeks and knows his moods and actions, let himself go. He had been dethroned by treachery to which Winston was a party – he could not resist the temptation. It had been his life's ambition, and with the prize dangling so near him he had seized it. I opened a bottle of champagne, Krug 1920, and we four loyal adherents of Mr Chamberlain drank his health, 'To the King over the water,' I said. Then we parted, but not before we had resolved 'to get him out' as soon as possible. Winston, with too much rope, is certain to crash one day.

I rushed home, by now in tears; dressed quickly, and joined Squadron Leader Wilkinson who was waiting for me in the Blue Amalienburg. He knew nothing and gulping champagne and crying at the same time I unfolded the tragic tale. Then, after innumerable telephone calls from Honor, the Romanian and Yugoslav Legations, Alan, Harold and others we went to the St James's Theatre where we arrived just in time to welcome Princess Olga and Lela [*sic*] Ralli.[1] The play *Ladies in Retirement*[2] was an absorbing thriller of a pathological nature. I whispered the news to Princess Olga who was amazed – Neville had seemed so gay and composed at luncheon. We talked, too, of the invasions and wondered whether London would be bombed tonight. The Air Ministry must have also wondered for the streets were inky black when we went on to the Savoy Grill, where I was horrified to see a little party of conspirators headed by Alec Hardinge, the 'Black Rat'; with him were Jim Thomas, triumphant at last – after two and a quarter years; Charles Peake, always a confirmed Edenite, and Sir Walter Monckton.[3] They were drinking champagne to celebrate; I ordered some to drown our sorrows. Diana Cooper was at a nearby table with the Rothschilds – I could not bear them in their triumph – why is it that anyone with a drop of Jewish blood so loathes Neville? Always Munich? – and avoided them until it was impossible to do so. Diana came up to our table, dropped a curt curtsey to Princess Olga, and attacked me for having neglected her. She had, she said, not a smile for me: I no longer cared. She looked worn, almost haggard, Grand

1 Julie Marie 'Lilia' Ralli. See entry for 14 December 1938 and footnote.
2 By Reginald Denham and Edward Percy: it had opened that spring and a motion picture was made of it by Columbia and released the next year.
3 Walter Turner Monckton (1891–1965) was a barrister who became a King's Counsel in 1930 and served as Attorney-General to the Duchy of Cornwall from 1932 to 1937, becoming King Edward VIII's closest legal adviser. Solicitor-General in Churchill's caretaker government of 1945 (without becoming an MP), he became Conservative MP for Bristol West in 1951, serving until 1957, when he was raised to the peerage as 1st Viscount Monckton of Brenchley. He was successively Minister of Labour, Minister of Defence and Paymaster-General between 1951 and 1957. He and Hardinge had effectively been on opposite sides in the abdication.

Guignol-ish; her phenomenal beauty fled she reminded me of her old mother. She was hurt and cold; I was not particularly gushing. I no longer care: she has withered away from me and interests me no more. How curious I am. We parted on bad terms. Princess Olga was v sweet and pleased to have her little daughter with her: the child at my suggestion arrived by aeroplane. Rodney and I drove the ladies home, and drank at B Square. A queer sly fish, we talked long and intimately. Miserable, thinking of Neville I went to bed at 2 a.m.

SATURDAY 11TH MAY

The war news is worse, the invasions of Holland, Luxembourg and Belgium proceeded. Will it be our turn next? Meanwhile what will become of Rab, and of me?
    There are four alternatives [sic]:

I   He will remain at the Foreign Office.
II   He will be offered another post which will be acceptable, even pleasant, i.e.: India Office, Admiralty or Dominion Office.
III He will be offered a very 'slum-ey' post – I shall have to give up my keys and suffer other humiliations.
IV   He will be offered nothing at all – we shall be properly *dégommés*.[1]

    At the FO I arrived before he did: there was no real news. We sat about restless, irritable, nervous, idle; it was impossible to get down to any real work. Every tinkle of the telephone might be a summons or a fresh piece of news. And nothing came. About one o'clock I heard that a terrific battle had been waging at the Admiralty where Winston had summoned Neville and Halifax; and it seemed that the Labour leaders, goaded and encouraged by Mr Amery and Lord Salisbury – has there ever been anything so treacherous or underhanded? – announced that not only would they not serve under Chamberlain, but not with him either. Winston was in a dilemma as he had offered a post to Neville last night, which he had practically accepted and announced in his broadcast.[2] Now Winston may be forced to choose between Labour and Neville, and may thus be unable to form a government at all. I sincerely hope so. He could not cast [aside] Chamberlain, for a govt composed solely of Labour and Glamour Boys would not command a majority. I went home to luncheon and when I came back about four o'clock the news was the same. The

---

1 Dismissed.
2 Churchill had wanted Chamberlain (who remained leader of the Conservative Party) to return to the Treasury, where he had been a much better Chancellor than Churchill himself; but Chamberlain, fearing this would be unduly provocative, declined, and was offered instead (and accepted) the post of Lord President of the Council, with a seat in the War Cabinet.

Labour leaders were putting up their price, and no decision had been reached. Tempers, Conservative ones, were rising against the 'Treachery' Bench.

I drove down to Kelvedon: the azaleas are out; all is green and luscious and lovely, but I feel ill and worn out. I explained the political position to Honor and we turned on the radio at nine. It was announced that the Cabinet changes had just been announced – so Winston, after struggling all day, was able to effect a last-moment compromise. Neville is Lord President of the Council, Leader of the House, and Leader of the Conservative Party – a position of immense power; Halifax remains at the Foreign Office; Attlee becomes Lord Privy Seal, and Greenwood becomes Minister without Portfolio: these five constitute the War Cabinet. Three other appointments have been made: A. V. Alexander returns to the Admiralty; Eden goes to the War Office – and how will the soldiers like that dolt? – and Archie Sinclair becomes Sec of State for Air. Considerable ingenuity is shown in this arrangement: Winston always has had imagination. How I hated hearing him referred to as the Prime Minister!

SUNDAY 12TH MAY

Another gloriously beautiful day but I didn't enjoy it. I slept badly, as I always do here . . . . In the night I heard mysterious rumblings, probably that of lorries transporting troops. And this afternoon as I dozed in the garden, I was awakened by the roar of planes and by what seemed to be distant gunfire.

The press is only lukewarm about Winston; *The Times* says that the PM's Norwegian policy was justified. No newspaper tells (or perhaps knows) the terrible truth, i.e. that Winston is responsible for the whole Scandinavian adventure, that he insisted on our laying mines near Narvik, that he delayed about sending the fleet when delay was fatal, was then instrumental in bringing back the whole Expeditionary Force. Norway was all Winston's adventure and poor Neville is unjustly the scapegoat. I wrote to him rather a sentimental letter.

I am really rather ill with fever and a throat: Honor sat with me all evening, and I dined in my grey and white beautiful bedroom.

MONDAY 13TH MAY

I woke feeling really ill and decided to make a bolt for London as I would rather be surrounded by the comforts of Belgrave Square . . . . and also I could not miss the meeting of the House. It was all so absurdly dramatic and very Winstonian. We were summoned by a telegram, signed by the Speaker, and asked not to mention the meeting of the House. Both Houses were convened, thus 1,300 telegrams must have been sent and seen by literally thousands of people.

I arrived at 2.15 and found an atmosphere of wonder, confusion and embarrassment. No one knew who had been reappointed, dropped or changed.

It was 'Crazy Week': I joined a group of bewildered ministers – ministers still – who stood in the Aye lobby. They chattered, amused, apprehensive, uninformed: Ernest Brown was the angriest and he inveighed against Winston: others did likewise and there seemed no enthusiasm. I was surprised and secretly pleased as I thought WC would have a triumph, at least today: but he very definitely did not. After prayers he went into the Chamber and was greeted with some cheers but when, a moment later, Neville entered with his usual shy retiring little manner, MPs lost their heads; they shouted; they cheered; they waved their order papers and his reception was an ovation so enthusiastic that Winston must have been alarmed, annoyed. He spoke well, dramatically in support of the new all party govt; but he was not well received. And all the mediocre speeches which followed fell on a cool audience. Only references to Neville received a shout. I met Winston face to face and murmured banal congratulations which he acknowledged very pleasantly, I must admit. He flitted about, enjoying his triumph, talking to everyone: Bob Boothby and Brendan Bracken, his faithful henchmen since many years, are now in for a spell of power, and I heard Brendan assure Ernie Brown that he would be given a post – it would be monstrous to leave him out. I am making a list for my private vendetta, of the traitors and in time will revenge myself upon them, one by one . . .

There was much whispering in the lobbies and people were giving it 'three months'! The lobby journalists varied, prophesied anything from three to six. The House of Commons resembled nothing so much as the Bullingdon[1] rooms after a blind: there was an obvious attempt to clear up the mess and wreckage and to be civil to those one had insulted . . . . But there was everywhere evidence of a 'hangover'. There was amusement too, over the seating quandary. If there was to be no Opposition, who would sit on the Opposition benches? Wedgwood, mad as your hat, attempted to proclaim himself a sort of leader of an official Opposition and sat in Mr Attlee's late place – that little gadfly looked smaller and more insignificant than ever on the govt front bench, dwarfed by Winston, who was next to the PM as usual. I mean Neville, who will remain PM to me forever! Alan went about raging; he is wildly indignant with the traitors, and yesterday changed his table at the Ritz so as not to murder Lord Cranborne who was nearby. Brendan came up to Alan, as I stood with him, and asked him what job he wanted etc. Alan made an offensive reply; and I begged him to go away before he did himself too much political damage . . . I sat for a time in the gallery, and chance put me near a little group of Quislings, the really worst ones, Jim Thomas, Paul Emrys-Evans and Cranborne. They snickered childishly when Neville was mentioned and showed no enthusiasm when a reference was made to his public-spirited resignation. Cranborne is too contemptible . . . . Hideous,

---

1 The Oxford University dining club notorious for its excessive and sometimes grotesque behaviour.

hysterical, humorous eunuch, ill-formed, unfortunately not tubercular, ill-dressed, unattractive and spoilt . . . . No one seemed to pay much attention to me: I don't suppose I am sufficiently important to be victimised. I want nothing; only to be left where I am; and I feel that Winston will not move Rab, although they are open enemies . . . . I hung about trying to pick up news, saw David [Margesson] closeted with Oliver Stanley who, I am delighted to say, is 'out'; they say he has been offered the Dominions Office;[1] they say that he wants to be a second lieutenant and fight. He cannot do right in my eyes, although I don't seriously dislike him. It is everywhere admitted that he has been a failure in every job he has ever held except, possibly, the Board of Trade. There are some consolations in this avalanche, but I fear also some unpleasant shocks coming. Anthony Eden had a poor reception.

Rab is down and depressed and even *distrait*. His position is undermined and he half-hoped that Winston would send for him. One hears so many rumours of impending appointments . . . and gradually they come out. Neville's last reshuffle at Easter finished him: it was a motley disaster. Poor Sam Hoare is out; but Simon, rather unexpectedly, goes to the Woolsack. Kicked upstairs. A dignified end to his political career. He is 67 and a priest at heart, a Jesuit really. In his frequent attempts to conciliate he always further wounds.

I felt so ill that I came home and went to bed. My temp. rose to 103° and I sent for a doctor. I have streptococcal fever and throat – the illness Philip Sassoon died of: but he rose in the middle of it and went to spend the weekend at Windsor.

My poor Fritzi rang up from the Normans' house at Much Hadham: he is to be interned today near Bury St Edmunds. All enemy aliens in the East Counties have been rounded up: it is all very sad and my heart bleeds for him; but I don't think that he will be maltreated. He was very sweet and gentle on the telephone, said it would be a new experience etc. But it is far from pleasant: luckily he is simple and makes friends easily; I have never known a greater gentleman nor a more charming character. How can I get him released? I must wait a little until the storms blow over.

Queen Wilhelmina has arrived at Buckingham Palace.

The division was victorious: 381 to none, as the two ILP members acted as tellers; but I had to pull Alan into our lobby and voted myself from prudence, not from conviction.

TUESDAY 14TH MAY

The war news gives great anxiety; Holland is as good as gone. In my bones I fear and expect the worst: it will be years before we recover, unless we can win and I don't see how that is possible. We shall be extremely lucky if England is not

---

1 He had turned down that office, but Churchill gave him a key liaison post in intelligence and he returned to the government in 1942.

enslaved by the Nazis . . . . The French are not playing up; they appear paralysed by the terrific German onslaught.

I lay in bed with high fever, but I persuaded Honor to move Paul from Kelvedon, which is too much in the parachute country, to Pyrford. He goes tomorrow. A wise precaution.

The tales of the bombing of Amsterdam and The Hague etc. are beyond belief for horror.

Alan was sent for by David Margesson last night and asked what he wanted to do; it was intimated that Winston would be prepared to keep him at the Ministry of Food. Alan retorted rather grandiloquently that he wished to join the Navy, that he could not promise to serve Winston with any loyalty etc. He rushed to me still in an heroic mood. I told him he was ridiculous and I bounced him into admitting that it is his fiendish cunning old mother who has been persuading him all the time to leave the govt, so that she could be near him at Folkestone where he will train. That grey slattern is a fiend incarnate and everyone except her brood of strange boys knows it!

Diana Cooper rang up and was gently affectionate and her usual old self: I am forgiven. Naturally she is cockahoop over Duff's appointment to the Min of Information: I think, and hope, it will smash him. Ridiculous little turkey-cock; but I love her still.

WEDNESDAY 15TH MAY

Still very ill: I lie in bed brooding about the grim future. The news for France is despairing: the Frogs will not play up and the line is badly broken near Sedan and north of Rettel.[1] There is talk of a total French collapse. Then we are done. There is something linked between that magnificent little Neville and England (like St George!). When he was harmed, England was bound to be hurt and perhaps go under. Louvain is taken: the Belgian govt, has or are moving [sic] to Ostend. Belgium will follow Holland in a few days' time. There is some consternation, almost amounting to panic in Downing Street. Harold and Alan came to see me and ring every few moments. Harold and Rab were both sent for by the Prime Minister and asked to continue in their present jobs: both gleefully accepted; fantastic government appointments are made every hour, so it seems.[2] I am reminded of Jock Colville's comment on Monday, 'Like a 50/- suit, cheap, spectacular and won't last.' Still nothing matters if we are really properly up against the Nazis, as it seems.

1 On the France–Luxembourg border.
2 Churchill was reluctant to squash the Chamberlainites as he was only too well aware of the modest level of popularity he enjoyed in the Conservative Party.

Rab tells me that he had a characteristic five minutes with Winston. Rab reminded him that they had often sparred in the past, disagreed on many things. 'Yes,' Winston stuttered, 'but you have invited me to your private residence.'

Beaverbrook returns to power and favour: he ought never to have been cold-shouldered by Central Office, Margesson *et Cie*,[1] and I often told David that. Attlee and Greenwood were last evening at Stornoway House I hear, and both rather the worse for champagne. Kitty Brownlow twitted them. This is a new world for Attlee, but not for Greenwood; both of these Labour leaders, their jaws loosened by Krug, talked too much and they repeated the telephonic conversations they had had with poor Neville on the fatal Friday afternoon. They were at Bournemouth and rang him up; he was presiding at a meeting of the War Cabinet, and went at once to speak to them. They now pretend that he clung to office, that he showed every reluctance to resign, insisted that the sudden situation created by the invasions of the Low Countries altered matters and that it was not the moment for a ministerial crisis. He was right; but they give the tale a bitter twist. Randolph Churchill, that obese horror, boasts that he composed the telegram to the TUC which so stiffened their resistance to Neville. I don't know what telegram he means; but certainly Conservative 'Glamour' influence was brought to bear upon the TUC, and they were encouraged to refuse to serve under Neville. Talk about Quislings! The shame, the filth, the treachery of Conservative gentlemen revolt me. Anything to do with a Cecil is contemptible.

I suppose the Nazis will take Paris by about June 1st. It has undergone two German occupations during the nineteenth century.

We expected Italy to declare war against us today or to spring some coup. She has hesitated again before taking the final plunge.

Duff spoke on the radio, and well. I was impressed: it is the sort of thing he can do.

THURSDAY 16TH MAY

I am beginning to recover and the fever drops . . . Harold came to see me; Alan flitted in and out, and he is beginning to regret his rather hasty foolhardy decision. The sweets of office linger in his mouth, and perhaps turn sour later . . . More appointments. Winston aims at an all-star cast: I fear he is overloading it.

The news from France was so grave this morning that Winston flew secretly and urgently to Paris to confer with Reynaud and his Cabinet. Defeatism is about, and the Germans are pushing their way towards Paris which they hope to have early next week. The Frogs are dazed and put up little resistance. The situation is extremely grave . . . . I am glad my little son is at Pyrford in comparative safety. I must send him to the USA. Why didn't I do so ages ago? . . . The govt depts are

1 French for 'and Co.'

being told that we may be obliged to fight on alone without allies although at the moment the Belgians and the French are still fighting. Winston calls the struggle 'The Battle of the Bulge' and such it is, a huge swollen bulge from Rettel to Sedan . . . . It is all like 1918 again. I am in despair, too about my Nattier:[1] will it be lost, or has Laura taken steps? It was in Seligmann's[2] cellars when I was there at Easter.

Euan Wallace has been [appointed] Regional Commissioner for London: he refused the Office of Works coupled with a peerage as he did not want to leave the House of Commons, and it was felt the appointment must go to a peer. Barbie, his wife, a delightful woman, but unwise in some respects, advised against the peerage. They say she didn't want him on her hands!!

And Jim Thomas, that amiable, deaf viper is to be an assistant whip.

Many conversations with Honor, Alan, Rab and Harold and Princess Olga who leaves tomorrow.

Queen Wilhelmina spoke on the radio last night; she was timid and uninspiring but I was surprised by the youthfulness of her voice. It was, however, very royal!

FRIDAY 17TH MAY

The seriousness of the war news increases and the fears of a French collapse are growing, although there is some little improvement in French morale, or so at least Winston reports, on his return today. But the air services to Paris were all cancelled today and Princess Olga, desperately anxious to get back to Paul at Belgrade, was in a quandary. She rang up and we had a sad, almost tearful farewell: God knows when I shall see her again, if ever . . . . She is afraid that Italy will attack Yugoslavia before she can reach Ljubljana and in her despair (she should, of course, have left a few days ago), she appealed to the King who has lent her his own private plane which flew her to Paris. She catches the same Simplon as I took. I believe Brussels is captured, and most of Belgium. The heads of the govt depts were sent for tonight and told that it could not be certain that France's resistance could be counted upon for more than a fortnight. It is expected that Paris will fall shortly. The Nazis are putting every ounce of their power into this [illegible] offensive and if they fail, which is possible, the war will be won for us.[3] They will then have nothing left: their reserves will have been used up. It is the Gauleiters' last throw – so our experts say, but I am not quite so sure – they are never right.

---

1 A painting by Jean-Marc Nattier that Laura Corrigan had promised to bequeath him and was keeping for him in Paris.

2 The gallery and art dealership founded in 1880 by Jacques Seligmann.

3 This was widely thought possible at the time: memories of the failed German offensive of the spring of 1918 remained fresh – though the German Army in 1940 was not worn down by four years of fighting, had better supply lines, and the Americans were not on their way to France.

I hear that the royal family are distraught over Queen Wilhelmina, who has settled down in the Belgian suite at Buckingham Palace for a long stay. They don't know how to amuse her as she has no friends here and cannot, of course, go out. It means a lugubrious family dinner party every night: she is very stiff and humourless, pathetic and intensely dignified.

The Germans are alleged to have lost 1,000 planes: and we have inflicted immense damage all over the Ruhr area, blown up bridges, munition works, oil stores etc., on a very grandiose scale.

My most astonishing visitor was Mrs Cresswell, who was sent by Queen Marie – she looked well and young and *bien servie:*[1] she wanted my advice: she and the Queen are living with only six servants in a Shakespearean cottage in Bedfordshire.[2] Her Yugoslavian Majesty is very odd, nervous, on the verge of a breakdown; and I asked Mrs Cresswell, who is her mistress, the reason. To my surprise she said: the Queen is having her change of life; she is only 40 and I am surprised. There is more in it than that.

SATURDAY 18TH MAY

I came down to the morning room today and I am definitely recovering. A lovely day . . . and far away in France this terrible battle is going on. I hear that Soissons and Rheims are gone . . . I have decided to send my child to the USA.

Duff spoke extremely well on the radio. There is a tiny lull in the great battle and the havoc we created last night and the night before in Germany is indescribable: fires are still burning in the Ruhr. Air raids are now expected here . . . It is now believed that the war will be over in September – the Germans will either win or be exhausted by this terrific effort which may go on for weeks, weeks of hell and anguish. If only the French can hold out . . . . The new tanks spitting fire caused much alarm but now our forces are getting used to them.

Brussels has been evacuated.

Lloyd George is jubilant by the turn of political events. He told someone the other day that the most disarming trait in Winston's character was his open avowal of treachery; he would boast amiably to the person of his intentions, and later when he had got what he wanted he would rush to his victim – as he does all day to Neville – and show him his spirits, his *quid pro quo* for his treachery. No one can resist such engaging charm, Lloyd George insists. It is a little surprising he was not offered a major job, or decorative sinecure, but even Winston, I suppose, realises how 'gaga' he is. But stranger people have drawn numbers in this mad lottery and it may be years before a Conservative govt comes in again.

---

1 Well served.
2 Actually Huntingdonshire.

SUNDAY 19TH MAY

The war news is slightly better: the Germans have eased their attacks – taking a 'breather' – and the French are putting up a more determined resistance.

Harold B says he doesn't know how far they have advanced, but somewhere south of Rettel. It all looks like 1914 and 1918 all over again. He was very against sending Paul to the USA; he said we should be criticised etc. I don't know what to do, and will probably delay matters for a bit. If the situation becomes too bad I don't see why he shouldn't go ... I have always minded criticism and yet always braved it: I am rarely deterred by it from a course of action I think right. There is a new feeling in the air that perhaps we can check the advance and thus defeat the Germans and crush them.

There is much submerged anti-American feeling at the moment: people think that the USA ought to come to our help. I have come up against it in Harold, in Alan, in my mother-in-law, even in Honor – all over my project of sending Paul there. Alan breezed in more than ever under the influence and spell of his silly, selfish sinister old mother. He spent the day with her and only came back to London at 8 o'clock when he came here. Patsy is at Pyrford where the Iveaghs have assembled their four grandchildren: they are to go to Paignton in case of emergency.

MONDAY 20TH MAY

I lay in bed: Harold B; Rodney Wilkinson, who I fear is becoming a bit of a bore; and Patrick Buchan-Hepburn came to see me. Patrick stayed three hours and was very charming, limited and inhibited. Harold breezed in: he says we shall be bombarded out of existence next week, then Mussolini will enter the war with his twenty submarines and we shall be defeated – the Mediterranean navy will seek refuge in some safe harbour. This may all be true but I am hoping still for a miracle and although the news is worse in that the German advance continues, nevertheless there are encouraging signs – the French are putting more vigour in their defence, the wastage of German aeroplanes is immense, they show some signs of slackening. I don't know .... The position is grave, as Winston himself said last night in his very excellent broadcast. I had a long talk with Diana Cooper, who miserable by the war, really miserable, has done everything possible within her power to bring it about. There is a mental gulf in our country which even war seems unable to budge.

Patrick and I gossiped: his servant threw himself in front of a train and was decapitated. It all came from some petty pilfering for which Patrick ticked him off. A pitiable tale.

The Germans have bombed Dieppe, Calais and are in the neighbourhood of Cambrai and Saint-Quentin and have even penetrated Arras.

Honor sent me up a mass of lovely flowers from Kelvedon which cheered and encouraged me. I lay back *en grand luxe* (for almost the last time?) in expensive *crêpe de Chine* pyjamas, surrounded by flowers and Government Boys and we listened to the bad news.

TUESDAY 21ST MAY

We are still here: I overslept and thus missed the news. The boys rang up; Dr Law looked in and said that I was better and could get up. I did: Honor came up from Kelvedon, and she, Lady Iveagh – looking like a ghost – and I lunched in the glorious lovely Amalienburg . . . . I wish I could get my child to the USA. If anything happens to me, nothing matters . . . And Honor suggested burying my diaries in the garden at Kelvedon. Where else can I put them? It seems incredible to sit in the calm and *luxe* of Belgrave Square and have such fantastic conversations. Perhaps they are unnecessary and we shall survive, even triumph . . . . Honor will not leave Kelvedon for obvious reasons.[1]

My wife after a v fleeting visit returned to Kelvedon. She talks of shooting the dogs. It is all so horrible: why must the world be subjected to such a scourge: . . . as I was writing Lord Iveagh accompanied by huge Alan came in. Alan said that he had been spending the morning attempting to arrange for his brother Francis to be transferred to France from Palestine – I pointed out to him that human folly could hardly stretch further. Signing his death warrant, but Alan blandly replied with that mad vacant look which occasionally comes into his eyes, 'Anyway he would be nearer to my mother!' That vampire would suck back her sons, let them be killed so that they were a mile nearer her hoary old heart. I am beginning to dislike her almost as much as I do Lady Astor, but with less reason. She is the more subtle of the two, and, at least her selfishness and wickedness is [*sic*] confined to her own family circle. The rest of the world leaves her cold, passes her by.

I did not go to the House, feeling too ill. I heard on the radio that both Arras and Amiens have fallen into Germany's hands.

WEDNESDAY 22ND MAY

I got up late, extremely depressed by the outlook, but Honor's appalling gloom on the telephone had the opposite effect and I decided to cheer up. All is not yet lost, even if they have, as Harold told me on the telephone, taken Boulogne. They have won the first round; but Weygand[2] may work a miracle . . . . And on the one o'clock news it was announced that the French have recaptured Arras, so perhaps

---

1 Presumably he refers to what he believes are her farming interests.
2 Maxime Weygand (1867–1965) was Marshal Ferdinand Foch's Chief of Staff during the Great War and although having retired in 1935 was recalled in 1939 and given command of French forces in the Middle East. In May 1940 he was brought back to become Supreme Commander as the Germans crushed the French Army. He worked with Pétain* after the Vichy regime was established but later protested about collaboration; the Germans arrested him in 1942 and he was tried for collaboration after the war, but acquitted.

he has! I thought that the news sounded slightly better. It may be a long struggle, but if the Germans didn't win through immediately they probably never will.

Brigid, looking pretty and gay, is staying with me. Honor prefers to sit broodily in the country. She is becoming increasingly eccentric and despondent and there seems little I can do to help her. Alan too, is dotty: he rushed down to see his mother last night, and came up this morning. If I were Patsy I should make the most unholy row . . . .

There was an air raid over Kent last night, but no damage was done. I heard continual buzzing here, a sinister hum, and I gather it was our planes defending us – but the Boche left us in peace.

The Irish Guards' casualties took place in Norway, not France: it is too early to know about France, except that General Gamelin[1] made a mess of it. There is a rumour that he has committed suicide. And I also hear very privately that Gort has lost his head and does nothing. We have been outmanoeuvred.

THURSDAY 23RD MAY   KELVEDON

We woke, the whole country, in a more cheerful mood: but I had for the first time for many months taken the precaution of sleeping with my gas mask and tank[2] next to my bed. The newspapers seemed more encouraging: but my private information tells me that the situation is definitely worse . . . . I drove here alone in a depressed mood and was almost overcome by the loveliness of Kelvedon which is all rather pointless now, I suppose: seas of azaleas and rhododendrons, white and mauve lilac . . . . The photographer for *Country Life* is much impressed and wants to do a special article with coloured photographs of the garden after the war. He has been here for nearly a week now doing the house and estate and has nearly been arrested several times as he was thought to be a spy.

I slept in the afternoon as I am still very weak: Honor twitted me and said that my gloom was a family joke: I trust it will be no more than that. We had a long talk and decided to bury my diaries in the churchyard. Honor and I slipped to the cellar, where they were kept, whilst the servants were at their supper, and we transferred them into a tin box, where I had kept my Windsor papers . . . . those I put into the safe. Honor and I crept up the staircase – carrying the heavy burden – into her garden, still unseen. We then deposited it in the deserted church where we left it for the night. Then I consulted with Mortimer and he promised to dig a hole tomorrow evening after the labourers and gardeners have gone home. Perhaps some future generation will dig it up!

---

1 Maurice Gamelin (1872–1958) was made head of the General Staff of the French Army in 1931, and was Commander-in-Chief from the outbreak of war in 1939. Blamed for the failure to counter the German invasion, he was replaced by Weygand in May 1940. He did not commit suicide, but was tried for treason by the Vichy regime.
2 Of oxygen.

The news on the radio was grave. Winston announced in the House that Abbeville had fallen and that Boulogne was the scene of a great battle, so my news was correct. It is maddening not to be in the House these momentous days.[1]

'Tom' Mosley[2] has been arrested, and rightly: this should have been done weeks ago. About twenty other of his Fascist henchmen share his fate. More surprising is the committal to Brixton Prison of Captain A. M. Ramsay,[3] an MP whom I know. I had long thought him mad: he is obsessed by the idea of a Jewish–communist conspiracy and has actually unearthed some valuable information. He is, however, hardly sane and I am surprised that the Home Secretary should have thought him sufficiently important – or dangerous – to bother about. He was always as far as I knew, anti-German . . . . But madly anti-Semite.

As I slept in the garden, a roar of planes immediately overhead woke me: and I counted twenty-one huge fighters rushing towards the coast. They were barely over the treetops. The war is at our door.

FRIDAY 24TH MAY

Rose late: the news was about the same. My secretary rang me from London: no cable from Peter; no letter from the bank about Arthur's cheque.[4] I am in a rage and feel frustrated and deserted . . . I went for a walk and on my return found two khaki-ed officers in battledress talking to Honor. One is so suspicious these days that I wondered whether they were German parachutists in disguise. They wanted us to put up 150 men and fifty-five motorcycles: we investigated the stables but they were considered inadequate for so many and they drove off.

It was announced on the radio that Boulogne has been definitely taken by the Germans. The situation is now extremely grave for the Allied armies – but,

---

1 He was still resting under medical advice.

2 Oswald Ernald 'Tom' Mosley (1896–1980) succeeded his father as 6th Bt in 1928. Mosley was Conservative and then Independent MP for Harrow from 1918 to 1924, failed to beat Neville Chamberlain in Birmingham in 1924, but became Labour MP for Smethwick from 1926 to 1931. He then founded his own party and became leader of the British Union of Fascists. His pursuit of fascist doctrine in the 1930s made him in equal parts a figure of fear and ridicule. He was interned during the war with his second wife, Diana Guinness (*née* Mitford, 1910–2003), who had been his mistress, and whom he married in 1936 in Joseph Goebbels' house in Berlin, with Hitler in attendance.

3 Archibald Maule Henry Ramsay (1894–1955) was Conservative MP for Peebles and South Midlothian from 1931 to 1945. A virulent anti-Semite, obsessed by the idea that the press was controlled by Jews, he was the only MP interned under the defence regulations during the war. He had attacked the internment regulations but was a critic of Mosley. An attempt to be released on the grounds that his arrest breached parliamentary privilege failed; he sued the *New York Times* for libel in 1941 after it accused him of treasonable behaviour. The paper could not prove it, but Ramsay was awarded a farthing's damages. He remained in detention until 1944.

4 The continuing saga of the £650 Arthur Hope owed him.

I should have thought, equally so for the invading Germans, as at one point our two armies are only twenty-five miles apart. Possibly General Weygand will make some swift move to attempt to cut off the spearhead of the German movement. If not, are we lost? There is still the fleet, and still France . . . I foresee weary weeks now of waiting, and victory pushed into the remote background. It was madness ever to have become engaged in this war . . . .

Neville seems to have made his exit just in time: otherwise he would now be blamed for this collapse. I suppose the fleet will protect us from invasion; but who knows? Eire may be used as a jumping-off ground. We cannot patrol the whole coast and the Mediterranean as well. We appear to be doomed, but the unexpected may yet happen to save this island and Empire.

Honor, magnificently dressed and bejewelled, set off for Southend to take my place at a political meeting in the Elm Hotel: I was supposed to have addressed it but Dr Law would not hear of it, and Honor sweetly deputised for me. I am wondering whether to bury my *bibelots* and jewels – the few that remain here – later this was done. Two tin boxes were put three feet below the earth's surface in the little churchyard under a tree near the brick wall – the west wall which divides the churchyard from Honor's private garden. They were put in about the only spot which could not be seen from the house. The larger, lower box contains my diaries for the British Museum, the smaller box my best *bibelots*, watches, Fabergé *objets* etc. Mortimer, who dug the hole, is discreet and he waited until all the gardeners had gone home. At 6.30 I crept out by arrangement and saw the earth cover them over. May they sleep in peace: Mother Earth must hold other secrets in her bosom.

Honor and I then drove into Ongar to the King's Head, the pub which has been taken over by the military. We had drinks with the officers, and amongst them were several we know slightly . . . They all seemed to think that there was something wrong somewhere and that our abandonment of Boulogne was a colossal mistake and misfortune. They seemed uneasy of our leadership. Has Gort really lost his head?

The evening news was no better and we went to bed depressed: I was very weak and could hardly walk as far as my room. I have overtaxed my strength today.

It seemed so queer to find little Ongar seething with uniforms, with mechanical units, soldiers strolling and smoking under the trees, girls leaning along the railings talking to them; every other person in khaki.

SATURDAY 25TH MAY

The newspapers are bewildering; they hint that Calais has been occupied and at the same time deny, according to the French reports . . . that Boulogne has been captured. No one now knows what to believe. Possibly Weygand will save the situation. Hitler has announced that he will declare peace and victory on August 15th and make new arrangements for the distribution of Europe.

I had a very charming letter this morning from Neville Chamberlain in which he thanked me for all I had done for him; I was much touched. My temperature however rose again and I stayed in bed until luncheon time. There were minor raids last night and bombs fell in Essex, in the North Riding and in Kent. Shall we have to live like this for months to come? If only America would rush now to our rescue. The 'military' yesterday think that Dover and Folkestone will be bombed out of existence any day now. Very probably . . . I am longing to return to my work and my routine life.

Honor rang up the Norman family and asked for news of Fritzi: Guy Norman[1] saw him for a flash at an internment camp and he seemed contented and well. It is sad to think of an ex-playfellow treated as a leper and a prisoner.

There is really no news; the whole outcome of the battle seems confused and uncertain.

SUNDAY 26TH MAY

One sleeps now oddly: I awoke in time for the midnight news, and then again for the seven o'clock bulletin. On neither was there any concrete news; but the newspapers this morning are more encouraging.

Harold B came; naturally buoyant and of an optimistic nature, he is dejected and fears that we shall have a very severe grilling or even worse during the next few weeks. He looked worn, almost haggard. Rab rang up, and concurs; but is confident, he says, of ultimate triumph.

MONDAY 27TH MAY

I motored up to London and the effort involved nearly killed me: I am exhausted.

The war news seems a trifle better, or at least, no worse. The German advance has been slowed down.

My bankers tell me that Arthur Hope's famous cheque has finally been cashed. Many letters, nothing from Peter. Alan rang up. I am retiring to bed.

TUESDAY 28TH MAY

It was announced at 8.30 on the radio by Paul Reynaud that King Leopold[2] had treacherously, so it seems, sold the pass to the invaders. He made peace with

---

1 I have been unable to trace this member of the Norman family.
2 Léopold Philippe Charles Albert Meinrad Hubert Marie Michel of Saxe-Coburg and Gotha (1901–83) was Duke of Brabant from 1909 until he succeeded his father, Albert I, as King Leopold III of the Belgians. His surrender of Belgian forces to the Germans was done without seeking ministerial advice and caused outrage in his own country, France and Britain. He was a prisoner of the Germans for much of the war and a regency was formed under his brother, Prince Charles, from 1944. His attempt to resume the throne in 1950 was met by a general strike, and in 1951 he abdicated in favour of his 20-year-old son, Baudouin.

Germany without informing either the French or English Allies and at four this morning the Belgians ceased fighting. The news had a numbing effect on London and came like a thunderbolt – but to me it was no news. I have always known that he was Wittelsbach in mind, vague, and unreliable; and his sentiments were always at least pro-German, if not pro-Nazi. But why did he ask for our help? Everyone seems dumbfounded by the blow which is a serious one for the Allied cause.

Then to the Foreign Office where everyone seemed pleased by my return. I slept for two hours at the H of Commons and then paraded for duty. Winston bowed his little grave bow which he keeps for people who are not his favourites; he was being bear-led by Brendan. The front bench resembled a nightmare one might have had a month ago; perhaps one will get used to it.

Long talk with Walter Buccleuch at the H of Lords: he tried to prevent the catastrophe of the war, the horrors and humiliations which we are now to endure: and his only reward is to be reviled by the unthinking.

WEDNESDAY 29TH MAY

The news gets gradually worse; but my mother-in-law shows no signs of moving her grandchildren and I have not the energy to interfere – for nowhere in England can really be called safe. Our troops are behaving magnificently in the face of superhuman odds and are retreating in an orderly manner. The Belgians' desertion is a grave blow and the manner of its delivery incredibly treacherous. Probably next week some move will be made towards the invasion of this country.

Then I went to the House of Commons; there was some amusement over Harold Macmillan's so very obvious enjoyment of his position;[1] he rushed frenziedly about.

I think there is a definite plot afoot headed by Winston, and perhaps Max Beaverbrook, to oust Halifax, and all the gentlemen of England from the govt, and even from the House of Commons. They hope to have a long reign of adventurers and traditionless middle [illegible] arrivistes like themselves. Sam warned Rab of this scheme only yesterday – today Sam left to be our Ambassador in Spain . . . . Already the Socialists have won a bloodless victory: they have attained almost their every aim in the course of a fortnight. They might now win the war.

Honor came up, had her hair done, bought a new dress and generally titivated herself as she only does when she is being admired: I drove her to the Brownlows where she said she was dining. Alan, however, told me that she was dining with Richard Temple at the Dorchester who has a party for her. What a curious tale: and why should she lie about it? She is always so transparent: it is obvious that that lecherous old man makes up to her, just as he used to do to Peter . . . . The world,

---

1 He had been appointed Parliamentary Secretary to the Ministry of Supply, his first ministerial job.

my world is becoming impossible, is collapsing like a house of cards. Life will soon not be worth living, or loving: I am making all my arrangements.

France is wobbly: there is always the danger of a separate peace since she never wanted the war, and was only dragged in by us, and we were led, or rather gulled by our extremists like Winston . . . . who has really destroyed our system and imperilled our independence . . . .

Will the blow fall next week? The Regent writes me that he fears so. I fear I am like Louis XVI: I, at least, see the gathering perils and surprisingly I sit back and do nothing drastic for the welfare of my adored son, nor for minor matters such as my precious possessions.

THURSDAY 30TH MAY

The war news is increasingly ominous from the point of view of the Allies. And Italy has rather jauntily announced that she will enter the war very shortly now. The English in Flanders are being pushed back to the sea.

I went to the H of Commons: we are now obliged to produce our passes. There was considerable indignation with silly old Roger Keyes, who has stoutly championed the King of the Belgians: I saw him surrounded by a group of jeering MPs. And the Lord William Scott[1] is also being much criticised as he spreads defeatist rumours and that we shall not retrieve our men in France. The French Embassy has complained about him.

To my surprise I saw Edward Rice[2] having tea with Maxton and I joined them on the terrace. What nefarious plot was this? I suspect a pro-peace conspiracy. Maxton wittily remarked that the Chamberlain govt was turned out for getting our men from Norway without loss: would this govt reign in perpetuity for having not got our men safely back from Flanders?

Nicky of Romania[3] rang up and invited himself to dine: I said I was delighted, but still ill – which I am, mysteriously and weakly ill and wobbly – and hinted that if he came, would he leave early. He came: drank and talked too much and stayed until 1.15 a.m. I was exhausted and finally turned him slightly ungraciously out,

1 William Walter Montagu Douglas Scott (1896–1958), Lord William by courtesy from 1914, was the second son of the 7th Duke of Buccleuch and Unionist MP for Roxburgh and Selkirk from 1935 to 1950. He fought in the war and rose to the rank of lieutenant colonel.

2 Edward Denis Rice (1899–1973), married in 1927 Marcella Duggan, daughter of Lady Curzon (qv).

3 Prince Nicholas of Hohenzollern-Sigmaringen (1903–78) was second son of King Ferdinand and Queen Marie of Romania, and an officer in the Royal Navy. He became Regent of Romania after his father's death in 1927 until 1930, though fell out with his elder brother, King Carol II, who exiled him from the Romanian court and stripped him of his titles in 1930 because he disapproved of his marriage to a divorcee: an act of stunning hypocrisy, since Carol himself had earlier (and temporarily) had to renounce the throne over his own adultery (see Vol. I, entry for 23 April 1935).

but he, fortunately too drunk to notice, and accompanied by Hector Bolitho, left for Claridge's. For three hours he talked against King Carol his brother, warned me that he was another Leopold, or worse; insisted that he, Nicky, would be a suitable candidate for the Belgian throne, and went on to say that in the event of Carol ever making peace with the Nazis, he Nicky would head the Allied movement in Romania and lead it to victory . . . .

A cable came from Peter at last: he is in hospital, has had a serious relapse, and is low, dispirited and suffers apparently from my disease – streptococcal fever. A curious coincidence.

FRIDAY 31ST MAY

It is now increasingly obvious that Italy will declare war next week: but it is a war with the gloves on, for the relations between Percy Loraine[1] and Ciano are still excellent . . . .

I rested the whole afternoon: Alan came to dine with me and we talked until midnight. He was very sweet and rather frightened by the appalling prospect of joining the RNVR[2] next week . . . . I shall miss him. If he comes out alive the months of training may sober him and cool and calm his passionate judgement, or rather lack of judgement. He is still madly, insanely, diseasedly in love with that grey hen of a mother.

Sir John Reith came in this morning to the office. A Dracula of a man, seven feet tall,[3] distinguished in dress and appearance, he is naturally shy, and suspicious of the Londoner: he told me he was lonely, praised me to Rab; said he wished he had a PPS like me. He was shocked and disillusioned by Quisling Tree's outrageous action in voting against the govt.

The retreat of our troops from France has been little short of a miracle.[4] Up to this morning 151-odd thousands had been rescued. There must be another 100,000 or nearly. As usual the Guards are bearing the brunt of the attack and the casualty lists, once they are made public, will make distressing reading. But the Germans have lost nearly half a million. 'Lou' of Hesse, or Grand Duke, as he has been since 'Doris's' tragic death in an aeroplane, has also died or been killed.[5] The whole Hesse family have now been wiped out. How right I was when I described them as ill-fated, and chosen by destiny. Of that house party at Wolfgarten only Honor and I and Miss Geddes (later Lou's bride) the three English are the only survivors: the Grand Duke; Grand Duchess; Don, and Princess Cécile [sic] and their three children, and now Lou – all gone, the whole family has been wiped

1 Britain's Ambassador in Rome.
2 Royal Naval Volunteer Reserve.
3 He was six feet six inches.
4 He refers to the Dunkirk evacuation.
5 Reports of the death of Louis, Grand Duke of Hesse, were exaggerated. He lived until 1968.

Chips telephoning to someone – or being telephoned to – in Belgrave Square, June 1943.

The Amalienburg Room and Library at 5 Belgrave Square, London.

Neville Chamberlain and Lord Halifax return
from appeasing Hitler.

Sir Nevile Henderson raises his
but not his game.

Sir Samuel Hoare, 'Soapy Sam'.

Rab Butler, the appeaser
who survived – just.

Winston Churchill and Anthony Eden,
mongering war.

Duff 'Turkey Cock' Cooper
and Lady Diana.

Winston's back – in Downing Street, May 1940.

Lady Honor Channon with Paul, aged nearly 4,
on the day war broke out – 3 September 1939.

Paul in Central Park, New York,
with 'Nannie', May 1942.

Lady Brigid Guinness and Honor in the Alps, 1939.

Alan Lennox-Boyd (standing second left) at his wedding to Lady Patricia 'Patsy' Guinness, December 1938.

The Earl and Countess of Iveagh in Coronation robes, May 1937.

Simon Lennox-Boyd's christening, February 1940. Lady Patricia is holding the baby, with Lady Iveagh to the right of her. Standing are (left to right): Alan Lennox-Boyd, Godfather Chips, Lord Iveagh and Patrick Buchan-Hepburn.

Chips and Lady Cunard, in one of
her lighter moments.

Harold Balfour attends to some paperwork.

Lady Pamela Berry,
keeping up appearances.

Viscount and Viscountess Duncannon,
taking it easy.

Sir John Simon, a man with no friends.

Sir Miles Lampson, genial proconsul.

Leslie Hore-Belisha: anti-Semitism
did not begin at Calais.

Lord Beaverbrook, a finger in every pie.

Rab outside
5 Belgrave Square
the day after it was
bombed,
7 November 1940.

The House of Commons takes a direct hit, 10 May 1941.

out. Don, for a brief few months, Grand Duke, was the most charming mortal I have almost ever met.[1]

Long letter from Fritzi in the internment camp, and he asked for many things, mostly food, which I have sent to him at once.

SATURDAY 1ST JUNE

I drove to Kelvedon and arrived exhausted.

I cannot get well; and the war horizon which darkens daily is too discouraging. The political news, whilst of lesser importance, is not satisfactory. Anthony Eden is playing a deep game to capture the Premiership and is responsible for the *dégommage*[2] of both Sam Hoare and Oliver Stanley, whom he looked upon as future potential rivals. Anthony wants to kill them all off politically and thus clear the decks for his own reign. I will thwart him . . . somehow.

SUNDAY 2ND JUNE

A glorious blue day . . . . I motored up early from Kelvedon to the Foreign Office to be 'on guard' for Rab. The newspapers were sensational and despairing; and the secret telegrams little better. General conflagration in the Balkans; Italy's entry into the war; even Spanish intrigues . . . . everything conspiring against us. The numbers of the rescued from Flanders is now 237[,000]-odd, and this great retreat, magnificently carried out against overwhelming odds, is an heroic feat and a relief to the whole country which is proud of its troops . . . . But how, or why our attempt to turn it into a victory, is a mystery to me. We are in an appalling position, that I foresaw last summer when I worked so hard and unavailingly even to the last moment to stave off the war . . . . The elaborate, almost elegant arrangements for the declaration of war between England and Italy are bewildering. The Italians are courteous, calm about it and offer Percy Loraine every facility for his comfort and convenience. His cordial conversations with Ciano continue.

I am all day at the Office. Rab is in Essex and I rang him up to give him the news. Halifax went to see the Duchess of Northumberland[3] and condole with her, and then lunched at Eton. The War Cabinet met at five, and he was back for that. The general atmosphere of the office is fairly calm; but everyone

---

1 Louis' mother, elder brother Prince Georg Donatus ('Don'), Princess Cecilie and their two sons were among those killed in a plane crash in 1937 on the way to Louis' wedding to Margaret Geddes. See Vol. I, entries for 13 May 1937 and footnote; 10 August 1937 and footnote; and 16 November 1937 and footnote.
2 Dismissal or removal.
3 Halifax was seeing Helen, Dowager Duchess of Northumberland, widow of the 8th Duke, whose son, the 9th Duke (qv), had been killed in France.

agrees that Paris will be the next German objective, either before, or subsequent to a peace offer. An offer which Winston will not consider! Then hell will be let loose . . . . I wonder as I gaze out upon the grey and green Horse Guards Parade with the blue sky, the huge silver balloons like bowing elephants, the barbed-wire entanglements and soldiers about, is it really the end of England? Are we witnessing, as for so long I have feared, the decline, the decay and perhaps extinction of the great island people? As I write the War Cabinet is meeting opposite, and other people are hastening about: I just saw David Margesson go into No. 12 [Downing Street]. Attlee and Greenwood, now high up in the Councils of the country, are as responsible for the war as anyone: they were bellicose, torpedoed appeasement and hampered rearmament. A more insane policy could not be imagined. And Neville, always right, is temporarily eclipsed, but he will be vindicated by History.

Long chat here with Sir Horace Seymour[1] whom I suddenly liked: I had always thought him hostile. I saw a copy of a letter from Roosevelt to the King which began 'My dear King George' and is signed 'yours faithfully, Franklin D. Roosevelt'.

Eden on the radio was uninspiring.

Much talk at the Office as to whether Cairo, in the event of Italy entering the war, should be declared an open town.

MONDAY 3RD JUNE

A longish day. I to the office; the news from Italy is still baffling: there are faint rays of hope she will not come in.

Sam Hoare's *frais de représentation*[2] are £8,000 a year as special ambassador in Madrid. This is a ramp.[3] I am delighted: his foolish predecessor, Sir Maurice Peterson, got only £6,500 including salary which was subject to tax. Sam has already assumed control in Spain.

I hear that Sir Horace Wilson is still powerful; he evidently 'eminces'[4] behind Neville, and has considerable influence at the Treasury, although Winston cannot abide him and does not consult him.

---

1 Horace James Seymour (1885–1978) was Assistant Under-Secretary of State at the Foreign Office from 1939, when he was knighted, to 1942. He had joined the Diplomatic Service in 1908 and from 1932 to 1936 had been principal private secretary to the Foreign Secretary. He was British Minister in Tehran from 1936 to 1939 and British Ambassador to China from 1942 to 1946.
2 Entertainment allowance.
3 That is, a substantial increase.
4 A verb Channon has invented from the noun 'eminence', which was how Wilson's position had been seen.

Mrs Coats[1] was coming to lunch with me but 'chucked' as her sailor son suddenly appeared from Dunkirk, worn out and weary. All our troops are now home, a most gallant withdrawal: something like 250,000 men saved. Many have been killed including John Erne:[2] he was a likeable fellow, gay but dull, handsome and uninteresting. Davina was alleged to be bored with him and flirted mildly with Anthony Eden, who is a very innocent swain, a sort of St Valentine lover. I liked John – all Crichtons have charm.

Ian Farquhar[3] came into my room at the office with a large packet which came in the bag from Princess Olga. He asked me to open it – a new precaution! It contained only a huge letter for the Duchess of Kent. Later I delivered it to the Palace and met the Halifaxes in the Palace Yard. He stopped to gossip. They were on their way to call on Queen Wilhelmina. As I walked away I reflected on Halifax's extraordinary character: his high principles, his engaging charm and grand manner (though he frightens people into fits, me sometimes), his snobbishness; his worship of titles and high position; his eel-like qualities and above all his sublime treachery which is never deliberate, always, to him, a necessity in a situation. Means are nothing to him, only ends. He is enchanting, flirtatious, but not loveable. He didn't become Prime Minister because he was shrewd enough to realise the intense perils of the position, and that he could not carry it off . . . yet he is largely to blame for the appalling turn of events, since the mad Polish guarantee was his child. At the time Rab wanted to resign as a protest, and I persuaded him that it means so little to be right and that he should stay on. I didn't regret doing so . . . . Rab and I had a talk, too, and agreed that we should be better advised to become reconciled with the Eden element, even become part of it, and later, to torpedo them when the occasion arose, if expedient to do so. There is a natural cleavage that would prevent our ever being firm allies.

I slept for an hour, worn out: and then dressed in my green velvet. Rodney Wilkinson, that dark *charmeur* and Hector Bolitho dined with me and we all

1 Audrey Evelyn James (1902–68) was believed to be the illegitimate daughter of Sir Edward Grey, later 1st Viscount Grey of Fallodon; and, through her mother, the illegitimate grand-daughter of King Edward VII. In 1922 she married Captain Muir Dudley Coats MC (1897–1927) of the Scots Guards. Having been widowed she married in 1930 Marshall James Field (1893–1956), an American department-store heir, investment banker and newspaper proprietor. They divorced in 1934. In 1938, she married Peter Pleydell-Bouverie. They divorced in 1946. She is referred to variously in the diaries as Mrs Coats, Audrey Field, and Audrey Bouverie. She was not the mother of Channon's friend Peter Coats, though had a son of that name.

2 John Henry George Crichton (1907–40) was for a month in 1914 Viscount Crichton by courtesy after his father was killed in action in Flanders; he then succeeded his grandfather as 5th Earl of Erne. He had been a professional soldier before becoming a Lord in Waiting from 1936 to 1939. Rejoining his regiment, he was killed in action in France on 23 May 1940. He married, in 1931, Lady Davidema 'Davina' Bulwer-Lytton (1909–95), daughter of the 2nd Earl of Lytton (qv).

3 This junior official is probably Ian Rupert Farquhar (1918-2003), whose father was Sir Harold Farquhar, a career diplomat who later became Ambassador to Sweden. The son would soon be commissioned into the Grenadier Guards and retire at the end of the war in the rank of major.

talked and drank too much. Alan joined us and soon he led Hector away leaving me alone with Rodney, who stayed until 1 a.m. I gave him a cigarette case as a parting present: tomorrow he rejoins the Air Force and will soon have his own squadron. Probably he will be killed.[1]

Paris was bombed at noon today. Duff Cooper gave a most ridiculous account of it over the radio – one cannot tune in without hearing him – in which he overstressed the luxury of the banquet he was attending.

A long, charming, witty letter from Peter who is still ill; he is soon to leave for Beirut to stay for a fortnight with the Ali Khans. In ordinary times he would have had a month's leave at home but communications are now too difficult. I am anxious lest his prolonged illness should force General Wavell to appoint another ADC in Peter's place.

I hear that Brendan Bracken is to be made a Privy Counsellor in the honours list:[2] it is almost incredible that Winston could carry favouritism so far – a most undignified action; but I should be pleased for Brendan's sake. Vansittart is one of the other new ones.

TUESDAY 4TH JUNE

I woke feeling so ill and old! Probably it was partly due to overindulgence at the table last night. I walked to the FO. Much talk about Italy and her intentions: it is thought now that she will not invade Yugoslavia. And Paul has had his infant daughter sent back to Belgrade; the King sent her as far as Paris in his private plane: there Queen Marie's private car will take the child to Belgrade. If Italy comes in, it will be 'by the big door' and she will attack the Allies. The Yugoslav Minister rushed up to me in the House of Commons and whispered that Maisky, the Russian Ambassador, had confided in him that it was his private opinion that Italy had no real intention of entering the war. That she was bluffing and punishing us for sanctions!

I slept for an hour at the House and then resumed my duties. Rab had several ticklish questions and cleverly contrived not to be drawn over the amount of Sam Hoare's *frais de représentation* in Madrid; nor did it get out that a private aeroplane had been chartered by the govt to send him and Lady Maud to Spain.

The Prime Minister made an important and moving statement.[3] I sat behind him (he was next to Neville who looked tiny and fragile). Winston was eloquent, oratorical and used magnificent English: several of the Labour members cried. But,

---

1 Regrettably, he was.
2 He was to be Churchill's parliamentary private secretary, but the recognition was unusual nonetheless.
3 In which he reflected on the miracle of Dunkirk, the need to take action against fifth columnists through internment, and the danger of invasion, including the peroration that 'we shall go on to the end ... we shall defend our island, whatever the cost may be. We shall fight on the beaches, we shall fight on the landing grounds, we shall fight in the fields and in the streets, we shall fight in the hills; we shall never surrender.'

whilst recognising a fine performance, he didn't move me. And I wondered whether it was a wise statement, for he hinted that we might be obliged to fight alone, without France, and that England might well be invaded. It is a very different atmosphere that reigns now! Only a few weeks ago idiotic MPs talked academic nonsense about our restoring independence to Warsaw and Prague. Is all England mad? I often seriously think so. Only Neville is the leader of the sane; and now there is a movement to blame him for the inadequacy of our supplies. I am beginning to be glad that he is no longer responsible for the conduct of affairs. How blamed he would be!

I saw David Margesson come out of the PM's room with him and overheard him complimenting him on his speech. David is digging himself well in with the new regime; but I don't think it is so to his taste as was the Chamberlain govt. His authority has been slightly shaken, but he is recovering it. Rab is worried about his political future and fortunes. He lunched with Alan at the Marlborough and came back unsettled.

I must get my child out of this country somehow. There is a short pause in the terrific fighting; but it cannot last. [Le] Havre was heavily bombarded – naturally, as it is the last remaining port for us to use in sending help to France. Also the French have bombarded Munich – not, I hope, the Amalienburg.

The Italian meeting has passed and no declaration of war.

The Sitwells are in London and asked me to dine and go to a film but I refused. I am having one of my quiet evenings which I relish and need. Peter, I suppose, is speeding towards Syria.

I told (and I felt like a lying Judas) Jim Thomas that I thought Anthony quite excellent on the radio. Later Anthony smiled at me and I knew that Jim had repeated my remarks. It is a very feminine coterie . . . . Jock Colville tells me that the Admiralty is fantastic now: people who were at each other's throats a few weeks ago are now intimate and on the best of terms. Winston darts in and out, a mountain of energy and good nature. The Labour leaders, Brendan Bracken and Prof. Lindemann,[1] sometimes Randolph, Beaverbrook, the Defence ministers etc. – the new racket – but no Neville and no Horace Wilson.

WEDNESDAY 5TH JUNE

The real news today is that the new offensive began in the early hours of the morning when a terrific attack was launched against the French. Will they hold

1 Frederick Alexander Lindemann (1886–1957) was an Oxford physicist (and, from 1919, professor) who became Churchill's principal scientific adviser. German in origin, his family had emigrated to Britain in 1871. Lindemann saw Churchill virtually daily during the war and had enormous influence over him. He was especially influential on matters such as strategic bombing and radar, and far from infallible. In 1941 he was raised to the peerage as 1st Baron Cherwell and joined the government as Paymaster-General in 1942, serving until 1945. He served in the office again, with Cabinet rank, from 1951 to 1953, and was advanced to a viscountcy in 1956.

out, or will the Germans be in Paris in, say, a fortnight from tonight? They have already broken through near Péronne.

Neville has had it out with Winston; he told him that he was aware of the recent intrigues and was prepared to resign: Winston must stand by him, take a firm line or allow him to go: he was prepared for either course. Winston assured him that his services were necessary to the present govt and that he would see to it that the plots ceased – Dunglass told me this.

THURSDAY 6TH JUNE

The Frogs are withstanding the attack which is violent: it may become more violent still. People, particularly in the defeatist Foreign Office, are openly betting that Paris will be taken within a fortnight.

I was on duty as PPS to Winston, Brendan being away. It is fantastic, the turn of the wheel! He was, however, agreeable, and easier in his manner – without, however, the great dignity of Neville. 'Have you two minutes, Chips?' he asked as he arrived. 'Yes,' I answered, and he went at once to the PM's private lavatory in his rooms. There were interesting Questions. And one was no doubt aimed at me – 'a grave indiscretion of an important member of the govt, harbouring a German guest?' I stood blandly behind the Chair pretending not to understand and barely brazened it out. After Questions I hung about the lobby in the hopes of catching the Chief Whip, and, this, I ultimately did. He took me into his private sanctum and there we gossiped for half an hour and I told him that Arthur Hope had repaid me; of my good relations with the new govt; of Rab's disgust at the cabal against Chamberlain. David reassured me on this last point and said that he had squashed this feeling, that both Winston and the Labour leaders agreed to be loyal to Neville etc. David, who is always wise and far-sighted, gave me excellent advice and also urged me to evacuate Paul to the USA ...

I gather that the men we saw at Ongar, Queen Victoria's Rifles, were suddenly dispatched to Dunkirk at barely an hour's notice and have been mostly all killed! Mown down. They were the victims. The whole rescue is epic, a tale of such heroism as has hardly ever been known in History.

A sad letter from the Regent hinting that communication will be severed between us from now on since Italy will probably come into the war! It may be years before we meet, if ever, again!

FRIDAY 7TH JUNE

Alan rushed in to see me before I was dressed to say 'goodbye'; he was *en route* for Hove[1] and seemed downhearted. His hair was cut like a convict's.

---

1 To begin his naval training.

I am disturbed about the news: can the French hold out, or will they accept a separate peace? And then what of England. There is a little friction between the two General Staffs. And the news from Egypt, as Peter long ago warned me, is far from reassuring. Italian propaganda has been as efficacious there as German has been in France during recent months.

I signed a codicil to my will in favour of Harold B, and Peter. If the system survives my child will be so colossally rich that he will not miss these few thousands.

SATURDAY 8TH JUNE

Alan rang me up in the wee hours to report on his first few hours at Hove: he seemed happy, says some of his fellow 'smellies' are publicans from Southend who admire me! He was treated well, with the respect due to an ex-minister. There is no beating of anyone, which seems a pity. It would have done that huge dear Alan much good.

I was on duty at the office; the radio reported fairly favourable news but I am weary, unhappy, and alarmed – and every telegram, every govt paper seemed to point to an ignominious defeat. The French might throw up the sponge! Italy still on the verge of coming in and certainly blackmailing us! Egypt wobbly, even considering neutrality! Franco and Spain not too certain! A combination of horror. These are, indeed, the dark days.

There is a corps of Defence Volunteers recruited from the staff of the Foreign Office to guard the building; every night they are on duty in shifts; last night they were searching the innumerable rooms and poking every sofa, they went into the Sec of State's room, the long one overlooking the Park. Someone jabbed the sofa and was startled by a piercing feminine scream. The surprised warden flashed his torch and found a couple reclining in flagrante delicto on Lord Halifax's private sofa: 'What are you doing?' he shouted. The question was superfluous as it was quite evident what they were doing. The culprits were a young typist and a young man in the cypher department. One wonders how long this affair has been going on? Surely such a thing has never happened in that room before – or perhaps I am wrong.

SUNDAY 9TH JUNE   *PYRFORD*

All night planes rushed past the house and it was almost like being at the Front. The news is worse.

To my relief and surprise I found the Iveaghs quite amenable to sending Paul abroad, anywhere, preferably to the USA. We practically decided to do so and then curiously the desire to do so died within me: I couldn't bear to be parted from him for so long . . .

Honor and I motored up to London and she left for Kelvedon. It is now decided to send the young man to New York: but the complications suddenly seem immense and I am almost regretting the decision.

My mother-in-law was divine, and so understanding. She is a very great woman: one of the finest and most intelligent I have ever met. She saw how upset I was about Paul, kissed me tenderly as I left – and I burst into tears. She is more affectionate than Honor, gentler .... She assured me that all would be well: that my child – whose welfare is all I care for – would survive happily.

MONDAY 10TH JUNE

The clouds are gathering .... The Germans are drawing nearer to Paris and Hitler's proud boast that he would be in the French capital on the 15th appears to be more than likely ...

All day I rushed about frantically trying to get papers etc. for Paul to go to the States: owing to a tightening up of the US regulations it is now difficult; indeed the complications seem almost insuperable. Still I shall proceed ....

This afternoon I was told that Mussolini would declare war at 6 p.m. One could hardly believe the rumour as he has threatened for so long. When the hour came we sat about the radio in the FO, listening; his voice was recognisable but owing to bad transmission it was difficult to understand. But it was war – war from tomorrow! And our Ambassador and the French emissary have been so informed. Appalling complications in the Mediterranean. I am now cut off from my Paul reigning still – by the skin of his teeth – in Belgrade; and how will Peter be affected? Shall I never see him again? He is recuperating in Lebanon. Now his armies will spring into action .... May he be saved.

Will England survive: triumph? capitulate? be annihilated? I don't know. Duff Cooper made a very fiery, tactless broadcast taunting Italians with Caporetto:[1] in other words rallying all moderate Italians around their leader.

I gathered at the Passport Office and at the American Embassy that there are masses of people trying to bolt to the US. Hundreds!

A typist came into my room about 4.45 with a message for Sir Orme Sargent who was with Rab in the adjoining room: 'Will you tell Sir Orme that Italy is declaring war at six o'clock?' she said. 'How do you know?' I asked. 'The Italian Embassy have been telling foreign journalists all afternoon,' she replied. I could scarcely believe my ears; but she proved right. Possibly if the Chamberlain govt had remained in power Mussolini might have stayed his hand; but he knew he could expect very little from a govt which is headed by many anti-Italians: this may have been enough – and I personally think it was – to turn the scales. There

---

1 Italy's humiliating defeat, and retreat, in October–November 1917.

may be, I am told, internal developments in Italy. How is my old pal, Prince Umberto,[1] tonight?

The King of Norway (and, so I hope in support Michael Rose) arrives in London this evening. Narvik has been abandoned.

TUESDAY 11TH JUNE

A wretched day: I am a cauldron of acid, a mass of nerves . . . I snapped at everyone . . . it is the long strain.

War began with Italy but until now I have not heard of any actual events of a war-like nature. Bastianini actually called at the Foreign Office: Halifax refused to see him but he was received by Alec Cadogan who listened to his complaints that Italians were being arrested and maltreated and then he told the Ambassador in icy terms what he thought of Mussolini.

This afternoon the Emperor Haile Selassie[2] came to Belgrave Square to tea: it was a v secret meeting arranged for him to meet Rab. Philip Noel-Baker[3] was also here. I met the Emperor at the door, and he entered gravely wearing a bowler hat and the famous cape. He has dignity . . . . He was attended by a very darkish individual who is his personal secretary . . . . I escorted Haile Selassie into the morning room – how many kings and queens have been thus led in – presented Rab, and Noel-Baker and left them to their own devices . . . later I returned to the house where I waited for Michael Rose, whom I had seen earlier in the day . . . . he got back from Norway last night after incredible adventures.

I spent the early evening alone, but Honor rang twice. She has been v sweet . . . . I am tormented by anxiety over my infant and the difficulties and sadness of sending him away, even to America, are overwhelming and have given me indigestion. The war news is slightly better: the Frogs are fighting valiantly against huge odds.

The H of Commons, so largely responsible for the war, was crowded; it was disappointed when the news got out that Attlee would speak instead of Churchill. Actually he did quite well; but his unemotional, crisp little voice is never pleasing

---

1 Umberto Nicola Tommaso Giovanni Maria di Savoia (1904–83), Prince of Piedmont, became King Umberto II in June 1946 after his father's abdication but reigned for only thirty-four days until a referendum declared Italy a republic.

2 Tafari Makonnen (1892–1975), Regent of Ethiopia from 1916 to 1930, reigned as Emperor Haile Selassie of Ethiopia from 1930 to 1974.

3 Philip John Baker (1889–1982) had been an academic at Oxford and Cambridge, and had been instrumental in the formation of the League of Nations. He was Labour MP for Coventry from 1929 to 1931, and sat for Derby from 1936 to 1950 and for Derby South from 1950 to 1970, holding office in Attlee's government. He hyphenated his name with his wife's on marrying Irene Noel in 1915, thereafter being known as Philip Noel-Baker. He was raised to the peerage in 1977 as Baron Noel-Baker (life peer).

nor inspiring . . . . There are still rumblings of a political cabal, probably an anti-Chamberlain plot.

Somehow I am more encouraged tonight without any good reason. Hitler said he would be in Paris on the 15th – in four days' time . . . . what has happened to Laura Corrigan? Will she have fled the capital, or remained? I imagine she will see it out in the Place Vendôme; she has a stout heart.

Alan L-B came in to see me just as I was going to bed: he was thinner, more handsome and altogether improved by his days in training. He was charming too; but resented my remarks about the antiquated parliamentary system. How can we fight a tank with a sedan chair?

WEDNESDAY 12TH JUNE

I went to see Leslie Belisha this morning and we walked for over an hour in the Park: it was a lovely morning but the people basking in the sun looked unhappy. No wonder. Possibly in a fortnight's time it will be no longer possible to sit on a bench in St James's Park and watch the ducks . . . Leslie gave me his views on the political situation; he thinks this govt worse than its predecessor (because he was not included in it?); he regrets that he voted against Neville and I rubbed that in. I told him that Chamberlain had been his staunchest supporter and we discussed the whole saga of his fall . . . He was interested, riveted even by what I told him; and he told me a few things about Alec Hardinge, 'the Black Rat'. Just the day before the King went to France last December Leslie was summoned to the Palace, where he was in audience for over an hour with the King, who then invited him to stay to tea. They were joined by the Queen and dogs and the atmosphere was exceedingly intimate and friendly. As he took his leave the King remarked 'I should like to see you directly I get back and tell you of my impressions,' etc. Leslie never saw the Sovereign again until he gave up his office some weeks later: this time the atmosphere was only civil but towards the end of the short audience the King unbent somewhat and made some perfunctory remark about their personal relations always having been friendly. Leslie replied, 'I only regret, sir, that Your Majesty didn't send for me when you came back from France!' 'But I did,' the King answered, 'and Alec Hardinge told me that you had said that you were too busy to come and see me.' Leslie was staggered, his astonishment was so great that the King must have been aware of it. The Black Rat takes too much upon himself: he rules the King, and has bamboozled the Queen. They are really a very inferior boring little couple: the institution is popular – the individuals are not. And if they allow Hardinge to interfere politically in their names, they will become unpopular. The Belisha incident harmed the throne and the more recent suspicion (which I know to be true) that

Alec Hardinge intrigued against Chamberlain in the attempt to get rid of him,[1] is doing the throne harm .... Leslie told me other stories of Hardinge's perfidy: he also knows that Ironside was treacherous to him, although he had appointed him – I was aware of that. I poisoned his mind as much as I dared against the Eden faction: he has lost his faith in them. He is a political Field Marshal without an army: politically poor Leslie is very down; but with his brains and ability and publicity value he will rise once more. As I left him an old soldier came up to me; 'Isn't that Mr Hore-Belisha?' I nodded: 'I thought so; we would be better off if we had him back.' The rabble is behind him. Rab was much interested and impressed by this whole story.

Later I attended a meeting of the 1922 Committee which was addressed by Ernest Bevin,[2] the burly, amiable, altogether terrific Minister of Labour. He drops his aitches, but is witty and has vision and much humour. I liked him and he successfully fascinated the 1922 Committee; all the old Tory colonels and knights (excepting that ruffian George Balfour)[3] applauded him. As I came out I met Rab who was just returning from his interview with the Archbishop of Canterbury[4] in the Lords. The old wicked 'Archbish' is full of plans for Christian revival. He won't succeed; the country hates him. Dined alone and at home.

How much more time have we in London? I don't propose to move things such as china etc. until after the first raid.

Beverley Baxter says that Beaverbrook is so pleased to be in the govt! He is like a great tart who has finally married the local Lord Mayor!

THURSDAY 13TH JUNE

Rumour is rife; first the Romanian Minister, my buddy Viorel, rang me up frantically and repeated what he had heard: that France had asked for a separate

---

1 Hardinge was a committed anti-appeaser. His only power would have been to turn the King against Chamberlain, and there is no evidence that he did; and Hardinge was too experienced a courtier to believe that 'intrigue' would get him anywhere in seeking to influence politics.
2 Ernest Bevin (1881–1951) was born illegitimate and orphaned at the age of 8. He left school at 11 and became a farm labourer in the West Country, and later a lorry driver. An active trades unionist, he was General Secretary of the Transport and General Workers' Union from 1922 to 1945. Churchill appointed him Minister of Labour and National Service in May 1940 and he held the post throughout the war. A parliamentary seat was found for him at Wandsworth Central, which he represented in Parliament for the Labour Party from 1940 to 1950; from 1950 to 1951 he was Labour MP for Woolwich East. He was Foreign Secretary from 1945 to 1951, and Lord Privy Seal for the last month of his life.
3 George Balfour (1872–1941) was a mechanical engineer who was Conservative MP for Hampstead from 1918 to 1941.
4 Archbishop Lang.

peace. I was able to deny this tale; but there is some small foundation for it. Later we were told that Paris had fallen: it has not. Winston, who only came back yesterday morning in time to preside over the War Cabinet, has returned to France, accompanied not by Anthony Eden this time, but by Halifax. That is sinister: there may yet be peace; but only an ignominious one for England. And an extraordinary communiqué appeared in the press supposedly from a German source, that all news in Germany would be stopped for twenty-four hours and that anyone circulating false news would be punished. No one knows what to believe.... The H of Commons was dull. I had this morning a longish talk and walk with Dunglass, who like me is suffering from streptococcal infection. And [a] tired heart. We discussed the political situation and Neville, who is broken-hearted about Italy: all his hard work lies in ruins. Leslie Belisha, that marshal without a battalion, lobbies too much in the House, and consorts with second-rate MPs. I must warn him.

We have made all arrangements for Paul's evacuation to the USA.

FRIDAY 14TH JUNE

Paris was occupied early this morning, although some advanced troops entered the capital late last night. Hitler's boast that he would have conquered the city before June 15th has thus come true. Little news has come through other than that both the Cardinal Archbishop and Mr Bullitt, the American Ambassador, have been taken into preventive custody. The French have retreated: the question is, can France hold out? M. Reynaud has asked to be released from his promise not to negotiate a separate peace: Marshal Pétain[1] is behind him. Winston and Halifax flew yesterday to see Reynaud at Tours and to try to dissuade him from giving up the unequal struggle. He was pleased by our offer to help and refused to consider peace negotiations; he said that he would make one more appeal to President Roosevelt for American help and if it were not forthcoming it was probable that the game was up. The army could not hold. Halifax and Winston are back and the situation is very grave indeed; meanwhile all hangs on Washington. What will Roosevelt decide tonight? If he refuses to come in it would seem that this war, which should not have taken place, will come to an end and this great Empire will have been defeated and humiliated. Tonight, tomorrow are probably the most vital days in our history...

---

1 Henri Philippe Benoni Omer Joseph Pétain (1856–1951) became a marshal of France at the end of the Great War, and was known as 'the Lion of Verdun' for leading the heroic defence of that fortress for nine months in 1916. However, his reputation collapsed when he acted as French head of state under Nazi occupation from 1940 to 1944; in 1945 he was convicted of treason and sentenced to death, but the sentence was commuted to life imprisonment because of his age (he was 89 on conviction) and his role in the Great War.

I was all day at the office which was extraordinarily calm for such a crisis. Rab even went to Essex to sleep the night. I wonder why!

SATURDAY 15TH JUNE

I was all day at the Office. The French are on the verge of collapsing and will soon ask for a separate peace. I see no hope for England or the Allies now.

We had better sue for peace now: that would be an unpopular view, I know; rumours floated in and out. At 6 p.m. I picked up Honor and we drove to Pyrford, discussing the war on the way. She is completely reconciled now to sending Paul to the US. I pray to God it is not too late. There has been no serious submarine activity really; but there are already signs of the dangers being resumed ... Rab and I were alone at the Office; he is increasingly affectionate; he tweaked my ears. He is really a lonely aloof creature who collects bores in his private life; and they rarely raise his infectious, fascinating hyena laugh ....

I felt ill, apprehensive and half-hysterical all day. Pyrford was calming. The Romanian Minister rang me up after dinner to say that a military dictatorship had been set up under Pétain. He is always ahead of the news. He also said that Turkey had definitely 'ratted' on her engagements and although his information is right, I denied it. We are living on the edge of a volcano.

Nicholas Lawford went into the S of S's room and hourly told me that Lithuania had been occupied by the Soviets. 'That leaves me quite cold,' Lord Halifax retorted. He was immersed in other affairs.

SUNDAY 16TH JUNE

A wet, grey Sunday spent in peace: I played with my child, concentrated on him. We listened to the radio: my parents-in-law came back from Elveden in the evening. Over thirty bombs have been dropped on their estate there, and none did any harm other than frightening sheep and causing holes which were filled in next day. My in-laws and their three daughters do not really take the war, or rather the situation, as seriously as they should. They think invasions an impossibility. I don't. Hitler will obviously attack England by air, by sea, and by blockade. The new govt which has been formed in France is a pro-peace one, and a complete surrender is now a matter of hours [away], if it has not already been done.

MONDAY 17TH JUNE

Honor and I drove up from Pyrford after taking an affectionate farewell of our son.

Pétain has formed a govt, and last night he asked Germany, through the agency of his old friend Franco, to negotiate an honourable peace. France has collapsed in twelve days, rather less time than it took Poland. England must now either fight on alone, or sue for peace. The latter alternative [*sic*] would be the wiser course but I fear that Winston would never consent: his emotions will always triumph over his reason.

I prophesy that Halifax will now fall: he will advocate a settlement after the senseless butchery of all these thousands of young men – and he will be dropped from the govt. Neville will go with him; so will Rab; so, in a descending scale, will I. But how can we blockade the whole coast from Norway to Gibraltar? And the Iraqi oil fields will be open to Italy and Germany. Halifax's successors, whoever they may be, will fight for a time and then they also will collapse and peace will be arrived at after more butchery and bloodshed when we shall not be in a better, but worse, bargaining position ... I listened to Pétain's singularly inept broadcast and came home to lunch. The Queen of Yugoslavia rang me up to ask if the speech had been really Pétain's or a piece of German propaganda; it seemed so incredible.

The govt have so whipped up the general public to a war frenzy that I don't see how we can now turn in our tracks and advocate a settlement – at least not yet. The public would not take it.

I signed a few letters, had a snack; the Romanian Minister, my Viorel, came in and we had a long gossip. He is a strong advocate of immediate peace. It is better to save a proportion of one's chattels, rather than lose all. Perhaps he is right. Winston made the shortest broadcast on record, about three sentences. And it was announced that Hitler and Mussolini would meet, probably tomorrow, to discuss the peace terms. Rodney Wilkinson came in and stayed some time: he had one night's leave and rushed to London. He has considerable attraction.

TUESDAY 18TH JUNE

A magnificent letter to his mother from a young airman who has been killed was published anonymously in *The Times* this morning: it is prose of immense strength and beauty.[1]

The Prime Minister made a statement to a crowded House: my usual place was taken, so Rab and I went to the gallery to listen. I wasn't very impressed, but suppose that the nation will be.[2] Hitler and Mussolini are meeting in Munich to discuss the terms which will be offered to France. Probably they will be generous.

1 The letter was written by Flying Officer Vivian Allen William Rosewarne (1916–40), co-pilot of a Wellington bomber, who died in the Battle of Dunkirk. It was subsequently published as a pamphlet and made into a short propaganda documentary film by Michael Powell and Emeric Pressburger.
2 This was the speech in which Churchill said that 'what General Weygand called the Battle of France is over. I expect that the Battle of Britain is about to begin ... Hitler knows that he will have to break us in this island, or lose the war. If we can stand up to him, all Europe may be free and the life of the world may move forward into broad, sunlit uplands ... let us therefore brace ourselves to our duties, and so bear ourselves that, if the British Empire and its Commonwealth last for a thousand years, men will still say, "This was their finest hour."'

Harold Balfour and I dined *à deux* and very happily and cosily at the Dorchester where we discussed the war, ourselves and everything else. The German planes, I gather, are now about 10½ to 6 of ours. But the quality of the planes and the skill of our airmen are superior ... The H of C is not happy under the new govt, which it considers a meretricious one, a govt of 'tarts' someone said. The country, however, is satisfied. Home to bed early, but tired.

WEDNESDAY 19TH JUNE

The big news today is that the French fleet is safe in Scottish waters; some parts of it escaped from Toulon to Oban and elsewhere in the Mediterranean. I was whispered the news by everyone directly I arrived at the House of C, and the secret spread. Miss Wilkinson[1] clasped her heart. This will make an enormous difference to the British Navy and greatly increase our chances of victory. The French govt at Bordeaux shows signs of losing control; people are rushing away from it: large nos. of the Air Force have deserted and flown to England. Meanwhile the German Army advances in France crushing all before it: there is little opposition, only dry rot everywhere in France. Nevertheless the French govt have announced that they will not accept a dishonourable peace. General de la Gaule [*sic*][2] who flew here with Spears rather melodramatically is trying to rally the French around him.

I spent three hours this morning at the American Embassy arranging for Paul's departure. The little boy and his Nannie came with me and he behaved well and charmed everyone except a Jap who was sitting near us. 'Good heavens. What's that?' Paul shouted out to everyone's embarrassed amusement. A little later when he was introduced to the doctor who was to 'vet' him Paul said rather saucily, 'If I had known about you, I'd have brought an apple!' I lunched with Paul and his Nannie in the Blue Amalienburg: his manners are nearly perfect, his charm colossal ... After Questions I rushed back to the House, giving Harold Nicolson a lift. Harold was affectionate, said he wanted me to meet a great friend of his, James

1 Ellen Cicely Wilkinson (1891–1947) was Labour MP for Middlesbrough East from 1924 to 1931 and for Jarrow from 1935 to 1947. Despite coming from an impoverished family she took a degree at the University of Manchester, was an active suffragette and became a communist. She was a junior minister throughout the wartime coalition and in 1945 became Minister of Education, a post she held until her death.

2 Charles André Joseph Marie de Gaulle (1890–1970) was a professional soldier who had had a distinguished Great War, in which he was taken prisoner, and, by this stage a *général de brigade*, had led an armoured division against the invading Germans in May 1940 before becoming Under-Secretary of State for War. He escaped to Britain as France fell and broadcast an appeal on 18 June to maintain resistance. Although he had difficult relations with the British government, he remained in London until 1944, when after the liberation of France he led the provisional government until 1946. He was President of France from 1958 until 1969.

Pope-Hennessy[1] who he thinks might be just my dish. *On verra*[2] . . . on the steps of the FO I met Noël Coward, very brown, but nervous, twitching and aged. We chatted and I told him about the French fleet. A little later Rab addressed twenty-four important Empire journalists on the present position. I received them and gave them tea. He is really remarkable and daily growing in stature; he handled them skilfully, said that the diplomatic situation in Madrid was the most delicate in Europe, paid a deserved tribute to my Paul at Belgrade etc. He hinted that the French fleet was here, and also that the French attitude was hardening.

THURSDAY 20TH JUNE

No news yet of the expected peace terms; opinion is divided: one school of thought anticipates that France will be tempted, indeed lulled by easy terms; another suggests that Hitler will demand complete capitulation. And there are signs of stiffening in the French attitude, insubordination and refusal to give up the struggle abroad, in the colonies etc. No doubt the Germans consider themselves tricked over the escape of the French fleet, which has visibly and enormously encouraged people here: the morale in London has been definitely raised. I came to the Office, beautifully dressed for the hot day. Then I rushed to the steamship offices to get Paul's ticket: it was a dingy place in Gerrard Street, which as I waited, seemed indescribably romantic and smelly! It had an Italian atmosphere. The Northern Transport Co. seems to be an apiary. I was startled, and shocked that so many lazing Ganymedes should be doing office work, rather than saving their country . . . However I got Paul's ticket and one for his nurse . . . . The departure will nearly kill me: I don't think that I can stand it. It means the end of Paul's babyhood – and I have been both father and mother to him, as Honor has never occupied herself in the least with him. This separation means the end of Paul's babyhood: he will be a big boy who has forgotten me when I see him next.

Lunched with Loelia Westminster at 8 Little College St. She was exquisite, cool, chic, *endiamantée*[3] and worldly, ever wise, and the house, with its *luxe*, a *Rosenbaum*.[4] She is letting it and evacuating to Dorset and burying her jewels.

---

1 Richard James Arthur Pope-Hennessy (1916–74) had just won the Hawthornden Prize for his first book, *London Fabric*. He had been in the West Indies as private secretary to the Governor of Trinidad but returned home to enlist as a private soldier in an anti-aircraft battery. He was eventually commissioned and served as a military attaché in Washington. He became a distinguished biographer, notably of Queen Mary, whose official life he published in 1959. A heavy drinker and a risk-taking homosexual, he died after an encounter with some young men who beat him up in 1974.

2 We'll see.

3 Bejewelled with diamonds.

4 A rose tree, but Channon seems to mean a rose garden.

Delicious food and *luxe* were soothing again, and we talked of the French refugees: there are thousands of them at Bordeaux struggling with the British to get aboard our ships. The Rothschilds are there; but not glamorous Kitty,[1] who with her usual shrewdness, got away to the USA just in time. The Windsors have arrived at Barcelona. Estoril, that dreadful Portuguese 'plague', has become the centre of fashion: all the foolish and *faubourg* French who could have fled there – of course, Lady Mendl etc. Laura Corrigan is supposed to be in Paris still at the Ritz with my Nattier and her fabulous jewels.

I am much encouraged about everything and my gloom has lifted; but we are living as people did during the French Revolution – every day is a document, every hour history.

The secret session[2] was exciting; but there were too many reminiscences, and tales of the past, personal accounts of the French front: not enough concrete suggestions for the future. There was, too, an ugly scene in which Neville was criticised: stung, he rose with dignity and some wrath and defended himself. The Chamber happened to be devoid of his more ardent supporters, who, at that hour, were drinking in the Smoking Room. I rounded some of them up: the atmosphere soon dropped. I was glad to see Jim Wedderburn, alive, dreamy and intact. He talked of defending Neville in the Chamber, and of demanding the resignation from the govt of everyone who had voted against armaments or conscription; this would have turned the tables on the Labour Chamberlain-hunters.

Winston wound up with his usual hilarious and out-of-place levity. His command of English is magnificent; but strangely enough, although he makes me laugh, he leaves me unmoved. There is always the quite unescapable suspicion that he loves war, war which broke Neville Chamberlain's better heart!

I feel so lusty and have no antler ....

FRIDAY 21ST JUNE

A more quiet day which began with a cable from Peter, and one returned to me from New York saying that Laura Corrigan was still somewhere in France .... At the office no news had yet come through about the peace terms. Lunched alone and slept exhaustedly for an hour afterwards. I am <u>spent</u>. We are sending off a special 'hush' aeroplane to Cairo tomorrow and it will take letters to Peter and my ruby and cabochon parure for him as an anniversary present, to mark a year of our friendship and axis. Nevile Henderson came in, tired and shabby, the glamour gone, even a touch common. He stayed too long, like all retired great men who find time hanging heavily on their hands.

1 Cathleen 'Kitty' Wolff (1885–1946) married in 1925 as her third husband Baron Eugène Daniel von Rothschild (1884–1976).
2 Of the House of Commons: with no press or public present.

I spent an hour in Westminster Cathedral this afternoon, burning candles, listening to a service, and praying for the welfare and safety of my beloved child on his transatlantic trip.

Rab and I met Vansittart in the passage: he was very wild and mad. He says that our leading statesmen will be tortured by the German Gestapo! And he foresees for himself a lingering death! Duff Cooper, Eden and Winston would be disembowelled and hung up in Trafalgar Square! I doubt it!

Rab was very licentious in the car: I dropped him at the Beefsteak Club. He had received seven ambassadors and ministers today and was weary but charming. I advised Tilea to send his children to Canada.

The French emissaries were received, after some delay, by Hitler and Göring at Compiègne on the same train, the <u>actual</u> dining car in which Foch delivered the Allied ultimatum in 1918. I remember those days and the Paris excitement well. The world does not yet know the result of this afternoon's talks. What a dramatic triumph for Hitler; what a German retribution!

SATURDAY 22ND JUNE

The terms are now known to the frenzied French govt which, after leaving for Perpignan, suddenly returned to Bordeaux. They have not yet been made public.

Bailey, my agent, rang up to say that Southend is now being evacuated: all the population is urged to leave immediately. This ruling applies to all seaside towns! As we talked he heard the distant thump of a bomb.

I was all day at the Office; sent off long letters to Peter and to Paul by the same miracle of a messenger. Rab and I are almost alone: it is grey and cheerless. Honor, as usual, spent the whole day at the farm. Honor and I motored to Pyrford.

A long conference about the future and dispersal of all our children:[1] Honor and I were only interested listeners as the die is cast for my adorable Paul – he leaves on Monday for New York via Montreal. He will be met by Serge Obolensky, escorted to Rhinebeck and be under the wing of Helen Astor until the end of the war. I am broken-hearted . . . . The little man had already gone to bed so I did not see him.

My mother-in-law told me a story which I had already half-heard; of how Gamelin, when he came here to a meeting of the Supreme War Council to discuss the Norwegian expedition, had stayed at the Dorchester: he had mislaid the plans, the highly secret plans. They were found by a housemaid who handed them to a paper-boy who turned them over to the manager – who is Italian! Thus they were seen by three people before they were restored to him. No wonder the Germans knew of our intentions!

---

1 That is, the Iveaghs' grandchildren.

SUNDAY 23RD JUNE

A dreadful day. The baby leapt onto my bed before I was barely awake and I played with that human dynamo for two hours. I adore him, love him beyond belief: he looks like me, acts like me, reacts like me. His energy is overpowering. There was an unfortunate scene as he refused to stay with Honor and insisted on clinging to me: there is a mysterious tenderness between us which unites us. I have never loved anything so much . . .

We all drove up, Honor, the Nannie, the chauffeur and maid, and I held the young man tightly in my arms all the way. Later here at Belgrave Square I crept up to say 'goodnight' and tried gently to break it to him that he was leaving me, perhaps forever . . . he didn't understand but looked back at me with my own eyes, my own little face and I wept and suffered . . . at last I left him. The Nannie, an exceptionally nice woman, saw me, and seized me, and for a second we were great friends. She knows how I love him . . . . Then Honor went to him. The Lennox-Boyds came to dine and we deplored the present position and the folly of the Polish guarantee and the decay and rottenness of the French and this mad, foolish war. I went to bed, wept . . . . I care more for Paul than for all France, and mind his departure more than France's collapse. For the first time in my life I felt a surge of remorse for my appallingly callous treatment of my own parents, who perhaps loved me as I love Paul.

MONDAY 24TH JUNE

The armistice between Germany and France is now in effect – and mad England goes on marching to her doom and oblivion.

I was called at seven, dressed and ate nervously; at 8.15 we set out for Euston. Honor and I had the child between us: he was gay and interested. At the station there was a queue of Rolls-Royces and liveried servants and mountains of trunks. It seemed that everyone one knew was there on the very crowded platform – Roberte Bessborough,[1] miserable at the extinction of her France, saying 'goodbye' to her youngest, George,[2] a handsome boy who looked extraordinarily vicious for so young a child . . . . Many others . . . we led our child to his compartment and clung hungrily to him until the whistle blew and then a feverish hug and kiss and we left him – oh! One second more, as we stood outside his opened window and kissed him once again. I am broken-hearted . . . . Honor and I came back to Belgrave Square, and I went to Westminster Cathedral to pray to St Anthony[3] for

---

1 Roberte Poupart de Neuflize, wife of the 9th Earl of Bessborough*.
2 George St Lawrence Neuflize Ponsonby (1931–51) survived the war only to be killed in a traffic accident in Germany when serving there as a lieutenant in the 9th Lancers.
3 St Anthony of Padua (1195–1231) was a Portuguese priest who is the patron saint of miracles, and of lost causes.

my Paul and then went to the FO. The telegrams and news were all depressing: I don't see a chance of victory, how can this small, haughty and rich island withstand the onslaught of a mighty Germany? It is very doubtful if the French fleet is ours: it seems that it was released and England has now only Admiral Darlan's[1] word that it will not be used against us.

The peace terms[2] are harsh; they might have been worse, might have been more lenient. Indeed they are very clever, clever, indeed . . . . shall we reach a settlement before we are defeated? Before the great bombing match begins, or ends us?

Harold Balfour rang me and asked me to lunch at the Diamond Corporation with his brother-in-law, Sir Ernest Oppenheimer.[3] It was agreeable, a rich lunch . . . . There was a Belgian present who had brought back the diamonds from Bordeaux; he recounted his adventures accenting the hopeless red-tape-ism of the French. After lunch we wandered into the anteroom where there were piles of what seemed to be sequins – they were literally piles of small diamonds, grey, white and yellow: they were mostly for commercial uses. 'They are worth £12,000,000,' Ernest Oppenheimer whispered to me. He is a plump, voluptuous, attractive Jew, who aches to be made a peer! I played with these piles of gems, and to the general amusement, licked a large uncut yellow one. A really thrilling lunch; but I was so nervously exhausted when I returned to the FO that I soon left, and went to the Baltic Club for a sleep, haircut and 'refresher' – anything to be alone!

My Paul is now, I suppose, *en route*. Roberte Bessborough rang up Honor at Kelvedon to tell her that he was well and happy and dominating the ship. She had been on board. And Olive Baillie[4] rang me, too, to say that she had looked after him on the boat. Everyone has been divine. If the capitalist system can transport him safely to Canada and the USA, I shall be deeply grateful to it, and to St Anthony. I am broken-hearted . . .

1 Jean Louis Xavier François Darlan (1881–1942) was head of the French Navy at the time of the fall of France. He then served Vichy until 1942, but went over to the Allies in late 1942 when the Allies invaded French North Africa, and took control of French forces there. However, he was assassinated on Christmas Eve 1942 by an anti-Vichy pro-monarchist who wanted to restore the comte de Paris to the throne.
2 The principal feature of France's capitulation was the establishment of the puppet regime in Vichy, which collaborated with the Germans. The Germans controlled Paris, and the north and west coastal regions of France themselves.
3 Ernest Oppenheimer (1880–1957) was German by birth, but went in 1902 to work in the diamond fields of South Africa in 1915 and raised a regiment to fight for Britain in the Great War. From 1924 to 1938 he was Kimberley's representative in the National Assembly. He ran De Beers and the Anglo-American Corporation of South Africa.
4 Olive Cecilia Paget (1899–1974) was daughter of the 1st Baron Queenborough (qv). She married in 1931, as her third husband, Sir Adrian William Maxwell Baillie (1898–1947), 6th Bt, and they lived at Leeds Castle in Kent, which she owned. She was a leading society hostess.

The Gamelin story is true; but there is a chance, as was hinted to me, that they were lost on purpose being false plans. A very remote chance indeed.

As the order to 'cease firing' between France and Germany came into effect at 12.25 this morning, we can now be prepared for the Battle of Britain – or rather on Britain.

Edward Rice came to see me: he is deeply involved in peace propaganda and is alleged to be strongly pro-Nazi. I don't know: he always praises Hitler in conversation.

Ernest Bevin took his seat, a huge bulk of a man, he was not intimidated by the ceremonies still observed in this, which probably History will call 'the Last Parliament'. After he had shaken hands with the Speaker he came towards the door, brushed past me and I saw Ralph Assheton advance to meet him. 'Yes. I should like to hear the Prime Minister's statement,' Bevin said and took his place in the already overcrowded front bench. Mabane got up and gave him his place.

Tuesday 25th June

I had hardly got to sleep last night when the sirens sounded: I woke Rodney [Wilkinson] but he refused to move and I went to the cellar alone where I was soon joined by the female servants in various stages of *déshabillé*. The scullery maid read the financial section of *The Times*! Soon the menservants arrived and I soon fell asleep in an armchair. About 2.30 (it was 1.05 when the sirens sounded) I went back to bed. A little later I heard another wailing noise but couldn't decide whether it was another alarm or the 'all-clear'! However this time I stayed in bed as did Rodney who slept through it all .... I woke very jaded and dull, but delighted that Paul had gone and that the raid had not come an evening earlier!

I went to the Office, and came home to luncheon here where I had the Duchess of Kent, radiantly lovely, Alice Harding,[1] Garrett Moore, Rodney Wilkinson, and Brendan Bracken. A pleasant but plain party. Brendan talked much and was most friendly: I subtly put Rab and me in his good graces so that he would make good blood for us with the PM. I drove him to Downing Street where he was to pick up the PM. I went on to the House. Winston soon arrived. He made a short statement about the French collapse and had a very lukewarm reception; he is not popular in the House. Nor is Leslie Belisha, who questioned him. As I came behind the Chair I ran into Neville Chamberlain who stopped, put his hand on my arm affectionately and asked how I was. I was much touched: I love him deeply. Winston bowed to me with his little smile ... Brendan told us at luncheon that he had been sitting in the garden at No. 10 last night with the PM when the sirens were sounded: they remained there drinking. From his conversational

---

1 Alice Astor had divorced Raimund von Hofmannsthal and recently married, as her third
   husband, Philip John Ryves Harding (1906–72), a journalist.

crumbs I gathered that all is far from well in Churchill's private paradise: there are endless squabbles amongst the new ministers! Brendan attacked Attlee and Greenwood, thus reflecting Winston's mind; and Herbert Morrison says that Harold Macmillan is a crook!!! I am enchanted . . . . The Duke of Kent left today for Lisbon to attend the celebrations.[1] The Duchess looked tired.

Tomorrow is Peter's birthday and I have sent him a cable. I had yet another one from Serge saying he is looking forward to Paul's arrival. I went again to Westminster Cathedral to pray for him.

The French fleet is lost to us. The govts have mishandled the situation.

If there is another raid tonight I shall arrange a *de luxe* shelter for my private use.

WEDNESDAY 26TH JUNE

Busy day: I arrived late at the House; I have been infuriated by a passport difficulty: the petty officials refused point-blank to give an exit permit to Susan Winn,[2] Olive Baillie's second girl, aged 17 because the regulations do not permit a girl of her age to go abroad. But the decision is an example of red tape and lack of imagination. Olive is paying and arranging for fifty children to go to Long Island . . .

A day and a half have passed and the dreadful hours pass, as my Paul speeds across the Atlantic. Every moment is a victory but I loathe the days and pray for next Monday when I hope to get a cable of 'all-clear'. I rushed this morning to Westminster Cathedral to burn a candle to St Anthony and was soothed by the stillness of the basilica.

Duff left yesterday for Rabat by seaplane, and, I hear, he was badly received after a longish exhausting journey. What a waste of govt petrol! He was bluntly told by the authorities that he was unwelcome and should leave at once before he was arrested!!

People are pouring in from France with appalling tales of being machine-gunned and losing their way and possessions. Anti-French feeling is growing here. Soon that country will be more hated than Germany.

Sat up with Rodney on this, Peter's 30th birthday! I gave him a table.

THURSDAY 27TH JUNE

Awoke a wreck . . . . and then to the Office. Lady Iveagh came to lunch, but I was distant and dull. I drove her to St James's Square, and then hurried post-haste to

---

1 The Portuguese World Exhibition was taking place, and the celebrations were of the 800th anniversary of the foundation of Portugal in 1140 and of the 300th anniversary of its independence from Spain in 1640.

2 Susan Sheila Mary Winn (1923–2001) was the younger daughter of Lady Baillie's first marriage. She married in 1946 Geoffrey Denis Erskine Russell (1921–2011); they divorced in 1971 and in 1973 he succeeded his father as 4th Baron Ampthill.

Westminster Cathedral to pray for my baby boy – from whom, thank God, no news. But all America and Canada are preparing to meet him with red carpets.

The House went into secret sessions but I was more occupied with the political position. There are rumours that Rab and Halifax are going – I, too, necessarily. I was put in to investigate these rumours . . . .

The session ended about eleven, and I walked home in the moonlight with Leslie Hore-Belisha and that firebrand ass, Hugh Seely.[1] Searchlights played the sky, and Hugh told us that a big raid was expected for tonight but that as an experiment no sirens would be sounded until bombs were actually dropped; we went with Leslie into his house in Stafford Place, full of mother-portraits and Wedgwood plaques and medallions etc. It is luxurious, Jewish, a tart's house, but attractive, even *gemütlich*. Hugh Seely, an argumentative ass, had had rather too much to drink and immediately began to attack Rab, and Halifax and quoted his leader; Archie Sinclair being his source and confederate. It was the Liberals' ambition to turn every Tory out of the govt. We were not really interested in the war, were bored by it and by the rising taxation. Only the Liberals could win it. Halifax must go – he would never wage war in France as they wished; Rab, too, who is a political menace, a pro-peace boy, a supporter of General Franco's etc. Kingsley Wood must be dismissed and he went on, that it was a plot which would succeed. Leslie, rather embarrassed, intervened with 'You can't expect Chips to agree with you about his chief, Hugh': Hugh became abusive about Halifax and Rab and rather irrelevantly said he hoped to shut up White's Club, abolish the aristocracy etc. I was riveted and kept my temper and we left together in the moonlight. As we came out into the passage which leads from Stafford Place to B[uckingham] Palace Rd [Gate] he collided with a post and nearly winded himself. The blow seemed to pull him together and he dropped me at 2.30 at Belgrave Square and we parted on friendly terms – I had learned a lot, just what I wanted most to know, i.e. the source of this campaign against Rab. I felt the chill in the Commons . . .

FRIDAY 28TH JUNE

Another nightmare is over – no raid, and more important, no news of Paul! In a few more days he may be safe! How glorious to have saved something from the wreck of European civilisation. Life from Vladivostock to Calais is impossible. And now Romania is the victim. I saw Tilea several times today.

A v sweet letter from Peter came via the bag. He is back in Cairo and wrote amusingly of 'the Foolish Wives' who married illicitly to get to Egypt – Mary

---

1 Hugh Michael Seely (1898–1970) was a Liberal MP from 1923 to 1924 and from 1935 to 1941, when he was raised to the peerage as 1st Baron Sherwood on becoming Joint Under-Secretary of State for Air, a post he held until 1945.

Roxburghe, Anne Feversham etc. – now they are anxious to get back to England and cannot. Moreover they are impoverished as they cannot get money out and are living on their husbands' pay. Peter stayed with Joan and Ali Khan at Beirut.

The situation in the Balkans is now charged with dynamite: anything may happen as the result of the Russian ultimatum to Romania which [she] has accepted – the rich provinces of Bukhovina to Bessarabia fall like ripe plums into the hungry Bolshevik hands. Among the developments may be the partition of Yugoslavia, further carving up of Romania, and a delay in the contemplated German invasion of England.

Lunched alone *en snack* at home. A day of intrigue really . . . . I went to the Air Ministry and saw Harold and warned him of the treacheries of Archie Sinclair, his chief. Harold was not surprised. In the afternoon I went over to No. 10 to see the Chief Whip and I told David my story of Hugh Seely's tipsy confidence. David said the plot was not really political but a Palace revolution, engineered by Vansittart who is regaining his former ascendancy. David often sees him gossiping with Winston in the little enclosed garden. He had hardly said this when he stood up and pointed to Winston, who was walking up and down, smoking a huge cigar, with an unknown grey-haired man. David watched him like a lynx. David said that he would report our conversation to Neville C, in the morning, and also to the PM. He took it seriously. As I came out I ran into Hugh Seely who was walking in Whitehall: I felt like Judas, but we had a few friendly words and I saw that he didn't clearly recall last night's conversation. We must nip this plot in the bud.

At 7.45 Rab and I left the Office and drove to Belgrave Square, where Walter Buccleuch was waiting for us; we met there quietly and directly and had a drink together. He is still strongly in favour of a negotiated peace whilst we have still so many cards in our hands.

Unfortunately he has burnt his fingers and is known as 'Public Enemy No. 1', a monstrously unjust accusation.

I found time to burn candles at Westminster Cathedral for the safety of my son.

When I came in late last night I was astonished to find a sleeping youth on a sofa in the morning room. I woke him, asked him what he wanted, and he shyly explained that he was Leslie O'Farrell[1] and was waiting for Rodney W. A dull unattractive shabby youth. I left him. At breakfast Rodney told me that he had not come in until 7 a.m. and his 'friend' had written and left a rebuking letter for him. What a story! I am relieved that I brought neither Belisha nor Hugh Seely back with me as the presence of this rather obvious pansy-boy would have been difficult to explain away! The little creature seemed pathetic, hungry and hideous. Rodney left (to my relief, really) to take up his command near Stamford: he now has a squadron. He is an intrepid airman and is attractive with his curious negro

1 Untraceable.

shuffling and debonair ways and sense of humour. He has wonderful eyes and a vicious mood. Can he have mulatto blood?

The S of S came to tea in the Secretary's room – the famous tea party – but looked harassed. He was about to see General de Gaulle whom we are today recognising as the leader of all the Frenchmen.

Corbin, the retiring French Ambassador, torn by conflicting loyalties, has resigned. He called to say 'goodbye'. I have never liked him: he was grey, correct, steel-like, civil, grave but unamusing. He always invited us to his grandest parties but he was never intimate. He was, I am sure, against the war. I remember him on the fatal night of Sept 2nd, trying to soothe us.

SATURDAY 29TH JUNE

No news of Paul, and no news is still good news.

I drove to Kelvedon, which looked so lovely, so distinguished. Honor and I lunched together and then I slept naked in the garden and later bathed. England looked its most glorious. About teatime the swans with their six cygnets left the water, crossed the lawn and approached the house. Honor fed them: a pretty sight.

The French fleet is the whole problem now:[1] has Winston muddled it, as I strongly suspect – not without reason. He trusted Darlan, indeed was overconfident of French support. He handled the French negotiations perhaps better than Neville would have done – but he failed lamentably. Now he has little to recommend him: he has not even Neville's quiet, reasoning qualities.

I have enjoyed my few hours 'off'. Honor is immensely distressed because poor Fritzi, languishing on the Isle of Man, has telegraphed and written for food; it seems that he is badly fed. I have, however, sent him three cases of food and can only suppose they have never arrived.

SUNDAY 30TH JUNE

I got up early, bathed in the Kelvedon pool, walked about naked followed by white dogs in the rose garden and then came to London . . . There have been no serious air raids now for several nights: are the Germans preparing some huge coup or are they delayed by the intensification of the Balkan situation? I think we shall have a brief respite now; but Rab, when I suggested this, scoffed. He thinks we are in for hell followed by probable defeat! Those are his secret fears. He is, I daresay, right.

[Hugh] Dalton is intriguing against the govt, of which he is a restless member: he is really angling for the Foreign Office for himself. He dislikes Halifax. I was all day at the Office, had a brief lunch with Hector Bolitho at the Carlton. In the

---

1 Britain wanted the French fleet to surrender and not on any count to fall into German hands. When it refused to surrender it was attacked by the Royal Navy at Mers-el-Kébir in Algeria on 3 July, with almost 1,300 French killed and several ships lost.

evening I bathed at the Bath Club, prayed at Westminster Cathedral, wrote to Peter and filled my car with petrol. I am tired of everything!

There seems to be an ominous lull: the German raids have not been intense, although they come every night . . . . I am feeling randy and restless and I look quite handsome. What a pity it is one is never good-looking nor attractive when one wants most to be. Early to bed: it is wise to rest and eat whilst one may.

I had ten brief minutes at Victoria Station with Alan who was returning to Brighton: he had been at Henlow with 'Mama'.

All accounts point to an invasion and bombardment of this country almost immediately; but I am not certain that it will take place so soon if at all.

At last, after two years or more, I am seriously attracted by Rab. We might, and may, have a great friendship! *Qui sait?* but he is fundamentally so impersonal and unattractive physically – at least so I thought a fortnight ago. Propinquity can do much: half Whitehall is in love with that jackanapes, Anthony Eden, so why shouldn't Rab have a *suivant*?[1]

I wonder, has my fat letter and its rich contents reached Cairo and Monsieur Coats?

MONDAY 1ST JULY

I had hoped for a cable from Canada announcing Paul's safe arrival; but nothing came!

A full day: I was at the FO by 10.15 . . . . Ambassadors poured in . . . and we forgot for a little the plot to oust us all from power. Harold rang me up and we lunched together at B Square as neither wanted to be seen with the other in public when there is a heresy hunt on. We are really living in an atmosphere like that of the French Revolution, rumours, plots, frenzy . . . Harold told me the astonishing news that Beaverbrook resigned last night. Winston asked Archie Sinclair to dine with him and offered him a seat in the War Cabinet with the Dominions Secretaryship, thus kicking out poor Falstaffian Inskip. It is a clever political move: to placate the rebels by throwing fat Caldecote[2] to the winds and the wolves, by giving Sinclair, and hence the Liberals, a seat in the War Cabinet and thus weakening the Conservative 5 to 3 element. Also it will free the Air Ministry from Archie who has been, from really no fault of his own, a shocking failure. The Air Ministry would be offered to Beaverbrook and the two ministries, the Air and the rather bogus one of Aircraft Production, would be merged under Max. Harold and Jay Llewellin would be, presumably, the two under-secretaries. Harold was very excited . . . Nothing is yet known; but Winston whispered the plan to Archie

---

1 It is unlikely that Butler, who would marry twice and give no hint of homosexual tenden-cies, would have reciprocated Channon's feelings.
2 Inskip had become Lord Caldecote the previous year on becoming Lord Chancellor at the outbreak of war.

Sinclair at the end of the Cabinet meeting this morning. We shall see . . . Possibly this also heralds the ultimate fall of Halifax (which Dalton is working for, in the fervent hope of succeeding him) and possibly also of Kingsley Wood and Rab – 'the men of Munich' – although Rab was at Geneva at the time; alternatively it may be a sop to the glamourist elements and be an attempt to save Halifax. I don't know but once attempts are made to save personalities politically it always means that they will go in a short time . . .

I heard much more today; that an Italian submarine surrendered at Malta – the heat was unbearable. We have now their codes and papers. It has been announced that a submarine has been sunk; but an aeroplane has been flown to Malta to bring back the Italian officers who engineered the surrender. And Dictaphones have been put in the dining room at Trent[1] where German air prisoners are kept. What would Philip Sassoon think? Probably he had some sort of contrivance himself as he always knew everything!!

Rumours are over-ripe and rife. Diana C[ooper] told me today that the Windsors genuinely believe that they will be restored to the throne under German influence: he will become a sort of Gauleiter and Wallis a queen. Perhaps!

Rab and I went at six o'clock to the Ministry of Information where he addressed a group of American journalists; it was really a feint to impress Brendan! Ronnie Quisling Tree was present with his red, warty face. Rab was too subtle for his hard-boiled audience but impressed them.

The Germans have landed at Guernsey and Jersey in large numbers: we have, however, evacuated these islands militarily. They killed twenty-nine people there in an air raid. A New York reporter has published a story that there are Germans on the west coast of England: it is, I believe, untrue. The French fleet is being saved or salvaged in many ways.

And also I hear that Basil Dufferin has asked Maureen to divorce him so that he may marry Virginia Cowles, the journalist. She is a blowsy girl who has had a long sequence of lovers – Seymour Berry for intermittent periods, and others. She is socially ambitious as I immediately spotted when we first met. What a fool Basil is; and how badly and caddishly he has treated both his wife and his [illegible] mistress! He will regret it. Maureen Stanley, who more than anyone, represents to me the decay of the system and collapse of old England, is encouraging this alliance. She is always an influence for evil.

TUESDAY 2ND JULY

Still no news of my child: the CPR[2] has heard nothing; but assured me that there was no reason to be alarmed as the boat is scarcely due.

---

1 Trent Park in north London, formerly owned by Sir Philip Sassoon.
2 It is not clear what organisation Channon refers to. The body overseeing evacuations to Canada was the Children's Overseas Reception Board.

The Commons is a curious place: MPs unexpectedly reveal high qualities. I had . . . . a long conversation with Lady Astor and disliked her less. Perhaps I was in a mellow mood: I was brilliantly dressed, and whispered with Anthony Eden for a bit – for the first time in my life I was aware of his charm. He has a flirtatious manner.

Arthur Greenwood, with his growing paunch, his very thin straight lips, gossiped with me and quoted the King, 'who last time I saw him – I see a lot of him – had said that Winston had told him that he could give him only five minutes'. The King was amused. Socialists love royalties always.

I hear that the Germans have taken over the Ritz in Paris and now it is their HQ. That hotel has seen much history and is now housing more.

We have had uninterrupted sleep for a week now: raids must soon come. Oxford has been awake for two nights . . . . is the world mad and are we not the maddest of all? I have lost all zest for living, and care little what happens once Paul is safe: but I should like a cottage somewhere with roses and my books, boy and *bibelots*. But where in this Armageddon can we hope for that?

WEDNESDAY 3RD JULY

An early telephone call told me the glorious news: my infant is safe and in Montreal . . . A later cable from Nannie confirmed that all was well. My relief passed all bounds . . . Now I care less what happens: my life is over, the rest is residue. I can live on in my dauphin who looks, acts, reacts, thinks, like me.

I walked jubilantly to the Foreign Office and during the luncheon-hour shopped – bought two dozen pairs of socks to celebrate, prayed (at Westminster Cathedral) to St Anthony to thank him. How relieved I am that our temporal quarrel has not affected him.

There were two stormy political meetings at the H of C, the first organised by that tiresome fanatic, Clem Davies,[1] who is I fear encouraged by Lloyd George and Hore-Belisha. The motive of the meeting was to dislodge Neville, but Conservatives packed it and shouted down any reference to him. The meeting broke up in disorder. Lloyd George is really wicked: he sees himself as a sort of Pétain, an old gentleman with a past rendered illustrious in the last war: he would make a peace, but a Lloyd George peace if he dared. The second meeting was the weekly one of the 1922 Committee and communism was discussed and the Home Secretary was pressed to make more arrests.

Bathed at the Bath Club, and refreshed and gay went to dine with Alice at Hanover Lodge – a pleasant party, the Kents: he fresh from Portugal; having got

---

1 Edward Clement Davies (1884–1962) was Liberal MP for Montgomeryshire from 1929 to 1962. He was leader of the Liberal Party from 1945 to 1956. He had played a leading role in the removal of Chamberlain from Downing Street.

back only yesterday, he looked breezy and debonair whilst his bleached hair was almost of a peroxide hue. In his aeronautical uniform he appeared tougher than usual and in much better spirits: she was lovely but tired, I thought, and wore a white two-piece number. The other men (except Garrett Moore, who was in uniform) wore black ties. The Duke told us amusing stories of Dictator Salazar,[1] and of the Portuguese President[2] who was deaf, and his wife who spoke only Portuguese, and of an endless but fascinating *Te Deum* . . . . The Duke referred to the Duke of Windsor slightingly and said 'My brother wants to be a Gauleiter!' They are hopelessly estranged and the D of Kent pursues the vendetta with all the animosity of one who knows he has been treacherous and has behaved badly . . . . We listened to the midnight radio which Osbert Sitwell[3] turned on, after they had left, and there was an account of the sinking of the *Arandora Star*; a huge ship which was taking 1,500 internees to Canada. It was torpedoed and there were indescribable scenes of confusion and fighting between the Italians and Germans many of whom were themselves probably refugees.[4] The Kents, he especially, seemed jubilant by this unexpected turn of fate, but I was horrified lest Fritzi be amongst them. The *Champlain*[5] has also been torpedoed: submarines are now more active and I doubly rejoice that we waited no longer to send Paul.

An agreeable dinner party. Alice is an incurable hostess and since the war an excellent one. But there was a defeatist undertone amongst some of the guests; some of the same people who a little while ago were clamouring for war and the removal of Mr Chamberlain. Talking of Mr Chamberlain, I called at No. 10 and had half an hour with Miss Watson who has been feeling lonely. She is a great character; an expert with parliamentary Questions, she was brought to No. 10 by Bonar Law, I believe, and has been there ever since, serving all the PMs. She liked Neville much the best after she had got to know him; it is always like that, no one can resist his quiet charm nor deny his cool judgement. His enemies are the people who don't know him.

---

1 António de Oliveira Salazar (1889–1970) was Prime Minister of Portugal from 1932 to 1968, in 1940 he was also Portuguese Minister of War, Minister of Foreign Affairs and Minister of Finance (he was a trained economist). He implemented a corporatist state, influenced by Roman Catholic ideals, and an authoritarian government, and kept Portugal neutral during the war.

2 António Óscar Fragoso Carmona (1869–1951) was President of Portugal from 1926 until his death; as an Army officer, he had helped orchestrate the *coup d'état* of 1926 that ended the First Republic and brought him to power. He married, in 1914, Maria do Carmo Ferreira da Silva (1878–1956), with whom he had already had three children.

3 Francis Osbert Sacheverell Sitwell (1892–1969), who in 1943 succeeded his father as 5th Bt. He was the elder brother of Sacheverell Sitwell (qv).

4 The ship was sunk west of the Outer Hebrides on the morning of 2 July. There were 805 dead and 868 survivors.

5 A French ocean liner that hit a mine off the Île de Ré on 17 June, but with little loss of life.

Louis Greig, with whom I bathed at the Bath Club, is pro-peace; and he added that the King must go to Canada. A whiff [*sic*][1] for the Court! He added that if Winston were to be 'bumped off' the heart of resisting spirit in this country would be pierced. Perhaps!

THURSDAY 4TH JULY

Cables poured in from Serge: Paul has arrived and he took him to Syosset, Long Island[2] to stay with Ailsa Mellon Bruce,[3] and to attend a children's party. Serge has been magnificent through all this, more than loyal; and I am deeply, deeply touched. Also one came from Peter from Cairo thanking me for letters and the rubies[4] ....

The newspapers announced the stirring story of our taking over the French fleet: I knew that this had been before the Cabinet for some days, and Vansittart, to give him his due, had advocated it: but [A. V.] Alexander had killed the idea originally. Alexander had been got around by Admiral Darlan. We have taken over the ships in Portsmouth and have won a great naval victory at Oran! But it seems sad and ironical that our first big victory of the war should have been over our Allies . . . Later Winston made his very characteristic statement and it was a theme after his own heart: he recounted the stirring story of the fight, how we had routed the treacherous French. At the end of his speech the House rose, cheered, waved Order Papers – as I have seen them do for Neville. Only it was not little Neville's turn now. Winston suddenly burst into tears for a second and then quickly recovering himself said that he had 'Spied Strangers' and the House, itself much moved, and semi-hysterical, laughed. A secret (and very boring) session followed. Secret sessions seem only to be occasions for MPs to pour forth their own adventures and their thoughts. Lloyd George addressed a nearly empty House and said that he approved of the action of the Navy, heartily endorsed it, and also said that in the autumn he had been in favour of opening peace negotiations; but now he was not for it would look too much like suing for peace. There are peace rumours about, Hitler has put out 'feelers' which to this government are a waste of time. Personally I am all for peace: why have a bombing match and more destruction? The H of Commons is deplorable, a club of dangerous and foolish eccentrics, they are responsible, along with left-wing journalists, for this shameless war. I hear that there is considerable dissatisfaction amongst our troops who declare that the German soldiers are better fed and equipped.

1 A slang usage of uncertain meaning: it is thus in the MS.
2 On the north coast of Long Island, just south of Oyster Bay, about thirty miles east of Manhattan.
3 Ailsa Mellon (1901–69) was one of the richest people in the United States, and a celebrated philanthropist; her father had been the banker Andrew W. Mellon (see Vol. I, entry for 13 July 1936). She married David Kirkpatrick Este Bruce (1898–1977) in 1926.
4 Channon had sent him some jewellery to mark the first anniversary of their meeting.

I saw Mrs Churchill come out of No. 10, wearing a curious blue hat with a sort of hanging veil behind. I hurried home from the secret session to give dinner to Viorel Tilea, the Romanian Minister who is in despair about the formation of a 'Quisling government' in Bucharest. He talks of resigning before he is 'sacked'. We had an affectionate dinner and then I returned to the H of Commons for the end of the secret session. Attlee wound up in his dull way.

The Yugoslav Minister, little Subbotić, called to see me privately: he had messages from Berlin via Belgrade that Hitler intended to launch another peace offer shortly. He is unusually well informed.

On reflection I fear I was not as sympathetic as I wanted to be with Tilea: I was anxious to get back to the House as Rab wanted me to be there and I was a little inflated after cocktails. He told me, *inter alia*, that the famous Mme Lupescu[1] is not a Jewess at all; he knows that she is the daughter of old King Carol I and a Romanian lady who was married off to a Jew when she became pregnant. The *maîtresse en titre*[2] is thus second cousin to her royal protector.

I am disgusted with Belisha and his plots; he is hand in glove with Lloyd George and they are trying to stage a sensational 'comeback' into the government. Yet I am fond of Leslie in a private way.

Friday 5th July

The lull before the storm is disturbing, and people are beginning to say that Hitler will never attack this country. And there are rumours that the Pétain government has broken off relations with Great Britain, but the Foreign Office had no knowledge of such a *démarche*.

Diana Cooper came to lunch and our reunion was only of a lukewarm character: she was civil, cordial but scarcely intimate or affectionate. I fear I have hurt her but I shall pursue the chase and still save our old friendship; but she bores me really, for all her brilliance and beauty. Her child, the highly precious John Julius,[3] left for America in the American ship today; the Coopers allege that he would be used as a hostage by the Germans. 'A marked child,' she said he was. Nonsense. Diana rushed away and the reconciliation was only half-baked, a half-hearted affair. I realised that it is up to me to make, to take the next step.

I was irritable all day, partly because of the summer weather I suppose. Everyone I met was cross; and there was a rumpus in the household here. The cook told the footman that he couldn't kill a louse much less a German! Fury resulted.

---

1 Elena Lupescu, known as Magda. See Vol. I, entry for 23 April 1935. She was Jewish, though her father converted to orthodox Christianity and her mother to Roman Catholicism.

2 Mistress.

3 John Julius Cooper (1929–2018) succeeded his father as 2nd Viscount Norwich in 1954. After a career as a diplomat he became a writer and television personality.

I hear that poor Francie Weikersheim[1] has been interned: Puppe, his silly doll wife, had wanted to marry Buffles Milbanke and even went to Rome to consult the Pope who was against it!

I heard today that Lloyd George is rather disapproving of Winston, finds him in an 'exalted mood' and doesn't want to serve under him. It is true that the PM has unlimited power and that Brendan Bracken rules the roost.

There are faint indications that the naval victories have had a heartening effect on some neutrals, except in Sweden, which is almost completely under Germany's thumb.

I saw the Queen, our cars passed, and as I raised my hat, she smiled. She was ridiculously dressed, in pale blue with an immense Gainsborough hat. She doesn't quite pull it off, but succeeds in looking gay.

Beaverbrook's resignation must have been reconsidered, as he is still in power, and Archie Sinclair still reigns ineffectually at the Air Ministry. Winston must be either staying his hand, or he has made peace between them, as he watches and awaits war and political developments.

I read [Sir] Ronald Campbell's account of his last days in France; it is a historic, sad dramatic document, and well told, but he lacks the vivid pen of Nevile Henderson – I am told that it was written by one of his staff. It is placed in the secret files of the Foreign Office; I also met him, sleek and correct and smiling. He is now back at the Office, joining the collections of *dégommé* ambassadors.

Dined blissfully alone on sole and hock! I had an irritating letter from that shameless beggar Lady Oxford, who asked me to give her £25 for her secretary's radium treatment.

SATURDAY 6TH JULY

A quiet day at the FO. Rab, who was to broadcast tonight, was told by the BBC that Winston had asked Attlee to take his place: is this a snub? Rab will have his turn on Monday night . . . He is not a good broadcaster, and I fear and dread a failure for him. I drove him to Liverpool Street Station, and he confided in me that he expects the great offensive to begin on Monday or Tuesday next: I do not. There will be a peace offensive first in my view.

Another boring letter from Lady Oxford asking for £25 . . . . it is monstrous one should be so blackmailed by that rather loveable old woman.

SUNDAY 7TH JULY

Everyone is now sending children to the US . . . . Honor and I were about two jumps ahead of everyone else.

---

1 Franz von Weikersheim (1904–83) was Austrian by birth. He married, in 1936, Princess Irma zu Windisch-Graetz (1913–84).

I meant to sleep late; but it was warm and lovely and I got up at seven, bathed and breakfasted by the pool, clipped roses, and spent a long, lazy morning in the sun. Too much lunch and then I slept. Honor went to the farm. She has been very sweet; we are both anxious to make some immediate financial provisions for Paul in the USA. But how? For all our joint wealth, it is complicated.

Honor remarked at lunch, 'There is no news!' There isn't today as yet; at least one thinks there is no news nowadays when neither a country nor a government goes crash.

MONDAY 8TH JULY   *PRINCE'S HOTEL, HOVE*

There is no news, except that Rab seems to think that the great offensive will begin this week but I rather suspect that action will be delayed until July 19th when we shall have full moon. Already however the air raids are increasing in activity and instead of killing three or five people we have fifteen or twenty casualties.

I came to Brighton and am staying with brother-in-law Alan in his luxurious suite at Prince's – where I came once before with Freddie Birkenhead. Alan is immersed in his sailor's life and is keen to go to sea. We dined at Sweetings and walked along the front; the seaside of the promenade is closed to people, but they are still permitted in the north side and are crowded with uniforms, naval and military.

Alan has a suite like one in a grand yacht. We are sharing a room and have had a long confidential talk. His charm remains immense and he has lost a slightly heavy look he was beginning to have. Happy evening, and how lovely to see and hear the sea again.

TUESDAY 9TH JULY

I woke with a headache as Alan insisted on sleeping with the blinds drawn and the windows only open a crack – he ought to have married Honor. Am I eccentric in my passion for air at night? He rushed off to his training ship and I dressed and came to London and went directly to the FO.

Harold Balfour dined with me alone and confided to me that he has been half offered a peerage; should he accept? I advised him to take it and we wondered how to clinch it . . . then he suggested that I have it. I should be glad of it really as I am becoming increasingly unsatisfied with my life. My talents, creative ones at least, are being wasted at the moment.

Rab's broadcast is at last fixed for Wednesday: but it has been an exhausting business as he cannot write and his English is ever jerky and inelegant. I shall be glad when it is over.

We have attacked the Italian fleet.

Another secret session and Dalton, although he never inspires trust, impressed the House with a too-long but highly vivid speech which was a complete picture of economic warfare. He was out to please and therefore less unpleasant than when in Opposition.

The Windsors have been appointed to reign in the Bermudas.[1] They will adore it, the petty pomp, the pretty Regency Government House, the beach and the bathing; and all the smart Americans will rush to Nassau to play backgammon with Wallis! It is an excellent appointment and I suggested it two years ago and have been harping upon it ever since . . . . I adored Nassau. The appointment shows real imagination on the part of the government although the idea is mine.

WEDNESDAY 10TH JULY

There was a big attempted raid when over a hundred German planes attacked this country with little result.

I approached David Margesson, against my better judgement, about Harold's peerage but was discouraged. It is sad as Harold has set his heart on becoming Lord Thanet.

I listened to Rab as he rehearsed his evening speech and he was really quite good; but I had carefully 'pruned' his English. Later I sat alone at B Square and listened in: as I had heard it, and half-written it, I was bored but I believe the public will like it.

The Third French Republic has ceased to exist and I don't care; it was an excrescence in the *monde politique*,[2] graft-ridden, ugly, incompetent, communistic and corrupt, it had outlived its day. Pétain is to be a sort of Hindenburg.

A pencilled note of thanks from Lady Oxford to whom I had sent £5 instead of the £25 she asked for. She is a shameless beggar but one should consider it an honour . . . . to send a cheque to so valiant an old dame.

FRIDAY 12TH JULY

Pétain has divided France into provinces, as she was before the French Revolution, and has appointed local 'Gauleiters'. The old France is dead.

There is much gossip about the attempted flight of three MPs, 'Bobby' Cunningham-Reid,[3] Captain Plugge,[4] who is supposed to have smuggled money

---

1 Thus in the MS. He means the Bahamas, where they were sent largely to keep them out of the way until 1945.
2 The political world.
3 Alec Stratford Cunningham-Reid DFC (1895–1977) had been a fighter pilot in the Royal Flying Corps in the Great War and in 1927 married Ruth Mary Clarissee Ashley (1906–86), through her mother (the daughter of Ernest Cassel, the financier) a prodigiously wealthy heiress, whom he would on their divorce in 1940 sue for half of her annual income, attracting him huge social opprobrium. He was a Conservative MP from 1922 to 1923, 1924 to 1929, and 1932 to 1945. It is unclear what prompts Channon to call him 'Bobby'.
4 Leonard Frank Plugge (1889–1981) was Conservative MP for Chatham from 1935 to 1945. He had started commercial radio stations, broadcasting from Europe, in the 1930s, notably Radio Normandy.

out of the country and Roland Robinson[1] are the offenders. I have trusted Roland, whom I have always found reliable; but the House considers them cads and cowards.

I have decided definitely to be a peer at the earliest suitable opportunity and hope it is not too late; for I suspect that this is the last parliament. The system is too antiquated, rusty and slow for the present world and its Blitz methods.

SATURDAY 13TH JULY

I sat to James Gunn and my portrait progresses; at the moment it is too hard, too grim and takes in no account of my light wit and gaiety; I appear a humourless politician with a determined expression and crooked smile. Definitely I am not photogenic!

Gunn has done a sketch of my Paul; it is enchanting. It helped him with the portrait but it portrays Paul as a baby with longish hair, which Gunn has altered in the portrait. I bought the sketch, had it framed and took it to Honor at Kelvedon. It was my anniversary present; but doubt whether she appreciated it as I do. She seemed only half-pleased and was not too gracious. She feels, I fear, that the child is not like her in any way; she is right; indeed it might be by some other woman so little does he resemble her. He is the very spit of me.

I drove to Kelvedon which looked lovely, but a touch unkempt. Honor was farming: she is preparing a lonely life for herself since she never troubles about anyone. She gave me green Fabergé links. Tomorrow we shall have been married seven years – indeed a phase of one's life. I have enjoyed it – on the whole, but wish I had been more tactful and understanding in 1936. Still the rift, while it might have been delayed, was, I am convinced, ultimately inevitable. We are both, particularly Honor, too independent, too egocentric ever to have remained yoked to another. Most men would have left her. She would have left most of them.

SUNDAY 14TH JULY

The French national fête day is no more: it is abolished, as is that tiresome motto *Liberté, Egalité, Fraternité!* Three absurd words really .... Here it is the anniversary of our wedding: seven years married. I bathed early, breakfasted naked in the rose garden and drove up to London and spent the day at the FO, where I had a long introspective conversation with Michael Rose, mostly about Alan. Came home at 6.30 and had an hour's heart-to-hearter with Alan <u>all</u> about Michael

---

1 John Roland Robinson (1907–89) was Conservative MP for Widnes from 1931 to 1935, for Blackpool from 1935 to 1945, and for Blackpool South from 1945 to 1964. He was raised to the peerage as 1st Baron Martonmere in 1964, when he was appointed Governor of Bermuda: he served until 1972. Had he been involved in the activities rumoured by Channon it is highly unlikely he would have been appointed a colonial governor or ennobled.

Rose. All this would bore anyone else but I find confidences riveting. Tea at the Office alone with Sir Ronald Campbell, and I asked him what would happen to his vivid account of his last days in France (I am told that he did not actually write it although he corrected and revised it): he said it had been originally intended to publish it but on reflection there was little point in further exasperating the French, and 'that Baudouin',[1] who is as clever as a barrel of monkeys would only deny the bits about himself and an acrimonious debate, which could only benefit the enemy, would ensue. Therefore the document must remain in the archives of the Foreign Office for some years until it becomes part of history. It is good reading. Horace Seymour[2] tells me that he has heard that Dalton will soon be Foreign Secretary: I have been aware of the Dalton plot for some weeks. It is the man's great aim and ambition and there is little he would not do to attain it. He is a sort of Mirabeau.[3]

The press has laid off Neville this Sunday and seems concentrating on ousting Duff Cooper. I am solidly with them there. He must be 'gunned' but he has a powerful and loyal defender in the Prime Minister, I fear.

Honor woke in a bad temper and I left Kelvedon, as I often do, with sagging spirits, for all its charm and beauty.

One is forgetting the invasion and the dangers. Is it a lull?

Alan came in again, and Patrick Buchan-Hepburn, a conceited fellow, dined with me. He is critical, carping, uninteresting but far from charmless. He is the typical public-school boy who cannot throw off his training: incredibly limited and dull really; yet he has a Scotch shrewdness. I ate meat as an experiment . . . later I walked as far as Hyde Park Corner with Patrick who was trying to be very agreeable; we watched the revolving searchlights sweeping the sky. They focused on a plane and we wondered whether it was one of ours.

MONDAY 15TH JULY

Awoke, gaseous and *congestionné*:[4] I must be mad to have devoured red meat, and all day I have felt ill and *gonflé*.[5] Much correspondence including letters from Serge and Nannie about Paul, who is happily at Martha's Vineyard.

---

1 Thus in the MS. Channon presumably means Leopold, the King of the Belgians, but refers instead to Leopold's son, then aged 9.
2 Assistant Under-Secretary at the FO.
3 Honoré Gabriel Riqueti, comte de Mirabeau (1749–91), was a French soldier and minor aristocrat who played a leading part in the early phase of the French Revolution and became a people's champion. Unusually for participants in that struggle, he died in his bed of heart trouble.
4 Congested or flushed.
5 Bloated.

The agreement with Japan about the closing of the Burma Road[1] is nearly complete: it will be a triumph for Rab who has all along struggled valiantly to prevent war with yet another country. If we avoid it, it will be thanks to his often unaided efforts.

Dined alone: talked much on the telephone as Alan has concocted some trumpery plot about an imaginary airman called Peter Fortescue, in order to annoy (and bring to heel) Mr Michael Rose with whom I had an astonishing conversation! He must be mad, and I fear he will end in the police courts, so sordid are his sexual habits. He says he has a split mind, whatever that means, and only gets sexually excited in public lavatories!! The more one lives the more one learns; but I admit his complex is a new one to me!

A wasted day owing to my indigestion. I rang Honor who seemed cheerful and sweet. I am bored, so bored for one cannot now go ahead; one can only save from the wreckage one's hopes, one's possessions, and some part of one's fortune. What a mess! .... I only want an oval library with doors leading into a rose garden by the sea ...

The raids continue killing a few people every night. Aberdeen had a baddish raid with thirty-three casualties but this has not been announced.

TUESDAY 16TH JULY

Rab, escorted by me, lunched at the Yugoslav Legation, 41 Upper Grosvenor Street, where there was a little festival to meet the Maiskys. I had arranged this capitulation to the new order, and found them both far better than I had expected: she[2] is *soignée*,[3] even chic and pleasant and very obviously not a communist; he is clever, charming, shrewd and humorous. After the ladies left the dining room we sat about the table drinking .... a little later Maisky and Rab retired into an adjoining room and continued their confidential conversations, while the others joined the ladies. Mme Subbotić[4] confided in me that she had asked Maisky at luncheon what he thought really of Hitler's triumphant progress? 'London may be his Moscow,' Maisky replied. 'Moscow may be his London, you mean!' Mme Subbotić retorted, which is a sly allusion to Hitler's boast that he will take Moscow in September .... Rab and I left only at 3.30. The new order is not so terrible as I feared; one could certainly get on with Beneš[5] and perhaps with Maisky, too.

1 The road linking Burma and China through which, to the annoyance of the Japanese, supplies were being moved to the Chinese, with whom they were at war.
2 Agniya Maiskaya was described in newspaper profiles as a talented pianist and needle-woman, and was the first Soviet Ambassador's wife to entertain a British prime minister, when Chamberlain visited the Embassy in March 1939.
3 Well groomed.
4 Wife of the Yugoslav Minister.
5 Edvard Beneš (1884–1948), the former Czechoslovak President and leader of the government-in-exile.

This week will bring a Hitler peace offensive; although people better informed than I think otherwise. They prophesy an attempt at invasion. We are not there yet.

Dined alone, read erotic literature – always an abortive pastime.

WEDNESDAY 17TH JULY

James Gunn came to Belgrave Square and sketched the library, which he is to use as a background for my portrait. He lunched, also Patsy looking v pretty like a Greuze.[1]

Rab made an interim, or rather preparatory, statement in the House of Commons today about our so-called concessions to Japan over the closing of the Burma Road. It was not well received. I arrived at 2.30 and at 2.40 came a telephone message to the effect that the agreement had just been signed in Tokyo. Rab had to make a Blitz alteration in his script, and breathlessly I ran to the House of Lords in order to catch Halifax, who came in from lunching with Queen Wilhelmina. He looked grave and ashen; when I told him the good news he seemed irritated (he had prophesied failure) and was not as pleased as he ought to have been. He refused to alter his answer to tally with Rab's and made the announcement as originally drafted; thus the Commons were a jump ahead of the peers! Rab had a rough passage and there were jeering cries of 'appeasement' from all the ardent warmongers . . . .

Later, feeling *désoeuvré* and not quite myself all day . . . . as if my brain missed a cog as it revolved – I rushed to the Bath Club to swim and sweat, and later returned to the House to give Honor and her jagger, Enid Raphael,[2] dinner. Honor looked divine, quite lovely and elegant. Why can't she always look so?

There was an acrimonious debate about evacuation of children to Canada and the USA. Much unfair and unsound argument about the rich fleeing and the poor remaining . . . . Duff Cooper roughly attacked, which is always salutary and to be encouraged.

THURSDAY 18TH JULY

Winston was superb, magnificent, in the House as he answered Questions and later made the very important statement about the Far East; and he successfully quashed the leftist Opposition for eagerness for war. The anti-Chamberlainites were puzzled . . . the House was crowded . . .

I dined at the Yugoslav Legation in order to say 'goodbye' to Alexander and Nicky who leave in the morning for Yugoslavia. Nicky, gay, clever and malicious, was in bed and I sat on it as he ate his supper; then I went down with Alexander

---

1 Jean-Baptiste Greuze (1725–1805) was a French portrait painter.
2 Enid Catherine Raphael (1901–42), daughter of Ernest Raphael and Flora Cecilia Sassoon.

who every day becomes more charming and handsome and better-mannered. He is sad to leave Eton, yet he hates work . . . I came home and found Honor alone reading that most riveting of all books, our passbook. We are a little over £25,000 overdrawn. I wonder where all the money goes . . .

Tomorrow, my mother's 71st birthday (I sent her a cable), is the day of the alleged Hitlerian offensive against England.

FRIDAY 19TH JULY

. . . . I have the office to myself, and prefer it so. A long day with ambassadors, the sulky, sly Chinese *qui en est*;[1] the lame dignified gentle Jap; the Finn, the garrulous Pole . . . . Walked at lunchtime to Christie's and watched the interminable Red Cross Sale. Nothing I wanted today. As I came out I ran into Cecil Beaton who is recently back from New York where he stayed with Emerald . . . . Emerald is not a success with New York society and has been much abused by the local press but she had a small admiring coterie on Long Island. Cecil and I discussed Osbert Sitwell's morals . . . .

At six o'clock, we turned on the radio to listen to Hitler, but the speech was badly relayed and Rab and I understood nothing except that he was less ranting, less hysterical than usual. Of course the Foreign Office made no attempt to take down the speech and we were indebted to Viorel Tilea, who rang up, for accurate information. He had heard it all and told us. It seemed more moderate than usual and was, in fact, both extremely clever and almost a definite bid for peace. Rab telephoned about 8.30 to the Dorchester and got on to Lord Halifax and retold Tilea's comments. I was a little shocked that he should so blatantly pretend that he had heard the speech clearly. However, when dealing with Halifax one must be clever. I am more than ever convinced that H is the greatest fraud ever perpetuated on the English race, although I admit all his charm and his many estimable qualities. But he hasn't a victory to show now after two and a half years here. I hope he doesn't go; but it might be better if he did. Probably most people would have done worse. Democracy is so constricted and is an absurd, and luckily declining institution! . . . . I drove Rab to an obscure flat in S. Kensington where he addressed a meeting of young people who are planning a better world in the future!! And at nine o'clock I listened in to the BBC commentary on Hitler's speech and went early to bed.

SATURDAY 20TH JULY

On duty at the office for the greater part of the day: am I never to have another holiday? Rab lunched with the Egyptian Ambassador, and although late insisted

1 Who is their ambassador.

on going by bus. He is extraordinarily mean financially and begrudges every spent sou. It is a curious trait in so balanced a character, who happens to be the possessor of an ample fortune. Halifax shares it: I have never shown any sign of it and I trust my son will not suffer unduly thereby. Rab and I discussed Hitler's speech: we both think it good stuff, but that is the minority now. I urged Rab that Halifax, not Winston, be selected to reply to it as Winston is so hated in Germany. Possibly his government, still popular with the masses, may one day be eclipsed and daubed 'warmongering'! The warmongerers [*sic*] are all in it. Look at Amery who more than anyone defended war, and wanted it: he has two sons under 30, one because he is 'delicate' lives abroad, the other is a press attaché in Belgrade. No fighting for them or for other Jews when they can help it.[1]

I drove to Kelvedon and we dined *à deux*. Honor drinks recklessly but as she works all day at her farm I suppose there is no great harm done, except that she is toughening. It is odd to be so easily influenced by one's companions.

SUNDAY 21ST JULY

I came up to London and spent the day quietly at the FO, as I like doing. Peaceful, profitable and pleasant. There is more trouble at Cairo and King Farouk continues to intrigue against us. And I fear a blow-up in Portugal. The PM sent a telephone message inviting Halifax to come to Chequers for the night. H[alifax] was attacked today by Atticus in *The Times*.[2] Our reign is ending, I shall regret its closure, although I have hardly ever been in complete sympathy with it.

The Budget on Tuesday next will be in the nature of a knockout blow to our class, and to everyone else. One can only live on capital, if it is worth living at all.

There are some terrors at the FO. The worst are Rex Leeper, G. W. Thompson[3] and old [Laurence] Collier. Orme Sargent and Vansittart are always wrong, and have been proved so, but are somewhat redeemed by their charm and good manners. Ivo Mallet amongst the smaller fry is despicable and liverish. I like Lawford immensely; but it is an incompetent Office, hopelessly old-fashioned, prejudiced, rusty and foolish . . . as I sat here I began a list of all the people I have

---

1 This is a particularly bizarre set of slurs, aimed at Leo Amery doubtless because of his consistent opposition to appeasement and Channon's resentment at the preferment this had now brought him. Amery's elder son John (qv) was living in France, was a fascist and would later work actively for the Nazis and be hanged for treason. The younger son, Julian (qv), had a distinguished war, fighting in Yugoslavia, Albania and China. Whatever Channon imagined their part-Jewish heritage signified for either them, he could hardly have been more wrong.
2 Thus in the MS. He means the *Sunday Times*.
3 There is no one of this name recorded in the Diplomatic List. Channon is almost certainly referring to Geoffrey Harington Thompson (1898–1967), who was serving in London from 1939 to 1941 and whose career culminated in his being Ambassador to Brazil from 1952 to 1956. He was knighted in 1949.

ever liked and it is staggeringly long . . . and then my mind moved back to the Foreign Office which I called 'Bourbon House' since they have learnt nothing and forgotten nothing. They are asleep, dreaming in a pre-Hitler, pre-dictator world, foolish, carping, finicky, inefficient and futile.

Alan came to see me: he is thinner, handsomer and improved. He has broken off with Michael Rose after a *Fledermaus*[1] comedy too complicated and petty to chronicle.

MONDAY 22ND JULY

Dr Beneš called and I had a word with him. He has been officially informed that he is the head of the Czechoslovak Provisional Committee or Government, and he smilingly told me that twenty-two years ago next month, Lord Balfour[2] had appointed him or recognised him and the Committee for the first time. History indeed repeats itself. I mistrust the man . . . .

Stayed late and when I came in I was soon joined by Alan, up again from Brighton. Rather an unexpected and tempestuous *soirée* with Alan!

TUESDAY 23RD JULY

The Budget which is to smash us has been fairly well received: there are even complaints that it is too mild. What an extraordinary animal is the English taxpayer. We personally are left with two bob in the pound[3] in the top bracket.

Kitty Brownlow, painted and pretty, came to lunch and then I rushed to the House and took up my important place directly behind Winston who was in roaring spirits. He gave slashing answers which he had himself drafted, to foolish questions and generally he convulsed the House. He is at the very top of his form now and the House is with him, as is the country, but it may be impolitic to be so disdainful. He knows little about foreign affairs. I sat behind him and later took his papers from him and in so doing scratched him: however he most graciously thanked me. But I am shy with him and cannot get it right: it is all the fault of that fiend Randolph.[4]

WEDNESDAY 24TH JULY

Lunched with Cecil Beaton in a tiny but super-attractive house in Pelham Place. I was envious of him and it: he has a curious flair for arranging rooms amusingly.

---

1 After the comic opera of 1874 *Die Fledermaus*, by Johann Strauss II.
2 A. J. Balfour (1848–1930), Foreign Secretary between 1916 and 1919.*
3 Slang for two shillings, or 10 per cent (there being twenty shillings in the pound).
4 Churchill's problematical son (qv).

I felt tired and dreaded my evening which was destined to be a long one with Leslie Hore-Belisha, for whom I have much affection. He dined with me here, and I poisoned his mind yet further against the Glamour Boys and Anthony's minions and methods. He says that he is unsuspecting. We went on to *Black Velvet* – a boring revue featuring Vic Oliver.[1] Last time I went was with Peter, from whom I have not heard for days, almost weeks.

Communications with Cairo are so complicated . . . . Leslie was everywhere recognised and conducted himself like a prima donna: he was even cheered by the crowds and the uniformed men in the packed theatre. Considerable war atmosphere at the Hippodrome. We returned to Belgrave Square and gossiped until, alas, 1.30. He is in fine fettle, our Leslie, and by no means considers that he is down. He is violently opposed to Winston: and repeated what Lloyd George recently said of him 'that he has made a mess, been a failure in every office he has ever held'. Lloyd George, whose affection for Winston has noticeably cooled of late, predicts that after the PM's first great blunder the country, now admittedly hysterically infatuated with him, will turn against him and remember his mistakes and possibly even his pro-war leanings. I wonder? Leslie thinks that his successor can only be Mr Chamberlain again reinstated. I hope he is right and I was tired, dull . . . Leslie confided in me that Winston had been responsible for Horabin's[2] election to the House, had arranged the by-election and was thus instrumental in bringing in another Opposition member last July.

I walked home with Leslie in the moonlight and sadly ruminated on the beauty of London in the blackout and on my own loneliness.

THURSDAY 25TH JULY

This morning as I sat at my desk in the FO there was a tremendous explosion and I rushed to the window. People in Downing Street were rushing about and soon someone emerged from the area windows. I thought it was an IRA outrage,[3] as did the War Cabinet already sitting. It was about 11.45. I rang up and got on to Miss

---

1 Victor Oliver von Samek (1898–1964) was from a Viennese Jewish family, served in the Austrian cavalry in the Great War and worked in finance before becoming a professional musician. He then realised he had talent as a comedian, and in the 1930s and 1940s was a big star on radio, in music hall and in some popular films. He married Sarah Millicent Hermione Churchill (1914–82), an actress and singer, in 1936 as the first of her three husbands and they were divorced in 1945. For Churchill's views on his son-in-law see Vol. I, entry for 27 April 1938 and footnote.

2 Thomas Lewis Horabin (1896–1956) was MP for North Cornwall from 1939 to 1950, as a Liberal until 1947 and a Socialist thereafter. He had been an active anti-appeaser. It is peculiar that Channon should accuse Churchill of having arranged the by-election, which was caused by the death from natural causes of the sitting member, Sir Francis Acland, Bt.

3 See entry for 3 February 1939. The last attempt at a bombing by the IRA had been the previous March.

Watson who had been frightened; but she laughingly reassured me it had only been a boiler bursting! And all ended in laughter.

At the House I was pumped as to whether Rab would like the Ministry of Information, as Duff is definitely going, as I always knew he would eventually. He has put the whole press against him.

Two cocktail parties, one at the Carlton Club given by Victor Raikes to meet Miss Wilson, his fiancée, a pretty full-blown girl who is evidently in love with him; and then I went to Loelia Westminster's where I found half London. Everyone was charming and affectionate to me; Daphne Weymouth as wildly attractive, vague and licentious as ever . . . . many more. All my past, my too-long past, seemed to be in that overcrowded room, and I liked them all except Maureen Stanley, who has done more to demoralise London than anyone.

Friday 26th July

Lunched with Harold Balfour at Buck's and we did ourselves well as he leaves tomorrow for the US by flying boat. I was tempted to go with him and it could have been arranged. I bought him a small dressing case . . . . Michael Beaumont[1] joined us for a little. He says that he mistrusts Winston, thinks him a greater menace than Hitler. Duff Cooper was alone with Brendan Bracken and both looked glum. I wondered whether Brendan was breaking it to him that he must go? I really think that he will weather this storm, but not the next one.

Saturday 27th July

The Office all day and then to Kelvedon.
  I fear that Neville is ill.[2]

Sunday 28th July

A gloriously hot day and I lay in the sun and got beautifully burnt while planes zoomed on high. I fell asleep, and woke with an uncomfortable feeling that I was being watched. I opened my eyes and found eight swans peering and hissing at me. I felt like Leda, Lohengrin or King Ludwig and hurriedly retreated into the pavilion. The grey, ungainly cygnets and their proud pompous parents then disported themselves in my swimming pool for some time.

1 Michael Wentworth Beaumont (1903–58) was Conservative MP for Aylesbury from 1929 to 1938. He had resigned his commission in the Royal Artillery because of ill health the previous January.
2 Chamberlain had been in continual pain and had been in hospital for exploratory surgery. His doctors discovered he had inoperable bowel cancer, but decided not to tell him. He resumed work in August, but the pain became too much for him and he resigned in late September.

I came up to London . . . . Alan came up from Henlow about eleven and rushed to the Dorchester where he found Patsy in the lobby talking with the Prime Minister and Brendan. The PM was most gracious to Alan: he had been dining upstairs with Duff – who is, I should imagine, soon for the high jump as the popular outcry, particularly in the press, clamours for his dismissal.

MONDAY 29TH JULY

A quiet day. I lunched at Hanover Lodge with Alice and three young Frogs, none of whom has any intention of joining de Gaulle, whom I saw in the passage at the FO.

Neville Chamberlain has been taken to hospital for a serious operation; and thus fades the last hope of peace. The 'War Party' is in complete control. I gather he has 'piles'; once again one man's illness will have influenced world events.

TUESDAY 30TH JULY

Lunched with Natasha Bagration in her tiny flat: excellent food. Profumo,[1] the baby MP, a bright-eyed, handsome youth in uniform was there and I detected an understanding, or at least an attraction between him and Natasha . . . . I went to the House as it was our big FO debate which began with an absurd Alice in Wonderland wrangle about procedure which lasted from 3.45 until 5.35 – in wartime. It was ludicrous in the extreme. At long last the debate began in secret session; Wardlaw-Milne opened with a surprisingly bitter attack on our Far East policy and on our closing the Burma Road in particular. Rab followed – the PM had just left the Chamber, and he was excellent, really first class, easy, informed, confiding and statesmanlike, and much of his inelegant jerkiness was absent. It was his most successful parliamentary performance so far and I was most impressed . . . . the debate continued. About 7.30, Winston returned to the Chamber and a hurried whispered consultation took place which I overheard, as I sat immediately behind him. At last he agreed to speak and rose at 7.55. We had then forty minutes of magnificent oratory and artistry, but he gave away no secrets and, indeed, talked from the heart rather than from the head. He was so eloquent and even amusing, that he had the House with him although he said little

---

1 John Dennis 'Jack' Profumo (1915–2006) was the youngest MP – the 'Baby of the House' – from 1940 to 1941 and again from 1944 to 1945. He was Conservative MP for Kettering from 1940 to 1945 and for Stratford-on-Avon from 1950 to 1963. He was Secretary of State for War from 1960 to 1963. He succeeded his father as Baron Profumo in the Italian peerage in 1940. His name is most associated with the scandal of 1963 in which he had denied impropriety with a woman who had also been intimate with a Russian naval attaché, and which forced his resignation from the government and the Commons. He had an immensely distinguished war, in which he fought in North Africa and France and ended in the rank of brigadier; after leaving politics he spent over forty years as a charity worker. He married, in 1954, Valerie Hobson (1917–98), a celebrated actress.

about foreign affairs. He did, however, develop a defence of our action in closing the Burma Road. Then he sat down, and left the Chamber after a wild ovation. I fetched Attlee in so that Rab might dine . . . . And we then had a communistic interlude. Russia is laying her plans for a communistic Europe, and will certainly claim Czechoslovakia as her peace prize when the war ends. Oh! the blindness of our statesmen!

The House rose at ten and I drove Rab home to rest upon his deserved but unheralded laurels! He was, however, much congratulated and went to bed pleased with a definite parliamentary success. He is growing every day politically.

Peter is much in my mind: I feel that I shall see him soon again, which would be an answered prayer. I have twice suggested to Rab that Wavell be summoned home for a conference as the military position in the Middle East is a touch precarious; and he might well by accompanied by his ADC. Who knows?

WEDNESDAY 31ST JULY

Rab's speech last night in the secret session has caused a parliamentary sensation . . . . when I escorted Rab through the lobbies today, many MPs including some temperamental, hostile Glamour Boys stopped to congratulate him. He was enchanted when I said it had 'been the greatest thing since the *Graf Spee*'!

I hear that some young man seeking to ingratiate himself with the Prime Minister and thinking he was an Old Etonian, said to him 'Well, sir, once again Eton is winning the war as it did in the days of Waterloo!' Winston saucily replied with his inimitable stutter: 'Far be it for Lord Gort and myself to compete with the claims of King Leopold and Captain Ramsay.'[1]

Honor up for the night and we went through her jewels and she returned them to the bank. A big collection but nothing of the first value. I had to leave her as I was dining at the Romanian Legation, a gay male sextet; Tilea, our host, who so soon leaves, and indeed has already given up his *lettres-de-créance*,[2] Drogheda,[3] Charles Peake, Gladwyn Jebb, Hector Bolitho. Lovely food: I ate and drank too much and bored them with accounts of my dinners with General Göring! I chatter too much when tipsy and always regret it.

THURSDAY 1ST AUGUST

A whole month has passed and no invasion yet, although there are constant air raids along the coasts and elsewhere. Norwich suffers severely.

---

1 Both the King and Ramsay were Old Etonians.
2 Credentials.
3 Henry Charles Ponsonby Moore (1884–1957), by courtesy Viscount Moore from 1892 to 1908 when he succeeded his father as 10th Earl of Drogheda. He would serve as Director of Economic Warfare from 1942 to 1945, and be given a United Kingdom peerage as Baron Moore in 1954.

This afternoon I wanted to be alone but Leslie Hore-Belisha insisted on my accompanying him out shopping. And we talked at the Bath Club: he is no maiden's dream when naked: he is portly and hirsute but what horrified me is that I weigh as much as he – thirteen stones dressed.

Raymond Mortimer[1] came to dine and we returned to the H of C, where an acrimonious debate was taking place in the form of a violent personal attack on the Ministry of Information and Duff Cooper in particular. I talked to him for a bit and found him jittery, even shaking with anxiety. He acquitted himself well to my deep, deep disappointment; but my press friends tell me he is now doomed. Leslie Belisha hopes for the job and is angling actively for it. Raymond and I went with Harold Nicolson[2] to Pratt's where we were joined by Tommy Lascelles,[3] a *sournois*[4] courtier, who, however, made himself agreeable.

I was rather shocked by 'Fruity' Metcalfe's[5] violent denunciation of the Duke of Windsor: 'Fruity' was in an adjoining cubicle at the Bath Club and he said that he had had no patience with a man who was always pining for his wife and rushed from the front to join her! In other words, Wallis Windsor has broken up this old and tiresome friendship which always irritated and bored her. Fruity's conduct is none too glorious – he only rushed to Le Havre in order to get a boat to England.

FRIDAY 2ND AUGUST

I learned that Wavell is coming back to London to be consulted by HMG. Perhaps Peter will accompany him? I pray it may be so. I sent him a cryptic cable asking him to stay here. It would be glorious to see him again. Glorious! Glorious!

I had my bottom cleansed today; I am so fat, furious and foolishly 40. How can I regain my youthful figure?

The *Evening Standard* printed a violent leader against Duff Cooper in its earlier editions; in the later ones it had been deleted. I was suspicious and afterwards learned that Winston had telephoned to Beaverbrook and asked him to join the War Cabinet – an announcement was made later in the evening, and

---

1 Charles Raymond Bell Mortimer (1895–1980) was a literary and art critic who eventually became literary editor of the *New Statesman*.
2 Nicolson and Mortimer were lovers.
3 Alan Frederick 'Tommy' Lascelles (1887–1981) was a cousin by marriage of Princess Mary, Countess of Harewood, the Princess Royal*. Having served in the Great War and won the Military Cross he joined the Court in 1920 and served as private secretary to the Prince of Wales until 1929. He was secretary to Lord Bessborough, the Governor-General of Canada, from 1931 to 1935, when he re-entered royal service as assistant private secretary to the King, and served Edward VIII and George VI in the capacity. He became private secretary to King George VI in 1943, and to Queen Elizabeth II in 1952. He retired in 1953. He was knighted in 1939. He declined a peerage. See also Vol. I, entry for 29 May 1925 and footnote.
4 Sly, or cunning.
5 Former close friend of the Duke of Windsor.*

at the same time, told him to lay off the Ministry of Information. Beaverbrook I hear is radiant. We now have all the crooks in power, but I am pro-Beaver.

SATURDAY 3RD AUGUST

Went by bourgeois train to Cambridge where I lunched with Sir Will Spens,[1] a pernickety, pleasant, important man, Master of Corpus Christi and Regional Commissioner for East Anglia. He was particularly agreeable to me, singled me out for attention and we adjourned from Hall to a business meeting of MPs. The news was disturbing and the outlook grim. After we had aired our complaints . . . . someone mentioned Duff Cooper and the Ministry of Information. Everyone went off like a rocket and there was a torrent of abuse. He must resign. Spens, whilst agreeing, was bored, and rose: 'The meeting, gentlemen, is now concluded. I am taking Channon away with me for a private talk.' I followed him to the Master's Lodge where, over whiskies and sodas, we had a long confidential conversation; he is anxious about Fritzi, languishing still on the Isle of Man and he is disturbed too, by the 'position'. He is anti-Churchill, and thinks we should have answered Herr Hitler succinctly. He is rather defeatist. He drove me to the station and confided in me that Rab had been too easily influenced by political currents. All hope for England ended when Neville resigned, he said . . . . I proceeded to Kelvedon in the great heat. The car met me at Bishop's Stortford.

Kelvedon is lovely. Dined alone with Honor who seems *désoeuvrée*.

A little surprised and considerably disappointed to hear nothing from Peter and Cairo.

SUNDAY 4TH AUGUST

A glorious day and I spent happy hours sunbathing. Aeroplanes buzzed on high. Last evening, apparently, about 10.30 there was a biggish air raid very near to us . . . . but we heard nothing.

Dined alone with H, who was depressed and depressing, 'difficult'.

MONDAY 5TH AUGUST

Came up by train: there was no reply from my cable to Peter and so I sent him another on hearing that Wavell is due to arrive on Wednesday. All day at the Office and with my secretary. About seven I took Rab, weary, worn, and overworked, to

1 William Spens (1882–1962) was a scientist; elected a fellow of Corpus Christi in 1907, he became Master in 1927 and served until 1952. He was Vice Chancellor of Cambridge University from 1931 to 1933. He was responsible for the Spens Report that recommended dividing secondary education into secondary, technical and grammar schools, a recommendation that formed the basis of Butler's Education Act of 1944.

the Bath Club to swim and later we looked in at Buck's for a cocktail. He was in high spirits. He is very hirsute. Buck's was deserted.

A very hot day, is this cancelled 'Bank Holiday'; crowds were lolling in the parks. It was disagreeable . . . . I wish I had stayed at Kelvedon.

TUESDAY 6TH AUGUST

A crushing cable from Master Coats: he cannot get back and Wavell has left alone. Ahead there are rumblings in the Middle East and Somaliland is being invaded by Mussolini's legionnaires.

WEDNESDAY 7TH AUGUST

Simon Harcourt-Smith[1] was very funny about his fleeting visit to Badminton.[2] Queen Mary, apparently, sat very straight in her white *moiré* silk, whalebones and massive sapphires. She talked of our dining room and asked whether we had put away the Meissen china. On being told no, she said 'Quite right, quite right. There will be no bombs over London.' Hours in the House: the Chief Whip, David, for the second time slept soundly beside me in the library; I think he is kept up late these nights by Lady Bridget Poulett,[3] who is too young for him.

I dined with Raymond Mortimer in his atmospheric Endsleigh Gardens, Bloomsbury, flat; he has such an alert mind. And also I listened with glee to Duff Cooper being heckled in the 1922 Committee. He had a chilly reception there: he is such a second-rate little bantam turkey cock, with the surface spurious culture which his really remarkable memory gives him.

The Italians continue to advance in Somaliland. Wavell has arrived safely.

I had a talk with Attlee in his room: he is quite agreeable and easy but small; he shook and trilled; I fear he is v nervous and fidgety.

THURSDAY 8TH AUGUST

A difficult day, as early the Post Office rang me on the telephone to say that my telegram to Fritzi in the Isle of Man has been returned undelivered as he 'left for Canada' on July 2nd!! I was terrified as I feel sure he was on the *Arandora Star*, the murder ship sent by Anthony Eden!! I rushed to the Home Office, after talking to Honor who had had a letter returned too, but I was reassured by Norman

---

1 Simon Guisbert Harcourt-Smith (1906–82) was a diplomat, an expert Sinologist, and a successful novelist who also wrote books on art.
2 The Queen Dowager had evacuated to Badminton House for the duration, staying with the Duke and Duchess of Beaufort. The Duchess was her niece.
3 Bridget Elizabeth Felicia Henrietta Augusta Poulett (1912–75), Lady Bridget by courtesy, was the daughter of the 7th Earl Poulett. She had been a model for Cecil Beaton (qv) and other photographers. She married, in 1948, Louis Robledo, a Colombian diplomat.

Brook,[1] Anderson's[2] capable competent charming secretary that Fritzi had sailed in the [illegible], the day after the *Arandora Star*, and that he had arrived safely in Canada. Poor boy, herded with a lot of brutal Nazis and dirty Jews; it must be terrible for him. My heart aches . . . .

Sad letters from Peter which Wavell brought with him; he is so disappointed at being left behind in what he calls 'that tart of a town' but there wasn't room in the aeroplane.

I took the six o'clock train to Brighton where I arrived in lovely weather: everyone was agog about the air battle over the Channel. German planes had been over Brighton several times. Alan – Sub-Lieutenant Lennox-Boyd, RN – rushed me off to dine on his stationary ship near Brighton. There were nearly 1,000 officers and ratings present, and it amused me to see Alan treated so cavalierly. He seems to have adapted himself, however, to his new life. But it is a shock always to come down a few strata and make contact with a lower class. For the first time in my life, I was not at the top table . . . . The function was ruined by what I thought an outrageous bit of sadism on the part of the Mess Chairman, or whatever the common little upstart calls himself. He rose and said: 'Will the officer who tried to smoke stand up.' An unfortunate sub-lieutenant . . . . of Spanish extraction got up. 'Leave the room,' he was brutally told. And the poor fellow, all eyes glued on him, walked silently but with hidalgo[3] dignity out of the hall. I was sorry for him.

We walked back together to an hotel where we drank Krug with Lord and Lady Carrick,[4] a dreadful couple, common and cheap: unfortunately they live in Essex and want to know us; I was cold as I knew that Honor would be terrible to them, if I encouraged them. Alan, a born democrat, was charming and enthusiastic about them. Alan altogether delightful. I am sharing his bed.

A vast number of German aeroplanes brought down over the coast. Our Air Force is sublime.

FRIDAY 9TH AUGUST

I woke with a splitting headache and listened to the throb-throb of the German planes on high: Alan will sleep (like Honor) in an almost hermetically sealed room

---

1 Norman Craven Brook (1902–67) was Sir John Anderson's principal private secretary from 1938 to 1942, Deputy Secretary to the War Cabinet from 1942 to 1943, Permanent Secretary to the Ministry of Reconstruction from 1943 to 1945, Additional Secretary to the Cabinet from 1945 to 1946 and Cabinet Secretary from 1947 to 1962. He was head of the Home Civil Service and Joint Permanent Secretary to the Treasury from 1956 to 1962. He was knighted in 1946 and raised to the peerage as 1st Baron Normanbrook in 1963.

2 Sir John Anderson, the Home Secretary.

3 A Spanish grandee.

4 Theobald Walter Somerset Henry Butler (1903–57), was by courtesy Viscount Ikerrin from 1909 to 1931, when he succeeded his father as 8th Earl of Carrick. He married in 1938, as the second of his three wives, Margaret Power (1903–54).

and I was stifled. I crept to his window and opened it; he heard me and woke up. Window argument . . . Alan later got up (at 7.20) in a distracted irritating mood. There is no one I love so much; no one who can infuriate me more, and waves of anger passed between us – and were soon forgotten. I left for London at 9 a.m.

Fifty-three German raiders, so the newspapers announced, were brought down during yesterday.

Rab at the Foreign Office in high spirits and pleased with his anti-baldness treatment which I had arranged this morning. I hung about Halifax's door and eventually caught a glimpse of Wavell when he emerged. He is a pocket Cyclops and seemed dwarfed by Edward the Confessor.[1] Wavell smiled at me as we passed, little knowing how obsessed by him I am. It was a Proustian *rencontre*[2] . . . As I drove Rab to lunch at the Russian Embassy he first inveighed against Duff Cooper, whom he considers deplorable, and then he lamented on the fall of England and our impending doom and death which has resulted from our obtuseness over a quarter of a century over Germany.

Saturday 10th August

I woke early and restless as one often does after a 'binge', and 'binge' is the proper description of my banquet last night. The house looked beautiful and brilliant; it is some time since I have seen it *en grande tenue*[3] – over a year.

Came:

Rab, the Romanian Minister, Harold Butler,[4] Hector Bolitho, Charles Peake, Alan, Peter Loxley, Brendan Bracken.

There was much drink, Krug 1920, but dull food. Brendan immediately dominated the scene and was in his most anecdotal ruminative mood and held us nearly spellbound with his tales of Winston etc. We left the dining room only at 11.15 and by then we were all more or less tipsy. I was irritated by the cook sending up tinned pears, although I had had fresh ones sent up from Kelvedon. A flash of annoyance crossed over me; but it was unobserved as the smoke, the chat drowned all else . . . . Rab, who is a sane and simple liver, did a Cinderella and left at midnight. The others, alas, remained on listening to Brendan. We drank much and my depleted cellar was further diminished. At 3.10 Brendan and Harold left, arm in arm, and went out into the blackout; Charles Peake and Peter Loxley left together. Alan had already left by car for Brighton. 'Violet' Tilea[5] in an excess of enthusiasm,

1 Channon refers to the pious, and tall, Lord Halifax.
2 Meeting.
3 In full dress.
4 No one of this name is traceable. It is highly likely Channon wrote 'Butler' in error for 'Balfour'.
5 His Christian name was Viorel.

kissed me 'goodnight' and 'goodbye'. 'Romania's farewell to England,' someone remarked.

I came to Kelvedon and found that the gardens had been opened to the public for some local charity.

Southend was considerably damaged by bombs last night: hundreds of windows were blown out along the Thorpe Bay frontage: no casualties. I saw a fantastic telegram from Sam Hoare, from Madrid, where he reports a rumour that England will be invaded this week and completely subjugated in three days' time. Half Spain believes it. The Führer has apparently said that England would be reduced to submission by August 15th. Only five days more.

SUNDAY 11TH AUGUST

Honor in great good looks and high spirits; but I suspect strange ongoings; she is an ostrich married to a lynx. However what I cannot prevent, I do not comment upon. It is foolish to snarl impotently – that has been the foreign policy of this country for too long. I sunbathed and watched the many planes and pruned roses. I am much in the press as the Fritzi story[1] has cropped up again.

MONDAY 12TH AUGUST

Breakfasted naked by the swimming bath, pruned more roses and sunbathed and then drove to London in a rather nervous state – constipation, I think, due to grouse eaten twice yesterday.[2]

A frenzied morning sending parcels of hair oil, many letters, a dressing gown and a Middlesex Yeomanry button containing a compass to Peter. General Wavell who flies back tomorrow will take them.

The battle for Britain has begun: there are mammoth air raids now every day. Tonight's bag was about fifty. Harold Balfour dined with me and we grew rather excited over religion: he is illogical about it. An enjoyable conversation, and I went back to the Air Ministry with him, and we went to the secret Map Room and I saw the little flags indicating where there had been raids and planes down. It was a big day for the RAF.

I have written a long letter to Princess Alice[3] telling her about Fritzi, who is an internee at Ottawa. It is dreadful to think that she, reigning at Rideau Hall, may not know of the plight of her young cousin. Still I appreciate she is in a difficult position, wife of the Governor of Canada, and herself the sister of

---

1 About the German Prince having been sheltered at Kelvedon before being interned.
2 And clearly shot out of season.
3 Cousin of George V and sister-in-law of Queen Mary. Her husband, the Earl of Athlone (*né* Prince Alexander of Teck, qv), had been Governor-General of Canada since earlier in the year.*

'Charlie Coburg'[1] as the Grand Duke of Saxe-Coburg-Gotha is called, and he a leading Nazi. Harold will deliver the letter on Friday, when he reaches Ottawa.

TUESDAY 13TH AUGUST

A busy day, pulling strings and arranging matters. I refused to dine with Rab as I wanted to be alone for a few hours. The calm of solitude is like velvet, soothing, rich and satisfactory.

Another big day along the Channel, with many planes down. It seems as if the big struggle has really begun. Shall we be invaded tomorrow? Rab and I received the overseas journalists at the Office and [he] spoke to them in his inimitable confiding way ....

Three Australian ministers were killed in an aeroplane incident: Winston referred to this tragedy in fitting terms at the end of Questions. I see that the Beneš have lunched today with the King and Queen. What a *rencontre!* .... All my parcels left for Cairo via Wavell. As I write, I hear the buzzing of planes on high: is London to be raided tonight? I feel that at long last we are entering upon a decisive phase of the war.

I had a sad mad letter from my poor mad mother: there is nothing whatever one can do for or about her.

I feel apprehensive about the future: what can happen? What will happen to us all during the next stupendous few weeks? Is the defeatism of the Americans justifiable?

WEDNESDAY 14TH AUGUST

The raids continue but today they were on a reduced scale.

Anthony Eden addressed us in the 1922 Committee; and made a fairly good impression but the growing habit of ministers of blaming their predecessors is irritating, and smacks too, of defeatism. He is a very moderate fellow.

FRIDAY 16TH AUGUST

Two raids; they are becoming a nuisance. One was late in the morning. I sat doing a crossword puzzle with Godfrey Thomas[2] in the Foreign Office cellar then I walked

1 Leopold Charles Edward George Albert of Saxe-Coburg and Gotha (1884–1954) inherited the Dukedom of Albany from his father, of whom he was a posthumous child. Educated in England until 1900, when he became Duke of Saxe-Coburg and Gotha, he was thereafter Germanicised, and fought for the Kaiser in the Great War, which caused him to lose his British titles and the style of Royal Highness. He first met Hitler in 1922 and became a committed Nazi.

2 Godfrey John Vignoles Thomas (1889–1968) succeeded his father as 10th Bt in 1919. He joined the Diplomatic Service in 1912, and served as private secretary to the Prince of Wales from 1919 to 1936 and as assistant private secretary to the King in 1936. He was private secretary to the Duke of Gloucester (qv) from 1937 to 1957, though seconded back to the Foreign Office from 1939 to 1944. He was knighted in 1925.

to lunch with Gladwyn Jebb at the Travellers. Had a Turkish bath, as I am getting so outrageously fat. On my return to the FO the sirens again sounded and I spent another hour in the cellar with Godfrey Thomas and we discussed the Windsors, and I gave him my version. He is charming and a great loyal gentleman – even if a courtier. Later I helped to dress Rab, who was going to dine for the first time at Stornoway House.[1] He felt nervous as a bride when I dropped him there.

A lovely evening alone.

SATURDAY 17TH AUGUST

A glorious hot day. but I awoke nervous and with feelings of foreboding. Rab had dined *à quatre* at Stornoway House: the *ménage* Maisky were the other two, which Rab described as an Alice in Wonderland evening. Beaverbrook was nasal, hospitable, *affairé* and constantly went to the telephone to talk to the Prime Minister and others.

I sat to James Gunn who is a bore with genius: and he is attractive and handsome but his half-baked political views are suffocating and I can barely stay awake as he paints me.

I drove to Kelvedon and felt irritated and ogre-ish: H greeted me with her ungracious detachment and foolishly furious I retreated in a rage to the gardens where I sat for an hour drinking in the soporific beauty of the evening. After dinner I went, still sulky, to bed, as Honor read *Northanger Abbey*.

Surprisingly few planes today: is there a lull in the Blitzkrieg?

SUNDAY 18TH AUGUST

The heat cuts me: I have never known such a day in England. I lay naked, pruned the roses and lazed. Honor very charming – contrite? About lunchtime Hector Bolitho rang me up to tell me that Rodney Wilkinson had been killed: he flew his Spitfire into a Messerschmitt, and crashed. I shan't forget his engaging charm, his curious shuffle and infectious gaiety; the strange Egyptian eyes, the highly sexed full mouth, the long limbs and natural elegance of this *charmeur* who had something negroid about him. He was fated to die; indeed he said so; but destiny, prompted by me, hesitated since the Duke of Kent offered to take him as ADC some weeks ago and Rodney, valiantly, refused. Later, he was given a squadron with the greatest difficulty, as being just 30 he was overage. He is typical of the type which is serving and saving England: and there will be many bleeding hearts in England tonight. He was all things to all men and women; slept with either with ease and carefree elegance. In character he was natural and normal but took whatever came his way with almost foolish nonchalance. He was a superb pilot. I wonder why I met him, and why we became such sudden friends?

1 London house of Lord Beaverbrook.

I heard the sirens sing about lunchtime at Kelvedon and later when I got back to the FO there was another raid. I sat with Nicholas Lawford in Lord Halifax's room and we refused to go down to the elegant bowels of the Earth. Halifax is at Chequers with Winston. Nicholas is the most simpatico of the FO boys; he is a man of the world, which many are not . . . .

I am haunted by Rodney. And the servants here at Belgrave Square who were fascinated by him, are all downcast and slightly excited.

MONDAY 19TH AUGUST

My beautiful darling Rodney – dead – and a hero. I seem to feel him everywhere, see him splashing naked in the bathroom; and his gay presence here in the morning room.

At 7.30 I went to Londonderry House – and how gloomy it seemed half-shut and dirty and I thought of other days and the ancient fun and splendour we had known there – Mairi Stewart, a provocative buxom girl, received me and soon Circe[1] appeared. She was in great good looks, *pleine de jus*[2] still: she is amazingly good-looking for one of her age which I suppose is more than 60![3] I was in a vague mood and could not concentrate on Circe, whom I am fond of; but she is always difficult *en tête-à-tête*.[4] She made me laugh when she repeated Mrs Greville's crack about Mrs Keppel:[5] 'To hear Alice talk one would think she had swum the Channel with her maid between her teeth.'

TUESDAY 20TH AUGUST

Since Munich we have had only four weeks' holiday. Two years of the strain and grind! I was tired and irritable and today behaved badly. Harold Nicolson asked that he might bring James Pope-Hennessy,[6] the young author of *London Fabric* to dine: he is a private in Teenie's [Cazalet] famous and much mocked anti-aircraft battery known as the *Batterie de Beauté*.[7] I was faintly excited by the prospect of meeting the v young and v gifted young writer. But he proved a disappointment; socially; and worse physically. He has a curious Jewish face, heavy dark hair, a tiny mouth and nervous fingers. I instantly took a dislike to him and was civilly hostile, and Harold, acting *entremetteur*,[8] was bewildered and annoyed. When he got up

1 Lady Londonderry, Lady Mairi's mother.
2 Literally, 'full of juice'.
3 She was 61.
4 One on one.
5 Alice Keppel, who had been mistress of King Edward VII. See entry for 10 July 1939 and footnote. She had managed to escape from France before the occupation was sealed.
6 See entry for 19 June 1940.
7 Battery of handsomeness, apparently because so many attractive young homosexual men were part of it.
8 Go-between.

to go, I suggested that Hennessy and I accompany him to the House of Commons, which we did. The evening, in spite of grouse and champagne, was a decided flop.

Winston made a great speech which lasted fifty-five minutes; but I was unimpressed.[1] It offered only years more of slaughter. However, he was eloquent even if he told us nothing. He made great play with a rather false peroration on Anglo-American relations. The House, and the country, were impressed but it was only another *tour de force*; not a new word, or fact, or hope. Archie Sinclair wound up for the government and he made the almost incredible and magnificent exploits of our airmen sound dull and trite. He was better in Opposition: his stammer, his trick of reiterated overemphasis are monotonous. Alan and I came back here together: Rab looked very tired. Winston did not remain for the debate which he had opened.

I rebuked my mad Alan for his foolish, childish mania about his mother. He is taking her to Bournemouth tomorrow for two days – much to Patsy's resentment. He is foolish.

Diana Cooper rang me up and was gentle and charming. I must not let this old friendship, which was v real, die from misunderstanding.

WEDNESDAY 21ST AUGUST

There are disturbing rumours about Neville Chamberlain: that he is unwell, that he will soon be out of the War Cabinet etc. These sly hounds who persecute him ought to be shot . . . . I lunched and dined alone, which was restful and blissful. All day at the House where I had two most affectionate conversations with Anthony Eden. I am almost reconciled to him!! He addressed the Anglo-Egyptian Committee and was v frank about the position in the Middle East; I also heard Harold Macmillan give a discouraging account of our munition and supply situation to the 1922 Committee.

Rodney's funeral is tomorrow at Margate at 10.30. I am 'on duty' so cannot pay him this last mark of affection. I found a lovely letter from Peter dated July 23rd, a nostalgic divine letter – it quite stimulated me.

Tomorrow we adjourn. Duff Cooper had a bad reception in the House today. He really must go.

THURSDAY 22ND AUGUST

Much political chatter. *The Times* has published such a slashing attack, which no Minister can survive, on Duff Cooper.[2] He is now for the high jump, yet Winston

---

1 Others were not; it was the speech about the heroism of Fighter Command, and how 'never in the field of human conflict was so much owed by so many to so few'.
2 The paper attacked the tone of Cooper's broadcasts as Minister of Information, comparing him with Goebbels.

obstinately shields him. I also think that the government, having got us into the war, into which it was rushed by public opinion, supported by left-wing propaganda, is at a loss as how to get out of it. That is my view; and the inclusion of Beaverbrook was a definite move towards peace. It was thought better that a settlement should be made by a gangster press lord than by gentlemen. Halifax and Chamberlain approved of Beaverbrook's entry into the highest political circles. But the moment has not yet come.

I drove Rab to Fortnum and Mason's where he bought a brace of grouse and an absurd leather belt as birthday offerings for his wife. Then I took him to Paddington and rushed back to the FO, to catch the two bags, the Belgrade and Cairo ones, as I had written long letters today to Peter and Paul. It takes weeks for letters to arrive . . .

Meanwhile the situation in Greece is deteriorating; an Italian invasion is expected there hourly. It is but the prelude to Egypt, which I fear is our most vulnerable spot. I tremble for Peter and for the Empire.

I had tea with Alec Cadogan and others. Cadogan is magnificent . . . . Now that the holidays are hanging over me, I am dreading them and am weakly arranging to be in London next week. I am too keyed up to relax unless there is great heat and nakedness; but one cannot pray for good weather since it would help the invaders! Today our convoys were attacked by gunfire in the Channel. There are giant guns all along the French coast.

FRIDAY 23RD AUGUST

I walked home last night about midnight. At four-thirty I heard the melancholy wail of the sirens and sleepily went to the cellar, where I remained shivering and sleepy, for half an hour. The servants maintain that they heard bombs! Certainly I did not.

I hesitated – go to Kelvedon or remain in London on some frivolous pretext? At last I left for the country: the house looked so lovely. Honor was in Norwich, where she had gone to a sale, on one of her mysterious jaunts. She did not come back until late, long after I was asleep. About 9.30, about in the study, there was an air raid: the distant bombs or anti-aircraft shook the house slightly.

SATURDAY 24TH AUGUST

I slept atrociously as I always do here; and as I lay awake I thought of many things, of the parliamentary session now ended; of how easily and well Brendan Bracken had taken control! He is so much better and altogether nicer, unlike some people, since he rose to power. I thought of Duff the despicable: why do I so dislike this man? I think it is charmless arrogance, his fatuous fanaticisms . . . planes buzzed on high. German or English? One is more conscious of the war in rural Essex than in London. And I thought too, of Rodney Wilkinson, now charred and dead and of the extraordinary letter his mother wrote to me in which she sympathised with me in losing a great friend; and then my mind wandered to Peter: it always goes back to Peter.

We heard planes off and on all day: I lay naked in the heat. About three o'clock Honor went to the farm and I fell asleep. I was, however, soon awakened by terrific noise of gunfire and I saw high above me seventeen or eighteen German planes. They were high, almost invisible and yet as they darted from under the gathering clouds, they glistened like silver. The bombardment began to be immense and my Bundi, lying at my feet, became very nervous. I saw that the squadron was headed for North Weald[1] and I ran to the other side of the Hall, to watch. Presently there was a great explosion: evidently the bombers had hit their mark, probably one of the pylons near Ongar or perhaps the aerodrome itself. It seemed so silly and unreal to be naked in a rose garden with a white dog. Later I came in and had tea: a man arrived on a bicycle with a scribbled note from Honor that she was all right. Later she came back with hair-raising accounts of bursting bombs.

I wrote long letters to Mrs Coats[2] and to Mrs Wilkinson. Why am I so painstaking with other people's mothers? Probably, because I am so beastly to my own impossible one, happily remote.

SUNDAY 25TH AUGUST

The newspapers and the fish were late in arriving as a bomb fell on the Epping–Ongar[3] road last night. They all told the same tale – extensive raids everywhere, particularly in Kent, although there were two over the London area.

I am burying another tin box, containing my Diaries for the first year of the war. Mortimer, the gardener, is my accomplice.

It has been a grey day, sombre and eventless. I wrote to Laura Corrigan in Vichy where she sips the Pétain waters. Here the gardens become more luxuriant, the cygnets have reached *l'âge ingrat*[4] and are hideous, a few planes roared by . . . I totted up my petty private fortune and find it comes to only £30,000 which is very serious!! I must economise and scrape together more.

MONDAY 26TH AUGUST

I went home [to Belgrave Square] to deal with letters; and how unlived-in can a house look after three days' absence. As I was dictating to Miss Sneath[5] the

1 A key fighter station in the Battle of Britain, about eight miles from Kelvedon.
2 Peter Coats's mother, not Audrey Coats (qv).
3 Ongar is a small market town three miles north of Kelvedon Hall and seven miles east of Epping.
4 An awkward stage.
5 Muriel Sneath (1899–1987) was Channon's secretary. She had previously worked for Paul Latham (qv).

sirens blew and we adjourned to the cellar to finish our work. I went on to the Foreign Office where I discovered that there are signs of a *détente* in the Italo-Greek situation: evidently Hitler has advised Mussolini to be cautious. But we fear a *coup de main* in Cyprus – long predicted by Peter.

I drove here [to Kelvedon] in the gloaming, untroubled by raids, but Honor tells me that there were about a hundred German planes over Kelvedon during the afternoon. On Saturday seventeen were killed at North Weald – in the explosion I saw. Walter Moyne says that Ford aerodrome near Bailiffscourt[1] has been badly knocked about. Yesterday there was a big fire in the City caused by bombs.

We had no fish or newspapers here today as the Epping–Ongar railway line has been blown up! It will take a few days to repair it.

The duc de Guise[2] is dead; a distinguished old gentleman in the *vieille école*[3] French manner. I never saw him but had been presented to 'the Duchesse'. They are very inter-married. The Duke of Windsor, as Prince of Wales, dined at the Manoir d'Anjou, the Guises' chateau in Belgium, at the invitation of the son, the ubiquitous comte de Paris. As the Prince left, he turned to the comte de Paris, asked 'Who is that old boy?' His host, the heir to France, the descendant of a hundred Bourbon kings! . . . The Prince, for all his flair and charm and success, never knew anything of practical continental politics . . .

Tuesday 27th August

Still no newspapers. I went to Southend and was stopped and asked for my military pass which I brandished. My poor constituency is deserted; it is a sort of Pompeii – long streets full of houses with boarded up windows. No cars, no gossiping women with prams, empty shops . . . desolation and despair. But the few people I met were all cheerful although they had been up all night with a severe air raid.

A letter from Serge says that my baby Paul goes to Newport to stay with Ailsa Mellon Bruce next week: and that he has been on Vincent Astor's[4] grandiose yacht, the *Nourmahal*. He is beginning his social career early and well! Poor mite.

Dukes are dying; the old Duke of Bedford[5] died today. He was a worn, thin, timid creature, like an ivory statuette, quiet, unassuming but feudal and utterly

---

1 In Sussex.
2 Prince Jean d'Orléans, duc de Guise (1874–1940) was Orléanist pretender to the French throne from 1926 until his death. He married, in 1899, Isabelle d'Orléans, his first cousin.
3 Old school.
4 William Vincent Astor (1891–1959), son of John Jacob Astor IV and elder brother of Alice Astor (qv), was a philanthropist who contracted mumps at his first wedding in 1914 and was rendered sterile as a result. He married three times.
5 Lord Herbrand Russell, later 11th Duke of Bedford. See entry for 19 March 1939 and footnote.

cut off from all reality, living in dreary, isolated splendour in his wonderful Woburn. Only my Alan could thaw him and even draw sparks from that decaying mummy. He kept fantastic state, and remained the eighteenth-century *grand seigneur* to the end with his Chinese Dairy, his private zoos, his legion of retainers, his lawns and vistas, his galleries and almost foolish formality.

WEDNESDAY 28TH AUGUST   *BELGRAVE SQUARE*

There is an air raid on as I write: the sirens blew a few moments ago and I have decided to while away what may be a long time by scribbling in my diary . . . . It is 9.20. For the first time in my whole life I have no premonition as to my future, have no plans and cannot foresee what will befall me. Is such a vapid, vacuous state of mind the prelude to death? Shall I be killed by a bomb, or will some strange destiny overtake me?

I drove up to London from Kelvedon in the morning: I left about ten. The butler told me, as I left, that he thought there was a raid. He proved to be right; for never a human being did I see for miles . . . the fields, the houses were deserted. The first human beings I came across were sentries at Stapleford aerodrome. The deserted, quiet countryside, lovely and lush in the green and blue morning, seemed bewitched . . . By the time I got to Rolls Park and later to Chigwell there were people about; and I gave a lift to a red-faced recruit who came from Tyneside. He smelt of khaki and straw and was going to London for the first time in his life!! I drove him into London and deposited him at a bus stop . . . I continued . . . went on to the Brewery where we had a formal meeting of the directors. It was decided to raise my small salary from £250 to £500 per annum. But this means only £25 net since we pay out 90 per cent of our income in taxation in the higher bracket! Lord Iveagh was flustered: they had had bombs last night in their garden at Pyrford, only a few hundred yards, if so much, from the house. Thank God my dauphin is idling luxuriously in the USA and yachting with the Astors . . . .

I went to the FO but all seemed quiet. People were only interested in their own raid adventures: everyone has become a hero; everyone enjoys the raids. I came home, dined lightly alone, counted my champagne, Krug 1920, like a miser would his gold. And me *voilà* waiting for the raid to end. I had been thinking of England and how much I love her, and of all her mad mistakes over the past few years – and I was perturbed to hear from Mrs Davis, my silversmith, that she had heard me attacked by a speaker in Hyde Park last Sunday. He was haranguing against the Fifth Column and said I had harboured German royalties! The fellow must be a communist. Still it is disturbing that there should be such malice; that such people should be allowed by the police to make subversive propaganda under the cover of staunch patriotism!! I am sad and discouraged and really not looking forward to a tiny gala I have foolishly designed for tomorrow night.

THURSDAY 29TH AUGUST

A ghastly night: I went to bed about eleven, and was soon rung by the Romanian Minister as he could not sleep for the bombs. And the searchlight flooded my room with a platinum glow: soon Lambert[1] rang me on the house telephone to say that bombs were dropping nearby (I discovered later that there had been two in St Leonard's Terrace and probably a delayed one in Cadogan Gardens). Sleepily, resentfully I went to the basement where I had rigged up a sort of shelter in what was formerly 'the room'. I reclined in a dilapidated armchair; it was midnight and I soon had the impression that I was cold, old and stiff. After a time I looked at my watch and was furious to see that it was 6.30. I had slept the better part of the night in acute discomfort, and of course never heard the 'all-clear'. I was frozen and cross all day.

Sat to James Gunn and the portrait made visible progress; Alan sat with me chatting gaily and later came with me as far as the Spanish Embassy where I was lunching. A *recherché*[2] little party: Alba, our host, deaf, anti-Semitic and debonair; Drogheda, a dried-up little man, prematurely aged by his exhausting marriages; Dr Dalton, now universally known as 'Dr Dynamo'; he has charm, is intelligent, and can, on occasions be more offensive than anyone I have heard – today he was delightful; also Vansittart. I chaffed Vansittart about his great love, his treacherous mistress, France, and he admitted that they had had a lover's quarrel. '*Vous portez des cornes*,'[3] I taunted him but he was obviously too downcast and discouraged to take up the challenge. He was in fact pleasant and I slyly got back into his good graces. He drove me back to the FO and he said how unhappy he had been all those years with Chamberlain and Halifax opposed to him but the real culprit, he said, was Horace Wilson whom he hates. He is charming, insinuating, handsome and a bit mad! I do not understand why Neville did not sack him as he often declared that he wanted to do: laziness or inability to cast off treacherous officials was Neville's weakness and ultimately one of the causes of his downfall. In the car 'Van' was reasonable, even about the Nazis!

FRIDAY 30TH AUGUST   *KELVEDON*

I drove here, where I was joined by Alan and Patsy who came from Henlow. Patsy in a possessive sulky mood verging on hysterics and frantic every time Alan left the room or her for five minutes. Honor was on one of her most mysterious Friday jaunts and had not come in when we went to bed at midnight. There were two raids here, one before, and one again after dinner.

---

1 His butler.
2 Desirable.
3 'You're wearing horns' – in other words, he had been cuckolded.

There was an air-raid alarm this morning; I was walking in Piccadilly, and one noticed a quickening of the pace for a moment, people suddenly walked as they do in New York, and some sought shelter but cars and buses continued normally. Later there was another alarm and this time it was in Whitechapel: I could not but contrast the behaviour of the two *quartiers*[1]. Terrified Jews rushed about, bumping into people; leaving their cars empty;[2] jumping off buses; slamming doors and pulling down shutters. What a deplorable race and it is for them, is it, that we are fighting?

SATURDAY 31ST AUGUST

A glorious, gorgeous day. We lazed by the swimming pool all day, played tennis and talked. Alan was absolutely enchanting and we are as intimate, I suppose, as it is possible for two men to be. We gossiped all day about our lives, our wives, the House of Commons and our past, sexual and political. Alan has had little of the former. I told him I kept a diary and that it was safely buried away, although there was much about him in it. He seemed apprehensive; he is maddeningly idealistic and gets carried away by every wave of popular emotion. I wish he had more judgement; he could not have more charm or fire. Yet there is a strain of weakness running through him; a lack of firmness. I think it springs from his dependence on his mother; only he fails to see how ridiculous is his behaviour with her.

SUNDAY 1ST SEPTEMBER

The heat continues but we cannot altogether appreciate it since good weather is the ally of air raids. We lazed again all the morning; Alan and I played tennis before breakfast, swam, gossiped . . .

The Lord Lieutenant and Mrs Whitmore[3] invited us to luncheon today at Orsett; but we could not accept as we had the Lennox-Boyds and Victor Raikes and his bride[4] come down from London. They were married three weeks ago yesterday and seemed in a haze of rather revolting lovemaking! She is dreadful,

---

1 Neighbourhoods.
2 George Orwell writes about this perception in his diary for 25 October 1940, in which he mentions a widespread belief that foreigners, notably Jews, panicked in air raids in a way that the British did not. Other than the odd anecdote, he had no more evidence of this alleged phenomenon than Channon. Orwell himself conceded this in a 1945 article for the *Contemporary Jewish Record*, in which he noted the dishonest propagation of anti-Semitic stories during the war, including about the Jews' entirely fictional responsibility for the 1942 Bethnal Green tube disaster.
3 Francis Henry Douglas Charlton Whitmore (1872–1962), a career soldier and landowner, was Lord Lieutenant of Essex from 1936 to 1958. He was knighted in 1941 and created 1st Bt in 1954. He married in 1931 as his second wife Ellis Christense Johnsen (1904–2001), of Bergen, Norway.
4 Raikes had just married Audrey Elizabeth Joyce Wilson (1921–2005).

very common, and talked about the 'grounds' and 'town', but she is a lusty florid creature rather in love with Victor, who is no beauty. He is perhaps lucky to have found anyone . . . Alan and Patsy left for Pyrford and I drove to London in blazing heat. Along Commercial Road I saw many paneless window frames and other signs of damage. Several houses were half-wrecked and there were holes, craters really, in the road. When I arrived at No. 5 I was told that a bomb had dropped in West Halkin Street but it did little damage, although it was an incendiary one. I looked in at the FO in search of news but there was none, and then I went to Hanover Lodge to pick up Alice Harding – I can never accustom myself to her new name nor really believe in the existence of a husband whom nobody has ever met. We drove to Coppins where we found the Kents who had obviously been sunbathing all day. The house is really hideous but so well arranged, so luxurious, so well appointed that one forgets the *mesquin*[1] background entirely unsuited to royalty! A drink chariot equipped with everything conceivable was wheeled in and the Duke mixed many cocktails. I had at least four, which was foolish. He curled up on a sofa and began to knit a blue scarf and somehow he suddenly seemed silly and even a touch pathetic. His great beauty is withering and his face is much lined; but he is very bronzed. The Duchess was lovely and as radiant as ever, and as gentle and affectionate to me as she always is. The others went up to dress and I remained with the Duke drinking; Lady Astor rang up twice and kept him talking. He complained that she gave him little peace! She is the arch snob of all time: I don't object to that but I deplore her hypocrisy, her absurd pretence of being democratic etc. I went up to dress and was late for dinner. I forget that all royalties dress in a trice. Last time I was late was staying at Polesden[2] a year ago, when I kept the Queen of Spain waiting! We served ourselves in the tiny dining room; excellent food, good wines, lovely flowers and *vaisselle*[3] – and no servants present. That is always a relief. After dinner the Duke played the piano in a desultory fashion, whilst I played backgammon with the Duchess. About eleven o'clock we went out onto the lawn to watch the searchlights as they swept the skies. In the distance was the chug of aeroplanes but we saw nothing and soon went to bed. Alice and I, however, gossiped until nearly 3 a.m. She told me how much she regretted that Serge left her and that she had done everything conceivable to induce him to return to her. I believe her. Her more recent husbands seem to mean little to her. She tells me that Vincent Astor has lent the *Nourmahal* to his mother, Lady Ribblesdale, who is entertaining Edwina d'Erlanger,[4] Emerald

---

1 Mean, penny-pinching.
2 Polesden Lacey, house of Mrs Ronnie Greville (qv).
3 Crockery.
4 Edwina Prue (1907–94) was born in New York but grew up in New Mexico, and worked for Ann Clare Boothe Luce (qv) on *Vanity Fair* before becoming a professional dancer. She married, in 1929, Baron Leo d'Erlanger, and became a prominent socialite in London.

Cunard, and 'some men and Paul Channon'. So my infant is yachting along the North Shore somewhere! It is fantastic.

The Kents *en petit comité*[1] are cosy and loveable. I enjoyed the change and the rich food. The passages and bathrooms are hung with royal photographs, and funny faded ones of Edward VIII, George V and the Tsar and all the others with their quaint nicknames. I suppose the Duke inherited the collection from his aunt, Princess Victoria. He has always been the family favourite. I looked at his albums, and there are many snapshots of 'David' and of 'Wallis' bathing etc. at Fort Belvedere. Ancient intimacy turned to hatred. The Duchess misses her mother, whom she has not seen for a year or more, nor of course Princess Woolly Toerring. The Duke was much more polite and amiable to his wife than usual. He is in better health, although looks aged and faded.

MONDAY 2ND SEPTEMBER   *KELVEDON*

I got up early and drove to London with Alice H. She is anxious about her financial position; having become English she is now liable for double income tax. She can have little left. It was hot in London, so I bought some oysters and came here in time to lunch with Honor. I felt dull and *congestionné*! There was a big short sharp raid about five o'clock. I watched the circling planes and heard much gunfire. I hear that Romford was badly hit yesterday.

I was depressed by a report I read yesterday at the FO. It was of a conversation recently held with Wayne Chatfield-Taylor,[2] head of the American Red Cross. I knew him as a child; he has travelled about Europe and says he has no doubt but that Germany can hold out indefinitely; and so can England, he admits. Therefore it seems the war can go on forever, the folly of it surpasses comprehension.

TUESDAY 3RD SEPTEMBER

The first anniversary of the war, if anniversary it can be called. I spent it by the swimming pool, naked, reading Lord Hervey's absorbing memoirs.[3] How wise he was, how shrewd; and how vivid his style. I can't put them down . . . . And when I did I wondered, what have we achieved in a year's time? Nothing. Norway, Denmark, Belgium, Holland and France gone, and against us. What will be added to the gruesome toll before next year? The war is utter folly and madness; but who can stop it?

1 In a small group.
2 Wayne Chatfield-Taylor (1893–1967) was, like Channon, born in Chicago. He served in junior government posts under President Roosevelt, and after the war became economic adviser to the European Recovery Program.
3 John Hervey, 2nd Baron Hervey (1696–1743) wrote memoirs of his life at court from 1727 to 1737 that were especially disobliging about King George II and his family.

About half-past ten a very severe air raid began and soon the blue heavens were dotted with aeroplanes, some of them with long smoking tails crashed. I watched three of them, one was ours and it came down with the pilot uninjured near Myles's.[1] The cannonading was severe and as I stood under an apple tree pellets fell all around me – I afterwards found three lumps of lead, of shell. And a parachute slowly floated to earth near Ongar: the man must have been twenty minutes in the air. A machine gun fired too nearby to be comfortable. Honor rushed across the fields, I following. The roar was deafening; in half an hour's time all was over. After lunch on the hottest day of the summer H went to London by train with Enid Raphael! I cannot imagine why . . . . There was another raid about three o'clock. There are always at least two now, a morning and afternoon one. What will the end be? I see no future for England or for me.

Wednesday 4th September

I called on my local Mr Mayor at Southend: he is a 'funker' and fears that the invasions will take place, and that it will be in the Bradwell country.[2] The landing would take place in the Blackwater country and the advancing armies would surround Chelmsford where their first big battle will take place. *Je m'en doute.*[3] Then London.

I rushed back in the great heat and slept, after an irritating episode of running out of petrol *en route*.

Raids and more raids.

Thursday 5th September

I drove up to London during a raid. Here I found mountains of letters . . . . Went to the FO, where there were more letters. Rab looks well and refreshed; he is gay, affectionate and friendly. He says he will break with the Churchill–Eden 'glamour' group as the country will tire – is already tiring of them. He is right: they represent nothing, are only a vehicle to continue and prosecute and win the war. There will be trouble later. But we must lie low, work openly with (and secretly against) them – perhaps for years. But true Conservatism will triumph once more in England. Baldwin-ism, and diluted socialism is the cause of all our troubles . . . To lunch at Hanover Lodge to meet the Kents who didn't turn up as they had been asked to lunch at Buck House. However we ate under the trees, a luxurious repast – could it be wartime? . . . . I left early to go to the House of Commons. I had no sooner arrived than the sirens sang their doleful wail. Questions had begun

---

1 Great Myles's and Little Myles's are two farms two miles north of Kelvedon.
2 Bradwell-juxta-Mare is a village on the north-east end of the Dengie peninsula, on the Essex coast and the River Blackwater.
3 I doubt it.

and continued until nearly 3.30 when the Speaker, on advice from the Military Command, adjourned the House and we wandered aimlessly to the cellars. I sat with Alan, who is still awaiting his summons to join a ship. Half an hour later a bell called us back to the Chamber. Winston rose – I had met him in the passage with Clemmie and two of his daughters – and spoke at some length. He was not at his best and invoked little enthusiasm; his speech was dry and dealt with facts .... Nor did he please the House which has become accustomed to his high-flown rhetoric. Nevertheless it is the Churchill reign and we are soon to have that cad, coarse libertine Randolph in the House. He has, I hear, successfully angled for Preston.[1] With such a serpent in the House, Westminster will lose much of its attractions for me . . . Winston promised brighter 'blackouts' which was rash as he has no assurance that they will be possible, and he deplored the sirens. He jokes too much, is rarely serious about even sacred things such as the loss of life, he betrays too easily that he is enjoying both his power and the war which gave it to him.

I look forward to his fall. Neville Chamberlain, contrary to reports which we had heard, was not present. I hear he may have cancer and if so, he is a doomed man. David has confided in several people that this tragic rumour is true . . .

Friday 6th September

Tilea woke me by the telephone – I had slept through three raids: the big one lasted until after five; and it was quickly followed by two more. Tilea was full of exciting news: King Carol of Romania abdicated in the night and has been succeeded by young Master Michael, who has summoned his mother to Bucharest. I am more pleased than otherwise, as Princess Helen[2] has always been one of my great loves. There is no woman alive with such charm and with such distinguished beauty. I am now *persona* extremely *grata* in Romania, and if it survives this endless Armageddon I shall go there after the war. As it was nine o'clock I rang up the Duke of Kent and told him the news. He was riveted. He adores advance information, and was affectionate and grateful. Then I put in a call to Queen Mignonne[3] but as there was a raid on it was some little time before I could get through. She took the news fairly calmly with her usual amused abruptness. I had never told a queen before that her brother had abdicated: it doesn't often happen in history. And by telephone . . . I didn't add that Princess Cilla (Helen)[4] had

---

1 Randolph Churchill would be returned unopposed at the Preston by-election on 29 September.
2 Formerly Princess Helen of Greece and Denmark.
3 Marie, former Queen Consort of Yugoslavia. 'Mignonne' is Channon's rendering of her family nickname.
4 Princess Helen of Greece and Denmark, later Queen Helen of Romania.

returned to Bucharest! They are not friends. Mme Lupescu who is not a Jewess, but the daughter of old King Carol, will follow her royal lover into exile . . .

To the Foreign Office. As usual they knew nothing of it and I broke the story of King Carol's abdication to all concerned! A raid warning was heard at one o'clock. I rushed back to Belgrave Square, in a bad temper and liverish . . . . I was irritated by Parker, our chauffeur, who has been too long with us and I sent him away. He has been useless, lazy and spoilt for months . . . . Then I came here. It is still dry and gloriously hot, and I slept for a long time before Alan arrived hot, handsome and breathless from Henlow. Honor and I twitted him at dinner about his Oedipus complex. He is besotted about his silly old mother and after dinner he tried in vain to ring her up, but no calls are allowed during raids! I talked to him very late.

Harold Balfour rang me up to say that he had got back safely: he was in Ottawa yesterday at luncheon time. He tells me that poor Fritzi is still in a labour camp in Canada, but he has been elected commandant: all the Jews and Nazis alike respect him! Harold didn't like Princess Alice who was frigid (as I knew she would be) about Fritzi; but she is a nice woman *au fond*,[1] and may do something to help her unhappy cousin – eventually.

SATURDAY 7TH SEPTEMBER

Tennis, and bathed with Alan and then he left for Pyrford. I prevented him motoring to Henlow to see his mother for ten minutes! It could not have been more as he was lunching with Brendan Bracken in London.

Queen Mignonne rang me up: she wanted more news of her brother! And she also complained that she had had no letter for weeks from King Peter (he was 17 yesterday). It is curious that these little boys, Peter and Michael, are both kings now!

Diana Cavendish arrived for lunch, in time for a very big raid. Dozens of German planes flew over us but we didn't happen to see any brought down.

A most disturbing letter came from Nannie in America. She is having a difficult time and I don't know what to do, nor where to send her, as she has most unfortunately quarrelled with Alice's [Astor] governesses – particularly a Miss Prendergast, a ghastly girl, sister to Lady Eden.[2] I shall revenge myself on this creature who has interfered with my child's happiness and welfare.

We dined *à trois*, Honor lovely in shimmering green and jewels, Diana Cavendish and I. We listened to the radio and heard that this afternoon's raid, which seemed severe, had been very serious and damaging to London and the estuary. We went out onto the lawns and saw the skies ablaze in the Romford

---

1 At heart.
2 Edith Mary Patricia Prendergast (1904–90) married Sir Timothy Eden, Bt, in 1923. She was born in Boston: I cannot trace a sister, but if there were one it would be realistic for her to be working as a governess in upstate New York.

direction and we heard the distant gunfire. The searchlights lit up the sky, and there was a stellar *battue*[1] such as I have never seen. *Götterdämmerung*[2] to the motif of the throbbing German planes. At times we could almost have read, so bright were the skies. Diana, whose yellow eyes not only resemble a cat's, but have a feline keenness, pointed out the planes caught in the beams of the sweeping searchlights which revolved above us . . . . suddenly she decided she must return to London to go back to duty at Guy's Hospital, where she has done strenuous work ever since the war started. Honor fetched the Packard and drove her to Brentwood. Diana was agreeable and nicer than usual . . . now as I write the anti-aircraft guns are going off and I run in and out to watch . . . what will happen? Can we survive such bombardments for long? I fear that London has been damaged . . . the windows rattle as I write . . . the dogs howl, the servants have scurried to shelter in the cellars, I creep about in the darkness wondering whether Kelvedon will be hit – yet I am curiously calm and fatalistic. How extraordinary life is.

Sunday 8th September

A disturbed night indeed. The bombardment went on for hours and about half-past one we retired to bed. I woke later as my bed shook violently and I went to the window. The skies were still bright with flares and gunfire; then I called Honor and we rushed into the barn opposite at Germains Farm and for miles behind there were literally hundreds of fires. The household was terrified and indeed, anything seemed possible in the darkness and the unreal light. We were surrounded by walls of flame. Someone said: 'They've landed. Those are camp fires.' Honor hurriedly dressed whilst I rang up the police and was told that the fires had been started by dozens of incendiary bombs. Honor rushed off in the car to investigate; but I remained behind to watch. Gradually the fires burned themselves out and Honor thinks they were flares . . . We had a little sleep, and after half-past five all was quiet. I have now heard on the radio that over 400 people were killed in London, 1,500 seriously injured, and that there is much damage and many fires in the East End of London. Two bombs dropped on the hospital where Diana was working. One cannot telephone to London as the lines are engaged. We shall hear more news later . . . All very dramatic and awesome.

This afternoon Honor and I went to Brizes' Hall[3] to return a call made upon us nearly three years ago. The house is gracefully built and has a braiding staircase: and there are a few fine pieces of furniture but the atmosphere is depressing and down-at-the-heel. The Hall is an imitation of this one, and possibly designed by

---

1 In game shooting a *battue* is the beating of birds out of cover and over the guns; Channon seems to be using it to represent the sound and illumination of gunfire.
2 'Twilight of the Gods', the title of the last of Wagner's *Ring* operas.
3 A house of the 1770s inherited by the Royds family in 1868; they sold it in 1949 and it became a school.

the same hand.[1] I should hate to live there as there is no outlook. Mr and Mrs Royds are a dull, harmless, shabby couple: he appeared rather argumentative. Never in our lives have Honor and I paid a call before; but I thought in wartime it was wise to be on friendly terms with our neighbours. Royds insists that the lights were incendiary bombs, and he extinguished many of them himself. We had a narrow escape . . . Diana Cavendish rang up from London. She had had a nightmare journey back last night and her train was machine-gunned. It took seven hours to get from Brentwood to London. She says that the havoc is deplorable. The Melchetts' house[2] in Smith Square was hit; and both Brendan Bracken and the Baillies, the first in Lord North Street, the latter in Grosvenor Square, had their windows broken. The casualties were appalling and there are rumours of an unexploded bomb in Belgrave Square! The outlook is not pleasant.

MONDAY 9TH SEPTEMBER

Honor was awakened at 7.30 by her swarthy bailiff, who came with the news that a 1,000 lb bomb had fallen on her farm. She rushed to see the damage. There is a crater only a few yards from the farm buildings, nearly sixty feet square and over twenty feet deep. About seventy bombs were dropped on this neighbourhood during the night. I slept soundly, with only one interruption when I got up at 2.45 and went out. German planes were everywhere; the heavens were clouded and noisy and swept by great arc lights: in the distance one saw the orange glow of the still-burning docks. Is it the plan to destroy London in the hopes of paralysing the nation? I drove in the afternoon with Honor to her farm: the crater caused by the bomb – it must have been a 1,000-pounder – is really immense. Standing at its edge were two old women who had lost everything; their pathetic wooden shanty nearby was demolished and a few dingy possessions and dead chickens were strewn about. The women refused to leave . . . no one could persuade them. All my suspicions and distrust of Honor's bailiff, a Mr Woodman,[3] were revived. He is insolent, swaggers about, and treats her with scant respect. She allows herself to be so familiar with that sort of people. I think I am wise in saying nothing; usually she tires of them. But I foresee trouble with that man; serious trouble, probably financial.

There is a *settembrile*[4] feeling in the air – going is the summer, going, indeed, is almost everything.

---

1 Architectural authorities such as Pevsner think not.
2 Mulberry House, home of Henry Ludwig Mond (1898–1949), 2nd Baron Melchett, and his wife Amy Gwen Wilson (d.1982).
3 Frank Ernest Woodman (1905–?) was a bailiff, horse dealer, riding instructor, farmer and land agent.
4 September-ish.

TUESDAY 10TH SEPTEMBER

I slept fairly well last night; although there were the usual noises I didn't get up. I left at 9.45 by car for Little Gransden:[1] appalling car complications and delays too boring to describe . . . . I gather that there was another severe raid over London last night, which did less damage than those on the two preceding nights.

The Queen of Yugoslavia and Mrs Rosemary Cresswell share a small brick villa house, 'The Old Mill House', and it is next to an old mill in Little Gransden. The house is horrible; 'Ye Olde' and unattractive and by the road. Rosemary received me and I was impressed by her chic and slender beauty. What an extraordinary woman. Almost at once the Queen came down; her hair is bobbed very short, but she is fatter than ever, and wore a flame-coloured *saut-de-lit*.[2] She was gracious; but had her luncheon sitting on the sofa – she is *malade imaginaire*,[3] and if there is anything wrong with her, it is a malady of the heart. I have never seen two people, of any sexual arrangement, so in love with one another. They are full of *petits soins*,[4] and little attachments and tender glances. Rosemary calls her 'Pingly' to her face, and referred to her so to me in conversation. Queens are not often called by nicknames by commoners be they ever so intimate!! The little princes, Tomislav[5] and Andy[6] (whose christening I attended years ago at Bled), lunched with us, as did their tutor. The Queen in her semi-recumbent position was served first: an excellent meal cooked and served by Yugoslav servants. About 1.30 the children and their tutor, a Mr Hughes of Sandroyd School, retired. The conversation had been largely about the inefficiency of the Secret Service and their difficulties. And I had the curious, yet very strong sensation, that Mr Hughes is an agent. He is a nice fellow, a touch grey and Civil Service-looking. He never once opened his mouth . . . . Then we settled down to a long conversation and gossip. Queen Marie asked a thousand questions and seemed rather *froissée*[7] that she has heard nothing from Bled and Belgrade for so long. Even little King Peter ignores her; then we got onto King Carol. She is very against him, and accused him of misappropriating Romanian funds, or more accurately of allowing Mme Lupescu to do so. The Queen dislikes the Lupescu, and would not definitely confirm the rumour that

1 In Huntingdonshire, near the border with Cambridgeshire, about fifteen miles west of Cambridge.
2 Dressing gown.
3 A hypochondriac.
4 Care for each other.
5 Prince Tomislav of Yugoslavia (1928–2000) was the second son of King Alexander I and Queen Marie. From 1941 to 1946 he attended Oundle School and in 1946–7 Clare College, Cambridge. He became an apple farmer in Kent and in 1992 became the first member of the Serbian royal family to return to his homeland after the exile of the communist years.
6 Prince Andrew of Yugoslavia (1929–90), youngest son of King Alexander I and Queen Marie. He studied mathematics at Clare College, Cambridge, and became an insurance broker. He committed suicide.
7 Hurt, or offended.

she is Hohenzollern – *main gauche*[1] – nor would she deny it. She seemed not really sure. The Queen dislikes her brother yet is disturbed by recent events in Bucharest. King Michael, she told me, had been corrupted by Mme Lupescu's agents; he is not yet 19 and yet he has already had affairs with several women, and men. He looks such a serious youth that I wonder whether she is romancing? Like all the Romanian royalties, she is a great and famous liar. One cannot believe more than a fragment of what she says. She lay curled up, exchanging *oeillades*[2] with Mrs Cresswell who fluttered over us with cigarettes and drinks. I sat at the Queen's feet: she was v friendly, a touch shrewd and sharp. She seems to have altered much since the old Bled days to which she referred. She has been living for more than six months in this semi-exclusion. At length I rose to go, as I had arranged to walk to Croxton,[3] the little princes accompanied me part of the way: Tommy, the elder of the two, complained that it was too hot and too far to walk but Andy gaily picked blackberries, which he gave me from time to time.

At last I arrived at Croxton to stay the night with the Eltisleys.[4] The long drive has fine trees and the house, whilst less beautiful than ours, has considerable atmosphere of *luxe* and the grand manner. A sumptuous tea: Lady Eltisley is deaf, handsome, beautifully dressed and rather like Isabelle Clow; in other words, rather my affair, although she must be 50 or more. He is a bore but an active agriculturalist. After tea he drove 'Pam' Fox (his son-in-law, Sir Gifford Fox MP)[5] and me over his farms. He has a large estate which reminded me of Elveden. Later we bathed in an icy outdoor pool. Lady Eltisley looked superb, a long lithe figure. I was definitely attracted by her. I have never before coveted an older woman but I could have seduced her with pleasure. Is this a new development in my character? Her pretty daughter, Lady Fox, left me cold. A most stately dinner, *grande tenue*,[6] with flowers, much plate and ceremony. I had almost forgotten how soothing Edwardian luxury can be; polite servants, gleaming silver, flowers everywhere. All very different from Kelvedon where everything, at the moment, is instead slipshod. But at Croxton they have never heard of the war! That is, none of them has seen a German plane, nor heard a bomb. It was peaceful, so like a dream of long ago that I felt soothed and envious of the Edwardian state and comfort still maintained. We played bridge in a yellow drawing room where there were five Romneys.[7]

---

1 Illegitimate.
2 Winks.
3 Croxton Park, near St Neots, seat of Lord Eltisley, was five miles' walk from Little Gransden.
4 George Douglas Cochrane Newton (1879–1942) was Conservative MP for Cambridge from 1922 to 1934, when he was raised to the peerage as 1st Baron Eltisley. He married, in 1905, Muriel Mary Georgina Duke (1888–1953).
5 Conservative MP for Henley.
6 Evening dress.
7 George Romney (1734–1802) was an English portrait painter, whose muse was Emma Hamilton, Nelson's mistress.

WEDNESDAY 11TH SEPTEMBER

I was loath to leave Croxton and its obliviousness to the war! But I did and got back at Kelvedon in time for luncheon. A delayed bomb exploded as I arrived. It must have been nearby. Honor looked tired and white. She had been up all night. The electric light was cut off and at about 2 a.m., the bombs caused so much noise that she feared we had been hit. The ARP people thought likewise as they rushed over to the Hall to see whether we had been killed! All this in my absence. The situation is becoming very serious. A bomb has badly damaged Buckingham Palace. I listened in at six to hear Winston Churchill. He made a good broadcast but it lacked his usual gusto and bombast, and he warned the country to expect imminent invasion; he said that there were boats, that a fleet was being assembled in the Channel ports which could only have one purpose, that of invading England!! There have been many casualties in London. And one cannot telephone as all lines are restricted. Is our day come at last?

THURSDAY 12TH SEPTEMBER

I drove to the Foreign Office. I had not long been there when the sirens sounded and we retreated to the cellars. Rab sat surrounded by a body of BBC journalists to whom he administered a heartening tonic. He is more optimistic about the war, now, although his house in Smith Square has been slightly damaged, and he has had several bombs in his village, Halstead,[1] in unfortunate Essex. At 7.30 Harold B came to see me, and he talked for an hour and drank Krug. He was lavish in his enthusiasm for President Roosevelt; evidently they got on, as they were closeted together for nearly three hours. The whole Blitz trip was a huge success; he went to Long Island, twice to New York where he saw Serge [Obolensky], and was four days at Ottawa. He didn't like Princess Alice, whom he found heartless and unhelpful about Fritzi (he had taken out my private letter to her). She did, however, tell him that Fritzi has been elected a sort of commandant by his camp and so is probably fairly comfortable. She refused to help him; but I wonder whether she will not cause discreet private enquiries to be made? She is a kindly woman and he is a near relation and a friend . . . Harold is happier about our air defences and says that the new barrage over London ought to protect it, at least by night. We went to the Dorchester together where I was to dine with Alan and Patsy. As I sat with them in the hotel foyer half London came in – Beaverbrook, smiling, younger and plumper I thought; he came up to me very cordially, took both my hands in his, 'Well, Chips, how is Honor?' and we had a talk. Perry Brownlow[2] was with

---

1 Halstead is, and was in 1940, a small town.

2 Peregrine Francis Adelbert Cust (1899–1978) succeeded his father as 6th Baron Brownlow in 1927. A close friend and equerry of the Prince of Wales, later King Edward VIII, and of Channon, he cut his ties with him after the abdication in the hope of remaining a Lord in Waiting, only to be sacked by George VI. His first wife was Katherine 'Kitty' Kinloch*.

Ursula Manners:[1] he always cleaves to that family. The dining room was full of well-known people and friends waiting for the raid which soon began. Somerset Maugham[2] was nearby . . . . Alan was tiresome at dinner: his genius is undeniable, his judgement deplorable. He is now intriguing to bring back his brother Francis from Libya, where he is stationed. He wants him for a complicated Lennox-Boyd reason to have a more dangerous job, and perhaps be killed . . . . The gunfire continued and when Alan and I stepped into the street we were almost blown away: the noise was terrific as there is a 'Big Bertha' nearby in the Park . . . The lobby was crowded, and people settled down for the night with rugs, etc. Johnny Churchill[3] joined us: he is a captain now, balder, fatter and more charming than ever. He never has plans and as usual wanted a bed, which Alan gave him. Just before midnight I left, and although warned not to do so, I walked home. It was inky dark and the incessant gunfire was alarming. It was like the battlefields . . . .

I am distressed to hear that Neville Chamberlain has cancer and can only live another fourteen months or so. The leadership of the party may then become Rab's – if there is a Conservative Party.

The invasion is expected any moment now, probably sometime during the weekend.

A letter from Peter dated June 3rd!

Everyone I have seen today was in the highest spirits. This island race is extraordinary: and certainly those, who have not been actually bombed themselves, are enjoying this Blitzkrieg. They are all convinced that an English victory now lies around the corner and that our Air Force is actually superior, not only in quality but in numbers, to the Germans. Rab says we are fighting a Punic war[4] and that Hitler, the modern Hannibal, will be defeated. Instead of elephants, we have Dorniers to contend with.

FRIDAY 13TH SEPTEMBER

A fiendish day. I slept in the morning room and woke with an acute headache because I had had no air; and I was contrite, too, for having needlessly crossed swords with Alan and perhaps offending him. The 'all-clear' sounded about six and I moved to my own bed . . . Another raid about seven and a third began about ten just as I sat down to dictate to my secretary, the incredible Miss Sneath. Bombs dropped nearby and I didn't go out: one terrific explosion, I afterwards learned, was on a house in Eaton Square, another on Buckingham Palace, where

1 Lady Ursula Isabel Manners (1916–2017), elder daughter of the 9th Duke of Rutland (qv).
2 William Somerset Maugham (1874–1965) trained as a doctor before becoming one of Britain's most popular novelists, short-story writers and playwrights.
3 John George Spencer-Churchill (1909–92) was son of John Spencer-Churchill, younger brother of Winston. Initially a stockbroker, he became a painter and sculptor, and founded an interior decorating company.
4 Fought between Rome and Carthage in the third and second centuries BC.

five bombs, evidently deliberately dropped damaged the chapel – the noise even now as I write is really terrific.

Then to the Office: Everyone had a headache and was annoyed by this morning's long raid, which continued until two o'clock. It was due to the clouds! There was soon a raid at the Office and after the 'all-clear' a huge bomb fell (or perhaps went off) in Regent Street. Alec Cadogan and Rab both, to my astonishment, crawled under a desk and a sofa . . . . At length I decided to come here [Kelvedon] as I didn't want to disappoint Honor, who had asked me particularly to take her out to dine . . . . However I found a note that she had gone on one of her mysterious expeditions, dinner she had cancelled. I was thus and am alone. This was not deliberate casualness – Honor is never that; but she doesn't think quickly and is never interested or concerned with other people. She could so easily have sent me a telegram, and didn't. She tried to telephone but all service is cut off.

I had felt so ill and discouraged today and so long for peace and plenty and Peter – and my adorable dauphin, happily so far away. Testing times will come this weekend for the invasion is probably now or never? Friday the 13th . . . the noise is increasing. Shall Kelvedon get through another night without a bomb on the roof? As the Cabinet have decided to adjourn Parliament indefinitely, I shall go to Devonshire for a few days.

SATURDAY 14TH SEPTEMBER

The day has passed and no invasion yet. There was a sequence of air raids in London but here at lovely Kelvedon – trembling between summer and autumn – we have had a peaceful day. Once or twice I heard the distant siren but paid no attention. Honor came back in the night and was in a delicious mood all day.

I walked around Germains Farm during the long raid and counted a convoy of twenty-seven of our planes flying in formation. I had momentary doubts as to whether they were ours . . . . I am in marvellous spirits having had a liver pill and now, *malgré la guerre*,[1] everything – almost – is *une couleur de rose*.[2]

The bombs on Buckingham Palace have made the King and Queen more popular; of late their stock had fallen. Everyone realises that they do their duty in difficult circumstances, but I have seen little love for them. She is still glamorous, unspoilt and gracious, but people whisper that she intrigues; and he is the dullest most boring, but well-meaning, little man on earth.

I was irritated to hear from Harold that Serge O is seriously considering marrying a ballerina in New York. He cannot really do that! It would be disastrous and really too Opera Bouffe! The Prince and the Dancer! . . . . I am told that Oliver Stanley, at long last, sees *en clair*[3] the deplorable situation at home

1 In spite of the war.
2 Rose-tinted.
3 Clearly.

and wants to rid himself of Maureen, that unmoral, immoral, termagant who has done more than any other individual to corrupt London society. She is an uneducated, soulless, selfish slut whose only quality is her capacity for making political speeches; but she contaminates everyone with whom she comes into contact. The court were very ill-advised to encourage her friendship with the Queen, who has been much criticised in consequence – I really must be more silver-tongued in conversation. But I wish that Alan's judgement was equal to his genius; no one has greater gifts or more charm.

SUNDAY 15TH SEPTEMBER

Honor and I drove to Langleys to luncheon. As we left our door the sirens sang, but we saw and heard nothing. Bill Tufnell was v pleasant, gave us three partridges, three gallons of petrol and ½ lb of butter. 'The Lord giveth to him who hath'... the house is untouched by the war, really, although there are a few military about and two young officers .... are billeted in the house. They make ideal companions for Bill .... Bill's only alleviation in wartime at Langleys is to build a large and attractive swimming bath.

I must go back to London and resume my usual life: I half look forward to it; but dread, in a way, the disturbed nights and perpetual bombardments. But what else can I do? One cannot remain here forever; so I will rush into the lion's mouth and hope for the best. I never cared to live so little .... yet I dread dying before Paul grows up. He must profit by all my mistakes, avoid the pitfalls into which I fell and emulate my successes and hope, really, for my luck, which I sometimes suspect is beginning to desert me now.

Tomorrow, we have been told, is the day fixed for the invasion. I am still somewhat dubious, but not as much so, nor so cockahoop as the other Government Boys in London who behave and talk as if they had already won this war, when half the world is still in arms against us. What madness.

MONDAY 16TH SEPTEMBER

I drove to London via the East End: it is a scene of desolation, house after house has been wrecked; debris falls from the remaining floors, windows are gone; heaps of rubbish line the pavements; a large hospital and a synagogue still stand windowless; some streets are roped off because of time bombs .... yet the people, mostly Jewish, seemed courageous but sad:[1] but the damage is immense. I gave many of them lifts. When I reached our part of London there seemed less damage obviously; nevertheless I raced along Constitution Hill as Buckingham Palace is

---

1 This illustrates the difference between Channon when he relies on hearsay and the prejudices of his circle to form opinions, and when he witnesses events for himself.

the most vulnerable spot. Tomorrow I prophesy that the Houses of Parliament will be the target – at home I found that the servants were cheerful but sleepy, and that Parker, my rather insubordinate chauffeur had, at length, left. I went to the FO; there were short raids; and during one of them I walked with Rab to Richmond Terrace where he attended a meeting of the Middle East Policy Committee. The Italians have captured Sollum, a desert outpost of no importance in Egypt; still one doesn't like these evacuations as they lower prestige. Everyone still seems cockahoop in the face of almost certain invasion. I am not. The German machine is very thorough, very successful; and there are ships of all kinds congregated along the French coast, enough to transport half a million men. Luckily a gale is blowing.

Patsy rang me up to say that Alan had left suddenly on Saturday. He was at Henlow when the message came and he had to rush at breakneck speed to report and arrived late owing to the delay in the delivery of the wire because of an air raid. But he finally caught his train and departed; God knows when we shall see him again. I am miserable. My great huge Velázquez,[1] all charm and genius and impetuous rash judgements. He and I have influenced each other considerably for three years now; unusual for two such dominant objective personalities. I was sorry for poor Patsy and hurried around to the Dorchester to console her, and I found her really remarkably calm and sensible. I then asked her to dine with Harold and me at the Carlton Grill, where we were going. She joined us, delighted; and we tried to cheer her first evening of sea-widowhood .... I had walked to the Hotel Carlton in the dark. All was well until just before I reached the Ritz when the sirens sang. I rashly decided to proceed on foot. Soon the anti-aircraft guns spat – and it was no doubt dangerous: but I dodged in and out of doorways and finally reached the Carlton, breathless, excited and hot. The Grill is well underground and we had a gay dinner à trois. Harold told us of all his American exploits; and also several amazing stories of spies recently captured .... [Harold] says that he is still out of favour with Max Beaverbrook. Nor does Harold see eye to eye with the Prime Minister .... About 10.30 we left the hotel and luckily Harold had his official car and sent both Patsy and me home in it. It was an exciting if short drive as bombs were falling and guns firing. The sky was quite lit up ... I decided to sleep in the cellar in the little room I have converted into an emergency bedroom.

There is a fresh poignancy in saying 'goodbye' and one never quite knows whether one will ever meet again; yet the number of actual bomb casualties in London every night is still small.

TUESDAY 17TH SEPTEMBER

I slept fairly well in my airless cubicle; only once was I startled enough to wake up when the bursting bombs were particularly noisy. The 'all-clear' sounded about six

---

1 Diego Velázquez (1599–1660) was a Spanish baroque painter.

... soon it was followed by another 'demonstration'. I heard that Berkeley Square, Bond Street, Londonderry House and other places had been hit, the Ministry of Economic Warfare had three fatal casualties ... I went to the FO, where work is largely suspended owing partly to Halifax's absence – he (a terrific heavy explosion has just happened and the room rocks as I write) has gone to Garrowby[1] for ten days. There were jokes about the probable attack on the House of Commons this afternoon. I went over early, and found everyone in the same mood: would the raiders come soon after prayers? Winston, who had been lunching at Buckingham Palace, wandered about without an escort and I chatted to him several times. The sirens blew about ten minutes to three but the Speaker did not adjourn the House until after 3.30, when the bells rang. Meanwhile, Neville Chamberlain appeared; he looked fairly well but lacked his usual colour and animation. He had an ovation as he always does when he took his place for the first time since his operation. So did Winston when he sat down beside him. I thought that Neville looked very small; has he shrunk? We all trooped down into the cellars, which did not seem very substantial: they are really only a shelter from splinters and shells. Yesterday one of our AA[2] shells crashed into a window in the library and went through the floor! As the Prime Minister afterwards said, 'The Houses of Parliament because of their size, their vulnerability and position are probably the most dangerous spots in London.' The 'all-clear' soon blew and the sitting was resumed. Winston spoke – after Edward Cadogan[3] and another new member had been introduced – and he soon 'spied strangers' which meant that we had to go into secret session. He then elaborated his suggestions for future meetings of Parliament; they would not yet be announced; and would be decided upon later. He also spoke of the imminence of invasion. He was neither long nor eloquent. Members went about chatting vivaciously, each recounting his own adventures. Many had had bombs in their houses or in their gardens. (I hear that the BBC was narrowly missed last night, and that the Langham Hotel was struck.) 'Dr Dynamo'[4] was being consoled on having had his Ministry struck .... no one seemed to appreciate the gravity of the situation. If this bombing continues London will be devastated in a few months' time, although the numbers of casualties are not serious ... I walked back to the F Office and later drove Rab home. In Berkeley Square and elsewhere we saw shattered glass and broken glass everywhere. At home I had time for a bath before the next raid began: it is usually punctually at about 8.20. It was, and is as

---

1 Garrowby Hall, seat of Viscount Halifax, in the East Riding of Yorkshire.
2 Anti-aircraft.
3 Edward Cecil George Cadogan (1880–1962), younger son of the 5th Earl Cadogan, was Conservative MP for Reading from 1922 to 1923 and for Finchley from 1924 to 1935; and was returned at a by-election for Bolton in 1940, holding the seat until 1945. In 1938 he chaired a committee that recommended the abolition of judicial corporal punishment. He was knighted in 1939.
4 Hugh Dalton.

I write, soon terrific. Served by two retainers, I ate in the dark . . . . The first week of the siege reveals the battle of London is probably the most comfortable siege in history – so far. But the din at the moment is considerable.

'Naps' Alington is dead of drink and dissipation in Cairo at the age of 44.[1] No living mortal had such charm or more gifts. Unbelievably handsome, faun-like, with tiny bright burning merry brown eyes, a figure like a ballet dancer (and a missing finger); a small provocative mouth, rich obedient hair; and a smile that no one has ever resisted, he carried the world before him. But he was not quite human; he was a centaur, a satyr. Pan *in excelsis* without morals, stability or ambition, but a warm loyal heart, he was an enchanting companion. But he was a spendthrift, he squandered his charm, his health, his fortune, and his time. He could never go to bed, and drank all night, was frequently surrounded by sycophants and went to bed with anyone and everyone he met. He was a half-classical creature, a sort of Hermes,[2] or more accurately benignant Eliogabalus [*sic*].[3] Years ago I saw much of him, indeed we went to Paris together, and again we motored across Europe together and his hacking cough kept me awake for nights for he insisted on sharing my room, and sometimes my bed. For he could never be alone . . . A little later I saw even more of him after he married 'Hula' Ashley.[4] A splendid couple they were (their vivid daughter[5] is the spit of her father); and his sister Lois[6] who was then a lovely bacchante was a friend too. The old mother[7] was a dark vicious rather magnificent Edwardian – Now they are all gone: Hula; Lady Alington; then Lois; and now, lastly, Napier, the most delicate of them all. He had a curious passion, that was his fondness for older women. Lady Crewe has been his mistress for fifteen years and she is about 60! There were others . . . . Naps was always my ally and friend; only recently has there been a slight cooling off as he was very anti-Chamberlain. He talked awful nonsense politically but I loved him really and shared many of his tastes. The whole family was vicious, colourful, romantic, stepped from the pages of the Renaissance. They loved *bibelots* and ballet, late nights and splendour, low cafés and sexual experiments, and were too aristocratic ever to feel the fetters of position or morals or standards. They were decadent, certainly, but rather in the grand manner; their glamour was such and their indolent ease of manner so fascinating that they could do

---

1 Actually he was still 43.
2 The messenger of the gods.
3 Also known as Elagabalus or Heliogabalus, he lived from 204 to 222 and was Roman Emperor from 218 until his death. He was chiefly remembered for flouting sexual and religious conventions, and is regarded as one of the most depraved Roman emperors. The praetorian guard assassinated him.
4 Lady Mary Sibell Ashley-Cooper (1902–36), daughter of the 9th Earl of Shaftesbury. They had married in 1928.*
5 Mary Anna Sibell Elizabeth Sturt (1929–2010).*
6 Lois Ina Sturt (1900–37).*
7 Lady Feodorowna Yorke (1864–1934), daughter of the 5th Earl of Hardwicke.

anything. Now the whole tribe is wiped out; only Naps's dark and vivid daughter remains. History will hear of her. She will inherit Crichel,[1] I suppose, a charming house and in his day kept up with *tenue*.[2] Life will be more drab without him, and every one of his legion of lovers will regret him. But perhaps it is better to be dead than to see poor London so scarred and battered and to watch all that is pleasant in life slowly fade out.

WEDNESDAY 18TH SEPTEMBER

A fairly quiet night, although I was rudely awakened twice. But at breakfast the bad news trickled in, brought by tradesmen – many buildings had been hit, a house in Hill Street, No. 32, a corner in Berkeley Square .... and large shops – stores in Oxford Street. I went to the office and found everyone still optimistic, foolishly so. Rab and I walked from the Foreign Office to the House where he had questions to answer. Winston walked about, frowning and unattended. I lunched with Peter Loxley at the Travellers Club – Rab went to the Spanish Embassy – and there I found half the Foreign Office as usual, all sitting separately and quietly at separate tables: many of them, and civil servants and other ministers are sleeping in.

This morning I attended a meeting of the 1922 Committee which was stormy. There was a discussion and argument about sending a congratulatory message to Mr Churchill and suddenly the old cleavage was bared once more; the Churchillians versus the Chamberlainites. It was quite heated and I was secretly on Neville's side – how he would have disapproved of such an undignified fray. There is a distinct mental schism which even the Blitzkrieg has not healed – and opposite was St Thomas's Hospital which has been twice struck! Have Members of Parliament no sense, no reality? Obviously St Thomas's and Smith Square were both missed: St Stephen's[3] must have been the target.

Rab and I drove about and saw the devastation, large houses completely wrecked! Can this continue? I believe there are secret peace *pourparlers* now in Sweden ...

Dined alone, now as I write these illegible, hurried lines a terrific bombardment is going on. Any moment we may be struck. Is all this a nightmare?

THURSDAY 19TH SEPTEMBER

I slept snugly in the small cellar: it is like a cell. Twice I was brusquely awakened by terrific noises, and later I heard that Dover Street – probably the Bath Club – had been hit. I drove to the FO but Rab had not yet arrived. After nearly two hours I began to be anxious about him and discovered that a time bomb had fallen in

1 Crichel House in Dorset.
2 High standards.
3 A synecdoche signifying Parliament, part of whose estate is St Stephen's Chapel.

Oxford Street; and that all the residents of North Audley Street had been turned out at very short notice. Rab managed to get into his clothes before being hurriedly escorted to Claridge's where he spent the remainder of his interrupted night. He arrived at the FO shaken, unshaved and untidy and announced that he would now stay with me. I was delighted and went home at luncheon time to order my depleted staff (six instead of fifteen!) to make the necessary arrangements.

Rab, Harold B and I dined in and Archie James,[1] home from Spain on short leave, joined us. We ate at the middle-class hour of 7.30 so as to start before the bombardment, which began with Teutonic punctuality at 8.10 – a pleasant dinner and good talk afterwards. Harold told us of his interviews with Roosevelt etc. and we all discussed the hour and are in agreement that the immediate outlook is grim; and that we are paying heavily for Baldwin's blunder, his ignorance about foreign affairs, his foolish trust in young Anthony; his susceptibility to left-wing opinions and his unwillingness to rearm actively. All these are contributory factors – a slightly academic conversation against the background of continual booming of machine guns and bombs. However . . . Rab is not anti-German; prefers the Saxon races to the Latin ones; says that as we were let down by France, so will Germany in turn be deserted by Italy. Rab always takes the long view, and thinks that the young German state has made many mistakes, has been too quick in its eagerness (as was France under Napoleon) to dominate the world and will be defeated by this, its primary object. He would be for peace immediately terms are offered that would be acceptable. The others agreed but added that there was no prospect of any such terms forthcoming at the moment. Rab was not quite so sure. He is more hopeful; but both he and Harold are 'invasionists' in that we think it will be soon attempted; I however do not quite agree, Messrs Hitler and Co. are too clever, too wily for that; they will wait until the autumn fogs, and until our alarms are allayed. Archie James doesn't think the plans for invasion are more than an elaborate expensive feint to detract our attention from Egypt and the Middle East generally. He was lavish in his praise of Sam Hoare's valiant efforts in Spain to keep that country out of the war. He had even taken him and Lady Maud to their first bullfight, a visit which added immensely to their popularity in Madrid. Franco is pro-British, or at worst, anti-war; his entourage is largely pro-Axis. There is actually a war going on there to decide their future course . . .

We broke up early, as is now the fashion; Harold drove Archie back in an Air Force car and they were nearly bombed *en route*. Rab and I decided to go to bed immediately; I lent him clothes and razors and whatnot. We looked at our beds and concluded the cellar was safest, so we shared my cell, he in the bed, I on an

---

1 Archibald William Henry James (1893–1980) was Conservative MP for Wellingborough from 1931 to 1945. He had served in the Royal Flying Corps and the RAF, rising to the rank of wing commander. He had preceded Channon as Butler's parliamentary private secretary from 1936 to 1938 and in 1940–1 was seconded to the British Embassy in Madrid. He was knighted in 1945.

Empire chaise longue which was comfortable. I was asleep first: he put wax in his ears and opening his red box, worked for a bit. Several times in the night I heard loud reports, but Rab, snoring slightly – and what a pleasant human reassuring sound when one is in sympathy with one's companion – waked not at all. The all-clear sounded before six and the most disagreeable moments were between 4 and 5 a.m. as one heard bombs whistling to the ground. I actually prayed at one moment.

FRIDAY 20TH SEPTEMBER   *KELVEDON*

We left our cell at seven and crept up to our bedrooms for a little rest and change. Rab is in high spirits and he walked to the office after our joint breakfast in the Black Room.[1] I remained behind to cope with my secretary but owing to a delay in the arrival of the post, I wasted my time . . .

King Carol has asked permission to live in Portugal as he is 'of Portuguese descent': it is true that old Ferdinand's mother was an Infanta of Portugal, but the plea is rather far-fetched. Is Carol angling for the empty Portuguese throne? Through his grandmother he has a claim to it . . . My adored Cilla, now known as 'Her Majesty the Queen Mother', is being treated with much honour and consideration in Bucharest. She is an angel, and a miracle of charm.

I drove here in the late afternoon, giving lifts to people all the way, 'Eastenders' and soldiers etc., chatted easily with them all. I am becoming very simple and democratic. H and I dined alone and went to bed early. Rab is by himself, which he quite likes, at Belgrave Square: I miss him. If only he didn't lack the one and essential quality[2] for perfect intimacy and understanding companionship!! No one ever lacked this particular kink more.

The East End, even the City, and a bit about the Monument have been sadly devastated.

Honor tells me that Kelvedon was immediately surrounded by incendiary bombs last night: she put sand [on them].

SATURDAY 21ST SEPTEMBER

The night was, at first, undisturbed; there was only the perpetual droning of distant German planes; but about twice I was awakened by two appalling thuds, worse, and nearer, than anything I had heard in London. Soon they began again and I retreated to the cellar (Honor sleepily refusing to budge); there I found the servants, gardeners and wives and children assembled in amusing *déshabillé*. They kept up a flow of conversation which I could hear. Every few minutes would

---

1 Presumably a darkly-decorated room in 5 Belgrave Square.
2 Channon presumably refers to Butler's lack of homosexual tendencies.

come another big bang! Before five I went out on to the lawn; there was a mist over the lake and one could just distinguish the swans; the house was lit up clearly by the moon; the bombardment continued. It was very Wagnerian.

MONDAY 23RD SEPTEMBER

Raids last night. Peter Loxley and I motored up to London through that tunnel of devastation, the East End. It is a shambles.

The Ministry of Information has been spattered with bombs; but there are no casualties. Halifax is back from his ten days' rest at Garrowby and is well, lively and amiable.

General de Gaulle has arrived at Dakar and even now a battle is in progress there;[1] I wonder whether this was a well-advised plan, or just a Winstonian scheme in his earlier, rasher manner?

Rab and I dined à deux and are sleeping together, but fitfully, in the converted cellar. I found two letters which both came by the Waynard bag; both gave me pleasure, and both were dated the same day, August 18th, one from the Regent, the other from Peter in Cairo who says we underrate the fighting qualities of the Italians.

The King broadcast a message at six. He is always embarrassing, shy-making: no enthusiasm or vividness and the painful pauses hurt. I suggested long ago that the Duke of Gloucester do the actual broadcasting – no one need ever know: their voices are very similar but Harry Gloucester has not those fatal hesitations. More and more I am bored by the monarchy; at least its present phase. She[2] is so gushing, so gracious, so winning but really at heart snobbish and insincere; he is just a well-meaning uninspiring dullard.

A really fantastic story. On Saturday after I left the Foreign Office there came a telegram 'very urgent' from Lothian[3] in which he said that President Roosevelt had known from a most trustworthy source 'that the invasion was due to start tomorrow, Sunday, at 3 p.m.' A copy of this telegram I myself saw today. Of course, the Service Departments were all informed, everyone was prepared. It only occurred to people here this morning that the cable and the President's kindly tip referred to the imminent Japanese occupation of Indo-China. An appalling and very inept and comic story; the machinery of the government thrown into confusion by a clumsily worded and more clumsily understood cable from Washington.

---

1 De Gaulle, with British naval support, was trying to establish Dakar, in West Africa, as a base for Free French activities; but it had already come under the control of Vichy forces, and the attempt failed.
2 Queen Elizabeth.
3 Philip Henry Kerr, 11th Marquess of Lothian, Ambassador to Washington. See entry for 13 December 1938 and footnote.

TUESDAY 24TH SEPTEMBER

A noisy night: Rab and I slept fitfully in our 'chamber' and went back to our respective bedrooms after the 'all-clear' sounded at six. The bombs seemed further away.

The newspapers splash General de Gaulle's sensational landing at Dakar: it will flop.

I ordered wine from Berry Brothers, the famous wine shop, still luckily intact. The owner begged me to dine in his cellar tonight as he is entertaining Anthony and Beatrice Eden, who are great wine connoisseurs. I could not face it. Possibly the Secretary of State for War in these days might have something better to do than sip famous vintages of an evening!

WEDNESDAY 25TH SEPTEMBER

A terrible night: I thought it would be my last; bombs, glare, incendiaries, the little room rocked but Rab, an excellent sleeper, and with wax in his ears, slept sublimely through it all until I called him at 3.30 after the 'all-clear'.

I got a builder in to see about our room and he is altering it and building a brick wall and making it gas-proof.

Rab and I drove to Cambridge at breakneck speed. He is a determined driver. We were forced to make many diversions as the roads are up in many parts of London owing to time bombs being in the vicinity, and to masses of broken glass. Rab and I gossiped all the way and agreed that Halifax is fundamentally a fraud and a failure; yet one cannot fail to admire his many great and redeeming qualities. But he is too theoretical, too much the sublime don. Japan is now slipping through our fingers. Perhaps Ribbentrop is, as Hitler said, the greatest diplomat since Bismarck. Certainly he has succeeded in isolating England.

Everyone is disturbed about Dakar, which is a rash, hazardous undertaking, almost certainly doomed. Why waste English lives and ships? We have had enough evacuations and retreats which were unavoidable; why create more?

Pembroke Lodge, the home of the Master, Sir Montagu Butler[1] and his very charming gracious wife, Lady Butler, is a pleasant, simple, comfortable house. No *luxe*; no ceremony; but everything adequate. Sydney Butler[2] is also here and I wondered whether she is having yet another baby – the best occupation for women in wartime, undoubtedly. We dined pleasantly and gaily and Rab's family was amused by my accounts of his sleeping so soundly through last night's raid.

THURSDAY 26TH SEPTEMBER

A breakfast in the bosom of the Butler family and then Rab and I, after looking at Pembroke Chapel and Hall and Pitt's room, drove back to London. We passed

1 See entry for 23 November 1938 and footnote.
2 Mrs R. A. Butler. She was not pregnant.

many houses that had been hit and even demolished by the recent bombing. Rab and I gossiped: he is shrewd, brilliant, omniscient; but he has not the aristocratic point of view, nor is there a trace of the trivial in his make-up; and he lacks a certain quality altogether which I find necessary for v deep friendship. Yet I like him immensely and admire him more every hour.

I gave Diana Cooper lunch at the Coq d'Or, and picked her up before at the Ritz where I found a few fashionables who cannot, I fear, keep away from London and the excitements. It is a sentiment I understand. Maureen Stanley was cool, I was icy to her: from now on I shall take the very rude, cutting line. I have several times offered her a chance to be more civil but she is a rude degenerate who will one day crash. Euan and Barbie Wallace were there: he is on a milk diet and has lost his spirits but regained his figure. Diana told me that she and Duff sleep in the Turkish bath at the Dorchester! In the restaurant was Lady Crewe in black – for Napier? Does that hard-hearted Jewess mind? I think that she does. She is almost one of my enemies, why I have never found out! . . . . Lady Camrose, always clucking and comic, was chaperoning one of her Berry brood . . . . She told us that Hackwood had been taken over by the Canadians as a hospital. 'They will not do it as much damage as the Camroses did,' Diana whispered to me. She was looking v lovely; all her old beauty was evident today. She is better now in the daytime and wearing big hats.

Harold dined with Rab and me here – excellent food, and pleasant company and conversation. We are all solidly and vocally against the Prime Minister: the failure – admitted now – of the Dakar expedition has revealed him to be as incautious as ever. It is a deplorable affair and feeling in the Carlton Club is running high against him.

Rab and I are sleeping in my new shelter which is now very comfortable indeed.

We had a long political conversation; attacking Churchill we nevertheless admitted that there was no one to take his place. Rob Hudson might become Prime Minister; he was so able and ambitious but I said he was without a soul and the others agreed. Who then? We are governed by a rum lot.

FRIDAY 27TH SEPTEMBER

We both slept soundly and well. Two nights of peace have done much for us.

The Japanese have signed a military pact with the Axis powers: this *démarche* shows our folly of not coming to terms with the Japs years ago; on the other hand the Americans, against whom it is primarily designed, will be enraged. It looks now as if the United States will enter the war soon after the presidential elections.[1]

I saw Joe Kennedy at the office; he is ever-smiling. Soon he returns to the United States on holiday – to avoid the bombing or to report?

1 Scheduled for 5 November.

SATURDAY 28TH SEPTEMBER   *KELVEDON*

I was alone at the Office all day. And I tried my utmost to prevent HMG opening the Burma Road on Monday. The agreement expires and is subject to renewal on October 16th. Under the circumstances the agreement cannot be renewed, but a hysterical, undignified renunciation of the Treaty now would do little good. A fortnight cannot make all that difference. The FO, always hysterical, takes the opposite view, and Halifax, ever academic, hedges! Eventually a cable was sent off to Craigie[1] in Tokyo asking for his advice. I am not sure that he represents us well but I am not convinced either of the contrary.

All day I had nervous indigestion. I drove here in peace through the East End without a raid. Kelvedon is cold and cheerless and Honor, as usual, out. When she came in I saw she had an appalling cold which she has contracted by sleeping in the icy stone cellar without making the proper arrangements. She sleeps on a sofa, *sans* carpets, curtains, *sans* anything. It is beyond her power to arrange even an air shelter attractively. We went to bed early.

I miss my huge Alan languishing on the waves. I hope he didn't go to Dakar.

SUNDAY 29TH SEPTEMBER

I slept for ten hours in my own room and heard never a sound. The Germans neglected us, probably because there was no moon. I have had several good nights this week now. One has a curious hunger for sleep and it becomes a luxury. Honor slept in the cellar.

The outlook is increasingly gloomy: the world, except America, against us. *Que faire?*

I am disgruntled with Peter, who now writes intermittently; and I resolved to punish him by not writing this week. For some days I resisted the urge, and then making excuses to myself, of course, I sent him a plump budget.[2]

Honor tells me that the local feeling runs very high over Dakar, which may indeed be the turning point of the whole war. Unfortunately, the real culprit, our verbose Prime Minister, is not blamed, yet who else sanctioned the madcap enterprise – he and only he, with, I suppose the connivance of the Alexander-controlled Admiralty.

As I was reading Lord Hervey's memoirs, and really one should read nothing else, Claud Phillimore[3] was announced. He is stationed at Box Hill. He is a clever

---

1 Robert Leslie Craigie (1883–1959) joined the Foreign Office in 1907. Having served as Assistant Under-Secretary of State at the Foreign Office from 1934 to 1937 he became the United Kingdom's Ambassador to Japan, serving until 1941, and in 1945 became Chairman of the United Nations War Crimes Commission.

2 Nothing to do with money, but an archaic usage meaning a wad of paper, in this case a letter.

3 Claud Stephen Phillimore (1911–94) succeeded his nephew as 4th Baron Phillimore in 1990. He was an architect.

and reserved, slightly hostile youth of tremendous beauty; I remember a weekend with him at Sutton Courtenay at Norah's years ago.[1] He wants us to lend Kelvedon as a hospital and we went over the house which he declared was too luxurious. I think, however, that I persuaded him to take it.

MONDAY 30TH SEPTEMBER

September closes without an invasion being attempted. Perhaps it was never seriously contemplated.

Raids all day and one now in progress as I write . . . Rab has just returned to bed in the chic cellar which we share. It is adequately protected and luxurious. We had a most *gemütlich* evening together, dining *en pajama*. He is the supreme companion when alone. We discussed politics and personalities. Sam Hoare will not be given India after all; and he seems to think that Anthony Eden will be made Viceroy, although Rab half harks after it himself. Sam Hoare will be broken-hearted: he has played politics so assiduously; but he is a tired man. I don't really mind Anthony going to India except that he is not up to the job; but his leaving would leave the way open to Rab; and perhaps the little glamour group, so ineffectual yet dangerous, might disappear. They have an ephemeral quality.

The Chief Whip's car was still at the Foreign Office steps at 7 p.m. – this must mean a Cabinet crisis. Rab says that Winston, whilst he had the final say in the matter, was not really in favour of the ill-fated Dakar expedition. De Gaulle is a *prétentieux*[2] and an ass.

TUESDAY 1ST OCTOBER

Rab and I went to bed before eleven, and after a little conversation were soon asleep. The barrage seemed light . . . . But I was rudely awakened by a swaying movement; so was Rab and we could not at first understand what had happened as there was no very unusual noise at the moment. Soon, however, chattering and frightened servants were heard rushing about the passage and I got up to inquire. It seems that – we were told that – two bombs had fallen on Belgrave Square, uncomfortably near. Later I walked over to see the damage; the old Austrian Legation, No. 18, had had its facade torn off, and the basement damaged: curiously enough the windows on the upper floors were intact and no one was injured and the garage at the back in the mews was completely wrecked. I thought of other days, of Mensdorff[3] reigning there in brilliant Edwardian days before my time

---

1 The Manor House, Sutton Courtenay, Oxfordshire, where Channon had been a recurring guest of Norah Lindsay (qv); see Vol. I, entry for 4 July 1923 and footnote.

2 Conceited man.

3 Count Mensdorff was Austro-Hungarian Ambassador from 1904 to 1914.

and the faded Franckenstein[1] parties, little distinguished boring lunches and countless concert parties with Dollfuss[2] and Princess Helena Victoria[3] etc. and latterly costume balls. At one, the Congress of Vienna Ball, Honor looked superb in an Empire creation. *Autres temps, autres moeurs*[4] . . .

I caught cold last night and spent the afternoon shivering in bed and hope that I have mastered the infection which I perhaps picked up from Honor over the weekend. There were raids all day but I ignored them . . . . People now believe that the invasion is either postponed or abandoned.

WEDNESDAY 2ND OCTOBER

A fairly peaceful night: Rab woke me to say the 'all-clear' had sounded and that it was three o'clock. I looked at our clock and saw that it was only 11.30 so we turned over and went to sleep again. We went upstairs at half-past five and slept blissfully until nine. Now we are going to Kelvedon for the night: our telephones here are still 'kaput'.

On the way to Kelvedon, I driving, Rab and I discussed the forthcoming Cabinet changes which, apart from the catastrophic resignation of Mr Chamberlain, are dull and faintly irritating.

> Sir John Anderson becomes Lord President in the room of Neville and goes to the War Cabinet.
> Herbert Morrison becomes Home Secretary in the room of John Anderson.
> Sir Andrew Duncan becomes Minister of Supply in the room of Mr Morrison.
> Oliver Lyttelton becomes Pres[ident] of the Board of Trade.
> Sir John Reith is given a peerage and becomes Minister of Reconstruction etc.
> Moore-Brabazon[5] becomes Minister of Transport in the room of Sir John Reith.

---

1 Georg Freiherr von und zu Franckenstein was Austrian Ambassador from 1920 to 1938.*
2 Engelbert Dollfuss (1892–1934) was Chancellor of Austria from 1932 until his assassination.
3 A granddaughter of Queen Victoria.
4 Other times, other customs.
5 John Theodore Cuthbert Moore-Brabazon (1884–1964) was the first Englishman to fly in England, in 1909, and served with distinction in the Royal Flying Corps and RAF during the Great War, winning the Military Cross. He was Conservative MP for Chatham from 1918 to 1929 and for Wallasey from 1931 to 1942. He was Minister of Transport from 1940 to 1941 and Minister for Aircraft Production from 1941 to 1942, when he was raised to the peerage as 1st Baron Brabazon of Tara. He had been forced to resign from the government for expressing the hope that, at the Battle of Stalingrad, the Germans and the Russians would destroy each other, at which the Russians took grave offence.

Lord Caldecote[1] becomes Lord Chief Justice of England in the room of Lord
Hewart[2] who retires.

Bobbety Cranborne[3] becomes Sec of State for the Dominions.

Bevin and Kingsley Wood, whilst keeping their jobs, are elevated to the War
Cabinet.

Oliver Lyttelton, a shrewd, slightly caddish fellow, gay, attractive really and a
bon viveur, is a surprise appointment. Presumably he will be given Southampton,
John Reith's seat. Oliver will be a House of Commons success undoubtedly. Reith
has been a failure, a flop. That huge granite Gibraltar, almost Brobdingnagian,
figure, who is so amiable and Scotch, has been a disappointment. I am angry about
Bobbety Cranborne: why should he be given a plum? He has done nothing to
deserve it. Except to have been a failure at the Foreign Office and to have advocated
policies which have led this country ultimately into war. He is weak, silly, petty,
unattractive, treacherous, anaemic and luckily has bad health.[4] His appointment
will please the Glamour element but will discourage the loyal Conservatives. The
wheel is turning full circle, certainly.

A long talk with Rab. He thinks that the war really began with Halifax's famous
visit to Germany where he met Hitler and decided that no real arrangement was
possible with him. Halifax decided on the Polish guarantee and really thought
that, as war was inevitable, it was better to have it now before than when Germany
was even more powerful. It was a terrible gamble which he made: of course our
country was behind him.

Feeling still runs high over Dakar and the reshuffle may be an unsuccessful
gesture to bolster up public opinion.

THURSDAY 3RD OCTOBER

Rab and I drove up early in the rain. Incendiaries were dropped all around us last
night: my room was lit up and I went to the window to see the trail of flares. Our
gardeners soon put them out although it was about four in the morning.

In London we discovered that the Cabinet changes are not yet out – they will
be tonight. My telephone has been put right. I shopped and ignored the many
raids.

1 Formerly Sir Thomas Inskip.
2 Gordon Hewart (1870–1943) was Liberal MP for Leicester from 1913 to 1918 and for Leicester
  East from 1918 to 1922. He was Solicitor-General from 1916 to 1919 and Attorney-General
  from 1919 to 1922, when he became Lord Chief Justice, serving until 1940. He was knighted
  in 1916, raised to the peerage as Baron Hewart (life peerage) in 1922 and advanced to a
  viscountcy in 1940.
3 Viscount Cranborne.
4 He lived another thirty-two years.

As I was attacking Cranborne's appointment he walked into my room and I congratulated him. He was friendly. Maisky and Rab were closeted together for nearly two hours!

The King has become known as RS, rubber stamp, as Winston has absorbed all power and is, in fact, a virtual dictator.[1] A telephone message was sent to the Palace to say that Dowding[2] was to be given a GCB immediately. It was done: Winston's idea was to placate him before the news of Newall's[3] removal and Portal's[4] succession should be made public.

As I came out of the office I saw the Chief Whip striding across the quadrangle preceded by porters, and the gate was opened for him to go to the Cabinet War Room. There is some speculation as to what will happen on Wednesday next when the Conservative Party meets to elect a new leader in Neville's place;[5] in all probability everything is rigged for Winston to succeed! He to lead the Conservative Party which does not trust him is, indeed, a sign of the times. Some pressure is being put upon Halifax to assume the role; he could have a watching brief until later; but I doubt whether the project will be allowed to advance. Winston is now all-powerful and, while he talks of resigning directly after the war, in order to make room for younger men, he nevertheless now wishes to taste the full fruits of power. It is a deplorable regime, nevertheless I wish I could be made Under-Secretary of Reconstruction under Reith! I might do it well. The

1 As was said of Lloyd George in the Great War.
2 Hugh Caswall Tremenheere Dowding (1882–1970) had been a professional soldier from 1900 before joining the Royal Flying Corps in 1918. He became an air marshal in 1933, and was knighted, and put in charge of RAF Fighter Command in 1936, being promoted to air chief marshal in 1937. He retired unwillingly in November 1940 but historians credit him with securing victory in the Battle of Britain. He was raised to the peerage as 1st Baron Dowding in 1943.
3 Cyril Louis Norton Newall (1886–1963) had begun his career as a professional soldier before transferring to the RFC and RAF. He served as Chief of the Air Staff from 1937 to 1940, and was responsible for the significant increase in manufacture of Spitfires and Hurricanes. He was knighted in 1935, promoted to air chief marshal in 1937 and marshal of the Royal Air Force in 1940, when he was also given the Order of Merit; these last two were consolations for his removal from office after arguments with Beaverbrook and his cronies. He served as Governor-General of New Zealand from 1941 to 1946 and was advanced to the peerage as 1st Baron Newall in 1946.
4 Charles Frederick Algernon 'Peter' Portal (1893–1971) had intended to be a barrister after Winchester and Oxford, but joined the Army as a private soldier in 1914 and became a dispatch rider. He was quickly commissioned, transferred to the RFC, qualified as a pilot, won the Military Cross and the DSO and Bar, and ended the Great War as a squadron leader in the RAF. He became Commander-in-Chief of Bomber Command in April 1940, was knighted that year and became Chief of the Air Staff, in succession to Newall (*vide supra*) in October, with the rank of acting air chief marshal. He instituted the programme of 'area bombing' in Germany and was promoted to marshal of the Royal Air Force in 1944. He was raised to the peerage as 1st Baron Portal of Hungerford in 1945 and advanced to a viscountcy in 1946.
5 Chamberlain's mortal illness had forced him to retire as leader.

Churchill regime will never offer me anything unless Brendan bestirs himself on my behalf. In any case I don't care.

I am surprised and perturbed by Peter's long, long silence. What counter-attractions are offered in *le Caire*?[1]

FRIDAY 4TH OCTOBER

Rab and I slept together saucily until 8 a.m. Not a sound disturbed us all night; a lull in the Blitzkrieg whilst the 'big boys' confer on the Brenner?[2]

Pamela Berry, who is supposed to be *en flirt*[3] with Oliver Stanley, told him of all his wife's many shocking infidelities. There is much indignation against Pam, but I am delighted that Oliver's stupid, sleepy, student eyes should be opened. A man so ignorant of the world is not fit to be a Cabinet minister . . .

Harold B came [to Kelvedon] for the night and as we were dressing the lights were fused and we had to dine in candlelight. Honor was overexcitable – in other words <u>drunk</u>, and argumentative. I am hurt when she behaves so.

Raids here continue; considerable noise. A letter came from Nannie, who is now happily installed with my Paul at Rhinebeck.[4] Helen Astor has angelically put them up in the tennis pavilion. It is a beautiful place.

SATURDAY 5TH OCTOBER

The air changes[5] were announced on the radio: they will improve the efficiency. Winston has been lavish with his honours and rewards, which is a pleasant trait in his character – it shows imagination!

Harold left early to shoot at Six Mile Bottom.[6] The weather improved: Honor was slightly ashamed of herself, I think, for her last night's inebriation.

Much publicity is being given to the Brenner meeting of Mussolini, Hitler and Ribbentrop and Ciano. Probably an invasion of Egypt was discussed. 'Methinks at such a meeting, Heaven stands still.'[7]

I was alone all day and felt dispirited by the noise, the wind, the grey clouds and stormy outlook. I wrote to Grace Curzon and to Mrs Neville Chamberlain, to Alan, and to Brendan Bracken. Then I walked with three white dogs to Bois Hall to call upon Master Phillimore but he was out. The v attractive rather Jane Austen house is bleak and undecorated within.

---

1 Cairo.
2 A meeting between Hitler and Mussolini at the Brenner Pass to discuss the possibility of encouraging Franco to bring Spain into the war.
3 Flirting.
4 The Astors' house in New York State: see Vol. I, entry for 3 December 1927.
5 Portal replaced Newall as Chief of the Air Staff, with Sir Richard Pierse (1892–1970) as head of Bomber Command.
6 A renowned partridge shoot in south Cambridgeshire.
7 A quotation by Jocasta from Act V of Dryden's *Oedipus: A Tragedy*.

Honor came back about eight; by then the raids had begun and we dined to the tune of machine guns. And we wondered shall we lose one or both of our lovely houses, so full of lovely possessions, the harvest of a lifetime of collecting?

SUNDAY 6TH OCTOBER

I slept in my usual grey and white George II chamber: Honor and all the servants and some of the dogs preferred the vaulted cellars! They were right, really as the house rocked. At 2.45 I was awakened by a terrific crash and thought for a brief second that Kelvedon had been hit! Then I went to sleep again – Honor told me that the impact had made the clock bells strike, but I did not hear them. After I was dressed we walked over to see the crater which fell in our field. It was a fairly big one and would have killed us had it dropped on the house! The footman, whom I had brought down from London, says it is noisier here than at Belgrave Square!

The newspapers give poor Mr Chamberlain a bad press on the whole:[1] there are some thinking exceptions.

Gloom; cold; grey; horror – it is like 'Wuthering Heights'.

MONDAY 7TH OCTOBER

I motored up and was caught in a traffic jam due to the dislocation caused by the weekend air raids. Many roads and streets are closed as a precaution against time bombs or 'DAs' – delayed action – as they are familiarly called. Impatient, panting, my over-full bladder threatening to burst, there was nothing to do, but to allow the tiny car to crawl tortoise-like to the FO. Two hours and a half *en route*!

Geoffrey Lloyd[2] proposed himself to dine at the last second, and was charming. He is intelligent, alive, keen and able but exhausting; as Harold B was dining I was a bit apprehensive as they are old enemies; however Rab's tact and my wine effected a reconciliation and they left together quite happily. A foolish complex had been dissolved; but perhaps more than tact and wine, was shared interest and political agreement! Four more stout and loyal Chamberlain supporters have never congregated before: all four were angry about Winston, and resented being 'bounced' into supporting his candidature as leader of the Conservative Party. Harold and Rab actively dislike him; Geoffrey knows that he is not *persona grata* (as I do) with the new regime and we made ambitious plans for the future. Rab eclipses them all by his brilliant intelligence. He has many ideas for the new England that will emerge after the war. He thinks that the whole system will be drastically modified and perhaps improved. Obviously he will be the architect

---

1 On his retirement.
2 Conservative MP for Birmingham Ladywood.

of the reconstruction. The Glamour Boys, now so prominent and powerful, after being fallow for so long, are a makeshift and shoddy lot, shallow and ineffectual. Their only merit has been long subservience and sycophancy to Winston. His court is disastrous: the new Cardinal, Morton,[1] is an Oppenheim character, and largely responsible for Dakar; his rival, Prof. Lindemann, the Berlin-born[2] scientist and snob, remains to his rage, Bishop-in-Partibus. Roy Harrod,[3] a theoretical, oriental-looking don, is a Monsignore.

Guns roared and our windows rattled as we drank Krug and discussed the future. Rab, unlike the others, is very abstemious.

TUESDAY 8TH OCTOBER

I am becoming increasingly attached to Rab and find him fascinating: his perpetual good nature, his shrewdness, his balanced views and lack of pose or pretence are amazing in one so young.

The House met in secrecy at eleven o'clock. Bombs dropped about nine on the War Office and the Admiralty and elsewhere. Usually the day raids are ineffective and more in the nature of reconnaissance. Rab and I had left our conjugal cubicle and gone up to our rooms to bathe. Geoffrey Lloyd came to breakfast and was very amusing: both he and Rab attacked Jim Thomas. Rab loathes him and says that he is ------ [sic].

The House was crowded and seemed indifferent to the air raids which occurred off and on all day. At the end of Questions Randolph Churchill was introduced by his father and David Margesson. They walked up together in military fashion and to my great surprise and infinite pleasure the House was silent; not a cheer; although a sunbeam from the high windows (the stained glass has been replaced) fell on Randolph as he walked up, he nevertheless looked old, dissipated and tough. He is enormously fat and his coarse face looks cruel and gross. He has not his father's warm heart, or other gifts and I prophesy a disastrous career for him. As he shook hands with the Speaker there was one faint cheer: the cool reception was significant and very striking as any ordinary unknown member is usually accorded the courtesy of a civil reception.

Winston then rose and spoke of the progress of the war. He was eloquent, in excellent form, and very adroitly handled the Dakar incident by refusing to

---

1 Desmond Morton (1891–1971) had been aide-de-camp to Field Marshal Haig. He was the main source of information to Churchill about German rearmament during his anti-appeasement campaign and became Churchill's personal assistant in Downing Street from 1940 to 1945, when he was knighted.

2 He was born in Baden-Baden.

3 Henry Roy Forbes Harrod (1900–78) trained as a historian but became an economist and disciple of John Maynard Keynes. He was a Student (that is, fellow) of Christ Church, Oxford, from 1924 to 1967, and advised, among others, Churchill and Harold Macmillan on economic questions. He wrote Keynes's biography and was knighted in 1959.

give it much importance. Skilfully he dismissed it as an error such as is bound to occur in warfare, and he rather dishonestly inferred[1] that the failure was due to the incompetence of the Foreign Office, which we know to be untrue. Rab knew nothing of it until he read of it in *The Times* except for a stray remark dropped to him by Alec Cadogan the previous evening. Cadogan was against the expedition but had not been informed of it until too late. Halifax was away. There was much unexpressed criticism in the Commons of the whole affair but few seemed courageous enough to challenge Churchill and he got away with it. But I should have enjoyed his speech had Mr Chamberlain been in power and Winston attacking the government! WC is fundamentally dishonest but he is unaware of it . . . . The lobbies hummed with gossip and Rab's name was bandied about as a potential Deputy Leader of the Conservative Party, a sort of insurance against Winston and the nomination of the Crown Prince.[2] Rab, whilst flattered naturally, was nevertheless aghast – the proposal, even the lobbying could only do him harm with Winston and the Edenites. I went about damping down the proposal, and reported to him my activities.

Roger Makins, long, dark, bald and brilliant, came to dine as did Gladwyn Jebb, a very FO evening. Rab startled them by his heterodox views on politics and foreign affairs. We argued until midnight and the bombardment was not severe; indeed there is usually a lull between 9.30 and eleven o'clock. Presumably the first big wave of German bombers returns to the French shores before the second starts out. Gladwyn is silent, secretive and discreet: he is the real head of MI5 and I am very fond of him.

I saw Randolph drinking in the Smoking Room; he was alone and looked depressed, and I thought it a good opportunity to break down my old vendetta, so I offered him my hand and murmured 'Congratulations.' He shook my hand warmly, muttered 'Hello. Thanks.' And I walked away before he could recover from his surprise. I shan't pursue this reconciliation. I had rather however that we remain on civil terms, as he is capable of doing me much harm, since his father adores him. But what a cad devoid of any redeeming quality he is: gross, vulgar, cruel, malicious, unsound, unstable and unkind, his future cannot be glorious.

WEDNESDAY 9TH OCTOBER

We slept fairly well, and I walked to the FO. The House met at eleven and several people, Rob Hudson, Shakes Morrison (he had much better be made a judge!) and other smaller fry asked me about the rumour of Rab's alleged candidature as Deputy Leader of the Party. I laughed and retorted that he had read it at breakfast! It was true that the newspapers talked of it but bracketed him with Anthony

---

1 He means 'implied'.
2 The Crown Prince being Eden.

Eden, which annoyed them both. However I soon saw that this political canard
had caused more excitement and comment than it merited and I warned my
chief. The 1922 Committee met at 12.30 and references were made to Rab and any
unfortunate divisions in the party; some members praised Winston; others abused
him; more took the line that he must be supported since there was no one else and
he could be more dangerous out than in. This is probably true ... Someone then
raised the controversial subject of David Margesson and the whips. Several people
complained that he was a martinet, spoke only to a small clique, was detached and
unsympathetic, and they urged that Tommy Dugdale[1] should be recalled from
the Middle East and reinstated in the Whips' Room. Mrs Tate was particularly
abusive of David and there was considerable smouldering resentment. Will he
weather this storm? I was reminded of a lot of naughty boys being insubordinate
when the prefect was away! Of course all the charges are true; but David is always
extremely loyal, has excellent judgement and is a magnificent Chief Whip. I pray
that he remains. In recent months I have suspected a lessening of his powers and
even a dimming of his capabilities; he could have managed the govt crisis more
shrewdly and one wonders whether he had not thrown in his hand? I really think,
however, that he is disturbed emotionally; Geoffrey Lloyd has superseded him as
Olive Baillie's[2] 'knight errant' and David himself philanders with Lady Bridget
Poulett who is half his age and no doubt exhausting and *exigeante*.[3] Few people
are aware of this romance ...

The 1922 Committee again revealed the curious but wide cleavage which exists
in the Conservative Party, and may, in time, unless successfully bridged, split it:
it is the old story of Chamberlain versus Churchill and although the leaders have
long since conquered their differences and are on terms of trust and affection,
their adherents are separated by a mental chasm ... However it was obvious too,
that there was nothing to do this afternoon but to support Winston's candidature:
any quarrel or discussion would be undignified. I went to the lobby, hoping for
no lunch, but was weakly persuaded to go to Prunier's with Paul Latham and
J. J. Llewellin, my very Saxon Conservative sensible friend! We had oysters and
much wine and became skittish and confidential. J confessed to me, what I had
already been told, that it was Beaverbrook, his busy boss, who was opposing
strong reinforcements for Egypt. Beaverbrook demands that everything be kept
for the defence of England and there is a serious division of view on this highly
important policy. Winston is cooling off a <u>little</u> towards 'the Beaver' .... Paul drove
me back to the Commons and *en route* told me the most extraordinary things
about J. J. Llewellin, things which I had only very faintly suspected and hardly

---

1 Dugdale had been a highly popular whip between 1937 and 1940; he would be recalled as
   Deputy Chief Whip the following year.
2 Olive Paget.
3 Demanding.

now believe.[1] Paul and I sat in the car in Great Palace Yard discussing life and Peter Coats, whom he knew so well of old. On the whole he was nice about him, but he couldn't resist a few malicious shafts. He is genuinely pleased by our 'axis' and yet slightly petulant about it. I was 100 per cent loyal about Peter . . .

Then, accompanied by Harold Balfour, I drove to the Caxton Hall meeting. Halifax was in the chair and looked more ecclesiastic than ever. The platform was crowded but the Hall not so; and I couldn't but recall the last party meeting three years ago when Neville had been elected amongst so much enthusiasm and hope. The atmosphere had been electric and wholeheartedly loyal; today many people were uncomfortable. Halifax in a finely balanced speech first praised Chamberlain, the retiring leader, and then proposed Churchill. He was supported by two old Tory fighting cocks, Sir George Courthope,[2] and Sir Eugene Ramsden.[3] Neither appeared to be enjoying his role. When the resolution had been agreed upon *nemine contradicente*[4] the Prime Minister, looking embarrassed, came in. He made a tactful, very tactful speech which was fairly well received but the atmosphere was chilly, almost frigid. Still it is better that he should lead us, than be against us in the future. I distrust him . . . he half-apologised for his attitude in the past but excused it by his love of England . . . there were titters in the audience and some people clapped without making any noise – a Jesuitical trick! The proceedings were quite quickly over and Rab and I returned to Belgrave Square, sad but resigned that this most brilliant, warm-hearted, courageous charlatan should now control the destinies not only of the nation but of the great Conservative Party. From his own point of view, Winston has made a mistake in courting the leadership, except that in the Commons one must have an army . . . .

THURSDAY 10TH OCTOBER

We were at the FO by 10.15 and attended the H of C for Questions at eleven. The House had that hangdog look which it assumes when it is ashamed of itself 'on the morning after'! It is remorse for having attacked David Margesson so scurvily yesterday! He looked quite downcast. The House is really becoming ridiculous

---

1 Llewellin was a discreet homosexual, though insufficiently so to prevent Latham, a promiscuous one, finding out about his proclivities.
2 George Loyd Courthope (1877–1955) was Conservative MP for Rye from 1906 to 1945, when he was raised to the peerage as 1st Baron Courthope; he had been created a baronet in 1925. He had fought with distinction in the Great War, winning the Military Cross, and was an expert on forestry.
3 Eugene Joseph Squire Hargreaves Ramsden (1883–1955) was Conservative MP for Bradford North from 1924 to 1929 and from 1931 to 1945, when he was raised to the peerage as 1st Baron Ramsden. He had been created a baronet in 1938.
4 Unopposed.

as its importance declines. It caused the war and now is impotent to stop it, or to guide it.

I lunched at the Overseas Club, a function to honour Polish airmen. Harold Balfour proposed their health in an adequate speech and was followed by Victor Warrender who said a few words in fairly fluent French .... Dollie Warrender[1] told me that they are 'very poor now'; yesterday she passed the Paymaster-General's office, or rather what was the office and from the rubble she saw a human arm protruding. She waited to watch the rescue of some unfortunate person imprisoned under the debris but none came out. The arm was alone and had no body attached to it. It is too surrealist for words.

Alan is in London and he left me a batch of messages which I did not receive until too late; now he has gone and I have not seen him. A very Blitz visit.

Jay Llewellin and Harold Balfour dined with us,[2] a merry quartet in the Black Room. The bombardment began at 7.20, dinner at eight, and we ate and drank to the usual din. We haven't taken to eating below yet; that will come, for there is really little one cannot do below ground. We are rapidly becoming troglodytes. There was more anti-Churchill conversation from the three ministers and myself; but we are resolved to serve him loyally. I am sure that he is aware of our resentful opposition. We agreed that David would probably weather the storm. I had a moment alone with Jay and he clumsily tried to tell me, or rather convey to me what Paul Latham had said yesterday. I wondered whether they had conferred? I pretended to half-understand, which is safer. I am amazed. He stayed until eleven when we practically turned him out. Indeed Rab got up and announced that he must write to Stafford Cripps in Moscow. He is lonely, our Jay, and garrulous and boring, but sweet, kindly, shrewd and able. More talk about the post-war new order which bores me. Rab is obsessed by it. I suppose I shall have to adapt myself to it.

Rab let out at dinner that Lothian has been told to hint to President Roosevelt that HMG disapproves of the Duke of Windsor's proposed visit to Washington, although for obvious reasons we cannot stop it. It is hoped that Roosevelt will pour cold water on the proposal, and perhaps the Windsors will remain at Nassau. An unkind story, but I fear inevitable.

I wonder why Winston always bows and withdraws into himself when he is aware of hostility. When he shakes hands with someone he dislikes, he seems to contract, to look small and his famous charm is overclouded by an angry taurine look. Now that Randolph has a son, born yesterday,[3] the race is perpetuated. I am fed up with Churchills and Cecils and some Cavendishes – not Eddie.

1 Dorothy Etta Rawson (1898–1975), daughter of Colonel Richard Hamilton Rawson MP. She and Warrender had married in 1920.
2 Channon and Butler.
3 Winston Spencer-Churchill (1940–2010) was born at Chequers. He was Conservative MP for Stretford from 1970 to 1983 and for Davyhulme from 1983 to 1997. He was actually born on 10 October; Channon must have been writing the following morning.

FRIDAY 11TH OCTOBER

At breakfast I was rung up and advised not to hurry to the office as there are delayed action bombs in the Horse Guards Parade, and elsewhere nearby. My poor secretary took three hours to arrive from Northwood, where she lives.

I shopped and for the first time was depressed: London looked appalling and all the diversions, particularly in Mayfair, were depressing. At the FO I saw Horace Seymour in golfing clothes and I asked him how he was. 'All right except for a direct hit last night.' He laughed. Luckily he and his wife had been in the cellar of a house in Carlton House Terrace where they have a flat. The house was almost entirely demolished. The front door of John Astor's[1] house had been blown in and they had taken refuge with the Astors for the night. Rab remarked that I looked dejected and tired and offered to drive me to Kelvedon, which I was loath to do. However at 5.30 we left and arrived easily and quickly. Honor looked lovely and she and Rab had a gay agricultural conversation until eleven. Then we all went to bed; but I peeped out with the dogs and saw that it was a starlit night, crystal clear so I feared yet another noisy night.

Rab went to Buckingham Palace to attend a meeting of the Privy Council, where he had a few words with the King, who sent me his love. I never know how I am with this regime, but I do know that they do not impress or thrill me at all. I suppose I know them too well for that. They are doing their job well but 'the divinity that doth a hedge a king'[2] is gone – or rapidly going.

Anthony Eden left early this morning on a very 'hush-hush' mission to Cairo and the Middle East. I almost asked him to take a book as a present for Peter; but decided not to as I am not supposed to know anything about it.

SATURDAY 12TH OCTOBER

An unexpectedly quiet night: I slept soundly. I am really lucky to have had so tranquil a week. All one's conversations now seem concentrated on where and how and with whom one has slept! Rab woke me up and I came down to see him off: Honor took him to visit Cow Farm and he went afterwards onto Stanstead where he could easily (but I am glad to say did not) have gone last evening.

A quiet day, I read and rested and raged against the servants who are all lazy and becoming slack in their manners as well as in their duties; the *ton*[3] of the house is going. It is partly the war, and partly Honor's inexperience and slackness with them. I ticked off two.

As I was dressing about eight o'clock in the evening there were two very loud bangs and I thought we had been hit; however nothing seemed to happen . . . by

---

1 John Jacob Astor V.
2 A slight paraphrase from *Hamlet*, Act IV, Scene V.
3 Tone.

ten o'clock the raiders seemed to have left and all was serene when I now am going to bed.

I am in despair about England and see little future, financial, social or political ahead of us. Am I really, as I have always sensed and expected, in at the kill?

SUNDAY 13TH OCTOBER

I walked over, accompanied by three white dogs, to Myles's to see the damage caused last night by three bombs, one was noiseless, an oil one.[1] The other two, which I had heard, made small craters but did little damage. The yokels with whom I talked thought that the cattle had been mistaken for camouflaged troops! They were most calm and had suffered nothing more than a few shattered windows.

Alan rang me up from Henlow where he is on leave; yesterday he was at Pyrford where there were two bombs last night in the garden. We shall be lucky indeed if we keep both our houses intact.

Planes roared on high making white trails of smoke with their exhausts.

MONDAY 14TH OCTOBER

The day dawned with a slight domestic fracas when I was disagreeable to our very annoying chauffeur at Kelvedon: I have infrequent flashes of irritation when I am hungry or overfed! I was driven to the crossroads where Rab and 'Madame' his wife, picked me up and we drove up to London remarkably quickly in an hour and ten minutes. The East End looked deplorable, the burnt-out houses, the broken windows, the many, many shops half-demolished and the occasional gaps which had once been houses and were now only heaps of debris . . . the sad, hurrying people, the yellow road signs with 'Diversion' on them to indicate the presence of time bombs, unexploded, all added to the gloom. It will be a terrible winter; taking toll of our nerves and lives and property and happiness and health . . .

Channon goes shopping with Lennox-Boyd.

We came back to drink. Later he and Patsy returned to dine with us. It was a memorable evening! Geoffrey Lloyd also dined as did the Butlers. It was Sydney Butler's first evening in London since the Blitz began! Alan has always disliked Geoffrey intensely but somehow lubricated by Krug they buried their ancient hatchet and became good friends: no one can resist Alan . . . . Dinner proceeded and suddenly Lambert[2] ushered in what appeared to be a Harlem n––: it was Harold Balfour, black from head to foot! He had been standing in the Smoking Room of the Carlton Club with David Margesson, Victor Warrender and Tupps

---

1 An incendiary bomb.
2 Channon's butler.

Ramsbotham drinking sherry before going into dinner. With a flash, the ceiling had fallen and the club had collapsed on them. It was a direct hit. Harold swam, as he put it, through the rubble, surprised to be alive. He soon realised that his limbs were all intact and he called out to his companions who all answered, so we know them to be safe. Somehow he got to the front door and found it jammed. At that moment he saw Lord Hailsham being half led, half carried out by his son, Quintin Hogg. A few other individuals, headed by Harold, rammed the door and it crashed into the street. By then a fire had started. Harold remembered that he had left his car, an Air Force one, nearby. He went to it and found only a battered heap of tin, but the chauffeur, an RAF man, was luckily untouched as he had gone into the building . . . Harold came here for a bath, champagne, and succour, and we gave him all those things. The noise increased and we foolishly went onto the porch, all of us, about ten o'clock. As we were standing there in the dark, a bomb dropped very near and was immediately followed by a whistling one. We all collapsed onto the floor of the vestibule and heard a crash! Later I found out that Seaford House[1] had been struck, that huge mansion where I have been to so many balls in old days! I wonder what happened to the famous green malachite staircase!! The noise continued for some time and then there was the usual evening lull. Geoffrey Lloyd offered to take the Lennox-Boyds in his car to the Dorchester where they are living and the party broke up. I meanwhile arranged a bed for Harold next to mine in the shelter . . .

TUESDAY 15TH OCTOBER

We were awakened several times by bombs dropping uncomfortably near; one fell in Motcombe Street, another in West Halkin Street. Rab and Sydney . . . . slept in one of my shelters. Harold and I shared the other; the door was open between us and we chatted sleepily . . . This morning a communal breakfast. The strain of the bombardment and sleepless nights is beginning to tell. I was a long time at the H of C, but I dislike raids there and the long fragile building is a death trap!

WEDNESDAY 16TH OCTOBER

Last night was the worst London has had but I slept well. Bombs, however, dropped near Whitehall etc. Belgravia got off lightly.

Later the water ran out in the Foreign Office and for the famous tea party in the Secretaries' Room, an attendant had to take a kettle into St James's Park to fetch water.

Rab, Harold and I drove in an Air Force car through wet and rain and fog to Ascot where we are staying with Evelyn[2] and Helen Fitzgerald: it is a small-ish

---

1 A detached, corner house at 37 Belgrave Square. It was repaired and stands to this day.
2 Evelyn Charles Fitzgerald (1874–1946), son of Baron Fitzgerald of Kilmarnock (a life peerage for a Law Lord), married in 1923 Helen Gascoigne Drury (qv).

cottage most comfortably arranged. We had an hilarious dinner – Ann O'Neill[1] (known as 'Idiot's Delight') came over from a nearby cottage where she is living openly with Esmond Harmsworth, whom she is trying to marry. For years their affair has gone on: it is almost a marriage and now Lord O'Neill is making a fuss: Ann, however, lives happily 'married' to two men. They are an abandoned group, the vivacious, dark attractive Charteris sisterhood . . . we had a great deal to drink and were merry – our first little fiesta since the Blitz. Rab, who is a touch strait-laced, was startled but amused by the *ton* of conversation etc. In the intervals Esmond talked politics and he declared that Leslie Hore-Belisha is the only alternative to Winston and he predicts that Leslie will be Prime Minister before the end of the war. He has a following in the country but too few troops in the House.

It is incredibly peaceful here; not a sound. Helen kissed Rab 'goodnight'; he seemed startled.

In the car we discussed the war and I said that I thought that the invasion was 'on' again. I have always felt and feared that November with its fogs would be the most likely time. No one agrees with them [*sic*].

THURSDAY 17TH OCTOBER

We breakfasted happily with Evelyn Fitzgerald and then drove to London, which, we soon heard, had had a fairly quiet night. But there was a dreadful message from Honor to say that Kelvedon had had two land mines which dropped in the field on the south side of the house. It was at 8.15 and she was in her bath, and was luckily unscathed. No one was hurt and by a miracle there was little or no damage to the furniture but the household is disorganised and the rooms are cold and windy. The dogs are miserable. I could telephone quite easily today. Evidently the services have improved. Hardly anyone one knows or meets has not had some bombing experience to tell. 'Bomb-bores' infect the body social.

I came home early feeling tired. The House rose at four o'clock. Several times I saw Winston who gave me porcine grunts and scowls.

I ran into Leslie in the lobby and I told him what Esmond said about him; he was pleased but laughingly said 'See how calmly I take it.' A little later I went to telephone and in the next booth I heard Belisha booming, 'Yes it is Mr Hore-Belisha. I want to speak to Mr Harmsworth.' My remarks must have struck home. He did not see me, nor did I hear the rest of the conversation.

London looked a mess today . . . . in the night four Treasury officials were killed when a bomb fell for the second time on that bit of the building immediately adjacent to No. 10 Downing Street. The Germans evidently think that Winston sleeps there. Actually he sleeps in the War Room.

---

1 Ann Charteris, wife of the 3rd Baron O'Neill, would in 1945 marry Esmond Harmsworth, 2nd Viscount Rothermere (qv). See entry for 20 January 1939 and footnote.

FRIDAY 18TH OCTOBER

Rab and I had wanted to sleep at Kelvedon but as the household is disorganised we could not do so. Instead we stayed here, and Harold came to dine. He twitted Rab, said he was priggish, or at best strait-laced. He is a touch [illegible]; or more accurately he has high standards of conduct allied to a lack of temptations. I don't think he is at all priggish. Sydney may be, as the Courtaulds are Nonconformists and wholesome.

I had an injection against typhoid, paratyphoid and tetanus as epidemics are feared.

I am sorry about Holland House,[1] gone beyond repair. I thought of that last ball in July with the crush, the Queen, and 'the world' still aglitter.

SATURDAY 19TH OCTOBER   *KELVEDON*

I drove here and gave lifts to people *en route*. One gave me a shilling and before I could recover from my surprise he had got out. Another was a soldier from Southend who knew of me and I didn't reveal my identity. As I arrived here I met Honor riding away with her agent, a dark horse-coper named Woodman whom I much mistrust. He is a dark stranger and no doubt mulcts her of much money. She is completely dominated by him, probably infatuated and I see serious trouble ahead. His manners are appalling. Honor always is a victim to outside influence and whilst it lasts forgets all else.

SUNDAY 20TH OCTOBER

Honor looks white and ill; she was shocked by the bombs falling so close. They made craters. I hope it is only that, but she seems so strange, and *désoeuvrée*; every year she becomes more eccentric and less tractable. I am desperately sorry for her; but she is so impervious to tenderness, so utterly uninterested in people or the world, that it is difficult to help her. Incidentally she has no moral sense, no idea of the obligations of friendship – but who am I, a Nero in embryo, to prate of people's morals? At least I am unselfish in small matters; Honor has never since I have known her lifted her finger to help or to please an individual. Her mind, too, is completely male.

In my bones I am alarmed about Egypt; but it would be no easy campaign – a dash across the Balkans, a hurdle over the Dardanelles, perhaps Iran and Palestine . . . could even Hitler do that?

A pleasant evening: Honor very sweet.

1 See entry for 5 November 1940.

TUESDAY 22ND OCTOBER

A remarkably peaceful night and I awoke refreshed.

At the House of Commons I picked up David Margesson for dinner and later called at No. 10, where I left a note for Brendan Bracken as all the Treasury telephones are still down and one can only use the few secret Federal lines; Brendan also dined, and he brought David with him in the Prime Minister's armoured car! It looks like a huge painted thermos bottle, and is supposed to be bombproof. Brendan drank a whole bottle of hock, David a bottle of Krug '20. A gay, interesting evening: these two are the most powerful men in England. Brendan offered Rab the presidency of the Board of Education, which Rab secretly covets; but I pray that they will leave him at the Foreign Office; but I know there is some plot afoot to oust both Halifax and Rab.

The raids seem to have diminished in their ferocity.

Hitler is meeting Pétain today . . .

David is slightly deferential to Brendan; he has had to be to weather the storm; but I think his power is re-established.

WEDNESDAY 23RD OCTOBER

Another quiet night due no doubt to cloudy weather.

The King came to the Office and was received by Halifax, Cadogan, Rab, Vansittart and Sir Stephen Gaselee.[1] I purposely kept in the background and only had a brief glimpse of him: he looked bronzed and fit and Rab reported that he was in good spirits. Rab likes him but actively dislikes the Queen, whom [*sic*] he says is an intriguer, and has not the detachment appropriate to her position. I fear she has become rather worldly; but she has immense charm.

FRIDAY 25TH OCTOBER

Another peaceful night. Rab got up and left my conjugal couch as he said that I snored!

SATURDAY 26TH OCTOBER

The blow, long foreseen, has fallen. Honor rang up that she was going to Pyrford and wanted to see me *en route*. She arrived late, looking sheepish; soon she bolted out the truth. She wants me to divorce her so that she may marry a Mr Woodman, a horse-coper, a dark, unscrupulous fellow of the yeoman class.

---

1 Stephen Gaselee (1882–1943) was Pepys Librarian of Magdalene College, Cambridge from 1908 to 1920 and a fellow of the college from 1909 until his death. From 1920 to 1943 he was Keeper of the Papers at the Foreign Office. He was knighted in 1935.

Apparently his wife[1] is about to sue him naming Honor. Poor darling, she has no moral or common sense, no *noblesse oblige* and doesn't realise what she is doing – social suicide. He is a penniless, tough adventurer after her money. I tried to move her without success and I saw that he has carefully trained her, schooled her in what to say. She will regret it to her dying day. She offered to make any adequate financial arrangements for Paul and me; swore that she would never have children by this fellow, declared that she didn't care what happened; was indifferent to the world's opinion and disdain. She were better dead . . . At last, after a three hours' conversation I promised to let her know my decision in January. Of course I shall give in – but it is the end of Southend, of a peerage, of my political aspirations, of vast wealth and great names and position – all gone, or going. Somehow I didn't care as I ought. Will I marry again? Or shall I live with Peter? I am almost relieved – complete independence and perhaps books and happiness. I fear my mother-in-law will be crushed; it may kill her. I have agreed not to tell them until December 1st . . . On reflection I think I shall do nothing – a policy of obstruction, delay and hope. Perhaps the *deus ex machina* will solve the problem. I shan't tell the Iveaghs, I think, for some time. It will take a year to obtain a divorce, I suppose. It would take some time before the preliminary decree were granted, and then before I asked for the *nisi* – all this will take months. And I am more hopeful. She has treated me so shabbily, so outrageously that I ought to hate her, but somehow I don't. Time is a great healer and may soothe out my problems. I am surprised how unmoved I am by my world crashing in ruins; of course, if England survives, I will be comfortable financially!

It has been announced in Vichy that there will be further collaboration between Hitler and Pétain. This doesn't mean that France will declare war upon England, though great pressure has been brought to bear on Pétain: telegrams from the King and from Roosevelt may have had some effect in preventing him from throwing in his hand with the Axis powers.

SUNDAY 27TH OCTOBER

I had a short mild attack of nervous prostration or indigestion brought on by this blow – I am to be deprived of my wife, my country home, and my position, financially and socially, will be seriously compromised. I could not sleep; and lay in utter dejection, as I have done several times before in my life – dreading the morning, hoping I would awake from a nightmare. The night, fortunately, was not too noisy after a bad beginning . . . And there had been raids all day. On mature reflection I realised that a parting of the ways is inevitable: I shall be free;

---

1 Raymonde Forster (1911–76) was an art and elocution teacher. She married Frank Woodman (qv) in 1934.

I shall become a Roman Catholic; I shall be vicious, unfettered – and perhaps, if I keep my head, great – *qui sait*? As the bitter hours passed I decided not to take the affair tragically but to be cheerful and surprise everyone by my gaiety! And dignity. Incidentally I shall get all I can, secure every possible penny for Paul and myself . . . I went to the Cathedral and burnt candles, as I always do when I am in trouble or doubt. I came away strengthened but I saw clearly that Honor, for her own sake, must be prevented from marrying this low fellow, this swarthy adventurer. All day I hesitated whether to tell the Iveaghs and at last decided to postpone breaking it to them for a little time. Why make them needlessly miserable? . . . and I toyed with the idea of a remarriage – can I afford it? I shall have roughly £8,000 per year gross . . . Belgrave Square would be impossible for long. I shall have a luxurious flat and a country cottage, or tiny house, shared, I trust, with Peter. That would be pleasant and consoling. But of course, the Germans may win the war and then nothing matters . . .

At the Office there were rumours of more German and French collaborations and hints of a huge peace offensive to be launched by the four great Continental powers, Germany, Italy, Spain and France. The blame for the continuance of the war will be given to Winston. It will be a clever move and will evoke considerable following.

I sat to Gunn for my portrait. He is really too loquacious and as I sat I ruminated that really my own difficulties were trivial compared to those of so many other people: the world crashing to atoms.

Honor arrived from Pyrford where she spent last night; she was funny about the discomforts prevailing there. The Iveaghs live in true wartime squalor . . . . Honor looked well and we had a friendly dinner, discussed the divorce and then a bantering conversation suddenly became bitter and acrimonious. She lost her temper after I remarked that the Dresden dinner service and gold plate would hardly be suitable to her in her new life; that she must have a sense of proportion!! She blazed at me with eyes of fury and flounced out of the room; luckily I called her back and we had a reconciliation and the tiff, if anything, brought us closer together, I thought. We both slept below. The usual booming didn't begin. All was quiet.

Coppins has been hit: there were four high-explosive bombs and some incendiaries but luckily no casualties. The *Empress of Britain*,[1] a beautiful ship in which I crossed the Atlantic in 1927, has been sunk. She was the pride of the Canadian Pacific, indeed of Canada.

---

1 Channon actually crossed the Atlantic in an earlier ship of the same name. This one was launched in 1930 and was serving as a troopship when it was first bombed and then torpedoed by a U-boat seventy miles off Ireland. It was the largest ship sunk in the war. There were very light casualties.

MONDAY 28TH OCTOBER

Apart from the pleasure my divorce will give to my enemies, I am looking forward to it now: I am not sure that it will come off, although Honor seems greatly determined. She is like a woman possessed by a poltergeist. Perhaps this Woodman individual is one. The night was curiously quiet and Honor had the most peaceful night she has had since June. I only once heard the guns and at 5 a.m. I went up to my own room. She followed later. This morning was all clear between us: we shopped, bought lovely little *bibelots* at Cameo Corner[1] and later met for luncheon at the Ritz where we saw many friends. A wise move which will allay gossip for a time. I dread the flare-up . . . .

Today is a historic one: Italy sent Greece an ultimatum at 3 a.m. that she would take over strategic bases at 6 a.m. unless Greece capitulated. General Metaxas[2] refused and now tonight the flame has spread to the Balkans, and Italian troops are pouring over the mountain passes into Greece. My poor Paul – what a position to be in – is holding a Cabinet meeting this evening to decide on Yugoslavia's role. She will remain, I suppose, neutral, but Turkey may rush to Greece's aid – and may not. What a difficult position for poor Princess Irene, married to Spoleto: I had thought that marriage a hopeful augury. The world is mad . . .

I have been thinking of my lonely future: I shall have roughly:

£5,000 per annum	marriage settlement
£1,000 " "	in Guinness shares which I own
£1,000 " "	from local investments and from the USA
£7,000	

In addition I shall have, for a time, at least £500 as a Director's fee of the brewery, and £600 as an MP. That makes over £8,000 gross. There may be more from various sources as I shall have the spending of Paul's money until he is 21; my American income may go up; either Honor or the Iveaghs will give me an additional sum; this house will be mine and I may be able to sell it; I shall inherit something from my mother no doubt; Honor's life is insured in my favour for another £27,500. I shall not want. So, at least, I imagine. But there may be unpleasant surprises ahead for me.

Paul, my alter ego, is deciding the destinies of his country and his dynasty, and perhaps Europe. But no man is more shrewd. I can't bear to think of his miseries now . . . . sitting in his library, which was once Lord Chesterfield's, tormented by doubts, scruples, deciding the fate of millions.

---

1 In the Burlington Arcade.
2 Ioannis Metaxas (1871–1941) had been a career military officer and was Prime Minister of Greece from 1936 to 1941.

I bought a pair of absolutely enchanting eighteenth-century buttons marked GM with a crown and shall give them to the Kents for a Christmas present.

Dined alone, nervously bankrupt: it is terrible to be alone too much, worse to be alone never and tonight I refused to go out with both Harold Balfour and Bill Mabane and also Leslie Belisha . . . . Instead I am scribbling these half-anguished notes; and preparing another memo on the bombing of Naples. It must be done. My first paper was sent up to Winston who, I am told, was impressed.

This will be a momentous week in world affairs. Meanwhile our brewery at Park Royal has been bombed and four men working there were killed. The buildings, which form a sort of city like Carcassonne, are so immense and cover so vast an area that I am surprised so tempting and easy a target was not hit before. It is a magnificent creation and shows much imagination. I only wish the management were equally inspired.

TUESDAY 29TH OCTOBER

The position in Greece is confused: the Italians advance; the Greeks resist. I hear that fur flew at the Cabinet as the Labour Party were particularly anxious to send everything possible – too much – to help Greece. Winston pointed out to them that had they been less obstructive over rearmament we should have had more to send. A stormy meeting. Winston sleeps in the tube station in Dover Street[1] which has long been disused and is deep underground. This is a secret known to very few.

I went to the much-abused Ministry of Information where I had an interview with Harold Nicolson who was v kind, courteous, and trouble-taking. He told us that Raymond Mortimer had been summoned to Chequers and had helped, and in fact largely written, the Prime Minister's French broadcast. I am pushing collaboration with Vichy: we should send a mission there to counteract the anti-British feelings there.

WEDNESDAY 30TH OCTOBER

I have a feeling that the Court feeling against me has been altered either by the Halifaxes, or curiously enough by Godfrey Thomas whom I now adore.

Wonderful letters from New York from both Helen Astor and Serge Obolensky who described a recent tea party at Rhinebeck: a message had come that the President of the United States was bringing Princess Alice (Athlone) to tea from Hyde Park. Helen told Paul that he must behave himself and be the host! The little fellow very gravely met the presidential royal party at the door and bowed. Later he sat on the President's knee and had a long talk with him

---

1 On the Piccadilly Line between Hyde Park Corner and Green Park.

about 'the international situation'. As the President left he patted him on the head and said he was a nice little boy. Paul retorted 'I hope you beat Mr Wilkie,'[1] to which the President laughingly remarked to Princess Alice 'He's beginning his diplomatic career young.'[2]

The Butlers' little Westminster house, No. 3 [Smith Square], has been damaged three times by bombs and today Sydney superintended the removal of their chattels – always a sad chore. Smith Square and the parliamentary quarter has been badly knocked about. Later she joined Rab and me at Belgrave Square and we drove to Polesden Lacey in a hired Daimler! It is dangerous and nerve-racking driving in the dark although we arrived before the raids began. We were shown into Mrs Ronnie's [Greville] boudoir where she was enthroned in an armchair. She was spiteful, witty, affectionate and amusing and dazzled the Butlers, who are *au fond* simple folk of high standards. For an hour we chattered and then went up to dress, dined, and more gossip, mostly reminiscences of royalty and the great. She is still intimate with the Queen, telephones to her most days and sometimes sends her malicious cuttings about the Duchess of Windsor from the American press; she . . . . told us that Queen Mary once admitted, but with extreme reluctance, that she would receive the Duchess of Windsor, were she forced to do so, but only if surrounded by the entire royal family; she gave us vivid 'close-ups' of her political past and of many of the great she has known. Her interests are partly political but fantastically social, and preferably royal. She was affectionate to me; said that I had been a loyal friend to her for many years . . . and when she attacked the 'Black Rat'[3] I joined in. She has lost the use of one eye and both legs but is surprisingly cheerful and still full of life . . . every word, every vitriolic pen portrait would be worth recording.

At eleven o'clock we went to bed: she was wheeled out like an empress. Rab and I browsed about the library, ate chocolates and then went up. The house is still *bien tenue*,[4] with an Edwardian atmosphere and *grande luxe*, although a bomb has dropped within a few yards of the front door . . . Mrs G thinks that the Anglo-French alliance was a mistake: she wanted friendship with Germany, Japan and Italy; she admires Chamberlain, dislikes Winston whom she thinks a charlatan. She says that the King does not trust him partly because of his role during the abdication crisis . . . . As I sat with Mrs Ronnie and devoured avidly her

---

1 Wendell Lewis Wilkie (1892–1944) was a lawyer and businessman who switched allegiance from the Democrats to the Republicans and was the Republican candidate in the 1940 presidential election, which he lost. An attempt to secure the nomination in 1944 failed and he died of heart failure soon afterwards. Like Roosevelt, he was keen to assist Britain in the fight against Germany.

2 Thus in the MS; Rhodes James has 'political career'.

3 Sir Alec Hardinge.

4 Well-kept.

velvety venom I felt like Walpole at the feet of Mme du Deffand[1] – only Mrs Greville is not in love with me. She let drop – purposely – that that Semitic courtesan and *grande dame*, Lady Crewe, is still hostile to me. She has always been, why I have never known except that her animosity was in some way connected with Napier Alington who, she once thought (and alas without cause), liked me too much. Also she blamed me for abetting his marriage when actually I tried to prevent it; it was as clear as daylight that it was doomed to crash. The fault was his.

THURSDAY 31ST OCTOBER

I had one of my dreaded *nuits blanches*,[2] tossed feverishly and at last turned on the light and frankly read. Was it indigestion, or the heat of Polesden? Like most Edwardian houses it is almost impossible to open the windows. My room was otherwise highly luxurious.

I got up early, and Rab came to my room as I was breakfasting – I am now utterly devoted to him – and we went for a walk under the beeches about the garden, now a vegetable allotment . . . We left early for London and saw a few wrecked houses on the way. *En route* we discussed Mrs Greville and the Edwardians; we agreed that they were more stalwart, courageous, granite-like than the Georgians; they stood up better to disasters . . . the Georgians (I suppose I am one) were weakened, undermined by the last war.

The Greek–Italian war seems not to be a war at all; a few skirmishes, desultory fighting on the frontiers.

I hope that I shall sleep better tonight; perhaps it was the utter silence at Polesden that kept me awake, or was it the divorce? I am beginning to think it will never come off . . . I care very little, really.

I had a long talk with the Duchess of Kent on the telephone. She is wretched about Greece, broken-hearted. She adores her native land . . . .

Much talk at the FO of bombing Rome; I pointed out that it was a city of parks, gardens and palaces. It would be a waste of bombs . . . . and antagonise the Vatican.

FRIDAY 1ST NOVEMBER

Only two months more – *avant le deluge!*[3] – *avant le divorce*. I am reconciled to the idea now. I shall be free, but shall be a long time recovering from Honor's selfishness; her treachery, her harlotry; her boredom with the war and with me;

---

1 Marie-Anne de Vichy-Chamrond (1697–1780) unhappily married the marquis du Deffand, her cousin, in 1718 and they parted after four years. She ran a major literary circle in Paris from the 1720s to the early 1750s, becoming close in later years to Horace Walpole.
2 Sleepless nights.
3 Before the storm.

and her complete indifference – cruel indifference – to her child. She has never cared for him and has always been casual and neglectful of him, and inclined to tease him. Never have I seen her smile on him affectionately, never have I caught a tender word or gesture between them. She has not, however, been actively unkind; but days would pass when she would forget to send for him, or see him when he was living with her at Kelvedon . . .

Lunched with David Lyon[1] at the Ritz; he has aged and has deep crow's feet at the ends of his eyes; but his charm remains. He is sly, pleasant, ever charming, and always delightful, as are all the Lyon family, but like the Queen he is indifferent, casual, and not painstaking. It was very nice seeing him again after too long a time and we were on our old footing again. I didn't say anything controversial; he however attacked Dalton, his chief, whom he accuses of being a war profiteer: that is, he is packing the Ministry of Economic Warfare with Socialists. David dreads the future, the Bevins and Labour lads. There is a vein of surface treachery in him which Mikey[2] lacks. Mike has had another baby recently, but David couldn't remember its sex – a curious lapse for so devoted a brother, I thought, but like him – casual.

I walked back to Berkeley Square with David and we agreed to meet again. I had a 'sinker' during lunch, a wave of mild despair but it passed. Curious, as these past few days I have been so well and witty . . . I walked back to the FO via Piccadilly. The recent damage to St James's Church etc. is dreadful to see.

Rab left for the country about five o'clock driven by his father-in-law, Sam Courtauld,[3] a young-looking man for his age. He is silent and lonely . . . . I went home and had a divine evening to myself, reading and writing. I am making so many arrangements for the future that I shall be almost disappointed now if the divorce doesn't come off! How astonishing are one's reactions. This morning I met David M by chance in Downing Street and followed him into his office. I offered to give up Southend in exchange for a peerage, as Oliver Lyttelton is looking for a safe seat. David was sympathetic, thought I was too young, hadn't been long enough in the House to be elevated – 'to be kicked upstairs' – still, if I insisted? I didn't. In any case it was too late for Oliver Lyttelton as a seat has been found for him . . . . David made a mental note and said he would willingly arrange for me to have a peerage later. Relieved, I left him; I don't really want to leave the House yet; but I fear that marital complications might later prevent me having a

---

1   David Bowes-Lyon (1902–61), sixth son of the 14th Earl of Strathmore and Kinghorne. He was the Queen's younger brother. He was working for a secret propaganda bureau in the Political Warfare Executive.

2   Michael Claude Hamilton Bowes-Lyon (1893–1953), fifth son of the 14th Earl of Strathmore and Kinghorne. He was the Queen's elder brother. He married in 1928 Elizabeth Cator (1899–1959), daughter of John Cator, of Norfolk.

3   Samuel Courtauld (1876–1947), industrialist, art collector and philanthropist, and founder in 1932 of the Courtauld Institute of Art. He was 64.

peerage – after a scandalous divorce case I would become *persona non grata* from that point of view. It would have to wait and by then the House of Lords might be abolished. However the seeds are sown, and in time I shall be Lord Chips. The future is now so problematical: I must exercise sense, dignity and shrewdness if I am to triumph. It is only for Paul that I mind, for my angel little boy whom I love so very much . . .

I had a note from the Duchess of Kent enclosing an open one from her mother in Athens. I half glanced at it and saw that she is broken-hearted by the invasion of her native land which she has always loved . . . and she hinted in no uncertain terms how offended she was with the Queen who had not written or made her any sign of life these days – they have never liked each other. Poor Princess Marina, who always is a stranger here – a royal Ruth in the alien corn[1] complex.

Saturday 2nd November

I made frantic, feverish arrangements all day; deposited my jewels, such as remain at Lloyds Bank in dangerous Berkeley Square; sent my four pictures – the Hickel[2] of the House of Commons; the Bonington[3] given me by Prince Paul; the Wouwerman;[4] and the Matisse[5] given me by my mother to the Pantechnicon . . . etc., etc.; At the FO I found a long typed, cold, or rather chilly letter from Pierrot.[6] He loves me no longer? Or is it discretion, or more likely, absorption in Cairene life? It would be too much to lose him too . . .

After a frenzied morning I drove to Julians, the lovely Hertfordshire seat of Reggie Cooper.[7] The house is small, a perfect tiny palace and I envy it. I covet it. I shall one day have it. There are great trees and a spreading park; it is idyllic, and I should be content living there with Peter and Paul. But would I? I suppose I could arrange to have it; but it would mean giving up so much – Belgrave Square etc. Perhaps I can find something smaller . . . perhaps I shall be killed by a bomb;

---

1 He refers to the Bible and the Book of Ruth, who picked up pieces of corn missed by reapers in order to feed herself. 'Let me now go to the field, and glean ears of corn after him in whose sight I shall find grace.' (Ruth 2:2.)

2 Karl Anton Hickel (1745–98) was a Viennese, and became court painter to the Holy Roman Emperor Joseph II.

3 Richard Parkes Bonington (1802–28) was a watercolourist who worked in France.

4 Philips Wouwerman (1619–68) was a Dutch landscape painter.

5 Henri Émile Benoît Matisse (1869–1954) was an innovative French painter distinguished not least for his use of colour.

6 Peter Coats.

7 Reginald Cooper (1885–1965) was a gifted amateur architect and close friend of Harold Nicolson (qv), with whom he was at school. The garden of Julians, near Baldock, the house he remodelled, were designed by Sir Philip Sassoon, but he was also close to Channon's friend Norah Lindsay (qv).

perhaps the divorce will not come about . . . Tonight I have a definite impression that I shall live here. It is gloomy tonight with the winds howling and the house rocking; and I can scarcely hear the guns. Honor is away with her dark stranger. I think she is a nymphomaniac. She said she was going to Shropshire for a cattle sale! I think he is trying to keep her from me lest my influence persuades her to give him up . . . it is so horrible in the country that I shan't mind, or shouldn't mind, giving it up were London habitable. The servants here were all pleased, obviously pleased, to see me. Do they know?

The beauty of Kelvedon, which I alone have created, overpowers one; but I now no longer love the house – Honor has spoilt it for me. It is an unlucky demesne.

SUNDAY 3RD NOVEMBER   *KELVEDON: BLEAK HOUSE*

All day alone and now it is nearly five and I am wondering whether Honor is returning. She went off without telling the servants and they are bewildered. I still hope that she is coming back for dinner so that we may talk. If she doesn't 'play the game' I certainly shan't. But I offered to be reasonable and understood that she agreed but she has a horrible character really, hard, mercantile, unsympathetic, uninterested. And my God, what a bore – no humour; no gaiety; no lightness of touch; no tenderness or *désir à plaire*.[1] I am beginning to hate this place, and fear the 'Kelvedon curse' is a real one; but it is supposed only to affect women. Nothing has gone right for me, however, since we bought it. Today it is wet, bleak, foggy and as yet we are free from raids. I haven't seen or heard a plane all day. I went for a long walk in what might be such beautiful woods and was sad and oppressed by them. The dripping leaves, the mud added to the gloom. I like the woods, but I love the baroque swimming bath and exquisite pavilion which I created. Something told me that I shall reign here again one remote day. But shall I want to? I wrote a long letter to Peter in Egypt: I mustn't expect too much of him, as he is only 30 – eleven months younger than Honor. Still I want and need and crave him now. I have no future, a bombed house probably in Belgrave Square, the loss of all my possessions, Kelvedon gone, my wife alienated, my child far away and perhaps forgetting me. All is bleak and dour indeed. I wrote to my child, who reigns at Rhinebeck, half-adopted by Helen Astor who is being angelic to him, 'mothering' him – he needs it now. The effort was too much for me and I broke down for the first time since all this affair and wept bitterly. I miss the lad dreadfully, desperately and for him alone I am grimly determined to fight this situation and secure and tie up every penny that I can for him, every penny, every picture, every acre, every ell.[2]

---

1 Desire to please.
2 An ell, a Viking measurement, was a foot and a half, or eighteen inches.

I spent the lonely day arranging my things; tomorrow I send the Rolls to Ledbury where I hope it will be safe; and more important I deposit my diaries, which I realise may have some interest for the future, into the hands of Sir John Forsdyke, Director of the British Museum; and I am also removing from the little graveyard here, where they too have been buried since June, a collection of watches, *bibelots* and jewels. I shall probably put them at my Oxford bank on the theory that it is safest to scatter one's possessions. My jewels are mostly in America; and some are at Lloyds Bank, Berkeley Square. I want Paul to have most of them, and a few for Peter ...

At about six o'clock Honor rang up from her secret *gîte*[1] and was pleasant, even sweet, but added that she could not get back until Tuesday. She agreed to be here next weekend and I swallowed it. I must swallow everything until things are settled satisfactorily for Paul. I am wretched tonight and lonely for the first time in my life, I think. Painfully lonely – oh! what shall I do? I am about to be deserted; am in love with someone who I suspect does not love me; my child is far away; life is a mess. The servants are all so assiduous in their attentions that I suspect that they know of and dread the change.

It has been v quiet all day; not a sign of an enemy plane or gun.

Monday 4th November

My spirits are indeed low, low, indeed. I am apprehensive, uncertain about the future, my future. The Greeks seem to be holding up the Italian advance with unexpected success. It is the new line that they can hold out for about three weeks, the usual resistance time put up by small nations against Axis pressure. One week has already passed.

I hear that Neville Chamberlain is very ill and will not survive until Christmas. Everything seems to come at once.

Lunched at Claridge's with *mes beaux-parents*,[2] Patsy, Arthur and Elizabeth Elveden – he has a week's leave and is well, immense and bouncing. I had arranged a quiet evening for Rab at Belgrave Square with Harold Balfour and Rab's Wykehamistical[3] secretary, the pleasant, unimaginative, common, competent Geoffrey Harrison, but Rab at the last moment decided to dine with Lothian who is still here ... I accompanied him to a small meeting of journalists held in the Ambassadors' Room. Lothian presided and spoke with astonishing frankness for an hour – he is confident of Roosevelt's victory,[4] thinks that the Americans, if they can be made to see the situation in its true light, would fight for us, when we wish. Lothian was rather scathing about Joe Kennedy, whom he describes as an

1 Refuge, or shelter.
2 My parents-in-law.
3 Harrison had been educated at Winchester.
4 Over the isolationists who wished to keep the United States out of the war against Germany.

Irish-American, much concerned with the preservation of property, his own in particular, since he has 'nine hostages to the future'.[1] The journalists were thrilled at this indiscreet peep behind the diplomatic screen. Lothian is an excellent Ambassador, understands America, is simple but remains a Liberal, I fear, at heart.

I dropped Rab at the Ritz about seven o'clock where he was to dine with Bobbety Cranborne and Lothian. Shortly after I left him the Ritz was *bombé*, glass flew about, windows and doors were shattered .... and Cranborne, arriving late from his father's house next door in Arlington Street, said that it, too, had been bombed. However they were all able to have dinner in comparative comfort in the cellar.

I am forgetting things: my mind works only at half-cock; my zest has gone with my digestion and my memory and keenness fail me. It is all this divorce situation. *Que faire?* I dread the scandal, yet almost relish the prospect of freedom. Letters from Peter which come now with regularity and frequency buoy me up ...

I had a busy day arranging matters: my huge green Rolls I sent to Ledbury to a garage for safekeeping; my tin box full of *bibelots*, watches and Fabergé ornaments I sent to Oxford to the Nat[ional] Prov[incial] Bank Ltd. More important packages, I deposited two tin boxes full of diaries and private papers at the British Museum where they will remain for all time – I hope! I have, however, the right to remove them later should I so wish.

Geoffrey Harrison, dull and inarticulate but sound, Harold Balfour, ever charming; and Nicholas Lawford, a clever, *mondain*, agreeable youth, a favourite secretary to Lord Halifax dined ... Lawford .... is very French, *très deuxième empire*;[2] he agrees with me that we have been stupid, extremely stupid and short-sighted in our policy and relations with Vichy. We have turned potential friends into almost certain enemies. It is the old English fault, the Whig tradition of always encouraging the left in other countries. Our backing of General de Gaulle was a colossal mistake – shall we have to fight him, too, in the end?

TUESDAY 5TH NOVEMBER

The day of the great presidential election – early reports indicate a victory for Mr Roosevelt. I met Lothian in the Foreign Office lavatory and told him that my baby boy was taking his place as chargé d'affaires since he had recently had such a success with the President at Rhinebeck.

I spent most of the day at the House of Commons. Winston gave his fortnightly review of the war situation and failed signally to please the House. Perhaps he was purposely *piano*;[3] I don't know; but there was scarcely a cheer

1 That is, his children.
2 Very Second Empire; that is, like a Frenchman of the mid-nineteenth century.
3 Quiet.

when he sat down and his prophecies for the future filled everyone with gloom. Talked about 1942, 3, or 4 . . . Of course he enjoys the war. I saw him sitting about talking with members as he always did before he was Prime Minister when he felt things were not going his way or was 'up to something'. I admire his pluck, his courageous energy and magnificent English. His humour too, although often in doubtful taste, is immense . . . One of his secretaries rushed up to me in the House and asked me where was the Prime Minister? He was due to lunch at the Palace and it was already 1.15. Luckily I had just seen him 'boozing' in the Smoking Room and so I volunteered to remind him. I went up to him politely, but unsmilingly, and said that his secretaries were anxious as it was so late and the Palace lunch was at 1.25. He got up ungraciously, after grunting at me. He can be very unattractive when he is in a bad temper. Neville, my poor dark dying Neville, was never like this . . . I walked away. I wonder how the King and Queen, whom alone he intrigued against, like him now.

There then follows a paragraph in the MS that is heavily crossed out and illegible.

Kenneth de Courcy[1] dined secretly at B Square with Rab. I arranged this tête-à-tête. Harold fetched me and drove me to the Dorchester, where we dined with the Elvedens . . . . Half London was there. The Coopers were next to us, entertaining the Walter Elliots; Walter Moyne, Cecil Beaton, Mlle Ève Curie[2] and Bridget Paget[3] made an incongruous quartet! Oliver Lyttelton, our new President of the Board of Trade, was throwing his weight and wit about. He, Lady Moira[4] and their very dark puppyish soldier son[5] were dining with the Lloyd Georges – Gwilyms! . . . indeed all London was there! It was exhilarating but fatiguing. I made a point of being particularly pleasant to Bob Boothby who must be unhappy as the scandal seems to be growing.[6] He was a touch tipsy and I gave him a champagne cocktail in the private bar, which looks, seems and smells like the rue Cambon Ritz Bar. Half the crooks of Europe almost . . . Knowing my dear brother-in-law's meanness about money, a trait which seems to go so often with millions, I left early to avoid paying his huge bill. We had four magnums of champagne. London

---

1 The editor of *Intelligence Digest* and the future convicted fraudster (qv).
2 Ève Denise Curie (1904–2007), younger daughter of Pierre and Marie Curie, was a jour-nalist and writer, her books including a biography of her mother. She worked as a war correspondent and served with the Free French during the Second World War.
3 Bridget Colebrooke (1892–1975), daughter of the 1st Baron Colebrooke, married in 1922 Lord Victor Paget, from whom she was divorced in 1932.
4 Moira Godolphin Osborne (1892–1976), Lady Moira by courtesy, was daughter of the 10th Duke of Leeds. She married Lyttelton in 1920.
5 Antony Alfred Lyttelton (1920–80) succeeded his father as 2nd Viscount Chandos in 1972.
6 Boothby had resigned from a junior post at the Ministry of Food a fortnight earlier for failing to declare an interest when asking a parliamentary question. It was one of his more minor peccadilloes.

lives well. I have never seen more lavishness, more money spent or more food than tonight. The dancing room was packed. There must have been a thousand people. Alec Hardinge, *sournois*, scornful, scoffing, sniffed as people passed. He was with James Stuart.

Harold and I wearing our tin hats – the cloakroom attendant said to me, without trace of a smile, 'There is a screw out of your hat. If you can wait I'll send for the electrician to mend it' – left the modern wartime Babylon and stepped quickly into his Air Force car. The contrast from the light and gaiety within to the inky blackout and the roaring guns outside is terrific. I was a little drunk and infinitely discouraged. People asked for Honor and I lied – I have no idea where she is; not a sign of life. Living in lechery with her dark stranger somewhere in Shropshire, I fear.

The government has had a bad day, and I am secretly pleased. Leslie Hore-Belisha, who is busy caballing against the Churchill regime, made a damaging attack on the Prime Minister: so did Archie Sinclair, but with less effect.

Nell Stavordale[1] was philosophic about Holland House; it had always been doubtful whether they could ever live there and since the war taxation they had sadly realised that they could never possibly keep it up. The bombs had solved their problem, the historic house has gone out in a blaze of glory. It can never be rebuilt. For the family it was an act of providence, of tragic providence. No rebuilt mansion could have the old atmosphere, the ancient Whig glamour. I have always found it gloomy, even ugly, but no one could deny its immense atmosphere and unique tradition. Parties there, however, have always been dull and flat.

WEDNESDAY 6TH NOVEMBER

A too full day. As the raids are very much increasing in intensity I am glad to be in the country .... With a waxing moon we must expect more severe bombardments. Shall we escape with our skins and our possessions? I wonder ....

The House met at eleven o'clock and we had the first lot of Questions, always a chore so early in the day. I cannot concentrate, am so upset nervously and fear that I do my work badly. I need a long rest and relief from my domestic Blitz. At three o'clock the House went into secret session by arrangement with the whips to discuss our future meeting place. Winston came in, 'spied strangers' and then made the government statement: we are to meet at Church House in Westminster Cloisters, or Abbey Square[2] as I believe it is called. The building which has recently been hit by a 1,000 lb bomb is thought safer than the Palace of Westminster and has been converted by the Office of Works. Winston was humorous but dictatorial,

---

1 Helen Elizabeth Ward (1907–70) married in 1931 Lord Stavordale (qv), whose family owned Holland House in Kensington.
2 He means Dean's Yard.

hinted at shutting down Parliament altogether if there was opposition to his decision, which on the whole seems a reasonable one. 'We must try the shoe, see where it pinches and perhaps return here later. This procedure will confuse the enemy.' Such was his line. The House took none too kindly to this announcement and there was chatter of 'funk holes' and 'bad example' etc. However, Winston stuck to his ground and at Church House we shall meet tomorrow, and probably nightly. Members are complaining openly that Winston trades on his position, on his immense following in the country. His popularity is on the decline but it is still high, very high. Yet the country would not tolerate a dictator. He is giving a peerage to Wolmer,[1] a freakish individual, to find a safe seat for Oliver Lyttelton. It is a clever arrangement as it obviates creating a new peerage since Wolmer will soon succeed his aged father, Lord Selborne, in any case.

At five o'clock, rather too late to my liking, and it was only by exercising much restraint that I concealed my annoyance, Rab and I set out in my little Ford to stay with the Turkish Ambassador.[2] Rab is unpunctual – his almost only fault. Darkness fell as we arrived,[3] but having found the gate, we left the car, carefully locking it since we had an FO bag with us containing many important secret papers, and went for a short vigorous walk on the adjacent golf course. It was romantic; the fading light, the heather and the stillness. We drank in the fresh air and talked of poor Mr Chamberlain dying of a broken heart . . . It quickly darkened, the gloaming was gone and we heard the distant gunfire, perhaps bombs in London, even on Belgrave Square and almost at once we heard the sirens. I felt like a priest of Baal high up over the tumult of the unhappy city . . . relatively safe, aloof, cut off for a few hours from Death. It was chilly, dark, [illegible] and I felt very near to Rab. I love him; yet there must always be that unbridgeable gulf between us which nothing will ever bridge [*sic*]. We laughed at the prospect of our visit, got into the car and drove up to the temporary Embassy of the Islamic Envoy. Sunningdale is a so-called safe area and here many of the *corps diplomatique* have taken refuge. This hideous house is large,

---

1 Roundell Cecil Palmer (1887–1971) was Viscount Wolmer by courtesy from 1895 until January 1941, when a writ of acceleration was used to elevate him to the House of Lords in his father's barony of Selborne; he succeeded his father as 3rd Earl of Selborne in 1942. He was Conservative MP for Newton from 1910 to 1918 and for Aldershot from 1918 to 1940. He was Parliamentary Secretary to the Board of Trade from 1922 to 1924 and Minister of Economic Warfare from 1942 to 1945.

2 Tevfik Rüştü Aras (1883–1972) was Turkish Ambassador to the United Kingdom from 1939 to 1943. He had been Turkish Foreign Minister from 1925 to 1938. His brother-in-law, Nazım Bey, had been one of the main architects of the Armenian genocide in 1915, and Aras was given the task of overseeing the disposal of the corpses, mainly by dumping them in wells and covering them with lime. During the Blitz he moved his Embassy to Sunningdale, where Channon and Butler visited.

3 During the war double summer time operated from May to August, and single summer time until mid-November, so at this stage the sun set in London just before 6 p.m.

completely vulgar and belongs to Lord Windlesham,[1] who ought really to know better. It is typical of a rich stockbroker's Californian villa, but the warmth and amenities are restful.

Rab and I were received by His Excellency, who is a garrulous, pathetic bronchial little man of energy and intelligence. For thirteen years he was Foreign Secretary to Atatürk.[2] We drank whisky in the 'Mission Style' drawing room and in uneven French discussed the situation. Aras advised an approach to General Weygand who is rallying somewhat to the English cause. Aras, himself, is pro-English, and pro-Russian, although inclined to be disillusioned about Stalin and his court. The Ambassador, who is very much a man of the people, of the professional class, talked excitedly with many gestures (there is a rumour that he was once an *accoucheur*[3]) and he hinted that Turkey would come into the war if Bulgaria attacked Greece. So much we already supposed. He was eloquent about the Greeks, and surprised that their resistance, which must have surprised the Italians, should have lasted so long . . . Rab has the grand bedroom and his connecting bathroom suggested the Chabanais![4] It is spacious and mosaic-ed with amber-coloured windows and little grilles through which the curious can peep. It is in the best brothel style. Rab and I had giggles; but we were touched and impressed by the Ambassador's painstaking hospitality. Dinner was terrific, seven wines and good food . . . . I was lyric in my fluent, funny imperfect French. The evening wore on and at length Rab was overpersuaded by the Ambassador to do what he had so resolutely determined not to do – to come back tomorrow night.

President Roosevelt has had a landslide, an even greater triumph than anyone had anticipated. I have yet to see anyone who is not delighted.

THURSDAY 7TH NOVEMBER   *POMPEII*[5]

I write amidst my ruins – to go back, Rab and I got up early in our separate bedrooms and it seemed strange sleeping without hearing either his gentle purr

1 George Richard James Hennessy (1877–1953) was part of the Anglo-Irish Ascendancy and had been a professional soldier before serving as Conservative MP for Winchester from 1918 to 1931, and was a member of the Whips' Office for most of that time. He was created 1st Bt in 1927, served as Vice Chairman of the Conservative Party from 1931 to 1941 and was raised to the peerage as 1st Baron Windlesham in 1937.

2 Mustafa Kemal Pasha (1881–1938), known from 1935 as Atatürk, was from 1923 until his death the first President of Turkey, and Field Marshal of the Turkish Army. He had played a key part in Turkey's victory at Gallipoli in 1915 and later in the Turkish War of Independence. He revolutionised and secularised Turkey, introducing equal rights for women, including their right to vote.

3 Obstetrician. Aras was an alumnus of the French medical school in Beirut, but there is no suggestion that he specialised in obstetrics.

4 From the 1870s to the 1940s Le Chabanais, in the *deuxième arrondissement*, was Paris's most exclusive brothel, patronised by (among others) Toulouse-Lautrec and King Edward VII.

5 A joke, as immediately becomes clear.

or the noise of the barrage. We breakfasted, took leave of the Ambassador and went again for a little hike on the golf course, and then left for London in my car. On arrival we went to the House of Commons, now at Church House. We met for the first time in our new premises which Winston has dubbed the 'Annexe'. It is a large building, astonishingly well arranged, and many members turned up to watch with sad curiosity the proceedings. It is the first time since the big fire of 1834 that the Commons have met anywhere except at Westminster and I believe for only the fourth time in their long history . . . . in the reigns of Edward II at Reading, Charles I at Oxford, William IV in London and now, year of our Lord 1940. The Speaker was enthroned under his usual canopy, the Serjeant-at-arms sat on a camp chair at the bar; members found places as nearly as possible equivalent to where they sit at Westminster. The Hall was not too crowded but the acoustics are indifferent and there was noise and muffled excitement, and ministers tumbling over one another. Winston watched the confusion amused. The atmosphere was gay; it is almost like the Dorchester. Outside in the cloisters, however, I ran into several clerics who seemed indignant that their building should have been taken over for so lay purposes as lawmaking and drinking – there are adequate bars and a Smoking Room. Proceedings followed their usual course with surprising ease. So strong is tradition among members that the usual forms and customs were observed. It was rather like a dream . . .

I walked home, remembered that Rab was returning without me to Sunning House and that I had invited Raymond Mortimer to dine. I ached for a long peaceful night by myself, yet could neither put him off nor face him alone in my distraught state – how ageing is an unshared secret and [I] feel my hair greying at my temples, and my digestive organs refuse to function – I rang up Hector Bolitho at the Air Ministry and he said he would be delighted to come, would face the barrage for the first time. Geoffrey Lloyd telephoned but I didn't invite him; a little later Bill Tufnell rang up to say that he and his young boyfriend, a sad-eyed silent soldier of immense charm, Richard Brabner,[1] were in London at Claridge's and would I join them? I invited them to dinner which was a success. The food was unusually good and I had two wines. Young Brabner, although he did not know it, was the secret *animateur*.[2] It is his last night before he leaves Langleys' palace; he has been moved to Oundle in Northants and is miserable to leave Bill. I have never seen two people so much in love: they were in [a] swoon of tenderness and watched each other's every movement; yet I should not be surprised if it were an innocent relationship. No one thinks so, of course. The barrage began towards the end of dinner and Hector nevertheless remarked that it was such a lovely evening, his first really, since the Blitz. It was soothing, the candlelight, and comforting, the food and the d'Yquem, a change from his usual sausages at the Air Ministry. Just

1 Brabner has left no trace; it is possible Channon had his name wrong.
2 Organiser, or host.

after nine we got up and as my four guests preceded me, still carrying their brandy glasses, into the morning room (we had dined as always since the Blitz began in the small Black dining room) there was an immense crack as if of lightning! 'That was somewhere near, let's go and see if we can see anything,' Bolitho suggested. I protested that there were usually two bombs in quick succession and that we had better wait a moment. As I spoke I heard the sound of breaking glass. There was a very brief pause, no one was frightened and then I heard the voice of Harold, the footman, shouting, 'We've been hit.' At this we all rushed into the hall and were half blinded by dust. In a second, as if we had invoked the Devil, from smoke in sprang an ARP warden, whom I recognised as the Archduke Robert![1] He was followed by a woman and several others armed with pickaxes. They had made their way through the falling porch and portico to dig us out! They seemed amazed, even a touch disappointed to find us intact and calm. 'But you've had a direct hit,' one of the wardens insisted. So it seemed. 'Are there any dead below?' they asked. 'I don't think so,' I answered, surprised by my own calm. I led them into the morning room, poured them out drinks and rang the bell. Lambert appeared. 'Are you all all right?' He nodded and I asked him to bring more tumblers and drinks. I nearly said 'Krug '20' but just didn't. We then stood about and the wardens put out the electric lights as we had by now no windows and the shutters had been blown in. I lit a candelabra and introduced my very variegated guests, the Archduke with his Habsburg chin looking longer than ever, his female companion, whom I discovered to be Mrs Harald Peake,[2] *née* Baillet-Latour, several chauffeurs from the mews, etc. A motley party. Soon we tried to go into the Square, but it was a feat to crawl over the fallen masonry and broken columns etc. The porch had gone, so too had the pretty balcony, only a heap of rubble and debris. My beautiful house so damaged: still we were lucky to be alive as the bomb fell within fifteen feet of where we had been standing. The house next door, No. 4, was even more ravaged. Then I heard that Shrimpton's Garage in Halkin Street had also had a direct hit. Luckily I had removed my car on Monday!

It was all so distressing but I tried to laugh and was polite to Robert the Archduke, who remained as grave as ever. In the candlelight I saw him exchanging addresses with Tufnell, as Hector did with Subaltern Brabner. Mrs Peake then declared that there was probably another bomb in the area and that I must not sleep at Belgrave Square. So I rang up the Ritz and reserved a room after sending out the wardens to investigate. They soon reported that there was no unexploded bomb, so I cancelled my reservation. Tufnell decided to leave for Essex via Claridge's, but when he went to his car, a handsome Alvis, he only

---

1 Archduke Robert of Austria-Este (1915–96) was the second son of Karl I, the last Emperor of Austria-Hungary. He was living in exile in London.
2 Comtesse Sophie Thérèse Ghislaine Marie 'Resy' de Baillet-Latour (1908–94) married in 1933 Harald Peake (1899–1978), who later became an air commodore and director of the RAF's public relations.

found its charred and battered *beaux restes*.[1] He was in despair and Brabner wailed that he would be court-martialled for being late. Bolitho went to the telephone, *mirabile dictu*,[2] it was still connected and functioned (when I rang the Ritz a few moments before we were still too dazed to remark upon this miracle), and asked the Air Ministry to send him a car, which they did. At length he left, dropping the others *en route*. Raymond Mortimer decided to stay the night, as our shelters, our underground bedrooms were in no way touched!! He and I, armed with torches, made a tour of the house. Every window on the south Square side had been blown in and most of the shutters lay on the floor. The dust and dirt were indescribable. I went to bed in my underground bedroom, took a sleeping draught, and thus is ending a very tiresome difficult day, and a fantastic evening which began by the Duchess of Kent getting me twice out of the bath to talk on the telephone.

FRIDAY 8TH NOVEMBER   *HERCULANEUM SQUARE*[3]

I slept well, forgot the horrors of a direct hit, and the complications of an impending divorce, and when I awoke a cold shiver crushed me as I sleepily wondered, could these things be true, were they happening to me? Raymond and I breakfasted together in the confused house – wind howled in, but luckily my upstairs bedroom was untouched. All day the house was in the throes of cleaners, builders, demolition squads – who very quickly removed the dangerous debris. Rab, sorry for me, invited me to luncheon ([for] which I paid!); and in the afternoon I rested at home whilst the house was put reasonably right. Foolishly, I had a flu injection this morning which depressed me further. And I had a frantic morning at the FO trying to catch up with much that I had neglected. Rab naturally assumed that my dejection was due to the bombing!, which it isn't.

Rab and I dined alone in the freezingly cold house.

SATURDAY 9TH NOVEMBER   *KELVEDON*

I slept fairly well last night but was told on waking that No. 12 Belgrave Square, the Bathursts'[4] house at the corner had been hit, and that four people had been killed in nearby Chesham Place. Our *quartier* has become a danger zone. I gave many orders; the fuss and confusion is almost as disturbing as the bombing!

---

1 An ironic use of a French idiom that means 'well preserved'.
2 Wondrous to say.
3 Herculaneum, like Pompeii, was left ruined and abandoned after the eruption of Vesuvius in AD 79.
4 Seymour Henry Bathurst (1864–1943), by courtesy Lord Apsley from 1878 to 1892, when he succeeded his father as 7th Earl Bathurst.

then deposited P's many letters in my strongbox at Lloyds, and joined Rab at the Foreign Office. Everyone was still being kind about my bombing! Ambassadors telephoned to enquire!

I delayed coming here as Honor was particularly ungracious when I rang her up to tell her what had happened. I am glad I delayed, for a very fat letter was sent around to me by special messenger from the War Office. It contained three letters for me, and others for his mother etc. from Peter. They had been brought back by Anthony Eden. I was immensely elated. The charming creature is constant still – then I went to Westminster Cathedral, prayed to St Anthony for help and guidance, but I felt it was no use. Yet I drew strength from the candlelit altar and came away knowing that I must be gentle and considerate with Honor; therein lay my only hope. I came here, but she was out – as usual with <u>him</u> at the farm. Angry and despairing I roamed about this lovely place which will so soon be taken from me, then I read and wept and waited. H came in at 6.30; it was already dark. She was nice, or tried to be: so was I. And she was sober and reasonable and agreed to many terms . . . . I pleaded with her to tell her parents as I am alone in this chasm-like crisis: ruin awaits us all. If it were not for Paul, and perhaps a tiny bit, too, for Peter, I feel I would cut the painter – and go – go anywhere in darkest despair.

SUNDAY 10TH NOVEMBER

A horrible sleepless night: a sexual explosion, cold, and the interminable drone of German planes on high kept me awake. I woke exhausted. H came to my room; she was backing out of the plan to make over this place definitely to Paul. On that I shall insist. That is my last line of defence. The whole affair is a plot on the adventurer's part to get control of Kelvedon and spend her fortune. The marriage cannot last, if it takes place – I am even doubtful of that. I had several long fatiguing arguments with Honor: I must be brave and stout and successful for Paul's sake. Later she went to join him[1] and I went for a walk with my beloved woolly white dogs. It was a beautiful autumn afternoon with a curious light and I felt strongly that although I might be forced to leave here, it will be only for a little. I shall reign at Kelvedon once more one day; of that I am strangely convinced. But perhaps by then I shall not want to . . .

Mr Chamberlain died in the night; and the dreaded news reached me here about noon today. I am glad he is dead: the shafts of malice, blindness had hurt him, probably killed him. Now the reaction, already begun, will have added impetus and his place in history will be secure. He had nothing more to live for; he was indifferent to his children; all his hopes had parted; this tough race, which is capable of great courage and strength, can be very cruel; he was against the war and would have done anything to prevent it. Now it will go on forever. The

---

1 Her *inamorato*.

world has lost its best friend. I shall miss him personally; his silly wife adored him; Horace Wilson will be broken-hearted . . .

Honor came into luncheon at three o'clock, having kept me waiting nearly two hours. She smelt of whisky and half-apologising, made some fatuous remark about 'her young man keeping her away from me as he was jealous'! A groom, a horse-coper whom she has known for a few months. The effrontery of it! She has no moral sense whatever; no sense of duty, no shame; but she is not fundamentally wicked – just abnormal, selfish and amoral. We had long financial conversations, as I wish to save what I can for the baby. She was not too gracious and seemed only concerned with the methods by which she could raise £15,000 to give to her paramour and more to buy off his wife. A horrible day. I must summon all my courage as I shall collapse, and that would defeat everyone . . . I am beginning to hate this place and to believe that there is a curse upon it.

MONDAY 11TH NOVEMBER

I drove up cold and half-heartbroken to London. Belgrave Square is depressing, but a few more windows have been replaced and the servants had tidied up things remarkably quickly . . .

It is a fortnight today that Italy attacked Greece and no progress seems to have yet been made. Perhaps Mussolini is surprised and disappointed by their heroic defence?

I lunched, as did Boss Butler, at the Belgian Embassy to meet members of the Belgian govt. The house is fairly intact, an atmosphere of *luxe* prevails, and the bomb which so damaged No. 5 broke the Belgians' windows, whilst the earlier one which hit Seaford House, next door practically, did not. Thus my blast was the more painful since it had to travel across the Square and gardens! I was next to Attlee whose French is appalling; but I was pleasantly surprised by the courtesy of the little man. He is a gentleman, or nearly so; no revolutionary he! We discussed *mémoires*, the eighteenth century and poor Mr Chamberlain, whom he once hated so much. Today he was kind about him, recalled his sympathetic speech on the Members' Pensions Bill, lauded his great qualities but shied off when I hinted that Munich had saved Christendom; but he did not contradict me. I think that I made a conquest of him: I hope so. He seemed curiously uninformed about the Chamberlains' poverty and family, and was unaware that the hat had been passed around after the deaths of Sir Austen and 'FE' Birkenhead[1] in order to raise sufficient funds for their widows and families to live . . . Attlee is narrow, nervous,

---

1 Frederick Edwin ('FE') Smith (1872–1930) was Lord Chancellor between 1919 and 1922, and raised to the peerage as 1st Baron Birkenhead. He served as Secretary of State for India from 1924 to 1928. He was advanced to a viscountcy in 1921 and to an earldom in 1922 as 1st Earl of Birkenhead. A lifelong heavy drinker, he died of cirrhosis of the liver. He married, in 1901, Margaret Eleanor Furneaux (1879–1968); their son was 'Freddie' Birkenhead*.

uninspiring and well meaning. He seems more Liberal than actually Socialist: but he could never hold nor direct the energies of his wilder followers . . . .

Harold B, Jay Llewellin dined at the Square where Rab and his wife Sydney (whom in my hour of crisis I am learning to admire more and more) are staying with me.

Honor was still asleep when I left Kelvedon this morning with sadness in my heart for all that was, and for all that might have been.

TUESDAY 12TH NOVEMBER

The House met at eleven and immediately after Questions Winston rose and spoke of Neville in measured, stately English. The general impression was that it was well done, that it might have been less restrained but that it was dignified, adequate and sincere. He looked grumpy enough. I sat next to Tupps Ramsbotham who cried a little, as I did. The scene seemed so strange in this new slightly shoddy 'Annexe'. Attlee followed and did his tribute on behalf of the Labour Party well, as did Archie Sinclair for the Liberals. Only old George Lambert[1] spoke after them and in praising Neville fulsomely he touched upon Munich which made our madder members squirm uneasily but no incident marred the proceedings until later on in the afternoon when on another motion that fanatic ass Vyvyan Adams made a vicious attack on David Margesson and his reign as Chief Whip; the time was unfortunate for it was an oblique attack, although perhaps not so meant, on Chamberlain and an indignant House snubbed him . . .

About five o'clock after showing my pass, I walked into King Charles Street and there met 'old Steepledick'[2] (as Mr Chamberlain's followers call Winston) face to face. He was wearing a fur coat with an astrakhan collar and his curious black hat: he was puffing a huge cigar and walked quickly, closely followed by one detective. He looked very cross, indeed, and half-grunted at me. He knows that we dislike each other. I cannot help but be suspicious of him and like all *Schwärmers*[3] he is sensitive about these matters and once asked me a year or so ago why it was that I always avoided him in the Smoking Room. When I got back to the Office I had to usher Kingsley Martin,[4] the editor of the *New Statesman*, into Rab's room. I pretended that I knew nothing of the vicious attack he once made on me in his filthy paper and was polite: he was disarmed. He surprised me by attacking the govt, and particularly Anthony Eden. He is untidy, shoddy and mad, and probably one of those people of whom there are so many in England, who always attack the existing govt, no matter what it does.

No news of Honor; curious unfeeling wench.

---

1 George Lambert (1866–1958) was Liberal MP for South Molton from 1891 to 1924, and from 1929 to 1945. He was raised to the peerage as 1st Viscount Lambert in 1945.
2 Presumably an insulting reference to the 'Church' in 'Churchill': it didn't catch on.
3 Zealots, or extremists.
4 Basil Kingsley Martin (1897–1969) was editor of the *New Statesman* from 1930 to 1960.

WEDNESDAY 13TH NOVEMBER

To the House early after a peaceful night. The raids have been easier for a few days in spite of the full moon. Are the Germans sending their squadrons southwards? I suspect so. At the House, where I arrived at eleven, there was soon an atmosphere of suppressed excitement and Victor Warrender whispered the good news to me that half the Italian battle fleet – three out of six capital ships and several cruisers – has been sunk or damaged beyond repair. Apparently our fleet arm caught the Dagos[1] napping in the Gulf of Taranto and practically annihilated them with only the loss of two seaplanes. Our own fleet was not engaged. This victory considerably alters the naval balance of power, frees our ships to go elsewhere and will greatly cripple and discourage Italy. I met the PM coming in from behind the Chair – we are still sitting at the 'Annexe' as Church House is glibly called. 'We've got some sugar for the birds this time,' he said; he even smiled at me. Questions seemed interminable and members who knew shifted uneasily. At 12.10 Winston rose and gave the electrified House the Nelsonian news. Philip Noel-Baker and Josh Wedgwood opposite could scarcely contain their delight: they hate Italy more than they do Germany, probably more than they love England. This announcement will restore the somewhat ebbing fortunes of the govt. It is an injection of vitality, a needed tonic; but I am not sure that it will not goad Germany into making some desperate terrific retaliation in an attempt to end this foolish war.

I had a reaction of immense fatigue from all this anxiety and worry: I am torn by doubts, should I divorce Honor or not? My own instinct prompts me to acquiesce: yet I might be better advised to ask for a judicial separation. I have two more months in which to decide. I longed for the sea, to sleep, for peace undisturbed and solitude, but where in this battered island can I find that?

I drove Rab to Albury[2] which he found easily in the blackout thanks to Alba's directions. It was a balm and tonic to my distraught soul to be in a *bien tenue* house once again . . . we were received by liveried servants (one notices details such as these now that so much is going) and ushered into a commodious drawing room where we were welcomed by an old Spanish female of distinction whom I recognised as Alba's mother-in-law, the Duquesa d'Aliaga,[3] a typical Spanish *grande dame* in black satin and many pearls. Next to her was the Duchess of Northumberland,[4] whose house Albury is: she is staying as a guest in her own house, having let it on friendly terms to the Duke of Alba who is alleged to want to marry her. She is tall, stately and calm, fair, a magnificent English rose. She

---

1 A term of racial abuse more usually applied to the Spanish than to the Italians.
2 A house near Guildford, owned by the dukes of Northumberland, but being used by the Duke of Alba, the Spanish Ambassador (qv).
3 The Duke's late wife's mother was María del Rosario Gurtubay y González de Casteljón (1878–1948), Duchess of Híjar. She was also Duchess of Huéscar and of Aliaga.
4 Lady Helen Magdalen Gordon-Lennox (1886–1965), widow of the 8th Duke of Northumberland (qv).

greeted us civilly but without warmth. I have known her slightly for years but Rab had never really heard of her before. He is curiously unworldly. I sat down on a sofa with her directly Alba came in, and we talked for an hour or more and made friends again. I like her enormously and find her gentle, sensible and sympathetic – the reverse of my Honor. Then we went up to dress. How I liked seeing lovely china in lit-up vitrines, pictures, *bibelots* and all the heterogeneous paraphernalia that is found in a distinguished country house.

After dinner I spent the evening with Helen Northumberland and she showed me her well-kept albums of Syon[1] and Alnwick,[2] both places I have been to. A wonderful ball at Syon years ago . . . . and in 1923. Grace Curzon and I, motoring south from Scotland, stopped for tea at Alnwick where we were shown over the castle by the late Duke,[3] a fox of a man. All Percies look like foxes, are vulpine, even Hughie,[4] the v attractive present one. His mother talked tenderly of George[5] who was killed at Dunkirk; and she ranted against the Socialists and even recent govts who have pillaged and destroyed the great families by crushing taxation. She is 52,[6] still beautiful and ought to remarry; but she is extremely ducal, and conscious of her position and dignity. She was interesting about the royal visit to Paris in 1938. As Mistress of the Robes she was in attendance and she said that it was obvious to anyone that something was wrong: lines of tanks, thousands of soldiers surrounded the royal party wherever they went, and they were far removed (as one heard at the time) from the French people; the whole visit seemed unreal and forced, and they only met Bonnet and Daladier etc. at every function.

We have come up to bed at eleven o'clock.

THURSDAY 14TH NOVEMBER

We, Rab and I, walked in the frost-coated gardens at Albury for twenty minutes, and then drove up to London. We hurriedly changed into short coats and striped trousers – not morning clothes or top hats – and after calling in at the FO walked to the Abbey to attend Neville's memorial service, which turned out to be his funeral.[7] The Abbey, as the proceedings had been kept so secret, was not crowded. He and I were put in the second pew, directly behind Lady [Austen] Chamberlain. There was some uneasiness lest the Germans would make a terrific raid onslaught in an effort to kill Winston and perhaps paralyse the nation. However, nothing occurred

1 The Northumberlands' house in west London, at Isleworth.
2 The ducal seat in Northumberland.
3 Alan Ian Percy (1880–1930), 8th Duke of Northumberland.*
4 Hugh Algernon Percy (1914–88), 10th Duke of Northumberland.
5 Henry George Alan Percy (1912–40), 9th Duke of Northumberland.
6 She was 53.
7 For security reasons, it had not been made clear to those asked to attend this ceremony in what form of service they were being asked to participate. It was common before the war and for some time afterwards for memorial services to be held very soon after death.

and there was no alarm during the actual service, which was long, dignified and moving. I sat exactly opposite to where I saw and watched Neville when he had attended a memorial service for John Tweedsmuir[1] last year. Today I was moved but angry for in the Abbey I saw a band of murderers, Attlee, above all Amery, Archie Sinclair, Boothby and Duff and Eden, all the little men who had torpedoed poor Neville's heroic efforts to preserve peace and had made his life a misery. Now they were there, gloating some of them. Winston, followed by the War Cabinet, however, had the decency to cry as he stood by the coffin. The Speaker and others seemed deeply stirred. The Duke of Gloucester represented the King. When I saw Maisky almost next to me I felt somewhat reassured – we should not be bombed as he would not risk his own skin. Yet the service was long, and it was cold, that terrible ecclesiastic cold known only in English churches . . . . At last the coffin was moved to another part of the church and the service was continued. I watched the choir and the very frightening, horrible face of the Archbishop of Canterbury: it is the most hard and terrifying countenance I have ever seen and it is alleged to bring one bad luck. After the official pall-bearers (and I am glad that Lloyd George had the sense to stay away, although I believe he was invited – it is a subject of controversy) and the royal representatives followed Mrs Chamberlain leaning slightly on the arm of her daughter. It was brave of her to come; but she has always been courageous and she looked magnificent and walked with dignity. It is an inhuman custom – as we filed out I ran into Dick Law, Ronnie Tree and Paul Emrys-Evans laughing, and they lighted cigarettes in the cloister. I gave them a glance of hatred and scorn; their demeanour was nauseating. I can never forgive their persecution of a great man; dirty flies buzzing about a god. As I ran into Emrys-Evans I asked him 'Did you send a wreath?' 'No, I fear I didn't,' he replied unconcernedly. 'Decent Judas blossoms are out of season,' I retorted and walked on. He looked amazed. I was seething with hate and anger: the atmosphere was akin to that in *Julius Caesar*.

I went home, hurt, humiliated and sad; the Iveaghs came to lunch and we talked at great length. I am on the edge of despair, the verge of a breakdown.

Harold B and Rab dined and I refused to ask anyone else. Harold prophesies a bad night re air raids as it is full moon.

I heard that after everyone had left the Abbey, poor Horace Wilson, the all-powerful *éminence grise* of the Chamberlain regime, was seen alone, his face contracted with grief, praying for his great friend.

FRIDAY 15TH NOVEMBER

Harold rang me from the Air Ministry to say that there had been a colossal air raid over Coventry and that there were over 1,000 casualties; the cathedral

---

1 John Buchan. The service had actually been held earlier that year. See entry for 22 February 1940 and footnote.

and half the town had been destroyed.[1] The misery and confusion there is indescribable.

A busy day, dentists and arrangements. How I hate life at the moment and now I am toying with the idea of a judicial separation rather than a divorce: Honor will be furious but I may be able to save her in this manner.

SATURDAY 16TH NOVEMBER   KELVEDON

I slept soundly but now am told that last night's raid on London was one of the worst that we have had. The Carlton and Savoy hotels were hit, as was Piccadilly and Wellington Barracks. Many people were killed but the country thinks only of the appalling havoc at Coventry.

I came here and discovered that a huge landmine had gone off opposite our lodge gates: our north windows including the ones in my bedroom were all blown out. This is the second irritation that Kelvedon has had. Honor has gone away mysteriously; the poor girl is mad, pathological, pathetic.

How bored one is with the perpetual raids, the disorganisation of life, the danger, the wailing sounds of the sirens. One longs for peace and permanency.

SUNDAY 17TH NOVEMBER

I rang up Rab at Stanstead and he told me that people had been killed on Friday in his village ... I am miserable that things are ending here; but they aren't really – I shall reign here again. I must induce Lord Iveagh to give it to [illegible][2] by some complicated arrangement to hold for Paul. There will be a tedious interregnum.

Two calves have arrived at Brentwood Station for Honor; they are unfed and unfetched. Perhaps she will be prosecuted for leaving them there.

A gloriously beautiful afternoon but I slept and took no exercise: I hate it more and more. Anyway life isn't really worth living and I shouldn't mind being killed; but I should like to see my child again. Too much hangs on my decisions during the next few weeks.

MONDAY 18TH NOVEMBER   5 BELGRAVE SQUARE

My house is now almost restored to its pristine beauty, comfort and grandeur. I was pleased to get back to it after my gloomy, semi-solitary weekend. I am straining every nerve to salvage from the domestic wreckage all that I can for

1   It is believed around 570 people were killed in the raid on this industrial centre, and over 1,250 injured, when 515 Luftwaffe bombers attacked the town. Two-thirds of buildings in the city were damaged and 4,300 houses wrecked.
2   In the MS it looks like 'you', which cannot be right; in his distress, Channon might have meant 'me'.

Paul. May God and he forgive me if I am sharp, deceitful, underhanded or even a touch dishonest: but I am dealing with a mad, unscrupulous enemy. The Duchess of Kent telephoned to me and we had a chat. And I hear that George Hicks[1] has been appointed Parliamentary Secretary to the Ministry of Reconstruction; curiously enough when I mentioned this to David Margesson a month or so ago, he denied it emphatically.

'The boys' dined here; Jay Llewellin as long-winded as ever – however he told diverting tales of how he shares a bedroom with Attlee; Geoffrey Lloyd, taut, complicated but intelligent; Harold, my ever buoyant Harold; and of course, 'Boss' Butler. Nostalgic talk of Neville.

TUESDAY 19TH NOVEMBER

The days pass and I feel a sense of doom. Despair, disappointment are my constant companions. My marriage has collapsed and I suspect that I might have saved it or, had it not been for the war and my peculiar temperament, at least prolonged it. But Honor has the most difficult character I have ever known.

This afternoon I had a sort of collapse and after a most exhausting day at the H of Commons interviewing tiresome members I came home to rest. I had not long been home when Alan burst in; he is handsome, slimmer, more effervescent than ever. He radiates energy and charm, gaiety and brilliance. Oh! May he be happy with Patsy! She is more in love with him than ever H was with me. So perhaps it will last; and she is an easier, less complicated character. We chatted until Rab and Charles Peake interrupted us. Then I went to the Dorchester, that temple of sin and squalor, where I joined . . . . 'Jack' Profumo, the dark, eager, young MP whose party it was. The Coopers were at a nearby table; Duff entertains too much for a minister; every night he has a dinner party (at government or Dorchester expense, I wonder?). We dined lavishly, danced a little and then I left, walking home in the mild 'barrage'. Rab, who had dined alone in order to catch up with his work – he is exceedingly eccentric at times which adds to his immense charm – was already asleep. I crept into our conjugal shelter.

WEDNESDAY 20TH NOVEMBER   *PYRFORD*

I am a man now of one idea, one thought: I can concentrate on nothing, am haunted by my matrimonial affairs.

Rab and I arrived here for the night – yet another of our very varied 'Wednesdays'; these expeditions offer him a change and an experience, for he

---

1 Ernest George Hicks (1879–1954) was a bricklayer by trade who was one of the founders of the Socialist Party of Great Britain and was General Secretary of the Amalgamated Union of Building Trade Workers from 1921 to 1941. He was Labour MP for Woolwich East from 1931 to 1950 and Parliamentary Secretary to the Ministry of Works from 1941 to 1945.

knows little of my stratum in England, really. The Iveaghs were charmed and charming; and the Lennox-Boyds are also here. Patsy has begun another baby, but only very recently. No one knows yet; gay conversation . . . . I am very sad here; is this the last visit that I shall pay to Pyrford as the premier son-in-law?

THURSDAY 21ST NOVEMBER

Rab and I walked about in the gardens before nine; but the Iveaghs had already left for London. Then we motored up; it had been a quiet night. On our arrival at the FO I heard that the Greeks had practically captured Koritza . . . I changed into a Westminster number and went to the Annexe for the opening of the new parliament. The King and Queen sparsely attended, walked into the Hall that is the temporary House of Lords. He was in an admiral's uniform; she in mauve velvet and fur, pretty and smiling. The 'Gracious Speech' was the shortest on record and he hardly faltered. The Hall was crowded with peers and a few MPs packed together. The ceremony seemed strange, almost nightmarish, stripped of its customary splendour; there were no peeresses; instead I only saw Lady Halifax, who was in-waiting. After the Sovereigns had driven away I went into Halifax's room where he was working, and he oozed personality and charm; and I persuaded him to address the H of Commons Foreign Affairs Committee next Tuesday.

I walked back to the H of C ruminating on . . . . my morning at Pyrford and how lovely the pictures looked. Lady Lade by Sir Joshua [Reynolds], the exquisite Watteau[1] and the famous Hogarth.[2] Some or one of those might have been mine had Honor not betrayed me.

Dined with Alan and Patsy who looked pretty with her rubies; we were seven men, Shakes Morrison; Harold Balfour; Jay Llewellin; Peter Loxley, who was affectionate and divine; Alan himself and Bill Mabane, whom Patsy fancies . . . . I hear that Winston at long last has reluctantly decided to get rid of Duff. I made a *mot*, 'You'll see, Winston may end up as a Conservative Prime Minister!' It may be so; for the glamour gigolos are letting him down, one by one; they are light metal. Harold drove me home after a very gay evening and I almost forgot my many miseries. Peter Loxley and I were side by side at dinner – he even embraced me when he arrived. He told me of his poor mother's death, and how she knew she was dying and how she had adored his baby Elizabeth, left her a Dresden clock and her pearls etc.; Peter is one of the most delightful of all mortals alive. Jay L was insinuating and nice but I avoided bringing him back to Belgrave Square lest he stay too long and bore Rab, who was on the point of going to bed when

---

1 Jean-Antoine Watteau (1684–1721) was a French painter in the rococo style.
2 William Hogarth (1697–1764) was an English painter and engraver best known for his satirical works.

I arrived . . . . Peter Loxley laughingly told me that he had come upon Alan and Michael Rose in the Travellers Club this afternoon deep *en tête-à-tête*. Shall we have a *rechauffé*[1] of that dreary friendship?

FRIDAY 22ND NOVEMBER

I am always exhausted on Fridays . . . . . H rang up fairly cheerful, but angry with her sister Patsy who had innocently proposed herself to stay at Kelvedon. Honor bluntly refused, said there were no windows etc. which is untrue. She can be horrible; there are strange depths in her complicated, cruel, casual, cold character.

As Rab and I left the FO and came out into Downing Street and passed the sentry box in the wet, fog and darkness we both thought poignantly of little Neville and how we had loved him. He seemed very near . . . Rab and I dined alone and I was gay and amusing; he seemed diverted and we put our feet up on the adjoining sofas and gossiped until ten; then we worked for two hours, and 'so to bed'.[2]

SATURDAY 23RD NOVEMBER   *COPPINS*

Arrived at about six at this always cosy, comfortable welcoming house: it is so gaily and charmingly arranged that one forgets the hideousness of the house and the suburban atmosphere. The Duke was in mufti and looked tired; he feverishly knitted as we sat gossiping in his study. The Duchess is a touch thin but doesn't think so; she wore many pearls and amazing jewels . . . . We drank and talked until 8.45 when there was the usual scramble to get down to dinner punctually since the Kents, like all royalties, dress quickly. The food was excellent and put on a sideboard at the end of the tiny dining room; the Duke helps the guests and the servants only appear with the coffee; thus confidential conversation flows, there is no *gêne* and an intimate atmosphere prevails. I ate like a pig for the first time since 'the trouble' which so haunts and perplexes me. After dinner I played half-hearted backgammon with the Duchess; he strummed prettily on the piano and looked still young in his wine-coloured velvet jacket and dazzling turquoise links. Bed about 12.30 a.m. after we had twice listened to the news. The Duchess is elated by the Greek victories and proud of them. They have heartened the British cause. Several times she made slight slips about names, incidents and facts and the Duke, rather rudely, I thought, snapped at her. She is on his nerves and wartime life throws them too constantly together.

I am deeply unhappy and cannot digest my food; I am usually sick after a meal. Oh! Honor, how could you behave so?

---

1 Reheating.
2 The phrase with which Samuel Pepys often ended his diary entries.

SUNDAY 24TH NOVEMBER

I slept fairly well and it is a relief to hear nothing! No alerts, no sirens, nor zooming noises. I lazed in bed, surprised by the absence of newspapers in so luxurious a household; then I walked in the warm sunlight – a summer's day – to an enchanting small house known as 'Bridge Head House'[1] in the village of Iver where the road bends. I have long coveted it and so boldly rang the bell and was admitted by a seedy individual who seemed pleased by my intrusion and showed me the tiny palace. It is down-at-heel but attractive, panelled and full of possibilities; curiously enough it is let to a Southend family who were away. My friend led me into the garden, told me that his wife had deserted him, and my heart almost stopped for a second; and his eyes filled with tears as he talked of his son, who he feared was half an Italian by now as he was with his mother and her second husband. A coincidence that spoilt my visit and I, too, was sad, and sorry for him as he lives alone in two cheerless rooms – what a contrast to the Kents' luxury and abundance. Gradually I realised that the pathetic little man was Martin Secker,[2] at one time a well-known publisher. We walked along the river towards Coppins and he must have thought me a frivolous fashionable creature. We parted warmly; then I sat in the summer house and wrote to Peter, whilst the Duke did his gardening. He busily pushed a wheelbarrow about and fed his pigs. The Duchess, who had gone to Windsor soon returned with the two children. They rushed up to me, and little Alexandra clung to me. I played with them for a little and then burst into tears of misery and loneliness; I ached so for my own child who is to be callously deserted by his mother – she is a heartless harlot. And I wished that I was married to Princess Marina. The royal babies are small Hoppners with engaging manners and that dazzling Hanoverian complexion. Both are rogues and Alexandra with her gay flirtatious manner is the more fascinating of the two; indeed she is irresistible and always smiles, particularly at men. She will be 4 on Christmas Day, but talks volubly. Edward is more silent, possibly prettier and has a rosebud pout. He seems to prefer his father whom he calls 'Papa' whereas the little girl likes everyone and smiles blandly all the time and roars with laughter. Somehow they made me utterly miserable. My Paul, after this coming scandal, will never be able to marry her as I dreamed ...

Tea ended in tragedy as little Edward became bumptious and knocked over a table, causing the kettle to pour hot water over his little pink legs. He bellowed. The Duke lost his temper, the Duchess was in a flurry, nannies rushed in, but little Alexandra, delightfully unconcerned, turned round and said 'I love soldiers, do you?' After peace had been restored the Duke showed me his jewels. I have never seen so many magnificent parures, quite twenty of every conceivable shape

---

1 Actually Bridgefoot House.
2 Percy Martin Secker Klingender (1882–1978) had been the publisher of, among others, D. H. Lawrence. His firm merged in 1935 to form Secker & Warburg.

and combination, the most attractive were the old-fashioned ones, an emerald set, a turquoise one, etc., which had belonged to the late King. Then he got out his many cigarette cases and snuffboxes; the best one is a square gold box inset with ivory figures of the Judgement of Paris. It came from the baron Henri de Rothschild's collection and he paid, he said, over £1,000 for it. It is unwise to have such treasures about when the house might so easily be hit or burnt. Already there are two yawning craters on the estate.

A lovely evening: the Duchess eats next to nothing and looks longingly at the lovely food. He was malicious about almost everyone who has ever lived since the reign of George III! – particularly royalties. He said, too, to my annoyance that poor Fritzi deserved his fate and he was glad that he languished in a prison camp in Canada! He has always been faintly jealous of Fritzi. I played more backgammon with Princess Marina whilst he again strummed and played Debussy. He is extremely intelligent, well informed, nervous and irritable and attractive, only I wish he didn't knit so much. It is touching to see her pride and pleasure in the Greek victories and advances; they are amazing.

I wish I felt assured that no invasions will come: I am not, indeed I feel it in the air again. In some foggy unsuspecting night it may be tried.

MONDAY 25TH NOVEMBER

I didn't sleep, neither drugs nor aspirin could banish my black thoughts. I wish I were not a man of one idea, obsessed by my boring problems. A letter to H raced through my brain and when I arrived at the FO I wrote and sent it off. A beautiful and clever letter. She rang me up cheerfully and we gossiped. She is an annoying creature.

TUESDAY 26TH NOVEMBER

Things took a better turn today: I was told that 'my' Canadian interests, that is if Honor makes them over to me, will amount to nearly a quarter of a million: I had counted on £40,000. But will Honor agree? I feel I am saving it for Paul and I must struggle to get it all done. Mr Bland lunched with me and was extremely kind and sympathetic.

I escorted Halifax to a meeting of the H of C Foreign Affairs Committee. He looked tired but was superlatively suave and gracious, and even affectionate to me. He drove me back to the Foreign Office and had some gay banter: he is amused by our *mercredis*[1] which I have arranged for Rab's *divertissement*.[2] H[alifax] handled the Foreign Office Committee with skill and success and assured them

---

1 Wednesdays – his and Butler's weekly excursions out of London.
2 Entertainment.

that Rome had not been bombed only because the Greeks had implored us not to do so, in the hope of saving Athens. He was also realistic about Russia. I nearly told him how much criticism there is of his continuing to live at the spy-infested, undignified Dorchester, but I funked it, dreading his scorn which can be very withering when aroused. Of course he lives there because it is cheap and he is notoriously careful: it is his cloven hoof.

There was a rumour that Leslie Hore-Belisha intended to attack both Rab and the Foreign Office in a big speech today: I hung about the lobby until he appeared and by a blend of flattery and veiled threats dissuaded him.

WEDNESDAY 27TH NOVEMBER

Questions early at the House. We have returned to the 'usual place' and everyone feels relieved and pleased to be home again.

Rab had a long conference with Maisky this afternoon; the filthy communist was rude, pessimistic and obstructive; then Rab rushed to a War Committee presided over by Anthony Eden. However he escaped at five o'clock and we drove in my car to Coppins where we arrived soon after the 'blackout' and before our hosts. The Duchess came in first and was v sweet and *accueillante*;[1] the Duke in uniform soon followed and they embraced affectionately. We had good conversation for two hours before dinner. The Duke told us that he had been kissed at Balmoral station by King Boris[2] and how amused his father, George V, had been. Rab was immensely impressed by the Duke of Kent, whom he found inspired and keen. So did Harold Balfour, with whom the Duke had an interview yesterday arranged by me. I am now launching him in ministerial circles.

[The Wednesday excursions] amuse and rest Rab and enlarge his experience. This has been the most successful and perhaps pointful of all: the royal family are not sufficiently in contact with ministerial circles as the Queen *au fond* remains aristocratic, snobbish and class-conscious. Real royalties are not.

THURSDAY 28TH NOVEMBER

My in-laws lunched and when she asked me for a photograph I burst into tears . . .

I am in an excitable hysterical condition certainly and must take a pill. I have however a conviction that the worst is over, and that I shall largely triumph, using my intelligence and playing my cards well. I want to safeguard Paul above all else, and secondly to save my poor deluded sick wife.

The House went into secret session and hardly had Anthony Eden got up to give an account of his visit to the Middle East when there was an air-raid warning

---

1 Welcoming.
2 Boris III (1894–1943), Tsar of Bulgaria from 1918 to 1943.*

and we trooped sheepishly to the cellar. The news was brought in by a whip, told to David Margesson, who whispered to the Speaker that planes were immediately overhead. Mr Speaker rose and suspended the sitting. Later we rescued our activities and Anthony was adequate and plausible: no more.

I had a dinner party at home: the plum was 'Peter' (Sir Charles Portal), head of the Bomber Command, and he is a man of granite and of ruthlessness; he is youngish, has a beak of a nose . . . . but one is conscious of an immense personality. He told us of his frequent visits to Chequers and was as funny and malicious about Winston as he dared be! The other guests relished his remarks. Rab, Harold Balfour, Geoffrey Lloyd, who, as usual with irritating frequency, proposed himself at the last moment and Jay Llewellin. All 'little ministers'. Portal said that he looks forward to his fishing, to living in a stone keeper's cottage in Scotland on £300 a year after the war. Meanwhile he is restive at the Dorchester!! He is Rab's brother-in-law's half-brother; and it is Portal who conceived the plan of consistently bombing German towns. The Germans are now imitating it and going for Midland industrial centres.

I had my bottom washed out. It takes two hours and does one a universe of benefit! Life takes on a new complexion.

Friday 29th November

A month has now closed and we do not seem much nearer a solution of either the war, or of H's and my domestic difficulties. She came to London and we lunched together, then shopped. She first signed a deed which gives me certain v valuable rights . . . . indeed made over [some of] her property . . . . to me for life with remainder to Paul. I hope, and indeed, am convinced that I was right to persuade her to do so. I sent off the papers immediately after having them photographed to the trustees . . . . Honor and I were alone all the evening and discussed further in the most amicable fashion possible our various entanglements. Just as we were leaving to dine at the Dorchester Charles Peake arrived, invited but forgotten by Rab – we took him with us to the Dorchester and he was very entertaining with his stories of Winston and Chequers etc. Winston received the Halifaxes in curious clothes[1] and wearing an Air Force cap! He seemed put out by Halifax's amusement and pointing to his strange garb said, 'Clemmie bought me these rompers!' When he went to Ditchley [Park] he took a suite of nearly thirty persons, detectives, guards, secretaries and glamorous sycophants. Ronnie Tree told Charles Peake that they had been 'over ninety' in the Servants' Hall. Winston went at the urgent request of the military authorities who believed that as it was full moon Chequers might be bombed!

---

1 Presumably his siren suit, rather like workmen's overalls.

Honor looked lovely and thin and chic and apparently enjoyed her dinner. How strange she is. I can scarcely believe that these things are real, are happening to me: but then I have never really believed in my life – it has always seemed to be someone else's.

Letter from Peter from Cairo: he says that Anthony Eden's visit flopped at the end. He also adds that he won't let me down; so perhaps we shall live together and I shall have the most charming of companions to *désennuyer ma tristesse*[1] and keep me young. My affairs are improving.

The Yugoslav Minister showed me a cable from his government to say that the Prince Regent would like me to go to Belgrade now.[2] I am tempted: I should make history; the destination allures me; the visits *en route* are dazzling; but what an uprooting, and what a fiendish journey . . . . Still, I shall go, if *les affaires*[3] permit. Meanwhile the situation in Romania is chaotic, massacres and assassinations. Antonescu[4] has lost control, and Queen Cilla has fled to Florence, possibly taking Michael with her.

This morning I wanted a private word with Halifax; Ralph Stevenson waved to me to go in and I did so quickly. I opened the door, saw him standing before the fire, a paper resting on his dummy arm[5] and he leaning on the mantelpiece. Occasionally he puffed at his cigarette holder and his ecclesiastic face seemed contorted by misery. He frowned, went to his desk, picked up a red pencil and made a few notes; then he picked up another document, returned to the fire, rested it on his withered arm and it all began again. I coughed slightly but he was too absorbed to see me. I became embarrassed and watched the ticking clock; after eight minutes I said 'I'm so sorry to interrupt you.' He looked surprised, smiled gravely and said 'Hello, Chips, I didn't know you were there. What do you want?' We had a little chat and he agreed, indeed was in favour of my going at once to Yugoslavia. How strange, silent and reserved is this really great man! I am, I know, uneven about him; for I realise his faults and forgive his frailties.

SATURDAY 30TH NOVEMBER

Honor and I talked and shopped and later I rejoined her for lunch and then drove her to Liverpool Street Station where she embarked on her melancholy unenviable expedition to Elveden, where she expects to break the news of her intending folly

1 Lighten my sadness.
2 Prince Paul was struggling to keep the Germans out of Yugoslavia; Channon was his best friend in England, and he needed messages taken back to London and to the Foreign Office by someone he could trust.
3 Business matters.
4 Ion Antonescu (1882–1946), military dictator of Romania and ethnic nationalist who aligned the country with Nazi Germany. He was tried for war crimes and treason after the war and executed.
5 Halifax was born with a stunted left arm and no hand.

to her parents. My heart ached for her; she is in a jam and no one can extricate her. Nor does she wish to be saved. I had a pang of conscience as I drove away and left her forlorn and alone, but grimly Guinness-ly determined. And I wondered whether, as I drove sadly away, I could have prevented this tragic debacle? Had I been more passionate, more affectionate, more tender, would things have worked out otherwise? My honest opinion is that I might have delayed a rupture, but could not *à la longue*[1] prevented one. And also it is fair to myself to record that most men would have been off long ago, as never was there so unsatisfactory a spouse from every point of view. Even her colossal fortune has only brought misery in its train.

Kelvedon looked lovely but is cold. My dogs are pleased to see me. Batsi is pregnant again; I fear she has had an affair with her handsome son and I have renamed her Jocasta.[2]

SUNDAY 1ST DECEMBER

An eventful, perhaps the most important month in my personal and the world's history has dawned. What will it bring me? Scandal? Death? Disappointments, or riches and triumph? Or deadlock?

Alice Harding rang up to complain of all her three husbands; Alan telephoned twice and persuaded me into going with him to Southsea tonight. Madness. Honor is still at Elveden, poor child. The fog is opaque and I wonder whether it is not a smokescreen; there was one in London yesterday. I must fuss now or leave for Southsea via Belgrave Square. I love this place and I am convinced that it will be mine. I am not done with it yet.

I drove up in the icy fog enchanted to be back in London. Really the country in the winter months is intolerable. Now I go to Southsea on my demented expedition.

MONDAY 2ND DECEMBER

There are some adventures too boring, too disastrous to relate[3] . . . . Last night's was one. Alan and I met at Waterloo at 9.30 just after the sirens sounded: there was a considerable barrage, and the big glass roof of the station seemed more a danger than a protection; it was dark; the platform was crowded with returning soldiers and sailors smiling freshly in the fog and cold . . . the train left two hours late: I curled up asleep between Alan's immense legs and we arrived at Southsea only at 3.30; there were no cars, taxis or buses; it was dark, increasingly cold and Alan didn't know the way. A wave of despair came over us, and we were told by a friendly policeman that there was a big raid in progress at Southampton, where

1 In the long run.
2 The Queen of Thebes, mother (and wife) of Oedipus.
3 He brings himself to relate it nonetheless.

martial law had been declared. We trudged through the dark and sinister streets, Alan carrying my Cartier dressing-case strapped to his back; an hour later we were hopelessly lost and luckily an air-raid warden took pity on us and led us to a garage where there was a fire. At long length a car took us to the Queen's Hotel where we arrived at 5.10 a.m. By then we had twice quarrelled and been reconciled and I fell asleep in an airless room – Alan hates air. At seven we were called, and his dark tousled [illegible][1] was next to mine; a snatched wartime breakfast, he rushed to his duties and I returned to London by a slow train. The *comble*[2] was having to share a compartment from Guildford to London with that amiable, courteous, nervous nannie goat, Eddie Winterton.[3] We were two hours late and thus endeth the worst night of my life.

Harold dined and both Butlers are staying here. I am increasingly devoted to Sydney. I fear I shall have double pneumonia after my adventures.

Sleeping upstairs.

TUESDAY 3RD DECEMBER

The Iveaghs to lunch: I was in tearing spirits; my terrible trip was a tonic and I have decided to take this terrific trek to Peter and Paul, Cairo and Belgrade. To do so I must fly across Africa – an incredible itinerary: Lisbon, Las Palmas, Freetown, Lagos, El Fasher,[4] Khartoum, etc.

Rab and I dined alone.

The Iveaghs agreed that Kelvedon should be Paul's technically, and mine to all intents and purposes.[5] I have asked for a twenty-one years lease which is sufficient: by then I shall want to live in Venice.

Sleeping below. Just as I was going to bed the Duke of Kent rang up to ask if he could dine here tomorrow night. I must collect a party.

The govt has had a bad day: it cannot last very long now. The House is seething with discontent and Churchill is not as popular as he was; however he still has a powerful hold on the country. But he will reconstruct.[6]

WEDNESDAY 4TH DECEMBER

A difficult, discouraging day, really. After Questions I rushed home to receive Honor who was as mad as a hatter: she was polite, readily agreed to surrendering

---

1 Presumably hair, or head.
2 *C'est vraiment un comble* is a French idiom meaning 'that's the limit': Channon uses the word to mean the last straw.
3 Edward Turnour, 6th Earl Winterton.
4 In Darfur, north-western Sudan.
5 After a conversation that appears to have taken place during Lady Honor's visit to Elveden.
6 A reconstruction is a ministerial reshuffle, which Channon thinks Churchill was planning.

Kelvedon; never wanted to see it, me, or her family again; was defeatist, escapist. She cares only for that creature. I watched carefully and neither the word 'divorce' nor 'Paul' was mentioned. I think that she is indifferent to them now; but she has been shaken by her mother's letter, which was, I am told, a very forceful one. So I am to have Kelvedon; I am to have Paul; I am to have Belgrave Square; I am to be rich; I shall have the world's sympathy . . .

Rab addressed a collection of National Liberals on Egypt. He was wily, sly and fascinating, and he scored a brilliant success. Several of them said to me afterwards 'Why look further for a Foreign Secretary or even a Prime Minister?'

The Duke of Kent, in Air Force uniform, arrived punctually; I saw at once that he was in high spirits. I had collected Nicholas Lawford [who] was a great success; Alan from Southsea, and Jock McEwen to meet my royal guest. The food was excellent; and we had Krug '20 and Château d'Yquem '01 which both inebriated and impressed everyone. Much gay chatter and when Rab came in at midnight he said that we were all 'lit'. The Duke left at 1 a.m. A successful evening; he ran down nearly everyone including the King of Greece, and particularly the Windsors.

THURSDAY 5TH DECEMBER

Arrangements for my fantastic journey are advancing . . . I leave on Monday, December 16th for Bournemouth and fly early next day from Poole. I am excited and it will be a welcome change and break from the hurt, humiliation which I have recently undergone. Actually they have hardened my character.

There was a three-line whip today in a debate to defeat an ILP proposal. The voting was 341–6. A satisfactory figure in a way but there is a feeling of malaise with the govt. Mrs Tate tells me it is more than the last one; that she thinks the Germans will land, and that she has bought fifteen grams of morphine to take when they do. I asked her where she kept it; she said on her person; where, I again asked, but she refused to reply. She was sitting in the Aye lobby with Ham Kerr and that Humpty Dumpty double fool Paul Emrys-Evans and they were all deploring the ineptitude of the govt, the bombing of our best coastal towns, the submarine losses, the attacks on our convoys. I was furious. 'You've got both the war and the government you wanted; why are you complaining?' I taunted them. They were silenced. All three had been pro-war, anti-Chamberlain and voted against him on that fatal day.

FRIDAY 6TH DECEMBER

Lunched with Harold at the Ritz: I have a severe cold which I fear may develop into flu. Perhaps I caught it from Rab, or is it a result of that madcap expedition to Southsea. Meanwhile I have made all arrangements for my journey, called to Paul and Peter, taken tickets etc.

Dined alone, which was bliss, in bed, after 'chucking' Hore-Belisha. I couldn't face him or any more people and above all conversation. I am so sick of conversation.

Just as I was going upstairs the Duchess of Kent and Zoia[1] walked in: they had gone down to the area steps[2] thinking the front door unpassable, as indeed it looks. They were v sweet; she said or rather reminded me, that *au fond* I had made her marriage; that she had remet him through me etc. Then she went on to say that she had sat next to the King at dinner, I think last night, possibly the day before; he seemed uneasy about the govt, thought that there must be changes etc. When she asked him whom he would send for, if ever Winston resigned, he said, 'Rab Butler.' She was riveted and led the King on; he said that there was a precedent, his father had sent for Baldwin who was not very well known at that time; they had much in common, Rab, and Stanley B. But the King thought that the moment had not quite come. Yet the country was demanding that youth should be in control. Rab was young, but the King wondered, was he 'sound' about Russia?

Saturday 7th December

Dictated and worked for hours, then had a snack lunch and drove Valentine Lawford (he likes to be known as 'Nicholas') here [Kelvedon]. He is most *habile*,[3] a man of the world . . . . He liked Kelvedon; we had much gossip; I feel differently about this place now that it is to be mine. I shall *soigner*[4] it. Honor is away sleeping at some Hogarthian[5] pub with her rustic paramour. What a woman: she is enough to turn one against the whole sex. She is also looking for a farm which she wishes to buy and live in with him. I now no longer care about anything. I shall be well rid of such a hoyden who deserts her home, husband and child so haphazardly.

---

1 Zoia de Stoeckl (1893–1974), daughter of Baron Alexandre de Stoeckl, had known the Duchess since the early 1920s and was now in exile in London. She married, in 1919, Captain Alfons Alexander 'Alik' Poklewski-Koziell (1891–1962), whose family had been known as 'the Siberian Rockefellers', such was the extent of their wealth in Tsarist Russia. However, they lost almost everything in the 1917 revolution. She had been a maid of honour to the last Tsarina, the Stoeckls having been in Russian service. Her mother, Agnes de Stoeckl (*née* Barron, 1874–1968), a writer, was known as 'Auntie Ag of the Courts of Europe'. They had lived at Łańcut from 1933 until fleeing a week before the German invasion in 1939; and, being friends of the Kents, lived with their son Vincent Poklewski-Koziell (1929–2017) in Coppins Cottage in their exile.
2 That is, to the servants' entrance in the basement.
3 Clever.
4 Look after.
5 Presumably the choice of adjective, after William Hogarth who painted *A Rake's Progress* and *The Harlot's Progress*, was to convey the depravity into which Channon thought his wife had pitched herself.

A long confidential talk with Nicholas Lawford in the course of which he confided in me – but I did not tell him that I was doing the same thing – that he keeps a diary. It ought to make good political-historical reading.

SUNDAY 8TH DECEMBER

I woke much worse with a burning throat; I am far from well, and fear it is more than a cold. Shall I now get off? Or shall I be in bed for a week? It is maddening; I must get well. Last night I thought I was all right again.

Lawford left for London; it is a beautiful day but there were no air raids over England last night, although it was a clear, cold, crystal night. I am up for a little but shall return to bed, as my fever is 99° and a bit. Long talks with gardeners. I must now take control of the estate, or rather shall when I get back.

MONDAY 9TH DECEMBER

Drove up to London, the car laden with flowers. I had slept very badly, partly because of my exhausted nerves, and partly because of the air raid which was severe – the house shook, and windows had there been any would have vibrated. My frightened Bundi jumped into my bed for comfort.

Today is Rab's 38th birthday: he looks much older. We had Tilea to luncheon and we tried to decide what to do with King Carol: I am rather against his coming here.[1] Tilea was very affectionate and friendly and confessed that when he first arrived here he had made a 'set' at me and had been told by the then Romanian government that I was the most 'useful man in London'. How flattering. I felt extraordinarily well, even gay for a man whose fortunes have floundered – of course, they haven't financially for I am now, or shall soon be, colossally rich! . . . We chattered in funny, fluent French. Then Rab and I returned to the FO. Luckily my duties took me to the House of Commons, where a friendly policeman told me that St Stephen's Cloister had been hit last night. I went into what was the members' cloakroom and saw a scene of devastation. Confusion, wreckage, broken glass everywhere. The loveliest, the oldest part of the vast building was in shambles. Suddenly I came upon Winston Churchill wearing a fur-collared coat and smoking a cigar; he was led by a policeman and followed by Seal,[2] his Semitic secretary. 'It's horrible,' he remarked to me without removing his cigar; but I saw that he was much moved for he loves Westminster, and I walked with him. 'They

---

1 As already mentioned, King Carol was hoping to be able to go to Portugal. He reached there eventually, via Mexico.
2 Eric Seal (1898–1972) had been an Admiralty civil servant since 1925 and in 1939 became private secretary to the First Lord. Churchill took him to Downing Street as his private secretary from 1940 to 1941. The word 'Semitic' has been added and crossed out, most probably by Coats; there is no evidence Seal was Jewish.

would hit the loveliest oldest bit.' 'Where Cromwell signed King Charles's death warrant,' he grunted. But it was an uneasy encounter for we openly dislike each other; yet I sensed the historic significance of the scene – Winston surveying the destruction he had long predicted of a place he loved. Then I walked back to the FO . . .

Leslie Belisha and Geoffrey Lloyd dined with us; both were late and inconsiderate and charming. Geoffrey talked too much Stendhal;[1] Leslie prattled of love. He is on a milk and sloppy diet as he is threatened with a gastric ulcer. He was gay, challenging, charming – and, *Dieu merci*, left at 11.20. We twitted him, and I laid on flattery with a trowel. Jews love it so. All day I wondered who we could invite to meet him: a year ago the world would have jumped to dine with the Secretary of State for War. And today, too, at tea at the FO, I mused on the melancholy business of ingratitude. I was in the Secretaries' Room at the world-famous tea party when John Simon emerged from Halifax's room. He was jovial, irritating and tactless; no one treated him with respect, or even civility. At last I said – after all, he is Lord Chancellor – 'Can we offer you a cup of tea in this palace where you reigned so long?' He was mollified, accepted a cup and was amiable but *cassant*[2] to Ronald Campbell,[3] Horace Seymour and others who clearly disliked him. And that famous smile – 'like the brass knocker on a coffin' – put people off. Personally I rather like him. Fallen idols.

My plans for this mad trip crystallise.

Tuesday 10th December

The wireless announced an important Egyptian advance in Libya: we are taking the offensive. I wonder whether all this is not a snare to inveigle our troops out to the Middle East – at the expense of Italy for Hitler could always restore order there – and then he would invade England.

There has been a fuss over my trip to Yugoslavia: I wrote, ill-advisedly, to the Treasury to ask if I might take out £60. Harry Crookshank,[4] whom I have never liked but really ignored, seized my letter as a pretext to make an attack on me and has been going about saying that I was rushing to America to get away from the war and that I had asked to take dollars. All quite untrue. Rab was unduly upset, as he always is, by criticism; he was loyal but fussy and my respect for him, but not my affection, slightly declined.

All day, every day this nightmare continues re H and arrangements. The deeds are now nearly drawn up. The Iveaghs came to lunch and were bitter, despondent.

1 Marie-Henri Beyle (1783–1842) was a French author who wrote under the name Stendhal.
2 Brusque.
3 Ronald Ian Campbell.
4 Financial Secretary to the Treasury.

WEDNESDAY 11TH DECEMBER

At the House, or rather at the Annexe where we now meet, I was very scathing to Harry Crookshank and made him as uncomfortable as possible. He lied to me; said he had never mentioned dollars or America etc. But I shook him. Later at dinner I got my revenge by telling Brendan, whom I put next to me purposely, that Crookshank was treacherous about Churchill – which is really half true – just as he used to be about Chamberlain. I sowed a seed. I shall not forget his interference.

Rab came into my room in the middle of the night to say that he and his wife were going down to sleep as there was a barrage. Lazily I turned over and fell asleep again.

Brendan says we need a Boswell; the Winston stories are fantastic. The other day he heard a noise, rang a bell and turned to the servant who answered, 'What was that noise?' 'I think it was a bomb, sir.' 'That is a platitude, sir,' the Prime Minister retorted.

Brendan left at 10.30 as he had to join the PM and he had his armoured car which is highly camouflaged and uncomfortable.

THURSDAY 12TH DECEMBER

Crookshank's interference has assumed the dimension of a scandal and I now learn that he wrote an obnoxious letter about me to Rab. Consequently Rab has sent a foolish and official telegram to Belgrade which will not please the Regent and probably my expedition will be postponed or cancelled. If only I had written to Kingsley Wood none of this would have happened. And apparently some of the FO are jealous of me . . . Henry Hopkinson[1] and even Cadogan.[2] It is all too foolish. I want to cash in whilst I may as I suspect that the present regime at the Foreign Office will fall during my absence!

Honor arrived here [Belgrave Square] at one o'clock; she was in an unattractive defiant mood, railed at her family and signed without a murmur a series of documents giving up Kelvedon to Paul, the life lease to me, etc., etc. She must love this foul drunkard desperately to be prepared to surrender her home which I thought she loved! She was uninterested, scarcely read the documents. The place is now mine for life to live in, to let, to sell or to dispose of as I like. I

---

1 Henry Lennox d'Aubigne Hopkinson (1902–96) joined the Foreign Office after Cambridge and was First Secretary to the War Cabinet Office from 1939 to 1940, before becoming Cadogan's private secretary and, from 1941 to 1943, Lyttelton's, posted to Cairo when the latter was Minister Resident in the Middle East. He resigned from the Diplomatic Service in 1946 to join the Conservative Research Department and from 1950 to 1956 was Conservative MP for Taunton. He was Secretary for Overseas Trade from 1951 to 1952 and Minister of State for the Colonies from 1952 to 1956, when he was raised to the peerage as 1st Baron Colyton.

2 Sir Alexander, the Permanent Under-Secretary.

hope I am behaving honestly and wisely: Honor is entirely in the wrong, therefore
I must protect Paul's interests, and incidentally my own. But I am unhappy about
it all and am conscious that my character is hardening. I have been materialistic,
even grasping: but only, really for my child's sake. My life is almost over . . . .
Honor and I (for the last time?) had guests to luncheon. Lady Colefax, pleasant
and friendly, Charles Peake and Peter Loxley, my beloved friend. We were all
gay and it went well. How little one knows of others' tragedies and our guests
must have thought us a happily married couple. My poor wife is half-demented;
my mother is more than mad: the outlook for my angelic child is not mentally
encouraging. My future is not really bleak as I shall soon accustom myself again
to liberty and I shall be prosperous, even opulent so long as my child lives . . .

Lothian died today; he had been suffering from some slight internal complaint
and being a Christian Scientist he refused to consult a doctor; he could easily have
been saved by a stomach pump or even a purgative. Lady Astor thus adds her
greatest friend, possibly her lover, to the long list of people she has murdered with
her proselytising – poor Alix Cavendish[1] years ago, and others. Her own daughter
Wissie Willoughby,[2] too, would have been a victim had she not rebelled. There
has never been so foolish, so conceited or opinionated a female. I frankly hate
her. Lothian, who was a Roman Catholic, was converted by her to her foolish
illogical religion – she goes to dentists. I came home early to rest and slept for an
hour before Rab came in: I then tried to urge him to intrigue for the Embassy at
Washington. He should get the post, and could if he made an effort. I was surprised,
even disappointed by his lack of imagination; perhaps he is more clever about
it than I supposed. Mrs Greville rang me up from Polesden and we chatted for
half an hour: the *but*[3] of our conversation was that Rab should go to Washington.
She adores him and sat next to him today at luncheon at the Egyptian Embassy
. . . . I don't think that I succeeded in moving Rab, and so I shall have to start
this intrigue on my own without his active help. Shakes Morrison, charming,
distinguished and the conversationalist par excellence dined, as did Harold
Balfour and Nicholas Lawford who is my new boy friend. He is v charming and
adaptable indeed. I couldn't like him more and unlike most of the Foreign Office
boys he is a man of the world. They all went to bed early. A lovely night, almost full
moon: I expect a big raid shortly – but perhaps I shall get away before it occurs.

Honor has bought a farm on the Hampshire–Wiltshire borders somewhere
nr Winchester for £13,000. There she intends to live in sin with her adventurer.
A police, or rather detective's report came in about him today: it made me ill.
It said that he was a well-known drunkard, a horse-coper, a man who had had

---

1 Alix Cavendish (1901–25), daughter of Lord Richard Cavendish (qv). She had suffered from
   tuberculosis, so her death was not inevitably down to pursuing Lady Astor's doctrines.
2 Nancy Phyllis Louise 'Wissie' Astor (1909–75), at this point Lady Willoughby de Eresby.*
3 Point.

the bailiffs in for debts of £4 – for this low fellow she is prepared to give up her position. How little I must have meant to her . . . . She has a sordid taste for low life, so why did she marry that exquisite orchidaceous cultured creature, Chips?

FRIDAY 13TH DECEMBER

No raid last night: I have slept upstairs for over a week now and the shelter is deserted.

I was irritable; perhaps this thyroid doesn't agree with me. I nearly snapped at Rab. Indeed I am annoyed by this journey, and the fuss and complications invented by the Foreign Office. I met Lord Halifax who was charming and advised me to go. All day I have tried to start the Washington hare; I whispered it to everyone I saw. Rab, about to go to the country, and I dined with Jay Llewellin; he asked where I wanted to go, so I said 'the Dorchester' as I knew that David Margesson was dining there. He was, and I managed to have a talk with him – he was with James Stuart and Helen Fitzgerald, and they were the only interesting people there. The hotel has lost its *ton* . . . . After many oysters and much woodcock I joined David and got in both my points, my dual purpose was thus activated – to poison him against Harry Crookshank and to enlist his support for Rab's candidature for the Washington Embassy. Then I came home here with Jay and talked much too late.

SATURDAY 14TH DECEMBER   *COPPINS*

I came here today after making my arrangements for the journey. The usual pleasant atmosphere: the Duke was grumpy at first, and then gave me a signed photograph, a snuffbox, and a clip. The Duchess very affectionate and lovely . . . . the Kents had just come back from Windsor where they had attended the film premiere of Charlie Chaplin[1] in *The Dictators*.[2] It was the King's birthday party.

SUNDAY 15TH DECEMBER

A long rest and I walked, read and rested. Then I helped the Duke of Kent arrange his Xmas presents – he has split a pair of rather ugly jardinières, one he gives to Princess Elizabeth,[3] the other to the Duchess of Gloucester. They made much fun of the poor Duchess of G, who is rather a sweet.

1 Charles Spencer 'Charlie' Chaplin (1889–1977) grew up in extreme poverty in south London, but after travelling to America in 1910 with Fred Karno's Army became perhaps the most famous star of the silent era. He became an innovative and experimental film maker once talking pictures were invented, left Hollywood for Europe during the McCarthy purges of the 1950s, and was knighted in 1975, having never relinquished his British citizenship.
2 He means *The Great Dictator*, Chaplin's satire on Hitler, which had just been released.
3 Not the future Queen, but his sister-in-law Princess Elizabeth of Greece and Denmark. See entry for 5 September 1939 and footnote.

When shall I write, if ever, in this diary again? I don't dare to take it abroad with all the customs and censorships and dangers ....

MONDAY 16TH DECEMBER

A funny day with parcels, messages, letters and luggage ... and at the last moment Rab very clearly showed that he did not want me to go: he put up a hundred objections and I was tempted for a moment to chuck the whole expedition: I should be criticised; I should not get back; I should be caught in Spain or somewhere the Nazis would undoubtedly invade; it was a risk. He managed to take the gilt off my travelling gingerbread and I went into the corridor of the FO to be alone for five minutes to make the important decision and concluded that I would go: I could probably always turn back if necessary, was my reservation. Of course he didn't know of my secret reasons for embarking on this great expedition, nor did he know that I shall prolong it as long as possible ...

I lunched with Harold Balfour at Prunier's for a farewell feast and he encouraged me to go. Not as intelligent as Rab, he is more a man of the world and his judgement about men, morals, money and politics is often the sounder of the two. Alan has none; he is a great flopping baby .... At 4.30 I left with few misgivings ... At the Bournemouth Hotel I found a telegram of '*bon voyage*' from Honor, and also a letter, a *cri de coeur*[1] begging me to divorce her. I sat down and wrote Lady Iveagh a long letter and before I had finished it Alan arrived gaily from Southampton to spend the night with me. We took a double room, and dined well in the restaurant. Nearby was a young man, handsome, but be-ringed who came up to us and said, 'Chips, don't you remember me, I'm Stephen Tennant.'[2] He has lived in Marseilles for years and become very chi-chi – always was. He sat with us, being the *terzo incomodo*[3] and later came up to our room – and I had only a few hours of sleep – my last night, possibly forever, in England – the Flight into Egypt has begun!

TUESDAY 17TH DECEMBER

Alan and I were called at five and he dressed first and left for Southampton by car in the dark. I was too sleepy to tell him how touched I was by this gracious act of devotion. Then I got up, bathed, and shaved in a sort of daze. About seven we left for Poole in several cars. Bournemouth looked colonel-y but not unattractive in the early morning light. There was much avoidable delay at Poole,

---

1 'A cry from the heart'.
2 Stephen James Napier Tennant (1906–87), supposedly the 'brightest' of the 'bright young things', was for several years the lover of Siegfried Sassoon (qv). See Vol. I, entry for 18 November 1928 and footnote.
3 Literally 'an uncomfortable third', idiomatically 'odd man out'.

with papers, passports and luggage, although no difficulties were made for me. Soon we were in a launch and speeded towards the harbour where the grand seaplane, the *Clyde*, looked like a great black swan asleep. We took off at 10.05 for Portugal. Lovely weather but cold in the plane and I was grateful for my fur coat, which will look silly in the desert. I slept most of the day, worn out, and lulled by the noise and wind. I didn't see the German plane which my fellow passengers observed near us. I have a feeling of *soulagement*,[1] of infinite relief, dozed and dipped into *La Chartreuse de Parme*[2] and dozed again. We saw the coast of Spain about four o'clock and were at Lisbon by seven – really six. The bay looked beautiful, like Naples and my spirits rose: how I have missed the sun and the operatic atmosphere. We were politely treated by the Portuguese officials and I drove to the Embassy in the dusk: a long drive but I liked the baroque houses, the urns, the gates and ironwork, the gaiety and the lights! Everything is a contrast to drab black-coated London. I couldn't stay at the Embassy because there isn't one! The house is being arranged during the interregnum between the 'sacked' Selbies[3] and the arriving [Sir] Ronnie Campbells. I didn't much want to go to Estoril where passengers are usually parked because Lisbon is crowded with rich refugees from all lands; and a chance meeting with William Hogg[4] (Hailsham's second son and a half-brother of my old companion Edward Marjoribanks) whom I knew solved my difficulties for he offered to put me up in the attractive flat which reminded me of San Francisco with a long view of the bay. Hogg and I dined at a crowded restaurant and the food was decidedly excellent and we drank a local wine known as 'Puss-in-Boots'. Then back to his flat where he was entertaining a polyglot party of bohemians whom I amused! I am in tremendous spirits once more – about midnight I stole away and went to bed.

WEDNESDAY 18TH DECEMBER   *LAS PALMAS, CANARY ISLANDS*

I was called at 6.15 and after an excellent breakfast I was driven by Hogg's chauffeur to the airport where, to my intense relief, I found my bag of papers which I had entrusted to the Embassy servant. It contains letters for countless people, mostly kings and captains! The sun was rising over the bay as we left and we saw a Yankee Clipper, larger than our Sunderland, take off for New York . . . . We took off at 8.40; and one of my fellow passengers – I haven't really taken them

---

1 Relaxation.
2 *The Charterhouse of Parma*, to give it its English title, was written by Stendhal and published in 1839.
3 Walford Harmood Montague Selby (1881–1965) joined the Foreign Office in 1904. He was principal private secretary to the Foreign Secretary from 1924 to 1932, Ambassador to Austria from 1933 to 1937 and to Portugal from 1937 to 1940. He was knighted in 1931.
4 William Neil McGarel Hogg (1910–95) was a junior diplomat.

in as yet, but gather they are all v hush-hush – was apprehensive of the reception the Spaniards will give us at Las Palmas. I was not. Again I slept.

We arrived at the port of [illegible: possibly Salinetas] about four o'clock; it looked like a Foreign Legion film, hot sand, dirt and dust. After a long, stifling wait we landed and grave untidy Spanish officials, polite but unsmiling, examined our papers. Then we drove for an hour across the island to Las Palmas, a smiling southern town. I went for a long walk, peered at the shops, the shabby palaces, the sea and wished we were staying here for a day, particularly as I have a room and bath over the sea and shall sleep and forget! Oh! My wife what you have done to me! But only forty-eight hours away from that appalling mess and smash I am beginning to recover from her blow.

THURSDAY 19TH DECEMBER   *LAS PALMAS*

I dined with my five fellow passengers early last night so as to ensure a good night's sleep. We had barely finished when we were told by the Captain, an immensely tall, Nordic-looking Canadian or Australian, that owing to the weather we should stay over a day. The others were irritated but I was enchanted and rushed to bed.

I slept well and long, but sometimes I woke and then, as ever, my secret sorrow was with me; it is on my pillow when I go to sleep, there, waiting when I awake. Nevertheless I had a long rest, a real night, the first for many wretched weeks, and came down at lunchtime. I decided to make friends with my travelling companions who are very nice and rather typical. They are:

David Keswick, an attractive semi-bounder but an Etonian who lives in Essex, has a brood of daughters and is doing hush work for the M of EW.[1]

Col Horne, of the War Office, pleasant, middle-class, middle-aged.

Commander Fearn, a typical sailor who is a friend of Bill Astor's and indeed once shared a house with him at Ismalia.

Col Burton, a jovial young colonel of the War Office.

We drank together in the local cafés, shopped mildly, and walked about happily until the evening when the news drifted in, picked up by one of the travellers at the bar of the British Club, that we had had a slight accident when lunching yesterday and that the left float of the *Clyde* was punctured. We may be here for several days, a depressing outlook as I am eager to get to Cairo yet I am soothed by the rest, and so really glad to get out of England and away from my horrors that I don't much mind. The other travellers, however, are frantic.

I ran into Francis Rodd[2] in the bar: he arrived in the *Clare*, the incoming plane from Lagos, and I gave him letters to take back to England to Rab, Lady Iveagh,

1 Ministry of Economic Warfare.
2 Francis James Rennell Rodd (1895–1978) succeeded his father as 2nd Baron Rennell in 1941. He was a staff officer during the Second World War, reaching the rank of major general. (On his father James Rennell Rodd, see Vol. I, entry for 16 May 1934 and footnote.)

and Harold. I have decided not to write to Honor on the trip, but to forget her: she has never appreciated any of my attentions . . . .

A fortnight today I gave up smoking and I see no good effect resulting from the sacrifice except that I cough less and am more irritable and perhaps more unhappy than before.

FRIDAY 20TH DECEMBER

I woke, wondering what would be my reception in Cairo? Will Peter be pleased, or only pretend to be? Will I complicate his life; will our great friendship have stood the test of nearly a year's separation? Something tells me that it will; I have such faith in his gentleness, his loyalty and his sweetness, and my love has not abated . . .

The mystery of our delay deepens; indeed there is a ghost train atmosphere, for the Captain and the crew rather avoid us, but they half admit that we may be here for a few more days. Everyone is angry: I am in two moods about it; but as the weather has calmed I cannot see why the Captain doesn't have the plane repaired. We shall never be in Cairo for Christmas now. I called to Peter that we were delayed and scribbled a line to Honor from force of habit and forgot after I had posted it. I watched the *Clare* take off for England from my balcony. She ought to be at Bournemouth tomorrow night all being well. Thank God I am not aboard her . . . but *en route* the other way, to sunlight, adventures and to Peter.

SATURDAY 21ST DECEMBER

I am sleeping, I am forgetting, I am basking in the sun and aching for Cairo . . .

The Captain, huge and inefficient, told us yesterday that we should get off today; of course we didn't. No one knows how we can, if ever, get away from this hot operatic island. All are frantic except me; they haunt the British Club, drink gin and read back numbers of the *Bystander*. I bathed and basked in the sun, and later we all, including the Captain, drove up into the mountains to spend the day. A long dramatic drive, massive cactus, acres of them; huge banana groves and bougainvillea of every colour. We arrived at an ex-monastery called 'Les Huiles', the most attractive hotel I have ever known, white, flowery, hot. Delicious food and Norman Douglas[1] atmosphere. Probably the most lovely drive of one's life.

We shall never be in Cairo for Xmas now.

SUNDAY 22ND DECEMBER

The mystery of our remaining here deepens and must really lie in the dilatoriness and inefficiency of the crew who seem unconcerned by the delay. They are

---

1 George Norman Douglas (1868–1952) was a travel writer, notably about the Mediterranean, though was perhaps best known for his 1917 novel *South Wind*.

garrulous, ill-mannered and given to drink. This is my fourth day and there is a ghost-train atmosphere of hopelessness. I woke, feeling liverish, had breakfast on the sunlit balcony and later had a few sharp words with the Captain, who blandly assured me that we should get off on Tuesday the 24th. I retorted that if we did not I should cable the Air Ministry and that Captain Balfour happened to live with me. He was impressed.

One should always avoid Sunday in a Latin town: the dancing, noise of extra buses and louder radios was appalling. And I spent most of the day on the lulu[1] seat. Took David Keswick, whom I am beginning to like, for a long walk amongst the pretty villas hidden by trees and bougainvilleas; I thought how lovely it would be to live in one with Peter and write books ... later David and I dined in a bistro by the seashore. He and all my companions call me 'Diputado'.[2]

MONDAY 23RD DECEMBER

My nerves are still shattered seriously and I cannot throw off the nightmare that is mine; nor almost as appalling – can I honestly say that I wish it never happened.

Colonel Burton, now nicknamed 'Licentious', burst into my bedroom before I was up to break the bad news (which I knew) that Halifax has been appointed Ambassador to Washington and that Anthony Eden is back once more at the Foreign Office. So am I jobless? I don't think I would serve under him, nor, I hope, would Rab. I quickly dressed and listened to the eleven o'clock news and was surprised and enchanted – there is always the correlation – to hear that David Margesson has gone to the War Office. No mention of Rab, or of his fate: I sent a cable to Harold at once to ask ... Perhaps Rab will be Chief Whip, more likely he will go to the Board of Education. He has been abominably treated certainly. And a dozen times he has said to me that he would resign if Anthony returned to the FO. I am dashed – yet another blow – 'they come like swans in a river'. My party here of four are three violently anti-Eden and one, David Keswick, who is rather a rake and certainly a *charmeur* is hysterically pro-Eden. He has the typical Eden mind.

We all went up again into the mountains to lunch again at 'Les Huiles' as the guests of the Captain, who is in disgrace with us. The place was a little less lovely in the grey light, and also there were some horrible Spanish mothers about smacking their children which made me indignant. Paul!! Perhaps I shall go to Washington now; at any rate he can go and visit his aunt, the Ambassadress.[3] Shall I take him away from Helen Astor and transfer him to the Halifaxes?

---

1 Lavatory.
2 An elected representative.
3 Viscountess Halifax was Channon's aunt by marriage, and Paul's great-aunt.

Eden back in his pansy paradise: it is monstrous. I was in the train on the way back from Sestriere when Harold Balfour and I heard of his resignation – in February 1938,[1] and now, hung in space, confined on a Canary Island, nearly three years later, I hear that he is reinstated. Winston Churchill, with a curious lack of timing, made an impassioned appeal on the wireless to Italy; does he think there is serious unrest there? Does he think by bringing back to his government the man who is anathema to all Italians, that he can make friends with them? Always his judgement is wrong, for all his great qualities.

On balance: I have lost at the FO; I have gained at the War Office; I have gained at Washington; in the Whips' Room I am in doubt . . . it depends whether it will be James Stuart or Tommy Dugdale who will succeed David.

Tuesday 24th December

We got up at 7.30 and left Europe. A glorious morning. There was endless hanging about at the port and we rose from the water at 10.05 in the now repaired *Clyde*. There seems something ill-fated about this great seaplane. We all hoped that we should not be shot down over Dakar by the French. Dakar looked white, even smiling in the sunlight; but no inquisitive raiders came out to snoop at us. We were in the sun.

At three o'clock we arrived at Bathurst.[2] The capital of Gambia was something of a shock and I, like Peter, am against Africa; incredibly crude, uncomfortable and uncivilised – but funny, almost too funny, and I was reminded of South Carolina. We were met by 'Empire builders' in shorts, and by negroes who piloted us ashore, and we are billeted in a filthy guest house and there are lizards and scorpions in my bedroom. [I] realise now, too late, that I should have made arrangements with the Colonial Office for me to stay with governors *en route*. I had thought it would be a bore but David Keswick, who is *débrouillard*[3] and knows his Africa, was met by a Government House launch. Still I am spared the strain and I need all the rest possible: people infuriate me. The negroes are incredible, a mixture of Ronald Firbank and Georgia. They are mild, smiling, lecherous-looking, fantastically dressed, and polite, and seem to be dancing a perpetual cake-walk and carry huge prettily arranged baskets on their black heads.

We went to the local club, drank gin with Sahibs and went early to bed. Decidedly I am a European.

---

1 See Vol. I, entry for 21 February 1938. Lothian's death had given Churchill the means to move Halifax, with whom he was deeply out of sympathy, to a job he could claim was vitally important: and to bring Eden in not just as Foreign Secretary, but as heir apparent.
2 Now Banjul.
3 Resourceful.

CHRISTMAS DAY, WEDNESDAY 25TH DECEMBER   *HMS* EDINBURGH
CASTLE, *FREETOWN, SIERRA LEONE*

Of all the Christmases this is the most exhausting and unpleasant. I didn't sleep last night for the noise of the lizards at Bathurst racing in my room . . . and I thought tenderly of my Paul hanging up his stocking – hung up by someone else. Oh! my sweet and faraway child, how I love and ache for you. Then I thought of his wayward mother – where is she? Hidden in some Hogarthian pub with her labourer? I wept and wept . . .

At nine o'clock we took off and flew in great heat to Freetown, where we were met by more Empire builders and 'n--s'. The harbour was crowded with ships and the might, the seafaring force of our great Empire impressed me. We are staying the night aboard the *Edinburgh Castle* – the most unexpected night of my life. It is a depot ship, used for everything and is crowded with handsome, bronzed drunken officers in white shorts – all lonely, no doubt, but all enjoying themselves. I contrived to get a cabin to myself and slept away the afternoon, thus missing the drive to bathe at the famous Lumley Beach. Meanwhile I had made friends with Commander Pelly who, curiously enough, lives at Ingatestone, only a few miles from Kelvedon; and I dined with him and another Essex man named Burton who is one of Rab's constituents! Turkey and Xmas pudding, all very English. I heard that the Essex regiment are stationed here and obviously I ought to go ashore and call upon them at the mess, and perhaps come across some of my constituents and George Judd![1] However I remained and had to listen to Pelly tell a much-garbled version of the drama at Kelvedon – how some smart and rich people had taken a place in Essex and the wife had run away with a groom! His wife had written him the story which he in no way associated with me.

BOXING DAY, THURSDAY 26TH DECEMBER   *LAGOS*

Wifeless, my child thousands of miles away and I perhaps jobless, but still rich. I again sobbed myself to intermittent sleep much interrupted by singing sailors and inebriated officers returning from shore . . . We were called at 4.30 and went by launch from the *Edinburgh Castle* in the dark to the seaplane which took off at 6.05. Much of the morning we were over land, Liberia, I suppose, and I thought of Lady Kemsley, and then the Gold Coast. All day in the plane, very hot now . . . . We flew over uninhabited lands for hours without end and I wondered what would happen if we came down? Should we starve? However, we landed safely at three and I soon saw my first crocodile. We were transferred into a launch and whisked ashore to an awful hotel . . . . The heat is intense, although the seafront looked cool, luxurious and inviting. After a bath we dined and went for a walk, all

---

1 Channon's land agent at Kelvedon, who had enlisted in the regiment.

annoyed that we are being forced to stay here tomorrow. Another wasted day – shall I ever get to Cairo?

My companions are more like Somerset Maugham characters every day.

A delayed Christmas cable from Rab, Harold and Jay was delivered to me here. It made me happier.

FRIDAY 27TH DECEMBER

Lagos is a hell of a place, too Kipling to be true. I woke early, it was too hot to sleep. Dressed, cashed a cheque and went to GHL,[1] where I sent a code cable to Peter and to Francis Lennox-Boyd, whom I hope to see at Khartoum where he is stationed. Lazed all afternoon, bored and unhappy and sweating. Fearn and I were invited to dine with General Hawkins,[2] who commands the Nigerian forces; he has an agreeable house, very Somerset Maugham-ish, over the sea and we had an excellent dinner. Civilisation again!

SATURDAY 28TH DECEMBER

Got up late, packed and sweated . . . . At two o'clock we left for the aerodrome (maddeningly inefficient the officials are at Lagos) and took off in a Lockheed at 2.35. The plane is comfortable and fast but, of course, not as quick as the Sunderland flying boat. The Captain, I think, is called Woodman of all names. And he has the same insipid insolence of that fellow. Struts about, pirouettes . . . We arrived at Kano[3] at 5.35, after exactly three hours in the air. And feels slightly less safe than in a seaplane. Kano is fascinating and we went out at once to the native city, which has a population of 90,000. It is sheer Arabian Nights. We called upon a certain Captain Sherwood-Smith, who is the local intelligence officer, and his wife. They live in a red mud cathedral sort of house with plenty of praying retainers. We were offered drinks and then led to the roof where we sat for an hour and gossiped. Opposite lives the Emir, who keeps up feudal state with wives and executioners, Hassan.[4] The town is well governed; elaborate mud houses and orderly people, Sudanese in type. I foolishly took quinine which made me feel ill and I fainted while talking to the Captain. I was escorted to the nearest house and slept.

1　Government House, Lagos.
2　Edward Brian Barkley Hawkins (1889–1966) joined the Army in 1909 and spent most of his career in East Africa, including as a consul in Ethiopia; he retired as a major general.
3　A Muslim city in northern Nigeria.
4　An untypically poorly cast sentence by Channon. He seems to mean the Emir was called Hassan, not an executioner. In fact, the Emir of Kano in 1940 was Abdullahi Bayero Dan Muhammad Abbas (1881–1953), who ruled from 1926 until his death.

SUNDAY 29TH DECEMBER

Called at 5.30 and after a good night I breakfasted with Major General 'Sammy' Butler[1] who joined us yesterday. He is an old dear and prattles about royalty! We were all sorry to leave Kano, the first stopping place that I leave with any regret. Kano is really fascinating. It is an old caravan town, as is El Fasher, and now air caravan routes are taking the place of camel ones. We took off about 7.30 for an 800-mile trek. Yesterday we did 700 miles.

Arrived at Fort Lamy[2] at 11.00 and left after changes of time at 12.40 – a few moments only. I walked about this Free Frog[3] aerodrome in the desert with General Butler discussing the Romanian royal family!! We passed near but not over Lake Chad, near enough however to see the haze of sludge rising from the lake. Everything was still and v hot. Fort Lamy, unlike our aerodromes, was Free French and thus dusty and slovenly. After Lamy we began to climb over this fascinating country, desert at first, then mountains – strange copper coloured peaks, and at last we came to an oasis, green and bursting with cattle and camels and at 4.45 we landed at El Fasher. We were immediately taken to the RAF mess where we are to sleep; but the v kindly general, who is staying with the local Governor . . . . soon fetched us in a cart and I sat with the Governor and he drove us to his house . . . . Glorious view from the roof; then we continued our drive, walked in the souks, where we were conducted about by the Sheik of the Souk, a dignified native. The Sudanese are charming. I foolishly bought a hyena skin for eight bob. The market was fascinating, particularly the grain one. The people are so friendly and handsome and apparently famous for their manners and dignity and bearing. The native quarters are primitive but tidy. The prison was the most exciting turn: hundreds of nearly black naked men, many wearing only their chains and manacles, were penned together like animals in the zoo; but they seemed happy and well looked after and their conditions are better than they would be in their own homes. The gallows occupies a conspicuous position in the courtyard but is only occasionally used. Prisons give me a curious mixed reaction, feelings of sadism and yet of pity are aroused. We were told that the natives regret being released as they prefer a lazy life with assured food. We walked back to Government House in the gloaming, a romantic walk, this my second peep into the East. It is evident that English rule is popular . . . . Suddenly sad and dejected I declined the [Governor's] invitation to dine and returned to the mess where we are billeted. I had supper with the crew and the Captain, I

1 Stephen Seymour Butler (1880–1964) joined the Army in 1897 and apart from service on the Western Front in the Great War and a spell in India and Romania spent most of his career in the Middle East and Africa. At the time Channon met him he was engaged in liaison work in Africa and would shortly become head of the British Military Mission to Ethiopia. He retired in the rank of major general.
2 Now known as N'Djamena, the capital of Chad.
3 That is, Free French.

discovered, is the man who flew Mr Chamberlain to Godesberg and is not called Woodman – who is another operating in the same service.

Bed at nine o'clock.

Monday 30th December

We took off from El Fasher at 6.45 in the growing light: the Governor came to see us off. At first more mountains and then flat desert. I am beginning to realise what a stupendous trip I am taking, and in the middle of the war, it is a miracle. I hate Africa, that is anglicised Africa, Lagos and Bathurst, but the desert has a fascination, magic and peace that is impressive although not for me.

Arrived at Khartoum at 10.10 in intense heat and there was some discussion as to whether we should continue to Cairo – then I should see Peter – but only perhaps: he may be at the Cape or somewhere on duty, but an inner voice tells me he will be waiting for me. I was irritable all day, overexcited and overate: is it suppressed anxiety or just too many thyroid pills? After a further display of inefficiency at the Khartoum aerodrome we proceeded to the Grand Hotel, passing the Governor's Palace where Gordon reigned and died (and, which is much more important, where Peter stayed last October). At the hotel I found Francis L-B awaiting me. He was cool, thin, angular, depressed, mild and faintly delightful. He lacks Alan's *joie*,[1] verve, brilliance and genius, but like him, he is in love with their old mother, a vampire of a woman, common and uninteresting. Alan worships Francis, who complains of his fate yet he lives in luxury at the Grand Hotel where others would give their eyes to be – and he has a balcony on the Blue Nile. He only wants to get back to Henlow and wallow in his mother's possessive affections. Indeed he impressed me as a drug addict from whom all drugs have been taken away, or a drunkard deprived of his drink . . . However he was pleased to see me because I had so recently been with Alan. At 11.35 we left the hotel and he came to the aerodrome to see me off, and I weakly promised to do what I could to get him back to England somehow. He seemed so sad and lonely that I was leaving so soon. We took off at 11.45 and flew over more desert, arriving at Wadi Haifa at 2.45 – a long drive, passing date trees and dirty Egyptian encampments to a most enchanting 'honeymoon hotel' on the Nile, cool breezy and luxurious. It was a joy to be civilised again, the first time since Lisbon, but after long baths and repacking the evening hung heavily on our hands . . . . General 'Sammy' Butler is the fine *fleur*[2] of the old-fashioned gentlemanly general, a most courteous, informed individual with lapis Nordic eyes. We dined early and went to bed. Wishing that he was P, I shared a room with Fearn. Oh! tomorrow, last day of a sad and terrible year, what joys and disappointments will you bring?

---

1 Joy, or vivacity.
2 Flower.

TUESDAY 31ST DECEMBER

Called at 5.30 – why? A quite absurd arrangement as we could so easily have flown on to Cairo yesterday. A hearty breakfast followed by a chilly drive of seven miles to the national aerodrome. General Butler sent a letter via me to the King of Greece. We took off after seven on the last lap of this long journey. Journey's End .... Oh! Cairo, what secrets hold you for me? What disappointments? What adventures? What pleasures? I could not sleep, I was too excited and eagerly ticked off the minutes ... saw the Pyramids, some of them, tiny below. At last arrived at Cytherea at 10.30. From the window before we landed I saw Peter, brown, amber, alert, handsome, distinguished, stupendous, waiting for me. I rushed out: he seemed enchanted: I was exhilarated, almost delirious with excitement ... there was too Digby Hamilton,[1] ADC from the Embassy who came with two cars to meet me. I am to stay there. I had to make a quick decision as Peter had arranged a suite, he whispered, at Shepheard's.[2] I went off with him, leaving Digby to cope with my luggage; and we had a glorious ten minutes and I knew then that our great friendship had survived twelve months' absence and separation. He drove me to Shepheard's, took me to the room, no. 203 – it was very 1880s – he had selected and so charmingly arranged. There were irises in bowls, books, a set of *Les Liaisons Dangereuses*,[3] his *Gepäck*,[4] a matchbox of my own, a hundred details, a pair of egg-shaped gold links he had had made for me set with dwarf turquoises. I could have wept for joy. He was so charming, so beautiful too, that I didn't notice he was a captain! A captain already. We had a rapturous reunion, and then wistfully we drove to the Embassy, I to wash and unpack and tidy and collect my thoughts, he to his office at Middle East [Headquarters] ...

The Embassy, the old Residency, is handsome, imposing and well conducted. The Ambassador and Lady Lampson[5] – Lampson and Delilah – are away at Luxor. It was a joy to be valeted and soothed again. Later Peter and I went back to Shepheard's. The wild delight of seeing him again – a most successful *réussi* reunion and not 'that sad little meeting' we had joked about.

Cairo is divine. All my dreams, my great expectations realised. I am glad I came ...

1 Arthur John Digby Hamilton (1912–80) retired from the Scots Guards in 1951 in the rank of major.
2 Shepheard's, Cairo's foremost hotel, was destroyed in the anti-British Cairo Fire of 1952.
3 A novel of 1782 about the decadence of the pre-Revolutionary aristocracy in France, written by Pierre Choderlos de Laclos (1741–1803).
4 Luggage.
5 Miles Wedderburn Lampson (1880–1964) joined the Foreign Office in 1903 and served in Japan, China and Siberia before becoming British Minister to China in 1926. From 1933 until 1946 he was successively High Commissioner and Ambassador to Egypt before serving as High Commissioner to South East Asia until 1948. He was raised to the peerage in 1941 as 1st Baron Killearn. He married, secondly, in 1934, Jacqueline Aldine Leslie Castellani (1910–2015).

1941

George Carlisle[1] is staying here and we are in and out of each other's rooms like in the old days of fifteen years ago . . . This morning Peter fetched me and we shopped gaily, rapturously and lunched together at Shepheard's. Everywhere one meets people one knows. It is warm; it is gay; it is lovely. Peter is so poised, so happy in his job, so exquisite in his manner and manners and has, it is already evident to me, created for himself an extraordinary position . . . . He is more charming than ever.

Life is overflowing. P and I dined in my Viennese room at Shepheard's, a luxurious dinner and talked until the early hours when I crept, blissful, and [illegible] into the Embassy. I hardly remembered that it was the New Year, a fateful one, no doubt, begun. A whole day of it over. The flight into Egypt is worth everything . . . even a divorce.

THURSDAY 2ND JANUARY

I am luxuriously established, and have made conquests of the Embassy staff. The Lampsons only returned today, which was heaven as it gave me time in which to establish myself. I adore staying in people's houses whilst they are away. I lunched alone with the Lampsons; he is a huge, magnificent man of about 60, of enormous physique and easy, flowing manners and in love with her. They were married in 1934 and have no children. I should say it was a *mariage blanc*:[2] at least now, as she is slight, and an old friend of Honor's. I liked her at once. She is a daughter of Sir Aldo Castellani,[3] the Italian doctor and scientist. After luncheon we went to the zoo, fed the ducks and sat about, he she and I. I became rather fidgety as P had arranged to fetch me at six to take me to tea with the Wavells, and they were late in getting back to the Embassy. However he hadn't arrived and I discovered

---

1 George Josslyn L'Estrange Howard (1895–1963), 11th Earl of Carlisle. See Vol. I, entry for 22 February 1923 and footnote.
2 Without the exercise of conjugal rights.
3 Aldo Castellani (1874–1971) was an Italian bacteriologist and pathologist. Between the wars he taught in London and built up a Harley Street practice, and was knighted in 1928. He supported the Axis against the Allies in the Second World War and this harmed his reputation, which he rebuilt before his death. He was widely connected among British and European royalty.

that people are always unpunctual in Cairo and Peter, partly because he is Wavell's slave, the most unpunctual of all. He is loved and respected and even feared by everyone. He whisked me off to Lady Wavell's[1] house where he lives: it is a modernist villa by the Gezira Club which the Wavells share with General Wilson.[2] Lady Wavell is a large lazy woman – with wonderful turquoise eyes. She is called 'Queenie' and was Quirk *geboren*.[3] She worships Peter and I saw at once that he rules the household with a Fabergé rod. He lives in a simple little room which he calls Longwood,[4] and there were five photographs of his mother about, and a few *objets* I had given him. He has grown in stature, improved in looks, but curiously enough his lovely hair is darker. He is elegant, *soigné*, and perfect. He came to dine at the Embassy (I rigged it) and we all drove in state with motorcycle police etc. to the Opera House, which was run up for the Empress Eugenie for her famous visit when *Aida* was first produced.[5] Tonight was a gala performance of *Middle East*, a revue for the troops, a charitable gala effort. We occupied the centre box and were received with considerable *éclat*[6] (I wore my rubies, Peter was in his 'blues'). King Farouk and his entire Cabinet sat to the left of the stage in a large box whilst opposite him were the little Queen Farida,[7] and her dazzling mother-in-law Queen Nazli[8] and the princesses .... The house was crowded with uniforms. A real gala. We sped home in state and gossiped and drank. I half wish I were staying at Shepheard's but on balance am better and happier here. I am *au mieux*[9] with the Lampsons and like them both immensely. She is nervous, highly strung, and sensitive, unattractive, and much criticised by the local English who are jealous of her, and because she is Italian find it easy to be malicious about her; but she holds her own easily and with a friendly dignity. I am definitely on her side. She told Queen Nazli, with whom she sat for an act, that

1 Eugenie Marie 'Queenie' Quirk (1887–1987) married Wavell in 1915.
2 Henry Maitland 'Jumbo' Wilson (1881–1964) joined the Army in 1900 and saw action in the Second Boer War. He finished the Great War with the DSO and three mentions in dispatches. He served in India and as a staff officer between the wars before becoming General Officer Commanding 2nd Division in 1937. He was appointed GOC Egypt in 1939, and had the Palestine and Iraq command from 1942 to 1943, when he became C-in-C Middle East. The following year he was appointed Supreme Allied Commander, Mediterranean. He was promoted to field marshal in December 1944 and headed the British Joint Staff Mission to Washington from 1945 to 1947. He was knighted in 1940 and raised to the peerage as 1st Baron Wilson in 1946.
3 Born Quirk.
4 The name of Napoleon's house on St Helena.
5 By Giuseppe Verdi: and first produced at the Khedivial Opera House in Cairo on Christmas Eve 1871 with Empress Eugenie of France in the audience.
6 Splendour.
7 Safinaz Zulficar (1921–1988) married King Farouk (qv) in 1938, and took the name Queen Farida; they were divorced in 1948.
8 Nazli Sabri (1894–1978) married as her second husband King Fuad of Egypt in 1919. She was Sultana of Egypt from 1919 to 1922 and Queen Consort from 1922 to 1936.
9 On the best of terms.

I was there and the gorgeous Queen half-inclined and stared at me through opera glasses. I met her in Coronation year at a large dinner party at Mrs Greville's.[1]

FRIDAY 3RD JANUARY

I am exultant, delirious, drunk with happiness: the Cairene scene is just my affair, easy, even elegant, corrupt, luxurious, trivial, worldly, me, in fact. People are pleasure-loving, and Peter is the [most] important Pasha of them all . . . . I should like to live here after the war in a luxurious, bad-taste palace overlooking the Nile . . . .

My telephone never stops . . . . I ring up 'Middle East' to talk to Peter every few minutes: he is now Personal Assistant to General Wavell who apparently adores him. He rules Middle East: this morning he told me that the Battle for Bardia is nearly won.[2] Wavell has been a superb tactician . . . . Lunched with Joan and Ali Khan[3] in their pleasant house: they still seem happy together but her dark Prince is unfaithful and she knows it: the East will out! They have two little boys, one dark like him, and other fair, sheer Yarde-Buller – almost Guinness. Ali has had a complicated war career, and was attached as ADC to General Weygand for some time in Syria. Now he is technically in the Wiltshire Yeomanry but does intelligence here. Peter picked me up and drove me to the Embassy . . . . After I left P I went with Freya Stark[4] to an Egyptian cocktail party in her flat over the Nile. Freya, who is one of my mother-in-law's greatest friends, is here officially to do propaganda for us, as she knows Arabic . . . . She is doing excellent work, has a charming flat, and is immensely popular with everyone except Lady Wavell, who calls her 'that Miss Stark'. Her eccentric clothes not unlike Norah Lindsay's and her habit of attaching any object or *bibelot* to herself in queer places infuriate Lady W, who, whilst she has a good sense of humour, is conventional *au fond*. The General, however, likes her . . . . Lavish tea, but Egyptians are not really easy to talk to. I had some conversation with General Catroux,[5] a small, able, wizened humourless Frenchman who commands the Free French here. He has Napier Alington's flat and in it he sleeps with the garrulous Mme Catroux[6] in Napier's bed – which must have harboured many strange people in his day before he died in September.

1 See Vol. I, entry for 24 May 1937.
2 A battle in Libya from 3 to 5 January, in which Australian and British troops routed the Italians; as a consequence, the Germans decided to intervene in North Africa.
3 Prince Ali Khan and Joan Yarde-Buller, the former wife of Loel Guinness.
4 See entry for 28 December 1938 and footnote.
5 Georges Albert Julien Catroux (1877–1969) was a five-star French general and the most senior to transfer his allegiance to de Gaulle. Sacked by Vichy as Governor-General of French Indo-China in 1940, he was appointed High Commissioner to the Levant by de Gaulle. From 1945 to 1948 he was French Ambassador to the Soviet Union.
6 Marguerite Jacob (1881–1959) married, as his second wife and her second husband, Georges Catroux in 1932.

After the Egyptian party I walked to Middle East and was received by Air Marshal Longmore,[1] who kept me for an hour explaining our air policy and the difficulties with which he has had to contend and surmount. Now things are easier as planes are beginning to come in: I gathered that he doesn't see eye to eye with Winston, who is always inclined to adventures. Longmore is against extending the lines of communication: we have been lucky, and it was partly bluff, to have done so well for so long. Now we are winning: he doesn't understand why the Italians didn't take, or at least bomb, the Sudan. Every day it is now less likely . . . . I told him my mission to Yugoslavia and he hopes that Yugoslavia will not come into the war until we are prepared to give her machines etc. Already we have captured 500 Italian planes but many of these are antiquated and damaged.

I went out to dine at Shepheard's with Bill Astor, who had come up to Cairo from Ismailia where he is posted, to see me. He seemed depressed and liverish and affectionate and enchanted to see me: he is a good friend, my Bill . . . . Peter, looking so *soigné* and distinguished, joined us for dinner and Bill made little attempt to conceal his annoyance. Political conversation became impossible particularly as P and I carried on a gay badinage *à double entendre*[2] throughout dinner: he suddenly tossed his head and said that he had only known happiness since a few weeks before the war. My heart contracted and I flushed with warmth and happiness, too . . . . Bill, annoyed, left for the Embassy alone and I sat on with the others until Peter took me back to the Embassy about 2 a.m. I told him of my conversation with Longmore, and how he deplores us sending too much materiel to the Balkans or elsewhere; I gather from Peter that Wavell shares Longmore's fears, but that he is, or has been, pressed from London. It would be utter madness to leave Africa unprepared and defenceless, especially now!

SATURDAY 4TH JANUARY

Peter I didn't see this morning, but he rang me up to say that Bardia had fallen!! Another great feather in General Wavell's hat. Bill Astor, <u>still</u> surly but sweet, made me promise to elude the others, and took me to Mena House to luncheon and there we had a satisfactory gossip and political talk . . . . Indeed we praised poor Neville Chamberlain and deplored the uninformed criticism of him, instead of talking of the Pyramids opposite . . . . After lunch Bill drove me nearer the Pyramids so

---

1 Arthur Murray Longmore (1885–1970) was Australian by birth and before the foundation of the RAF had served in the Royal Naval Air Service. He was a veteran of the Battle of Jutland, and won the DSO in 1919. An air chief marshal by the outbreak of war, he was Air Officer Commanding Middle East from 1940 to 1941, but did not enjoy Churchill's confidence. He concluded his service as Inspector-General of the RAF from 1941 to 1942. He was knighted in 1935.
2 With double meanings.

that I might have a *coup d'oeil*[1] of them! Then we went to the races to join the Ambassador and Lady L in their box. 'God Save the King' was played as we all arrived. The paddock was crowded and it reminded me of Newmarket, with Ali Khan leading his horses, and Charles Wood[2] (in Cairo at least) wandering about with Hughie Northumberland.[3] There were masses of friends and acquaintances but I looked for Peter in vain. We betted and won and I escorted Lady L about and later she, Hughie and I went to the Mousky[4] to shop. Hughie bought a round French tortoiseshell box which I am to take back to his mother. I bought Peter a cat – 26th dynasty, I think: he is collecting cats, cats and jewels!!

About seven o'clock we, the Lampsons, Hughie and I drove in state to the Wavells' where there was a mammoth cocktail party of over a hundred people, all carefully selected and invited by Peter, who is their Lord Chamberlain as well as everything else. The joke in Cairo is that until about three weeks ago he looked after General Wavell and now Wavell looks after him. I nicknamed him the 'Eminence Rose' and everyone calls him that! In the crowd of fashionable Cairenes, Australian nurses, and officers I had my first glimpse of the great General Wavell. He is like his photographs! He is grey, gracious, and smiling but is alleged to be more silent than Coolidge.[5] I avoided him at the party as I was to stay to dine. He has a queer expression due to having only one eye and doesn't seem to focus accurately, as do most people with only one eye after a time.

After the guests left we went into dinner, everyone in the highest of spirits over the Fall of Bardia. Even the pusillanimous Egyptians are bellicose now; but one fears that the bumptious little King, whose secret sympathies were always with Italy, is furious .... At dinner there was only General and Lady Wavell, one of their three daughters, Peter and I. I knew from the food – kedgeree and soufflé – that P had ordered in. He does all the housekeeping .... Dinner was gay, and I was relieved that the General laughed at all I said and I soon found him easy, even a cataract of conversation. After dinner he led me into a corner of the rather bare drawing room whilst Peter talked to the ladies, and we talked for over an hour standing up. He asked me dozens of questions, first about London, then David Margesson, whom he has never met, other politicians etc. I gathered that he agrees with Longmore on strategy, which is fortunate. Then he switched off on to books and I found him charming, one of the most rare, gentle, detached, good people I have ever met with an insidious charm. I quite understand Peter's passion and devotion to him, which P told me was of gradual but now of very deep growth.

1 A look.
2 Channon's cousin by marriage. See entry for 29 June 1939 and footnote.
3 The 10th Duke of Northumberland was serving in the Royal Artillery as a lieutenant.
4 The Cairo souk, or shopping district.
5 John Calvin Coolidge (1872–1933) was the 30th President of the United States of America, as Vice President succeeding Warren G. Harding on the latter's death in 1923, and being elected in his own right the following year. He was legendary for his taciturnity.

The Victor of Bardia hardly mentioned it: all goes according to plan; he does his thinking alone, walking, or on the golf course. His staff is excellent . . . . A very cosy evening with the beam of history on that house, and I alone with Wavell for an hour and a half. He is very modest and seemed surprised when I told him how famous he was at home, and that a grateful nation would no doubt present him with 'a second Blenheim'. 'I hope not,' he laughed, and when I said that he was a second Nelson (a foolish remark) he retorted, 'Why? Because I have only one eye?' We made friends, possibly because there was a secret link between us of which he is probably not altogether unaware, and, also, I was all out to captivate him. Peter, when he drove me back in his car to the Embassy, said that I had had quite an unprecedented success with the General, who was often bored and 'not easy'. We found the Lampsons still up and after a whisky-soda said 'goodnight' to them and then I took P back to his car: but the Cairene witchery was over us – full moon; champagne, ecstasy of being together, victory and we walked along the Nile for an hour and a half up and down, arm in arm. The city was silver. Peter said that we were 'happy together' which was the secret of our friendship. He always does things well and economically . . . . Bed about 3 a.m. after another rapturous day. How I wish I was a Pasha!

SUNDAY 5TH JANUARY

Peter picked me up late . . . . and drove me to Air House where Longmore lives. A pleasant luncheon party with Gambier-Parry,[1] the General, as the other *pièce de résistance*. The glare and heat intense . . . . After lunch went on until 3.30 Longmore suggested going for a hike in the desert but I had other plans . . . and I walked to see Freya Stark who had arranged a luncheon party for me and which I had been obliged to chuck because of Longmore. I found her on her balcony watching the barges floating on the Nile.

I had a short siesta which was interrupted by the Ambassador, my dear courteous comely mammoth Sir Miles, coming to my room to say that Bardia had completely capitulated. That we knew, or almost knew yesterday, but I knew there was some outpost or group or garrison which held out until today.

Then I went to dine with Peter at Shepheard's and we took the same room and were served in the candlelight. After the waiter had left us, I told him my story, my tragic tale. He listened attentively, and took it well: I wonder whether he isn't secretly pleased, which is flattering. I pray so. Certainly he advised divorce, said that obviously neither H nor I would be happier until we were rid of each other.

---

1 Michael Denman Gambier Parry (1891–1976) was a professional soldier who joined the Army in 1911 and won the Military Cross at Gallipoli. He became General Officer Commanding 2nd Armoured Division in 1940, but was captured by the Italians in April 1941; however he escaped in 1943. He retired the following year in the rank of major general.

He agreed to live with me after the war, and to share my house, houses, or flat: we should travel together and be happy. I think he is right and I long for the day.

MONDAY 6TH JANUARY

My Cairo operetta is drawing to a close and I shall be wretched . . . . P and I drove to the desert gossiping happily all the way until we came to the Oasis of Fayoum, a heavenly place. Everything seemed biblical, the shepherds with their donkeys and goats, the camels, the primitive peasants. The green and the salt lake were a relief from the desert. The tiny hotel which reminded me of San Vigilio on Lake Garda is attractive. We lunched, had a siesta, and then went for a walk along the water's edge and dined, divinely happy.

We went early to bed: it is peaceful, it is paradisiacal: one of the happiest days of my life.

TUESDAY 7TH JANUARY

A glorious morning and lovely drive through the desert. I was tired. There was a pompous dinner party at the Embassy originally arranged for me. I was next to the immensely fat wife of the Minister of Defence and later I went out shopping with Jacqueline [Lampson] buying presents for her, Peter, and the two Embassy ADCs . . . . I am utterly wretched to be leaving Cairo . . . . it has been a glorious release, a glamorous week, a sonata of complete perfection due primarily to my private Khedive, Peter.

WEDNESDAY 8TH JANUARY

I was called at 5.15, which is a frequent occurrence in this aeronautical age, and dressed gloomily. When I came down there was Peter, cool, distinguished and perfect. He drove me to the aerodrome, looking amber and handsome, and was affectionate and divine . . . . After some delay we left the ground at 7.45 in an antiquated machine. My companions were [*sic*] General Gambier-Parry, a sympathetic, social sort of general who had enjoyed a partial success in Athens. Our first stop was at Faka, a blazing Egyptian aerodrome where we breakfasted and waited: I wandered about in the blazing sun . . . . We came down again at Crete, where the General was received by several Commandos; the new suicide-squad of daredevils: they looked terrific; and most bloodthirsty. The General and I parted, and he sent many messages to the Greek royal family. Crete is now an English island: nothing to eat procurable at the aerodromes except a few oranges. Soon we were over Greece, smiling in the clouds and came down at Tatoi.[1] There was no car

---

1 Around twenty miles north of Athens.

to meet me but a message explained that the Legation – which is rather a muddled and muddling institution – had sent the car to the wrong aerodrome: there were two. I was, however, given a lift into Athens and saw our airmen everywhere; and oranges in the churchyards. Athens seemed smaller than I thought. The Legation is a pretentious, conventional house which formerly belonged to Mme Venizelos.[1] The minister, Sir Michael Palairet,[2] has had it painted a lollypop pink. Tea with him, Lady Palairet and Lord and Lady Dunsany,[3] an antiquated comic pair. He is a glamorous, bewhiskered old gentleman – how could he have written such lovely plays? And she, the Irish, bony chatelaine of the housekeeper type. A message came that the King[4] had been waiting for me, so unchanged I rushed to the Palace escorted by Harold Caccia.[5] We were received by Colonel Levidis,[6] his pompous chamberlain whom I had known in London. The King seemed overjoyed to see me: he is thin, lovely and conventional, and sees few people. He is convinced of victory – if only we would send him more things, and if only Paul of Yugoslavia (they telephone to each other nearly every night) would come into the War now! He gave me more tea and showed me over the unattractive Palace which is mostly under dust sheets.

Then we went to Lelia [*sic*] Ralli's[7] for a cocktail . . . . Lelia, the most *mondaine*, Parisienne of people, is happy in her tiny flat, and does hospitable work. She was enchanted by presents and letters I had brought her from the Kents . . . . Lelia's 'salon' is the smartest in Athens and she acts as liaison officer between the royal family and Athenian society. Which rarely, I gather, mixes. I tried to walk back to the Legation but the blackout is complete – one is not allowed to light a match and it is far darker than London. Dined at the Legation with the foolish Palairets. Lady P is a half-sister of Neville Chamberlain, is younger, better-looking,

---

1 Helena Stephanovitch Schilizzi (1873–1959) was a British-based philanthropist who in 1921 married as his second wife Eleftherios Venizelos (1864–1936), the Greek Prime Minister from 1910 to 1920, and 1928 to 1933.

2 Charles Michael Palairet (1882–1956) joined the Diplomatic Service in 1905 and served as Minister to Romania from 1929 to 1935, to Austria from 1937 to 1938 and to Greece from 1938 to 1943, from 1942 as Ambassador. He was knighted in 1938. He married, in 1915, Mary de Vere Studd (1895–1977).

3 Edward John Moreton Drax Plunkett (1878–1957) succeeded his father as 18th Baron Dunsany in 1899. He married, in 1904, Beatrice Child Villiers (1880–1970), Lady Beatrice by courtesy, daughter of the 7th Earl of Jersey. Dunsany was part of the great Irish literary renaissance in the early twentieth century, making his name as a writer of short stories and then as a playwright. In 1940 he was appointed Professor of English at Athens University.

4 King George II of Greece (1890–1947): see Vol. I, entry for 29 August 1924 and footnote.

5 Foreign Office official; see entry for 17 January 1939 and footnote.

6 Dimitrios Levidis (1891–1964) had served in the Balkan Wars and in the war between Greece and Turkey from 1919 to 1922. He had been a courtier since 1917, becoming Master of the Household, Chamberlain and ADC to George II. When King George had to go into exile Levidis accompanied him.

7 Lilia Ralli (qv).

perhaps more intelligent, but not as endearing or vague. I rather disliked her
. . . . Dunsanys also at dinner. Afterwards we sat in a horrid little room which
Lady P described as cosy and she made tea into which she put honey. Even that
didn't keep me awake and I at last withdrew. I dislike Lady P for abusing Neville
Chamberlain who, I happened to know, insisted on their appointment.

I am a touch disappointed by Athens – so far. But my welcome from the King
was very warm: I have known him well for twenty years; he is lovely, sad, thinner
and rather a mild bore; but he is kindly, gentle, loyal, and stingy. He is deeply in
love with Mrs Brittain-Jones, (*née* Joyce);[1] and is miserable away from her. He
would almost have given up his kingdom for her; but it is she who would not hear
of it. They are a simple, domestic couple – and she is languishing in London. He
talked of her so gently, with such affection that I was moved and thought of my
own complicated love life. He is living officially at the Tatoi Palace at the request
of General Metaxas for reasons of security; but he comes up to Athens nearly
every day and picnics in the town palace. He asked me shyly to share his tray; but
I refused, pleading the Palairets . . . his uniform cut like an English one, makes him
look more English than ever. Like all deserted husbands whose marriages have
been failures or frustrated, there is something incomplete about him. I am feeling
it myself now.

THURSDAY 9TH JANUARY

Got up late and made my arrangements for the appalling journey on to Belgrade
tomorrow. I don't like the Balkans. Then Lelia Ralli, witty, frivolous, sweet, hideous,
chic and annoying as ever fetched me and we shopped . . . . I bought some silver
cigarette cases, a handsome ring for Peter, and other things . . . . we drove up to the
Parthenon: it is a superb amber-pink (not beige as Lady Mendl is alleged to have
said), staggering in its quiet splendour.

I had to hurry away as the King had announced his intention of coming to
tea at the Legation to see me. The Palairets were in a frenzy and did it awkwardly
indeed. Tea in the dining room, a brass kettle and candles: it was ridiculous,
ten people sitting around a table making conversation. The King, next to Lady
Dunsany, was very bored . . . . Later he and I talked for nearly an hour, but
standing – a trick of royalties when they are on parade! The party waited, slightly
piqued, whilst HM again asked my advice and assistance about arranging for
Mrs Joyce Brittain-Jones to come to Athens. He pines for her so, and being well

---

1 Joyce was her Christian name, not her surname. Joyce Henrietta Wallach (1902–74) married
  John Brittain-Jones, an officer in the Black Watch, in 1924. She had met the then-exiled King
  George II of Greece in 1930 and, following his separation from Queen Elisabeth in 1935, and
  Mrs Brittain-Jones's divorcing her husband for adultery, the two effectively cohabited, with
  her living at the royal family's summer palace.

disposed towards lovers I promised to do all I could to help. It won't be easy to fix up; but I am writing back to the Foreign Office at once.

I am apprehensive about something the K of Greece hinted to me – that Paul .... is having a sort of nervous collapse. The Germans are putting it about that he is mad. I don't believe it. The King and Paul have not actually met since they came for a cocktail in my house in Belgrave Square three years ago. They are v old friends but mildly hostile and amusing about each other. Now they talk every night on the telephone and the line is certainly tapped! The King said *inter alia* that he was aghast at the disastrous appointment of Eden to the Foreign Office but as it was an accomplished fact there was no use making such a song and dance about it as Paul was doing.

Friday 10th January

A really rather dreadful day. I packed, said 'goodbye' to the Palairets and caught the 12.10 train to Belgrade. Then Athens Station was crowded and I saw many hundred soldiers, some limping, others on stretchers. The courier switched me to the one first-class compartment, and I was much burdened with luggage and three diplomatic bags. When I got there I found to my dismay that I was next to the German courier who had more bags than I, and a wife and companion. There was a sudden and frantic move to another compartment which I shared with six Greeks, one of whom spoke a little French. I sat in discomfort and watched the lovely Greek countryside slip by: we proceeded very slowly. There is only one railway and it crosses many bridges. Why the Italians have not blown it up, I cannot imagine: supplies, reinforcements, in fact the whole Greek effort would have been checked, or, at least, seriously delayed, had they done so. At Tatoi I looked in vain for the Royal Palace; instead I saw very English faces of some of our grand airmen and I called out to them. The hours passed; I was cold, uncomfortable, apprehensive for my bags and the journey generally and occasionally had desultory conversation with my well-meaning, high-smelling companions. The little stations where we passed were crowded again with wounded! Everything looked bare except the blue Greek skies and the olive trees. Sometimes we were greeted with frenzied cheers – Klisura had fallen into Greek hands, and lovely church bells pealed in triumph. The Greeks in my compartment kissed each other. It was joy triumphant. Then I remembered Lady Palairet's picnic basket, and I brought out her bottle of wine, and .... passed it to my fellow travellers! They all had a good gulp and toasted England and victory!! I thus ingratiated myself – and was able to leave the bags for the *besoins de la nature*.[1] At last I fell asleep, huddled in my fur coat, but clutching my diplomatic bags all the while.

---

1 Call of nature.

Saturday 11th January

Another uncomfortable day, sitting hard-arse in the train . . . . At 7.30 a.m. we reached Salonika where the Levantine courier of the Consulate met me . . . . He told me that I had missed the connection and must spend twenty-four hours in Salonika where he had engaged a room at a hotel for me. Luckily one of my Greek friends assured me that this was quite untrue: there was a wild dash to another train, where after settling down for half an hour, we were again forced to change trains. In the confusion I lost *War and Peace*, my constant companion on this dreadful journey: how I hate trains and this is the first one I had been in since going to Bournemouth – soon the German courier with good manners came up to me and handed me my book and addressed a few words to me in English! I thanked him civilly . . . . Another change, and this time a wait of three hours . . . . There was no one to meet me: the Regent in his desire to keep my visit a secret has sacrificed my comfort. I had nothing to eat all day except some milk chocolate . . . . Another change at Skopje; in Nish I tried to get a wagon-lit in a car added to the train, but failed.

Sunday 12th January

Half-dead with fatigue, hunger, thirst and a sore bottom I arrived at Belgrade at 6.30. A courtier came to meet me and I was whisked to the Palace: grave sentries saluted me and the ADC on duty conducted me to my room, the same as I had last Easter. I went at once to bed and rested for an hour whilst my things were unpacked and breakfast was brought. *Luxe* again is soothing. About nine o'clock there was a knock on my door and the Regent walked in, half-dressed, wearing a dressing gown. We fell into each other's arms and hugged each other tightly. He looks well; but has a cold: he seemed cheerful, but said he was distracted with work and complications. I was overjoyed to see him. He left me to dress; soon there was another gentle tap at the door and a 'Can we come in, your enemies?' The Toerrings walked in, both looking thin and worn. She is an angel of sweetness as ever and Toto silent, evasive, elusive with a strain of the Wittelsbach charm. More hugs. It took me a long time to get up with those interruptions and then the boys Nicky and Alexander both came in. I rang up the Legation and sent them their bags and then distributed the many letters, parcels and presents which I had brought from the Kents and others. Everyone was delighted. Princess Olga seemed preoccupied but gentle and grave and said she was worried about P's health . . . The Palace is smooth-running, perfect, luxurious, too much food and drink. The Regent's children are improved: Alexander is a manly fellow, honest and slothful and the least-liked; Nicky is more gay, intelligent and quick, but he is a touch treacherous and very much spoilt by his father who worships him;

the baby 'Pixie'[1] is 5 and is the most alert and engaging child I have ever come across – Honor adored her years ago! She is full of charm and conversation and curiously enough in no way resembles her mother or her family: she is the spit of the Regent . . . . After luncheon the Regent and I had a long talk. He is violently anti-German, cannot abuse them enough, and is well-on to their intrigues and double-dealing, so he says. He has turned against the whole race; but he is in a difficult position politically and geographically and cannot enter the war – yet! But he says he is helping Greece as much as he can in little ways. He mistrusts the Croatian advisers who at any moment are prepared to break away from him and certainly would not follow him into a world war. He is playing for time; until we are more powerful. He prayed that England would not do anything rash like sending troops to Greece: that would only bring the Germans southwards further into the Balkans. King Boris was a rogue. Carol a fool.

At six o'clock Ronnie Campbell,[2] the Minister, came to be received in audience. They were closeted in Lord Chesterfield's library for a long time and as I went off to dress the Regent rushed into my room shaking with rage. A proposition had come from the Foreign Office that a united Balkan front be proclaimed, and Wavell, so Campbell told him, would be in Athens tomorrow . . . . The Regent and Campbell had rather a heated argument, the highly strung Paul eventually shouting 'This stinks of Anthony!' I could not understand his anger but I appreciated his reasoning. He believes, and so does General Metaxas, that such a declaration might be a challenge to Germany, and that she would invade Yugoslavia at once – perhaps bomb Belgrade tonight. It seems at all costs that he wants to preserve peace at least until he hands over the country, which he rules as trustee, next September to young Peter.

Later in the evening after the Toerrings went to bed, he had calmed down; and he complained bitterly of our Foreign Office, and of Anthony and of the mistakes we had made in the past. He blames Anthony for almost everything and says that if the British Empire falls the architect of its destruction will be not so much Adolf Hitler as Anthony Eden.

MONDAY 13TH JANUARY

It is very cold and there is snow everywhere: however the Palace is hot and the food is incredibly luxurious . . . . I went into the town with Alexander, everywhere they seem silent, taciturn, bowing Serbs. In the afternoon the Regent took me for a drive and we skidded in the snow: he can never learn to drive, and after all these

---

1 Princess Elizabeth of Yugoslavia (b.1936). Actually she was still 4. See Vol. I, entry for 24 August 1936 and footnote.
2 Ronald Ian Campbell (qv).

years! I have the impression that he is personally unpopular: he, who has more charm than anyone on earth when he exerts it, which he almost always does, is ungracious with his boorish Serbs who think him 'too English'. He says himself, that he is the English Minister to the Court of Belgrade and that Campbell is a nice noodle.

TUESDAY 14TH JANUARY

I feel *congestionné* by the richness of the splendid food . . . . The King[1] came to lunch and got [the] giggles over some silly jokes . . . . Went to tea at the Legation with Campbell and we were tête-à-tête: he has the highest respect for the Regent and is unaware that it is not reciprocated. He told me that General Wavell arrives today in Athens.

On my return to the Palace the Regent told me that he was sending a special courier to Athens with a letter for Metaxas; so I sent one by the same man to Peter c/o the Legation. The Regent gave me a black and gold evening-watch as a belated Xmas present: he had had it sent out specially, he said, but I half-suspect, but dared not ask, that it came from Cartier in Paris? More abuse of the Germans . . . . When anything of the sort is mentioned Toto Toerring gets up and quietly leaves the room: what else can he do? I wonder whether he is a Nazi agent? He is so silent, shy and *chétif*[2] and irritates the Regent. She is an angel, really the gentlest of the three famous sisters. I often wonder what will be the fate of their daughters, Alexandra of England,[3] Elizabeth of Yugoslavia, and Helen Toerring,[4] all amazingly attractive children?

WEDNESDAY 15TH JANUARY

I feel I ought to think about my return arrangements: how I dread the long trek and my arrival back in England. The Regent I find more vague: he seems to have somewhat lost his grip on things; but remains loyal, loving and attractive. He is much interested in Peter C. He keeps asking me to take various things back to London for safekeeping as he foresees a tremendous bombardment of the Palace. Princess Olga showed me the air-raid shelter, a subterranean affair of immense size with bathrooms, its own electricity, kitchens etc. There is an ominous atmosphere of feckless politicians, and, in the evening with the lights still blazing,

1 The regent's nephew, King Peter (qv).
2 Puny.
3 Princess Alexandra Helen Elizabeth Olga Christabel of Kent (b.1936). She married, in 1963, Angus James Bruce Ogilvy (1928–2004), second son of the 12th Earl of Airlie.
4 Countess Helene Marina Elisabeth of Toerring-Jettenbach (b.1937), married in 1956 Archduke Ferdinand Karl Max of Austria. She and her two cousins mentioned by Channon became exceptionally close all their lives and called themselves, in old age, 'the Widows' Club'.

one wonders on what night the enemy will decide to fly over? Will there be a short ultimatum or none?

Albrecht von Bayern[1] came to lunch; he is a very mild, slightly deaf little man, is the heir to Bavaria and the 'rightful' Stuart King of England! He doesn't speak English. He is the *maître des chasses*[2] of the Regent and lives in a villa here, whilst his wife is at present at Budapest. He and Toto Toerring and the King of the Belgians are all first cousins, being sons of sisters. Prince Albrecht is anti-Nazi, being a Wittelsbach and a Roman Catholic. Toto Toerring left for Munich tonight.

THURSDAY 16TH JANUARY

King Peter and a Greek editor came to luncheon. The editor told me that Wavell is definitely in Athens; and that he arrived on Tuesday; and the situation here seems to darken: the Regent is so angry over Wavell's visit that he has retired to bed – also he has a cold in his left eye [*sic*]. He is convinced that by our actions we should draw the Germans south in the Balkans: he is unprepared for them and doesn't want a war. It was Paul's idea to have a pact of friendship with Hungary.

Queen Helen rang up from Romania to gossip; she is lonely in Bucharest. She has only King Michael. Her German lover is a doctor at Dresden, but I am told that he had been replaced by a young Italian. She complained to Princess Olga that Spoleto,[3] once her lover, and now married to Princess Irene, her sister, is no use as a lover, and is practically impotent.

Beli Dvor is a perfect house: it is too exquisite to be a palace, for palaces often are hideous. Lying about, too, are many of my presents, a Lamerie gilt coffee pot, always used; snuffboxes; a silver seal-box sent out this Christmas, whilst on the table are always four Adam silver candlesticks which I wish I owned. I gave them to the Regent in 1935.

Too many films. The King asked me over to Beli Dedinje to see one this afternoon but I refused. He is Hollywood-mad and seems uninterested in world politics. The Regent got up for dinner having been resting most of the day.

FRIDAY 17TH JANUARY

This morning as I came down the staircase I met the Mistress of the Robes, a dignified old girl with white hair and the usual pearls. She saw me and curtsied

---

1 Albrecht Luitpold Ferdinand Michael, Duke of Bavaria (1905–96) was the grandson of the last King of Bavaria, who was deposed in 1918. He refused to join the Nazi Party and was forced into exile to Hungary. He and his family were arrested when the Germans invaded Hungary and were sent to Sachsenhausen concentration camp, and then to Dachau, whence they were liberated in 1945.
2 Master of the Hunt.
3 Prince Aimone, Duke of Spoleto (qv).

to the ground: as my visit has been kept a semi-secret the curious courtiers who don't have to know me think I am a Greek royal relation. We went out: Princess Olga and I walked, followed by sentries and detectives – she and the Regent are like Honor, they never smile or say 'good morning' to their subordinates and I have a sneaking suspicion that they are disliked, or at least, unappreciated. And how unjust, for the Regent has slaved for years for his horrible country – to Beli Dedinje to see the famous Holy Relics. They are kept in the King's private chapel and were given to the late King Alexander[1] by the Dowager Empress of Russia in whose possession they were at the time of the Bolshevik Revolution. They are of incredible value; and they are three:

I. The hand of St John the Baptist, his finger bent, as if blessing.
II. Portrait of the Virgin by St Luke.
III. A bit of the true cross.

They are all magnificently mounted with heavy gold frames richly encrusted with mammoth ruby and sapphire cabochons and ruby spinels. They are v heavy and the gold alone must be worth a fortune. These extraordinarily holy objects were for centuries owned by the Knights of Malta: when Malta was threatened by Napoleon the relics were sent secretly to Russia to the Emperor Alexander who happened at the time to be Grand Master of the Knights of Malta. Ever since, until 1917, they remained with the crown jewels of the Romanovs, and about a hundred years ago were framed in their splendid settings. 'Pray,' Princess Olga suggested. We were alone, except for an orthodox priest, in the tiny mosaic-ed royal chapel, and I knelt, and putting my finger on the bit of the true cross (there is a glass over it) I murmured a few words of prayer for the safety of my son and the preservation of Peter. Then in the silence Princess Olga and I tiptoed out into the cold sunlight . . . . A royal car took me to the Legation where I lunched *en famille* with Ronnie Campbell, the Minister . . . . A most pleasant party and I was treated almost like a royalty myself and asked a hundred questions about the Regent's intentions next September.[2] In a world crisis, with war threatened, it would be unwise, almost impossible to turn over the reins of power to a boy of 17, the Minister insisted.[3] I agreed to try and persuade the Regent to stay on. Campbell wanted to know why he had reacted so violently to Wavell's visit to Athens and I explained his point of view with which, I half-suspect, Campbell agreed. When I got back to the Palace the Regent was up and fretting for me. He was in a most

1 King Alexander I of Yugoslavia (1888–1934) was assassinated by a pro-Bulgarian revolutionary when on a state visit to France.
2 Rhodes James wrongly has this luncheon happening the previous day, which according to the MS it did not.
3 King Peter would be 18 in September and the Regency would end. He was 17 as Channon wrote.

affectionate mood and offered me either his 'wagon', as he called his train, or his private Lockheed to take me to Greece. But he wants me to stay on, although he seems to think that the climate of crisis is approaching. Again he said that nothing would really happen to him, nor to the Balkans generally until March. He has so informed the Legation, who repeated it as their view to me at lunch. The Regent repeated that he is His Majesty's Ambassador[1] to Belgrade and after the end of the Regency he is thinking of applying for the job officially. Nevertheless he is alarmed by the decision of the Hungarian government to suspend all railway services for three days beginning tonight: the official reason given is the snow, but P knows it is because Germany is using the railway lines to order troop movements into Romania. The Regent attacked the Foreign Office with some violence: yet he has supplied us with secret and highly valuable information for years. It was he who first warned us of the impending rapprochement between Germany and Russia and he is convinced that it was King Boris who acted as broker. The Regent mistrusts Anthony Eden, whom he accuses of being a drawing-room communist, the *âme damnée*[2] of English politics and wrong in every subject. Above all, don't send him abroad, he advised, as foreigners are never impressed by one so young, so fashionable, and so foolish! I fear that I agree with all of this . . . .

Saturday 18th January

After luncheon the Regent took me for a drive all around Belgrade; everyone stood to attention, and he drove recklessly his Mercedes car. We stopped at last at the Royal Palace in the town where he lived for many years in terror of his hated old uncle, King Peter.[3] We got out and the Palace had been prepared for our reception, and he led me through many rooms all ugly and hardly imposing French genre [circa] 1920. Then he showed me his own rooms, King Alexander's and others. The decoration is somewhat Germanic. He laughed when we came to a bedroom where he had once stood guard whilst within King Alexander, then himself Regent, had raped an Austrian Lady who was enamoured of him.

Sunday 19th January

I spent the whole day with the Regent, and felt sad, lonely and affectionate: we are still on our old basis of firm friendship and trust. After lunch he rested a little and sat on his bed: he talked of England so poignantly and of his old and many friends there and of all our fun together and youth and of Doris Gordon-Lennox,[4] and

---

1 Coats, in the MS, has glossed by writing 'our real' in pencil, having crossed out 'His Majesty's'.
2 Lost soul.
3 See Vol. I, entry for 25 December 1935, where the late King is 'beloved'.
4 Lady Doris Hilda Gordon-Lennox (1896–1980), daughter of the Earl of March.*

Elizabeth (the Queen now) and Walter Buccleuch ... his heart is there he says, and immediately he can he will go and live in England; but he is worried about the income tax. Will he be rich enough? And, too, he wonders, does England really understand the war and its problems and Hitler's terrific armies and powers?

The splendour prevails, the overeating goes on but I have the curious empty vacuum sensation of waltzing on the edge of a volcano which may erupt tonight.

None of the royal family has asked me about Honor and yet I am sure that they do not know: it is the old story – she never makes an impression on people, they never love her or even like her because she takes no trouble or interest in them. It augurs sadly for her future.

Monday 20th January

Last evening the Regent tried to persuade me to stay another week; but it is always a mistake to alter one's plans and perhaps spoil a perfect visit: besides I must get back to England, and I want to see Peter. So reluctantly I got up this morning still surrounded by the *luxe* and splendour of the Palace, sad to go and yet a touch relieved as I have premonitions that it will not be long before Belgrade is attacked. I was packed, dressed and had tipped [the staff] and breakfasted before ten. Then there were the 'goodbyes': the children first . . . . then the sisters, and I wept too for a second as I saw tears come to Olga's fine eyes: she is usually so undemonstrative. They came down to the entrance hall with me and I was miserable: what will they – and I – go through before we meet again? We have each our problems, and are cast in too many positions to be left alone by destiny . . . . Then the Regent came running down the stairs and he clasped both my hands in his, and we walked out onto the portico and were surrounded by their eternal grave, unsmiling, bowing sentries. 'Goodbye, Chips. I fear I may never see you again,' he murmured. I burst into tears, but he smiled and came to the car. There was an instant's delay then we started and I heard him call out again 'Goodbye, Chips.' Alexander was standing with him – and I drove away from my greatest friends with a heavy heart. At the Terminal Aerodrome I was met and conducted to a comfortable Lockheed, a luxurious one which is used sometimes by the Prime Minister, but belongs to the King. We took off after 10.30 and I was fairly apprehensive both of the pilot's capabilities and of Greek gunfire . . . . We passed directly over Beli Dvor and below I saw, I suppose, Princess Olga and Princess Elizabeth and the boys waving their handkerchiefs frantically. The weather at first was wet and cloudy but it soon cleared. I had a crew of eight including two secretaries: I can't think why there should have been so many. We flew fast and crossed the Greek frontier without incident although there seems some doubt as to whether the government had been warned. The plane might have been mistaken for an Italian one! About two o'clock we were at Salonika and the heat was intense. The authorities refused to allow the plane to proceed to Athens without the permission of the Minister concerned, which in wartime would take several hours to get – to telephone to Athens etc. As they were debating I suddenly decided to go into Athens by train. We drove through pleasant Salonika, along the very blue sea. I saw no traces of recent air raids.

The railway station at Salonika seemed as confused as ever; however I got a corner seat and had no hostile courier to contend with, and so slept peacefully with my diplomatic bag stowed above me. When I awoke, the train was crawling: it goes v slowly now and, of course, there is the risk of bombardment or of bridges being blown up.

TUESDAY 21ST JANUARY

Bored, bearded and travel-stained, I arrived at Athens, where Legation officials awaited me. I lunched in, a nice officer called Blunt and his wife gave me letters to deliver and commissions to do in London. My postbag is enormous: I am, indeed, as Princess Nicholas[1] called me, 'a private Hermes'. The Regent gave me letters and presents and jewels for the Kents, the kings of England and of Greece etc. Directly after luncheon Princess Nicholas, wearing her famous widow's weeds which enhance even her dignity and magnificence, fetched me at the Legation; she was accompanied by an aged *hof-dame* (someone ought to write a book about ladies-in-waiting). They would not come in as they are not on friendly terms with these silly Palairets, who make tea and rush to Mass. I am so ashamed by the Legation painted a tart pink. I drove with Princess Nicholas to Psychiko[2] where we had two hours together and I gave her all the news from Belgrade. Later I picked up Lilia[3] Ralli (one doesn't dress in Athens) and dined at Nelly [blank]'s[4] pretty home, a most enjoyable party. Philip of Greece[5] was there; he is extraordinarily handsome and I at once recalled my afternoon's conversation with Princess Nicholas – so he is to be the Prince Consort and it is for that he is serving in our Navy!!? He is here on leave for a few days with his more than mad mother. He is a *charmeur*; but I should deplore such a marriage: he and Princess

1 Formerly the Grand Duchess Elena Vladimirovna of Russia (1882–1957), widow of Prince Nicholas of Greece and Denmark (1872–1938).

2 About three miles north of central Athens, a residential suburb that in the first decades of the twentieth century was an elite neighbourhood, not least because of the presence of houses belonging to the royal family.

3 A rare incidence of Channon rendering her nickname correctly. He later uses both variants interchangeably.

4 Nelly Eliases, wife of a leading Greek banker.

5 Prince Philip of Greece and Denmark (1921–2021) was the son of Prince Andrew of Greece and Denmark and Princess Alice of Battenberg (qv). He served in the Royal Navy from 1939 to 1952 in both the Mediterranean and Pacific theatres. He married, in 1947, Princess Elizabeth of the United Kingdom (qv), who succeeded her father as Queen Elizabeth II of Great Britain and Northern Ireland in 1952.

Elizabeth are too inter-related and the Mountbatten–Hesse family are famous for their ill-luck and madness. Disaster pursues them. Like Princess Nicholas I should prefer Alexander[1] who is more manly.

Athens is warm and lovely and I like it better this time. I even like Lady Palairet . . . . The Palairets have an inverted snobbery and detest anyone important; in other words they cannot patronise. The usual inferiority complex.

WEDNESDAY 22ND JANUARY

Shopped all morning . . . . Lelia and I drove to lunch in the Legation car to Psychiko, passing the German Legation . . . . Princess Nicholas received us warmly, and although we were not late, the King was already there, and also the Crown Prince Paul,[2] who in Naval uniform was over-bejewelled, wearing several bracelets and rings. The Crown Prince has improved and is pretty but tentative. I like her, and see that she has immense character: her role may become extremely difficult. We were just the six. I reminded the Princess that the last time we met was a dinner party in Berlin at General Göring's where I sat next to her. She remembered. She is madly in love with her large husband who was formerly a friend of Peter's – in 1937. I was very amusing and in gentle, excellent spirits: everyone laughed and we stayed on until 4.30. The King never left me and gave me a huge photograph of himself signed in white ink. Then frantic shopping, and got my basuki gold links which I had had made. A cocktail party at Lilia's where Prince Philip came. He is very attractive.

All during luncheon we talked of Peter to my delight but somewhat to the Crown Prince's embarrassment. I said that Peter was known in Cairo as the 'Eminence Rose'. The King said he would arrange a meeting for me with General Metaxas: I didn't encourage him as my journey is not supposed to be 'official'. The King again talked of Mrs B[rittain]-Jones and I promised to do all I could to get her to Greece; but the Palairets were horrified and unhelpful when I mentioned it to them. However, I have sent back a letter to the FO which I hope will do the trick and send her out post-haste. The Monarch wants his morsel and must have it.

THURSDAY 23RD JANUARY

I sent P a cable in code that I should be returning to Cairo tomorrow and added 'try to arrange Palestine' as an inspired afterthought. He is such a wizard with people that he can do anything. Then I went back to the Legation to pack up and say 'goodbye' to the Palairets before going out to a huge dinner party arranged for me by Nelly Eliases and in her handsome house. Her rich husband is Governor of the

---

1 Of Yugoslavia.
2 Prince Paul of Greece (1901–64) succeeded his brother as King of the Hellenes in 1947.

Bank of Athens. It was a grand spectacle, about fifty people, some were bores. Good food and I was amusing – my high spirits continue – and then tomorrow there are Coats and Cairo. Mr Eliases wanted a résumé of the whole Windsor tapestry which I told him. At one o'clock I left . . . . My Athenian interlude has ended.

FRIDAY 24TH JANUARY

Got up early . . . . Drove to the Port of Piraeus, and how lovely it was, white against the blue sea. We soon boarded a Sunderland, a crock-plane: there was a crew of ten including four gunners. I was taken up to the cockpit and allowed to pilot the machine for a few moments – we rushed across Mitos and other islands. Constantly on the lookout for Italian – and even German – planes. We flew over Crete and I thought of Gambier-Parry reigning below. The most lovely flight of my life: and we came down in Alexandria about two o'clock. We were to leave for the grand aerodrome at four, and I drove about the town. When I returned one of my bags had disappeared and there was an appalling scrimmage and search. Inefficient ground staff had mislaid it; but at last it turned up and I was rushed at breakneck speed to catch a Lockheed which in no time whisked me to Cairo, where waiting below I saw the green Peridot[1] and Captain Coats, auburn and handsome.

He drove me to the Embassy . . . . Then we went to have a bath: there was the usual bother about dinner: would I dine with Their Excellencies, or out as I wanted to? The ADCs are vague but very helpful and they try to be tactful. At last I decided to have two dinners, shared one with the Ambassador and [his wife] Jac[queline], and when Peter came to fetch me – he had sent them a charming note meanwhile – I went out with him and dined again at Shepheard's.

Peter and I had a rapturous reunion and gossiped and I gave him a cornucopia of presents from Athens, basuki links I had had made for him; a handsome cornelian ring; an ikon, and, of course, the case earlier . . . . We sat in my huge room in the Embassy until all hours of the night and he told me that he had fixed it for Palestine: General Wavell had given him ten days' leave and Peter and I are off at dawn on Sunday. The world is a lovely, lovely place. Tobruk fell yesterday, and he had tried to delay its surrender, Peter laughed, to coincide with my return! Captured Italian generals, nine, I think, have poured in all day.

SATURDAY 25TH JANUARY

Spent most of the day fussing, packing, repacking and making arrangements for our flight out of Egypt tomorrow. About noon I walked out to the nearby Middle East Headquarters to have a drink with Peter and he arranged for me to see

---

1 Coats's name for his car, after the green gemstone.

General Wavell: he was shy this time and silent and made me so: yet I felt a wave of sympathy between us. He sits in a spartan office, Peter's room being the anteroom through which all must come . . . . The General curiously enough advised me to go to Palestine, said that Peter was going and then sat down and wrote a letter of introduction to General Neame,[1] the VC, who has the Palestinian Command. Lunched alone with the Lampsons who were charming. Jac . . . . complained of the meanness of Lady Wavell . . . encouraged, she hinted, by Peter. I defended him stonily. Tonight is the big gala of the Red Cross and troop comforts: Jac sent Lady Wavell a hundred tickets to sell and she returned all but four! The Wavells are simple folk, I explained, and not yet accustomed to *largesse*. However, I gave Jac a cheque for £100 to make up for Lady Wavell's delinquency and the Lampsons were impressed – I slept in the afternoon, wrote a few letters and cables. Hughie Northumberland arrived and we shopped and drank together.

I am looking forward to this expedition more than to anything in my life . . . . It will be a test of friendship.

SUNDAY 26TH JANUARY

The Departure for Cyrenaica began at dawn . . . I had come in, drunk, exhausted, and had to make some more frenzied arrangements at 4 a.m. and at 5.15 I was called and gobbled an excellent breakfast . . . . Then I crept down the stairs of the still dark and silent Embassy, and feeling like an eloping virgin, I stole into the drive. Peter drove up in his little green car which he gaily calls the Peridot; and our luggage was transported into a police car . . . . I promised to send it back immediately, as it was to take Hughie Northumberland to his watch. I said 'goodbye' to him as he bathed; he was vulpine and voluptuous and charming. P and I drove to Heliopolis and we soon embarked on a Lockheed . . . . We came down at Port Said where there was some delay and we walked about in the shiny sunlight and had a drink. Eventually we landed at the Jerusalem Aerodrome, which is some eighteen miles from the town; and we were met by untidy, officious Jews who spoke Bowery English. As I was not travelling officially, we were to be anonymously received. Soon we got into a car and drove through High Palestine. It seemed a fascinating country with its vineyards, sunlight, orange trees, goats, and hills, and the cypresses and towns reminded me of Calabria. At length the pale pink town of Jerusalem was before us with its dust and donkeys, its dark-eyed women and walls. We drove up to the

---

1 Philip Neame (1888–1978) joined the Army in 1908 and won the Victoria Cross at Neuve Chapelle in December 1914 after holding up a German advance single-handedly. He was awarded the DSO in 1916 and several times mentioned in dispatches. In 1924 he won a shooting gold medal in the Olympic Games, the only VC ever to do so. He was appointed General Officer Commanding Palestine in 1940 in the rank of lieutenant general, but in February 1941 was posted as GOC to Cyrenaica, and was taken prisoner by the Germans and sent to Italy, whence he was liberated in 1943. He was knighted in 1946.

King David and at once I fell in love with it: next to the Ritz in Paris it is the world's best hotel. We have a comfortable cosy suite overlooking the walls: it is warm, even balmy and there are precocious blossom trees already in bud. Opposite us is the Garden of Gethsemane and the Mount of Olives .... We had a delicious late lunch, then slept a little before going out into the town. It is bewildering, noisy, Arabs arguing, Jews bargaining, the Mouskys are a hive of life. We wandered about until the evening light fell upon the walls which seem to glow[1] .... I was moved .... Peter who has been here before, and who anyway always knows everything in the *guide de livre*,[2] and makes everything romantic, beautiful and glamorous with his gay erudite enthusiasm.

P and I dined in our sitting room. I shan't really keep a diary: I am too happy.

MONDAY 27TH JANUARY

We dawdled with our baths and had breakfast on the balcony in the warm sunshine, then dressed slowly, and went to the Mosque el Sharif:[3] the most peaceful place in Jerusalem, it is impressive and splendid. And we saw the Wailing Wall, and as I saw the unattractive Jews lamenting I wondered what would Hitler do to them, if he took Jerusalem, which I think quite probable.

Peter was busy on the telephone and has arranged with the Transjordan government for us to go there tomorrow to be their guests for three days. He is a skilled organiser. We dined *à deux* in our suite and talked of the Jaffa Gate and the imperial stillness of the Church of the Holy Sepulchre.

TUESDAY 28TH JANUARY

We left at 9.30, leaving our suite with some regret, and drove across part of Palestine, crossed the famous Allenby Bridge and were in Transjordan which is even more romantic – no Jews, less sophistication, and wilder country. [We drove] for many miles through wild and almost untouched country, occasionally we came upon a caravan – to Jerash, the ruined city. It is splendid in its decoration, and the ruins and remains are immensely impressive. We clambered about amongst the once stately temples, saw the mosaic-ed floors and frescos, took photographs and, at length, had an excellent picnic lunch in the Forum. Not a sound or a human broke the warm peaceful silence – what bliss was this .... We drove on to Amman, the old Philadelphia and were given drinks by a Transjordan grandee, then went for a drive, were shown the Emiral Palace (outside) .... Amman is primitive.

P and I slept together in the little hotel overlooking the Forum.

1 Coats has added 'with history'.
2 Guidebook.
3 He means the Al-Aqsa Mosque, on top of the Temple Mount, in a compound known as Haram esh-Sharif.

WEDNESDAY 29TH JANUARY

Peter and I got up early, had an icy bath together, and a huge breakfast . . . . After driving about the disappointing town [we] left for Shouneh to lunch with the Emir of Transjordan.[1] He is camping with his followers near the Dead Sea in a lovely position but the actual camp was disappointing, only a collection of a few tents. We were received by an ADC, and the Prime Minister, and conducted to the largest tent where His Highness awaited us. He is about 58, a large genial man with a beard and dressed in a blue robe. He is a great gentleman and has the grand manner!! We were placed on chairs, he occupying the centre one and conversation – and orange juice – flowed for an hour. The Minister of Education acted as interpreter and thus we had a time to think up the next compliment! The Emir is violently pro-British and was riveted by my accounts of the air raids etc. We made immediate friends and finally rising, before going off to pray, he removed a cornelian ring from his finger and put it on mine. 'Young man: this ring has been in the family of the prophet. Wear it: it will bring you luck.' I was thrilled but poor Peter looked dejected at getting nothing. Soon we walked to an adjoining tent, the Emir taking me by the hand, like a bride, the others following. Awaiting us were several sheiks who were presented to us! And a sumptuous repast began, the Emir and I were seated opposite each other and served simultaneously. Peter was on his left. Next to me was the local chieftain, a very grand Arab with a lustful face and painted eyelids, a character from Lawrence[2] . . . during lunch the conversation turned on to daggers and I said that Peter had tried to buy one whereupon the Emir with Eastern cunning and quickness ordered the ferocious and very virile Sheik next to me to present his to Peter, which he politely (but reluctantly) did! It is an old silver and gold one. P was enchanted and his day made! After luncheon the Emir took us into the sunlight once more and we inspected his Arab stallions . . . . He was delighted when I told him that the Egyptian Embassy had been bombed in London! He loathes Egyptians . . . . He tried to persuade me to stay on, said that Petra, which he had only once visited, was an appalling disappointment, etc. But P was not to be detained – and we took leave of His Highness who was all smiles and charms, and drove back to Amman where a curious trolley, a two-seated affair, awaited us. P and I sat on one seat, the Minister of Education on another: behind us crouched an armed guard – and we were off! The trip took four hours or more and was cold and dark. P and I huddled together We were actually on the famous Amman–Ma'an railway made so famous by T. E. Lawrence (who seems to

---

1 Abdullah I bin Al-Hussein (1882–1951) was Emir of Transjordan while it was a British protectorate from 1921 to 1946, and King of Jordan from then until his assassination in 1951. His father, Hussein bin Ali, had led the Great Arab Revolt against the Ottoman Empire in 1918 and Abdullah played a significant part in it.
2 T. E. Lawrence ('Lawrence of Arabia') (1888–1935). See Vol. I, entry for 25 May 1935 and footnote.

be an exploded myth in these parts). At Ma'an we were welcomed by fifty natives including the great Sheik and driven in the dark to the RAF mess where a fair young man, Pilot Officer Johnson, received us. P and I have a room, the Minister has another next door. It is cold and dark but we had an excellent dinner and much to drink and talked of England. It is a very outpost of Empire, this tiny remote aerodrome.

THURSDAY 30TH JANUARY

Peter and I woke early: it was cold; there was a frost. We dressed hurriedly, and after an excellent English breakfast of eggs and bacon we took leave of Pilot Officer Johnson. We motored for nearly two hours . . . . At last we arrived at a Foreign Legion-looking outpost of a place, a high white fortress . . . . Here we were given coffee, coffee, always coffee in the East, and then mounted our horses. No one hates horses as much as I: I even prayed that I should not fall or be terrified and I wasn't. We left at nine, a strange caravan. The country was lovely, but the road was winding and stony. We descended the whole way, and came at length to a sort of gorge where it was colder still. The overhanging rocks were pink-ish: I was, however, prepared to be disappointed. After some minutes in the tunnel we turned into the sunlight and before our eyes was a pink baroque basilica of great beauty. I gasped and pointed and we dismounted. It is breathtaking: sixteenth-century baroque in manner and recalls the Salute[1] or any grand Venetian church. Peter and I then photographed and photographed each other, scrambled about like goats, went into raptures: at last we left and continued our journey, passing more ruins, until we were *en plein*[2] Petra. To the right was a hill of carved out houses, resembling Pueblo ones, and there were more palaces, more temples. All was pink. The sun was out, the houses shone like tourmalines.[3] There was a vastness, a stillness, something frightening and yet a gay, aristocratic air of disdain and plenty and perfection . . . . I felt that we had reached the end of the Earth: the summit of earthly peace and paradise . . . . Again we dismounted and went for a longish walk, exploring more temples, doorways, caves and arches. We came upon a few natives who handed us coins and fragments and we, ourselves, found more. Meanwhile luncheon was being prepared for us, as we were the guests of the local Sheik by the orders of the Emir, who had himself telephoned last evening to Ma'an to inquire after our comfort. The Emirical splendour followed us. At last, a bit awed and amazed, we sat on a carpet surveying the classic scene – and we heard strange and plaintive shouts from high. They came, it was explained to us, from a fugitive from justice, a murderer who was pleading for mercy. He shouted from a high inaccessible rock

---

1 Santa Maria della Salute, a Venetian basilica of the seventeenth century on the Grand Canal.
2 In the heart of.
3 A gemstone displaying a spectrum of colour.

and I was sorry for him and frightened, too, that he might shoot us! At last he went away and we devoured a sheep – a very tasty dish, I thought. We plunged our fingers into it and made the best of the feast prepared in our honour. Then I took P aside and we had a little conference: it had been arranged for us to sleep at Amman where we should arrive at about 10 p.m. – a considerable feat. Why, I whispered, if we could get to Amman, why shouldn't we go to Jerusalem and sup at midnight in the King David? Peter, patient, perfect, and pleasure-loving, instantly agreed . . . . Reluctantly, we left Petra, its pinkness, its queer atmosphere of elegance, and light-hearted disdain, its remoteness, and rode back – and I wondered, should I ever come to Petra again, and would it be, as I should like, with Peter? Somehow I saw my son in the picture, perhaps I should bring him . . . . We paused before the pink cathedral . . . and then continued. All was arranged like clockwork. We left on horses, got into the car for an hour's drive, went in Ma'an to the Sheik's house – a voluptuous affair: (the doorknobs of the houses in Ma'an are shaped like hands), found the trolley awaiting us, and started off in the gloaming for Amman. We were told it was dangerous as we had so small a guard. It was v cold: Peter and I snuggled together and fell asleep. For four hours we jogged, mostly in the darkness. At Amman we found a huge car, we bought whisky and food, and set forth to Jerusalem. The Palestinian–Transjordan frontier had been kept open for us and we raced over the Allenby Bridge and arrived safely and gaily at the King David by about midnight. No one, we were told, ever has got back to Jerusalem from Petra in one day: it was soothing to be luxurious, to have a bath, and we sank blissfully into bed . . . ecstatically content and pleased with our fantastically successful expedition – the happiest day of my life is ending . . . .

FRIDAY 31ST JANUARY

We slept until ten and woke with the sun pouring in. I nudged P who laughingly, tauntingly remarked that he would sleep all day. We had a merry bath, went out onto our bedroom balcony and wallowed in a luxurious breakfast. The walls opposite were drenched in sunlight and we took many photographs of each other . . . . No two people can ever have known such happiness, such blissful content . . . We walked about the town and did some amateur shopping – Peter is a professional. He is a professional at everything and gladdens the atmosphere as he delights the eye and entrances the mind. For over forty years I have searched for such a companion and now I have him, and mean to keep him . . .

We lunched late, ran into a pleasant friend of Peter's, and in the afternoon drove to Bethlehem. The scene of the nativity disappointed me but there was a lovely wrought-iron gate leading into a small disused sunlit cloister; and there were little houses and poor shops where we bought trinkets, a nacre box etc. Then we drove around Jerusalem in the gloaming and – surprise – signed the book in the Government House.

Dined alone in pyjamas and made plans for after the war – decided to do nothing for a very long time, indeed.

SATURDAY 1ST FEBRUARY

We went to the Garden of Gethsemane and to Mary's tomb, and later we drove to the Dead Sea where we lunched, after bathing in the curious buoyant water . . . . Drove back to the suite and slept, and after tea went for another walk. We dressed and drove to Government House to dine . . . . The MacMichael[1] family I found, at first, boring, even hostile which may have been due to my day clothes – I left everything in Cairo . . . later he [the High Commissioner] led me into his study and I discovered to my great surprise that he is Lord Curzon's nephew. We sat and swapped Curzon stories until midnight whilst Peter chatted with the MacMichaels – then home. Other people are bores. Why see them?

SUNDAY 2ND FEBRUARY

A long, long day. We drove to Tel-Aviv which I thought horrible, a Jew-infested resort overlooking the lovely blue sea, it reminded me somehow of Berlin in 1928 with its squalor and rude, unattractive people. I am anti-Semite.[2] We lost the car, had drinks, found it again, shopped in vain, saw nothing but a plate of my Dresden dinner service, which I bought, and then drove on to Haifa where we lunched at Spinney's after running into a few friends including Linley Messel,[3] who is now a colonel. Peter showed me where he had been stationed those first few anxious days when he arrived in the Middle East before a magic wand had wafted him to the Wavells – the luckiest thing that has ever happened.

About five we left to look up Henry Weymouth,[4] who is stationed with the Wiltshire Yeomanry in a wadi[5] near Nazareth. As we drove up an orderly addressed me by name and I recognised little Donald, his ex-servant, who asked us into the officers' mess, where we warmly received and given drinks whilst we waited for an hour for Henry who did not come . . . he was out duck shooting. As he

---

1 Harold Alfred MacMichael (1882–1969) served in Sudan for almost thirty years until 1933, when he became Governor of Tanganyika. He served until 1938, when he became High Commissioner of Palestine, where he served until 1944. His mother was Curzon's elder sister. He married, in 1919, Agnes 'Nesta' de Sivrac Edith Stephens (1888–1974). He wrote extensively on Sudan. He was knighted in 1931.

2 See note for 1 November 1938.

3 Linley Francis Messel (1899–1971). From 1942 to 1944 he was General Staff Officer at GHQ of the Mediterranean Expeditionary Force. He was the older brother of Anne and Oliver Messel (qqv).

4 Henry Frederick Thynne (1905–92), by courtesy Viscount Weymouth until he succeeded his father as 6th Marquess of Bath in 1946. In 1927 he married Daphne Vivian (qv).*

5 Valley.

didn't arrive we drove back to Jerusalem and dined late and well on Guinness and champagne.

If ever the Germans take Tel-Aviv, and I think that they will, it will be a holiday for them – what would become of the thousands of Jews who think themselves so secure?

MONDAY 3RD FEBRUARY

Our last day, and slightly overcast by the sadness of parting and separating .... We made arrangements. Shopped and entertained Henry Weymouth, who motored three hours to see me on hearing of our visit to his barracks yesterday .... P and I had a rapturous afternoon .... blissful yet wretched. Nothing can even touch this Palestinian episode . . . And we went back to the Holy Sepulchre where I prayed on the tomb of the Saviour, prayed for my little faraway boy, and prayed that Peter would be safe, unscathed by the war – this horrible war which I had forgotten for a fortnight.

We dined and packed and wept and went to bed.

TUESDAY 4TH FEBRUARY

We left the hotel at 10.15 .... In intense heat we drove to the aerodrome .... At Cairo there was no one to meet us, and I had a sulker that we were not expected. I longed to stay at Shepheard's. However, I rang up the Embassy and was told that a room had been prepared and that the ADCs had muddled the meeting. So I returned there and found a house party arriving .... I dined in, a dull dinner party. As I arrived I ran into the Lampsons, who are charming to me and I accompanied them to the zoo.

When P and I arrived we commandeered Joan Khan's car and had no compunction in being driven to Shepheard's! There we had a last nervous lunch together: I was distraught at leaving there. He returned to his office and later rang us up to say that all was well. He had been much missed.

I have indigestion and am liverish. Running into Joan Khan I noticed how pale and unhappy and harassed she looks: I fear that her brave and unorthodox marriage is breaking up. Ali, her dark Prince, has long been notoriously unfaithful to her but until recently he was kind, and on the surface, devoted; now I fear he is trampling her on all sides and is rude and irritable at home, bored with her. What can the future hold for poor Joan, an English girl, a Guinness divorcée, now caught in the toils of the East?

WEDNESDAY 5TH FEBRUARY

Got up late, dressed and wrote letters and talked several times to Peter, who sounded *affairé*: it is amazing that he is not spoilt (and the Ambassadress assures me that she has heard on all sides that he is: I doubt it); but he gets tired nervously and has immense responsibilities. There is some friction between the two rival courts: the Wavells and the Lampsons. The Lampsons have more *habitude du monde*,[1] but inefficient but very wise ADCs. Peter said he would meet me at Shepheard's at 3.30 but sent a frantic message that he was on duty. I lunched in with the Lampsons. There was only Lord Oxford,[2] a stormy intellectual youth whom [*sic*], I heard, is in love with Miss Palairet[3] who is as tall and ever more tiresome. Both ardent convert Catholics . . . . Jacqueline and I went shopping and later we drove in some state to a cocktail party given on a barge by General and Lady Blamey.[4] Here I met many Australians and Egyptians etc., and I was warmly received by Lady Wavell whom I like. She is a vague, motherly, bosomy, lazy, humorous creature with turquoise eyes: the General calls her 'Queenie' because her name is Eugenie and she is a god-daughter of the old Empress . . . . The General is more charming, more cultured, more silent – a very rare bird, indeed, and a genius.

There was an immense dinner party at the Embassy to meet Mr Menzies,[5] the Australian Prime Minister. He is jolly, rubicund, witty, only 46 and has a rapier-like intelligence and the gift of a raconteur.

I didn't see Peter alone all day and missed his gay insouciance. But it was lovely to be in the luxury of the Embassy again, and Spencer the butler is my slave. He is the nicest man I ever knew and the most efficient. P and I are going to have him after the war at Kelvedon.

It is so soothing, so pleasant to be luxurious, to have twenty-four people to dine with wines and rich food. Decidedly I was not made for simple life. I had a talk with the Egyptian Prime Minister[6] and liked his Edwardian manners and pro-English sentiments . . . I bought knick-knacks for Peter and pressed them

---

1 Familiarity with society.

2 Julian Edward George Asquith (1916–2011) succeeded his grandfather as 2nd Earl of Oxford and Asquith in 1928. He served in Egypt with the Royal Engineers from 1940 to 1942 and then as an Assistant District Commissioner in Palestine until 1948, before spending the rest of his career as a senior colonial administrator.

3 Anne Mary Celestine Palairet (1916–98) married the 2nd Earl Asquith (*vide supra*) in 1947. During the war she worked for a time as a code breaker at Bletchley Park.

4 Thomas Albert Blamey (1884–1951) joined the Australian Army in 1906, was a staff officer in the Dardanelles and ended the Great War as a brigadier general. In the Second World War he commanded the Second Australian Imperial Force in the Middle East and would soon play a key part in the Allied defeat in the Battle of Greece. He returned to Australia and fought in the Far Eastern campaign, signing the Japanese surrender document in 1945. He was promoted to field marshal in 1950. He was knighted in 1935. He married, in 1939, as his second wife Olga Ora Farnsworth (1902–67), a fashion designer.

5 Robert Gordon Menzies (1894–1978) was one of the towering figures of twentieth-century Australian politics. He was Prime Minister from 1939 to 1941, Leader of the Opposition until 1949, and then Prime Minister until 1966.

6 Hussein Serry Pasha (1894–1960) was three times Prime Minister of Egypt, from 1940 to 1942, from 1949 to 1950 and for three weeks in 1952. I have been unable to find any details of his wife, whom Channon mentions later.

into his pockets at the cocktail party on the barge. The Lampsons took me on to another party at the [Gezira] Club where we met the Wavells arriving, escorted by Peter. They were cheered. They were like two rival royal parties.

Sun, oranges, corruption, ease, bad taste, heat, dazzling shops – how I love Cairo. It is the occidental-ised East, without the filth of the usual Eastern town. I should live here after the war, if we win it, which I think extremely doubtful in spite of the thousands of Italian prisoners, including generals, captured every day.

THURSDAY 6TH FEBRUARY

I walked around to Middle East Headquarters and we[1] had a drink together in the officers' canteen. He was charming, very charming. Had taken a liver pill from what he calls 'the Cat' – laxative pills which he takes about with him in an exquisite Dresden cat .... Then I went .... to lunch at the Yugoslav Legation. An airy spacious house on the other side of the Nile. A huge party, the Prime Minister of Egypt and Mme Serry, General and Lady Wavell, many more including P. I was next to Longmore, which I liked: I made him roar with laughter. Food excellent .... Then I was closeted with the Prime Minister for some time as the Yugoslav Minister .... hovered about me. I was treated (as usual) like a Yugoslav royalty .... Lampson agreed to send me to Tobruk and Sidi Barrani[2] in an RAF plane .... I am not sure that I want very much to go; but I ought. Then I went back, after some shopping, to the Embassy to sleep for a little ....

Cocktails with Freya Stark in her apartment over the Nile. She is an original ... speaks Arabic well, is popular amongst the natives; dresses eccentrically; hasn't a hair on her head;[3] dances with pansy young men.

P fetched me at nine o'clock and we went to dine .... at Shepheard's. Peter drove me home and we made a detour and parked the car for a little in the moonlight by the Nile and he made a curious confession. Back to the Embassy at 1 a.m. If only this glorious sunlit love life could go on forever .... But I must get back to England. I have had no news, only cables from Alan, my father-in-law and Rab. What strange surprises await me in London, what horrors, and what loneliness.

I wish I were back in Jerusalem.

FRIDAY 7TH FEBRUARY

My departure seems delayed again: I feel and fear that I ought to get back to England. Meanwhile the victories continue and we become correspondingly more popular .... I walked to the Middle East Headquarters, stayed and had a

---

1 He and Coats.
2 Not in that order, as one reaches Sidi Barrani first when travelling west from Cairo.
3 Miss Stark (qv) lost her right ear and part of her scalp in an accident while visiting an Italian factory when she was 13.

drink with Peter, and then went shopping, and had some drinks at Shepheard's Hotel with 'the Boys'. I didn't tell them that Benghazi had been captured late last night – at ten to twelve. Peter had whispered the news to me as I arrived . . . . I forgot for several minutes to tell Lady Wavell about Benghazi. Nor could she believe it! 'But Archie doesn't know,' she said . . . . And it was true that the Generalissimo did not know as he had left at 4.30 a.m. A dispatch rider had been sent off by Peter to tell him the good news . . . .

Afternoon drink in Cairo . . . . Suddenly I felt nervous and liverish as I did once at Salzburg and the room went a bit black. I decided to walk home to the Embassy via the Wavells' where there was a cocktail party for Mr Menzies and to celebrate the fall of Benghazi. However I lost my way, got very hot and confused and increasingly bad-tempered, and got back to the Embassy only at eight o'clock where I met the Lampsons coming in . . . . We dined late, Charles Wood; Hughie Northumberland with whom I am very *lié*,[1] – he is just my affair were it not for P – . . . . Charles Wood long, lazy, charming, gently treacherous like his father. A pleasant evening: I like diplomatic life at the top. This Embassy is extremely well staffed.

I had a whiff of annoyance with Peter both yesterday and today but realise, or at least should, that I am to blame. I am so jealous, so possessive of his friendship and forget how hard-working and important he is.

SATURDAY 8TH FEBRUARY

The capital is *en fête* celebrating the fall of Benghazi. Already there is much Italian loot about: Chianti is bought quite cheaply. I had my morning drink with P, shopped, and met him again at Shepheard's where we had a cocktail . . . . We spent the afternoon there gossiping and planning our new life.

SUNDAY 9TH FEBRUARY

We drove to Air House to dine with Longmore, who had a banquet which began by being a small dinner for me. I was next to Tedder[2] and Wavell who was silent

---

1 Close, friendly.
2 Arthur William Tedder (1890–1967) had fought with distinction with the Royal Flying Corps during the Great War. He held a number of senior posts in the RAF between the wars, becoming Air Officer Commanding in the Far East in 1936. He joined the Ministry of Aircraft Production in 1940 but fell out with Beaverbrook and was thus disregarded by Churchill; when Channon met him he was Deputy Air Officer Commanding RAF Middle East Command, with the acting rank of air marshal. He took over the command in June 1941, was knighted in 1942 and was promoted to air chief marshal the following July. He was instrumental in the victory at El Alamein and was given charge of Mediterranean Air Command in 1943, helping plan the invasion of Italy and then the following year the Normandy invasion. In 1945 he was promoted to marshal of the Royal Air Force and was raised to the peerage as 1st Baron Tedder in 1946.

and bored at first. He sits quietly and then thaws. I noticed that he focuses badly unlike most people with one eye, and he upsets things. He was charming, almost affectionate to me . . . . A most distinguished party indeed! The whole Middle East and yet I would rather have dined with Peter – who regretted not being asked. After dinner we listened to the Prime Minister's broadcast[1] which was well received, particularly the references to the Middle East. Wavell, who knew what was coming, hid behind a doorway. As the Churchillian compliments were handed out that magnificent language seemed rather forced, almost comic. I was embarrassed as the only English politician present. When the broadcast ended Wavell came and sat down next to me and we had a long conversation and I saw how loveable and gently distinguished he is . . . . He began about Peter . . . . Could I not get him a seat in Parliament, he asked. I didn't say that I had long ago decided to do that! People, particularly the great, like to foster their own ideas so I pretended to be surprised and agreed that it was an excellent plan. Together, surely, we could do it, the General said . . . . His charm completely engulfed me. After an hour Menzies rose and the party broke up, General Wavell offering to drive me back to the Embassy, but I refused politely as I was already going with the Prime Minister of Australia . . . .

MONDAY 10TH FEBRUARY

Only a few more days . . . it is decided: I am to fly with Menzies and Donovan.[2] I ought to be thrilled; instead I am bored by the prospect of such close proximity with the great. We leave on Thursday, probably. I am broken-hearted . . . . The entire Egyptian episode has been enthralling and successful beyond every expectation . . . . I dressed luxuriously, having had breakfast overlooking the sunlit Nile, I wept. Perhaps the happiest phase of my life is ending and I must return to the nightmare of my English existence, my horrible wanton wife; the absence of my child; the threat of invasion; Eden at the Foreign Office and Churchill all supreme – what a vista. Perhaps I shall be killed *en route* . . . . I read in the newspapers that we have broken off all diplomatic relations with Romania. . . . . To [the] Gezira Club where Peter was awaiting me. He showed me over the famous Club, led me through the notorious changing rooms. Then it came on to rain and we retreated to Caliban's Cave for *un quart d'heure* before driving

---

1 In which Churchill exhorted the United States to increase its supplies of materiel with the phrase 'give us the tools and we will finish the job'.
2 William Joseph Donovan (1883–1959), an American, had been highly decorated in the Great War, which he finished as a colonel. He practised as a lawyer between the wars and in 1940 became an informal envoy of Roosevelt's to key foreign theatres of war, and from 1942 to 1945 he ran the Office of Strategic Services, the forerunner of the Central Intelligence Agency.

to Prince Mohammed Ali's[1] Palace, where we were received like royalty. The Prince is nearly 70, was formerly the Regent, and is now the Crown Prince of Egypt. He is noted for his Anglomania. The Palace is in the Egyptian-Turkish style and he keeps up considerable state. Several secretaries bowed us in and His Highness welcomed us. He was in morning dress but wore his tarboosh[2] and a Scottish tartan tie and socks which lent a fantastic note. He led us into a little room where we had coffee and then he began to talk and gossip. There seemed no limit to his garrulity. He knew the old Iveaghs, Mrs Greville and King Edward; he thinks Lampson weak with the present King, his cousin, whom he loathes, and in general attacked the Cairo Court as upstartish and pro-Italian. Nor does he like the Prime Minister or the Serry influence. He is out of the picture at present but is well aware that His Majesty's Government might at any moment dethrone young Farouk and make him king. After an hour's astonishingly frank monologue he led us into his well-kept gardens to the museums he has built at great expense. He is immensely rich. One houses china, silver, and a fine collection of carpets (and how I hate carpets: I can hardly be in the room with one) while the other is a palace which recalled the Mad Ludwig[3] for he has built a throne room, ballroom and sumptuous bedrooms with silver bedsteads etc. None are ever used. I was a bit *ébloui*[4] by their lavish hideousness, but really liked them. Then we returned to the palace which he occupies, and on the first floor in a series of vitrines are his most valued treasures, his mother's jewels, ruby and emerald cups, snuffboxes and *bibelots*, mostly Turkish. I thought at one moment he was about to give Peter and me a present; but his Scottish instinct goes further than a penchant for tartan! Dazzled and tired, P and I at last took leave of the Prince, this great gentleman, the *grand seigneur* of the East.

Tuesday 11th February

Lunch with Freya Stark alone at Shepheard's. She had come from Alexandria to see me and was quaintly dressed – she had pushed her car, run into a lorry etc.... She is an extraordinary woman, and English eccentric certainly with an Italian touch from having lived so long in Italy. She is devoted to my in-laws. We made great friends.... Eventually P came back to the Embassy with me. We dined in (at the Embassy), a disreputable party, I thought, as I was annoyed with Mrs Fuller[5]

---

1 Mohammed Ali Tewfik (1875–1955) was King Farouk's heir presumptive, and in 1936–7 had been Regent during Farouk's minority. He was the son of Khedive Tewfik I.
2 Tasselled hat resembling a fez.
3 King Ludwig II of Bavaria (1845–86), known for his extravagant architectural projects, and on whose family Channon had written his 1933 book.
4 Dazzled.
5 I can find no trace of Mrs Fuller: no diplomat of that name whose wife she might have been was in Cairo at the time, nor a senior soldier; nor is anyone of that name mentioned in Coats's memoirs.

who was rude about Peter to me. She was vitriolic about everyone . . . . We all went on *en bande*[1] to a film and came home late. I was exhausted. She calls Peter 'Peter Pansy!'

An unexpected morning: I was still in my bath when the Crown Prince of Egypt was announced. I flung on some clothes and came down to receive His Highness who was in a frock coat. *Une visite de cérémonie*,[2] indeed. But he stayed for two hours and as he left begged me to send him Scottish socks and ties from a Kensington shop . . . . All Cairo is talking of Prince Mohammed Ali's paternal visit to me!

WEDNESDAY 12TH FEBRUARY

It is still a secret about Anthony [Eden]'s arrival;[3] and now Donovan declares that he will wait over and see him. Anthony arrives at any moment . . . He is making a mistake in not cabling me to remain, as I could help him in consolidating his Balkan front, an improbable scheme, I fear. The Regent loathes him; the King of Greece dislikes him; the Romanians and Bulgarians are gone – will he knobble the Turks?

THURSDAY 13TH FEBRUARY

My last day was correctly 'Coats Day'. He has been angelic, a miracle of tact and sweetness . . . foreseeing, anticipating my every wish and falling in with my every scheme or whim . . . . I didn't meet him until luncheon time as I packed, wrote letters until 11.15 when, accompanied by Mme Serry, the gay alert wife of the Prime Minister, Bob Menzies (the Australian Prime Minister) and I went shopping in the Mousky. We had two amusing hours together and I piloted them to the best shops. Menzies wanted to buy a present for his wife and at last decided upon an emerald brooch in the shape of a peacock. There was much Eastern haggling and at last I got him for £45. He was enchanted and roared with laughter as I was called 'Excellency' everywhere . . . Mme Serry dropped me at Shepheard's where I met Peter and we lunched sadly together. Charles Wood was at the next table . . . . Then we went to Caliban's Cave for our farewells; both were in tears. When shall I see him again, or ever be so happy? This fantastic Egyptian expedition is coming to an end, the gayest, most exquisite, most elegant episode in my life . . . . Went to the Wavells' and had a brief tea with Lady Wavell and said 'goodbye'. Peter rushed off on some mysterious commission and I was sent back to the Embassy alone in the C-in-Chief's car. Peter soon joined me, and looked at my things. We drank

---

1 In a gang.
2 An official visit.
3 Eden visited Turkey, Egypt, Greece and the Balkans to try to construct an anti-Axis front in the region: German momentum and local weakness were too powerful.

with Donovan and the ADCs. I returned to my room and put my platinum and diamond cylindrical links in my pocket and Peter drove me to the Wavells' as he wanted to fetch his coat. I pressed the links, which Laura [Corrigan] gave me years ago, into his hands . . . and then we drove to Meira House where we dined dramatically *à deux*. Had champagne and pleaded eternal fidelity. He said that he was a member of the Church of England and in old days dyed his hair – he has had *une jeunesse scabreuse*,[1] I fear. Now he is domesticated which he always was *au fond*; and he remains gay and distinguished and delightful. We came out of the hotel about 10 p.m. and it was full moonlight. We drove the car to the barrier of the Pyramids and left it. Then we walked about for an hour in the silver moonlight, arm in arm, panting, affectionate, a bit drunk . . . and came to the Sphinx with its terrible, sinister beauty, alone, immense in a deserted sea of moonlight. I went cold with emotion and horror. It was stupendous . . . sadly, coldly, we left and wandered back to the car and drove to Caliban's Cave for another hour – the last, perhaps, for all time. Shall I ever see him again, except perhaps in the morning?

I crept in at the Embassy. It was 2 a.m. and everyone, Menzies, Donovan, the Lampsons had all gone to bed. The most terrific day of my life.

FRIDAY 14TH FEBRUARY, ST VALENTINE'S DAY

I got up at five, after a brief nap, and in my dressing gown went along to say 'goodbye' to Miles Lampson who was already having coffee in his little sitting room. He was going out shooting: we said an affectionate farewell. We like and understand each other, certainly . . . . then I dressed and breakfasted, packed, gave Spencer £10 and came down. Peter, sleek and sleepy, was waiting for me and I decided to go away in his car . . . . A few frantic notes of farewell had to be written . . . . I stepped into P's green car, and he, pale, silent, and fascinating drove me slowly to Heliopolis . . . . No farewell has ever been so horrible. 'Put your hand in my pocket,' he said; and I found a gold pencil engraved 'St Valentine's Day 1941', and a tiny religious box he had bought in Bethlehem which contained a coin we had found in Petra and two seeds from Jarash. 'Plant them,' he said. At Heliopolis Aerodrome we found Menzies and his suite of two . . . . and Longmore, the A[ir] C[hief] Marshal lined up to see us off . . . Before eleven we were off. P saluted smartly and I saw the khaki figure which soon became a pathetically tiny speck – as the Lockheed sped away. I collapsed, and tried to doze . . . . I had left Coats and Cairo and my [illegible] behind me . . . . We passed over the Pyramids and I thought of how I had seen them in different circumstances only a few hours before.

---

1 *Scabreuse* is literally 'dirty', but Channon implies a reckless or misspent youth.

About 2.30 we arrived at Khartoum where we were met by the Governor, Sir Hugh [*sic*] Huddleston[1] .... We were whisked off to the Palace and rested for two hours and then had tea on the lawn of the Palace. It is huge, Kitchener's demesne, but there is no real splendour. Kitchener lived here for years, on the actual site of Gordon's house, with his hand-picked ADCs. The heat is terrific. In the evening we walked, Their Excellencies, Menzies, and I along the Blue Nile ... and then I darted into the hotel to inquire of Francis Lennox-Boyd but he had gone. He left me a sad note and many letters to take back.

A pompous dinner party of about thirty. I was bored, distracted. I would never accept a governorship: it is the soul of horror. Not even India, I think. Honor is right for once. Bed exhausted.

SATURDAY 15TH FEBRUARY

Their Excellencies left at dawn today on a long-ago arranged tour of their Empire which they had delayed for one day to welcome us. We thus had the cool huge barracky place to ourselves. At ten o'clock I came down as the Crown Prince of Abyssinia[2] and his younger brother – Peter's friend – the Duke of Harar,[3] called upon me. They were in white duck suits and v polite and distinguished, and spoke good English. The younger one was at Wellington.[4] Actually I liked the elder better: they looked like a couple of overdressed piccaninnies from Carolina! Then I wrote long letters to P and other favourite Pashas in Cairo, and sent them back by the military bag.

Lunched in, and then slept until four o'clock when Howell[5] and I drove to the great market at Omdurman. We wandered about the Bazaar and I bought a silver cigarette box for Honor, a cigarette case for P, which I left for him with Howell 'in case' he passed that way – as he often does, and an ashtray for myself ... I have the bedroom usually assigned to General Wavell overlooking the Blue Nile. In it I found *The Widow and Her Son* by Hector Bolitho.

1 Hubert Jervoise Huddleston (1880–1950) joined the Army in 1898 and fought in the Second Boer War and the Great War (winning the DSO and Bar, and the MC) before becoming General Officer Commanding Sudan in 1924. He served in India from 1934 to 1938 and was briefly GOC Northern Ireland in 1940, when he was knighted, before being appointed Governor-General of Anglo-Egyptian Sudan, a post in which he served until 1947. He retired in the rank of major general.
2 Asfaw Wossen Tafari (1916–97) became Crown Prince of Ethiopia when his father, the Emperor Haile Selassie (qv), succeeded in 1930. He remained in exile until his father's restoration later in 1941; abroad for medical treatment when his father was overthrown in 1974, he succeeded him as Emperor-in-Exile with the name Amha Selassie, holding that title until his death.
3 Prince Makonnen Haile Selassie (1924–57) became Duke of Harar on his father's accession. He would be killed in a car crash.
4 Wellington College, in Berkshire.
5 Paul Howell (1917–94), a young officer from Epping, near Kelvedon, who was serving as Sir Hubert's ADC.

SUNDAY 16TH FEBRUARY

The Crown Prince of Abyssinia and his little dark curly-haired ducal brother again called this morning . . . . They entrusted bulky letters to me to deliver to the Ethiopian Empress[1] living still at Bath. And I shopped. More people to lunch . . . it is really extraordinary that not one of them, not even the government ADC, should ever have heard of Francis Lennox-Boyd who was stationed at Khartoum for months and months . . . he is dull, a bore and inoperative and resembles Alan only physically and his foolish adoration of that awful vampire of a mother.

We took off at 1.40, and the Sudanese government lined up to see us off: I read and finished the first vol. of *Les Liaisons Dangereuses* which P had given me. The PM dozed all afternoon. I thought of my appalling problems. Menzies is sympathetic, highly intelligent, but he looks much more than his 47 years.[2] He overeats and drinks.

At 4.20 we landed at El Fasher where I had been – again on a Sunday – on Dec 29th. We were met by the local Governor, Mr Ingleson[3] and taken to his house to tea and then walked through the souks. This time I did not buy a gazelle carpet. Dined with the Inglesons and heard over the excellent wireless that the *Clyde*, the Sunderland in which I flew out, had crashed in a hurricane at Lisbon. Shall we be delayed, perhaps for a fortnight at Lagos? We were unable to communicate and went to bed hoping for the best. Menzies thinks that the government will send out a special Sunderland, or perhaps that the secret plane bringing out Anthony will come around to Lagos for us. I am sorry about the *Clyde*, my Cupid's Chariot – but the Captain, Travers, is hopeless . . . .

The Inglesons gave us an excellent dinner and we are in the midst of nowhere. El Fasher is a romantic and attractive place. Menzies has the only guest room and I am sleeping, as before, in the guest house. The heat is intense. Ingleson is a success and I mean to push him . . . .

MONDAY 17TH FEBRUARY

We left El Fasher at six and flew across the desert, coming down at Fort Lamy in Free Frog Land.[4] I fear I am v anti-Free Frogs. We lunched with the Governor at Kano in great heat and I drove with Menzies into the highly picturesque native city. He took many photographs and then we left for Lagos.

---

1 Empress Menen Asfaw, *née* Walatta Giyorgis (1891–1962), married in 1911 as her fourth husband Ras Tafari, later Haile Selassie (qv). She was the niece of the then heir to the Abyssinian throne, Lij Iyasu.
2 He was 46 (as Channon correctly states in the entry for 5 February 1941).
3 Philip Ingleson (1892–1985) joined the Sudan political service in 1919, having fought in the Great War (in which he won the Military Cross). He was Governor of Darfur Province from 1935 to 1944. He married, in 1921, Gwendoline Fulton (1896–1986).
4 Chad.

We were met by the Governor . . . . and whisked off to bathe and shave and rest. I slept for three hours. The heat is unbelievable . . . . The disaster to the *Clyde* doesn't affect us, as we leave by the *Clare* at dawn.

TUESDAY 18TH FEBRUARY

We left, or were supposed to, at 7 a.m. directly it was light. Government House muddled and nearly spoilt the departure: cars and launches were late and took off at 8 a.m. All day in the air: I dozed . . . we came down at Bathurst to refuel and there was some doubt as to whether we should go on. We took off again at 6.45 with only five minutes of light left. We were soon over Dakar; and I dined well with Menzies and finally fell asleep. The *Clare* is comfortable and well run by Captain May. Menzies is genial, garrulous, given to whisky and gossip . . . . He has a rapier-like tongue and is a raconteur of some merit. I like him definitely . . . . he abused Eden and poor Brendan Bracken. He doesn't intend, he repeated, to be 'blitzed by Winston'; but he will be!

WEDNESDAY 19TH FEBRUARY

A dreadful day, really, overcrowded and exhausting . . . and I am reluctant to return to beleaguered Britain. We arrived in the Lisbon bay before nine o'clock, having dozed most of the night. Lying like a dead swan was the *Clyde*, which overturned in a tempest a few days ago. I had almost an affection for that boat! As we landed I saw at once that <u>no</u> preparations whatever had been made to receive us. Everywhere else there had been officials and red carpets, but here, as usual, the Lisbon Embassy did nothing. The Prime Minister of Australia was allowed to land like any ordinary traveller. Luckily I had my *laissez-passer* given me by the Portuguese Ambassador in London: thanks only to it our luggage was not examined. Menzies, hungry, unshaved and affronted, was in a bullish rage. I tried to calm him by ringing up the Embassy: there was no reply. At last we got into a car, Menzies and I, and drove to Estoril where no rooms had been reserved. I made a row and procured one which we shared for a few hours . . . whilst he bathed I slipped below and rang up Noel Charles[1] and told him the situation. Later Menzies and I had breakfast together and Charles, sleek and chic and apologetic, arrived. The Embassy had been caught napping. I slept for a little and then drove to Lisbon to shop and to pray but did neither. The churches are dank and dark, the shops denuded of anything good. The Estoril Hotel is full of spies,

---

1 Noel Hughes Havelock Charles (1891–1975) joined the Diplomatic Service in 1919 after serving in the Great War (in which he won the Military Cross and was twice mentioned in dispatches). He was Minister at Lisbon from 1940 to 1941, Ambassador to Brazil from 1941 to 1944, High Commissioner to Italy from 1944 to 1947, and Ambassador to Turkey from 1949 to 1951. He succeeded his elder brother as 3rd Bt in 1936 and was knighted in 1941.

impoverished grandees and nondescript people, including Rothschilds and rich refugees trying to get to England or America. I ran into Bertha Michelham[1] who seemed more mad than ever; she was surrounded by a covey of grandees, Spanish and French . . . . Half the Embassy is here, too, and all seemed pro-British.

. . . . I wanted to see Queluz[2] and drove there. The Palace is a dream of pink paradisiacal beauty, like a seraphim asleep . . . The sophisticated garden, the tiered statues, the tiled canals, all too Rococo and beautiful: it makes the Trianon[3] tawdry, even Bruchsal[4] seem rough. Aged Infantas still inhabit the wings. I was in a daze, the heat, the pinkness, the faded splendour . . . back to bathe and drink cocktails with the Australian Prime Minister and then I drove him to the Embassy. He was still angry, but Sir Ronnie Campbell mollified him. Lady Campbell greeted me as an old friend and we had a delightful dinner party: I was between the Ambassadors and Lady Charles,[5] a blonde *mondaine* woman who begged me to get them moved on . . . . After Rome and the Palazzo Colonna they are bored by Lisbon.[6] Menzies twitted me throughout the evening and Campbell joined in. 'I hear that Firth had to leave Cairo when Chips conquered it,' he laughed. Firth is the American Minister here. A little man whom I met in Cairo dining with Wavell and Lampson: he has only just been transferred!

Lisbon is rather lovely but dull and it is ablaze with light. We drove home in the cool evening air – our great trek is over.

THURSDAY 20TH FEBRUARY

I was called at five and drove alone to [the] airport as Menzies was not yet up. A long wait for him, the luggage and the light. There was some doubt about the matter and whether we should get off. However, we did before eight – and all the way back to England I wondered, what disappointments, what problems, what difficulties will I find awaiting me? No matter what happens – and it may be much – I shall have had one of the happiest most successful and glamorous trips of my life. And I owe it to Peter who was the *animateur* and to both Rab and Harold who made it possible . . . .

The excitement of Menzies' Australian entourage was touching to see as they approached England for the first time. We came down at Poole and were met by the same officials who saw me off on December 17th. The Kangaroo party

1 Bertha Isabella Susanna Flora Capel (1874–1961), married in 1919 Herman Alfred Stern (1900–84), who that year succeeded his father as 2nd Baron Michelham. Her name is sometimes cited as 'Berthe', which it was not.

2 A seaside palace of the Portuguese royal family, built in the eighteenth century.

3 An opulent palace near Versailles built by Louis XIV in 1670–2.

4 A massive baroque palace in Baden-Württemberg, near the German border with France, built as the seat of the prince-bishops of Speyer.

5 Grace Edith Bevir (1890–1955) married in 1915 Sir Noel Charles (*vide supra*).

6 She had her wish; her husband would soon be posted to Brazil.

disappeared and I chartered a car for £8 to drive me to London. I had no luggage difficulties but paid voluntarily £2 duty on Greek cigarettes, which the King of Greece had given to me for the Duchess of Kent. All my letters, parcels, safely in a diplomatic bag, were untouched. England was cold and dark – blackout again – and the gaunt woman driver drove recklessly. I was wretched to go back, and I heard the siren as we approached London. Rab and Harold were dining at my house and the warmth and affection of their welcome cheered me: but my heart, my faith are in Cairo.

THURSDAY 20TH FEBRUARY   *5 BELGRAVE SQUARE*

This page is another entry for the same day, written by Channon in the diary he had previously used for the latter part of 1940; that volume then continues to 22 March 1941 when he starts a new diary.

I got up at five o'clock in the Hotel at Estoril, and was awakened, not by the concierge as arranged, but by the indignant protests of the Duquesa di Santona[1] in the next room to mine who had been telephoned to by mistake instead of me .... No breakfast. Nervous and irritable I drove ahead of the Australian party to the aeroport [*sic*]. Lisbon looked romantic in the early dawn. We took off at 7.30 – all day I dozed, read *War and Peace* and wondered what my homecoming would bring, what horrors, what complications and disappointments? Poole was reached at about 5.15 after an easy flight and England looked grey, wet and uninviting. For the first time in my life I was sad to return to her bosom, and was reluctant to get to London. However as a last extravagance I chartered a car (£8) and drove up, my papers and baggage not having been examined; but I voluntarily paid £2 customs for cigarettes for the Duchess of Kent .... At Belgrave Square where I arrived in the dark about ten o'clock I found Harold Balfour, and Rab Butler, my little ministers .... still dining. We drank champagne and had a gay-ish evening and I went to bed.

There are mountains of letters and an endless list of things to be done ... and a handsome china clock from Loelia [Westminster] as a Xmas present and a blue fish vase from my bewildering wife ....

FRIDAY 21ST FEBRUARY

The morning was feverish and I did many of my duties, and wrote letters. Eventually I went to the FO. Rab is now acting Foreign Secretary: there was an atmosphere of gloom, indeed of disappointment with the recent attitude and activities of the Prince Regent. I walked along the passage to the Colonial Office and there in Walter Moyne's ante-chamber I met Mr Bland, who later called to see

---

1 Carmen López de Carrizosa y Martel (1894–1979), wife of the 3rd Duke of Santona.

me here. He tells me that Honor is in a rage, wild and violent with me . . . . I feared as much . . . and my spirits sank.

I worked, wrote, went to bed early. My homecoming has been a disappointment in a way . . . . Talked to both the Kents twice and called to Peter.

SATURDAY 22ND FEBRUARY   *PYRFORD*

Overworked, and am nervously tired and perhaps on the verge of collapse. I refused to go to Coppins until tomorrow and came here instead where I found Lord and Lady Iveagh . . . . Elizabeth Elveden, Patsy . . . . I had a long talk with Patsy and discovered that Honor has made her confidante in this scandal! Patsy is rather pro-her, which dashed me. H is living in a pub near Basingstoke where she and her lover are known as 'Mr and Mrs Woodman'!

I related tales of my travels and regaled the party.

Raids seem to have ended . . . .

So many people have died in my absence – that iron-eyed, short-sighted Lady Chamberlain whom I always liked, John Rathbone,[1] Euan Wallace etc. The Butlers have been to stay at Coppins!

SUNDAY 23RD FEBRUARY   *COPPINS*

A disappointing, disquieting morning with the Iveaghs, who are definitely less well disposed towards me; perhaps they are tired? They looked ill and worn and seemed uninterested by the drama . . . . I was nearly sick, but I know that occasionally they are like this . . . . Alan breezed over from Gosport and I told him the whole tale. He was horribly shocked and pro-me naturally.

In the afternoon I drove to Coppins and had a warm welcome from the Kents. Freda Casa Maury[2] is also there: I sat for two hours with the Duchess and gave her all the news of Athens and of her admiring sisters in Belgrade. The Duke was irritable and made the adorable children cry with one of his flashes of discipline!! Roddie Wanamaker[3] is also here. We dined late, and for five minutes or perhaps less, there was considerable gunfire – a sharp raid somewhere nearby. I was tired and not amusing, nonetheless I chattered on. The Duchess admired my new parure, Peter-given! The Duke wore his lees-of-wine smoking jacket and strummed prettily at the piano.

I cried myself to sleep with loneliness, with love, and anxiety . . .

---

1 John Rankin Rathbone (1910–40) was Conservative MP for Bodmin from 1935 to 1940. Serving in the RAF as a fighter pilot, he was killed on 10 December 1940.
2 Formerly Freda Dudley Ward; see entry for 3 February 1939 and footnote.
3 Rodman Wanamaker II (1899–1976), of Philadelphia, was the grandson of John Wanamaker, founder of the Wanamaker department stores in America. He ran a flying school, competed for the United States polo team in the 1924 Olympic Games, and served in the US Navy in the Second World War.

MONDAY 24TH FEBRUARY

I came up to London early, driving Roddie Wanamaker to the FO, where I tidied up matters, then I came home to luncheon by myself and suddenly feared a nervous collapse . . . I took bromide and slept and recovered about 6 p.m. I am anxious financially, matrimonially and physically now . . . .

I had a telephone message to say that Fritzi is back in London: I must try to see him tomorrow. I am desperate . . . and yet realise it is quite silly for me to be so. Everything is wrong, and I am so unhappy, so wretched: only one face, only the love and companionship of one person could cheer me; and I must wait interminable years for <u>that</u>.

I dined alone and am going to bed.

TUESDAY 25TH FEBRUARY

Lady Iveagh came to lunch and was a touch aloof: her usual affection seemed absent. I sat with her until 3 p.m. I went to the bank, and that, too, was depressing: I am overdrawn to the tune of £14,000 – and my accounts have been separated. How can I pay that off? Honor is angry, Peter remains silent. London is grey, grim and cold . . .

Harold B, and Rab and I dined à trois, the 'Three Belgrave Musketeers' – David Margesson came to see me later and I gave him the Egyptian gossip. Bed only at 1.30 and I was so tired that I was stupid with David instead of scintillating.

Had a drink with Diana Cooper at the Dorchester who was charming; Venetia Montagu was here and George Gage – how cold and indifferent he left me: I was not even glad to see him. Could I ever be like that about P? . . .

WEDNESDAY 26TH FEBRUARY

Dined at the 'No. 10 Annexe'; in other words, at the secretaries' mess. I was next to Brendan Bracken, my affectionate auburn host. All the secretaries, all the Churchillian court except the PM, who dined alone composing his speech for tomorrow . . . .

I felt that the gloom is lifting in my private life but that life here will be unendurable for months . . . A friendly letter from Honor which is encouraging. Oh! God, what a life . . . .

I am shocked by the Churchillian court, the rather bogus flashy coterie who flatter and cajole him; occasionally they show flashes of imagination but on the whole they are unsound.

THURSDAY 27TH FEBRUARY

A pleasant, almost affectionate chat with Lady Astor: I am going to make up with all my enemies. She was charming, as she can be: her lapis eyes are still beautiful . . . I lunched alone, went to and from the House of Commons. Winston made an excellent, engaging speech, about Malcolm MacDonald's appointment to Canada, on the Immunity Bill.[1] In reality he has banished Malcolm, who once stood against Randolph: there is an obvious plot to get rid of anyone who might be a rival to Anthony Eden's succession to the throne . . .

Winston did not speak to me which I thought strange: I am not sure that he saw me. The House was crowded and, I thought, irritable.

I went to the Oratory Schools where I was allowed half an hour with Fritzi, returned at last. He is still interned, and was charming; very manly, philosophic and said that however terrible the whole experience had been, he would not have had it otherwise . . . He doesn't realise his complications, or the mess he is in. My heart bled for him: the Commandant . . . . was present at our interview. Will this prisoner of Chelsea one day be Emperor of Germany?

FRIDAY 28TH FEBRUARY

The dreaded day has come and it is nearly done . . . I lunched with H, who was on the whole very nice, certainly charming and beautiful . . . . I told her frankly that I could not, and would not face divorce proceedings now. She seemed not to mind, and I think it is probably true that the wife, Mrs Woodman, shows reluctance to divorce him – (as we were informed by the woman detective). Perhaps there may be a reconciliation after all one day. We got on well but I feared a breakdown on my part. I handled her well on the whole and nothing, it is so true, is as frightful as one expects . . .

Sandy Vereker[2] has killed himself: an appalling tragedy. I am in the know – few people are. He left his wife for love of a fellow officer, one Howard: it was the great love affair of the war. I knew all about it. Now I gather Howard has left him – this is the neurotic result. Sandy was plump, pretty and attractive and Lord Gort's only son – the heir of the Commander-in-Chief of the Army!

I called on Mrs Joyce Brittain-Jones at 36 Montpelier Row; a tiny house, well arranged but too many photographs of the King of Greece about. We have arranged for her journey out to Athens and she leaves next week. Will she arrive before the Germans?

SATURDAY 1ST MARCH   *FARNHAM PARK*[3]

I am worn out utterly by my complications and accumulated arrears of work . . . . refused to lunch with the Coopers, who rang three times, and also with Rab – who

---

1 When enacted, this measure regulated diplomatic immunity and privileges.
2 Charles Standish Vereker (1912–41) was the only son of Lord Gort (qv). He was a lieutenant in the Grenadier Guards.
3 At Farnham Royal in Buckinghamshire, home of Lord and Lady Kemsley (qv).

naively offers me £14 per month peppercorn towards the expenses of B Square! His Achilles heel is his famous meanness. He costs me at least £30 a month to keep. In the afternoon I came here to stay with the Kemsleys at this hideous grandified villa, all in the most handsome Hollywood 'grand style': still, it is pleasant to be comfortable again. Coopers are here and Duff was vituperative about the Germans, yet very nice and gentler than I have ever known him. Portia Stanley, immensely improved, is sweet: she says that Diana looks like an underfed barmaid! Diana whispered to me that Portia is more 'Hogarthian' than ever. Both are wrong. I played bridge with the Kemsleys, who after ten years of marriage are still desperately physically in love. His daughter, Pamela Berry, has just got engaged to the Marquis of Huntly,[1] the biggest matrimonial coup yet pulled off by the House of Berry. Much abuse of Eden and of Beaverbrook . . . . Bridge, champagne, no raids. The Kemsleys have lost their yacht and had bombs within a few yards of the house here.

Bulgaria has announced her adhesion to the Axis: Anthony Eden has done that, first he brought in Italy, now Bulgaria (not quite a fair charge, the latter one); still if he had stayed at home it would have been wiser. This, the Regent always predicted.

SUNDAY 2ND MARCH

Spent an entrancing morning alone in my room writing to Jacqueline Lampson and to Peter . . . long, loving, longing letter to my gay Cairene companions . . . . I found Duff much mellowed, softer and gentler, and he bit nobody . . . Much bridge and foolishly I played backgammon with Diana and lost £25 to her – in my present state of lean finances this was foolish. Yet I mustn't become ridiculously mean: I am still well off. Portia Stanley was charming and after we had put the Coopers to bed I followed her to her bedroom and we had a long talk. She lunched yesterday with the K[ing] and Q, who had only one real course which was excellent, and they wore napkin rings – like those awful Palairets.

I am a little happier; comforts, Coopers, and cocktails contribute to one's content.

MONDAY 3RD MARCH

. . . . My dinner guests, Diana Cooper; Rab and Mrs Rab; Harold; Jay Llewellin and Mrs Menzies and the Prime Minister of Australia arrived . . . . The dinner party was a huge success from the start, one of the gayest and most *réussis* festivals I have ever arranged. There was a round table; little to eat and much to drink,

---

1 Douglas Charles Lindsey Gordon (1908–87) succeeded his great-uncle as 12th Marquis of
  Huntly in 1937. He married, in 1941, Mary Pamela Berry (1918–98).

the three supreme ingredients of gaiety. Menzies told lengthy stories with gaiety and gusto and imitated me in the Mouskys of Cairo etc. Diana and Sydney left before midnight, but the others remained until 2.30 – Rab curled up on the sofa slept and snored for an hour. The Duchess of Kent rang up and he accused me of 'planting' the call .... Menzies is immense, a raconteur, conceited but full of sense and charm. Shakes Morrison came in for a drink and added his curious flavour to the banquet of the banquets .... Almost dead with fatigue I was pleased when the party broke up just before 3 a.m.

TUESDAY 4TH MARCH

There is a much unkind speculation as what exactly Paul will do, and his enemies call him 'Palsy': I am enraged and indignant for he will do the right thing; of that I am convinced. It will be wonderful to refute the charges ....

All day I felt ill, worn out by my banquet. A siesta somewhat rested me (I am on the verge of a breakdown) and I went to dine at the Savoy .... I got rather tipsy: I drink too much: I love too much: I am pining away.

WEDNESDAY 5TH MARCH

The 550th day of the war. We broke off relations with Bulgaria ....

Dined at the Dorchester with a group of seventeen MPs in a private room, a gathering to fete Brendan Bracken. He spoke, sitting down, for nearly two hours and warned us to expect reverses in the Balkans – hinted at the loss of Greece, and said that there would be a further rise on income tax! My elegant England is fading. Everything is so grey and grim .... Alan picked me up, joined rather too acrimoniously in the discussion and then he, Brendan and I adjourned to Alan's room. More drink, more conversation and Brendan promised him a job in in the government shortly.

THURSDAY 6TH MARCH

A birthday cable from Captain Coqueluche[1] filled me with rapture. My mother-in-law to lunch, and she was dispiriting. I took her and Lord Iveagh (who was a touch 'hard' and unsympathetic) to James Gunn's studio to see the portraits of their sons-in-law. Alan's is striking but I don't like it: it is too good, but soulful and he is handsomer than Gunn portrays him.

David Margesson made an excellent impression in the House when he presented his first estimates. He will be a successful minister (there is talk of his marrying Bridget Poulett).[2] He was assured, humorous and human.

---

1 Coats. The word is French for 'darling' or 'heart-throb', though its primary meaning is 'whooping cough'.
2 He and Lady Bridget (qv) did not marry.

Dined with Cecil Beaton at 8 Pelham Place in his attractive house. I wish he would sell me Talleyrand's desk which Juliet[1] put up at Christie's some years ago: he uses it. A curious little dinner party. Henry Hopkinson and his metallic American wife;[2] Nicholas Lawford whom I like so much, Ava Wigram[3] and Juliet – 'There's always Juliet'.[4] Gay conversation mostly about my trip and General Wavell. Hopkinson dropped me in the rain; my 'Boys', Balfour and Butler had both gone to bed. They gave the house warmth and companionship.

FRIDAY 7TH MARCH   *KELVEDON*

Never have I had so depressing a centenary![5] Only a sweet note from my mother-in-law to cheer me.

I came here with Christopher Hussey, the editor[6] of *Country Life*, and he took notes for the articles which he proposes to bring out in April – the Kelvedon *jadis*.[7] We talked of Edward Marjoribanks with whom he once shared digs, and of . . . . my beloved Ivo Grenfell[8] . . . .

Kelvedon is Heartbreak House with its loveliness. Am surrounded by all the objects I collected with such loving care but there is an atmosphere of desolation, the piles of unopened letters, the untilled fields, the bewildered servants, the neglected gardens and dogs forlorn – after Hussey left I had a breakdown. I love only the two Pauls, and Peter, my baby and the Regent, all so, so far away. I can't bear to live anymore; there is only void, separation, loneliness and disappointment ahead of me. Oh! What horrors will this new year bring in its train?

Later I had a birthday telegram from Honor from Alton where she lives in squalor and sin. And a cable from my poor mad mother.

SATURDAY 8TH MARCH

I drove to Cambridge, sad to leave my beloved Bundi, and even Heartbreak House, to attend a meeting at the Regional Commissioners at Corpus Christi.

1 Lady Juliet Duff.
2 Alice Labouisse Eno (1903–53) married in 1927 Henry Hopkinson (qv).
3 Alix Yveline Ava Courtenay Bodley (1896–1974) married in 1925 Ralph Follet Wigram (1890–1936), a Foreign Office mandarin who in the years leading up to his death provided secret information to Winston Churchill about German rearmament. In 1941 she married Sir John Anderson (qv).
4 The title of a 1931 comedy by John Van Druten (1901–57).
5 His birthday, satirically.
6 He was in fact architectural editor.
7 Once upon a time.
8 Ivo George Grenfell (1898–1926), son of Lord and Lady Desborough*, was killed in a car crash. In a letter of November 1920 to his father, Channon describes Grenfell as 'my best friend in Oxford . . . he is as big as a great Greek god and looks like a Viking'.

Sir William Spens is a pleasant little don, a snob and a conservative. He seemed bored but warned us, a group of MPs and regional officers, solemnly enough that we might expect invasion at any time, probably towards the end of March. Precautions have been taken and coastal towns are to be semi-evacuated again shortly. A most gloomy meeting, and I left wondering why one bothered about anyone or anything: one's financial and domestic trials seemed so trivial. I drove to London quickly enough along the empty roads, and found Harold at Belgrave Square. I wrote letters, sent a cap etc. to Peter in the War Office bag, and then dressed. As I left the house in the moonlight (about eight o'clock) I heard the wail of the sirens; nevertheless I walked, hearing nothing, to Claridge's, where I dined with Arthur and Elizabeth Elveden, and John and Nancy Hare.[1] Much talk of my trip! Bill Tufnell with his non-escaping Casanova was at an adjoining table! *Quel ménage*[2] ... About eleven I walked home; there was the purr of planes.

SUNDAY 9TH MARCH

I heard this morning that last night's raid was really serious and severe. Buckingham Palace was badly hit, and at the Café de Paris over thirty people, including Poulsen[3] the manager, were killed.[4] Another bomb fell on Sloane Street. Breakfast with Harold Balfour who is more helpful about Yugoslavia .... how can we defend Greece unless both Turkey and Paul fight?

After talking with Harold I dread Anthony's return.[5] Harold says that Rab is absolutely loyal about me and will stand no nonsense from AE. I hope so; but I also hope to get around AE; there is still the bridge of old affections.

London presented a melancholy appearance this morning – *un vrai visage de lendemain!*[6] I came to Kelvedon in the afternoon and now regret doing so as it is

---

1 John Hugh Hare (1911–82) was a younger son of the 4th Earl of Listowel. His sister was Elizabeth, Viscountess Elveden. He fought with the Suffolk Yeomanry in the war and was Conservative MP for Woodbridge from 1945 to 1950 and for Sudbury and Woodbridge from 1950 to 1963, when he was raised to the peerage as 1st Viscount Blakenham. He held a series of ministerial and Cabinet posts between 1955 and 1964, finishing as Deputy Leader of the House of Lords from 1963 to 1964 and, from 1963 to 1965, Chairman of the Conservative Party. He married, in 1934, Nancy Pearson (1908–94), daughter of the 2nd Viscount Cowdray.
2 What a household.
3 Martinus Poulsen (1890–1941), from Denmark: he also ran the Hotel de Paris in Bray and Poulsen's Club in Datchet.
4 The bombs on the Café de Paris fell down a ventilation shaft – the club was in a basement and considered safe – and killed thirty-four in the nightclub and injured eighty-two. Among those killed was the bandleader Ken 'Snakehips' Johnson, decapitated by the blast, and members of his West Indian Dance Orchestra; an event that provoked another musician, Ralph Vaughan Williams, to write his Sixth Symphony.
5 Eden was still touring the Mediterranean and south-eastern Europe. Channon is starting to fear for his job.
6 That true morning-after look.

so very noisy; planes are everywhere and bombs falling – 10.05. It is maddening and nerve-racking. The raid has decided me to let this house to the RAF. I can no longer cope with it – an awful bang! Are we the target? Is the beam bent over Kelvedon? The dogs are fretful.

Monday 10th March

All day in Southend where I received many people and attended an important luncheon of prominent businessmen – are they of the same race and sex as I? Had a long talk . . . . about dividing Southend into two seats so that Peter might have one.[1]

Soon after I got back to London Honor rang me up and I went to see her at the Dorchester: I was shocked by her appearance and thought I had never seen so despicable and unattractive a young woman! She is hard and has no sense of honour or duty: there is a substratum of perceivable hardness running through her and I wonder how had I put up with her for so long?

Dined alone with Harold: I am so ill and down, depressing and despairing. The tales of the 'Café de Paris' disaster are, indeed, horrible. Eighty [sic] were killed: some were blown by the blast against the wall and dashed to death.

Honor sent me a birthday present: a bit of china, Leda and the Swan.

Tuesday 11th March

I am dreading the return of Eden who has <u>not</u> done so well in the East and he irritated everyone. But the Regent is holding fast to him and refuses to be 'jockeyed' into an alliance of friendship with Germany. It's monstrous that Anthony should take credit for that! – but he will. There are moments when I actually hate the Prime Minister. I can see little to be said in his favour, other than his magnificent flow of oratory. He is usually wrong, always impulsive and worse, he adores the war – the war which brings such misery to us all.

There is a raid on now: I care so little whether I am killed that I shan't go down to sleep . . . . Declension, declension, all is going.

Mrs Brittain-Jones came to see me this morning and I gave her messages for Peter and the K[ing] of Greece, then I rushed her to Heywood Hill, the booksellers, to buy books for Peter which she will read *en route*. She is courageous to take this great expedition. She is dull, unexciting, loyal and in love.

Wednesday 12th March

I am on the very verge now of complete collapse . . .

---

1 From 1950 onwards this was the case, but Coats was not the beneficiary.

Lady Kemsley rang up to invite Rab and me down to Farnham for the night but I contrived to take Jay Llewellin instead as he has been on my mind. Boring evening really . . . . The Kemsleys kept us up until nearly one whilst we were all drooping with fatigue or longing to go to bed for one reason or another. Much too much food; there are always backwaters from the war.

Winston made a statement in reference to the Lend and Lease Bill;[1] he sat up late last night redrafting it. He spent much valuable time drafting. Words are his delight. He looked cross enough.

THURSDAY 13TH MARCH

I slept badly at Farnham and rushed up to London with Jay Llewellin, who is my clumsy admirer! At Belgrave Square I found Harold B supine on a sofa recovering from influenza and we shared a tray. I went to bed at 2 p.m. and slept deeply until seven, the sleep of exhaustion.

I had a brain wave this morning at the House and suggested to Rab that he cable to Anthony Eden urging him to stay in Cairo: the longer he is away the better. He is dangling for an invitation to Yugoslavia which will not be forthcoming!! Rab was sceptical of the success of my *démarche* but will contact Alex Cadogan.

FRIDAY 14TH MARCH

Really today has been surprising. Rab came into my room last night but as the window was open we could not have a long talk.[2] However he said that the PM wanted Anthony to come back at once, needed him, wanted to 'exhibit' him . . . . Now today the position is reversed. Rab lunched at the Mirabelle and ran into Winston and Max Beaverbrook, who were in high spirits and *à deux*. He sat with them for some time, noticed that the PM had two whiskies and sodas and two Kümmels – now a rare commodity. They all thought it would be an excellent idea if Anthony were to remain in the Middle East and orders are being sent off immediately for him to remain, that is if he has not already left!! The PM and Max were vituperative about everyone, attacked Lady Halifax for trying to torpedo the Washington appointment.[3] . . . . But he kept his gems for Wavell, whom he likened to a man one would propose as president for the local country golf club. He abused him roundly and even Rab believes that his motives are based on jealousy . . . . All this was told me by Rab who came into the FO after

---

1 An act of Congress that allowed America to supply Britain and the Allies with arms, food and oil during the war, ending America's effective neutrality.
2 Butler, like Lennox-Boyd, had an aversion to fresh air.
3 Of her husband.

four o'clock slightly overexcited – he must have had a Kümmel too – he has left the others still there. It is fantastic that Winston could spare two hours for lunch luxuriously. I am angry with him for nicknaming my Regent [Prince Paul] 'Palsy' and for being abusive about Wavell.

SATURDAY 15TH MARCH

Today is the dreaded Ides of March but it is ending quietly.

The Duchess of Kent rang me up and begged me to go to Coppins for the weekend and, if possible, to bring Rab. But I had business at Kelvedon. I spent the morning at Belgrave Square 'working' and Dr Law came to see me: he said that I would not have a nervous breakdown, that my physical health was excellent but obviously I was living under extreme nervous strain and asked me why: I told him the tragic tale. He is a sensible man, and has treated Honor for years: he says that she is not mad, but extremely abnormal, a sort of border case. He thinks that she will regret her rashness and recover from it: I wonder. In any case I have made up my mind that I do not want her back. She told me on Monday that she would not surrender her rights over Paul because they were her only counter to fight her mother and me – my child to be made a pawn! She has an extremely unpleasant character and that remark made openly, even amicably, lost her my friendship for life. She doesn't know it yet; but I shall fight her until the end. We are enemies now. She killed carelessly then any remaining remnant of affection or even of pity.

Later I drove to Kelvedon where I showed over the house to Colonel Churchill[1] who is probably taking it for the Red Cross as a convalescent house; the arrangement would save me much money and responsibility. After he left I dressed and drove to Langleys to dine with Bill Tufnell who was alone with his 'boy-friend', David Cazenove,[2] a fair youth known as 'The Lily of Langleys'; he is a sort of cousin and was on a short leave. There are a few traces of the war; Langleys, which has ever an immense 'Pelleas'[3] charm and is now beautifully arranged. A beautiful burgundy at dinner. At eleven I left, but the park was wrapped in a blanket of fog and I went back to ask [for] hospitality for the night. Both Bill and Dave are very *aux petits soins* . . . . they delight in each other, they exchange presents, their domestic jokes all hurt me – I was a St Sebastian and thought of the days when I, too, was happy, blissfully so . . . .

---

1 It is not clear who this soldier was.
2 David Michael de Lérisson Cazenove (1921–88) served in the Army during the war and retired in the rank of major.
3 In legend, Pelleas was a knight of the Round Table.

The cause célèbre of the week is the extraordinary murder of Lord Erroll[1] by Sir Delves Broughton,[2] a dull squire, respectable and a bore. It must have been jealousy goaded by drink as Jock Broughton was very recently married to a young girl. Josslyn had immense charm, although he was fat, 40 and 'porky'. He was always rather sexual 'two-way traffic' and lived for the fleshpot. This case will add squalor to Kenya's deplorable reputation. It is a ghastly story yet I can now understand desperate action, and might even take it under similar circumstances; but perhaps I shan't be let down!

SUNDAY 16TH MARCH

Dressed in my dinner jacket, I drove back to Kelvedon where I spent a peaceful day resting, recuperating and writing. Now that I am about to lose Kelvedon, or rather to let it, I am beginning to love it. Spent an hour with the gardeners.

MONDAY 17TH MARCH

The Yugoslavian crisis continues! How well I can imagine the chaotic hustle, the confusion, the *va-et-vient* at Beli Dvor . . . .

Dined in: Rab, Harold and Peter Loxley, ever charming. Before dinner I rang up Honor, who was staying at the Dorchester with Patsy: she sounded, or seemed, intoxicated and was rude and difficult as she sometimes is. Any relations with her always spoil my day – they have for years and were it not for the scandal I should rejoice at the turn of events. Only have I enough cash to live luxuriously? Will anyone?

The Duchess of Kent again rang me up and begged me to come to Coppins and bring Rab. I have persuaded him to go tomorrow. He says there is more in it than just an ordinary invitation, for the Duke has privately approached him and asked his aid in arranging a trip to America, he wants to embark upon a huge propaganda tour there. The truth is that he is bored to death. Rab approached Winston who was adamant: the Duke could not go, but he might, if he liked, go on a trip to the West Indies – a most malicious suggestion since it would invite

---

1 Josslyn Victor Hay (1901–41) was Lord Kilmarnock by courtesy from 1927 to 1928 when he succeeded his father as 22nd Earl of Erroll. Impoverished, he sought to make his fortune in Kenya, where he became part of the so-called 'Happy Valley' set; and after the death of his wife in 1939 began an affair with Diana, Lady Delves Broughton. He was murdered on 24 January 1941 by a shot in the head; Sir Jock Delves Broughton (*vide infra*) confessed to the murder.

2 Henry John 'Jock' Delves Broughton (1883–1942) succeeded his father as 11th Bt in 1914. Ruined by gambling debts in the 1930s, he moved to Kenya in 1940 having married Diana Caldwell (1913–87). He was acquitted of Erroll's murder because of the failure to match the murder weapon with Delves Broughton's own revolver. He returned to England after the trial but killed himself with a morphine overdose in December 1942.

'Windsor trouble' and a meeting with the Duke of W. Winston is against the Kents as he thinks they have behaved treacherously towards the Windsors, which is, of course, true.

TUESDAY 18TH MARCH

I rang up my wayward wife and she later came to the House of Commons to meet me: she was dressed like Puss-in-Boots, no hat, snowshoes, wild hair, nicotine-stained fingers and looked as if she had just emerged from the stables, except for her expensive sable coat. We lunched, and luckily several people saw us including Brendan Bracken, and Mollie Buccleuch who was lunching – as usual – with her cold paramour, James Stuart. Walter Buccleuch is the cuckold of all time (next to me, but no one knows about me yet!) – Honor was rather unbending but we were soon on rational terms together and I told her that if she wanted me to divorce her she must first ascertain that her lover would be free – that Mrs Woodman would divorce. Honor lied slightly: the woman was willing to take steps and would be induced to do so in April. Lord Iveagh's detectives assured him that Mrs W will do no such thing. *On verra.* Then Honor and I went out shopping, looked at silver (I am keeping the plate for Paul – and anything else that I can lay my hands on – as it belongs to me): soon we were chatting amicably. She has no idea, no suspicion even that she is behaving badly and gets angry when it is hinted to her that her behaviour has been so scandalous. We parted on friendly terms . . . but I rushed to B Square to sleep for an hour to recover from her. She is a vampire and I long really to be rid of her . . .

About 6.30 I picked up Rab and we drove to Coppins. *En route* we talked: he is happy as acting Foreign Secretary; he is respected, if not liked, by Winston; he attends all the Cabinet meetings. He is disappointed in Anthony, who has succeeded in making himself so very unpopular at the Foreign Office during the short time he has been back there. It was always known as 'The Garden of Eden', his paradise, and now he is detested. For one thing he insists on bringing back Oliver Harvey as his private secretary and both Alec Cadogan and Rab had protested in strong terms. Anthony is technically in the right: the Sec of State has obviously the right to select his own private secretary, but he is being pig-headed about it since the idea is so unpopular with all concerned. Harvey is a dangerous fellow, the mandarin of the mandarins . . . Meanwhile Anthony is philandering in the Moyen-Orient[1] and is flirting with the Turks, with some success. He has sent a message – a fortnight or so ago – to the Regent that he would like to go to Yugoslavia and until now the hint has been ignored! Paul won't receive him! I could have told him that . . . All this and more, Rab and I discussed. He was rather

---

1 Middle East. 'Philandering' should not be taken literally.

dreading the inevitable tête-à-tête with the Duke of Kent, and breaking it to him that Winston won't hear of the American project.

Alec Hardinge, the King's sinister secretary, formerly known as 'The Black Rat', is now called 'The Red Rat' since he goes about saying that the Russians were right to invade Finland! . . . I have quoted this statement which he made to Sydney Butler to everyone . . . We arrived, and found the couple waiting for us in his study. We had drinks and went up too late to change – they had already gone in to dinner when I came down. I haven't the royal trick of dressing in five minutes. Good food and drink and a new butler . . . . Afterwards the Duchess and I played backgammon whilst the Duke and Rab had a confidential talk. Rab broke it to him about the USA, whereupon the Duke said that he would then like to go to the Middle East to 'do the sort of trip Chips did'. That, Rab thought, could be arranged and would really be an excellent thing. I am for it . . . The Kents (to me) were very funny about the Gloucesters, who are arriving tomorrow and they asked me to stay on to amuse them! There is no love lost between the two couples and both agreed that Alice Gloucester is an awful bore: I like her, and she is popular in the country, very popular with ATS and WVSs[1] . . . but I can see that she has no message for the v sophisticated, society-jewel-loving Kents.

It is very noisy here at Coppins and the house actually shook from the impact of nearby bombs.

WEDNESDAY 19TH MARCH

Rab and I motored up from Coppins to London in the early fog . . . Anthony Eden is restive in Cairo and wants to come home: he can never remain long out of the political 'racket'. Winston's motives are missed in now wanting him to remain on the Nile. Perhaps he wants him to have the credit for Yugoslavia stiffening: but if Belgrade comes over to us, it will be my victory, not Anthony's obviously: but this will be one of the things I cannot say!

Diana Cooper rings me up nearly every day asking me to give her and her young ladies – Pam Berry[2] and Pamela Churchill[3] – lunch. I refused to do so again today: I should be so loved, and also I am convinced that Pamela, the most outrageous and dangerous gossip in London, wants to 'pump' me about Honor's squalid activities.

---

1 Auxiliary Territorial Service and Women's Voluntary Services.
2 It is unclear whether this was Lady Pamela Berry, daughter-in-law of Lord Camrose, or Mary Pamela Berry, daughter of Lord Kemsley (qqv).
3 Pamela Beryl Digby (1920–97) was the daughter of the 11th Baron Digby. She married, in 1939, Randolph Churchill (qv), whom she divorced in 1946. Her third husband was William Averell Harriman (qv), the American diplomat; she served as American Ambassador to Paris from 1993 to 1997. She had a reputation as one of the leading courtesans of her age.

David Margesson proposed himself to dine and was super-charming: I also asked Eddie Devonshire, who was gay and amusing but became Hogarthian, in fact, uproariously drunk before he finally left for the Mayfair Hotel where he lives. He was quite inarticulate but affectionate: I like him. I fear he is lonely now: there is so much loneliness in the world, luckily Rab, Harold and I all like one another and live happily together.

THURSDAY 20TH MARCH

Brigid Guinness, looking like a Grecian damsel, and reminding me of the 'Ode on a Grecian Urn', came to lunch; she told me much: she has refused Hugh Euston[1] for the nth time and so will never be a duchess; and, more, she went to Hampshire yesterday to see Honor and her swarthy paramour. She is affectionate with me but sides entirely with Honor whom [sic] she says will be a second Lady Ellenborough![2] A charming prospect! She upset my nerves and I had to retire to bed to recover from her visit: I am better but still in a weak state.

No Blitz disturbed us. Bed by midnight. I have not slept in a luxurious shelter since November, but as the raids are increasing in severity once more I suppose I shall soon resume conjugal life with Rab in the cellars.

I was rung up by the Home Office and told that poor Fritzi leaves tomorrow for the Isle of Man. His release has been refused and he has been shockingly treated – only because he is a prince! Actually I have discovered that Princess Alice personally requested that he be sent away from Canada, where his presence in an internment camp was an embarrassment to her. Perhaps Harold is right in saying that she is a cruel spiteful woman: I have always liked her. I managed to get F's transfer delayed until Tuesday.

In the MS, half a page of the entry for 20 March has been cut out.

FRIDAY 21ST MARCH

A frantic day. I saw Reginald Cockburn,[3] my solicitor, who told me that he had broken off negotiations with Honor, and would refuse to handle her affair. He is horrified by the story and advised me to begin immediate divorce proceedings which I refused to do. I must have time . . . I think in a way he is right. But I must

---

1 Hugh FitzRoy, Earl of Euston.*
2 Jane Elizabeth Digby (1807–81) was Lady Ellenborough after the first of her four marriages (three of which ended in divorce) to the 1st Earl of Ellenborough. As well as proceeding to marry a German baron, a Greek count and a Syrian sheikh she also had an affair with King Ludwig I of Bavaria. She spent the last thirty years of her life in Damascus, where she died of dysentery.
3 Reginald Stapylton Cockburn (1889–1971), a partner in Baileys Shaw and Gillett, Solicitors, of Mayfair.

first settle my financial affairs and later convince the Iveaghs – it will not be easy to do . . . . I shall do nothing, take no steps or decisions until after Easter.

I went to see Fritzi at the Oratory Schools where he is detained. It was a pathetic meeting and he was crestfallen indeed to learn that he is not to be released – he, perhaps, the future Emperor of Germany. I smoothed his path as much as possible.

SATURDAY 22ND MARCH

The Yugoslavian crisis worsens daily: I am sure that the Regent is also playing for time as every day his army is being prepared and mobilised. He has now turned his old 'Stoya' – Stojadinović to us.[1] I know the old ruffian well; a dark, huge man, not devoid of charm, he was pro-Axis in his leanings and dishonest financially. He was personally pleasant, and was obsequious with his dealings with the royal family. Later his head was turned by Italian flattery and he saw himself as a second Mussolini. Paul told me that after discovering his treachery one morning – the man was Prime Minister – he waited until the evening, when it was quiet in Belgrade and Stoya had gone to bed, when he dismissed him from his post and had him arrested. This was some time ago. The poor Regent was considerably shaken by the man's treachery: but no Balkan can ever really be relied upon . . . . Eden is still fuming in Cairo.

I went to the Home Office and was shown the Fritzi file . . . . There were copies of cables etc. and I read in black and white that he was shipped back to England, against his own declared wishes, at the urgent intervention of the reigning authorities and with the promise, a definite one, of immediate release. It is monstrous. Prince don't eat Prince – but they do!

SUNDAY 23RD MARCH

Now that I am proposing to shut Kelvedon I am loving it and using it more than ever before. I shall miss it . . . A very foggy night and hence no raid. I slept uninterruptedly for eleven hours. Now it is a lovely day: I have written many letters and am now awaiting with some resentment the arrival of Simon Harcourt-Smith, who has proposed himself to luncheon here. I am convinced that he writes for gossip columns and has come here to spy upon me – or rather upon us. I should never have made friends with him. One is always paid out for any social *bassesse*.[2]

---

1 Milan Stojadinović (1888–1961) was Prime Minister of Yugoslavia from 1935 to 1939, serving simultaneously as Foreign Minister. He was also three times Finance Minister between 1924 and 1935. Famously corrupt and untrustworthy, he was sent into exile with British help to the colony of Mauritius on 17 March 1941, the British having been warned that he might help mount a coup to support the Axis.
2 Baseness.

The situation in Belgrade is chaotic: Paul is still holding out against any form of pact with the Axis. I forgot to record that on Friday evening the Yugoslav Minister rang me up to say that he had had a telegram from the Regent asking that his love be sent to me. And his thanks for my recent letter. Was this a code, a message that all would be well? In any case I was much touched.

.... [Harcourt-Smith] came only to pry and probe into my matrimonial affairs. I was icy and soon got rid of him.

MONDAY 24TH MARCH

I came up from Kelvedon late in the afternoon and as I drove through the streets I realised how badly battered the capital is: the raids are beginning to show. At the Foreign Office I found the atmosphere tense about the Yugoslavian situation. I cannot yet believe, I shall never believe, that the Regent, whom I love more than anyone on earth after my two Ps, could do anything either dishonourable or against the interest of England, which he loves as I do. England has been beyond all else the passion of his life .... Even now I have not yet abandoned all hope. Rab came in from the Cabinet looking pale and tired, and when I said the news is bad, he answered, 'Let's not talk about it.' Later in my car, driving home through the wet and the blackout, he explained that he knew how much grief and disappointment the denouement would bring to me. Tonight the Yugoslav Prime Minister, Cvetković,[1] and his Foreign Minister, Marković[2] who has ever been the Bonnet[3] of Belgrade, are leaving for Vienna to sign a pact with the Axis. There are reported risings and disturbances in Yugoslavia. Something will come out of this. My heart aches for my poor Regent: I know his minor weaknesses, his occasional sudden unreliability which is Slav; but his character is loyal, affectionate and fine *au fond* ...

TUESDAY 25TH MARCH

A dreadful day. We heard confirmation of the news that the Yugoslav delegates left last night ... and when they arrived at the station there was no crew, the engine-driver and others had vanished. A slightly comic note in the drama. Eventually the emissaries left on their sinister errand. I went to the H of Commons and was immediately surrounded. Jay Llewellin remarked that my 'Garter had

---

1 Dragiša Cvetković (1893–1969) was Yugoslav Prime Minister from 1939 to 1941. Two days after he signed the pact he was arrested after a military coup against Prince Paul in favour of King Peter. Cvetković fled to Bulgaria in 1944 and spent the rest of his life as an exile in Paris.
2 Aleksandar Cincar-Marković (1889–1947) was Yugoslav Foreign Minister from 1939 to 1941. He had been Minister in his country's embassies to London (1934–5) and Berlin (1935–9).
3 The former French Foreign Minister.

gone west'; I felt an unfriendly atmosphere. Harold Nicolson gave me a drink in the Smoking Room – always a depressing symptom, for he makes a point of being kind to his friends when they are down. But I didn't care: my heart only bleeds for Paul, my poor distracted Regent. The Duchess of Kent rang me several times on the telephone but I had no real news. It was only in the evening that we heard that Yugoslavia had definitely signed the pact; has the Regent collapsed? Has he gone back on all his sentiments and declarations, or as has been told me, has he had a complete nervous breakdown? I am distracted – can destiny deal me any more blows? I feel like Marie Antoinette . . . .

Honor rang me rather chirpily from Kelvedon: she has decided to remove most of the furniture. The lovely schloss will be denuded. I am too dejected to care and weakly agreed, knowing later I will regret my weakness.

Anthony Eden and Co. left Cairo today for England and expect to be back by Monday.

WEDNESDAY 26TH MARCH

The news is official: in spite of risings, protests and serious demonstrations in Belgrade and elsewhere, the emissaries have signed the pact and returned today to their capital. The Regent's name is mud in this London which he loves: he is ranked as a Leopold,[1] as a traitor.

The bank rang me to say that Lord Iveagh had dispensed £6,425 – *quel soulagement!*[2] But I hoped for more. I have now economy mania.

THURSDAY 27TH MARCH

News reached the Foreign Office of more extraordinary events in Belgrade. There was last night, or rather this morning, at 2.20 a *coup d'état*. Little Peter was proclaimed King, the ministers who signed the pact have been arrested and the Regents[3] have all three resigned: Paul is reported to have fled; some say he has been arrested. No one knows what to think but there is jubilation here which is perhaps premature, this is something we did not intend. I can see the dramatic happenings in the Palace which I know so well; the generals taking control; the Regent at bay; the King awakened – it is all Ruritania,[4] and no doubt a blow to German prestige. I rang up the Duchess of Kent to break the news gently to her

1 The King of the Belgians, who had also done a deal with the Germans.
2 What a relief!
3 There was a Regency council, the two other members being Radenko Stanković (1880–1956), a leading cardiologist, and Ivo Perović (1881–1958), a lawyer and former provincial governor.
4 Channon refers to the fictional country in Anthony Hope's 1894 novel *The Prisoner of Zenda*. Prince Paul was considered to have caved in to the Nazis – in reality it was either that or be overrun – and forgiveness by the British would be slow.

but she was out and so I told the Duke who seemed delighted and laughed! Then I telephoned to Queen Marie of Yugoslavia and told her that her son had assumed powers, sacked the government, and entrusted the formation of a new one to General Simović[1] whom I remember . . . Rumours all day . . . . I was relieved and yet so anxious for my poor Regent. My report is that he has fled . . . .

[During dinner] Rab was twice summoned to the telephone . . . . about the tone to be taken by the press. I had primed Rab and pleaded with him that we should not be too hasty or severe in our judgement of the Regent and he emphasised that this was the line to be taken with the press . . . . All day my loyalties have been stretched and my emotions engaged. The Regent, a fugitive, perhaps assassinated. Late tonight came a report that his train taking him to Brdo had been stopped and that he had been arrested; later we heard that he had left for Greece at his own request. I am in despair about his future as Winston told Rab at the Cabinet that he would not allow him to come to England. Where else can he go? Where on earth? Perhaps to Cairo where he will meet Peter? . . . .

Queen Marie's stock is now 'up'; but she has a despicable character, really, like all the Romanian royal family. After all she is Hohenzollern. Still we have always been friends . . . .

Winston has suddenly shown great interest in royalties and wants them restored wherever possible: the comte de Paris's chances are better and perhaps – who knows – we shall see once again a French monarchy. I read Winston's strong minute on the subject; he is an ardent royalist, he says, and also believes that kings are a bulwark against dictators . . . .

What a *chute*;[2] now all my Yugoslav fun is over; no more Bled, Brdo and Belgrade, no more palaces and pomp, sunlight and happiness with the Regent whom I may never see again. I dread every wireless bulletin lest it tell that he has been butchered in the best Balkan manner.

Before dinner I dropped in to see Mrs Greville, who was affectionate, kissed me, and said she had been my ally for twenty years. I am devoted to this scheming jewelled-tortoise. She is working to oust Alec Hardinge whose days at the Palace are, she says, numbered. She told me that she always kept her promises: I think she does. Only one has she left half-broken: it seems that immediately after the abdication, whilst the K and Q were still living in Piccadilly, that they sent for her and she dined with them *à trois*. They embraced her, each took her arm and said, 'Dearest Mrs Ronnie, promise us to tell us always the truth; for no one else ever will.' She admits that she has failed in this trust: she has always told them the truth when asked but has never volunteered it for she would only make trouble for others and enemies for herself. She showed me a letter from Queen Mary from

1 Dušan Simović (1882–1962) had been Chief of the General Staff of the Yugoslav Air Force. He was Prime Minister from 1941 to June 1942, though for much of that time was in exile in London, where he stayed until 1945.
2 Downfall.

Badminton in which she asks for news, says she hears 'nothing' – in other words, is bored at Badminton. Queen Mary always has her letters registered!

A terrible day, indeed. I had a snack lunch with the Iveaghs who were v friendly – but they haven't paid off my overdraft.

FRIDAY 28TH MARCH

I woke early and eagerly turned on the wireless. I was relieved to hear that there has been no bloodshed in Belgrade, and that the Regent left last night by train for Athens 'with his family'. Later Princess Marina rang up, whilst I was drinking my coffee, to say that she had had a cablegram from Belgrade via the FO that the Regent and his family were well. It was not until the evening that I read that actually he left this morning by air – which he abhors: no doubt in the same Lockheed which took me to Greece. But he will have a horrible reception in Greece, and where is he to go afterwards?

SATURDAY 29TH MARCH   *COPPINS*

I put more things away in the safety deposit vault . . . . Then to the Foreign Office where I gathered the feeling against the Regent is growing. He has done worse, they say, than Boris, Carol or Leopold:[1] he sold out England. I cannot yet believe it and am distraught about him. He arrived in Athens today, I understand, and the King of Greece reluctantly went to meet him. It must have been a frigid and dramatic meeting: last time they saw each other was in my house. At seven o'clock Poppy Thursby came to Belgrave Square . . . . and I then motored her here. The Kents have both severe colds and he has been in bed a week. She is disheartened and wretched about the Regent and Olga. I tried to comfort her and gave her good advice, particularly as they are lunching tomorrow at Chequers, a meeting arranged by Rab, and the subject is bound to be raised. I want Paul to come here – I would so willingly have lent him Kelvedon! After dinner the Duchess and I went into the music room ostensibly to play backgammon but really to talk. She cried, she smiled, she sniffed and I soothed her until midnight: then she went to bed and I talked to him for another hour. He is more loyal about the Regent than I dared hope; but he is always like that, treacherous on the surface, but *au fond* a good friend. It has been a terrible week for them and for me.

SUNDAY 30TH MARCH

I take drugs in increasing quantities in order to sleep and did . . . This morning I wrote letters and then had an hour with the Duchess of K, who has partly recovered,

---

1 The kings of Bulgaria, Romania and Belgium respectively.

and looked a dream of beauty. I have never seen her so glamorously beautiful. Steeled by my advice, they both left for Chequers . . . apprehensive, I thought. They have not seen Winston to talk to since the [start of the] war . . . . I dozed in the afternoon after too much food; and our hosts returned before six o'clock worn out. Lunch at Chequers had been fairly successful – the Duchess sat between Winston and Winant,[1] the dark American Ambassador to whom she quite lost her heart. She handled WC as an ally, not as an enemy and he reacted and was pleasant. He added, however, that of course Prince Paul couldn't come here now! It was being arranged to send him either to India or to S America! (It will kill him, I fear.) Then Winston changed the subject and harped on monarchy, which is his new and pet theme and talked first of freeing Fritzi and eventually establishing him as King of Prussia, and then of the comte de Paris. Curiously enough I had told the Duchess that these would be the subjects and she praised them both and encouraged him in his theories. Later the Duke and Winston had a long conversation during which he was more firm about the Regent and said that a most unfortunate telegram had been sent by him to the Emperor of Japan[2] which had been intercepted in Cairo! Can it be genuine? The whole story is a nightmare!! He went on to say that efforts would be made to make him comfortable wherever he was sent – a sort of semi-prisoner-of-state. It is too terrible. Winston added that 'he has very loyal friends'! Meanwhile the Duchess was with Bobbety Cranborne,who told her that he had known Paul most of his life and was now championing him and trying to pacify Winston! The other guests were Averell Harriman,[3] Jock Colville . . . . and Menzies, the PM of Australia who talked of me . . . . The Duchess retired to bed when she returned with a streaming cold and nerves; but not before she gave me an account of her visit. The Duke is not at all tender with her, always cold and snubbing and betrays his boredom.

Bed at midnight. Life holds little for me now: in five months I have been betrayed by my wife and my greatest friend, one a millionairess and the other a reigning Sovereign! I have now only my child, myself, and Peter.

MONDAY 31ST MARCH

I came leisurely to London: nothing much to report. Portia Stanley, much calmer and improved, dined. As did Poppy Thursby, David Margesson, and my

---

1 John Gilbert Winant (1889–1947) was twice Governor of New Hampshire (1925–7 and 1931–5), and served as United States Ambassador to the United Kingdom from 1941 to 1946. He formed close relationships with the King and Queen and with Churchill, and a closer one still with Churchill's daughter Sarah, with whom he had an affair. It was partly because of the effect of the affair that he shot himself in November 1947.

2 Michinomiya Hirohito (1901–89) was Emperor of Japan from 1926 until his death.

3 William Averell Harriman (1891–1986) was a diplomat and Roosevelt's special envoy to Europe. He was United States Ambassador to the Soviet Union between 1943 and 1946, to the United Kingdom for five months in 1946, and held senior positions in the Truman, Kennedy and Johnson administrations.

much-loved-lodgers, Harold Balfour and Rab .... David was loyal about the Regent, as were Poppy and Portia. But Harold warned me that anger with him, and hence with me was growing. The Duchess of K rang me up during dinner and I confided in her that P had cabled from Cairo that he would do everything possible to help him when he arrived there – a much appreciated cable. The boy is so understanding and gentle and good: I am exceedingly lucky .... I felt *congestionné* and irritable and dull and sent off two pairs of very Scottish socks to Prince Mohammed Ali by the bag.

TUESDAY 1ST APRIL, ALL FOOLS' DAY

Rather nervous about my reception at the H of C, I was relieved and surprised to be received as a sort of hero: several members congratulated me on the recent coup in Yugoslavia: it seems that someone has started the hare – and there is nowhere on God's wicked Earth where hares start and run so quickly as in the lobbies of the mother of Parliaments[1] – that the Belgrade revolution is a result of my trip to the Balkans!! I had many long talks about the Regent, and all favourable, beginning with Jack Balfour, who says that the very existence of Yugoslavia, its survival and its present government are due to the Regent's skill and cunning. Lady Astor rushed up to me – screaming, 'I don't believe that Prince Paul did anything wicked.' So did others .... But the Prime Minister, whom I happened to run into several times, did not smile at me: he never does. It is because of my feud with Randolph, really.

The time of the House, and it made me despair of democracy, was entirely taken up by a discussion of whether or not theatres should be allowed to open on Sundays. An acrimonious debate revealed the deep Nonconformist strain still existing in this antiquated England. The proposal was defeated, although it was a government measure, by eight votes. Of course, all the gay sparks and soldiers were away on service so only the old fogies, prejudiced and much lobbied by their constituents' votes [were there]. Many abstained and I was disappointed that Rab was one of these. He has that strain running through him and is not a man of the world, really.

The Bath Club has been burnt down almost to the ground and not by enemy action: no one knows the cause but they employed four fire-watchers who observed nothing until too late. One more of my haunts is now no more: how transitory everything is. I am in despair: H deserted me; my baby in America; now the Regent dethroned and cut off from all communication with me. Perhaps we shall never meet again now. Gone too are the glamorous Chamberlain–Halifax days when I basked in the high favour of the great. Twice today I was next to Winston (he is rather better-dressed since he was made PM); and neither time did he make any advance towards me, nor even smile. Perhaps he, too, half-blames me for the Yugoslavia debacle.[2] Nothing could be more unjust.

---

1 Channon assumes the establishment at Westminster is the Mother of Parliaments. England, according to John Bright in a speech in 1865, is the Mother of Parliaments.
2 Clearly, not all applauded Channon for his efforts with Prince Paul, and it fed his paranoia.

One wants only to kill time now. I have no other ambition; my life is over, ended: I may have an autumn summer of happiness with P I don't know, nothing else, other than my child, matters. My world is being split into fragments. Except that I have a new mania, economy and investments!

When I came in Rab was still working – 11.40. He loves work, but overdoes it and his health will collapse one day. At 38 he looks 50. Before dinner I went to see Menzies at the Dorchester: he was charming; no one has ever enjoyed himself more: he is even thinner. His note about 'robbing Paul to pay Peter' has gone around London; and the Regent's enemies still refer to him as 'Palsy' which infuriates me.

WEDNESDAY 2ND APRIL

Jay Llewellin came up to me in the H of C and said that he wanted to talk to me; I went with him to the Smoking Room and over a drink he warned me that both Jean Norton and Maureen Stanley are campaigning against me, saying that the Regent's collapse, his signing with Germany was due to me, that I had so advised him. It is monstrous! Jean, whom I thought a friend, openly accused me of such action last Sunday night at Cherkley[1] in front of Max Beaverbrook. There was a large party there: Jay defended me. I didn't know quite what action to take, probably none would be the wisest course.

There are rumours that Germany will now definitely invade Yugoslavia; I shouldn't be surprised. Victor Warrender thinks that the Regent will be . . . . proved innocent: so do I.

Dined alone – talked again to my wayward, wicked wife.

THURSDAY 3RD APRIL

Several heartbreaking telephone conversations with the Duchess of Kent who is even more distraught than I about the fate of the Regent and his family . . . . I am convinced in my heart that he behaved as he thought fit for the welfare of his country, and a long perusal of the telegrams confirmed this theory: but I shall not forgive our Consul-General at Zagreb who sent in a malicious . . . . anti-Regent report of his meeting with Paul . . .

My mother-in-law came to luncheon and we discussed our own particular problem and Honor's peculiarities: she cannot believe that Honor is really her daughter, so disgusted is she. She may live to forgive her, but never entirely . . . Then I retired to the House of Commons, where I had several conversations with members inducing them to remove questions: I have never had failure yet all these years.

---

1 Cherkley Court, Beaverbrook's neoclassical Victorian house in Surrey, just outside Leatherhead.

I had a most charming letter from Leslie Hore-Belisha saying that he was returning to London today, so I sent him a message and asked him to dine. He came and was charming. He is still suffering from a duodenal ulcer and eats only steamed food; but he looked better and was in good spirits. He is against the government, although he added that the Prime Minister had enquired two times [*sic*] after his health during his recent illness . . . . Paul Latham also dined and was untidy, a touch 'whiney' but charming, impressed and pleased by the political party – Rab and Harold. We were all in high spirits and Rab said that in opposition to Wavell and Winston he had advocated an advance to Tripoli: it would have been better tactics than going for Abyssinia so soon . . . . Now the German shadow looms over Cyrenaica. After Paul had left my little ministers retired with their red boxes whilst Leslie and I went to my study, lit a fire and had a long talk about politics and love and he told me that Violet Trefusis[1] has proposed marriage to him and that he had refused her. He wants someone younger, a child-bearer and not a lesbian. I think Violet, to whom I introduced him, would suit him admirably. He has been staying with her for some weeks recuperating.

Rab told me that the Cabinet discussed little except Fritzi. Winston has become obsessed by him and advocated his immediate release; indeed a Cabinet paper has been circulated about him which mentions me and his sojourn at Kelvedon.

Friday 4th April

Grievous news – Benghazi has been retaken:[2] the newspapers splash it. Its loss after its glamorous capture on February 6th – the day I lunched with the Wavells – is a definite defeat and may mean a prelude to big battles. I am downcast and apprehensive about Peter. If he were killed I should have really little motive in living other than my remote child. And I have sometimes a horrible feeling about him . . . that he will not come back unscathed, such an Ariel, such a golden-amber Ganymede is too rare for this world . . . .

I am so sorry for Wavell, for the fall of Benghazi must be a disappointment to him, so far his only setback – if only Abyssinia had fallen a week earlier!! If the Germans can so easily cross the Mediterranean why shouldn't they cross the Channel, too? People are depressed today . . . Mr Stephens of Coutts bank rang me up: he had had direct news from the Regent: the first person who has – it was a cable asking him for £200 to be transferred to the account of the King of Greece, and also to know his present balance in dollars and pounds!! He apparently is staying with the King of Greece.

I gather that Fritzi is to be released shortly.

---

1 Violet Keppel (1894–1972), daughter of George and Alice Keppel (qv), married in 1919 Denys Robert Trefusis (1890–1929). She is best remembered now for her long affair with Vita Sackville-West*; she was also a novelist and memoirist.
2 The British had taken Benghazi from the Italians on 6 February. The Germans recaptured it.

Virginia Woolf[1] is dead, or rather she drowned herself: a grey, very highly-strung woman of dignity and charm, she was unstable and often had periods of madness. She led the Bloomsbury movement, did much indirectly to make England go left – and look at the result. She undermined it, yet she always remained a lady, and was never violent. She could not stand human contacts and people fatigued her.

SATURDAY 5TH APRIL

It was pleasant to awake after restful sleep and no very shattering news: there is only the *coup d'état* in Iraq[2] which, whilst important, is too remote to excite me. I went to the office, and Rab soon arrived from Stanstead. My house is the only occupied one in all London.

SUNDAY 6TH APRIL

I turned on the early wireless and heard that Germany has declared war on both Yugoslavia and Greece: I foresee terrible complications, the spreading of war, and perhaps another Gallipoli. The Cairene scene alters . . . . I am anxious about Peter and everything else.

Kelvedon is sad: H. has removed many of our most precious possessions, things I collected with loving care and the house looks derelict. I shall miss these things: that is if we ever have possessions after the war, which I doubt . . . .

I drove in the cruel cold, which numbs the spirit and dulls one's wits, to Langleys and lunched alone with Bill Tufnell: he was charming and lives still in luxurious loneliness. Then I drove to London, dined alone with Harold Balfour. We had a brace of trays . . . . I gather that Belgrade has been bombed already and I thought sadly of beautiful Beli Dvor with its exquisite contents and the Sèvres Buffon dinner service made for Mme du Barry: it was last used when the Regent entertained for Count Teleki,[3] the Hungarian statesman who has recently committed suicide. Life becomes increasingly drab and horrible; and still no letter from Peter.

MONDAY 7TH APRIL

There are alerts in Athens and more bombing of Belgrade . . . . I walked in the cold with my snow-white hound to the Foreign Office where there is an atmosphere of

---

1 Adeline Virginia Stephen (1882–1941) was a novelist, literary critic and publisher, who suffered throughout her life from mental illness. She married, in 1912, Leonard Sidney Woolf (1880–1969).

2 A pro-Nazi coup overthrew the pro-British regime, led by the Regent Abd al-Ilah. Britain soon invaded and occupied the country until 1947.

3 See entry for 26 August 1939. He had committed suicide three days earlier.

great depression attributable to the invasion of Greece and Yugoslavia, which has begun; and also to the now imminent return of Anthony Eden, who is due back on Wednesday when the Prime Minister wishes to exhibit him in triumph! It will be a nauseating spectacle.

My in-laws came to lunch and were jolly and we didn't much touch upon the tragic situation! . . . . The Duchess of Kent rang up in the middle of lunch hoping for news which luckily I was able to give her, as a cable had just come from Princess Nicholas in Athens to say that 'all were well – love': this, of course, is an inspired message from the Regent and I am infinitely relieved . . . The House of Commons was boring, and the Budget dull; but actually on further reflection it will prove a sound one. Taxation has now reached 19s 6d[1] in the highest bracket – confiscation in other words. England is being quickly socialised. It is really robbery. However there were not 'irritating' trimmings in Kingsley Wood's Budget and it was well received. We are practically ruined now! He is a colourless speaker and the Chamber was restless, many members left before he sat down. Everyone was bored, no one was angry or disappointed.

Dined in: Harold B; Rab; and Leslie Hore-Belisha, who after the others went away to see a secret film with the Prime Minister at the Air Ministry, confided in me that he wanted to marry a Miss Nadine Pilcher,[2] who came up to him at the Oxford Union begging him for a ticket so that she might hear him. She is 22; he asked her and discovered that she was half-Greek and the daughter of an old acquaintance.

Rab was depressing about the immediate future; he had just come from the Cabinet and I drove him back to Belgrave Square – the Italo-German forces are advancing . . . . and Wavell's forces are retreating. General Wavell, apparently, had advised the Cabinet that a German advance was impossible in this season; and now even Egypt was threatened whilst our position in the Balkans is very grave as there is evidence that the Yugoslav morale is already slightly cracking up after the heavy bombardment of Belgrade; and the Croats may 'rat', just as the Regent always said that they would. I was against sending a huge army to Greece – the secret is out now – as I fear another Dunkirk, and think it would have been wiser to make our stand in Africa. In Abyssinia the position is better.

Brendan Bracken talked to me about the poor Regent; in time he will be allowed here, but not until after the war, nor will President Roosevelt let him into the States. He must go to the Argentine, or to India, Brendan thinks: both Anthony and Winston are very much against him. It is heartbreaking. The Regent would die of boredom.

1 Or, 97.5 per cent.
2 Nadine Marie Cathryn Pilcher (1919–2011), daughter of Vice Admiral Cecil Pilcher, did not marry Belisha, but, in 1946, Graham Curtis Lampson (1919–96), who in 1964 succeeded his father as 2nd Baron Killearn.

TUESDAY 8TH APRIL

I slept fitfully, disturbed by the siren's wail; but I did not move: I care so little whether I survive ... and this morning with much to do, I was frayed and nervous. Wrote and dictated, lunched alone, and shopped a little, returning to the office about four, as Rab had an important conference of Menzies, Walter Moyne, and Bobbety Cranborne – that maddening siren has just gone (10.02) and it is really a most depressing noise. Perhaps we shall have a severe raid since last night Kiel was so heavily hit. The news from the Balkans is not encouraging: the war looks bleaker. I am depressed by the outlook, and in any case peacetime conditions in England will be horrible.

WEDNESDAY 9TH APRIL

A gloomy, dejected day. The earlier news from the Balkans front was discouraging and I hear that Salonika had been captured, that the Serbs were demoralised and scattering and their government was in flight.

I hurried to the House in order to hear Winston make a statement on the cause of the war. The moment was ill chosen, indeed: he had tabled a resolution thanking the armed services for what they had done in Africa – and now news of defeat pours in. I arrived late, just in time to hear him refer to Paul as 'a weak and unfortunate prince' which infuriated me .... He made a grave speech, and I looked up at the Diplomatic Gallery where Winant was the most conspicuous figure. With his stoop and strange, inspired, yet slightly idiotic smile, he reminds me of poor Edward Marjoribanks.

Then I came home here to luncheon as I had invited Jean Norton to come .... She came, kissed me, was sweetness and gentleness itself; said she was lonely, hated the war – I didn't remind her that she had wanted it so desperately, had criticised Munich and reviled Mr Chamberlain – and we parted on the most affectionate terms.

Patsy, pregnant and pretty, came to dine with me and stayed until midnight. She told me much of Honor's squalid life and was remarkably sensible: she is against Woodman who she says is embarrassed by the unusual situation. Who wouldn't be?

Rab and Harold were dining out, and Rab, still acting Foreign Secretary, went to a late Cabinet. The situation is very grave now, and there is a tendency to blame Wavell who, after all, only obeyed – and reluctantly, I have reason to believe – orders in withdrawing his forces from Libya and sending them to Greece. Already in two days the Yugoslavian forces have retreated disastrously, and Salonika was reoccupied this morning at 4 a.m. Meanwhile the Italo-German forces rush on in Libya, and whilst Rab says that we shall hold Tobruk and that Egypt will be safe, I wonder? General Neame, that valiant VC, the sad anxious man whom I liked so much in Jerusalem, has disappeared and has probably been captured, as has General O'Connor,[1] who was chiefly responsible for the former desert victories – how far away they seem . . . I am thinking now only of Peter.

The Duchess of Kent rang me up: the King has told her that the Regent and his family are going to Coppins to live for some time, and that a cruiser has been sent to the Yugoslav coast to rescue the government, and to take King Peter to Egypt. I arranged to get confirmation of this from the F Office. Everyone is sad and uneasy . . . .

THURSDAY 10TH APRIL

Much correspondence . . . . Things to do and the news is increasingly depressing. Lunched alone and eventually retired to the FO, having passed Berry Bros, the jewellers, and got a valuation of a wooden Fabergé case for the Duchess of Kent which she wanted to sell. I sent her a cheque for the same amount and am keeping the case for Peter as he said he wanted one 'more than life'. The FO was in a state of excitement as Anthony Eden . . . . and Co. all arrived back from their great trip which was certainly a failure: their bag is empty: everything they did turned to ashes: why not leave the prosecution of the war to the generals and not to interfering politicians? I did not see AE. The Prime Minister sent a special train, which cost the taxpayer £250, to Plymouth to bring him to London. An ordinary train was leaving within an hour! I cannot think that a special train was worth £250! – to save Eden an hour's boredom when he has been away for two months. Rab says that he is extremely nervous of criticism here – no wonder. Rab (and, indeed, the whole FO) regret his return, Rab because he will now diminish in importance; he will no longer be acting Foreign Secretary, nor attend cabinet meetings. Yet he is far abler, subtler and more balanced than that overrated dandy. Ralph Stevenson said that there were no letters for me which almost broke my heart. Perhaps Peter put them in the bag?

Rab and I drove back to Belgrave Square, and dined peacefully *à deux*. He was *piano* and depressed and had fears that we may lose Greece and Egypt! General Gambier-Parry is also a prisoner in the hands of the Germans: he was such a social, amiable creature – I flew to Crete with him: it is v sad. Wavell feels the lack of generals now, all his best men gone . . . . Oh! What an outlook.

---

1 Richard Nugent O'Connor (1889–1981) joined the Army in 1908, served with distinction in the Great War being awarded the DSO and Bar, and in 1938 became Governor of Jerusalem in the rank of major general. In 1940 he became commander of the Western Desert Force. He played a leading part in the defeat of the Italians in North Africa in 1940–1, and was knighted in recognition of his leadership. He, with Neame, was captured by the Germans on 6 April. He escaped from a camp in Italy in 1943, was promoted to lieutenant general and given command of an Army Corps in time for D-Day. He finished his service as a full general and became a Knight of the Thistle in 1971.

Erskine-Hill[1] told Rab that the Tory Party would never take Anthony Eden as Prime Minister: I wish I dared to agree with him. Rab is so changeable, but sound *au fond*, and Scotch and shrewd. He confided to me this evening that what he finds difficult to forgive in the Regent was his silence about his meeting with Hitler:[2] he never mentioned it to [Sir Ronald] Campbell, and we only discovered it later. This secrecy, this deception of his alleged allies and his telegram to the Mikado[3] and others have darkened his name here forever – I trust that it will be forgotten.

GOOD FRIDAY, 11TH APRIL

A noisy night: I was awakened frequently by the gunfire and flashes of light lit up my room. Bundi with canine sense and obstinacy refused to come up to me and slept in the hall below. However I care so little whether I live or die that I didn't bother [to take shelter]: but I should rather survive until all my affairs are in order . . . . Rab came cheerfully into my bedroom about 9 a.m. Later I went to the FO and found that Rab had accompanied Anthony Eden to the Cabinet to hear his apologia: certainly he has brought back nothing but disaster in his train. The military were much criticised, particularly by Menzies who was present. Wavell is down, and is, so AE reports, dejected. He must be ever more so now since he has no generals . . . . Slightly hostile atmosphere – or did I imagine it – at the Office, due perhaps to Anthony's unwelcome return. A letter, a sweet one, came from P, but dated March 11th: it must have been sent off on the original return of AE and Co. – before they turned in their tracks and went back to Athens. There was one, too, from Jac Lampson dated April 7th. Surely P could have written again, or has the War Office a letter for me, as yet undelivered. I broke down, and came home, a wave of *Heimweh*[4] came over me and I cried, and ached for P. I am alone and lonely now: life is barren and increasingly sombre. Rab went off gaily to lunch with Bobbety Cranborne, who is becoming more sensible and less glamorous.

Dined alone with Harold and we deplored the depressing news.

SATURDAY 12TH APRIL   *ESPLANADE HOTEL, DOVER*

Talked with Harold this morning: he thinks that the government will have to be reconstituted, for the defeats in Libya will shake it. He fears the collapse of

1 Alexander Galloway Erskine Erskine-Hill (1894–1947) was Unionist MP for Edinburgh North from 1935 to 1945. He was created 1st Bt in 1945.
2 The Regent and Hitler had met in Berlin in June 1939, and the acquaintance had been secretly renewed at the Berghof, at Berchtesgaden in the Bavarian Alps on 4 and 5 March 1941, where Hitler had sought to press him to support the Axis; the Regent, who had attended fearing immediate attack if he did not, promised only to consult his advisers. Churchill interpreted this as a sign of weakness and perfidy.
3 Emperor Hirohito of Japan.
4 Homesickness, or in this sense nostalgia.

Egypt – as I do – and a drive to the [Suez] Canal. I can think of little else . . . yet Rab, when I drove him to Liverpool Street last night was more encouraging. He has always said the German advance would be halted at Tobruk, and he strongly supported the sending of an expeditionary force to Greece, a move I disapproved of – as did the King of Greece, the Prince Regent, Wavell and Longmore in their various conversations with me. Perhaps Wavell changed his view (I believe he was over-persuaded by AE, the *âme damnée* of English politics); but Dill defended Wavell yesterday at the Cabinet. P writes approvingly of Dill but doesn't like AE. I thought it madness to risk another Dunkirk and imperil thousands of lives – luckily mostly Australian and New Zealand . . . I am dejected beyond measure. I looked in at the FO, found another letter from Peter which must have come in the FO bag. He was in Benghazi on about the 20th of March with Wavell and describes Graziani's[1] Palace and Cyrenaica generally – no suspicion then, apparently, of German advances which took place only a fortnight later. Is our intelligence then so bad? I was told at the Office that the Regent had been sent to Egypt yesterday or today. Had a chat with Ralph Stevenson, who was vitriolic about him, said he must be put out of harm's way, that he was completely under the spell of the Axis etc., all this reflects Anthony's views. Ralph is unaware that Anthony has been plotting and planning to get rid of him and to reappoint Oliver Harvey as First Secretary in his place; but both Cadogan and Rab have protested and tried to persuade Anthony not to make so grievous a mistake. Eden is down now, having returned with an empty bag – indeed created havoc and blazed a trail of failure wherever he went – perhaps the Egyptians will be put in cold storage for a time. But what a record of a trip: war declared against Greece and Yugoslavia by Germany; the 'ratting' of the Turks; the *coup d'état* in Iraq; the defeats in Libya! Foreigners never take AE seriously and think him a silly doll: he is better than that; but he makes that impression and loses us friends wherever he goes.

I came down to Dover to see Alan. The town is full of military, and many houses have been hit by shells. The Lord Warden Hotel, so famous as a honeymoon hotel, is now the headquarters of HMS *Wasp*, the torpedo boat in which Alan is serving. Alan leads a dangerous life: last night he was sent to France, shelled Boulogne and got back safely. I cannot imagine a more horrible existence; and he doesn't look well, or enjoy it. We dined together and later sat about with his companions; all v middle class and boring. Some were Free French serving under assumed names. Alan was very sympathetic about H and my entanglements and difficulties. He has never liked Honor or been intimate with her. He is as charming as ever but looks aged and untidy. No wonder. I am staying at this ghastly little

---

1 Rodolfo Graziani (1882–1955) was a marshal in the Italian Army, a dedicated Fascist and Governor of Italian Libya from July 1940 to March 1941. After the war he was sentenced by an Italian court to nineteen years' imprisonment for being a Nazi collaborator, but served only four months.

pub alone: it has been shelled and there are no windows in my room. Every few minutes there seems to be an *alerte*: the atmosphere is much the most warlike I have come across.

The news from Libya is hardly more depressing: my thoughts are only of P, and how these developments will affect him. If he were killed I couldn't go on living now: everything else has been taken from me. I am so frightened for him, and fear that he may be made a prisoner. That would mean an endless separation and misery for me; but he is so *débrouillard*[1] that he would [be] content.

EASTER SUNDAY, 13TH APRIL

I am fated to celebrate the festivals of the church in unexpected places! Christmas morning I awoke in Bathurst, and dined at Freetown! Today I woke at Dover to the sound of sirens. As I was dressing Alan burst in: he is on a quarter of an hour's notice and must be by his boat. I breakfasted and followed him to the Lord Warden Hotel, where we gossiped. About eleven o'clock we went to the jetty where his torpedo-boat is moored, and at that very moment planes appeared, guns roared, everyone ducked, a balloon came down, and in the mist of the excitement – my *baptême de feu*[2] – I saw thirteen parachutes descend: they were mine-laying ones. It was one of the most exciting five minutes of my life. Alan jumped aboard leaving me on the quay as he called out 'goodbye', and I sadly left him. Fighting, most decidedly, is not in my line! Then I took a train to London, and came here [Kelvedon] by car.

The wireless announces that battles are in progress as far east as Bardia and the Italian communiqué claims its recapture. Is the drive to the Suez begun, and can Wavell hold it up?

My gay companions of only a few weeks ago are dead, dying or being captured. It is heartbreaking.

MONDAY 14TH APRIL

The hateful wireless early announced the capture of Bardia, and said that fighting was taking place near Sollum on the Egyptian frontier. Tobruk was evidently bypassed. The excitement, chaos, and, I fear, defeatism in Cairo must be terrific. I am in despair . . . and cabled to Peter advising him to put his possessions in the hands of Kirk, the American Minister. I am so uneasy about him and fear that he will be captured.

It is still cruelly cold, ten days of feverish weather. Oh! To be out of England now that April is here;[3] but on balance it is a godsend as the raids are less severe.

1 Resourceful.
2 Baptism of fire.
3 A parody of Robert Browning's 'Home-Thoughts, From Abroad' – 'Oh, to be in England / Now that April's there'.

The one o'clock news announced that Belgrade has been occupied.

I spent an hour settling gardening and estate affairs with Mortimer, my manager and head gardener, who leaves tomorrow to join the Air Force. I shall miss him. Honor bungles the matter; as I believe I could have had him classified as 'reserved' had I been consulted earlier. She rang up and we talked jauntily, even amiably.

TUESDAY 15TH APRIL

A full, formal, foolish day of functions and interviews in Southend: and I addressed a luncheon-club . . . Then I drove up to London to dine with Bob Menzies, the Prime Minister of Australia. I went with Jay Llewellin and Harold, but not expecting so brilliant a gathering. There were fifty men, all the government mostly – Simon, and Portal[1] etc. A very distinguished yet gay gathering. David Margesson whispered to me before dinner 'The Yugos have packed up'; and when I asked him how 'my lover' was, he answered 'Oh! Wavell (he always calls him that) has taken a second breath. You had better get out and satisfy him!' he laughed. I had half an hour with Bobbety Cranborne re Paul, and he told me that he still believes in him and has done everything possible to plead his case (not very successfully so far) with Winston. I confided in him that the Regent always hated Anthony Eden and that a deep antipathy existed between them: he was unaware of that, and I thought it a wise move. He was impressed and promised to meet me in six months' time when we could review the situation. Meanwhile Paul is going to S Africa and has already arrived safely at Cairo, he added. I did not tell him that I already knew this both from the Foreign Office and also from a cryptic cable which Peter angelically sent me today via the War Office. Menzies was most affectionate: he made a brilliant speech . . . .

Dill seemed more optimistic: but on the whole there was an atmosphere of intense gloom re the Libyan and Balkan situations. Jay Llewellin told me that he had said to Beaverbrook, as he went to the fatal War Cabinet meeting when it was decided to send troops to Greece – to back up Anthony's pledge given at Cyprus on March 20th without reference back to the Cabinet – 'Remember three words: Gallipoli – Narvik – Dunkirk.' Beaverbrook had been impressed but later reported that it was hopeless to stand up to the Prime Minister, that no one except Portal and Wavell ever did. It was a terrible error in strategy and I am in a deep heartbroken rage about it . . . . There is some hope of holding Egypt I gather. I

---

1 Wyndham Raymond Portal (1885–1949) was Parliamentary Secretary at the Ministry of Supply from 1940 to 1942 and Minister of Works and Planning from 1942 to 1944. He had served in the Great War, winning the DSO and retiring in the rank of lieutenant colonel. He became Chairman of his family's paper mill company and later was a major investor in the Rank Organisation. He succeeded his father as 3rd Bt in 1931, was raised to the peerage as Baron Portal in 1935 and advanced to a viscountcy in 1945.

rejoiced to get a cable from Peter for it proved that he is still all right . . . . When it came before dinner I rang up the Duchess of Kent to tell her. She said that Rab, who was staying at Coppins for the night, had already told her that they were safe and in a villa at Heliopolis; the whole family. Peter's cable said 'fine'. I cannot make out why Rab went to Coppins: I refused.

Home with Harold and Jay and we continued to criticise the government for their folly in sending an expeditionary force to Greece, thus leaving Libya undefended . . . . Apparently we lost six Blenheims yesterday on their way to Greece; and also the Germans have already flown our captured generals, Gambier-Parry, O'Connor and Neame, to Berlin. Why, I wonder? Such a flight disproves the theory that they are short of petrol.

WEDNESDAY 16TH APRIL

Got up early and drove to Southend for more interviews and saw many constituents. Spent the latter part of the afternoon with Mr Fenn, the agent, making decisions about Kelvedon and its future . . . much is going from me. I sent some silver to Honor, and her Bessarabian carpet from Belgrave Square, and chandelier she wanted – one of a pair. She is inconsiderate in little ways.

The news in the Balkans continues to be alarming; in Libya there is apparently a welcome lull, with nothing fresh to report.

THURSDAY 17TH APRIL

A most disturbed night: the house [Kelvedon] shook as an uninterrupted wave of bombs came over us: I lay awake, philosophic but really apprehensive as the drone never ceased . . . there was no lull – as there usually is. I fell asleep finally about 4 a.m.

All day in Southend attending to constituency matters. Reports kept coming in of the really appalling Blitz in London last night. Belgrave Square was hit again, Charing Cross Hotel wrecked and much worse.

Home, here, exhausted about 6 p.m. and found the furniture removers taking away some of our lovely things to H's Sin-Box. 'When the bulldogs go out, the housebreakers come in.' It was remarkable how little I cared; but did until I saw the huge van drive away. The carters told gruesome stories of last night's raid on London. The Victoria area was the worst.

FRIDAY 18TH APRIL

A quiet night and woke refreshed. I spent the day arranging my papers, writing to the Iveaghs, and drafting a new will. The news from Libya is nil – a pause, evidently, on both sides, although we have sunk a convoy. The Greek news is worse: Yugoslavia has caved in; and it is only a matter of time before Greece does likewise.

I wrote, I worried, I went through various things . . . . And waited for the wireless. The six o'clock bulletin announced that whilst the situation was obviously deteriorating in Greece, it was perhaps improving in Libya: at least there was a lull and our forces had taken the offensive. Oh! Peter I prayed for you at the tomb of the Holy Sepulchre, and I prayed for you on a bit of the true cross in Belgrade – perhaps my prayer will be answered after all.

How sad is this English spring, late in coming, and cold, but lovely nonetheless. The blossom is out, the chestnuts are in bud – and far away in Greece young Englishmen are giving their lives for Anthony Eden's foolishness!

SATURDAY 19TH APRIL

A long wet morning along the Thames Estuary [visiting] the Anti-Aircraft sector, the huts, bases, Bren guns etc. Many of the men came from Southend and are brave strong fellows: for a year and more they have lived in these conditions in all weathers, wet, fog, dangers. I marvelled at them and appreciated my own shortcomings.

The news seems slightly better; at least it is not worse now: the Greeks are fighting desperately but I foresee an eventual withdrawal; but it looks as if we may hold in Libya. It is Libya that I am most [concerned] about, caring more for the fate of Cairo than that of Athens. Is it curious?

I walked unhappily about and fished frogs from the swimming pool. And I thought of my lonely future: I am domestic *au fond*; and now I am becoming a miser, collect pennies, await dividends, save stamps . . . . The future holds v little and yet I hope to outlive a few people – I want to see my son once more.

As I write the raid has begun . . . Harold Balfour rang up to say that the damage in London has been appalling, and that he had caught cold putting out incendiary bombs. Arlington Street, Jermyn Street, St James's Square, the RAC have all been hit badly . . . a few moments ago my Cyclops-butler[1] Church rushed in to advise me to go to the cellar, which, for a few moments, I did. There I found a group of huddled, terrified servants: then – in pyjamas – I went out on to the lawn. It was as bright as daylight as the flares fell. Some were red, some white, and a dreadful din of droning planes. Now I am going to bed, perhaps, for the last time. I must put my affairs in order . . . .

SUNDAY 20TH APRIL

A long day by myself which soothed me . . . and I wrote to my mother-in-law a clear budget of my position and complications. I hope I am wise to send it. Its

---

1 It may be that Church had, or gave the impression of only using, one eye, like the giants of mythology.

composition and letters to P took most of the day. Then I wandered about the gardens, read, and lazed away the hours, still safe . . . . The news from Greece is gradually worse.

TUESDAY 22ND APRIL

To the House of Commons, or rather, to Church House where we now meet as the Palace of Westminster has been damaged again. Winston announced that the Navy had bombarded Tripoli and he did it deftly, thus disarming a somewhat hostile House. Anthony E came in, looked bronzed and even attractive; but he was given a bad reception. Questions were put to the Prime Minister and we were urged by the *franc-tireurs*[1] to have a debate on the situation in Greece and Libya. Opposition to the government is growing, but it is chiefly confined to scattered groups, Winterton; Clem Davies;[2] Hore-Belisha and others . . . . I wonder what will be the outcome? There are rumours of a change in government, or rather of changes. Certainly this one has had its first great shock . . . and Belisha was only saying what Churchill would have said had he been in his place.

A long talk with Rab, who tells me that Greece has come between Eden and Churchill: both were for the mad campaign, now each blames the other and accuses the other of lack of judgement. This is the first time that they have both been right.

Erskine-Hill came to dine: he is a huge man of 47 and looks 60 or more. As chairman of the 1922 Committee he holds a certain position in the party and yields some influence. Jay Llewellin also here and we had the usual political discussions. They all think that John Anderson will be the next PM; I suggested Menzies.

Honor rang up in the most friendly manner.

WEDNESDAY 23RD APRIL

To the House of Commons quite early and in our room I met Anthony Eden and we had almost a rapturous reunion; he as charming, said 'Bless you' three times, gave me messages from the Lampsons etc. I asked him to get a Privy Counsellorship for Miles Lampson and he agreed to do so: he hadn't thought of it (later, reinforced by this morning, I went to see Alec Cadogan who agreed to do it). Thus the meeting, which I somewhat dreaded, passed off extraordinarily well: I shall pursue it. The day really went well for me personally for when I went back to the offices – after hearing murmurings of disapproval of AE and that there was a hunt on against him etc. – I find a brace of divine letters from Peter . . . . P writes

1 Mavericks.
2 The Liberal MP for Montgomeryshire.

that Wavell was against the Greek campaign, as I am sure he was, and fought against it unsuccessfully: he had to give in to Churchill's orders and the decision once taken had to be undertaken with all possible energy. P's letter, dated the 9th of April, gives the impression that Cairo is frightened and very nervous. He, poor boy, has had to dissimulate; but he has taken steps about his possessions and money. He will probably get away with the General. Later in the day a cable came from him to say that he had been in Greece with Wavell and only just returned – he added that Paul and Princess Olga leave tomorrow for Kenya, where they will occupy Erroll's house. Too macabre.

. . . . I went back to the House of Commons. Yes, there is an Eden hunt on and his position is perhaps precarious.

So many people are dead or killed. Poor mild dull Ronnie Balfour[1] was dining out on Wednesday; when he returned to his flat in Charles Street he found that it had vanished; so, somewhat shaken he went during the bombardment to the Admiralty which was struck as he arrived and he saw the building cut in two; somehow he got a car and was killed on the way to the country. Then there is Jack Kimberley;[2] he dined on Wednesday at the Ritz . . . . he walked back to his *garçonnière*[3] in Jermyn Street and was killed a few minutes later. Now Mrs Rupert Beckett[4] is dead – and although I haven't seen her for years, her death recalls the glamorous days of my rich youth. There was a fantastic night – I think in 1923 – Paul of Yugoslavia and I dined with the Prince of Wales and went onto the ball in Grosvenor Street: it had extraordinary and strange *Stimmung*. A terrific tempest – I only remember another such in London, the night before we declared war – broke out and for hours thunder roared and lightning flashed. The ball continued . . . and it was nearly six before P and I decided to go back to our flat in Mount Street. We waded through inches of water: there were no taxis, and tiaras glistened in the lightning. There was something oppressive in the atmosphere . . . I slept late, the breakfast newspapers announced that a murder had been committed at the Savoy

1 Ronald Egerton Balfour (1896–1941) had served in the Royal Navy during the Great War and fought at Jutland. He was married in 1930 to Deirdre Hart-Davis (1909–99), a niece of Lady Diana Cooper (qv) and a muse for Cecil Beaton. He was killed after falling asleep at the wheel of his car.

2 John Wodehouse (1883–1941) was by courtesy Lord Wodehouse from 1902 to 1932, when he succeeded his father as 3rd Earl of Kimberley. He played polo for Great Britain in the 1908 and 1920 Olympics, winning a silver medal at the former and a gold at the latter. He won the Military Cross serving with the 16th Lancers in the Great War and was twice mentioned in dispatches.

3 Bachelor pad.

4 Muriel Helen Florence Paget (1878–1941), daughter of Lord Berkeley Paget, married in 1896 Rupert Evelyn Beckett (*né* Beckett-Denison) (1870–1955), a leading banker and for thirty years Chairman of the *Yorkshire Post*.

during the storm. Mme Fahmy[1] had killed her Egyptian husband: the storm and murder were later described by Edward Marjoribanks in his life of Marshall Hall … Later that day Paul gave me some jewels! I have them still.

The Greek government and royal family have retired to Crete: it is the beginning of the end for poor gallant Greece.

THURSDAY 24TH APRIL

The political atmosphere grows more tense … there are rumours that old Lloyd George will be brought back into government, that Anthony will leave the Foreign Office etc. As Eden is down I thought this an opportune moment to make him an advance and so – meeting him in the passage – I asked him to dine next Wednesday and he has accepted! Rab was irritated but he has no social sense, although his judgement is excellent. The House of Commons is restive and the government's popularity is declining, but the Prime Minister's personal position seems secure, even supreme, although he has been responsible for two major disasters of the war, Norway and Greece. There was a leader in today's *Daily Mail* attacking Anthony: it must have been inspired by Winston – perhaps as a *ballon d'essai*[2] as I discovered that Esmond Harmsworth dined with him at Ditchley on Sunday night. Is Winston preparing to throw Mr Eden if the going becomes too hot? – and to keep him if he can get away with it? So it seems.

I went back to the FO, talked to Anthony, who is so disloyal about me (but I am determined to bring him around), and it may be easier than I expected since he is down, and drove Rab home here …. Rab calls the Glamour Boys 'The Pansy Division'! – a dangerous but witty remark.

Rab thinks that Cairo will fall … it may.

I am alone, always alone, always anxious. But I have had a happier week with many missives and cables – sometimes two a day – from Cairo.

FRIDAY 25TH APRIL

All day Kelvedon, colder than charity, and bleak and heartbreaking.

The Greek royal family, or some of them, are at Crete. I got back to London about four o'clock and hurried to the Foreign Office, where I found a letter from Peter which made me almost collapse. I read and reread it, his descriptions of

---

1 Marguerite Marie Alibert (1890–1971) was a Parisian courtesan who counted the Prince of Wales (Edward VIII) among her conquests. She murdered her husband of six months, Ali Fahmy Bey, at the Savoy in 1923, by repeatedly shooting him; the judge forbade mention of her prostitution and the defence, led by Edward Marshall Hall (1858–1927), emphasised Fahmy's sadism. She was acquitted.
2 Literally a trial balloon, metaphorically to put out feelers.

the Regent's arrival at Heliopolis made me weep. Later I drove Rab to broadcast and in the taxi as I read him the letter I broke down and cried like a child: he was astonished and embarrassed and put his hand affectionately on my knee – I like him so much, but I don't love him like the Regent or P[eter]. Here is part of P's letter:

GHQ 12th April
Dear Chips,
   Your 'son',[1] wife and three children arrived yesterday. I was deputed to meet them and they came in a British plane, landing at Heliopolis, where I saw you off to Greece with General Gambier-Parry. As the Egyptian government did not want them here and it was the Egyptian Sunday, no official arrangement could be made. The General was away – so luckily I had time to be at their disposal. We took them to a house in Heliopolis – an English Colonel's and really it was not nearly as bad as it might have been. P[rince] P[aul] said, as he stalked from the plane, 'I felt sure you would be here.' She [Princess Olga] was pale, beautiful as never before, travel-stained. The children had been sick over Crete. PP at once said where could he buy presents for the airmen who had wafted them across. No guard of honour . . . all slightly underhand and Anthony Hope. I stayed with them until dinner, making the hot-water work, putting the house straight, ordered the milk for the little girl. They have an armed guard till their situation is regularised!! I am taking them to the Pyramids this afternoon. Neither of them has been to Egypt before! What an incredible meeting it has been. The last time I saw him was at your luncheon, do you remember, when he came back to No. 5 afterwards? [July 1939]. He recalled it – and we spoke of the book he had sent me. I find him really charming . . . . I have, of course, not spoken of politics at all . . . . If you have any idea as to their future, write me.
   Bless you
   Peter

It is a heartbreaking letter to read for one who loved them as I do, and who knew them surrounded by all their pomp and circumstance. Thank God! Peter was with them to help with his gracious kindness . . . .
   I broke down: I am a hysterical sentimentalist – and wrote P a hurried line of thanks.
   The news from Greece seems to be now – a total collapse of the Allied–Greek forces; but Libya looks like being held.

---

1 Code for Prince Paul.

SATURDAY 26TH APRIL   *KELVEDON*

I rushed to the FO at nine o'clock to catch the outgoing bag with my letter to P and I cabled asking him to send the Regent a birthday cable on Monday[1] from me . . . . Honor rang up proposing that we should lunch together, but I was already engaged to the Willingdons; she said that she would come to No. 5 at 2.30 punctually . . . . I excused myself at 2.30, pleading a train to the country, and rushed home to see H. She was not there. She came at 3.30, nearly an hour late and smelling of drink. She was friendly, unattractive, shabby and most ungracious. The hour's wait had thrown me into a rage – she is so inconsiderate always. The meeting was scarcely a success and gave me indigestion. She kept plaguing me for things – *bibelots*, etc. She lacks all sensitivity . . . Then I drove here in a melancholy mood. It is arctic and I am hating the place today.

It is six months today, and, curiously enough on a Saturday, that Honor came up to London from Kelvedon to tell me that she wished to marry her swarthy ostler! I told her then that she could not, would not be able to jump into another so unsuitable an alliance so quickly. She was [illegible], selfish, impatient and said that she would – well, she hasn't. Had she even evinced any graciousness I should have been easier. Perhaps that is beyond her limited capabilities: she is always rude and oblivious of the feelings of others.

SUNDAY 27TH APRIL

I am turning against this place and Essex altogether. Perhaps I won't live here after the war. Begin again from scratch elsewhere, and let Kelvedon and sell Belgrave Square, live on a smaller scale, more happily, and, I trust, with P. Vancouver or Venice?

The Germans occupy Athens this morning. All our efforts only delayed their progress by a fortnight. Is the Suez next, or Libya and Cairo, or all three? The government have committed a major blunder which may lose the war.

The Prime Minister made a magnificent broadcast: I was moved and impressed.

MONDAY 28TH APRIL

Woke ill-tempered and fretful and drove to London: my will to live is atrophied and dulled. Dictated letters . . . at 3.30 the Duchess of Kent [arrived], looking curiously Russian with a red velvet bandana instead of a hat on her head. We sat on my sofa and talked of Paul for an hour; and she referred to the Queen's laziness; her inability to answer letters; her neglect in not sympathising with her about Paul and Princess Olga. There is no love lost between them. I said that I knew that the

---

1 His birthday was in fact the 27th.

Yugoslav party arrived in Nairobi today and would stay at Erroll's house . . . . She admitted that the Duke is disappointed and dismayed by the decision not to send him to the Middle East: but, of course, it is impossible now.

Discouraged, dumb, dull, deserted, I went to bed.

TUESDAY 29TH APRIL

To the House in the morning. There is some political unrest and much intrigue but the Eden hunt is perhaps postponed.

Anthony Eden, Jay Llewellin, Harold, Rab, and I dined. The feast was by way of a reconciliation between Anthony and me: I was determined to be decent to young Daniel as he entered the lions' den. He walked here from the FO with Rab, and was immediately charming, even jocularly with his long eyelashes, his fluency, his glib descriptions of his Blitz expeditions to Greece, of Wavell – but never once did he mention Peter nor Paul – I was rather thankful for that, really.

We had Krug 1920, claret – AE drank much and rarely drew breath. It was a perpetual flow of conversation for which he apologised: but he did the trick: we were reconciled and agreed without saying so to support him next week when he will need it most. He called me 'Chips dear!', said 'Bless you' – a mannerism of his caught from Jim Thomas – half a dozen times. Rab says that AE has a political nose like Sam Hoare, but that whilst Sam is a eunuch, Anthony is a wily woman. I found him fluent and facile, almost fascinating, certainly amiable and affectionate. The evening was a huge success but more than ever was I convinced that it was an unforgivable fault on the part of the government – or rather of Churchill's, since he is the government – to send him abroad on so important a mission. No doubt he did his best but he came back with an infamously empty bag. Foreigners find him frivolous, foolish and light-metal. It is only in England that he has a following.

The Greek royal family have escaped: the King and others are at Crete – and presumably Mrs Jones, whilst both Princess Nicholas and Princess Andrew deliberately chose to remain behind in Athens. When shall we have news of them again? The Regent and his family arrived safely at Nairobi and have been installed at Erroll's house. They are being treated as prisoners, but prisoners allowed every luxury and privilege. Later they will be sent further south. I am distressed beyond measure by the treatment meted to them. No one hits a man so hard when he is down as do the English – but no one does for so short a time. In a few months' time Paul may be a hero, or, at least, forgotten.

WEDNESDAY 30TH APRIL

There was a rumour that we shall be raided tonight as a reprisal for our recent attack on Berlin. I walked a bit in London and was horrified . . . . The capital looked like a battered old war horse! St James's Place is the worst and the most poignant

.... The Camroses' – No. 25, which I made them buy, wrecked! But Lady Camrose, whom I saw today, tells me that all her possessions except the silver in the plate-room and the wine cellar had long since been removed to Hackwood. There were three servants in the house, who had luckily retreated to the basement, and they are all alive and tell the harrowing tale – and the plate and wine cellar are saved. Only the Rothschilds' house escaped: Divine Providence seems to have signalled out the English Rothschilds for protection! Our poor old house, No. 21, known as Moira House, and one of the loveliest and most romantic in London is no more! .... Honor and I lived there from February 1934 to February 1936, and Paul was born there – gone, gone. All the big houses overlooking the Park in this road, Spencer House, Bridgewater House .... Stornoway House, Esmond Rothermere's – all badly battered. The press lords seem almost to have been singled out for attack.[1]

Later I went in some state to represent the Foreign Office at the Greek 'do': long and tedious and pathetic. The Duchess of Kent was the Chief Guest; and I refused to be 'presented' as I thought it would be too foolish. Suddenly during a long speech .... she caught my eye and we had *foux rires*![2] She looked lovely and was received with much state; I could not help contrasting her position with the present one of Princess Olga, now practically a prisoner in remote Kenya.

Winston made a statement to the House about the evacuation of Greece: it has been less of a disaster than Peter feared, for over 45,000 men have got away. The House, whilst restive, was relieved. Anthony also made a statement reading out a message from the Greek government agreeing, indeed suggesting the withdrawal of our troops.

I am very downcast; dined in with Harold and we had trays by the fire and talked schoolboy filth instead of *Weltpolitik* – what a relief.

THURSDAY 1ST MAY

I went to the House to do some lobbying for Anthony Eden, to smooth his path for the big debate when we will be under fire on Tuesday.[3] My dinner party, if it did not heal, certainly went a long way to patch up a wound in the Conservative Party. I walked from the House of Commons to the Dorchester with Leslie Belisha and flattered him, as I know how so well to do; and prevailed upon him not to mention Turkey, as the situation there is still tense and tricky. There remains a faint chance of them remaining loyal to their alliance .... Meanwhile the news in Iraq is increasingly severe. We are being attacked on all sides.

Harold came in before dinner and whispered to me that the government changes are to be announced tomorrow! Max [Beaverbrook] goes from the

---

1 Rothermere ran the *Daily Mail* and Stornoway House was Beaverbrook's.
2 The giggles.
3 A debate seeking the House's approval for the policy of assisting Greece. The motion was passed 447 to 3.

Aircraft Production and becomes Minister of State,[1] a sort of moving commission which is scarcely a promotion, nor does he so regard it. Brabazon succeeds him. Jay Llewellin becomes Parliamentary Secretary to the new Ministry of Communication, which will combine both transport and shipping; and he is made a Privy Counsellor. An unknown Mr Leathers[2] is created a peer and made a Privy Counsellor and becomes Minister of Communications. Poor Ronnie Cross[3] is sent to Australia as High Commissioner! *Dégommé*. I told Rab that he would soon be sent to the Falkland Islands and he was annoyed . . . .

Peter Loxley, Geoffrey Lloyd, Rab, and Harold and I dined: we talked oil and Iraq. The situation is even more gloomy since a heavy attack has been launched against Tobruk. Will it hold?

SUNDAY 4TH MAY   KELVEDON

A delicious day, warm and balmy . . . . I had not seen the sun since I left Cairo.

Honor's rude farm labourers still strut about the place, insolent and overbearing. I am having them out soon.

MONDAY 5TH MAY

I came to London, my car full of flowers and vegetables: London, I found, depressing, no exciting post, no letters from Cairo. I walked to the Foreign Office and was surprised by the number of couples kissing in Green Park.

Dined at Hanover Lodge and Sibyl Colefax was there: this valiant old war horse told me that she was married in 1901. She was malicious all the evening: I drove her back to Lord North Street and as we arrived there was an air-raid alarm, but nothing followed it. Delicious food, but *manqué* evening.

TUESDAY 6TH MAY

The first day of the great debate: and I wonder will Anthony Eden survive it, or rather would he have survived it had it not been for 'our' sudden and unexpected

---

1 He would be appointed Minister of Supply in June.
2 Frederick James Leathers (1883–1965) left school at 15 but worked his way up to become Managing Director of the Steamship Owners' Coal Association by 1916. As a director of P&O shipping he came to the attention of Churchill, who was also on the board, and who appointed him Minister of War Transport, having him raised to the peerage with a barony, in 1941. He served until 1945 and joined Churchill's second government as Minister for Co-ordination of Transport, Fuel and Power from 1951 to 1953. He was advanced to a viscountcy in 1954.
3 Ronald Hibbert Cross (1896–1968) was Conservative MP for Rossendale from 1931 to 1945 and for Ormskirk from 1950 to 1951. His performance as Minister of Shipping had been attacked by the newspapers and thus he was sent to Australia as High Commissioner from 1941 to 1945, though created 1st Bt on his appointment. He was Governor of Tasmania from 1951 to 1958.

decision last week to support him? He opened the Debate with an appallingly bad speech, thin and light .... Anthony rose but no cheers greeted him and he gave a dim account of his travels and failures. He sat down amidst complete silence. I have never heard an important speech so badly delivered: it was so silly and ineffectual. He was followed by a series of speakers, all of whom attacked him and the government. Leslie Hore-Belisha was eloquent and damning, Maurice Petherick[1] said that he wanted a 'Panzer government, not a Pansy government', a sly allusion to Anthony and his minions. The whole debate was acrimonious, rude, and even ill-tempered rather than particularly damaging ... I rushed about hypocritically doing yeoman service to Anthony, who called me 'darling' and said I was 'angelic'. I wanted to be friends with Eden but could not help taking some secret delight in his, or 'their', discomfort. Winston looked uncomfortable and aware of Anthony's shortcomings. Duff Cooper took me into his room and laughingly remarked that the most damaging speech against the government was Anthony's! Trouble in paradise!

The government is wobbly, or rather would be, if there was any alternative. I despaired of England and of democracy all day and yet I never enjoyed a day more thanks to the intrigues.

WEDNESDAY 7TH MAY

Indeed a big day. I was early at the House as I was in attendance on Anthony Eden and he was markedly cordial, affectionate, ingratiating, even grateful. He took his Questions and at twelve o'clock the big debate was resumed. Lloyd George got up and I rushed to Anthony's room to fetch him. LG spoke, or rather fulminated for a full hour: he was weak at times, at others sly and shrewd, again he was silly and senile, and often vindictive as he attacked the government. No one could make out what he was driving at, nor why he should abuse Eden and Churchill. I sat immediately behind these two gentlemen of Westminster and watched Anthony chew his nails as he whispered to Winston, who was very obviously shaken and enraged for he shook, twitched and his hands were never still. He kept up a running flow of commentaries and, indeed, was right, for LG's attack could help nobody except the enemy as he was rude about Turkey and America. Several times the P Minister rose and contradicted him; and several times, too, Anthony and Winston turned to me for confirmation of statements mentioned by L George. I spent the morning tripping along the PPSs' bench to the official gallery to ask for advice and information, and notes and red boxes were frequently handed to me. I was very conspicuous. I enjoyed the role, for it is a year ago today that we had the great Norway debate, which brought about the

---

1 Maurice Petherick (1894–1985) was Conservative MP for Penryn and Falmouth from 1931 to 1945.

fall of Mr Chamberlain. Today was different; again the government was attacked, but the personal position of the Prime Minister is not to be questioned: Anthony was the victim and he was rattled, even pathetic. I served him well and loyally. Yet I could not but experience a rather subtle mixed pleasure in the proceedings: he was my chief, so I was loyal; he has been my friend so I was indignant; he has also been my enemy so I was enchanted and half agreed with his attackers.

Before 1.30, when LG sat down and the debate was turned over to backbenchers, I went along to the Strangers' dining room and gave Georgia Sitwell, Alfred Beit, Alan [Lennox-Boyd], and 'Peter' Mallaby[1] lunch. It was a gay festival and I was excited as I always am when on the point of making a conquest! The conversation was frivolous, and we all agreed that David Margesson was more 'beddable' than Anthony with his rabbit teeth. Mallaby was astonished by such conversation! He is a brigadier and we were soon Peter and Chips! Then I returned to the Chamber. Soon after four o'clock Winston rose, and never have I heard him in such brilliant (although irrelevant) form; he was pungent, amusing, cruel, hard-hitting and he lashed out at Lloyd George, Winterton and Hore-Belisha with irritable venom and wit. He was soon at his ease and began to enjoy himself: it was a magnificent effort and he completely captivated the House. He tore his opponents to shreds and when the division came the figures were 447 to 3.[2] A triumph on paper, but in reality the government has been seriously shaken and both Anthony and Winston know it. These two days are the thunder before the real storm, which I predict will blow up again in July. Everyone went away exhilarated . . . .

THURSDAY 8TH MAY

The Palace of Westminster today reminded me this morning of grand houses in the old days, the day after a ball when one came upon caterers moving out the gilt chairs, the palms, and servants in aprons eating the leftover quails . . . . It looked headachey and was nearly empty. I stayed only a short time. Lunched at home and slept and later retired to the Office. It is a long time since I have had a letter from Peter – April 26th. But I know he has been to Greece and [is] fantastically rushed. Talked several times to the Duchess of Kent as usual.

1 Aubertin Walter Sothern 'Peter' Mallaby (1899–1945) was a regular soldier in the Indian Army who served at the War Office from 1938 to 1942, reaching the rank of brigadier. Channon had only recently met him and had some homoerotic interest in him. After the war he was sent to Java, during a revolution, to find and repatriate British prisoners of war taken by the Japanese, but was killed within days.

2 The motion on which the government had this overwhelming victory was 'That this House approves the policy of His Majesty's Government in sending help to Greece and declares its confidence that our operations in the Middle East and in all other theatres of war will be pursued by the government with the utmost vigour.'

FRIDAY 9TH MAY

Still no letter from Peter but this morning a cryptic cable came. 'Mrs Woolly well now at Berchers' – I tried to understand. It can only mean that Toto Toerring is attached to Hitler and is staying at Berchtesgaden. After all he is a German and has always been a Nazi at heart. So why shouldn't he? I am not surprised. I shall tell nobody.

A secret: Vansittart is to be made a peer quite shortly and he will retire and his office lapse, a course I have been urging for three years. A[nthony] E[den] is making himself unpopular in the FO . . . . the usual English 'head-on-a-charger' complex![1] And he has selected the American Department to receive the full blast of his spleen. He knows that his position politically has been severely shaken by the recent debate and wants to 'take it out' on someone but unfortunately he chooses that Dept which has been the most supportive. It really is monstrous: he will have us out before long; but I shall no longer care.

Lunched alone; Elizabeth Elveden dined with Harold and me. He went back to the Air Ministry and she then talked to me of my matrimonial entanglements. She hates Honor and advises me to divorce her: she told me that H is the most selfish, unsympathetic and unpopular woman in London! She loves nobody and is loyal to no one! I fear this harsh criticism is true.

I ran into Julian Amery[2] in the street and later he came to No. 5 for a drink. He is an insinuating Jew boy, but intelligent. As he is going to Jerusalem I rang up Queen Marie and told her that I knew of a secret means of getting a letter to her son in record time.

If Anthony pursues his present course of sacking the members of the American Dept. and almost everyone else he will end by fighting the USA. Much as I now like him I cannot forget the Regent's[3] Cassandra-like prophecy: 'If the British Empire falls the architect of its destruction will be Anthony Eden.'

SATURDAY 10TH MAY   *KELVEDON*

It is still very cold and here the blossom is scarcely out. There has never been so cold, so backward and depressing a spring.

---

1 In the Bible the phrase, relating to John the Baptist, is 'head in a charger'. Channon appears to be referring to a culture of searching for scapegoats when mistakes were made.

2 Harold Julian Amery (1919–96) was Conservative MP for Preston North from 1950 to 1966 and for Brighton Pavilion from 1969 to 1992, when he was raised to the peerage as Lord Amery of Lustleigh (life peer). His father was Leo Amery (qv); his father-in-law was Harold Macmillan (qv), who appointed him Under-Secretary of State for the Colonies in 1958, Secretary of State for Air in 1960 and Minister of Aviation in 1962, a post he held until 1964. He also served as a Minister of State in the Heath administration from 1970 to 1974. He would serve in the Middle East, as a liaison officer with the Albanian resistance, and in China during his military service.

3 Prince Paul of Yugoslavia.

We had a big raid over Germany last night and I suppose there will be a reprisal either tonight or tomorrow. I wrote letters for Egypt, and bought a pair of white enamel and ruby and sapphire ball links for Peter and sent them to him by Julian Amery, who is leaving for Cairo in a few days' time; and who dispatched letters by the same courier including one for King Peter in Jerusalem from his mother.

Lunched with Harold Balfour at Prunier's and he confessed to a very youthful affair with 'Peter' Portal twenty-three years ago in France!! We had dinner at the Carlton Club where we ran into David Margesson reading the description of Kelvedon in *Country Life*. He was amused by my sudden, and much talked-of axis with 'Peter' Mallaby! Jay Llewellin, now a full-fledged Privy Counsellor, was there and later came back to Belgrave Square to gossip . . .

I drove here. Honor has been staying here but left me no note. I shall miss this place: it will not be the same with a Convalescent Home established here.

Sunday 11th May

I slept badly last night: the perpetual drone of the planes kept me awake. This morning I was not surprised to hear that London had had a very severe attack.[1] The windows are out in my bedroom in Belgrave Square.

A quiet day here lying in the sun and reading and writing. I feel well, and have lost a stone these past weeks and so am handsome although my hair is greying (like Mr Chamberlain's) at the temples. I am happiest, since I cannot be with Peter, alone. I think only of Egypt, of Egypt and of money. Something of my old grandfather's miserly instinct is coming out in me: I pounce upon pennies, and have almost an orgasm over cheques.

The nine o'clock wireless has details of the appalling raid last night on London and the fires at the House of Commons and Westminster Abbey – they are seriously damaged, and, I fear, [so] is the British Museum. My poor diaries: I kept them for twenty years: are they, too, gone? . . . even as I write I again hear the sirens wail in anger. We are about to have another raid. All last night my beloved Bundi lay in my arms and I could feel his canine heart beat fast . . .

Monday 12th May

I left the lovely May countryside with regret and drove up to London; at first it appeared normal; but by the time I had arrived at Belgrave Square I realised the havoc and devastation. The servants here were jittery; the Alexandria Hotel in Knightsbridge almost immediately behind us was hit on Saturday night, and rumour says that 150 people were trapped and many killed. There were burnt

---

1 This was the worst, and last, night of the London Blitz. Over 1,400 were killed and 2,000 injured. The next serious bombardment of the capital would come with the V-1s in 1944.

bits of paper fluttering in the street, broken glass everywhere, and rubble and debris are heaped high in the streets. Yet Belgrave Square looks normal! Bombs fell on Chester Square, Eaton Square, Grosvenor Crescent and elsewhere. The din lasted until 5.30! I tried to get to the House of Commons but the crowd was so large I didn't fight my way through; but I could see the huge hole in Westminster Hall roof. I met Jim Thomas who tells me that the Chamber is <u>gutted</u>: no more shall we have fiery and futile and dangerous and inciting speech there . . . gone is that place, as I always foresaw it would be. Itself the cradle, the protector of democracy, in the end it has gone a long way to kill what it created – a more antiquated assembly one could not imagine . . .

Lunched with Bill Tufnell at the Mirabelle restaurant, delicious food; all seemed normal. Then I had an attack of nerves and came home to rest. Nothing pleasant today – no letter from Peter; no surprises or attentions from anyone. The appearance of London is depressing . . . I am lucky to have been away and that my house has survived yet another colossal attack.

Europe, Archie James says, is divided into two parts: the occupied and the pre-occupied.

I met Leslie Belisha and he walked with me for some time; he was vitriolic about the government. The country will soon wake up and realise that speeches are not victories, that we are drugged with Winston's oratory. He is gloomy about the future, sees little hope if we continue as we are now doing. He is very anti-Russian. Rab, curiously enough, is not and still flogs his red horse.

There is an extraordinary rumour in the office that a German peace envoy[1] has arrived and that he has some connexion with the Duke of Hamilton![2]

TUESDAY 13TH MAY

The early wireless announced that Rudolph [*sic*] Hess,[3] the third most important personality in the German Reich, arrived alone by plane in Scotland on Saturday

1 This is Rudolf Hess: *vide infra*.
2 Douglas Douglas-Hamilton (1903–73) was by courtesy Marquess of Douglas and Clydesdale until 1940, when he succeeded his father as 14th Duke of Hamilton and 11th Duke of Brandon. He was Unionist MP for East Renfrewshire from 1930 to 1940. A distinguished aviator who made the first flight over Mount Everest in 1935, he reached the rank of air commodore in the RAF.
3 Rudolf Walter Richard Hess (1894–1987) had been the second most important Nazi, being Deputy Führer, a post he had held since 1933; but in 1939 Hitler named Göring as his successor and Hess was next in the succession. Hess was from a mercantile family and had fought, and been wounded, during the Great War. He met Hitler in 1920 and was one of the early recruits to the Nazi Party. Like the Duke of Hamilton, Hess was a committed aviator, which was one of the reasons why he flew to Scotland on his peace mission. He also wrongly believed that Hamilton led a party opposed to the war. Hess was tried at Nuremberg and given a life sentence, and repeated attempts to release him were blocked by the Soviet Union. He hanged himself in 1987.

night. A hazardous and remarkable performance. All day people talked of a crack in the Nazi government and system: I don't believe it. He once invited me and Honor to Berlin when we were there for the great festivities at the time of the Olympic Games; but we refused – but I remember that 'Duglo' Clydesdale, as he then was, went as did Pat Jersey.[1] I think the world doesn't know that 'Duglo' is concerned in the story. He came to the Foreign Office yesterday and spent an hour with Anthony telling him the tale.

The Duchess of Kent came to see me for a moment. Rab and I dined . . . . at Claridge's, a dreadful old girls' evening: I was next to that horrible old harridan Mrs Arthur James[2] who whispered to Rab before dinner that I was 'the most man[3] in London'. How I have always hated her. She is 84[4] and all too healthy. However we chatted merrily at dinner (I didn't know then that she had so abused me). She ran down everyone and everything; and she boasted that throughout the seventeen years that a one-legged beggar woman had stood on the corner opposite Mrs James's house in Grafton Street (I knew the poor thing by sight) she had never once given her a farthing. And Mrs James has £40,000 per annum. I repeated the story to Lady Hudson[5] (Lord Northcliffe's amiable and distinguished widow) who retorted with horror. She used to send the poor creature home in her Rolls-Royce. The Willingdons drove Rab and me home and justly and roundly abused Mrs James *en route*. A horrible evening . . . . Here I found Harold had been entertaining Alan, Bill Mabane and Hector Bolitho to dine. Alan showed me an ecstatic letter from Eric Duncannon arranging his engagement to Mary Churchill, the Prime Minister's youngest daughter![6] It is to be announced on Wednesday. I thought this strange as he was proposing to my sister-in-law Brigid less than a month ago. A coup for the Churchills after Vic Oliver!

Depressed, drunk and world-weary I went to bed; the boys, I left in the morning room, still chattering about Hess. The appalling devastation in the House

1 See Vol. I, entry for 15 August 1935 and footnote.

2 Mary Venetia Cavendish-Bentinck (qv). Her meanness was legendary, and included inviting only Roman Catholics to dinner on Fridays as fish was cheaper than meat. See entry for 2 May 1939 and footnote.

3 Thus in the MS. Coats, on what authority one cannot be sure, has added 'dangerous' before 'man'.

4 She was not quite 80.

5 Mary Elizabeth Milner (1867–1963) married in 1888 Alfred Charles William Harmsworth (1865–1922), who founded the *Daily Mail* and *Daily Mirror* and became proprietor of *The Times*. He was raised to the peerage as 1st Baron Northcliffe in 1905 and advanced to a viscountcy in 1918. For voluntary work with the Red Cross and Order of St John during the Great War she became a Dame Grand Cross of the Order of the British Empire in 1918. In 1923 she married, as her second husband, Robert Arundell Hudson (1864–1927), with whom she had collaborated on war work and who was knighted for it in 1918.

6 They never married. Mary Spencer-Churchill (1922–2014) married in 1947 Christopher Soames (1920–87), who became a Cabinet minister, diplomat and the last Governor of Rhodesia. She became a DBE in 1980 and was made a Lady of the Garter in 2005.

of Commons is forgotten – nothing remains of the Chamber, of that Tower of often foolish battle. There are angry crowds outside the building and they gaze wondrously at the Abbey. I met Winston in King Charles Street . . . . he stopped me for a second and exchanged banalities. He is more friendly in tone. Is it the engagement of his daughter Mary, or does he know that Randolph is having a roaring affair in Egypt . . . .

WEDNESDAY 14TH MAY

Woke ill and depressed, and walked to the H of C[1] . . . . Anthony took the Questions as he does now on Wednesdays rather than Rab, a sort of rhythm. Harold told me, as I dressed, that Rab is jealous of my rapprochement with Anthony and I am reluctantly bound to record that he is probably right! Lunched with Jim Thomas, Anthony's alter ego, his slave, his jackal, his mental Ganymede . . . Then I went back to his windowless flat in Lansdowne House to talk . . . I am depressed by the treachery about[2] . . . . there are very hush rumours that Longmore will be sacked: Winston doesn't like him. No one who is not his blind adorer has a chance of survival in this racket dignified by the name of government! Shocking but true . . . I was exhausted by my *3 à 4* with Jim and went home to sleep and recover . . . Then I returned to the FO about six, where I found a stupendous letter from P from Cairo describing in vivid melodramatic language his trip to Greece with Wavell, the day before Greece cracked and collapsed. It is one of the finest letters in the . . . . collection; indeed in any language; and he gives riveting details of the visit from the Robinsons (as the Regent and Princess Olga are called) to Cairo! My heart throbbed and my temperature went up as I read it . . . as I devoured it – but I am ahead of my story. I found several letters from Princess Olga for the Duchess . . . . and rushed back to No. 5 to deliver them, as both the Duke and Duchess were awaiting me. I had not seen him for several weeks, and he has been in Scotland for a fortnight. He is sunburned and much improved, he was charming – so he has got over his fit of petty surliness with me. I then returned to the Office, hurriedly, with P's long document still only half-read and as I was devouring it again a telephone call came from Anthony Eden asking whether he might dine? I was irritated as I was socially bankrupt and longed to be alone. However, I agreed and collected Rab. He and Anthony walked home to Belgrave Square. I drove, thinking only of Peter's letter and its burning contents. Anthony and I both drank too much – champagne, burgundy and Kümmel and got heated, argumentative, even tipsy . . . Rab tried to stop us . . . in the midst of a conversation about royalties which bored Anthony – and he betrayed both his ignorance and shallowness – the Duchess of

---

1 Which was then sitting in Church House, following the destruction of the Commons' chamber.
2 He implies there was a habit of ministers blaming officials for their mistakes.

Kent rang up and I told her that AE was with me. She was staggered! Then I came down, and we had more conversation. AE left to join Winston at 11.30. He keeps his henchmen up until all hours! Then Rab and I gossiped and he told me that I had talked too much, that he had feared an unpleasant scene because I defended the Regent!

I put him to bed and we reviewed the evening. AE had been v against monarchies, but I retorted that they were bulwarks against both dictatorship and socialism. He has been much influenced by Oliver Harvey's rather Girondin[1] mentality, and blunt in mind – advanced, polite radicalism. Rab added that Loelia Westminster had abused me to him – which I didn't believe. But he has destroyed my old friendship with her. He has an irritating habit of repeating unpleasant things and so destroying one's happiness. He is unworldly as I told him; and I pointed out that the higher one moves in the social scale the more malicious people become. Malice is the currency in all high civilised, aristocratic circles – in which he has never moved. He is also extraordinarily mean and Scotch: he offered to pay me peppercorn bed and board of £3.10.0 per week; but makes it for the month, thus gaining three days each time – and he rarely pays that. It requires a sharp reminder from my secretary to his to get it: I suddenly dislike him tonight, but think it was drink.

Bed at twelve, miserable and melancholy. I read Peter's letter to Rab who was moved and impressed.

THURSDAY 15TH MAY

I woke early with the dead doomed feeling that I had been foolish the night before, and Rab quietly confirmed my fears: I had shouted at Anthony, been too garrulous and argumentative altogether. So it was with some trepidation that I waylaid him at the House: he was affectionate and said that he had never enjoyed himself more. Rab admitted that AE too had been a touch tipsy. So that passed off . . . A ridiculous scene in the House of Commons over the Allied Maritime Bill . . . . I sat nervously, bored and angry and wondered how long we shall be able to sit here in peace – before Church House is bombed? We are looking for alternative accommodation and the House of Lords has been suggested . . . . Anthony made a brief statement about our relations with France, which have become acute during the past forty-eight hours, as the Vichy government have agreed to allow the Germans to use the Syrian air bases. Is this the prelude to war with France? . . .

Early this morning I was rung up by Arthur Longmore who asked if he might dine, and I spent most of a harassed day trying to collect a suitable party – and

---

1 An anti-monarchist faction during the French Revolution, which originated in the Gironde in south-west France.

didn't. The Defence Committee was meeting at 9.45 and everyone, including Longmore, had to be there. Rab much against my advice insisted on going to the country, and was already *en route* to Stanstead when he was summoned to attend. I rang him, but it was too late for him to return – but I managed to spoil his evening, as in a way, he spoilt mine. Nothing went well today . . . I tried to get 'Peter' Mallaby to dine but he refused and said he would look in afterwards – and again didn't because of the blasted Defence Committee meeting. Finally I had only Jay Llewellin; Harold [Balfour], the ever faithful, and Allan Chapman[1] whom I picked up at the last moment at the Carlton Club. Dinner was moderately successful but overshadowed by the knowledge, shared by Harold and me, that Longmore is <u>not</u> going back to the Middle East as ACM [Air Chief Marshal]. He is going to be Governor of Southern Rhodesia instead![2] From Longmore's depression I concluded that he, too, had half-guessed . . . . However he rushed off to the Defence Committee and is not *dégommé* yet – at least not officially . . . . He was charming about Peter.

I was left alone with Harold and Jay, who is a shrewd, loveable old Blimp but bores me to distraction. Unfortunately he is rather in love with me – an added and unneeded complication in my life.

Black Rod is dead, old Pulteney,[3] a most amiable old bird with the manners of a courtier. No more shall we hear him rattle the doors of the Commons with his wand – for the doors are gone, too.

Friday 16th May

We are nearer to a war with France.

I walked . . . . in this battered London and tried to buy General Wavell a Black Watch scarf. There is hardly a good shop left standing or intact. London looks deplorable.

Rab returned to the country for the night: he is genuinely afraid of raids, and rightly. I dined alone – at last – and am going now to bed. Harold has just rung up to say that the decision is taken: Longmore is <u>not going back</u>, but becomes Governor of Southern Rhodesia.

---

1 Allan Chapman (1897–1966) was Unionist MP for Rutherglen from 1935 to 1945. He was assistant Postmaster-General from 1941 to 1942 and Under-Secretary of State for Scotland from 1942 to 1945.

2 He did not go to Rhodesia; he became Inspector-General of the RAF and retired the following year.

3 William Pulteney Pulteney (1861–1941) served in the Army from 1878 to 1920, retiring in the rank of lieutenant general. He served with distinction in the Great War, commanding III Corps on the Western Front from August 1914 to February 1918. He held the office of Black Rod from 1920 until his death. He was knighted in 1915.

SATURDAY 17TH MAY   KELVEDON

I drove here. It is lovely, but still cold. Honor has now removed almost all of her things – but not quite. I shall always remember later that she has not kept one of her promises to me, not one, whereas I have kept all of mine. She is selfish and mad and cares for nobody or anything except the obsession of the moment. I am getting used to being without her and would <u>dread</u> her return; yet I fear that one day she will want to come back. And being both mercenary and a fool I shall probably take her.

I wrote out long letters of instructions for Peter etc., about my will.

The story of the Duncannon–Churchill courtship is astonishing. Mary Churchill accepted him, the Churchills were enchanted – after Vic Oliver,[1] the comedian, what a contrast, for Eric is very handsome, aristocratic, suitable and charming. Suddenly the PM changed his mind, decided that Eric was ambitious etc., and demanded delay. Mary meanwhile turned against him and the engagement is off. Clarissa C[2] hinted to me that Eric was thought rather 'pansy'. I don't suppose that they knew he had proposed to Brigid Guinness less than a month ago?

SUNDAY 18TH MAY

I spent the day writing to P, a long but inadequate reply to his magnificent missive ... It is warmer and hence more agreeable: and the gardens are still lovely. Rab rang up chattily and pleasantly and we were reunited: he was a bit on my nerves this week, but was *entêté*[3] and spiritually bankrupt.

What will this week bring us? The past one brought the destruction of the House of Commons, the exciting arrival of Herr Hess and the Vichy surrender to Germany over Syria. Oh! Why cannot we have peace?

Later.

The news has begun: the Duke of Aosta[4] has asked for the terms of surrender to his troops in Abyssinia. And the throne of Croatia has been accepted by the King of Italy who has nominated the Duke of Spoleto – (my old (and Honor's) boy-friend) as King. His wife is Princess Irene. They will probably live at Brdo in my Paul's beautiful Palace. Every hour something exciting happens; unhappily

---

1   Churchill's son-in-law; see entry for 24 July 1940 and footnote.
2   Anne Clarissa Spencer-Churchill (b.1920) is the daughter of Winston Churchill's younger brother John (qv). She married, in 1952, Anthony Eden (qv).
3   Stubborn or pig-headed.
4   The 4th Duke of Aosta, since 1937 Viceroy of Italian East Africa. See entry for 26 May 1939 and footnote.

change and vigour is [*sic*] more spellbinding than the struggle of the status quo diluted by prattle about democracy which I, for one, detest.

In my loneliness I have been brooding over P's letter: the Regent, he tells me, seems to have little idea, little realisation of what he did: is he then mad? He sent me a hundred messages and as his plane took off, leaving Europe and the past, for Africa and obscurity, he was still talking of me ... The letter almost broke my heart. P goes on to say that little King Peter is now in our room, where we were so happy, in Jerusalem.

I have devoured the letter twenty times and each time it brings tears to my old, tired, eyes .... What have I done to deserve, to win so devoted and perfect a friend as Peter? All my life I have dreamt about and asked for such a person ... gay, gracious, handsome, distinguished and debonair, gentle, affectionate, loving and whimsical with a flair for people and a genius for life, he combines everything that I love, admire, covet and am attracted by.

MONDAY 19TH MAY

The Duchess of Kent came to me at three o'clock and stayed for two hours: we read out to each other our recent riveting letters. One from Princess Olga from Athens goes a long way to vindicate the Regent but she admits that her mother, Princess Nicholas, soundly hated him on his arrival at the villa at Psychiko. The whole Greek royal family had, however, gone to the station to meet the party on their arrival from Belgrade and I now gather that there was no real difficulty about their departure; they took most of their belongings and travelled in their own train in dignity, safety and splendour. Princess Olga's long letter, which is an historical document of importance, describes how young King Peter had been with her throughout the day of the *coup d'état*, and knew nothing of the proclamations which he was supposed to have signed. Nor did he broadcast: the new government had arranged for someone with a voice slightly like his to speak. It is a fantastic story. I had the letter copied by my secretary, and the Duchess is sending a copy to the King tonight: I kept one which is in the bank. She was much moved by Peter's accounts of Paul and Olga in Cairo .... Then I went back to the Foreign Office to lend Rab my car as he drove to Coppins to stay the night.

TUESDAY 20TH MAY

Rab returned gaily from Coppins: his fellow guest was the Princess Royal,[1] whom he found almost idiotic. He alleges that somehow he exchanged vests with her, or rather the servants did.

---

1 Princess Mary, Countess of Harewood (1897–1965), the daughter of George V and Queen Mary.*

The long-expected attack on Crete has begun . . . Parachutists and airborne troops are arriving in large numbers. No one knows what the outcome will be . . . The King is still there; Mrs [Brittain-]Jones has arrived at Alexandria as has the Crown Prince and others . . . It has been decided to send them to South Africa, rather than to bring them here . . . The invasion of Crete is regarded in some quarters as a dress rehearsal for the invasion of England. General Freyberg[1] is out of date and nearly mad. I have never liked him . . . .

I rushed to my solicitor, signed my will in duplicate, left one copy with a letter of instructions for Peter in his keeping, and put the other in my Safety Deposit box at Lloyds where I went through my possessions, jewels and otherwise. Peter is now provided for. This is the fourth will I have made; the first was fifteen years ago when I left everything to my mother with remainder to my friends . . . . The second was done at the time of my marriage when I left everything to Honor; the third was drawn up in 1939 when I made my baby my heir . . . Now that he is to be so rich, I have provided primarily for Peter, and Paul to have the remainders.

Going for a long walk before dinner in the evening light, I was appalled by the devastation, particularly in Ebury Street; old George Moore's[2] house, where I used to go and see that old pink petulant walrus, still stands; and curiously enough as I passed it I heard – there are no windows and the door was half-broken – I heard the tinkle of a telephone. A telephone was the one thing he would never tolerate: messages had to be sent in from a neighbouring chemist's. He used to say that a telephone disturbed him at his work, others were convinced it was to prevent Lady Cunard from ringing up . . . Chester Square is badly damaged.

Just as I came in, and was about to go to bed, David Margesson rang up from the War Office proposing himself to dine: I hesitated, told him that there was no party but he insisted on coming as he wanted to see me alone. He was fascinating, showed his immense charm, and intelligence and I had him to myself for nearly

1 Bernard Cyril 'Tiny' Freyberg (1889–1963) trained as a dentist in New Zealand, and came to Britain when war broke out in 1914 to join the royal Naval Division. He served at Gallipoli where he won the Distinguished Service Order, to which he would add three bars. At the end of the Battle of the Somme, having risen rapidly to the rank of temporary lieutenant colonel, he won the Victoria Cross for taking a strongly defended village and 500 prisoners, despite having been twice wounded. Promoted to brigadier general in April 1917, aged just 28, he was the youngest general officer in the Army. Although retired (as a major general) in 1937 due to health problems stemming from the nine wounds he had sustained during the war, he rejoined the Army in 1939, and Churchill put him in charge of Allied forces during the Battle of Crete. He commanded the 2nd New Zealand Division in North Africa, including at El Alamein, and then in Italy at Monte Cassino. He was knighted in 1941, reached the rank of lieutenant general, served as Governor-General of New Zealand from 1946 to 1952, and from 1953 until his death was Deputy Constable and Lieutenant-Governor of Windsor Castle. He was raised to the peerage as 1st Baron Freyberg in 1951.
2 George Augustus Moore (1852–1933) was an Irish novelist and dramatist. For many years he had a relationship with Lady Cunard (qv). See Vol. I, entries for 9 March 1925 and footnote, and for 12 June 1925.

four hours before Harold and Rab came in from their different dinner parties . . . Then I read him Princess Olga's letter. He advised me not to send it to Winston, who is so prejudiced against Paul, and in any case is too busy. I built up Wavell tremendously, said that he was adored in the Middle East and that to change him would almost cause a revolution amongst our troops. He listened, admitting all I said, but added that Winston and Wavell didn't hit it off, that Wavell came off v badly in Committee etc. He seemed to infer[1] that no immediate change is contemplated, and that Wavell might be summoned home next winter – will there be one – to confer?! I rhapsodised until he said that I was blinded by love – perhaps I am, but not for Wavell. David thinks that we may hold Crete: I am defeatist about that. The newspapers have over-stayed the battle. The sacking of Longmore is an unfortunate precedent . . . . Harold and Rab were impressed and surprised to find me cloistered alone with David.

WEDNESDAY 21ST MAY

No raid now for ten days . . . .

Lunched with Lady Colefax, a tedious, terrible affair but I enjoyed being rude to Sir Kenneth and Lady Clark and was so icily *hauteur*[2] that they both made me advances. Archie Sinclair, ever foolish, ever fascinating with his queer green eyes – [several words blacked out] – and his dull wife, and that red harlot, Lady Violet Bonham Carter, Loelia Westminster and others. Harold Nicolson . . . . arrived uninvited. A *directoire*[3] atmosphere – the Girondins. Sometimes I think that England is doomed: the driving force is dead . . . I was exhausted by luncheon and my day and slept for hours, dozed the whole afternoon and thus missed Winston's second announcement about Crete[4] . . . .

I went to inspect the House of Commons – there is little left, but our room is intact. It is heartbreaking, yet I had a certain secret satisfaction as it has contributed largely to my world's chaos.

THURSDAY 22ND MAY

I woke dreadfully depressed; went to the House of Commons to arrange for Anthony to make a statement about our relations with Vichy, which are deplorable . . . And there was a further question about Hess in the House. He has a striking personality and his escape to England is the most entertaining, unexpected and exciting episode of the whole war. What fools Honor and I were not to have lunched

1 Channon means 'imply'.
2 Grand.
3 The Directoire ran France from 1795 to 1799, between the Reign of Terror and the advent of Napoleon.
4 About the continuing fighting there.

with him in Berlin in 1936! I rang up my mother-in-law and came to Pyrford, where the Iveaghs are living frugally. They are very sweet, even sympathetic and very against and angry with Honor! She has hurt them horribly. I found them towers of strength, courageous, splendid and wise – if a little slow. Both have aged over this appalling affair. Actually, Honor rang me up on the telephone very early – only she rang her own private number and thus awakened the Butlers who were asleep .... She did not apologise and only explained that her no. was the only one she could remember! She is madder than ever.

SUNDAY 25TH MAY   *KELVEDON*

No raid. Seven nights have passed since London was even disturbed.[1] I slept well. Smith, Honor's faithful maid, talked to me openly. She cried and is v unhappy about her mad mistress. I gave her £5 . . . she is going to Honor's love-box as housekeeper and will regret it.

The newspapers announce the sinking of 'The *Hood*', one of our largest ships.[2]

Honor has behaved dishonestly here, and rather underhandedly. She has not kept a single one of her engagements or promises; she is semi-demented.

George Clutton,[3] a *charmeur* from the FO, came down for the night; he is a relation of the Petre[4] family, who often in ages past intermarried with the Wrights and lived here – unhappily. It is a doomed house, I fear. George is highly clever and sophisticated, quick and determined, a Roman Catholic, impoverished. He has great blue eyes, looks older than his 31(?)[5] years and has immense and stubborn charm.

MONDAY 26TH MAY

Drove Clutton up to London, the car laden with flowers and vegetables. Lady Iveagh came to luncheon and we got on famously: she is magnificent, but broken-hearted about Honor, whom she disowns but I detected a lingering affection for her which I share ....

The battle for Crete continues; but it is a foregone conclusion.

---

1 Presumably by a false alarm.
2 HMS *Hood*, launched in 1918, was the last battlecruiser ordered for the Royal Navy. It was sunk in the Battle of Denmark Strait on 24 May, going down in three minutes with only three lives saved; 1,415 died.
3 George Lisle Clutton (1909–70) worked in the British Museum before joining the Army in 1939, whence in 1940 he was seconded to the Foreign Office. From 1952 to 1955 he was the FO's liaison officer with MI6; he then served as Ambassador to the Philippines from 1955 to 1959 and as Ambassador to Poland from 1960 to 1966. He was knighted in 1959.
4 An Essex landed family, whose seat is Ingatestone Hall, a few miles from Kelvedon.
5 He was 32.

I had a *réussi* dinner party: Loelia Westminster (I gave her petrol for the journey); Lady Colefax; Lord and Lady Willingdon; Rab; Harold; and Jim Thomas who made an ass of himself. He began attacking the Munich settlement, which goaded Harold Balfour into retorting that Jim knew nothing of the condition of the fighting services ... Jim calmed until Lady Willingdon reminded him that but for the Munich settlement [crossed out] appeasement Jim would now be dead and therefore the conversation would never have taken place ....

TUESDAY 27TH MAY

Mrs Greville to lunch: she arrived in a wheeled-chair, was vivacious, witty, and malicious beyond belief. I was a *tour de force* ... She kissed Alan and me, so elated was she by the news of the sinking of the *Bismarck*:[1] I had been in the House and was able to tell her how Winston had made an announcement at the end of Questions, a guarded statement to the effect that the *Bismarck* had been disabled, was a wounded mallard etc. A few minutes later Brendan Bracken rushed into the Chamber (Church House still) with a bit of paper which he handed to the PM, after he climbed over PPSs, including myself. The PM fidgeted and at last, after a brief delay, owing to procedure, got up for the second time and told of the sinking of the crack German battleship. The House cheered ... and forgot Crete.

Alan is staying with me. He had a cocktail at the Ritz and then went to Soho which looks badly battered: there we went into a pub, the York Minster which recalled Marseilles, being frequented by the French sailors etc. Much atmosphere. We dined in Soho and Alan went off and left me: I walked home in the dark, after talks with that dark sinister Tom Driberg[2] ('William Hickey' of the *Express*). Alan came in at 6 a.m.

WEDNESDAY 28TH MAY

Alan is gay, in terrific spirits; indeed he is exhausting.

1 Launched in 1939, the *Bismarck* was with her sister ship the *Tirpitz* the largest European battleship ever built. She had helped sink HMS *Hood* days earlier, sustaining damage. Heading for occupied France for repairs, and pursued by numerous ships of the Royal Navy, the *Bismarck* was attacked by aircraft from HMS *Ark Royal* and scuttled in the North Atlantic several hundred miles west of Finisterre.
2 Thomas Edward Neil Driberg (1905–76) left Oxford without a degree, joined the Communist Party, and became a journalist. He started the William Hickey society gossip column in 1933, and bought the house at Bradwell-juxta-Mare in Essex that Channon had considered some years earlier (see Vol. I, entry for 27 November 1936). He was Independent MP for Maldon (the constituency in which Bradwell was situated) from 1942 to 1945 and Labour MP for the seat from 1945 to 1955, when he stood down. Bored outside the House of Commons, he returned as Labour MP for Barking from 1959 to 1974, and was raised to the peerage as Baron Bradwell (life peerage) in 1975. He sat on the party's NEC for many years, was a promiscuous homosexual with a penchant for rough trade, but is thought to have been expelled from the Communist Party for passing on its secrets to MI5.

Harold showed me a most bitter letter from Longmore who is vindictive and miserable that he has been superseded by Tedder. Longmore indignantly refuses the governorship of Southern Rhodesia and vents his spleen against Winston, who has treated him shabbily.

THURSDAY 29TH MAY

I have heard that at last Fritzi has been released.

Mrs Greville rang me this morning and told me that Lady Crewe had rung her up and told her about Honor and me – so the news is out!! The dreaded news has struck. I now no longer care. I took Harold and Alan to the Dorchester to dine with Mrs Ronnie who was gay and affectionate and gossipy. Home about 11.30, and we are all rather tight.

The Cabinet have decided to clear out of Crete; but the news is not yet out.

FRIDAY 30TH MAY

Alan left for Henlow: how he dislikes matrimony and I fear that one day his marriage will crash as mine has ...

Lunched and dined alone and feel wretched and exhausted. Alan stimulates, exhilarates but exhausts one.

SATURDAY 31ST MAY

I came here and Kelvedon looked beautiful but brooding . . . I walked to the Joneses[1] at Kelvedon Grange and we talked of Honor. They knew the whole story but added dramatic touches – a neighbour one evening last winter had heard a terrific fuss going on and went to the door to investigate. He saw a herd of cows being driven by Woodman who was roundly abusing Honor, calling her a 'bloody witch' etc. She was hatless in the rain, wearing a red jumper, and patiently trying to help ... it is too pathetic. Woodman, so the Joneses allege, is part gypsy (no scholar, he!);[2] and wholly drunkard. He frequents pubs, boasts of his money, is a professional womaniser; and had an earlier affair with a lady. Apparently he goes to the pub, plays the Lord, swaggers, offers 'drinks all round' to everyone, adding 'plenty more money where that came from'. He is a low horse-coper: that my wife should have fallen so low is an undying humiliation. My poor child, I fear, will be vicious and lustful – how can he be otherwise?

---

1 John William Bertram Jones (1883–1963) was a near neighbour of Channon and a previous owner of Kelvedon Hall. He married Cynthia Harriet White (1889–1974) in 1918.
2 A reference to Matthew Arnold's poem of 1853 'The Scholar Gipsy'.

WHITSUNDAY, 1ST JUNE

The big news this morning is clothes-rationing. Oliver Lyttelton is changing England! He issued fairly drastic orders and the whole population is limited to sixty-six coupons per annum. A suit takes twenty-six. Luckily I have forty or more. Socks will be the shortage. If I am not bombed I have enough to last for years...

I went to Much Hadham to see F[ritzi], released at last. I returned to him his possessions and was struck by his gaiety, and good health. He said it was paradise to be 'out'. He is now to work on an estate near Carlisle.

The greyness passed and towards evening it has become clear, lovely again, which means sunbathing and raids! I am happiest alone and am rarely lonely; but I wrote to my little boy in faraway America. Poor pet: yet he is one of the lucky ones, really, and I don't regret his going. Nor does Honor really: she always teased him. Yet the sight of a pretty pink-faced child stabs me and I think of those fleeting months I had with my baby boy before the war intervened.

The old Kaiser is supposed to be dying. What an immense failure he was. I once caught sight of him driving at Doorn[1] in an American car – an elderly patriarchal figure with a white beard looking not unlike Bernard Shaw.

Planes roaring overhead: I believe they are American.[2]

The tiresome, sadistical common snobbish old Hugh Walpole[3] (he wasn't old really, only 57) is dead at last. He was an arch bore and a flagellant *in excelsis*. There is much vice in England certainly.

MONDAY 2ND JUNE

All day alone, arranging the house, reading *War and Peace* which I can never tire of.... making plans for the installation of the Red Cross.[4]

The evacuation of Crete is announced and we are told that over 15,000 men got away in our ships. I doubt whether the defence of the island was ever worthwhile. It may have delayed the attacking forces on their downward march but it means also a further decline in our prestige. The BEF are now known as 'Back Every Friday'!

---

1 Channon's memory tricks him: he was at Amerongen, not Doorn. See Vol. I, entry for 22 August 1927.
2 An interesting supposition, as America would not be in the war until the following December.
3 Hugh Seymour Walpole (1884–1941) was a protégé of Henry James and became one of the most renowned English novelists of the 1920s and 1930s, his best-known work possibly being *Rogue Herries* (1930).
4 The Red Cross was about to take Kelvedon over as a convalescent home.

TUESDAY 3RD JUNE

It has been cold and grey for a week and I shiver still – in June.

The removers have come to pack up the furniture. 'When the children go out, the hunchbacks come in.'[1] It is very sad; but I find, to my surprise, that my wounds are healing. I have been so outrageously treated that I now care little for Honor, or what she does. Bertram Jones said last night that he hoped she would not only regret what she has done, but [be] made to suffer. I was indifferent . . . and am determined not to take her back under any circumstances. She is too selfish, too unreliable, too demented – <u>and</u>, the original <u>cause</u>, too <u>dirty</u> in her personal habits.

WEDNESDAY 4TH JUNE

A hellish day of arrangements and packing and fuss. Bitterly cold.

The Kaiser is dead. What a disturbing factor in world politics! He is individually responsible for much that has happened.

THURSDAY 5TH JUNE

A full, fretful, feverish day. Early interviews with Red Cross people and I sold much of the furniture, and kitchen equipment to the organisation and probably netted £500. I am money-mad . . . . Then I drove to London, the car laden with asparagus and strawberries . . . . Harold, Rab, and Alan all rang up immediately and I asked them to lunch but all were engaged. However, I had the Duchess of Kent, Natasha Bagration and Nicholas Lawford. A cosy *partie-carrée*;[2] and we talked much of the ex-Regent, his flaws and his family; and of political news generally. The Duchess was jealous of my letters and I read out snippets to her – all that I dared. I didn't want to tell her <u>all</u> P said of their fantastically rude treatment in Kenya etc. It would make her too unhappy.

At the FO, and from talking to Alan, I gathered that there is much afoot. Winston is <u>v down</u>; much criticism of Crete and of him personally. The Kemsleys say that he is miserable and for the first time his position is assailable. Alan and I had a Turkish bath at the RAC. He talked too loudly and is indiscreet politically and sexually. I foresee a scandal one day.

FRIDAY 6TH JUNE

All day, exhausted and only spent at Southend interviewing my constituents. Back to Kelvedon which I found eerie, empty and re-echoing – as sinister and haunted as ever it was when we first entered it.

1 If this is a literary reference I have been unable to trace it.
2 Foursome.

A nice letter from H.

On all sides one hears increasing criticism of Churchill: words, however magical, are not victories ... He is undergoing a noticeable slump and many of his enemies, long silenced by his personal popularity, are vocal once more.

Sunday 8th June

Cleaned out cupboards, bathed, wrote. There seems little to report. The hope of reopening the route to Tobruk seems not to materialise . . . But Imperial forces have invaded Syria with the intention of occupying it. Does this mean war with France? The British counterpoint is under the command of fat 'Jumbo' Wilson.

I wrote a long letter to Cairo. I have been here for eight nights alone and have been fairly happy. I don't need human companionship much: I find my own company, since I cannot have Peter's, enough. But I ache for my child sometimes, particularly today when I gave away some of his toys.

Monday 9th June

A complicated morning at Kelvedon making further arrangements, which wore me out. I now weigh only eleven stone and am haggard and handsome, fagged-out and foolish.

Tuesday 10th June

The Big Debate about Crete all day at the House of Commons: I rushed in and out, listened, intrigued, dropped poison or honey as it suited the situation and me. The government is very unpopular and people are even beginning to criticise Churchill openly – all his enemies, silent so long, are vocal again. He was not cheered today; seemed tired and rattled and handled the House clumsily – for the first time .... The government is on its last legs in its present form, I think.

Long talk with Rupert Brabner, the MP for Hythe who returned from Crete and Cairo on Saturday. He is vituperative about the government, and told me that there were only ten aircraft at Crete – never more, and yet we attempted to hold the island; indeed might have succeeded if the Air Arm had been reinforced sufficiently. I asked him to dine. Seymour Berry and David Margesson also came. A *réussi* dinner party, indeed. Brabner told us enthralling stories of the campaigns in Crete and Greece. Apparently we never had more than thirty fighters in Greece. This is scandalous, and probably Longmore was rightfully removed. I am horrified and told Harold so.

Osbert Sitwell tells an amazing story of how he was driving recently with Queen Mary and the Princess Royal from Badminton in an old-fashioned car. Seeing a soldier tramping along the road the Queen ordered the car to stop and the man was invited in and offered a lift. He was garrulous and uncouth and after a bit the Queen turned to him and said, 'I am Queen Mary, this is the Princess Royal, and who are you my good man?' Undaunted, not to be taken in, the man retorted, 'I am a patient in a Maternity Ward.' There was a terrible and long silence which became more acute as slowly the fellow began to wonder whether, after all, it might not be the Queen Mary. He began to squirm immensely. A wonderful episode. Mrs Greville told me the tale on the telephone. Also that Anthony [Eden] had been sick at a distinguished luncheon party yesterday which broke up in confusion. He suffers from diabetes. She was present.

WEDNESDAY 11TH JUNE

Very tired . . . . The weather is blue and I fear that raids will begin again.

I rushed out like a lunatic and attended the 1922 Committee, which was addressed by David Margesson who held his audience enthralled for an hour and ten minutes with secret statements about the army.

A letter came from P written in Athens on April 21st – a sort of farewell note in case he didn't get back to Cairo. His death is too awful to contemplate.

The Duchess of Kent looking a vision came to see me at six o'clock, and luckily I had a letter for her, too, from her mother written in Athens on April 22nd. She wept . . . and gave me letters to send to Peter and to Princess Olga. She has tremendous hatred for Winston, a gnawing deep dislike, distrust and dread.

Dined in alone with Harold.

Still no news of Honor now for nearly a fortnight. Is this ominous, or just the usual inoperativeness?

THURSDAY 12TH JUNE

The honours list is out . . . . there is considerable indignation that too much favouritism has been shown to the Churchillian entourage – indeed it is a scandal. [Frederick] Lindemann, the Berlin-born [sic] bore and scientist, a lord! What an age. All Winston's cronies are rewarded . . . and not a Tory amongst them. The feeling against the government is growing: some steps towards a reconstruction must be taken.

I am disturbed by Honor's silence. But I had a letter from Peter.

FRIDAY 13TH JUNE

Sinister day.

I tire so easily now. I dictated all the morning, and later Rab confided to me that there is a plan afoot to make him Minister of Information. I have urged him to refuse the post and stay at the FO. Duff Cooper and Anthony have had a rather violent row and Winston does not know which of his favourite sultans to back.

The Duchess of Kent came in wearing cherries in her hat; she had had a pathetic letter from Princess Olga complaining of their appalling living conditions in Kenya. One's heart bleeds for them . . .

Yesterday I went to see Mrs Greville and spent an hour with her. She kissed me several times, told me that Winston is finished . . . . I dined last night – I was too tired to chronicle it – with a coterie of MPs . . . . The little gala was in honour of the recently unearthed and created Lord Leathers, who talked 'shop' to us for two tedious hours. He is like a bank manager in appearance and manner; is lower middle class and has a genteel voice. Yet somehow he reminds one of Horace Wilson, might be his son. Then Harold [Balfour], Jay [Llewellin] and I came home and sat up too late. I cannot stand much human companionship . . . . But I am stimulated by 'Mrs Ronnie' . . . .

I passed the French Embassy today, shut and gloomy and I thought of the old splendour, the grand dinner parties there, royalties and rich food, footmen and Frogs . . . .

There are rumours of a political change and the inner circle is in the excited nervous state which is usually a prelude to a reshuffle.

FRIDAY 13TH JUNE

This is the second entry dated thus. It includes some of the events already detailed, which have been edited out.

An unlucky day? I spent it dictating and working at home and at the Foreign Office. I am so easily tired. Harold [Balfour] went to Shoeburyness in a special train with the Prime Minister, Beaverbrook, Archie Sinclair and others, and they inspected tanks and new anti-aircraft guns and devices. The PM lives luxuriously, a most lavish lunch and grand train. 'Baron Berlin', as Lindemann is called, was there, too . . . Harold was back before dark and we dined *à deux*. I am somewhat domestic *au fond* . . . The fortunes of war seem to be more kind to the British these last few days, as the *Deutschland*[1] has been hit and colossal air raids have been made over the Ruhr industrial areas.

There are rumours of a Russian–German war and huge German concentrations of troops have been reported all along the Russian and Romanian frontier – I, for one, do not believe in this theory. I saw Stafford Cripps yesterday and he looked thin and shabby for the first time.

---

1 This ship, renamed *Lützow* in 1940, had been badly damaged in 1940 and just brought back into service when its electrical systems were paralysed by British aerial attack. She remained out of service for another six months, and eventually was sunk on the Baltic coast in 1945.

SATURDAY 14TH JUNE   *KELVEDON*

Nothing. Came here; the emptied house is eerie, but my suite is luxurious. The place is luxuriously lovely and green.

Worn out.

SUNDAY 15TH JUNE

A lovely English day but my miseries are many. I am haunted by the miseries of poor Paul and Olga languishing seventy miles from Nairobi in an uninhabitable house. The pathetic letter took only a month in which to arrive; and it was written on Lord Erroll's coroneted notepaper – too macabre.[1] People in Kenya, and Government House have been beastly as only the English middle class can be! What can I do to save their position?

The usual green luxuriance of Kelvedon is intoxicating: I lay in the partition garden, plunged in and out of the water, dozed and basked until an SOS in the form of a telephonic call summoned me back to London. Alan had sent a message to Portsmouth that he was leaving within forty-eight hours for America on a hush-hush mission … and I rushed up to the hot, deserted capital, driving through the City, which looked appalling. One saw the devastation created by the raids … Alan was waiting for me, the huge, great wolfhound, gay, brilliant, inspired and half-mad in many ways. We dined together at La Belle Meunière and came back to B[elgrave] Square where we pledged eternal loyalty and love and had a tempestuous evening.

Yesterday Lord Iveagh's detective sent me a recent report of their further investigations. Woodman is reported to be dispirited and anxious – and probably bored to death. There is nobody on this troubled world who can be more boring than Honor. I feel that their liaison is breaking up – still I have nothing to go by.

MONDAY 16TH JUNE

A gloriously blue evening half-promised a raid but we slept undisturbed. I shared Alan's bed so as better to talk …. He says he loves me less than Francis, his youngest brother but more than George the eldest …. He rushed off to lunch with his menacing mother at Henlow and on to Elveden to say 'goodbye' to Patsy, pregnant and pathetic …. I collected letters of introduction for him to the Vanderbilts, the Roosevelts, etc. He was back in time to dine and Harold, Jay Llewellin, and Rab were here: later Hector Bolitho brought in the Archduke Robert and we sat up too late drinking and gossiping. Alan is an exhausting guest; he breaks chairs, telephones all day, causes confusion and exudes life and exhilarates us all. There is a plot afoot to turn out the present government, which is perfectly hopeless and

---

1 Erroll having just been murdered: see entry for 15 March 1941.

has suffered defeat after defeat ever since it took office. I had not agreed to join this junta but of course, am interested. Harold and I have written an article for *The Times* which may have considerable repercussions . . . .

I was cross and tired and nervously exhausted. No letter from Honor. I imagine that her solicitor has advised her not to communicate with me.

TUESDAY 17TH JUNE

An Alan day – he fills the hours with his arrangements, appointments and frenzied life. I love him . . . . The Iveaghs came to lunch and we had a jolly family party. No news from Honor: no one misses her. It is terrible, the fate she has chosen for herself.

The Ruhr has been raided by our bombers nearly every night. And there is much talk of the expected attack on Russia by Germany. If Hitler does attack Russia it will be the cleverest act of his whole career since he will smash up the Russian war machine, thus liquidating the liability of 'the bogey' of a war on two fronts which has always haunted the German General Staff; and he would cause division of opinion in the USA, and even here; and, of course, obtain wheat and oil. His position would then seem impregnable.[1] Will Stalin give in? I don't think that Hitler will allow him to do so; he is determined on a Russian invasion . . .

Alan and I were to have dined alone, but Godfrey Winn[2] who is my fervent fan – and God! what a bourgeois little bore – came here for a drink and insisted on dining with us, thus spoiling our farewell tête-à-tête. I was furious and had difficulty in repelling his ardent advances! Has the world gone mad?

The battle in Libya is still indecisive.

Lord Iveagh took me aside and – to my surprise and embarrassment – gave me £200 in £1 notes. Why?

WEDNESDAY 18TH JUNE

A rushed day. Woke utterly weary: Alan drains my vitality . . . . Then to the House, the dentist, and finally to Euston to take leave of Alan who looked frenzied and untidy. He left at 4.55 for Belfast and embarks tomorrow in a C[anadian] P[acific] R[ailroad] ship for Montreal. Shall I ever see him again?

. . . . The Russian campaign seems imminent.

Rab and I dined with Mrs Greville at the Dorchester. She showed me the recent letter from the Queen of Spain from Rome etc. She says that Winston will not last for six weeks and that he was booed in Plymouth. Can this be true? Rab

---

1 A serious misjudgement by Channon: it was the attack on Russia that lost Hitler the war.
2 Godfrey Herbert Winn (1906–71) had been a bit-part actor, but became a highly successful newspaper columnist and popular novelist. He served in the Royal Navy during the war until invalided out.

told us that Baldwin told him recently how much he now regretted his decision to throw over Sam Hoare over the Abyssinian affair! It was the greatest mistake of his life – as even I, newly elected then, saw and said. Now he realises it.

THURSDAY 19TH JUNE

Harold's article appeared in *The Times* today and has caused a sensation.[1] Rab said that it 'was weak, probably written by Mrs Greville', he added laughingly. Anthony Eden thought it excellent and asked me to find out who wrote it!!

A treaty of non-aggression has been signed between Turkey and Germany. I am not surprised; but it is another blow for Anthony Eden.

No news of Honor – but she wrote out of the blue to her mother asking for family news. I think a crisis is being reached soon – that the man will run out on her.

I dined alone, the summit of bliss, and went wearily to bed.

FRIDAY 20TH JUNE

A disturbing day fraught with difficulties.

D'abord a bill for £377 – one of Honor's 'leftovers' – then the joy of hearing Alan's voice on the telephone and hearing that he had not gone, but returned to Henlow, as his ship has been delayed, and was coming to London to see me. We arranged to go to Pyrford and I sent a message to say that I and 'a friend' would be coming, not mentioning his name .... I went home to lunch, after being disturbed by a letter from Terence Shone,[2] which I am transcribing here.

I went to King's Cross at 6.26 to meet my immense Alan – a rapturous gay reunion after his *faux départ*![3] We dined [at] Chez Auguste; a bistro in Soho with a Marseilleseian [*sic*] atmosphere. Free French soldiers, and one expected bouillabaisse! Then A and I drove to Pyrford where we found the Iveaghs; Brigid; Patsy – very pregnant; awaiting me – but they were astonished to see Alan, the prodigal returned. The countryside looked very lovely and it is hot.

I told them that Russia would be invaded on Sunday by Germany – a very clever move which, if it succeeds, will make Hitler Master of Europe.

Terence Shone's letter to me –

---

1 The article, bylined 'From a correspondent', is entitled 'Organizing for Victory', and argues for a better strategic plan and for a strengthening of the gene pool of the War Cabinet. It is unlikely Churchill sanctioned Balfour to write it. Channon appears to have helped in the composition.

2 Terence Allen Shone (1894–1965) joined the Diplomatic Service in 1919 after service in the Great War. He was British Minister in Cairo from 1940 to 1944, and later UK High Commissioner to India. He was knighted in 1947.

3 False start.

Cairo – The Embassy, May 31st

.... You ask about Prince P. It was indeed a sorry business and a very disappointing one. He got himself – or thought he had got himself – into the position of splitting the country whatever he did; and as you know the 'trustee' idea was what weighed with him most. He was unfortunately surrounded by a number of bad advisers and neither he nor any of his Cabinet were capable of taking a really sharp line. His Minister of War and Chief of Staff were old women and had not done what might have been done – however little it may have been – to put the country into a state of defence. They and the majority of his Cabinet, especially the Croats, were in favour of signing the pact; and I suppose he would argue that as a constitutional Head of the State, he had no other choice. But I doubt whether he realised what a black thing he was doing – though we all did our best to make it plain! I doubt whether he had even realised either how unpopular his government had been. The *coup d'état* was really against what the majority of the people – Serb at any rate – regarded as a repressive regime. Even if he had had the courage to tell his Cabinet to go to hell and refused to sign the pact, I doubt whether the people who led the *coup d'état* would have accepted his leadership. The saving clauses which the Yugoslav government attached to the pact were poor little things and there were secret clauses – as I know for a fact – which were quite disgraceful. Dislike of Russia may also have played its part. Anyway, it was pretty clear that he had suffered from being bottled up with his own problems for so long, without enough contacts with the outside world or with the people who could put some stuffing into him and that he was just about at the end of his tether and lacked the guts, or whatever you like to call it, at the critical moment. And yet he seemed to expect that everyone would understand his action and treat him as before ...

A horrifying letter, and probably the truth.

SATURDAY 21ST JUNE   *PYRFORD*

I slept – or rather tried to sleep – with Alan, but his snores were Wagnerian! A glorious hot day. We lazed and bathed and walked amongst the rhododendrons.

Harold rang me up from Ascot where he is staying with the Fitzgeralds to say that David Margesson told him that Winston thinks that Lord Trenchard[1] wrote

---

1 Hugh Montague Trenchard (1873–1956) developed the Royal Air Force out of the Royal Flying Corps and the Royal Naval Air Service in 1918. He had begun his military career in the infantry and had fought in the Second Boer War, but by 1915 was Commander of the RFC in France. He was knighted in 1918 and was the first Chief of the Air Staff. After retiring in 1930 in the rank of marshal of the Royal Air Force he was raised to the peerage as 1st Baron Trenchard. He served as Commissioner of the Metropolitan Police from 1931 to 1935 and was advanced to a viscountcy in 1936.

the recent article in *The Times* which caused so much talk. I hope that the secret never leaks out.

SUNDAY 22ND JUNE

Alan left in a frenzy this afternoon. It is a year ago today since my baby left Pyrford. Honor and I drove him to London on that sad Sunday.[1] What a horrible year it has been!

The wireless announced that Germany attacked Russia this morning at five o'clock. What will this new development mean?

Winston made a big broadcast.

MONDAY 23RD JUNE

I miss Alan already . . . . I motored up to London with the Iveaghs and found a casual letter from Honor. Whitehall is jubilant over the German invasion of Russia: I am not. He[2] wants a Full Dress Debate tomorrow in the Commons and Anthony has spent the greater part of the past twenty-four hours trying to dissuade him. I don't yet know the result.

Dined in alone with Harold; feeling cross and discouraged. I am very down. Perhaps I am going mad?

Rang up Circe Londonderry at Mount Stewart to ask if Harold and I could stay with her next weekend – but she is coming to London on Friday. Instead we are going to Clandeboye to stay with Maureen Dufferin.

TUESDAY 24TH JUNE

I fell ill with nervous indigestion. Ate nothing all day. This morning the House met at eleven in the House of Lords. I always knew that I should end up on those benches – but not so soon, nor indeed in such circumstances. Anthony made a statement about Russia to a crowded house. Maisky and Alba sat side by side in the gallery!! The PM rebuked that goat-like Winterton. Anthony dressed in coal grey delivered badly his speech which has been drafted by the office with Rab's help. Not a cheer greeted him and he sat down in silence.

The government is increasingly unpopular . . . . I went into the Smoking Room and sat with Jay Llewellin, who abused the powers that be, as did Maurice Petherick. The Commons are bewildered by the turn of events and have lived through so much these past years that they – like everyone else – have lost the faculty of reacting quickly.

---

1 It was in fact Sunday 23 June 1940.
2 This is Churchill, as is made clear by the subsequent entry.

Mrs Greville rang up: she is intriguing furiously against the government, but pretends a deep loyalty to Winston. Anthony won a considerable victory over him today, or rather last night, by persuading him and the War Cabinet that a full-dress Foreign Affairs Debate today would be a mistake. Instead we had only the statement and a few desultory speeches. A few MPs aired their dreary news in order to be able to tell their grandchildren that they had spoken in the House of Lords![1]

WEDNESDAY 25TH JUNE

A secret session about shipping in the Commons. Winston was grave and informative and was severely attacked afterwards in a vitriolic speech by Shinwell. Winston's popularity is waning.

Ralph Assheton, Rab and Harold dined. Ralph, who is so charming and gentle, surprised me by the violence of his attacks on Anthony Eden, whom he dismissed as a 'pup' and 'a doll' and 'no good'. I encouraged him, I fear.

From what I hear I fear that Wavell is doomed.

THURSDAY 26TH JUNE

Tilea and Rab to lunch and we discussed Romania's problematical future. Fortunately I drank in the Smoking Room and was suddenly very popular and a wave of gaiety passed over me – but this fleeting episode spoilt my afternoon as I was sleeping in consequence.

An unfortunate muddle about our Ulster visit.[2] Basil Dufferin rang up Harold Balfour on another matter and Harold let slip that we were going to stay this Sunday at Clandeboye, thinking it natural since it is his own house. Whereupon Basil immediately proposed to accompany us: I saw complications as the Dufferins, whilst not even legally separated, are on the very worst terms. Harold was mortified and rightly put through a call to Maureen who was upset and asked for a few hours in which to consider the situation . . . Basil also brings bad luck to aeroplanes and I am afraid to travel with him.

Tilea told me that he had seen much of Queen Marie of Y[ugoslavia], and told her how the Archduchess Ileana[3] had managed to get her tiara away from Coutts bank, have it put in the Romanian bag and later she sold it in Venice for £30,000. The Regent told me this story. Tilea also met the Archbishop of Canterbury who asked him where Prince Paul was living; when Tilea told him,

---

1 Where they would meet for much of the next nine years until the Commons was rebuilt. The Lords met in the Robing Room, a matter that was kept secret during the war.
2 Channon and Balfour were planning a visit to Lady Dufferin and Ava in Northern Ireland.
3 Princess Ileana of Romania (1909–91), daughter of King Ferdinand I, married in 1931 Archduke Anton of Austria, Prince of Tuscany. They divorced in 1954.

His Grace – the hypocritical sodomitic old ecclesiastic – was horrified; said that it was bad taste to have the Regent in the villa of a murdered man, and that he intended to complain, to bring it to the notice of both Winston and the Foreign Office – as if they didn't know it. I am glad but it shows the crass stupidity of the old Cosmo.

A little gala in the evening. Geoffrey Lloyd gave a party: we met at Lady Baillie's house, sombre and dismantled as it is, and had caviar and champagne. Olive Baillie; Miss Harriman[1] (Averell's daughter, a typical American debutante); and Pam Churchill, 'the Crown Princess of England'. She is an auburn wench, intelligent and apparently in love with Randolph. I made up to her rather and drove her home and made plans to meet again.

Paul Latham has had an appalling crash on his motorcycle.[2] I don't like the sound of it. His head is fractured, skull broken etc.

FRIDAY 27TH JUNE

The Duchess of Kent rang me up and we were disconnected during an indiscreet conversation. Do the MI5 people listen in to conversations with the royal family? I know that Edward VIII's every conversation during the abdication crisis was listened to – and I suspected ours, too, at the time.

This morning I went to the bank, deposited some things and took out some jewels which happened to be on the top – ones the Prince Regent had given me .... Harold then rang up to say that Maureen Dufferin definitively did not want Basil to go to Ireland with us and an awkward position has arisen. We have put him off now ... he will be angry, and, I fear, blame me.

I am not taking this diary to Ireland, and will leave it here until my return and copy into it any notes that I might make.

As I was preparing to leave Harold rang me up urgently from the Air Ministry to go at once to the Carlton Club with all the luggage, as he feared that perhaps Basil Dufferin would not have had his message and might turn up at Belgrave Square. I hurried away, and only just in time, for Basil did come to No. 5 with his bags expecting to go. Luckily he didn't ask for me and was told that Harold had already left ... This awkward drama and reception cast a shadow over our hurried

---

1 Harriman had twin daughters and it is unclear which of them this was: Mary Averell (1917–96) or Kathleen Lanier (1917–2011). Channon comes to socialise much with the latter, so it was probably she.

2 Latham, a serving officer in the Royal Artillery, was shortly to be court-martialled for indecent conduct for having committed homosexual acts with three gunners and a civilian. He attempted to kill himself by riding his motorbike into a tree at high speed, and was court-martialled for that too. He was sentenced to two years' hard labour and resigned his parliamentary seat.

departure. We drove to Hendon accompanied by Wakefield,[1] Harold's hefty PPS, and soon embarked on the King's Flamingo,[2] taking off at 6.45 exactly. A comfortable plane and we raced across England as I unpacked a picnic basket and we dined over the Irish channel. At 8.46 exactly we landed at Belfast aerodrome and were received grandly by air vice marshals and officials, and looming large amongst them was my lovely Alan and we had a rapturous reunion. He had been three days at sea in acute discomfort until an accident caused the ship to return! He drove with us to Clandeboye, where I had not been since New Year's [Day] 1933! Maureen Dufferin was v pleased to see us and had taken great trouble to put us up. She is immensely improved but sad . . . Whilst the others walked in the garden she and I had a two hours' talk and laid out cards on the table: Basil suffering from DTs,[3] is in debt and hopelessly dissipated and is in love with Mrs Virginia Cowles; Maureen refuses to see him. I told her of my difficulties of which she had been informed by Eddie Devonshire – who was told, of course, by Diana Cavendish, that arch gossip and snake in whom Honor always confides! Maureen is definitely pro-me and told me how shocked she had been by Honor's strange behaviour whilst our child was at Clandeboye – apparently Honor never once wrote to her, or to the Nannie, and never thanked her afterwards. She thought that Honor's whole attitude had been scandalously selfish and that poor little Paul ached for affection which he had never had . . . . My heart almost broke to hear her . . . . she had even believed that I was indifferent to him. I, the most doting of fathers. I fear that the secret is out now and that I cannot now long delay action.

There were three rooms prepared, but none for Alan; so he and I stuffed Harold into the smaller room and decided to share the big bed. We sat up until 2.30 . . . . We are in gay spirits. Much talk about the Londonderrys who are away. They are highly unpopular and suspected locally.[4]

SATURDAY 28TH JUNE

Harold went off pompously to inspect the aerodromes, whilst I accompanied Alan to Belfast where we shopped and made arrangements . . . . Alan v charming. I am sending Nannie a brooch, and Serge [Obolensky] a gold Fabergé cigarette case which I bought in London yesterday; and am also entrusting my gold watch and chain and my entire sapphire parure to Alan to take to my child. We went back to Clandeboye to lunch and sunbathed all the afternoon. The house is

---

1 William Wavell Wakefield (1898–1983) was Conservative MP for Swindon from 1935 to 1945 and for St Marylebone from 1945 to 1963. He was 'hefty' as befitted a man who had captained Cambridge University, Leicester Tigers and England at rugby union. He became 1st Bt in 1944 and was raised to the peerage as 1st Baron Wakefield.
2 A model of civil airliner made by de Havilland.
3 *Delirium tremens*: shaking brought on by alcoholic excess.
4 Possibly for Lord Londonderry's pre-war Nazi sympathies.

shoddy, down-at-heel but has still a certain grand air – there is an enthralling library and the park with the distant lake is green and lovely. Maureen and I had several talks: she is angry with Honor; and she has financial as well as domestic worries as she has many debts and her reduced income prevents her paying them off. She is much developed and improved since the old gay tiara tipsy days and I genuinely love her now.

I was sleepy all day, the soft Irish air, and the wild night punctuated by Alan's snores was disturbing. How I hate sleeping alone.

SUNDAY 29TH JUNE

Alan snored less and we had a pleasant night together. Maybe I am made for matrimony – with anyone except my wife. Lazed all day and in the afternoon we drove to the lake where we bathed and had a picnic tea and afterwards went to see Helen's Tower.[1]

MONDAY 30TH JUNE

The morning in Belfast where we lunched and then, after saying a sad goodbye, we took off for London again in the King's private Flamingo. Harold had a ham, I an old master,[2] under our arms. We took Alan with us as he has several more days on his hands. Just as we left I read of the Cabinet changes: Beaverbrook becomes Minister of Supply in the room of Sir Andrew Duncan who returns to the Board of Trade whilst Oliver Lyttelton becomes our Minister in the Middle East and a member of the War Cabinet, a curious and unconstitutional appointment. In the hope that Alan may be saved an unnecessary crossing to America, I telephoned to Rab and asked him to circulate the news that he was returning with me to London for twenty-four hours.

A quick flight back and we flew over Blenheim. I thought of July 7th, 1939, the happiest night of my life,[3] and I thought, too, of the parties there long ago.

London was hot and depressing and I found a rude and inconsequent note from Honor which disturbed me and dampened my spirits. Anything to do with her fills me with repulsion and malaise . . . I went to the FO for news. The German and Russian communiqués both reporting colossal losses and victories are bewildering. One doesn't know what to believe. The biggest battle of all time may well be in progress . . . Alan dined and then rushed to Pyrford to see Patsy and the Iveaghs. To my surprised delight he came back about 1 a.m. He says that Patsy had run into Honor accidentally on Friday and that she was bitter against me. Patsy says her affair cannot last.

---

1 A nineteenth-century folly at the highest point of the Clandeboye estate.
2 Channon had bought a picture in Belfast.
3 The night he met Coats.

TUESDAY 1ST JULY

A depressing day. I tried somehow to get Alan into the government all day and failed. There is no job going yet. I had hoped – and indeed there seemed just a chance – that he might go to the Ministry of Supply under Beaverbrook . . . .

All my correspondence was disturbing: I have spent too much money this quarter etc. . . . . I drove Alan once more to Euston and we said yet another 'goodbye'. When I got back to the FO I heard that General Wavell has been removed but I couldn't get the rumour confirmed, and came home miserable to dress.[1] Dined with Mrs Ronnie Greville who was alert and malicious and affectionate. She asked me about Honor and I glossed over the situation . . . So it is out! Harold [Balfour] left [the dinner] early and Mrs G and I had a long talk. She was full of the Queen, who had spent two hours with her on Wednesday whilst her lady-in-waiting, Lady Helen Graham,[2] waited in the bedroom.

I shall miss Alan desperately and wonder whether he will really leave this time . . . I walked home alone sadly and thought of Miles Lampson's letter. The baby comes in September. Will everyone think that it is mine?[3]

Harold said at dinner how much he hated Winston personally; Mrs G despised him and she enumerated his defeats: I. Gallipoli; II. Invasion of Russia;[4] III. Gold standard; IV. Narvik; V. Dakar etc. He has never had a success in his long variegated career.

WEDNESDAY 2ND JULY

The dreaded blow has fallen: I awoke and saw 'Wavell removed' in large letters on every newspaper. I am horrified, indignant and revengeful. From now on any remaining loyalty to the government has gone and I shall work secretly – until I am caught, and then openly to overthrow it. It is Winston's most foolish and disgraceful act. The House was restless and Winston arrived late; he was bad-tempered and seemed uneasy when cross-questioned by Belisha. I feel this blow acutely. First the Regent shorn of his pomp and power – and now Peter. Wavell has been sent to India and I suppose, and pray, that Peter will go with him . . . or

---

1 Wavell was swapping jobs with Auchinleck (*vide infra*), to become Commander-in-Chief, India.

2 Helen Violet Graham (1879–1945), Lady Helen by courtesy, was the daughter of the 5th Duke of Montrose. She was lady-in-waiting to the Duchess of York from 1926 to 1937, Woman of the Bedchamber to the Queen from 1937 to 1939 and Extra Woman of the Bedchamber from then until her death in 1945.

3 Lady Lampson was expecting a child, conceived around the time of Channon's visit to Cairo.

4 After the Great War, when a short-lived expedition of the British Army went to fight the Bolsheviks. Churchill was then Secretary of State for War, and responsible.

will he be sent back to his regiment, or asked to remain under Auchinleck.[1] The whole story is monstrous; he has been sacrificed to Winston's personal dislike. No general in all history has had so difficult a role fighting on five fronts and harassed daily by contradictory cables from Churchill . . .

That little squirt Cary,[2] the MP for Eccles, tried to draw me about Honor, but I snubbed him. Later Mary Baker[3] came to see me and she had been told the story by H. G. Wells. I am thought, she said, to have behaved with great dignity.

Dined alone with my thoughts. How sad my poor Peter must be tonight; he is dethroned, distracted and devoted to his General. I loathe Winston and the shady Churchillian clique.

Cairo and the whole Middle East will be sad tonight. I cannot get over it. Lady Wavell will miss her grandeur; the General will be saddened by the injustice of the world; Peter will be wretched. Everything is gone, or going: my world is hardly recognisable now.

THURSDAY 3RD JULY

Every day something simply horrible seems to happen . . . Last evening Rab dined with Anthony Eden in his small flat at the top of the Foreign Office. The other guests were the Prime Minister and Mrs Churchill, Beatrice Eden, and Beaverbrook. In the midst of the war they have so little to talk about that I was the chief subject of conversation. Anthony began by saying that he had sat next to Queen Marie of Yugoslavia at luncheon at the Legation and that she had abused me, said she didn't wish King Peter to see me etc. as I was a friend of the Regent's. And wasn't she, for God's sake? Can treachery go further, or *mauvaise foi*?[4] The Regent always said that she was the biggest bitch in Europe: the Romanian royalties are notoriously unreliable. Anthony was rather bored and nice about the tale and merely repeated it to Rab, who has no social sense and always gets overexcited by *potins* and attached too much importance to them . . . He told me the story immediately I arrived this morning. A few moments later Peter Loxley, recently appointed Alec Cadogan's private secretary, burst in, puzzled and angry. Cadogan had had a

1 Claude John Eyre Auchinleck (1884–1981) joined the Indian Army in 1903 and became its Commander-in-Chief in 1941 briefly before moving to the Middle East; he returned and commanded it again from 1943 until 1947. In the Great War he fought with distinction in Mesopotamia and won the DSO. Knighted in 1940, he was promoted to field marshal in 1946 but refused a peerage.
2 Robert Archibald Cary (1898–1979) was Conservative MP for Eccles from 1935 to 1945 and for Manchester Withington from 1951 to 1974. He was knighted in 1945 and created 1st Bt in 1955. He fought in both world wars.
3 A childhood sweetheart of Channon from Chicago, originally. See Vol. I, entry for 2 February 1918 and footnote.
4 Bad faith.

monstrous letter from Alec Hardinge from Buckingham Palace, in which he said that the King (George VI) did not wish Mr Channon to be in any way mentor to King Peter of Yugoslavia! Is the Black Rat mad as well as wicked and Red? I had no intention of being the Boy-King's mentor; nor had I ever communicated with him, which is perhaps unnatural as I have known him since he was born! It is a fantastic tale – I had meant to ask him [King Peter] to stay here, but I shall never speak to that fat lesbian Queen and Judas again. For years I have done kindnesses for her, and how they are appreciated! I think that she always sails with the wind and had hoped to ingratiate herself with Anthony, whom she has abused for years. I will revenge myself upon her – only she isn't worth it. Only this morning before this episode came to my knowledge I received a letter from P from Cairo dated June 17th in which he says that King Peter told him how fond he was of me, and that he would ring me up the moment he arrived in England! P's letter, in view of what has since happened, is poignant. Rab, to return to the dinner party, was over-impressed by all that they said; that Mrs Greville was intriguing against the Prime Minister etc. . . . and by Winston's repeated declarations of how pained he was by Wavell's fall (for which he was, of course, entirely responsible). Wavell had asked to fly home for ten days to see his son and Winston had even refused that concession – at the Viceroy's request that Wavell proceed to India immediately – but he added, 'Why shouldn't I send the boy out to him?' Will he? Only if someone, probably I, make the steps . . . . How I hate the whole horrid lot of [illegible] and flashy opportunists who are running – and indeed got us into – the war. What blows I have had:

I.   The abdication
II.   Fall of Chamberlain
III. Honor's desertion and scurrilous love-affairs
IV.   The Yugoslavia debacle
V.   Wavell – and hence, for me, Cairo – gone.

What have I left? My child, and some talents and perhaps a few years of life. I now no longer care what happens; but I needn't have unnecessary insult from the Palace. Am I to get more buffeted by fate?

Dined with Lord and Lady Kemsley in their private suite at the Ritz . . . . Bridge and delicious food. The general trend in the conversation was abuse of Churchill and the government. I was surprised: there was the old familiar note of criticism such as one used to hear *ad nauseam* of Neville Chamberlain! London society, whilst always wrong, is usually two jumps ahead of everyone else. Everyone seemed agreed that if a choice had to be made between Winston and Wavell that they would choose Wavell. Lost £7 and walked home.

Peter Loxley is staying – instead of King Peter!

FRIDAY 4TH JULY

Harold [Balfour] flies in a bomber to Canada next week and may take me. I'd adore to go . . . . I am tired of London and of life and care little what happens to me . . . . Rab is still angry with Alec Hardinge, and Cadogan wrote him a rather snubbing answer. I wonder if there is a vague chance of Peter and Wavell paying us a Blitz visit next week – I wouldn't go to Canada if I thought so.

A friendly casual even affectionate letter from H – what a mysterious woman.

Maureen Stanley is really desperately ill with galloping consumption. What a good thing if she died for she had always been my enemy incarnate; and moreover she had for years been a demoralising influence in London society, contaminating and bringing down all those with whom she came into contact. I hate her: and she me – for no real reason.

My mother sent me a present of $100. She is behaving better and is gentler in her old age.

Hardinge should not be a courtier since he is really a left-wing politician, ungracious, almost communistic.

SATURDAY 5TH JULY

To the FO in the morning and then I drove to Pyrford after carefully packing up a basket of Paul's little dresses and clothes – I had had them cleaned and arranged prettily – for Patsy Lennox-Boyd. However she received me ungraciously (but friendly) and this reminded me of Honor – it is difficult to make any impression on Guinnesses. They are hard and impervious to affections, attentions of gentleness. For years I have suffered from it . . . She refused the prepared present so I bathed and drove away to Polesden, which is still kept up with Edwardian splendour. The Amerys[1] are here . . . . I was depressed particularly as I overheard people whispering about me and a probable divorce. Everyone knows it now; I am pitied, perhaps despised, and often maligned. However my conscience is clear, but I am beginning to hate my wife with increasing venom.

Mrs Greville came down to dinner and was less affectionate than usual. She said that she was tired and seemed so. Conversation and bed. Unfriendly atmosphere.

SUNDAY 6TH JULY

Intense Cyrenaican[2] heat: I sunbathed and made up to the Amerys . . . . The Lord Chancellor of England and Lady Simon came to lunch. Mme is Irish, garrulous and common and always prickly with Mrs Greville as she is aware that Simon

---

1 Leo Amery married, in 1910, Florence 'Bridie' Greenwood (1885–1975), of Canada.
2 That is, like North Africa.

tried to marry her! James Stuart attacked the Jews again and was supported by Mrs Greville; both Amery and Simon were uncomfortable. All these people who wanted the war are bored with it now. Mrs Greville never did – nor did Simon. There is a feeling of false respite, of relief, that the war is receding. On the contrary I am convinced that we shall all be dead in September. Götterdämmerung – with a Russian *entr'acte*. I don't believe the Russian communiqués.

I am wretched . . . . All I love is going. P is in India, or arrives there in a day or two; Alan is on the high seas; the Regent languishes in Kenya; Harold goes to New York this week; and my beautiful beloved boy is far away; and my wife wallows in lustful gipsy embraces.

TUESDAY 8TH JULY

Channon was becoming increasingly concerned about the financial settlement with Lady Honor, which she persisted in trying to reopen.

To the House and then I rushed to see Mr Bland who, wise old owl and wonderful friend, is vigorously opposed to any compromise with Honor, or any concession. He insists that her threats to institute legal proceedings are blackmail, bluff and spite. We have agreed to hold our head now, and to do nothing. Lady Iveagh has refused to see Honor and has written her a sharp letter setting forth her views. I don't know what will be the result.

All day I tried to summon up the courage to go to the USA tomorrow with Harold in his 'bomber' – a perilous and uncomfortable flight, but thrills, escape, and my darling Paul awaiting me there. Only I should never come back, probably.

WEDNESDAY 9TH JULY

There were raids over England last night but I slept sublimely and heard nothing . . . . I went to the H of C. Winston made statements about Iceland and Syria. He looked surly and aged and I saw him make that curious little bow, which he reserves for those he dislikes, to Harold Balfour. He ignored me but Anthony was affectionate and called me 'Chips, dear!'

Harold came in hurriedly to pack his bag and I felt *émotionné* and *attendri*[1] towards him as he rushed off for the USA in a bomber, for I shall miss him and perhaps he won't come back? He will see my boy and Alan and his love, the first Mrs Jimmy Roosevelt.[2] He flies to Scotland this evening, and takes off in a

---

1 Tender.
2 Betsey Maria Cushing (1908–98) was from a leading Ohio family. She married, in 1930, James Roosevelt II (1907–91), son of the President, and they were divorced in 1940; and in 1942, Jock Whitney (qv). Like her second husband, she was a philanthropist and prodigious art collector.

converted bomber tomorrow and lunches in Atlanta tomorrow.[1] All my loved ones are scattered.

I no longer bite my nails which is something … I spent a quiet evening, eating nothing, collecting my thoughts and scribbling these lines. I must have peace and quiet and human beings, particularly in the heat, exhaust me. But I wish I were literally 'on the wing' to the USA to see Paul: instead I shall have a lawsuit, a scandal, a divorce, mild ostracisation [*sic*] and eventual social recovery – and no doubt the invasion.

The Duchess of Kent whispered to Rab last night at dinner that the Queen of Yugoslavia had [illegible][2] our King against me: that I was discussed all over dinner at Windsor. Is it conceivable? The Duchess is v angry and sent me a message to lie low, that it would blow over and was monstrous. It is her [Queen Marie's] self-seeking mania …

THURSDAY 10TH JULY

Nothing very terrible has happened today – but it is only 6.37. I felt ill, went to the House of Commons and found people anti-Winston. The lobby is much against him; undoubtedly he has been saved by Russia. His satirical announcement re Ireland yesterday[3] fell flat: irony can be dangerous. Then I came home, saw my doctor who says that I am not really ill at all, but have weak digestions and my pressure is only 92? He wants me to eat more and I hate food ….

A letter dated July 1st from Peter still in Cairo: he says that he feels like Josephine[4] after the divorce. He and Wavell were in Abyssinia and returned to Cairo after various adventures to find Auchinleck already there and in control. P thinks that Auchinleck is not up to it and looks forward to a triumphant return to the Middle East next year. He is angry and hurt and sorry for Wavell; he didn't hesitate when Wavell asked him what he wanted to do – but I fear and feel that he will be bored in India far from the sophistication of Cairo. I also had a letter from Lady Halifax saying that they are returning shortly to London; there is some criticism of this trip in the H of C. I am hesitating, should I get myself appointed to their staff, say as Honorary First Secretary? Then I could live in Washington and be with my child. There will soon be political changes: I smell it in the air and we may leave the Foreign Office.

Godfrey Winn dined with Peter Loxley and me at No. 5. He was tipsy and enthralling, sloppy and confiding. He told me strange stories of his feverish

---

1 Logistically impossible, but thus in MS.
2 Possibly 'turned'.
3 In reply to a parliamentary question, Churchill had said he couldn't work out whether or not Éamon de Valera (qv), the Taoiseach, thought Ireland had Dominion status.
4 Napoleon's empress.

friendship with David Bowes-Lyon![1] Everything in this too small world gets known.

SATURDAY 12TH JULY

All day at Southend: a pompous luncheon party given by the Mayor[2] to meet A. V. Alexander, the First Lord of the Admiralty. I spent the day with him in the intense heat: he is gay, garrulous, easy-going and amusing in the way he imitates Winston's mannerisms: the funny little bow, the dramatic sidelines as he speaks. We sat on the dais as a long procession organised to inaugurate the War Weapons Week passed by. The Archdeacon[3] was charming because he wants a bishopric, the Mayor because he hankers for a knighthood; how well I know these self-seeking Southend bourgeois. I don't think that they have yet heard of my tragedy as several people asked politely for Honor.

SUNDAY 13TH JULY   KELVEDON

All day here, reading, resting, brooding on its beauty. I am not nuts on Mrs Nimmo, my auburn-haired neighbour who is the commandant of the Red Cross convalescent home. They have rather taken over but have not yet moved in. Many irritating little problems.

The Russian–German war, fought on a large scale with many casualties on both sides, began three weeks ago today. Forecasts varied; it was thought that it would take Germany anything from a fortnight to three weeks to finish off 'The Bear'.

MONDAY 14TH JULY

The eighth anniversary of my ill-starred marriage, and the first time that we were not together. I was never happy, once the flush wore off. H was always selfish and a bore, never willing to do anything or assume responsibility. Perhaps, however, I wasn't tender enough . . . . But Honor never showed me any tenderness, any affection or graciousness and I cannot conceive why she married me.

I drove to London and had a chat with Rab at the FO. He thinks that there will be government changes this week and that he will be involved. I shall certainly not follow him to the Board of Education if he is offered so lousy a job.

---

1 Bowes-Lyon, like Winn, was homosexual.
2 William Miles (1875–1960) was the Mayor of Southend-on-Sea three times: from 1922 to 1924, 1936 to 1937 and 1939 to 1945. He remained un-knighted, but did receive the CBE in 1946.
3 Ellis Gowing; see entry for 10 May 1939 and footnote.

I heard again today that Paul's [Latham] 'fallacious' motoring accident was really an attempt to kill himself.

TUESDAY 15TH JULY

Our days at the Foreign Office are ending . . . I am wretched, yet relieved! I came there on March 7th, 1938 full of hope and promise and happiness. I have learned much, been considerably disillusioned, and owing chiefly to neglect of my work since October 26th when my wicked wife informed me bluntly that she was leaving me, I have not been an outstanding success recently – not enough to qualify for the office which normally I should have had. Life is a disappointment.

Micky Renshaw and Rex Whistler, both slim and smart in their Welsh Guards uniforms, dined and we gossiped.

The shoddy, shabby government is doomed by its own ineptitude and the arrogance and personal unpopularity of the Prime Minister. Nevertheless it will survive for a time for two reasons, i.e. there is no body substantial enough to supersede it and the Russian campaign has been repressive. Already the optimists go about saying that the war will be over in March, which, I fear, is nonsense.

Called on the Amerys and sat with him for an hour. He listened as I praised Wavell and told me that after Lampson had broken the sad news to him, he added banally: 'They could have knocked me down with a feather.' General Wavell's only comment on his dismissal was 'some feather'! Terse and true.

WEDNESDAY 16TH JULY

Went to the H of C with Rab in his car; he drives badly and we had an argument with another car, thus making us late. However, Anthony had already arrived and took the Questions. We await the summons now from No. 10. If Rab goes to the Colonial or Dominions Office I remain with him – or a Service Department. If, however, he goes to the Ministry of Health, Labour, or Board of Education I leave him as the boredom would be too terrible. I really could not cope with schoolmistresses and children in provincial towns . . . I stayed at the H of C, attended a meeting of the 1922 Committee which was addressed by Attlee! He made a favourable impression. Then I fell into a deep coma: I must sleep every day now for an hour after luncheon. When I woke it was 3.30 and I dashed to Belgrave Square to receive the Duchess of Kent, who stayed with me for an hour before going on to the Buckingham Palace Garden Party held in honour of the Allied governments! We talked of Paul and Princess Olga still languishing in Kenya. She was riveting about Queen Marie, who stubbornly refused to see her, made excuses and prevented King Peter from going to Coppins. Eventually the Duchess drove to Little Gransden to lunch with her, whom she found dominating and disagreeable. The Young King was affectionate and charming, but whenever the Duchess asked him a question about the Regent, the Queen always chipped in with a disapproving reply. The visit was not a success and now the Duchess has persuaded Queen Elizabeth to invite Peter to Windsor without his mother, whom they consider a bore, a lesbian and an *intriguante*.[1] I added fuel to her rage and we both decided that the Romanian family are the most caddish, *cabotin*[2] race alive.

George Gage, now a *sournois* major and quite unchanged physically since the last war, Leslie Hore-Belisha, Loelia Westminster, Ann O'Neill and Virginia Cowles came in for a drink before I took them to Noël Coward's ghost-play, *Blithe Spirit*.[3] I drove with Ann and she confessed to me that Shane[4] was anxious to divorce her, but that Esmond Rothermere refused to be cited and urges a three-year plan, the desertion ticket. Ann says that she hasn't the patience to wait for so long and might even go back to Shane. What a muddle all our lives are in. Victor Warrender is bringing a case against Dollie for a judicial separation . . . . I am left hanging in mid-air, deserted, miserable and ridiculous! The play was amusing and a brave bit of writing as it might so easily have been absurd and a flop. Noël Coward unfortunately was sitting immediately behind us with Ronnie Tree and David Lyon, so we could not discuss the merits of the piece. We dined at Quaglino's and I felt dull and *gêné* with Loelia for the first time; however I quite liked Virginia Cowles and even found her attractive. We had a long talk and she confided in me that she had no intention of marrying Basil Dufferin as he is too dissipated. Incidentally, he has gone to Clandeboye to be with Maureen! after the Palais Royal farce of a fortnight ago. Leslie and I dropped the girls and walked home.

THURSDAY 17TH JULY

Woke exhausted and nervous after a *nuit blanche*. I walked to the Office – for the last time? Soon it will not be mine to go to. However the break will come at a psychological time. Secret session on Home Defence at the House.

Peter [Loxley] and I dined alone and I went early to bed, exhausted and bored. I stayed with Rab until 8 p.m. He is still living at Eltham Palace and is reluctant to leave the Foreign Office early lest a summons come from No. 10 offering him a new job. He was loyal and affectionate tonight and we both know that we shall so soon separate.

An interesting report from Miss Hunt, the remarkably brilliant detective of Searle's Agency: she went to Shalden Park Farm[5] and chatted with Honor who was quite unsuspicious! Miss Hunt reports that Honor 'looked as though she might

1 Intriguer.
2 Ham actor.
3 Having 1,997 performances, it set a record for the longest West End run by a non-musical.
4 3rd Baron O'Neill.*
5 Lady Honor's 'love nest' in Hampshire.

be in the early stages of pregnancy'. It is known in the countryside that Honor was a Guinness and that she is rich and has furnished her farm luxuriously to look like 'a rich town mansion'!! (the lovely things she took away from Kelvedon, no doubt, and chosen by me).

FRIDAY 18TH JULY

I went to the F[oreign] Office: I am beginning to be nostalgic about it now. Rab had had no message, no summons from the obese Almighty, and had been told by Tommy Dugdale that after all the changes might be postponed. However, just before I went gaily off to Pyrford to see my in-laws a telephone message came asking him to come to No. 10 (the Annexe, really) at 5.40. I drove down to the country agog with excitement and despair and later I rang him up. Winston offered him the Board of Education and he accepted willingly. A mistake obviously, as he is now in a backwater.[1] The PM added that nothing was to come out until Monday as [Herwald] Ramsbotham had to be moved, 'a sheep on the line', as the PM put it, and persuaded to go to the Unemployment Assistance Board. Dick Law, that humourless turnip who was so eager for war and has sat in a cushy job ever since, is to succeed us [sic], but who will take his place at the War Office I have not heard. Brendan Bracken goes to the Ministry of Information to replace Duff who is being sent – so I am told – to Singapore. What will happen to me?

My in-laws are charming but she looked tired and ill and cross. We discussed the eternal situation and they have agreed to meet Honor's solicitor, a most unusual proceeding next Wednesday . . . . They are dreading the visit and it has made Lady I[veagh] ill. They are much against Honor and tired of the whole performance. No wonder. Patsy, very pregnant, is immense and quite unruffled. She was friendly but has been used as a go-between by Honor, which irritated their mother.

Pleasant evening. But the Iveaghs are ageing and no longer so quick on the uptake. This tragedy has affected them.

SATURDAY 19TH JULY   *KELVEDON*

A most unpleasant day. It began by me smoking too much last night, not sleeping, thinking of my lost job at the FO, and wondering what I shall do . . . Then for the first time in my life my mother-in-law was uncordial, even cross, and spoke sharply to me. Looking back upon it I realise I was to blame, as she was tired and had been ill for a week. However the moment passed and I left after luncheon in

---

1 Not quite; Butler would use his time at the Board of Education to bring in the 1944 Education Act, improving access to secondary schooling, one of the most important reforms of the war years.

a happier, but still not contented mood, really. She is distressed about Honor, distressed and ashamed. No wonder! And I was boring and long-winded. Lord I was charming – but they can be hard where their interests are concerned and whilst they have been divinely loyal to me through this crisis, they have not done much except to prevent a divorce. I promised him this morning that I would do nothing for some time without his permission. The Brewery, he told me, is flourishing; making a fortune.

In London I found annoying letters. Then I came here. Rab rang me up affectionately from Stanstead to say that his appointment has been confirmed, and will be announced tomorrow. He is lunching with Tommy Dugdale to see whether I can be made a whip, and he too also arranged an appointment for me with Sir Gerald Campbell[1] at 3 p.m. to see about going to America. I am torn by conflicting interests ...

I am a little angry with the Iveaghs about these financial matters: they have not [paid off], and show no sign of paying off, the overdraft with which Honor saddled me.

My mother is 72 today. She is more gentle in her old age and I have to see her. But I have decided that I hate all women: I understand them too easily.

Sunday 20th July

A beautiful day. I went through my possessions. Bertram Jones called and he tells me that Woodman (Honor's dusky paramour) got a hold of a rich woman who owned horses and ruined her about three years ago. I shall try and trace her.

The Russian–German war has gone on now for four weeks and only now do the newspapers begin to refer to the Battle for Moscow. Meanwhile we have had a false peace, a dangerous lulling respite and our doom may come in September.

Brigid rang up from Pyrford to say that a cable had come from Alan that he had arrived safely in Montreal. I was beginning to be anxious about my big ebony boy who has been eighteen days at sea in a monstrous convoy.

I wrote to my remote Regent: it is difficult to be interesting at such a distance. I told him in basic English what I thought of the Queens of Yugoslavia and England, one is a bitch, t'other only treacherous and snobbish for all her charm. The Queen of England might really be above snobbery. Queen Mary is: she likes the *Gotha*,[2] which English people never read.

---

1 Gerald Campbell (1879–1964) was Consul-General to the United States from 1931 to 1938, High Commissioner to Canada from 1938 to 1941 and British Minister at Washington from 1941 to 1945, though serving as Director-General of British Information Services in New York from 1941 to 1942. He was knighted in 1934.

2 The *Almanach de Gotha* was published in Gotha, though written in French, from 1763 to 1944, and was a directory of all European royalty, nobility and high officialdom.

The changes are to be announced tomorrow: They have just been given to me:

Duff Cooper to be Chancellor of Duchy and to proceed to Singapore.
Harold Nicolson to be appointed a governor of the BBC.
Brendan Bracken becomes Minister of Information.
Ernest Thurtle as under-secretary.

Rab goes, of course, to the Board of Education and is succeeded by Dick Law, who is succeeded by Duncan Sandys,[1] Winston's aloof, tawny-haired, silent, attractive son-in-law.

Harold [Balfour]
Gwilym Lloyd George
Tom Williams[2] are made Privy Counsellors.
Harvie-Watt[3] becomes PPS to the Prime Minister.

It is a second-rate list; the appointment of Duncan Sandys will lead to considerable criticism; people will say that it is nepotism, and rightly. I ought to be on this list and had the debacle over Honor not occurred I should be.[4] I have played my cards badly, evidently. Still there is now a vacancy in the Whips' Room.

Another scandal is the promotion of Hugh Seely[5] to an under-secretary at the Air Ministry. He has been PPS for only one year. Tupps Ramsbotham goes to the Unemployment Board with a peerage and £5,000 so he doesn't do badly. I am rather fired to go on, to advance, to succeed . . . if success comes so easily.

MONDAY 21ST JULY

After leaving Kelvedon and saying farewell to Mrs Jarvis, my loyal housekeeper, I drove early to London and spent the day at the Foreign Office packing up and

---

1 Edwin Duncan Sandys (1908–87), Conservative MP for Norwood from 1935 to 1945 and for Streatham from 1950 to 1974. A former diplomat, he married in 1935 as her second husband Diana Bailey (*née* Spencer-Churchill) (1909–63), daughter of Winston Churchill.*

2 Thomas Williams (1888–1967) was a coal miner from the age of 11 who served as Labour MP for Don Valley from 1922 to 1959. He was a junior Agriculture minister from 1940 to 1945 and Minister of Agriculture from 1945 to 1951. He was raised to the peerage as Baron Williams of Barnburgh (life peerage) in 1961.

3 George Steven Harvie-Watt (1903–89) was a barrister who served as Conservative MP for Keighley from 1931 to 1935 and for Richmond from 1937 to 1959. He was parliamentary private secretary to the Prime Minister from 1941 to 1945. He was created 1st Bt in 1945. On his retirement from Parliament he became Chairman of Consolidated Gold Fields.

4 What almost certainly counted more against Channon in failing to have him promoted was his record as an appeaser and his friendship with Prince Paul of Yugoslavia, and the view of him among Churchill's set that he was not entirely serious.

5 Hugh Michael Seely (1898–1970), Liberal MP from 1923 to 1924 and from 1935 to 1941, when he was raised to the peerage as 1st Baron Sherwood.

saying farewell. Dick Law, a humourless bloke, came to take over Rab's office. I was wretched: could not bring myself to say goodbye to anyone. Jim Thomas was charming and gave me an excellent lunch at Boodle's, and then I proceeded to the Ministry of Information where I ran into Ronnie Tree, who is staying on there. I also saw Duff drive up – his last day there. I had a short interview with Sir Gerald Campbell and his secretary Wheeler Bennett[1] apropos of my joining the American Propaganda Mission to the USA. I am tempted to go there and see my son. It was left indefinite . . . Then back to the FO to take my things away . . . . I have loved the Office, which in my ironic moods I called the 'Bourbon House' . . . . Back to Belgrave Square, depressed and down. Rab dropped in and remained for an hour and was wise and affectionate. He advised me to go [with] Jay Llewellin as PPS, and I have almost decided to do so. I told him about Honor and, to my surprise, he hadn't heard the talk but instantly guessed that it was Woodman, whom he had once seen at Cow Farm where Honor took him. 'The man is a sort of hypnotist,' he said and he had been struck by his rudeness and the way he treated her!

I am alone, wretched and miss my child and Peter . . . But not Honor whom I am beginning to hate.

TUESDAY 22ND JULY

I went to the House, delightfully late; but I was embarrassed by the many questions, 'Are you still at the Foreign Office?' or 'Are you going to look after little boys and girls?' etc. . . . when actually I am to do neither. I hedged, pretended to be gay . . . and took the pulse of the House which was distinctly anti-Churchill. Everybody was bored and bitter about the changes. Pickthorn[2] said that Anthony had been plotting since December to get Dick Law at the Foreign Office; Erskine-Hill[3] said that the PM's annoyance and autocratic methods were worse really than those of a dictator . . . . As he spoke (we were sitting in a corner of the sitting room) the PM came in, surly and unsmiling, and sat silent and alone. Nobody spoke to him and he hid behind a newspaper, and some got up and left. His popularity has slumped. Jay Llewellin slyly said that he had heard that Vic Oliver was to be made Minister of Munitions! Harold

1 John Wheeler Wheeler-Bennett (1902–75) was a historian specialising in German history but who is now best remembered as the official biographer of King George VI. From 1940 to 1942 he worked as a government official helping to persuade the United States to enter the war; and from then until the end of the war worked in the Foreign Office's political warfare department, and then provided support for British prosecutors at Nuremberg. He was knighted in 1959.

2 Kenneth William Murray Pickthorn (1892–1975) was Conservative MP for Cambridge University from 1935 to 1950 and for Carlton from 1950 to 1966. A historian, he was a fellow of Corpus Christi College, Cambridge from 1914 until his death.

3 Alexander Galloway Erskine Erskine-Hill (1894–1947) was Unionist MP for Edinburgh North from 1935 to 1945. He was created 1st Bt in 1945.

Nicolson, who is *dégommé*, was pathetic and sarcastic. I made it clear to him that the PM had never been pro-him. At last I could bear it no longer and came away with Jim Thomas. At home all was still and I thought over my abortive conversations with Jay Llewellin: he had pleaded with me to be his PPS and had asked Rab in the spring to release me, but we both refused. Now this morning when I hinted he said it was, he feared, too late as he had taken on Douglas Thomson,[1] which I knew but had momentarily forgot . . . So that, too, is out! Shall I go away and write, and bury my shame? . . . As I was ruminating Lady Iveagh rang up very cheerfully and gaily to say that Patsy had had a son at 1.30, a huge boy weighing nearly eight pounds. I am relieved and glad. Alan will be delighted. He is to be called Simon Francis [*sic*], and Harold [Balfour] and Francis Lennox-Boyd are the godfathers. Mr Chamberlain and I were to the first one! Lady I[veagh] sounded and seemed years younger. Thank God that is over. I wish I had a second child: I am envious and frustrated.

Over-obsessed by my own troubles I have neglected to chronicle how happy I am about Harold's P[rivy] C[ounsellorship]. He longed for it and it is quick promotion indeed. Peter Loxley and Jay Llewellin – dear funny slightly dowdy Jay – dined and we gossiped and ran down the government.

I seem to be in an unlucky vein. Perhaps next year 1942, when the numbers add up to 7, my star will rise again.[2]

WEDNESDAY 23RD JULY

I went to the House, felt *dépassé*:[3] I am no longer a PPS. I am no longer anything: I am a genius at finding other people jobs and advancing *them* but I push myself clumsily or inefficiently out of the racket, which is a bore . . . I came home discouraged, and received the Iveaghs. They were charming, loyal, even gay and affectionate and they went away to their quite unorthodox and dreaded meeting with . . . . H's interfering solicitor. I was relieved and she was particularly sweet to me and gave me to understand that she regretted having spoken somewhat strangely on Saturday when she was ill, dyspeptic and worn out with worry. I felt a wave of love and pity for this fine old couple being dropped into litigation and the mud because of H's follies . . . .

Duff told me that he is enchanted to leave the M[inistry] of [Information] and ever looks forward to Singapore, where he goes next week – will the Japs be there first?

---

1 James Douglas Wishart Thomson (1905–72) succeeded his father as 2nd Bt in 1935. He was Unionist MP for South Aberdeen from 1935 to 1946.
2 Because 1+9+4+2 =16, and 1+6 = 7.
3 Past it.

THURSDAY 24TH JULY

Woke at seven and after asking for coffee, dressed and drove to Pyrford .... I crept in to see Patsy who was jolly and comfortable and really looked very lovely. She is pleased to have another boy but seemed distressed not to have heard from Alan. Luckily, however, a cable soon came from New London where my own baby is – so Alan has gone to see him.

The Willingdons came to lunch and were charming. She bustled with energy and attacked Alec Hardinge with violence. He ought to have gone to Madras and stayed there when he was offered the Governorship. He does infinite harm to the monarchy and 'Tommy' Lascelles is better, Lady Willingdon thinks. I could not agree with her more. She added that Lord Wigram,[1] who recommended Hardinge, confided in her that he much regrets his choice and can do nothing. Considerable criticism, too, of Winston and his growing arrogance and nepotism. Everyone agreed. The country is tiring of him quickly now ... Lady Willingdon told me how King George V had telephoned himself to her husband whilst they were reigning in Canada,[2] asking them to go to India as Viceroy. They had refused it a few months previously but they could not resist the royal request. She also said that her son[3] was not impotent, although he might have 'lost fertility'. We teased her and had fun.

Geoffrey Harrison, Rab's secretary at the Foreign Office, with whom I have shared a room for nearly two years, came to dine. He is a nice creature, unimaginative, efficient, and very Wykehamistical. Peter Loxley who was also here, 'and is a charmer' and a gentleman and delightful, compares favourably with him; in a sense they are rivals, both held the same position with Rab. I was always much more intimate with Peter and a certain jealousy developed between them; but that is now over .... We discussed the Foreign Office and to my mild surprise they both attacked it as an institution. They both believe that Oliver Harvey is determined to rule the office as firmly as he did during his previous reforms. He is an extreme, but able, 'left-winger' and always wants war wherever he can get it. He is a desperate character and these two private secretaries are convinced that he intrigued against Rab – as I warned him – and probably 'hoofed' him out of

---

1 Clive Wigram (1873–1960) served in the British and Indian armies before becoming assistant private secretary and equerry to King George V, posts he held from 1910 to 1931. In 1931 he became the King's private secretary, retiring on the King's death. He was raised to the peerage in 1935 as 1st Baron Wigram; and as a Permanent Lord in Waiting from 1936 until his death, and Deputy Constable of Windsor Castle from 1936 to 1945, he retained influence at court long after his retirement.

2 The 1st Marquess of Willingdon had served as Governor-General of Canada from 1926 to 1931.*

3 Inigo Brassey Freeman-Thomas (1898–1979) was by courtesy Viscount Ratendone from 1931 until he succeeded his father as 2nd Marquess of Willingdon in 1941. Twice divorced by 1939 he would marry a third time in 1943, but never have children.

the Office.[1] He has made sly insinuating remarks that now Rab has left, Anthony Eden intends to run his own office – in other words he means to ruin it; and I foresee trouble between him and Alec Cadogan, who may be the next to go. Something of the sort has crossed Cadogan's conventional, however Edwardian, mind: but both Harrison and I warned Peter Loxley, who may pass it on to his chief – he is now private secretary to him, having succeeded Henry Hopkinson who has gone to Cairo with the Lytteltons.

Miles Lampson writes long lyrical illegible letters hinting to me that I get an intrigue going to make him Viceroy of India! Another came today, somewhat flattering but beyond my powers, I fear, with this regime, which cannot be long-lived. This new idea of making Hugh Seely a peer is yet another piece of scandalous nepotism ... We three recalled how right we had been: how we had fought and worked against the Polish agreement which caused the war, and we recollected too the very hush and tentative advances made to Rab by Dalton and other leaders of the Socialist party over a year ago: they had approached him with the idea that he should persuade Halifax to become Prime Minister and then overthrow Mr Chamberlain. Rab refused to touch it or to be disloyal to Neville C. What would have happened, I wonder? There might not have been the preponderating Churchill influence ... Rab went to Buckingham Palace to see the King and kissed hands on his appointment as Pres[ident] of the Board of Education.

I didn't go near the House of Commons and revelled in my brief holiday.

Lady Willingdon told me that there was a ball at Windsor Castle two nights ago: the first ever attended by Princess Elizabeth[2] who danced with Guards officers and the King. She is now 15. I remember George Gage bouncing into my bedroom at Buckingham Street saying 'listen to the guns. Elizabeth [Duchess of York] has produced ...' as we counted the booming and knew it was a female heir.[3]

FRIDAY 25TH JULY

In nine months I have lost

    I.   My wife and home
    II.   Yugoslavia and the Regent debacle
    III. Now the Foreign Office
    IV. To a certain extent the fortune.[4]

1 According to Harvey's published *War Diaries* (Collins, 1978, p. 18) he had not inspired Butler's move, which was apparently done on Churchill's orders. But Harvey does note with joy that 'at least we get rid of Chips', so there was no love lost between them.

2 Elizabeth Alexandra Mary Windsor (b.1926), from 1952 Queen Elizabeth II.

3 See Vol. I, entry for 21 April 1926.

4 Investments the proceeds of which he had had to make over to Lady Honor as part of their separation settlement.

What further blows can fate hold for me? I don't really want very much to live now.

Rab rang up; he is determined to be loyal and is bored at the Board of Education! No wonder. He came to lunch and was charming. He advises me now, after reflection, to go to Washington and he will help me arrange it. He told me that the Duke of Kent had hinted to him of my marital entanglements and said that he had heard that Honor was 'fed up' with social life, which is true. Rab then described his audience with His Majesty, who had been most friendly and kept him for three-quarters of an hour, thus upsetting the programme. He asked Rab whether Oliver Harvey was very left and had, so Rab said, actually danced with delight when he heard that it was true! Evidently he had had arguments on the subject with someone, perhaps Alec Hardinge. When Rab left, the King had said, 'Well, goodbye Rab,' which startled him.

I had a Turkish bath this afternoon which always soothes and refreshes and restores me ... but I thought over the Latham scandal; he was caught apparently, [blacked out][1] maybe. His motorcycle accident was an attempt to kill himself – a sort of Ethan Frome![2] What he must have suffered! And how [blacked out] are [blacked out] in this country.

SATURDAY 26TH JULY   *THE BOTHY, CULHAM COURT, HENLEY*

Elizabeth Elveden called upon me this morning and we discussed the vagaries of my rampant wife whom she frankly hates ... She says Diana Boothby (always Honor's *âme damnée* and trusted confidante) dines out with Honor and tells funny stories wherever she goes about her. I am not surprised.

Drove here to this dwarf Thames-side Trianon to stay for a simple Sunday with Raymond Mortimer. It is pink and pretty and costs £10 a year in rent: I bathed in the Thames: it looked very Corot.[3] Eardley Knollys[4] is here; we have rarely met since Oxford days. He is Greek and handsome but his sad blue eyes made me miserable. His alter ego, an Australian to whom he has been intensely

---

1 It appears to be Coats who has gone to lengths to black out three phrases about the Latham incident. It is only conjecture, but the first of these could be something like 'in flagrante' and the last two something like 'how homosexuals are persecuted in this country'.

2 Ethan Frome is the eponymous central character in a novel of 1911 by Edith Wharton. With the woman he loves Frome enters into a suicide pact, to drive a sled head-first into a tree. However, he survives, badly injured.

3 Jean-Baptiste-Camille Corot (1796–1875) was an innovative French landscape painter.

4 Edward Eardley Knollys (1902–91) was a member of the Bloomsbury group, as an art critic, collector and dealer. In his late forties he began to paint and held his first exhibition in 1960. His partner in life and in business, Frank Coombs (1906–41), joined the Royal Navy and had been killed in the blitz on Belfast the previous April, after which Knollys closed down their Knightsbridge art dealer's shop.

devoted for nearly ten years, was killed by a bomb in Belfast a few weeks ago. Eardley is broken, his hair has turned grey, and he is like a piece of cracked china.

The Bloomsburys stimulate me with their eager quick alert intelligence and their new books and bitter detachment from life.

SUNDAY 27TH JULY

This Jack-in-the-Beanstalk cottage belongs to Cecil King,[1] the sinister owner and editor of the *Daily Mirror* which is doing much to undermine the fabric of English life . . . a terrible man.

A sad Sunday: it rained and later the sun shone. Eardley wanders disconsolately about like a lost soul, desperate, bereaved, anguished. His other half, as he puts it, is gone . . . . There was melancholy music on the river. Bridge and too good food.

Berlin was raided last night, which means, I suppose, a retaliatory raid on London soon. Is this wise?

MONDAY 28TH JULY

A pleasant cable came from Alan and signed by him, my baby Paul and Helen Astor saying that the child was well and magnificent!! *Quel soulagement!* A king of *savoir faire*, brown as a berry, plays the piano and rides – accomplishments denied to his father.

A long dreary day: I snatched luncheon at home, and Jim Thomas and Nicholas Lawford dined with me and I was nostalgic for the Foreign Office again. I wondered whether I could have made more of it? Bed late. There was a small air raid last night which I survived.

TUESDAY 29TH JULY

To the House of Commons which I now dislike: it has an opaque glow and I seem to see it through different lenses, out of focus. The PM, sober, annoyed, grim and determined made one of his more important speeches since the war [began]: the theme was production and was meant to be a reply to his critics. He held the House, which was interested certainly but not enthusiastic, and there were few of his usual oratorical tricks. He has been told that we are universally weary of his

---

1 Cecil Harmsworth King (1901–87) was Lord Northcliffe's nephew and cousin of Esmond Harmsworth, 2nd Viscount Rothermere (qv). With Hugh Cudlipp as his editor King turned the *Daily Mirror* into the largest selling newspaper in the world, selling almost 5.3 million copies a day by the late 1960s. This in turn fed King's megalomania, and after using the *Mirror* to call for the resignation of the then Prime Minister, Harold Wilson, and trying to get support for a military coup to overthrow him, the board of King's publishing company, IPC, sacked him.

eloquence .... I hear that Randolph Churchill is to be made liaison officer between Oliver Lyttelton and the Prime Minister – yet another plum for the Churchillian court; but a plum that may well become a nail since the country is dissatisfied with such flagrant nepotism .... I drove Rob Bernays to the Savoy, glad to do him a courteous act as I have been cold to him for a year or so. I don't like him, really. Then after a snack, I slept for an hour. I seem to need an afternoon siesta: I am far from well; am exhausted by events and emotions. Then to James Gunn's studio: my portrait progresses. What a bore he is with his uninformed political opinions; however he is notably anti-Anthony Eden which is something.

I had a dinner party, Adrian and Olive Baillie; Freda Casa Maury – clipped and staccato and charming; Kay Norton;[1] Geoffrey Lloyd .... all went well but both Kay and Olive took me aside and asked me about Honor and I had to tell the humiliating truth.

WEDNESDAY 30TH JULY

I had a lazy morning; more and more I miss the Foreign Office. Alec Cadogan, who, I fear, will be the next victim of Oliver Harvey and his camarilla,[2] wrote me a charming letter on my departure from the FO. I had also a somewhat mysterious communication yesterday from Prince Nicholas of Romania who writes from Saint-Moritz telling me how much he espouses the Allied cause: it must have come in the Yugoslav bag, as it was sent on to me by Mrs Creswell, Queen Marie's – well, her everything. Is this a slight climbdown? I wrote and thanked Mrs C and at the same time suggesting that we meet as I had something private to tell her ....

Jay Llewellin gave me dinner at Claridge's, which was crowded and gay; and we came back here to talk. He is a bore but a dear.

THURSDAY 31ST JULY

The great event was Harold's [Balfour] breezy return. He was in Newfoundland last night, or rather yesterday afternoon, and arrived in England this morning. He is well, happy, pleased with his P[rivy] C[ounsellorship], important and full of 5th Avenue and Halifax news. He had flown to Washington to lunch with them [the Halifaxes]; seen both George [Gage] and Alan [Lennox-Boyd] in New York, and reported well of Paul. Better: he brought me letters from Alan written at Rhinebeck in which he gives me graphic and glowing accounts of the little man who is now a dream of beauty, *savoir faire* and charm ....

---

1 See entry for 18 December 1938, and footnote.
2 A group of cronies forming a corrupt and unaccountable court around a ruler. The term was first used of the circle around King Ferdinand VII of Spain, who reigned from 1814 to 1833.

Harold and I met at Claridge's for a drink with Eric Dudley[1] – much aged, greyer and fatter – and Virginia Cowles, and then dined. I told him the whole Honor story, which he already knew. He was horrified. Nannie writes me that 'I have at last heard from Lady Honor who addressed her letter to Miss Pearce'! Her name is Waite. She doesn't even know the name of the Nannie who has been with us for more than three years.[2] Harold was loyal and a 100 per cent-er.

This morning at the House was indeed dramatic. I had a talk with Rab who is becoming more donnish and conceited . . . Then I went into the Chamber for the end of Questions. David Margesson got up and said that he had a statement to make: it was a message from the King to the effect that Paul Latham had been arrested and court-martialled.

We were electrified: few people knew of the scandal and those, like myself who did, hoped that it would be hushed up! Of course, he must be very guilty, caught probably in flagrante delicto, otherwise he would have been allowed to hand in his papers. It is the end of Paul: he will resign his seat, be sentenced to imprisonment and probably succeed next time he attempts to kill himself – very tragic! I don't know all the details. MPs, never men of the world, think he has committed some breach of the military regulations and struck a colonel or cashed dud cheques . . . The news reached the Ritz Bar about one o'clock and caused consternation in high [blacked out]. I am told there was a *sauve qui peut* from the Bar . . . . I had to break the sad news to Miss Sneath, Paul Latham's secretary [blacked out]. She is devoted to him [blacked out]. She has no idea of the charges and anyway would not understand. Every day something desperate happens.

I had a Turkish bath at the RAC, and as I took my place on the marble slab I saw prone, naked and being pummelled, the too fat figure of the Crown Prince of Norway.

SATURDAY 2ND AUGUST

Group Captain A. H. Willetts[3] dined with me last night in London . . . . Willetts was in Greece throughout the campaign . . . . and he had thus many opportunities of observing conditions: he lived at Psychiko next to Princess Nicholas, whom he adored; the Crown Prince was – well, his fervent ally; and he saw much of the King . . . . He said much that was interesting. He and the whole RAF in Greece

---

1 William Humble Eric Ward (1894–1969), by courtesy Viscount Ednam until 1932, had been a Conservative MP from 1921 to 1924 and from 1931 to 1932, when he succeeded his father as 3rd Earl of Dudley.*

2 The nanny in fact joined the Channons' staff two years earlier.

3 Alfred Henry Willetts (1904–71) went on to command a Pathfinder squadron during the bombing of Germany, but was shot down over Berlin on 23/24 August 1943 and taken prisoner. He won the DSO in 1942 for planning and leading a raid on the Norwegian island of Vågsøy.

were strongly against an intervention there. Metaxas, as everyone knew, had held out against it and his successor, Papagos,[1] a weaker man pursued the same policy because his Master Metaxas had, but he forgot the reasons! The only people who knew anything about the Balkans, Willetts said, were the Prince Regent and Metaxas and they saw eye to eye. To send an English expeditionary force across the Aegean was to invite the Germans down. Probably they would have come anyway; but we could do little and by doing nothing might have delayed for a few days – even weeks with luck – the German invasion. Willetts insists that my Paul was perfectly right and he heard Papagos remark that the much-heralded 'Yugoslavian *coup d'état*' was really a disaster for Greece! Willetts was present at the famous meeting of ministers and generals – Dill, Eden, Wavell etc. – when the Greek government held out strongly against Allied assistance. The conference broke up in disorder but was convened again and a few hours later, that evening, I think. Meanwhile Eden, egged on by Palairet, had been to the Palace and over-persuaded the weak, tired and desperate King to back them up. When they met again Papagos gave in and an ill-starred, foolish and fatal defence of Greece was decided upon. The Greek government was induced to ask the English government for assistance – telegrams had poured in from Winston – which was over-willingly promised. Willetts deplored the whole arrangement, as I think, does Longmore. He saw the Regent who looked worn out, bewildered and broken. The populace of Greece, naturally, did not share these views and looked upon Paul as a traitor and an enemy to their cause. He confirms what the Duchess of Kent told me: that Princess Nicholas had had a violent quarrel with her son-in-law.

Godfrey Winn called to see me: he is under my spell but I have no room for him in my strange life. We gossiped for an hour mostly about poor Paul Latham. A wall of anger and filthy gossip has swept over London. Heresy-hunting and talk of 'purges': one might be living in the Wilde period. I am told that the Ritz emptied in five minutes' time on Thursday when the news reached the Bar, which has a bad reputation. And that night the girls at the Maurier[2] did a roaring (face-saving) trade. It is cads' week and every malicious tongue is wagging. Patsy Latham, who treated Paul so wickedly and selfishly, will now be put in the right.

Kelvedon looked a dream as I arrived: it is humming with life and well appointed. There are about thirty females living here: everything is in order except that there are no patients!

I heard yesterday that the Duchess of Gloucester is at last really pregnant: it has been a long business, treatment and minor operations. One baby was begun at the beginning of their honeymoon and lost in Kenya: since then nothing has taken. This child might become King of England one day: who knows?

---

1 Alexandros Papagos (1883–1955) was a general commanding the Greek Army who led a resistance organisation after the German invasion in 1941.
2 Presumably a nightclub in the West End frequented by prostitutes.

SUNDAY 3RD AUGUST

On s'habitue à tout.[1] I am looked after by a parlourmaid, which I always thought could be the end, the *coup de grâce* of elegant living . . . And I am comfortable enough. There is something to be said for the simple life. All my dogs except Batsi are gone [from Kelvedon]. Bundi reigns supreme in Belgrave Square. His seven children have separated, and have different destinies.[2]

This afternoon nearly 300 people came to Kelvedon and I stood for two hours receiving them. There were the grander farmers from the county and the Bishop of Chelmsford. An immense tea was provided by the Red Cross . . . everyone looked at me askance since they were all aware – as Mrs Nimmo assured me – of the scandal. It was embarrassing but I blandly carried it off. Only the Bishop,[3] who is notoriously tactless, inquired after her – and in booming voice. I fear that we have made an appalling impression on the indignant county.

I have been given many things in my long harlot-esque life; but nobody has ever given me a church until today. I conducted the Bishop into the disused Church of St Nicholas, which was abandoned in 1894 and he said at once that it should and would shortly be mine. I shall be buried there. It is attractive with hatchments to the Luther family who once lived at Myles's . . . Three dreadful, exhausting hours of strain but at last they left. The county are all dowdy, squirearchical and funny – a dying order. I missed Honor, at least what she stands for; it is unnatural her not being here. However, it was nice to have the gossip and I was charming to everyone. One lady rang me up and asked if H would be back as she didn't wish to meet her.

MONDAY 4TH AUGUST

A rainy Bank Holiday – Michael Parker[4] drove down for tea and we talked in the Chapel Room whilst farmers and their wives wandered about the gallery and peered through the windows. He is quick and corrupt, intelligent and charming, but, I fear, a tart. Yet I like him although he has treacherous eyes.

It is six weeks today since the German campaign opened and now the real plan is revealed: they are driving towards Ukraine, always their ultimate goal, of course.

---

1 One can get used to everything.
2 Most had been given to friends, including Lady Dufferin, Lady Baillie and Alice Harding.
3 Given Bishop Wilson's view that a 'landslide in sexual morals' threatened the continuance of Christianity in England, he and Channon could have had an interesting conversation.
4 John Michael Avison Parker (1920–2001) joined the Royal Australian Navy in 1938 and then the Royal Navy, fighting at Narvik in 1940. At this time he was a sub lieutenant. In 1942 he met Prince Philip of Greece and Denmark (qv) when they served together, and in 1947 became his private secretary when the Prince married Princess Elizabeth (qv). Parker worked for the Prince until 1958 when Parker's divorce forced his resignation; however, the two men remained close friends until Parker's death.

Harold is ill at Belgrave Square: I talked to him a couple of times; and I wrote to Honor describing the party yesterday. I knew I should annoy her and perhaps make her contrite. I thought that she loved Kelvedon; but she doesn't: she loves only herself, not a man, woman, object or dog – or even her child – means a thing to her! I read *Anna Karenina*[1] and thought how like my own life it is.

TUESDAY 5TH AUGUST

I drove up, my car filled with flowers and vegetables, to London where I found Harold still ill, recovering slowly from his blitz flight across the Atlantic: people take days to recover. This morning he had been to Buckingham Palace to be sworn a member of the Privy Council, one of his life's dreams. The King had been amiable but had not talked sense, he thought: he kissed the royal hand, and was given the little hard Bible by Sir John Anderson. We lunched together: the household was maddening – everything went wrong and I was irritable and harangued the servants and sacked the silly cook. Then we both slept – but I went for a moment to the House of Commons when the serious coal situation[2] was being debated. The government had a bad day.

WEDNESDAY 6TH AUGUST

Lunched with Rob Bernays who complained that Churchill had lost his popularity, his hold over the House. Lloyd George had fallen under similar circumstances – when he was at the height of his personal popularity in the country. Shakes Morrison echoed the same views, hinted that Winston considered himself a dictator. Geoffrey Lloyd grumbled, said that the honeymoon was over; that the rapture was past; that the government was unpopular. Then much gossip about Sir Paul Latham, silly gossip . . . .

I left [the Commons] hurriedly to come here [Belgrave Square] and receive the Duchess of K. Instead I found Harold and Helen Fitzgerald *à deux* and *en flirt*. In a few minutes, however, the Duchess arrived looking worried and lovely. She still has had no news from Kenya and is anxious, so wretched about her poor sister and brother-in-law. Princess Nicholas writes from Athens that she is well, and that conditions are not too bad. The Duchess stayed for an hour: the Duke is in Canada. She goes to Badminton for a fortnight tomorrow to stay with Queen Mary.

I have decided to sack my footman, Dudley MacDonald, who is pert, cheeky; he pries, goes into the secretary's office, uses her typewriter etc. Under the circumstances I cannot risk having someone untrustworthy in the house.

---

1 Epic, doom-laden 1878 novel by Leo Tolstoy.
2 There were fears that because 75,000 miners had joined the services in the preceding year, and with productivity poor, there would be coal shortages in the coming winter.

A closely guarded secret still: the PM accompanied by Harry Hopkins,[1] Dill, Dudley Pound and others including Alec Cadogan sailed on Sunday very secretly in HMS *Prince of Wales* for America: he will meet Pres[ident] Roosevelt, a sort of second Tilsit[2] on the high seas. The Pres is supposed to be cruising in the yacht *Potomac*. No one knows yet, and I was only told yesterday.

THURSDAY 7TH AUGUST

A disagreeable letter from Honor began a bad day – she is completely under the domination of this ostler and is turning against everyone . . . . She is madder than ever.

I went to the House, after a very nervous and anxious morning here due to the curious activities of the footman who apparently goes through all our letters, snoops and pries – is he in Rollo's pay?[3] A spy? Or what? I feel uneasy and even frightened – but what would he find out? He goes every night to the secretary's office, borrows the typewriter, and always keeps his bedroom door locked. It is disturbing, indeed. I have sacked him.

At the House of Commons I found that a few, the favoured few, now knew about the Churchill–Roosevelt meeting which rivals Napoleon and Alexander's, or Caesar and Cleopatra – possibly he has wishes to emulate, to eclipse Mr Chamberlain's sensational flight to Berchtesgaden and at the same time to revive his waning popularity.

FRIDAY 8TH AUGUST

I am less tormented today after a long sleep. Possibly I was overdramatic about the footman; but the whole household hates him! And he goes today! Life is becoming increasingly unpleasant.

I had a private appointment with Mrs Cresswell at the flat, Cramer Court, Sloane Avenue, which she shares with Queen Marie. She was charming and sensible and seemed unaware of any atmosphere between the Queen and me. I told her frankly the story: that I was deeply wounded (which I am not) by the Queen's treachery and malice towards me. There has never been such a bitch,

---

1 Harry Lloyd Hopkins (1890–1946) had been a social worker in America and became one of the architects of Roosevelt's New Deal, designed to bring America out of the slump in the 1930s. During the Second World War he became the President's most trusted adviser on foreign affairs.

2 A conference at Tilsit, then in East Prussia, in July 1807 between Napoleon and Tsar Alexander I of Russia, ending the war between their two countries.

3 William 'Bill' Rollo was Lady Honor's solicitor. See Vol. I, entry for 4 July 1927 and footnote.

really, as the Regent often warned me. Rosemary promised to put matters right and to let me know . . . . One should never let friendships go by default: at least I have tried.

More and more I am convinced that Oliver Harvey is a sinister influence and my – and Rab's – irrevocable enemy!!

Beaverbrook flew the Atlantic today in a last-minute attempt to join the presidential party. People say that he gatecrashed, was uninvited. I don't know.

Anthony Eden sent a message to an agent in Birmingham that he would be pleased to speak there towards the end of the month provided that he was guaranteed an audience of at least 25,000! Does he think that he is a film star?

Miss Sneath[1] confided to me startling and disturbing facts about Paul Latham's life. She is distraught and devoted to him.

Thank heavens our sinister footman has left!

SUNDAY 10TH AUGUST

I drove over to Pyrford to call upon my in-laws this morning. Lady Halifax, who 'bombed' over from the States is staying there but I missed her as she had gone to the station to meet her favourite son, Richard. She is well and suffered no ill effects from the crossing which took nine hours to Scotland, where a Flamingo met and brought her to London. In-laws charming, a touch vague, the new baby, Christopher,[2] has much hair and is colossal.

Peter Quennell, an angular weedy young man arrived . . . . in time for luncheon. He has had three beautiful wives and must be much sexed . . . We overate, slept and then drove to Sutton [Place] to bathe. Geordie Sutherland is deafer than ever! I had not seen him for over a year. Eileen is at Dunrobin.[3] As usual he was surrounded by second-rate females . . . . Geordie asked me to spend this week at Sutton with him. I dread the boredom but if the weather improves I may accept.

Quennell, who is a gifted writer certainly, is working at the Ministry of Information. He, too, knows all about Winston's great trip which has not yet been announced. I wonder why the delay? We listened in to the Queen who made an adequate broadcast: it was full of clichés but will be a success in the USA. I thought of our old intimacy. She has fooled everyone, really, for she is a frivolous but friendly fraud and I cannot help but admire her although she has not been loyal to me.

---

1 She had been secretary to the unfortunate Latham (qv) before working for Channon.
2 Christopher Alan Lennox-Boyd (1941–2012).
3 Dunrobin Castle, seat of the Duke of Sutherland.

MONDAY 11TH AUGUST

Lunched at Boodle's Club with one of Alan's sugar-daddies, Sir Malcolm Stewart.[1]
I am hoping that he will make me a director of one of his cement companies.

London is wet and dull; but where else can I go? I am tidying up my affairs
and am more than mad about money. Malcolm Stewart is a common old kindly
thing, rich and rather naif. I liked him and hope that I shall recognise him next
time we meet.

TUESDAY 12TH AUGUST   THE CAMP, WINDLESHAM

I came to this hideous house in Sunningdale to pay a duty visit to Mary Baker. She
is touchingly loyal and gay and amusing and practically asked me to marry her!
Clive Bell[2] is the only other guest and the atmosphere is similar to that of *Ladies in
Retirement*. Mary's aged mother, a white-haired madwoman, is more selfish and
sinister than ever: she has hallucinations and imagines that there is a young man
in the house who wants to kill her. I never met anyone who didn't want to escape
after about five minutes of her company. She dresses like an orthodox bishop
and speaks slow elegant English with an American accent. And her sentences are
a blend of Henry James[3] and Macaulay.[4] Before dinner I heard a wild wailing and
discovered that she was singing hymns seated in an armchair facing the setting
sun. She does it from loneliness but she isn't really lonely, for she has a day and
a night nurse. She has spent the past forty years wallowing in selfishness ... And
has ruined her adoring darling daughter's life. I have known them since I was 15
.... Clive Bell is still, and always, in love with Mary and wants to marry her, thus
releasing Vanessa Bell to marry her lover Duncan Grant,[5] the artist. Shall I sell
my two Grants – the lovely Venetian one of the Julienne given to me by [George]

---

1 Percy Malcolm Stewart (1872–1951) was a cement and brick magnate, who became
   Chairman of the London Brick Company in 1923 when his own concern was amalgamated
   into it. He built a model village, Stewartby, in Bedfordshire for his brickworkers, and was
   created 1st Bt in 1937.
2 Arthur Clive Heward Bell (1881–1964) was an art critic and a key member of the
   Bloomsbury group. He married, in 1907, Vanessa Stephen (1879–1961), sister of Virginia
   Woolf (qv).
3 Henry James (1843–1916) was an innovative American novelist who moved to England and
   took British nationality, being awarded the Order of Merit. His most famous works are *The
   Portrait of a Lady, The Golden Bowl* and *The Wings of the Dove*.
4 Thomas Babington Macaulay (1800–59) was a Whig statesman and historian, most notable
   for his *History of England*, which dealt extensively with the Glorious Revolution of 1688 and
   its aftermath.
5 Duncan James Corrowr Grant (1885–1978) was an artist, a core figure in the Bloomsbury
   group, and despite being an active homosexual the lover of Vanessa Bell (*vide supra*) and
   father of her child Angelica.

Gage and the smaller one of Firle given to me as a wedding present by Ld Ivor Churchill.

Much clever talk and too late – always too late to bed.

WEDNESDAY 13TH AUGUST   *SUTTON PLACE, GUILDFORD*

The newspapers this morning announced the death of Lord Willingdon. I saw him about ten days ago . . . . and watched him go off rather reluctantly to play golf in the rain with his indomitable, indefatigable wife. It was how he caught cold. He was a *grand seigneur*, to the fingertips; amazing appearance, careful impressive clothes, marvellous manners, *désir à plaire*[1] carried almost to a flirtatious degree with everyone he met, he was the great Whig of the eighteenth century. He was the proconsul par excellence, yet dominated all his life by his overpowering and delightful wife. Now he is dead: Inigo, his heir, is impotent, so the marquessate will lapse and Lady Willingdon will probably marry again . . .

I left the Camp, taking cuttings of an exotic hydrangea brought from Japan, to my mother-in-law, and posting others to Kelvedon: a white and blue blossom, delightful . . . I lunched at Pyrford and spent the afternoon with my in-laws, both charming, a touch impersonal, and affectionate . . . . I went on to nearby Sutton to spend the night with Geordie Sutherland. He had asked me for the whole week but I couldn't face the boredom of it. He was out when I arrived, having motored to Taplow to see Lady Desborough;[2] for that old sphinx still exists, still likes young men, especially dukes . . . . I wrote to Peter and to Lady Willingdon. It rained; Geordie returned and we had a pleasant evening.

THURSDAY 14TH AUGUST

The newspapers this morning announced that Mr Attlee would make an important statement on the wireless at 3 p.m. Of course it would be relevant to the Churchill visit to Pres[ident] Roosevelt and all day tongues wagged and the world was in a state of eager expectancy . . . I had breakfast with Geordie and later drove Billy Ednam[3] to London. He is staying with me here.

My mother and father-in-law came to lunch: he pressed £200 into my hands, in £1 notes. I was both insulted and pleased. A curious habit but one to be encouraged. Later we listened to Mr Attlee, who at three o'clock addressed the world. He would make anything sound dull and dull it was; perhaps the most sensational meeting in all history sounded and seemed like a Sunday sermon. A dreadful little bore, but fairly friendly. This second Tilsit has fallen rather flat

1 The desire to please.
2 See entry for 6 July 1939 and footnote.
3 William Humble David Ward (1920–2013), by courtesy Viscount Ednam from 1932 to 1969, when he succeeded his father as 4th Earl of Dudley.

partly because the result seemed illusory and also, in London at least, everyone had known the news for a fortnight. We were all disappointed: only an idealistic 'declaration of war aims' which would have been negotiated by Halifax or even by the transatlantic telephone. Somehow this very great and dramatic event has fallen flat[1] ....

Elizabeth Elveden, Jay Llewellin – bringing me two bottles of rare old brandy – Godfrey Winn, Harold and I dined and bridged. Godfrey Winn, no longer sycophantic and insinuating, was rude and witty and I liked him less. He and Jay went home together about midnight .... As we were playing bridge Harold was summoned to the telephone and told that there had been another air crash in Scotland and that Arthur Purvis,[2] with whom he had today lunched, was one of the twenty-two victims. It is one horrible and mysterious story. Harold, already looking grey and ill, paled and rushed off to the Ministry.

FRIDAY 15TH AUGUST

No letter from Honor: She no longer answers my notes about business and other matters. And the recent report finished by the detectives depressed me deeply: it told of Hogarthian revels, that Honor had become a drunkard and 'when in drink Her Ladyship sank to the level of the low and surly fellow with whom she went about'! They had been turned out of a pub for noisy and drunken behaviour! My wife! I am wounded beyond words and we all are agreed in thinking that this is the worst report which has come in ... Well-bred, fastidious Honor involved in a drunken brawl: it is revolting, indeed.

Billy Ednam woke me up with his banging of doors: he came in at 6 a.m.! And at about seven Harold burst into my room, just after I had again fallen asleep, to say that he was flying to Scotland to make a personal investigation into the aeroplane smash. Then Godfrey Winn telephoned to boast of his success with Jay Llewellin: it is an unexpected axis.

Had tea with Alice Harding: she has moved into her mother's chauffeur's cottage to save rates etc. All her gloomy but expensive furniture has been transported to Dorset where she has taken a farm, Fornstar nr Dorchester. With her was Freddie Ashton,[3] the dancer, now in the Air Force, whom I met for the first time. She wanted to marry him at one time but he refused as he has other inclinations. He is common but I liked him.

---

1   Attlee was announcing what came to be known as the Atlantic Charter, a joint declaration by Britain and America on their aims for the post-war world.
2   Arthur Blaikie Purvis (1890–1941) was a British industrialist based in Canada who ran the government's war purchasing programme in North America and had excellent top-level contacts in American business and politics. He was killed when his plane crashed just after take-off from an RAF base in Ayrshire.
3   Frederick William Mallandaine Ashton (1904–88) was one of the most celebrated ballet dancers and choreographers of the twentieth century.*

Harold flew back from Scotland in time to dine: he looked ashen and worn. His descriptions of the accident and of the mangled bodies were horrible. Early to bed.

SATURDAY 16TH AUGUST   *LEEDS CASTLE*

I sat to Gunn; and my beloved Bundi also posed.[1] I fell asleep: he is such a nice muddle-trained bore. Then I registered for national service with the '44s'[2] and after a snack lunch followed by a nap – I have two daily now as I am so tired – I drove here. The castle, rising grey, amongst the green looked impressive, indeed. Most of it is a military hospital but the Baillies have kept a wing for themselves and have large weekend parties.

A charming general – how I like generals! – named Allfrey[3] dined and we played bridge and I won with him as my partner. He seemed surprised when I told him that I was in love with General Wavell!

Olive Baillie is an unusual woman, vague, unpunctual, mean; she has a warm heart, is sound and sensible and has considerable charm. This is her third and most successful (so far!) marriage; for some years she has loved David Margesson and he, in his way, her; now she has transferred her affection to Geoffrey Lloyd who improves every day. He is reflective, intelligent, intellectual and able: the Birmingham bourgeois manner has gone.

This half-hospital runs smoothly and I am happy here. But today's happiness was somewhat clouded by a long letter from Jacqueline Lampson in which she tells me that Peter (letter dated July 26th) was still in Cairo. It seems that the Wavell sisters caught chickenpox and he has remained. But he never told me: occasionally he has flashes of a certain lack of consideration and they disturb me, yet bind me more closely to him, I suppose.

MONDAY 18TH AUGUST

Drove . . . . to London and was arrested for speeding, or rather given a summons. Everything goes wrong, 'There comes [*sic*] a tide in the affairs of men . . . . '[4]

---

1 For his portrait, which was still being painted.
2 That is, other men such as himself who were 44. The maximum call-up age was 41, but this exercise was for the purpose of marshalling manpower in the gravest emergency and for domestic needs.
3 Charles Walter Allfrey (1895–1964) was twice wounded in the Great War and won the Military Cross in 1917 and a Bar in 1918. He served in Iraq in the early 1930s, where he was awarded the DSO; and he fought in the Battle of France in 1940. From 1942 to 1944 he was General Officer Commanding V Corps in North Africa and Italy and from 1944 to 1948 GOC of British troops in Egypt. He retired in the rank of lieutenant general and was knighted in 1946.
4 Channon is quoting Brutus's observation to Cassius from *Julius Caesar*, Act IV, Scene III, which when rendered in full is not entirely relevant to Channon's feelings: 'There is a tide in the affairs of men, which, taken at the flood, leads on to fortune.'

And no good news greeted me. Nothing from Honor and she owes me so much money.... I found a letter from Peter dated 27th July: he was still in Cairo waiting for Felicity Wavell[1] to recover from chickenpox. He didn't even say when he was leaving but I sensed that Cairo had 'died' on him. He added that Paul and Olga had moved to Johannesburg – can it be true? In any case, I repeated it to the Duchess of Kent when she rang me up about seven o'clock.

I am not happy about Harold [Balfour]: I have an uncanny feeling about him. Can it be that he will be killed in a flying accident? He looks grey.

'The Big Uns' are back. Winston and Co. landed at port today. He will be disappointed by the coldness of his reception – that is if he expected a sort of Chamberlain-after-Munich arrival.

TUESDAY 19TH AUGUST

Sat to Gunn and he took two hours to do my right hand. Alice Harding came to lunch and we gossiped about old days at Bled and Rhinebeck and she convinced me that she still loves Serge Obolensky and always would, and that she regretted her divorce from him ... The Duchess of Kent came to tea .... also Alice who was charming.

I feel a little lost being out of the racket, but am enjoying the peace: shall I ever be in it again? A dearth of domestic and personal news of any kind; yet I feel something sinister or ominous is working up. The Prime Minister returned to London this morning and the press is working up a publicity popularity stunt of it, without much success.

Dined alone with Harold Balfour who was in a trite, reminiscent mood; insisted that Fate would soon deal him – and me – a new hand, for better or for worse destiny would soon move us. I think that he is right.

WEDNESDAY 20TH AUGUST

A curious August, almost ominous silence, which disturbs me. Am I dropped? Paul Latham resigned his seat: the announcement appears in this morning's press. Why has he done this, which is tantamount to a confession of guilt? I suppose that my Essex neighbour, a Mr Spearman[2] who lives at Rolls Park,[3] will succeed him as he has long been nursing the division of Scarborough. I am sad about it all.

1 Felicity Ann Wavell (1921–94), from 1947 Lady Felicity by courtesy, was the third of Wavell's four children. She married, in 1947, Captain Peter Longmore, son of Sir Arthur Longmore (qv).
2 Alexander Cadwallader Mainwaring Spearman (1901–82) was by profession a stockbroker. He won Scarborough as a Conservative at a by-election in 1941 and served until retiring in 1966. He was knighted in 1956.
3 In Chigwell in Essex: a fine Queen Anne house so damaged after being requisitioned by the Army in the Second World War that it was demolished in 1953.

The Treasury are being difficult about Prince Paul's finances. They insist on requisitioning his dollar holdings since he now lives in a 'sterling area'; this seems unjust since he is forced to do so. He is a virtual prisoner and so they confiscate his American holdings. It is having it both ways, and is un-English and unjust. I shall take steps with the Chancellor of the Exchequer. Blame it on Eden again.

Harold Balfour very against the rather Hollywood performance of the Prime Minister yesterday on his arrival! Many people are; but I see no harm in it.

For the first time in my life I should be indifferent to death: my glamorous life is over and it may be years before I recover. *Qui sait?*

This morning I attended the funeral of Lord Willingdon. The Abbey was crowded, all the familiar faces and many military. I thought of much we had lived and put up with, and perhaps we were not a bit battered by life as we had been spoilt by power and position and money. But it is a valiant order, brave courageous, strong and a touch hard. And in the crowded chancel I felt, feared that I was an object today of pity and curiosity as my marriage has proved a failure. Perhaps there was no speculation. Why? . . . but everyone smiled at me and was pleasant. Most of the congregation stood since there were few seats, and I happened to be next to the clergy as the procession followed and I found myself cheek by jowl with the infamous Archbishop of Canterbury, that is if he has either cheek or jowl. For quite three minutes I leered at his wicked, sombre face with its tiny compressed inquisitional mouth, his billiard-ball cranium, his cruel eyes. His profile is one of the most horrible I have ever studied. With him was the Dean of Windsor,[1] another old sinner, but he is warmer and more kindly *et quelqu'un*.[2] The procession moved up the aisle, [Lord] Simon, bland and smiling was a pall-bearer, John Anderson another, so was Buckie De La Warr, looking not more than 20 – later he told me that his aunt[3] had had over 3,000 letters . . . . All the ambassadors, the government, society, the many friends filled the nave. An impressive tribute to the most charming man I have ever met. I came away more infatuated with England and saddened by what may be her fate in September; for people here are behaving just as did the French in the spring of 1940. And the war doesn't progress. England only bombs and blockades and neither will crush Germany with whom we should many years ago have come to terms.

John Beith,[4] who was at the Legation in Athens, confirmed what I had heard so often – the reluctance of the Greeks to accept our aid. The whole affair was

1 Albert Victor Baillie (1864–1955) was a godson of Queen Victoria. He spent much of his early life as a clergyman in deprived parishes in the north-east of England and south London before becoming vicar of St Michael, Coventry, and was Dean of Windsor from 1917 to 1944. He was wont to travel widely in Europe during his holidays, which may be connected to Channon's 'sinner' observation.

2 And somebody.

3 Lady Willingdon.

4 The diplomat. See entry for 22 March 1940 and footnote.

an unthought-out whim of Anthony Eden's. Beith slightly blames Wavell for not being firm; he should have refused to undertake the Greek campaign. At Athens, whilst they were all deliberating, a curious cable had come to Wavell from Winston hinting that the whole project should be abandoned. The Legation repeated it in Cairo to Eden who had left Athens several hours before. Eden answered 'go ahead' . . . . Beith says that the Legation assumed that the PM was hedging; in any case he had sent off a cable which he could much later publish in his history of the Second World War, and thus prove that he was against the campaign and our intervention, that is if it failed. He was having money on both horses. Beith is Anthony Adverse, indeed and said that the Balkan front and its ramifications had never been thought out. Anthony was a film star. This opinion is growing in the country.

THURSDAY 21ST AUGUST   *KELVEDON*

Woke, feeling operative and dictated to a secretary for some time and wrote endless letters, mostly Southend ones.

Drove here in the afternoon. All is lovely and peaceful. I finished *Far From the Madding Crowd*:[1] it is practically Honor's story. She is Bathsheba, Sergeant Frank Troy, Mr Woodman; Mr Boldwood – isn't quite me.

The Germans are advancing at Leningrad. Perhaps September will be horrible here, as I always prophesied.

SATURDAY 23RD AUGUST[2]

A wet day. Few letters to relieve my boredom; but one came from the Colonial Office to say that the Regent and Princess Olga were still in Kenya but had moved to a more suitable house and that the boys were now at school. Princess Olga had changed her mind about going to Johannesburg: it looks now as if they were treated with more courtesy and consideration.

All day alone and I feel immensely better: no people to take a toll of one's nerves. It has been wet and the rain always leads me out of doors and I went for a walk in the woods, overgrown and alive with pheasants and partridges and stinging with nettles! Will it ever be an enchanted wood . . . well, I remember five minutes there. A feverish, fascinating, foolish five minutes long ago. The views are surprisingly rural still and much as they were centuries ago. I got soaked, picked roses and plums and gazed at my fields which with their pretty cattle looked like a

---

1 Thomas Hardy's 1874 novel partly about a young woman and her suitors from different social classes.
2 Dated 22 August in Rhodes James, thus in MS.

picture by Paul Potter.[1] Then I came in and read *Anna Karenina*. In my dejection I like only gloomy fine books such as this, or *Far From the Madding Crowd*: both have poignant and appropriate passages that move me.

Is my life really over? Have I reached the end of my development? I don't think so, really: after a blow one must have a pause, one must mark time and that I am doing. Harold is right: there will be some unexpected change. I am sorry that they would not make me Governor of Bermuda.[2] Perhaps I shall marry again for I should like children about me, more and many children. Seryozha, Anna Karenina's little boy, reminds me of my own faraway Paul with his craving for affection. In Paul's case, however, his mother has always denied it to him, poor mite.

SUNDAY 24TH AUGUST

Mustering my courage, I drove to Southend to have a confidential conversation with my ever loyal agent, Bailey. He had heard no hints or rumours of my marital difficulties. But he spoke out frankly: said that Honor was no loss to me in the constituency as she was personally unpopular, even disliked: many people had asked him whether she drugged.[3] Her rudeness and vacant expression had offended and puzzled people.

I finished *Anna Karenina* and went sadly to bed. Mrs Nimmo tells me that old Sir Drummond Smith,[4] a decayed farmer of 80 who lives nearby at Suttons, is courting her 18-year-old daughter. I advised her to encourage the marriage.

Winston Churchill made a long, weighty and excellent broadcast about his journey across the Atlantic. Bailey tells me that the trip 'fell flat' in Southend.

The Battle for Leningrad has begun. It is eight weeks since Germany invaded Russia.

MONDAY 25TH AUGUST

A dull and disappointing post. Why does nobody write to me? Am I dropped by all? Only Bill Tufnell on guard at Windsor Castle sends a line of sympathy.

Ten male patients arrived here this morning. They seemed hale and healthy and I hope that they will do no damage, or be difficult or destructive. They are privates.

---

1 Paulus Potter (1625–54) was a Dutch painter of bucolic landscapes, and the animals within them.
2 The post had been vacant, and was given to 2nd Viscount Knollys; this is the first hint that Channon had been interested in it, or had applied for it.
3 *Sic*: he means, 'whether she took drugs'.
4 Drummond Cunliffe Smith (1861–1947), succeeded his father as 4th Bt in 1905.

I have been feeling slightly better these past few days; but people exhaust me and this afternoon after lunch I had a mild collapse again, reaction from yesterday. I really must get better again. At 4.30 Roland Robinson, MP for Blackpool, who is acting as intelligence and liaison officer with the American Eagle Squadron who are now stationed at North Weald, arrived here escorting six very young American Eagles.[1] I gave them tea, drinks, put them on the tennis court and into the pool. The pretty young nurses helped to entertain them and a successful and happy time had by all!

Early to bed after reading *Jane Eyre*:[2] the world is a sad place and I am in the depths of a very un-Chipsian storm.

TUESDAY 26TH AUGUST

Another grey Essex day; and I so want to sunbathe. Eleven patients, all privates, arrived here: nice polite hale and hearty soldiers and I dread damage or destruction to the house. They are sleeping, some of them, in the drawing room.

I am slightly off Rab. He is a bourgeois and a don at heart, and I only like princes and great gentlemen and *flâneurs*,[3] and even, if need be, pansies!

I had a slight flare-up of rage against the Red Cross people here because they gave me so little to eat ... and made a silly scene. I am nervy.[4]

THURSDAY 28TH AUGUST   *5 BELGRAVE SQUARE*

I am so glad to be back in this still lovely comfortable house with its *luxe* and my books and baths. Godfrey Winn came in this morning, then Anne Feversham, who is proving herself a loyal ally; we talked of Honor and she promised to help me get a job with the Halifaxes etc. She will see Honor in ten days' time. Honor wrote me a long plaintive, impatient letter asking for many objects etc. She deigns, *enfin*,[5] to write! I wrote thirty-one letters today .... A lovely, affectionate letter [came] from Peter who only left Cairo on Monday, August 18th. The naughty boy has been idle for a month, sunbathing and learning Hindustani! The less he has to do, the more infrequently he writes. Still I love him always. He also sent me one for Paul Latham which I destroyed .... Anne Feversham came back at seven and

---

1 Fighter squadrons of the RAF formed with US volunteer pilots in the early days of the Second World War.

2 Novel of 1847 by Charlotte Brontë, often regarded as a precursor of the novels of the 1920s describing the idea of consciousness.

3 Literally a stroller or lounger, a *flâneur* is a person who saunters or swans around observing society.

4 It seems that in return for letting the Red Cross use Kelvedon as one of its convalescent homes, Channon was allowed to keep his private space there and would be fed from the charity's kitchen.

5 'At last'.

we talked for another hour about Honor. Anne is shocked and distressed by the tragic tale ....

Harold, Godfrey Winn, Jay Llewellin and I played bridge. After the others left Harold confessed to me that he had broken with Helen Fitzgerald, and that whilst he felt he was both caddish and cruel, he was relieved: she, apparently, is wretched. We sat up until 2.30.

FRIDAY 29TH AUGUST

The Iveaghs came to lunch and were charm, affection and amiability itself. She was gay and gracious and horrid about Honor; he was not at all pleased by the recent rise in Guinness shares and said that were he to die now, it would cost his estate another million or so.

I had a Turkish bath which soothed me: I am still in a desperately nervous mood and go off like a rocket at times.

Patsy tells me that she is going down to Shalden Park Farm, nr Alton, to spend the night with her adulterous sister. Naughty of her, but perhaps a good thing really.

SATURDAY 30TH AUGUST

It was a lovely day and I am here, too inert to make an effort to go away, even to Kelvedon. Shopped, felt liverish, paid bills and ordered turquoise buttons for Peter, and lunched alone at Buck's, which was deserted.

This afternoon a wave of despair swept over me and I fell asleep weeping, weeping; when I woke my mood had changed and I was gay and greeted Brigid, my ravishing sister-in-law, eagerly and tried to fascinate her and her pretty gracious swain, the rather eighteenth-century young Lord Euston, and I succeeded. They are both staying with me for the night. I tried to persuade them to marry each other ... and was insinuating and subtle. Then they went out and I felt old again until Harold Balfour arrived back from Margate where he had made a speech. Over duck and champagne we listened to a résumé of it on the wireless and then went early to bed, Messieurs Bouvard and Pécuchet.[1] We slightly abused Rab, each of us much as we dared to the other: we both know him to be ambitious, inhuman but withal loyal and honest.

SUNDAY 31ST AUGUST

Nine weeks ago today the German–Russian war began, one of the most sanguinary in all history.

---

1 Eponymous principal characters in Gustave Flaubert's satire *Bouvard et Pécuchet*, published posthumously in 1881. The two friends try a number of schemes to advance their lives, and they mostly fail.

A glorious day, and I got up early, found that Hugh Euston had already left for Windsor, and that Harold B, and Brigid were still in their beds! I drove to Kelvedon, still fulminating against the Red Cross. The gardens were bright with the blue uniforms of the patients wandering about and I am glad that that lovely place is being put to good use. Went on to Langleys, which the war never changes: Bill Tufnell had a weekend leave and we lunched, he, his senile mother, and his cousin . . . . by the swimming bath and sunbathed. His young cousin, whom he loves, David Cazenove arrived at teatime: Bill's adoration of him is innocent and pathetic. The house is immaculately kept by a devoted housekeeper about whom there was once a lawsuit and nearly disinheritance – a sordid story. Went back to my Kelvedon where I found the American Eagles, nine of them, playing tennis and bathing. One of the ones who came over last week was killed a few days ago; and the boys there today had bombed Lille this morning. I gave them drinks, made tentative advances (ill-received!) to Mrs Nimmo, who is offended with me; and came back to Belgrave Square which was welcoming but empty – Harold is staying with Lord Beaverbrook. Suddenly as I write I am lonely, desperately lonely. And I am such a cad *au fond*; for seeing a cable on the front hall table my heart beat faster . . . but it was not from Simla, but Chicago, a long, disjointed telegram from my dotty, old mother – and I was ashamed of my disappointment. Peter has treated me shabbily of late.

MONDAY 1ST SEPTEMBER   *COPPINS*

I drove here, reading *en route* that the Duchess of Kent had had a slight eye operation, but when I arrived she seemed well and greeted me very affectionately. She was wearing dark glasses and was doing a jigsaw puzzle. Her left eye is to be drained tomorrow as it is infected; some jot of poison which comes from being run-down and fatigued: she is desperately anxious about her loved ones so faraway and so scattered . . . Garrett Moore, tappering [*sic*] and unimaginative soon arrived as did Alice Harding. The Duchess pointed out to us that just a year ago today Alice and I had driven down to Coppins together and stayed for the night. I remember it well, leaving Honor at Kelvedon to cope with the *ménage* Raikes. What a year for all of us it has been, a horrible one for the Duchess and me. At tea there was a wild joke about swellings apropos of the Duchess's eye and Alice said '*À qui le dites-vous?*'[1] I shot a quick look at her and realised that she is pregnant, very. None of her other babies ever showed: this one must be immense! A very pleasant evening *à quatre* but I ate and drank too much. Coppins is such an agreeable place, friendly, comfortable and effortless! We gossiped cosily and talked of old days. The Duchess got out a sketch she did of me, a huge charcoal drawing done in about 1926 at Bled. She has talent, certainly. The Duke is still in Canada.

---

1 'To whom do you say that?'

Bed now about midnight. Garrett Moore, perhaps not unexpectedly, was not kind about his ex-brother-in-law Paul Latham: his sordid tale opens on Thursday next and he has briefed Patrick Hastings[1] to defend him – a poor choice, I think. The man has a somewhat warped class-conscious brain and a bitter tongue.

A crushing cable came from Captain Coats that he is not coming on leave with Wavell.

TUESDAY 2ND SEPTEMBER

Slept atrociously and woke feeling liverish and awful. The Duchess came to say 'goodbye' to me and then left for London to have her eye operation. I drove up with Alice . . . . Harold rang up to say that there had been yet another disaster to a Liberator and that ten people had been killed as the plane crashed against a Scotch hill . . . . The plane was on the way back. It is the third crash since a fortnight.

The Duchess of Kent rang up to say that she has quite recovered from her operation and that she had had a letter from Princess Olga with one from the Regent for me enclosed.

WEDNESDAY 3RD SEPTEMBER

We have now entered the third year of this boring war!

Much publicity about the Liberator disaster: the queue awaiting passage from Newfoundland to Scotland will shorten.

Dined with Harold and Jim Wedderburn who impressed me as being madder than ever. He denied being in love with Brigid and dared to defend Honor – he attacked her selfishness and her unchristian behaviour but he said that I should take her back, be reconnected to her. I retorted that I had been deserted in distressing circumstances and would never do so. He replied that I was unchristian. He didn't seem to realise the true situation and I saw at once that H had got hold of him: for a flash I was angry but then controlled myself and instead wheedled him a bit. Jay Llewellin came in late and we played bridge. The Duchess of Kent rang up saying that she had a note for me from Prince Paul. At midnight it came but it is only a scrawl and I can make nothing of it.

THURSDAY 4TH SEPTEMBER

I woke at nine and was reading Paul's pathetic pencilled scrawl, with his photograph next to mine, when the telephone rang: it was the Duchess of K and we discussed it. It is illegible and a touch incoherent: I felt nostalgic. Then I went, got up, wrote

---

1 Patrick Gardiner Hastings (1880–1952) was one of the leading criminal and defamation barristers of his era. He was Labour MP for Wallsend from 1922 to 1926, and Attorney-General in the first Labour government in 1924, when he was knighted.

letters – one, a long one, to Peter at Simla, and took it to the India Office to be sent out in the Viceroy's bag. Walked on to Coutts bank where I was shown into the waiting room hung with royal engravings of the Orleans dynasty, and then the manager, Mr Stephens, received me uncertainly. We discussed the Regent's affairs, his finances, and his private fortune etc. It has some jewels still, many in fact, both at Exeter and at Chester. Stephens confided in me that he had made over many of the tin boxes to the Duke of Kent, and that they are now in his name: it is now too late to do more as the Regulations are strict and rigid. He showed me a stiff, indeed curt letter from Anthony Eden refusing to help: hardly a civil letter. AE's spite is v deep; for the failure of his absurd proposed Balkan Bloc he must find a scapegoat and he blames the Regent. I walked away in the August[1] heat feeling depressed and nostalgic, and longing for Paul. Usually at this time of the year I was either at Bled or setting out for there . . . . The evening newspapers print in full the sordid details of Paul Latham's court martial. There are thirteen charges of indecency against him, and one of attempted suicide. A horrible squalid affair. Batmen and servants. Ripples of the scandal will travel far . . .

I forgot to record that during dinner last night Max Beaverbrook rang up Harold in person and invited him to accompany him to Moscow on the military aeronautical missions. Harold was enchanted especially so when Max told him that he had secured the Prime Minister's authorisation. I have an uncanny instinct that he will be killed somewhere soon. One by one they go, my loved companions. It is Paul of Y[ugoslavia] that I am thinking of mostly today . . .

Maureen Dufferin, Elizabeth Elveden, Micky Renshaw, Jay Llewellin and Harold dined and we played bridge. Much talk of poor Paul Latham who has been so caddishly treated. There are thirteen counts of gross indecency, five against Gunner 'A', his batman; six against Gunner 'B', also his batman; one against Gunner 'C'; and the thirteenth is against Mr 'D', a civilian whom he is alleged to have picked up in the Ritz Bar. There is an additional accusation of attempted suicide on June 24th, making fourteen in all. Jay Llewellin, who is a barrister, said that he will be acquitted on the last charge and that he will be sentenced from anything from two to twenty-six years – the terms to run concurrently – for the indecency charges. Probably about five years with some remission for probably good behaviour. My heart bleeds for him; and Patsy, his selfish bitch of a wife, is largely to blame.

FRIDAY 5TH SEPTEMBER

A friendly, even agreeable letter from Honor was a welcome surprise this morning.

A grey day which opened well. I went through Honor's things, mostly nostalgic muck but came upon a few illuminating papers! There were Anne Feversham's letters to Honor written in Nov[ember] 1933 about her flirtation and ruptured

1 *Sic*; either Channon has forgotten it is September, or he felt it was hot enough for August.

engagement to the Duke of Kent. I have kept them: everything else I sent on to H – boxes full of old letters, cheques, receipts, rubbish and hats! It all makes one miserable and <u>very dirty</u>.

Dined with Bill Tufnell at Claridge's and he asked me about Honor: he seemed uninterested in her and still in love with Brigid. Wonderful food and wines as Bill is a famous gourmet. We became a touch mellow and he told me that he hated P[eter Coats], whom he roughly described as 'a little gold-digger with a bad reputation'! I controlled my annoyance: I am v good at concealing my feelings.

The Latham case is a revolting one and the details too squalid for description. He has been acquitted on three of the thirteen charges of indecency. The result of the remaining ten charges and the one for attempted suicide is yet to be known. What he must be suffering!

SATURDAY 6TH SEPTEMBER

All day in front of me, alone and empty, but I don't mind really. Many people rang up. Alice H[arding] has a tiresome letter from America in which her governess complains of my Nannie who is very tiresome and difficult, indeed.

I have made a firm resolution to be nicer – and more discreet – in the future. The world can be v unkind, indeed: nobody is loyal to Latham, but everyone seems sorry for him. I shall never be involved in a scandal: I must pull myself together.

Dined with Bill Mabane whom I found charming, at La Belle Meunière. Eleanor Smith,[1] rather dishevelled and dirty, was at an adjoining table with a grubby friend.

SUNDAY 7TH SEPTEMBER

Away all day, and back only at midnight to sleep. I should have gone [to Sunningdale] yesterday but waited for Harold who – as often happens – at the last moment had to stay over to see Max Beaverbrook who rings him up every second hour. They leave soon for Russia. However Harold sent me to Sunningdale to 'Earlywood' in his car this morning. The house is hideous but Winnie Portarlington has arranged it with skill: it is a triumph; many of the things inherited from George IV etc., masses of boxes, *bibelots* and books attractively arranged. I long for a house again to play about with. Rex Whistler, Micky Renshaw and General 'Boy' Brooke[2] were there,

---

1 Eleanor Furneaux Smith (1902–45), by courtesy Lady Eleanor Smith from 1922, daughter of the 1st Earl of Birkenhead*. Previously a gossip writer, she became a highly successful popular novelist, notably with *The Man in Grey*, which like her other novels was made into a film.

2 Bertram Norman Sergison-Brooke (1880–1967) fought in the Second Boer War and the Great War, and in the 1920s commanded the 1st Battalion of the Grenadier Guards. He was recalled from retirement in 1939 to be General Officer Commanding London District, a post he held until 1942. He was knighted in 1937.

and old Lionel,[1] more portly, deaf and boring than ever. Winnie is a sensational ass and angel, affection and disarming. I sunbathed, overate . . . . I gorged. Harold drove me back. There is much speculation about the presidential broadcast announced for tomorrow.

I am haunted by the startling discoveries which I made about my wife. She is so deceitful – a really despicable and filthy character, much given to lechery.

I adored 'Boy' Brooke; I have a weakness for generals, obviously. Long walk with Winnie who told me many tales of the jealousy existing between Windsor and Coppins! There is no real love between the Sovereign and the Kents.

MONDAY 8TH SEPTEMBER

Old Mrs Roosevelt,[2] the President's mother, has died suddenly and his broadcast is postponed until Thursday.

Nicholas Lawford, Peter Loxley, Jay Llewellin and Harold dined and we played bridge; or rather Nicholas wandered about fingering my books. He is a delicate, exquisite creature, cultivated and charming; but he is treacherous about Eden whom he dislikes.

Lady Iveagh writes to me that she has failed to persuade the Halifaxes to take me on at the Embassy in Washington: there were too many objections, an MP, a relation: the currency restrictions etc. I am disappointed but not surprised for Halifax never does anything for his subordinates. He likes nobody, really; and for all his idealism, his lofty sense of duty, I think he hates humanity. In the end nobody trusts him.

A curious leader appeared in *The Times*: it discussed the succession to Winston. Was it an Edenite manoeuvre?

TUESDAY 9TH SEPTEMBER

Walked to the H of Commons and had an hour with Rab. He was really charming and even affectionate. I warned him against Anthony Eden, who is not his friend. He tells me that the PM has definitely turned down Sam Hoare as Viceroy [of India] and will prolong the Linlithgows'[3] term for another year.

Winston spoke endlessly and rather dully: people walked out – for the first time. I sat in the Smoking Room and everyone plied me with drinks and there was a gay atmosphere, like the first ball of the season. Everyone most friendly, I thought. Lunched with Jim Thomas and as we came out of the dining room I read on the tape Jacqueline Lampson has produced a son! A son. Another son.

---

1 6th Earl of Portarlington. See entry for 6 July 1939 and footnote.
2 Sara Ann Delano (1854–1941) married James Roosevelt I (1828–1900) in 1880.
3 Victor Alexander John Hope (1887–1952), 2nd Marquess of Linlithgow, served as Viceroy from 1936 to 1943. He married, in 1911, Doreen Maud Milner (1886–1965).*

My emotions are mixed but I am delighted for her and for Miles ... I came home with my thoughts to rest: Jim Thomas soon followed and had a bath.

WEDNESDAY 10TH SEPTEMBER

Felt ill, but walked to the House, lunched with [Jack] Profumo and lingered on for a bit. Brendan Bracken in a slight light superficial speech addressed the 1922 Committee. His easy brusqueness was a success.

Bed about 10.30. I am rereading Trollope's *The Prime Minister*.[1]

My annoyance with Mrs Nimmo grows daily. And the Red Cross are infuriating. There is general indignation that too much publicity was given to the Latham trial and considerable regret that it was ever brought at all.

THURSDAY 11TH SEPTEMBER

Went to the H of C, taking a brace of eggs to Jim Thomas: he is living at the Foreign Office with Anthony who complains that Jim eats his eggs!

Wavell is back: so probably he brought my very quick letters [from Coats]. I reread them: P[eter] seems happy and already absorbed in his new life. His mother came to see me today: she is so extraordinarily like him and he is the blue-eyed child. When she left I hurried to the Dorchester to see Mrs Greville who has ulcers on her tongue, laryngitis and other ailments. She is very loving but with a viper's tongue and attacked everyone, particularly Lady Willingdon for dining out so soon. I told her that I had seen Halifax today. He addressed an old Party Meeting at the House with his usual urbanity. He was very gracious to me; kindly; flattered me. But he is an elegant elongate [*sic*] eel. I sat with my father-in-law who is the more honest of the two.

Gave a rich lunch to Jim Thomas and managed to extract from him that *The Times* leader on Monday had been inspired. I always get everything out of Jim.

At the Dorchester I ran into Lady Camrose, who had been visiting her new granddaughter, Sheila Birkenhead's baby born on Tuesday. Mrs Greville asked me if Honor had eloped with a cow man. What can I say to this gossip?

FRIDAY 12TH SEPTEMBER

A lyrical characteristically Chipsian day: my real role. I was up early and went to bed late, and not once during the seventeen hours that I was awake did I venture out! All day people poured in; the telephone buzzed; messages were sent. I had a *réussi* and rare little luncheon party: the Prince Consort of Luxembourg,[2] dark

---

1 Published in 1876, the fifth of the 'Palliser' novels.
2 Félix Marie Vincent of Bourbon-Parma (1893–1970) married Charlotte, Grand Duchess of Luxembourg, his first cousin, in 1919.

and Bourbon-looking he talked French – the Grand Duchess was in the country and unable to come; the two Habsburg boys, the archdukes Robert and Felix[1] – the latter never left me all day and indeed, he came here four times; Sir Noel and Lady Charles, our newly appointed couple to Brazil; Audrey Bouverie[2] and Peter Loxley. The Charleses are so fashionable and social, a welcome contrast to the usual FO appointment. The Prince of Luxembourg told me that he had lost all his possessions as he only just got away so I gave him an *almanac de cour*[3] which belonged to the comte de Chambord (his great-uncle) and had both the handwriting and arms of his grandmother, Louise, duchesse de Parme. He was enchanted. Gay party . . . After lunch Rab looked in and was affectionate and amusing – said that Audrey Bouverie talked of my lunch – 'so many royalties that she had a sore knee!' Rab was followed by Herlihy,[4] the lobby correspondent, who stayed too long – even outstayed Godfrey Winn who is just out of hospital – but he told me much. There is, he assured me, a growing anti-Churchillian feeling in the House, particularly in the Labour Party. He gives the government only until Xmas. Greenwood, Attlee and particularly Bevin are Anderson adherents, and Bevin remarked to him 'sunshine comes out of John Anderson's arse'! Herlihy hates Eden; says that the Erskine-Hill party will support Anderson, too. Eden is light metal, a mental pansy etc. etc. An interesting conversation certainly.

SATURDAY 13TH SEPTEMBER   *PYRFORD*

Mrs Greville tells me that she will refuse to be a godmother to the Lampsons' child. I had a cable from Miles saying that mother and child were flourishing which is a relief.

Harold is very excited about his great trek to Russia which begins next week. I am not, and feel uneasy, have a Kitchener feeling about it.[5]

I drove here for luncheon and spent the afternoon in the bosom of the family: they are pleasant and affectionate and really rather bored and tired of the Honor affair. Brigid Guinness tells me that she wants to go to the Middle East to serve as a nurse instead of marrying Hugh Euston. The more fool she!

[The Duke of] Alba told Harold that he had news from Rome that Tassilo Fürstenberg died recently in Italy. Poor, gay, attractive, wild, wayward Tassilo, who likes every girl he meets, and clicked teeth and sang and told amusing stories. I am so sorry for him. I made his marriage: they met in this house – Clara

---

1 Archduke Felix of Austria (1916–2011) was the third son of the last Habsburg Emperor, and brother of Archduke Robert (qv). He would soon move to the United States.
2 *Née* Audrey James. See entry for 3 June 1940 and footnote.
3 A French royal and courtly directory.
4 John Gerard Herlihy (1903–74) was lobby correspondent of the *Daily Graphic*. He later worked for Reuters and the *Daily Sketch*.
5 1st Earl Kitchener of Khartoum was killed when the ship taking him on a mission to Russia in June 1916 hit a mine off the Orkney Islands.

Agnelli – and soon married, but not until I wrote and urged him repeatedly to propose to her.

SUNDAY 14TH SEPTEMBER

A pleasant day. The Halifaxes arrived at Pyrford early and I spent much of the day with him: he is so long, so lean, so distinguished and so bored he looked more clerical than ever. I pleaded Paul of Y[ugoslavia]'s cause and he advised me to write and say not to worry; 'all would in time be forgotten and probably forgiven'!! Halifax was friendly, even affectionate and she was smooth, simple and gracious; but it is always difficult to make any impression upon her. He was riveted by *Dorian Gray*[1] and came looking at an old copy and quoting from him, discussing the famous ritualistic passage with his youngest Richard,[2] an immense auburn young subaltern. What a strange book for Lord H to read now after all these years! After a picnicky lunch he returned to work (or to sleep, as I suspected) but kept saying 'Chips, don't let me miss anything! Come and call me if there is any fun!'

Channon comes across a pile of clothes collected for evacuees in Pyrford's old laundry.

Amongst them was Lord Lothian's entire wardrobe, which had been sent to her [Lady Iveagh] by his sisters.[3] I went through it and bought – *sans* coupons – three ties and a pair of evening shoes. It is as near as I shall ever be to being in an Ambassador's shoes! When I brought the things back to the house Edward Halifax pounced on them, tried on the shoes, found that his predecessor had smaller feet than his own and decided to let me keep them. But he insisted on buying one of the new ties from me for five shillings. It was all rather macabre, poor Lothian's 38 shirts, his underclothing and coats!

TUESDAY 16TH SEPTEMBER

Woke feeling *désoeuvré* and lonely and I went to Kelvedon for a whiff of country air. It looked lovely and still has many traces of my strange personality. I loaded the car with roses and returned . . . . A pile of messages and letters cheered me. One

---

1 *The Picture of Dorian Gray* was Oscar Wilde's only novel, published in 1890, in which after a mephistophelean pact a young man's portrait ages but he does not.

2 Richard Frederick Wood (1920–2002), youngest son of Lord Halifax, served in the King's Royal Rifle Corps during the war, losing both his legs after they were crushed by an unexploded bomb in North Africa in 1942. He was Conservative MP for Bridlington from 1950 to 1979, when he was raised to the peerage as Baron Holderness (life peerage). He was Minister of Power from 1959 to 1963, Minister of Pensions from 1963 to 1964 and Minister of Overseas Development from 1970 to 1974.

3 The 11th Marquess of Lothian had died while Ambassador to Washington. See entry for 12 December 1940.

from Peter from Cairo dated July 19th – must have been long delayed *en route*. It contained a heartbreaking epistle from the poor lonely discredited Regent: it had no end, no beginning. Here is a copy of it:

'How can I thank you for your three letters. It is almost worth going through such ordeals when one has friends like you and Kitten [i.e. the Duchess of Kent]. Bless you! I'll keep your letters always. Please tell Steph to invest all my $ in USA Gov. bonds and if that is impossible in Canadian Gov. bonds. I have also got a small sum in New York with the Hanover and Something bank. Could he ask them to invest it in Gov. bonds for me. I am horrified at all the untruths published about us in papers. Why is that necessary? In one I saw that we tried to go to Romania . . . . !! All love.' The heading of the note paper had been cut off. It is all *déchirant*.[1]

WEDNESDAY 17TH SEPTEMBER

Harold [Balfour] came to my room early this morning. He had been up until nearly 3 a.m., and had sat in Beaverbrook's long room at No. 12 Downing Street with him, David Margesson and Brendan Bracken. About midnight there was a tap at the door and a muffled throaty voice was heard, 'May I come in?' It was the Prime Minister dressed in his famous purple siren suit over which he wore his heavy coat and he was smoking the inevitable cigar. He was in an angry mood and whilst not drunk he was certainly a bit enflamed. He began to abuse everybody and everything, said that he was at war with about every country 'including Australia'! Then he attacked the Army, said that it always refused to fight and this raised David M to a spirited defence of his department! Winston went on, 'The Army won't fight'; 'The Army always want more divisions, more equipment.' Said that he had 'sacked Wavell' and now would 'sack Dill or go himself'. Dill was no use, little better than Wavell etc. etc. He ranted, roared and walked about the room. Brendan and Beaverbrook were not in the least surprised, David was annoyed but Harold, new to this technique, was amazed . . . .

I walked to the Reform Club to lunch with Herlihy: the magnificent building crowded with left-wing radicals and intellectuals and a wave of despair came over me. These are the people of the future, polite revolutionaries who always want war and preach world revolution but never fight themselves. A wave of communism is sweeping over England, a distant echo from the Russian steppes.

We are back now to batteries and blackouts, and soon – who knows? – we shall have basements and bombings again? I walked to the Dorchester to call on Mrs Greville, who was in a gentle and reminiscent mood. She is ageing fast. Then

1 Heartbreaking.

I dined at Claridge's with Peggy Dunne[1] and Evelyn Waugh (just back from the Middle East) and his quiet twee wife.[2] Dinner cost Peggy £8. It is inflation.

When I came in Harold was undressing: I have a dread, a premonition that he may never return from what may prove an ill-fated expedition to Russia. Who knows? He was amused by Beaverbrook trying to apologise for the Prime Minister's strange conduct last night. The PM had said to him, 'I hope I didn't go too far in front of Balfour,' and Beaverbrook reassured him that all is well . . . Everyone thinks that the Anglo-American mission to Russia will go by plane; actually they go in a small cruiser soon.

Patsy L[ennox]-B[oyd] tells me that she stayed with Honor for two days: there wasn't a servant. H had to cook, do the washing up and it was all comic and disorganised. However she seemed well, preoccupied and happy – and *Dieu merci!*, no baby on the way. I wonder how it will all end? . . . . Her judgement of people is appalling.

Evelyn Waugh tells me that Randolph Churchill is as argumentative and noisy as ever and that he abuses Halifax, whom he will call 'the Holy Fox', all day.

THURSDAY 18TH SEPTEMBER

I took my in-laws out to luncheon and then went with him [Lord Iveagh] for a long walk; we went over 11 St James's Square, a rather fine house which they have ruined and now emptied. Then he and I came here [Belgrave Square] . . . . Lord I has apparently forgot his promise to pay off my indebtedness . . . However I am not too badly off. As we were sitting together the telephone buzzed and I was flattered and embarrassed to hear Archie Wavell's voice. I rushed around later to the Service Club to see him and actually met him in Waterloo Place. He looked rested and well and his face lit up with his charming shy smile. I sat with him [and] his son Archie[3] . . . . for an hour; we drank whisky and chatted, and I found Wavell, the great soldier, the war hero, as quiet, modest and as unassuming as ever. He told a tale or two, said how bust he had been, and asked whether anybody knew that he was in England? I laughed, told him that half of London was aware

---

1 Margaret Anne Walker (1908–2000) married in 1930 Philip Dunne (see Vol. I, entry for 1 February 1937 and footnote). They divorced in 1944. She had only one hand.

2 Arthur Evelyn St John Waugh (1903–66) had become famous after the huge success of his first two novels *Decline and Fall* (1928) and *Vile Bodies* (1930). Although mainly a satirist, he became perhaps best known for his novel *Brideshead Revisited* and for his *Sword of Honour* trilogy. In 1937 he married, as his second wife, Laura Letitia Gwendolen Evelyn Herbert (1916–73), daughter of Colonel Aubrey Herbert, who reputedly died of the Pharaoh's Curse after being in the party that opened Tutankhamun's tomb in 1923.

3 Archibald John Arthur Wavell (1916–53) was by courtesy Viscount Keren of Eritrea from 1947 to 1950, when he succeeded his father as 2nd Earl Wavell. A professional soldier like his father, he lost his left hand in the Burma campaign, won the Military Cross in 1947 and was killed fighting the Mau Mau in Kenya in December 1953.

of his visit since he lunched out and walked in the streets. He is unaware that he is a popular hero. I quite understand why the PM dislikes him: he is too silent for Winston's taste which is more flamboyant! Young Wavell, on whom his father lavished much affection and calls 'Archie John', asked me many pertinent questions as I drove him to the Air Ministry. Incidentally, he said that he was a Socialist and when I asked him why he retorted that he wanted to be able to ask his batman to dine. I pointed out that he could do that now if he chose – people might think that he was Paul Latham, of course – but it didn't really require a social revolution, and overturning the existing order to do something silly which he could do now. The lad is spoilt, is not quite accustomed to the glory and glamour which has come so deservedly and characteristically to his family, but he is intellectual and honest at heart. He has charm, freckles and theories and his hair is very long and very red. I found him inoperative and vague and bullied him into ringing up Mrs Coats, Peter's frail and devoted mother . . . . I finally got the number and the General himself spoke to her: she was enchanted. The General said that he was lunching with Portal and perhaps the Prime Minister tomorrow, but would Mrs Coats and I meet him for a drink about one o'clock, and if he could get out of his engagement he would give us lunch. Then, thrilled, I walked home.

Patsy, Jay Llewellin, Alice Harding and Peter Loxley dined here, a sort of farewell party for Harold who leaves at any moment for Moscow. We had a magnum of champagne and got rather mellow, even tipsy. I was sleepy indeed and dozed as the others played bridge. About midnight young Wavell arrived and cut in; the bridge went on until 3 a.m. and he, I gathered – I slept through it – was rather pugnacious and annoyed the others by his too frank criticism of their awkward play . . . then he and I walked with a torch around the Belgrave Square Gardens and I took his arm. After a little he withdrew it; seemed annoyed (so was I) that he had been kept up so late. By then taxis somehow had been produced and Jay Llewellin drove him to Dill, the CIGS's,[1] flat.

I feel a hundred: I can no longer sit up like this.

The Mission to Moscow goes off tomorrow or Saturday or Sunday very secretly and probably by destroyer. I have vague Kitchener forebodings about it all – this expedition which is fraught with disappointment, frustration and considerable danger. Harold was sad and sentimental. I was to have all the things that I want and am to give the others to Ian,[2] his very delightful handsome son.

FRIDAY 19TH SEPTEMBER   *LEEDS CASTLE*

I went to sleep about 4 a.m. this morning and woke feeling ill and dreadful. Honor rang up in one of her leonine moods: she raved and was rude, accused me of stealing two pepper pots which belong to me; said she wished that she had

1 Chief of the Imperial General Staff.
2 Ian Balfour (1924–2013) succeeded his father as 2nd Baron Balfour of Inchrye in 1988.

taken the carpets from Kelvedon in order to spite me etc. However, I soothed her somewhat and after forty minutes she calmed down and we parted on fairly friendly terms. I was at once sick twice: anything to do with her makes my heart pound, I feel ill and the room blurs. I want never to see her again but fear and feel that would be foolish. I got up at last, washed-out and aged, dressed, went to the bank .... and then sauntered slowly to the Service Club where Mrs Coats had already arrived from Wiltshire. She was touched and thrilled to meet the General, who soon came in accompanied by Archie John .... We lunched somewhat silently .... and few people in the crowded ladies dining room of the Service Club seemed to recognise General Wavell. I felt ill after the late night and Honor's repugnant conversation – she has become so rude and rough – that I was dull. However the party was a success and we all talked gloriously of Peter ....

Channon then drives to stay with the Baillies at Leeds Castle.

Leeds looks romantic and lovely .... There was a late tea at 6.30 and we dined on partridge and champagne at nine o'clock.

Geoffrey Lloyd has the room next to me: he travels with a large library – about fifty books, mostly classic which he marks heavily. Stendhal is his favourite. He is an extraordinary youth. The castle, whilst a hospital, is still sumptuous but there is an absence of books, *bibelots* and *Gemütlichkeit*.

Saturday 20th September

Went to bed in the hope of a long rest but was awakened by a distant siren at eight o'clock. A lovely long lazy day: I walked, talked, overate and sunbathed. Most of the time I passed with Geoffrey Lloyd who is an extraordinary creature, so gifted and intellectual with amazing theories and inhibitions on love. He is more of a *littérateur* than a statesman; and he is gay, provocative, fun and amusing. Does our hostess love him?

The news from Russia is confusing but Kiev has been occupied by the Germans.

The grey castle rising out of the rich green in the evening sunlight looked more than ever like a tapestry. And my hostess with her slim, thin little figure and smokey turquoise eyes is becoming increasingly eccentric: her hours are late and later and one dines about ten. There is a touch of Mad Ludwig about the place.

Sunday 21st September

Harold rang me early: he had come to London from Cherkley, where he had spent the night with Beaverbrook. The newspapers had announced the departure of the mission by air yesterday: actually they go tonight by a cruiser. H[arold] told me last week that Pres[ident] Roosevelt had had information that the Germans would make every attempt to catch the party and imprison them.

A glorious green lush tapestry day: the grey castle against the green; the shiny sunlight. Geoffrey and I stripped naked and lay for three hours by the swimming bath – I had a handkerchief, he a copy of Lord Chesterfield's letters – to cover our parts.

All day with Geoffrey Lloyd who looks brown and Greek stripped. He told me how a group of Conservatives headed by Neville Chamberlain had sent a memo, later known as 'The Black Spot' soon after the 1929 disastrous election to Baldwin, declaring that they thought he could never win another election and might perhaps [wish] to resign the leadership of the Conservative Party. Baldwin refused to budge (Geoffrey was his private secretary) and asserted rather stoutly that it would take two years of unemployment and a Labour government to make the country see sense and vote Conservative. And so it proved. Geoffrey also described how he gave Jim Thomas (long since now his enemy) his first chance on the political ladder. Jim has done everything through women.

MONDAY 22ND SEPTEMBER   LONDON

My secretary told me that whilst I looked sunburned I seemed weary. So I am and no wonder, for Geoffrey Lloyd sat on my bed until the early hours. We discussed the political frontier and agreed and feared that when Churchill ceases to be PM that the King will call upon Eden to form a government. He will first send Alec Hardinge to 'sound' different statesmen and ask for their guidance. Of course, Hardinge will recommend Eden and the indignant but helpless Conservative Party will meekly submit and elect him leader. Thus the Palace will direct politics. For this reason probably the Prime Minister will leave Hardinge at his post, although he is alleged to dislike him.

The Greek royal party arrived here and were received with much pomp by the King and Queen, the Prime Minister and others. John Beith, who dined here tonight, was present. He is in love with little Princess Alexandra[1] and was so moved by her arrival that tonight he had a sort of collapse, was sick and disappeared. The others were Peter Loxley and Geoffrey Harrison, an otherwise cosy FO evening.

Poor John Beith, is he really so in love with the ravishing little Princess? I fear so. She and her mother, the Crown Prince and Mrs Brittain-Jones all arrived together. It is exactly five months since they 'started on their travels'.

---

1 Princess Alexandra of Greece and Denmark (1921–93); not the daughter of the Duke of Kent, who was only 4. She was the posthumous daughter of King Alexander of Greece and his morganatic wife, Aspasia Manos. In 1944 she would marry King Peter II of Yugoslavia (qv).

TUESDAY 23RD SEPTEMBER

Anne Feversham rang me to say that she was seeing Honor this afternoon. I sent Honor her gilt dressing case which I originally gave her: she has already the grand gold one I had made for her years ago. I lavished thousands of pounds on presents for her and little did she appreciate them!

John Beith rang up to apologise for his curious behaviour last night. He had covered the floor of the lavatory with vomit. What love.

Dined with Mrs Greville at the Dorchester, and on the way ran into Mary Marlborough dressed as a general! She looked remarkably handsome and was v pleasant, as was Audrey Bouverie. But a brace of worldly girls! . . . Mrs Ronnie reminisced about old days, Lady Ripon,[1] King Edward and Queen Alexandra . . . etc. Then she let drop a bombshell, indeed, Ava Wigram is going to marry Sir John Anderson! This lovesick doting old widower warned Mrs Ronnie against his fiancée in June: in September he is madly in love with her. Mrs Ronnie thinks that they will both regret it. No doubt. I cannot help but admire Ava's despairing persistence. She has always been ambitious, and now may achieve 'Downing Street' or at least Delhi.[2] What an adventurous life! She is a minx, a schemer, a Becky Sharp[3] but with an assured position she may make him an excellent wife and surround him with a salon and stoke him with delicious food. Still it is sad to see a man fall into so obvious a snare. Mrs Ronnie is disgusted and defeated . . . . As we left and rang the lift bell, the lift flashed by and I saw the Prime Minister with his inevitable cigar. He was wearing a dinner jacket and was accompanied by the manager of the Hotel, who was seeing him to his car. He had been dining with the Halifaxes. He smiled at me for a brief second. I walked home in the blackout.

This afternoon I bought two pairs of salt cellars and two pepper pots and sent them to Honor as 'an advance Christmas present'!

[George] Gage keeps ringing me up: he is like a voice from the past, and I cannot stir up an enthusiasm or even affection for him. Just bored tolerance. *Autres temps, autres moeurs.*

WEDNESDAY 24TH SEPTEMBER

The newspapers announce that Paul Latham has been sentenced to two years' imprisonment without hard labour; as he was arrested on July 28th and nearly

---

1 Constance Gwladys Herbert (1859–1917), daughter of the 1st Baron Herbert of Lea, married Frederick Robinson (at that point by courtesy Earl de Grey) who in 1909 succeeded his father as 2nd Marquess of Ripon. Lady Ripon was a noted patron of the arts and close friend of Oscar Wilde.

2 In other words, if her prospective husband did not become Prime Minister, he would be Viceroy of India; in fact, Anderson achieved neither.

3 The leading female character from W. M. Thackeray's 1848 novel *Vanity Fair.*

two months have passed, which are deducted, perhaps he will also have a further remission for good conduct. I shall go and see him.

A letter in Honor's handwriting filled me with dread, but surprisingly enough it was pleasant and even contained an apology. 'I am sorry I was cross about the silver'! Strange, wayward woman!

Lunched at Brooks's with George Gage who is remarkably thin; he looks younger and handsomer and I felt slightly *attendri* towards him again. We talked of old days together and mentioned our expeditions to Herstmonceux in the distant days when Claude Lowther[1] reigned there. I said that it must be an unlucky house but Gage thought not; said it was a bogus, ersatz place, even originally built after the days when fortified castles were constructed. He thinks that people who would be attracted by it are unlucky – Claude Lowther, the next owner, Lawson[2] who shot himself, and now Paul Latham who squandered half a million on it and evidentially tried to commit suicide and succeeded in committing social suicide. We wondered what will happen to it when the Hearts of Oak Society[3] leave it. Paul can never live there. He is to be confined in a civilian gaol. Eddie Devonshire was at lunch and said that he would do something about Pratt's for me shortly. I should like to join it.

Hector Bolitho and Tilea, the gloomy ex-Romanian Ambassador, dined here to my annoyance as I had wanted – but was invited too late – to go to David Margesson's little dinner at the Savoy, which was to celebrate Olive Baillie's birthday. However, I joined them afterwards, and we went over to Warner House, Wardour Street for a private view of a new American film .... Geoffrey dropped me here at 1 a.m. and I have taken a sleeping draught.

THURSDAY 25TH SEPTEMBER

Slept well and late and passed an agreeable lazy morning with little post to cope with. Mrs Greville tells me that John Anderson [is] actually ardent and Ava Wigram coy and indignant about last night. Anderson whispered to his hostess that he had not yet proposed but would do so! What a quaint alliance.

Lunched at the Carlton Club. David Margesson advised me to be an independent member, to speak and ask questions. He is right; but I prefer the jewels of office. Then I walked to Claridge's where I left a letter for the King of

---

1 See Vol. I, entry for 8 June 1936 and footnote. Channon must have visited the castle with Gage when he was not keeping a diary; his account of it is during Latham's occupation. In 1946 Latham sold it to the Admiralty and it was used as an observatory.

2 Reginald Lawson (1892–1930) and then his estate owned the castle from 1929 to 1932, when Latham acquired it. Lawson was a member of the family who owned the *Daily Telegraph*, and his wife Iva, an American, liked castles; he also owned Saltwood, in Kent, later the home of Sir Kenneth Clark (qv), and it was in the grounds of Saltwood that he shot himself in December 1930.

3 A friendly society whose staff were evacuated from London to the castle during the war.

Greece and ran into the Crown Prince of Norway and others. Then to a bookshop where I ordered a whole library sent off to Kenya to my poor lonely Robinsons.[1] Feeling against them has risen high . . . . the band of conspirators who were responsible for the *coup d'état* wished to shoot him. It would have been in the Serbian tradition as they have always shot their kings!

FRIDAY 26TH SEPTEMBER

Eleven months since H[onor] broke the bad news!

I was alone all day . . . . pottered about in my long neglected library, rearranged the books, lunched and dined alone; talked to Anne Feversham on the telephone: she had seen Honor and reports that she was well, handsome, calm and determined to stick to her ostler, but was in no way vindictive against me. Can one rely on the flighty Anne?

SATURDAY 27TH SEPTEMBER   *KELVEDON*

Continued to sort my books, then . . . . drove here to Kelvedon. It looked entrancing in the golden autumn heat. There are thirty-eight patients. As I lay asleep in the swimming-pool garden which I created and love, a telephone message came that Jim Thomas was at the Foreign Office and could he come for the weekend? Reluctantly I consented and met him at Brentwood, after making some frantic arrangements here. On the way back from the station we met the old Kelvedon van driven by Mr Woodman and Honor. They saw me but Jim didn't notice. I felt sick and saw the van turn up towards Cow Farm. What a *rencontre*.

Pleasant evening with Jim who slept in Honor's bed in the Chapel Room.

Suddenly with a feeling of released energy or *soulagement*, I decided to write a volume of long short stories and will begin immediately. I lay awake thinking them out.

SUNDAY 28TH SEPTEMBER

A morning of almost Sudanese heat. Jim and I lay naked in the swimming-pavilion garden and sunned our tired bodies. He is greying, he is ageing and is duller and deafer. To think he once attracted me. He had to be on Home Guard duty – fire-watching at Westminster tonight, so I took him into Brentwood, I was sad but not sorry to see him go, as I came here to be alone.

Read and finished *Jane Eyre*, a fantastically improbable but powerful book, and wrote to Prince Paul, Peter and Jacqueline [Lampson].

---

1 Prince Paul and his family, compared with 'the Swiss family Robinson', from the 1812 novel by Johann David Wyss about a shipwrecked family.

George Balfour, the Tory MP for Hampstead, is dead. He was the leader of that band of businessmen in the House known as 'The Forty Thieves'.

Thought much of Honor and how monstrously she has treated me.

MONDAY 29TH SEPTEMBER

Returned to London and did chores. Two agreeable letters from Honor awaited me.

Anne Feversham dined and confessed to me her love of Peter Laycock[1] and I advised her to be cautious. Anne had seen Honor and reported that she was well, in good looks and grimly determined to continue her present life. She asked affectionately for me and even spoke of Paul with some interest: she apparently never mentioned divorce and is uninterested in it. What a woman.

I hear that my 'mother-in-law' – the richest woman in England – had no cook and was obliged to do it all herself at Pyrford over the weekend.

TUESDAY 30TH SEPTEMBER

Walked to the H of C; Winston gave a brilliant review of the war situation in inimitable language: but he said nothing one didn't know. Platitudes were cloaked in gilded Macaulay-like language and he impressed the House. Whilst warning against optimism he seemed nevertheless sanguine. Everyone very pleasant. When I came home I found that the King of Greece had twice telephoned; later he rang again and is lunching here on Thursday. I was in a frenzy to collect a party and invited Lady Willingdon and then put her off because there wasn't room at my tiny table. I ought really to open the grand dining room for these royal banquets.

WEDNESDAY 1ST OCTOBER

To the House of Commons. I felt ill and didn't stay long. Archie James took me in a corner and gave me much unsolicited advice about my matrimonial affairs. He advised me [not] to be so lazy with Honor and divorce her immediately. I then asked him who had talked to him about my affairs and he said, to my surprise, that it was Rab. Rab is often indiscreet socially: he is so shrewd and able and yet so clumsy and innocent in affairs of the world.

Walked to the Dorchester in the bright sunlight meeting many people *en route* including Loelia Westminster, and lunched also with Helen Fitzgerald. She was charming and plump and pretty and didn't admit to me that Harold Balfour

---

1 Peter Laycock (1910–77) was then a major in the Army.

has broken off his liaison with her. She asked me much about Honor whom she considers mad and a good riddance.

THURSDAY 2ND OCTOBER

It is seven o'clock and I am nervously bankrupt. A long day beginning with a massage at seven; then I got up, and soon received a Southend deputation; then strolled over to see my mother-in-law who was depressed and *enrhumée*,[1] and then I had a luncheon party which was highly successful: the King of Greece, gentle and good-mannered; the Crown Prince of Greece, bejewelled and aged;[2] Olive Baillie, sweet and simple . . . . Winnie Portarlington; Joyce Brittain-Jones; 'Bill' Cavendish-Bentinck[3] . . . . Food excellent. Mrs B-J, whom Peter and I call 'The Morsel', was charming, well dressed and much improved – more *distinguée*. Good food and gaiety. They all stayed until three and the Crown Prince and I went out and spent the afternoon together. We shopped, but bought little. We went to Wartski's, saw Fabergé objects, and elsewhere, drank at Buck's and at last I left him at Claridge's. In Piccadilly we ran into [Sir Michael] Palairet, an asinine Minister to Greece – we had been abusing him. He bowed gravely to us. The Crown Prince who is a rake *reformé*[4] (?) looks old, wrinkled and obese. He was once one of P[eter's]'s admirers! I like him but he is not amusing and gave forth no sparks! No wonder that General Wavell said that he was a 'poop'!

My mother-in-law is very down and dejected and I suspect feels somewhat secretly conscience-stricken about Honor. She must know in her heart that she is somehow responsible for Honor's curious character, which cannot be altogether disassociated from her bringing-up. The Guinness girls were appalling[ly] brought-up. Bad-mannered, antisocial, off-hand, aloof and ungracious they all are *au fond*, but Brigid's immense natural charm triumphs over these handicaps . . . . The Crown Prince was sweet but he could be a great bore *à la longue*.

The institution of marriage is foundering, certainly at least with the *jeunesse*. I cannot think of a happy marriage. Perhaps old Pétain is right – the world is dissolving. As I was writing these lines the King of Greece rang up to say that he would like to dine here next Wednesday, and would I arrange *un petit dîner*[5] and a film afterwards. I have already taken steps. Then I rang up Mrs Greville, who is staying, at my suggestion, at Swanage. She was merry and malicious.

---

1 Afflicted with a cold.
2 Prince Paul of Greece and Denmark (see entry for 22 January 1941) was not quite 40.
3 Victor Frederick William Cavendish-Bentinck (1897–1990) served in the Grenadier Guards in the Great War and then in the Foreign Office. He was Ambassador to Poland from 1945 to 1947 but had to resign from the service over his divorce of his first wife. He then had a career in business and succeeded his brother as 9th Duke of Portland in 1980, having by courtesy become Lord Victor Bentinck in 1977.
4 Reformed, though Channon seems to doubt it.
5 A little dinner.

FRIDAY 3RD OCTOBER   *BULLANDS, WATFORD, HERTFORDSHIRE*

The King of Greece rang me early and later I talked with his loved-lady, Mrs Joyce Brittain-Jones. Am I to become involved again as I was with the Windsors? She is not unlike the Duchess of Windsor physically and in her style of dressing; also she too, is *à côté*, and perhaps – if I cultivate and encourage her as I did the Duchess – might become social[ly] ambitious. Actually she is less amusing and certainly a nicer character.

I drove here with my beloved long, lanky, distinguished Peter Loxley: it is a queer rambling house, rather more than a cottage, and Lavender his lovesick wife looks highly pregnant again. I envied them their domestic happiness, their obvious delight and absorption in each other, the double bed and enchanting Hoppner child, Elizabeth – a more charming, calmer more English child I have never seen. The Loxleys are touchingly pleased with a Coalport dinner service which they recently bought at the Faudel-Phillips sale at Balls Park.[1]

Early to bed and to rest.

SATURDAY 4TH OCTOBER

The death of Mrs Ernest Simpson[2] is announced; a strange tiresome little woman, she played a great role in the abdication drama and was sent here for that purpose by a syndicate of American newspapers. She was called Raffray and I met her only once and that was at a very grand dinner given by Emerald at the height of the Edwardian [illegible] reign. There was the King, the candlelights, and several dukes, and this curious little Yankee who had been a girlhood friend of the then Mrs Simpson's[3] . . . .

I drove to Cambridge, lunched at Corpus Christi College with the Master[4] after attending a Regional meeting of East Anglia MPs. We would talk of invasion and alarms. Then I drove to Stanstead, but my car broke down *en route* and I had appalling adventures too boring to enumerate. Here I found Sam Courtauld,

---

1 The Faudel-Phillips family owned Balls Park – an early classical house of the 1630s in Hertford – from 1901 to 1946.

2 Mary Kirk Raffray (1896–1941). See Vol. I, entry for 3 November 1936.

3 Bessie Wallis Warfield (1896–1986), daughter of Teackle Wallis Warfield of Baltimore, married as her first husband Earl Winfield Spencer Jr in 1916. They were divorced in 1927 and in the following year she married Ernest Simpson. She met the Prince of Wales in 1931 and became his mistress early in 1934, at a time when her husband had encountered financial problems. They holidayed together in 1934 on Lord Moyne's yacht and thereafter became largely inseparable, despite her marriage and his position. By the time of King George V's death in January 1936 it became clear that the new King intended to marry her: and when he made these intentions clear to his prime minister, the Abdication crisis was set in train. They married in 1937.

4 Sir William Spens. See entry for 3 August 1940.

the young-looking father of Sydney Butler; Rab's cousins, Mr and Mrs Nevile Butler,[1] who are back again at the Foreign Office after their outstanding failure in Washington.[2] They are an agreeable but perhaps over-English couple....I was tired and bored and inclined to be irritable and felt perhaps that my Rab and Sydney were hostile. I asked them to dine on Wednesday with the King of Greece but they were engaged; later the atmosphere changed and they were more affectionate than ever before. Several chats with Rab, who is fatter and seems refreshed by being at the Board of Education. He told me that he now hates Halifax, whom he considers a bad and dishonest fraud: he has never liked them and obviously the Halifaxes took little trouble with the Butlers, whom they considered socially unimportant. Their standards are always social and snobbish – like mine. I tried to defend them but weakly . . . . Good food, a simple atmosphere. These Butlers are ambitious beyond anybody and will succeed. Sydney is anti-Catholic and notably anti-Eden and anti-Semite.

SUNDAY 5TH OCTOBER

Much reading and later Rab was affectionate and considerate and suggested making me a Deputy Lord Lieutenant of Essex![3] He was so subtle and trouble-taking with his youngest boy, James aged 4,[4] a sturdy little boy and not so quick as the Polish cuckoo[5] they have more or less adopted.

No newspapers and no news.

Rab is tactless at times and repeated to me remarks better left unmade. He is so shrewd and sly politically but a child in the ways of High Society.

MONDAY 6TH OCTOBER

Left Stanstead at ten and my car again broke down; and I had to taxi on to Kelvedon which was bathed in sunlight. I swam, collected flowers and plates and drove to London. All day I have wondered about my party on Wednesday night for the King of Greece: as usual I have perhaps spoilt it by asking too many

1 Nevile Montagu Butler (1893–1973). He had been Minister at the British Embassy in Washington from 1940 to 1941 and had returned to lead the North American Department at the Foreign Office, which he did until 1944 when he became an assistant under-secretary. He was British Ambassador to Brazil from 1947 to 1951 and to the Netherlands from 1952 to 1954. He was knighted in 1947. He married, in 1923, Oonah Rose McNeile (1898–1979).
2 I can find no evidence of such a failure, and Butler's subsequent promotions suggest that, had he made a mess in Washington, it was quickly cleared up and forgotten about.
3 Channon means Deputy Lieutenant.
4 Samuel James Butler (1936–2015).
5 Kris Balinski (b.1933) was, with his parents, a refugee from Poland who arrived in the early days of the war.

people. This time the Vsevolods of Russia.[1] So I gave orders that the dining room should be reopened .... And sent out messages. Already the house looks lovely and luminous.

I asked Princess Aspasia,[2] King Alexander's morganatic widow who is really nameless, her dark quick daughter, the pretty Princess Alexandra, Nicholas Lawford, Peter Loxley and John Beith to dine. As I was coming down the Crown Prince rang up and proposed himself: he came very late after keeping us waiting for twenty minutes because he could not find a taxi. There is no love lost between him and his niece and sister-in-law. The young Princess, I thought, knew too much, was quick and rapier-like and a touch malicious. The evening was a success as my dinners always are, and it was the Cinderella hour[3] before the *heterae*[4] left and I was alone with the Crown Prince: he stayed until 5 a.m. and we discussed Peter, the [illegible] himself, jewels, Fabergé, the [*Almanach de*] *Gotha* and all the things dear to a royal heart. I was weak when he left.

TUESDAY 7TH OCTOBER

Woke late and worn out. Worked and stayed away from the House of Commons as I had the Crown Prince on my hands all day. To amuse him and rest myself I took him to the RAC for a Turkish bath and we shared a cubicle for two hours and slept the sleep of the guilty.[5] I pretended to be engaged for dinner and am now at last alone – I like him; he is a conquest but I find the boredom and the bulk almost unendurable – and yet, and yet . . .

WEDNESDAY 8TH OCTOBER

An incredible day. The Crown Prince fetched me and I escorted him to the House of Commons and put him in the Distinguished Strangers' Gallery. He was soon bored and we went along to the Robing Room, where the Lords are now sitting since we usurped their Chamber. The little room was crowded with peers and I presented several, including the impressed lawn-sleeved Bishop of Chelmsford, to HRH .... Eddie Devonshire came up to me and whispered that he had arranged

---

1 Prince Vsevolod Ivanovich and Lady Mary 'Maimie' Lygon; see entry for 1 June 1939 and footnote.
2 Aspasia Manos (1896–1972) married King Alexander of Greece morganatically in 1919, being styled Mme Manos. After he died the following year, and King Constantine I was restored in 1922, she was styled Princess Aspasia of Greece and Denmark. She lived mostly in Venice but spent the war in exile in London. In 1944 her daughter married King Peter II of Yugoslavia (qv).
3 Midnight.
4 Others.
5 The Crown Prince was an active bisexual; the reader must judge what Channon means by this remark.

Osbert Sitwell, 'with venom and malice'.

Rex Whistler, another of Chips's lodgers.

Sir Thomas Beecham, who conducted
himself badly towards Lady Cunard.

'Bosie' – Lord Alfred Douglas – in
retirement, with a pension from Chips.

Peter Coats, with whom Chips found happiness.

Chips in Cairo, December 1940.

Field Marshal Viscount Wavell at Chips's desk.

Chips's diplomatic passport.

Princess Olga, the Regent's wife, before their exile.

Prince Paul, Regent of Yugoslavia, in bad company in Berlin, June 1939.

King Peter of Yugoslavia (standing, centre) with his mother, Queen Marie, and fiancée, Princess Alexandra of Greece and Denmark, seated.

Prince Philip of Greece, destined for greatness, 1939.

Kelvedon in the first winter of the war. From left to right: Unknown, Chips, Honor, Brigid and Prince 'Fritzi' before his internment.

King George II of Greece – 'that gossip'.

Prince George, Duke of Kent, 1940: 'Enchanting, and so handsome and treacherous, but sweet.'

Princess Marina, Duchess of Kent, 1940: 'Glamorously lovely, slender and glittering.'

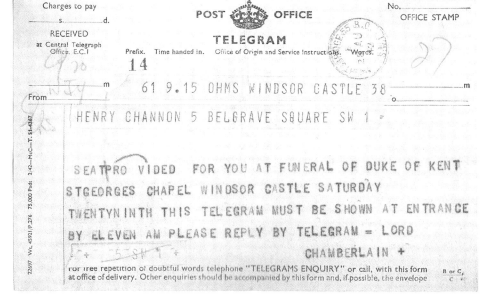

Chips summoned to the Duke's funeral, 1942.

'Dickie' Mountbatten, 1943;
a questionable hero.

Field Marshal Smuts, 1942:
the best sort of old Boer.

Charles de Gaulle,
Chips's least favourite 'Free Frog'.

Chips's travelling companion,
Robert Menzies, declares war on
behalf of Australia, 1939.

Lady Londonderry – 'Circe' – 'amazingly good-looking for one of her age'.

Loelia, Duchess of Westminster, 'intelligent but ludicrously lacking in logic'.

The Dufferins at Ascot before the war.

'Eddie', Duke of Devonshire, in scholarly attire, 1938.

Chips, master of all he surveyed, by Cecil Beaton.

Pratt's for me![1] Then I took the CP into the bar, presented various people to him and I showed him the really appalling mess that was once the House of Commons. A tangled debris of rubbish and burnt panelling stone and rubbish .... We lunched *à deux* at the Ritz, where we saw many people and much curtseying went on. Jim Thomas watched us uneasily from a corner table.

I had a splendid feast for King George: the blue dining room was opened and candlelit and I got out such Dresden as is not packed up. The lovely room shimmered and looked so eighteenth-century and beautiful that once again I fell in love with it and vowed to cling to it at all costs. It is my castle, my citadel. Came: Mrs Brittain-Jones, who is really very Anglo-Indian; the Crown Prince; Brendan Bracken who drank hock; Mrs Randolph Churchill, Crown Princess of Downingstrasse; Lord and Lady Portarlington; Olive Baillie; Audrey Bouverie; the Secretary of State for War [Margesson]; Geoffrey Lloyd; Micky Renshaw; Prince Vsevolod and Princess Pavlovsky.[2] The King and Crown Prince arrived in day clothes: the others were in dinner jackets. He sat between Audrey Bouverie and Maimie Pavlovsky. He particularly asked that the film should be short and cheerful and I asked Olive Baillie to arrange it accordingly. We all drove off (minus Brendan, who had to go to No. 10) in the blackout and crept up to the tiny theatre. A magnificently produced but interminable film in colour called *Bomb Diving*[3] was produced. It lasted two and a half hours and we were all worn out . . . David [Margesson] drove them home after. Much curtseying in the dark. I came home with the Crown Prince and we sat until Micky Renshaw came in: I left them to their own devices . . . and went to bed wondering, since the news is dark and discouraging,[4] whether I had given a sort of limited Duchess of Richmond's ball on the eve of Waterloo.

THURSDAY 9TH OCTOBER

I awoke a wreck and was so tired that I didn't go to the House of Commons, deliberately stayed away for almost the first time since I was elected. Lady Iveagh came to lunch and talked openly and honestly about Honor – about whom she

---

1 The Duke of Devonshire was, and his descendant still is, the proprietor of Pratt's Club in St James's.
2 Lady Mary Lygon had been granted the title Princess Romanovsky-Pavlovsky by Grand Duke Vladimir Kirillovich, the head of the Romanov family, at Prince Vsevolod's request.
3 He means *Dive Bomber*, a film starring Errol Flynn and Fred MacMurray, released by Warner Brothers the previous August.
4 Channon's main fear, like that of many of his peers, was that the Germans were about to take Moscow and eliminate the government of the Soviet Union, allowing them to turn their full attention once more to invading Britain. Hitler had announced the start of the Battle of Moscow a week earlier; Stalin declared the city was in a state of siege on 19 October, but the snows came early and on 25 October the German advance on the city was paralysed by bad weather.

was bitter and disillusioned and I had the impression that our long tête-à-tête was a success. She was sympathetic and helpful.

Dined with the Portarlingtons at Claridge's and we were joined by the Crown Prince of Greece with whom I had spent most of the day. I had a small cocktail party for him in the afternoon, which included Mrs Coats[1] whom he much wanted to meet. Bed late again worn out .... Royalties are a heady wine and leave one a wreck. I had a rest.

Lady Iveagh encouraging about my overdraft and the prospects for it being paid off. We drank to the health of my darling little boy who is 6 years old today .... My remote, much-loved angel.

FRIDAY 10TH OCTOBER

At 10.30 this morning Harold [Balfour] fresh from Moscow burst in .... with caviar and vodka. He looked simply terrific. I rushed off to the Air Ministry. In the evening we dined together at Claridge's with his wife and swilled his vodka – we gave two glasses to the King of Greece who was sitting nearby, and devoured a huge tin of caviar which Harold had hugged all the way from Moscow. I was soon quite tipsy and only by force of will remained tolerably sober ... But the huge restaurant waltzed before me as Harold told his tremendous tale of his meeting with Stalin, the banquets in the Kremlin, the gala performances of *Swan Lake* in the old Opera House etc. ... Never has there been such a three weeks! Stalin was tidy, friendly and quite accessible. The communications were conducted mostly by Beaverbrook and were short, secretive and businesslike. Nobody in Russia smiled; nor was much said and little was revealed; the commissars remained taciturn and guarded.

SATURDAY 11TH OCTOBER   *LEEDS CASTLE*

I drove alone: the castle looked enchanted in the sunlight and it was so warm that I sunbathed with Geoffrey Lloyd, whom I like more and more. Much conversation with him about love and I am now convinced that he is Olive Baillie's lover and that Adrian [Baillie] resents him and is consequently unhappy and given to tippling. David Margesson was enchanting and teased me about Peter Mallaby and General Wavell etc. A very gay evening, Kay Norton the only woman.

MONDAY 13TH OCTOBER

I drove Kay Norton up to London and we gossiped *en route*. She told me the story of Olive's many marriages (she is alleged to have broken up the first two: but I

---

1 He seems to be referring to Audrey Coats (qv): it is not clear why he should have the urge to meet the mother of Channon's friend.

don't know) and is against Geoffrey Lloyd whom she dismisses as a Birmingham bourgeois – ' . . . . out for what he can get. Undoubtedly Olive's lover!' Then she discussed Honor, who apparently has told her friends – and they are few and far between – that she only wanted to marry her swarthy lover but that I refused her a divorce! If Honor really said that it is monstrous as she had never mentioned divorce to me since last February, and the man is himself tied up. Kay Norton didn't even know that he was married. Honor has either herself been deluded or was being dishonest; for our detectives have frequently reported that Mrs Woodman, whom they interviewed, flatly refused even to entertain the idea of a divorce. When she takes steps I shall do so.

Appalling car complication on the journey and I was forced into a suburban garage to ask for help. I had rather a surprise: the manager and mechanics were extremely rude and unhelpful and when I commented upon their behaviour to Kay she replied that 'the people' were uncaring like that: and that we, who only swished through the Ritz and Cartier and were still surrounded by the remaining remnant of class privilege and riches were unaware of the new prevailing conditions, which our recent alliance with Russia has gone far to increase . . . Perhaps she is right. The news from Russia incidentally seems to indicate that the Germans will soon take Moscow . . . . Harold B tells me that the Russian government was secretive and . . . . really told our mission nothing. They are as isolationist and as wicked as ever. Nothing will ever make me pro-Russian. Their victory in many ways would be a disaster.

John Anderson's engagement to Ava Wigram has been announced. Nicholas Lawford rang me up to say that he had been to see her and she had laughingly remarked that she had done it only to please Chips 'and so that he will come and see me and talk about life'!

WEDNESDAY 15TH OCTOBER

Much to do, and I spent the day alone which was balm. Nor did I go to the House of Commons . . . . I walked to Maimie Pavlovsky's for a drink and there met Mrs Brittain-Jones: she discussed a plan for a weekend at Leeds [Castle] and she suggested the 24th and that the King and Crown Prince both be invited, and she and I, naturally.

Harold went off to America with Averell Harriman: I felt nervous and envious of these many expeditions but he may not return. He has some of the earmarks of an abrupt destiny and I am over-anxious about him. He sleeps in the house tonight, tomorrow he will be at Azores and on Friday in Washington.

Meanwhile isn't it too late to send this aid to Russia? Won't it be collared by the enemy?

Just before Harold left a present, a gold and silver cigarette case, came to him from Beaverbrook in memory of the Moscow mission. Max is very disarming, indeed endearing with his princely gestures. It is a Cartier case and Harold is boyishly pleased with it.

Thursday 16th October

What a day and yet nothing breeds energy like activity. I was up early and went by train to Southend, where I addressed a banquet of businessmen and did it well. I had almost an ovation; and I gathered that it was felt in the Borough that I had been too long away from it, and that Socialism is growing there. I don't know. Back by train and found that a dinner party had collected itself here: the Crown Prince; Godfrey Winn, whose 35th birthday it is (I twice said that it was his 30th and he did not contradict me); Jay Llewellin, Jim Wedderburn and Peter Loxley. Jay and Godfrey are boon companions now and have established a lasting and unexpected axis. Jay is entranced by all that Godfrey says or does. The sex matters little once a middle-aging [*sic*] man is infatuated!! They all left about twelve o'clock in a tipsy mood and I was left alone and *planté*[1] but in the highest spirits with the Crown Prince, who stayed until nearly 5 a.m. Certainly everything this week has been more than Greek to me.

Friday 17th October

It is amazing how much a little thyroid will do, a few pills and one radiates charm and good looks and energy. I woke this morning still full of high spirits after a brief and complicated Casanova night, and was soon dictating .... The in-laws to lunch. And at five I went to Joyce [Brittain-]Jones's for a drink and there were the King and Crown Prince of Greece and Maimie and Vsevolod. We gossiped and drank and talked.

Dined alone with Barbie Wallace at the Dorchester in her suite. She looked astonishingly young and pretty. We had a confidential conversation and I talked to her about Honor. Barbie was always against her. Barbie is a Bolshie at heart, a confirmed Edenite, destructive and difficult.

There is a jam about next weekend. The King of Greece has refused to go to Leeds; has put his foot down firmly because Francis Queensberry[2] has made mischief. He was next to him at the St James's Club dinner last night and apparently told him that high gambling etc. went on at Leeds – which never happened except when Francis is there! And I am in a difficult position as Mrs Jones, the Crown Prince and I had all accepted. Olive is in a rage. One should really leave royalties alone as in the end they always let one down; and yet who can resist their fascination?

1 Stuck.
2 The 11th Marquess of Queensberry.

My mother-in-law, who has a certain genius for living uncomfortably, is having acute servant worries and has now a motley crew at Pyrford.

SATURDAY 18TH OCTOBER

Alone the whole day, wrote many letters, rested and caught up. Met Enid Raphael in the street; she is half-mad and has recently tried to kill herself. She is Honor's only friend and confidante; but she seemed friendly to me.... London is extremely immoral, certainly.

The Crown Prince rang up from Claridge's where he is staying. He and 'Timon'[1] are going to Badminton to spend the weekend with Queen Mary. What gossip will they pick up there?

The railings in Belgrave Square have now disappeared. Yet another link gone with the fast-fading past.

How I like being alone. But where shall I go tomorrow?

SUNDAY 19TH OCTOBER

I thought of my new book: but it does not progress. Or shall I wait a bit and write a Trollopian semi-social, political novel? Am I ripe for it? The past two years have been a panoply of pain, disappointment, triumph, passion, ecstasies and sadness ... I went to Kelvedon for the day: the place has an atmosphere of decay which depresses ... I have loved it much; love it still but I have never really liked it. Perhaps I shall shed it.

Winnie Portarlington said to me on the telephone this morning that the Crown Prince of Greece would be the death of me: now, what exactly did she mean by that?

Secretly I rang Honor's Essex farm – Cow Farm, Doddinghurst, her first love-box. A woman around said that she was the tenant and had not seen 'Lady Channon' for six months. So she doesn't go to Essex. I don't really care where she goes, and only wish it was to hell –

A cable came from New York signed by Harold, Serge and my own boy.

MONDAY 20TH OCTOBER

Woke feeling congested, discouraged, dyspeptic and unpopular. About luncheon time the telephone started and I was inundated with messages, invitations etc. I am only happy alone and yet I crave for company and surround myself with life-takers. Take the Crown Prince of Greece, who never leaves me: he came in the afternoon straight from the station and stayed for two hours, and was amusing

---

1 The King of Greece: the nickname is from Shakespeare's play *Timon of Athens*.

about Badminton where he and King 'Timon' spent the weekend with Queen Mary. She was magnificent, bejewelled and gay. One night it was sapphires, the next it was pink pearls . . . . We talked much of the King, his brother, who is, he said, a difficult inhibited character. (I have never found him so.) He only loves Joyce Jones whom he 'protects'; indeed 'keeps'.

Dined alone with Peter Loxley – oh! This morning I lay half-awake and felt a wave of annoyance with the Kents and the Butlers pass over me . . . . I felt embittered and dropped by them. On my breakfast tray were two letters from the Duke of Kent and Sydney Butler. The Duke's enclosed one from the Regent for me.

Lunched at Buck's with Freddie Birkenhead, whom I found fascinating as ever, not a touch coarsened . . . He told me that on the formation of the present government Winston sent for him, and after keeping him waiting until 2 a.m. offered him the Paymaster-Generalship which F foolishly refused. Had I been there, F laughingly added, he would have been forced, bullied into accepting it.

TUESDAY 21ST OCTOBER

To the House, and after lunched with Patsy and Francis Lennox-Boyd who at long last is back from his travels. He is slim, handsome, silent and a colonel. At 3.30 the Crown Prince picked me up (he had been lunching with the Kents) and we shopped. He bought a pair of jewelled Victorian birds at Cameo Corner for his wife. I gave him a pale turquoise blue Fabergé case from Wartski's. In the evening I had a few people to dine to meet him: Leslie Hore-Belisha, Hector Bolitho, Jim Thomas . . . They all stayed too late. A message came during dinner inviting me to dine and sleep at Coppins on Friday; am I returned to favour, or did I imagine that I was out?

Rab Butler sent me a brace of partridges.

WEDNESDAY 22ND OCTOBER

This Leeds drama is really too bad. First the Greeks accept for the weekend arranged by me, then the King 'chucks', and now the Crown Prince is afraid to incur his displeasure by going and he wrote – from here – a line of regret. It was polite, since I dictated it and in the wee hours this morning we drove to Grosvenor Square – I in my red velvet and the Crown Prince in uniform – and we dropped it in the letter box. Olive Baillie will be in a rage.

All day today I acted as PPS to Jay Llewellin and learnt much about the railways. He handled the House tactfully. Godfrey Winn was in the Peeresses' Gallery to hear him. Then I came home (worn out from the lack of sleep) and was resting when the Crown Prince was announced. He handed me a tiny *seicento*[1] St George

1 Seventeenth century.

on a white horse. A delicious *bibelot*. Winnie Portarlington soon followed as did the Archduke Robert. In the course of conversation the Diodach[1] told me a tale against King Ferdinand of Bulgaria whom he called 'an old Jew'; Robert gravely remarked that he was his uncle. In the midst of conversation Godfrey Winn arrived and as Winnie left she got confused and curtsied to him, too.

Patsy Lennox-Boyd, silent and slim, Jim Wedderburn, more silent, and rather irritating, and Bill Mabane dined. Bill was enchanted to have had a cocktail on Saturday at Maureen Stanley's with the King and Queen. So that deplorable friendship continues!! I was either angry or depressed or drunk or all three for suddenly could bear my guests no more and was rude and surly to Jim Wedderburn . . . . I fear that I was rude and inhospitable to him . . . However nothing could evict my guests who were joined by J. J. Llewellin and Godfrey Winn. About midnight the Crown Prince arrived and I literally turned the others out! I am now shocked by my boorish behaviour. But I cannot entertain from 6 p.m. to midnight without a break.

The Crown Prince stayed until 4 a.m. He is a 'sweetie', really – gentle, canine, a touch trivial, affectionate and ambitious.

THURSDAY 23RD OCTOBER

Woke worn out. A pleasant little note from H[onor], who has been actually invited to Pyrford for the weekend! Does this denote a change of heart or tactics by the Iveaghs? I walked around to see my mother-in-law who seemed afraid and anxious.

Dined with the King of Greece and an immense affair afterwards chez Captain Plugge,[2] the round, absurd MP for Chatham. At dinner were the Crown Prince, King, Winnie Portarlington, Joyce B[rittain]-J[ones] ('The Morsel'), Harold Caccia and his wife;[3] Col Lendis, the suave chamberlain to the King, and two silent swarthy ADCs. We met in the huge foyer of Claridge's but nobody offered us cocktails, and there we marched into dinner to the corner table reserved for the King. Dinner good, but only lager drunk and hence a certain flatness of conversation. I was next to Mrs Caccia. Afterwards we piled into a royal car and drove to Captain Plugge's in the blackout. The whole Greek government was lined up to receive us plus our fat and fawning host. Captain Plugge is a curious individual, an adventurer, common, insinuating, rude and rich; and he lives in a vulgarly arranged house, No. 5 Hamilton Place, which formerly belonged to one of the Rothschilds. He had collected a crowd of 'second-raters'; but we, the royal party, were herded off from the others; but I recognised Maimie and Vsevolod of

---

1 The word is from the Greek, meaning a successor.
2 See entry for 12 July 1940 and footnote.
3 Mrs Caccia was the former Anne Catherine Barstow (1910–2005), whom Caccia (qv) married in 1932.

Russia and Robert of Austria .... and was able to bring them in. We were then, after drinking Dubonnet, taken up to the top floor – five flights up – where there is a private cinema theatre, for a film, really too vulgar, showing the Plugges' yacht in the South of France .... This lasted an hour or nearly! Then a recently captured film made by the Germans: the capture of Crete. It was thrilling and apparently taken off a German ship, which the Navy captured. It must have been harrowing for the royal party. Then a Western film, quite good. We then filed downstairs, and the King whispered to me, 'Let's go away – arrange it.' But the efficient Captain Plugge produced soup, which detained us five minutes more. The King dropped Winnie Portarlington and me in Chesham Place. He tripped as we got out in the blackout and luckily I caught him in my arms. He then drove Joyce Jones home, the C[rown] P[rince] accompanying them tactically, I thought .... No sooner was I in bed than the Crown Prince rang me up for a goodnight chat. He is surprisingly enchanted with the turquoise-encased Fabergé cigarette case which I gave him.

FRIDAY 24TH OCTOBER   COPPINS

The house is icy: the Duke has a streaming cold and abused everyone, principally the Halifaxes, who he says neglected or rather bungled his visits to the USA. He was rabid about them or rather against them. Indeed he abused everybody. The Roosevelt *ménage* is a joke, he laughed, and the party assembled at Hyde Park[1] to meet him – hardly credible!!

     Delicious food: we served ourselves as always at Coppins. I played backgammon with the Duchess and won forty-two shillings. She was not attending: her thoughts are always of Princess Olga and the Regent languishing in Kenya.

MONDAY 27TH OCTOBER   LONDON

Lunched alone, but the Crown Prince of Greece arrived at three, leaving me little time in which to work and do my letters. He stayed until eight and then we separated for a brief bath. I dined with him and his brother the King at Claridge's, *à trois*, in the famous corner table reserved for the King. The King was particularly charming and we had a confidential conversation which lasted for two hours, and mostly about the Regent whom he despises but is sorry for certainly. He told me too much. He believes (and for the first time I am shaken) that but for Paul's indecision and vacillating and pusillanimous policy, Greece would have won. They would have driven the Italians from Albania before the Germans arrived and, as the King said, we shouldn't be here now! Nevertheless, he stood up for Paul to Winston Churchill, when he entertained him at luncheon the other day, and advocated, and indeed pleaded that P should be accorded

1 Roosevelt's country house in upstate New York.

lenient treatment. A riveting evening and I was suddenly gay and amusing as I always am with kings . . . .

To bed early and mused over what the King had said. He attacked Eden and the Foreign Office with some asperity.

TUESDAY 28TH OCTOBER

Woke slightly refreshed and lingered in bed. Walked to the India Office where I left a letter for the bag for Peter, and the Colonial Office where I deposited nine for the Duchess of Kent for Princess Olga and Paul . . . . I gave luncheon to Vsevolod of R[ussia]. Delicious food and afterwards we shopped. He bought her [his wife] on my advice a ruby cabochon bracelet . . . . Then I came home to sleep. I must rest every afternoon or I am a wreck. I picked up Winnie Portarlington and we drove to Claridge's to dine with the King of Greece. He, the Crown Prince, Joyce Jones, Maimie of Russia, Lionel Portarlington, and me. A gay dinner. I never now leave the Greeks. It is a set . . . . After dinner we went on to a private theatre in Wardour Street to see a film – German, Russian, American and English ones! . . . . The King dropped Winnie and me at General Brooke's flat in Chesterfield House. He was in bed but received us in pyjamas. What a character!

WEDNESDAY 29TH OCTOBER

Woke *désoeuvré* and had to face a little luncheon party, which was a success. The King of Greece; his 'morsel', Joyce Brittain-Jones; the Crown Prince; my mother-in-law, and Mrs Greville; and Harold Nicolson, whom I collected at the last second . . . . Much gay chat about the Anderson nuptials tomorrow. They are going to Polesden Lacey for their honeymoon. Mrs Greville says that they are divinely happy and he is drivelling with love! It may be a success. Sam Hoare is furious. My mother-in-law was very sweet, shy, but I suspect secretly pleased by her unexpected party! She left to catch a Woking train but the others remained until nearly five o'clock.

There are rumours that Max Beaverbrook has quarrelled with the Prime Minister, which I doubt.[1] Certainly he has asthma and may resign, and perhaps Jay Llewellin will be given his job! If so, I hope to get Alan a job in the government. I shall press his claims and he returns at the psychological moment.[2] I instantly rang up Jay to ask him to dine alone with me on Friday.

Went to bed early, rang up my mother-in-law and talked, Honor went to Pyrford for one night last Saturday. This was the first time that she had seen her father for eleven months exactly, and only the second meeting with her mother.

1 Beaverbrook and Churchill were always quarrelling, but rarely seriously. Beaverbrook's main antagonist at this stage in the war was Ernest Bevin.
2 Lennox-Boyd was on his way home.

The visit passed off peacefully and nothing controversial was discussed; I was not even mentioned, the chief subjects were agriculture and cattle – there was no intimate talk at all. What a curiously impersonal family are the Iveaghs!

THURSDAY 30TH OCTOBER

Woke after a long night, anything but refreshed. In fact I must be ill as I feel so dejected and odd. And I have the D[uke] of Kent's cold certainly.

There is real nervousness always so noticeable in Whitehall before a reshuffle.

Rab came to lunch alone with me and stayed for two hours. We were frank with each other about the political position: we are being outflanked by the Garden Party, the Pansy Division, or Edenites. They are manoeuvring and have somehow been responsible for a quarrel between Beaverbrook and the Prime Minister . . . . Anthony told Mrs Greville that Max was impossible to work with.

I took the Crown Prince to dine with Mrs Greville at the Dorchester in her private suite . . . . Mrs G was magnificent, immensely garrulous and with wicked venom destroyed Lord Lloyd,[1] whom she hated. Hardly anybody escaped her malice. The CP was deeply impressed by her brilliance. It was the eighteenth century, he said. He came back with me here and stayed, oh! Much too late gossiping. He could not get over the tales of Lloyd's treachery and immorality and how, although Lord Willingdon had once saved him from an open scandal in India,[2] he had nevertheless ungratefully attacked him!!

I am a touch aggrieved by the Guinness family, or rather by the lack of imagination with which they have handled the Honor crisis. They are mercantile, mistrusting and hard at heart really. I hope that Paul will inherit only their sterling substantial qualities.

FRIDAY 31ST OCTOBER

Lunched at the Savoy with Francis Lennox-Boyd who made me nostalgic with his tales of Peter darting in and out of Shepheard's . . . Slept all the afternoon. I am on the verge of collapse, had to hurry away rather rudely from lunch and fell into my bed. The telephone rang the whole afternoon but I pretended to be out until 7 p.m. when my 'salon' re-opened. The Crown Prince, quickly followed by Michael Parker arrived: I sent them out to dine, as I had Peter Loxley, Jay Llewellin

---

1 George Ambrose Lloyd (1879–1941) was Conservative MP for West Staffordshire from 1910 to 1918 and for Eastbourne from 1924 to 1925, when he was raised to the peerage as 1st Baron Lloyd. He was Governor of Bombay from 1918 to 1923 and High Commissioner in Egypt from 1925 to 1929; and from 1940 until his death Leader of the House of Lords and Secretary of State for the Colonies.

2 Lloyd was married, but homosexual.

and Bill Mabane dining here for bridge.[1] The others returned later and kept me up too late . . . .

Never now have I a moment.

The political scene is set for a drama. Beaverbrook is the big actor and what exactly he is up to I don't know – but something. He has been seeing Lloyd George. There are rumours of Cabinet reconstructions, even of a pro-peace group.

Called in at the Colonial Office with masses of Christmas parcels from the Regent and Princess Olga for me and the Kents. I got them all in the bag for Kenya.

SATURDAY 1ST NOVEMBER

A parcel of sugar and butter has come from my mother. Does she think that we are starving here? It is sweet and pathetic of her. Something tells me that she and I will never meet again. I have been ruminating, too, on the mysterious and profound friendship which links P [Coats], me, the Crown Prince and the ex-Regent together. It is curious: P born near Glasgow, I in Chicago; the Regent in Belgrade; the Crown Prince in Athens. And now a pact. But both the ex-Regent and the Crown Prince like me and P better than they like one another.

The King of Greece has gone to Windsor Castle for the weekend. The Crown Prince however is here and in my hands: he showed me a cable which came today saying that his family are safe and even some of his possessions have been saved.

We lunched, gossiped, separated for an hour for siestas, met again – I called for him at Claridge's, and then dined *à deux* at La Belle Meunière in Soho. Delicious dinner and came back to B Square where he promised he would remain only an hour. However he stayed until nearly three o'clock. And we heard the first air-raid alarm for many months. We went out into the cold of the square, waited and walked but nothing happened and the 'all clear' soon sounded.

The Crown Prince was very frank and illuminating about his brother, the King, whom he rather dislikes and is jealous of. I don't agree with his summing-up of the royal character: he says his brother is a bit mad, inhibited, narrow, vacuous, with the redeeming qualities of Anglomania etc. He likes second-rate people, listens to nobody, is opinionated, *entêté*, etc. He gets ideas in his head which are impossible to dislodge, takes dislikes . . . and whilst in love with Joyce Jones, whom he keeps, he is totally uninfluenced by her. He painted rather an unpleasant picture of his elder brother and walking up and down the bedroom gave me 'close-ups' of the other members of his family.

---

1 Two days earlier Channon had intended a dinner just with Llewellin; the expansion of the dinner appears to have been typical of the management of his social life.

SUNDAY 2ND NOVEMBER

Woke late and refreshed. I have regained my strength and health after a few days' depression due in a measure to a chill and probably more to too much expenditure of energy . . . I dressed luxuriously and sallied forth in a triumph of tweeds to Claridge's to pick up the Crown Prince, who returned from a memorial service. I watched the mammoth change: the royal surroundings, the silk coroneted pants, the rolls of fat, the eyeglass, the rings, the many bottles of Houbigant[1] and the immaculately put out clothes. Then we drove in my small Ford to Eaglewood, W. Sunningdale, to lunch with the Portarlingtons. Glorious food cleverly converted as an ice-cream made with chestnuts. I ate so much that I had to sleep an hour afterwards! We drove back . . . . before the blackout: I had a deep longing to be alone but the CP persuaded me to dine with him at Claridge's. Maimie and Vsevolod of Russia joined us . . . . and then I came home to bed at midnight.

MONDAY 3RD NOVEMBER

A disturbed night with dreams . . . Dr Law came to see me early and after examining me reported that I had very low blood pressure and needed an injection of glycerine and arsenic! This, he proceeded to give me in the bottom! Then I felt a glow of reaction and got up.

The political crisis has eased somewhat and the P[rime] Minister is alleged to be against any major changes in his government. My ploy to reinstate Alan on his return from the USA progresses. *Peut-être*[2] . . . I want his affection and loyal help as I feel a touch carted by 'the family'. Their odd impervious hardness hurts but I realise that I exaggerate it.[3]

Will Hitler invade these islands in March? The Ides again?

TUESDAY 4TH NOVEMBER

The Duchess of Kent rang up early and we chatted. Tiny Princess Alexandra talked to me and said 'Hello, Chips!'

Yesterday, I somehow felt, reached the zenith of my axis with the Crown Prince: the tempo must now fall a little and keep the matter solid. Actually I have had every meal with him for nearly a month . . . My nerves must be in a frayed and dangerous state, or is it my liver? I worked happily alone all day until Jay Llewellin, one of the busiest of HM's ministers, drove here to see me and I gave him tea. He is so friendly and affectionate and well disposed yet in a tactless second he

---

1 Cologne from the shop in Paris, founded in 1775 by Jean-François Houbigant, who was Marie Antoinette's favoured *parfumier*.

2 Perhaps.

3 He refers to the Guinnesses, and what he imagines is their lack of sympathy for him.

irritated me and it used up all my nerves to control myself: however I refused his errand, which was to ask me to dine with him at Pratt's, and he went away slightly crestfallen or chilled – yet I am devoted to him. I felt contrite and at that moment the Crown Prince rang up and he, too, invited me to dine; again I refused. He was very sweet, said that his brother's weekend visit to Windsor had been pleasantly uneventful but 'cold, very cold'. I had had a premonition that mischief might have been made but evidently I was wrong. He asked me to go with him to one of the Overseas League teas and I quickly said that I would join him there, and did. It was an immensely crowded affair with officers talking every known language. I could not mix with them, felt contained and had claustrophobia yet everyone was particularly nice to me, indeed, the CP winked his monocle-eye every time he looked at me.

Lady Willingdon with her usual gusto pounced upon me and led me up to General Simović, the Yugoslav premier. I backed away and whispered to her, 'I don't want to know him.' Very foolish, and I have committed a gaffe which may or may not have repercussions. It would have been so much more politic to have shaken his hand and walked on; as likely as not he would never have remembered me. But somehow I couldn't bring myself to do so – shaken hands amiably with my greatest friend's arch enemy! And moreover I am convinced that he is an opportunist and a crook. I hope that Lady Willingdon, who is never malicious, will not make a story of it: I could ring her up and ask her not to do so, but think it better not to. It may simply pass over but I feel ill inside. A depressing day, indeed. I wrote at length to P in India advising him not to return, not to exchange the solid substance of a Wavellian job for the shadowy lot of a subaltern posted God knows where!

I am against everyone today, particularly myself and Jim Wedderburn who so infuriated me the other day.

Jay told me of his weekend at Cherkley with Beaverbrook: the supposed 'crisis', if ever there was one, has passed. He [Beaverbrook] was asthmatic but all smiles. Even the Sinclairs[1] were there. Dinner at nine, a long film and conversation until 2 a.m. or after . . . I couldn't stand it. Sam Hoare arrived on Sunday from Ditchley where he had stayed the Saturday night with the Trees, who produced a film for the amusement of their guests. It was so boring that finally the Prime Minister got up and ordered it stopped. The Prime Minister always weekends away from Chequers, and usually at Ditchley, the Sunday of the full-moon as a precaution against being bombed there.

Now the blank evening faces me, having turned down two pleasant plans. I am increasingly despondent about the future, my future most of all.

The Crown Prince rang up and I said that I was out!

---

1 Sir Archibald Sinclair (qv) and his wife Marigold Forbes (1897–1975), whom he had married in 1918.

WEDNESDAY 5TH NOVEMBER

Slept soundly and was massaged at 7.30. Lovely long morning luxuriously recumbent in my bed. The doctor at ten who gave me an injection of glycerine and arsenic!

A letter came from Nannie at Rhinebeck discussing Paul's birthday party. He had fourteen books, a telegram from me, his grandparents, Alan etc. – but nothing, of course, nothing at all from his neglectful mother. Her indifference enrages me. She is almost criminally negligent, her selfishness is monstrous . . . My in-laws lunched and were easy and affectionate and amiable, [and] asked me to use whatever influence I may have in trying to get Alan a government job on his return next week from America. I have enlisted Mrs Greville, who has already approached Sir John Anderson who agreed to do what he could . . . My mother-in-law for the second time hinted – very lightly and gently, indeed no fly was ever so gossamer – about a divorce. I was non-committal. I cannot make up my mind yet.

When they left I slept a little and then the Crown Prince arrived, handsome and debonair and demonstratively affectionate. He said that both Harold Nicolson and Leslie Hore-Belisha had gossiped about me, but only nicely, to him. They were devoted friends of mine, he added. At that moment the Duchess of Kent, looking superb, arrived. She had been to a function with the Queen, and was divinely beautiful and charming and wore a green hat like drooping spinach. She didn't stay long, and the CP remained until dressing time. People rang up on all sides and wanted to dine, but I had ordered food enough for only eight. The dinner in the Blue Room was a success, certainly. Came: the Crown Prince; Vsevolod and Maimie of Russia; Alice Harding; Natasha Bagration; Bill Tufnell, handsome in his blue uniform, and accompanied by his Ganymede Dave Cazenove. All ate and drank too much. Viorel Tilea arrived late, after dining with Mrs Greville and Sam Hoare . . . All my guests left at midnight except the Crown Prince who remained – alas – until 3.30 a.m. But he was very sweet and said I was the dream of his life, 'the sunlight' and most loyal and painstaking friend he had ever known and always wanted; talked of his past loneliness and even of his one-time prejudice against me as being too *intime*[1] with the Regent. He was so charming that I burst into semi-alcoholic tears . . .

The gossip in Whitehall is that Kingsley Wood will go soon to the Lords, thus retiring from the Chancellorship, which will be given to Anthony Eden: thus paving the way in the usual tradition for the premiership. Bobbety Cranborne will be offered the FO. I don't know whether any of this is true, but in any case it is premature.

1 Intimate.

THURSDAY 6TH NOVEMBER

Awoke a wreck after a short and shadowy night . . . . I am now really approaching, on the brink of breakdown – except that people who have breakdowns never know beforehand?

A year ago today No. 5 B[elgrave] Square was bombed.[1] I have survived another full and varied year. The servants here are much excited by the anniversary.

FRIDAY 7TH NOVEMBER

The Duchess of K rang me up early for a talk . . . . I felt somewhat better. Got up late and arranged my Roman Catholic luncheon party . . . . all arrived punctually and I met the Cardinal[2] at the door: the Catholics knelt and kissed his ring. He is a dignified, deaf, somewhat Yorkshire man, of, I should suspect, humble origin, who has acquired the sanctity of the Roman prelate. He was gracious and benign as he sipped his sherry; then we walked into the blue dining room and lunch proceeded most successfully. Its object was for His Eminence to meet young politicians and Rab was today's 'dish': good, rather Irish conversation. Eventually His Eminence and Rab withdrew to the morning room and had a private conversation the nature of which has not been divulged. The Cardinal is very anti-German, but is far from being pro-Russian. He talked the realistic point of view; he . . . . doesn't like 'Franco who was an adequate general but amateur administrator'. Party over at four o'clock and I have promised to invite His Eminence again soon. He was charming . . . Then I walked to Claridge's to see Mary Baker for half an hour before tea there with the Crown Prince. Mary is grey, a still attractive – to many – spinster. Her mad mother was crooning in their private sitting room. The old lunatic has a young man; a spiritual suitor and talked of his youth, intelligence and beauty! And she is 74 or more . . . Mary, too, has a new suitor, and an extremely earthly one in the unappetising person of Mr Leslie Hore-Belisha who has proposed to her. She declined the offer and wonders whether she was wise? She asked my advice . . . .

SATURDAY 8TH NOVEMBER

I am desperately down and ill . . . Walked to Claridge's to lunch with the Elvedens and Patsy. Elizabeth Elveden remarked upon my wan appearance and nervous manners; certainly I am in a parlous state. We had [a] message that Alan had arrived in this country and Patsy and I waited for him impatiently at No. 5. She actually shook with emotion: she is so in love with him and he is only tolerant of her advances. At last he came, embraced us both and gave us glorious accounts

---

1 He was presumably writing the following morning, as it was bombed on 7 November.
2 Arthur Hinsley (1865–1943) was the son of a carpenter, born in Yorkshire, and ordained in 1893. From 1917 to 1928 he was Rector of the English College in Rome; and in 1935 was appointed Archbishop of Westminster, being created a cardinal in 1937.

of America! He bounced in gaily, un-tired by eight hours and forty minutes in a bomber. He loaded me with presents, food, wirelesses etc. Arriving here at four o'clock, he didn't leave until eight. Meanwhile the Crown Prince appeared cold after a long day at Cambridge where the King, his brother, was invested, made a doctor. He was fascinated – who isn't! – by Alan. His accounts made me nostalgic, particularly the stories of my angel little boy who remembers me, talks of me . . . tears came to my eyes. I love that child so much . . . . Alan says that the Windsor visit[1] was a flop, that American society behaved badly etc. . . . The Duke of Kent rang up and I passed on the news to him: he was in a sweet mood.

The Crown Prince tried to persuade me to dine with him and the King but I lied [and] said I was going out with Alan. But I decided to leave the couple alone, and am now by myself, feeling unwell. I half-fear that the Crown Prince twigged. He is such a sweetie but exhausts me. He and Alan both rang up late to say 'goodnight' which warmed me.

MONDAY 10TH NOVEMBER

Dr Law gave me another injection of glycerine and arsenic. Then Lady Iveagh rang up and afterwards the Crown Prince. I had a charming letter from the Cardinal thanking me for Friday's lunch.

The Crown Prince gave me luncheon at the St James's Club, which was crowded with unknowns: John Beith was the only man I knew. He has been posted to the Embassy at Buenos Aires and leaves for the Argentine next week; he puts his appointment [down] to the gossip about him and little Princess Alexandra of Greece. He is madly in love with her and she submits to his attentions, but she is a worldly minx and a flirt and would never marry him. The move, whilst making him unhappy now, will save him much misery later.

Alan, the Crown Prince and I had a Turkish bath at the RAC. We lay naked on marble slabs and were pummelled; we gossiped and we sweated. Later we dined, plus Peter Loxley, with much gaiety at Claridge's. Excellent food, but I was shocked by the bill which came to over £20 – for five people.

Although the Crown Prince was with me from noon until 1.30 a.m., as I now write, I nevertheless managed to snatch odd moments in which to gossip with Alan. He told me much that delighted me; how Paul is flourishing in the USA, is adored by everybody and is keen, affectionate, polite and intelligent. And he told me more that was distressing – that Duff had dined out on me in New York, told stories of the wreck of my marriage etc. . . . had even hinted I did not care for women. I hate them[2] now. He defended me valiantly and warmly. I am uneasy.

---

1 When the Windsors had visited Washington in September the press had been most interested in the fifty-eight items of luggage they had felt it necessary to take with them; Lord Halifax complained that he had been sent a bill for £7 10s for the hire of the lorry needed to transport it all (Philip Ziegler, *King Edward VIII*, p. 467).

2 That is, the Coopers.

The Prime Minister made a storming speech at the Mansion House today: Rab attended wearing my clothes.

TUESDAY 11TH NOVEMBER

Parliament met today. I walked to the House with Alan and we were soon surrounded by a small court in the Smoking Room. I was very short indeed with Jim Wedderburn and refused his advances as I am still smarting under his tactless behaviour the other evening, and also his lack of loyalty in seeing Honor sometimes. He met her through me and she never liked him. She likes nobody.

In the Commons Winston C was in a bellicose mood. He answered Questions ungraciously and annoyed the House. Alan and I went along to the Smoking Room and ordered brandy and ginger ale. Nearby sat Sir Waldron Smithers,[1] an ass of a man, alone. The Prime Minister attended by Harvie-Watt[2] entered and they too, sat down. Suddenly the PM, shaking with anger rose, crossed to Smithers and bellowing at him, like an infuriated bull, roared, 'Why the hell did you ask that question? Didn't you know that "he" (Lord Cherwell) is one of my oldest and greatest friends?' The unfortunate member for Chislehurst tried to defend himself – but the PM still shaking, refused to listen or be pacified, and went on: 'You make protestations of loyalty – however – I won't have it! The President was most impressed by him.' So forth . . . . It was an extraordinary scene.[3]

The Prof., 'otherwise' Baron Berlin, or correctly the Lord Cherwell, has long been the subject of speculation to the House and from time to time there have been questions and veiled innuendos reflecting on his tentative origin. Today there was a barrage of them. Winston's almost blind loyalty to his friends is one of his endearing qualities.

WEDNESDAY 12TH NOVEMBER

Alan fetched me and we walked to the House, arriving just in time to watch the King open the new parliament. He scarcely stuttered at all and looked well enough in Naval uniform. The Queen was at his side dressed magnificently in deep purple velvet, pearls and flowers on her shoulder. She looked better than

---

1 Waldron Smithers (1880–1954) was Conservative MP for Chislehurst from 1924 to 1945 and for Orpington from 1945 until his death. He was knighted in 1934.
2 Churchill's parliamentary private secretary: see entry for 20 July 1941 and footnote.
3 Smithers had asked a question (Hansard, Vol. 374, Col. 2036) about a government committee on inventions, which Churchill answered in full. There was then a question by Sir George Broadbridge, Conservative MP for the City of London, about 'whether, in view of the fact that we are fighting for our existence, he will consider removing from government service all persons of German education and of German origin?' Churchill asked whom Broadbridge had in mind, which prompted him to ask what Lord Cherwell's (i.e. Churchill's scientific adviser, formerly Professor Lindemann's) duties, qualifications, salary and support staff were. It is possible Channon has confused Broadbridge and Smithers; the volley of abuse Churchill supposedly launched at the latter is not recorded in Hansard.

usual; and was smiling her famous fixed – yes, and fascinating smile. [John] Simon[1] presented the address on bended knee. The Duke of Kent was not looking distinguished as a group captain and sat next to Lord Crewe. All this happened in the Robing Room. I was soon next to Lady Anderson – the bride, Ava! She is more chic, prettier than ever and very friendly. I walked with her, some yards behind the Sovereigns [sic] in the Prince's Chamber. She said that I had made her fantastic marriage, I had suggested it (which is true, but it was a joke) . . . A few bishops and peers stood about chatting until the K[ing] and Q[ueen] drove away, and I went to the library to snatch some sleep. At noon our House reassembled and Pilkington,[2] the MP for Widnes, whom I had always considered a [illegible] ass, moved the address. And he did it with a calm dignity and success which I envied and admired. He was in uniform and stood immediately behind the PM in my old seat. Fred Marshall,[3] a Labour member for Sheffield followed and was too long and less effective. A touch of sectarianism crept in, as it always does in Socialist speeches . . . As Winston rose I left lest I should be late to the luncheon with Lady Willingdon who had the King of Greece. I was in time . . . . The King soon arrived and was genial but looks ill . . . . After lunch Lady Willingdon took us up to the drawing room, which she has filled with china and furniture which she has recently removed from Walmer Castle. I am buying twenty-four lovely Nymphenburg cups from her collection. She gave me a pretty Crown Derby Cornucopia which I hugged and took back to Belgrave Square, where I found my mother-in-law and the Lennox-Boyds still discussing Alan's future. I am intriguing to keep him in this country as it will suit him better. My Alan is madder than ever, wild, gentle, restless, self-centred, adoring everybody, loving no one except his absurd old vampire of a mother who by pretending to prefer Francis, her youngest one, keeps Alan like a lover. He telephoned to her today in my presence: it was embarrassing, indeed. The endearments, the declarations of passion, the silliness passed between them could not be believed by anyone who had not heard it.

Mrs Greville rang me before dinner to tell me that she had entertained the King and Queen to lunch today in her suite at the Dorchester. They had proposed themselves, and she collected [Ambassador] Winant, Lady Cranborne and Osbert Sitwell to meet them. She was enchanted with her party and gurgled with pleasure.

---

1 In his capacity as Lord Chancellor.
2 Richard Antony Pilkington (1908–76) had been a professional soldier before becoming MP for Widnes in 1935; he held the seat until 1945, and was Conservative MP for Poole from 1951 to 1964. He won the Military Cross at Dunkirk in 1940 when he was one of the last men evacuated. He was knighted in 1961.
3 Fred Marshall (1883–1962) was Labour MP for Sheffield Brightside from 1930 to 1931 and from 1935 to 1950. From 1938 to 1945 he was Chairman of the National Union of General and Municipal Workers.

THURSDAY 13TH NOVEMBER

Alan breezed in and blurted out that he had been offered an operational job in London but he seemed doubtful about accepting it and will, no doubt, ask everyone in London for his advice. He quickly proceeded to ask me, [and] the Crown Prince, and a few moments later we had the whole story again as he retold it to Rab who dropped in. Alan has really decided but wishes to be bolstered up. I begged him not to cheapen himself by talking too much – he always does.

Dined with Mrs Greville, who looked superb with her many jewels and green feather boa. The Simons again,[1] Lord Ilchester, Shakes Morrison; Alan and Patsy; Lady Willingdon; Clarissa Churchill, who is a remarkable lovely and inspired girl – a milder Diana Cooper, more of a Brigid Guinness – and me. Lady Simon told the same anecdotes as she did last evening, one was in Erse, the others in Hebrew. She is a tremendous Zionist, an anti-Edenite and a champion of the slaves for whom she has really done much. She challenged Shakes Morrison in Celtic and he retorted in Gaelic. An amusing and unexpected duel in the Dorchester! But it was a friendly passage-at-arms, which a dialogue I overheard between Mrs Greville and Lady Willingdon was not!

> Mrs G: 'I hear, Bee, that you had the King of Greece to lunch with you yesterday.'
> Lady W: 'I'm so sorry, Maggie, I didn't ask you. I can only have six – just a tiny party.'
> Mrs G: 'Quite right, my dear. I had the King and Queen of England to lunch with me.'
> Lady W: 'But you will come again, won't you, when he comes again?'
> Mrs G: 'I always have the King of Greece to lunch with me alone. He likes that best.'

After dinner – two magnums of champagne – Lady Willingdon talked of her glamorous past. She has done up seventeen government houses and spent millions of government money. She has been a great and valiant servant of the Empire.

She drove me home and we dropped Shakes Morrison *en route* at the Carlton. She was rather testy with him (I think she fancies me!). She is called at 6.30 a.m. every day of her life and is full of energy.

Bed early.

FRIDAY 14TH NOVEMBER

A long, cold day at Southend too boring to chronicle. But one gets used to the war in one's division: the cold, the blackout, the distraction and misery of people . . .

1 Channon had been at the same dinner as them the previous evening.

The sacrifices and separations. I live still in a gilded world. I haven't been so happy since before I married as I have been these past weeks, except of course during my incredibly glamorous flight into Egypt last winter.

The American House of Representatives last night passed a bill amending the Neutrality Act by 18 votes. Does this mean America's actual eventual entry into the war?

SATURDAY 15TH NOVEMBER

Decidedly I talk too much, and about royalty.

TUESDAY 18TH NOVEMBER

Walked to the House of Commons, still feeling tired even after another injection of glycerine and arsenic. The House friendly . . . I went along to the Lords to see 'Niggs' Willingdon[1] take his seat . . . . Walked home and slept. About five Alan [Lennox-Boyd] arrived: it is his 37th birthday and I gave him an engraving of the Speaker Onslow.[2] He told me much of Harold's [Balfour] amorous activities in America . . . . When Harold arrived from America by clipper an hour later I was able to twit him unmercifully and did. Harold's trip was a huge success; he saw the President twice; stayed at the Embassy, which he described as 'chaotic' and far from a success. He brought me two bot[tle]s of French vermouth and a dozen oranges. (There is a new snobbery now – the provenance of edibles – people chat of sugar from Montreal, caviar from Moscow, socks from Panama etc. etc.)

Auchinleck has begun his offensive in Libya; if he fails the government will be discredited and Wavell will, in a way, be whitewashed. It is still a deep secret but is a major offensive.

WEDNESDAY 19TH NOVEMBER

Dill is made field marshal and appointed Governor of Bombay[3] to succeed Roger Lumley.[4] His departure is made easy but he has spoiled the show by saying that he leaves 'without bitterness' which, of course, suggested that he is embittered. There are various other changes.

---

1 Inigo 'Niggs' Freeman-Thomas, 2nd Marquess of Willingdon, qv.
2 There have been three Speaker Onslows: it is not clear which one featured here.
3 He was not: he was posted to Washington. Lumley (*vide infra*) remained in post (see entry for 12 October 1942).
4 Lawrence Roger Lumley (1896–1969) served in the Great War and was Conservative MP for Kingston-upon-Hull East from 1922 to 1929 and for York from 1931 to 1937, when he was appointed Governor of Bombay, where he served until 1943. He then rejoined the Army (in which he held a reserve commission) in the rank of major general until the end of the war. He succeeded his uncle as 11th Earl of Scarbrough in 1945. He was Lord Chamberlain from 1952 to 1963 and was made a Knight of the Garter in 1948.

Walked to the H of Commons after talks with Harold [Balfour] and Peter [Loxley]: it is lovely having them both back. H is gay, the peripatetic Ambassador, indeed. He is a great success, but a touch *exalté*[1] and has made – he doesn't know it – enemies. Today is the golden wedding anniversary of the Speaker, and the Prime Minister in an amusing and graceful speech paid him a tribute which pleased the House. He is a master of that sort of thing, certainly.

And not a word has come out about the Libyan offensive, still a deep secret. Nobody knows how it will develop.

Slept the whole afternoon. The Crown Prince woke me up about six and stayed for an hour. I am tiring of him quickly: *le jeu ne vaut pas la chandelle.*[2] He told me that the King of Greece has begun to comment on our friendship. The CP is a touch second-rate and Germanic, but he is devoted, dependent and endearing. I was irritated by him today because he stayed too long – everyone does – and from now on shall unload him gradually.

A note from Honor, short but friendly.

After the Crown Prince left Godfrey Winn burst in and he, too, stayed for too long. He is a 'second-rater' and never knows when to leave. Who does? I shall write a pamphlet about guests who sit on . . . Patsy dined, as did Peter Loxley and it was with the utmost difficulty that I got to bed at eleven o'clock. Patsy is pathetically in love with Alan, who is kind to her but she knows, I think, in her heart that she doesn't really hold him. The affair of the letters is on his conscience; how a love letter, the outpourings of his exaggerated love for his mother, went to Patsy by mistake. She cherishes it, carries it about, thinking it was for her. She is intelligent, a sweetie but limited.

I hinted to the CP that the government here think that he and the King, Timon, should leave for Egypt.

THURSDAY 20TH NOVEMBER

Slept for ten hours and yet awoke ill and tired. I am 'cracking up'; and I am irritated with the King of Greece who is jealous of my axis with his brother. Perhaps I am liverish.

The news of the offensive in Libya is out: our troops advance . . . . If the campaign should prove to be a failure, it will be a bitter blow for our government. And an oblique compliment to Wavell! I dreamt of both Wavell and Winston last night.

Breakfast with Harold who has immensely broadened; but he is bored by his Air Ministry job and is restless. He is now known as 'The Peripatetic Ambassador'. As I waited for Alan in the Smoking Room of the House of Commons – he is temperamentally unpunctual always – I sat with Herbert Williams, the rather

1 Grand.
2 The game isn't worth the candle.

downright, hard-boiled and sensible MP for Croydon; and I gathered from him that he is intriguing against the government. Indeed he is beginning a *frondeur*[1] movement against Winston, whom he dislikes and disapproves of. As he is bound to fail, I shall not become in any way identified with such a group. The Prime Minister made a statement about Libya in the House, and he clearly showed his interest and excitement. There is always the suspicion that he enjoys war and campaigns and that trait sickens me – all the slaughter is, no doubt, a necessary evil but why revel in it? And also it is too soon to be sanguine about the outcome of the desert advance.

I felt wretched – am I ill organically or is it only indigestion? I slept all afternoon after a quick Turkish bath cum snack with Alan. The Crown Prince rang up every few minutes and I pretended to be out! At length he arrived here, as did Alan . . . . and I was obliged to come down and receive them. I was cold, even rude to HRH as I wish to unload him. Now that Harold is back, I can no longer bear the burden, the boredom and the silly royal stupidity of my new friend. However, he waited as I dressed and dropped me at the Dorchester where I dined with Mrs Greville in her private suite. She was v affectionate and made me host: the others were the King of Greece, Joyce B[rittain-]Jones, Sacheverell and Georgia Sitwell and Clarissa Churchill. I was gay again, amusing, and made a set at the King who was most agreeable – so that silly Diodach was wrong. Champagne and chat . . . and at 10.15 the King rose and we left the old lady. He seized my hand warmly: and I walked home with the Archduke.[2] When I got in I felt remorseful – and perhaps a tiny touch tipsy – and so telephoned to the Crown Prince who had dined alone. He was uncommunicative on the telephone and conveyed that he was not alone. Later he rang me and said that when I called him the King had just come in and was sitting on his bed and he naturally couldn't discuss him over the telephone . . . Bed early; and I have decided to be nicer to the C Prince but at the same time to allow our friendship to cool slightly – preferable tactfully without a breach.

FRIDAY 21ST NOVEMBER

I awoke after an almost sleepless night feeling like death, and was cross and impossible all day.

All day I avoided the CP and let my private telephone ring unanswered. At 4.30 I walked to Lady Willingdon's for tea; a complicated boring evening and I went as I wanted to meet young Lord Wharton,[3] who was expected. However, he had run out. Tea with Her ex-Excellency and the Greigs, Sir Louis and Lady. They were

---

1 Rebel.
2 Not previously mentioned; presumably Archduke Robert, his neighbour.
3 Charles John Halswell Kemeys-Tynte (1908–69) succeeded his father as 9th Baron Wharton in 1934. He served in the RAF during the war.

[illegible] about Eloise Ancaster,[1] who lives near them at Richmond;[2] for two years she has not seen them and she lives a life of complete seclusion and is believed to be more than a little mad. We went to a film – how I loathe them – and then to the Mirabelle restaurant to dine with Alan, who had collected an incongruous party: Patsy, Lady Willingdon and me; Michael Parker, who is a sharp and engaging youth; Elizabeth Elveden and the Crown Prince, to whom I was 'sarky'. Once relations between two people get out of gear or become self-conscious it is almost impossible to put them right. Elaborate dinner and I escorted Lady W home early so as to avoid the Crown Prince.

Lady Willingdon says that my laugh is vulgar.

SATURDAY 22ND NOVEMBER   *THE OLD RECTORY, ELVEDEN*

Harold fetched me and we drove to Eton where we lunched with his wife and son, Ian, a very tall, pleasant youth to whom I gave £1. As there was a mock gas attack at 3 p.m. Harold and I drove away early . . . . and came here. Nobody had arrived so after tea I went to the nursery to see the children. Benjamin[3] and Eliza[4] are pure happiness, fair and plump, English and very lovely and attractive children. Indeed I don't think that I have ever seen such fascinating infants. The house is attractively arranged and warm and comfortable. The big house . . . . is shut, but the Duke of Gloucester[5] is living in the servant's wing with his unit. Both Patsy and the Iveaghs have arranged squalid little cottages on the estate.

Gay evening, Alan and Patsy, Harold Balfour, Elizabeth and I. I still feel ill and only alcohol seems to help.

SUNDAY 23RD NOVEMBER

The day was pleasantly futile. Got up late and then walked to see my in-laws, who seemed aged and vague, kindly but detached and absorbed by their collection of entrancing grandchildren. Simon, the red-haired heir of the Lennox-Boyds, and my godson is the favourite certainly. He is not yet 3[6] and is a grave, strange, healthy

---

1   Eloise Lawrence Breese (1882–1953), of New York, married in 1905 Gilbert
    Heathcote-Drummond-Willoughby, from 1910 2nd Earl of Ancaster*.
2   The Greigs lived at Thatched House Lodge, later the home of Princess Alexandra of Kent
    (qv).
3   Arthur Francis Benjamin Guinness (1937–92), by courtesy Viscount Elveden from 1945 until
    1967, when he succeeded his grandfather as 3rd Earl of Iveagh.
4   Elizabeth Maria Guinness (b.1939), by courtesy Lady Elizabeth from 1967.
5   The Duke had been a professional soldier between the wars but had retired after his
    brother's abdication to take on more ceremonial duties. He rejoined the Army in 1939 and by
    late 1941 was second in command of the 20th Armoured Brigade, in the rank of lieutenant
    general.
6   Either Channon's arithmetic or his famous misestimation of people's ages asserts itself
    again: the child was in fact not yet 2.

child. The Iveaghs seem cut off from reality: they have spent nearly forty years together and are cut off from the world. He seemed more friendly than usual, she possibly less. I don't know. We lunched at the Old Rectory where we were joined by Mrs Lennox-Boyd, the Queen Vampire, and her other surviving sons, George and Francis. It is some queer love-club, a cult I don't know. Then came the christening[1] which was a long-drawn-out and hideous affair, ill-managed. It lasted an hour and the infant Christopher bellowed naturally enough. I held Eliza in my arms and she smiled slyly, and I carried her home. My old heart ached for my own child; I worship children . . . . I gave the new baby, who was christened Christopher Alan, a silver-gilt Georgian rattle.

Drove back to London with Harold: we slept *en route*, took only two hours for the journey and dined happily together in pyjamas and went early to bed after hearing Averell Harriman on the wireless.

MONDAY 24TH NOVEMBER

Said 'no' to a variety of dull invitations and wondered why the Crown Prince didn't ring up – relieved but perhaps piqued? He spent the weekend at Windsor and today was going to Bomber Command. To my surprise I had a box of food from Quebec from the Empress Zita[2] of Austria, maple syrup, tea and orange conserve. No doubt a gesture of thanks because of my kindness to her sons. Still I am touched, certainly.

The Germans now look like capturing Moscow; and the Libyan battle rages.

I am being a touch sadistic and short-sighted about the Diodach. He bores me to a frenzy: four times he rang up and wanted to come and see me or to dine and I put him off . . . . Dined instead at Pratt's with Harold and a collection of amusing people. Basil Dufferin was there and looked drunk and dissipated.

TUESDAY 25TH NOVEMBER

The Crown Prince rang up and said that I had dropped him and he was offended: I denied the true charge in a way that would convince him that he was right.

The Libyan campaign obsesses everyone: I fear that Randolph Churchill has had his interfering finger in this sand-pie. Old 'Josh' Wedgwood[3] who is

---

1 Of the Lennox-Boyds' baby son, who had been born in July.
2 Zita of Bourbon-Parma; see Vol. I, entry for 1 February 1936 and footnote. The sons of hers to whom Channon refers were the Habsburg archdukes Robert and Felix (qqv).
3 Wedgwood was speaking in the debate on the King's Speech about the importance of mobilising the Jewish people against Hitler; and argued that one reason why a special Jewish army had not been formed to fight Nazism was that Britain's Arab allies would not like it; he said the Arabs were being 'appeased', and that the centre of this appeasement was the British Embassy in Cairo. He named, and blamed, Lampson as the agent of this (Hansard, Vol. 376, Col. 675). Lady Lampson was attacked only by inference of her Italian ancestry.

mad, ill-informed and whose career is to be wrong, attacked Miles Lampson in the House of Commons and made sly allusions to Jacqueline – from whom, *en passant*, I have heard nothing recently.

The Duchess of Kent rang up, but she had had no news from Kenya. And I have had little really from Peter recently. I have neurasthenia and am against almost everyone and everybody; but this mood, I know, is only a passing phase. I am so whimsical, impossible, moody, and frivolous . . . .

THURSDAY 27TH NOVEMBER

Today was the last of the [debate on the] address and Anthony Eden wound up and did so rather more convincingly than usual; he had the House with him and was on an easy wicket. The result was 326 to 2 on some futile amendment of the ILP.[1] I then went to the Ritz to a cocktail party given by the Americans, talked to Averell Harriman who tells me that . . . . there is now much bitterness in New York society; a feud between the Interventionists and the Isolationists threatened to break up society. It smacks of the 'Glamour' versus Chamberlain vendetta which overshadowed and poisoned London for years . . . . Then home, had a visitation from Godfrey Winn, who is a cross and a bore. Dined at the Ritz with the Crown Prince who gave me champagne and oysters . . . . The Ritz was almost empty but rather distinguished. I startled Ronnie Tree by being overwhelmingly charming to him – poor fellow, no wonder that he can never make me out! Perhaps I was a touch tipsy. I presented him to the Crown Prince. The CP and I walked home together in the damp blackout, sat and drank. Bed at twelve.

Alan tells me that Brinsley Plunket[2] was addicted to filthy practices. He was a c[blank][3] of shit and always made messes in Aileen's[4] bed which she was forced to clean up – pink crêpe de chine sheets too! I didn't know this. She stood it for years and then suddenly left him. I didn't blame her, if she no longer loved him. Alan is now known as 'The Eel'.

FRIDAY 28TH NOVEMBER

Typical Alan day – he rushes to the country, is back to give Godfrey Winn late lunch and goes at three o'clock to Henlow to stay with his old mother. He rang me up this morning but was still glacial: perhaps he feels ill which, as he never goes to bed, nor rests, and drinks too much, and worse is depressed by Patsy, is not surprising. The Guinnesses are a v heavy family of terrific personality and they get one down usually in the end. I refuse to be beaten by them for my gifts are greater, if different, from theirs.

---

1 Independent Labour Party.
2 Brinsley Sheridan Bushe Plunket (1901–41), who had just been killed in action.
3 It seems Channon alludes to coprophilia.
4 Plunket's wife Aileen Sibell Mary Guinness (1904–99), a cousin of Lady Honor Channon.
   Aileen and Plunket had divorced in 1940.

Basil Dufferin was ruined by his marriage;[1] Brinsley Plunket likewise; Philip Kindersley[2] broke away in time. But what will happen to Alan, to me, and to the unfortunate husbands of both Grania[3] and Brigid? . . . The Iveaghs were in the same restaurant and very affectionate. I seem to be in favour. But I was distressed by Mrs Greville, who repeated to me gossip she had picked up from Lady Camrose, who is never ill-natured. Lady C said that Honor was seen in every pub in Basingstoke with her low lover who was rarely shaved and that they consorted with the Camrose employees and were usually drunk and made scenes! Can any woman have fallen so low?

This is unfortunately reliable information since Lady Camrose always liked Honor, whom she knew well. True she opposed H's marriage to her Michael.[4] Lady Camrose thought that I ought to be told, and should divorce her at once. She asked Mrs Greville to repeat the tale to me. Depressing news indeed . . . .

I picked up the Crown Prince and we shopped a little and then had a Turkish bath together at the RAC, and slept soundly side by side for two hours. I am loving him again; at times I am bored by him and cannot take the strain. We returned to Belgrave Square, which the CP describes as the best and most distinguished club in London.

SATURDAY 29TH NOVEMBER   *KELVEDON*

A quiet day. I drove here: the garden is depressing, all debris and decay. The Home noisy with soldiers. I alone and I reread the famous 'Esteban' chapter[5] in *San Luis Rey* and wept and thought of my Manuel – far away.

I fear that Micky Renshaw may have read my diary as I found him yesterday alone in the morning room with the case unlocked. I don't recall ever having left it unlocked for long before.

Terrific battles continue in Libya. I dread the casualty lists that are bound to come.

SUNDAY 30TH NOVEMBER

Slept badly and got up late. Kelvedon is icy but pleasantly calm and it is a haven of refuge from people . . . Wrote long letters to Peter [Coats] and to Diana Cooper,

1 To Maureen Guinness (qv), Aileen's younger sister.
2 Kindersley (see Vol. I, entry for 17 January 1935, and footnote) married another of Lady Honor's cousins, Oonagh Guinness (1910–95), youngest sister of Aileen, in 1929. The marriage was dissolved in 1936.
3 Grania Maeve Rosaura Guinness (1920–2018), daughter of Lord Moyne (qv), married in 1951 the 4th Marquess of Normanby (1912–94), who was created a Knight of the Garter in 1985. They had seven children and remained married until his death.
4 (William) Michael Berry (1911–2001), younger brother of Seymour Berry (qv). He married in 1936 Lady Pamela Smith (qv), daughter of the 1st Earl of Birkenhead. He became proprietor of the *Daily Telegraph* and was raised to the peerage as Baron Hartwell (life peer) in 1968.
5 The third chapter of Thornton Wilder's 1927 novel *The Bridge of San Luis Rey*, in which Manuel, twin brother of the eponymous Esteban, dies.

and Jacqueline Lampson. Now I am frozen and bored and tempted to return to London; but a let-down is restful. Nobody has rung me, not Alan, not the Crown Prince, but I haven't rung them.

The Battle in Cyrenaica continues. Thank God I am not there, nor is P. It will be expensive. I went for a long tramp and consequently felt well; perhaps it is only exercise and air that I need. I hate both. Read Rosebery's *Pitt*;[1] and Cyril Connolly's[2] *Enemies of Promise* and began to be happy with a quiet life when Harold, Alan and Micky [Renshaw], all at Belgrave Square, rang up to disturb my brief retreat, and I wished I was with them. Alan, very sweet, has recovered his temper.

MONDAY 1ST DECEMBER

Drove up to London, my car laden with chrysanthemums and vegetables.

Dined in: Alan and Patsy; the Crown Prince; Peter Loxley and I. The Libyan battle continues; and I hear (a deep secret still) that the HMS *Barham*[3] has been sunk in the Mediterranean with all aboard. There will be no announcement as the Italians have not claimed this sinking and are apparently unaware of it.

Josh Wedgwood, Wedgwood Benn[4] and Comm[ander] Fletcher[5] are soon to be made peers as Winston wishes to reinforce the Labour bench in the Lords. Possibly this is a wise move. On Saturday this week Anthony accompanied by Alec Cadogan, and one or two other officials, leaves for Moscow. The trip will not be announced for some time. These are all secrets.

Alan in glorious spirits again: he is bored, hampered by matrimony.

---

1 Lord Rosebery had published his book on Pitt the Younger in 1891; it was written while he and the Liberal Party were in opposition to Lord Salisbury's administration.

2 Cyril Vernon Connolly (1903–74) was one the foremost literary critics of the twentieth century, but a man who disappointed himself in his own output. He analysed this disappointment in *Enemies of Promise*, a part-autobiographical work of literary criticism published to great acclaim in 1938.

3 HMS *Barham* was a super-dreadnought launched in 1914. It fought at Jutland in 1916 and was escorting the Malta convoys in 1941. It was sunk off the coast of Egypt by a U-boat on 25 November with the loss of 862 men; around 500 survived. The Admiralty imposed an order of secrecy on next of kin when they were informed, and the news was not formally announced until 27 January 1942.

4 William Wedgwood Benn (1877–1960) was the younger son of Sir John Benn, 1st Bt. He was Labour MP for Aberdeen North from 1928 to 1931 and for Manchester Gorton from 1937 to 1942. He was Secretary of State for India from 1929 to 1931 and for Air from 1945 to 1946. Having been decorated for service in the Royal Flying Corps and RAF in the Great War he rejoined the RAF in the Second World War, becoming its director of public relations; he also flew several combat missions over Germany as a gunner, despite being aged 67. He retired in the rank of air commodore. He was raised to the peerage as 1st Viscount Stansgate in 1942.

5 Reginald Thomas Herbert Fletcher (1885–1961) was Liberal MP for Basingstoke from 1923 to 1924, then Labour MP for Nuneaton from 1935 to 1942, when he was raised to the peerage as 1st Baron Winster. He was Minister of Aviation from 1945 to 1946 and Governor of Cyprus from 1946 to 1949.

I am reading *Endymion*[1] with immense pleasure.

Rex Whistler is staying with me. I shall see less of the Crown Prince this week; slightly but tactfully let him down.

More distressing news about the condition of poor Paul Latham and the treatment accorded him at Maidstone Gaol.

TUESDAY 2ND DECEMBER

An extraordinary conversation of a masochistic character with Rex Whistler, with whom I dined. I went to bed early. Rex is mildly malicious, gently gay, a pleasant Pierrot.

WEDNESDAY 3RD DECEMBER

Pam Churchill tells me that Randolph in Cairo writes the Libyan communiqués, which have been much too optimistic now for nearly a fortnight.

THURSDAY 4TH DECEMBER

Spent the morning with Alan, who is the world's perfect companion, and we lunched together at the H of Commons where I afterwards slept for an hour. But I heard Ernest Bevin wind up on the Manpower Bill; it was an extraordinarily able and balanced parliamentary performance. Winston came in late, well dressed and seemingly depressed. Apparently the news from Libya has made him downcast. I don't know. Certainly the newspapers are playing up the recent small successes of the Russians . . . But I wonder. I always wonder. I voted twice. We were like sheep in the overcrowded Peers Content lobby, and then [I] went to the RAC to join Alan and the Crown Prince for a 'Turker': we were very gay and I felt better and firmer than I have been for many weeks.

Godfrey Winn gave a gala dinner at Claridge's to repay all our hospitality. I went with some dread, but it was beautifully done and a great success. I was on his right; opposite was John Gordon,[2] the editor of the *Sunday Express*. A most pleasant man, not dour as I had heard. A v good and successful gala. Harold, Jay Llewellin who was rather emotional; Alan, Peter Loxley and self. Home at 12.30, and still in uproarious spirits I am now going to bed.

Rex has returned to his regiment after his brief bit of London.

---

1 Presumably the poem of 1818 by John Keats; though Wilde and Longfellow also wrote verse with this title.
2 John Rutherford Gordon (1890–1974) was editor of the *Sunday Express* from 1928 to 1952, and thereafter a widely read columnist on the paper, whose circulation increased nearly eightfold under his editorship.

FRIDAY 5TH DECEMBER[1]

Slept badly and woke late. Harold, who comes to my room every morning, says that I 'enjoy being out of office like Disraeli'. I worked, wrote, and shopped. A let-down day. Little news from Libya and what there is seems bad. We have fought for a fortnight and the net gain is nil, and I fear that there may be immense casualties. The country may be in for rather a rude awakening.

Yesterday I had one of my usual 'dust-ups' with Lady Astor. How I loathe that interfering termagant. She came up without the slightest provocation and attacked Geoffrey Lloyd for not being in the services – in uniform. 'This bill will get you now, you ought to be ashamed of yourself.' Geoffrey was mute and cowed but I sang out to her: 'Well you are nearly 70 so they can't get you!' She flushed with rage, and grabbed Kathleen Harriman[2] and walked away. Later she accosted me and asked why I always attacked her! I retorted that I was flattering her as she didn't look a day over 60! She hates and fears me.

I gather that the sinking of the *Barham* is to be kept a close secret. The City is mildly apprehensive and the recent boom seems to be faltering . . .

The Crown Prince came and sat for an hour and we talked of Peter, from whom came a most glamorous brilliant letter detailing his achievements in Malaya, Calcutta (which he liked) and Burma, about twenty pages of brilliance, wit and sensitive writing. I was much *attendri* towards him . . . The CP and I walked to the Vsevolods, where we had a drink and they urged me to stay and dine – but I was promised to Harold, whom they all roundly abused. I was irritated. They said he was ruthless and an *arriviste* and other unpleasant things.

Harold and I dined happily on two trays, ate a wild duck. Early to bed.

The Far Eastern affair is blowing up . . . .

SATURDAY 6TH DECEMBER

Went early to Burwood to attend a meeting of the Kelvedon Hall Estates. I was upset to learn that it is £7,400 overdrawn and I see little hope of paying it off. Luncheon at Pyrford with my in-laws who were gentle, detached and affectionate. They seem to want me to spend Xmas with them at Elveden . . . Then a nightmarish journey to Leeds [Castle] via London where I wrote a quick note for Peter, which the FO party will take to him in Russia. They go tomorrow, Anthony Eden, Oliver Harvey and Alec Cadogan. They are to meet Wavell at the end of the week.

Everyone is disappointed by the lack of success in Libya, particularly as we were given so much encouragement, even grounds for elation, by the PM and others. The overoptimistic communiqués drafted by Randolph Churchill in Cairo have done much to destroy that confidence. There is a feeling of 'hangover'

1 Rhodes James attributes some of these events to 4 December; thus in MS.
2 One of Averell Harriman's twin daughters.

and lassitude in the country and confidence in Churchill is somewhat shaken by the clumsy manner in which he handled the Libyan campaign, referring to it as another Blenheim or Waterloo!

I am dazed and dazzled by my Peter's peregrinations in Malaya last month and now Moscow. Coats in the Meridian . . . .

MONDAY 8TH DECEMBER

As I lay awake in bed [at Leeds Castle] last night something prompted me to turn on my little *de luxe* wireless. I was flabbergasted to hear that Japan had declared war on the United States and Great Britain, and that bombing of Honolulu etc. has already begun. So it is *Götterdämmerung* and the vast war spreads. America's participation, of course, ensures final victory for the Allies . . . . I rushed to Geoffrey Lloyd's room and awakened him with the startling news. Then I told Adrian and Olive Baillie who were still up . . . . Much talk and finally to bed again about 1 a.m. this morning. It was an historic hour . . . .

I drove up to London in my car . . . . There is excitement in the air, nervousness . . . . The Duchess of Kent rang up for news, but I know none: everything is on the wireless. Shanghai, Hong Kong attacked etc. . . . Parliament meets at three and I wonder whether – since for the first time in years now – our meeting is publicly announced – Hitler will bomb Westminster.

Will Anthony Eden's hush visit to Moscow be continued? Will he be rushed back to appear today? Will Wavell be ordered to return to India, which it is possible he had not left?

The House of Commons so quickly summoned, was crowded. I was there at 2.30 and procured a ticket for Lady Kemsley, who failed to turn up. There was an immense queue and I rescued Pam Churchill and led her into the inner lobby. She looked most attractive and I am a little in love with her – the complexion and skin texture I admire etc. Coming back into the main lobby I actually collided with Winston, who closely followed by [his wife] Clemmie and Harvie-Watt was pushing his way through the crowd! I don't know why he had chosen to come by the crowded way. He was smiling: she, however, looked older. I made way for them, and they seemed smiling and friendly. Lady Simon was rushing about. There was the usual scramble for tickets and after prayers the PM rose and made a brief and well-balanced announcement that the Cabinet had declared a state of war to exist at one o'clock with Japan. The House was full and moved: nobody seems to know whether this recent dramatic and undoubtedly clumsily contrived development was helpful to the Allied cause or not. It means immense complications, but probably America's immediate entry into the war. Geoffrey Lloyd whispered to me how lucky Winston was and now Libya will be forgotten. Russia saved the government in July; now Japan will do likewise . . . The PM was followed by

Lees-Smith,[1] old Percy Harris (who is always known as 'The Housemaid' since he empties the Chamber), and finally by Leslie Hore-Belisha. Then we rose and I drove away with Alan after a talk with Rab, who told me that his funny old father, Sir Montagu Butler, the Master of Pembroke, had a serious accident in Cambridge yesterday. His condition is grave.[2] I told Rab about Anthony's flight into Russia and he was amazed. The secret has been well kept. I wonder whether Wavell will return to India or go on to the Moscow conference now that the whole Far East is in flames. It is a *Götterdämmerung* certainly: civilisation is now at stake, and perhaps may perish. Only South America is still at peace.

Lady Kemsley rang me up and asked me to Farnham tonight but I could not face the long cold black drive. I rang the Crown Prince for once – he always rings me – and I thought that he was depressed. Has someone made mischief? So sudden and feverish a friendship is subject to fluctuation and coldness, and probably we are both a bit tired of each other. I shall do no more about it or him for a time.

The war has taken a tremendous leap forward and deepens in intensity. As I write I am listening to Pres[ident] Roosevelt's address to Congress . . . it is remarkably clear and audible.

How curious that at Leeds last evening we were discussing Diana Cooper during dinner! Even now she is being attacked, raided and anxious in Singapore. It will not be comfortable for her: possibly she will be killed.

TUESDAY 9TH DECEMBER

Woke ill, as usual. Went to the House agog with rumours of the Far East. Took Alan out shopping and later had a Turkish bath. All day I have dodged the Diodach, who is beginning to be a burden beyond endurance, from all his surliness . . . his ticks of saying 'Honestly; Good Heavens' etc. and all *à la longue*.

Dined in: Harold; Pam Churchill; Kathleen Harriman and her dark handsome father, Averell; and the Baillies, and Geoffrey Lloyd. I was over-gay and expansive and we had champagne, one of my last grand magnums of Krug 1920. Averell is sallow, distinguished and pleasant. Much talk of Japanese invasions of California etc. Averell hopes that the American cities will be badly blitzed so as to awaken the people!! Pam C is auburn, with soft skin and charm, but is, I suspect, hard at

---

1 Hastings Bertrand Lees-Smith (1878–1941) was Liberal MP for Northampton from 1910 to 1918. In 1919 he joined the Labour Party and represented Keighley in its interest from 1922 to 1923, 1924 to 1931 and 1935 to 1941. He was Postmaster-General from 1929 to 1931 and President of the Board of Education from March to August 1931. He was Leader of the Opposition from May 1940, when Labour joined the coalition, until his death, but strongly supported Churchill's policy as Prime Minister.

2 He lived another eleven years.

heart. She is alleged to be having an affair with Averell Harriman.[1] He attacked the American isolationists . . . .

WEDNESDAY 10TH DECEMBER

A dreadful day of despair and despondency. I woke feeling ill, but wrote letters and worked until time to go to the House. The Prime Minister slathed[2] in and seemed anxious to speak: after a preliminary parley and getting up and sitting down twice, he announced the sinking of the *Prince of Wales*[3] and the *Repulse*[4] at Malaya. A most shattering blow for our Pacific fleet and naval prestige . . . A wave of gloom spread everywhere. The House was restive; the government suddenly unpopular . . . I came home and gave luncheon to the Iveaghs who had been at the Lords. They, too, were dejected. I could have cried.

Dined with Mrs Greville . . . . Mrs G says 'If only the Prime Minister could have permanent laryngitis we might win the war.' She was alluding to his unfortunate reference on Monday to the moving to the Pacific of our battleships at a convenient moment. A heartbreaking remark viewed in light of subsequent events. The thousands of lives lost . . . it is terrible.

Averell Harriman suggested last night that there was a strain of amusement in our reaction to the air raids and alerts on the California coast. Perhaps he is right. It all sounds unbelievable. And that will happen now?

The CP, who delights in repeating despicable things, says that the King of Greece had told him that my correspondence with Peter [Coats] was read and that it gave much amusement to people at the FO. I don't [think] this is [so], there may have been a leak somewhere but is disgusting, certainly.

THURSDAY 11TH DECEMBER

Early to the House, where I put the Crown Prince in the Distinguished Strangers' Gallery. A rumour, which afterwards turned out to be true, swept over the depressed house that over 2,000 men had been saved from the sunken ships. Our spirits recovered a little . . . Just before twelve o'clock the Prime Minister, looking somewhat worn, entered the Chamber. There were some preliminary questions put by Lees-Smith. The PM explained that Members of Parliament would be allowed a free choice between entering the armed services or attending

---

1 She was, and it helped cause the end of her marriage to Randolph Churchill. She and Harriman married in 1971.
2 He means 'slathered', to move in a sliding fashion.
3 The battleship HMS *Prince of Wales* had only been completed the previous March; it had been sunk that day in the South China Sea after an air attack by Japanese planes, with the loss of 327 lives.
4 HMS *Repulse* was a battlecruiser launched in 1916, sunk that day off Kuantan in the South China Sea, also by air attack, with the loss of 508 officers and men.

to their parliamentary duties. I was relieved, for I know how utterly hopeless I would be in uniform, although at times I hanker for it. I am too old, too unfit and too temperamentally hopeless . . . Besides I am gun-shy . . . Then he began his very long, perhaps overlong statement with a spirited yet slightly defensive explanation of the recent Cairene communiqués which were, everyone realises, overenthusiastic, and misleading. By putting too much emphasis on this feature of this extraordinary week, the Prime Minister increased the very suspicions which he wished to allay, and I watched members shift uneasily as they do when they are irritated and think that they are being imposed upon. Then the PM turned to the larger theatre of the war and he had his usual exhilarating effect on the House . . . And I soon read on the tape that the City quickly reacted. Yesterday shares fell dramatically and Guinness dropped to 90 from 96. Today they are recovering.

A 'Turker' with Alan who, whilst as charming as ever, is becoming more selfish and self-assured. Perhaps wealth is unwholesome for him? However as I made the marriage I must do everything possible to make it a success. But I noticed a cooling in the Iveaghs' affection and regard for Alan recently, due, I think, to his mad rushing about, his almost insane passion for his mother and his selfishness. He is a divine, brilliant puppy really. As I sweated in the steam room the evening newspapers were brought in and I read that both Italy and Germany had declared war on the United States. It must be v galling for that great Republic to be treated like Poland and Czechoslovakia. So now the world is in flames and seems no longer worth living. Even young Archie Wavell writes to me that he thinks 'The war will last fifteen years or more.'

I am haunted by the Crown Prince story of my letters being read. I wonder?

Nothing has been mentioned of Anthony Eden's visit to Moscow: how wonderful really (heartless as it may sound) if he suffers the fate of Kitchener, as he is a menace to the future of the world. This secret has been well kept; but the Belgian Ambassador has twigged.

I forgot to chronicle a curious incident which happened to me on Tuesday. Wine and spirits are almost unprocurable and as I was entertaining the American, Averell Harriman, I went to Fortnum and Mason's in the hope of buying some brandy. There was none and as I was being told so by an attendant in the shop I ran into Lady Aberconway,[1] whom I have always considered an affected absurd pretentious *poseur*[2] with her wide eyes and mannerisms. She instantly collared me, drove me to her vast empty mansion in South Street, led me to the wine cellar and presented me with a bottle of beautiful Berry Bros 1860 brandy. I was surprised and touched. The war certainly makes people more considerate and gentle and I am still impressed by this gesture. Sydney Butler, however, rather spoilt the story tonight by saying, when I told it to her, that 'Christabel evidently

---

1 Christabel Mary Melville Macnaghten (1890–1974) married in 1910 Henry Duncan McLaren (1879–1953), who in 1934 succeeded his father as 2nd Baron Aberconway.
2 It should be *poseuse*. See entry for 22 March 1939, and footnote.

knows how important you are!' Sydney's deep dislike of her is due to her father's friendship with Christabel which, were they not so old, would be called a liaison. I shall never be spiteful or even amusing about Christabel again.

FRIDAY 12TH DECEMBER

I felt suicidal, so ill and depressed ... And stayed in bed until ten, having *un petit lever*[1] of Rab, Harold and Sydney Butler. Shopped a bit, and spent most of the day avoiding my friends, particularly the Crown Prince. And in a queer mood I chucked the Rotary Luncheon Club meeting next Tuesday – and I shall go to the Belgian Embassy instead! Naughty; but what does it matter? One must live from day to day ....

What will happen when the loss of the *Barham* is announced? How long will it be possible to keep the ghastly secret?

Honor came up for the day and met Patsy. She did not ring me. The news added to my gloom and I was sick several times.

Why do I tire of people so quickly? I need months of peace and recovery. Tomorrow I go to Southend for three days of sea and speeches and discomfort.

I am thinking of Diana Cooper. Will she escape to India? Will Wavell remain there?

Harold dashed in, invited me to dine, but I declined, and also sent a curt message to the Crown Prince that I could not see him this evening. His sweetness and affection are as touching as they are exhausting. I am *un être solitaire*.[2]

This afternoon I went on a shopping expedition and ran into Anne Rosse[3] who was affectionate and gushing, and much improved. She is a kitten at heart; but I really genuinely like her today. Am I becoming more tolerant, more mellow, as the war and the weary wretched world complications gradually engulf me?

I thought of my will – I have left legacies to Serge Obolensky, Paul of Yugoslavia, Harold Balfour, and to Peter whom I look upon as my four greatest friends. Shall they all four survive me?

SATURDAY 13TH DECEMBER

I am closing this diary in a few moments' time and going to Southend for three dreary days of 'do's'.

---

1 He mocks the ceremonial morning audience a monarch would give to his courtiers while dressing.
2 A solitary being.
3 Anne Messel (1902–92), married first, in 1925, Ronald Armstrong Jones, from whom she was divorced in 1934; and second, in 1935, Michael Parsons, 6th Earl of Rosse. Her brother was the distinguished stage designer Oliver Messel (qv), and her son by her first marriage was Antony Armstrong Jones, who became 1st Earl of Snowdon on his marriage in 1960 to Princess Margaret. Lady Rosse was known as 'Tugboat Annie', as she 'drifted from peer to peer'.

Averell Harriman, Sir Charles Portal, Beaverbrook, Dudley Pound and others left for the US last night in great secrecy. There is even a rumour that Winston went with them, but I think this is untrue.[1] Certainly he considered going. Now the country is ripe and ready for invasion with its many chiefs away ...

I slept eleven hours last night and feel refreshed this morning.

MONDAY 15TH DECEMBER

After two crowded days in my not very delectable division of Southend I returned to London. I discussed myself with an unknown man on the train who was unaware of my identity. He said that I was known as being 'democratic' and 'not a snob' etc. in my constituency. I was tempted to get him to put this unorthodox rather startling view on paper – since obviously no one would believe the story – but refrained.

No taxi at Fenchurch Street Station but after a longish wait in the cold blackout I shared a cab with a friendly Canadian soldier, whom I invited in to No. 5 for a drink. He accepted but afterwards declined when he saw my menservants helping out with my luggage etc. Class trouble again! The Crown Prince was waiting for me; he had rung up and been invited to dine by my butler. We had a merry dinner *à deux*, and as I was so tired, drank champagne. Later we went to the Dorchester to see Alan, who had been dining with Patsy, who is ill. We were joined by Pam Churchill and Kathleen Harriman. Really fun ... I walked back to Claridge's with the Crown Prince, who complained plaintively that I was dropping him gradually and tactfully – but he knew that I no longer cared to see him, and that my early enthusiasm for our friendship had waned; I protested; but it was in vain as he is right.

TUESDAY 16TH DECEMBER

A mass of correspondence to attend to as a result of my Southend visit!

Lunched at the Belgian Embassy: Lady Pembroke, the Moore-Brabazons, Loelia Westminster, Mrs Greville, others. Rich food and the very delightful suave septuagenarian host.[2] Mrs Greville first told me that she feared that Hector Bolitho had lost his mind or balance, as he writes her obscene letters – curiously enough he telephoned to me this morning and was rather odd and disjointed! Later she was exceedingly provocative and remarked that the only good result of the Japanese intervention was that they might kill Duff Cooper at Singapore – at least she hoped so! (she has always hated him). Loelia Westminster was loud in his defence and Mrs Greville retorted that she 'hated him more than she hated

---

1 Churchill had left on 12 December accompanied by Beaverbrook, his daughter Mary and a secretary, among others.

2 The Belgian Ambassador, baron Émile de Cartier de Marchienne (1871–1946).*

even the French!' It was brilliantly done, and one had expected her to say 'The Germans!'. I went to the House of Commons where I found that many people knew that Winston went to the USA last Friday with Max Beaverbrook and that Anthony Eden is in Moscow. The best kept secrets are thus out! Dined with Alan in his suite at the Dorchester. Also Godfrey Winn, who gets on my nerves with his barrage of flattery. Avoided the Crown Prince all day.

Both the Gloucester and Harding babies are due this week. And there is another Kent infant on the way, due towards the end of July. Nobody knows; she[1] whispered it to me on the telephone.

WEDNESDAY 17TH DECEMBER

Went early to the House for questions: felt sparkle-less – have I lost my charm? Gave Anne Rosse and Nicholas Lawford lunch at the crowded Ritz where I met de Gaulle and many others. Later shopped etc., returned to the house and heard Harold [Balfour] address the 1922 Committee about Russia. He was voluble, vivacious and gay and held his audience enthralled. Then I listened to Winant, who was shy and brief, speak to the Anglo-American Committee. He was uncommunicative and saved only by his personal charm and obvious embarrassment.

Drinks with Helen Fitzgerald in her flat at the Dorchester. James Gunn, who is always muddled politically, thought that Winston Churchill should be shot. Esmond Rothermere, too, was critical of him and of this complicated American Democratic Charter which he hopes to bring back from Washington. All the women chatted state secrets indiscreetly! Vere Harmsworth,[2] Esmond's unattractive, Jewish-looking! (why?) heir was with him . . .

Dined in, a scratch party arranged at seven o'clock which was, however, very successful. Rob Bernays hideous but delightful; the Crown Prince; Tilea, the Romanian. Later we were joined by Harold and the Vsevolods of Russia. Everyone was horrified by a speech made today by King Peter of Yugoslavia at the Dorchester in which he attacked – with violence and ingratitude – the regime of the recent Regency. Nobody knows better than I how devoted the young King was to the ex-Regent: they were on the most affectionate and kindly terms. It is monstrous, this treachery and the boy King, never clever, but always amiable, is like poor Louis XVII[3] influenced by his gaolers! Vsevolod thinks that he had not even bothered to read the speech (since we read it), and may have been surprised or at least indifferent or ignorant of its treacherous contents. I am horrified. From

1   The Duchess.
2   Vere Harold Harmsworth (1925–98) succeeded his father as 3rd Viscount Rothermere in 1978. He had taken control of his considerable newspaper interests, which included the *Daily Mail*, in 1970.
3   Louis XVII of France (1785–95) was gaoled and manipulated by his captors after the executions of his parents, Louis XVI and Marie Antoinette, in 1793.

now on I shall work for the overthrow of the Karageorgevich dynasty. This is all the doing of Queen Marie or 'The Fat Cow' as the Greeks call her. All the Romanian family are low, Judases. Will Michael[1] escape the taint?

Honor sent me a humble, touching and quite useless little gold Christmas present; still it is a gesture. I sent her silver wine coasters and a set of *Anna Karenina* which I hope will give her a salutary sermon, if she reads them.

The Far East is in flames!

Thursday 18th December

Lunched with the Prime Minister of Greece; a party of about thirty MPs etc. to meet the King and the Crown Prince who arrived regally and pompously! I was amazed by my Proustian relation to them both – after last night. They were correct and unsmiling!! Harold Nicolson proposed the King's health with much grace and distinction . . . . But I kept thinking of how surprised the assembled company of staid puritanical MPs would be if I told them – well, all!

As I was dressing for dinner young Archie Wavell arrived unannounced from Scotland and begged a bed. His long red locks, his untidy appearance, his freckles and vagueness are not attractive and yet somehow he is. He is intellectual and even intelligent with perhaps more character than charm. He is a touch uncivilised. Harold B doesn't like him; says he is wet. He dined as did Barbie Wallace, Helen Fitzgerald, Harold and Peter Loxley. Barbie, usually so in the political 'world', was unaware that the PM is *en route* for Washington, and that Anthony Eden is already in Moscow. Barbie Wallace is very Red, as Socialistically minded as anybody who has recently inherited a million[2] . . . . She has always been so, and tonight attacked Eton and hoped that Rab would abolish it. I fear she was a little nettled when I retorted that, on the contrary, he had just decided to send his own son there.

A son[3] was born to the Gloucesters: he is third in line to the throne. A caesarean. The Kents' child is due in June.

Friday 19th December

Woke *désoeuvré* and chatted with Wavell about Kipling and Browning, whom he admires! Then to the house where we sat in secret session. There was continual criticism, of the government, a barrage of questions, bickering and obvious

---

1 King Michael of Romania.
2 From her husband, who had died the previous February.
3 Prince William Henry Andrew Frederick of Gloucester (1941–72). After Cambridge, Stanford and a spell in merchant banking, he joined the Diplomatic Service. He was killed in a flying competition. At this stage he was actually fourth in line, after the princesses Elizabeth and Margaret Rose, and his own father.

dislike. The government is doomed: I give it another month. No government can survive such unpopularity for long. It was another Narvik night. Of course, the members behaved rather like schoolboys with the Headmaster away, and no doubt Winston on his return will harangue us and possibly pacify the house once again for a short time. But its days are numbered. I walked home rather wistfully and found Archie Wavell awaiting me and took him around to the [Leo] Amerys for a drink. Harry Crookshank was there and to my surprise was almost amiable . . . Archie and I went on to a terribly boring film and then dined with Alan at Postina's where to our amazement we found the Dufferins *en ménage* dining together!! Maureen gave me to understand that they are temporarily recommitted. He looked appalling, with a red face covered with scabs and emptiness. Later we looked in at Pratt's and I noticed that Eddie Devonshire had NOT put my name down as he promised. Perhaps he has forgotten to do it. I was disturbed. Anyway I am nearly nervously bankrupt.

Patsy Lennox-Boyd is ill with a tired heart. She lives under perpetual strain. For anyone in so low a key, so glamorously indolent, to be married to a vital vivacious fellow like Alan must be a risk and I think she is worn out with watching and waiting and loving. He is being gentle and sweet but is bored to death with her.

Archie Wavell kept me up until all hours gossiping about his father, whom he adores.

SATURDAY 20TH DECEMBER

Patsy is worse. I shopped in the fog, completed my Xmas list and lunched with Alice Harding . . .

Dined with Harold and Alan and we discussed the political outlook, which is confused. Everyone says that the government is doomed; but Winston is capable of defying the House of Commons by insisting on a division – a three-liner[1] – which he would presumably win. I want him to remain Prime Minister certainly, but he should reconstruct his government.

The arrival of the Gloucester Prince will irritate the Duke of Kent. It will be a dull boy for the Duke of G is nearly half-witted and Alice, his mother, whilst sweet and nice, is no bluestocking. She is still as shy and retiring as ever.

Difficulties this morning with the Colonial Office to induce them to send the Kents' parcels – yes more of them – to Kenya for poor Olga and Paul. I cannot get over the outrageous speech of little King Peter. The 'wet' fool . . . . I hope that he marries a film star, which is the sort of thing one expects of him.

---

1 That is, a three-line whip on a vote of confidence, compelling government supporters to attend and expecting them to vote for the government.

SUNDAY 21ST DECEMBER

A lazy cold day. Read Osbert's [Sitwell] new book, a tiny classic, *A Place of One's Own*: it is a lugubrious ghost story. Delivered Xmas presents, revelled in the absence of the Crown Prince who is at Tredegar, and did little . . . Played with my possessions, came [up]on some nostalgic photographs and oddly enough a letter from King Peter written when he was still a decent boy.

Patsy has developed jaundice and now bullies Alan to her heart's content: she is a selfish creature with her apple-like looks and her untidiness. Alan is weak and always gives in to her. Lunched with him at the Dorchester and we wondered whether Winston will arrive at Annapolis tomorrow according to schedule.

Dined with Alan and talked too late. Patsy is worse and he enjoys the rushing and flurry of illness and remained tender and devoted.

TUESDAY 23RD DECEMBER

An odd day. I woke fuming with rage against the Crown Prince and decided to cut the friendship as it is too exhausting . . . . I worked, I wrote, and I shopped and eventually went to earth at the RAC where I was massaged and slept for three hours. Then I felt better and came home to arrange my dinner party, the last of 1941; perhaps the last ever in the Amalienburg? Came: the Crown Prince; Londonderrys; Loelia Westminster; Ann O'Neill; Esmond Rothermere; Alan and Harold. Gay and a success and the CP impressed – as royalties always are by 'high society'. Loelia brought me a lapis and coral china *bibelot, très bon goût*.[1] The CP brought a pair of red John Derbyshire Spar vases [*sic*][2] and an immense black pearl and diamond stud which I am enchanted with. I have had lovely presents this year. After dinner there was bridge and then they left. (I gave Loelia three gallons of petrol for her car.) The CP stayed on, said I had 'made' his London, been so sweet to him and he kissed me with tears in his eyes and I felt a beast for all the treacherous thoughts I had harboured all day against him.

Harold Balfour's immense son, Ian, aged 17, is staying here. He is a gay and delightful lad. The CP was much attracted by him.

A mass of cables, cards and presents poured in all day! So <u>far</u> I like best:

1 emerald tiepin from Peter in India
1 lapis box from the Duchess of Kent
1 pair ormolu and crystal ornaments from Alice Harding
1 pair ormolu and red enamel pots from the Duke of Kent

---

1 Very good taste.
2 Channon has conflated two synonyms: the material Derbyshire spar, also known as Blue John.

1 huge black pearl and diamond stud from the Crown Prince
1 blood-stone Russian egg from Vsevolod of Russia.

Eric Kennington[1] dressed as a Home Guard called here again this morning bringing an immense portrait, over lifesized, of General Wavell. I don't think that I like it. Kennington talked of T. E. Lawrence and said that Henry Williamson,[2] who had just produced a book about him, was insanely in love with him.

WEDNESDAY 24TH DECEMBER   *THE OLD RECTORY, ELVEDEN*

Alan and I, after stopping at Baldock to meet his vampire of a mother, arrived here about five. A tree and the children ... I was miserable and missed Paul. Benjamin Guinness is a beautiful boy, sensitive and dreary; his plump 2-year-old sister is flirtatious and a character. Simon Lennox-Boyd, who has fiery red hair, is most independent (I don't like him yet) and pushes Alan about saying 'Go away, Daddy!' The Iveaghs very sweet and pleased to have four of their five grandchildren with them, and all three in-laws, but none of their children curiously enough.
    Tired.

THURSDAY 25TH DECEMBER

A year ago I was flying between Bathurst and Freetown on my famous flight into Egypt.
    Got up late, exchanged presents – Alan gave me a handsome blood-stone seal – and went to church with him, the Iveaghs and Elizabeth Elveden. A crowd of gay officers, stationed at 'The Big House', dropped in for drinks, all gay and attractive and I, feeling well for the first time for months, went all out to amuse them.
    Arthur [Elveden] came home rather unexpectedly from Felixstowe where he is stationed in acute discomfort. We dined with the Iveaghs in their tiny cottage and drank some champagne which Honor had sent them. I unpacked the box, the Iveaghs are firm and fixed in their attitude towards her.

FRIDAY 26TH DECEMBER

Walked to see the Iveaghs in the sunny cold and they took me to the Hall, now closed, and we wandered about the deserted passages looking at the Kenwood

1 Eric Henri Kennington (1888–1960) was a sculptor and painter and an official war artist in both wars.
2 Henry William Williamson (1895–1977) was a naturalist and writer on the countryside, best known for his 1927 novel *Tarka the Otter*, which was read by Lawrence and sparked their friendship. He went out of favour when war came for his earlier espousal of Oswald Mosley. In 1941 he published *Genius of Friendship: T. E. Lawrence*.

pictures[1] – the Rembrandts, the famous Vermeer and the enchanting portrait of Beau Brummell. The home may never be opened again – who knows? The servants' wing is occupied by the military; the Duke of Gloucester amongst them. Last night he produced two crates of champagne and they had a gala dinner to celebrate both Christmas and the birth of their son.

Elizabeth and I lunched alone and in the afternoon the Brigadier, who turned out to be an old acquaintance, and a charming one – a very social soldier, Evelyn Fanshawe[2] – fetched us, took us to the Hall where we drank cocktails, and after attended a pantomime produced by the men . . . . A very coarse performance. Elizabeth and I dined at the mess and made a whole new batch of friends . . . .

Tipsily we all walked back to the rectory. Hong Kong is forgotten . . . . Wavell is flying back probably with Peter, from Chungking to Delhi . . . . I miss Paul.

SATURDAY 27TH DECEMBER

Evelyn Fanshawe, it transpires, has an Egyptian wife! He came to see us this morning. We lunched with the Iveaghs who were gay and affectionate and then Elizabeth bullied me, drove me to Ickworth, which she had never seen. It is an immense Palladian pile in the Brenta manner[3] built by the eccentric Bishop of Derry.[4] We were rather apprehensive about our reception, not knowing the aged Lord and Lady Bristol.[5] Luckily however Lady Marjorie Erskine,[6] the daughter, whom I have long known, received us and with two studious, weak-looking but humorous sons,[7] conducted us over the house. It is a palace, a Fun-Palace! Many good pictures: Eight Zoffanys,[8] one . . . . done at Holland House showing

---

1 Pictures, including some by Rembrandt Harmenszoon van Rijn (1606–69), the legendary Dutch Baroque master, and his younger contemporary Johannes Vermeer (1632–75), from the collection at Kenwood House in London made by the 1st Earl of Iveagh, and which had been evacuated to Elveden for their protection during the war.

2 Evelyn Dalrymple Fanshawe (1895–1979) was in command of the 20th Armoured Brigade. Promoted to major general in 1942, he commanded the Royal Armoured Corps Training Establishment until he retired in 1945. From then until 1952 he directed relief work for refugees in Germany.

3 A neo-Palladian style noted in the region of northern Italy through which the Brenta river flows.

4 The 4th Earl of Bristol (1730–1803) was Bishop of Derry from 1768 until his death. He travelled extensively in Europe, and took inspiration from Italian architects especially in conceiving Ickworth, which he did not live to see finished: it was built between 1795 and 1829.

5 Frederick William Fane Hervey (1863–1951) succeeded his uncle as 4th Marquess of Bristol in 1907. A career naval officer, he retired in the rank of rear admiral. He married, in 1896, Alice Frances Theodora Wythes (1875–1957).

6 Marjorie Hervey (1898–1967), from 1907 Lady Marjorie by courtesy, married John Francis Ashley Erskine (1895–1953), by courtesy Lord Erskine, in 1919.

7 The Erskines had four sons, and it is not clear which two these were.

8 Johan (or Johann) Zoffany (c.1733–1801) was a German-born painter who settled in England and was noted for his portraits of high society.

Stephen Fox![1] Another of the wicked Lord Hervey,[2] who has always so obsessed me since I lived in his house (now destroyed by a bomb) at 21 St James's Place; and a fascinating portrait of the Bishop [of Derry] by Mme Vigée Le Brun,[3] who was his mistress.

An enthralling afternoon and luckily we never saw the Bristols at all. What will happen to this vast pile? The heir, the 'Mayfair Man',[4] is in prison.

SUNDAY 28TH DECEMBER

Lady Iveagh says that all the lovely exciting Bristol possessions will come under the hammer when the old man dies – probably I should love to own the Vigeé Le Brun.

Elizabeth and I said goodbye to our new military friends and drove up to London where I found a mountain of Christmas cables etc. – none from my mother, Peter or the Regent, still languishing in Kenya. But two from my baby . . . .

Elizabeth, Harold, Alan and I dined and I felt ill again. Alan is in dejected spirits; he is bored, becoming a touch spoilt and cynical and is curiously detached from his attractive children. He is only in love with his old mamma really.

Archie Wavell writes that he doesn't like the Kennington portrait; he has taken it to Scotland. Heroic in size, it is at first sight somewhat disappointing but it grows on me.

Harold is disapproving of my new royal jewel; says it is too big to wear – but is it? And Elizabeth, who dislikes Honor, thinks that H is very happy in her new favourite life.

I have enjoyed my Christmas and the respite from London life – but my heart was at Rhinebeck with my child. For whom my whole heart aches . . .

---

1 Stephen Fox (1704–76) assumed the additional surname of Strangways in 1758 to comply with the terms of an inheritance for his wife. After parliamentary and government service he was raised to the peerage and eventually became 1st Earl of Ilchester. He was the lover of the 2nd Baron Hervey (*vide infra*).

2 He refers to the 2nd Baron Hervey (1696–1743), who served as Lord Privy Seal from 1740 to 1742 at the end of Robert Walpole's premiership. Bisexual like Stephen Fox (*vide supra*), the two were lovers for around a decade.

3 Élisabeth Louise Vigée Le Brun (1755–1842) was a prominent Parisian portrait painter. One of her main patrons was Marie Antoinette.

4 Victor Frederick Cochrane Hervey (1915–85) was not the immediate heir; first his father, Lord Herbert Hervey, succeeded his brother as 5th Marquess of Bristol in 1951, at which point Hervey became, by courtesy, Earl Jermyn; he succeeded as 6th Marquess in 1960. Channon's reference to him as the 'Mayfair Man' refers to Hervey's conviction for the robbery in July 1939 of jewels and furs with a total value over £5,000 from two premises in Mayfair: he was sentenced to three years. He had already been declared bankrupt in 1937 having failed in an arms-dealing business, selling weapons to both sides in the Spanish Civil War. Channon misremembers in one respect: he was not one of the 'Mayfair Boys', a group of ex-public school criminals with whom he was associated who were sentenced to prison and flogging for an armed robbery at Cartier's in 1938.

Monday 29th December

Anthony Eden's great visit to Moscow is now announced. He must be back. I gather that there was disagreement between him and Stalin over the future of the Baltic States, which Russia annexed.

I feel ill and didn't sleep – my four-days interlude wasn't long enough. A cable came from my mother; nothing from Peter – there would hardly be time and anyway he cabled last week; nothing from the Butlers. But a nice letter from the Duchess of Kent. She rang me up and we gossiped. Nobody knows about the baby, already three months started. Alice Harding produced a daughter, a 7½-pounder last night at 19 Bentinck Street – the nursing home.

Spent a happy day in bed reading, resting, and telephoning and didn't really get up until dinner time, when I entertained Elizabeth Elveden, who is still staying here; the Crown Prince; Alan and the Vsevolods of Russia. I managed to get rid of them by eleven o'clock – a triumph. Prince Bundi (as we call him, named after my faithful dog) was in high spirits having been made an admiral of the Greek fleet today. King Timon was given the English DSO by the Monarch today at luncheon.

Intense and terrible cold. Nice letter from Honor, thanking me for the silver and *Anna Karenina*. I hope she enjoys it!

Tuesday 30th December

Alan confessed to me how bored he is and is making secret attempts at the Admiralty to return to sea! He cannot be late for a moment: has no sense of leisure.

Anthony Eden's words when he returned to London this morning have caused some amusement. His talks with Stalin he described to the press as being 'full, frank and sincere'! Good God!

I am desperately anxious about the poor Regent and fear that he may do something terrible, perhaps suicide. His gloom increases. Oh, will this awful year be followed by a better one? It could hardly be worse. The digits of 1942 add up to 7 which is something.

The Coopers are being bombed at Singapore and are in a tight corner.

Dined with Maimie and Vsevolod and we discussed the Yugoslav dynasty and decided to dethrone it. There has never been so malicious or wicked a bitch as Queen [Marie]. Came home early as I cannot face sitting up gossiping until all hours with the Crown Prince. Harold bets me that Wavell is to be appointed Supreme Commander of the Pacific Forces. Another Foch![1] He will have his headquarters at Surabaya[2] in Java. Another leg up for Peter, yet this means yet another move? Or will he return as Comptroller at Delhi?

---

1 Ferdinand Foch (1851–1929), Commander-in-Chief of the French and Allied Armies in the Great War.
2 The capital of the province of East Java.

WEDNESDAY 31ST DECEMBER

A desperate incoherent scrawl came from the Regent forwarded to me by the Duke of Kent. I am now severely alarmed for my poor old friend and dread his future.

The in-laws came to lunch; they were affectionate to me but abused Alan, his extravagances and eccentricities. He has gone with his old momma to York to see his dark brother Francis who has had an accident – on course to travel for a few hours with his ageing ma! He asked me to spend New Year's Eve with him and I promised to do so, and kept myself free. At eight o'clock he rang up that he had missed his train – probably purposely, a manoeuvre engineered by Mrs Boyd. And the prospect of a sweet and lonely New Year's Eve faced me: I was not unhappy. But Vsevolod of Russia rang up and insisted on coming here bringing Maimie, Natasha Bagration and Arthur Leveson,[1] a handsome debonair sailor who is in love with her. I had little food in the house, having said I should be out. However they arrived laden with caviar, champagne and a turkey, and we had a gay *tovarisch*[2] evening half-looking after ourselves. The Crown Prince went to the Horlickses.[3] I have hardly seen him and am quietly, tactfully freezing him off.

Sent off long letter to the Regent, my child, and to Peter.

I feel somehow that the New Year will benefit me and bring *soulagement*.[4] A year ago tonight I was with Peter in Cairo.

---

1 Arthur Edmund Leveson (1908–81) came from a distinguished naval family; his father was Admiral Sir Arthur Leveson, who from 1922 to 1925 commanded the China Station.

2 Comradely.

3 James Nockell Horlick (1886–1972) succeeded his nephew as 4th Bt in 1958. He had met King Alexander of Greece while serving in Salonika in the Great War. Before that war he had played some first-class cricket; from 1923 to 1929 he was Conservative MP for Gloucester, and later became a distinguished breeder of rhododendrons. He married, in 1909, Flora McDonald Martin (1888–1955).

4 Relaxation.

1942

The New Year began with a bang: a horrid little letter from Honor asking that I bring an action against her for divorce. Probably I shall do so, and possibly it is the wiser course; but I shall play for delay. I should like to be rid of the whole business, the letter upset me, and then I walked to Bond Street and *en route* dropped a tortoiseshell and piquet box given me by my mother-in-law at Christmas. I was taking it to be repaired. I hate tortoiseshell and piquet and was horrified to learn that it cost £28! I would sell it for ten bob! Depressing adventure . . .

I have decided not to answer Honor for about a week – not until four things have happened will I take action:

I.   Income tax paid
II. My appointment to the Air Ministry[1] announced – if it is
III. Wavell's [appointment] made public
IV. and, if possible, the departure of the Greeks.

Lunched with Garrett Moore who is stupid, tactless but nice.

Oh! Where am I drifting? I am an ill-natured, wicked old thing; yet I have kept my head fairly well over the horrid debacle. I must go carefully from now on.

Reading Michael Sadleir's[2] fascinating *Trollope*. Mrs Trollope[3] must have been an outstanding woman and I admire her more than anybody.

Until now (and it is 5.26 p.m.) I have avoided the Crown Prince. I am killing the intimacy fast. Also I am irritated with the King of Greece – bored with the lot;

1 This is the first mention of this possibility. Either Harold Balfour had suggested Channon might be his parliamentary private secretary, or had even raised his hopes of a junior ministerial job there.
2 Michael Thomas Harvey Sadler (1888–1957) varied the spelling of his surname to differentiate himself from his father. He spent most of his working life with the publisher Constable and Co., ending up as Chairman in 1954. His best-known work was the 1940 novel *Fanny by Gaslight*: his two books on Trollope, the first a commentary and the second a bibliography, were published in 1927 and 1928.
3 Frances Milton (1779–1863) wrote over a hundred books under her married name, Frances Trollope, many of them novels, and is prized by some modern critics for her work detailing the lives of the industrial working classes.

but it would be foolish and short-sighted to break with them completely. I doubt whether they will ever be restored; yet I hope so.

I must write a book this year somehow. The honours list this year is a very pedestrian affair; it is the first time for years that I didn't happen to have my finger in it, too. A few KBEs for soldiers and dull industrial people. Billy Rootes[1] is now Sir William!

At six the Crown Prince came and stayed until 8.20, and as I didn't invite him to dine he had to leave! But he came back with Alan at eleven and they remained chatting with my dinner party until 1 a.m. Dined: Jay Llewellin; Garrett Moore – to whom we were particularly pleasant and discreet since he transmits everything to Oliver Lyttelton in Cairo; and Harold B[alfour]. Bridge, burgundy, boredom and eventually bed.

FRIDAY 2ND JANUARY

Slept like a child, deeply, druggedly, and woke to no unwelcome news. Wrote letters and tidied up my affairs generally and then went for a walk, but not before Patsy L[ennox]-B[oyd] had rang up frantically to inquire the whereabouts of her semi-mad husband. Alan, apparently, had slept at the Dorchester and gone out early without saying 'Good morning'! ... and she feared he was lost. He is becoming increasingly eccentric and reminds me slightly of Edward Marjoribanks. I suspect that thwarted sex is at the bottom of it.

Rab rang me up gaily and affectionately: he has just returned to London after a fortnight at Stanstead. He drives down to Coppins this afternoon to dine and sleep. The Kents rely upon his judgement and advice and they are extremely perturbed about recent attacks, personal and political, on the Regent.

Peter Loxley tells me that there is now no doubt but that Wavell will be put in Supreme Command in the Far East; his headquarters, however, are in doubt.

The Crown Prince rang up repeatedly but I pretended to be out. I must have some sleep and independence. I am unloading him quickly now: a fast feverish friendship rarely survives its furious beginnings and nothing cools more quickly than intimacy once blown upon.

SATURDAY 3RD JANUARY

Slept late and there were no horrors on my breakfast tray. Later I went through my possessions, wine, store-cupboard etc. and now at noon I have nothing to do, which is delightful. I am becoming antisocial, anti-royal, mean, avaricious and live from day to day *sans* much *but*.[2] But no letter yet from Peter; the last

---

1 William Rootes, the industrialist. See entry for 3 February 1939 and footnote. He had played a leading role in the reanimation of Coventry after the Blitz.
2 Without much aim in life.

was on December 15th. I am always half-ill and frequently irritable – *que faire*? My grievances against the Diodach are not great, yet they are tangible: he bores me to distraction; he keeps me up at night; he says tactless things by repeating ill-natured and unimportant remarks; he is a noodle; he has destroyed my very ancient friendship with the King of Greece. Decidedly *le jeu ne vaut pas la chandelle* . . . . But if only he would go to the US before we become definitely hostile to each other I would be infinitely relieved!! So far I have behaved abominably! He telephones four or five times a day and I ignore the messages but am fairly friendly when we meet. He behaves well and his pathetic devotion touches me and makes me ashamed.

I have been in a fiendish mood all day: angry, foaming and probably liverish. Everything conspired to plague me . . . . Alan, wildly impulsive as ever, said he could come here before seven and never turned up. I took umbrage . . . after dinner the Crown Prince rang up and persuaded me to go around to Vsevolod where we passed a merry hour and I was nice, but distant to HRH. We turned on the wireless and heard of Wavell's appointment now made public. He is to have Supreme Command. What a wonderful war Peter will – and has – had [*sic*]! Or will he now be discarded? It is possible. The CP walked me home in the rain, accompanied me to the door; but I didn't ask him in. Bed by 12.30 but found a sweet letter of apology from Alan.

SUNDAY 4TH JANUARY

Slept late; dreamed of H[onor]. Harold has gone down to Leeds [Castle] to fish. I am going to Kelvedon. Recovered my lost temper and had a rapturous reconciliation with Alan whom I adore more than anyone. He, the Crown Prince, Maimie, Vsevolod and I drove down to Kelvedon where we went for a walk and had tea. Then they left me to my loneliness and I read Saint-Simon[1] and am going early to bed.

The beauty, silence and sadness of this place are heartbreaking. I wrote to Honor, thought of the miserable mistakes I made. Divorce this year is inevitable, I fear.

MONDAY 5TH JANUARY

Drove up in the cold. An inconclusive report has come in about Woodman's wife, who seems to have abandoned hope of ever regaining her husband. I am veering towards a divorce now, but Alan . . . . counsels delay. And procrastinate I shall.

---

1 Louis de Rouvroy, duc de Saint-Simon (1675–1755), was a soldier and diplomat renowned for his memoirs.

I felt invigorated and was in high spirits for our most *recherché* dinner party, which was a huge success, one of the most *réussi* dinner parties I had ever given. The *clou*[1] was Stewart Menzies[2] who is 'C', head of the entire Secret Service. He is an old acquaintance and greeted me warmly; the others were Harold; Peter Loxley; Air Vice Marshal Medhurst,[3] who is the Head of Air Intelligence. Wine and conversation flowed . . . and I found Stewart sympathetic and sensible and very pro the Regent. I had feared otherwise. He is balanced and Conservative in his outlook. As we were finishing dinner Bill Mabane arrived, accompanied by Mr Attlee, who is always pleasant in society! Much talk and badinage about [Reginald] Fletcher's peerage. He is to be called Lord Windermere[4] and I said I should be 'Lord Windermere's fan'! etc.[5] Then I sat on a sofa for an hour with 'C', and discussed the Balkan dynasties etc. He was impressed. Bridge, Bill Mabane and I playing against the Lord Privy Seal [Attlee] and Harold. We won. The Acting P[rime] M[inister] left about 1 a.m. saying that he was going back to sleep in his 'dugout' and to read the latest telegrams, which ought by now to be arriving from the USA. 'Winston will be getting up again from his Washington nap,' he laughed. He was extraordinarily amiable and liked the orchids that I had brought up from Kelvedon. I seized the occasion to put a few nails in Queen Mignonne's [Marie] coffin.

An enchanting evening.

TUESDAY 6TH JANUARY

Woke feeling like death after the excitements – and drink? – of last night . . . Even Mr Attlee had seemed a bit gay . . . Alan soon fetched me and we went to see Kay Norton's enchanting flat at 8a Hobart Place. It wasn't a flat but a Charles II house with a large garden behind St Peter's Church. It would make, and no doubt has often been, an enchanting and convenient love box. I feel somehow that I shall one day live there – and with? I hope with 6d. The place has immense charm and could be made absolutely ideal.

---

1 In this context he means the central figure at the dinner party.
2 Stewart Graham Menzies (1890–1968) was head of the Secret Intelligence Service (MI6) from 1939 to 1952. He won the DSO at the first Battle of Ypres in 1914 and was so seriously wounded at the Second Battle of Ypres in 1915 that he was honourably discharged from combat duties. He joined military intelligence following this and, after the war, the Secret Intelligence Service.
3 Charles Edward Hastings Medhurst (1896–1954) fought in the Royal Flying Corps in the Great War and from 1941 to 1942 was Assistant Chief of the Air Staff. By the end of the war he had the Middle East Command for the RAF. He retired in 1950 in the rank of air chief marshal.
4 Sadly, he was called Lord Winster. See footnote for 1 December 1941.
5 An allusion to Oscar Wilde's play of 1892, *Lady Windermere's Fan*.

Alan tells me that Honor is coming to London on Friday and is to stay the night. Very probably we shall meet to discuss the divorce which I am increasingly inclined to look upon as inevitable.

Mr Stephens of Coutts bank telephoned and asked me to call upon him tomorrow to arrange for the investment of the Regent's fortune: I shall advise half in industrials half in govt securities. The two Elvedens, the Crown Prince, and Maimie Pavlovsky dined; later we were joined by Harold, and Vsevolod – dressed as a fire-watcher and in high spirits. Harold had dined at the Apéritif where he saw Randolph – that fiend! – with his wife, Pam, who looked rapturous. Randolph arrived back today by plane . . . . They left Gibraltar this morning. I gather that the *Valiant* and *Warspite*[1] were recently badly damaged in Alexandria harbour by an Italian submarine. Have we any fleet left?

Everything is Russian now, even the arctic weather.

WEDNESDAY 7TH JANUARY

Arthur Elveden came to see me and remained for an hour whilst we discussed Honor and her vagaries and *amours*[2] . . . he is firmly, determinedly on my side and says that nothing will ever induce him to meet Woodman, and he doesn't care to see her. He advised me not to divorce her; to play for time. He is probably right. Then I went to 19 Bentinck Street to see Alice Harding and her tiny daughter who is to be called Emily Sophia! Alice herself looked well. She is having financial difficulties and is now suddenly confronted with a demand for [an] extra £17,000 in income tax. Her mad marriage to an uninteresting Englishman is costing her – and her children incidentally – millions. I ordered her oysters at Buck's for her dinner and then sauntered in the icy cold to Coutts bank where I had an hour with Mr Stephens, the manager, as we discussed the ex-Regent's financial affairs. I recommended several investments. He has in all accounts probably over £100,000 – in addition he has a fortune in jewels and pictures.

What a jam I am in about the future and the divorce . . .

Lunched at Pastori's with David Lloyd[3] and his fiancée Lady Jean Ogilvy, and Alan. David is a gay attractive satyr and not much in love: she is an intelligent alert girl, dark and pleasing. Rather impulsively I offered them the use of No. 5 for their wedding reception on January 24th; but I foresee difficulties and regret my

---

1 HMS *Valiant* was damaged by mines placed by Italian frogmen; she was repaired and survived the war. HMS *Warspite* had been damaged months earlier in the Battle of Crete. She too was repaired and survived the war.

2 Love affairs.

3 Alexander David Frederick Lloyd (1912–85) succeeded his father as 2nd Baron Lloyd in 1941. He served in junior posts in both the Churchill and Eden administrations in the 1950s. He married, in 1942, Victoria Jean Marjorie Mabell Ogilvy (1918–2004), Lady Jean by courtesy, daughter of the 12th Earl of Airlie (see Vol. I, entry for 14 February 1936 and footnote).

rashness as the Airlies will obviously oppose such a gesture. I have always openly be[en] rude to Airlie who is a conceited ass – or rather hidalgo. Jim Thomas telephoned suggesting that we dined together tonight, and I hypocritically told him how brilliant I thought Anthony Eden's rather absurd broadcast was![1]

THURSDAY 8TH JANUARY

Went with Alan to the House where the war was discussed: the govt had another bad day. Without Winston it would not last a week; and I wonder whether he will be able to save it? Randolph was mooching about but did not speak .... Attlee was dull and could not hold the House; later I saw him surrounded by Conservatives in the Smoking Room. He is usually now in their company. Is he about to 'cross the floor'? I came down to give my mother-in-law lunch and we discussed the problem of divorce – the eternal problem. She is set dead against it and entertains no illusions about Honor. As we were talking, Honor rang up rather jauntily and suggested meeting me tomorrow; luckily I am going to Coppins and I used that as an excuse. Lady Iveagh sat on the sofa winking at me in a conspiratorial way as I chatted with her daughter!! who of course, could not guess that her mother was there. I hated the whole horrid deception ... Later I walked back to the House as much for the air as to hear Anthony, who was utterly deplorable! He wound up so amateurishly that many members got up and left the Chamber; others began to whisper ... what is England coming to?

Teenie Cazalet told me of his former days of constant bombing in Malta, of his peep at Tobruk, his trip to Cairo. Malta is bombed every day now.

At the House I went into Rab's room where on his desk lay a note addressed to Mark Patrick[2] who is a friend of his. An hour later I read that he had died very suddenly at the age of 48. I wonder why? He was pompous, a fool and an Edenite; but one could not help liking him. I succeeded him at the FO in 1938 and he was always rather jealous but polite, well-mannered and friendly. Perhaps I shall die soon: my mother-in-law is 60, she tells me, born in 1882.[3] She was affectionate but she is ageing.

Early to bed: I am going now and taking two sleeping pills.

FRIDAY 9TH JANUARY

Honor rang up in a reasonable mood, talked for an hour and reduced me to practically pulp. I vomited afterwards and had hysterics ...

---

1 On 4 January Eden broadcast on the BBC about his meeting with Stalin.
2 Colin Mark Patrick (1893–1942) was Conservative MP for Tavistock from 1931 until his death.
3 Lady Iveagh was born on 22 July 1881.

Seventeen MPs dined last night at the Dorchester, collected by Erskine-Hill, who sees himself as a sort of Lord Younger.[1] Anthony Eden was present and was grave and upset by what he was told. Every MP present told him that the government was doomed and that it was no use the PM coming back and making one of his magical speeches. It would serve no purpose as the govt must be reformed, and that soon.

Later at Coppins.

Drove here in the icy cold and arrived as the blackout fell – the Duchess was alone and looked less glamorous than usual; the baby is beginning to show. We chatted for an hour very intimately and affectionately, first of Paul and Olga and then of Honor, whom she admitted to always disliking! She tells me she hears frequently from her mother languishing still at Athens. Apparently the Crown Princess of Sweden,[2] who acts as postmistress to all the royalties in Europe, forwards the letters and news. She reported to the Duchess that all the ex-Regent's magnificent possessions both at Brdo and Belgrade have been carefully preserved and are intact. When the Duke [of Kent] arrived I saw at once that he was in an exceptionally amiable mood. We all abused Queen Marie and little King Peter, who has had the audacity and cheek and ingratitude to ask to be relieved of that old ruffian, General Simović, who was responsible for the *coup d'état*! The boy is an ass . . . Excellent dinner *à trois*. Then I played backgammon with the Duchess and after she went to bed I had two hours' confidential conversation with the Duke. I advised him to consult Walter Moyne and ask his help on the plight of the Regent. (Rab has already appealed with some success to Bobbety Cranborne.) He agreed to do so. Today the Duke went to Coutts's bank and in Mr Stephens' presence opened the Regent's boxes, which were disappointingly poor in contents. However there were a few things, including the famous diamond garter star which I gave him. (It came originally from the Somerset family who sold it to the Cadogans. Grace Curzon bought it from Lady Cadogan for Lord Curzon. I bought it in 1939.) Then the Duke proceeded to abuse the King and Queen: says that they are inept, ineffectual and inexpert and had no influence in Whitehall, Westminster or anywhere. They never answer letters or messages and are treacherous friends[3] and hopelessly lazy. The Queen's ladies-in-waiting

1 George Younger (1851–1929) ran the Scottish brewery that bears his family name. He was Conservative MP for Ayr Burghs from 1906 to 1922 and the following year was raised to the peerage as 1st Viscount Younger of Leckie. He was Chairman of the Conservative Party from 1918 to 1923, raised and contributed a great deal of money to the party, and was a considerable force within it until his death.

2 Formerly Lady Louise Mountbatten: see Vol. I, entry for 29 June 1923 and footnote. She was able to convey news to and from royal families on different sides during the war because she was related to several of them and Sweden was neutral.

3 The Duke was especially angry that the King and Queen, doubtless on Churchill's advice, refused to communicate with Prince Paul of Yugoslavia, a once genuinely close friend.

are terrified of her! How the Duke hates them, but I suspect jealousy is at the back of him. I was riveted but nearly fell asleep – and now at 1.40 a.m. (tomorrow as it were) I am at last going to bed.

SATURDAY 10TH JANUARY

The Duke brought little Prince Edward[1] to my bedroom whilst I was shaving. He is a dear, rather pretty, rather petulant, little boy – no longer a baby. And I thought of my remote Paul, born the same day. He is less good-looking but more intelligent, taller and better-mannered than Prince Edward. I listened nostalgically to the patter and chatter which Alexandra made as she rushed about the house and I noticed in the guestbook that I have been the Kents' most frequent guest.

Drove up to London before luncheon and am half-frozen and wretched.

It is announced that Duff Cooper is soon returning from Singapore. His appointment has come to an end; and I wonder what cushy job Winston will invent [for] or allot him. I hope he gets away before the Japs capture Singapore where he has been a flop.

I am in the very depths of depression and cold. Refused to dine with the Crown Prince and the others; dined in instead with Harold and Jay.

Long talk yesterday with Rab, who is helping us over the Regent and his difficulties. Rab added that my salon was undoubtedly the first in London now and he congratulated me.

SUNDAY 11TH JANUARY

Slept for eleven hours. The Crown Prince rang me early and fetched me about one o'clock and I walked with him to Claridge's, where he gave us an excellent lunch: Maimie, Natasha Bagration – and her young man whom she calls 'The Pie', his real name being Arthur Leveson, and Prince Philip of Greece, an absolute 'charmer' aged only 20. He is about the best-looking boy I have ever seen, fair, a touch languid but with good manners. No wonder that he has been selected as the Prince Consort of the future! He is much improved and more mature than he was in Athens last winter. Dickie Mountbatten, his uncle, and Noël Coward, the Kents etc., see much of him!! I was impressed and attracted. Later I took Patsy for a drive in the Park; she is improving and was sweet and sensible.

The Japs have begun their assault on the Dutch East Indies. Where will Wavell establish his headquarters? Peter has not again cabled: he may even now be *en route* for Singapore, and will he contact and make allies of the Coopers?

---

1 Prince Edward (b.1935) succeeded his father as Duke of Kent in 1942.

Reluctantly (like Byron in his middle age I have taken to avarice)[1] gave dinner at the Ritz to the same collection of people who lunched with the Crown Prince at Claridge's. It cost me £7 15s and I was enraged, especially as Harold Balfour and Llewellin, my no longer so very 'little ministers', were anxious to entertain me.

This may be an anxious and full week.

MONDAY 12TH JANUARY

Alan is behaving badly, like a selfish lunatic, saved, however, as always by his colossal charm. He promised Patsy to be back from Bedfordshire yesterday before five; he turned up at home not having been able to tear himself away from his mother's siren charms! This morning he was off to see her again before five o'clock and came back only at two to take Patsy by car to Elveden. They looked in on me for a moment at 3.10 and she looked cold and cross – I don't wonder – I had a sort of premonition that they would have an accident on their way to Elveden since he drives atrociously.

A very cold and lonely day. I thought out a speech for tomorrow and [illegible] and sulked the whole day. The Duchess of Kent rang me early; at long last she had had a Xmas cable from Princess Olga, but only yesterday.

This week I must meet the Iveaghs and a decision must be agreed upon . . . . And I should like to know Peter's plans before I agree definitely to any course of action.

Dined in alone with Harold, who quite unintentionally offended me deeply: lies never hurt me; it is only the truth.

Prince Philip told me yesterday that Billy Hartington (a weak boy, really) has broken off his engagement to Sarah Norton.[2] 'Moucher' Devonshire[3] has won – for months she has worked against the projected marriage and she is in the right and successful.

TUESDAY 13TH JANUARY

All day in the cold of Southend, Russian trains, wails, shuntings, speech and interviews. How much suffering and unhappiness there is in the world . . .

Arrived back at 8:30 to find four messages from the Crown Prince asking me to ring him. I was too exhausted to do so – He came here at 10.30 and stayed until midnight. Dined with Peter Loxley before – he is a sweetie but becoming becalmed and a bore. Harold perhaps aware of his unfortunate shaft of last night was particularly sweet.

1 Presumably a joke; Byron died at 36.
2 Sarah Kathleen Elinor Norton (1920–2013) was the daughter of the 6th Baron Grantley and Jean Norton (qqv). She married the 3rd Viscount Astor in 1945.
3 Wife of the 10th Duke and mother of the Marquess of Hartington (qqv).

A tiresome letter that the Kelvedon gates are to be requisitioned: they were very expensive and I shall regret them. All iron is being collected and the first drive is to be made in Essex. The gates are very splendid, black with fasces with gilt heads and my monogram on shields ...

WEDNESDAY 14TH JANUARY

Woke feeling *congestionné* but naked. It is v cold. All last winter I was in sunlit lands and so escaped the bitterness of an English winter: now I suffer and shiver.

Letters for my mother and me, a brief one from Lord Iveagh, in which he declares that he has written firmly to Honor that he will not tolerate a divorce. So that is that! And the matter is again in abeyance; I am relieved but I shall know no peace until it is settled and we are finally separated.

Harold thinks that Anthony Eden may go to the US either as Ambassador or on a special permanent mission; in that case perhaps [Archie] Sinclair will succeed him at the Foreign Office.

I cannot get warm; I shiver and shake from the extreme cold. Did little; wrote my Southend letters, walked in the snow which reminded me of my American childhood, to the Ritz where I gave luncheon to Lady Kemsley, Maimie and Vsevolod . . . and walked back. Harold has had much publicity today after his speech. He rang up several times and has been so sweet and gentle these past two days: I never liked him more.

I have gleaned that the PM has not yet left the American Continent as I happen to know that Anthony Eden spoke to him on the telephone last night – whether he was still at Washington, or in Newfoundland or even Iceland, I don't know. I also heard that the Germans have concentrated all their available submarines on the Atlantic coast and they are lying in wait for the *Duke of York* in the hope of torpedoing her and sinking the Prime Minister. Another Kitchener. Perhaps he will after all fly back.

THURSDAY 15TH JANUARY

Can nothing pleasant ever happen to me? Life seems a rosary of horrid disappointments ...

Lady Airlie,[1] looking extremely young, her daughter Jean, and David Lloyd lunched here: all charming. And I spent the afternoon shopping with David who somewhat surprised me by his outspokenness about his bride whom he dismissed as being stupid but in love with him; and of his determination to make the marriage a success ... we had a long talk; I don't think the marriage will really work out

---

1 Lady Alexandra Coke (1891–1984), daughter of the 3rd Earl of Leicester, married the 12th Earl of Airlie in 1917.*

well? . . . David hates Randolph Churchill more than any human being (as I do); he was v tiresome, turbulent and difficult in Cairo and generally unpopular. His own regiment refused to have him back! . . . . I left David at Buck's Club, where it took us thirty minutes to get a cup of tea, and came home. Harold soon arrived: he has made yet another speech and is again on the wireless tonight . . . . I refused several invitations to dine and am alone . . . I am always alone. Harold is hardening but he is being very sweet.

FRIDAY 16TH JANUARY

A muddled morning of crossed messages . . . I was undecided and at last decided to go to Leeds [Castle], thus chucking both Harold and Jay Llewellin with whom I was to dine . . . Made very complicated plans, walked to Buck's Club, and on the way ordered twill shirts in order to use my coupons. Actually I had masses of clothes. At Buck's I awaited the Crown Prince who was late but charming: we are very friendly but I have snapped the cord. He is off to Madresfield for the long weekend. Lunched at home with Elizabeth Elveden and her divine sensitive beautiful boy Benjamin, who is not yet 5, and is already witty and fascinating. Although prettier than Paul ever was, he reminds me of him nonetheless. He still smells like a baby. Elizabeth was taking him to Pyrford to stay with the Iveaghs. They have rather dropped me since the divorce question recently arose. Have I committed a gaffe? I don't know.

After lunch I rushed to the Reform Club to find Herlihy, who is one of my best-informed agents: I found him closeted with Clem Davies, always an intriguer, but an honest, good-intentioned one. Herlihy says that the govt will be radically reconstructed within the next ten days. He thinks that Winston will be coming back in about a week's time (I didn't tell him that he is due tomorrow). Herlihy showed me a copy of a memorandum which is being sent to the PM by a group of his well-wishers: it is a weak non-constructive document and left-wing in spirit. It emanates from 'Glamour' certainly . . . it will be released to the press tonight.

I drove to Leeds in the icy cold; there were Olive and Adrian Baillie, my hosts, who are both ailing, her second daughter Susan Winn.[1] An enchanting, gay girl of 18 with wide grey laughing eyes. She is by far the most fascinating young female that I have ever known and I am already rather in love with her, as is Billy Ednam,[2] also here . . . . Geoffrey Lloyd is as usual here. I was gay, witty and in high spirits: this comes from not eating last night. One should rest one's 'senses' occasionally.

The old Duke of Connaught is at last dead, aged 91. He was handsome, amiable, courtly, stupid and inclined to attach too much importance to etiquette and

---

1 Susan Mary Sheila Winn (1923–2011) married in 1946 Geoffrey Denis Erskine Russell (1921–2011), who succeeded his father as 4th Baron Ampthill in 1973. They divorced in 1971.
2 Viscount Ednam (qv).

military detail, such as buttons and decorations. I used to meet him at luncheon parties long ago at Lady Essex's[1] house – in the early '20's. Of recent years he has been semi-gaga and ailing. I wish that my child had seen him – I could easily have arranged such a meeting – as it would have been a link with time since the old Duke sat on Wellington's knee.[2]

SATURDAY 17TH JANUARY

Winston is due back today by air . . .

A lazy day. I walked on the ice all around the castle on the moat: others skated . . . . Did nothing but read Trollope.

Later; the Prime Minister arrived by air, accompanied by Beaverbrook, Dudley Pound and Portal, and they had a sensational and warm welcome; but the newspapers hint of political unrest and the necessity for reconstruction.

SUNDAY 18TH JANUARY

The newspapers splash the Prime Minister's return and his rapturously warm welcome . . . Everyone here at Leeds is cold and has one and I had decided to go up to London after luncheon. Alan L-B rang me up to say that he couldn't possibly leave his mother tonight as she has a cold!! The old shrew! So I am carted; having arranged my plans accordingly I am justifiably annoyed. Alan never keeps an appointment and is always unpunctual and inconsiderate. I think that he is going mad.

Later – Drove up to London; the countryside looked like Russia. I brought dark young Vaughan[3] with me. He is in the Welsh Guards. Here I did a bit of telephoning and am reliably informed that the PM has decided to defy his critics and that he is determined not to make any sensational changes. He will face the House on Monday with the brief statement that he has not yet had time to prepare a review nor present his case to the House. I smell a political crisis and possibly a Churchillian victory. No new developments before next weekend.

Now shall I meet Honor on Wednesday next or ask her to postpone the meeting?

Harold v friendly and affectionate: so that is all right! I feared that he might be annoyed about Friday night. He didn't go to Paddington to meet the PM but

---

1 Adele Beach Grant (1866–1922), heiress to a New York engineering fortune, married in 1893 George Devereux de Vere Capell (1857–1916), 7th Earl of Essex. After Essex's death she was the mistress of the Duke of Connaught, and they were briefly engaged.
2 This is just possible: the Iron Duke died when Connaught was two years and four months old, and was regularly in the society of Queen Victoria.
3 John David Malet Vaughan (1918–2014) was Lord Vaughan by courtesy until 1963, when he succeeded his father as 8th Earl of Lisburne. He had been staying at Leeds Castle for the weekend.

Jay did. Apparently the PM praised Harold in a bantering spirit to Beaverbrook all the way across the Atlantic, found there wouldn't have been a clipper to bring him if it hadn't been for Balfour etc. All this Max repeated magnanimously enough to Harold today. Jay has gone down to spend the night at Cherkley with Max.

All my agents report that the Prime Minister will defy, or at least stall his critics by playing for time; he will ask the indulgence of the House and plead pressure of work, etc. before making an important statement. A wise course. Probably he is unaware of the extent of the prevailing anxiety in political circles.

Monday 19th January

Nothing this morning of interest. I slept late; walked to Prunier's where I lunched with Geoffrey Harrison and Nicholas Lawford, both ever charming. Then I took Nicholas to the RAC for a sunbath. He was amusing about the FO; said that Molotov had to tick off Anthony on his arrival in Moscow about his hat. '*À Moscou, Excellence, on ne porte pas la casquette de fourrure blanche.*'[1]

Tuesday 20th January

Still no news of the Iveaghs: are they avoiding me, am I a disgrace, or are they, as so often has happened in the past, just absorbed in their own lives, and ageing? . . . Walked to the House with Alan and we stopped to buy a black tie because of the mourning of the Duke of Connaught. At the House the Prime Minister arrived and was given a cheer, barely could his welcome be called enthusiastic – civil perhaps. And I watched the whips below. He looked fat and cross and when he rose to answer his Questions it was obvious that he was displeased with his reception and that he had a cold, since his voice was husky. Such is the return of the great hero and I was almost sorry for him; but it is perhaps well that his natural and growing arrogance should be dampened. The House took his suggestion for a broadcast of his speech, which he has announced that he will make next Tuesday, ungraciously; indeed, members were querulous but I remembered Rab's words last night when he warned us that Churchill is the greatest asset the Conservative Party had and we had best exploit it – not antagonise it. Rab said many wise things: how impossible it is for him to co-operate with Winston; how much he really dislikes Anthony Eden whom he considers 'absolutely ruthless' and 'bad with ambassadors' and 'not a Conservative' etc. Alan and Harold and I agreed with much that he said whilst the Crown Prince, impressed, listened silent and spellbound.

Alan and I went to Cameo Corner and spent too much money buying a Fabergé silver cigarette case for David Lloyd's wedding present; and other things. I bought a pair of platinum and diamond links for Vsevolod who is 28 years old

---

1 'In Moscow, Your Excellency, you don't wear a white fur hat.'

today. Then home in the still-numbing bitter cold. I was to have gone to Vsevolod's cocktail party but I could not face going out again and put my feet up and tried to get warm, and soon fell asleep, only to be awakened by the arrival of Michael Duff from North Weald. He gave me amusing gossip. The telephone kept ringing with different invitations to dine and I finally went to Claridge's and dined alone at the corner royal table with the Crown Prince, who was v sweet and gentle and really divine. He ate oysters and carrots: I had oysters, burgundy and roebuck. The restaurant was crowded; indeed all London seemed to be there. I left at eleven and trudged through the snow to the Dorchester to keep an assignation with Alan who was at his very best! I stayed too late with him.

Winston is in a defiant mood and declared in the House that he would put down a vote of confidence in the govt next week. He will win, but it will not be an altogether secure victory.

WEDNESDAY 21ST JANUARY

Snow and slush everywhere. Honor rang up in a cheerful mood and we chatted and decided not to lunch together today as she says that there is too much snow to come up. I am not surprised. After some hesitation I made an overture to the Iveaghs and asked them to lunch; they were already engaged, now I shall do nothing more for some time to come. I walked to the House. Winston bowed to the will of the members by withdrawing his motion for his speech to be broadcast direct – the feeling of the House was strongly against it; and in deciding not to challenge it, he acted wisely. It was better to placate Parliament on a small matter than to have a row on a minor issue. The boys – the naughty boys – have won a round! I talked to Randolph who was almost amiable; how I hate him, even more than I hate [blank].

The most hopeful individual incident since the war occurred today: the Archbishop of Canterbury has resigned. This aged, cruel prelate has done irreparable damage to the Church of England: narrow, snobbish to a fantastic degree, cold, calculating, political, vengeful, lazy, he has emptied the churches and alienated thousands of people. He has never been right on any issue and is hated by laymen and ecclesiastics alike. His evil face, thin lips, hard, small, terrible eyes, are enough to frighten an adult. Only his voice redeems him.[1]

Lunched at home as the House rose unexpectedly early . . . I am down and cold and disinterested. Jim Wedderburn said that he had heard from Harold that I have become a hypochondriac. I was enraged. Still no news of Peter and meanwhile the Dutch Indies are being increasingly bombarded. I have a queer dual-hunch: either he will soon return, may even now be *en route*, or that he will be killed or

---

1 Channon's loathing of Archbishop Lang dates back to the abdication: see Vol. I, entries for December 1936 *passim*.

captured. I am unhappy about him . . . The more I think about the resignation of the bigoted Archbishop the more I rejoice. If I were rich I should send a fat cheque as a contribution to some charity to celebrate this auspicious event. Hard, relentless, pompous he is a dreadful creature. He is, however, an able speaker and had dignity – the dignity of a Grand Inquisitor. The Prime Minister loathed him, Neville Chamberlain respected and consulted but disliked him; the royal family are divided about him. Queen Mary supported him, as do the present K[ing] and Q[ueen]. He often dined at large parties, particularly at Mrs Anthony James's[1] – to meet them; but the Kents and naturally the Duke of Windsor hated him. There was an old feud dating long before the abdication between the Archbishop and the then Prince of Wales. The Archbishop's reception of Perry Brownlow was almost unbelievably absurd and aggravating.[2] He has driven hundreds into the Roman Church and made maybe millions of agnostics.

The Crown Prince came for a drink and took me back to Claridge's to dine with him, the Vsevolods and Prince Peter of Greece, whom I found pleasant, simple and v French. He has the curious scientific interests of his Bonaparte relatives, is 32, madly in love with his unsuitable morganatic wife, eats only vegetables and fruit neither drinks nor smokes and looks 45. I don't really like him: he is un-royal . . . . I saw the King of Greece and Joyce [Brittain-Jones] waiting – like everyone else – for a taxi; but I pretended not to see them. Later I was sorry as Maimie told me how much Joyce liked me! The King is obviously jealous of my friendship with the Crown Prince!! Maimie, Vsevolod and I had to walk home in the bitter cold and snow: no taxis, not even buses.

At Claridge's I had a long conversation with Mrs Neville Chamberlain who almost fell into my arms. She looked well, in great good looks and rested. She seemed less vague and nervous and foolish . . . talked affectionately of Neville and of his fondness for me. She said that she would like to come to lunch here one day and meet some of his faithful admirers and I agreed to arrange it. And she suggested that I approach Keith Feiling,[3] who is writing Mr Chamberlain's official Life, and ask him, too, to dine, and give him local colour or rather atmosphere. I shall.

THURSDAY 22ND JANUARY

Didn't sleep for the cold and woke too early. Now I feel too ill to go to the House of Commons which is silly. A little line from Lady Iveagh, friendly and easy, but no word about anything important. So contact is re-established, if, indeed, it had ever

---

1 I have been unable to trace this lady.
2 See Vol. I, entry for 21 December 1936.
3 Keith Grahame Feiling (1884–1977) graduated in history at Oxford in 1906 and with the exception of his war service taught there until 1950, being Chichele Professor from 1946. His *Life of Neville Chamberlain* was published in 1946. He was knighted in 1958.

been broken. She says they have only twice been to London in ten days because of the snow and cold – all true.

I should like some word from the Far East, which is in flames. Every day the position there worsens. Jay Llewellin, who ought to know, told me yesterday that we shall soon lose Singapore.[1] A radio-ed photograph appeared of General Wavell in this morning's press. He is known as 'Supreme Allied C-in-C in the South-West Pacific'.

It is too cold to live! . . . However, one must lunch even if one doesn't love or live, and I trudged through the slushy snow to Soho where I joined the *ménage* Loxley for an excellent *déjeuner*[2] at the Escargot. She is pregnant and plain: I am to be godfather . . . then to the House of Commons to hear Harold wind up in the aerodrome defence debate which he did with ease, good humour and fluency. And I picked up the gossip. No. 10, now known as the Dixième Bureau,[3] is in a flap; the 1922 Committee sent an ultimatum, or at best, a strongly worded request, to the Prime Minister asking him not to insist upon a vote of confidence in the coming full-dress debate, as many Conservative members would be obliged by their consciences to accept the challenge. Many more might abstain. The PM was originally adamant but is now alarmed, yet he still refuses to reconstruct his govt. He may climb down but he is in an angry mood: messages rush to the Cabinet Rooms, 'the Annex'; the ineffectual whips are in a frenzy; and a crisis, no doubt chuckled over by the enemy, is at hand. I walked home. Geoffrey Lloyd rang me from Leeds Castle for the news, as he is in bed with a chill.

Dined in and talk turned onto the dullness of diaries, especially when nobodies chronicled their doings and dinner guests! I agreed – and smiled that little inward smile of mine which used to so delight the Regent.[4] Harold, Alan, Hector Bolitho and Helen Fitzgerald were the party. Everyone was excited politically. Alan told me that he had had a word at the Dorchester with Randolph Churchill who asked him sarcastically: 'How is the saviour of Yugoslavia?' – meaning me. Alan retorted: 'He had about as much chance of saving Serbia as did Duff when your father sent him to Singapore!' – a brilliant and loyal retort discourteous [*sic*].

FRIDAY 23RD JANUARY

The political clouds are gathering . . . nobody knows what to do or think.[5]

---

1 For once, Channon's intelligence was unfortunately correct. Singapore would be overrun by 15 February.
2 Luncheon.
3 In fact, he first makes this reference on 7 May 1940 (qv).
4 It is unclear how an inward smile can be visible, even to a Regent.
5 The disquiet about the impending loss of Singapore would lead to a confidence vote in the Commons and possibly the greatest threat to Churchill's leadership during the entire conflict.

Fritzi came to lunch: he has had three days' leave from his secret address. Very charming and improved. He asked the news of everyone: then we talked of Honor for whom he has a great affection. He thinks she is more than a little mad; is oversexed and strange but sweet *au fond*. Perhaps he is right.

The Duke of Connaught was buried today with four kings[1] at his bier. The Crown Prince told me that he was too gaga to speak, much less recognise him and King George [of Greece], when they drove over to Bagshot a few weeks ago.

The Japanese have landed at New Guinea. And still nothing has come from Peter. His mother writes to me for his news and his whereabouts. The news seems grave, indeed . . .

Drove with Alan (as usual nearly an hour late: Harold declares that Alan's inability to keep engagements, his mad rushing about, his unpunctuality have a sexual origin?) to dine with David Lloyd for his bachelor dinner at the Savoy . . . . Dinner was gay without being licentious or debauched and I enjoyed it. Went home – we had to walk in the snow – with Alan to the Savoy.[2]

Loelia Westminster got me out of the bath to talk on my telephone for half an hour: she is anxious for political news.

SATURDAY 24TH JANUARY   *FARNHAM PARK*

Woke *désoeuvré* . . . Harold Nicolson has sent me a revolting pamphlet written and circulated by the Yugoslav government. It attacks the ex-Regent [who] cannot defend himself; it is full of lies, innuendoes but there is an undercurrent of truth running through it which lends weight to it. I was so angry that I rang up the Duchess of Kent, who was indignant; she doesn't, however, want to see it. I am boiling with rage and indignation. As she and I were chatting Fritzi came in and I gave him £5! He goes back to Cumberland tomorrow.

David Lloyd rang up and asked me to take entire charge at his wedding today; it is amateurishly arranged, obviously, and I shall have to pull it together.

Harold has said this morning that he thinks the political clouds will pass, and that some compromise will be effected. The 1922 Cttee are frightened a bit by what they rashly did and show signs of withdrawing. He [Balfour] dined alone last night with the Chairman, the obese intriguing ambitious Erskine-Hill.

Wore a short coat, striped trousers and lots of *bijoux*, and walked to Buck's Club where I had a snack with (Charles) Rutland;[3] he is one of the more debauched dukes and looks dissipated. Then on to St Martin's-in-the-Fields where I ran, organised and directed the Lloyd wedding. Few preparations had been made but the church filled up quickly with the Scotch, the *jeunesse dorée* and the great.

---

1 George VI, Haakon of Norway, George II of Greece and Peter of Yugoslavia.
2 He probably means the Dorchester, where Lennox-Boyd was living.
3 Charles Manners, formerly the Marquess of Granby, since 1940 the 10th Duke of Rutland.*

Old Lady Airlie,[1] our gracious and *grande dame*, was particularly pleasant . . . I ushered people into all the right pews . . . . it was like [the] old days to open pews again and I tried to recall how often I have done it before.

Today's bridegroom, David, was in a gay but indifferent mood; it is obvious that he doesn't love her at all. She looked well, red and round like an apple and had only one attendant, her youngest brother James Ogilvy,[2] who looked sweet in a tiny kilt. Only the Amerys and the Shakespeares [Morrisons] represented the govt. As the cortège came down the aisle Lord Airlie stopped, advanced several paces to thank me for offering my house and generally helping. He was most cordial and courtly. He has certainly immense charm and looks . . . went on to Claridge's Hotel with Eric Duncannon. A large reception was held – no champagne, only dry martinis and whisky. Lady Lloyd, the mother, thanked me properly. It is just about a year since he died. I sat for half an hour with Portia Stanley, discussing the political situation which is involved and almost despairing. Then I came here with Harold Balfour to spend the weekend with the Kemsleys, who are as anti-Churchill as they dare to be! They deny it but all their remarks and comments reveal their disapproval of him. They are Chamberlain-minded still. At dinner there was a boring and terrific argument between Lady Ridley[3] who championed Winston (her first cousin), whilst Harold and Kemsley led the attack. I sat silent and distressed. Messages kept arriving and more and more discouraging news: the Japs advance; the Axis-offensive in Cyrenaica is becoming serious. And yet we are here, in the lap of luxury still, with excellent food, drink and footmen to serve it! . . . . Much bridge and I won!

I noticed at the wedding that David L[loyd] was carrying the attractive and *recherché* Faberge cigarette case which Alan and I gave him last night! I coveted it!

SUNDAY 25TH JANUARY   *FARNHAM PARK*

The balmy weather is a welcome change from the cruel cold of the past fortnight . . . I slept late and laughed a bit about the duel last night between the two old ladies who are evacuated here: Rosie, Lady Ridley, and that dark Mrs Elliot[4] whose large gay son, Gilbert[5] (a friend of Honor's) was killed in the Air Force as the result of an accident. The two ladies hate each other and both murmured disparaging remarks about the other. Lady Ridley is a *passée* hostess, but still extremely

---

1 Mabell, widow of the 11th Earl (see entry for 6 July 1939 and footnote).
2 James Donald Diarmid Ogilvy (b.1934) was the youngest child of the 12th Earl of Airlie.
3 Rosamond Cornelia Gwladys Guest (1877–1947) married in 1899 the 2nd Viscount Ridley (1874–1916). She was Churchill's first cousin, her mother having been Lord Randolph Churchill's sister.
4 Marguerita Barbey (1876–1955), daughter of Henry Isaac Barbey of New York. She married in 1910 Gilbert Compton Elliot (1871–1931).
5 Gilbert George Elliot (1911–40) was a pilot officer in the RAF and was killed during a training accident.

intelligent; Mrs Elliot is one of those four famous Barbey sisters, half-Swiss, half-American. I knew the other three well in my Paris days – comtesse de Jumilhac,[1] Mme de Neuflize,[2] and Mme de Pourtalés.[3] The Elliot girl, Cynthia, a dark beauty, is a prisoner in Germany.[4] I admired the broken-hearted mother, her only son[5] killed and her adored daughter in a German camp, and yet she is here and even gay . . .

Won nearly £20 at bridge and went to bed early, and reread with a feeling of nausea the revolting pamphlet written about my poor exiled Regent. I admit to being a touch shaken by it, but not seriously. It is the doing of that fat fiend Queen Mignonne.

I am nervously exhausted and have aged: I don't really care now whether I live or not; but I should like to see Paul and Peter again and to put my finances in order etc. . . . and I sat, dejected and shivering . . . . and dictating to Miss Sneath the while – a cable came from 'Master Fenton Coats', from Delhi. He had consorted with the [Duff] Coopers and liked them; he is still attached to Wavell and hopes soon to proceed – this means Java.

MONDAY 26TH JANUARY   *LONDON*

Here all is bare and barren – no letters, disturbing or otherwise; no messages. I rang up James Gunn and was rather cold to him as it is five months since he has given me a sitting for my portrait. Still no letter from Peter; where can he be?

The Times and other newspapers are genially pushing the Prime Minister to change his govt or get out! I cannot prophesy what he will do.

Immensely cheered by Peter's cable.[6] I went up to dress and later dined with Jay Llewellin at Claridge's . . . . He gave me an expensive dinner costing £6 and indeed I felt like a prima donna. We discussed the political developments, in which he takes not much interest as he says nothing will happen; wishes Winston were less arrogant and more placating . . . [Sir Stafford] Cripps was offered (either yesterday or today) the Ministry of Supply but under Beaverbrook who would remain as roving ambassador or Chief Director of Production, moving between Moscow, Washington and London. Cripps declined the offer, as he dislikes Max particularly since he was so overshadowed and snubbed by the mission to Moscow in the autumn.

1 Ethel Barbey (1873–1959) married as her second husband Odet Chapelle de Jumilhac (1887–1980).
2 Eva Barbey (1879–1959) married in 1903 André Poupart de Neuflize (1875–1949).
3 Hélène Catherine Barbey (1868–1945) married in 1891 Hermann de Pourtalés (1847–1904).
4 The future wife of Leslie Hore-Belisha was working as a Red Cross Nurse in a prisoner-of-war camp. (See entry for 10 July 1939 and footnote.)
5 In fact Mrs Elliot had another son, Alexander Henry Elliot (1913–86), who was serving in the Royal Artillery and ended the war in the rank of major.
6 Which seems to have arrived later in the day after the morning's disappointment.

Ann O'Neill rang up, to gossip: said that she would join the Japanese Red Cross if Anthony Eden became Prime Minister. I assured her that that was unlikely.

TUESDAY 27TH JANUARY

American troops have landed in Ulster, obviously with the intention of preventing a German occupation of Eire. Canada has given this country a present of £200,000,000. Big events are announced in simple sentences.

One of the great days in parliamentary history is over.[1] It was a splendid spectacle. I went early to try and get tickets for the Crown Prince, Prince Peter of Greece, Lady Kemsley and a sailor friend of Alan's, who implored my help. Throughout the question hour I cajoled, intrigued and at last – although half England was attempting to get in – put my four important protégés in the different galleries. A triumph. As I was rushing about I met the whole Churchill family coming in, Mrs Churchill, her hair grey now, was with Diana Sandys[2] and both were hatless. Clarissa was with her father, Jack Churchill;[3] Pam was not far behind and she pressed my hand in an affectionate conspiratorial way. Immediately behind them accompanied by his secretaries, was the Prime Minister. He had his angry full manner and seemed to charge into a rope barrier which he did not see; indeed, he very nearly toppled over; however this little incident was unnoticed even by the large crowd who was watching him, and he made a tiny detour and walked boldly towards the Lords' Chamber where we still sit . . . The great lobby was packed and having placed my guests I was unexpectedly given an extra ticket and I looked about for a friend to whom I could offer so precious a prize! And I saw old Coalbox[4] looking dark and angry. 'Have you a ticket?' I asked her. 'No – but I've been promised one. I've just seen Lady Kemsley go in. Why should she have a ticket and not me?"

'Well, she's the press and a peeress,' I answered, fingering my extra ticket.

'She was the queen of the appeasers and shouldn't be allowed in,' Sibyl snarled.

'For that argument, I suppose you would keep Maisky out? The Russians were the greatest appeasers of all,' I retorted and walked away. Lady Colefax didn't get her ticket!! The PM was greeted with perfunctory cheers but he quickly revealed that he was in high fettle, his voice was clear, his manner confident, if slightly whining. I watched the House; there was not an empty place, and I had to sit on the steps between Anthony Eden (who looked evil but well dressed) and Brendan Bracken, who was smiling, pale and friendly . . . . The PM's carefully prepared

---

1   This was the great debate on the conduct of the war. A motion of confidence was put down the following day and passed after two days' discussion by 464 votes to 1.
2   Churchill's daughter.
3   John Strange 'Jack' Spencer-Churchill (1880–1947), brother of Winston and father of John George and Clarissa Churchill (qqv).
4   Lady Colefax (qv).

and brilliant speech was like a vivid film; sentences were well constructed and he held, almost captivated the House, for ninety minutes or more. I was won over, as were many others. Opposition was dead, or so it seemed. Perhaps he was too long, or his finale failed since members left before he sat down, and when he did the atmosphere had chilled. A great parliamentary hour had passed into history . . . and the House emptied. The lobbies buzzed: one's first impressions were entirely favourable but I soon detected an undercurrent of hostility, and of criticism. He had mollified nobody and perhaps he knew it. I was sorry for him and impressed by the grandeur of the panorama he had painted. Members whispered in groups, intrigued in pairs . . . Erskine-Hill recanted and tried to insinuate himself in governmental good graces; Herbert Williams openly attacked Winston, who was sitting benignly in the Smoking Room, surrounded by members and his ogre of a son, Randolph . . . It is always a bad sign when the PM comes to the Smoking Room: he is uneasy, angling, or anxious. At 4.30 I left the Chamber, gossiped a bit with Nicholas Lawford, and peeped once more into the Smoking Room. The PM was drinking and his full neck bulged over his collar, Randolph was hanging on his father's words. And I knew that I hated them, hated them both! – and yet I shall not vote against the govt on Thursday, if vote there be. I don't think it would be in the interests of the country to do so. Why is the PM so unpopular, he a lifelong House of Commons man? I don't know; but it is a fact. Perhaps his intolerance, his rudeness, his arrogance and his unfailingly bad judgement are the reasons; yet his many magnificent qualities are obvious to all.

WEDNESDAY 28TH JANUARY

The second day of the dramatic debate is over . . . . The most colourful moment was an excursion by Randolph Churchill. He was quick, witty, and amusing and made the House laugh, although he added fuel to the fires of bitterness. As he insulted everybody, men old enough to be his father, I thought of the wise passage in the *Chartreuse de Parme*, in which Stendhal advises young men not to make enemies . . . Randolph made half a dozen today, and, of course, I was secretly pleased. For one second I thought that he was going to attack me. Earlier Alan and I sat in the Smoking Room together drinking; when he left I found myself opposite the Prime Minister, who was alone reading the *Manchester Guardian*. He looked up and smiled at me and I had a few words with him and conveyed that I would support him tomorrow: he became amiable and gracious at once, and we talked of Diana's [Cooper] homecoming and I suggested giving them a party; he half-intimated that he would come, if he could. Several people watched me maliciously and Harold twitted me later about 'being as one with Winston'! Yes: I have decided to go over to HMG as I see no alternative but my heart is not with them.

The 1922 Cttee was like a bear-garden today: packed and overexcited, member after member attacked the govt; the most vindictive was Lady Astor, who was as hysterical as usual; she said *inter alia* that Winston had drawn tracks [*sic*] around all of us! Winston remarked to Harold, whom he met in the Smoking Room, that the House is in an odd mood. Randolph had quite a rough passage!! He did.

THURSDAY 29TH JANUARY

An exhaustingly nervous day ... woke weary and old. My right foot gives me such pain: it is flat and surgeons say that they can do nothing at all as it is caused by a deformity. I went early to the House; it was crammed; but I could bear no more, the noise, the futility, excitement, detachment from reality, hypocrisy, or so it seemed, so I came away as soon as ever I could, and gave my father-in-law lunch here [Belgrave Square]. He had rung me early this morning. He stayed for two and a half hours and abused Honor and everything she ever did; later Lady Iveagh came in. They are firmly fixed against any divorce proceedings, and gently intimated that they would withdraw their support and friendship if I defied them. Worn out I went back to the House: the Lords' Chamber, which we continue to occupy, was packed. Half a hundred members had to stand; the Prime Minister was already speaking and he held the vast audience enthralled. He was conciliatory, tactful – and, of course, successful. I looked about me: George Gage was sitting next to Mrs Churchill; the Crown Prince came into the Distinguished Strangers' Gallery on a ticket I had procured for him; there were many peers; Ava Anderson was in the Peeresses' Gallery – she rarely misses a debate <u>now</u>. The PM spoke for forty-two minutes and sat down, after glancing at the clock. The Speaker, in his tired voice, put the question twice and called a division. The 'Aye' lobby, or more accurately, the 'Content' lobby, since it is in the Lords, was at once so crowded that many of the members were forced to remain and wait in the Chamber. The six-minute rule was suspended and it was a quarter of an hour at least before we filed through: one good bomb would have destroyed the whole democratic apparatus of this country but I shouldn't be surprised if Hitler thinks that the House of Commons is doing that on its own. When at last the figures were announced – 464 to 1 – there was a faint cheer and yet another one when the PM, bowing slightly, walked out triumphant, followed by his more ardent supporters ...

The Crown Prince, Alan and I adjourned to the RAC for [a] Turkish bath and rest. Alan told me that Basil Dufferin, who has behaved so badly to Maureen with his drinking and his many mistresses, apparently attacked both Honor and me! He has always been jealous of us. His face is covered with pimples, one eye is shut and he looks terrible .... The Crown Prince accompanied me to Belgrave Square and sofa-sat until I asked him to dine, which we did *à deux*. Suddenly I had little to say to him, but he told me too much of his secret past. Bed at 11.

As I undressed, before writing these final lines I thought of the govt victory and what it means. It is a triumph for Winston – there was no alternative and he knows it. Nevertheless, he is the most inspiring leader we have and the masses and the Americas both adore him . . . . I was fed-up, *énervé*,[1] and wish seriously and sincerely that I were a peer.

The outlook for the Allies is serious: the Libyan campaign is going the other way with General Rommel's[2] armies about to enter Benghazi; the Far East looks temporarily doomed; invasion is imminent. What then? Beaverbrook, meanwhile, is to be made Minister of Production and there are rumours that Cripps may reconsider his decision and accept the Ministry of Supply after all. He could be a damned bad one.

The Crown Prince remarked to me tonight 'You were formerly very intimate with the Queen, weren't you?' 'She has always been a friend of mine,' I retorted: I did not add that somebody, and I suspect Arthur Penn and Alec Hardinge, has long since made trouble between us.

Friday 30th January

A mixed, very mixed day. The day dawned and I woke ill and was irritable to Harold; found a chatty letter from Miles Lampson and so there is no ill feeling there, which I half-feared. I am conscious of my growing unpopularity, but as it is in a certain over-dynamic group, it will be transitory and I care little: Churchills, Birkenheads, etc. It will pass. Then I read that Guinness shares had slumped heavily (and this evening the fall continued dramatically, so every hour I am poorer). *The Times* administered a sharp rebuke to Randolph, which is decidedly on the asset side of the day! and I met Eddie Devonshire in the street who was charming; said he hadn't put me down for Pratt's but had given orders that I was to use the club as much as I liked; that I would be elected etc. next month – thus possibly that bogey has passed? I shall be more confident when I receive an official notification. Then to the Dorchester where I waited for Honor in the Lennox-Boyds' suite. I had a trickle of vanity, wished I were looking better, and did, indeed, take the step of having my hair cut and nails manicured this morning *en route*.

Eventually Honor did come, and she, too, had had her hair done and looked well; but she was fatter, and her face had hardened. There were lines in her neck and wrinkles on her face. She was fashionably, if unattractively dressed. She kissed me and was immediately friendly. We had a drink and ordered oysters and beer, and began to gossip gaily for a time before getting down to brass tacks – I told her of my communication yesterday with her father and of how adamant he was about any divorce proceedings. I promised her that I would reconsider the

---

1 Angry or irritated.
2 Johannes Erwin Eugen Rommel (1891–1944) was one of Germany's leading generals in the war, who fought successful campaigns in France and, initially, North Africa, and led the resistance to the Allied invasion of France in 1944. He had a reputation for chivalrous conduct towards his enemies that was rare in the German Nazi-era army. He was forced to commit suicide after his involvement in the plot of 20 July 1944 to assassinate Hitler.

situation at the end of three years' time, and then might bring a case against her for desertion. We talked for two hours and I think that I mollified her, won her over, even touched her: she did, however, make one threat: she said she would soon be obliged to alter her name by deed poll to Woodman: she said, with some truth, that life was becoming too difficult with ration cards etc. The confusion of two names was awkward for her. Perhaps it is. It would be a clever move on her part, almost fiendish, and, of course, cause scandal. No mention was once made of Paul – I watched and waited for her to speak of him. She told me that she was still £13,000 overdrawn which I didn't know . . . at length we parted and my emotions were considerably disturbed and my digestion upset. In tears I walked home, only to read that Benghazi has again been recaptured, and that Guinness shares have slumped heavily. Now I am alone with my troubles, my thoughts, my aching foot, and my loneliness . . . it is indeed grievous to meet one's wife under such circumstances, and after nearly nine months. It was a miserable marriage and now we find ourselves in even a crueller situation. Yet she [was] showing flashes of affection, even of loyalty to me, and being tender weak and sentimental I was sorry for her, and regretted the past. At one moment she looked mad, her face contracted strangely and she had that vacuous look of the drug addict, which has been commented on before. Of course she isn't one.

Early to bed.

Saturday 31st January

Wakefield's appointment as Director of the Army Training Corps has been announced; he thus vacates his PPS-ship to Harold at the Air Ministry and it is proposed that I should succeed him. My instinct is against it; yet it would be a solution of some difficulties. There may be objections; Harold, however, is seeing James Stuart[1] on Monday to discuss, or suggest my appointment. I care very little . . . no letter, no news from Peter: the last letter came on January 8th. He has since lived in a whirl of world events, yet has sent me three or four cables. I suppose that the Coopers are bringing me back messages, letters and perhaps parcels. I must not be impatient.

We are anxious about the outlook, since the Battle for the Island of Singapore has begun, and the advance against our forces continues in Libya.

Sunday 1st February

A dull month has faded without any terrific developments other than Honor's expected offensive to obtain a divorce which failed . . .

---

1 Stuart had succeeded Margesson as Chief Whip and therefore had a strong say in such appointments.

Alan, Patsy and I drove to Eton in heavy snow, lunching at the Hind's Head at Bray on the way: an atmospheric 'Pub' with succulent food. At Eton we called upon Mrs Snow[1] and the Lennox-Boyds entered their small sons: Paul [Channon's son] is no. 3 on the list for January 1949: I rather hope that he will go the previous half ... Patsy was hit by a snowball and lost her temper: in a wild angry mood she snapped at Alan and tried to strike him. He behaved with dignity and moved to the front seat of the car. I watched her anger subside and gradually give way to tenderness as she gazed worshippingly at the back of Alan's neck, and after some time she leant forward and kissed it. It was a tempting target. She is so desperately in love with him – Guinness girls are oversexed – and he is a helpless, hopeless (but heavenly) husband. Later there was another outburst: it is [illegible] desire and she hasn't Honor's pride, who used to hide her emotions. I see the whole drama re-enacting itself again and yet I can do nothing to help them ...

I am back in London lonely but at peace. The wireless reports further Axis progress in Libya and the beginning of the battle for Singapore: everything is depressing.

It is only lately as the world plays *Götterdämmerung* that I have been lonely; it is a new and distressing emotion and I realise that it will be my future fate, and a cruel one. Only a few years ago I was handsome, lustful, a favourite at Court, a protégé of Mr Chamberlain's, a millionaire, happy at the Foreign Office: now I am none of those things .... As I write Alan has rung me from King's X to apologise for Patsy's boorish and nervous behaviour. I hinted that she is pregnant; is she? Of course he has already left her to go to Henlow to spend the night with his old ma – he has been there most of the week only flitting to London now and then. The old lady is really the fundamental cause of Patsy's occasional outbursts and constant misery and jealousy. It is an irrational relationship .... Now I shall finish *Doctor Thorne*[2] which I am devouring for the second or third time. I am a tremendous Trollopian ...

I wrote to my mother and my son, crises of loneliness. I only live now to see him again and to complete the three years (from December 1940 to December 1943) when the property I signed away will be Paul's free of death duties – for his sake, and also to clear my estate of encumbrances.

I much miss my correspondence with Peter and will be glad to have it reopened when I know where he is. The news of a KLM Dutch passenger plane crashing in the Far East gave me a fright; as did Alice Harding telling me that Paul had had a chill at Christmastime, which I didn't know until yesterday. This morning Alan gave me two records of Paul's broadcast on Christmas Day, 1941,[3] when he spoke amongst other English children in New York to his parents in

---

1 Mrs Snow was the wife of John Snow, an Eton housemaster.
2 A novel of 1858 by Anthony Trollope, the third in his Chronicles of Barsetshire series.
3 Thus in the MS. He means 1940.

England. Of course I didn't know and was in Freetown, of all terrible places; and Honor was in a pub with her dirty paramour and didn't listen in. She has the decency to be ashamed, at least, of that action.

I must get some sort of semi-war job. The appointment at the Air Ministry won't come off: I would take it, if it did, as it would be a solution of some problems; yet I fear it might wreck my friendship with Harold, who might be a hard taskmaster? . . .

MONDAY 2ND FEBRUARY

Belgravia is still wrapt in snow: no communication from the Crown Prince for several days: Vsevolod says he is mislaid or something . . . it is certainly mysterious. Vsevolod has had an SOS from Badminton for more hock: Queen Mary, it seems, drinks a half-bottle of hock with her dinner and has done so all her life; sometimes she does the same at luncheon. And the stock of hock is running low in this country. She still keeps up some exhausting state, even splendour at Badminton where her tireless energy quite exhausts her long-suffering but devoted entourage.

Lunched alone and went to the RAC to meet the Crown Prince and we had a Turkish bath together; we were soon joined by Alan who was in exceptionally high spirits. He, Patsy, Harold and Peter Loxley dined and we were all uproarious – why? – when the war news is so utterly sombre? The future so drear, the outlook devastating . . . for the first time I should not mind dying[1] and perhaps I shall.

TUESDAY 3RD FEBRUARY

Snow everywhere – it is like America. I walked to the Dorchester to take leave of Alan, who was frantically packing and again in uniform. He assumes command of a motor boat at Portsmouth this afternoon and I shall miss him. Patsy's misery is touching: she loves him desperately . . . and I can sympathise with love and the void it can create.

I happened to overhear Tommy Dugdale offer the vacant PPS-ship at the Air Ministry to Ham Kerr, who gave no answer. At least, although I didn't want it much, I expected to be offered it. I was depressed . . . walked home in the wet and found that Anne Feversham had not turned up as she had promised. She never does.

I fear that my judgement is not as good as it was; I do silly unpremeditated things, impulsive and weak. I really need a long holiday to recover and regain my self-reliance and equilibrium. I can no longer even spell.

---

1 He has mentioned this before, so it is not for the first time.

In the mud, blackout, cold and snow I trudged, hitting my head against an invisible Belisha beacon *en route*, to Maimie Pavlovsky's at 36 Montpelier Walk, where I dined cosily with her, Vsevolod and the Crown Prince. I was cross and tired and left early after somewhat brusquely declining the Crown Prince's offer of a lift. I loathe going out at night. When I came in I found Harold Balfour depressed: he had had an interview with James Stuart, who told him it was now the practice and the Prime Minister's wish that PPSs attached to Service Departments should be serving members.[1] A sensible regulation really, but one which prevents me going to the Air Ministry. I am annoyed, relieved yet disappointed, too, Harold seems much downcast.

WEDNESDAY 4TH FEBRUARY

Walked to the House where I quickly picked up the government changes [that] were rung tonight, and I congratulated Jay Llewellin. Surprised, he turned to me and said, 'How did you know? I have only just left the Prime Minister!' So Jay is now President of the Board of Trade. Perhaps I might go to him? Rab told me on the telephone that Chuter Ede[2] was going to War Transport and would be replaced at the Board of Education by Philip [Noel-]Baker but tonight when the various and highly unsatisfactory reshuffle of under-secretaries was made public, I saw that Philip Noel-Baker was given War Transport. He must have refused Education – the second in command there is necessarily very small fry. I stayed at the House, attended the 1922 Cttee after lunching with John Findlay[3] and Somerset de Chair.[4] The Committee was crowded and was addressed by Beaverbrook who, with his curious Canadian accent, his small physique and very dominating personality, soon captivated his audience. He was confiding, charming and sought to please – with the Ministry of Production in his pocket, I knew. Left the House in a despondent mood and walked to the Dorchester to call upon Mrs Greville, whom I found aged and vituperative against the govt, particularly the Prime Minister and 'his ill-advised and fatal boasts'! The Dorchester is still popular and I went on to another suite to have a drink with Helen Fitzgerald, where I found

1 That is, serving in the Armed Forces.
2 James Chuter Ede (1882–1965) was a schoolmaster who became an active trade unionist. He served in the Great War and reached the rank of acting sergeant major. He served briefly as Labour MP for Mitcham in 1923, then for South Shields from 1929 to 1931 and from 1935 to 1964. He was Parliamentary Secretary to the Board (from 1944 the Ministry) of Education from 1940 to 1945; Home Secretary from 1945 to 1951, and simultaneously Leader of the House of Commons from March to October 1951. He was raised to the peerage as Baron Chuter-Ede (life peerage) in 1964.
3 This is the same man (Unionist MP for Banffshire) whom Channon refers to in Vol. I, entry for 19 February 1937, as Edmund Findlay.
4 Somerset Struben de Chair (1911–95) was Conservative MP for South West Norfolk from 1935 to 1945 and for Paddington South from 1950 to 1951.*

Esmond Rothermere who was even more critical of Churchill than was Mrs Greville! Said he was a dictator! and that Lloyd George had told him privately that Winston had a 'Hitler Complex', whatever that may mean . . . Harold picked me up and we dined with Lord and Lady Kemsley – more political talk (I am tiring of it, certainly) and speculation and criticism of the very unpopular govt. Victor Warrender was told only at noon today that he is to be made a peer.[1] People are pleased that Beaverbrook is to be Production Minister and nobody minds Malcolm McCorquodale's[2] promotion; but the consensus of opinion is that the reshuffle is inadequate and reminiscent of Mr Chamberlain's last, and fatal, attempt to reorganise his govt. The changes were announced on the wireless, I think: I didn't listen as I had the list. The early edition of tomorrow's *Daily Sketch* was sent to Lord Kemsley (where I was dining) and it contained a short, sharp leader story offensive to Mr Churchill. We persuaded Kemsley to eliminate it and he rang up his editor, or rather I did for him. Old Lord Iliffe,[3] rather a Dickensian character, dropped in and we played bridge, Harold and I won. Iliffe's visit, immediately twigged, was to do with his aviator son[4] who is in Cairo and wants a commission. Harold promised to do what he could. Harold and I walked home in the cold discussing our thwarted project of working together, the startling and alarming reverses in Libya, and Malcolm McCorquodale's mountain [*sic*]. Malcolm is an ally, an Oxford pal, a huge hulk of a man, generous, good-natured and altogether likeable, certainly.

Thursday 5th February

Had my bottom washed out but alas the treatment did not stimulate me as usual . . . . Then I rested, and deliberately stayed away from the House of Commons, being in a bad humour. At five o'clock Mrs Coats was coming to tea; just before a thick letter from India was brought to me. *Enfin* – Peter wrote it on January 9th; it has taken under a month. It was a touch impersonal but contained, along with rings for his mother . . . . a handsome pair of links for me; they are *en suite* to the

---

1 He became Lord Bruntisfield.
2 Malcolm Stewart McCorquodale (1901–71) was Conservative MP for Sowerby from 1931 to 1945 and for Epsom from 1947 to 1955. He was parliamentary private secretary to Ernest Bevin (qv) from 1942 to 1945. He was raised to the peerage as 1st Baron McCorquodale of Newton in 1955.
3 Edward Mauger Iliffe (1877–1960) was a newspaper proprietor, owning several regional papers and being a part-owner of the *Daily Telegraph* with Lords Camrose and Kemsley (qqv) until 1937. He served as Conservative MP for Tamworth from 1923 to 1929. He was knighted in 1922 and raised to the peerage as 1st Baron Iliffe in 1933.
4 Edward Langton Iliffe (1908–96) became an RAF intelligence officer. After the war he returned to the family business but devoted his life to the restoration of his Palladian mansion, Basildon Park in Berkshire, which he presented to the National Trust. He succeeded his father as 2nd Baron Iliffe in 1960.

ones he gave me in Jerusalem, from coloured stones and moonstone centres. I was touched and impressed and *attendri* . . . . Mrs Coats, too, was delighted with her present.

I am depressed by my matrimonial failure: the vast wealth I have forfeited, for I might have kept the marriage going for a little longer? I wonder. It was the abdication autumn of 1936 that was fatal and foolish. Honor was impossible but I was tactless, too.

I wish I had a career, a war too, something, anything to relieve my depression.

FRIDAY 6TH FEBRUARY

All day in fiendish temper – why? Even Peter's gay letter and present of yesterday have failed, for the first time, to restore my spirits.

James Gunn, Alan, and the Duchess of Kent rang up to talk and gossip. She tells me that Alexander of Yugoslavia had to be removed from his school in Kenya (he is 17) because of the unkindness and bullying of the other boys who accused him of being an enemy. How monstrous. Poor fellow. I love him. The ex-Regent discovered what had happened and was in a rage . . . a parcel came from the Regent containing Kenyan coffee.

SATURDAY 7TH FEBRUARY   *QUEEN'S HOTEL, PORTSMOUTH*

Every day brings more disturbing news: General Rommel continues his advance and people are talking of a Cairene collapse; and Singapore seems doomed . . . .

I sat to James Gunn and was pleased that the long-neglected portrait at last progresses.

Caught the 4.45 train to Portsmouth, reading Violet Trefusis's brilliant sketchbook, *Prelude to Misadventure*,[1] and bits of *Framley Parsonage*.[2] I lose myself now in Trollope as I used to do in Proust . . . . Alan met me at the station and we came to this crowded, icy cold hotel. It is full of RNVR officers and some soldiers. A scrimmage to get food etc. . . . I don't know how Alan stands it. I admire and not envy him.

It was so cold that Alan and I decided to sleep together.

SUNDAY 8TH FEBRUARY

Slept with Alan who snored . . . we got up late in the freezing cold, breakfasted, bathed and went to see his boat at Gosport. Drinks with some of his fellow officers . . . . and then drove on to Bosham, that quaint village which our father-in-law owns. The sun came out; there was a lovely light; and we had an excellent lunch

---

1 A memoir by Mrs Trefusis published in 1941.
2 The fourth in Trollope's Chronicles of Barsetshire series, published in 1861.

at the Old Ship inn and then mooched about the village, peeping at 'The Slip', the house the Iveaghs usually occupy .... We saw the yacht, *The Cat* rusting in the mud and sun – I always hated that yacht ....

We went on to Hayling Island and called on Princess [Catherine] Yurievskaya, whom I had not seen for seven years.[1] She greeted us cordially, pleased, I think, by our surprise visit. This daughter of an emperor, descendant of all the Romanovs, lives in squalor and poverty which my £300 per annum makes possible. Otherwise she would starve! Her little house is dirty, horrible; she has no servant of any kind; looks after herself in this cold and is lonely and over 60. Somehow she still exuded a certain atmosphere of grandeur and had her pearl earrings, the only tangible trace of her opulent days. She chatted of her royal relatives, her various nieces and nephews, reigning still or exiled! She is an historic link since she is actually the daughter of the Tsar Alexander II, great-great granddaughter of the luxuriant Empress whose name she bears. It was a depressing visit, but she was so cheerful and self-possessed that we realised she has achieved a certain philosophy of life and we left her to her loneliness; we drove away [and] I remarked that she is one of those people to whom every misfortune falls. She found her last servant dead in bed a few weeks ago; her three beloved Pekinese all have died recently ...

MONDAY 9TH FEBRUARY

Slept with Alan who didn't snore: I like sleeping with people – with anybody except my wife!

Returned to London and the cold train was over an hour late. The Iveaghs and Patsy to lunch. They were very hard about Honor and rightly; but when I told them that she intends to change her name by deed poll to Woodman, they were considerably shaken. They both said that she is mad. I retorted that I agreed and whilst I dreaded the preliminary scandal and publicity which a change of name would necessarily mean, I nevertheless welcomed it in the long run – which I do. She has so disgraced my name that the sooner she discards it the better. The in-laws were affectionate, but aged and detached; and I had to listen to a long digression about barley at luncheon. I am smarting with a feeling of injustice.

Dr Law says that I have an enflamed gall bladder and I am alarmed. My poor father had his out at the age of about 60. We are bad about bladders ....

I am really ill and the news makes me worse.

TUESDAY 10TH FEBRUARY

Woke, unelated and *congestionné*; I am really liverish or worse ... walked to Claridge's, shopped with the Crown Prince and then went to the H of C. Winston

---

1 See Vol. I, entries for 8 February and 24 and 26 August 1935. The Princess had previously been a 'dependant' of Serge Obolensky (qv).

had made a statement, which I missed, about the duties and functions of the recently created Ministry of Production. House dull, and I soon rejoined the Crown Prince and Vsevolod and we shopped. Vsevolod bought a pair of baroque pearl and diamond earrings for a birthday present for Maimie.

More Japanese landings at Singapore but Rommel's advance in Libya seems to have slackened. Cyrenaica has become a sort of no man's land.

There is too much pro-Cripps talk. The dying order kisses the hand of the revolutionary!

The King of Greece told me last evening that Turkey will become difficult if Singapore falls, I fear he is right.

General Wavell, it is announced, has returned safely from Burma to Batavia, no doubt accompanied by Peter, or is he entertaining General Chiang Kai-shek[1] in Delhi? Will he win the war, or is it already lost? Anyhow the world is hell.

A ghastly evening: my dear sisters-in-law, the Ladies Brigid and Patsy proposed themselves to dine and reluctantly enough I agreed as I felt ill. Jay Llewellin, our new President of the Board of Trade, rang up and I asked him; but he made a bad fourth. Conversation flagged; I was tired and the Guinness girls, with the lack of manners which characterises them and infuriates me, ignored Jay and sat in stony, sulky silence, which I could pass over. Brigid was tired, hostile, and just risen from her jaundiced couch (she has been ill for weeks) and last night foolishly celebrated her semi-recovery by dancing until six at 'the 400'. With Lord Euston! I have always adored Brigid but tonight she was maddening; and I suddenly hated the whole tribe for their dullness, bad manners and lack of graciousness. I have done all I can to love and placate them . . . but the sands of affection are running out. Soon I must stand on my own flat feet.

The war bulletins are increasingly depressing.

WEDNESDAY 11TH FEBRUARY

I woke feeling a little better but still very angry with my *Schwägerinnen*[2] for their boorish behaviour. I practically had to turn them out. Jay told us of his audiences with the King, who was in one of his shyest moods and could not get out the one necessary word 'Approve' for some sixty embarrassed seconds.[3]

---

1 Chiang Kai-shek (1887–1975) was a generalissimo and Nationalist politician who led the Republic of China from 1928 to 1949 and, after his overthrow by Chairman Mao, from Taiwan until his death. He married, in 1927, Soong Mei-ling (1898–2003), who took an active part in politics and in raising international awareness of the brutalities of the Japanese invasion of China, notably in the United States.
2 Sisters-in-law.
3 The King was shy, but that was not the reason for his inarticulacy, which was caused by his stammer.

I thought about my involved, complicated finances: I shall never be really rich again, but must eke out, spread out, an adequate income and small capital over the remaining, perhaps thirty, years of my life. I hope not to begin drawing upon capital say until my 43rd birthday – next March 7th.[1]

The astrologers predicted a very successful week for those born on March 7th. So far every week has been completely purgatorial; cold; illness; atmospheric[2] lunch with the Iveaghs; ghastly evening yesterday; no favourable financial developments; a more than mad letter from my mother this morning – she must be demented; a discouraging one from my American lawyers; no offer from Jay to be his PPS. Nothing yet on the asset side except a reconciliation, if such there ever was needed, with the King of Greece, and some social success. But there are three and a half days exactly – it is noon as I write – still to go. By then, I suppose, Singapore will have fallen. Jay thinks so.

A sweet conciliatory note from Brigid mollified me and I feel affection towards her. Patsy tells me that Brigid is . . . . disturbed by the imminent departure of Lord Euston, who goes with his regiment, the Grenadiers, 'to foreign parts' almost at once and feels he will be killed . . . the world is crashing, crashing.

All day I felt ill and *désoeuvré* . . . . at six o'clock I felt so ill that I sent for Dr Law who examined me and pronounced me 'fit', not suffering from any complaint, without fever but generally stale and run-down. 'What you want is another love affair and a winter in Egypt – like last year,' he said. I was somewhat startled, the man is a tonic certainly and I felt better immediately and will resume my interest in life soon again . . .

Freda Casa Maury and her Cuban Marquis of a husband – now a wing commander; Olive and Adrian Baillie; Michael Duff; Geoffrey Lloyd and the Crown Prince dined with me. The Baillies brought champagne; the Crown Prince produced a brace of [illegible] bottles. Gay dinner, and we went on to a dreadfully boring film. I loathe films, almost always.

Bed about midnight, really feeling more myself.

THURSDAY 12TH FEBRUARY

Woke in high spirits, inappropriate to the war outlook, and walked to the House of Commons. Are my troubles, digestive and emotional, really only caused by constipation and liver? Met Brendan Bracken in the lobby who at once offered me a drink; I sat with him for a time in the Smoking Room and wished that perhaps I was ripe for some sort of job. He was very friendly and helpful; but he promises overmuch always . . . Then half an hour closeted with Rab, who was amused by my gaiety and chatter. As I left him I read on the tape that Singapore

---

1 He would, of course, be 45.
2 By which he manifestly means there was an 'atmosphere' at the lunch.

had practically fallen; only perhaps a few more hours left to it of British rule. Already there are celebrations in Tokyo. It is the most grievous single defeat since the fall of France . . . and now what will happen to the East, and the Far Eastern command? Will Peter return or languish in Australia?

Walked home and stopped in at a newsreel in the hope of seeing Peter; but I didn't recognise him really, although there were several 'close-ups' of General Wavell.

Today is Maimie Pavlovsky's (as well as Abraham Lincoln's) birthday and I am arranging now a supper party here in the famous Blue Room; perhaps the last that there will ever be.

Later . . .

My 'Singapore Supper' was an astonishing success in spite of ill-luck, royal unpunctuality, scarcity of servants and highly depressing news. I was still in the bath when Maimie Vsevolod, the Crown Prince and Joyce Brittain-Jones, Natasha Bagration and Arthur Leveson arrived at 8.15. We waited for a time and at last went into supper. The Blue Room shimmered in the candlelight and looked more lovely than ever, since it is a touch tawdry now. I provided oysters, eggs and bacon and champagne – all rarities now. At 9.30 the King of Greece arrived . . . . Supper proceeded; everyone was gay, but I kept wondering, with inward conviction of impending doom, would this be our last little gala before the deluge? Harold rushed in at ten o'clock and whispered to me that the *Scharnhorst*[1] and *Gneisenau*[2] and other ships had got away from Brest and that there had been today a big naval-cum-air attack on them which had failed. Can we never do anything right, or even have a stroke of luck? I told nobody . . . At 10.15 the Duchess of Kent, looking like a very lovely Laocoon,[3] coiled with pearls, came accompanied by Mary Herbert. They had been to an official function. Once more all the guests stood up . . . but before they entered the dining room I showed them to the lavatory and just stopped the King of Greece from going in! He, I piloted upstairs. Then more conversation and champagne and slightly fuddled gaiety. About midnight we began to break up, and Harold sent the King and the Duchess in his car to Claridge's where they are staying. It was really like the last gasp of the *ancien régime*.

When the others left Harold told me in halting phrases of the extraordinary sea-cum-air battle that took place off Dover all afternoon; the three huge German ships apparently slipped out of Brest, where they have been kept in by our fleet for over a year, last evening after dusk. Everything helped them,

---

1 A German battleship, launched in 1936, which would eventually be sunk at the Battle of North Cape on Boxing Day 1943.

2 Sister ship to the *Scharnhorst* (*vide supra*), also launched in 1936. She escaped back to Germany but was damaged *en route*, and while being repaired was far more badly damaged in a British raid, and never saw service again.

3 A Trojan priest in Greek mythology.

the clouds, the morning's obscurity, and even the failure of instruments in one of our reconnoitring planes; this accident prevented the signalling to our forces for some time. Nevertheless, all the afternoon the fierce battle raged: the German ships were escorted by 200 Messerschmitts, and yet our planes and our destroyers fought and bombed and torpedoed – with little or no success. And HMS *Worcestershire*[1] caught fire.

FRIDAY THE 13TH (INDEED!) OF FEBRUARY

Woke ill and very sleepy, indeed, and my first thoughts were of last night's party, and then sleepily I stretched for the newspapers which were emblazoned with '*Scharnhorst*' and '*Prinz Eugen*'[2] and '*Gneisenau*' – and the whole story . . . I got up, wrote letters, but felt confused, as one does after a late night when one has overindulged, and also I was emotionally flurried. Is the war lost? Everything seems to be going against us. Harold rushed into my bedroom. 'Read this,' he said. He referred to a violently anti-Churchill, anti-government leader in the *Daily Mail*. It is the first that has ever appeared . . .

The Duchess of Kent called. She was in a rage against the Prime Minister, and then everybody I met during the course of the day echoed the same sentiments. Rage: frustration. This is not the post-Dunkirk feeling, but one of anger. The country is more upset about the escape of the boats than over the imminent, but not yet, fall of Singapore . . . Sat to James Gunn who bores me almost to madness. He attacked the PM with violence, abused him even personally . . . The Capital seethes with indignation and were Londoners Latins there would be rioting. I have never known so violent an outburst, and so deep feeling. I looked in at the Amerys in the hope of picking up news, but he was out, and the womenfolk knew, or said, nothing. I found Herlihy, my Reuters friend, waiting for me at home, and he had seen Attlee and others. Apparently there is a flap on at 10 Downing Street. Winston, angered by the *Daily Mail* leader, is in a defiant, truculent mood. Attlee hinted to Herlihy this afternoon that 'outside men' would be brought into the government, that is non-parliamentarians.

A touching, refreshing personal sidelight on the situation is Rab's dependence upon me. He rang me four times on the telephone today, and is now at Stanstead where he begged me to join him tomorrow. I refused from laziness. Perhaps tomorrow I shall change my mind.

---

1 The ship was HMS *Worcester*, a destroyer launched in 1919. Although badly damaged with the loss of twenty-six officers and ratings the ship returned to Harwich for repairs. In December 1943 she hit a mine off Great Yarmouth and was decommissioned.

2 A heavy cruiser, launched in 1938, that escaped from Brest with the *Scharnhorst* and *Gneisenau*. She surrendered to the Royal Navy on 7 May 1945 and was given to the United States as a war prize in December 1945.

There is some talk about the formation of a so-called 'Centre Party' composed of Liberals, disgruntled Conservatives etc. with Beaverbrook at the head. He, unscrupulous as ever, is alleged to be intriguing either for the Premiership or a negotiated peace. It may be all rumour but curiously enough, the name of David Margesson has been mentioned as being implicated. I can scarcely credit that.

SATURDAY 14TH FEBRUARY

The country is dejected, affronted and anxious . . . the newspapers are almost unanimous in condemning the govt.

Harold and I drove early to Hendon, flew in a small plane to Duxford Aerodrome, where I waited, whilst he flew the new terrific still secret 'Typhoon' plane, which has a speed of over 400 miles an hour. Then we flew, Harold piloting, which he does gracefully, to North Weald, circling over Kelvedon. My lone house looked red and beautiful and one could see the bomb holes, frozen over now, in the Park. At North Weald we lunched with the CO, Group Captain Pike;[1] the Crown Prince, [and] Micky Renshaw joined us. Michael Duff, now attached to the American Eagle Squadron, received us. Gay party and then Harold and I drove back to London.

The news from Sumatra now is disturbing: the Japanese are near Batavia!! Singapore has not yet fallen and the battle continues; and meanwhile reinforcements are rushing to the rescue. Probably they will arrive too late.

I am alone now and thinking of the gallant, gay pilots whom I met today who had fought in the great Channel battle on Thursday; some of them had actually seen the ships; most of them had not owing to the poor visibility. And again my thoughts are of Peter and the fantastic war he has had; how different is bombed and threatened Batavia from the delights of Cairo. It is a year ago this morning, St Valentine's Day, that he drove me to Heliopolis and I caught the aeroplane accompanied by Bob Menzies, and sadly I watched a brown speck disappear as we flew away . . . and arrived a few hours later at the Palace of Khartoum where we stayed so comfortably with Governor Huddleston – how wretched I was. A ghastly year has passed . . .

I packed off the two Michaels to drive with the Crown Prince, wishing above all else to be alone tonight, alone with my news, my books, and now I shall read *Framley Parsonage* before going to bed.

---

1 Thomas Geoffrey Pike (1906–83) joined the Royal Air Force in 1924. He won the Distinguished Flying Cross in 1941 while commanding a squadron of night fighters, and was awarded a Bar just over a fortnight later. He took command at North Weald in February 1942. In a distinguished post-war career he was knighted in 1955 and became Chief of the Air Staff in 1960. Promoted to marshal of the RAF in 1962, he served as Deputy Supreme Commander Allied Powers Europe from 1964 until his retirement in 1967.

SUNDAY 15TH FEBRUARY

The press echoes the country's anxiety, and the possibility of defeat, which I long ago envisaged, is dawning upon the nation. I wish sometimes that I had had the courage to vote against the govt in the recent vote of confidence – but it would have been probably both foolish and futile to have done so.

The hero of the battle of the Channel seems to have been Colin Coats,[1] who commanded the *Worcestershire* [*sic*]; he is, I think, Peter's brother. He has five.

Life .... may soon suffocate me altogether. My political, financial, love and domestic problems are all increasingly appalling.

My agents report confusion and consternation in No. 10, with the Prime Minister defiant and truculent; and I am told that Beaverbrook is intriguing for the job for himself. I cannot vouch for the accuracy of that.

The Crown Prince arrived here at noon and was with me until midnight; no one ever had so faithful a follower. We lunched *à deux* [and] went to the RAC for a prolonged Turkish bath, dozed, and I felt more rested than I have been for many months. We rushed to dine early at Claridge's before Churchill's broadcast .... The broadcast was moving, and was an eloquent and successful appeal for national unity, the PM having had general tilts at Socialists who in the past were against rearmament. and also against his present political critics and opponents. Carefully wrapped up in his oratory was the given and far-reaching defeat at Singapore. It has gone, unconditionally surrendered; moreover the Japanese have now attacked and landed – at Sumatra, thus blocking the entrance to Singapore. Sumatra is dangerously near to Batavia and my thoughts flew to Wavell's staff, which presumably will evacuate to Australia now.

MONDAY 16TH FEBRUARY

I awoke today in a fiendish temper, but full of energy .... [I] Galvanised the household, did my alarming accounts – all accounts are alarming – and wrote many letters. My suffering secretary had a field day, indeed.

It is still icy cold.

Dined at the St James's Club with Nicholas Lawford whom I like increasingly; he is a sad, cultivated creative, but an excellent Second Secretary to Anthony Eden. He likes his chief but is not in sympathy with his pinkish politics; and he thinks his superior, Oliver Harvey, who is First Secretary, a danger to the community since he is a communist at heart.

---

1 Ernest Colin Coats (1902–71) joined the Royal Navy as a cadet in 1916. He was captain of HMS *Worceste*r from May 1941 until July 1942; he commanded HMS *Campbell* from 1942 until 1944. He was awarded the Distinguished Service Order for his part in the battle with the three German ships, and later the Distinguished Service Cross, and retired in the rank of commander in 1947.

London is seething with political talk and unrest; what will happen nobody knows. The PM is alleged to be in a defiant mood and talking of a general election etc. He is disillusioned with the House of Commons ...

TUESDAY 17TH FEBRUARY

Early to the House, and dispatched letter by bag to Peter, now, I presume, at Batavia; to the Regent, and others.

The House was restless, crowded and angry: It did not seem to know its own mind ... I got places for the Crown Prince – to whom I introduced Averell Harriman, who is dark and very good-looking; and Lady Kemsley. The PM came into the Chamber and I saw him scowl. No cheer greeted him as he arrived, nor as he answered questions. He has lost the House. At twelve o'clock he rose and in a curiously nonchalant, indeed as if uninterested, manner read a prepared statement about the passing through the Channel straits of the German ships. He convinced nobody, and particularly his attempt to turn an inglorious defeat into a victory displeased the House. There was soon a barrage of questions, and a debate as to whether or not there should be a debate began. Several times the PM intervened and each time his reception was increasingly hostile; never have I known the House growl at a prime minister. Can he ever recover his waning prestige? He is ever such a *Schwärmer* that he basks only in approval; smiles and praise encourage him; criticism irritates and restricts him. Today the august assembly nearly blew up; he was at last saved by several dull speakers who so bored the House .... that members began to file out in dozens. It was a disgraceful scene which lasted an hour; there was no disputing that all sense of reality seemed to have left the elected representatives of the people. I could not help thinking how much better the country would be if the Chamber were abolished or suspended; other people thought so, too. I believe we are entering in[to] a political phase that has had no equal since Cromwell; that we shall see a struggle between the executive and Parliament. We have the first dictator since Cromwell. If such an issue arises I am undecided which side to take and much as I distrust Winston (and I fear that he has the evil-eye, or ill-luck: certainly nothing that he has ever touched – Dardanelles, abdication, India Bill, has come off well), I have even less faith in the Commons – a more moribund collection of old fogies and nitwits I have never met. Alan whispered to me; 'You think we are a doomed decadent race? Don't you?' I refused to reply; but I do in my heart; I have always thought so, that is for quite ten years; yet nobody has ever loved this country more than I have ... Eventually the House resumed its ordinary business after having extracted a promise for a two days' debate next week from the Prime Minister. He was obviously disgruntled and shaken by his reception. I felt sorry for him ...

Called on the Coopers, who came back last night from Cairo via Malta. Poor Diana who loathes flying, and is always terrified, has flown around the world, in itself almost a record. She was looking lovely, slim and glamorous and embraced me affectionately, and Duff was amiable. They were surrounded by a group of highly exhausted people whom I have known for twenty years, and am now heavily tired of, and exhausted by; Randolph Churchill – who has once again postponed his departure to Cairo and is being freely criticised for doing so; Brendan Bracken, whom I really like . . . . etc. etc. Diana never mentioned Peter, although I know that she has seen him . . .

There is much afoot politically and a wholesale reshuffle will shortly take place: of that I am convinced.

WEDNESDAY 18TH FEBRUARY

To the House, but feeling ill. The lobby was seething with rumour. Then I came home and rested for a time. A letter came – a glamorous, glorious affectionate one from Peter which touched me very much. The Coopers brought it back with them.

Sydney and Rab Butler arrived to stay with me and we dined with Mrs Greville, who was amusing, but ill and fading slowly . . . Rab had attended a meeting of ministers presided over by the PM, who told them little really; but I gather the War Cabinet is being reconstructed today and that the changes will be announced tomorrow.

Everyone is uneasy, unhappy and restless. Attended a crowded meeting at the House which was addressed by Cripps. He was skilful and moderate in his talk. Somehow he has caught the fancy of the public because of his recent association with Russia. The public doesn't know that all his predictions were falsified by events; that he knew nothing about Russia's entry in the war – which he repeatedly warned the Foreign Office would never take place, that he was not trusted by Stalin, that he was actually in Sweden at the time, etc. The English public is illogical, unstable and easily imposed upon.

THURSDAY 19TH FEBRUARY

All day London and later the lobbies seethed with stories . . . . I realised that much that I had earlier heard on the telephone was true: the War Cabinet has been reconstructed. Kingsley Wood, who is an excellent Chancellor, but too weak and unworldly for War Cabinet rank, is to be dropped, and so is Greenwood, who is now rightly known as 'Deadwood'; more surprising is the emission of Max Beaverbrook, who is not only giving up his so recently created post of Minister of Production, but also his seat in the War Cabinet. There were difficulties over this and I gather friction between him and 'The All Highest'. These major changes will be announced tonight and more are to follow shortly.

Spent the afternoon with Leslie Hore-Belisha; he tells me that overtures have been made to him by HMG to join it; even said that he had 'feelers'. He is quite confident of a reinstatement, but both Harold and Rab say that in view of some articles which appeared in *Truth*, which he has never taken the trouble to deny, that he can never come back. I think he will and soon.

Sent P a cable asking where he was.

FRIDAY 20TH FEBRUARY

Woke so ill and wretched that I chucked a Southend engagement and have been alone all day.

Can nothing pleasant ever happen to me? My life seems 'all winter' now and my hair is alas! greying over the temples. I look 100 and feel more but I still care, which is something, I suppose.

Quiet dull day; the country is jubilant over the Cabinet changes and once more Churchill is the nation's hero. I cannot see how Cripps can ever save the war.

Harold had a long telephone conversation with Max Beaverbrook, who seems disgusted at being dropped from the govt, which, I presume, he will soon turn against. It is a doomed affair. Max is going to America on some trumped-up mission, but really to heal his asthma and soothe his pride, in Florida. During the recent crisis, which is far from being over, he and Lord Camrose have supported Churchill, whilst the Kemsley, Rothermere and Astor press has been hostile and as critical as it dared.

SATURDAY 21ST FEBRUARY

A better morning ... many telephone calls, a huge, fat brilliant epistle from Peter, a telephone chat with Diana ... and the prospect of further political changes ...

Dined on a tray with Harold Balfour who has a fever: he was exacting and pernickety to his secretary on the telephone. Now I have just finished *Framley Parsonage* and am going to bed; but before doing so will reread for the eleventh time Peter's brilliant, colourful and rich budget. What a lad! What a pen!

Enid Raphael, an unlucky, neurasthenic half-crazed, drugged girl has at last killed herself after many attempts. She looked like a tortured Greco and I was sorry for her until she became Honor's *âme damnée* and self-appointed sycophant and lady-in-waiting. Honor began by impressing her and ended by boring her – the usual sequence in H's case. Of course Enid was a Semite and a lesbian although she had a passionate affair which lasted for years with Liam O'Flaherty[1] who treated her shabbily.

---

1 Liam O'Flaherty (1896–1984), a novelist, was one of the key figures in Irish literature in the twentieth century. He fought in the Irish Guards in the Great War and was a founder of the Irish Communist Party.

SUNDAY 22ND FEBRUARY

A desperate day: I early heard of the proposed changes and all – so far – are disappointing, indeed. David Margesson has been kicked out, literally,[1] and for no good reason.[2] He has been a brilliant success at a job which he accepted only under pressure; he has been the best War Minister for many years; he has been efficient, painstaking, energetic and even loyal to Winston. Now he is thrown to the wolves. First it was Wavell, then Dill; now this – I am in a rage. He is to be replaced by Sir P. J. Grigg,[3] the Permanent Head of the War Office, a brilliant man, I believe, but about whom I know little; but it is a dangerous experiment, or rather precedent to elevate civil heads of departments to the Supreme Command. If the Civil Service is to rule us, then why not abolish Parliament? To cripple it, render it both impotent and unpopular seems to be the Prime Minister's design. The other appointments leave me cold; but the idea of sending Wolmer[4] to MEW[5] is fantastic. He is half-gaga. All of this adds to one's general gloom and rage. I seem to sink further into the mire of despondency.

Drove in cold weather to Pyrford where I lunched with the in-laws, who were charming. Nothing was said of my affairs, and little reference was made to Honor. They have so really treated me well . . . meanwhile the communistic wind blows stronger and England is being semi-Bolshevised. David [Margesson] must regret advising Mr Chamberlain not to go to the country after Munich in October 1938, when he would have had an immense triumph and half the people now in power would have lost their seats. Mr Chamberlain, ever honest, thought that it would be taking an unfair advantage to do so . . . now we are hopelessly divided and on

---

1 Of course, metaphorically.
2 The 'good reason' was that he was a scapegoat for Singapore, and it gave Churchill the opportunity to get out of the Cabinet a man who had merited a place there but who had been entirely loyal to Chamberlain.
3 Percy James Grigg (1890–1964) was the son of a carpenter who won a scholarship to St John's College, Cambridge, took a double first in mathematics, came first in the Civil Service Examination and joined the Treasury in 1913. From 1921 to 1930 he was principal private secretary to successive Chancellors of the Exchequer, including Churchill. He then became Chairman of the Board of Customs and Excise and the Board of the Inland Revenue, and spent the period from 1934 to 1939 in New Delhi, as Finance Minister in the government of India. In 1939 he became Permanent Under-Secretary at the War Office, and when he replaced Margesson as Secretary of State he had to tell the outgoing Minister the news himself. He remained Secretary of State until July 1945. From 1942 to 1945 he was National MP for Cardiff East.
4 Roundell Cecil Palmer (1887–1971) was Viscount Wolmer by courtesy from 1895 to 1941 when he was called to the House of Lords in his father's barony of Selborne by a writ of acceleration. He was Conservative MP for Newton from 1910 to 1918 and for Aldershot from 1918 to 1940. He held junior office under Bonar Law and Baldwin between 1922 and 1929 and served as Minister for Economic Warfare from 1942 to 1945. He succeeded his father as 3rd Earl of Selborne in 1942.
5 The Ministry of Economic Warfare.

the edge of defeat. I fear that my glorious England is mad, illogical and expiring. Nobody ever loved her as I have done.

I should like to live until about April but really care very little. Meanwhile, I have written David Margesson a touching little note: I shall ask him to stay here, since he is penniless and depressed.

MONDAY 23RD FEBRUARY

The changes have been announced and a wave of indignation has swept over London at the dropping of David M. It is monstrous, unnecessary and unfair – the present govt is a ramp and a racket. I now hear that Randolph has been given permanent leave. The press is favourable to David.

I am reading Rousseau's *Confessions*[1] with enjoyment.

I fetched Diana Cooper and took her out to lunch; I much wanted to see her; even more I ached to hear her speak of Peter. She was looking a vision of nacre loveliness – all her great beauty was returned; and she was gay, gentle and affectionate. I adored her. She told me riveting tales of Singapore and elsewhere and finally I got her with difficulty onto Delhi. She liked Peter, found him pleasant but suspects his morals. She seemed unaware of our particular axis . . . we talked long but I was *congestionné* and dull and then I dropped her. She was not angry about David; thinks that Winston can do no wrong etc.

My agents report that David's fall was largely engineered by Erskine-Hill and the caucus of the '22 Cttee; but that the real villain of the piece is Master Randolph [Churchill] who is one of the most desperate and unscrupulous men it has ever been my misfortune to meet. Today I <u>loathed</u> the Prime Minister, and Olive Baillie echoed my sentiments on the telephone. I gather that the changes have pleased nobody, really – only a small unimportant anti-Chamberlain group.

TUESDAY 24TH FEBRUARY

Walked, although feverish and ill, in the freezing cold to the House of Commons. Talked with Randolph, whom I hate more than I do anyone; he was arrogant and proud to have dislodged David, I am told he is responsible. Winston got up in silence; at first he looked cross but the mood passed and warming to the more friendly atmosphere of the House he proceeded to read and deliver his speech with gusto and gaiety; but it was a valedictory affair and he as much said so – in the future Cripps[2] would do the speaking; now and then the Prime Minister might come down to Westminster – but rarely. He is to be a sort of invisible

---

1 The autobiography of the first fifty-three years of his life by Jean-Jacques Rousseau (1712–78), published posthumously in 1782.

2 Who had just been appointed Leader of the Commons; but he would hold that post only until November.

dictator, a lama of Tibet. The House of Commons so hates him at the moment, is so affronted by his rudeness and his flaunting of our susceptibilities that we, too, were glad to separate . . . He almost waved 'goodbye' as he left the Chamber. The more recent changes have had a tepid reception and everyone agrees that Margesson has had a rough and raw deal.

My cold is worse; perhaps I am to have the flu? I slept most of the afternoon, dined *à deux* with the Crown Prince, whom I turned out at 9.45, and now am going to bed. Sent off a long letter to Peter to Batavia . . . .

WEDNESDAY 25TH FEBRUARY

I have mild flu and a passing temperature . . . . [I] took my temp[erature] which was under a hundred and so I decided to dine out. Walked in cold blackout, since there were no taxis, to the Dorchester to dine with Mrs Greville. There the King of Greece, who said that he could barely look upon the food since it made him think of his starving compatriots; Dickie and Edwina Mountbatten, both cool, chic and completely charming; Sir John and Lady Anderson and Lady Brabourne,[1] who was so fashionable and handsome that I didn't immediately recognise her. She has immensely improved. I was between Edwina and Ava and was gay and amusing and quite dominated the dinner . . . . Mrs Greville, old and ill, sat silent and as ancient-looking as some venerable Buddha. After dinner a confidential conversation with the dejected King of Greece, who feels that he is neglected here and that the Foreign Office and Anthony Eden dislike and disapprove of him. Actually the BBC attacked him in a recent broadcast; unobtrusively I led the Lord President [Anderson] into our conversation and he took a note and promised to investigate. I hope he will. Lady Brabourne and I said that Rab ought to be made Viceroy: but she thinks that Sydney would not go down [well]. Very probably she is right. The party, well dressed and gay, broke up at eleven. It was lovely to have champagne etc. again. Edwina M is a confused Socialist, which for anybody in her position of a millionairess, a semi-royalty, and a famous fashionable figure, is ridiculous. She works very hard at the WVS, or Red Cross. She looked a dream of slender beauty and seemed fond of Dickie. I went to their wedding years and years ago[2] . . . *Chacun s'amuse de son côté*[3] in that glamorous *ménage* and how!

The King of Greece told me indignantly that Somebody in the Foreign Office had confided in him that letters exchanged between the ex-Regent and Walter Buccleuch had been held up in Cairo by the censorship. Can this be true?

1   Doreen Geraldine Browne (1896–1979), by courtesy Lady Doreen from 1903, was the daughter of the 6th Marquess of Sligo. She married, in 1919, Michael Knatchbull (1894–1939), who succeeded his father as 5th Baron Brabourne in 1939. She was murdered by the Irish Republican Army when she died of injuries after it blew up the boat of Lord Mountbatten (qv) off the Sligo coast in August 1979.
2   They married in 1922.
3   Each amuses him or herself according to his or her own tastes.

THURSDAY 26TH FEBRUARY

Awoke with a temperature. I stayed in bed until three o'clock. Now up, but not going out.

Dressed late and waited for the evening which was a huge success. My chief guest was Keith Feiling, the Oxford don and historian whom I had known in 1921 in my undergraduate days. He has aged very little. Mrs Neville Chamberlain suggested my inviting him and he was grateful for a chance to meet some of the ministers whom Mr Chamberlain liked best; those he was proudest of and much intimate with – came: Alan Lennox-Boyd; Rab Butler and Harold, who were both staying with me, and Peter Loxley who saw much of the PM because of Foreign Office questions. We talked affectionately; even wistfully of Neville and it was a sentimental, nostalgic evening; but more of interest and value to F[eiling] who was surprised by the evident affection and admiration we all expressed for Mr Chamberlain. He was the modern St George, and England is paying now for its ingratitude to him: this rotten, gangster, regime is a disaster. Rab said tonight that it could not and will not last; that Randolph has been intriguing and doing a lot of dirty political work and is much to blame. He is his father's *âme damnée*. Perhaps we shall have a Conservative govt again in the summer. We cannot go on as we are doing.

I hear that Geoffrey Lloyd will be the next to be dropped. We all agreed tonight that we detest the Prime Minister, deplore his lack of judgement, disapprove of his henchmen; and yet we can do nothing – yet!

FRIDAY 27TH FEBRUARY

Went out for a walk and that sent my fever up again – or perhaps it was Peter's cable that he is still in India and would I write there?

London awaits the announced political changes; I feel that they will be unpleasant. A dull day for a dull day.

I am becoming increasingly obsessed and absorbed by my finances. The next few months will bring me in much money; but I intend to economise severely, pay off my indebtedness, and if possible reduce my overdraft considerably.

Channon goes to Farnham Park to stay with the Kemsleys.

SUNDAY 1ST MARCH

Slept late and did little all day; made friends with John Manners,[1] who is handsome, and even more precocious than his brother Charles.[2] Both are full of theories and are astonishingly conversational. John is 20; Charles 23; both are soldiers; both

---

1 John Martin Manners (1922–2001), Lord John by courtesy, was the second son of the 9th Duke of Rutland (qv).
2 The 10th Duke of Rutland. Both he and his brother were a year younger than Channon thought.

are dark, very un-English looking. We were joined by Esmond Rothermere, who yesterday became a grandfather, Ann O'Neill and Evelyn Fitzgerald. There was more bridge. I thought and read a lot. Somehow I feel that I shall enter a new era, have increased luck during the coming year – at least my awful depression and the many causes for it will lift. The digits of 1942 add up to 7; but until now this year has brought me nothing but boredom, disillusion and dejection . . . Too much conversation and bridge. Much criticism of the Churchillian Dynasty, and particularly of fiend Randolph, who yesterday attacked Lord Chatfield in a violent speech, delivered, at all places, at Retford at the opening of a 'Warships week' – to attack a distinguished admiral is anyway a tactical mistake, but to do so at a Warships week must be the very zenith of folly.[1] Chatfield, a calm, considerate, sailor, made a blunt reply in the press. Everyone incensed by Randolph's growing arrogance and intrigues . . .

MONDAY 2ND MARCH

A better day – *déjà*.[2] I drove up to London in milder weather and feel *enfin* that my bones are thawing. Lunched at the Belgian Embassy, where Alec Cadogan was particularly agreeable to me; I never liked him so much. He crossed the room to speak to me several times.

A notice came that I had been elected to Pratt's Club last Thursday. How silly of me to have had apprehensions on this score when I was proposed by the Duke of Devonshire. Buck's, Bath, Carlton and now Pratt's. Shall I also join the Turf, the Travellers and White's? . . . .

Rex Whistler has arrived to stay for a few days; elegant, vague, gentle and strange, he is a most delightful satyr, and full of charm. His newly grown moustache lends him a French air. He is in the Welsh Guards, and is in charge of a tank. Anyone more unsuitable I cannot imagine. After some conversation, he left me; and I was then handed a long typewritten letter from General Wavell! It was written at Batavia: a most friendly, chatty missive, beginning 'My dear Channon' and ending 'Yours Ever, Archie Wavell'. It is like having a letter from Napoleon and I was touched, exhilarated and enchanted all at once. Indeed, a much better day.

Poor old 'Nealey' Vanderbilt[3] is dead; he was 69.[4] He looked like George V, drank like a fish and was the most bored man I ever met. He was thin, bearded

---

1 Churchill called Chatfield 'a man of Munich', which was far from the truth and caused widespread outrage. Chatfield had regularly warned about the Nazi threat from 1933 onwards.
2 Already.
3 Cornelius Vanderbilt III (1873–1942), of New York, was a soldier and yachtsman: in 1896 he married, greatly against his father's wishes, Grace Graham Wilson (qv). His sobriquet was normally spelt 'Neily'.
4 He was 68.

and had bloodshot blue eyes and quiet, detached manners. For thirty years he was maddened by his wife, maddened by his wealth and disappointed with his children. He loved little Grace;[1] and had a certain affection for Mrs V, but her foibles, her royal obsessions, unpunctuality and frenzy for entertaining exhausted him. Nor did he share her Anglomania, although he was not hostile to us. A weak heart long served him as an excuse to live almost altogether on his yacht.

Everybody rang up; Leslie Hore-Belisha, Barbie Wallace, Alan; the Crown Prince but I have done nothing about any of them. Oh! God give me a new and happier phase in life; preserve my child; help me; and bring me Peter, happiness, and perhaps the end of the war.

Patsy Lennox-Boyd and Harold dined with me here; a cosy conversation and once again I was soothed by the beauty and the *bibelots* of this house. The Crown Prince has given me a piece of French furniture, a tall, slender cabinet with many, many drawers, for my jewels or my private papers.

Tᴜᴇꜱᴅᴀʏ 3ʀᴅ Mᴀʀᴄʜ

Mad morning of telephoning and messages and then to the House of Commons where I stayed for some time. An undercurrent of Churchillian criticism; the Prime Minister's unpopularity is immense and increasing. Randolph now known as 'Major Error',[2] is one of the causes for it.

Poor Geoffrey Lloyd was in despair as he seemed to think that he is to be thrown to the wolves by Winston in today's reshuffle. I tried to reassure him having heard that the Prime Minister had decided to sack both Grenfell[3] and Geoffrey; but when the Labour Party made strong representations about Grenfell he gave in and then decided to keep both. I hope the story is true; true at least that Geoffrey will remain at the Ministry of Petroleum where he has done well.

I walked home, after leaving a fat letter at the India Office to be sent in the Viceroy's bag to Peter . . . . I went to the Dorchester to see Mrs Greville, whose 75th birthday, I think it is.[4] She is slowly fading out, she was weak, almost inarticulate and pathetic; yet her courage remains and she was elegantly arranged with jewels and a feather boa and surrounded by flowers. I promised to lunch with her tomorrow to meet the Kents.

Peter Loxley, Geoffrey Lloyd, and Harold dined here but I capriciously went to Claridge's to dine *à deux* with the Crown Prince, who was very sweet. We had a long intimate conversation, part of which had to be in half a whisper since

1 His daughter (1899–1964).
2 He was at this point known as 'Major Churchill', hence the joke.
3 Dai Grenfell was Secretary for Mines at the Board of Trade, and held the post from 1940 to 1945.
4 She was 78, but in fact her birthday had been on 20 December.

Prince Bernhard of the Netherlands[1] was at an adjoining table. He seems rather a flat-goblet[2] and I overheard his high voice talking rather American-English very fast. He walks, too, so quickly and without dignity: indeed he almost minces and looks like a small Chinaman ... I dropped the Crown Prince at the RAC, where he was to have a Turkish bath and then came home, where I gossiped with Harold Balfour and Rex Whistler who is like an exquisite goat.

Apparently Geoffrey Lloyd has also heard that he is now safe, for a time at least.

The Duke of Aosta has died in Kenya from his hereditary illness, tuberculosis; it is rife in the Orleans family. He was immense, attractive, manly and courteous and a great lover. (Princess Olga was secretly in love with him and so were many, many more – probably Queen Helen of Romania.) He was alleged to be pro-British, but I know this to be untrue. He was anti-British, anti-German and very pro-Italian. I often met him and he reminded me of the Grenfells with his huge body always carelessly dressed. He had a slight, very slight snow flirtation with Honor at Sestriere; he picked her up on a slope, where she fell skiing and took her back to the hotel named for him, and called her by name. Of course she didn't recognise him, since she never knows anybody, until he presented himself and then she talked of me. I know Spoleto, his brother, better; he is the less intelligent of the two, and rather a pleasure lover and *coureur*[3] – but impotent. His relations amuse me – I thought otherwise – once! Both these giants were immensely ambitious and not very loyal to Prince 'Beppo', the Crown Prince, my ancient ally.[4]

WEDNESDAY 4TH MARCH

Warm but wet ... and I went to the House of Commons and sat through Questions. There were rumours of the reshuffle but nothing definite. Jim Wedderburn, with whom I spent an affectionate half-hour, completely burying our small hatchet, confided in me that he has been relieved of his office.[5]

Lunched with Princess Alexandra of Greece ... [she] has taken a flat at 37 Grosvenor Square belonging to Paris Singer;[6] it is quite attractive with views over

1 Prince Bernhard of Lippe-Biesterfeld (1911–2004), from birth Graf von Biesterfeld, was raised to the rank of Serene Highness in 1916 by his uncle, Leopold IV of Lippe. He married Princess (later Queen) Juliana of the Netherlands in 1937. He acted as aide to his mother-in-law, Queen Wilhelmina, during the war, and also saw active service with the RAF, repudiating Hitler and Nazism in his native Germany, even though he had briefly been a member of the party. He became Prince Consort in 1948 when his wife became Queen, and was one of the founders of the World Wildlife Fund. In the 1970s he was seriously implicated in a bribery scandal involving Lockheed, the aircraft manufacturer.

2 It is not clear what Channon means by this, unless it is to compare the Prince's squat form with that of a short, wide wine glass.

3 Womaniser.

4 He has not referred to the Crown Prince of Italy (qv) by this nickname before.

5 He had been joint Under-Secretary of State for Scotland since the previous year.

6 Paris Graham Singer (1892–1953), grandson of Isaac Singer who founded the sewing-machine company and son of Paris Singer, the 22nd of his 24 children.

the square and I wondered, would it not suit Peter, Paul and me after the war as a *pied-à-terre*? Yes, decidedly. (I shall give up Belgrave Square as its upkeep is too great a drain on my income.) Returned to the House of Commons where after a long talk with Leslie Hore-Belisha, I attended the 1922 Cttee, which Rab was addressing about post-war planning. It was meaty; and my God, how boring! I could scarcely listen; I can no longer concentrate.

The changes have been rung and very dull and unsatisfactory they are, too. [Richard] Pilkington goes to the Admiralty as Civil Lord in place of dull dreary Austin Hudson;[1] Pilkington is a lightweight. More astonishing is Arthur Henderson at the War Office as Under-Secretary; suddenly yanked out of the Army, he now assumes high office. He is a dear but very, very stupid and will not be a success – oh! Why, oh!, why Mr Chamberlain did you not go to the country after Munich? These people would not have been re-elected (Arthur got in by only 17 votes).[2] The *comble*,[3] however, is Paul Emrys-Evans at the Dominions Office as Under-Secretary with Cranborne; the wheel has now turned full circle; he is a silly, a humpty-dumpty, a noodle, Chamberlain-hating, anti-*Munichois*; and his only contributions to parliamentary life have been an undue absorption in the posteriors of his superiors, and his prolonged attacks on the late Prime Minister. Winston has now come out in the open; he reviles any supporter of the old regime, and refuses to give them office. He is bitter, unscrupulous, *rancunier*,[4] and I wonder how much more the Conservative Party, the Commons and the country will put up with. I hate him bitterly and think that he will ruin England and the Empire for personal aggrandisement.

Not, so far, at all a pleasant day and Monday's little spirit has not been sustained. Can nothing now go right?

Mrs Greville is now so ill that she has cancelled her royal luncheon for tomorrow; she must be a-dying to do that!

THURSDAY 5TH MARCH

The astrologers all are unanimous in predicting that today would be my 'lucky' day; so in a way it has proved for it brought me a short letter from Peter from Agra, dated February 2nd, and with it a splendid parure of emeralds, carved ones. More jewels! He is too touching and I am *attendri* indeed by his devotion.

---

1 Austin Uvedale Morgan Hudson (1897–1956) was Conservative MP for Islington East from 1922 to 1923, for Hackney South from 1924 to 1945 and for Lewisham North from 1950 to 1956. He held junior office from 1931 to 1942, and on being sacked from the Admiralty was created 1st Bt. He served again briefly during Churchill's 'caretaker' administration from May to July 1945 as Parliamentary Secretary at the Ministry of Fuel.
2 He in fact beat his Tory opponent by just 16 votes out of almost 42,000 cast at the 1935 election.
3 Limit.
4 Vindictive or spiteful.

I walked to the House where I remained all day, since my royal luncheon party with Mrs Greville was cancelled. There is India in the air and I attended a special meeting of the 1922 Cttee to hear Mr Amery, who whilst lucid was cautious and did not reveal the government's intentions, which are shortly to be announced.

Rex Whistler stays with me still; silent, strange, friendly but vague, he flits unobtrusively in and out of the Peterhof[1] – I like him.

I didn't wear Peter's emeralds as I am pretending that they came tomorrow, or Saturday, my 45th birthday.[2]

FRIDAY 6TH MARCH

A bitterly cold and rather empty day. A premature birthday cable came from Peter from Delhi: he is being very attentive these past months. Is he anxious lest our friendship cool – he need not be, as I am devoted, utterly devoted to him – and a long letter from Jacqueline Lampson from Cairo.

Java is all but taken by the Japs. Another day or two and the Dutch East Indies must be written off.

Lord Chatfield has written a crushing retort to Major Error Randolph Churchill in *The Times*. My agents tell me that there is a movement to get rid of him, to send that firebrand back to Cairo at the earliest opportunity and that even the Prime Minister wants to be rid – for a time – of his blue-eyed boomerang of a son.

Batavia has been evacuated.

Tomorrow, for me, begins perhaps a new, and less luxurious regime since I shall be 45.

Dined in alone with Harold; he had attended the lobby luncheon today where the PM, in a taurine but apologetic mood, had made a speech and been only moderately applauded. Harold hates him intensely.

SATURDAY 7TH MARCH

My 45th birthday: the *ancien régime* after a fashion has lasted me until today. I woke early and refreshed but was quickly dashed by having no news from Paul, nor from my mother-in-law; their silence hurt me – still, how could the child know. So far, as I write: cable and present from Peter; a telegram and telephone call and promise of a present from Alan; a note from Mr Bailey, my loyal henchman at Southend; telephone messages of congratulations from Maimie Pavlovsky and Diana Cooper and Natasha Bagration.

---

1 A jocular reference to 5 Belgrave Square.
2 A rare burst of honesty on this subject.

From now on I shall live a grimmer life, spend less, be kinder, devote more time to my diary, my health and the House of Commons. My youth is over, faded, and I am kept alive now by a desire to see Paul and bring him up well; and hankering to be nice more, at least with Peter; and an ambition to put my affairs, financial and otherwise, in order. To save death duties for Paul I want to live until about Christmas 1943. For the same reason I hope that my wicked, wayward, unfeeling wife will survive until that date . . . . I want and need this money for Paul and perhaps for Peter's use during his lifetime? Obviously it will never be mine . . . Strange too is my mother's silence. I am anxious about her, and know in my bones that when my next birthday comes round that she will not be on this unhappy planet.

I am half-conscious of a cold wind blowing from Pyrford; perhaps I am wrong. Yet I think that they have treated me rather roughly in some ways; but the Iveaghs, like their children, are astonishingly impersonal and are cold to everyone, and are uninterested and reserved with their progeny. Mr Bland, who has known them for fifty years, says that they are the hardest couple he has ever met. I wonder!? Is lack of warmth necessarily hard? I really believe, however, that they think only of their money, their many millions, and how to save them. Lord and Lady Midas. Why is it that when people behave badly to anybody, they usually turn against their victims? . . . But I am, I know, always too quick to report slights where none are meant.

All the London ladies rang me up but didn't cheer me much – Lady Willingdon, Loelia Westminster and others. The Coopers asked me to lunch . . . instead, I went, perhaps unimaginatively to the Vsevolods and thence to sit to James Gunn. My famous, long-delayed portrait is about finished. He is a magnificent painter but his backgrounds are dull, and dark, and I am somewhat uncertain about his taste.

The Crown Prince fetched me, and was very sweet. Later he organised a gala dinner at Claridge's to celebrate my birthday – Maimie, Vsevolod, Arthur Leveson and Natasha – but I, unable to throw off my depression, was dull and downcast and kept thinking of my faraway child and of the crumbling Empire and my blasted life . . . home at midnight where I found consular cables from my mother, and Laura Corrigan, still in Vichy.

On the whole an unsatisfactory birthday and no presents except emeralds from Peter. Perhaps more will come.

SUNDAY 8TH MARCH

There is a nip of spring, *enfin*, in the air and I am tempted to go to Kelvedon.

Java has gone, and the Battle for India is about to begin. Already the Japs are laying their plans for the occupation of Madagascar. We are caught . . . caught – and I am like a trapped beast but still in a gilded – or is it pinchbeck – cage?

Lunched with Maimie, Vsevolod and the Crown Prince; and was prepared and packed to go to Kelvedon for the night when the CP rather pathetically pleaded with me not to go, not to desert him during his last few days here; it seems he is to leave at long last on Wednesday next. The Foreign Office and the Court – particularly 'the Black Rat', Alec Hardinge, who is so violently anti-monarchical, although the King's private secretary – have been unhelpful, even obstructive about the Greeks' visit, arrangements and their departure. The CP remarked, 'What has come over England? What is the matter with this wonderful country?' Both he and his brother the King are seriously disillusioned and despondent and in their hearts deeply offended. Only I have taken real trouble with them . . . and so I changed my plans, drove him and the Russias to Kelvedon, where we spent the afternoon and had tea. The place saddened me, as it always does now . . . Whilst they browsed over my albums I sent off cables to my mother, my son, my alter ego; and to Laura Corrigan. Then we drove back and I dined here *à quatre* in Belgrave Square. I thus spent eleven consecutive hours with my friends and am now going to bed, relieved to be *enfin* alone.

MONDAY 9TH MARCH

Woke early, refreshed . . . no personal news on my breakfast tray. World news continues to be momentous: the Japanese have landed at New Guinea, Australia is threatened. We have bombed Paris again; evidently HMG are goading Vichy into declaring war against us . . .

Wrote to Peter and Prince Paul, and then walked to the Apéritif where I lunched with Patsy. Felt ill, and rather flushed by *vin rosé* I retired to the RAC for a Turkish bath. Dined in alone with Diana Cooper, who shimmered loveliness although she has a cold. She was charm and gentleness itself and asked me about Honor. I told her the story and was startled when she told me that my marriage had been broken up, or at least seriously unsettled, by Diana Cavendish – I always suspected something of the sort. Diana advised me against divorce etc.

Much irritation and fuss about the departure of the Greeks for the Middle East as the Air Ministry, goaded, I think, by the Foreign Office, refuses to give the royal party the requisite number of places! The King, however, accompanied by his Prime Minister, M. Tsouderos,[1] his Secretary, his Chamberlain and Humphrey Butler,[2] leave on Friday in the *Clare*, the flying boat which brought me back from Cairo. Cripps – this is still a secret – goes by the same plane.

---

1 Emmanouil Tsouderos (1882–1956) was Prime Minister of Greece from 1941 to 1944, for almost the entirety of the Greek government-in-exile. He was a Cretan, and had been Governor of the Bank of Greece.
2 Humphrey William Butler (1894–1953) was a professional soldier who had won the Military Cross in the Great War and who reached the rank of colonel; he became equerry to Prince George, later Duke of Kent.

TUESDAY 10TH MARCH

Walked to the House and back as I had a luncheon party: Loelia Westminster, the Crown Prince of Greece; Cecil Beaton; and Nicholas Lawford – all charming and I was gay and even witty – I still have flashes of my old power and today for an hour was brilliant – then something snapped and I dried up. Loelia, whom I have always regarded as one of the richest women in England . . . . heralded her poverty. The Treasury have demanded years of back taxation and she is ruined – temporarily. However, she glittered with jewels and seemed well . . . . Alan, delightful and affectionate, is back from Portsmouth for a few days. His old mother has been with him for a fortnight at Brighton and Portsmouth. It is a scandal.

WEDNESDAY 11TH MARCH

Today . . . . indigestion and the prelude to a cold added to my despair, as did a discouraging conversation with dear old Mr Bland, who fears that Lord Iveagh is not now prepared to pay off my indebtedness, which is disappointing and almost dishonest since he several times promised to do so.

Winston rose and without a preliminary cheer announced that important decisions had been made about India and that Cripps was going there at once (which I knew). The House appreciated the solemnity of the moment and that the great Empire of India was being bartered away; that Churchill was going back on the policy which he championed for five years in the House. The Empire is ending . . . I was in a frenzy to get a letter to Peter via Cripps . . . . Then I attended a crowded all-party meeting of MPs and peers which was addressed by Duff Cooper. Never has he been so dull – and what a theme, the fall of Singapore. He scarcely held his audience, which was restive, even hostile. I was sorry for him and indeed, since when has he lost his eloquence? He was tired, listless and dull – Lady Astor, who was unfortunately next to me, kept up a running commentary of rude remarks about him. At times she almost hissed like the serpent she is!

Later

Harold [Balfour] tells me that Cripps had laughingly remarked to him that he had been trying to avoid the King of Greece for five months; now he will have him as a companion for five whole days.

The Crown Prince dropped in; he and his brother, the King, had lunched with the King and Queen at Buck House. Just the four. The Queen, he remarked indignantly and royally, hadn't kissed either of them. 'She doesn't know yet,' he added. All royalties over-kiss. I was not mentioned in this little festival. Later he gave tea to the Kents, who sent me many messages and were sweet. Her pregnancy is now obvious; but few people know of it as yet.

Going to bed now at 9.30. I am really ill. I am sure the Iveaghs avoid me because they owe me morally at least, if not legally, £16,000! Shall I ever get it?

THURSDAY 12TH MARCH

Woke dazed after drugs and aspirins, but dressed hurriedly and rushed to 11 Downing Street which is now the Lord Privy Seal's Office and there I deposited letters for General Wavell and for Peter which Cripps, who leaves tonight, has promised to take. A fighter escort has been laid on . . . trust that the King of Greece will think it is for him! Then I came home, avoiding the draughty House of Commons. Now I shiver and shake and must have people to lunch. Sometimes I wish I were dead. Only Paul and Peter to live for; one in Delhi, and the other in New York. And my beloved, immense, affectionate Alan is becoming rather spoilt – as perhaps I once was. The break-up of my marriage is a salutary lesson to him, he is determined to avoid any such catastrophe for himself. He is lunching with the Iveaghs today; their silence is wounding, almost ominous? Why? What can they have heard? I think it is embarrassment about the money. My mother writes that she has made a new will and hints that it is in my favour. I trust so. She must have at least £150,000; the income will be a great help. She will be 73 on July 14th next, but looks 100 at least. She has always been old, unkempt and half-mad, but fundamentally honest and well-meaning.

Patsy lunched with General de Gaulle yesterday and was thrilled – why? I wouldn't meet him if invited!

My little luncheon party, which consisted of Mrs Keppel; her daughter Mrs Trefusis, who is cruelly nicknamed 'Violet Le-Duc',[1] Leslie Hore-Belisha and Tilea . . . Much chat. Mrs Keppel is magnificent, untruthful and *grande dame*, and will be to the end. She is still stately and her hair is a pale blue – powdered blue. She gave me advice; said that I had behaved with restraint and dignity and that the Iveaghs and Halifaxes praised me on all sides to everybody – she had often heard it! I hope she was being rather more accurate than usual. Certainly she was when she added that Honor had always been the rudest girl she ever met – 'a barbarian', that I was too good for her etc.; and she advised me to divorce her, not perhaps tomorrow, but at my leisure. I promised to think about it and I fear somehow that she may be right . . .

Rested all the afternoon: I feel ill and have a temperature; perhaps flu is coming on. Then I dressed, was fetched by Lady Willingdon, and we went to the Ritz where she gave an immense, too-large dinner party: the King of Greece (who is leaving tomorrow), the Crown Prince, Mrs Brittain-Jones; Sir Philip and Lady

---

1 Eugène Viollet-le-Duc (1814–79) was a leading French architect of the nineteenth century who restored many of the country's medieval monuments. The joke was presumably a slight on Mrs Trefusis's masculinity.

Game[1] of the Police! Sir 'Pug' and Lady Ismay;[2] the Spanish Ambassador;[3] June de Trafford;[4] Sir Eric Miéville;[5] Lady Hudson;[6] and the *clou* of the dinner party which was Sir James and Lady Grigg,[7] the new regime at the War Office. I have never met a more undistinguished-looking couple. They might come out of a pawnbroker's shop in the East End. Yet perhaps they aren't Jewish,[8] and only look it. Dreadful clothes, no manners; but intelligence and good intentions. I was not impressed by either, really yet didn't dislike them. He seemed rather overwhelmed by so much high society. More than she was; she over-curtsied, he didn't 'bob' at all ... I was host at this quaint dinner party and was next to Joyce Brittain-Jones, whom I like rather less each time I see her. I wonder whether she is not secretly married to King George? She had many new bijoux, bracelets and other loot ....

Lady Willingdon and I dropped Eric Miéville at Buckingham Palace, and then I came home, resisting Violet Trefusis's pleas to join her in the 'Rivoli', where she was with the Archduke and Leslie Hore-Belisha! The Greeks thoroughly enjoyed their evening and the King of Greece paid me an affectionate adieu. He leaves at dawn tomorrow.

FRIDAY 13TH MARCH

I woke with fever; was obliged to 'chuck' my weekend at Leeds [Castle], and rang up Lady Willingdon. I feel 100 and so ill.

---

1 Philip Woolcott Game (1876–1961) fought in the Army in the Second Boer War and the Great War, and in the Royal Flying Corps and RAF, from which he retired in the rank of air vice marshal in 1930. From then until 1935 he was Governor of New South Wales and then served as Commissioner of the Metropolitan Police from 1935 to 1945. He was knighted in 1924. He married, in 1908, Gwendolen Margaret Hughes-Gibb (1882–1972).

2 For Ismay, see entry for 12 January 1940 and footnote. Lady Ismay was Laura Kathleen Clegg (1897–1978), whom he married in 1921.

3 The Duke of Alba.

4 June Isabel Chaplin (1899–1977) married Rudolf de Trafford in 1924 but divorced him in 1938.

5 Eric Charles Miéville (1896–1971) joined the Consular Service in 1919. He served as private secretary to Lord Willingdon during the latter's service as Governor-General of Canada and as Viceroy of India. He was appointed assistant private secretary to the Duke of York (later King George VI) in 1936 and served him until 1945. He rejoined the government service in 1947 to assist Lord Mountbatten (qv) with Indian independence and partition. He was knighted in 1936.

6 Margaret (Peggy) Broadbent (1901–78) was the wife of Sir Austin Hudson (qv), whom she married in 1930. In the 1970s, when widowed, she hired as a butler one Archibald Hall, who had murdered his previous employer (the former Conservative MP Walter Scott-Elliott) and his wife. He planned to murder Lady Hudson and steal her jewels but decided he liked her too much. Hall died in prison in 2002, aged 78.

7 Gertrude Charlotte Hough (1885–1968) married Grigg (qv) in 1919.

8 They were not. In fact, Lady Grigg was the daughter of an Anglican clergyman.

SATURDAY 14TH MARCH

Still ill. We have been decidedly defeated in a huge naval battle off Java.[1] Why must England always be on the wrong side? . . . Harold has gone down to Cherkley to lunch with Beaverbrook.

SUNDAY 15TH MARCH

Harold reports that Max Beaverbrook is still in favour with the PM (who, by the way, had a small operation yesterday): they talk constantly on the telephone. Winston is annoyed because the American and Canadian newspapers give him only three more months as Premier. He is turning against Anthony Eden.

Harold is beginning to irritate me deeply. I think his character is deteriorating in some ways and his outlook is so limited. He is frightened of himself, unsure . . .

The sirens sounded last night; but, whilst they recalled the old raids, it was a technical accident. A huge German merchant cruiser got down the Channel yesterday, out-going:[2] it escaped. This added disgrace has been hushed up; but it will leak out! So England no longer rules the waves? We are defeated at every turn, particularly at sea wherein our strength was supposed to lie.

The newspapers make the official announcement that the Duchess of Kent cannot undertake any public engagements during the next few months. It [her baby] is due in June and already – but only recently – she shows.

Alice Harding and her erstwhile admirer, Freddie Ashton the dancer, who is now a Flying Officer, called, and stayed too long; as did the Crown Prince after dinner. He was sweet, silly, stupid and in a frenzy about his clothes and his packing. He doesn't seem to understand the difficulties of air-flying.

MONDAY 16TH MARCH

I am definitely better; but not yet recovered. However I got up, am up . . . Harold dined last evening with Duff, Oliver Lyttelton, David Margesson and 'the girls'; much political talk. OL very against Randolph, who was nearly court-martialled in Cairo, and had been threatened with immersion in the Nile by his enraged fellow officers. Three times Oliver, as Minister of State, had been obliged to send for him and rebuke him. The authorities in the Middle East are doing everything within their power not to have him back; meanwhile Winston is determined to send him there since he is doing the govt infinite harm here. Yet here he remains . . . They all agreed that he had no future (I could have told them that, and did, years ago) but, that he would always lead a party, a party of one! The boys all say

---

1 The Battle of Java, which had been fought since 28 February, ended in defeat for British, American, Dutch and Australian forces on 12 March.
2 That is, away from Germany.

that Winston's little operation yesterday [*sic*] was actually circumcision! Can it be true? Everyone swears that it is. The appointment of a minister in the Middle East has not yet been made and may never be filled.

No letters of importance. I talked to Diana, who also has flu and is in bed; and slowly got up. Nothing from *mes beaux-parents*, Honor, or anyone else. I suppose that every day gained is a victory. I want to live until about Xmas 1943 when the various settlements will be free of estate duty. By then the necessary three years will have elapsed.

Harold is perhaps going to America this week and I am hoping that he will. Wrote to my baby boy and to my mother. Paul's school report, which is the first I have ever had, is excellent and I am delighted and proud.

Alan and Patsy breezed in, gay, high-spirited, and rather animal. Alan gaily let down his trousers and revealed that he was wearing a pair of Patsy's palest, pinkest pants, a rather *dix-huitième* garment, lace etc. It seems he had none, and when he came up unexpectedly today from Ramsgate he borrowed a pair of his wife's!! . . . I thought the performance indecent and faintly exciting!

TUESDAY 17TH MARCH

Walked to the H of C, which I found singularly lacking in distinction. Dalton announced a reduction in the clothing coupons. Luckily I have an immense wardrobe.

Dined with Helen Fitzgerald at the Dorchester; Kathleen Harriman, Harold and I. Much political conversation and I attempted, but warily, to poison Kathleen against that fiend Randolph. No caution was, I soon discovered, necessary – she loathes him. She is a shrewd observer, a typical American girl of the more intelligent type; and whilst much in the Churchill clique is by no means blinded to its imperfections, and thinks it is soon to be doomed. After dinner she went up to Pam Churchill's bedroom to gossip and I accompanied her as far as the door and was creeping away when Pam called to me; and I went in. Randolph is luckily away at Chequers conferring with his father. Pam was sweet, attractive, soft and seductive: I could be in love with her; perhaps I am . . . . She unburdened herself about Randolph, prays for his departure, which will be her 'deliverance', and generally attacked him in the most disloyal and outspoken manner. I give that marriage until a fortnight after Winston falls or dies, whichever happens first! She was revelling in her short separation from him. I was startled, relieved and inordinately pleased.

WEDNESDAY 18TH MARCH

Still feeling ill: I fear that a malignant bug has got hold of me. However I walked to the House . . . . Slept, and attended two Cttees, the 1922 which was addressed by Archie Sinclair. He stuttered; he was verbose; he was fustian but towards the end improved and probably on balance just got away with it. Nevertheless the proceedings, like those in the Chamber, impress me as unreal and futile: such an institution is *démodé*,[1] out of date and slightly ridiculous. A later meeting of the Anglo-American Cttee was addressed by Averell Harriman who gave a pleasing and competent performance to a crowded house.

Came home. Eric Duncannon has arrived to stay with me. Very beautiful still with his aristocratic features and gay smile . . . . Jay [Llewellin] rather spoilt my evening by telling me that Basil Dufferin has been abusing me; did so in his hearing. This tactless sally spoilt my evening! Will I never learn not to take offence? Am I oversensitive? Usually these stories when never too grand prove harmless.

THURSDAY 19TH MARCH

Perhaps a luckier day. Woke early, still feeling dispirited; nice letter from my mother-in-law. Got up; rang Basil Dufferin on the telephone and he was charming. We agreed to lunch together; then I rang his wife, for she is still his wife legally, at Grosvenor Place where she is staying with her father. Basil lives at the Savoy. Walked to the House which Attlee again mishandled; met Winston in the passage and he half-smiled. In an attempt to court his lost popularity he himself announced to the House that he had appointed Casey[2] to be Minister of State in Cairo. I soon left and walked slowly towards the Ritz to meet Basil. In Jermyn Street I ran into Gerald Palmer[3] and asked him to dine tonight and then he confided in me that he is leaving this evening for India to join his master, Cripps. In fact he is leaving London at 3.15. It was then nearly one. In a frenzy I rushed to a bookseller's, bought several, came home, wrote a hurried scrawl to Peter and to General Wavell, and rushed to the Ritz. Basil, his face oozing pus, his jaws enflamed, and wearing bedroom slippers was half an hour late and I was in a rage because I could have written a longer letter to 'my other self' [Coats] . . . . I attacked Basil, told him I had heard these stories etc. He denied everything, said he barely mentioned me, and had always been loyal. I don't quite believe him; except that for all his faults, he has never been a gossip. We parted on the most amicable terms, and I rushed to Brooks's Club to find Gerald Palmer, who was waiting for me. I gave him two books and a letter for Peter; two books for himself and one for General Wavell, and then envying him as I have never envied any man before I left him sadly. In ten days' time he will be with Peter in Delhi: it is almost incredible.

---

1 Out of fashion.
2 Richard Gavin Gardiner Casey (1890–1976) had been Australian Minister in Washington since 1940.
3 Gerald Eustace Howell Palmer (1904–84) was Conservative MP for Winchester from 1935 to 1945. He was Cripps's parliamentary private secretary. After leaving Parliament he became an authority on the Greek Orthodox Church. He also played minor counties cricket for Berkshire.

He goes in the plane tomorrow along with Beaverbrook . . . . I took a taxi to the House of Commons in order to hear P. J. Grigg address the all-party committee, his debut was a dramatic disaster; he rose rudely and said that he would attempt to answer any questions. No speech; no remarks. He offended the largely attended Committee; most of the audience got up and left as a protest. No minister can live down a performance like that. Why he was not warned or advised, I don't know. I walked away with Ernest Brown, who said he thought that Grigg could never recover. And he also made sly little innuendos against the Prime Minister. Randolph, he said, was fast undermining his father's already precarious position.

The Home Secretary has finally warned the *Daily Mirror* that it is in danger of being suppressed.[1] It is a petty rag . . . As I walked back from the House I contrasted the fine, finished speech yesterday of Averell Harriman with the gauche and boorish behaviour this afternoon of P. J. Grigg. Perhaps I am prejudiced, but I am prepared to think him a farouche and dreadful person.

I hear that Dickie Mountbatten is to have a new and most important appointment.[2]

FRIDAY 20TH MARCH

Slept well and woke sleepily. Eric Duncannon came in at 3 a.m. I wrote letters and dictated all the morning; and wondered whether I should become PPS to Jay Llewellin? Could I stand the boredom? . . . Everybody rang up. The Coopers are laid low by flu and are lying, Diana tells me, prostrate side by side . . .

Channon spends a quiet weekend at Kelvedon.

MONDAY 23RD MARCH

Walked in the Kelvedon gardens early this icy sunny morning, before leaving. The many trees and shrubs I have had planted are growing and the yews are doing splendidly. Even the copper roof to the swimming-bath pavilion is at last turning green – one day this place will be a Paradise I trust, for Paul. Then, my car laden with orchids, I drove to Southend, which was blue and sunlit. Bombs were dropped last night at Thorpe Bay.[3] Has the spring offensive begun again?

All day I had interviews, and then drove to London where I found many letters but none of importance except one from Peter. Cripps has arrived in Delhi, where the excitement must be immense.

1 Churchill was especially angry with David Low, the cartoonist, whose drawings goading the government were also deemed defeatist.
2 He was about to join the Chiefs of Staff Committee, and would have a hand in planning the raids that summer on Saint-Nazaire and, disastrously, Dieppe, where three-fifths of the 6,000 men who took part were killed, wounded or captured.
3 A modern suburb of Southend-on-Sea, to its east.

Dined with Ham Kerr at 11 Westminster Gardens and almost envied him his small, sunny, attractive flat. Home early in buoyant spirits. I must try and never smoke again since I now feel so well, clean and clear.

TUESDAY 24TH MARCH

Many letters, the Butlers arrived to stay for a few days, and the Crown Prince called. He is actually leaving now on Thursday morning and I shall miss him. Almost congenital,[1] his brain barren, he is nevertheless so sweet, so trusting and dependent that there will be a void in my life. A vacuum . . . after he left this morning I walked across the Square to lunch with the Spanish Ambassador just the six, Alba himself, sleek, fashionable, deaf and debonair, even dashing; the Archduke Robert, Rab . . . . and Mr [James] Garvin, who is a colossal man, both in age, physique and mentality. He was brilliant; he was anecdotal, he repeated many of the more worn Curzon stories, but was nevertheless riveting. He has only recently resigned the editorship of *The Observer* owing to differences with Lord Astor. He maintained that 1942 is a year in the history of the world, the year that will decide the future for generations, perhaps centuries to come. He thinks that Germany has had in Russia a blow from which she may never recover; the flower of her youth sacrificed, killed and frozen? He compares the German campaign with the Russian defeat in 1915 at Tannenberg.[2] He was interesting, and optimistic, and intensely critical of Lord Baldwin, whom he dismissed as a dangerous mediocrity with a fatal touch of talent. Had he been a greater man, either he would have been all right, or so unpopular that he would have been soon defeated; had he been completely incompetent, he could never have kept his high position; it was the fatal touch of talent and England and the Empire and the world are suffering now in consequence . . . so he went on.

Rab drove me to the House of Commons and later I walked home. I found Sydney Butler in and really genuinely liked her quite immensely. She has improved, thawed or mellowed. I dined with them at the Ladies' Carlton Club, the ex-Iveaghs' house. There is still an atmosphere of space and splendour, although the vast and hideous mansion has been considerably modernised. I thought of the old Iveagh magnificence which prevailed in the days of Honor's lavish grandfather (I went there to a ball); and I felt sad at all that had happened, that I had perhaps forfeited by a defeat of character . . . Roy De Maistre,[3] the painter, dined with us.

---

1 He seems to mean 'a congenital idiot'.
2 Tannenberg, which was a colossal defeat for the Russians, actually took place in August 1914.
3 Roy De Maistre (1894–1968) was an Australian abstract painter, heavily influenced by cubism. He moved permanently to London in 1930 and during the war was attached to the Foreign Relations Department of the British Red Cross Society.

Rab was so gay and charming; I really love him. We gossiped . . . De Maistre said that he knew that the King had recently summoned Winston to see him, and when the Prime Minister arrived at Buckingham Palace he was surprised to find both Baldwin and Lloyd George with the Sovereign. They were there, at his command, to tell Winston how to behave in the Commons, etc., that he needed guidance in his manner and behaviour. De Maistre swears that his story is true. I shall find out.

Walked home, arm in arm with Sydney Butler, a delightful evening had it ended there. However the Crown Prince rang up and insisted that I go to Claridge's to say goodnight to him. I did: he gave me two handsome photographs of himself – but nothing else.

WEDNESDAY 25TH MARCH

A full day, I woke early, was massaged and waited for breakfast. My house is full since Harold Balfour, both the Butlers and Eric Duncannon are all staying here. On my tray were many boring-looking letters and one from my bank I almost didn't open; however, I did languidly enough. I was startled to see that Lord Iveagh had given me a present of £8,000 to pay off my overdraft. It is a year I have waited; a year I have been anxious! Will I never learn to be patient; and that the Iveaghs, whilst admittedly slow, are always right in the end? Of course I am immensely relieved; for this sum regularises my affairs and I am determined not to be extravagant; but to keep within my income, and if possible to save . . . Enchanted with this present, which had been so long delayed that I had begun to think it would never come, I walked gaily to the House of Commons, sat through the Question Hour and then accompanied by Ham Kerr went to the Savoy to attend the 1922 Cttee annual luncheon in honour of the Prime Minister.

He arrived, seemed mincing, shrunken and apologetic; yet I was surprised by the warmth of the reception, and he seemed much touched by it. I noticed that he saw I was not applauding – his eyes are often on me – and I hurriedly beat the table with my fist. I was between Ham Kerr and Adrian Baillie who told me that he could do nothing, nothing at all with his obstinate wife, the incredible Olive, who is ill. The PM spoke for half an hour and apart from attacking the *Daily Mirror* (and I am with him there) told us very little. He wound up well; and made a dramatic bid for more loyal support. Indeed I was almost moved until I remembered it was only his artistry which was impressing me. He is a *Schwärmer*, certainly, a supreme artist: nothing more, except a disaster for England. I came away disillusioned; walked to a jeweller's and bought for £50 a set of five sapphire and diamond buttons for the Crown Prince which I knew he hankered after. My good resolutions about finance seem to have lasted about six hours. Then I called on Mrs Greville who has somewhat recovered; she was sitting up and full of venom and malice and wit. She attacked Lady Willingdon whom she described as a 'selling-plater'.[1] The Andersons have both been to see her and the Queen was expected. She was, in fact, herself again . . .

Came home where I found the Archduke Robert and Sydney Butler waiting for me. Cocktails. Rather tired I went up to dress for my little dinner party, which was a farewell gesture to the Crown Prince who leaves tomorrow. He was very late and I rang him up and was almost rude but he explained that he had difficulties about his packing and his suit-cases. Came; Lady Willingdon, the Butlers; Basil Dufferin; Harold; Maimie and Vsevolod, and of course the round guest of honour, who whilst unpunctual was very sweet and infinitely touched by the jewels. He ought to be . . . Dinner was excellent: caviar, roast beef, ice cream and champagne. Diana arrived about 9.30, looking like a golden goddess and wearing a long ruby necklace she had ordered in Delhi which Peter had sent to her, she breathed beauty. A most hilarious evening which went on too long . . . but the blue dining room looked lovely and shimmering and the champagne was excellent; and we were gay and the war almost forgotten. Much chat about Cripps, who is bound to fail in his India mission. Basil thinks so; and so do Lady Willingdon and Rab. Cripps has made one ridiculous remark about solving the difficulties in a fortnight! A fortnight in India is like a drop of rain.

I had a drink with Jay Llewellin in the Smoking Room but he made no offer; perhaps he has been prevented by James Stuart, ever mine enemy, from doing so. I wonder.

In the Strand I ran into Nancy Cunard who looked 50.[2] I had heard that she was here, the horrible, degraded creature. Wearing white shoes, appalling clothes and too thin, too tall, she looked the distracted hunter she is, and yet about her features were traces of her mother!

THURSDAY 26TH MARCH

Woke early with a slight headache. The Crown Prince rang me at 7.20 to say 'goodbye' and I felt ashamed not to have gone to Claridge's to see him off; but I was so tired and it was so early! Now, later, I am sorry. A more quiet day . . . . went to the House, came home and entertained my mother-in-law to lunch. She was charming, affectionate and well and I felt ashamed and sorry that I had ever doubted her loyalty or her promises. I thanked her for the £8,000 . . . and we

---

1 A selling-plate is a race after which the winning horse is auctioned; it does not imply a high-quality horse.

2 Nancy Clara Cunard (1896–1965) was daughter of Sir Bache and Emerald, Lady Cunard (qv). She lived in France for most of the inter-war period and had a series of affairs with notable men, including Aldous Huxley. She became a campaigning anti-fascist and anti-racist, and worked herself to exhaustion during the war working in London on behalf of the French resistance. After the war her mental health degenerated – she had been an alcoholic and drug user since the 1920s – and she ended up being committed to an asylum. When Channon saw her she was 46.

discussed Honor and Paul and love and life . . . . She had in no way changed. I glowed towards her . . .

Arthur Longmore has been defeated at Grantham by a narrow margin.¹ The Socialists have done it! Of course it is a disgraceful proceeding since Longmore has the official backing of all parties and the coupon from the Prime Minister. It is the first defeat for the govt since the war and a rather serious reverse for Winston, who, Rab reports, made an unpleasing speech at the Conservative meeting today. I am fed up with his oratory and couldn't be bothered to go. Is Oliver Lyttelton aiming at the succession? Has he shrewdly understood the paucity of talent, the weakness of democracy, the futility of the almost degraded House of Commons, and does he mean to capitalise [upon] them all for his own personal advancement? I shouldn't be surprised if he succeeded in doing so.

The Andaman islands in the Bay of Bengal have been evacuated. Another and serious defeat, and the dangers to India grow. Will the Japs bomb Delhi and take Calcutta in their stride?

There was a most indecent scene in the Commons this afternoon once again demonstrating the ineptitude and selfishness of the Labour Party. This time it was a battle and a very rude one, between the Socialists who are in power and those who are out of the racket. Once in power they sing a very different tune. Morrison was exposed and badly battered. He is an embryonic dictator. The Socialists have ruined this country, lost the Empire and caused the war – and today they have defeated Longmore, a most distinguished serviceman, at Grantham by their treacherous tactics. Kendall,² the victor, is also the seducer of the Lady Ursula Manners and, I am told, her acknowledged lover!

The House has now risen for over a fortnight. We are in a state of eviction. I am in a state of exhilaration because Randolph has left. Auchinleck was at last persuaded to have him back, and the wicked boor left this morning by the same flying boat as the Crown Prince, much to his [the Crown Prince's] annoyance.

---

1 Longmore (see entry for 3 January 1941 and footnote) had fallen out with Churchill and been recalled from the Middle East. He stood as a Conservative candidate in the Grantham by-election, caused by Victor Warrender's (qv) elevation to the peerage, but lost by 367 votes to a socialist, despite Attlee's having endorsed Longmore's candidacy. The vote was seen as a verdict on Churchill's conduct of the war. Denis Kendall, the winner (*vide infra*), stood as a notional independent.

2 William Denis Kendall (1903–95) had a colourful life before becoming the Independent MP for Grantham, which he represented until 1950. He ran away to sea aged 14 and spent his youth earning a fortune by helping police raids on opium dens in China. He also ran a cabaret in Shanghai. He moved to America and worked as a steeplejack and in a car factory. Eventually, he became the works manager at a Citroën plant in Paris. By 1938 he was managing director of a factory near Grantham making aircraft guns; but became of interest to MI5 because of his supposed fascist sympathies; they were also convinced he was a black marketeer and currency smuggler. After losing his seat in 1950, and being defeated again in 1951, he returned to America and set up a series of engineering businesses.

FRIDAY 27TH MARCH

Berners[1] rang me in the night to gossip . . . however, I slept well. I don't miss the Crown Prince yet; instead there is a feeling of relief. I am thinking of Longmore and sorry for him: he has had a year of disappointments.

The Butlers have left for the country. A petulant letter came from Nannie! I hate all nannies, this one less than most. A quiet day. Went to a play *Old Acquaintance*,[2] featuring Edith Evans,[3] with Alice Harding and Gerald Berners, and they came back here for supper. Both sweet and in superlative spirits – Gerald was gentle and pleasant and in an almost touching mood. He is living at Oxford where he is lonely; but his great passion, friendship or *tendresse*, for the Mad Boy, Robert Heber-Percy,[4] still goes on.

Early to bed.

SATURDAY 28TH MARCH

Slept magnificently: my health seems to be recovering definitely. Harold came into my room early as he is going flying for the day. The Duchess of Kent rang me up and we gossiped and talked of my loved absent 'Robinsons';[5] it is a year ago today or yesterday since they fled from Belgrade. What a ghastly year for them. No recent news.

David Margesson has been made a viscount; Moore-Brabazon is a baron.

MONDAY 30TH MARCH

Two books arrived from Honor – 'With best Birthday wishes!' – over three weeks late. Typical. And boring books, too: still it is a gesture. And gestures are so important. Are all women mad? I suspect so.

The Indian proposals[6] were announced by Cripps last night at Delhi and today splash the newspapers.

---

1 Gerald Hugh Tyrwhitt-Wilson (1883–1950) succeeded his uncle as 14th Baron Berners in 1918. He was a composer, painter and writer.
2 A play by John Van Druten, first seen on Broadway in 1940, and made into a film starring Bette Davis in 1943.
3 Edith Mary Evans (1888–1976) was one of Britain's leading stage actresses of the twentieth century, though also made a name in films, most notably as Lady Bracknell in Anthony Asquith's 1952 film of *The Importance of Being Earnest*. She became a Dame Commander of the British Empire in 1946.
4 Robert Vernon Heber-Percy (1911–87), known as 'the Mad Boy', was like Berners a wild eccentric, who became his partner in the early 1930s and lived with him until Berners' death in 1950.*
5 Prince Paul and his family.
6 Cripps sought complete support from India during the war in return for self-government after it; but Churchill thought this too radical, and Gandhi (qv) and his colleagues wanted independence at once.

After some reflection I have concluded that I am still comfortably off, if not actually rich ...

The Indian proposals have not been well received.

The Palace telephones to ask the address of the Crown Prince of Greece urgently! I trust that nothing has happened to the Crown Prince on his journey. It would be sad never to see that round smiling face again, never to be bored by 'nothingness' – that is the cruel world which best describes his fatuous character. Not a word from him since he left England on Thursday.

TUESDAY 31ST MARCH

I have changed my mind again; I am not rich, far from it and must continue to economise and to do so for a long time.

The Duchess of Kent rang up and we talked; she is coming to tea tomorrow. The newspapers defeatist about the acceptance by the Indian leaders of the new plan. So I always was. It was sheer Churchillian folly to suppose that Stafford Cripps could solve these time-old problems in a fortnight's time. Folly.

The joy and relief that the Crown Prince's absence has given us is like a balm. Perhaps I am liverish as I am so tired of and bored with Harold; he is becoming conceited, and perhaps Vsevolod is right in saying that he has an evil 'on the make' character. Or is it just I who am impossible? – Wrote letters, totted up my Himalayan accounts. How can I reduce my expenditure and avert eventual ruin?

Gave Circe Londonderry lunch at Pastori's; she looked handsome and was good company. Talked of the days when she governed England through Ramsay MacDonald ... they had been offered both Canada and India at different times. How the grand, the great, and the gay have fallen. The Londonderrys live now in a converted flat on the Hertford Street side of Londonderry House, and very squalid and sordid it is. Bleak bedrooms, skimpy plumbing, drab walls, cold corridors, few servants . . . . And I thought of their old days of splendour. It is depressing. Eric Duncannon is staying with me and bores me to distraction; is he a bit cracked? So he seems; but many people are . . . . I ached to be alone, alone; but had to take Eric out to dine at Pratt's; a motley crew – that rogue Ivan Cobbold,[1] who is a *faux bonhomme*[2] and a *poseur* and braggart, and a [blank]. Still he is attractive.

From all accounts the Cripps mission has been a failure. We are living in a Gibbonian age, Fall and Decline – but the Prime Minister still repeats to his

---

1 John Murray 'Ivan' Cobbold (1897–1944) was such an unruly child that his parents called him 'Ivan the Terrible' and the name stuck. He was wounded in the Great War, became Chairman of his family's Suffolk brewery, and rejoining the Scots Guards in the Second World War was one of those killed when a V1 hit the Guards' Chapel on 18 June 1944. He reached the rank of colonel.

2 An imitation of a good fellow.

immediate circle that when he signed the Atlantic Charter the war was won – only a matter of time. This, he believes.

WEDNESDAY 1ST APRIL

Irritating letter from James Gunn who is the biggest bore I have ever met. He muddled the frame of my portrait and so now it will not be exhibited at the Academy this year. It is a pity, and entirely due to his inoperativeness and casualness – sent a telephone message through his *charmeur* and was surprised when the frame turned up the wrong size. I am in a rage.

Harold suggested this morning bringing Paul back at once and by clipper. I am tempted to do so; but must first consider the complications here . . . I am in a fiendish temper despite the lovely spring weather . . . . However I walked to the India Office where I deposited a letter for Peter, on to the Colonial Office where I left another for Princess Olga and Paul . . . . walked to the Dorchester, still in a bad temper, and waited in the foyer for Vsevolod and Maimie who at length arrived; but I ran into General de Gaulle who came in with great panache. He is an irritating *poseur* . . . and with amusement I watched the hotel proprietor wait for and then escort Mr A. V. Alexander and Mrs to the lift. When I went up Mr and Mrs Ernest Bevin were in the lift. They, as had the Alexanders, looked bloated and self-important and pleased with themselves as Socialists in power always do. Luncheon was with the Kemsleys – a young verbose Frenchman attacked de Gaulle throughout the meal: He had formerly been attached to him. I twitted this garrulous Gaul with being a Free-Free-Frenchman but he had no humour and didn't smile. Lovely food, and the party would have been pleasant had the Frog not turned the festival into a harangue, a further-meeting. It was amusing as I knew that de Gaulle, whom I do not admire at all, was lecturing at that very instant in the same hotel a few floors below . . . when de Gaulle was selected by us, I wrote a memo advising against such a course since I knew he would not appeal to the majority of Frenchmen; but I don't know what became of it. He is a *poseur*, a dictator and according to my noisy fellow guest at lunch, capable of every trick.

The Duchess of Kent came to tea; she is enormous, colossal and had to be propped up with pillows. I had not seen her for more than a month. She was sweet, gentle and we talked of our poor friends in Kenya . . . She is so unhappy about them. Yesterday she received Nincić,[1] the Yugoslav Foreign Minister, at Coppins: he stayed for two hours and they discussed the poor Prince Regent. Nincić was hostile but not violent towards him; and even he abused Simović. The Duchess has just gone, and I feel so lonely, so *désoeuvré* with the path of failure hanging heavily on me – oh! What can I do? I am wretched. She said that

---

1 Momčilo Nincić (1876–1949) had been president of the League of Nations in the 1920s and was Yugoslav Foreign Minister from 1941 to 1943.

Rab had been charming about me last night at Coppins. He was there for one of his periodic 'dine and sleep' visits when he reports the news to the Kents. They dote on him and owe this friendship to me; as I originally took him there. The Duchess said he praised me lavishly.

Dined alone.

THURSDAY 2ND APRIL

Woke in better spirits: the sun is out and I am seriously tempted to bring back my boy from the Bronx! Shopped, fussed, wrote letters, and had a dinner party: Diana Cooper, lovely but *enrhumée*; Diane Abdy, petite, pretty, pregnant, provocative and unpunctual; Maureen Dufferin; Patsy; Harold; Leslie Hore-Belisha, and Geoffrey Lloyd. A little farewell before the Easter break. I was tired and lifeless but perhaps liverish. Jay Llewellin later dropped in . . . Bridge and burgundy. Maureen drank too much as usual and couldn't cope with her sentences . . . all stayed too late. I smoked again and drank a bit – I feel so much better when I do neither. Diane was sweet but maddeningly illogical; attacked our unpreparedness etc. – and her very pro-war, pro-French husband is very strange and idiotic. Bertie[1] has been sacked from the Army for being 'incompetent' – 'mad', as Diane said. And he, too, criticises Mr Chamberlain for not fighting before.

GOOD FRIDAY, 3RD APRIL   *WEST COKER MANOR, NEAR YEOVIL*

I fetched Leslie Hore-Belisha, as arranged, at 10.30. With much verbosity he kept me waiting for an hour whilst he packed, talked, telephoned and dictated to his famous secretary, Miss Sloan, who is one of the well-known Whitehall timers. I met her; and I suspect she is a semi-Semite. At last we started on our Somerset jaunt . . . and talked all the way to Yeovil. Leslie is charming, affectionate, French, stimulating and gay. He is rabidly anti-Churchill, who, he says, is quickly losing both the Empire and the war. He is right. He regrets having voted against Mr Chamberlain and wishes he were today alive and still Prime Minister . . . Then we talked of Miss Sloan who adores and bullies him and refuses to allow him to see his passbook; sends back things he has ordered when she thinks that he has been too extravagant etc. And he asked me for my matrimonial advice; he decided not to marry Mary Ravensdale,[2] and now, our hostess Violet Trefusis, should he – or should he not marry her? I advised him, with some reservations, to do so and soon. He promised to consider the proposition; but I feel he won't. Of course we

---

1 Sir Robert Abdy, her husband.
2 Mary Irene Curzon (1896–1966) was Lord Curzon's eldest daughter. On his death in 1925 she inherited the barony of Ravensdale as it had a remainder to descend through the female line. She was more generally known as Irene, her second name.

arrived late at Bulbridge to lunch with Juliet Duff. (I had arranged it!) But she was charming and pleased with our visit. The little house, so skilfully arranged with exquisite Regency and French furniture inherited from her mother, the famous Lady Ripon,[1] is charming. Juliet is a fool but a cultivated one and has immense taste; .... Leslie was impressed by our luncheon, and our interlude. Then we came on to Yeovil where I had not been since the old Curzon, Montacute [House] days of my platinum-ed youth. Now we are staying in a cold, uncomfortable little house belonging to Sir Matthew Nathan,[2] which Violet has taken. The west country is cold, wet and uncomfortable and horrible. I wish I were back in Belgrave Square.

Saturday 4th April

Violet Trefusis is an extraordinary woman: she is a well-known lesbian, yet has had lovers, including myself in the Florentine days (Ambellino *circa* 1930 or '31). Last night she proposed, and not for the first time, to Leslie H-B, who refused her again. She is quick, clever, a raconteur who has inherited Mrs Keppel's gift for inaccuracy. In fact she is a liar, and an embarrassing one; yet she is a good writer, and a bilingual one having written several competent novels in both English and French. I am sure she tosses them off ...

We drove to East Coker Manor, picked up Mrs Keppel, very Edwardian with her jewels and gloves, and then drove to Wells passing Glastonbury Abbey, or rather the dreary remains *en route* ... At Wells we went over the cathedral and then went to the adjoining palace where we lunched with the Bishop.[3] It is a magnificent building outside, thirteenth century. Within it is an untidy and unattractive mess. Awful lunch .... Much talk of *Barchester*. 'There is nothing I like better than to lie in my bed with my favourite Trollope,' the Bishop said to everybody's consternation. Mrs Keppel looked up and in a stately voice said, 'His Lordship has been reading *The Chronicles of Barsetshire*.' Leslie H-B and I exchanged glances and half-giggled. We were then shown over the large and hideously arranged palace. The Bishop took us to his spartan bedroom and confided in us that it was impossible for him to live upon his present income of £5,000 less tax. He is a sweetie; he then conducted us in person to the Close, which at Wells, is called 'The Liberty' and proceeded to show us over the cathedral, which from that approach is magnificent. An interesting two hours, then we drove home. Mrs Keppel full of *vivre*,[4] charm and lies even more than her daughter! She sees much of Winston but considers him 'bust'.

1 See entry for 23 September 1941 and footnote.
2 Sir Matthew Nathan (1862–1939) had a distinguished career in public service that included being Governor of Sierra Leone, the Gold Coast, Hong Kong, Natal and Queensland.
3 Francis Underhill (1878–1943) was Bishop of Bath and Wells from 1937 to 1943.
4 Life.

Quiet evening – I am so cold and homesick. I feel I shall never go away again, but I am amused by Leslie Hore-Belisha's airs and grand mannerisms. He stops to talk to everybody, is widely recognised and with the meagrest encouragement he offers his autograph. He has a surprising following in the country, certainly, particularly with the young. The aristocracy, however, hate him.

EASTER SUNDAY, 5TH APRIL

Last Easter I was with Alan at Dover and we were shelled; the Easter before I was with the Regent at Belgrade, staying at his magnificent palace . . . now I am here. We went to lunch at East Coker Manor,[1] a honey-coloured house of great antiquity which belongs to Mrs Dorothy Heneage, *née* Hilgar [*sic*].[2] A fine house. lived in since about 1400 and full of treasures. The hostess, a stepdaughter of old Lord Savile, is 63, and has known everybody always – she is a half hunched-back, hideous, but witty and a widow. She took to me at once and showed me her treasures – the Sir Joshuas [Reynolds] in her bedroom, the Fabergé objects, the two rooms full of Hilgar and Heneage muniments etc. . . . A wonderful old house, damp, well kept, with many years and the accumulation of centuries. Mrs Keppel *élégante*, Edwardian, and affectionate kissed me several times, and told us many lies and extravagances!

Mrs Heneage, who has had a rich life full of lovers, was coy about my father-in-law – was he ever *en flirt* with her?

There was a large cocktail party of neighbours and 'locals'; but I was bored. Went to church this morning for a beautiful service, gay and high. The organ was a delight.

The house is cold and uncomfortable.

EASTER MONDAY, 6TH APRIL

Leslie confided in me that Violet followed him to his bedroom last night and proposed to him again! She is mad keen to marry any politician, preferably him. Lady Anderson has set the fashion! . . . We lunched at Yeovil at the Mermaid Inn; the others went to a film whilst I waited for two dreary hours in the squalid hotel lounge ruminating about my child, my past, Peter and the depressing war outlook.

(The Indian negotiations spin out; Cripps is still at Delhi and confers with the Viceroy, who may be succeeded by Wavell. That is the last report.)

---

1 The house, which is a manor house, is known as Coker Court. T. S. Eliot visited the village, from which some of his forebears came, in 1940 and its name became the title of the second of the *Four Quartets*.

2 Dorothy Margaret Helyar (1879–1947) was the widow of Godfrey Clement Walker-Heneage (1868–1930).

Drove to a pretty cottage at East Coker to have a drink – hock, and eat plovers' eggs with the young Heneages, David[1] who is in the Grenadiers and a pretty wife. They have a charming cottage on the estate. I was amused when shown the voluptuous conjugal bedroom to see only one photograph and that of that *faux beaux sabreur*, Geordie Lennox-Boyd.[2]

TUESDAY 7TH APRIL

Leslie and I left at 11.30: he is maddeningly unpunctual. It was grey, wet and cold, and we stopped at Salisbury to look at the cathedral and I wandered about the Close; and we had a picnic lunch. He drank milk as usual. Then we continued: the great trunk road was deserted and we raced along. I began to think of my will – why? – Leslie dozed and chatted occasionally. Suddenly, turning out of a side road I saw a military lorry approaching at breakneck speed: I knew at once that an accident was inevitable. I tried to slow down, blew the horn – but it was too late. I swerved into the ditch, first avoided the lorry and brought the car back onto the road, but it skidded and overturned. First I thought we should be killed, but in the second during which we avoided the approaching car, knew we would live but probably be hurt. It was a ghastly, sickening second. However with great *sangfroid* Leslie and I climbed out unscathed, intact but perhaps shocked. Altercation with the driver, followed by apologies when Leslie was recognised. He drew himself up: 'Not only am I an ex-Secretary of State for War but also an ex-Minister of Transport, so I have you on both counts,' he declared dramatically. The stupid dazed driver and the three soldiers with him were impressed and obsequious and were able to lift the car up – and we continued. I asked where we were and was told near Alton – where Honor lives in sin. This added to my emotions. Belisha behaved well; so did I, he kept repeating. We continued on our way in the very battered car until Sunningdale, where we had a sumptuous and reviving tea with Maimie Pavlovsky at Earlswood. She had aged twenty years with her recent illnesses.

No bad news awaits me here; exhausted I went to bed for supper.

WEDNESDAY 8TH APRIL   *SEND GROVE, WOKING*[3]

Slept atrociously; the room seemed to overturn and waltz and I could not put the accident from my mind ... this morning much fuss with the garage and insurance coupon. It will take a month or maybe more to put my poor car right. Meanwhile I have hired a Ford. Long day with constituency letters and lunched alone .... Loelia

---

1 John David William Graham Walker Heneage (1905–50).
2 Alan's brother. See entry for 23 December 1938 and footnote.
3 Send Grove was a country house of the Duchess of Westminster, in Surrey.

Westminster, Violet Trefusis, Raymond Mortimer and Winnie Portarlington came to tea. The first three and I drove here in my hireling where we dined and are spending the night. Delicious dinner and the lovely little house is ever a delight. It and Bulbridge[1] are in the acme of perfect taste. Gay chat . . . I am sorry for Loelia and all other impoverished duchesses. One midnight conversation with my old ally, Raymond Mortimer.

THURSDAY 9TH APRIL

Drove up to London with Violet. Many letters and much accumulated work. I am now, my returned passbook reveals, overdrawn only £113. Never for twenty years have I been in so healthy a state financially: but I must continue to economise. Quiet day still recovering from the shock of my accident. I wrote to Honor and told her: will she reply? I doubt it . . . .

Lady Willingdon; Peter Loxley – so very charming; and Leslie Hore-Belisha dined. When Harold returned we had a slight dust-up about Russia as I accused him of sending too much materiel to Russia thus endangering the Empire. He was annoyed but I am right.

It is announced that both HMS *Cornwall* and *Dorsetshire*[2] had been sunk off Ceylon. Have we any ships left?

Since the smash that night[3] so easily could have been fatal I have taken to nail-biting and smoking again. Life is very precious.

FRIDAY 10TH APRIL

Reconciled with Harold . . . Wrote endless business letters. Called on Patsy, had doubts for the very first time of Alan's complete loyalty, and had a Turkish bath. The collapse of my marriage has served as an object lesson to Alan and he is determined now to make a success of his lucrative marriage; in so doing he has grown more fond of Patsy and she of him. Formerly he was so bored with her, and indifferent. She goes to Portsmouth tonight to spend a weekend honeymoon with him. She spent Wednesday night with Honor at Shalden Park Farm, and reports that she was well and totally immersed in her farming. Mr Woodman was away – 'in Essex'! Was he on the loose, or had he gone to see his wife who is living now near Brentwood? Honor was apparently well and happy as indifferent to the world as ever.

---

1 A house on Lord Pembroke's estate at Wilton in Wiltshire.
2 *Cornwall* was a heavy cruiser launched in 1926; *Dorsetshire* was a heavy cruiser of the same class launched in 1929. They were both sunk by the Japanese on 5 April, 200 miles south-west of Ceylon, with a total of 424 men killed; but another 1,122 survived, being picked up after thirty hours in the water.
3 It actually happened during an afternoon.

Yet another ship gone, HMS *Hermes*,[1] one of very few remaining aircraft carriers. It is the fourth which we have lost since the war [began].

SATURDAY 11TH APRIL   *KELVEDON*

Still nothing, not a sign of life, from the Crown Prince since he left London. He is like that; incapable of putting pen to paper. Still it is depressing, such bad manners and I am annoyed and regret having given him diamond and sapphire links as a farewell present. He is very common really, and Teutonic, yet loveable ...

Micky Renshaw came to lunch, and then I drove here. Kelvedon is looking almost its loveliest, brooding and beautiful. I read Simon Harcourt-Smith's very exquisite extravaganza *The Last of Uptake*;[2] it is lovely and then I went for a solitary walk in the dusk. Uptake reminds me of Kelvedon.

Cripps reports failure in his attempts to negotiate with the Indians and tomorrow he leaves for England. I never believed he would succeed. He will bring me letters .... from that dark land which is even now in my thoughts.

An extraordinary letter from Mary Baker which is really an offer of marriage ... after all these years, is it possible? Shall I accept? An antidote to my growing loneliness, and increased financial security since she offers me her fortune which is in America. Two proposals in one week! But my heart and future are pledged.

SUNDAY 12TH APRIL

A glorious vernal day and I spent it out of doors, gardening and roaming about, tying trees and almost watching them burst unto bud ... and I ruminated on the immense fatigue of the English, only they don't know it. They are the most baffling race on Earth, much. But all their women are neglected and hence demonic and repressed. Now there is another scandal in high-life – the Weigall heiress, Priscilla,[3] who married Richard, Lord Curzon[4] – the Howe's handsome mild heir, in 1933, has already presented him with two bastards, which she admits publicly. Nevertheless Richard has acknowledged the boy as his son, and eventual

---

1 When launched in 1919 *Hermes* was the world's second purpose-built aircraft carrier. She too was sunk off the Ceylonese coast, on 9 April after an attack by over thirty Japanese dive-bombers, and with the loss of 307 lives.

2 A novella, published in 1942 and illustrated by Rex Whistler, about the relationship between two spinster sisters in a Victorian country house.

3 Priscilla Crystal Frances Blundell Weigall (1914–96) married Viscount Curzon (*vide infra*) in 1935; they divorced in 1943. Her father, Sir Archibald Weigall, 1st Bt, was Conservative MP for Horncastle from 1911 to 1920; her mother was the daughter of Sir John Blundell Maple, 1st Bt, and the heiress to the Maple furniture fortune.

4 Edward Richard Assheton Penn Curzon (1908–84) was Viscount Curzon by courtesy from 1929 to 1964 when he succeeded his father as 6th Earl Howe. He had a distinguished naval career during the war.

Earl Howe![1] Priscilla not long ago went off with her lover and seducer, who was the agent at Penns[2] – an agent again! – now the man is in prison. And the climax to this sordid tale is that Richard, usually so quiet, so gentle, and mild-mannered with his quiet fogeyish charm and on the surface at least his mother's sweetness, has run away with his stepmother![3] Lord Howe's second wife, whom he picked up in Africa.

I feel that I am on the edge of a decision or precipice! I must be cautious, careful and plodding.

I have read much today and aborted life: I am only happy alone. People intoxicate or infuriate me so.

The news tonight is depressing; the Japanese are advancing quickly in Burma and I fear that Calcutta is doomed and perhaps India. It is announced that Cripps is already at Karachi on his way back.

MONDAY 13TH APRIL

My car literally laden with blooms, I drove to London for the reopening of Parliament. The PM, uneasy, halting, almost inarticulate, made a short, and far from comprehensive, brilliant, or even elegant statement about Singapore, Cripps and the recent loss of the three ships. He has lost his self-confidence and the House listened rudely. He was much questioned and was ungracious and uncompromising. Henry Studholme,[4] elected last week for Tavistock, took his seat. He was a friend of mine, indeed an intimate in Oxford days. Kendall the new independent Black-leg[5] member for Grantham was also introduced. He looks a wiry, large, cocksure, troublesome little upstart. I promised to stand behind the Speaker's Chair to welcome Henry S after his ordeal of taking his seat, and did so. I led him into the lobby and as we chatted the Prime Minister came up for a second and stopped to smile at him. I at once introduced them and they shook hands. There was a flicker of a smile on the poor PM's face; but he looks haggard and harassed and much careworn and thinner. I was almost sorry for him. Henry Studholme is dull, a bore, but rather an old 'sweetie'; certainly he will not cause much excitement in the House. I must try and nobble him; prevent him from becoming an Edenite! I saw Jim Thomas make his usual advance to every new member.

1 The illegitimate boy never became Earl Howe. When the 6th Earl died in 1984 his second cousin succeeded him, as was inevitable under English peerage law.
2 Penn House, near Amersham in Buckinghamshire, is the seat of Earl Howe.
3 Joyce Mary Mclean Jack, of Johannesburg, married Lord Howe in 1937 and they were divorced in 1943. She and his son did not marry.
4 Henry Gray Studholme (1899–1987) was Conservative MP for Tavistock from 1942 to 1966. He served as a whip from 1951 to 1956, when he was created 1st Bt.
5 Channon uses this term in this context to allude to Denis Kendall's supposed activities as a black marketeer, currency racketeer and fascist sympathiser.

Patsy rang up and proposed herself to dine which she does too frequently. She is developing[1] and more balanced than Honor and may perhaps never come such a cropper. I trust not.

TUESDAY 14TH APRIL

I walked to the House, which met at the unusual hour of two o'clock, because of the Budget. There were more members than usual but I had no difficulty in getting a comfortable and convenient seat on the bench, which is on the steps of the Throne. I was next to Jimmy Maxton. Punctually at two, since there were no Questions, Kingsley Wood rose and opened his colossal, astronomical Budget. He spoke clearly and calmly, and whilst there were many clichés – he is a cliché king – and he has little humour and no wit, he was nevertheless easy to listen to, and remained good-tempered in spite of foolish interjections by the irrepressible communist, Gallacher. The speech lasted 137 minutes, and he did not break the news of the dreaded [tax] increases until towards the very end. They were a relief: it is indeed a people's Budget. Heavy increases on spirits, wines, beers, and tobacco and the purchase tax to be raised. The community as a whole will have to bear the burden of this war which the Socialists were so determined to have, and so determined not to prepare for ... When it was over I walked home where I found that both Micky Renshaw and Duncannon (who is becoming a bit of a cross since he invites himself constantly and never seems to realise that he might be unwelcome) had turned up, unasked and unwanted.

WEDNESDAY 15TH APRIL

Walked to the House, and sat for a time in the Smoking Room. Everybody says that the Prime Minister has regained his high spirits, that he is enchanted by Cripps's miscarriage. And so he seemed! For when I walked into the House I saw him sitting by the Throne, beaming. He was there with Attlee waiting to introduce P. J. Grigg, who has just been elected for Cardiff East. At the end of Questions, this very unattractive, un-me-ish little man was presented – an odd trio they looked. Attlee was embarrassed; the PM all smiles and Grigg, badly shabbily dressed and too-possessed. I am prejudiced against him; he is ill-mannered, rude and rough ... When he approached the table there were ironical cheers, particularly from the Socialist benches, and I must say that the new Mars looked most unmartial. As he took the oath he kissed the Bible, an old custom, but I have never seen it done. He looks Jewish ...

I attended a crowded all-party panel meeting which was addressed by Harry Hopkins.[2] Angular, amusing with rather an Irish sense of humour he spoke

---

1 From the context, one presumes developing emotionally.
2 Roosevelt's foreign affairs adviser. See entry for 6 August 1941 and footnote.

amusingly [*sic*] for forty minutes and held his rather dull audience enthralled. Early on I twigged that he was making propaganda for Winston and his method was cleverly but fairly transparent. First he told us that the USA would soon be turning out 8,000 aeroplanes a month, and promised every support for the war effort. His auditors by then pleased, he gently led up to the PM; began by ridiculing him gently; told us that at the White House Winston occupied an adjoining room to his, and how in the morning, no matter how late they had gone to bed – and it was always very late – there would be a knock at his door, and before he could even say 'come in!' the Prime Minister wearing a garment which certainly wasn't pyjamas, and bore some resemblance to a nightshirt, would barge in, preceded by a huge cigar. Then over coffee and newspapers they would talk. The PM apparently has a prejudice against bedroom slippers – in other words he was always barefooted. Mrs Roosevelt was away from Washington at the time and one morning she returned early to the White House. (She too, apparently, is in the habit of 'barging in' to Harry's bedroom without waiting for a welcome.) She went at once to hear about Winston whom she had never met, opened the door and entered, Harry Hopkins was still in bed and after a second's pause he murmured, 'Mrs Roosevelt – Mr Churchill!' It was an extraordinary meeting, the wife of the President of the United States, still in her travelling clothes, and the Prime Minister in his nightshirt smoking the inevitable cigar, and Harry Hopkins in bed! However it was a great success. Nobody was embarrassed and all were amused. Hopkins is a sort of benevolent *éminence grise* to the President.

Came home: my house is overcrowded since Micky Renshaw and Duncannon are still staying whilst Harold, of course, lives here. I can never be alone . . . And I ordered dinner for me, which owing to the great good nature of my household and the elasticity of the kitchen arrangements had to stretch to seven since Maimie and Vsevolod, Clarissa Churchill, Rob Bernays, Eric Duncannon and Nicholas Lawford all proposed themselves during the cocktail hour. Clarissa Churchill like a water lily, or perhaps gardenia, is calm, intelligent and independent. I like her enormously. She is the young girl of the present age, a milder Diana Cooper. She is about 21. (Diana rang me up from Bognor) . . . . The weather is lovely, *ce diable du printemps*[1] gets hold of me! . . . Rob Bernays, the ugliest man alive, is to be married next week and I do not envy the bride her marital duties. He asked me to give him a Regency chandelier, an expensive affair; and I was annoyed. *Il s'est le juif toujours*,[2] but isn't, I believe. Eric is maddening and inconsiderate in the house and arrives unexpectedly and gives the servants many and conflicting orders.

I can understand the Prime Minister's obvious elation over the India failure of Cripps. He realises that the public never have quite the same ardour for a politician who has failed. He becomes like a woman who has miscarried.

---

1 Literally, the devil of springtime; metaphorically, 'the sap is rising'.
2 He is always the Jew.

Anyway, Churchill has always been dead against any concession to India. The whole expedition was largely arranged to placate America, which more and more attempts to dictate English policy.

I hear that Elizabeth Elveden is going to have a baby. I am so glad.

THURSDAY 16TH APRIL

A horrible day really. My weekend arrangements have all gone askew due to various causes . . . Chats with Kingsley Wood, whom I complimented on his excellent 'people's' Budget; and with Anthony Eden, more insincere than ever but pleasant, almost affectionate to me but he knows what I think of him really . . . On Tuesday afternoon I was walking in the lobby with Walter Buccleuch, who began as usual to talk about Paul, when we met Anthony and I quickly changed the subject. Walter and I then sat on a remote bench and chatted; I warned him that his harmless letters to the ex-Regent are opened, read and probably undelivered. He was not surprised, certainly . . .

The Iveaghs came to luncheon and I was determined not to mention anything controversial but of course both Honor and the various financial arrangements cropped up and I felt I was being tactless but couldn't somehow stop . . . . Honor had been over to Pyrford for the day on Monday, I think, and they reported that she seemed well and impersonal. Oh! I am so sick of it all. I gathered, too, that they are very against my bringing Paul back at the moment; they hate action or decisions; and so to avoid having to do anything themselves, they urged me to go to America. Oddly enough they had no sooner gone than an airmail letter came from Bill Buny.[1] He told me bluntly enough that my mother was ailing, failing and not quite in her right mind. I've always known that. Yet she is only 73. He says that she looks greatly aged. Should I go to the US?

The country is disturbed by the recent accident; whilst on manoeuvres many officers and men, including Robert Cecil,[2] were machine-gunned by mistake, seventeen have been killed including the Brigadier and scores wounded. Robert Cecil, a huge dark fellow, more Cavendish probably than Cecil, is supposed to be very seriously injured. His bitch Betty[3] of a mother [sic] will probably not much mind although she has rushed to Warminster to see him. Their youngest son[4] is usually supposed to be a product of her long liaison with Sidney Herbert.

1 Presumably a friend of Channon's mother in Chicago.
2 Robert Edward Peter Gascoyne-Cecil (1916–2003), by courtesy Viscount Cranborne from 1947 until 1972, when he succeeded his father as 6th Marquess of Salisbury. Whatever his injuries, he recovered to take part in the invasion of Normandy in 1944. In the combined air and infantry exercise at Warminster twenty-five men were killed when a Spitfire pilot opened fire on spectators, thinking they were dummies placed as targets.
3 Elizabeth Vere Cavendish.
4 Richard Hugh Vere Gascoyne-Cecil (1924–44) was killed in action while serving as a sergeant pilot in the RAF.

Archie Wavell,[1] gentle, greyed and erratic, arrived. He is strangely untidy, no smartness at all. He is staying with me and to make room for him, I had to turn out Eric Duncannon. People dropped in but my spirits did not rise – Alan and Patsy, Peter Loxley, Harold, Archie and I dined and played bridge. We didn't do too badly, scallops, fried eggs and tongue and a chocolate mousse! Alan was in teasing spirits, affectionate and bronzed. He now affects black side whiskers which Harold, who always teases him successfully, calls 'bugger-grips'! Alan, however, was defeatist in his talk; this is the first time I have heard him speak so but he is right when he says that most people are but dare not admit it. There is little spirit left, barely any enthusiasm for the war. We are living through one of the convulsions of history which happens to be an extremely disagreeable one for England. Harold was staggered but he has no historic sense, and not much *aperçu*,[2] only acumen and shrewdness.

Archie came into my bedroom and talked to me until I fell asleep. He read me a long historic letter from his mother in which she writes how Winston cabled that he [General Wavell] should hold on to Rangoon until the middle of March. Where will the Japanese drive end? Is Delhi their objective? Laval[3] is now all supreme in France. That means that England and France will soon be at war? Probably. We now excel at nothing, certainly not diplomacy.

SATURDAY 18TH APRIL

I wish that I had decided to go to Kelvedon. Idle day, but I need rest . . . had my hair cut, an incoherent letter from my mother. Lunched with Alice Harding in her converted garage flat: Phyllis de Janzé,[4] looking a hundred, was there; dressed in *démodé* black satin dripping with immorally acquired diamonds and wearing a gold wristwatch (Cartier no.), which I remember once giving to Hubert Duggan, and carrying a pretty gold snuffbox which I gave him years ago. With her carelessly dyed hair and rouge she looked like Boule de Suif[5] . . . . She talked of the appalling disaster which occurred near Warminster early this week when an aeroplane flown by a Czech pilot during an exercise, test-fired on a group of officers, killing twenty-three [*sic*] and wounding many more. Hubert

---

1 Son of the General (qv).
2 Insight or percipience.
3 Pierre Jean-Marie Laval (1883–1945) was Prime Minister of France from 1931 to 1932 and from 1935 to 1936. From 1942 to 1944 he was head of the French government under Marshal Pétain (qv). At the liberation he was arrested, tried for treason and shot.
4 Phyllis Meeta Boyd (1894–1943) in 1922 married vicomte Henri Louis Leon de Janzé. She later became the mistress of Channon's uncle-in-law, Lord Moyne, and of Hubert Duggan (qqv).
5 Literally 'butterball', Boule de Suif is the name of a prostitute in a short story of 1880 by Guy de Maupassant.

Duggan escaped miraculously unscathed, Harry Stavordale[1] was slightly wounded; it is a dreadful disaster. Then she rather ranted against the Queen, who she says is known as 'grinning Liz' by canteen workers etc. Certainly the King and Queen have lost any popularity they ever had, but I think this story exaggerated. People know that the royal pair do their duty earnestly enough, but also realise that they are a rubber stamp, eclipsed and bullied by Winston, and are a brace of very unbrilliant, uninspired bores. What the people don't know is that they are unimaginatively inspired; that the fault lies with Alec Hardinge and his entourage. There was atmosphere between Phyllis and me, but it was quickly dispelled.

Tokyo, Yokohama and Kobe have been heavily bombed, presumably by American aeroplanes, and last night there was a big raid on Germany with Augsburg as the chief target. I hope that the magnificent Bishop's Palace is spared. It is also announced that the *Surcouf*,[2] the largest submarine in the world, which was part of the Free French Forces, has been lost. It was not, however, added that it was sunk by the Americans. Another deplorable accident! The news had long been held up.

Irritated by my companions I tried to be alone. Dined with Maimie and Vsevolod; Natasha Bagration lay in bed upstairs, as she is still ill. Vsevolod is fast becoming a character, a raconteur, *un original* . . .

SUNDAY 19TH APRIL

Drove to the Carys, Windlesham, a ghastly red house surrounded by pretty verdant grounds to see Mary Baker. It is twenty-five years since I nearly married her; and again twenty-three . . . since she proposed to me; and my old grandfather, wise and brilliant, and my parents urged me to accept her! The wheel has turned almost full circle now. She gave me a volume of Shelley and many flowers and we talked of old days. Her aged and slightly mad mother[3] more than ever reminded me of an ancient orthodox priest. She is 76. She told me amongst other high-flown absurdities that she had squared the circle; had invented or discovered the fifth dimension and was still partial towards the figure 36!! Mary is 41 and still a shy bride.

Mary is still anxious to marry me and I promised to consider it seriously – but shan't. She isn't nearly rich enough. I walked in the gloaming through the Green Park, passing what was once my lovely and historic house, 21 St James's

1 Edward Henry Charles James Fox-Strangways (1905–64), by courtesy Lord Stavordale until he succeeded his father as 7th Earl of Ilchester in 1959.
2 Launched in 1929, the *Surcouf* was the largest French submarine. It is thought to have sunk after colliding with an American freighter in the Caribbean.
3 Mary Corwith (1866–1953), married Alfred Landon Baker in Chicago in 1894.

Place. I saw the vacant aching void of what once had been my magnificent residence . . . . where my little Paul was born. Now all that remains are bits of rubble, remnants of the basement and some persistent daffodils which I myself planted in a once so charming garden where we used to sit on summer afternoons and entertain half London. Dined with Harold Balfour at Pratt's and walked home with him.

MONDAY 20TH APRIL

Called on Mrs Greville who was resilient, wicked and witty. She sits back, telephones, intrigues and terrifies both society and the government. Dined in with Harold and Patsy, and later we were joined by Bill Mabane who is in love with Miss Sheila [*sic*] Duggan,[1] who refuses to marry him because she is a Roman Catholic – he has a divorced wife somewhere. Patsy pretty but slow and stupid, unimaginative like all Guinnesses.

I weigh only 10 st 12 lbs! A triumph due to Lord Woolton.[2] Harold is divine . . .

PS Mrs Greville showed me a long letter which the Queen of Spain had written her from Lausanne. Her Majesty wrote rather indiscreetly and complained that the food in Rome was uneatable and had given her colitis. She seemed anxious . . . . to put on record that she is anti-Axis. She is now living in Switzerland.

TUESDAY 21ST APRIL

George Gage dined with me. He came and went away on a bicycle and I wondered the while, as we chatted, of the old magic he had for me! Yet he still has traces of his old fascination. He went to a party at Windsor last night given by the Grenadier Guards; the King and Queen and Princess Elizabeth were present and danced. The Princess is now to take her place in English life. George says the Princess is dull and mouse-like looking; I have heard otherwise! He is as simple, [illegible] and as strange as ever. He remarked *inter alia* that I had once been in love with Diane Abdy but never with any other woman. Perhaps he is right! A very curious and strong bond unites us still . . .

George thinks that the German war will be over this year. I don't. He says that Europe cannot survive another winter of war. I wonder.

I am toying still with the idea of going to the States; shall I?? It would be enjoyable, but rather difficult to arrange; but I ache so for my child, for my blond beautiful brilliant boy. Sometimes I am tempted to do a 'bunk'; to live there with him; never bring him back; for England, this great England is done.

1 Stella Jane Duggan (1908–?), born in Buenos Aires, married Mabane (qv) in 1944. He had been divorced in 1926.
2 The Minister responsible for food rationing.

WEDNESDAY 22ND APRIL

I walked to the House half-hoping to find Gerald Palmer, who would be my Mercury and would bring me letters from Peter.[1] He was sitting on the PPS bench where I lorded it so long and proudly, and looking up he caught my eye. His face lit up and he made frantic signals to come to him. I climbed over dozing dull members, got to him and he handed me an immense packet, weighing, I should think, a pound! I rushed with it to Rab's room but he came in just as I was undoing it, so I fled to the library and wallowed in the luxury and fun of opening it. There were several letters for various people and a huge one for me. It was an historic account from Peter of his trip with Wavell to Maymyo and Mandalay. Potted history and then more about the beginning of Cripps's visit, of the dark Metternich prowling about avid for power but he clearly foresaw failure at the end . . . the letter also contained a handsome pair of sapphire links made in the shape of H and C. I was infinitely touched and a wave of loyalty and affection came over me, and there were six packets of razor blades too.

. . . . Lunched with Harold and Diana Balfour – almost pretty for once in a new hat – at a bogus club. And back to the House where I attended two enthralling committees. The first, the weekly Wednesday meeting of the 1922 Committee, was addressed by Vansittart, who was persuasive and less violent than we expected. Still he preached for nearly an hour about the iniquities of the German race, how they can never be trusted, nor treated with. A doctrine of despair, I thought. A large audience was interested, since he has charm and speaks engagingly, but was not especially enthusiastic. There was an interval during which I reread my letters and then I went back to the big Committee Room this time to hear Oliver Lyttelton speak to the all-party panel. He was gay, cynical, cheery and rather over the heads of his many hearers. He painted a vivid picture of the Middle East, the complications, the Cairo Court, the troubles in Syria; his rows and reconciliations with de Gaulle etc. He was followed by Casey his successor in Cairo. This Australian, too, spoke well and has no trace of an accent but he is less than Oliver who, I think, has sized up the weakness of political life, institutions, and the paucity of ability in the House of Commons. He has decided to capitalise on all this and make himself Prime Minister but it is a pity that he always must turn a facile, cynical phrase at the expense of our friends and allies and indeed of everyone. An enthralling afternoon.

The Duchess of Kent rang up, rather depressed I thought she was.

THURSDAY 23RD APRIL   *THE LAST HOUSE, ALDWICK, BOGNOR REGIS*

On my frugal breakfast tray were letters from General Wavell and Peter; and they gave further close-ups of negotiations which were doomed from the first since no

---

1 Palmer had gone to India with Cripps, and Coats had given him letters to bring back to Channon.

one except Cripps himself wanted them to succeed. However, American opinion is placated, which is something.

The House went into secret session at noon and Winston rose majestically and had a polite reception. He then began his long review of recent events. He painted a magnificent canvas. I rushed to the gallery and sat next to Ronnie Brocket, and I looked down on the crowded House. Every seat was taken, black-coated dullards, they looked; only a light sprinkling of khaki among them . . . . For very nearly two hours the PM spoke with almost no interruption. It was a *tour de force*. No humour or wit, little oratory, no *mea culpa* stuff; a straightforward, very brilliant and colourful, yet factual résumé of the situation. Only at 1.30, when MPs began to think of their stomachs and their luncheon engagements, was there any restlessness and not much. At 1.50 he had finished, and his prate was definitely encouraging and heartening, and we left the Chamber confident that the war would be won thanks chiefly to the stupendous American production. Alan and I crossed over Parliament Street to a sort of Hogarthian tavern where we lunched badly and gossiped. Returned to the House, Cripps was speaking to a thinner House and finally I came away. Picked up a bag and came to Bognor on the 5.30. It was cold but the countryside looked green and lovely in that curious English vernal haze. Arundel looked magnificent. I suppose I have not been in a train, except to go to Southend, since I was in Greece last January 1941.[1] Diana [Cooper], wearing amber slacks, met me in her little car and drove me here, where I have so often stayed. (Many weekends *au temps jadis*[2] with the Coopers and then for nearly two months when I shared the cottage with Freddie Birkenhead when we were both writing!)[3] She looks a dream of gold and amber beauty and like Honor, she is obsessed by farming. Still in my London clothes I helped her to drive pigs, seven little creatures and feed the rabbits. The little place has been converted into a farm! And we walked to the water's edge which is framed by barbed wire, spikes, railings and whatnot against a possible invasion. It looked formidable. 'If only poor Singapore had been like that!' Diana sighed . . . She showed me her poultry with pride, and her swill – the world's most beautiful woman coping with swill! Then we dined quietly *à deux*, with a glass of vodka each instead of a cocktail. Delicious meal cooked by her maid: onions and eggs and then we hovered over the fire and gossiped. She was beautiful, delicious, fragile and affectionate. I gave her the Cairene chatter which one of my chief agents, Jac[queline] Lampson the Ambassadress, had just written me: that Randolph Churchill was now known as 'the problem child' and is living in idleness in Cairo . . . . Bed late in this cold, charming uncomfortable house.

1 He forgets a recent train journey to Portsmouth and back: see entries for 7 and 9 February 1942.
2 'Once upon a time', or 'in the old days'.
3 This would have been in 1931 or 1932, a period for which there are no diaries. The first of Birkenhead's two volumes on his father, and Channon's book on the Ludwigs, were published in 1933.

FRIDAY 24TH APRIL

The modern Helen, the loveliest woman of all time, up at dawn, milking her cows, 'Edith Kemsley' and 'Princess' she calls them .... We breakfasted together later and heard the aeroplanes buzzing overhead – only about thirty feet high, practising. Then she drove me to the station and I caught the 10.20, a long luxurious nearly empty train. I read The Claverings[1] .... Home before one o'clock, changed my country clothes, reread Peter's letters and am no longer irritated by one of them, and then entertained a luncheon party – the Duchess of Kent, cleverly dressed in green and brown and her pregnancy not too obvious; Natasha Bagration; Juliet Duff; Alice Harding – who arrived as usual with her maddening American tick of unpunctuality; the Archduke Robert, long and lonely ... and Gerald Palmer who is unaccustomed to royalty and was shy but sweet. The food was delicious, but I was not at my very best and possibly the party was not a huge success. One never knows. However all seemed to go well; the Duchess whispered to me sweet things, looked lovely and didn't 'poop', so the presence of the Home Secretary and the doctor was not required!! What if she had begun her baby! Gerald had to rush off to Mr Cripps. Everybody liked his great blue eyes ... Quiet afternoon.

SATURDAY 25TH APRIL   PYRFORD

Up early, talked with Harold. A photograph of the Gunn portrait has arrived and it is excellent. Sent off letters to Princess Olga and to Peter by various means. It is lovely but cold today. Lunched with Vsevolod and Maimie and drove here. The Iveaghs are so friendly and affectionate that I could never let them down in any way – and shan't.

Brigid is here, very sweet, plump, tired and generally divine. I gave her petrol coupons and so won her wayward heart (she is somewhat under Honor's influence)! Hugh Euston writes her passionate and poetic love letters but she spurns him. She thinks that he will marry Princess Elizabeth, who likes him.

SUNDAY 26TH APRIL

Cold but beautiful day. The richest family in the world lives simply, almost frugally. I managed to have my coffee and toast in bed – toast made from the new national loaf which immensely increases one's energy and is an aphrodisiac.

Last night I dreamt of fire, a long intermittent dream; dreamt that Honor and her paramour were burnt to death. This afternoon there was a huge fire on a nearby heath. Lord and Lady I and I walked to see it and helped to stamp it out. An extraordinary sight.

---

1 A novel of 1867 by Trollope.

TUESDAY 28TH APRIL

To the House; heard Cripps make his statement on the abortive trip to India. He was clear, concise and convincing, but the House was bored in spite of his eloquence, as it always is with the *fait accompli*. I left at last, to lunch with Lady Kemsley at the Ritz. She had her buxom, luxuriant daughter Ghislaine Dresselhuys[1] and Iliffe niece[2] and a most amusing and intelligent boy called Ali Forbes,[3] who cannot be more than 25. Clever and attractive I thought him. Back to the House for Amery's wind-up. He was authoritative but dull . . . . . Later had a chat with Ava Anderson who has become, at the age of 47 or 48, a beauty. Pretty and provocative, she is really attractive now. Success does much to improve a woman's looks.

When I got home I found Hughie Northumberland waiting for me. He is just back from Cairo and came by boat – a six weeks' journey. He is highly attractive, gay, gentle, [illegible] and vicious. But he stayed two hours and drank a whole bottle of my precious sherry, yet complained of a feeble digestion.

WEDNESDAY 29TH APRIL

Harold came into my room somewhat sadly, I thought, and we said goodbye; he left for America via Bournemouth, Lisbon and Lagos at luncheon time.

Dined with Jay Llewellin at Claridge's. He is an old Red pet. Earlier in the day, he had addressed the 1922 Committee and his speech was a masterpiece of restraint. He told us nothing at all.

THURSDAY 30TH APRIL

Woke gay and high-spirited, and made household and social arrangements before proceeding to the House of Commons and thence returned to No. 5 [Belgrave Square] to receive Elizabeth Elveden and her enchanting little boy, Benjamin, who has immense charm, and is certainly beautiful, almost bewitching. He seems

---

1 Ghislaine Marie-Rose Edith Dresselhuys (1922–2000) was Lady Kemsley's daughter by her first marriage to Cornelius Dresselhuys, who was the Dutch Consul in London. She would marry three times, become a leading socialite and a television personality.

2 Kathleen Iliffe (1904–88), daughter of the 1st Baron Iliffe (qv), married in 1926 Leslie Frederick Laurence.

3 Alastair Cameron Forbes (1918–2005) was a cousin of President Franklin Roosevelt and from a grand Boston family; but he was born in Surrey, educated at Winchester and Cambridge, and joined the Royal Marines at the outbreak of war. He was invalided out and decided to become a journalist. Rather like Channon, he chose to befriend the great and the good, and soon became a habitué of Chequers, with the Churchills, and also a friend of royalty. He wrote for *The Observer* and the *Daily Mail*, and stood unsuccessfully as a Liberal in the 1945 general election. In later life he was a noted, if vicious, book reviewer, and an entertaining raconteur.

delicate, a touch effeminate et *peut-être quelque chose*[1] in character. The Iveaghs and Patsy also lunched but I was obliged to rush away and leave them as I had promised to lunch with Mrs Greville. The old lady was sitting in her bath chair at the door to receive me – in her suite at the Dorchester. She looked well but was actually in pain; and many jewels lent her impressiveness. Pleasant party: the Kents, she lovely, rather amber in colour, he in an Air Force uniform and slightly shabby and aged; both Mountbattens; and what a dazzling couple they are! I sat between them and found Dickie slightly grown in stature since he took up his highly important, indeed vital, command; but he remains simple and unaffected and only when I talked of his nephew, Prince Philip of Greece, did his sleepy strange eyes light up with an affectionate, paternal, almost adoring light. Molly Buccleuch, recovering from a tonsil operation, looked radiant but pretended to have caught a cold from walking for an hour in the Downing Street gardens yesterday, with Winston. Brendan Bracken, bombastic, imaginative and kindly, his teeth are blacker than ever and his red hair is greying now: and the Duke of Alba. We stayed until three and I felt sleepy after the rich food and Moselle wine. Then home, played in the Belgrave Square gardens with Benjamin and half-pretended to myself that he was my Paul.

Walked across the Park – full of life and gaiety I felt – to dine with Bill Mabane, Miss Duggan with whom he is in love (I find her tiresome, a touch affected, almost common) and Lord and Lady Woolton.[2] They are an amazing couple, bustling, dynamic, the new order indeed: they are immensely, comically impressed by their peerage and position and we talked coronets and ration cards the whole evening. I was amusing. Apparently before they made their great wealth, he was a Socialist, he even canvassed and spoke for Victor Grayson,[3] the first Socialist MP, who later (according to Woolton) offered to sell his services to the Conservative Party. Nobody could be more Conservative or realistic than the *ménage* Woolton now. He had wanted to keep his family name but the King had demurred at creating a Lord Marquis! I enjoyed them and their vulgar prattle and childish and disarming delight with their titles and grand position. We discussed the new vitamin bread, the national loaf, and I asked whether it was really an aphrodisiac (it is certainly) and the Minister of Food looked startled.

---

1 Perhaps something.
2 Maud Smith (1883–1961) married in 1912 Frederick Marquis, later 1st Earl of Woolton (qv).
3 Albert Victor Grayson (1881–1920) was Labour MP for Colne Valley from 1907 to 1910. He was not the first Socialist MP. He became a serious drunk; he fought in the New Zealand Army in the Great War but in 1918 was under surveillance from Special Branch for suspected communist and Irish Republican Army sympathies. In 1920 he threatened to expose Maundy Gregory, Lloyd George's 'honours broker', and was beaten up; shortly afterwards he left a hotel in London where he was drinking with friends, but never returned and disappeared without trace. It was speculated that Gregory murdered him, or had him murdered.

Wondering the while whether Oxford was being bombed I walked across the Green Park, since there are no longer any railings, in the bright blue moonlight and to the Park Lane Hotel where I found Michael Parker, known to Alan and me as 'The Clanger'; waiting for me. We sat talking and drinking until 2 a.m. I find him enchanting. Then home cold and somewhat ashamed.

Norwich was again bombed last night and one hears that both Bath and Exeter had been badly battered.

Off and on all the week I have read Barbara Cartland's[1] Life of her brother Ronald; it is an infuriating book since it makes him out a sort of Greek god, a hero, the epitome and symbol of young England. I knew him so intimately and liked him but he was anything but that, conceited, priggish, common, narrow, bigoted and limited but not without charm, he was extremely vicious in his private life (I know much, and all of it fact); and he was prejudiced, unfair and muddle-headed. I never heard him make an intelligent remark, and many idiotic ones. With the years he became increasingly pompous and self-opinionated. The whole book, written by someone who loved him, but who is even more vulgar, is out of focus and whilst it recalls incidents, gives no picture of the man. Little is mentioned of his terrific friendship with Tony Muirhead.

FRIDAY 1ST MAY

Got up rather late. Geoffrey Lloyd dropped in, as he so often does before I finished my letters, and I walked with him through St James's Park. He loves trees, beauty and books and longs for a cultured leisurely existence. He is a rare creature.

Left with Alice Harding, after she had shown me her round dark 4-months-old baby, Emily Sophia, for Coppins. The Duchess [of Kent] awaiting us: she was very sweet, beautiful and a bit boring as women often are when they are having babies. The Duke soon joined us and at first, was garrulous; but a few drinks soothed him. He whines, is rarely tender to her. Dinner was excellent and we had a delicious evening: backgammon and gossip. The Duke kept me up in a very cold room until 2 a.m. He attacked all his brothers, Anthony Eden and almost everybody else. I was glad to hear that the Yugoslav government have restored Paul's appanage, which amounts to £7,000 per annum. He will now be well off, especially as life in Kenya cannot be expensive.

This house is most *gemütlich* and full of rich treasures: gold boxes, *étuis*[2] and pretty expensive objects are always being exchanged or moved about. The Duke's possessions and collections of furniture and china are colossal. He lives really for nothing else.

---

1 Mary Barbara Hamilton Cartland (1901–2000) wrote over 700 romantic novels which, rather like her biography of her brother, were not of the highest literary merit. Her book on Ronnie Cartland was a whitewash, with not even an allusion to his homosexuality; but Churchill wrote the preface. She was created a DBE in 1991.
2 Boxes.

I am completely devoted to the Duchess of Kent; her loyal graciousness, her gentle sweetness and charm, which equals her beauty and her saintly character, make her an outstanding woman.

SATURDAY 2ND MAY

I slept badly at Coppins and after breakfast I had a long gossip with the Duke before he went out gardening. He is genuinely distressed about Paul and is harassed by his conscience that he doesn't do more for his brother-in-law. However he roundly abused Queen Mignonne and young King Peter who have behaved so treacherously . . . . Alice Harding and I left about noon to drive to London. At Belgrave Square I found both Elvedens, their dauphin Benjamin, and also Brigid Guinness all staying. To ease the household and because I wanted to be alone, I came here. Kelvedon looks very beautiful but it is cold. The fruit trees and tulips are out.

Mandalay, I fear, has fallen to the Japanese, and probably the Burma Road has been shut. Will this mean Wavell's return – and Peter's?

I went for a preprandial stroll in the blue and green loveliness of Kelvedon and I was assailed by strange and deep longings, longings almost unmentionable! I am becoming more sexual. I thought that I would have done anything, given anything, to be taken into the woods here, stripped and then whipped by a fat middle-aged severe woman! Why does one have such urges? Such strong, impossible desires. Do all men have them?

SUNDAY 3RD MAY

A superlatively lovely day. Blue and green. I sunbathed for three hours, after an unpleasant interview with Mrs Harris, who, mother of four children and wife of my gardener, lives in one of the lodge-cottages. She has become a hoyden or perhaps harlot in her husband's absence and the soldiers here are quite out of control and run after her like dogs after a bitch on heat. The Red Cross insist on my turning her out, which is rather a ticklish task.

TUESDAY 5TH MAY

To the House early as I had heard privately that there would be fun and frolic; so it ensued – a deplorable scene occurred. Brograve Beauchamp[1] asked that the House go into secret session to hear charges of a serious nature against a

---

1 Brograve Campbell Beauchamp (1897–1976) was National Liberal and Conservative MP for Walthamstow East from 1931 to 1945. He succeeded his father as 2nd Bt in 1925.

member. Geoffrey Shakespeare[1] also made a statement naming McGovern.[2] Most members assumed that both charges applied to the same Hon. Member, but such was not the case . . . . I was sitting between Douglas Hacking[3] and Geoffrey Lloyd at the time and we were discussing the growing numbers of independents elected and I referred to Charles Rutland's very pertinent apposite letter which appeared in today's *Telegraph*, in which he castigates independents. Those in the know realise that he was really rebuking [Denis] Kendall, the independent recently returned for Grantham thereby defeating the lonely unfortunate Longmore. Kendall has seduced Lady Ursula Manners, Charles's [illegible] sister, whom I had secret[ly]considered marrying. Kendall hopes to marry her;[4] his wife is the obstacle . . . . As we were talking of this *cause pas encore célèbre*[5] and joking about an announcement which appeared in this morning's press, about the arrival of an infant to Mrs Tom Dugdale (on the front page of *The Times* it is described as a son, and on another page as a daughter) . . . . Brograve Beauchamp rose and intimated that he wished to bring a charge against a member of having revealed what happened at the last secret session. There was a momentary sensation, and he was followed by Geoffrey Shakespeare who made a similar charge naming the Honourable Member for Shettleston [McGovern]. The House was soon in an uproar, and we went into secret session. An interminable foolish, farcical wrangle over procedure followed. I despaired of democracy or parliamentary government and longed to remind the demented, so it seemed, assembly, that there was a war on, that Madagascar had that morning been attacked by our forces (will war with France follow?). However, the scene dragged on, tempers rose, and even the imperturbable Speaker seemed confused, since there was no possible precedent to help him, and we were indeed, making history. Another page in this most historic and fantastic of all Parliaments ever elected. Cripps several times intervened and was at least once contradicted, by the irritated Speaker, who as usual tried to lower the atmosphere. The charge was finally made by Bro Beauchamp who related how he had been telephoned to by one Doctor

1 Geoffrey Hithersay Shakespeare (1893–1980) was a barrister and political journalist who became Lloyd George's private secretary. He was Liberal MP for Wellingborough from 1922 to 1923, and for Norwich from 1929 to 1945. Between 1931 and 1942 he held a succession of non-Cabinet ministerial posts. He was created 1st Bt in 1942.

2 John McGovern (1887–1968) was the Labour MP for Glasgow Shettleston from 1930 to 1959. He was an active pacifist and enjoyed a turbulent relationship with his own party.

3 Douglas Hewitt Hacking (1884–1950) was Unionist MP for Chorley from 1918 to 1945. He held junior office in Baldwin's administration from 1924 to 1929 and again in the National Government between 1933 and 1936. He was created 1st Bt in 1938 and raised to the peerage as 1st Baron Hacking in 1945.

4 She married twice, on neither occasion to Kendall.

5 Not-yet-notorious case.

McManus who reported that Edgar Granville,[1] the little busybody member for Eye, a National Liberal, and Leslie Belisha's devoted jackal, had on last Thursday attended a cocktail party where he had quoted in front of five other men, remarks alleged to have been made by the Prime Minister. The Doctor, who met him on that occasion for the first time, had denounced him. The House was silent with stupefaction for a second since most people supposed that McGovern would be brought in and had not realised that there were two separate charges! Granville, looking very red and uncomfortable, rose to make his statement, and did it clumsily, convincing nobody of his innocence, which he did not even proclaim. He harped too long on the Gestapo methods employed in spying on Members of Parliament etc. and soon lost whatever sympathy he may have had. He then withdrew, as is the custom; once more there was a wrangle, too tedious to chronicle, that he should be brought back. To this the Speaker consented and I saw Alec Cunningham-Reid dart from the Chamber to find him. (A few minutes later I met them together in the lobby hurrying back.) More argument and then I left; meeting Duff [Cooper] in the corridor I told him the story and he was amused: he is very charming now and we have tacitly agreed to bury our ancient political hatchet (I think he has mellowed and is gentler). Then I rushed off to lunch with Lady Willingdon, dreading to be late as she is such a martinet.

I had made a muddle about tonight; asked the Kemsleys to dine and had nobody to meet them. However I 'Houdini-ed' out of the engagement and instead dined with them in their private suite at the Dorchester. A hedonistic meal – caviar, duck and Welsh rarebit. Delicious. Kemsley was irritable and launched an attack of considerable violence against the King and Queen, whom he accuses of ineptitude, incompetence and lack of all imagination. I fear he is right, and he blames the Black Rat. He says that the Lords Cromer and Wigram[2] are considering going to the King and demanding Hardinge's resignation, warning the Sovereign that the monarchy is in peril. It is certainly true that the Royal Family have lost ground and whatever popularity they may once have had has faded, waned to nothing. The King should never be allowed to broadcast: it is deplorable and he sounds almost idiotic . . . . Victor Cazalet dropped in; he had been entertaining Margot Oxford to dinner: she is eighty and as amusing and *pointful* as ever, he said. I must ask her to something soon.

---

1 Edgar Louis Granville (1898–1998) was Liberal and then Liberal National MP for Eye from 1929 to 1951. After losing his seat he joined the Labour Party, and was raised to the peerage as Baron Granville of Eye (life peerage) in 1967.

2 Rowland Thomas Baring (1877–1953), 2nd Earl of Cromer, had been Lord Chamberlain between 1922 and 1938, and Wigram (qv) had been George V's private secretary for the last five years of the King's reign. Both men retained huge influence at Court.

WEDNESDAY 6TH MAY

To the House, where I stayed all day, and listened to much of the debate, attended the 1922 Committee, had a snack lunch with Gerald Palmer in the tea room and then went with him to the Lords to watch David Margesson and Moore-Brabazon take their seats. David looked handsome, dignified and determined in his robes; he smiled at me and once during the ceremony he caught my eye . . . . He has taken the title of Viscount Margesson of Rugby. Watching was Kakoo Rutland, very charming and young-looking. She came out with me and we talked for some time (I had not seen her since the war and was impressed by her youthful appearance). Somehow, although an old friend, her nervousness and quick clipped laugh always makes me a touch foolish and shy, and has done so for twenty years! She is living at Belvoir and never comes to London now.

David, the new Viscount, joined us and we walked through the lobbies; David wondered why on earth Victor Warrender had taken the ugly name of Bruntisfield (which is an Edinburgh Park which he owns). 'To spite Dollie!!'[1] Kakoo laughed.

THURSDAY 7TH MAY

A big House of Commons day. First another long wrangle and investigations into an alleged indiscretion supposed to have been made by McGovern. He made a manly and spirited defence and when the division finally came, the voting was 148 to 115 against him. A very thin majority. I voted with the noes as I have always had a sneaking sympathy for the ILPs[2] who are usually sensible, always eloquent and often charming. Then Winston suddenly appeared in the House and rose at the end of the division and made a colourful statement about the British seizure of the Island of Madagascar, which practically capitulated today. He was cheered. I think he only comes to the House now when searching for kudos.

Chatted with that firebrand Mrs Tate, who says that the government will be out in three months' time, that Winston will have a general election – for sheer spite against the Conservative Party for attempting to act as a brake upon him; and that afterwards we shall have practically a Bolshevik government. There is, of course, that danger, but English politics are always unexpected.

[Hugh] Dalton followed and explained the proposed fuel rationing, which I suspect the HMG of intending to 'bounce' us into. I wonder what Oliver Lyttelton thinks of it all, since he is now slated by No. 10 to be the future Prime Minister – much to the disgust and disillusionment of the Edenite faction. Eden's shares are very down just now.

---

1 Dorothy, his wife.
2 Members of the Independent Labour Party, which had not followed Attlee into the coalition in 1940.

Clarissa Churchill, looking more and more like a gardenia – lovely, clever and glib, with her little caustic clipped phrases – came in for a cocktail. Rab was attracted and impressed by her. He is angelic. I refused to dine with him and went instead to Maimie's and Vsevolod's. They are a sweet couple, have an excellent cook but they put me off my food by their disgusting trick of picking their teeth with their toothpicks. Home early: Rab sat on my bed and I tried to persuade him to intrigue a little to push himself back into the Foreign Office, since everybody says how much he is missed there.

FRIDAY 8TH MAY

Busy day doing nothing; I wrote a long letter to the ex-Regent, and finished what amounted to a document for Peter, and walked through the St James's Park – lovely now with tulips – and deposited them at the India and Colonial Offices, and then I lunched with Lady Colefax. She is the Queen of the Churchillians, a rabid anti-appeaser and anti-Municher, and hence her society is unpleasant. Her position, like that of many others who share her views, is untenable. She has done nothing for the war, apart from a vague spot of charity work, and she continues to give luncheon parties and to entertain. She has two sons of military age; the elder Peter[1] calmly remained in the US and has done nothing; the second, Michael,[2] has been sitting for two years in the Ministry of Information in a cushy office job. One day I will point this out to her. Luncheon however was very pleasant: Gage, Margesson, Garrett Moore, and I remarked that I had never seen so many viscounts in one room. And what was the plural[3] for viscounts? Was it a virtue? No, a vice, David Margesson retorted. Others – Barbie Wallace who wants to marry David; Sylvia Compton;[4] Virginia Cowles; an American who is Lady Beatty's[5] lover – good food. We were all asked to sign the guest book and clapped David as he signed 'Margesson' *tout court*.[6] George Gage arrived and left on his bicycle.

I walked away with David and basked in the luxury of his society for half an hour. And I both learned and told him much. He was honest to me as ever and made no pretence about not being badly treated by Winston. We had, he particularly, a long run of power: for nine years he was Chief Whip, and fourteen months Secretary of State for War. Now it was over ... The brusque manner of his dismissal rankled and the reason for it was still to him a mystery. I told him that

---

1 Peter Anthony Colefax (1903–79) had become a naturalised American in 1930, and lived in Santa Barbara.
2 Michael Arthur Colefax (1906–89). He was by profession a banker.
3 He means 'collective noun'.
4 Sylvia Farquharson (1899–1950) married in 1918 Edward Robert Francis Compton (1891–1977).
5 Dorothy Carlotta Power (1902–66) married in 1937 David Field Beatty (1905–72), 2nd Earl Beatty. They divorced in 1945.
6 With no addition.

Randolph had done it, that whilst I could not prove my statement I nevertheless knew it to be true. He looked surprised, stopped for a second – we were by then opposite the Guards Memorial facing the Horse Guards Parade – and he said with an air of conviction: 'I think you are right. It must have been Randolph!'

I had long wanted and waited for this conversation. I was rather emotionally spent by it all and went into the RAC for a Turkish bath and a rumination. I laughed, too, to myself over Lady Colefax's gaffe at the length of luncheon when Gage, being fidgety, tried to leave. She had turned to her parlourmaid and said, 'We must let Lord Gage out, and see that he doesn't steal the spoons!' Gage had been obviously affronted by this silly sally and I had afterwards explained that his father, the old Lord Gage, had been a famous kleptomaniac; that he always went away from parties with other people's silver and that on the following day his devoted servant would always return it . . . . This proves the theory that one's worst *faux pas* are often unobserved by the person who commits them . . . .

Mr and Mrs Amery . . . . dined: a quiet successful evening. I managed to do Arthur Hope a great deal of harm – in retaliation for sending me a dud cheque. I told Amery the story of the £600. Amery is ageing; he is a touch deaf, but very nice and a raconteur, if a bit too anecdotal!! All went to bed early.

Fear I talked too much tonight. Mrs Amery remarked affectionately that the two quickest brains in London were Mrs Greville's and mine! . . . Leo Amery made an apt remark to the effect that Anthony Eden had joined that growing group of ex-future prime ministers along with Walter Elliott, Shakes Morrison and Oliver Stanley.

SATURDAY 9TH MAY   *QUEEN'S HOTEL, PORTSMOUTH*

Woke realising that I had been too talkative and indiscreet last night; perhaps it does not 'signify' as Trollope would say. Lunched with Circe Londonderry and her fascinating sensible daughter Mairi Bury[1] at Pastori's and then we walked to the Palace Theatre to see the revue. They wanted particularly to see it as the leading lady Cicely Courtneidge is supposed to look like Maureen Stanley. So she does. I caught the 4.45 for Portsmouth and slept all the way. Train punctual . . . . skies grey and grim. Alan, who was starting his MTB[2] from Weymouth soon arrived, and I was impressed how dark and well and handsome he seems and is. We dined in the crowded hotel, talked of Ronnie Cartland, of what an untrue bit of pious picture the recent book about him gives! Then we went up to his sitting room and I was amazed to hear that he has offered £40,000 for Lulworth Castle. Only the shell remains. The Iveaghs will be furious. Sat up late.

---

1 Formerly Lady Mairi Stewart (see entry for 20 June 1939 and footnote); in 1940 she had married Derek Keppel, Viscount Bury (qv).
2 Motor Torpedo Boat.

SUNDAY 10TH MAY

Breakfasted in pyjamas with Alan. He then went to Gosport and I dressed slowly and lazed. I read Trollope's *American Senator*[1] and finished *The Romance of a Nose*[2] by Gerald Berners. We lunched, philandered and came up to London about 6.30, where we were joined by Michael Parker, an enchanting engaging Pierrot. Supper together and then we listened to Winston, who made a magnificent broadcast. It is a double anniversary in a way; it is two years ago today that he became Prime Minister. I remember every detail of that dreadful day: Alec Dunglass rushed into my room at the Foreign Office soon after six, to say that Winston had been summoned to the Palace where Chamberlain had preceded him . . . Rab and I were thunderstruck! . . . . Princess Olga had lunched that day with the Halifaxes and had sat next to Neville Chamberlain, then still Prime Minister, and he had complained wistfully of L[loyd] G[eorge]'s bitter and personal animosity against him, and had talked later to Dill, then just appointed CIGS. How that world has scattered since. Olga a prisoner, Dill in Washington, ditto the Halifaxes, Neville dead . . . . and a year ago today was the last appalling heavy air raid over London. I missed it by having gone to Kelvedon.

MONDAY 11TH MAY

Woke, but unnaturally rather spent. A loving little letter from Diana Cooper whom I so love. Lunched with the Grand Duchess of Luxembourg.[3] I sat on her right and next to me on the other side was her husband, the Prince of Luxembourg . . . . The Grand Duchess is extremely *grande dame*, possibly a touch shy and her inadequate English falters; but she is altogether fascinating, and I fell for her charms. We gossiped about old days and her relations, the Toerrings . . . . A most *réussi* party, and I was at the top of my form as I am invariably with real royalty. We sat for two hours in the Coq d'Or restaurant and I was sorry to leave them . . . . we discussed Winston's terrific broadcast last night: she, too, thought it colossal but we were both in agreement about the ~~wisdom~~ [crossed out] prudence? of talking of poison gas.[4] Was it wise, or really necessary? I cannot believe that the German government would countenance its use against a civilian population and a public reference to such a practice by the Prime Minister of Britain may have a propaganda value to the enemy.

1 Published in 1877.
2 A novel of 1941.
3 Charlotte Adelgonde Élise of Nassau-Wellburg (1896–1985) succeeded her sister, who had abdicated, as Grand Duchess of Luxembourg in 1919. That same year she married Prince Félix of Bourbon-Parma (qv). She abdicated in favour of her son in 1964.
4 The government feared at the time that the Germans would drop canisters of poison gas on British cities; and Churchill had warned in his 10 May broadcast that if they did, Britain would retaliate.

TUESDAY 12TH MAY

Alan burst in to see me at seven o'clock and I was still asleep. He looked immense, bronzed and majestic and altogether irresistible.

The newspapers announce that the long-expected German offensive against Russia has actually begun.[1]

In the evening I took Violet Trefusis to a revue – a drab affair, and later we supped at the Ritz and discussed the unimaginative present! So far the war has not yet produced a poet, a sonnet, not even a play, or a *Chu Chin Chow*![2] One wonders whether this wonderful island race has not lost a little of its genius. Actually I am increasingly convinced that England and the English are mad and now that the lower orders are more in control the ailment is more obvious and dangerous.

WEDNESDAY 13TH MAY

Walked to the House, where I lingered most of the day listening to the debate and gossiping in the lobbies. The German spring offensive in Russia seems to have really begun . . . . Everybody was particularly charming to me today and I felt a breeze of the world's warmth. I wonder why? Shakes Morrison, white-haired and so beautiful in a negroid way, was demonstrative and affectionate, as was Brendan Bracken. We talked of poor Edward Ruggles-Brise,[3] who died yesterday, aged only 60.[4] MPs are dying like flies now. Perhaps I shall be the next to go? In any case my affairs are in order. Walked to the Dorchester meeting Eleanor Smith, fat and maternal, friendly and dirty; Winnie Portarlington and others. Called on Mrs Greville who was again not so well. She has been badly burned by her doctor! English doctors, particularly the expensive ones, are clumsy artisans, and often murderers. Mrs Greville kissed me and remarked to the Belgian Ambassador who was there 'Chips is my only vice' – Mrs Amery added that she adored me, and I purred, a whiff of the world's warmth once more. Everybody is being divine to me and I wonder why? The Ambassador, the most charming old gentleman on earth, drove me home and came in for a while.

Jim Thomas, surprisingly enough, thinks the Cartland book 'a vulgar disaster'. So it is.

---

1 It would be this campaigning season in the East that ended with the Germans cornered at Stalingrad, and the Soviets' fierce beating back of the German forces thereafter to their final defeat.
2 A musical comedy by Oscar Asche, based on *Ali Baba and the Forty Thieves*, and premiered in London in 1916. It was notable for running for five years, a then unheard of feat.
3 Edward Ruggles-Brise (1882–1942) was Conservative MP for Maldon from 1922 to 1923 and from 1924 to 1942. He was created 1st Bt in 1935.
4 Actually he was still only 59.

THURSDAY 14TH MAY

Spent a quiet day . . . . 'Bill' Tufnell dropped in and I foolishly gave him a Fabergé matchbox, a red heart of beauty, and worse, persuaded him to stay to dinner. He was boorish, boring and rude to Lady Willingdon, who took offence. Others: Clarissa Churchill; Sylvia Compton; Gerald Palmer, who is nicer and commoner than I thought. Afterwards Rab, Jim Thomas, and the Archduke all looked in. We ridiculed Tufnell – after he had rushed to catch the last train to Windsor where he is on duty. He is intolerable! He remarked that I had made mischief between him and his oldest friend; when I asked whom he meant, he said 'Hugh Euston'! I promptly retorted that Hugh a year ago had never heard of him! . . . I shan't invite Tufnell again – the squirearchy doesn't mix with high society; it is too gauche and clumsy.

Rab very charming and he borrowed my coat to wear tomorrow at Ruggles-Brise's funeral. He was a dull, pleasant, agricultural man and will be regretted in the House. Already there is a queue for the vacant seat. I put the Kemsleys on to it and he is already intriguing with Rab as they want it for Neville Berry,[1] the most intelligent and able of the Kemsley basket.

SATURDAY 16TH MAY   KELVEDON

Another MP is dead! Old Somerville,[2] and I am sorry. He was always a courteous old cock. The Commons is indeed a dangerous profession.

Drove here. The Duchess of Gloucester, very late, having been delayed *en route* from Barnwell, by a motor breakdown, arrived . . . . at two o'clock. We lunched eleven strong in the tiny Empire dressing room! As we waited I overheard Lady Whitmore, the Scandinavian wife of the Lord Lieutenant [of Essex], ask what the figures on the great clock meant (they are Honor's name which I had put there) – there was a low laugh – 'She'd be enough to stop any clock!' I overheard someone say. Stabbing. The Duchess looked prettier than she used to, was well dressed and reminded me of a mignonette, very English. She asked many questions; we talked of Paul [Channon's son], and to my horror she sent her love to Honor! She must have forgotten – could she be ignorant still? – and as about a dozen people surrounded us, I could do nothing but answer monosyllabically. But I felt a hypocrite with so old and sweet and simple a friend. Shall I write and explain?

The beauty of Kelvedon this late afternoon almost broke my heart. I am so lonely, and so in love. The fruit trees, the tulips and the lilac against the lush green

---

1 William Neville Berry (1914–98) did not pursue a political career.
2 Annesley Ashworth Somerville (1858–1942) had been a schoolmaster, latterly at Eton where he taught mathematics, before becoming Conservative MP for Windsor in 1922, at the age of 64. He was knighted in 1939.

background bewitch me. And all afternoon, after HRH left an ENSA[1] band played popular music – Puccini can be extremely poignant.

Maimie and Vsevolod begged me to dine with them in London, a little party for King Peter; but I refused as I am uneasy with that royal stripling now. He is weak and silly, not normal; and I cannot like him, although I have known him since he was born, because of his treachery to Paul. Mrs Greville has an unkind story about Paul which she is spreading; it is to the effect that he persecuted the duc d'Aosta with his attentions in Kenya before he died. I wonder?

Sunday 17th May

Alone, one thinks. I feel the stirrings, the urge, once more to write. Shall I? And then I realised that I have been corroded by wealth. I am Midas, I am a horrible Harpagon[2] and think only of money – but money for Paul.

I slept fitfully: simple food always gives one indigestion! .... [I] almost decided to write a book in the Trollopian style. A semi-political, social theme .... Indeed, I wrote several lines and defying the blackout regulations jotted down notes. Shall I persevere? I have the talent but have I the application?

A gorgeous day and Kelvedon bewitching with its vernal beauty. May is a miracle here. I wanted to stay on but Alan sent me a peremptory message to come up to London, which I did. We dined *à deux* at La Belle Meunière, and later frolicked here where he is staying.

Monday 18th May

Alan got up at 3.15 a.m. and took my car to Paddington to meet Adrian Liddell Hart,[3] a young naval officer who is the writer's son. He brought him back here and they slept the remainder of the short night in my great Empire bed. We all breakfasted together. A dark boy and rather a lecherous one, methinks. I only half-liked him. They looked amusing in bed but I am not sure that the servants thought so!

I called at Gunn's studio to see my portrait, at long last completed. He tells me that his two portraits, one a rather sugary affair of Lady Errington,[4] and a

---

1 Entertainments National Service Association, set up in 1939 to entertain troops and other service personnel during the war.
2 The title role in Molière's *L'Avare* (*The Miser*), first performed in 1668.
3 Adrian Liddell Hart (1922–91) served in the RNVR during the war and unsuccessfully fought seats for the Liberal Party at the 1945 and 1950 general elections. He then spent a year in the French Foreign Legion, wrote a book about the experience, and then worked in industry and in a hostel for the rehabilitation of young offenders. He was the son of Basil Liddell Hart (1895–1970), military historian.
4 Esmé Mary Gabriel Harmsworth (1922–2011), daughter of the 2nd Viscount Rothermere (qv), married in 1942 George Rowland Stanley Baring, by courtesy Viscount Errington until 1953, when he succeeded his father as 3rd Earl of Cromer.

conversation piece of Geoffrey Dawson[1] were refused by the Academy, so perhaps after all it is for the best that my portrait was not exhibited. This shows the wisdom of never sending off angry letters – I kept back and later destroyed the 'snorter' I had written him. I think that Gunn is going off in many ways.

Dined alone and am going soon to bed.

TUESDAY 19TH MAY

All day I was in a receptive mood, made notes for my new novel – shall I call it 'Declension'? Went for a drive with Rab, and listened to the debate on the war. Unreal as ever. Attlee dull and the Chamber emptied. The PM not present, and criticised for not being so. Various members, principally Wardlaw-Milne, attacked the government with some violence. The temperature is rising again against it.

Five MPs have died this week; and there is a scramble for the seats led by the Berry family.

There is talk of intrigue. Beaverbrook is alleged to be intriguing against Winston and to have joined forces with Cripps. Their aim is to overthrow the present government and if possible, force an election. The result would be an extreme left-central government.

Dined in alone; I am worn out and must try to recover and recuperate. All day I made notes for my new novel; and also decided to speak in Thursday's debate.

Maureen Stanley is desperately ill and may die; I most certainly hope so. A dissolute unfaithful wife, a notoriously neglectful mother, a vampire, nymphomaniac, a drunkard and even a degrading influence, corrupting every-body with whom she came into contact, she has exerted a deplorable role in London society. Oddly enough, both the King and Queen are amongst her intimates and go frequently to her house in spite of warnings not to. She is a corrupt creature without the good qualities of either parent[2] except that she speaks well, even extremely well. I daresay that Oliver will remarry.

WEDNESDAY 20TH MAY

The big debate continued. Leslie Belisha made an effective and smashing speech against the government. The Tory Party seems indeed doomed. I attended the 1922 Committee which was addressed by Tommy Dugdale, who was pleasant last week.

Dined in with Rab and Sydney Butler; Lady Londonderry who arrived in Red Cross uniform . . . . Leslie Hore-Belisha, relaxing after his heroic effort this afternoon, and Jay Llewellin, my poor dear dreadfully ponderous Jay who

---

1 The former editor of *The Times*.
2 Lord and Lady Londonderry.

yesterday sent me salmon and tonight arrived carrying a bottle of excellent brandy, which is expensive and all but unprocurable. He is an angel, shrewd, but a colossal bore; and worse, he is lonely. Dinner flowed easily but Circe Londonderry refused to have much conversation with Leslie, who[m] she dislikes. The *haut monde*[1] hates him. Both Butlers very charming indeed. They are sleeping in the Josephine bed, where so many other orthodox (and otherwise) couples have consorted and frolicked, loved and wept . . .

I wonder whether I shall speak tomorrow.

THURSDAY 21ST MAY

Molotov arrived secretly in Scotland last night where he was met by the royal train, and brought to London, where he has been hidden.[2] Nobody knows of this, hardly anyone. I had much pleasure in telling Rab this evening, who was astonished.

I went early to the House after playing for a little with my intoxicating niece, Liza Guinness who is 2½ years old, and is staying at Belgrave Square with me. It is soothing to hear a childish voice and noises in the house; but those pleasures are finished for me I fear, as everything else . . . the House was crowded but uninterested and uninteresting; it is sad to see democracy slowly committing suicide and every debate, I think, lowers parliamentary prestige. And there is so much filth and dirty political plotting at the moment, and of course the chief instigator is Max Beaverbrook, who cannot bring himself to forgive the Conservative Party . . . . When the adjournment about retail shops came on I went to my place and waited to be called. Member after member spoke, but the Speaker ignored me! Suddenly I became shy and only wanted to bolt and after someone opposite got up I thought that the little debate had ended and fled, relieved, from the Chamber – but I was wrong, as it was reopened by a handful of experts and, disillusioned, cowardly and disgusted, I came away and walked home.[3] The Butlers came in: Sydney has improved in looks, she is greying and Rab is gayer and more *homme du monde*.[4] He said the days he had spent with me formed him! So they did.

I dined with Helen Fitzgerald and David Margesson at the Dorchester. Gossip and politics, hock and seagulls' eggs. Then I joined Alan and Patsy who were at a nearby table and drove home with the Butlers who had been dining with Sybil Colefax upstairs. She had a gala, at 10/6d a head – for the Mountbattens etc. Both Rab and Sydney had been bored. We discussed the mysterious arrival of

1 High society.
2 Molotov had flown to Scotland at enormous risk and would come to London to conclude the Anglo-Soviet Treaty, the formal alliance between the United Kingdom and the Soviet Union that would last until the end of the war.
3 Channon had not made a speech in the Commons since 9 February 1937.
4 Man of the world.

Molotov. I am sure that Anthony Eden has done this and that the Anglo-Russian Treaty will be sprung on the House and the country – during the Whitsuntide recess. It would be a dreadful mistake, a calamity for the future of sinking England. Immorality in politics never pays, and to wink at the annexation of the Baltic states by Soviet Russia is too Jesuitical and shocking. Rab does not agree and told me so. Victor Cazalet however, threatens to vote against the government if need be . . . . He stopped me in Constitution Hill today and told me that he had recently given lunch to Queen Marie and King Peter and that they had been fairly decent about Paul, me and altogether more conciliatory.

FRIDAY 22ND MAY

The Butlers left for Stanstead . . . Later lunched with the Lennox-Boyds and Mr Bland at the Ritz. Alan is beginning one of his *grandes amitiés amoureuses*[1] with Adrian Liddell Hart. Will it lead to trouble?

Diana Cooper rang up and asked whether she could stay the night and I was enchanted and made arrangements accordingly. Then I walked to the Dorchester to have a cocktail with Ghislaine Dresselhuys, Lady Kemsley's large, florid baroque ambitious daughter. She is attractive and [illegible]. A group of young people and I made friends with the Duke of Connaught[2] (he is alleged to be afflicted with gonorrhoea, but I noticed that he drank several cocktails). He looks very like the Duke of Windsor did at that age but has not quite the pretty attractive freshness of his double cousin. Perhaps the desert has dried him up! He is a friend of Francis Lennox-Boyd . . .

Diana duly arrived, lovely and radiant. She, Duff and I dined and talked . . . . He wrote to Eden recently to protest against the proposed Russian Treaty and he was indeed startled when I told him about Molotov being hidden somewhere in the suburbs. Duff was charming tonight and seemed very *à côté* politically; didn't know that Gwilym Lloyd George is being heavily tipped for India, nor about the Beaverbrook plots. I liked him quite enormously and we were suddenly at ease. They were both fascinated by my story, which I had from Circe Londonderry, who swears it is true, that Anthony Eden is really the son of that bounder FitzGerald,[3] who afterwards deserted Lady Eden and eventually married Millie, Duchess of

---

1 Big love affairs.
2 Alastair Arthur Windsor (1914–43), *né* Prince Alastair of Connaught, by courtesy Earl of MacDuff from 1917 until 1942, when he succeeded his grandfather as 2nd Duke of Connaught and Strathearn and Earl of Sussex. He died in Canada of exposure after falling out of a window while drunk.
3 Percy Desmond FitzGerald (1873–1933) was born in Melbourne, Victoria, but came to England and became a cavalry officer, fighting in the Second Boer War and Great War and becoming a brigadier general. He married the Dowager Duchess of Sutherland in 1914, but their marriage was annulled in 1919.

Sutherland![1] If the tale is true it explains much. Certainly FitzGerald was Lady Eden's lover at the time . . . Diana's simplicity is so surprising. She arrived with a tiny bag containing only a toothbrush and a nightdress. She unpacked herself and was *sweetness* and simplicity itself.

SATURDAY 23RD MAY

Breakfasted with Diana in the Empire bedroom. The Empress Josephine's bed has had a mixed bag week. Then I walked to the Ritz, where I met Charlie Londonderry, who advised me to back his horse for the Derby, which I did. Gave lunch to Mairi Bury, with whom I am slightly *en flirt*, and then walked home and almost collapsed. I ought not to be so tired that a stroll followed by a light lunch almost kills me. I slept for two hours and then drove here. Kelvedon is as lush as ever, but the fruit blossom is fading.

Maureen Stanley is luckily much worse but her illness is dragging on; as she is only 42[2] I fear she may last a bit.

SUNDAY 24TH MAY

I decided that the effort of driving to Stanstead to stay with the Butlers is too great and I have sent a message chucking.

It is a cold cruel day, with wild winds whining through the surprised trees, so lovely in their vernal beauty and there is a touch of the sea in the air . . . . All day it has been like a monsoon here, pelting with rain. No sunbathing, and much changing of shoes.

Wrote all evening, now to bed. Through the walls I hear the soldiers chattering as they undress in the drawing room, which is now a ward. I envy them their companionship. But perhaps, I too, will have happiness again when Peter gets back.

Listened to Duff's broadcast;[3] he was late, and, I suspect partly 'tight' but the broadcast itself was excellent and moving.

WHIT MONDAY, 25TH MAY

The war has become quite unreal. The distant Kharkov[4] fighting is so remote and probably so exaggerated.

1 See Vol. I, entry for 1 January 1918 and footnote.
2 Actually she was still only 41.
3 It was Empire Day, and Cooper broadcast about the British Empire being one held together by the common aims of its people, rather than by military force.
4 Kharkov, in Ukraine, was captured by the Germans in October 1941; a Russian offensive to recapture it was under way, but failed badly, and the city was not finally retaken until August 1943.

Here there is a perpetual monsoon and it is too melancholy for words, for wild winds hum of happier days and add to one's misery . . . . A message from Belgrave Square that there was a telegram awaiting me threw me into a ferment but I was doomed to disappointment, as it was only from Alan about a gold cigarette case he wants me to buy for him to give to Adrian Liddell Hart. Other people's love affairs are of such secondary importance and my hopes were dashed![1] Yes, certainly Peter is on his way back: since he ignores cables it must mean that he doesn't get them. He ought to arrive in England DV[2] about June 21st, or perhaps before. The tediousness, the melancholy of his long journey is despairing. My emotions towards him are peculiar; for he always seems to be a bit of myself chopped off. There is nothing of him that isn't me – can he really be my other half as he suggests? And we are so close. Today I could hear the waves that must be buffeting him, and smell the tang of the sea that soothes him . . . later, is this all imagination? I cannot think so; but I am now told that his poisonous second-rate sister has had a recent letter from him and that he is a major. That enchanting Pierrot a major!

Tuesday 26th May

A telephone talk . . . . convinces me that Peter is not now returning . . . It seems he called from Delhi two days ago. He, who writes so gracefully, is a clumsy cabler.

I collected baskets of flowers and drove to London in the May moisture and wet. I sent one huge bouquet to Mrs Coats at her nursing home,[3] and the other I gave to Patsy.

Unfortunately I found a horrible little pencilled scrawl from Honor, which came in an unstuck envelope. She merely stated that she was changing her name quite shortly to Woodman. She doesn't realise the complications, all the unfortunate and inevitable publicity which will ensue – it is ungracious and inconsiderate to my faraway child certainly.

I rang Lady Iveagh who was remarkably calm about it; took the line that there is nothing whatever that can be done with Honor and there it was . . . . Of course I dread the announcement, since it will cause unpleasant enquiries and chat . . . . Lunched at the Ritz with Alan and Patsy . . . . we met half London and everybody seemed particularly friendly except Perry Brownlow, who, I suppose, takes Honor's side, although he is really my friend, or was originally. Alan takes a gloomy and serious view of the name-changing affair and got quite heated and furious with Honor, and implored me to try to persuade her not to do anything so rash. I am almost indifferent. He rushed off to Ramsgate and then telephoned frantically that he was coming back and arranged to meet Adrian Liddell Hart

---

1 Channon was convinced Coats was returning to England, as he did not reply to any of the cables sent to him.
2 *Deo volente* – God willing.
3 Coats's mother was recuperating from an illness.

here at midnight. He – perhaps they – stayed here all night. I dined in with Nicholas Lawford who is staying here and Millard[1] of the Foreign Office, a most charming and gay young man who is also one of Anthony Eden's secretaries.

Teenie Cazalet has played a great role these few weeks; he has prevailed upon the FO and the government not to include the Baltic States in the proposed Anglo-Russian Treaty, which will soon be announced. The treaty will be anodyne, I am reliably informed. I don't know. The secrecy surrounding Molotov's visit still persists but Lawford tells me that it was he who went to meet him in Scotland and brought him back on the royal train. Incidentally, Molotov has stayed with the King!! The mind can hardly take it in. He is now going to the USA, apparently. Everybody says how pleasant he is.

WEDNESDAY 27TH MAY

Much upset still by Honor's letter, I am down and *désoeuvré* ...

Called on Mrs Greville, who was brilliant and anecdotal. She had lunched at the Spanish Embassy to meet Winston, who was genial. He sat between Alice Wimborne and Mairi Bury – both his relatives. A successful party! .... Then I had cocktails with Helen Fitzgerald, Esmond Rothermere and Ann O'Neill and Lady Kemsley.

There are two[2] royal romances which are thriving: the first is little King Peter of Yugoslavia, of whom Princess Alexandra of Greece (a merry, intelligent slightly *méchante*[3] minx) is in hot pursuit. She has even gone with her mother to Cambridge, where they have taken lodgings so as to be near the young King. This marriage will probably come off,[4] and it may save both the throne and the future of Peter, who is an ass.

This morning Alan had breakfast in my bedroom. I sold him a cigarette case which I had bought from the Crown Prince of Greece, to whom the Duke of Kent gave it as a Christmas present! Alan gave it to Adrian Liddell Hart, who was enchanted by it, although of course ignorant of its travels.

THURSDAY 28TH MAY

Still very cold. Patsy called on me and we discussed Honor's latest move in the war of words – this wild idea of changing her name. Patsy is going to see her today

---

1 Guy Elwin Millard (1917–2013) joined the Diplomatic Service in 1939. When Eden became Prime Minister in 1955 he asked Millard to be his private secretary for foreign affairs, and Millard was heavily involved in the Suez crisis. He later served as Ambassador to Hungary (1967–9), Sweden (1971–4) and Italy (1974–6).
2 He does not mention the second.
3 Nasty, or vicious.
4 It did, in 1944.

and will try to persuade her to abandon the idea. Cable from Laura [Corrigan] from Vichy.

I fear that the proposed Russian Treaty will revive the Eden shares and that Anthony's political stock will rise, although he has been forced to climb down and surrender over the immoral proposal about the Baltic States. That, however, will not get out.

Walked to Queen's Gate, taking my blond, snowy, obstinate Bundi, and called upon Mrs Coats who is beginning to recover from her long illness. She looked pretty, hale and exquisite with her white hair – like Marie Antoinette. She was affectionate and her somewhat common daughter gave me tea and was amiable. We talked of Peter . . . . and then I called on Maimie Pavlovsky, where I found a nest of White Russians – one had recently arrived from Brussels, Paris, Vichy and Aix-en-Provence and told us her experiences and was thrilling. She said that the Germans behaved well in France and were mystified by the scoffing attitude of the French population who have not collaborated with them. Wine is unprocurable. The *faubourg* has behaved well etc. and life in Paris is not unpleasant, certainly interesting.

Lady Londonderry, and my new girl-friend, Mairi Bury, Nicholas Lawford, and a silent, mysterious Norwegian dined. We talked of the last war and Circe Londonderry said that the atmosphere was far more Red and extreme than now. She was not alarmed for the future of England, as I am.

Nicholas is altogether delightful, cultured and sad.

The Axis offensive in Libya continues.

FRIDAY 29TH MAY

Patsy rang me early to say that she had not succeeded in persuading Honor to abandon her idea of changing her name. Apparently the complications, legal and otherwise, of living under an assumed name are considerable. I see that.

Old Miss Fox, the governess of the three beautiful sisters,[1] came to see me and stayed for an hour. Her loyalty to the princesses, Marina and Olga, is very great. She is over 80 and quite tireless in her efforts to help Prince Paul and Olga. (Their money, £7,000, has actually been paid into Coutts bank by the Yugoslav government, which is a great relief to all of us.) She hates Queen Mignonne . . . and Mrs Cresswell. Alas! She gave me a distressing account of my poor friends. Paul, apparently, does absolutely nothing but mope and he is too thin and his almost bald head is turning white with worry. My beautiful Fabergé distinguished Balkan Prince, yes Sovereign, now an old crushed and unhappy exile is terrible, terrible . . . . Had my hair arranged, and so looked handsome, even dashing when I went to the Ritz for a drink with Elizabeth Elveden, who is really very nice. She

---

1 The three Greek princesses.

is anti-Honor but pro-divorce; she admits that I am in a strange position since the male members of the family, Lord Iveagh my father-in-law, Arthur Elveden and Alan my brother-in-law, are violently on my side. Women have no moral sense . . .

I wanted to go to Kelvedon; instead I gave a rather *réussi* dinner party: Natasha Bagration . . . . had her two *suivants*, Arthur Leveson, who is now Flag-Lieut to Dickie Mountbatten, an important job; and the Duke of Connaught, whom I liked immensely. He is tough, royal, but shrewd and said smart and penetrating things. Ghislaine Dresselhuys also dined, who adores dukes and wants to marry them all; Mairi Bury again; and Nicholas Lawford. Afterwards we were joined by Vsevolod and Maimie. To her I rather impulsively gave a heliotrope enamel Fabergé cigarette case and now regret its loss . . . . I twitted her, told her she was like her imperial ancestress with so many lovers!!

Bed late, and perhaps a tiny weeny touch tipsy.

SATURDAY 30TH MAY   *KELVEDON*

Came here to write, but my pen is slothful. However I have finished Chapter One of 'Declension'.

SUNDAY 31ST MAY

All day at Kelvedon and then drove up in the gloaming. Found many letters, one, a long one from Harold Balfour described his meeting with my Paul. It brought tears to my eyes. The child is well and happy and 'obviously highly intelligent'. Thank God. There was also one from that fraud Rollo[1] who informs me that Honor has definitely decided to change her name. I suppose she has no alternative but it is a smack in the eye.

The house is full of flowers. I am well, calm, but not writing as easily as I did last week. Why?

Lawford has left and Loelia Westminster arrives tomorrow.

Dined with Michael Parker; *par arrangement* we met at Boodle's Club; but he arrived late and no dinner was available. We wandered about, somewhat at a loss as to where to go until he suggested the Café Royal. It sounded excitingly old-fashioned and there we went – I had not crossed its doubtful threshold since my marriage. We were ushered into the very 1890 dining room and put by a glass screen in a sort of semi alcove. There was a lady opposite to us and unfortunately it [the other side of the screen] was occupied by Basil and Maureen Dufferin. There was immediate atmosphere since they were having a somewhat drunken reconciliation, and I was on the prowl . . .

1 A legal adviser to Lady Honor, qv.

Tremendous excitement to those in the know. Anthony Eden has been forced to climb down over the proposed Russian Treaty and the Baltic States are not to be included. Molotov has agreed and will so report to Stalin. Eden, chagrined, is to be allowed his triumph over the treaty, which is largely spiritual, and he will get much kudos.

There has been a mammoth raid on Cologne, in which a thousand planes took part. And foolish people now believe the war to be ending. A silly view?

MONDAY 1ST JUNE

I woke exhausted and had to face a bleak evening with only one or two people dining. However I got busy with the telephone and the cook and produced a festival, an almost pre-war dinner party –

Self,
Maureen Dufferin,
Lord Kemsley,
Duchess of Westminster,
The Argentine Ambassador,[1]
Lady Kemsley,
Lord David [sic] Margesson,
Alan Lennox-Boyd,
Helen Fitzgerald,
Dufferin,
Patsy Lennox-Boyd,
Jay Llewellin.

There was candlelight and Krug and witty political chatter. Loelia said that she would stand for Parliament on an anti-feminist ticket – and would certainly get in. I bet her a hundred pounds that Rab would be in Downing Street before June 1st, 1962. Other bets flew about. Gomer Kemsley is much annoyed that his son Lionel Berry has not been adopted for Windsor, although he is on the shortlist still. His rival is Charles Mott-Radclyffe,[2] a dark amiable youth whom I knew in Athens. He was once private secretary to Sam Hoare, but is now in sympathy with the Edenites and was recommended by Central Office through the intervention of Jim Thomas.

---

1 Miguel Ángel Cárcano (1889–1978) was Argentinian Ambassador to France from 1938 to 1942 and to the United Kingdom from 1942 to 1945. He served as his country's Foreign Minister from 1961 to 1962.
2 Charles Edward Mott-Radclyffe (1911–92) was Conservative MP for Windsor from 1942 to 1970. He had previously worked in the Diplomatic Service. He was knighted in 1957.

Dinner was successful, even brilliant. Everyone dressed and was cheerful. The party had the atmosphere of a London season, which, indeed, in a small war way we are having. Maureen D got very drunk and was I fear sick, but everybody is accustomed to her weakness. The Argentine Ambassador who is dark, friendly and saturnine, seemed bewildered; particularly so when we talked of future prime ministers! We all agreed that there were several at the table!

Loelia Westminster, fulsome, florid, gay and dignified has arrived to stay with me for a few days.

At long last a very witty but vaguely unsatisfactory epistle from Peter.

TUESDAY 2ND JUNE

Woke early, as one invariably does after a champagne night; and felt vigorous and stimulated. I am in my old form . . . . I walked to the House with dear Alan, who looked young and handsome, even boyish. Towards the end of Questions the PM somewhat unexpectedly appeared and was given a warm welcome (I am pro him now). At twelve o'clock he rose, and how big and ungainly his bottom looked, and proceeded to read out rather inarticulately for him a lengthy detailed dispatch from General Auchinleck, describing the drama of the desert campaign, the whole Libyan saga. It seemed on balance moderately hopeful. Then the PM turned and in his own words described the recent devastating raid on Cologne, which has been followed up last night by an aeronautical armada of 1,036 planes (of which we lost thirty-five) over western Germany, particularly the Essen environs. Both the Prime Minister and his announcements were well received.

I then walked home to meet my dear mother-in-law and we lunched *à deux*. She was pretty, discreet, but detached and rather shocked me by her casual attitude towards Honor's decision to change her name. It will be announced on Tuesday next, today week. No man has ever had to submit to such a humiliation; and I am doing it only to curry favour with my *beaux-parents* since I think it to Paul's advantage to do so. People might well ask, what could I do about it? Easy. Honor sent me a private message via Patsy that if I would agree to institute immediate divorce proceedings she would wait. But the Iveaghs are adamant and I can do nothing but acquiesce reluctantly to their wishes in the hope that they will treat my boy tenderly in their arrangements . . . .

Dined with Esmond Rothermere at the Dorchester. A pleasant party: Kemsleys; Margaret [illegible][1] with whom I discussed Mr Chamberlain, and suddenly, I burst into tears about him; Ann O'Neill . . . . Loelia Westminster; others. Afterwards we adjourned to the Kemsleys' suite where we played bridge

---

1 In the MS the name begins with an H but is then an indiscernible scrawl. There is a possibility it may have been Rothermere's first wife, whom he divorced in 1938 but with whom he remained on good terms, and whose married name was Margaret Hussey.

and I won £11 . . . . Others dropped in including Duff Cooper, who had been dining
à deux with Winston Churchill, who confided to him the details, or rather the
spirit of the recent Anglo-Russian Treaty, still so deep a secret. The PM whispered
that not even 'the Cabinet' knew of it; and Duff retorted (or so at least he repeated
to me), 'Chips told me about it days ago!' Eventually the evening, as evenings
however eternal they may seem, ended and Loelia, Duff Cooper and I drove home
together. We discussed *en route* the O'Neill divorce which has only just begun.
Shane is suing Ann, naming Esmond Rothermere as co-respondent. He has
waited six years to do it.

There has just been an alert and I wonder whether a thousand German planes
will come over London? I was alarmed about the divine Elveden children, who
are staying with me.

WEDNESDAY 3RD JUNE

There is still idle chatter that the war is over. A few spectacular raids over
Germany and the country becomes optimistic. I went tritely [*sic*] in the intense
heat to the House and then back to Lygon Place to lunch with Lady Willingdon,
where I am always wholly welcome! I was gay and triumphant and sizing up the
company felt justified in cutting old Mrs Arthur James[1] dead. The party were all
my supporters: Audrey Bouverie; Edwina Mountbatten . . . . Buck De La Warr;
Prince Lobkowicz,[2] the Czech Ambassador; 'Niggs' Ratendone, Teenie; others. A
gay party which I much enjoyed. 'Niggs' Willingdon[3] – I always forget that he is
a marquess now – drove me to the Lords where I wandered about after he went
into the debate. I must really become a peer! I sat for some time with Geordie
Sutherland in the library and introduced him to Mungo Mansfield.[4] One might
have thought that these Scottish grandees needed no introduction from me. Then
I walked home and slept for a bit. About 5.30 the Duchess of Kent, accompanied
by Zoia Poklewska[5] and Natasha Bagration, her two devoted henchwomen,
dropped in and I gave them tea. The Duchess is very, very impressively pregnant.
She wore no hat, and wore an amber *imprimée* dress and was as delectable and is
as affectionate as ever.

Jim Thomas dined with me *à deux* and we discussed the proposed Russian
Treaty. He attacked Teenie Cazalet and I pretended to know nothing. Later
Loelia returned and we twitted him further.

1 Mary Cavendish-Bentinck.
2 Maximilian Lobkowicz (1888–1967) served as ambassador from the Czech
   government-in-exile throughout the Second World War.
3 The former Viscount Ratendone was now 2nd Marquess of Willingdon.
4 Mungo David Malcolm Murray (1900–71), by courtesy Lord Scone from 1906 to 1935, when
   he succeeded his father as 7th Earl of Mansfield and Mansfield.
5 See entry for 6 December 1940 and footnote.

I don't think that the Libyan news is as encouraging as before. Russia is now back-page news.

How soon shall I be going to Eton on this day to see my altogether adorable dauphin?[1] His portrait, his and mine, by Gunn, now hangs here and is much discussed. Everyone agrees that I look severe, if not actually senile. Abraham and Isaac! Otherwise it is an excellent portrait.

Had old Colefax, who is still anti-Chamberlain . . . . to lunch, also Nicholas Lawford and of course Loelia. Sybil Colefax remarked that Sir John Wardlaw-Milne should be shot. She is so prejudiced and violent.

I gather that the royal romance between little Peter of Yugoslavia and Alexandra of Greece is going very well and that there may soon be an announcement! I wonder?

At six I picked up Teenie Cazalet and Grace Curzon and we went to the Aldwych Theatre to see *Watch on the Rhine*,[2] a most moving and frightening play about a refugee family in America. We went back to the Dorchester with Kakoo Rutland to have a merry *souper à quatre*.[3] Kakoo has not aged; she told us amusing tales of her dinners at Sandringham with King George V etc.

I was moved and pleased by the meeting with Grace Curzon after all these months, almost years. We talked sadly of old grand days . . . and then I left, escorting Kakoo home. We stopped here and I showed her my house and the pictures and then we walked in the starlight to Eaton Square. She is v sweet.

Had a luncheon party which was super successful: Grace Curzon; George Gage; Victor Cazalet; Barbie Wallace; Rab and Sydney Butler; all dear and devoted friends. I have had a tremendous social success recently. I wish I could have lunched today with Bernhard of the Netherlands but I had to refuse. My party was gay and witty but I was sorry that the Duchess of Rutland 'chucked'; she rang up this morning to say that she couldn't come . . . .

Loelia, dignified and charming, but like all well-bred English people inclined to be somewhat on the make, left me to go to Highclere, the Carnarvons' still-inhabited castle. I covered her with kindness, presents and petrol, etc.

Grace Curzon still looks superb in spite of all her tragedies and financial worries. I told her that we all had them, which seemed to console her slightly.

1 The anniversary of the birth of King George III, and Eton's annual day of celebration.
2 A play by Lillian Hellman, first seen on Broadway in 1941, about the need for an international alliance against Hitler.
3 Supper for four.

There is another lull in my correspondence with Peter. Hardly anything has come for a month or more.

SATURDAY 6TH JUNE   WESTON HALL, NEAR TOWCESTER

The heat is Libyan! I slept late and arranged to go to stay with the Sitwells. I am giving one Billy McCann[1] of the Ministry of Information a lift down. I am told that he is charming.

Left London at noon accompanied by McCann, a tall, prematurely aged Australian, who now works at the Ministry of Information. He is passionately pro-Spanish and an ardent Francophile. We took a picnic lunch, stopped near Buckingham, sat, ate, and undressed and sunbathed in a field. Then drove on here to stay with Sachie and Georgia Sitwell. We are the only guests. Both Sitwells charming; the house tawdry but full of atmosphere and quaint *bibelots* and old books. A magnificent border of irises. Good food and amusing conversation. Sachie is a Home Guard, and looks well and rather red in the face. I had the best bedroom, and I recall that I slept in it once before – with Honor in 1934! Last time I was here was for the Blenheim Ball – July 7th, 1939. Georgia asked me if I could remember the date (as if I could ever forget it): there were Ali and Joan Khan and Peter Coats, and a new phase of my life began. I was nostalgic tonight instead. Nearly three years.

SUNDAY 7TH JUNE

Sunbathed all day and sipped cider. Georgia is an efficient wonderful wife and mother and cajoles Sachie. At six we drove in my faithful car to Chadshunt,[2] a rather unattractive house belonging to Peggy Dunne, who gave us a warm welcome and a most delicious dinner with champagne. Much talk and gossip and poring over albums. We brought back two baby pigs who were wrapped in sacks and reposed contentedly on the Sitwellian laps. The intelligentsia have all taken to farming pursuits. Much laughter about the porcine companions whom I named Romulus and Remus.

There has been a big naval engagement at Midway between the Japanese and American fleets and from all accounts, it has been a smashing victory for the Yanks.[3]

1 William 'Billy' McCann (1910–?) was head of the Spanish Division in the Ministry of Information. He was a lifelong friend of the Sitwells. He spent the latter part of his life in South America, and appears to have died there.
2 In south Warwickshire.
3 The Battle of Midway, fought at the atoll of the same name to the west of the Hawaiian Islands, was a crushing victory for the United States against the Japanese Navy and is regarded by military historians as one of the most decisive and significant naval battles of the war.

MONDAY 8TH JUNE

Drove up with Billy McCann who is amiable, intelligent and psychic. He read the lines on my wrist and predicted that I should now have five gloriously glamorously full years of love and success beginning last Monday, June 1st. He said that an affair crystallised next August would last ten years – between eight and ten, etc.; that I would have honours too and success. I felt quite cheered.

Lunched with Grace Curzon at Claridge's. Marcella and Edward Rice and their daughter Caroline,[1] who is my godchild .... At the corner table were Lord Derby much aged; Circe Londonderry and Charlie, Oliver Stanley and his dark son.[2] It was a family party and they were relieved by better news of Maureen who will now live, so Charlie assured me.

Loelia looked in to pick up her luggage. She is v sweet and loveable. We gossiped about Daphne [Weymouth] who is compromising herself with Robert Cecil to such an extent that the Cranbornes are seriously alarmed. I hear that she has had a miscarriage, or perhaps an operation. Poor Henry languishing and wilting in Palestine!

Nothing from Peter; he rarely writes now, and is thus endangering my affection for him.

A more than mad letter arrived from my mother in which she begs me not to go to Italy. Does she not realise that we are at war? It was crazy, incoherent but affectionate. I hope she will do nothing rash! And I have an intuition this year will be her last, poor demented creature.

McCann says that No. 17 is my lucky no. I thought it was 7. 1+9+4+2=16 + 1+6=7. So far nothing pleasant has happened to me this year. He didn't mention tomorrow's scandal – which may not prove to be one.[3] But he warned me that I should have six months of litigation; and also that my affairs would steadily, even dramatically improve.

This last night before the bomb falls, before the public announcement of Honor's outrageous perfidy I seem to be spending alone; and perhaps it is just as well since I cannot concentrate on other people, and am almost dreading Pyrford with its chatter, discomfort and rhododendrons.

Jay Llewellin rang up and asked me to dine but I refused. Gay little note from Michael Parker who is beginning to intrigue me.

TUESDAY 9TH JUNE

Today is *Der Tag*;[4] my humiliation is now public property, or will shortly be in a few hours' time. There was nothing in the morning press; and at 1 p.m. as I write,

---

1 Caroline Helen Rice (1931–2016). She married the 3rd Earl of Plymouth in 1950.
2 Michael Charles Stanley (1921–90).
3 Lady Honor's plans to change her surname.
4 The day.

no newspaper has as yet rung up. However I avoided the House of Commons and made a catalogue of my pictures instead . . . .

Lady Iveagh, Alan, Mr Bland, Clarissa Churchill and Maimie Pavlovsky telephoned. It is grey: I am alone: I am horrible . . . . no letter from Peter: and I am too nervous to write although I tried. How could Honor treat me so?

Pyrford
Later

The Iveaghs fetched me in their big car and we drove here: they were most charming and affectionate . . . . Then I fetched Alan at Woking station: he had come from Portsmouth to be with me on this difficult day. We scanned the newspapers – nothing.

WEDNESDAY 10TH JUNE

A full important day. We all had a somewhat nervous breakfast; but again nothing. Patsy then rang Alan to say that the dreaded dreadful notice had actually appeared last Friday in the *Gazette*. No notice was taken of it; so it seems we have escaped. Great relief; but the Iveaghs are saddened and angered by the whole story. Lady Iveagh remarked to me 'Chips, you may one day get rid of Honor, but we've got her for life, the problem child,' and she sighed. Honor has killed all their love for her . . . .

The Iveaghs, Alan and I, drove to Send Grove to call on Loelia. (The Iveaghs think that I shall marry her!) We went all over the house and then visited the adjacent church where Lady Iveagh was surprised to come on the tombs of her great-grandparents, Thomas Cranley Onslow and his wife. The visit was a great success. Lady Iveagh remarked: 'Only Chips could make us pay a call.'

THURSDAY 11TH JUNE

Alan left at 7.30 after waking me. We slept together and he did not snore. He returned to Portsmouth and I drove up to London with the Iveaghs.

I went to the House, voted in the crowded 'Aye' lobby for the fuel arrangements. Afterwards at about 5 p.m. Anthony Eden rose on the adjournment and in most stilted tones announced the terms of the Russian Treaty. Nobody was impressed. 'It isn't worth the paper it's written on' was the general verdict. Poor man with his genius for miscarriages. Walked home. Mr Lloyd George however rose and in a mischievous postscript, felicitated the government.

Dined with Maimie, Vsevolod and Bill Tufnell. All delightful and affectionate.

Natasha Bagration looked in before dinner; she won't marry Alastair Connaught in spite of my injunctions that she should. Bill Tufnell and I dined with Vsevolod and Maimie . . . .

I hear that Lloyd George is to be married very soon to Miss Stevens [*sic*], his ageing mistress and mother of his child.[1]

Mrs Greville is very ill again: she has had another relapse, is exhausted and I fear, is dying really.

A letter, number 7, came from Peter today. He is Military Secretary to Wavell and a major.

FRIDAY 12TH JUNE

Went to bed at 10.30 exhausted by emotions . . . . The Sitwells telephoned and woke me. Just as I again got to sleep I found Jay Llewellin in my bed and he stayed and loved me for an hour – now this morning I am tired.

Mrs Coats came to tea; she looked frail. We discussed Peter's amazing career! PS to the C-in-Chief! It is little less than fantastic.

A horrible wet day; I wrote and rested and ruminated on my rich post. Patsy rather spoilt the day by telling me that a brief notice did appear in the *Telegraph* on Wednesday; but I doubt it since nobody has remarked on it. Now after writing a little I am going to bed.

SUNDAY 14TH JUNE   SEND GROVE

Slept until ten, and then scanned the newspapers – still no publicity and probably we have escaped. It is cold and horrible . . . . And the Libyan news is disturbing. We've perhaps been living in a false paradise for some months.

Drove here in time for luncheon. Loelia Duchess [of Westminster] is alone except for Sylvia Compton, who is v charming. Lovely food followed by a sunbathe and a gossip, and then we drove over to Clandon and walked in the park and went through the huge house which is now used as the Record Office. Clandon to me is one of the most attractive seats in England. It has an enfilade;[2] it is spacious with fine ceilings and the trees are magnificent. In happier days when everything seemed possible, even probable in my prospering affairs, I coveted the place since it is unlikely that Cranley[3] will ever be able to afford to live in it. The Onslows have retired to a small villa at Farnham for 'the duration'; he[4] is ill . . .

---

1 Frances Louise Stevenson (1888–1972) had been at Clapham High School with Lloyd George's eldest daughter, Mair, and later became governess to his youngest, Megan. She became Lloyd George's mistress in 1913, served as his private secretary, and in 1929 gave birth to a daughter, Jennifer. The girl was almost certainly fathered by a Liberal Party official, Thomas Tweed, with whom she also had an affair, but she persuaded Lloyd George that Jennifer was his. Lloyd George's first wife died in 1941 and he married Miss Stevenson, much to his children's dismay, in 1943.

2 A corridor that passes through a succession of rooms, linking them.

3 William Arthur Bampfylde Onslow (1913–71), by courtesy Viscount Cranley until 1945, when he succeeded his father as 6th Earl of Onslow.

4 That is, the 5th Earl.

MONDAY 15TH JUNE

I read a horrible much-discussed book, *No Orchids for Miss Blandish*[1] until 3 a.m. so woke late. I disliked leaving Send and wished I had the courage and the patience to have an affair with Loelia. She has such perfect taste; her small house is really a dream . . . .

A short news cutting sent to me from the *Telegraph* of last Wednesday announces that Honor is to take on the surname of Woodman. It is fairly discreetly worded but the fact remains that the cat – or at least a kitten – is out of the bag. How many people have seen it? I don't know. I only care now about the financial provisions for Paul which will amount to over £500,000 which will grow to three-quarters of a million even perhaps a round million or more before he comes into the property. This conservative estimate does not include his mother's share of his interests!

Peter Loxley dined and Geoffrey Lloyd looked in afterwards. We chatted about the Molotov visit and all agreed that the new Anglo-Russian Treaty is an anodyne, harmless and valueless document. Beaverbrook is trying to boost it and make it a major issue, thereby praising Eden and building him up as a future Prime Minister. Since all that 'The Beaver' does is doomed to failure, I am not seriously alarmed.

TUESDAY 16TH JUNE

I went early to the House which I found depressed and dejected because of the Libyan news which is discouraging. Shall we be able to hold Egypt?

Rab opened the debate on education and made a moderately successful speech which hinted at much but promised little. His old 'stalling' trick again. Dined at Claridge's with Olive and Adrian Baillie and Geoffrey Lloyd. It was the first night of the new austerity regulations which limit food consumption to the value of 5/-. The result was that we had less to eat than ever but it cost more, i.e., £6.15.0. for four people. The others went on to a film but, *ennervé*,[2] I fled home in order to see Alan [Lennox-Boyd] who arrived about eleven in a desperate and hysterical condition. On Monday night he had had an unfortunate experience; whilst patrolling the Channel in the dark but with a calm [illegible] his boat came upon a collision, and the cries of drowning men were heard all about them. Alan, evidently thinking – (or tight?) that his first duty was to his own men ordered his boat to withdraw; he hoped to avoid becoming entangled in the collision but in

---

1 A crime novel of 1939 by James Hadley Chase, controversial because of its depictions of sex and violence. It was the subject of a 1944 essay by George Orwell, *Raffles and Miss Blandish*, in which he noted how the ethics of the crime novel had changed over the years. What seemed to offend him most was not the subject matter, but that the novel, by an Englishman, had been written in what he considered to be 'American'.
2 Irritated, upset.

so doing he abandoned, as it were, dying sailors. His own crew was so incensed that it became insubordinate and insisted on returning; and Alan agreed. Here he made a mistake, for by returning he actually admitted that he had probably made a mistake in ever leaving the watery scene of disaster. Twenty minutes must have elapsed and they only came on one man, evidently dead, but still clinging to a log of wood. He was not brought aboard and I cannot think why as he might have been resuscitated. An appalling drama and I cannot help thinking for all my love and loyalty to A that he behaved without either sense or judgement. They again went away and he sensed that in the opinion of the crew he was seriously at fault in refusing even to attempt to rescue the men . . . . I don't understand the tale. I tried to console him; failed, and let him go.

Rex Whistler is staying with us for a few days.

The PM has gone again to the USA. The secret is well kept and I don't know exactly when he went.

WEDNESDAY 17TH JUNE

To the House, cool and beautifully dressed, but still depressed by the Libyan news. It is the same story. Save Bolshevism and lose the Empire. Too much has gone to Russia, too little to the Middle East. It is heartbreaking . . . .

Lunched with the Amerys. Camroses; Clauson,[1] whom I had wanted to meet particularly since it is he who copes with my bag letters to India; and the dark, gay, garrulous Egyptian Ambassador.[2] A most successful function. Clauson I tried to captivate, and, I think, did. He is a weary, dried-up old maid of a man who must have once been attractive. Etonian; good eyes; shabby clothes; some gentleness and a little humour. An English male virgin with a weakness for the lad, methinks. But exceedingly useful to me. Slept soundly for two hours and a half this afternoon. Why?

THURSDAY 18TH JUNE

A peaceful day and I neglected my parliamentary duties: the House, now that I am of-out [sic] the racket, has lost much of its old glamour for me. Had, however, a gay private conversation with Rab in his room. He seems devoted to me: I certainly am to him.

---

1 Gerard Leslie Makins Clauson (1891–1974) was a brilliant linguist and orientalist who joined the Diplomatic Service in 1919 after fighting with distinction in the Great War; and, from 1940 to 1951, was Assistant Under-Secretary of State at the Colonial Office. He was knighted in 1945 and published several books on the Turkish language.
2 Hassan Pasha Nashat (1895–1964) was Egyptian Ambassador to the United Kingdom from 1938 to 1945.

A dinner party here which was a success. Londonderrys – and twice they rang up the Clinic for news of Maureen Stanley who is such a long time a dyin'!; Helen Fitzgerald, who says that she hates the PM but thinks he should remain in control for the duration of the war. She is right. He is a bully, an irritating tyrant, unfair, unkind, wrong, but strong...he hates all of us, me, Alan, Rab, Harold [Balfour], and she added 'Both Max [Beaverbrook] and Walter Monckton'!; Clarissa Churchill, so clever and like a camellia; Gerald Berners. After dinner James Gunn dropped in and I was surprised by his sudden shyness and commonness – perhaps it was his *endimanché*[1] clothes. We discussed the portrait, which was embarrassing as nobody agrees about it. Charlie Londonderry remarked that he never liked portraits of people he knew, and that nobody did. One only admired pictures of the dead or of people one had never seen. Alice Harding dropped in; and I am beginning to regret that I ever gave her my diamond and gun-metal cigarette case. A merry evening.

It seems my agent Bailey has been charged at Southend with indecent assault on a girl of 8! The Baileys are prostrated with shame.

FRIDAY 19TH JUNE

The visit by the PM to Washington has been announced and the press splashes it; it will arouse less interest this time. The news from Libya is dreadful; and I fear that by supplying Russia we have weakened the Middle East and may thus lose Egypt.

Rex Whistler, gentle and faun-like, but maddeningly vague, inefficient and feckless, has left after a badly muddled departure – frantic messages, 'chucked' engagements etc. – to stay with the Edens in Sussex. I was infinitely relieved when he went. Lunched alone, wrote etc.

Libya is worse.

### SATURDAY 20TH JUNE					*UPTON HOUSE, POOLE, DORSET*

At 12.30 Jay Llewellin fetched me in a grand government car and we drove to his house here, picnicking *en route*. The house, which was formerly a minor seat of the Tichborne family, is a 1760 affair, yellow Palladian,[2] attractive and has much atmosphere and traces of the excellent taste of that elegant age and of the good taste of its former owners such as an enchantingly arranged little library with cunningly contrived bogus revolving doors, let-in bookcases and fine mahogany doors. There are long views over Poole Harbour, extensive gardens and much sunlight and sea air. The house however is down at heel but far from dull and has immense atmosphere. The house is run by Jay's gaunt maiden sister, Miss Mary Llewellin[3] .... Jay and I stripped and sunbathed for three hours totally naked, but

---

1 Formal.
2 The house was actually built between 1816 and 1818 and is therefore Regency in style.
3 Mary Margaret Llewellin (1897–1983) was Llewellin's younger sister. She never married.

as we revelled in the glorious heat, our thoughts turned to those unfortunate men defending Tobruk which has not yet, I gather, fallen. Egypt is now in danger and I take a most gloomy view of the immediate outlook.

England at its loveliest today.

SUNDAY 21ST JUNE

A roasting day of sunbathing. We lazed, dozed and overate, but Jay ever a diligent minister, worked at his papers, sitting cross-legged and naked with a red box on his lap in the rose garden . . . . We drove up to London after tea and found Harold Balfour just arrived (last night actually) here from the USA. He flew over in a Liberator in under ten hours and was fit and gay, vigorous and well, full of American news. He had seen everybody. Winston, the Duke of Windsor, stayed with the Halifaxes, prosecuted his amours with [illegible],[1] and thoroughly enjoyed his trans-American flight to Vancouver and Los Angeles. Most important to me were his reassuring reports about my son who he says is tall, charming, amazingly intelligent and healthy and like me. He has two front teeth missing. He is happy, well looked after and I have no grounds for worry or alarm. He remembered Harold, was delighted to see him and talked affectionately of me. All this was balm to my aching old heart . . .

Jay, Michael Parker and I dined *à trois* and we were later joined by Harold. We all agreed that the appalling defeat, the surrender of Tobruk, may endanger or even bring down the spineless government. Certainly it would if there were any alternative. I doubt if silly Attlee will be able to hold the House tomorrow. The war outlook is bleak. Libya gone, Egypt and Suez threatened, Malta isolated and starving, the whole of the Middle East in grave danger and the shipping problem desperate. The public seems unaware of all this and complacent and meanwhile we continue to reinforce the Bolsheviks. Madness –

Maureen Stanley died yesterday, an able, attractive gay woman, I had always hated her. She was heartless, hard and an evil influence on all with whom she came in contact. Sordid love affairs, drink, wicked lovers and misery that was her contribution to society. And she was intelligent!! She died as Tobruk fell.

Michael Parker rang me late to tell me that after Jay had dropped him at his hotel he ran into a murder party! A drunken harlot hit an American soldier over the head with a whisky bottle and fractured the man's skull (she had stolen £5 and his passport). A Hogarthian brawl which Michael avidly witnessed. The man, who will die, was taken to hospital and the whore to prison.

This country is mad, madder than ever before with its Soviet celebrations and ranting about a second front – with Tobruk gone and the war half-lost. It is heartbreaking.

---

1 In the MS the Christian name is blank and the surname illegible.

MONDAY 22ND JUNE

It is v hot and everything is depressing; Egypt is threatened: Winston is losing the war if he has not lost it. He is the most dangerous man in England, a wild *Schwärmer*, without reliability or [the last two words crossed out] stability . . . resentment grows. I gave Lady Willingdon lunch at the Apéritif and we gossiped; for the first time she mentioned Honor and wondered how I reacted to the sordid drama which is of her making? I explained.

Had my dog clipped and instead of a hearth rug he looks like a poodle. 'Drinks' with Juliet Duff in her enchanting flat at 3 Belgrave Place: I almost envied it for it is compact and elegant. Raymond Mortimer dined and stayed – why will people do so – until midnight. We had a terrific and long confidential gossip about various matters.

TUESDAY 23RD JUNE

Harold came early to my bedroom: he takes no long or profound view of the war . . . all day I have been depressed, even desperate. Libya gone, and the whole Middle East once more threatened and this time more seriously. The country is aroused at last by Winston's follies . . . . I walked in the heat to the House where I found an atmosphere of disappointment, bewildered rage and resentful uneasiness. There were all the signs of a crisis. Anthony Eden, who even more than the Prime Minister is responsible for the present position since he created the Mediterranean problem and was chiefly responsible for the folly of the Greek campaign, remained at the House all day testing public opinion . . . . There was first an unreal hour during Question Time but everyone knew that all that really mattered was Attlee's statement,[1] which he made in his usual colourless style. He really handled the House well, which was unexpected. Questions were restrained, given the dramatic and consequential [the last two words crossed out] circumstances and he almost got away with it. Towards the end of a wild barrage, John Wardlaw-Milne rose and demanded that a debate should take place immediately, suggesting Thursday as an appropriate day. Attlee refused and intimated that it would be better to await the arrival of facts before finding who was guilty and that next week would be time enough. It was obvious that the delay was made so that the Prime Minister might get back. This ruse whilst it pleased many deceived nobody. Wardlaw-Milne then threatened a vote of censure, and the House was electrified and cheered. The lobbies soon hummed, everyone I saw was as excited as an aged virgin being led to her seducer's bed . . . . Everybody agreed that Winston should either cease to be Minister of Defence or go altogether, and Belisha said to me in the lavatory, where I met him: 'When your doctor is killing you, the first thing to do is to get rid of him.' Ernest Brown whispered to me 'It is never the last day!' and went on to say that it was

---

1 About Tobruk and the Libyan campaign.

extremely difficult for 'those in the family', as he described the government, to be loyal to Winston. The House was in a ferment. I left at last and toyed with the idea of going to Kelvedon. Instead I had my hair cut and then called on Mrs Greville who is again, indeed, failing. Winston had always been wrong, about the Dardanelles, wrong about Antwerp, the Russian campaign which cost us £100,000,000, the gold standard, the abdication and has mismanaged everything since he came into power two years ago.[1] What a sorry scroll of defeats and humiliations. She insisted that he is losing the war. And I agree with her.

Dined alone, having wriggled out of giving the Sitwells dinner. I am too frightened about the future . . . .

Coming out of the Dorchester, I met Virginia Cowles who was effusively cordial and I saw at once that now we were allies: we chatted and she said that when we sent that mad expedition to Greece, that it was 'the turning point of the war'! I heartily agreed. She thinks the Middle East as good as gone. She added that Churchill and the government ought to go, but echoed the eternal cry 'There is nobody else.' Always that – there is nobody else – if only Mr Chamberlain was alive. Many a member who voted against him would willingly now withdraw his vote. When Winston was made Prime Minister I said it was the end of England; and so it seems. Now perhaps this shoddy government is doomed: it may go. Wardlaw-Milne and other Honourable Members have tabled a vote of censure. I shall probably vote with them.

Dined divinely alone on Virginia ham brought over from America by Harold.

WEDNESDAY 24TH JUNE

The House is still in a turmoil and people intrigued in corners. Wardlaw-Milne will put down his motion; the government will survive, but scared and shaken. Alan will abstain; I am still hesitating, I want to vote against it and I have been right about everything so far, Wavell's dismissal, the foolish expedition to Greece, etc., yet caution, or is it cowardice wedded to self-interest warns me not to. Perhaps I too will abstain . . . . I cannot make up my mind. I don't want to be a pariah. Meanwhile there is a pause in the battle in the Middle East. Rommel is massing his troops against the Egyptian frontier, which he will no doubt soon attack. Much can happen before the debate next Wednesday. Meantime the PM is flying back, today, I believe, to take charge of the crisis. It will be a big battle certainly, but one always gets back to the old problem, there is no alternative.

---

1 Antwerp refers to the disastrous decision by Churchill, when First Lord of the Admiralty in the autumn of 1914, to raise an inexperienced Royal Naval Division and send them to keep the Germans out of Antwerp. They were heavily defeated, with many of them rounded up by the Dutch for violating neutrality and interned until 1918. His desire to send troops to Russia to fight the Bolsheviks in 1919 also proved ill-fated, and his decision to put Britain on the gold standard in 1925 helped worsen the slump after 1929.

I picked up Alan at 8b Hobart Place where he and Patsy are living in the attractive little house I found for them. I think that it is haunted. Patsy was agitated as I arrived and whispered to me that Honor was expected at any moment. I retorted that I didn't mind meeting her – why should I? However she failed to turn up with her usual casualness. Thank God I am free of her and every night now I pray that she will soon die – for Paul's sake. Lunched with the Lennox-Boyds at the Apéritif, and Alan and I attended a meeting of the 1922 Committee, which was addressed by Brendan Bracken. He is usually such an able and amusing speaker that I was amazed by the shortness and feebleness of his speech. He said practically nothing and was coolly received. He seemed to be aware of the lack of cordiality and sat down after ten minutes. Nothing was achieved. Alan and I hurried away to Belgrave Square. I am dejected. I cannot decide how to vote; I cannot quite summon the courage to vote against a world leader and figure; yet he leads England to destruction.

Rab rang me twice as he always does when there is a crisis; early this morning he was inclined to tone down the situation – he is ever cautious, even against coming out into the open; but this evening he is somewhat alarmed and shaken by the rising tide of anti-Churchillian feeling. I hear that both Ritchie[1] and Auchinleck have been 'sacked' and that Montgomery[2] has already been

---

1 Neil Methuen Ritchie (1897–1983) joined the Army in 1914 and fought on the Western Front and in the Middle East during the Great War, winning the DSO and the Military Cross. Rapidly promoted during the early phases of the Second World War, he was given charge of the 8th Army by Auchinleck in 1941; and it was Auchinleck who sacked him after Tobruk, holding him responsible for the defeat. However, Sir Alan Brooke (qv), the CIGS, valued Ritchie so highly that he had him recalled to command an Army Corps in the Battle of Normandy, which Ritchie did successfully, retaining the command until the German defeat. He was knighted in 1945 and retired in the rank of general.

2 Bernard Law Montgomery (1887–1976) became perhaps the most famous British soldier of the Second World War, following his victory with the 8th Army at El Alamein in the autumn of 1942, but was also one of the most controversial. Descended from Ulster gentry, he was commissioned into the Royal Warwickshire Regiment in 1908 and fought with distinction in the Great War, winning the DSO, and was badly wounded. By 1938 he had been promoted to major general and had attracted Wavell's attention. Although he managed to evacuate his division from Dunkirk with minimal casualties he soon crossed swords with Auchinleck when answering to him in Southern Command. Auchinleck had been replaced as Middle East Commander by the time Montgomery arrived there in August 1942, to assume command of the 8th Army after its intended leader, William Gott, was killed in a plane crash. Montgomery had been planning to attack French North Africa. His victory at El Alamein in 1942 turned the tide of the war, and started the expulsion of the Germans from North Africa. Montgomery then led his men into Italy, before returning to Britain to help plan the D-Day landings; his combustible personality caused great tensions with General Eisenhower throughout the campaign. After the war he served as CIGS and as Deputy Commander of NATO's European forces. He was knighted in 1942; became a field marshal in 1944; was created a Knight of the Garter in 1946; and raised to the peerage as 1st Viscount Montgomery of Alamein in 1946.

appointed as C[ommander]-in-Chief. There have been too many changes in the Middle East Command. Perhaps now Peter will return, as surely Wavell might be promoted to being either CIGS or Minister of Defence.

Winnie Portarlington looked in; she wants me to find a seat for Sergison-Brooke,[1] and I promised to take steps tomorrow. She was sweet, sincere and intense. She said I was the most popular individual in London society and perhaps, she added without a ray of malice, it was because I am so easily and constantly imposed upon. I wonder? My enemies are alas legion or am I wrong? I have been much more popular since the separation; and nobody, except possibly the Brownlows, has deserted me.

That scheming woman, Diana Boothby, ex-Cavendish, has snared Ian Campbell-Gray into marrying her. He will regret it. She is feline and she smells so strongly that I once nearly fainted when sitting next to her. They had a long liaison ages ago which he broke off and she consoled herself by her brief and disastrous marriage to Bob Boothby. This is a *rechauffé*[2] and Ian, who is so serious, will tire of her as he has had a series of elegant affairs with exquisite ladies .... and beautiful young men. I have never liked him at all, although we were at Oxford together. I hated him then. Will Honor, I wonder, attend the wedding? Would she dare?

Went early to bed to recover from the day's excesses. The battle for Egypt is about to begin.

A sweet letter from Princess Alexandra of Greece about her engagement to King Peter.

In spite of what the quidnuncs[3] prophesy, I think that Tom Driberg will be elected to Maldon. He has a forceful personality and the Tobruk defeat will enhance his chances. But even Winston is more unpopular than he or the government supposes.

THURSDAY 25TH JUNE

The House was still excited but the movement against Winston is subsiding and I have now almost decided not to take part in it, and yet I should be pleased if the old lion gets a good smacking!! Rab was affectionate and asked me to lunch with him and Sydney at La Coquille, which I did. I had also a conversation with Brendan Bracken, who was obviously currying favour: I pretended to be pro-Winston and put in a plea for a peerage for Wavell. He promised 'to see about it'. Perhaps he will. He lied about one thing, said that the PM liked 'Archie Wavell', which we know to be untrue.

1 He did not have a political career.
2 Reheated dish.
3 A quidnunc is a nosey person and gossip.

Rested this afternoon for nearly an hour and ruminated licentiously. I am lusty, vicious, depraved and hungry for sensations and sex.

.... Rab suddenly decided to stay the night here – as Sydney was doing so. And he did; I lent him pajamas and a razor. Both he and Harold urged me to support the government next week. I suppose I must ...

The House went into secret session for an hour today to discuss the alleged misdemeanours of Edgar Granville, the independent Liberal MP for Eye: he is supposed to have quoted remarks made by the PM in secret session at a cocktail party! The affair was reported to the Committee of Privileges which has returned a verdict of 'non-proven'. Considerable haranguing about procedure and eventually he was entirely absolved, and secret copies of the report, all but one, were ordered to be destroyed. I hear that one was found in the Smoking Room! Typical.

FRIDAY 26TH JUNE

Peter is 32 today, and I saw him ... but I am in advance of my tale. I woke feeling exhausted yet somehow energetic and dictated until twelve, fled to a Turkish bath, and then attended a private view of an Indian film .... The Indian films were enthralling since they gave me an insight into Indian life and there were welcome glimpses of General Wavell; and I thought I saw Peter twice but may have imagined it. Walked home ... finished off masses of letters and gossiped with Harold. Mrs Harold, a maddening, pathetic garrulous woman prematurely aged through neglect, dined and early to bed. Harold remarked that he was a 'last-ditcher' and would, for instance, stand by me through anything! Alan says that he is sure that Harold wouldn't ... Harold said that Rab was not overly reliable. I was amused.

Both the Butlers, Rab, who had no toothbrush, and Sydney looked into my bedroom this morning and they had the obvious ear-marks of *une nuit orageuse!*[1] Perhaps Rab is more sexually inclined than we supposed.

Driberg had an astonishing, even an alarming victory – a majority of 5,993 at Maldon over the official candidate. He is an attractive but sinister character, rather desperate, certainly unhappy and of course *quelque*;[2] indeed he was once charged by the police but acquitted.

SATURDAY 27TH JUNE

A maddening morning of muddled arrangements: anything to do with Leeds or the Baillie boutique is like that – messages, delay, telephones and fuss ....

---

1 A stormy night.
2 No literal translation of this French word, meaning 'a little' or 'around', will suffice: it is a euphemistic reference to Driberg's promiscuous and reckless homosexuality.

No news from Libya except that the Battle for Mersa Matruh is about to begin. Winston has taken a nasty shock over Maldon. And Tom Driberg, who owns Bradwell-juxta-Mare, the enchanting Adams'[1] 'cottage' which Honor and I once nearly bought, will be a stormy and difficult member. Nevertheless I propose to make friends with him for a variety of reasons.

Now that Maureen Stanley is dead my old enemies are less powerful. Harold tells me that Kathleen Harriman confided in him here the other night that she hopes – and obviously she was echoing Pam Churchill – that Randolph will be killed. He is such a dreadful creature and Pam is worn out by him and actually, I gather, hates him.

The Kent baby was expected any time yesterday ....

Leeds Castle

After a feverish morning of telephone calls and frantic fuss I drove here, taking Adrian Baillie, my host, with me. He was a touch tipsy and is unhappy and frustrated. I think that he resents Geoffrey Lloyd's unusual relationship with Olive Baillie. Are they lovers? I am inclined to [think] so ...

The Middle East news is increasingly worse. I am in despair.

MONDAY 29TH JUNE

The battle for Egypt is in progress ... and there is no real news yet. Sunbathed and breakfasted by the pool with Geoffrey Lloyd to whom I am increasingly devoted – then drove .... up to London. It is so gloriously hot I was reluctant to come. Masses of messages and correspondence awaiting me. I attended to them and now am on the wing for

Later: Farnham Park

I arrived to stay with the Kemsleys and find to my surprise and delight that they were just leaving for London; instead it is a young party given by Ghislaine Dresselhuys, who is, I suspect, a little in love with me. She is a voluptuous wildly worldly girl with a penchant for jewels and the *corps diplomatique* and is bent too obviously on a great marriage. John Stanley,[2] who is here, would be suitable certainly, as she would like to be Lady Derby .... We sunbathed and I was amusing.

The Middle East seems as good as lost.

---

1 There is no evidence any of the Adam brothers had a hand in Bradwell Lodge, though the style is similar. Pevsner attributes it to John Johnson, a prominent Essex architect of the period, who built the Shire Hall in Chelmsford.
2 Edward John Stanley (1918–94), from 1938 Lord Stanley by courtesy until he succeeded his grandfather as 18th Earl of Derby in 1948.

TUESDAY 30TH JUNE

Drove up to London and went to the House. Winston had been and gone, having made his first appearance since his rather dismal trip to America and he announced that General Auchinleck had now taken over full command of the 8th Army, thus sacking the unfortunate Ritchie, who has managed to lose one of the most decisive battles of the war. Attended the 1922 Committee, where member after member expressed the view that the big debate should be cancelled, since never were we in more peril. Public anxiety is growing and intense. The House was in a hubbub but I now see that the PM will come down on Thursday, do his stuff, that is make a magical speech, a sheer *tour de force* for an hour, and he will get a huge vote of confidence. He always does and I shan't vote against Winston to make Anthony Eden king. Many members feel likewise. There is growing resentment against the Greek campaign; its folly I proclaimed and deplored at the time.

Geordie Sutherland has arrived here at No. 5 to stay with me. He is deafer, but looks younger than ever. He is an old sweetie really but a colossal bore, and worse, he knows it. I took him to dine at the Argentine Embassy opposite where we found a gay and pleasant party: the Ambassador, who is dark, social and a touch saturnine . . . . Virginia Cowles; Esmond Rothermere; Ann O'Neill; Helen Fitzgerald; the *ménage* Casa Maury etc. The Embassy looked lovely with its rich French furnishings and luxurious atmosphere and I again realised how cloying and delightful and important to me wealth is for what it can command. Exquisite food and many wines and Meissen dinner service and footmen – like an echo of the not distant past. I was next to Freda Casa Maury and we talked of old days, and she told me that Serge [Obolensky] had once raped Princess Olga at Bohin.[1] Now I was there at the time and whilst well aware of the situation – she was infatuated with him – I don't think that anything serious ever really happened. It was the summer of 1929 . . . Ann O'Neill tells me that she is marrying Esmond Rothermere as soon as possible and yet she still regrets Shane, her husband, who is miserable, and as she admits, 'the nicer man'! She would have liked to continue as she has done for the past seven years – being married to both!

The news grows steadily worse and the Nile is now, I fear, doomed.

I hear – and this is super-hush – that the Mediterranean fleet has been withdrawn and has passed into the [Suez] Canal which is to be blown up in case of total defeat. Meanwhile Auchinleck is playing for time with his delaying tactics.

Talked with and congratulated Tom Driberg who took his seat. An unhappy, tortured, tormented and unhappy [*sic*] creature with communist leanings: I cannot help but like him.

---

1 In Slovenia: there is no diary extant for 1929, so this was probably a party with Prince Paul.

WEDNESDAY 1ST JULY

The big dramatic rather dreadful debate has run one day. I walked to the House with Alan and Geordie Sutherland and we found Westminster packed . . . . John Wardlaw-Milne moved his much publicised vote of censure in strong and convincing language and I watched the front bench squirm with annoyance. Winston looked cross and harassed as he glanced at the crowded Chamber. People were emotional and uneasy, exhausted. I hated it and thought it horrible . . . John Wardlaw-Milne rose to move his vote of censure and at once held the House. He was fair, calm and dignified and was listened to with respect until he made an unfortunate suggestion – that the Duke of Gloucester should be made Commander-in-Chief of the Forces. The House roared with disrespectful laughter . . . . and I saw Winston's face light up as if a lamp had been lit within him and he smiled genially. He was saved and he knew it. Poor Wardlaw-Milne undoubtedly had a blind spot and the suggestion, however ridiculous, was sincere. He never quite regained the hearing of the House. He was followed by Roger Keyes, who made a rambling contribution during the luncheon-hour. People began to say that the debate was over; that Winston had won again. That there would not be twenty in the lobby against him. I rushed away reluctantly to give my mother-in-law luncheon at No. 5, and when I got back Oliver Lyttelton was speaking for the government, and he made, as he afterwards remarked to Somerset de Chair, 'a proper balls of it'. His canvas was too large, he was too diffuse and altogether unconvincing, and he and HMG have suffered a parliamentary setback. I didn't wait to hear him finish and so missed Clem Davies's novel suggestion that he should be impeached!! Hurried to the Lords which were also crowded. I really must be made a peer; I was surrounded by all my friends. Camrose, Kemsley, Gage, David Margesson and my father-in-law all rushed up to ask how Oliver was doing, and for news of the by-election. I had the figures: a majority of 2,740 for Mott-Radclyffe at Windsor . . . Max Beaverbrook rose and the Lords shivered a little. He very rarely puts in an appearance. He looked puckish . . . . in his dark clothes and seemed aged. He spoke with punch and his usual exaggerated Canadian accent, and disregarded the usual polite forms of address to their lordships and seemed to be making a tub-thumping speech. He was effective and spoke at great length to an enraptured audience . . . . About five o'clock Alan and I went to the RAC for a 'Turker' and later he, Patsy, Geordie Sutherland, Vsevolod, Maimie and I went to a revue and came back to No. 5 for supper. Meanwhile as we fiddled (and what else can we do?) – the Germans are rushing towards Alexandria and one wonders will anything ever stop them? Is the archway of the Middle East doomed?

At supper tonight in the rococo candlelight we were discussing the declension of things. I said how much had gone when Alan chimed in 'All lost – save Honour!' and then he flushed crimson with embarrassment at his supreme gaffe. I laughed until tears rolled down my cheeks but he was contrite.

THURSDAY 2ND JULY

On my arrival at the House I was told that last night's sitting had been prolonged until near 4 a.m. when McGovern called a count. Only thirty-seven members were present, although there were others who did not hear the call asleep in the libraries ... Everybody seems to have been angry. A. P. Herbert[1] called insulted McGovern in the lobby and they began to fight but were immediately separated by attendants and the whips. A curious parliamentary situation had developed since by the count the numbers had lapsed. Thus after Questions, and after some amendment, Wardlaw-Milne formally moved his vote of censure – for a second time.

We rushed back to the House, and found we had missed little. Belisha had just begun what was to prove to be a brilliant, eloquent and damning attack on the govt; as well as a summary on the Libyan campaign. He was at ease; he was skilful and deadly and I admired his courage and accurate marshalling of the facts. Surely Churchill, I thought, could not answer him. But answer him he did, and for over an hour we had all the usual Churchillian gusto, the panoply of almost meaningless phrases ... I hated him more and more: his music has no magic for me – might as well have made Macaulay or even Caruso Prime Minister.[2] He skated around dangerous corners and by clever evasion managed to ignore the question as to whether he had ordered Tobruk to be clung on to? He never decried his misleading statements in the past etc. Nevertheless he was moving, and had his usual effect of intoxicating his listeners. I left before he sat down and went to the library, put my head into my hands, took a deep breath and prayed for advice – to vote against him, as I longed to, or not? The arguments against voting against the govt are strong and on balance I decided I hadn't 'the guts': I would give Churchill the benefit of the doubt, and slowly I walked into the very crowded 'Aye' lobby to the derision of the few abstainers, perhaps twenty in all. I met Winterton and Archie Southby leaving the Palace, muttering to one another. They abstained. Lady Astor, Megan Lloyd George[3] and others sat silent on the benches. As I walked into the lobby that Welsh Judas, Jim Thomas,[4] came up to me and laughingly said 'I am surprised to see you in this lobby!' So suddenly my deep-rooted disgust with the govt is known. I nearly retorted that I wasn't going to kill Churchill to make Eden king. I waited until the fatal final figures

1 Alan Patrick Herbert (1890–1971) was a comic writer who made his name in the 1920s writing for *Punch* and as the librettist for some light musicals. He was elected as the independent MP for Oxford University in 1935 and held the seat until it was abolished in 1950. He was knighted in 1945.
2 Enrico Caruso (1873–1921) was the most celebrated Italian operatic tenor of his day.
3 Megan Arvon Lloyd George (1902–66), by courtesy Lady Megan from 1945, was the daughter of David Lloyd George*. She was Liberal MP for Anglesey from 1929 to 1951 but moved to the Labour Party in 1955, and was Labour MP for Carmarthen from 1957 to 1966.
4 The Conservative MP for Hereford, and earlier a close friend of Channon.*

were announced. 475 to 25, a government majority of 450. The PM rose, looked up at the Speaker's Gallery and smiled at Mrs Churchill and then walked out of the Chamber and went to the Smoking Room. As he left everyone rose and gave him a polite but lukewarmish ovation. I felt sick . . . . and fled – home.

Exhausted, emotional and uneasy I tried to rest but was interrupted by the arrival of my old Darby,[1] George Gage. We gossiped; Leslie Hore-Belisha rang up and asked me to dine but I was already engaged to go to the Somerset de Chairs. A boring house and a common party of unknowns. We waited for some time before I realised that Honor was expected!! I made vague profuse apologies and he went on about it, his rudeness etc. They must be very out of the world; yet I think he will go far politically and prophesied as much five years ago. He is young, able, intelligent and has much energy. He showed me a curious huge Janus head which he had bought in Palestine. I left as soon as I dared and came back to B Square where I found young Michael Parker up – at Alan's invitation from ~~Portsmouth~~ Chatham, and soon we were joined by <u>Alan himself</u>. He was somewhat tipsy and unattractive. We sat up too late, drank, talked, and eventually the orgy ended by a raid on the larder below. Michael had nowhere to sleep; he shared Alan's bed – a Hogarthian evening; perhaps a fitting end to a desperate and dreadful day.

Once more Churchill has triumphed and he will presumably lead us on to our doom. Always wrong about everything . . . words, words, follies – foolishness – why has England so taken him to her heart – hasn't she?

There was a slight wave of hope for Egypt this afternoon. The German advance has slackened.

FRIDAY 3RD JULY

Hesperus case all day. I was a wreck;[2] first I had to get up to get the poor sailor [Parker] packed off to Chatham; then I snapped at Alan who was in one of his monumentally selfish moods; they are rare and usually induced by alcohol . . . Didn't go out all day; dictated etc.

We are holding the Axis forces in the El Alamein area. A pause in their triumphant march, or a turn of the tide?

SUNDAY 5TH JULY   *KELVEDON*

All day sun-bathing and recovering from a too hectic life. Smoked only four cigarettes and drank nothing. Now bronzed and energetic. I feel virile and re-vitalised but am saddened by my silvering hair. *Que faire?*

---

1 An allusion to the notion that he and Gage were like Darby and Joan, the mythical devoted
   married couple from the eighteenth-century poem by Henry Woodfall.
2 *The Wreck of the Hesperus* is a poem of 1842 by Henry Wadsworth Longfellow.

A son[1] was born to the Kents last night – I had a telegram from the Duke saying that 'both were well!' The infant prince is now 7th in succession; he arrived in the world a week or so late.

WEDNESDAY 8TH JULY

To the House, and then lunched with Hughie Northumberland at the Ritz. He reminds me often of Charlie Cavendish, the same gentle wit . . . . He has vast estates, a stupendous income and no money. After lunch we walked to Cartier's where I bought a tiny brooch for Prince George[2] who, I am told, is a delightful baby. Both he and the Duchess are well. Then home where I fell asleep for half an hour, worn out because Jay Llewellin walked in last night after I had gone to bed, and insisted on my getting up and gossiping with him for a reluctant boring hour. He is an 'old sweetie' but lectures . . . Hurried back to the H of Commons and listened to Reggie Dorman-Smith give a vivid account of the invasion of Burma. He is no orator, not even a finished speaker, but was listened to with respect since his sincerity was obvious . . . . Peter reports unfavourably of him and 'his hideous brood' who are still in Delhi.

THURSDAY 9TH JULY

I was in a minor key having had a sleepless night, the after-effects of drinking a 'hooch' cocktail at the Ritz yesterday. The gin there is known to be poison. Went to the House of Commons where there were no excitements really. John Morrison[3] has held the seat at Salisbury and was returned with a comfortable majority. The last two elections have been strongly pro-government.

Dined in . . . . Rab is disturbed, flattered and amused by an article which appeared in the *Daily Herald* on Tuesday: it tips him as the future Prime Minister – which he undoubtedly is. Before dinner Julian Amery, who is the cleverest young man I have ever met, dropped in. He was scathing about the Egyptians and gave me much local Cairene gossip . . . . Randolph, the eternal 'problem child', is still in plaster of Paris in a Cairene hospital . . . . Julian thinks that Auchinleck is a greater personality than Wavell, but has nothing like Wavell's popularity with the troops, or prestige. There was a plot to bring Wavell back to Cairo.

---

1 Michael George Charles Franklin, Prince Michael of Kent (b.1942). He married, in 1978, Baroness Marie-Christine von Reibnitz (b.1945).
2 He means Prince Michael.
3 John Granville Morrison (1906–96) was Conservative MP for Salisbury from 1942 until 1965, when he was advanced to the peerage as 1st Baron Margadale – the last hereditary barony created. He was chairman of the 1922 Committee from 1955 to 1964.

Jennifer Fry,[1] only child and heiress of Sir Geoffrey Fry, is to be married on Saturday to Robert Heber-Percy, known as 'the Mad Boy'. For eight years he has been Lord Berners's adored Ganymede and has led him a tormented existence with his escapades and infidelities . . . . The boy is delinquent, and to me, highly unattractive. He was brought by Gerald to stay with us at St Martin[2] in September 1933. We all hated him, particularly Honor, and she was right . . . . It is a long and romantic cause célèbre which I may one day write . . . of course their freak marriage will not last: it is a wartime sensation.

FRIDAY 10TH JULY

All day alone until Mrs Coats[3] came to tea. Harold [Balfour], who is becoming increasingly tactless and cross and difficult (the truth is I am tired of him), happened to come in unexpectedly and fell asleep on a sofa, thus spoiling our tête-à-tête. His manners are appalling.

The position in Egypt seems the same. We hold the enemy at El Alamein and the battle wages furiously.

Alan and I avoided that gay Pierrot, Michael Parker who telephoned constantly to us.

A horrible letter from Honor, undated and casual, to say that she is changing her name by deed poll. *Tant pis*.[4]

TUESDAY 14TH JULY

I was married nine years ago today – Friday, Bastille Day. At the time I thought the marriage would not, could not last. Later I changed my view. Nine years is a long time. I had an appalling letter from Bill Rollo – she is determined, my wayward, woeful, vicious wife, to change her name by deed poll. I cannot stop her . . .

Went to the House, it was the production debate and Oliver Lyttelton spoke for the government. He was inaudible; the clipped fashionable voice is not suited to the senatorial atmosphere of the House. However it was generally admitted that he had acquitted himself admirably and somewhat retrieved his reputation after the recent fiasco. I left the House to lunch at the Allies Club . . . . It is in

---

1 Ann Jennifer Evelyn Elizabeth Fry (1916–2003), daughter of Sir Geoffrey Fry, 1st Bt, was already pregnant when she married Heber-Percy (qv): their daughter was born the following year. She lived in a *ménage à trois* with Heber-Percy and Berners (qv) for a year before moving out with her child. They divorced in 1947.
2 There are no diaries extant for 1933, but this would appear to be St Martin im Innkreis, where the Channons had spent part of their honeymoon.
3 Probably Peter Coats's mother rather than Audrey Coats (qv).
4 Either 'too bad' or 'never mind'. Since Channon minded very much, probably the former.

the old house of the Rothschilds where I once went to grand balls! Many people about; foreigners and Free Frogs etc. It is the intention of the founders to emulate the Inter-Allié in Paris, of which I was long a member. I doubt whether they will succeed; nonetheless I said that I would join. But as one should never be proposed for a club except by the President, I asked Buckie De La Warr to arrange it for me, and he said he would.

Lord Halifax addressed a crowded mixed meeting room at the House of Commons. He seemed aged, tired and silly and began dully but later warmed up. Made a moderate impression and answered his questions well. He seemed sleepy and a little deaf. Then I came home to arrange my dinner party which had been originally arranged in honour of Reggie Dorman-Smith, at home on leave. He is an old ally and I like him (but Peter with his penetrating insight reports unfavourably of him and his hideous brood; says that he was a flop in Burma and wildly foolish and indiscreet). I collected a party consisting of:

Self
Reggie Dorman-Smith
Rab – MP, President of the Board of Education
Brendan Bracken – MP, Minister of Information
Harold [Balfour] – MP, Under-Secretary of State for Air
Jock McEwen – MP, Whip
Jay Llewellin – MP, Minister of Aircraft Production
Brograve Beauchamp – MP, Parliamentary Private Secretary to Richard Law
Robert Cary – MP, Parliamentary Private Secretary to Amery
Ralph Assheton – MP, Parliamentary Secretary to the Ministry of Supply
Alan Lennox-Boyd – MP
Harvie-Watt – MP, Parliamentary Private Secretary to Winston.

A most distinguished group. All the important younger government set. The Blue Room was candlelit. The 1920 Krug (my last remaining magnums) flowed. Much conversation, and I was dimly aware that this was a memorable memoir-evening. HM's Government dining with a gilded diarist in Belgrave Square in the middle of a war!! ... and I noticed, too, that Brendan, who arrived in high spirits, was irritated by the presence of his successor, Harvie-Watt .... He did not greet him nor even reply when Harvie addressed him directly. He is increasingly jealous of Harvie's growing dominion over Winston. Harvie is dull, honest, manly, red-headed and Scotch in look as Rab remarked, 'Like a Scotch shepherd who has gathered in his flock and is sitting down to two bottles of whisky.' I tried to talk to Reggie, who was too impressed with the party, to concentrate on me. He wanted to talk to them all ... nevertheless I wormed it out of him that he disliked Peter – I said he was charming: 'Much too charming!' Reggie retorted. He argued with everybody, laid down the law, was perhaps a touch tiddly. Rab whispered to me 'He is like a proconsul returned to the dissolute society of Rome!' Rab and Brendan remained closeted in the dining room until midnight; the others drank and gossiped and debated the seamy subject of who should inherit Winston's mantle. Nobody (except Brograve Beauchamp, who is one of the glamour Edenite group) wanted Anthony Eden; yet the consensus of opinion was that he would get the premiership and that it would be a mistake. All concerned. I said I hoped we should have a stop-gap in John Anderson. This possibility was admitted. Others thought that Oliver Lyttelton would recover from his setback . . . Reggie and Brendan had a long boring argument in which Reggie, who repeated himself too much, was worsted. Wine and words flowed and it was a bit disagreeable for a moment. Rab roared with laughter, his famous cackle. A truly great success. He said my best effort . . . at last they left. Rab, Harold and Alan all are staying here. Boys' dormitory life which I love, it reminds me of Oxford and happy gilded semi-monastic months with the Regent . . . Alan kept me up late: his company is an insidious drug, indeed.

WEDNESDAY 15TH JULY

Absolutely worn out by last evening's excesses – many headaches in the Commons. Notes of thanks etc. My governmental gala is the talk of the town.

I flitted between the two houses and attended two committees – Malcolm McCorquodale addressed the 1922 boys in surprisingly forceful language and his booming voice suited his massive frame. Later General de Gaulle addressed the French Parliamentary Committee. He strutted in, gave himself immense airs, and was enthusiastically welcomed . . . . People stood up to sing 'La Marseillaise'. He was introduced by Anthony Eden in a brief speech in which he employed every known possible cliché. Gaulle [sic][1] rose and spoke in quiet, fluent French for forty minutes. Many members remained because (it was obvious) to leave would infer [sic] that they didn't understand French. I can't bear this [illegible] creature and soon fled – home, and am going early to bed.

A charming letter from the Duchess of Kent telling me of her new son etc. and thanking me for a tiny brooch I sent him.

THURSDAY 16TH JULY

A foolish morning with Alan and I only reached the House at 11.30, feeling shadowed and half-cock-ish, which was a pity. After a wrangle about procedure we went into secret session, but I was obliged to rush home to entertain a little, but distinguished, luncheon party, which consisted of Mrs Neville Chamberlain,

---

1 The rule in French is that the 'de' is dropped at second and subsequent mentions of a name, but only if that name contains two or more syllables: so it is always 'de Gaulle'.

her stepmother[-in-law], the aged white-haired but exceedingly spry Mrs Carnegie,[1] and Lord Halifax, bland and insinuating, the hard old hypocrite, Alan and Patsy; Portia Stanley; Ralph Assheton and Geoffrey Lloyd. Mrs Chamberlain talked of Neville; said I was perhaps his favourite amongst the young MPs and he used to chuckle in the evenings and repeat to her the silly things I had said … he was affectionate and much touched by my loyalty and was well aware of the love I bore him. Mrs Carnegie, who must be nearly 80 since she was married in 1888 to Joe Chamberlain, described Austen Chamberlain's maiden speech in 1892. She had been present and saw Mr Gladstone, who was her political enemy, cross over to him and mutter something about it being a speech that must have gladdened a father's heart. She is very Boston, sheer Henry James. An impressive lunch, like peeping at history. Halifax had to hurry away to see Archie Sinclair and Geoffrey Lloyd went to call on the Baldwins – the old days! Mrs Chamberlain, Mrs Carnegie and I drove with the Lennox-Boyds to Hobart Place to see Patsy's babies. Simon, the red-headed one, who is a godson of both Mrs Chamberlain's and mine, behaved well. I went on to the House where I slept for a solid hour before returning to the Chamber where I heard Sir Arthur Salter[2] wind up in excellent form. He gave a brief résumé of the shipping position which he described as being more serious than in 1917. It was a businesslike competent performance which impressed the House. I gave tea to John Morrison, newly elected for Salisbury. He is very nice ….

Dined with Mrs Greville: she is discouraged; said she would like to die. She cannot sleep or eat anymore. She sat like a jewelled idol and was amusing and alert. Others: Sir John and Lady Anderson, who confided in me that I had made the marriage etc.

John Knebworth[3] has been killed in Libya. A terrible tragedy – the poor Lyttons:[4] that rather glorious Anthony Knebworth killed in a flying accident

---

1 Mary Crowninshield Endicott (1864–1957) was the daughter of William Endicott (1826–1900), of Salem, Massachusetts, who served as Secretary of War in President Grover Cleveland's first administration. She married Joseph Chamberlain as his third wife in 1888; after his death she married, in 1916, a clergyman, William Hartley Carnegie (1859–1936).

2 James Arthur Salter (1881–1975) was a civil servant and transport expert who from 1919 to 1930 worked in the League of Nations secretariat. He was knighted in 1922. In 1934 he became Gladstone Professor of Political Theory at Oxford. He was Conservative MP for Oxford University from 1937 to 1950 and for Ormskirk from 1951 to 1953, when he was raised to the peerage as 1st Baron Salter. From 1939 to 1945 he was Parliamentary Secretary to the Ministry of Shipping.

3 Alexander Edward John Bulwer-Lytton (1910–42) had been Viscount Knebworth and heir to the Lytton earldom since 1933, when his elder brother Anthony had been killed (see Vol. I, entry for 9 June 1935 and footnote). The heir presumptive to the title became the 2nd Earl's younger brother Neville Stephen Bulwer-Lytton (1879–1951), who succeeded as 3rd Earl in 1947.

4 Victor Alexander George Robert Bulwer-Lytton (1876–1947) was by courtesy Viscount Knebworth from 1880 until he succeeded his father as 2nd Earl of Lytton in 1891. In 1902 he married Pamela Chichele-Plowden (1874–1971).

a few years ago; then John Erne, their son-in-law, killed at Dunkirk; and now, their only surviving son, John, lost in Libya. Actually he is the son of the Duke of Westminster as everybody knows. He even looked like him; but Lord Lytton recognised him and was fond of him. The heir to the title is now a descendant of Byron's, a son of Lady Wentworth's.[1]

Letters pour in from India. One came today in just ten days. Everything else is depressing – I have not yet answered the letters about Honor's deed poll and the contemplated change.

FRIDAY 17TH JULY

A wretched wet day – on Fridays I recover and do my chores and accounts. Last Friday I wrote to Paul Latham, languishing in Maidstone Prison, offering to go and see him there if I could obtain permission, for which I did not anticipate much difficulty. A few days ago came a reply from the prison governor, polite but firm to the effect he was not seeing anybody or even writing to people. At least my conscience has been sated. It is tragic: but he is not a gentleman. The choice to cut himself off completely from the world, whether a wise one or not, is his own.

I detect signs of exhaustion: I am irritable and I slept for two hours this afternoon. Then Maimie and Vsevolod of Russia came to dine and we had a quiet evening gossiping *à trois*. They are apprehensive of and hostile to Queen Marie of Yugoslavia (the arch bitch of all time) and to her lesbian lady-of-the-bedchamber, that middle-class *poseur*,[2] Rosemary Cresswell. I incited them further against these Ladies in Retirement.[3]

Harold left B Square about six this morning to fly to the Isle of Man in appalling weather.

Gerry Herlihy, my lobby spy, called. He said that John Anderson is the only hope as a successor to Winston, since the Labour Party would never serve under Anthony. Herlihy thinks that Winston's usefulness ended in 1940 and that he should now go – but he is carrying on, so Herlihy, assures me, a rather dirty intrigue with Beaverbrook to force an autumnal election.

SATURDAY 18TH JULY

We seem to have had a minor success in Egypt.[4]

Harold flew to the Isle of Man and back yesterday and he brought me back welcome additions to the larder, butter, eggs, ham and kippers. There were two

---

1 This was not so; the heir was the 1st Earl's younger son Neville (*vide supra*).
2 As elsewhere when applying this noun to women, he means *poseuse*.
3 An allusion to a successful Broadway play of 1940, made into a *film noir* in 1941.
4 The first Battle of El Alamein, which ended indecisively on 27 July.

accidents – he was surrounded by death – for two planes crashed killing many people. One was the actual plane in which we crossed last year to Belfast.

Master Michael Parker came here and said 'goodbye': his ship HMS *Despatch* is due to sail shortly, perhaps on Monday. He is a most engaging and extremely intelligent child of 22. I gave him a birthday present and was sad to part with him. Very likely we shall never meet again.

Beechwood, Lavington Park, near Petworth

Drove here to spend the weekend with Barbie Wallace. The 'big house' is an Army headquarters; and she has arranged this small place with skill and taste: it is charming and cheerful. She is v lively now and I am sure will, and ought to, marry again.[1] She is, I fear, a confirmed Edenite; wars with everybody!! She actually defends the mad expedition to Greece, although she admits that everyone now says it was a mistake. How I campaigned against it. Even the Prime Minister was against it. (It was entirely an Eden adventure and cost us Libya) . . . . Norah Lindsay [is] here. Norah is the same, but aged. She must be 70[2] and at first I found her hostile, boring and tactless, and she told us all the old stories which date to the Sutton [Courtenay] days, and I hated her for an hour; and then I realised that she is only lonely, impoverished and unhappy and we re-became allies and friends which we had been for many years . . . . Glorious food; too good and too much. The champagne flows; the house is extremely comfortable.

SUNDAY 19TH JULY

A lovely day which I revelled in. Good weather, exceptionally hot. Barbie, Norah and I went for a long walk on the Downs. Barbie says that the generals and CIGSs have to fight <u>two</u> wars: Winston and the Germans. Wavell was a brilliant general against the enemy, but weak against Winston – no good there – Alan Brooke,[3] the next CIGS, is hopeless against the enemy but brilliant (acquiescent?) with Winston.[4] Winston, I am deeply convinced, is losing the war for us, if anyone could. I hear, too, that Randolph has been invalided out of the Army and is about

---

1　Euan Wallace had died in February 1941.

2　She was 69.

3　Alan Francis Brooke (1883–1963) was Chief of the Imperial General Staff from 1941 to 1946. He joined the Royal Artillery in 1902 and ended the Great War as a lieutenant colonel and with the DSO and Bar, having made a great reputation for military planning. He held a number of senior commands and staff appointments between the wars and by 1938 was a lieutenant general. He was knighted in 1940, raised to the peerage as 1st Baron Alanbrooke in 1945 and advanced to a viscountcy the following year, when he also became a Knight of the Garter.

4　Anyone reading Lord Alanbrooke's published diaries will soon realise that he was anything but acquiescent in his relationship with Churchill. He was particularly appalled by how Churchill, in his own account of the war, frequently took credit for innovations and ideas that were the work of officers on the staff.

to come back to London. It is dreadful news: we shall have him on our hands and backs now forever. He poisons the House of Commons for me . . . I think that Pam will leave him, and probably divorce him. She hates him utterly – told me so, herself.

Alan rang up from Brighton every hour, and I arranged for him to meet us at the [illegible] house, bound chez les Coopers. We drove there and had tea and mint juleps in the garden. Diana, too thin, but very lovely; Duff, gentle and pleasant and polite; little John Julius, to whom I gave £1, is perfectly delightful. He is and has always been the nicest little boy imaginable. His two years in America have broadened him, and he has filled out. He is astonishingly charming and alert and good-looking. Duff worships him . . . Diana leads an agricultural life, surrounded by pigs and rabbits and cows. Alan was very big and engaging: he dominates an atmosphere. Then we drove back to Beechwood and had a hilarious evening. He and I talked too much! He should have been back at Brighton by midnight but I refused to drive him 40 miles (and back) in the dark. He eventually stayed the night in the room where Oliver Stanley was to have slept – he 'chucked' the weekend, to my great relief. Barbie is so competent and gay and an ideal wife. She is much upset by John Knebworth's death. 'Officially' he is her first cousin. The eventual heir is now a Lytton-Milbanke, a priestly young man who is a descendant of Lord Byron's. The Lytton family seem doomed.[1]

My aged mother is 73 today. I sent her a cable.

John Julius is more like an actor playing the role of a little boy, than an actual little boy! He is so mature in mind, and calmly confident that he gives the impression of being 40.

Monday 20th July

Called at 6.30 a.m. to drive Alan – that power he has over me – to Brighton and onward to Newmarket[2] where he joined his boat. I parted from him at eleven after a gay drive and good breakfast.

Much to do in London, but no news, good or bad – Harold fetched me: (he is being so very charming and considerate now) and we had a drink first with Helen Fitzgerald and then with Esmond Rothermere and Ann; NO couple is so married. They are touching together; and I hope it will be a success. Already it has gone on for seven years.

I am feeling well and lusty.

---

1 Channon is right, unlike above, to say the 'eventual' heir: Noel Anthony Scawen Lytton (1900–85) would succeed his father, the 3rd Earl (*vide supra*), in 1951 as 4th Earl. He changed his name to Lytton-Milbanke by deed poll in 1925 in recognition of his mother's inheritance of the barony of Wentworth, to which he succeeded as 17th Baron in 1957.
2 He means Newhaven.

Dined alone; thought about the current currents. Beaverbrook is intriguing against Winston,[1] playing a dirty game, indeed but that they are still friendly, even intimate. Max Beaverbrook who has no convictions but a desire to become Prime Minister, and at second best, if he fails, at least he can cause endless mischief. That is the game, deep and unlovely. He is out to destroy the Tory Party, which he can never forgive for its somewhat foolish treatment of him, and I suspect that Brendan Bracken is behind him. The other current is Randolph Churchill's imminent return. What will happen? Pam Churchill wants to get rid of him, but can a divorce be rushed? Could even Randolph even dare name Averell Harriman? Wouldn't the scandal and international repercussions be too grave? And yet Pam, if she waits (and as she admits) brings matters to a head until after the inevitable fall of the Churchill regime, would she not be accused of time-serving? Of only waiting until there are no more plumes of power to be plucked, whilst in reality she was activated by patriotic motives? Nobody knows what will happen!

TUESDAY 21ST JULY

Walked, as usual, to the House. To everyone's surprise Winston walked in and took his Questions. He was not well received and apparently sensed the atmosphere as he answered awkwardly (I think he is courting favour in view of Randolph's expected return) .... Grace Curzon, still remarkably lovely, Irene Ravensdale and Victor Cazalet dined with me – Rab joined us for a brief bit. Then we went to see *Mrs Miniver*,[2] a most magnificent film about the war. I was much moved in spite of a few glaring inaccuracies! We had to walk back to the Dorchester, since there were no taxis. We grouped in Victor's suite .... The lobbies today hummed with the Churchill vs Harriman situation and romance. Anglo-American relations could not tolerate a divorce; and besides there is Mrs Averell Harriman sitting in New York.

WEDNESDAY 22ND JULY

A year ago I left the Foreign Office – and what, if anything, have I accomplished since? A year ago today Christopher Lennox-Boyd was born, and his grandmother Lady Iveagh was 60. She is 61 today, I think.[3]

---

1 Beaverbrook had spoken at Birmingham on 21 June, the first anniversary of the invasion of the Soviet Union, critically of the Allies' reluctance to mount a second front. His ability to remove Churchill was highly limited; but Churchill was sufficiently worried about Beaverbrook to offer him the Washington Embassy, to get him out of the way.
2 Hollywood's 1942 take on the life of a Home Counties housewife during the war, directed by William Wyler and starring Greer Garson and Walter Pidgeon; it won six Oscars.
3 She was.

Walked to the House; lunched twice, firstly alone with Rab at the House and gave him the news of the prevailing intrigues and advised him to accept the Viceroyalty of India, unless his growing chances for the premiership develop. He is playing, he explained to me for the fortieth time, 'a waiting game'.

The whole afternoon with Mr Wilder, my accountant. We 'did' the income/surtax return for the past year. Neither his forecast of what my assessment would be, nor the bank return for the Scotch Bank were as discouraging as I feared. If I continue to be sensible and careful I ought always to be rich! During the past fifteen months I have extricated myself from debt, curtailed my expenses, and thanks to Lord Iveagh, paid off my overdraft of about £15,000!

I warned Ernest Brown that he is the object of a Beaverbrook plot; he told me with some heat that he was aware of the machinations of this 'Satan incarnate'; he was affectionate, angry, wounded, apprehensive. It seems that Max has selected Chippenham, Teenie's seat,[1] in which to begin his campaign for Second Front and a general election.

Alan has had a mad but typically Lennox-Boyd day – came up from Newhaven; is motoring to Elveden and Henlow and returns here to sleep. I dined alone and shall finish Trollope's *The Eustace Diamonds*[2] as I await him.

Thursday 23rd July

Alan came in during the night but did not awaken me and I was unaware of his presence: we had breakfast together, dawdled, and he left for Portsmouth and his mother. He is in her clutches again.

I feel completely exhausted nervously and sexually and can barely cross the room, so lacking am I in energy. I went to the House of Commons . . . . had my hair cut; called on the Kemsleys and Mrs Greville. Jay Llewellin came to dine, and he brought me a handsome bottle of old brandy now as rare as happiness in the mad world. He was in high spirits as he had lunched with the King and Queen at Buck House. The only other guest was Archie Sinclair, a good luncheon and talk, the King and Archie stuttered at each other and the Queen had been charming. He told her that he was dining with me. Peter Loxley and Harold also dined and we played amateurish bridge.

Bed at midnight.

Friday 24th July

I am still utterly exhausted and too feeble mentally to make up my mind about anything. I couldn't decide whether or not to go to Kelvedon. Lady Crewe

---

1 Victor Cazalet had been MP for Chippenham since 1924.
2 Trollope's novel of 1872, the third of his political, or Palliser, sequence.

decided for me; she rang up and we gossiped. A peace offering? Never before has she telephoned to me in her life . . . what does it mean? She asked me to tea to meet the [de] Gaulles and I accepted . . . . All day I rested, and did little else except to sign letters; then, refreshed and recovered, I walked to Argyll House to have a cocktail with Lady Crewe who received me with much and marked cordiality. Talked to Mme de Gaulle,[1] a dim little woman whom I shall never recognise again; spent an hour with Eileen Sutherland whom I had not seen for two years. She looked remarkably well, slim and handsome . . . . [I] dined alone. George Gage came and talked to me for an hour. He seemed depressed; said that his blood pressure was too low and that he was going to Cornwall to recuperate as 'a rest from his family' who, evidently, love him. He thinks that Beaverbrook is the Laval of this country; that he ought to be shot etc.; that he is exploiting the war only to serve his private ends. His insatiable ambition wedded to his impish sense of mischief may easily land this country in a serious plight!

SUNDAY 26TH JULY   *THATCHED HOUSE, ASCOT*

Harold drove me here, and we stopped *en route* at Farnborough to inspect the huge, growing, sprawling aerodrome there. We were shown a German fighter . . . . which came down by mistake recently and the pilot surrendered. It is wonderfully made . . . In the distance one saw the Napoleonic mausoleum . . . then we came on here to stay with the Fitzgeralds in their tiny manor of a house: it is beautifully arranged, and the food is excellent, although they have only three or four servants . . . . the King of Greece and Joyce B[rittain-]J[ones] had been with them all day . . . I was much ragged as ever since it was known that I was coming here the telephone has buzzed with invitations asking us everywhere. At last Helen Fitzgerald weakly consented to go to Farnham to dine with the Kemsleys. A pleasant party . . . . two kinds of champagne, bridge – a very Edwardian evening. And long conversations about Beaverbrook and his wicked plan for a second front. Everybody thinks one desirable at the proper moment but the country must not be 'bounced' into doing it prematurely. What is the Beaver aiming at? No. 10? Or a separate peace?

MONDAY 27TH JULY

Helen, Harold (they are *au mieux*)[2] and I drove up to London in the wet dawn. None of us had slept (the first two for obvious reasons, but I was kept awake by

---

1 Yvonne Charlotte Anne Marie Vendroux (1900–79) married Charles de Gaulle in 1921. An ultra-conservative Catholic, she was known as 'Tante Yvonne' – Aunt Yvonne – for trying to persuade her husband, when president, to roll back the permissive society, even to the extent of urging him to ban mini-skirts.
2 Literally 'on the best of terms', by which he means sleeping together.

indigestion and the Germans!) Two air raids! I felt very old and ill and down and after working for an hour, went to the RAC for a 'Turker' and resumed.

A brilliant gay letter from Peter, no. 14, came; and also a cable. He has a tremendous dominion over me.

Gave a gay and distinguished dinner party and Cecil Beaton came: Lady Crewe, cold not unbending, in a *très grande dame* mood; Loelia Westminster who is staying here – she looked well; the Argentine Ambassador; Harold; Helen Fitzgerald . . . a most voluble evening and Cecil Beaton held us entranced for five hours with his descriptions of caves in the Middle East from where he has so recently returned. He was scathing about . . . . Walter Monckton, who has become *un grand amoureux*;[1] but he is pro-Lampson . . . till the press astrologer predicted a fortuitous development for me this week. And so it seems, for His Argentine X [Excellency] invited me to accompany him to the Argentine as his guest. We would fly out; attend a series of galas and banquets – a glorious trip and I am certainly considering it.

TUESDAY 28TH JULY

A few frantic twits from Alan who is bronzed, debonair and exciting in appearance. He laughingly confessed to me that his mother returns to her bed for a week after one of his lightning descents on Henlow. I am not surprised.

The Russians continue to retreat. There were air-raid alarms so had a somewhat disturbed night as Bundi barked and was terrified.

WEDNESDAY 29TH JULY

Again the sirens sounded . . . Loelia is still staying.

I returned to the H. of Commons which was in an uproar. All about the lobby was crowded with earnest dreadful-looking youths who demanded a 'second front!' A communist agitation! . . . I have almost persuaded myself (and others!) to make the effort of accepting the Ambassador's amiable invitation to go to the Argentine. Should be an exhausting but an enviable experience and I secretly know that I might get to New York to see my child on the way back. I began to pull strings today.

THURSDAY 30TH JULY

Today is Honor's 33rd birthday! May she never live to have another one! Her deportment is so deplorable. I went to the weekly Guinness meeting and signed the usual transfers and discovered that she is selling her shares – for drink, no doubt. Soon she will be ruined. She has only 173 shares left! Old Bland was there

---

1 A great lover; Monckton was supposedly conquering the women of Cairo, where he was head of British Propaganda and Information Services.

and said that she has not even acknowledged his letters about business, and an affectionate one – he has known her all his life and done her 1,000 'good turns'. It is scandalous and ungrateful. My mother-in-law is right: she will be a thorn in all our flesh for the rest of our days.

A dull short letter written hurriedly from Peter.

FRIDAY 31ST JULY   *KELVEDON*

Worn out . . . before coming here I heard that Winston, accompanied by Bobbety Cranborne, the CIGS, and others are flying very secretly to Cairo today. It is fantastic. I came here, exhausted but in a highly vicious lustful mood. I think that Alan is coming tomorrow.

I had a luncheon party before I left. Lady Willingdon, Norah Lindsay and my poor dear old Gage who I think is *désoeuvré* and unhappy.

SATURDAY 1ST AUGUST

Alan could not get away from his doting dotty mama! I am here alone.

MONDAY 3RD AUGUST

A fête – a fête worse than death at Southend and then I came to London and dined with Harold *à deux*. Winston arrived safely at Cairo today. This still very <u>hush</u>.

The third Bank Holiday Monday of the war.

TUESDAY 4TH AUGUST

To the House of Commons where we went into secret session. Cripps clumsily announced to an astonished House that Winston and Co. are in the Middle East *en route* for Russia!! Everybody gasped. The House of Commons is already several laps behind London society which is aware of the trip.

Dined with Alan and Patsy at the Polonac. Alan came back here with me to gossip and frolic. I showed him a touching and friendly letter which came from Honor this morning. It was by way of thanks for two books I sent her for her birthday, *Reflections in a Golden Eye*[1] and *The Last of Uptake* by Simon Harcourt-Smith. (He, by the way, I met last week in the street and he cut me dead for the third time, all because I refused to lend him money. How disillusioning people are!)

Looked in at the Overseas Club to have a cocktail with the Crown Prince and Princess of Norway whom I found delightful. She[2] has improved, more chic

---

1 A 1941 novel by Carson McCullers, eventually filmed in 1967.
2 Princess Märtha Sofia Lovisa Dagmar Thyra of Sweden (1901–54), niece of King Gustav V of Sweden, married in 1929 the Crown Prince of Norway, later King Olav V (qv).

and less Nordic than hitherto; she had an immense hat, as she had just come from Windsor Castle where the christening of the infant Kent . . . . had taken place. Roosevelt is a godfather! It was my suggestion originally and I have been pushing it for some time. He is called 'Michael George Charles Franklin' and has an imposing list of sponsors, two kings, Roosevelt, and the Duke of Gloucester. What a closed fraternity the royal racket is!

WEDNESDAY 5TH AUGUST

I lunched with Alan and we returned to the House of Commons to hear Ernest Bevin address the 1922 Committee which he did with eloquence and skill. Is he the herald of the horrible new world? Alan and I returned to frolic here . . .

THURSDAY 6TH AUGUST

Lunched at the House of Commons where I was most of the day. Long talk with Rab who is toying with India. Then home, fetched Violet Trefusis and took her to a brilliant film *The Young Mr Pitt*[1] which I enjoyed. It was Mr Chamberlain's ambition to be like him; he often said so in conversation and his speeches. Violet T . . . . came to a candlelit supper here. Violet openly remarked that Winston is in Cairo *en route* from ~~the Middle East~~ [crossed out] Russia. I denied it. The news is out! London society is always pips ahead of the House of Commons.

FRIDAY 7TH AUGUST   *KELVEDON*

A full day. I picked up Gaston Palewski,[2] the amiable Polish Frog and drove him to Coppins – the Duchess received us animatedly, and she looked bewilderingly lovely, thin, and her amber eyes seemed sadder than ever. I saw them flush with tears as Palewski told his sad tale of the Regent's despondency and of Princess Olga's bravery, and how they realise that there is no future for them. Nothing but exile and boredom . . . The Duke was gay, young, slim and most friendly, but his face seems more lined, and more and more – I suspect – *quelque chose*.[3] We lunched *à quatre* and Palewski was tactful at ease and excellent, and quite unembarrassed even when TRHs served him his food.

---

1 A 1942 film with Robert Donat as Pitt, with propagandistic use made of his struggles against the French.
2 Gaston Palewski (1901–84) was of Jewish descent and from Belarus, not Poland. He escaped to London from French North Africa in 1940 and de Gaulle, whom he had known since 1934, appointed him Political Director of the Free French; they enjoyed a very close association for many years. A notorious womaniser, he had Nancy Mitford as one of his many mistresses. He had recently seen Prince Paul in Africa.
3 'Something'. Channon may allude to marital difficulties, though it is not clear on what grounds.

I left him alone first with her and then later with him. She left us over the coffee and reappeared half an hour later carrying the new Prince, whom she had just fed. He is very royal-looking already; has wide flaked very blue eyes, and no chin. The Duchess laughingly said that she found him the image of Queen Victoria! He was silently muzzled in the arms of his father, who smiled tenderly at him. He adores his children. The . . . . Duke was funny about President Roosevelt's letter which began 'My dear Kent'! – He showed me various things he had bought at Bagshot at the recent auction of the Duke of Connaught's things.[1] I find him friendly, not at all whining – he didn't seem to know about Winston, and certainly the Duchess didn't. The secret of the Cairene trip has been well kept.

Palewski and I drove back to London and we talked of the fall of France. He insisted that only five families in all of France had been collaborationists, the Paul Morands,[2] Beauvaus, Melchior de Polignacs, Pierre de Brissacs, Chambruns, and Madame Charles de Noailles, the famous Marie-Laure [Bischoffsheim].[3]

SATURDAY 8TH AUGUST   *LEEDS CASTLE*

I drove into Brentwood, made some inquiries re a retreat for Catholic priests, and then drove on here, crossing by the Gravesend ferry without any difficulty. On the way I decided definitely to go into a monastery next week, and I wrote to Val Elwes[4] who is himself doing a retreat now with His Eminence at Buckfast, asking him to arrange one for me. I shall fast and be flayed and adhere strictly to all the rules.

Leeds is remarkable. There is no host since Adrian is in Scotland, and Olive is confined to her private apartments with an imaginary (?) chill . . . . Delightful party and I am in tearing spirits after sleeping from 3.30 until eight o'clock, soundly.

1   The late Duke's pictures, furniture and porcelain were sold over several days at Bagshot Park in late July. The prices they reached were thought to be disappointing.

2   Paul Morand (1888–1976) was a diplomat and novelist, an ambassador for Vichy, and in his ideology a white supremacist and anti-Semite. He was eventually admitted to the Académie Française in 1968 despite heavy protests from de Gaulle.

3   He means, of course, families of note. The Beauvaus and Melchior de Polignacs (see Vol. I, entry for 19 November 1936 and footnote) were from ancient French nobility, as was Pierre de Brissac, who became 12th duc de Brissac in 1944. Mme de Noailles (1902–70) was a leading patron of surrealist art. Her father was a banker of Jewish extraction, which may or may not cast doubt over Palewski's accusation of her collaboration.

4   Monsignor Valentine Elwes (1898–1966) was private secretary to Cardinal Arthur Hinsley (qv), the Archbishop of Westminster, and later a Roman Catholic chaplain at Oxford University.

SUNDAY 9TH AUGUST

Only the flapping of the swans on the moat disturbed me and I slept eleven hours[1] and awoke like a pigmy refreshed. We sunbathed, overate, drank champagne, gossiped. All day I was gay and amusing and I forgot the war, forgot H[onor] and all my anxieties. I feel that things for me will get better? On the mend ...

Gandhi[2] has been arrested in Bombay and there is rioting in India. We sat in the peaceful sun, ignored the war, and chatting with Freda [Casa Maury] I remembered my old, and now happily outworn hostility towards her! She is entirely responsible for the *dégringolade*[3] of the poor Prince of Wales; for her influence was always, while not corrupting, cheapening. I like her now and appreciate her pointful lilt. She seems to adore her slim Cuban ersatz Marquis.

MONDAY 10TH AUGUST

I brought Loelia Westminster to London in my car, along with my footman Peter who came from Bagshot. I deposited her at Waterloo and then came home little expecting the Himalayan pile of momentous letters and news. *D'abord* a cable, encrypted (but clear to Chips) from Peter. It is obviously from Cairo and he says that he has seen Winston, Auchinleck and others and is going on to Moscow, where he is probably tonight! What a war the boy has had ...

Lunched with Violet Trefusis at the Mirabelle; a recondite party: the old Princesse de Polignac[4] who grunted at me in her deep guttural Grenadier's voice, Lady Crewe (now my 'buddy'), Leslie Hore-Belisha, Peter Quennell . . . . and Gaston Palewski. Later in an ecstasy of happiness and prosperity I took Violet to a shop and bought her a Georgian diamond butterfly. Leslie H-B was jealous. He is such an old sweetie. He begged me to go with him next week to the Western Isles to stay with Compton Mackenzie[5] but I refused. Instead I shall do my retreat.

---

1 He must have gone back to sleep until after lunch if he had woken at 8 o'clock, as he claims in the previous entry.
2 Mohandas Karamchand Gandhi (1869–1948) trained as a lawyer in London and practised for a time in southern Africa, where he developed a hatred of racism and colonialism. Back in India from 1915 he preached the politics of non-violent change, campaigning to acquire independence from Britain, and changed his lifestyle to live frugally among the urban poor. He argued forcefully against Indian involvement in the Second World War, and in 1942 organised the Quit India Movement to try to drive the British out. He was assassinated by a Hindu Nationalist.
3 Tumble.
4 Formerly Winnaretta Singer (1865–1943), an heiress to the sewing machine empire and a patron of the arts. She and Mrs Trefusis had been lovers.
5 Edward Montague Compton Mackenzie (1883–1972) identified as a Scot (and was a founder of the Scottish National Party) but was born and educated in England. He was a prolific author – including ten volumes of autobiography – and although had a huge success as a young author with the semi-autobiographical *Sinister Street* (1913–14), is best remembered for his 1947 novel *Whisky Galore*, which was filmed by Ealing Studios. He was knighted in 1952.

A frenzied afternoon of fuss and detail; wrote to Peter, to my mother and to my child; sent off letters to the Regent, and the Queen of Spain etc. etc. Refused to dine with Harold, and also with both Geoffrey Lloyd and Jay Llewellin who all rang up. I am busy doing up huge packets for General Wavell and Peter etc.

TUESDAY 11TH AUGUST

Val Elwes writes lengthily from Buckfast, and has arranged for me to go there next Tuesday for a contemplative week with the Benedictines. I am greatly excited and shall go.

Jay Llewellin, rather tactlessly, called about eleven and woke me up. He stayed too long.

A lovely summer's day, fitful and showery: I spent it rearranging my life and writing – all day I was busy. A letter came from a monastery near Bishop's Stortford asking me to go there. Is all Catholicism a freemasonry?

Dined angrily alone, avoiding invitations . . .

FRIDAY 14TH AUGUST

Two very quick letters from Cairo from Peter, one dated August 9th. He had seen Winston, etc., and was leaving with him and Wavell on the following day for Moscow. Gay, brilliant letters . . . Lunched with Lady Willingdon, a large dull party . . . . Wrote – worked. Caught up – sent off over thirty letters. Took Lady Willingdon to the boring Astaire film[1] and we dined *à deux* afterwards at the Potomac restaurant . . . Alan wants to come for the weekend to Kelvedon to frolic!!

MONDAY 17TH AUGUST

All day with Archie Wavell [Junior]; he gave me books; we exchanged presents. He adores, worships his great father. And he has, I think, and half-fear, a sentimental regard for me. We talked of Archie Wavell's future; will he return from India and become Prime Minister? We discussed the whole Greek episode; how the General (accompanied, of course, by Peter Coats) went to Greece in January, 1941 (whilst I was in Greece) and offered a certain amount of help to suffering Greece. General Metaxas politely refused it saying that it would not be enough to save Greece, and would only serve as the bait to the Germans. (Did I ever record that Paul of Yugoslavia summoned me to his Chesterfield library at Beli Dvor and in a towering rage said that Eden and Churchill with their mad schemes would end by Germanifying the Balkans (he has been proved right); and how he sent a special courier to Athens with a strong letter to Metaxas which I read

---

1 The most recent Fred Astaire film was *You'll Never Get Rich*, co-starring Rita Hayworth. It did not bask in critical acclaim.

(at the same time I sent off a *billet-doux*[1] to Peter).) A little later, according to young Archie, the Greek government enquired whether the offer was still open (February 8th?) and the War Cabinet here replied that it was. Meanwhile Wavell was ordered to remain in Cairo to await Eden's arrival there with Dill and was thus prevented, as he confided to his son, from going to Cyrenaica to inspect his forces. Bad weather contributed its share, for Eden and Dill were held up four days at Plymouth; consequently Wavell, too, was held in Cairo. That is his great regret, and nobody can be blamed. But for the delay he would have flown to Cyrenaica and probably, he says now, reduced his offer of reinforcements to Greece, as he would have realised how necessary they were in Libya. The result might have been the abandoning of the madcap Greek campaign for which Wavell, although he never opposed it, had little enthusiasm. Once ordered to go on with it he did so with his usual energy. This is his explanation to his son and is probably the true one. I believe it. History might have been different. Wavell, however, always tries to belittle himself and shields himself – always. He also told me another story about him. He was once flying to France at the beginning of the war to confer with Gamelin etc. He got into his plane at Croydon and settled down to the difficult Torquemada crossword puzzle which he solved. It took him just forty-five minutes or so ... young Archie hopes that he [Wavell] will be Prime Minister. So do I ...

Now what clothes does one take to monastery? I am off in the morning and tormented by what to take ...

TUESDAY 18TH AUGUST   *ST MARY'S ABBEY, BUCKFAST, DEVON*

My new volume opens surprisingly enough in a Benedictine monastery, where I came this afternoon after a most uncomfortable journey from London in an overcrowded train. Travelling is discouraged – luckily I found a seat and read Aldous Huxley's *Grey Eminence*[2] and ruminated on yesterday, which was 'Wavell Day' and on last evening's dinner party, when I 'entertained' Patsy and Alan (she had just returned from staying with my wayward wife and had been bored), Alice Harding, Freddie Ashton, a common bore, a Sadler's Wells dancer and Alice's Cicisbeo,[3] and Maimie and Vsevolod! The German radio today had just announced that Winston is reported to have offered him the Russian throne. So there was much Imperial chaff, etc.

I drove here from Newton Abbot in a taxi, rang the bell, was admitted by a lay brother, and soon the Abbot himself received me. He is a fine-looking German,

1 Love letter.
2 *Grey Eminence: A Study in Religion and Politics* (1941) is a biographical study of François Leclerc du Tremblay, Richelieu's adviser.
3 A man, usually homosexual, who dances attendance on a woman who is married to someone else. Ashton fulfilled all those functions.

aged about 46. His name, Don Bruno Fehrenbacher, OSB;[1] and he is, he told me, a Württemberger. Fine eyes, a large aquamarine ring set with diamonds, a pectoral cross, spectacles and greying hair . . . Already I have been to Vespers and Compline. I sit next to the Abbot at meals and occupy the best bedroom, vacated only this morning by Cardinal Hinsley, who left me messages and blessings. I could be very happy here, and only a few times has my mind wandered back to the world which I have temporarily left . . . . today the Duchess of Kent wanted to come to tea; but I said I was going away.

The monastery is not in the least frightening. It is simple, sweet and peaceful. I wonder whether I can induce the Abbot to whip me. I shall try.

The news of the Churchill–Wavell visit to Moscow was released last night; of course half England knew of the Prime Minister's junketings, I was anxious to read of General Wavell's forced landing near Teheran for Peter was his passenger. However they proceeded after a short delay.

It is now nine and I have just come in from Compline. The great silence has begun.

WEDNESDAY 19TH AUGUST

The almost uncanny silence made me long even for an air-raid siren. I slept fitfully, haunted by vicious thoughts of which I was ashamed and impeded too by indigestion. The strange rather heavy Rhineland food lies heavily on me.

Went to early Mass at 6.50 and remained in the cathedral until eight. Then breakfast and returned for High Mass, which took only an hour . . . . The programme for visitors here is:

Low Mass at 7.30
Breakfast at 8.10
High Mass at nine o'clock
Dinner at 12.45
Tea 4.30
Vespers 6.30
Compline 8.15 – a complete day.

The Abbot has just been to see me but I got no forwarder with him over my secret plans for abasement and humiliation. He was out to luncheon and I made friends with another monk, who has lent me his key to the well-stocked library where I read for two hours. Then a long walk.

1 Hermann Bruno Fehrenbacher (1895–1965) was one of many German Catholics of his era who came to Buckfast, not just to pray but to engage in the rebuilding of the ruined Abbey. He was ordained in 1919, became a naturalised Briton in 1935 and was installed as Abbot in 1939, serving until his resignation through ill-health in 1956.

The military changes have been announced. I don't understand the delay, as I was told of them a fortnight ago. Alexander[1] succeeds Auchinleck; Montgomery follows Ritchie. I shall have the greatest pleasure in rubbing that in: the removal of Wavell was a wicked disaster. Winston at his worst. The loss of Libya is the result of that change and the grotesque Greek campaign.

. . . . after Compline during the Great Silence the handsome, rather charming Abbot fetched me from my room and we crept not too surreptitiously to his spartan room and we listened to the forbidden wireless, heard about the commando raid at Dieppe and smoked *verboten*[2] cigarettes. He is an attractive German, a Württembergerian of about 44.[3] Today he wore a peridot ring. I am making friends with the other monks who are all gentle, with the viciousness drained out of them. One has given me a key to the remarkably well-stocked library where I browse. He told me that the monks are all flogged on Fridays after he sings the 'Miserere'. I must try and see that.

THURSDAY 20TH AUGUST

I slept beautifully, the viciousness gone from my soul, the indigestion from my belly. I was late for Low Mass and slipped outside and ran to the cathedral, entering, I hope, unobserved. Then breakfast. Then High Mass for an hour (and I wickedly thought of Peter the whole time). I have made friends with a young man, also a guest, who is studying for the priesthood. He is funny about the monks, and more especially the novices who get, as he put it, 'a hell of a time, and it serves them right'!

The early afternoon I spent dawdling with the Abbot, and he took me up the high tower, showed me over the monastery where I envied the rather spartan cells of the monks – not really. Then I went for a walk and met a long way up the river one of the older Fathers whom I had once seen eating alone. He is an extraordinary old bird and came here in 1886. He is the last of the French émigrés, and my French is now more fluent than his. For fifty-six years with few breaks

---

1 Harold Rupert Leofric George Alexander (1891–1969) joined the Army in 1911. By the end of the Great War, in which he saw action in most of the major battles on the Western Front, he had won the Military Cross and the DSO, and was a lieutenant colonel, even though still aged only 26. After a series of staff appointments and other commands he became the youngest general in the Army in 1937. He took part in the evacuation at Dunkirk and by late 1940 was a lieutenant general commanding Southern Command. In taking over from Auchinleck in 1942, having managed the retreat in Burma, he took charge of British forces in North Africa and then in Italy. He was knighted in 1942, promoted to field marshal in 1944 and raised to the peerage as Viscount Alexander of Tunis in 1946. That same year he became a Knight of the Garter, and joined the Order of Merit in 1959. He was Governor-General of Canada from 1946 to 1952, returning to become Minister of Defence in Churchill's administration, and serving until 1954. He was advanced to an earldom in 1952.
2 Forbidden.
3 He was 47.

he has lived here – one of the few breaks was, of all places, Kelvedon Hall! For some years, off and on, he lived there as chaplain and adviser to the rather fishy nunnery, from which we bought it! He even occupied my actual room and I made him laugh by saying *'Vous avez dormi là plus que moi, mon père!' 'Et toujours seul,' il a repondu.*[1] I have made a date to walk with him tomorrow at the [his] usual hour of three.

Friday 21st August

Rain. I am a touch bored and was disappointed of receiving no morning post. The old priest, Father Milletus .... spent the afternoon in my room proselytising me heavily. Enthralled and gradually restless I encouraged him and hinted that I might give Kelvedon to the Benedictines. He produced a tiny pamphlet for me, and wants me to be an oblate. I should if I was free to do as I choose; but the Iveaghs would be annoyed. I think all springs from the influence of Kelvedon, so long a Roman house. This old priest loved my house, slept in my room.

A heavy post brought back the world! Elizabeth Elveden is all right and the baby daughter (my second niece, and for the fifth time I am an uncle) flourishes at 19 Bentinck Street. I rang up Patsy, who had had Honor staying with her last night: she was, Patsy says, well – and never once mentioned me .... Michael Parker writes that he is alone and bored in London. I was half-tempted to rush up to see him – in one flash I felt all the charm of monastic life today; it was as we walked into supper, the scuffling feet, the bells, yet the silence moved me much.

After Compline I crept up to my room to await the Abbot, but I doubted whether he would come in view of it being Friday. I found the door to the cell corridor unlatched and crept in unobserved. The doleful 'Miserere' had just begun and I listened entranced. The flogging seemed severe, frightful whacks against obviously bare flesh. Each monk gives himself the discipline in the privacy of his cell. His zeal is thus left to himself to decide ... The Abbot and I joked a bit. He doesn't take it necessarily now, and I listened later, since our rooms adjoin, and heard nothing. We turned on the wireless, and whispered because of the great silence, and then returned. It is now 10.05 p.m. and the lights have just gone off and I am writing by candlelight.

Saturday 22nd August

The last half of my retreat, and I am regretting it. I should really be happy here for a year; and probably one day when I am an oblate I shall come every year, work and write, as the great worldlings of Paris society did in the eighteenth century. I am too wise, frivolous, witty and wicked to enjoy this life permanently, yet I think

---

1 'You have slept there more often than me, Father!' 'And always alone,' he replied.

I could do it . . . I crept out after lunch in order to avoid the Abbot and went to the distant moors, a long trek and there I sunbathed in fitful weather, intermittent showers and sunlight. I rested by a boulder and 'meditated', as one is advised to do. My hand stung with nettles and I thought about mortification. Madly, insanely, I scarified my body with stinging nettles and the effect was electric, exquisite pain, exciting sensation: and then I came in. I felt I was in disgrace with the Fathers, having been out from two until seven. Also, worse, I imagine that I had a chill. I went to bed before Compline – going now at 7.55.

SUNDAY 23RD AUGUST

A ghastly night. I itched terribly: the nettles stung and tormented me all night. I alone cried out with pain . . . at last I got up and took two aspirins and fell into a coma, resolved to be normal hereafter. I have had more than enough of mortification and mummery. Reaction had set in. I long to get out . . . I am fed up; have claustrophobia. I slept, however, twelve hours, missing Matins and God knows how many other services or obligations. Late for breakfast, but nobody noticed . . . now I am going to have a bath. I am bored by religion and long for the luxury of Belgrave Square.

Later – a gorgeous operatic touch, Tosca High Mass. Then, I fled to the distant woods where I stripped and sunbathed (wearing only a huge crucifix). For nearly five hours I lay naked in the warm August sun, listening to the rushing Dart, thinking of my man-child in America, and of his unfortunate godfather languishing in Kenya, and of Peter and his triumphs; and I read, and finished Lord Rosebery's brilliant sketch of the Younger Mr Pitt.[1] I felt happy again and shall be wretched to leave on Tuesday. The temporary depression I had must be common to all monks. Once more I am soothed and happy here.

Read Lord Acton's weighty tome on the French Revolution.[2] The lights have now gone out: and I am writing by candlelight.

Brazil has declared war on the Axis.

MONDAY 24TH AUGUST

My last day at the monastery and I am very sad . . . . The world once more beckons me. I have written (and prayed for) my son, and to Peter . . .

The following entries were recorded in a separate exercise book covering the period 25th August to 18th September. These books were in an envelope attached to the diary for August to December 1942.

1 A short biography by Rosebery of his predecessor, published for the centenary of Pitt's death in 1906.
2 Acton's *Lectures on the French Revolution* were published in 1910.

TUESDAY 25TH AUGUST

A frenzied morning in the monastery with many monks coming to say 'goodbye' to me. Dear Father Milletus who is 70, a pet, who tried to proselytise! He brought me photographs of himself and other pathetic little relics. Obviously I had fascinated him. And then came the Abbot, suave yet somehow heavy and Teutonic . . . . and lastly little Father Isodore who is only 28 and wedded now for life to the church. He is gentle and affectionate and it makes me weep to think of his solitary life. However he seems happy . . . I drove in after luncheon to Newton Abbot where I caught the train and found a seat. I like long train journeys. At Paddington the usual wartime wait for a taxi. Then home where I found masses of letters including a more than mad one from my mother, and two brilliant epistles from Peter in which he describes a vast banquet at the Kremlin where Wavell, speaking in Russian, was the success of the dinner, and rather eclipsed Winston . . .

WEDNESDAY 26TH AUGUST

Lambert woke me at eight, saying 'A message has come that the Duke of Kent has been killed!'[1] I cried out in astonishment and a few minutes later he returned with the newspapers which speak the dreadful news. My first thoughts were of the Duchess, that glorious, glamorous tragic creature whose life, although she is not yet 36, is over. No Conroy[2] will ever intrude there. It is ghastly . . . I rang up Natasha Bagration for news but she didn't even know of it. And all morning I was telephoning or being telephoned to. Geoffrey Lloyd dropped in to pay his condolences; others did likewise. It seems that the experienced pilot, Wing Commander Moseley, must have mistaken his route and crashed into a mountain, the only one on the horizon. (I have seen the Air Ministry report) . . . . Death must have been instantaneous . . . a shudder seems to have come from the

---

1 The Duke was one of fifteen men on an RAF Mark 3 Short S.25 Sunderland that left Invergordon at 1305 GMT on 25 August and crashed thirty-seven minutes later into a headland at Dunbeath in Caithness. Only a rear gunner survived. The Duke was on a mission to Reykjavik in Iceland in his capacity as an air commodore. The plane crashed in fog because of a navigational error. There have been several conspiracy theories about the crash, none of them plausible.

2 John Ponsonby Conroy (1786–1854) had been the equerry to the previous Duke of Kent – Queen Victoria's father – and after his death became Comptroller to the last Duchess; and rumour had it that they were lovers. He and the Duchess devised an educational system designed to make Victoria compliant, so that they could exercise power through her when she succeeded her uncle, William IV, as Sovereign. Victoria hated him, dismissed all suggestions of his having had an affair with her mother, and sacked him from her service the moment she became Queen – albeit with a baronetcy and pension of £3,000 a year. He appears also to have siphoned off a substantial amount of money from the Duchess's household.

country for today everybody is shocked and depressed. I could think of little else, and telephoned to the Duchess and to Queen Mary. Still stunned, I had to get up, dress and go to the Brewery for the annual meeting . . .

We all lunched together and I sat between my in-laws who were very sweet and affectionate. They had had no news of Honor and were bitter about her . . . I drove Alan and Patsy back to London . . . a melancholy afternoon. I talked to the Poklewskis[1] several times and they tell me that the Duchess is practically prostrated! It seems that for some hours nobody knew of the accident, as it happened in a remote and wild part of Scotland – why do these tragedies always happen in Scotland? – and when finally it was definitely known that the Duke had been killed the Air Ministry telephoned the news to the King who was [with] the Queen, at Balmoral. Nobody there knew what to do, but it was obvious that the Duchess must be told before the midnight news announced it. Just before 10.30 the King ordered Eric Miéville[2] to telephone to Coppins and 'somehow to tell her!' (He ought really, I think, or at least the Queen, to have done it himself.) Miéville behaved with tact, for after getting on to Coppins he asked who was there etc. Booksmith,[3] the excellent butler, told him that the Duchess had just gone up to her room, but could not yet be asleep. And, he added, that Miss Fox was there. Miss Fox is the octogenarian old nurse who brought up these tragic sisters. I know her well: she is one of my many crosses, for she is tiresome, and a pertinacious bore, but her devotion to the whole 'Nicholas' family is deep and dates from over half a century. She sent me a note today telling me the story . . . she could not bring herself to go up to her lifelong charge and break the ghastly news, so she telephoned to Zoia Poklewska, who luckily was living at her little cottage at the end of the garden, and she implored her to come up at once to Coppins, which she did. Old 'Foxey' met her at the door and whispered the story. The Duchess overheard something from the landing above and called over to them, 'What are you two talking about? Is there anything wrong with the children?' (Edward and Alexandra are at Appleton at Sandringham.) Poor Zoia had to go up, and tell her. Decency draws a veil over what happened between these wretched women . . . but Zoia remained the night with the prostrated Duchess, who first collapsed and then became strangely calm. Almost immediately she put through a telephone call to Angela Lowther,[4] John's wife,[5] and told her that they were widows together

---

1 Alik Poklewski and his wife Zoia, *née* de Stoeckl. See entry for 6 December 1940 and footnote.
2 His assistant private secretary.
3 His name was in fact Henry James Bysouth (1896–1966). He remained in the Duchess's service until shortly before his death.
4 He must have misheard her name. She was Priscilla Lambert (1917–45), and married Lowther (*vide infra*) in 1937.
5 John Arthur Lowther (1910–42) was a lieutenant in the Royal Naval Volunteer Reserve and the late Duke's private secretary. He was the grandson and heir of the 1st Viscount Ullswater.

... John's death is a tragedy in itself. Only at the last moment did he decide to accompany the Duke and when the party arrived at the aerodrome there were not enough places. Somebody had to drop out, and it was a choice between John Lowther or the detective Evans. John insisted on going, although he felt ill. The old Ullswaters[1] are grief-stricken, and so is his mother Ti Cholmondeley.[2] His baby boy born last summer is now the heir. Michael Strutt,[3] Eva Rosebery's[4] second son, who was married to a *richissima* American, Miss Frazer, was also killed. He had gone instead of Ferguson, the usual ADC, who was ill ... I remember being sad about Rodney Wilkinson who was killed two years ago, and thinking at the time had he only accepted the Duke's offer to be his ADC he would have lived – lived until now!

All day messages poured in and people consoled with me (I wasn't aware that my friendship with the Duke was so well known) and asked for more news. I am really most anxious and upset for my poor Paul languishing in Kenya; for he loses not only one of his greatest friends, his brother-in-law, and a link with England; but he will be quick to realise that now his chances of ever returning to this country are slimmer than ever! Hope is taken away from him; and people will be nastier than ever: for there were some cads and snobs who dared not be invective [sic] for fear of offending the Duke. I fear that he may not survive this fresh blow ...

I half thought of going to Coppins, but know that the Duchess is surrounded by her loving affectionate Poklewskis and others ...

Harold returned from Scotland with a huge salmon. He, Geoffrey Lloyd and I dined off it and discussed the Duke. What a day it has been. Old 'Foxey' behaved well, certainly, in summoning Zoia, a great friend, and near the Duchess in age. I am surprised that 'Foxey' didn't do it herself as she is inclined to push herself, but with the most devoted and best of intentions. The Court thinks her a persistent bore.

---

1 James William Lowther (1855–1949) was Conservative MP for Rutland from 1883 to 1885, for Penrith from 1886 to 1918, and for Penrith and Cockermouth from 1918 to 1921. He was Speaker of the House of Commons from 1905 to 1921 when he was raised to the peerage as 1st Viscount Ullswater. He married, in 1886, Mary Frances Beresford-Hope (1854–1944).

2 Ina Marjorie Gwendolin Pelly (1885–1969) married Christopher William Lowther in 1910; and, having divorced him, married secondly George Hugo Cholmondeley (1887–1958), Lord George by courtesy, in 1921.

3 Michael Strutt (1914–42) was a pilot officer in the RAF. He was the son of the 3rd Baron Belper. He married, in 1939, Arielle Frazer.

4 Eva Isabel Marion Bruce (1892–1987), daughter of the 2nd Baron Aberdare, married firstly, in 1911, Algernon Henry Strutt, 3rd Baron Belper, and secondly, in 1924, Albert Edward Harry Mayer Archibald Primrose, by courtesy Lord Dalmeny until he succeeded his father as 6th Earl of Rosebery in 1929.

THURSDAY 27TH AUGUST

One thinks, talks and telephones of nothing but the Kents. The whole nation mourns him and sympathises with the sorrowing Duchess. She has [given] queer orders that the children, still happily at Sandringham, are not to be told. She sent me a message of thanks for my telephone [message] and hopes soon to see me; but I didn't offer to go down today after I heard that Queen Mary is spending the day there. I wrote many letters with my secretary, sent off one to Peter, and another to Princess Olga, and then went shopping with the King of Greece who was much moved and upset, for he was fond of the Duke (the Crown Prince hated him!). He had telephoned to the Duchess this morning and they had had an unsatisfactory conversation in Greek – she had sobbed, been hysterical and finally slammed down the receiver . . .

I spent an hour with Elizabeth Elveden who exuded malice about everyone. She looked well and has made a rapid recovery, and the baby was born only on September 19th.[1] She was born before the doctors or anaesthetists arrived, and in only two hours – she seems a bonny baby, fair and grave, and somewhat Guinness in appearance! Actually like all babies she looks like Winston and the Duke of Windsor.

Natasha Bagration came to see me, stayed for two hours, and wept for the Duke. She remained to dine; and I had a successful, extremely so, dinner party . . . . A gay evening. One seems to survive anything, but one more chain which bound one to the world, one more brick, and an important one, in my own splendid position, is gone . . . all is going.

Lunched with Maimie and Vsevolod who think that the royal romance, the engagement between Princess Alexandra and King Peter, is <u>off</u> – certainly very little has been heard of it recently.

FRIDAY 28TH AUGUST

The Duchess is no better today. The Queen is with her. Arrangements have now been completed for the funeral which takes place very quietly tomorrow in St George's Chapel at Windsor. I had a telegram from the Lord Chamberlain commanding my presence. (Honor was not mentioned in the invitation so supposedly the Court are officially 'aware' of our separation.) I rang up Ulick Alexander[2] at Windsor and suggested that Rab be invited and an invitation was immediately sent to him. He is the only member of the government invited, and I the only other Member of Parliament. Queen Mary sent me a gracious telegram.

---

1 He means August.
2 James Ulick Francis Canning Alexander (1889–1973) was a professional soldier who in 1928 had become the late Duke's Comptroller of the Household.

Had a Turkish bath, the only real remedy for tired nerves and an exhausted body. Michael Parker came to see me: he is an attractive Pierrot.

Dined with Juliet Duff in her exquisitely arranged flat at 3 Upper Belgrave Place . . . . Sidney Herbert, who was very charming [was there]. He had obtained a week's leave from the Southern Command to assist the Duchess with her arrangements. Everything, since poor John [Lowther] is dead – he was so tactful and efficient – is in chaos. Sidney had spent the day between Windsor and Coppins. He went into the Duchess's sitting room early this morning to fetch something and came on her sitting on the sofa, holding the Duke's service cap, weeping like Niobe.[1] She says that her life is over. So it is. We talked only of the tragedy. As the Duke died on active service his estate will be lightly taxed – and he was rich, although grossly extravagant. The late King left him over £1,000,000, I think. Queen Mary threw Windsor into some confusion by bringing nine people with her for three nights. The staff was at Balmoral, and then on holiday and the castle was practically servantless. I walked with Sidney as far as Hyde Park Corner where we stopped and talked for a long time pacing the pavement. I suggested that either Princess Nicholas should be brought immediately from Greece, or Princess Olga from Kenya, or perhaps both. He foresaw endless complications, said that the Duchess would never make such a request. I agreed, and hinted that the idea should come from the King himself. I don't think that at this moment even Anthony Eden would refuse to help. Sidney was impressed by my arguments and agreed to pass on the suggestion to the King via someone. I left him, came home, and found that Jay Llewellin had waited for me for an hour, and left me a brace of grouse. How I hate grouse![2]

Queen Mary, contrary to one's expectations, is bearing up stoically, although the Duke was beyond doubt her favourite child. She is a magnificent, brave but hard old girl.

SATURDAY 29TH AUGUST

An exhausting, emotional, hot day. Slept badly, and got up at 7.30, and dressed in my funereal garb, top hat and all. Maimie Pavlovsky, Vsevolod, Natasha and I drove down together in a hired Daimler. We left over early and so arrived at the White Hart[3] by 10.30. There was half an hour to wait. We tidied ourselves and started through the small crowd to the chapel. There was no guard of honour, few police. Indeed the extreme simplicity of the arrangements was impressive,

---

1 In Greek mythology, the daughter of Tantalus; her fourteen children were slain as a punishment for her hubris.
2 In fact, Channon has earlier said how much he likes the bird: an indication of what a bad day he was having.
3 He means the Harte and Garter, a hotel opposite Windsor Castle.

I ran into Walter Buccleuch and Eric Dudley[1] and a few others and we went in. I was next to Alice Harding . . . . opposite me sat Catherine Carnarvon,[2] recently widowed. Her ex-husband 'Porchie'[3] was wandering about. In all some forty people had been commanded and we all chatted – Poppy and Peter Thursby[4] (what a shattering blow for her, since she always loved and nearly married him. Years ago I overheard a long telephone conversation between her and the Prince of Wales in which he promised 'to help [her] over it'); Sheila and Buffles Milbanke; Jean and Richard Norton – all the semi-separated couples who came on this royal occasion together. And I thought of Honor – why could she not, too, behave decently? Noël Coward in ordinary clothes . . . Portarlingtons, Buists,[5] etc. [Soldiers] lined the nave, there was a pause and I saw the Duke's servants, his chauffeur, Booksmith [*sic*] the butler, and Evans the detective who had so miraculously escaped, others. The Duke's old Nannie sat with Miss Fox who was in tears . . . at last the procession appeared headed by a beadle and prelates. Middle-aged air marshals carried the coffin clumsily, and they were followed by the mourners. The King looked unhappy, [and] was in the middle in Air Force uniform, on his left was Halsey[6] in Naval uniform, representing the Duke of Windsor, whilst on his right in khaki walked the Duke of Gloucester, who was in tears. Immediately behind them came the cortège of kings . . . Haakon of Norway in Naval dress towering over the King of Greece on his right who was in General's uniform, and little sickly Peter of Yugoslavia in Air Force blue on his left. 'Uncle Charlie', as King Haakon is called by his relatives,[7] was grave, dignified and tall; Peter grinned sheepishly, King Timon[8] was correct and ashen. Then the princes, Olav of Norway, with Bernhard of the Netherlands – who minced . . . The others followed, Alastair Connaught,

---

1 The 3rd Earl of Dudley; see entry for 31 July 1941 and footnote.
2 Catherine had divorced the 6th Earl of Carnarvon (qv) in 1936. Her second husband, Lieutenant Commander Geoffrey Seymour Grenfell, was killed in action in 1940.
3 Prior to succeeding to the earldom in 1923, the 6th Earl had been styled Lord Porchester.
4 For Thursby, see entry for 4 December 1938 and footnote.
5 Colin Buist (1896–1981) reached the rank of commander in the Royal Navy, was for many years part of Edward VIII's circle as Prince of Wales, and became his equerry. He married, in 1928, Gladys Mary Nelson (1890–1972).
6 Lionel Halsey (1872–1949) joined the Royal Navy in 1885 and in 1914 was appointed a naval aide-de-camp to the King. He fought at Jutland and was mentioned in dispatches, and was present at the German surrender at Scapa Flow in 1919. In 1920 he became Comptroller and Treasurer to the Prince of Wales and was promoted to admiral in 1926. He disapproved of the relationship between King Edward VIII and Mrs Simpson and left the King's household in 1936, being appointed an extra equerry to King George VI the following year. He was knighted in 1918.
7 He had originally been Prince Carl of Denmark: see Vol. I, entry for 17 October 1923 and footnote.
8 George II of Greece.

'Drino' Carisbrooke, young Lascelles[1] in battledress, Harry Harewood[2] etc. The coterie stopped where I happened to be, and for a minute I was surrounded by sovereigns. The King caught my eye, but I averted it. He looked wretched, as he always does in public. Later he cried. The coffin was carried up to the altar where a group of at first unrecognisable ladies waited. Dressed like Malta women completely covered with crêpe we could not make them out. Gradually, however, I realised who they were – from their movements. The Duchess stood half a pace ahead of the Queen and of Queen Mary, whose white hair was visible even through the veils. She carried a stick and made many of those Teck gestures peculiar to herself. She towered magnificently above the others, looking like the mother of the Gracchi.[3] In the background were the Duchess of Gloucester, Princess Mary, Irene Carisbrooke ... Mary Herbert was actually in attendance on the Duchess, who very visibly showed her grief. I feared she would collapse and when she knelt over the sinking coffin, one wondered whether she had the force to get up. By then, as the short simple service slowly moved to its end, the King cried openly. Tears rolled down his cross little face ... the Queen leant over and graciously helped poor Princess Marina to her feet; and the royal procession passed out by the side chapel door to the castle. It was all over; half an hour of sweet singing, and cold psalms. I thought how much better the Buckfast monks would have done it; and yet the very simplicity, the lack of pomp surrounding the cortège of kings, and group of black-hooded queens was striking. Queen Wilhelmina looked a picture of Dutch dowdiness ... there are times when Protestant services stripped of theatricality, as they are, can be very impressive. The Garter King read out in a fine voice the splendid array of the Duke's titles and orders. Airmen blew the last post awkwardly; and the Duke's forty friends, if so many, filed out into the intense heat. No member of the government was present; none, except Rab, who was invited. I was the only MP there; and there was some surprise that Winston had not been included as a personal friend (he wrote the Duchess a splendid letter). I didn't even see Archie Sinclair – coming out I talked to Sheila [Milbanke], and to Perry Brownlow who was friendly .... The one exception to the decision to limit the attendance to friends and relations was Dr Beneš, President of Czechoslovakia. The heads of other states were all relatives! Queen Marie of Yugoslavia, I am told,

---

1 George Henry Hubert Lascelles (1923–2011), by courtesy Viscount Lascelles from 1929 to 1947, when he succeeded his father as 7th Earl of Harewood. He was captured in Italy in 1944, fighting with the Grenadier Guards, and sent to Colditz. He became a substantial figure in the world of English opera, twice being director of the Royal Opera House.

2 Henry George Charles Lascelles (1882–1947), by courtesy Viscount Lascelles from 1892 to 1929 when he succeeded his father as 6th Earl of Harewood. He married, in 1922, Princess Mary, the Princess Royal*.

3 The mother of Tiberius and Gaius Gracchus, tribunes of the plebs in second-century BC Rome, was Cornelia, daughter of the second Punic War hero Scipio Africanus. Her elder son was murdered and her younger committed suicide before the mob could get him.

was not invited. The royal family dislike her and rightly: she is wicked, obese, obscene, evil-speaking and smelling, as well as being an [illegible] and a lesbian . . . the Court looked old and somewhat moth-eaten: glamour is gone from it. And that is what is irreplaceable about the Duke: it is the end of an epoch. All elegances are over. Our royalty will become increasingly civic, duty-doing, dour and glamourless . . .

We drove to the Hind's Head, the famous hostelry at Bray and there I gave them an excellent lunch. Old Lady Milford Haven,[1] who is a sort of noble *Dame des Pleurs*,[2] having known every conceivable tragedy, was there with Edwina Mountbatten, her daughter-in-law, and Patricia[3] her granddaughter. Lady Milford Haven has had an exhausting life full of tragedies – two of her sisters, one the Empress of Russia, were assassinated by the Bolsheviks.[4] She is a German, erudite, over-educated, garrulous almost to madness, and extremely anti-Hitler. Her sole surviving sister Princess Hen of Prussia[5] lives in Silesia. Humphrey Butler soon joined us. He looked worn out and unhappy, and even more ashen than usual. He was devoted to the Duke and carried, along with Sidney [Herbert], his decorations on a cushion in the cortège. Humphrey's great good looks remain, his famous cat's eye still smiles . . . we drove on to Coppins. It was quite unguarded, and we went on to the front door which was wide open. There was nobody about and I thought of what an Axis household would be like on a day like this! The new baby Michael was asleep in a pram, and we peered at him. His nursemaid smiled sadly – Natasha [Bagration] went in to spend the rest of the terrible day with the Duchess; but I decided not to. I would have gone in had not Maimie and Vsevolod and Humphrey been with us. We returned hot and nervous to London where I went at once to the RAC for a swim. Then I came here [Kelvedon], bringing Master Michael Parker with me. He is companionable and quite astonishingly sophisticated for one so young . . .

---

1 Victoria Alberta Elisabeth Mathilde Marie, Princess of Hesse and by Rhine (1863–1950) was the eldest daughter of Louis IV, Grand Duke of Hesse, and Princess Alice, Queen Victoria's second daughter. She married, in 1884, Prince Louis of Battenberg (1854–1921), and among her children were Princess Andrew of Greece and Denmark, mother of Prince Philip, Duke of Edinburgh, and Earl Mountbatten of Burma (qqv).

2 Lady of the Sorrows.

3 Patricia Edwina Victoria Mountbatten (1924–2017), by courtesy from 1947 Lady Patricia, married in 1946 John Ulick Knatchbull (1924–2005), who succeeded his brother in 1943 as 7th Baron Brabourne. She succeeded her father in 1979 as 2nd Countess Mountbatten of Burma, his earldom having been created with a special remainder.

4 The Tsarina, Alexandra Feodorovna (1872–1918), was murdered in Yekaterinburg with her family; the other sister, the Grand Duchess Serge, born Princess Elisabeth of Hesse and by Rhine (1864–1918), was murdered the following day by being thrown down a mineshaft.

5 Irene Luise Marie Anne, Princess of Hesse and by Rhine (1866–1953) married in 1888 Prince Henry of Prussia, younger brother of Kaiser Wilhelm II.

Kelvedon is soothing with its loveliness . . . a cable of sympathy came from Peter in Delhi.

MONDAY 31ST AUGUST   WOOLPACK INN, CHILHAM[1]

Had a message from the Duchess of Kent that she would like to see me tomorrow, but that is difficult. And also she sent me a very cryptic one to say that the King had suggested that arrangements be made for Princess Olga to come here.[2] She was much touched that the move came from the Monarch; little guessing that it is the result of my *démarche*! I hope we shall succeed.

I dropped Michael 'Claridge's' Parker[3] at Brentwood and crossed by the ferry to Gravesend where I went into the church and found the tablet put up to Pocohantas,[4] my Indian ancestress who died there as she was about to embark for Virginia. An unexpected 'bracket' was a plaque to General Gordon . . .

I drove on here through hop fields and brown khaki country . . . The Woolpack is a fascinating inn with marvellous fantastically fine French food . . . . Alan arrived about five . . . . I am ending up in bourgeois middle age with my brother-in-law as my huge and horrendous alter ego, my Damon.[5]

WEDNESDAY 2ND SEPTEMBER

Alan and I visited Chilham Castle; at first, charmed by the situation and place, he half-decided to buy it; but the restored over-panelled, Jacobean interior is so depressing that he changed his mind.

We picnicked by the pool at Leeds (as Olive is in London) sunbathing, a heavy day of sun and peace. Shopped in Canterbury. Was sorry to miss John Lowther's memorial service at the Chapel Royal.

Rommel has begun another offensive in Egypt.

Honor is staying with Patsy in London. Is she tiring of her yeoman rogue?

---

1 A village in Kent, just south-west of Canterbury.
2 Plainly the government were not prepared to treat Princess Olga with the severity they accorded to her husband, Prince Paul, so she could be with her sister in her bereavement.
3 The only plausible explanation for the sobriquet can be that Parker had become an habitué of the hotel.
4 Pocahontas (1596–1617) was from one of the native American tribes in the Tsenacommacah in Virginia. She was kidnapped and held to ransom by settlers in 1613, converted to Christianity, married a tobacco planter, John Rolfe (from whom Channon claimed descent), and they had a son, Thomas Rolfe. She was brought to England and achieved some celebrity but died at Gravesend when about to sail for America.
5 In Greek mythology, Damon was the friend of Pythias, who was sentenced to death for plotting to kill Dionysius. Pythias asked to be allowed to settle his estate before dying, which Dionysius agreed to do provided Damon was held hostage in his absence, to be killed if Pythias did not return. When he did return, Dionysius was so impressed by the act of friendship and trust that he freed them both.

The mysterious mixture of melancholy and masochism is growing in my character: I like silence, solitariness and long to be humiliated and whipped. It is most ridiculous and quaint but <u>there</u>.

THURSDAY 3RD SEPTEMBER

Drove Alan into Ramsgate, where we saw much military preparation. Nobody stopped our car! How easy it would be for a fifth columnist to flit about! . . . . Drove up to London where I heard that poor Mrs Greville is, this time, dying. Everything is going now . . . I wrote letters, had my hair cut and made arrangements. I miss Alan. And there was no brilliant letter awaiting me from Peter. I heard, however, that my child is all right.

Dined alone – world-weary, but handsome and sun-bronzed.

FRIDAY 4TH SEPTEMBER

All day in Southend . . . . entertained thirty constituents to tea and read them the riot act.

Dined in; Natasha Bagration, Alice Harding, Harold [Balfour] and Sidney Herbert, who was absolutely charming.

It was such a shock to sleep alone last night – the first time for nearly a week – I like sleeping with Alan; he snores, grunts, groans . . . His huge warm body is a solace. If I could arrange my life as I like, I should never see anybody during the waking hours, but never sleep alone.

SUNDAY 6TH SEPTEMBER

A lovely sunny morning. I woke refreshed, replenished with energy. I have been thinking about the poor Duke of Kent: his death is a loss to me and to the country. Nobody knew him better than I of recent years – particularly the past six or seven . . . Fundamentally frivolous, he was fitful, fretful, both moody and unreliable in small matters. Yet his painstaking kindness was immense and equalled, even surpassed, his surface treachery. For he could be very treacherous: no man was ever more disloyal in conversation, and no man was a better friend in action, or at heart (this curious and often disturbing contradiction in his complex character was the reverse of the habits of the Prince of Wales who always ferociously resented conventional condemnation, or even gossip, about his friends yet was never known to do anything for anyone except the reigning favourite, whether it was Freda Dudley Ward, Audrey Field,[1] Fruity Metcalfe, or Wallis Simpson). But it was this puzzling trait to the Duke of Kent's Franco-Semitic [*sic*] make-up

---

1 Formerly Audrey Coats, since 1938 Audrey Bouverie. See entry for 3 June 1940 and footnote.

which first stopped people from loving him wholeheartedly, for as one began to be fond of him, he would do, or say, or commit some little act that chilled one; and again, just as one began to mistrust or be indifferent to him, he would be so thoughtful, affectionate and disarming that one would genuinely like him once more ... unstable, sensitive, volatile he had beauty, wit and worldly wisdom as well as considerable culture. He read, collected and was a musician, but only people were of real importance to him. He was good and gracious with people, and avidly interested in their morals, incomes, food and vices. (He happened to sit next to old Mr Bland, the Guinnesses' trustee, at a banquet in Swansea and spent an hour trying to find out my exact income.)

Fair, with the extravagantly youthful figure and looks common to the male members of the royal family, he always looked and seemed ten years younger than he was. The Duchess and he must have been the most beautiful and dazzling couple in the world! It was only recently that deep lines began to show under his prominent turquoise eyes. And his *tics nerveux*[1] had grown: his exquisite hands knitted incessantly as he talked quickly and irritably. He was plagued by boredom. His walk was an impressive shuffle. Being an ardent sun-worshipper, his small and trim figure was always bronzed and bleached. Naked he was magnificently gold and copper. And his head – his fair, untidy hair in the rain! – was aristocratic, even *fin-de-race*[2] . . . He liked jewels, *bibelots*, snuffboxes, expensive china, Georgian furniture, pictures and *les élégances*. But more than the actual *objets de vertu* he collected, he liked buying, selling and exchanging them. His life was a long tussle with antiquaries; for he was a dealer at heart. He was a gourmet, even a connoisseur of food, and always personally supervised every domestic detail of his establishments. Alone of the royal family he had social sense and a flair for society and entertaining. His parties were always enjoyable and usually brilliant ... In his off-time he would garden relentlessly, or he curled up for hours in the sun! Extremely *soigné* he was nonetheless unsuccessfully dressed.

Of course he had a secret of which he rarely talked and was ashamed. I was long aware of it. Later his conscience, too, tormented him about his eldest brother, whom he treated very shabbily, indeed. To lull his conscience he ended by hating the Duke of Windsor who was *au fond* the only person he cared for deeply. (He was even jealous of my spasmodic intimacy with Edward VIII who occasionally telephoned to me.) In his cups the Duke talked of little else, and it was a mixture of abuse and love and *Schadenfreude*. Latterly he was also extremely unhappy and haunted by the tragic position of Prince Paul, his brother-in-law. Except for Queen Mary, who admired him, and to whom he was devoted, the Duke had no feelings for his other relatives. From her he inherited his love of collecting, his artistic bent and his methodical habits of correspondence. He liked writing letters,

1 Nervous twitches.
2 Degenerate.

which he always answered punctually, in his beautiful handwriting. He actively disliked the King, and more particularly the Queen. He said that they were little more than civic functionaries now and was sarcastic about her to anyone who would listen, calling her 'grinning Liz'. Although since the abdication crisis they were rather more intimate, he secretly resented her non-royal origin. Once he said to me, 'Do you know what Bertie does with his money? Why, he invests it!', and his high voice trembled with scorn. The Gloucesters, he thought, hopeless bores, and his sister, the Princess Royal, a somewhat pathetic turn. The more remote relatives were a constant target for his gibes and eighteenth-century malice . . . . He was flirtatious in manner and in his conversation which was always good and stimulating. He could never hide his deep and infinite desire to please and to carp. Probably he felt frustrated and cramped in his position. He hated Alec Hardinge, whom he accused of trying to poison the King against him. He said that he was not given sufficient scope for his latent and many gifts . . . He proposed himself recently to lunch with old and dying Mrs Greville (I was present). Next day he attacked her soundly in my hearing, and did not add that he had sent her a pair of white satin cushions on that very morning, which I knew to be a fact. He had many weaknesses and peculiarities: he drank to excess during the long pre-dinner interval, usually gin and fruit mixtures; at dinner and afterwards he drank nothing at all. He gave a somewhat effeminate impression by his furious knitting, his too many bracelets and rings. He was wildly extravagant in his purchases, lavish with his presents, but shrewd with finance generally. Often he exchanged or sold or passed on presents that had been given to him. Sometimes he would select his Xmas presents and send me the bill afterwards: it was the safest course.

Devoted to his attractive children, particularly to little Alexandra, to his dogs, he was often embarrassingly querulous – less so, of late – with the Duchess who idolised him. His brain was quicker, better-informed and more instinctive than hers. Somewhat out of focus for this prosaic age, he was nevertheless extremely popular and had a Perrault[1] quality for the people at large which is lacking in other members of his family. The Duke's sad and dramatic death is the end of an epoch: London and life will be more colourless and less gay without him, that elaborate, eager, excited elf. And I shall miss his gossip, his maniacal laugh, his rich presents, his haunting personality, coral and lapis.

MONDAY 7TH SEPTEMBER   *PYRFORD*

Wrote letters naked on the terrace at Pyrford in the warm sunlight. All night planes buzzed on high; probably American flying fortresses setting forth on bombing expeditions.

---

1 Charles Perrault (1628–1703) was a French author credited with the invention of the fairy tale in its modern form, developing them from predominantly rural tales.

My in-laws delightful – told many quaint tales of the old Lord Halifax; and of the wickedness and eccentricities of the half-demented present Lady Onslow[1] who rang up in the middle of the conversation.

My in-laws so sweet and affectionate that I was much touched; and left them with regret. Masses of correspondences, the MP's cross, awaited me.

Michael Parker arrived for the night . . . . intelligent, gay and provocative and acquiescent – an extraordinary child and very devoted to me. I took him to dine with Nicholas Lawford at the Allies Club, which is an amusing locale but ill-run; it won't last unless the committee are more far-sighted. At the moment Buck De La Warr and Mrs Churchill are the leading spirits in it. Natasha was dining with . . . . Alastair Connaught, who tells me that he is going to Canada as ADC to his cousins, the Athlones. They all came back here, after listening to a nostalgic French programme of songs. Imitated Laval and other French politicians.

Harold is becoming difficult . . . . he is rude to Michael Parker.

TUESDAY 8TH SEPTEMBER

Parliament reassembled and was unusually crowded. Many members were dressed in black, and black ties were everywhere to be seen! Motions slowly rolled on until noon when the Prime Minister rose. Contrary to my expectations he had no reception. He first moved votes of condolences and sympathy to the King and to the Duchess of Kent in their loss; and then proceeded to give his war résumé. He fairly plunged into it. I watched the House . . . Clemmie Churchill was in the gallery with Pam, who was dressed in WVS uniform. Diana Sandys was in another gallery. Randolph, horrible to look upon, was in mufti. The new reigning family, I fear! Winston proceeded without either fireworks or interruptions to give a pedestrian account of his journeys and junketings. He seemed fit, full of vim and vigour, and perhaps a touch surprised by his tepid reception and the lukewarm interest of his audience. He always expects to captivate the House, and never does, although he usually dominates or terrorises it. Many people hate him. I have a deep and bitter loathing of him which dates from many years; yet I see his great and many qualities: but he remains a selfish, paranoidical [*sic*] old ape, charmless, arrogant, grumpy, disagreeable, bullying, irritating, indeed infuriating . . . He spoke for just under an hour; but before the end many members left the Chamber, an unprecedented occurrence . . . I ran into the whole family. Pam smiled, so did Clemmie, but coldly, I thought. I used to like her so much, and lent her Honor's tiara on several occasions to wear. Squabbling and general rudeness. I was revolted, but rather pleased that Cripps should be rebuked by the entire House for his injudicious castigation of absent members yesterday. He is increasingly

1 Lady Iveagh's sister-in-law, wife of the 5th Earl Onslow: see Vol. I, entry for 1 September 1935 and footnote.

unpopular. I returned here and worked. Miss Fox called and spent an hour with me gossiping about the despondent Duchess and Princess Olga's possible return. Then Michael Parker looked in. This weak but enchanting Pierrot is having an affair with an Austrian countess, who was formerly his father's mistress.

Had a dinner party: Helen Fitzgerald, Harold, Adrian and Olive Baillie and Sir William Wiseman,[1] a somewhat mysterious baronet who looks a Jew. He was 'high up' in the secret service during the last war.

The Archduke borrowed my top hat to wear at the Duke of Kent's memorial service.

THURSDAY 10TH SEPTEMBER

Sent letters and a book to my child by Sir William Wiseman who flies over tomorrow.

Alan and I attended the general meeting of the Guinness Brewery. I stayed on to luncheon.

Alan rang up the Admiralty about Michael Parker and was privately told that reports about him are <u>appalling</u>. Poor boy.

Alan and I attended a crowded meeting addressed by Sam Hoare. He was glad to see me, and very friendly. He is whiter and aged, but still infamous and gave an encouraging account of his ambassadorial activities. Only once did he refer to Lady Maud! I cut Jim Wedderburn, or perhaps he cut me! He recently proposed himself for a weekend with Honor. He is the only friend of mine who has done so. <u>All</u> London society has come here; only he has gone to her. An announcement has been made that he goes to China soon on a goodwill mission. And yet he is more than mad. Once he loved me.

Dined alone: all my affairs seem to be improving, certainly financially, and yet I am in a fiendish mood.

I fear that I have upset the abbot-cart at Buckfast. He has come again to London, and dodges my footsteps . . .

FRIDAY 11TH SEPTEMBER   *LEEDS CASTLE*

To the House where the Indian situation was being debated. The PM made a brief statement. The House is 'bothery' and has not had sufficient holiday. Long talks with Bill Astor, just returned from Syria, and others. Chatted coldly with Jim Wedderburn early this morning, snapped at Harold who is becoming pompous

---

1 William George Eden Wiseman (1885–1962) succeeded his father as 10th Bt in 1893. He had a successful career as a banker and was a territorial soldier before the Great War, in which he served as lieutenant colonel. After being seriously wounded he moved to military intelligence, and set up the Secret Intelligence Service's office in the United States, and became a liaison officer between President Wilson and the British government.

and inconsiderate. Last night I took castor oil and today feel thinner. But I am unwell.

Drove here with Olive Baillie, my non-witted, tender-hearted, blue-eyed hostess. Her very young curiously attractive sister, Enid Paget,[1] aged 19, and looking like a tired Velázquez infanta, attracts me very much. The young Warwicks[2] are also here, and her adoration of this somewhat swashbuckling debonair young man is pleasing and nostalgic to see.

SATURDAY 12TH SEPTEMBER

Fulke Warwick attacked his uncle, Anthony Eden: says that if AE ever became Prime Minister it would be a disaster. All the Eden family, including his own mother, he says, are unstable, more than mad. Anthony barely speaks to him when they meet.

I am much struck by the hauteur beauty of Enid Paget. What a triumph for old Lord Queenborough, to have produced her at the advanced age of 62. There is even a younger one.[3]

SUNDAY 13TH SEPTEMBER   LEEDS CASTLE

A strange set-up here, really. The major part of the castle is a hospital full of wounded officers, nice, brown young men who limp and play croquet and watch the private wing, retained for the Baillies, and the guests with interested amusement. Spent the day amusing the Archduke Robert, whom I invited here for the weekend. Long talk about Stendhal with Geoffrey Lloyd. I like him almost more than anybody I know.

In a few days' time Princess Olga will be here: it was remarkably secretly arranged. Geoffrey Lloyd, although 40, has the brown lithe body of a beautiful boy. Donatello.[4] His mind is brightly polished and informed, yet playful and provocative. He reads for some hours every day, Stendhal and Tolstoy.

1 Enid Louise Paget (b.1923), second daughter of the second marriage of the 1st Baron Queenborough (qv) to Edith Starr Miller (1887–1933). She married, in 1947, Roland, marquis Paulze d'Ivoy de la Poype (1920–2012).

2 Charles Guy Fulke Greville (1911–84) was by courtesy Lord Brooke from 1924 to 1928 when he succeeded his father as 7th Earl of Warwick. In the 1930s he had been an actor in Hollywood under the name Michael Brooke, notably with a leading role in *Dawn Patrol* in 1938, which starred David Niven and Errol Flynn. He had married for a second time, in February 1942, Mary Kathleen Bell (*née* Hopkinson) (1916–82); they divorced in 1949.

3 Cicilie Carol Paget (b.1928).

4 Donatello di Niccolò di Betto Bardi (1386–1466) was a leading sculptor of the Italian Renaissance.

TUESDAY 15TH SEPTEMBER

Early this morning I heard that Mrs Greville had died in the night. Faded out after a stroke on Saturday night from which she never fully recovered consciousness – a cruel blow . . . Only Victor Bruntisfield[1] and Osbert Sitwell, her two most devoted adherents, were with her . . . Again an epoch ends, for with her death the Edwardian regime definitely closes. She stood for grandeur, the magnificence of the Empire, kings and splendour. Never beautiful until her extreme old age, and never amorous she nevertheless was surrounded all her life by male adorers of all ages who were fascinated by her raillery and pulverising conversation, her eminent social position, which she had created for herself, and her vast wealth, which she inherited and lavished on her many friends. She was a staunch and stout ally and a ferocious enemy. Her tongue was the most mordant I knew; she could annihilate anybody with a sentence – 'Dear little Lady Cunard. I am always telling Queen Mary that she isn't nearly as bad as she is painted!' Her malice was magnificent; her judgement shrewd . . . . her loyalty unquestioned; her fascination immense. She inspired even more hostility than desolation, for necessity the number of people she snubbed or ignored was greater than the circle of intimates. The Empress Catherine without her sexual tastes, Madame du Deffand without her literary qualities, she was really an eighteenth-century character transplanted into the Edwardian era. She was alleged to be the illegitimate daughter of a cook. Who knows? She was both Everyman and *une grande dame*. She expected to be treated as an empress, and was everywhere she went . . . I am depressed, indeed. This world is fading . . . will she leave her vast wealth to the various queens who were really her ladies-in-waiting? They think so; but I rather imagine not . . . and she mocked at the world she loved and dominated for so long.

Lunched at the Spanish Embassy . . . . Sir Edward Peacock;[2] Mr [James] Garvin, 80,[3] garrulous and staggeringly intelligent. A mammoth man of shining granite, and prodigious memory; Sir Stephen Gaselee! The Duke of Alba[4] is a courtier, a conversationalist and a connoisseur. He has been ill, and is still subject to fits of giddiness, he must be over 60,[5] lovemaking has exacted its toll, and he has been the *amant*[6] of so many duchesses in different countries. Rich food, good talk – an entrancing meal. Esmond Rothermere was the only

1 Victor Warrender. See entry for 10 September 1939 and footnote.
2 Edward Robert Peacock (1871–1961) was a Canadian merchant banker who acted as a liaison man between the United States government and the Bank of England during the war. He was also Receiver-General of the Duchy of Cornwall, for which he was knighted in 1934.
3 He was 74.
4 The Ambassador.
5 He was 63.
6 Lover.

'younger' guest, and he seemed pale and depressed. All London now knows the astonishing development in his private life. Ann O'Neill, after being his mistress for seven years, has at length persuaded her husband to divorce her, so that she might regularise her position by becoming Lady Rothermere! The divorce was all but completed: the guilty couple talked of it and accepted congratulations. And now Ann has suddenly and dramatically returned to her husband: the divorce is off; and Esmond is deserted – but only temporarily, I think, for Ann will try and get him back and have the best of both worlds as she has done these many years. She is a universal minx, but a most attractive, gay and disarming one. She is so affectionate, witty and loveable!

Crossed the square, I found Michael Parker waiting for me. My private little Sinbad, he is a mass of charm, feckless [illegible] and cultivated intelligence – and absolutely devoted to me. Some curious coincidence always brings a letter from Peter at the moment Michael flits into my life. And a fat, colourful Delhi budget was here, which waited until after Michael's departure, to devour. He has gone to Aberdeen to join a Free *Grenouilles*'[1] ship – we hope at least – as a liaison officer. I managed to get rid of him just before Diana Cooper arrived with her son John Julius to stay here. She is so cool, calm, adorable and classically loveable – she is the Supreme Companion No. 2, and often reminds me of Peter. Her wit and touch on life is similar, and so is her epidermic texture, which plays so powerful a role in attraction and friendship. John Julius is the nicest lad, next to my own, that I know. Fair, funny, gay, he is like an old man playing a boy's part . . . I gave them, and also Marjorie Anglesey,[2] who is still delightful, still seductive, tea. Duff dropped in. He is gentle now and in a swoon of life for his son, who is the passion of his selfish life, just as he is Diana's. They took the boy, whose 13th birthday it is, to a play. I awaited them here and we all had a candlelit supper together afterwards. Helen Fitzgerald and Harold joined us. Both Diana and Helen read out most depressed letters from Emerald Cunard, who with shingles and forsaken by her wicked old lover, Thomas Beecham, is alone and wretched in New York. John Julius stole up to bed; and when Diana and I went up some hours later we found him, not in his room, but in her bed – the great Napoleonic one which has seen so much history these five years. It is his last night as a little boy for tomorrow he goes to Herbert's[3] house at Eton. He was asleep, and looked a golden little angel with a seraphic smile. I was much moved, as I always am by sleeping children, and thought sadly, nostalgically of my own faraway lad . . .

---

1 Free French: *grenouille* is French for a frog.
2 Victoria Marjorie Harriet Manners (1883–1946), daughter of the 8th Duke of Rutland, married in 1912 the 6th Marquess of Anglesey (qv).
3 Mr Herbert, of whom I have failed to find further details, was manifestly to become John Julius Cooper's housemaster at Eton.

Princess Olga, accompanied by Lelia[1] Ralli, is flying across the jungle and will soon be here. It will be <u>wonderful</u>, and a godsend for the Duchess, that 'stricken and beautiful Princess', as Winston happily put it.

Daisy Fellowes is giving a farewell gala dinner party tonight for Walter Moyne who leaves on Friday to take up his new duties in the Middle East.

I talked to Helen F about Harold and she agrees that something ought to be done. He has been difficult – is already better – and impossible with everybody. He told me today that the flying boat *Clare* sank suddenly off Bathurst.[2] I am indeed sorry, it is the flying-ship in which I returned last year with Bob Menzies, and we, too, took off from Bathurst. The Captain, a most amiable, breezy Canadian called Musson,[3] has been drowned, with all the crew and passengers. The boat has simply disappeared but not, Harold is certain, from enemy action.

WEDNESDAY 16TH SEPTEMBER

Gossiped with Diana, and her dauphin and Duff. She remarked that it must be some comfort to me to know that all London society in a phalanx, all my old friends, have stood by me in my troubles. I wonder? . . . I walked to Boulestin's where I lunched with Perry Brownlow, who was most friendly. We talked of Honor; he is in no way on her side, but hinted that Kitty is so, as I thought and even hoped. He said that there had been gossip re finances – that I was still living in splendour, whereas Honor was 'pigging' it on a farm; but it was all long ago. I explained the situation to him and he was surprised to hear that Honor's yeoman was married and had a child. Honor had lied about this to Kitty, and pretended that he was free and single. She is quite unscrupulous. Diana thinks that she has always been feeble-minded, or perhaps has had a diseased mind. Came back in time to see the three Coopers leave in their ministerial car to Eton. John Julius was pleased, even gay about it, as was Diana, but Duff was sombre and testy.

THURSDAY 17TH SEPTEMBER

Caught up with my chores, wasted a delicious hour gossiping with Diana in her bedroom. She brought the minimum of luggage, which she packs herself, to the irritation of the servants. Then I fled to the Turkish bath, which I like better than anywhere else; and nothing so clears the brain, just as it cleanses the pores! Diana returned to Bognor, and the Imperial pints[4] arrived to stay. A most domesticated

---

1 As he often spells her name: it was Lilia.
2 A Short S.30 'C' Class flying boat, it caught fire on 14 September shortly after leaving Bathurst, heading for Lisbon *en route* to Poole. There were nineteen fatalities.
3 The captain of the flying boat to whom Channon refers on 18 February 1941 was named May, not Musson.
4 His nickname for this scion of the Russian Imperial family and his wife.

and lovesick couple are my Maimie and Vsevolod. They dined in and I collected Georgia and Sachie Sitwell; Lord and Lady Warwick; and Leslie Hore-Belisha to meet them. A gay impromptu party which was later joined by Harold, who is busy being charming and courts me with presents! My guests stayed too late – 1.30 a.m.

Osbert Sitwell telephoned and hinted that I ought to go to Mrs Ronnie's funeral tomorrow. I want to have an axis with Osbert; unfortunately he is *casé*[1] with David Horner,[2] an *amitié amoureuse*[3] which has persisted for fifteen years.

Princess Olga has actually arrived at Coppins. The Duchess of Kent rang me up and I talked to them both. It is a blissful reunion. I go there on Saturday.

A wonderful letter written in his own clear hand has come from General Wavell, my hero.

FRIDAY 18TH SEPTEMBER

Went for a walk with Osbert Sitwell, and then went to lunch with Leslie Hore-Belisha in his attractive but bad-taste little house in Stafford Place – No. 16. It is heavy with books, portraits of his mother, and Wedgwood plaques. We drove in my little car to Bookham[4] church, arriving as the coffin was being carried in. The small church was not crowded; and it was a motley assortment of people who came. Eric Miéville representing the King; Lord and Lady Simon; Sir John and Lady Anderson, Jock in tears; Beaverbrook, unshaven, crying and looking wicked! What a malevolent fellow he is! The Abingdons[5] and others. Peggy Crewe[6] looked seductive and whispered to me, 'I hear you corrupted the Abbot in the monastery and taught him to smoke cigarettes.' John Anderson gave Leslie and me a lift from the Bookham church to Polesden and we stood in awed silence around the opened grave in the garden. Gargoyles in the walls seemed to mock us. It was a very beautiful afternoon and I thought of how often Mrs Ronnie had looked out on that view. The butler collapsed, the other servants wept; so did we all. And afterwards we trooped in the house to a melancholy tea party. The hospitable but hideous house saw us for the last time; it has been left to the Nation, generously endowed, and will become a kind of country Kenwood – a Surrey Villa Mansion. I was quite miserable all day. Another epoch has ended. Indeed I have lost two of my most intimate friends within a month. Leslie and I stopped at his

---

1 In a relationship.
2 David Stuart Horner (1900–83) wrote detective novels and was for decades the lover and companion of Osbert Sitwell.
3 Love affair.
4 Great Bookham, in Surrey, was the parish in which Polesden Lacey, Mrs Greville's house, was situated.
5 Montagu Henry Edmund Cecil Towneley-Bertie (1887–1963), by courtesy Lord Norreys from 1919 to 1928, when he succeeded his grandfather as 8th Earl of Abingdon, married in 1928 Elizabeth Valetta 'Bettine' Montagu-Stuart-Wortley (1896–1978).
6 See entry for 20 June 1939 and footnote.

Wimbledon villa, Warren Farm. It is attractive, but could be more so. It reminds me of Fontainebleau with the rides and glades.

On my return to No. 5 I found two rather dashing young American airmen drinking with Harold! They had just arrived from San Francisco, and had been lunching with the Churchills at Chequers! From California to Chequers in thirty-six hours is a feat. Harold had brought them over for the purpose! They had a quick drink, and after I had asked them about Peter in Moscow – they remembered him quite well – Harold bundled them in his ministerial car and they returned to Chequers to dine and sleep. The Prime Minister, apparently, insisted that they should. He was graciousness itself.

Dined in with Maimie, Vsevolod and Patsy – Alan is still at sea somewhere.

I hear that Eloise Ancaster is dying[1] and doped at Prince's Hotel at Hove. A lecherous woman, she had charm and point. One by one the hostesses of my youth have faded out or died. Leslie Hore-Belisha said much the same to the Belgian Ambassador. 'All the great houses are finished!' 'There is only Chips left,' His Excellency smilingly replied.

SATURDAY 19TH SEPTEMBER

I have found this diary, temporarily mislaid, and will resume writing in it.[2]

Woke refreshed after a long night, and breakfasted on the Imperial Russian bed containing Maimie and Vsevolod of Russia – my Napoleonic bed which came from the Borghese collection in the British Embassy in Paris. Whether Napoleon ever slept in it, as I believe he did, it has seen much life and turmoil and history since it has been in my possession!

Leslie Hore-Belisha rang up to say 'goodbye!' He returns to his Cistercian monastery near Leicester today for a further 'cure'.

I drove to Coppins; Mary Herbert and Zoia in deep black received me; the butler seemed sad; 'Muffy' the char was disconsolate, for it was to have been today that the Duke of Kent was due to return from Iceland. In a few moments the two sisters drove up, on their return from Windsor. They have spent yesterday with the King, and again today . . . I was ushered into the Duchess's little sitting room, and there they were, beautiful, tragic, still lovely and glamorous. We all half-wept. The Duchess looked pale and plump, and was rather gayer than I had expected. Her sister's return has been a tonic to her. Princess Olga immediately took over the conversation, and in dull, sad tones, talked to me for three hours, interrupted only by the arrival and departure of the tea things! She first recounted her adventurous trip across the desert and the jungle . . . and how she had been sitting with Paul in their hated house when the gubernatorial messenger arrived in a grand car

---

1 Her death was manifestly protracted: it happened in 1953.
2 He refers to the foolscap exercise book he had been writing in until late August.

bearing her an invitation from His Majesty the King to come to England! It was a miracle. A sort of answered prayer. Paul immediately said 'Of course you must go!' She hesitated and replied that she could only decide on the following day. All that evening they debated whether she should leave him in that lonely, forsaken place with only natives, servants for companions . . . The house is horrible, isolated and surrounded by wild animals, roaring hippos, etc. A Piero di Cosimo[1] background . . . next day they drove into Nairobi, took leave of Alexander,[2] who has joined the RAF, and made arrangements for her fantastic flight. She was accompanied by Lelia Ralli. One annoying week over desert and jungle, sleeping in government houses, received royally by governors, staying in their palaces, and, *enfin*, they arrived in England. She is still tired, startled and discouraged. Her stories of the horrible humiliations to which they have been subjected were heartbreaking. My poor Paul is a broken man – ill in body, crushed in mind. He only wants to die; but is kept alive by a burning sense of injustice. His conscience is completely clear; he thinks that he took the only possible course and that history will vindicate him . . . as I have always said . . . now and then she digressed to talk of her family and several times I made them laugh – my Duchess looked so lovely, and so sad; but better than I had dared to hope! She roared with hysterical laughter once or twice, and was so sweet and affectionate to me. I was infinitely touched by their sweetness, and actually she the less tragic of the two. Princess Olga has somehow deepened, is broader, and more human than she was; but traces of her royal, abrupt manner remain. I left the house of mourning with regret, much *attendri* and depressed. My poor, aching, lonely Paul, how I long for him . . . drove back to London, where I found a fascinating letter from Peter from Delhi.

Lelia Ralli, Cecil Beaton and Alice Harding dined as well as Harold and 'The Russians'! Harold was full of Chequers from where he had just returned. Winston was in his most gracious mood, and charming about both the sorrowing sisters. Harold sat up with him until 3 a.m. this morning discussing aeronautical matters long after the impressed pilots had gone to bed. Cecil Beaton, who is fast becoming the King Tabby Cat, was most malicious about everybody. A dull evening, I fear.

I long for the truth to come out about the ex-Regent. He will be vindicated. I tried and succeeded in poisoning Princess Olga's mind against that arch fiend Queen Mignonne. Maimie archly remarked that she[3] had had a letter of condolence from every member of the government she knew, except Anthony Eden, whom she had known – and disliked – for years. A strange and tactless omission on the part of the Foreign Secretary. The King has been considerate and charming. There

---

1 Piero di Cosimo (1462–1522) was a Renaissance Italian painter noted for his depictions of mythology.
2 Her and Prince Paul's son.
3 'She' appears to be referring to the Duchess of Kent.

is much excitement in Yugoslav circles over the unexpected arrival of Princess Olga. Queen M is almost apoplectic with rage, I hear.

Meanwhile, the days and weeks pass. The threatened 'big raids' have not yet begun again; nor has Stalingrad been occupied – nor Russia collapsed. What will happen, I do not attempt to prophesy.

SUNDAY 20TH SEPTEMBER   *KELVEDON*

Slept late . . . Diana Cooper rang up, inviting me to Bognor today, and Alan begged me to join him at Ramsgate. I hesitated and decided to come here for a 'let-down'. I must occasionally be alone. Kelvedon is melancholy. It is 'Bleak House', and for the first time I didn't love it, and didn't much want to live here without Peter . . . Finished *Le Rouge et [le] Noir*,[1] and wrote to P[eter], Jacqueline Lampson and my mother.

MONDAY 21ST SEPTEMBER

I drove up to London in the wet afternoon, after being desperately bored at Kelvedon. I feel frustrated, impotent . . . *désoeuvré* but in high spirits.

Stalingrad is somewhat of a mystery. The Russians seem to be putting up a terrific defence.

I have been thinking over some of Princess Olga's remarks; she is convinced that the *coup d'état* in Belgrade was no more than a Palace revolution on the part of some ambitious hot-heads, animated by treachery, ambition and communistic propaganda. It had nothing to do with pro-Allied sentiments, so she says. One of the ministers now in London, who goes about abusing the ex-Regent, said in her defence to Prince Paul in the Palace in Belgrade, 'If you go to war against the Germans, it will only be because you have a Greek wife.' The Yugoslavs are all villains . . . The tide is turning and the truth will one day come out.

TUESDAY 22ND SEPTEMBER   *PRINCE'S HOTEL, BRIGHTON*

I caught the four o'clock train to Brighton, where Alan was to have met me. But his convoy was late . . . however I was not stopped, and indeed, went for a long walk along the promenade and made some amusing *achats*.[2] . . . . The town is crowded with soldiers, sailors and airmen. Delicious air. Alan and I dined at Sweetings and then attended the first night of Beverley Baxter's war play *It Happened in September*.[3] It was very nearly a fine play – and will probably prove a success, if pruned.

1 A novel of 1830 by Stendhal.
2 Purchases.
3 Baxter was the Conservative MP for Wood Green. The play was not a success.

WEDNESDAY 23RD SEPTEMBER

Slept with Alan, and lay awake for a long time listening to the waves – and, alas, he snores! He rushed to his boat at seven o'clock, as I dressed leisurely. Then we came to London, and went with Patsy to St Martin's Church to attend a memorial service for Mrs Greville. It was crowded with ambassadors etc. I invited the Sitwells, Sachie and Georgia, and the Carisbrookes and the Lennox-Boyds to luncheon at Claridge's which was very crowded, but good food. Irene Carisbrooke, a great lady, very gentle and charming, was lovely and affectionate. Her silly drivelling husband Drino was as trivial and malicious as ever, nevertheless I quite like him . . . . we talked of Mrs Greville and of her famous *mots*. A few are worth recording: when Lady Chamberlain returned from Rome in early 1940, Mrs Ronnie remarked 'It is not the first time that Rome has been saved by a goose!' Apropos of another lady, she said 'I didn't follow people to their bedrooms, it is what they do outside them that matters!' . . . . Irene seemed to think that the monarchy would very shortly be restored in France,[1] and that her nephew's[2] coronation might take place even before Easter. She suggested that we all go to Madrid for it. Luncheon cost me £10 including tips and three bottles of Moselle. Exhausted I came home: people poured in, among them Sydney and Rab Butler – he was very gay; and danced in, coming on from a visit to Maisky: we all agreed that the Soviet Ambassador is a most crafty old fox, and no friend to this country.

Maimie and Vsevolod, Sachie Sitwell and Lady Dashwood[3] dined. I have always secretly liked this most unpopular woman and this evening she was charming. At one time she was so anti-Chamberlain (she is always anti-everybody) that I couldn't bear to see her. I described the memorial service to her, which she had not attended; all the familiar funeral faces were there and Grace Curzon looked extremely handsome, even young.

Vsevolod was delighted by Rab remarking that he prophesied the restoration of all monarchies after the war.

Bobbety Cranborne has been offered the Viceroyalty of India, but hesitates to accept because of his own and his wife's delicate health. If they go I shall record my reactions.

THURSDAY 24TH SEPTEMBER

Wrote letters and worked. The Russians have left after a most successful week. They and I are disturbed by strange tales of Natasha's eccentric sexual behaviour!

1 Thus in MS. He means Spain.
2 This was the Count of Barcelona, Juan Carlos Teresa Silverio Alfonso de Borbón y Battenberg (1913–93), whom his father Alfonso XIII had designated his heir, and had been pretender to the Spanish throne since 1941. However it was his son, also Juan Carlos, who became the next King of Spain in 1975.
3 See entry for 8 May 1940 and footnote.

Alan and I had a Turkish bath together; he then returned to Newhaven. I am well, if bored, and everyone says that I look handsome, which is something . . . George Gage, also dropped in for an hour's gossip, thinks that Cranborne [is] too ill to accept the huge plum offered him.

FRIDAY 25TH SEPTEMBER

A full moon last night, yet the Junkers did not come. It makes getting about much easier.

Lunched with Lady Kemsley at the Dorchester . . . . I escorted her afterwards to Cameo Corner where she spent several hundred pounds on jewels! I found a crumpled ten-shilling note in a taxi which I spent on drinks at the theatre where I went with Lelia Ralli, Alice Harding, Sidney Herbert, Juliet Duff . . . . The play was *Flare Path*,[1] a remarkable topical play about the Air Force. We dined afterwards at the Ivy, and I had two astonishing conversations. The first was with Lelia Ralli, who attacked the Poklewskis savagely; says that they are feathering their own nest, and are intriguing to get complete control of the Duchess . . . and that they have been ungracious (which I doubt) to Princess Olga etc. She hinted that they had 'gone over', or were over-[illegible] by the King and Queen. It is jealousy, and Zoia is really a better, saner influence than Lelia herself, who is too foreign, too Parisian for the English taste! I walked back with Sidney Herbert and he made some amazing admissions which I had never even expected!![2] Piccadilly was moonlit and crowded with tipsy Americans and soliciting sailors and airmen. A most vicious atmosphere. Sidney and I ran a gauntlet of imposturing [*sic*] military – what has come over London? I like Sidney Herbert more and more – and yet once, according to Honor, he was my enemy?

Olive Baillie invited me to Leeds, and Lady Kemsley to Farnham this weekend. I shall, however, go to Kelvedon as arranged. At least I think so.

Jim Wedderburn has sent me two brace of partridges from Scotland. Are they a peace offering? Shall I acknowledge or ignore them?

SATURDAY 26TH SEPTEMBER

Harold slept at a fighter command last night. It was a *volupté*[3] to have my own house to myself; but I put it to no use, other than to sleep alone. My dog was cross and unfriendly.

Lelia Ralli lunched alone with me at home, and I was immediately aware that she had come to attack Zoia Poklewska, whom she loathes. It is jealousy; and I

---

1 Written by Terence Rattigan, who would shortly become close to Channon: this is
  Channon's first mention of his work. The play was written in 1941.
2 Herbert was fundamentally homosexual.
3 Luxury.

am savvy that internecine strife has broken out at Chequers! She and L – Mrs Freeman and Mrs Masham[1] – are contending for the Duchess of Kent's favours and each wishes to rule the royal roost. Lelia finds herself somewhat supplanted and accuses GR [the King] of being pro-Pole and anti-Paul. She says that the whole family of Poklewskis are intriguing for position, power and money and are poisoning the Duchess! There may be just the touch of truth in all this, but I think it is exaggerated. However I am *bien*[2] with both sides. As we were talking the Duchess herself rang up and suggested that we go down to Coppins for tea and spend the afternoon. It seemed complicated with petrol and cars, and I reluctantly refused. Instead came here [Kelvedon] where I am cold and bored, I wish that I had accepted either of my weekend invitations to Leeds Castle, or to Farnham Royal. Kelvedon is lovely in warm weather, but cheerless and bleak in the autumnal fuel-less days. One must get used to shivering – it is only the 26th of September. I read all the evening, and thought too much about money. Am I really so material and mercenary? I am a mixture of my four grandparents and see all their qualities coming out in me at times.

Lelia repeated such charming things that the Regent had said of me, that I wept. He hoards all my letters, reads and rereads them. Lelia insists that I am, and have always been, the greatest thing in his life. He is moody, nervous, ill, and cannot concentrate for long, nor even hold a pen at times. He forgets his present position, harks back with bitterness, blames Eden, is terrified of Bolshevism etc. He is thin, almost white-headed and bald and pitiable. I can hardly bear to think of it . . . our glorious, glamorous, rich and powerful group is disintegrating, almost gone, and certainly shorn of power.

SUNDAY 27TH SEPTEMBER

I shivered all night, slept fitfully, and got up early and wrote a long letter to my hero, Archie Wavell. I am bored now, and have lost temporarily my power and enjoyment in being alone.

Must it always rain in Essex?[3] The eternal wet of the eastern counties! Only for a brief hour did the sun come out, and I fled to my woods . . . those woods where once I gambolled so happily with a Scotch nymph . . . and came on a herd of cows, trampling on the nettles. They must have strayed from some neighbouring farm.

---

1 A reference to an intrigue at the court of Queen Anne between the Duchess of Marlborough ('Mrs Freeman') and the Queen's dresser (Abigail Masham) who competed for the Queen's favour.
2 In good standing.
3 Essex is in fact the driest county in England, and was then.

The old Archbishop,[1] heaven knows, was foolish and wicked enough; but the new obese one[2] is positively dangerous! He now preaches socialism from a platform which he shares with Cripps! On the same day the fatuous Eden says that we are all revolutionaries now. Is England mad or doomed; or is it as well that the revolution should come from the top, rather than the bottom? Almost everything that I loved has disappeared in under three years. I have only my adorable dauphin, Peter, and a few other friends, my money and, as Cyrano[3] put it, '*mon panache*'![4]

MONDAY 28TH SEPTEMBER

All day at Southend listening to the grievances and difficulties of my constituents: it is like turning the pages of Balzac, their sufferings and dramas are poignant.

Drove back to London in the cold, wet and even fog. A dreary arrival, chores and cadging letters.

TUESDAY 29TH SEPTEMBER

Woke bristling with life and energy, and went to the House which I found restless, leaderless and uncertain. The PM, answering Questions, was received without enthusiasm. Lunched with Alan and Patsy at Claridge's where we saw all London. The King of Greece sulked with a book at a corner table. Patsy was in one of her difficult indignant moods which was quite understandable as she – so Alan later whispered to me – has just begun her third baby. She is enchanted really, as is Alan!

Diana Cooper arrived to stay with only a tiny handbag. She found Lelia Ralli and Rab sitting here, and we gossiped over cocktails for two hours. Lelia was most amusing and yet I was saddened by her accounts of my poor Paul languishing near Naivasha,[5] friendless, wretched and failing. Diana said that he must see himself as a galley slave, another Cervantes. She, George Gage, Cecil Beaton dined cosily,

---

1 Cosmo Gordon Lang, whom Channon had loathed since his remarks on the abdication, had retired the previous March. See entry for 22 February 1940 and footnote.

2 William Temple (1881–1944) was ordained in 1909 after several attempts, his ambition thwarted by his progressive religious views, but possibly also by his political ones. He was headmaster of Repton from 1910 to 1914, but felt unsuited to the work, and left to become incumbent of St James's, Piccadilly, and in 1919 a canon of Westminster Abbey. He joined the Labour Party in 1918. He became Bishop of Manchester in 1921, Archbishop of York in 1929, and was translated to Canterbury in 1942. He died of a heart attack after just over two years in the post. He had on 26 September addressed a Christian rally in London, demanding that the Church put itself fully behind a programme of social reform after the war.

3 Savinien de Cyrano de Bergerac (1619–55) was a French playwright, usually interpreted to modern times by the 1897 play *Cyrano de Bergerac* by Edmond Rostand.

4 'My style'.

5 A town in Kenya, around 50 miles north-west of Nairobi.

and we were joined by the mysterious and ubiquitous Colonel Palewski, and Harold. Gay, friendly, intimate evening which pleased Diana.

Regret having frolicked with Alan as he leaves me so exhausted.

The Randolph Churchills have parted with a view to a furtive divorce, which will be lengthy and complicated to arrange; as obviously Averell Harriman cannot be named as co-respondent. Pam Churchill loathes her bombastic, absurd, choleric, pimply consort; and I didn't blame her for that. How she even tolerated him for a night, I fail to understand. He is sad, down, dispirited, and discredited.

WEDNESDAY 30TH SEPTEMBER

Shopped with Alan, but felt like death. Drank at the House of Commons with Ben Smith[1] and Jay Llewellin, and then went to lunch with Lady Willingdon . . . . I was next to James Grigg, the *sournois* Secretary of State for War; but he unbent after I had turned my artillery on him (although I felt so ill). Said that he thought 'L[loyd] G[eorge]' the greatest man he had ever met; then he named eleven others . . . 'You have omitted the Prime Minister,' I said. He looked startled; and I gather there is little love lost between them. Probably he is for the high jump? He is devoted to Lady Willingdon. I walked home, went to bed, took my temperature, which is 101F. Natasha and Harold sat with me. I feel I am dying. But am happy for Alan! All goes well with him now. And he deserves it.

THURSDAY 1ST OCTOBER

Dr Law, my fascinating medico, says that I am not ill, really. So I got up, and gave lunch to George Gage (once more my shadow and my henchman), Maureen Dufferin and Diana Abdy. From my window I watched Princess Mary take the salute at a Red Cross review. She is the most ridiculous (and harmless!) woman in public life. Charmless, cross, stiff and square, her shyness makes her frigid, and she plays no part in contemporary life, social or otherwise. Her son, Lord Lascelles, has become involved in a romance: it seems that he met a young Jewess in a bus, made friends with her, and has escorted her frequently to dance halls and now wishes to marry her.[2] It has been explained to him that the descendants of George III cannot marry without the Sovereign's permission and that it would be withheld: so the precocious demi-royal is thwarted.

Maureen Dufferin very affectionate and sweet. Eddie Devonshire rang up to trace her! He is so very nice and likeable. Maureen admitted that he has

---

1 Benjamin Smith (1879–1964) was Labour MP for Rotherhithe from 1923 to 1931 and from 1935 to 1946. He was Minister of Food from 1945 to 1946, when he became Chairman of the West Midlands Coal Board. He was knighted in 1945.
2 This is probably a reference to Marion Stein (1926–2014), who married Lord Harewood (qv) (as he had by then become) in 1949. She later became Mrs Jeremy Thorpe.

refused India again and hinted that it was because of his love for her! He is madly infatuated with her and has been for some time.

Natasha Bagration and Lelia Ralli dropped in for drinks. Much Coppins talk! The Duchess of Kent is learning to use a typewriter and wants me to give her one for Christmas.

FRIDAY 2ND OCTOBER

Slept badly and woke worse. Had I been poisoned? Am I dying? Undoubtedly I am dull and dreary and *désoeuvré* and my famous light touch, once so fastidious and fascinating, has deserted me.

Half London telephoned me this morning: Duchess of Kent and Princess Olga, who are 'entertaining' Queen Mary this afternoon at Coppins, Cecil Beaton, Diana Cooper, Lady Kemsley and Peter Fleming,[1] who has just arrived from India and brings me fresh news of Peter Coats. Shall I make friends with him? Alan has left to join his old 'ma' at Callander.

A communication came from Honor, harmless and uninteresting in itself, the handwriting on the envelope was decidedly drunken and careless. Queer demented girl.

The bishops are interfering too much! Dr Blunt, Bishop of Bradford who brought about the abdication, now advocates a revolution.

The day, as I idled and tried to recover from my recent ridiculous indisposition – its cause too shaming for me to chronicle even here – was long. For the first time in my life I was bored. Bored by people; bored without them. I walked to dine with the Russians; their house is dirty, slugs and toothpicks, and my stomach rises, yet I love them. Leslie Hore-Belisha, recently returned from his second retreat, was in high spirits; he is beginning to resemble Louis XVI in appearance.

I fled into the night. The walk back seemed fraught with danger as there were so many drunks and male prostitutes about; and many pedestrians have been attacked and robbed.

I hear that Cripps is leaving the government and will lead a small party of '*frondeurs*';[2] but he has no support or following.

---

1 Robert Peter Fleming (1907–71), the elder brother of Ian Fleming (qv), had made a name for himself before the war as a travel writer in Brazil and Central Asia. On the reserve of the Grenadier Guards when war broke out, Fleming became a specialist in military deception operations in South East Asia, based in Delhi. He married, in 1935, Celia Johnson (1908–82), the actress most famous for her starring roles in *This Happy Breed* (1944) and *Brief Encounter* (1945). She was awarded the DBE in 1981.

2 Rebels. Cripps was not leaving the government, but he did on 22 November move from being Leader of the Commons to become Minister of Aircraft Production.

SUNDAY 4TH OCTOBER

Harold and I dined opposite each other last night, and feeling tired and down went early to bed ... this morning I awoke with a temperature of 99 or so, and my throat feels weak.

It is frightful the tragedy of the Sussex school near Petworth where twenty-six boys were killed by a stray bomb.[1] Sussex sounded and seemed so safe and secure.

My temperature goes up and down and I have decided to go to Coppins *quand même*.[2]

My agents tell me that P. J. Grigg is going the Margesson way; that there is a cabal against him, and that pressure is being brought upon the Prime Minister to dismiss him; already their honeymoon is at an end. In fact, I smell a reshuffle when Parliament is dissolved, or more probably during the short recess. With Cripps and Grigg both out of the government, drastic moves and changes will be necessary.

Just before one o'clock the Duchess of Kent, Princess Olga and Lelia Ralli came here and fetched me. They were using the magnificent black Rolls-Royce which the Duke had ordered for their Australian reign.[3] The Duchess has decided to make use of it on 'grand' occasions. We drove to Coppins, and they were childishly pleased with the chocolates which I gave them (I had bought them yesterday with my monthly ration). I sat with Field, the chauffeur, who praised the Duke all the way down. He had been with him for fifteen years, and seems touchingly devoted to the widowed Duchess. I found her *déjà un peu élargie*[4] – more poise and self-assurance than ever before. I somehow half-suspect that she isn't quite as miserable as she thinks: widows rarely are. At Coppins I noticed a few small changes, but the general atmosphere and even the food were as the Duke would have liked it ... We discussed the eternal problem of Paul. Princess Olga is broken by it all; but she is lovely and charming and loyal. She says that most of the stories are libels and lies; the *coup d'état*, far from being Yugoslavia finding its soul, was a Palace revolution organised from the lowest motives of self-interest by a crowd of opportunists, traitors and adventurers! Even King Peter had begged them to take him with them to Athens, but Paul had insisted that his duty to his country and dynasty demanded that he remain behind in Belgrade. Paul's whole behaviour had been scrupulously correct all along .... the

---

1 As part of the Luftwaffe's strategy of destroying Britain's heritage, a lone Heinkel 111 sought to drop three bombs on Petworth House on 29 September 1942. He missed his target, but one bomb, having ricocheted off a tree, hit the town's boys' school and killed the headmaster, a schoolmistress and twenty-eight boys.
2 Nonetheless.
3 For his governor-generalship, cancelled when war broke out.
4 Already a little more expanded – not in the physical sense, but in terms of coming out of her grief.

young King, after asking the advice of both the kings of England and Greece, has made a sign of life; and is lunching with them on Tuesday. It will be a difficult meeting . . . and I wonder whether the weak noodle will not run out when the day comes? He has behaved so shabbily about money and everything else! He is an unliked little skunk, if ever there was one! Princess Olga is much wounded by their behaviour and contrasts it with the attitude of the English royal family. We all attacked Alec Hardinge. The King of Greece had invited the sisters to lunch with him in his suite at Claridge's but they had refused because of me. We gossiped much, and I regret that I was not much more amusing. I gave Princess Olga a Victorian bracelet of gold and garnets as a Xmas present; and she was touched. I really love her.

The car drove me into Windsor where I caught a crowded train back; how ugly are the *hoi polloi*!! I still feel ill and think I have some suppressed 'bug'. Dined with Maimie and Vsevolod at the Ritz.

I held Prince Michael who gaped at me with his father's blue eyes; he is a quiet, grave, pretty baby very like his father's family.

I am re-reading Molière.[1]

MONDAY 5TH OCTOBER

Harold has given me a basket of hydrangeas, seven partridges, a brace of pheasants and some vegetables; all of which will be useful additions to my larder. We had a dinner party consisting incredibly enough of Leonard Brockington,[2] the Canadian KC who is a well-known broadcaster (he is an intelligent sandy-haired man, stooped and a challenging incarnation; he reminded me of old Mr Garvin) . . . . Diane Abdy, who I thought would fascinate Rab, but didn't; Harold; Rab and Sydney Butler, who are both staying with me; and Jim Wedderburn, who rang up and proposed himself. He has not been with me for months and I mean to speak sharply to him about his visits to Honor at Shalden Farm. Dinner was a success; and later I sat up for some time with the Butlers gossiping: it is obvious that they have high hopes of going to India; certainly their name is on the shortlist for the Viceroyal stakes. Rab hankers for it, but fears that he might miss the premiership by becoming a peer! It is doubtful, however, whether, as he said, Winston would ever offer him so important a post.

---

1 Jean-Baptiste Poquelin (1622–73) took the name Molière when he was a strolling player in the 1640s and went on to become one of France's, and the world's, greatest playwrights. He is best remembered now for *Tartuffe* (1664), *Le Misanthrope* (1666) and *Le Bourgeois gentilhomme* (1670).

2 Leonard Walter Brockington (1888–1966) was born in Wales but emigrated to Canada in 1912, where he became a distinguished lawyer. From 1936 to 1939 he was the first president of the Canadian Broadcasting Corporation. He was adviser on Commonwealth affairs to the Ministry of Information from 1942 to 1943.

Winston is an elephant and the only lapses or slights he ever forgets or forgives are his own! Rab put me to bed: he is ageing, he is nearly bald, he is inelegant, but very charming and gay and cautious.

Peter Fleming and his wife, the actress, Celia Johnson, dropped in for drinks. He has just got back from Delhi where he is attached to Wavell's staff. He is dark, dull, handsome, and has an attractive silent masculine manner. It is obvious that his wife adores him (Imogen Gage was once much in love with him, too). He gave me news of Peter; they see each other constantly, and I gather that Peter is bored but busy in Delhi.

Tuesday 6th October

Rab sat on my bed as I dressed, and were soon joined by Harold: the *lever de Chips*![1] I went to the House of Commons which I thought in an odd mood. Winston looked surly and disgruntled and answered rather brusquely embarrassing questions about Stalin's recent pronouncement.[2]

My mother and father-in-law lunched and were charming. Their visit to Eire had been a success; they had invited de Valera,[3] whom they call 'the antique shop'! (because his Irish title sounds like that), to luncheon at the brewery, which he had never visited. He came accompanied by Mr Walshe,[4] his Minister for External Affairs, and was most agreeable, even attractive; he made polite conversation to Lady Iveagh and to Elizabeth Elveden and was afterward conducted over the brewery! They returned a few days ago. Lady I . . . was bitter about Honor; and funny about her second daughter, Patsy, and her new pregnancy. We call her 'Bunny Boyd' . . . . . Then to the 1922 Committee which surpassed itself in fatuity.

Jim Wedderburn came to see me, and we spent an hour together, I found him less mad than usual, yet I wonder whether he's sane enough to get to China? He leaves tomorrow morning by clipper . . . . on a goodwill mission . . . . He was contrite about his weekend at Shalden; says that Honor wrote and invited him, and that he had no idea that I would object, and resent it. He is so mad that I suspect he is telling the truth! I parted from him affectionately, after lending him an overcoat and two suitcases . . . he is melancholy, detached and more than mad.

---

1 He mocks the ritual of the monarch rising and dressing in the *ancien régime* in France.

2 One of Stalin's many complaints about the Allies' refusal to open up a second front in the West.

3 Éamon de Valera was Taoiseach, or Prime Minister, of Ireland three times between 1937 and 1959, and President of Ireland from 1959 to 1973.*

4 Joseph Walshe (1886–1956) was Secretary of the Department of External Affairs from 1923 to 1946, the equivalent of the Permanent Under Secretary of the British Foreign Office. He was an official and not a minister; the ministerial duties were discharged by de Valera.

Rab, Sydney and I went to see *Flare Path*. The author, Rattigan,[1] was at Cambridge with my future Viceroy! There were seven MPs in the audience; the foyer was like the 'Aye' lobby. We walked in the blackout to Pastois where Rab gave us an excellent supper. Charlie Londonderry joined us for a bit and was amusing about his house, [which] had been recently searched by prying Food Office Officials. Lelia Ralli and the Caccias were at a nearby table. Mrs Caccia has a sharp tongue! Rab and I joined them for a time which resulted in Sydney being left alone, and a marital tiff ensued in the car. They made it up later – Rab put me to bed.

WEDNESDAY 7TH OCTOBER

The Butlers left this afternoon as I had Diana Cooper coming to stay. Rab wanted to remain. He sat on my clothes this morning, delayed my dressing as we discussed the Indian deadlock and his viceregal ambitions. Harold Balfour came in as did Jim Wedderburn, again, whose plane had been held up for a day. I like dressing surrounded by ministers and felt like Catherine the Great.[2] At length to the House, after disposing of Jim, which took three hours. He came shopping with me and I sent out to Peter, a gold cigar-lighter, and a photograph of the Gunn portrait; whilst to Jacqueline Lampson I sent a tiny Cartier brooch. Will Jim ever deliver them? I much doubt it!

At 4.30 I fetched Leslie Hore-Belisha to go to a Free French concert: he is maddeningly unpunctual and kept me waiting for an hour whilst he changed, signed letters, drank tea and fussed. Then we picked up Violet Trefusis, who had asked us to be ready at five. She kept us waiting too. It was nearly seven before we arrived, and the French fête was almost finishing. I had an ovation when we arrived; everybody rushed to me and I felt that glow which comes from fashion's favour. Joyce Brittain-Jones, much improved in looks, was selling programmes. She was friendly but I shan't take any steps *envers elle et le roi Timon*[3] until they invite me to something, which will be never as they are mean and don't entertain. I like the King of Greece but cannot be bothered to take trouble over him as I did last year! . . . Diana, as lovely and fascinating as ever, and I walked in the

---

1 Terence Mervyn Rattigan (1911–77) became one of the most celebrated British playwrights of the mid-twentieth century, with a string of successes including *The Winslow Boy*, *The Browning Version*, *The Deep Blue Sea* and *Separate Tables*. Many of his plays were filmed, and he wrote a number of successful screenplays, one of which, based on *Flare Path*, was *The Way to the Stars* (1945). He was an unhappy, bibulous homosexual and much of his writing reflects his internal turmoils. He was not at Cambridge with Butler: he was nine years younger, and was educated at Trinity College, Oxford. He and Channon would become exceptionally close.

2 Coats has crossed this out in the MS and, one presumes for consistency, written 'Louis XIV'.

3 Towards her and King George.

wet blackout to dine with Leslie H-B. Violet Trefusis was there; food excellent and Violet's stories as outrageous and as apocryphal as always. Still she is always amusing, but her appearance is now grotesque, and her inaccuracy too fantastic. Diana loved the evening but hated her! Leslie Hore-Belisha was full of his luncheon with Randolph Churchill, which was of gargantuan proportions. Randolph has managed to get out of the army and spends his days overeating and drinking at White's Club. He looks fifty . . . Rab rang me three times and I transmitted the political news and lobby chatter to him. Robert Cary thinks that I should reign in Madras, and should succeed Arthur Hope.[1]

Much political chatter. Robert Cary thinks that Rab will be either Viceroy or Secretary of State for India before Christmas. Cripps is believed to have become ~~temporarily~~ [sic] reconciled to remaining in the government, temporarily at least. Edgar Granville says that we shall have a Conservative government in January, that Labour, all except Attlee and Bevin – will drop out. I trust so: a division in the Labour Party would play into our hands. I also attended another meeting of the 1922 Committee. Anthony Eden had a rough ride, was much criticised and even hooted! . . . I was enchanted, indeed. After an acrimonious discussion, Oliver Lyttelton addressed the crowded meeting. He was inaudible and irrelevant and had a poor reception. It was an astonishingly bad speech. If Hitler could overhear our discussions I fear he would smile. Everything is so unreal and irrelevant and fatuous.

Full day, ending with unjustified flashes of irritation against Harold Balfour for his rigid, bourgeois refusal even to help people procure places in the clipper.[2] Princess Olga telephoned early this morning to say that King Peter had spent the day with her yesterday: That at first he had been shy and embarrassed but had melted. She had managed him; but it had been sad and nostalgic for her. He ended by asking affectionately for 'his uncle Paul'! The weakling.

THURSDAY 8TH OCTOBER

Breakfast with Diana who slept in the Great Napoleonic bed where the Butlers gambolled last night. Then I walked to the local Figaro in Knightsbridge to have my hair cut, and returned home to await my little luncheon party which was most successful. Maimie and Vsevolod, Victor Cazalet arrived punctually, and Princess Olga soon came. She looked magnificently beautiful, calm, distinguished and tragic; however she was in a gay, gracious mood and we discussed during lunch the iniquities of the present Serb government, their treacheries and disloyalties! The stories are scarcely believable. Victor Cazalet,

---

1 The Governor of Madras.
2 Presumably Channon had sought a favour from Balfour for another friend, which had not been granted.

who had really only heard the Queen's and King Peter's account, was much impressed. Alice and others looked in after luncheon, including that trite little Australian, Freddie Ashton, who is in the Air Force. He insisted on accompanying me as I walked to the House of Commons; and I found him extremely tiresome. Apparently, however, he is honest, since he told me how he had neglected Alice's advances, and refused to marry her, as he is in love with a man! He told me that Philip Harding, Alice's dark and mysterious husband, whom I had never seen, is of the same ilk!

At the House the big Indian debate was ending – Amery and Oliver Stanley (the most irritating of dried-up men) had made good speeches. There was an overwhelming vote in favour of the government. As I came out I met Alan who had missed it by five minutes, due to his extreme unpunctuality and inability ever to be anywhere on time. We came home here where I 'entertained', a small cocktail party of the Coats family . . . . and Mr and Mrs Peter Fleming. I was bored by them and showed it; and felt for the first time in over three years a lessening of my affection for Peter; but I eagerly seized his letter which was given me. It was dull and short and increased my irritation.

Dined in alone with Harold who was compassionate and pleasant. Alan rang up; he was philandering at Boodle's Club with his arch enemy, Jim P. L. Thomas.

FRIDAY 9TH OCTOBER

My faraway little man's 7th birthday and I am nostalgic for him.

All day I thought of him and could do nothing. The Duchess of Kent rang me from Windsor where she was with little Edward who was also celebrating his 7th anniversary; and I was much touched.

I did nothing all day . . . . went and had my bottom 'cleaned out' – always a refreshing experience; and dined alone and went to bed early.

SATURDAY 10TH OCTOBER   PRINCE'S HOTEL, BRIGHTON

Took a morning train to Newhaven where Alan, dark and handsome, met me. He showed me a vast armada of small ships, tank carriers, landing boats, minesweepers, MTBs etc. – surely over a hundred, which had been assembled in Newhaven harbour as another raid, such as the Dieppe one, is about to take place; but has either been cancelled or postponed. I was cold, wet and disagreeable. He drove his car carelessly and burst a tyre on the kerb at Peacehaven, outside an antique shop where we made amusing *achats*; he bought a medieval man-trap from the Seaford museum, and we went on to icy Brighton to this famous hotel which is closing so soon, as it has been requisitioned! The war is closing its clutches on us, on everything, on civilisation. Every day something goes . . . Alan and I had a quick hot bath and then frolicked, dressed – how I love this huge puppy-ish creature – and drove to see Lord Alfred Douglas,[1] whom neither of us had ever met. He lives in a tiny semi-basement flat at 1 St Anne's Court, Nizells Avenue, Hove. He opened the door, was gracious and friendly and ushered us into his small sitting room where there were books, and a few pathetic *bibelots*, relics of his youth. He is 72,[2] looks much younger, is lithe, lean and smiling and has pleasant eyes, but he no longer listens to what one says, scarcely took in our conversation, and rattled on. We had resolved not to mention Oscar Wilde, prisons, Winston, Robbie Ross[3] or Frank Harris.[4] We were soon embarked on all. He told us much of Wilde, after giving us some sherry; and said that although the Wilde story had ruined his life, he didn't regret him; that throughout his [Wilde's] imprisonment he had only waited for his release and had received him in his villa at Sorrento where they lived together until his family ordered them to separate, threatening to cut off his allowance if they did not do so. 'Bosie' wrote to his mother Lady Queensberry asking for £200 to give to Wilde, refusing to leave him utterly penniless, and really also playing for time. The old lady, old then (she died only recently) sent the money; and the two famous lovers parted for all time. He made no secret of his not[5] being Wilde's catamite; and he showed us photographs of a drawing of himself taken about that time. It was Dorian Gray – a young man of almost unbelievable good looks; so staggeringly handsome that I thought of Peter. But he must have been more beautiful even than Peter. He went on to tell us that Ross and Harris behaved like the scoundrels that they were; that his whole life had been poisoned by the association; that he served six months in Wormwood Scrubs in the 2nd Division for having libelled Winston Churchill[6] – to whom he

1 Alfred Bruce 'Bosie' Douglas (1870–1945), Lord Alfred Douglas by courtesy, was the third son of the 9th Marquess of Queensberry. He was the lover of Oscar Wilde, a relationship that sealed both their places in history when Wilde was imprisoned for gross indecency after unsuccessfully suing Lord Queensberry for criminal libel, in 1895. Later in his life he turned against Wilde's memory and became virulently anti-homosexual: he also became a rabid Roman Catholic and an anti-Semite. He wrote some poetry, and became a serial litigant, being bankrupted at one point and imprisoned at another.

2 He was still just 71.

3 Robert Baldwin Ross (1869–1918), a Canadian critic and journalist, is believed to have been Oscar Wilde's first male lover, and supported him after Wilde's release from prison in 1897 until his death in 1900. He was Wilde's literary executor. Douglas hated him and tried persistently to have him prosecuted for homosexual offences.

4 Frank Harris (1855–1931) left Ireland for America as a teenager, studied law, but began a career as a journalist, and on moving to London in the 1880s edited various magazines and periodicals before becoming a low-grade novelist. He published four volumes of memoirs that scandalised those who read them because of their boastful accounts of his sexual experiences (a fifth appeared after his death); he was a pathological liar and much of what he wrote was the work of a fantasist. He was an early biographer of Wilde, whom he knew.

5 Thus in MS, but crossed out by Coats, which he was clearly correct to do.

6 He claimed, wrongly, that Churchill had suppressed an account of what really happened at Jutland in 1916, something Churchill was powerless to do, having left the Admiralty more than a year before the battle.

has recently (and with the Prime Minister's permission) written and published an ode. It was all most pathetic for he is alone, poor, almost friendless, and married to a woman[1] whom he rarely sees, who, however, lives in another flat in Brighton. Alan and I melted towards him, especially when he told us that he can no longer afford to keep his flat for which Francis Queensberry pays the rent – I don't know what will become of him. I think that I shall give him an allowance; and then perhaps somebody will be kind to me in my advanced age! (He is notoriously unreliable about money!)

We left him reluctantly, as we were pledged to dine with Sir Roderick and Lady Jones[2] at Rottingdean in a house where Kipling long lived. Although it was pitch-black we found it and were warmly welcomed. Lady Jones is a buxom, vital blonde who writes plays and books under her maiden name of Enid Bagnold. She is highly sexed, highly sociable, full of fire and energy – and rather common. Obviously she was considerably impressed by us, and she remarked that she had heard of me for upwards of twenty years and often wondered what I was like! Sir Roderick is a little man, ineffective, overshadowed by his wife, and I should have thought, scarcely up to his former important job of being Chairman and Managing Director of Reuters, a position he relinquished a few years ago. He told us the whole story of Reuters and we reminisced about old days when I knew Mrs Gordon Bennett[3] so well. I used to go out to her villa at Versailles with Cecile d'Hautpoul where we would meet 'Papa Joffre'[4] in the last war. I am getting old and anecdotal! Mrs Gordon Bennett was formerly Baroness de Reuter and she has long since been dead![5] . . . We ate rabbit and washed it down with a vintage burgundy . . . . We talked first of Alfred Douglas, and then of young Julian Amery and I related tales of his brilliance which surprised them, as the Jones family had known him as a precocious and tiresome child! We left at last after a most appalling few hours, and went back to Prince's Hotel . . . . Bed about 12.30 – now.

1 He had in 1902 married Olive Eleanor Custance (1874–1944), a poet, but they had separated in 1913.

2 Roderick Jones (1877–1962) became a Reuters correspondent in South Africa in 1895; by 1919 he was the agency's Chairman and Managing Director. From 1916 to 1918 he was Director of Propaganda in the Ministry of Information. He was knighted in 1918. In 1920 he married Enid Algerine Bagnold (1889–1981), who had earlier worked for Frank Harris (*vide supra*) and become one of his many conquests; during the Great War she had been a nurse and a driver and begun to write, and wrote numerous novels and plays, the most famous of which are *National Velvet* (1935) and her play *The Chalk Garden* (1955).

3 Maud Potter (1866–1946) married as her second husband James Gordon Bennett Jr (1841–1918), publisher of the *New York Herald* and one of the English-speaking world's leading press magnates. She had previously been married to George de Reuter, son of the founder of the Reuters news agency.

4 Joseph Joffre (1852–1931) was Commander-in-Chief of French forces on the Western Front from 1914 until sacked in 1916.

5 Her death was in fact reported in February 1946, in Paris, so Channon was wrong about her being dead already.

A full day full of new personalities. Alan very charming but a bit mad. I begged him to buy Clandon, a glorious house.

SUNDAY 11TH OCTOBER

A horrible day; Alan, with whom I shared a small single bed, kept me awake with his snores. And although it was cold, he sweated . . . I woke unstrung. We drove into Rottingdean, inspected the little hotel known as 'The Little Place', and he decided to move his things there. Then we drove on to Newhaven; *en route* he confirmed my suspicions that James Stuart is intriguing against me, and is determined to prevent my political advancement. I don't know why he hates me so! It is recent, or rather has intensified lately. I must get to the bottom of this mystery; but I fear he is adamant, and relentless. He is not a very good Chief Whip since he has no imagination. Unfortunately, he likes all the people whom I most hate – Arthur Penn, Alec Hardinge etc. Perhaps they will go before I do . . . At Newhaven I sat on the deck of Alan's MTB in the sun, but it was chilly. We went to another neighbouring boat, a minesweeper, where we had drinks with Peter Scott,[1] the artist who does first-rate sketches of animals and particularly birds. His father discovered the South Pole[2] and his mother is Lady Kennet. Alan bullied me into staying over for a couple of hours, and when he put me affectionately in the train at Newhaven Harbour and accompanied me to the next station, I lost my temper and was most disagreeable. I am contrite now, for I love him: but his selfishness is colossal and almost but not quite equals his warm generosity of spirit and the lavishness of his expansive nature. He is so disarming, so unpunctual, so supremely selfish! He will sacrifice someone's whole day from a second's whim, and because he is so fascinating is speedily forgiven.

I crossed through London, had a snack at my Belgrave Square house and then drove here. Kelvedon is blue but icy. The Duchess of Kent rang me up and we chatted; then I talked to Alan who was at Brighton and we buried our tiny hatchet; and now I feel better.

I must get ahold of James Stuart somehow – all day I have been desperately unhappy; I think I miss my child, Peter, and even, possibly Honor!! Certainly I am lonely although aggravated by human beings. I foresee a dreary old Alfred Douglas-ish old age. *Que faire?*

---

1 Peter Markham Scott (1909–89) was the only son of Robert Falcon Scott, 'Scott of the Antarctic'. He represented Britain in sailing at the 1936 Olympics, and his expertise on wild-fowl led to his forming the Wildfowl and Wetlands Trust at Slimbridge in Gloucestershire in 1946. He became a famous painter of wildlife, a leading conservationist, writer and broadcaster. He was knighted in 1973.

2 Captain Scott explored the South Pole, but did not discover it and was not the first man to reach it.

Now that Maureen Stanley is dead, my remaining enemies are:

James Stuart
Randolph Churchill
Alec Hardinge
The Queen? – I didn't know
Mrs Arthur James.

I am alone now, still haunted by that sad solitary leftover, Alfred Douglas, eking out a solitary existence surrounded by his few remaining rather pathetic possessions. How clumsily he must have arranged his life to be placed in so awkward a position now.

MONDAY 12TH OCTOBER

A glorious rich autumnal day at Kelvedon: I had slept twelve hours and woke refreshed, younger, and reinvigorated. The morning I spent gardening and planting out trees in the cool sunlight. Alan rang me twice – of course he lost his train up to London by two minutes, due no doubt to faulty organisation! Then Diana rang up from Brighton to tell me what a success we had both been, Alan and I, with the Jones family and 'Bosie' Douglas. I sent off cards to Peter, Prince Paul, Michael Parker and to my mother. And soon I might go up again to London.

Later I fetched Alan and we were rapturously reunited; I was speedily forgiven for my loss of temper yesterday and as I drove him to Liverpool Street he hinted to me that I had better make my plans to marry the Duchess of Kent. I told him that I thought that Princess Elizabeth will marry Philip of Greece – Philippe le Bel, indeed.[1] I have long watched that royal romance grow. Alan retorted that I must concentrate on my own affairs, that he would relish Lady Astor curtseying to me! So, indeed, would I!

I had a successful dinner party; little Leo Amery, Lady Willingdon who brought her son, Niggs Willingdon, who is a gay and gracious, smiling eunuch; Jay Llewellin who amused us with his stories about himself; Sadie Rodney;[2] and Mrs Massey[3] who came without her husband, the Canadian High Commissioner, who has a chill; and Harold. Over the port I chatted with Leo about the

---

1 This was the name given to Philip IV of France (1268–1314), known in English as Philip the Fair.

2 Gladys Cecil Hamar 'Sadie' Greenwood (1896–1966), married in 1922 Charles Christian Simon Rodney (1895–1980), son of the 7th Baron Rodney. The Rodneys were neighbours of the Channons at Kelvedon.

3 Alice Parkin (1879–1950) married in 1915 Vincent Massey (1887–1967), Canadian High Commissioner to the United Kingdom from 1935 to 1946 and Governor-General of Canada from 1952 to 1959. She undertook considerable charitable work in Britain during the Second World War.

Viceroyalty; he hopes to induce Winston to settle the matter before Christmas. I tried to put a nail in the Cranbornes' coffin and pleaded for the Lampsons or the Butlers but without much encouragement. He asked me whether Rab was sufficiently mature and I replied that certainly he was; he was now the same age as Lord Curzon had been when he became Viceroy. Amery then put an astonishing query to me, Would Rab accept Bombay with a view to Delhi later? I thought not, but evidently such an arrangement was in Amery's mind. Perhaps Cranborne had been induced to accept Delhi for two years with the promise that he would later be relieved? Leo then asked if I had any suggestions for Bombay, as Roger Lumley must come back after having been abroad for nearly seven years. I hadn't. There is nobody anywhere for anything.

TUESDAY 13TH OCTOBER

Woke with a temperature. Am I developing consumption too? Walked to the House of Commons. Winston, just returned from his Edinburgh triumphs and speech, looked glum, as he answered a question about the chaining of our prisoners in German hands.[1] The country is moved by this dastardly development and opinions are divided as to whether it is wise to retaliate . . . . Walked to Claridge's, where I lunched with Tante Winnie, as the aged Princesse de Polignac[2] is called. She is old, wicked in a way, but brilliant still. Her voice is hard and crisp and she smiles in a severe way. She is living in two rooms at 55 Park Lane, this musical millionairess, whose parties and lesbian love affairs – and kindness, too, to young artists, are famous. Her salon, her soirées in Paris, her palazzo and concerts in Venice were unique . . . . I was between Lady Crewe and Lady Rosebery.[3] Peggy [Crewe] and I chatted of the Belisha–Trefusis romance and whether it will ever culminate in matrimony. She is opposed to it: I am in favour. Eva Rosebery travelled down last night from Scotland in the special with the Prime Minister and others. She had spent two days in his and Cripps's company and said it was amusing to watch Winston twit him. The whole party ragged Cripps and he seemed to resent somewhat the chaffing! He was treated like a schoolboy and his alderman's habits, so different from Winston's own, were much mocked. Winston had been in tremendous form! Eva said that Harry Rosebery immensely admired Wavell and was glad that the General and PM had got on better this time at Moscow! This again confirms Peter's report – and Mr Amery's! I like Lady Crewe immensely now.

---

1 In his diary of 11 October, George Orwell mentions that the Canadians had chained up 2,500 German prisoners in their country, in retaliation for the same number of Canadians, captured at Dieppe, and being kept in chains by the Germans.
2 See entry for 10 August 1942 and footnote.
3 Qv: wife of the 6th Earl.

WEDNESDAY 14TH OCTOBER

I spent the whole day at the House of Commons, listened to the Welsh Debate, lunched with Jim Thomas, went for a walk with Rab, attended the 1922 Committee. And, alas, heard that arch four-letter man, [Alec] Cunningham-Reid,[1] ask a question about Prince Paul which he followed up with a supplementary about Princess Olga, demanding to know whether she, too, was a political prisoner, and if not, why not? There was indignation in the House, and if anything my poor friends benefited by such a question being put by this low much-hated individual. I was indignant.

Jim Thomas and Nicholas Lawford dined and we discussed what should be done about Cunningham-Reid, who threatens to raise the matter again on the adjournment tomorrow. It is monstrous. And curiously enough Anthony Eden and Co. have rallied and are furious, and intend to snub him roundly. Nicholas is much the most charming creature I know.

I had a private talk with Cranborne today apropos of Paul and Princess Olga, and he has arranged to see her very privately.

THURSDAY 15TH OCTOBER   WEST HOUSE, BOGNOR

Lelia Ralli rather spoilt my morning by repeating one of the King of Greece's minor *mesquineries*[2] to me on the telephone. It seems that at Coppins last Sunday he remarked to the sisters that Princess Olga had been criticised for lunching out – with me, as it happened. And that I had rung up people and told them! This mild-mannered Monarch can never resist making minor mischief; his mind is *mesquin* and his knowledge of England, for all his residence here, extremely limited. He combines snobbery with a preference for common people. This is not the first instance of his prattling . . .

I went early to the House, conferred with the whips, suggesting that Cunningham-Reid should be counted out when he rose to ask further information on the adjournment. Anthony Eden, however, wanted the matter to go through as he had prepared an extremely tart 'hot' reply – he is now almost on our side? I met Winston face to face and he smiled said 'How are you?' and passed . . . We were in secret session for a few minutes to make business arrangements. I then lunched with Somerset de Chair and we discussed his new book, *The Golden Calf*,[3] which with little humour he describes as the best book since Lawrence.[4] As we were still at lunch the tinkle of a bell told us that the House was up! The whips

---

1 See entry for 12 July 1940 and footnote.
2 Meannesses, or pettinesses.
3 Thus in the MS. It was actually called *The Golden Carpet*, and was a book about the Desert War. It was published early in 1943.
4 The allusion is to T.E., one imagines, not to D.H.

had pulled a fast one and managed to curtail the speeches. Not long afterwards Cunningham-Reid, carrying a bag with his brief, no doubt, came in, and looked discomfited indeed. He had been foiled of his prey. James Stuart was even agreeable to me as we discussed our victory! He roundly abused Cunningham-Reid who has no rival in unpopularity! I walked back triumphant and loyal and delighted that my poor friends should have escaped this further ignominy. At home I found an immensely long letter from Jacqueline Lampson full of news of the boy etc.; one from Lord Alfred Douglas from Hove, and one, no. 26, from Peter from Delhi. It was shorter, and more curt than usual – is there a diminishment in our terrific friendship? Did Cairo adversely affect him? I suspect it was the Crown Prince – I don't know. Perhaps I imagine it, and also it is probable that letter has been lost in the sunken *Clare*!

Mrs Roosevelt's visit has been postponed.

Later, at Bognor. I travelled down here by fast, comfortable, empty train to stay here with Diana. We are alone: she is more lovely, fair, splendid than ever; and her great talents are harnessed now to farming. She milks her cows, feeds her rabbits, sells swill! A happy evening together, gossiping – Chianti and cheese.

FRIDAY 16TH OCTOBER   *GREAT SWIFTS*,[1] *CRANBROOK, KENT*

Diana drove me into Bognor in her dirty, disreputable-looking car with a trailer of swill behind. We bought large lobsters. I was some hours in London, dictating and 'catching up'. I sent off a long letter to Peter, dropped it at the India Office, and after signing a dozen letters came here by car. It took me nearly two hours. Victor Cazalet's modern house is surprisingly attractive, and arranged with skill and taste. The appointments are American, the taste a touch flamboyant. High eighteenth century, things the Duke of Kent would have liked. The house was built by 'Paul' Hyslop[2] and sits in an old park full of fine trees; there is a long, lovely view. Here are . . . . Virginia Cowles; Esmond Rothermere and Ann O'Neill. These last two lovers have decided not to marry after all, and her divorce proceedings have been cancelled. She ought really to know her own mind after eight years.[3] She loves Esmond, but complains of his cold temperament; that he is clumsy and too [illegible] in bed. He is hypochondriacal and looks amazingly young for a grandfather. He and I are sharing a suite – Virginia Cowles seems tired and

---

1 The estate was known as Swifts Park; perhaps at this time the new house was known by a different name. It is thus in the MS.

2 (Charles) Geddes Clarkson 'Paul' Hyslop (1900–88) had a number of Channon's circle as his clientele in the period around the Second World War. Cazalet had bought Swifts Park in 1936, demolished the Georgian house there the following year, and had Hyslop build a pastiche of a Georgian house on the site – which was Hyslop's forte. Paul was his nickname.

3 Over two years earlier. Channon said the affair had lasted for seven years. If so, it had been running for more than nine by now.

depressed. The house is comfortable, the food quite excellent, the servants expert, and the atmosphere one of enjoyment. Much bridge and I am winning.

SATURDAY 17TH OCTOBER

I am enjoying my pre-war weekend and the weather is gloriously warm. Didn't sleep well as we were all kept awake by the lowing of cattle, who were yesterday deprived of their calves. I walked into Cranbrook, shopped . . . Bridge, books, conversation. There seems little news. I am enjoying it all, like a whiff of the past, and I am inspired to return to Kelvedon and live there surrounded by objects and books. The quasi-rural life may be my solution. Unfortunately I have a foreboding sense of impending doom again and was frightened almost apprehensive when my butler rang up from London that there were several telegrams for me. All were anodyne; one from Peter from the Himalayas; another from my mother etc.

I continue to win at bridge. I am unable to understand Virginia Cowles's point of attraction: she seems just a tired plain girl. Much talk and indignation about a recent leader which appeared last week in *Life*; America is seething with anger. Of course it was written, or at least inspired, by Henry Luce's wife, Clare Boothe Brokaw Luce whom I have always detested, loathed and abominated.[1] When she came to this country I warned the Foreign Office and everyone else of her extreme anti-English views. As usual nobody listened. Unfortunately, General MacArthur[2] is alleged to be in love with her. Her visit to Delhi was disastrous and she was disliked by everybody.

MONDAY 19TH OCTOBER

I am cross, liverish, and perhaps I suffer from haemorrhoids again. I must have my sphincter inspected . . . . Harold says that there is difficulty about Princess Olga's return passage to Africa, owing to parliamentary questions about Paul. The Foreign Office and the government are frightened. What cowards people are! She may have to go by sea. It would be monstrous since she came at the personal invitation of the King: Harold will never help people over their matters.

TUESDAY 20TH OCTOBER

Alan walked to see me; and then I went to the House, asked Kingsley Wood a question; walked to the Ritz where I gave Diana Cooper and George Gage

---

1 See entry for 22 June 1939 and footnote.
2 Douglas MacArthur (1880–1964) lost, and then won, the Philippines during the Second World War, fulfilling a famous promise when retreating in 1942 that 'I shall return'. He became a five-star general and the most senior soldier in the US Army. It was he who accepted the Japanese surrender in 1945.

lunch – we had cocktails with the Pembrokes. Lady Pembroke is now Mayor of Wilton!! The Stanleys of Alderley[1] joined us for a bit: they are divorced but often lunch together. That seems very fashionable now with divorced couples. Perhaps Honor and I will be like that one day.

I spent most of the day with Diana Cooper, radiantly lovely, gentle and sweet, and we deplored – she his friend, I his enemy – Randolph's genius for making enemies. His roughness, tactlessness and general objectionableness. He is the only individual of my vast acquaintance for whom there is nothing whatever to be said; not a redeeming quality, unless it is a certain pride and affection for his father – even that is past – or his arrogance. Diana, George Gage and I had drinks and [a] long talk at home where we were joined by Peter and Mrs Fleming. He leaves shortly for Delhi and I sent Peter a book and a pair of scarab links. Dined with Maimie and Vsevolod: Bridget Parsons[2] and Teenie [Cazalet] there and we walked home together in the bright moonlight. But I feel cold and ill … after lunch as I was walking up St James's Street with Geordie Sutherland we saw de Gaulle, accompanied by Palewski, strutting along insolently. We crossed over to avoid them. Nobody can stomach de Gaulle; his intolerable swagger and conceit infuriate everyone.

Wednesday 21st October

Feeling rotten I drove to Southend, where I inspected the damage done on Monday by the German raiders.[3] Clarence Street is a shambles and my offices almost totally destroyed, but not quite. The Conservative Club likewise. There were four fatal casualties and thirty-nine injured, of whom seventeen were seriously. The town was rather excited, even stimulated, and seemed like a woman who has just been ravished! There were rumours: for instance, I was told that Cecil Jones[4] was killed – and I sat next to him at luncheon. Then I heard that my Treasurer had been badly injured, and I met him in the street with only a scratch on his neck! I walked about and showed myself generally, and then attended a Trafalgar Day luncheon at which I both spoke and presided. At three o'clock I leapt into my little car and drove brilliantly to Westminster where the Smuts[5] meeting had just

---

1 Edward Stanley, 6th Baron Stanley of Alderley, married in 1932 Victoria Audrey Beatrice Chetwynd Talbot (1910–94), from 1921 Lady Victoria by Royal Warrant, as sister of the 21st Earl of Shrewsbury. She and Stanley were divorced in 1936; he would have three more wives.*

2 Mary Bridget Parsons (1907–72), from 1908 Lady Bridget by courtesy, daughter of the 5th Earl of Rosse.

3 A light air raid on the town had brought a direct hit on the Conservative Party offices.

4 Edward Cecil Jones (1884–1967) was a prominent local philanthropist and charity worker in Southend.

5 Jan Christian Smuts (1870–1950) had fought the British in the Second Boer War, but then allied with them and led South African troops against Germany in the Great War, before joining the Imperial War Cabinet. He was Prime Minister of South Africa from 1919 to 1924 and from 1939 to 1948. In 1941 he was made a field marshal in the British Army.

opened. The Royal Gallery was crowded, cold and cordial. At the end seated at a table, were the Speaker, Lloyd George, Smuts, Winston and the Lord Chancellor. Lloyd George, in clear but a touch affected Welsh tones, introduced the Field Marshal who was warmly received. He looked trim and fit, bronzed and wiry. He spoke, or rather read out his text, for forty-four minutes and it was all intolerably long; his stuff was no doubt excellent (it was a résumé of the whole war and so bromidic that I guessed that Anthony Eden must have written most of it, and later I heard that such was the truth!), but there was nothing new in it and his accent is too <u>Afrikaans</u>. The truth is that the speech was a most disappointing flop and failure locally, that is in the packed gallery, packed with peers and MPs and the press; but, to the outside world, it will be a tremendous triumph. For the scene was inspiring and the text moving. I understood little that he said and he rarely looked up; a low drone which might have been in Chinese, variously broken by a familiar word. People nearer to the table, although they heard better, confirmed my impressions. I was between Maureen Dufferin and huge Alan. At the end of the applause, there was a polite silence, since everybody appreciated the historic importance and indeed solemnity of the occasion, which was broken by Winston, who made a few adequate and well-chosen remarks – his clear voice was a relief after the Field Marshal's mumbo jumbo. The PM then called on the assembly to cheer Smuts, which we did, and sang with some constraint 'For He's a Jolly Good Fellow'; there was then a little procession and the Big Five trooped out. I was in the aisle and compared Smuts's ruddy, bronzed complexion, his wiry taut little figure, with Lloyd George, Winston, the Speaker . . . all of whom seemed greyer, paler and years older than our distinguished guest. Winston's face, often impish, looked intensely bored during the speech, as no doubt he had read it. He and Simon exchanged little notes, and each time Winston went through all his pockets, as he does when he is irritated, searching for his spectacles. I drove Alan to the station; he is a touch less fulsome to me, and I think I wounded him when I rebuked him for his selfishness at Newhaven. I am so sorry.

I much wanted to dine in alone and had arranged to do so, was even in pyjamas, when both Geoffrey Lloyd and Bill Tufnell telephoned, proposing themselves. Thus a dinner *à trois* was unavoidable; but they got on better than I had expected. Geoffrey Lloyd looked old and ill, but is charming.

The Smuts function, whilst interesting, was a disappointment. Very cold I fled from the Royal Gallery directly Winston had finished and I rushed to the Smoking Room to order a drink. It was nearly deserted but sitting at one table together were those three 'grand old men' who had just been speaking: Winston, Lloyd George and Smuts. And there were glasses before them. Winston, who had once fought Smuts in the Boer War. Only the bronzed South African looked fit. As I was standing by the cigarette case Leslie Belisha looked in, and I was amazed to see Winston leap up and, taking him by the arm, lead him up to Smuts and introduce him. Smuts rose politely and I left them in conversation.

THURSDAY 22ND OCTOBER

Of course I woke with a high temperature, 102, and have remained all day, bored and irritable in bed. A cable came from Kenya from Prince Paul to cheer me, as well as a reassuring letter from Nannie posted on October 10th, the day after my boy's birthday, which he had enjoyed. Nannie says however that the American doctors advise removing his tonsils and adenoids. Yankee medicos always want to pull out everything. I don't know what to do. Princess Olga and the Duchess of Kent rang up. Lelia Ralli, Rab, and Micky Renshaw called; and my doctor, too. I have a severe chill.

FRIDAY 23RD OCTOBER

Feeling slightly better. Harold is being most affectionate and kindly as he always is when I am ill. He goes today to stay at Lavington with Barbie Wallace. I doubt it was a 'Love Club', for Barbie secretly wants to marry David Margesson who will be there; Harold still fornicates with Helen Fitzgerald; and James Stuart has begun a liaison with Sheila Milbanke, which may in some measure explain her apparent coolness to me in recent matters? Or is it a good thing?

Diana, my lovely, looked in. In bed one hears everything: to be ill is a shortcut to knowledge; for the world comes to see one and is confiding. (People always prattle confidentially to someone in a prone horizontal position.) Today I heard that Winston insists on sending back the Halifaxes to India – 'Edward can jolly well reap what he has sown,' he is alleged to have remarked. India bores Winston.

I heard that another offensive has opened in Egypt.[1]

SATURDAY 24TH OCTOBER

Alfred Douglas now writes to me by every post! Poor leftover! I got up for a time, feel 'shaky' but better.

Mrs Roosevelt, looking more like 'Tookie' Zoppola[2] than ever, has arrived to stay at Buckingham Palace (Tookie and she are first cousins). The visit is almost a state one, and the King and Queen met her at Paddington. Diana rang me up to say that Emerald Cunard is actually arriving too. I wonder!

Cecil Beaton dropped in: he is greying and ageing, but is more sensible. Yesterday in the country he received a sudden summons to Buckingham Palace! He arrived breathless and was at once received by the King and Queen, and led by them to Mrs Roosevelt's sitting room, and told to photograph her. It was the

---

1 The Second Battle of El Alamein, this one decisively victorious for the British and Allied forces.
2 Edith Mary Mortimer (1891–1976), of Newport, Rhode Island, married in 1919 Count Mario Panciera di Zoppola; they divorced in 1929. She was a first cousin of Mrs Roosevelt.

Queen's idea as they had to amuse her! Cecil said she was a difficult, restless and unpromising subject. She had barely arrived, was still in her travelling get-up; talked incessantly, moved about, said she had had no powder on her face since she left New York etc. etc. An enjoyable but difficult hour. Cecil is much attracted by Alan Lennox-Boyd.

Sydney Butler spent an hour with me, and we discussed India. She half hankers for it; but what should she do there for five years? 'Have another baby – and a daughter,' I retorted. She was much taken with the idea.

How I long for my own little lovely lad; his face, from fifteen photographs in this room, stares at me everywhere.

SUNDAY 25TH OCTOBER

I got up as I was so bored in bed and my fever had subsided . . . Lunched with Alan in Soho, and later dined with him at the Ritz. He stayed the night. A Boyd day, and Chicanery. He is so mad, disarming, endearing, engaging and untrammelled. I let him whip me which he loves doing. The newspapers tell of nothing but Mrs Roosevelt's activities, and of the offensive in Libya. Both seem successful.

MONDAY 26TH OCTOBER

A wet, pelting day, and the siren sings as I write . . . .

A dull, petulant missive, no. 27, has come from Master Coats. I fear a *diminuendo* in his intense interest and our feverish friendship; and I attribute it to the Crown Prince of Greece whom he saw in Cairo. P describes him in this letter as 'really too much in many ways, stupid, mischievous, boring, tiresome – and yet there is something that I will always be fond of . . . .' Apt.

I listened in to the accounts of the Egyptian offensive. Meanwhile I hear much Indian gossip and speculation as to the future Viceroy. Winston says to everybody, 'Let Edward reap as he has sown'; thus it may be the Halifaxes after all. They would go, after a polite protest, for Edward Halifax always pretends not to want preferment, always refuses, and only after some urgings and inducements he accepts.

Dined at Argyll House with the Crewes. Revolting food but several wines. I was between Daisy Fellowes and Lelia Ralli. Daisy looks her age; is over-made-up and her face has been so often lifted that it now rivals the Eiffel Tower. There was a sort of scene between her and Vsevolod; after she had read out an intimate, almost amorous letter, from Walter Moyne, who is Deputy or Assistant Minister of State in Cairo, she announced that she intended to join him in Egypt where she would act as hostess and give balls. Vsevolod lost his temper and rated her soundly; said it was typical of a frivolous Frenchwoman to suggest such a thing. Such reasoning had brought about the fall of France! . . . . The Crewes live very much in shabby grandeur and their butler must be nearly as old as Lord Crewe himself. Lady Crewe says that her husband puts the butler to bed and calls him. The Russians drove me home early; and I slipped quickly to bed so as to avoid Adrian Liddell Hart, son of the strategist, and Alan's latest infatuation. I was forced to put him up for the night. 'They' came in later.

This afternoon I dropped in at Barbie Wallace's (she is living at the Dorchester) for a drink; there I found little Pam Churchill who was gay and friendly. She tells me that she has left Randolph permanently and taken a flat at 20 Grosvenor Square for herself. She is slightly red-head[ed], but attractive and provocative and deeply in love with Averell Harriman. That arch super-King Cad Randolph has returned, *Dieu merci*, to the Middle East.

TUESDAY 27TH OCTOBER

I feel so ill still. Went to a haemorrhoid specialist who subjected me – gently enough – to various sphincteral indignities. He gave my piles an injection etc. Lunched at Buck's Club with George Gage and spent the afternoon with him. People, all uninvited, poured in for drinks. Cecil Beaton, still imitating Mrs Roosevelt, whose photograph he had taken at Buckingham Palace – (actually I saw her this morning in Grosvenor Square about 10.40. I was walking to see Medico in Harley Street, and watched her arrive briskly enough, and surrounded by a small crowd of fans and press photographers. She went into 23 Grosvenor Square); Sam Courtauld; Lady Aberconway; Oggie [Olga] Lynn;[1] Duff Cooper; Tilea; others. Diana Cooper has arrived to stay. She dined with Lady Colefax. I went with Ghislaine Dresselhuys, to dine with Maimic and Vsevolod, a small party for Prince Bertil of Sweden.[2] He is dark, big, oversexed, and friendly; and in his Bernadotage.[3] Dark and Gallic and French, he is unroyal and un-Nordic in manner. After dinner Vsevolod fainted and I put him to bed; then walked home in the dangerous dark streets.

Confusion last evening as Harold, awakened in the night, suspected burglars. He rushed to my room and we searched the house carrying torches. I was half-hearted knowing it was probably the lovers; and so it turned out; but Harold, luckily, suspected nothing. A ridiculous and comical performance, indeed. I am bored with Boyd's marine 'legions'!

WEDNESDAY 28TH OCTOBER

Philandered the morning away with Diana Cooper; Duff and others dropped in. I gave her £20 as an anonymous contribution to 'Bosie' Douglas as I cannot bear

---

1 Olga 'Oggie' Lynn (1882–1961) was a noted singing teacher.
2 Prince Bertil of Sweden, Duke of Halland (1912–97) was the third son of King Gustav VI Adolf. During the war he was Swedish naval attaché to London.
3 A pun on the name of the Swedish royal house, Bernadotte.

to think of that aged historic creature semi-starving and totally lonely, in Hove
... She went to Eton for the day to visit John Julius who apparently adores it. He
is the most *débrouillard*[1] little dauphin .... I walked to Regent's Lodge[2] to lunch
with Alice Harding and Lelia Ralli. They roundly, soundly abused Zoia Poklewska
who has become the Queen of the Limpets and clings [to], crushes and eclipses
the Duchess of Kent, whom she smothers with ribald affection – but she is, no
doubt, secretly aggressive and even more possessive. Princess Olga fetched me at
2 p.m. and I escorted her to a matinee – a horrible thing to do. The Savoy Theatre
was crowded with provincials and unknowns; the play, *The Man Who Came to
Dinner*[3] was amusing and bitter. Princess Olga, looking sadly distinguished,
enjoyed it. Then we drove back to Regent's Lodge and had tea with the Duchess of
Kent. Those lovely sad sisters, whom I love so very much, depress me.

Loelia Westminster, self-invited, has arrived here, and I have had to put her
in the Nursery as Diana Cooper is in the best room. We dined in – both Coopers
(Duff is so charming and friendly these days), Loelia, Nicholas Lawford, who is
the most friendly and cultivated and altogether charming of the FO boys. Went on
to a gala given jointly by Bridget Paget[4] and David Herbert,[5] in a darkened studio,
which is part of Lady Crewe's house! There were sailors, singers, Americans,
'pommies', and others. I sat with Lady Crewe, Hore-Belisha and afterwards with
Natasha Bagration, and Lelia Ralli .... people did stunts and imitations of Queen
Mary, Lady Colefax, Lady Cunard, and others. Quite an amusing atmospheric
evening, the late arrival of Beatrice Eden put an end to the festivities. She is a
queer girl. Duff drove us home, and my house party (all except Harold Balfour,
who had dined with Alba at the Spanish Embassy and then gone on to Max
Beaverbrook's to a supper party) went to bed. It was 3 a.m. I am doomed, fated,
to be over-surrounded or lonely. No. 5 is now crowded – telephones tinkle;
messages come in, people arrive . . . and I have claustrophobia but I half, I
suppose, enjoy it. Loelia Westminster can be irritating and even hostile; she is
over-Liberal-minded, intelligent but ludicrously lacking in logic; and worse, she
is anti-Chamberlain, and resents my wealth and luxurious background. She is
an Edwardian at heart with her worship of wealth and material comfort. Diana
Cooper is, on the other hand, a miracle of sweetness, beauty, wit and gentle
simplicity. The greatest woman of all time.

As we emerged, hilariously, in the blackout from No. 5 about 10.30 we ran
into Bill Rollo, and we stopped and teased him. Duff asked him what 'dirty work'
he was up to? I was especially cordial to him – nobody, I suppose, except him
and me knew that he is Honor's agent and solicitor and that he gives her most

---

1 Resourceful.
2 This must be a slip of his pen: he knew Alice Harding's house was called Hanover Lodge.
3 A comedy by George S. Kaufman and Moss Hart; it ran on Broadway from 1939 to 1941.
4 See entry for 5 November 1940 and footnote.
5 See entry for 14 December 1938 and footnote.

amateurish and yet rather shoddy advice. I think that the solicitors' *rencontre* did good. Perhaps he was a-spying here?

THURSDAY 29TH OCTOBER

Gay worldlings in this democratic, austere age have lost their talent for sitting up late and this morning we all feel like wrecks. 'Hesperus cases'. Headaches all around, James Gunn called and stood for an hour on a pair of steps, touching up, or rather redoing my left hand in the now famous portrait. Loelia Westminster, Diana Cooper and I chatted with him as we sipped our port, and gossiped about last night's gala. It was an eighteenth-century scene. The coal fire, the modern Sir Joshua drawing, the Duchess and Diana – great beauties, and I, the diarist, wit, bean [*sic*] or leader of fashion, or whatever I am, chatting. My mother-in-law, looking none too well, came to lunch. She was bitter about my wife who has been ill. The hatred one can bear one's child or parent is of a very special brand.

I walked to the dentist's, where I fell asleep as he excavated amongst my molars, and then came home. Tilea, the Romanian, dropped in; he says that that scoundrel, General Simović, is intriguing now against King Peter and the Yugoslav government. He is a horrible man. However I hate Peter and his mother so much that I am delighted. I don't think that any of the Balkan kings will be restored, at least not permanently; and Tilea agrees. Lawford and Georgia Sitwell and others looked in. I pretended to be dining out, and slipping up the backstairs I am now undressing and going to bed. My house guests have all separate plans for the evening, thank God!

I have a sinister intuition that the offensive in Egypt is not going too well; at least, not up to expectations. And in ten days' time – a grim secret – our landings against the French will probably begin. Therein are far-reaching and great and grave risks.

FRIDAY 30TH OCTOBER

I slept for eleven hours and yet feel dejected and cold and ill. Refused to go down to Brighton with Alan to dine with Alfred Douglas and to stay the night.

Diana Cooper and Loelia Westminster have left. I am now alone with my cold and dejection and generally low spirits. I have fever and shall now undress and go to bed . . . . Alan rang up from Newhaven, persuasive and engaging and overwhelming; but I resisted his wiles. I haven't the energy to go traipsing to Brighton for no real purpose. Instead I dined alone in bed on the excellent *beaux restes* of my luncheon party. I am definitely middle-aged, and clearly a bore; as for the first time in my life I am bored. And I have noticed a dramatic diminuendo in my sexual powers, prowess and appetite recently – only since last August. Desire is dormant, lust is asleep, and luckily Peter is far away.

How charming Diana Cooper is with her easy wit, gaiety and gentleness. Loelia Westminster is less so: she is a *malintentionée*[1] matron and talks only of her money – and lack of it. Her standards are Edwardian. I like her less every time I see her and shall soon hate her.

Saturday 31st October

Woke undecided whether to stay in London or flee to Kelvedon ... it is icy and autumnal and I have a heavy cold. No news. Harold went out early to receive Mrs Roosevelt somewhere. I must really invite both her and Smuts to dine one night soon! She talked much.

I walked to the RAC where I had a Turkish bath followed by a violet-ray light bath in the hope of curing my cold. Of course it didn't. Dined in with Harold, whose 45th birthday it is tomorrow. He looks nearly 100 with his greying hair, increasing baldness and lack of youthful lustre. Luckily I look much younger. I don't understand his fascination for women. Jay Llewellin looked in after dinner and bored us for an hour: I was horrible to him, rude and perverse, for I had a desperate longing to be alone. Nothing can assuage these fits except solitude. I hinted to Harold that he was becoming ungracious, particularly about air passages.

Sunday 1st November   *KELVEDON*

To get away from people, bores and friends, I came here. The cold is intense as the Red Cross, to economise fuel have not yet turned on the central heating. I wrote to everybody.

Read Pepys. He kept a diary for only nine years and it filled only four volumes. Is mine then so much longer already? He began it at the age of 27,[2] ending at 36.

Went early to bed. In winter I am half-bear, and have hibernating instincts.

Monday 2nd November

Came up to London after a morning in the icy [weather], gardening. Kelvedon looked very lovely, indeed in the autumnal sunlight. I dreamt last night that Honor died. Today Alan tells me that she is seriously ill. I trust it is not pregnancy; probably it is her old pancreatic complaint from which she so often suffered – once acutely at Brdo in 1936 when we were staying with the Regent at that gloriously beautiful place which I shall never see again.

Talked with Lelia Ralli on the telephone. She's angry with Zoia Poklewska who never allows the Duchess out of her sight, and really overdoes the Cerberus

---

1 Ill-intentioned.
2 He was in fact 26 when he began his diaries.

act.[1] Lelia is jealous and understandably so, and being a Greek she must make mischief. This quality she shares with her Monarch, who always repeats malicious rumours and makes trouble when he can. He has the tactlessness without the charm of his mother, the Hohenzollern Queen Sophie, whom I adored.

I went through my finances; they are in a fairly buoyant state. I owe nothing to anybody; my nest-egg capital is still intact; my income flows in; but I fear I shan't be able to live for long as I now do – on a reduced scale. I am spending about £9,000 per annum which is more than I receive, since taxation is so ruinous. Of course additional money may come to me from various sources in time. A lot of ageing females must leave me something; and I should bank another £10,000.

I cannot thaw off my depression and fear that I betray my irritability . . . . Diana tells me that Duff is laid up with flu and an Himalayan temperature at Send. Loelia will be in a flutter about it, probably none too gracious.

The secret of the contemplated attacks against France is only half-out. There are rumours, but few people seem to know the date – November 7th or 8th – or place as yet. What will Weygand do?

TUESDAY 3RD NOVEMBER

I read in the newspapers – it was the first news any of us had – that Peter Wood,[2] the Halifaxes' second son, has been killed in the Middle East. He was only,[3] and a most attractive gay ne'er-do-well; and always gave the family trouble and anxiety. The wild, wayward Gardner blood, or taint, which is so strong in Honor, and Anne Feversham, came out in him.[4] He was extravagant, unsatisfactory, gay, unreliable, handsome and licentious – and, worse in his parsimonious parents' eyes, always in debt. He once tried to borrow £5,000 from Honor which she would willingly have lent him, but I stopped it. He was half-engaged to Lady Mary FitzRoy,[5] but the Halifaxes disapproved since she is penniless. He was the least like his relations, didn't care for them much; but was always my favourite. He dined with us just

---

1 In Greek mythology, a three-headed hellhound who guards the underworld.
2 Francis Hugh Peter Courtenay Wood (1916–42) was a major in the Queen's Own Yorkshire Dragoons; in civilian life he was training as an architect. He was killed at El Alamein on 26 October.
3 Left blank in the MS: he was 26.
4 Lady Honor and the Halifaxes' children were first cousins. Their maternal grandmother was Florence Coulston Gardner (1853–1934), who in 1875 married the 4th Earl of Onslow. Lady Honor's great-great grandfather, Admiral Alan Hyde Gardner, 2nd Baron Gardner, had had a scandalous divorce in 1805. Her great-uncle, Herbert Gardner, became 1st Baron Burghclere in his own right, being unable to inherit his father's barony because he was born out wedlock after the 3rd Baron's affair with an actress, whom he later married.
5 Mary Rose FitzRoy (1918–2010) was the posthumous daughter of Viscount Ipswich, killed four months before her birth on active service. When her brother succeeded as Duke of Grafton in 1930 she was accorded the rank of a duke's daughter, as Lady Mary Rose. She married Francis Trelawny Williams (1915–77) in 1945.

before the war for[1] some big drinks party here – the King and Queen were dining that night in Eaton Square with his parents, but he refused to attend and came to us, which I thought commendable really. Honor and her sisters didn't care for him, but they care for nobody really.

I was distressed by Harold's demeanour this morning. He said that he was on my nerves, he well knew. That is true enough, I fear, at times, but I regret having shown it – and that he would shortly move, perhaps after Xmas, unless I persuaded him to stay on. I cannot understand why this has come to boiling point; except that he, too, is highly strung and extremely sensitive, and has lost his glamour for me. But I am fond of him. Why do people 'die' on one? Why are friendships of such short duration? I don't know. Both he and Loelia Westminster, although they maddened each other, succeeded in infuriating me last week, and probably I was to blame: it is the war and the claustrophobia it creates. We have all been cooped up too long in this little island. I long at times more than anything for Peter's return . . . and yet, and yet, I might snap at him and tire of him, too. I trust not. I am a cad at heart, I daresay: but an unmeaning, or at least, unwitting one.

Alan, accompanied by Adrian Liddell Hart, called on me this morning. It is a nervous, uneasy, uneven, emotional friendship. I was alone for a bit with the young man who confided in me that he was terrified lest Alan came some sort of cropper as he is so incautious and indiscreet. The young man is right.

Will those hard bland Halifaxes be crushed? I doubt it.

Lunched alone, had my hair cut and went to Cecil Beaton's enchanting distinguished little house, in Pelham Place, where I found Ava Anderson, insinuating and infuriating; Lady Crewe, morose and mournful; Bridget Paget and the Cárcano girls, daughters of the Ambassador[2] and others. I drove with the girls to another cocktail party and finally dined with Bill Tufnell at Pratt's Club (he asked me to propose him for membership). I held forth about Trollope to a learned judge present . . . Harold drove us home in his impressive government car. He was charming and we were reconciled and closer than before. I behaved badly as I had accepted to dine both with Lord Willoughby, and the Baillies; and had to send several frantic 'chucks'.

WEDNESDAY 4TH NOVEMBER

Everybody in London rang me up and I decided to give a dinner party, and wasted the long day arranging it. The Argentine Ambassador rang me . . . others. Bill Astor says that the only people who enjoy the war are Winston, Professor

---

1 Presumably Channon means 'after' the drinks party.
2 He means the Argentinian Ambassador, Dr Cárcano (see entry for 1 June 1942 and footnote). The Ambassador had two daughters, Stella Cárcano y Morra (b.1924) and Ana Inéz 'Chiquita' Cárcano y Morra (1918–92). Stella married, in 1946, Viscount Ednam (see entry for 14 August 1941 and footnote); Ana married in 1944 John Jacob Astor VII (qv).

Joad[1] and Peter Coats. In the end, after too much telephoning, cadging and rearranging, and refusing people, we were sixteen –

Chips,
Lelia Ralli,
HRH Prince Bertil of Sweden,
Mademoiselle [Ana] Cárcano,
Lord Gage,
Aleco Matsas,[2]
Alice Harding,
Cecil Beaton,
Guy Millard,
Ghislaine Dresselhuys,
Nicholas Lawford,
Vsevolod of Russia,
Mlle Stella Cárcano,
Archduke Robert,
Princess Natasha Bagration,
Ben Kittredge.[3]

My depleted, attenuated but patient and kindly staff played up: dinner was excellent and well served. Immediately, there was *Stimmung* and atmosphere terrific [*sic*] of young people enjoying themselves hugely. Prince Bertil, who is a dark, lively, boisterous boy, a burlesque of a prince, arrived at eight – before I was down. We had a confidential conversation before the arrival of the others .... He says that family life in the Palace is a touch strained since his father and stepmother[4] (and the old King)[5] are

1 Charles Edward Mitchinson Joad (1891–1953) was a popular wartime radio personality as a member of the BBC's Brains Trust. He had been a career civil servant but in 1930 became Professor of Philosophy at Birkbeck College, London. His life collapsed when convicted of fare-dodging on a Waterloo to Exeter train in 1948; the BBC sacked him and the peerage he was hoping for from the Attlee government became out of the question. He became bedridden and died, many thought, as a result of the scandal.
2 Alexandros Matsas (1911–69) was a Greek diplomat and also a poet. Later in his career he was Greek Ambassador to Turkey and to the United States.
3 Benjamin Rufus Kittredge (1900–81) was an officer in the US Navy during the war, and acted as an American attaché to the governments-in-exile in London.
4 His father was Oscar Fredrik Wilhelm Olaf Gustaf Adolf Bernadotte (1882–1973), Duke of Scania from birth, Crown Prince of Sweden from 1907 to 1950, when he succeeded his father, Gustaf V (*vide infra*) as King Gustav VI Adolf. He was a serious intellectual; with a strong expertise in archaeology, botany, oriental art and history. He married, in 1923, as his second wife Lady Louise Mountbatten (qv).
5 Oscar Gustaf Adolf Bernadotte (1858–1950), Duke of Varmland from birth, Crown Prince of Sweden from 1872 until 1907 when he succeeded his father, King Oscar II, as King Gustav V.

definitely pro-English, but Princess Sibylla,[1] his sister-in-law, being a Saxe-Coburg, is a touch pro-German, whilst violently anti-Nazi. Bertil is dark and French-looking. The Marseillais blood, and that of the Empress Josephine must be very strong, as there is nothing of the Victorian strain in his appearance. All the young people were impressed by the beauty of the room, the wines, and excellence of the food!! Harold, Bill Astor and his fair brother 'Jakey'[2] (who was in the Dieppe raid) dropped in afterwards and added to the general gaiety. They drank much; the Argentine girls are gay and highly attractive ... all stayed until one o'clock, and they eight of them left for a nightclub, with Prince Bertil as host. I was exhilarated and pleased by my success. The lonely, long, lank Archduke was a trifle tipsy with happiness and was pathetic. Gage was in a hiatus of bewildered gaiety. One of the most *réussis* fêtes I have ever had. I foresee that the Argentine girls will take London by storm. I half-arranged the party to please and impress their parents, who have been so kind to me. I was particularly pleased to see my old friend, Ben Kittredge, the most sympathetic – he is the son of a very old man – of my American friends. Honor and I stayed so happily at his famous plantation, Shanberry something,[3] near Charleston, in 1934, January.

THURSDAY 5TH NOVEMBER

Woke well and lively but later had a relapse and had to indulge in somnolence and a siesta. The telephone tinkled all day with messages of rapturous thanks and numerous notes arrived. To the dentist and then walked to the Andersons' to have a talk with Ava as arranged but I found her pleasant tiny house in Lord North Street packed with people – Cárcanos ... and many more. Went on to the Kemsleys for a cocktail, being driven recklessly by an Argentine in his powerful car in the blackout, dropping Lady Brabourne on the way.

Rab arrived to stay and he, Harold and I dined in *à trois* – political and personal gossip. Rab says that my position is unique: I lead London society, my house is the loveliest – indeed the last and only stronghold remaining of the aristocracy and *ancien régime*! I should not be politically ambitious (which, incidentally, I am not) as I should never get anywhere important in that arena, whereas in society I am unrivalled. He says that I shall never be the Governor of Madras! But when he is Viceroy he will certainly insist on my going as his Comptroller to cope elegantly with the Indian princes ... etc. I put him to bed; his conversation, due to years of repression, was highly licentious. He was a virgin, he confessed, when he married.

---

1 Sibylla Calma Marie Alice Bathildis Feodora of Saxe-Coburg and Gotha (1908–72) married in 1932 Prince Gustav Adolf of Sweden, son of King Gustav VI Adolf, who predeceased both his father and grandfather. Their son eventually succeeded as King Carl XVI Gustav.
2 John Jacob Astor VII (1918–2000), son of the 2nd Viscount and Viscountess Astor (qqv), served in the Life Guards and the SAS in the war, attaining the rank of major. He was Conservative MP for Plymouth Sutton from 1951 to 1959, and was knighted in 1978.
3 The plantation was called Cypress Gardens.

The victory in Egypt is being over-heralded and crossed over; but it looks like a rout. I suspect that the enemy is up to something else.

Emerald [Cunard] is arriving: she is already in Lisbon and I have engaged a suite for her at the Ritz for Monday. The future looms great and fraught with possibilities which do not preclude the end of the war. The Egyptian campaign continues brilliantly . . . and the Yankees will attempt to land (and no doubt, succeed) in Morocco and northern Africa, within the next four or five days . . . . Peace but no goodwill by Christmas?

FRIDAY 6TH NOVEMBER

At six I went to the Argentine Embassy where I had a drink with Their gay and charming and very social Excellencies . . . . I was fascinated by the Ambassadress,[1] who is still young, amorous, of *châtain*[2] colouring and social distinction; she is aware of her social importance. In general, she was scathing of the French, to whom she had long been accredited, and in particular of the Third Republic, of its follies, *grossièretés*[3] and graft. She always refused to receive either Madame de Portes[4] or Madame de Crussol,[5] the *maîtresses en titre* of Reynaud and Daladier. Madame Cárcano had raised nearly 3,000,000 francs in the Argentine for French charities and she presented the money to Daladier not long before he fell. No trace of it can be found: the money simply disappeared – she thinks it found its way into Madame de Crussol's corrupt hands. The only pleasing phase of the Pétain regime was its scornful treatment of the ladies of the Third Republic! We supped at Claridge's . . . . chatted with many people. A most delightful evening and I shall 'run' the Argentines, even if Rab says I am wasting my time with them!

Someone told me a story about old Bowles, Mrs Greville's pompous, efficient, but slightly alcoholic butler. There was a grand weekend party at Polesden, attended by the King and Queen. Royalty was too much for him, and towards the end of dinner Mrs Greville scribbled on the back of a menu card 'You are drunk – go to bed at once, M G', and slipped it to Bowles who very politely put it on a

---

1 Stella María Carlota Morra y Victorica (1893-19?) was daughter of Carlos Morra Manhes, marqués de Monterochetta. She married Miguel Angel Cárcano Sáenz de Zumarán (qv) in 1914.
2 Chestnut, dark brown.
3 Vulgarities.
4 Hélène Marie Jeanne Rebuffel (1902–40) had met Paul Reynaud (qv) in the early 1920s, but later married an Italian count, Henri de Portes; but she became Reynaud's mistress in 1938 and exerted what his colleagues considered to be a malign influence on him. She was a fascist sympathiser and deeply anti-British. She was killed in a car crash in southern France, with Reynaud (who survived) driving, as they were trying to escape to North Africa after the German invasion.
5 Marie-Louise Frédérique Jeanne Amélie Béziers (1904–91) was the wife of the marquis de Crussol d'Uzès, whom she had married in 1924. She was Édouard Daladier's (qv) mistress from 1934 to 1940.

salver, bowed and presented it to Lady (Austen) Chamberlain who flushed with rage. Nobody knew what to do!

Madame Cárcano said to me at the play, '*Monsieur, je vous trouve très beau!*'[1] – what do I do now?

SATURDAY 7TH NOVEMBER   *LANGLEYS, ESSEX*

I should have attended a meeting of East Anglian MPs at Cambridge under the chairmanship of Sir Will Spens, the Regional Commissioner, but I 'funked' the early start. Messages from everybody. Emerald arrives on Monday. I had arranged a big dinner party for Tuesday, for the Butlers and Cárcanos, but now Winston has sent out invitations which are tantamount to 'commands' for a governmental dinner that night; thus no member of the government, no minister, will be able to dine with me. I have had to reshuffle and spent a frantic morning telephoning everybody. The whole party, more or less, has been shifted to Wednesday now – but what a waste of effort; only I am 'landed' with Lady Willingdon on Monday, and Lady Brabourne on Tuesday, these ladies could not rearrange. The boredom of it.

A most welcome letter came from Nannie that Paul is in school in New York and well. Nothing lately from Peter: is that side dying? The ardour is abated, and only since three months, or even less. I have an intuition that it is mutual? But at the sight of him his old witchery would probably exert its usual dominion over me? Who knows?

Lunched at the Ritz, with Elizabeth Elveden; we drank with John Fox-Strangways[2] who is very fat, still on crutches. He had been taken prisoner in Libya, kept at Benghazi, and later transferred to Caserta, where the Italians treated him well. Finally he was exchanged, got to New York, and is now here, gay, amusing, and eager as ever. His adventures have not sobered or soured him. Last time I saw him was in Cairo at the height of my passion! I lunched with him etc. there.

Drove here to Langleys via Kelvedon. This lovely house is very cold; there is no central heating; it is highly uncomfortable, but there are beautiful things and much atmosphere. Bill Tufnell is an excellent and generous host. We are all rather enflamed by the Egyptian victories and it seems that Rommel's forces have had to retire as far as the Libyan frontier – at least. It is a rout for Rommel, so far.

SUNDAY 8TH NOVEMBER   *KELVEDON*

Suffered acutely from the cold all last evening and was so numb that I slept badly; also there was the hum of aeroplanes on high – all bombers on the way to Brest, and perhaps Genoa.

---

1 'Sir, I find you very handsome.'
2 John Denzil Fox-Strangways (1908–61), son of the 6th Earl of Ilchester, and grandson of the 6th Marquess of Londonderry.

I heard the news about eleven! It has happened. There have been successful American landings near Algiers and in Morocco; meanwhile, General Montgomery advances in Libya, and has perhaps bypassed Mersa Matruh. I felt exalted, as if emerging from a long tunnel, for now, surely, the war is at last ending; or at least entering on a happier phase which must lead to victory. Peace and Paul! Peter – and socialism, elections, new troubles and frustrations.

Drove here to Kelvedon. A most lovely, autumnal day, glorious East Anglian light, the shedding trees, the colours ... Here an affectionate cable from my mother, and Jay Llewellin rang up from the Ministry of Aircraft Production asking me to dine tonight. But I must stay here in the blackout. I also refused Matsas. Jay Llewellin is the King of Bores, but a most devoted and painstaking friend.

My days of idleness and peace are now over; I have a full week ahead of me. This brief excursion is my last respite ...

Last night I dreamt vividly of Honor; I wrote to her eighteen days ago commiserating with her on her illness from which I hear she has now recovered; and am not surprised to receive no reply for she is too drunken and dissolute to attend to her correspondence. It is 9.35 and I sit alone in my solitary, sympathetic green study; I have been listening to the wireless: the sound of it came through the heavy doors (my own set is broken) and, I heard, too, the chatter and comments of half a hundred soldiers who are lounging and reading so near to me! (one of them to whom I gave a lift yesterday told me that Kelvedon is the best-run and most comfortable convalescent home in England: he did not know me). The news was immensely encouraging. American landings, risings in Morocco, four Italian divisions almost surrounded, Rommel's army on the run and expelled from Egypt. Mersa Matruh probably in our hands ... so it goes on. A very different tune from a few months ago. Mrs Roosevelt gave the postscript, too long, but quite good and in a very English voice. One would never have recognised her as an American except for her pronunciation of the word 'tempo-rá-r'ily.' The soldiers listened politely .... But I feel that the long nightmare is drawing to a close. Soon I shall be living here with my little boy once more.

MONDAY 9TH NOVEMBER

Today is my father's birthday; he would be only 74. Almost the only thing one remembers about him is his birthday!

A dense fog delayed me; I was over two hours *en route* from Kelvedon and several times I stopped the car and almost gave up the trip. Arrived at one o'clock: the absurd Lord Mayor's show caused the traffic to be diverted. Imagine holding such a carnival in the middle of a war! Here no bad news. Emerald's plane was delayed and she is now expected tomorrow.

The excitement and atmosphere is tense: Rommel on the rout; more American landings; the Mediterranean almost freed; Hitler declaring that he will not capitulate . . . my butler says that the war is won. So may the people believe. I don't; not yet. Hitler will attempt one more big coup, an unexpected invasion or something on the grand scale . . .

Lady Willingdon, Sadie Rodney, Harold and I dined in. A terrific attack on the Black Rat (Alec Hardinge) which was launched by Lady Willingdon, who said that he was endangering, jeopardising the monarchy. Harold and I agreed; she gave instances of his limited experience, his lack of imagination, his conceit, and left-wing bias etc. I recalled Mrs Greville's dying injunction to the Queen, 'I am an old woman, and believe me, if Alec Hardinge is still with you when you reach my age, you won't be on the throne.' Sadie weakly, but loyally defended him. He is in a stronger position since Mrs Greville and the Duke of Kent, his two powerful and implacable enemies, are dead. And Winston, whilst he loathes him personally, is not hostile to him politically since he serves Winston's interests.

The American attack on Africa is an amazing success. Capitulations everywhere.

TUESDAY 10TH NOVEMBER

Walked to the House. It was crowded. Winston appeared, answered a few questions in that irritating manner of his, which is most pronounced when he is triumphant, and then left to attend a Guildhall luncheon. I went to the Lords, accompanying an American colonel, whom I picked up, and we heard the King's Speech read out clearly by [John] Simon. It had more body and 'guts' than is usual.

Long talk with Rab who reaffirmed his advice to me; that I shall never go far myself politically since whatever talents I possess lie in other directions; but that I can – and have – considerable political influence. But it is in London and society that I shine: I can, and already do, lead and rule a larger section of London society which takes its colour and life from me.

I want to be a peer: there are many ways of becoming one. The quickest would be for Leslie Hore-Belisha to become Prime Minister. To do that he would first have to be a Conservative – so I had a confidential chat with him and later walked from Westminster to Stafford Place with him, trying to persuade him by every weapon in my armoury to go over to the Tory Party. He was surprised; he had never considered it but promised that he would do so seriously. I suggested January as a psychological moment. Such an action would embarrass or annoy Winston, but why not; for Leslie's talents are too great to be thrown away as a freelance in Opposition.

The temperature of my affection for Peter is falling – falling, and it is my friend's fault – or is it my own fickleness? I am offended by the tone of his more recent letters; but I secretly know that this is but a passing phase; for it is a 'lifer' really.

Emerald's return has been again postponed this time until tomorrow.

Lady Brabourne, cold, aristocratic, lovely and sad[1] dined; so did Ben Kittredge and Sydney Butler, and the Lennox-Boyds .... About 10.30 Rab, Harold, Geoffrey Lloyd and Jay Llewellin arrived; they had all been dining with Winston at No. 10. There had been seventy-one people, speeches by Winston and Smuts, beer and little food, but an enjoyable evening. Winston is cockahoop. How Rab hates him. The HMG boys all stayed too long and too late. Only Rab, much the shrewdest of the lot, slightly denigrates the African landings and thinks, as I do, that Hitler is far from being done!

WEDNESDAY 11TH NOVEMBER

Today, the anniversary of the Armistice, Hitler has announced that he is to occupy all of France, and that the Pétain government is being removed to Versailles. All of lovely France gone – I am not surprised.

The telephone never stopped; all London rang me up, people wanting to dine; to stay; to sleep ... The fog is so impenetrable that I couldn't get to the House of Commons, where the King and Queen were opening Parliament. I am sorry.

Peter's letter, no. 29, dated October 22nd, is more cheerful and I feel *attendri* to him again. But all human relationships are unsatisfactory *au fond* certainly.

Today was the Great Fog, the most impenetrable in human memory. There were accidents, delays, late trains, and general dislocation; of course it quite threw my day out of joint. I tried to walk to the House of Commons since taxis were unobtainable, but I couldn't see and so turned back, thus missing the formal opening of the new session by Their Majesties.

Channon manages to get to the House in the afternoon.

As I stood in the lobby I saw Winston approaching, led by Harvie-Watt. They both smiled genially. After, the usual ritual of the King's Speech etc. It was moved tediously by Walkden,[2] a white-bearded, earnest honest Socialist: he was too long and inaudible: then Peter Thorneycroft,[3] looking a mere boy, rose and with very little shyness – just enough – he held the House as he seconded the

---

1 She had been widowed three years earlier, aged just 43, when her husband, the Governor of Bengal, died in India.

2 Alexander George Walkden (1873–1951) was Labour MP for Bristol South from 1929 to 1931 and from 1935 to 1945. From 1906 to 1936 he was General Secretary of the Railway Clerks' Association. He was raised to the peerage in 1945 as 1st Baron Walkden, and served as Deputy Chief Whip in the House of Lords from 1945 to 1949.

3 George Edward Peter Thorneycroft (1909–94) was Conservative MP for Stafford from 1938 to 1945 and for Monmouth from 1945 to 1966. He was President of the Board of Trade from 1951 to 1957, Chancellor of the Exchequer from 1957 to 1958, Minister of Aviation from 1960 to 1962, Secretary of State for Defence from 1962 to 1964 and Chairman of the Conservative Party from 1975 to 1981. He was raised to the peerage as Baron Thorneycroft (life peerage) in 1967. He was a gifted watercolourist.

gracious speech. It was an admirable performance. Winston followed and for seventy-six minutes we had a dramatic treat, as he explained and described the African landings, the victory in Egypt, etc. But, whilst vivid and boisterous, he said nothing, or little, that one had not heard on the wireless or read on the tape . . . Indeed, events seem to happen with such dramatic celerity and frequency these past few days that we are breathless. The Germans have occupied Tunisia, the Italians have taken the Riviera . . . Darlan[1] is rumoured to be treating with us. We listened enthralled – at last I crept away and slept solidly in the library for twenty minutes, and when I returned Winston was winding up. It was a creditable, indeed amazing performance, for an overworked man of 68.[2] He was cheered when he sat down and the House emptied, or almost. Cabinet ministers met their wives in the lobbies, ambassadors stalked out: everybody was jubilant and gay. The announcement that the church bells are to be rung on Sunday in celebration of the Egyptian victory was enthusiastically received; (I am not sure that it is a wise decision) and I was reminded of the Greek bells that I heard announcing the victory of Klisura when I was in that ghastly train between Athens and Belgrade in January 1941 . . . I chatted in the lobby with various ambassadors (the Corps is always friendly to me!) and met Clemmie Churchill face to face and she cut me again. That fiend Randolph has evidently made mischief between us as she was at one time most cordial; she lunched and dined at Belgrave Square in old days and I twice lent her Honor's tiara and jewels to wear at a Court function.

Then by chance I wandered back towards the emptying Chamber and there I met Col. Carver MP[3] (a Yorkshire gentleman) who rushed up to me, saying, 'I have been looking for you everywhere. That cad, Cunningham-Reid, is attacking your friend, Princess Olga.' I crept into the Chamber and stood behind the Speaker's Chair. It was true, that low rat, smiling, and his black hair shining, was on his feet and haranguing an almost empty House. He made the wildest charges, wild misrepresentations and clumsy untruths. James Stuart, Dick Law, Jim Thomas and one or two others squirmed uneasily on the front bench. I then rushed – my heart breaking and full of indignation, yet feeling sick, to the Thrones and stood behind the screen and listened to that shit's foul inaccuracies.[4] Should I interrupt him? Should I speak? I feared to cause more excitement by doing so, and perhaps start a debate or discussion. Jim Thomas, in the uniform of a Home Guard, found me. 'Do nothing. Keep still. We will ignore him. Dick thinks it is best.' Bill Astor stalked out and passing me, remarked: 'I'm going away before I vomit!' Not a word of what Reid said was true; his rigmarole was a dishonest tangle of semi-facts. But it was horrible

1 Admiral Darlan, of France. See entry for 24 June 1940 and footnote.
2 He would not be 68 until the end of the month.
3 William Henton Carver (1868–1961) was Conservative MP for Howdenshire from 1926 to 1945.
4 Cunningham-Reid referred to Prince Paul as 'a traitor to his country and to the Allied cause generally' and asked why 'the companion of this dangerous traitor, his wife, Princess Olga, who incidentally has a dominating character' was allowed to move freely around England.

to hear one's lifelong friends abused in this way. At last he sat down .... There were only a dozen people in the Chamber luckily; but the lobbies buzzed with anger and indignation. I met Lady Astor running towards the Chamber: 'It's over – you're too late,' I told her. 'Why didn't you find me?' she screamed. I didn't know where she was ... Feeling nauseated, I came out, found a taxi and made for Belgrave Square. The fog had thickened; it was really almost impenetrable but I got home at last. Princess Olga, unaware of the revolting attack on her, was on the telephone when I arrived. We chatted cheerfully. She was awaiting Walter Buccleuch, who delayed by fog, never turned up. I told her nothing, and remembered that I must cope with my dinner party, really arranged for Emerald: I checked the list. We were thirteen. And Emerald was in Portugal. Diana Cooper arrived and offered to help. She is staying at No. 5, as are the Rab Butlers. Loelia Westminster rang up the Ritz where I am putting her up. She is there as my guest since she cadged so obviously that I had no alternative ... I sat down for a long gossip with Diana as the telephone buzzed. Loelia says that buses and taxis have been ordered off the streets; Duff rang up that his car had had an accident; but he agreed to dine and once more we were fourteen. Then I invited Daisy Fellowes and Juliet Duff, last-minute inspirations since they live in the quarter, I thought they could walk. They gladly accepted. And so we were sixteen. And I thought I need bother no more ... However, Lady Crewe rang up saying that she had no means of transport and would I excuse her? She was rather rude, as she always is. I tartly agreed. We were fifteen. Half an hour passed ... Harold telephoned that he had had to abandon his car and couldn't see a yard and was attempting to walk home. Next it was Duff who rang from White's, said it was 'impossible', he couldn't get here. We were fourteen. And then I went up to dress. Daisy Fellowes sent a message that she was unable to come, although she lives in Chapel Street, and at 8.30 we were thirteen again. By that time the Duke of Alba, accompanied by Juliet Duff, had arrived. Desperate, I ran into the dining room, rearranged the placement and put a small table at my place, dashed back to the drawing room to receive the Argentine Ambassador and Madame Cárcano, who said she was overcome by twin emotions, i.e. the experience of the fog, and the beauty of my house. They had walked preceded by two footmen carrying torches. It was like the Middle Ages. I went to the front door; it was cold and milky without and one heard the voices of people lost and struggling to find their way. Presently David Margesson and Loelia Westminster turned up in day clothes. They had taken the Underground by the Ritz and somehow managed to walk from Hyde Park Corner. I hardly dared to admit that we were thirteen. However, I was saved by a message from the Londonderrys that they, too, had lost their way; had attempted to walk from Londonderry House, and had missed their bearings and were somewhere off Oxford Street. I again reshuffled the placement, and eleven strong we marched into the blue and silver dining room. People talked only of 'the Great Fog' and it had exhilarated everyone. Diana said it must go down in history like 'the Great Frost' of Jacobean days, which Vita Sackville-West describes in *Orlando*.[1] High spirits at dinner, animation and excellent food. I was between the Ambassadress and Loelia. Rab's famous pheasant cackle was heard again and again, and I knew that all was well. A brilliant party in spite of every adverse elemental condition. After dinner Rab and David remained behind in the dining room chatting *haute politique*[2] with Miguel Cárcano, as I led Alba to the morning room to join the ladies. He had had an important telegram from his government which was being deciphered as he came out to dinner. This handsome hidalgo is ageing and he is subject to sudden attacks of giddiness. Of course we all discussed the victories, the landings and the confused situation in North Africa. Darlan is the mystery man, and it now seems that he has joined forces with the Americans, and indeed is collaborating with us. From once being the villain of the Vichy piece he is now almost a hero. He has not fought the invading American troops and has deserted Pétain and is hoping for the French fleet to join him. For once events are ahead of gossip and one cannot keep pace with them. German paratroops have landed in Tunis …

After Alba's departure we settled down to a gay evening; David Margesson was in high spirits; Rab laughed until I feared he would be sick, as he is sometimes; Diana egged him on; whilst Madame Cárcano, who is *une grande amoureuse*,[3] sat flirting with Harold on the sofa. She is young, vital, bronze and voluptuous and rich …. Just my affair. I have rarely been so attracted by a woman.

I only heard afterwards that Walter Buccleuch, whom I had invited by telephone in desperation, had arrived and hearing that we were thirteen[4] had gone away again. What trouble he would have saved me.

The recent quickly accumulating victories have sent up the government's and particularly Churchill's stock; thus a reshuffle is now less likely.

THURSDAY 12TH NOVEMBER

We went to bed at 2.30, Diana and I following the Butlers to their bedroom to continue gossiping, and I watched Diana's famous charm subjecting [*sic*][5] Sydney. This morning Sydney praises her lavishly. Rab came into my bedroom as I was breakfasting and asked somewhat shyly if he could live at Belgrave Square for a few months and I said that I would be delighted, as indeed I am.

---

1   Thus in the MS. *Orlando* was a novel of 1928 by Virginia Woolf, in which a great frost is depicted.
2   High politics.
3   Literally 'a great lover', though Channon is referring more to what he perceives to be her appetite for men.
4   Channon must mean twelve, as the Duke realised he would make thirteen.
5   He may mean 'subjugating', or putting her in an attitude of subjection.

A frenzied morning; handicapped by a headache I tried to 'catch up' with various matters. Diana was in and out: people telephoned. I told her that Alan and I are prepared to allow Alfred Douglas £25 per annum, and we will sign a covenant. Incidentally Osbert Peake[1] has written Alan a pompous and absurd letter in reply to his request that a manuscript poem written [by Douglas] whilst he was in Wormwood Scrubs be returned to him. Osbert Peake is a professional 'no-man' lacking in courage, and never stands up to his Department: he is putty in the hands of the civil servants. In many ways he reminds one of Edward Halifax, to whom he is remotely related, the same bland insincerity, coupled with fundamental honesty, and the inability to refute his advisers, or to take trouble for his friends. Consequently he has none. I never liked him at Oxford and don't trust him now . . . In fact I was so busy this morning that I didn't get to the House of Commons at all. Diana and I went to lunch with Oggie Lynn in her delicious little Lowndes Street flat. Exquisite and trouble-taken food. I was next to old Princesse de Polignac, who at 80[2] has become both a beauty and a siren. She is much easier and more anxious to please than in her grand Parisian or Venetian days. Cecil Beaton and Madame de Polignac's girl-friend, Alvilde Chaplin,[3] completed the party. Alvilde is about 30, and a daughter of Tom and Flossie Bridges,[4] and the wife of Chaplin. She is dark and not unattractive and she lives quite openly with her old female lover in a tiny flat in 33 Park Lane. It is really extraordinary and nobody seems to mind or notice. Much talk of France and its appalling predicament.

All afternoon we expected Emerald's return but a message from the Air Ministry finally informed us that she would not arrive before nine, so there was nobody to meet her . . . . I then escorted Loelia Westminster, who has arrived at No. 5, to the Argentine Embassy opposite, where we dined in considerable state. Fair footmen, rich food, fine wines. I was on the right of the Ambassadress; the elder and less attractive daughter was on my other side. These girls will go far. The whole family is attractive and are [illegible] and extremely social. An old-style evening of much splendour and pleasantness in the gaily-lit Embassy. Afterwards the daughters showed us a collection of fantastic hats . . . Later Loelia . . . . and I took a taxi to the Ritz and went up unannounced to Emerald's suite. She

---

1 Peake at this stage was a junior Home Office minister.
2 She was 77.
3 Alvilde Bridges (1909–94) became a noted gardener. She married in 1933 Anthony Freskyn Charles Hamby Chaplin (1906–81), who succeeded his father as 3rd Viscount Chaplin in 1949. They divorced in 1950 and the following year she married George James Henry Lees-Milne (1908–97), an authority on country houses, writer and diarist, and former lover of Harold Nicolson (qv).
4 George Tom Molesworth Bridges (1871–1939) was a career soldier who lost a leg at Passchendaele but remained in the Army to lead important missions, notably military liaison with Greece and Russia. He was knighted in 1919, reached the rank of lieutenant general, and was Governor-General of South Australia from 1922 to 1927. He married, in 1907, Janet Florence Marshall (née Menzies) (1868–1937).

was undressing but we forced our way in; she seemed not at all tired after her first flight, and received us in bed. She was like an old but very chirpy canary and we listened to her brilliant conversation, or monologue of her travels, for two hours. She is more amusing and witty than ever before, and I realised how much we had missed her all this time. Her ambience is fascinating . . . She was scathing about the Americans, liked only Glenway Wescott[1] and his tribe of indigent writers, or so she said. I realised sadly how much we had missed all these sad, empty years without her brilliance and tremendous spirits. We left her reluctantly at 2 a.m., and luckily found a taxi. Loelia and I went up to her adjoining rooms. I am beginning to hate her, which is a pity.

The past two days have been too full.

FRIDAY 13TH NOVEMBER   *PALACE HOTEL, SOUTHEND*

An ominous date! The world was closing in on me and I feared that I should do scant justice to my speech tomorrow or myself if I remained in London. So I decided to drive here in the late afternoon, and go to bed early and awake sufficiently refreshed tomorrow to cope with a heavy constituency day!! My mother-in-law rang up from Pyrford to say that she and Rupert are both ill, and would I please deputise for them tomorrow at two hospital functions? I agreed.

Prince Fritzi came to see me this morning and I found him immensely improved: he looks young, vigorous and fit and seems reconciled, even to like his hard, agricultural life. I tried to prevent Loelia Westminster, who is an arch gossip, from seeing him but she unfortunately found out through my own stupidity! She left for Send and I was glad to be rid of her.

Fritzi has been staying at Shalden with Honor, whom he has always liked. I was somewhat amused but tried to hide it. He said she was well, but was drinking; and as for Mr Woodman, he is drunk every night. Honor, apparently spoke of me with much affection. Poor mad, deluded, muddled woman. There is some link between Fritzi and her, forged no doubt during those long months passed together in the loneliness of wartime Kelvedon. I was unable to make any plans with or for him as I was leaving for Southend. He is enchanted by the victories. He said *inter alia* that he thinks that Honor will not marry Woodman. Isn't he wrong?

I think we are ill-advised, indeed idiotic, not to use this young man more as he may well be Emperor of Germany one day. I love him, and his visit brought back old days, and lost happiness. The wheel seems to be turning full circle. Then I turned to my Hansard and read with pleasure and surprise of Dick Law's strong snub to Cunningham-Reid yesterday, when Law answered for the government. He

---

1 Glenway Wescott (1901–87) was a poet and novelist, originally from Wisconsin, but living in Manhattan by the time Lady Cunard met him.

said that evidently 'the Honourable Member wished to regain his lost reputation by attacking a defenceless woman'! And I now hear that C-R was completely routed and looked most uncomfortable. He has made in me an enemy for life and I shall do my utmost to unseat him in the next election.

At last after signing many letters I drove here, dined in the hotel, which is gay and crowded with young officers with their real wives and otherwise, and now I shall go to bed.

SATURDAY 14TH NOVEMBER

Attended and addressed three large meetings, the first at the Hospital, the second a gathering of the Conservative Association at Garon's,[1] and thirdly a smaller one held here [Palace Hotel]. I rang mother-in-law, who was lonely but affectionate. Sometimes I adore that steely-grey woman. Lord Iveagh is in bed, suffering from an attack, not the first, of gallstones.

Today is the seventh anniversary of my election for this Borough. Someone at the meeting handed me this quotation from Genesis: 'And Jacob served seven years for Rachel and it seemed but a short time unto him, for the love he had unto her.'[2]

SUNDAY 15TH NOVEMBER

A cold and foggy day. I attended a celebration service in state with the Corporation at St Mary's Church, Prittlewell. The church bells here and all over England rang out, and pealed the victory. I thought of the bells that I had heard in Greece for the short-lived victories there, and how beautiful they had sounded then.

How shall I get back to London? I must be there for luncheon on Tuesday. This morning the Duchess of Kent and Princess Olga rang me up. Princess Olga is leaving towards the end of the week on her return trek to Kenya. Poor woman, when shall we see her again?

MONDAY 16TH NOVEMBER   BELGRAVE SQUARE

All day interviewing constituents in Southend and drove home, arriving at six. Dined with Lady Cunard and Harcourt ('Crinks') Johnstone[3] at the Ritz. Gay, exquisite, full of life and fun and wise witty Emerald talked, as we sat enthralled, for three hours. She is an amazing, dazzling creature. She calls 'Crinks' 'le

1 A sports and social club in Southend.
2 Genesis 29:20.
3 Harcourt Johnstone (1895–1945) had twice been a Liberal MP, from 1923 to 1924 and from 1931 to 1935, and would sit for Middlesbrough West from 1940 to 1945. He was a junior minister at the Department of Overseas Trade at this time.

Misanthrope', and rightly, for this obese bachelor is a disappointed, middle-aged, rather boring and hideous creature. But he is friendly and ever lonely now. He has eaten and drunk too much all his life and overindulged and spent. At last he left and I had an hour alone with my favourite woman; her spritely gaiety is infectious. She kissed me affectionately 'goodnight' and I admired her courage for I know her heart to be broken over Thomas Beecham's dastardly desertion.[1] She has loved him for thirty-four years.

TUESDAY 17TH NOVEMBER

Today this house has been the modern Hôtel de Rambouillet.[2] [After lunch] I rushed to the door to receive the Duchess, Princess Olga and old Miss Fox, their antique duenna. The Duchess is thinner, and looked lovely; she was in deep black and wears a half-veil: I found her subdued, whilst Princess Olga is sad and regal. Her departure has been once again postponed (it had been arranged for her to go with Smuts this week, flying with him as far as Cairo, but Lelia Ralli's illness has prevented them at the last moment from going). I gave the ladies tea, and entrusted a book and a little gold money-clip to Olga to take back to my poor languishing Paul as Christmas presents. Harold Nicolson dropped in and immediately Princess Olga beckoned him to sit next to her, and I overheard her thanking him for his article about Prince Paul, which appeared (inspired by me) in the *New Statesman* last year. Alice Harding, very *piano*, and Rab, also arrived. Princess Olga led Rab into the Black Room, where they had a confidential talk for about half an hour, and as they talked Princess Marina whispered to me about the Cunningham-Reid attack; in spite of her precautions Princess Olga had heard of it. I explained that coming from such a source it would only have a ricochet effect; and in any case it was not worth worrying about since it was over and done with.

Princess Marina decided it was time to go back to Coppins because of the blackout, and interrupted them. A sad, nostalgic little tea party indeed and I thought of how splendid and glamorous these beautiful sisters had once been. They left about 6.30 and I had a short time, a brief respite in which I arranged the house for our evening party which was really a Balfour benefice. Harold, Rab and I dined *à trois* rather hurriedly. At nine o'clock sharp I went to the front door and a moment later a huge military car drew up and out stepped Captain Smuts,[3] who is acting

---

1 She had just learned that Beecham planned to marry Betty Humby (1908–58); she was twenty-nine years his junior. She was a pianist of some renown and, having met Beecham in the 1930s, had gone to America during the war with her young son of her first marriage, and was reintroduced to him. Although he had an affair with Lady Cunard for nearly forty years, Beecham did not think to tell her about his marriage. He and Miss Humby married in 1943.
2 The Hôtel had been a leading Parisian literary salon; Channon may have meant the Château de Rambouillet, a political salon.
3 Jacob Daniel 'Japie' Smuts (1906–48).

as ADC to his father. He was followed by the Field Marshal and I led them in. Smuts is breezy, bronzed and remarkably fit; he has a boyish complexion, fine clear sky-blue eyes, and gentle, excellent manners and he radiates charm. He refused a drink, but chatted most amiably of the Lampsons and of the Crown Prince and Princess of Greece for a few minutes, whilst the MPs, all junior ministers, arrived: Sir James Edmondson; C. U. Peat[1] – who reminded me of how we had dined together with Honor, in February 1940, when we made our maiden speeches against socialism (Honor was with us!): he is a junior minister now and I am a dumb member; Malcolm McCorquodale, Allan Chapman, Ham Kerr (Harold's PPS) Geoffrey Lloyd, Bill Mabane, Jock McEwen, Harold Macmillan, Harry Strauss,[2] and Charles Waterhouse. When they were all more or less assembled and had taken drinks and sandwiches, the Field Marshal sat on a sofa and began a sort of monologue punctuated by some rather amateurish questions asked by the junior ministers. I was immensely and immediately impressed by Smuts's simplicity, his sweet smile and his incisive way of speaking, yet there is a pronounced accent; and his charm is colossal. He has an old man's charm, an affectionate manner which is most endearing. He gave us his views of the past few years and of the future; thinks that Baldwin deserves a high place in history for his management of England in a difficult period but regrets that SB was uninterested in Europe – hence his mistakes; says that Hitler, indeed the whole German race, is pathological! Was grateful to Mr Chamberlain, etc.; admits to being frightened of Europe and its eternal entanglements and suggests that the war, or struggle may last hundreds of years. Germany has always been a destructive power; it broke the Roman Empire and nearly, but not quite, broke the British! – then he described in dramatic phrases the fatal division in his Parliament, the decision to support the war, which he won by only 13 votes and after a long struggle and tremendous debate. The Opposition was largely isolationist, not anti-British. If the voting had gone the other way South Africa would have remained outside the war, neutral like Eire, and the war would have been lost. England could never have hoped to have won without her help etc. Harold Macmillan, who is so intelligent and pleasant, asked searching questions. Someone mentioned the dreaded subject of Munich and Harold Macmillan lost control; for he is obsessed by it, and was always violently hostile to it. Bill Mabane, as everybody stirred uneasily, asked a most tremendous question: 'Did the Field Marshal think that this famous all-important division which he had described so

---

1 Charles Urie Peat (1892–1979) was Conservative MP for Darlington from 1931 to 1945. He had been a first-class cricketer for Oxford University and Middlesex before the Great War, in which he fought with distinction, winning the Military Cross. He would serve as Churchill's parliamentary private secretary; he was an accountant by profession.

2 Henry Strauss (1892–1974) was Conservative MP for Norwich from 1935 to 1945, for Combined English Universities from 1946 to 1950 and for Norwich South from 1950 to 1955. He was a junior minister of Town and Country Planning from 1942 to 1945 and at the Board of Trade from 1951 to 1955, when he was raised to the peerage as 1st Baron Conesford.

vividly, would have been won had we gone to war at the time of Munich?' I was embarrassed. Smuts smiled kindly. 'Certainly not. There would not have been a chance of it', he replied, and he explained once more how far away Czechoslovakia, Danzig, and Poland are from South Africa. At that moment Germany had done little to estrange or frighten South Africa and if anything opinion was pro-Sudeten. It was only the later betrayal of Mr Chamberlain, the occupation of Prague, etc., and the actual invasion of Poland which swayed the doubtful votes. This is the most tremendous vindication of Munich that I have ever heard, and Harold Macmillan was silenced. Gloomy Smuts Junior sat in complete silence drinking whisky and soda. At 11.30 the Field Marshal rose, shook everybody genially by the hand and left, Harold and I seeing him to the door – as he got up he mentioned Runciman[1] and how sorry he had been for him at the time of his mission, but was he sorry for himself? Rab chipped in; he had been present at No. 10 with Mr Chamberlain when the offer was made to Runciman, who had said: 'I am a lone man whom you are putting to sea in a little boat on a big ocean and I shall drown.' Everybody laughed. At the door the Field Marshal whispered to me that he is leaving tomorrow for Cairo in his private plane. I hope that the fine beautiful old gentleman will arrive safely . . . . I came back; the MPs had gathered about the drinks table and were drinking and eating. Harry Crookshank was affable, even friendly to me; was it good manners or a change of heart? The evening was a huge success and I am only sorry that Dick Law and Jim Thomas, whom I invited, did not come. They would have been impressed. Here endeth one more great evening in Belgrave Square . . .

Really Smuts is so charming that I should like to have him for a Christmas present.

WEDNESDAY 18TH NOVEMBER

Slept beautifully; I am in high spirits and excellent health once more. Diana Cooper rang up to hear about the Smuts gala. Rab came into my room in his dressing gown and we talked Smuts and smut! He is sex-obsessed, probably from repression. Walked to the House of Commons, where everybody was discussing only last evening's party; but I learnt to my horror that that filthy scoundrel Cunningham-Reid had returned to the charges against Princess Olga yesterday afternoon, and probably at the very moment that I was reassuring the Duchess that it was all over!! Leslie Hore-Belisha collared me and we went along to the Smoking Room, where Oliver Stanley gave us sherry. Sitting with them, I asked: 'Has either of you ex-Secretaries for War a gun?' 'What for?' Oliver asked. 'In order to shoot the gallant member for Marylebone,' I explained. Both agreed that I should be another

---

1 Walter Runciman (1870–1949), son of the 1st Baron Runciman, had led a mission to Czechoslovakia to see whether mediation was possible between the Sudeten Germans and the Czechs. His report recommended the Sudetenland be ceded to Germany.*

Charlotte Corday,[1] only that I should probably get off. Walked back to 16 Stafford Place with Leslie to lunch and we spent three hours together; I begged him to join the Conservative Party. Would I, he asked me, make him Prime Minister if he did? Only I could have that power, he said in all seriousness and I recalled Max Beaverbrook's famous message to Honor when he wrote asking her to see Sam Hoare with the idea of making Sam Prime Minister in succession to Mr Chamberlain! Honor was immensely flattered and amused at the time; it is true that our house was then – as it is now – the centre of political, or at least of Conservative London! Leslie Hore-Belisha told me much; described once again how he had been ousted from the government; how he had sent for Brendan Bracken who had been indignant, and how they had put a call through to Winston then staying at the Embassy in Paris, and how Winston had promised to reinstate him etc. (He was First Lord of the Admiralty at the time.) Later Winston wrote him a charming, commiserating letter in which he 'looked forward to the not distant day when once more they should be colleagues in the Cabinet'. A few months later Winston was Prime Minister and did not offer him a portfolio. Leslie loathes Winston; he is supremely ambitious still and even hopes to supplant or succeed him one day – but will he?

Worn out and sleepy from too much monastic sweet wine, I came home and slept for two hours. Then I had a bath, as Cecil Beaton watched me dress, and went to fetch Jim Thomas at the FO and drove him in the blackout to Argyll House where I had a cocktail with the Crewes. There were fifty people there, *le tout Londres*,[2] an interesting party. Ava Anderson introduced me to her stepson[3] saying that I had made her marriage to Sir John . . . I left the party with regret . . . . And drove to the Baillies' house at 25 Eisenhower[4] Platz, as Grosvenor Square is now called. I was the last to arrive: David Margesson, Dickie and Edwina Mountbatten, Geoffrey Lloyd, Jock Whitney,[5] Audrey Bouverie and others. We had a glass of champagne and some sandwiches and then all went in various cars, I between Dickie and Edwina [Mountbatten], to the Queensberry Club to attend a crowded boring and too long drawn out charity variety performance. I was bored: it was cold and dull

1 Marie-Anne Charlotte de Corday d'Armont (1768–93) was executed after she assassinated Jean-Paul Marat, the leader of the Jacobins and one of the most radical figures in the French Revolution.
2 All the people who mattered in London.
3 David Alastair Pearson Anderson (1911–90) succeeded his father in 1958 as 2nd Viscount Waverley. He served in the RAF during the war and was a cardiologist.
4 A reference to David Dwight (later Dwight David) Eisenhower (1890–1969), at that stage a lieutenant general who had just been posted to London as Commanding General, European Theater of War for the American Army. From 1953 to 1961 he would be 34th President of the United States of America.
5 John Hay 'Jock' Whitney (1904–82) was born into one of America's richest families and built his wealth up further by shrewd investments in business, and in motion pictures and bloodstock. He was in military intelligence, serving in London, during the war, and was one of Eisenhower's major backers in his presidential campaigns. He was rewarded by being made Ambassador to London, where he served from 1957 to 1961.

although there were many friends. Lady Castlerosse, that *démodée courtisane*,[1] was sitting directly in front of me . . . . Harold joined us . . . afterwards we had supper on the stage and met many of the stars. Drove back with Jock Whitney (whose new wife, Betsey,[2] ex-Roosevelt, was recently Harold Balfour's mistress!). More fun, frolic, gossip and champagne at the Baillies'. Olive whispered to me how much she loved me and wished that we had not wasted so many futile years hating each other. So do I.

Miguel Cárcano told me at Peggy Crewe's party that Laura Corrigan is actually arriving tonight at Claridge's. I could scarcely believe it, and telephoned to the hotel where I was told that a suite has been reserved for her. Well done Laura: she has triumphed over the Foreign Office and English officialdom certainly. I am enchanted. Madame Cárcano, the Ambassadress, accused me of abandoning her. '*Monsieur, vous me négligez*,'[3] she said. Rab hates her. To me she is divine.

I am so sorry for the Amerys; their eldest son, John,[4] an eccentric ne'er-do-well, has managed to get to Berlin where he has joined a small 'intellectual' colony of Englishmen who are living at the Adlon [Hotel] and making propaganda for the Germans. He has always been an unsatisfactory son – careless about other people's chequebooks and that sort of thing. Now, however, he has gone over to the enemy, and his poor parents' hearts will be broken. I am not surprised for if I believe in anything at all, it is that those people who persecuted Mr Chamberlain, hounded him to his death, will and should be punished. And they are, one after another. But I happen to love both the Amerys and an exception could have been made in their sad case. What unhappiness children bring one!

Oliver Stanley is a sad and disappointed man. Evidently he hates Winston, thinks him volatile and unreliable; he especially criticised him for his crowing too soon – he always does – over our victories. The ringing of the bells was a major mistake, he thinks; why not wait until the Afrika Korps was completely defeated

---

1 Old tart. Jessie Doris Delevingne (1900–42), daughter of Edward Delevingne, haberdasher, married in 1928 Valentine Browne, Viscount Castlerosse (qv). She conducted a number of affairs, sometimes with homosexuals whom she hoped to 'cure', and the marriage ended in 1938. Within a month of this entry, Lady Castlerosse committed suicide.

2 Betsey Cushing, former wife of James Roosevelt II, the President's son. See entry for 9 July 1941 and footnote.

3 'Sir, you neglect me.'

4 John Amery (1912–45) had been expelled from Harrow after a year for refusing to conform with the rules, went bankrupt in his early 20s through bad investments in the film business and, aged 21, married a prostitute. He became a fascist sympathiser in the 1930s and joined the *Cagoulards* in France, finding himself there after the Nazi occupation in 1940. He was allowed to travel to Germany in 1942 where he suggested forming a British anti-communist legion. He tried to recruit members from among British prisoners of war but only two volunteered. He broadcast propaganda from Berlin before being captured in north Italy in April 1945, where he had been supporting Mussolini. An attempt was made to construct a defence for him but he pleaded guilty to eight charges of treason, and was hanged in Wandsworth Prison in December 1945.

and Rommel really routed. Until now he has merely retreated, as we have often done. I thought him improved, and he has seemingly recovered from Maureen's death; and he is much more friendly towards me. But he leaves me indifferent; *il me laisse froid.*[1]

THURSDAY 19TH NOVEMBER

The retreat of the German Army continues. We are almost at Benghazi!

Walked to the House, where I asked a question quoted later in all the newspapers about the recent and growing outbreak of lawlessness in the West End.[2] Snack lunch with Gerald Palmer and later returned to Belgrave Square for a deep siesta. Rab came in and in a male, moody state of mind; he was tired and irritable, and I left him to his bath and his box and went around to Londonderry House to have a drink with Charlie and Circe [Londonderry] – Mairi Bury was there. Charlie was most affectionate and demonstrative; tomorrow he goes into a Nursing Home, Prince Arthur's, to have a minor operation for a hernia.

Dined with Emerald Cunard at the Ritz, and I was in a scintillating humour . . . .

Laura Corrigan has been again delayed by fog or something and is still *en route* from Lisbon.

FRIDAY 20TH NOVEMBER

We have re-taken Benghazi.

A quieter day *enfin* . . . . I refused all invitations, and I had many; and spent the day with my diaries and books and letters. Lady Cunard rang me up to say that Leslie Hore-Belisha had remained behind with her last evening and had praised me with 'exaggerated lyricism' for two hours. He adores me, and is, I think, although he doesn't know it, in love with me. Alan came to London for a moment and telephoned. He is having a boring holiday as Patsy talked him into going to Brighton and Chilham for his leave. He is henpecked, certainly!

Prince Fritzi came to see me and we spent a nostalgic hour together talking of old times. He has had news – letters came on Friday – of the Crown Prince and Crown Princess [of Prussia][3] and his adored sister Cécile. Fritzi had improved,

---

1 He leaves me cold.

2 Herbert Morrison, the Home Secretary, replied that there had been 181 incidences of robbery with violence in London in the first ten months of 1942, 124 of them in the streets. He added: 'I have been in consultation with the Commissioner of Police and can find no evidence to suggest that the situation in any particular district need give rise to apprehension.' (Hansard, Vol. 385, Col. 503, 19 November 1942.)

3 For the Crown Princess, see Vol. I, entry for 10 August 1936 and footnote. She married, in 1905, Friedrich Wilhelm Victor August Ernst (1882–1951), eldest son of Kaiser Wilhelm II. He spent the war in Germany, but after the failed assassination plot on Hitler in 1944 was kept under surveillance by the Gestapo.

developed physically and in character, we talked much of Honor with whom he stayed on some days at Shalden last week. He says that she is well physically but *désoeuvrée*, and rather drunken; she speaks of me with affection! The man, Woodman, is, Fritzi believes, to be half-Dutch, half-gypsy. He is always drunk but Fritzi never saw him violent or quarrelsome. He [Fritzi] is devoted to her but desperately sorry for her and his original loyalty to me remains unshaken. He says that she has no future.

Both Harold and Rab are away for the night: it is a *volupté* to be alone for a change. Talked three times on the telephone to the Duchess of Kent.

Will Fritzi ever be Emperor of Germany? Perhaps.

Tomorrow I must go to Send to stay with Loelia Westminster: I would give a good deal to wriggle out of it, especially as there are 'changes in the air'; and nothing so excites me as a Cabinet reshuffle. This time Cripps and Jay Llewellin are for the '*haut-saut*'!;[1] or so I think.

SATURDAY 21ST NOVEMBER   *SEND GROVE, WOKING*

I slept long but fitfully and twice I was telephoned, and refused to speak, during the night; by Lady Cunard and Leslie Hore-Belisha. People really shouldn't telephone to their friends after midnight. I dreamt of Honor and of Peter....

No news this morning. The position in France is increasingly confused and unhappy. Captain Cunningham-Reid has circularised his last speech attacking Princess Olga to all MPs. Edwina Mountbatten told me the other evening that he had twice induced the Duke and Duchess of Kent to accept his hospitality; that they stayed there for a shoot at Six Mile Bottom: this makes his conduct even more despicable ... His horrible circular came in this morning's post and as I sat here reading it Prince Fritzi looked in. He is still a philosopher, saying what does anything matter in these troubled times ... and democracy must always demand a victim. Once it was him; he is now fortunately forgotten, working incognito at .... Rockcliffe, Castletown, near Carlisle;[2] now it is Princess Olga .... He says that Honor will never marry Mr Woodman; that he will drink himself to death; doctors have already warned him against whisky because of his concussion. Perhaps Fritzi is right: I don't know.

I spent a fitful futile day, half-waiting for Laura Corrigan whose plane, as planes always are, was delayed. Eventually I came here, driving down the Baillies. I hate weekends and am temporarily *agacé*[3] by Loelia Westminster, my plump Edwardian-minted old friend and hostess. The Duchess stoops to cadge! Alfred

1 High jump.
2 An estate in Cumberland owned by the Mounsey-Heysham family since 1802.
3 Irritated.

and Clementine Beit[1] – she much *en beauté*[2] – are here. Pleasant party; I was amusing but bored.

I hear that Eddie Devonshire has been offered Delhi and that John Colville is going to Bombay.

Laura Corrigan telephoned to me here after dinner; she had arrived safely from Vichy via Lisbon. Diana Cooper is staying with me in London.

Sunday 22nd November

Woke angry and bored and anxious to return to London. It took me all day to arrange it and I succeeded, alas, in annoying and offending my hostess. It is very cold; and when I announced that I was leaving everyone else followed suit. Got back at six just as the blackout began and I rushed to Claridge's to call on Mrs Corrigan. I ran into that gossip the King of Greece in the corridor, and he was most friendly and proposed lunching here next week. Laura I found unaltered, voluble, gay, eager and vibrating. She tells long stories of her adventures in Germany, Paris and Vichy, and of the very great work she has done to alleviate human suffering and boredom. She is pro-Pétain; and went to call on him the day before her departure – thirty-six hours before the Germans entered. She spent an hour with the old gentleman, who gave her sufficient petrol to drive to Lisbon. She says that he is pro-British[3] and is misunderstood in this country and that we have treated him tactlessly and stupidly. That I have always thought. American policy has been wiser and more realistic! Laura was followed by the Gestapo, insulted by the Germans etc. She says that all Roman society is pro-Ally.

Dined with Emerald Cunard: Duff and Diana; Diane Abdy; Cyril Connolly and Dingle Foot,[4] whom I have never before met *dans le monde*![5] Dull evening. The Coopers and I had to trudge to the Ritz in the cold moonlight. Harold Balfour rang me this morning at Send and gave me the government changes which were announced this evening on the nine o'clock news. Cripps is *déformé*[6] and relinquishes the leadership of the Commons at which he was so conspicuous a

---

1   The MP for St Pancras South East. He married, in 1938, Clementine Mabell Kitty
    Freeman-Mitford (1915–2005), a cousin of the Mitford sisters and of Mrs Winston Churchill.
2   Looking beautiful.
3   This was a serious delusion.
4   Dingle Mackintosh Foot (1905–78) was Liberal MP for Dundee from 1931 to 1945, and
    Labour MP for Ipswich from 1957 to 1970. He was a junior minister in the wartime coali-
    tion, and Solicitor-General for England and Wales from 1964 to 1967. He was knighted in
    1964. His younger brother was Michael Foot, leader of the Labour Party from 1980 to 1983.
    He died after choking on a chicken sandwich.
5   In society.
6   Literally 'deformed', but presumably a metaphorical reference to what had happened to his
    career.

failure, ceases to be Lord Privy Seal and goes to the Ministry of Aircraft Production, replacing poor Jay Llewellin who is kicked upstairs[1] and made Resident Minister of Supply in Washington, with diplomatic status. Neither of these moves, or 'polite sackings' cause any surprise; but putting Oliver Stanley at the Colonial Office is most unexpected, particularly as he is notoriously disloyal to Winston and highly critical of the government. He succeeds Bobbety Cranborne, who becomes Lord Privy Seal without a portfolio, but remains Leader in the Lords. Is this a stepping stone to India? Will he win the Delhi sweep? I pray not: the Devonshires would be a more sound appointment.

MONDAY 23RD NOVEMBER   *COPPINS*

Diana announced her intention of staying another night in order to dine with that woolly old bore, Lady Colefax. I was in a quandary as I expected Rab back from his weekend; however I induced him to go down to Eltham Palace for the night.

Lunched with Laura Corrigan, who is most exhausting but affectionate and loyal. She talks a thousand words to the minute. Later I drove here and found the royal ladies quite alone. But Zoia Poklewska soon joined us; she is becoming a menace; she is large, buxom, good-humoured and brave and undoubtedly devoted to the Duchess whom she bullies, coddles and patronises; but she is tactless, sometimes, and is always there; indeed the *ménage* Poklewski are cashing in on the Kent tragedy to rehabilitate their lost social and financial position. Courtiers are ever the same regardless of the situation; and royalties never see through them, although they often turn against them . . . Princess Olga and I were discussing my tragic domestic affairs, and she recalled how she had come to 21 St James's Place (our lovely house, now bombed and destroyed) to see Honor soon after Paul was born. Honor was in bed, beautifully arranged and smothered with pearls and never once mentioned the baby until at last Princess Olga had asked to see her husband's godson. She thought Honor unnatural to say the least . . . as we were deep in conversation Zoia came in and interrupted us with her schoolboy jokes and prattle. She is friendly and well disposed. The Duchess of Kent and I settled down to backgammon which we played for two hours; I thought that she looked tired, and rather drawn. For the first time in her life her radiance seemed gone. She was gay yet subdued, and gentle and loving as ever. She has rearranged her sitting room, kept the Duke's as it was; and has shut up the music room. Dinner *à trois*, was delicious . . . but before little Edward came to play with me for a time. He is a vigorous, noisy, manly boy, and extraordinarily like his father; the same pouting lips and hair. Both he and Alexandra have a touch of a lisp,

---

1 Llewellin was made a peer, but in 1945. Until the end of 1943 he was on the Combined Policy Committee discussing the development of the atomic bomb, something of which even Channon did not know.

and enchanting rather naughty smiles. They seemed so well and gay, boisterous, that I couldn't help but reflect upon the cruelty of children; for they have already forgotten their father, who worshipped them ... And my thoughts flew to my own dauphin, born on the same day as Edward ... After dinner we played elementary pencil-games such as one did at Taplow twenty years ago; but the Duchess is enchanted with them and showed me with pride a Cartier box made especially to hold pencils and blocks; it was given to her by Noël Coward who, for a time, was in favour in the Kent household.

About 10.30 Alik Poklewski joined us and I was not surprised as I did not think that they would leave the Duchess out of their sight for long. He is a fat, intelligent, well-informed, overfed, anti-Bolshevik creature and I have always liked him, but, of course, he spoilt the *Gemütlichkeit* of the evening. The royal ladies are depressed by Bobbety Cranborne's removal from the Colonial Office as he had been kind about Paul and Kenya; I tried to reassure them, and Princess Olga asked me if Anthony Eden is really the monster she thinks him? Tomorrow Anthony acts as Leader of the House, a difficult task; and, I ask myself, why has Winston given it to him? Is it to groom him for the leadership of the Conservative Party, as is popularly supposed, or to finish him off, as Cripps has been ruined? I suspect a bit of both .... We went up to bed about midnight; and I was haunted by the spirit of the Duke. Every room and *objet* is so inspired – so <u>him</u>. I met him on the staircase, 'saw' him sitting at the end of my bed, as he so often used to do, and constantly aware of him in this house, which still vibrates with his vivacious personality ... one half-expected to meet him coming out of his sitting room and went in to look at it – I wonder whether the Duchess will ever imprint her personality on the place? I doubt it; and I don't think that she will ever be happy here ...

Before I came to Coppins I had to make up my mind what attitude to adopt with Jay Llewellin and his American appointment, so I rang him up, and heartily, heavily congratulated him on his adventuresome mission. He was pleased; says that he is handing over to Cripps tomorrow.

Harold, and Diana Cooper are at Belgrave Square tonight; I am here, and Rab has gone to Eltham. Emerald remarked last night that [Salvador] Dalí, the surrealist painter, has the evil eye and always brings people bad luck. Curious. Once Harold and I and Diana Cooper travelled out to Sestriere, Harold shared a wagon-lit with Dalí, whom I knew slightly; and three days later Harold broke his leg skiing, being out with one of Honor's lovers at the time – the instructor.[1]

TUESDAY 24TH NOVEMBER

Alik Poklewski asked me to drive him to London and I did so. The royal ladies left Coppins at ten o'clock, just before we did. Alexandra rushed to my room,

---

1 See Vol. I, entries for 17–20 February 1938.

she is a whirlwind of a girl – and told me that she had 'prayed' to be taken up to London for the day; and was to have a 'perm'. She is most flirtatious and attractive, although a little less pretty than before.

Lunched with Circe Londonderry at the Ritz; Laura Corrigan, Robin Castlereagh and I. I saw Alba, who is always optimistic and hopes to have a skiing holiday at Saint-Moritz shortly! I returned to the House; listened to the desultory debate and at length left and went to Claridge's to call on Eileen Sutherland who has long been ill. She received me in her 'bed-sitter' and was gently affectionate and rather wan and in good looks; a certain coarseness of middle age has left her and I never liked her more. We discussed the Kent tragedy, and she told me harrowing details. She had been in bed with asthma, but not yet asleep when the news came, and an RAF official asked whether bodies could be sent to Dunrobin,[1] and casually the man informed her that the Duke of Kent was amongst them, little knowing that Eileen and he were lifelong friends. The battered corpse, which she wisely refused to see, lay in a sitting room at Dunrobin for nearly two days whilst many and often contradictory messages poured in! Both Buckingham Palace (actually Balmoral, where the King was staying) and the Air Ministry seemed to lose their heads and the arrangements fell on poor Eileen. It was she who saw to the ordering and sealing of the coffin, of finding a shroud, etc.; of putting flowers in the little sitting room which she had converted into a *chapelle ardente*.[2] The strain and shock made her very ill and she has not yet recovered. I promised that some of these details would be conveyed to the Duchess of Kent whom she has not yet seen.

Emerald Cunard and Loelia Westminster fetched me, arriving before I was dressed, and we all dined chez Cecil Beaton at his attractive candlelit house in Pelham Place. A dreary collection of people really, Eddie Sackville-West,[3] wise, wizen[ed] and sap-less; James Pope-Hennessy, a clever Jewish-looking 'bitch' who writes admirably, Lelia Ralli and David Eccles,[4] who has made a name for himself in Spain, as he was the favourite protégé of Lord Halifax. I rather coquetted with this surprisingly attractive and young individual. He attacked Anthony Eden: to

---

1 The Duke of Sutherland's seat in the Highlands of Scotland.
2 In French the phrase means literally 'burning chapel'; it alludes to the candles that would burn around the coffin of a high personage while it rests there awaiting the funeral.
3 Edward Charles Sackville-West (1901–65), from 1962 5th Baron Sackville, was a music critic and novelist.
4 David McAdam Eccles (1904–99) was Conservative MP for Chippenham from 1943 to 1962, when he was raised to the peerage as 1st Baron Eccles. He worked in the Ministry of Economic Warfare from 1939 to 1940 before becoming economic adviser to the British ambassadors to Portugal and Spain from 1940 to 1942, when he returned to London to work at the Ministry of Production. He helped organise the 1953 Coronation as Minister of Works, for which he was knighted; and served as Minister of Education from 1954 to 1957 and from 1959 to 1962, and as President of the Board of Trade from 1957 to 1959. He was Minister for the Arts and Paymaster-General from 1970 to 1973. He was advanced to a viscountcy in 1964.

do so is now the fashionable pastime . . . . about midnight I induced Emerald to leave, and we dropped Loelia Westminster at the Argentine Embassy opposite. A moonlit night, and a too-full day.

I rang up Oliver Stanley at the Colonial Office where he took over his new duties today, and asked him to lunch tomorrow to meet Princess Olga. He was very nice but refused as he is engaged; he suggested another day. I am disposed to make friends with him now that his drunken harlot-hoyden of a wife is dead. There is much criticism of his appointment because he has been so disloyal and critical of the government and hostile to Winston.

WEDNESDAY 25TH NOVEMBER

At Westminster I found everything in a turmoil; people were still gossiping about the recent changes, and inclined to think that Cripps was definitely finished; his handling of the House has been too awkward and tactless; and now there is a suspicion that Winston is trying to finish off Anthony Eden by giving him the same thankless difficult job; and thus prepare the way for Oliver Lyttelton.[1] I wonder? Jim Thomas, ever Anthony Eden's transparent jackal, confided to me that he feared Anthony's health would not stand the strain; and today, apparently, at Question Time he had a rough ride. Actually the House, when I arrived, was debating equal compensation for women and members were in a critical truculent mood, many being forced to vote against their convictions as a defeat on the address technically would call for a general election, an unthinkable procedure. It was hoped that Mrs Tate would not force a division, but she is a determined minx, quite unscrupulous and a publicity-hunter. She did: the voting was 95 against the government, 229 for the government. After slight hesitation I voted with the government, but I was not displeased that it had a smacking. The Prime Minister was not present.

Everybody is bewildered by the French position and the Free Frogs refuse in any way to help or to recognise Darlan etc. The American government has been more realistic all along, and more sensible. Perhaps Laura Corrigan is right, for she insists that Pétain is really our friend.

Dined with the Kemsleys at the Dorchester . . . . After dinner Emerald and Francis Queensberry, who is indeed an eighteenth-century figure, had a long duel. For three hours I sat entranced. Emerald was in her most enchanting mood, and won. She slyly asked him 'Aren't you some relation of Oscar Wilde's?' This provocative sally evoked the whole history of the Wilde trial etc. David [Margesson] and I sat gaping and riveted. No diary writer could do justice to the scene, the slightly tipsy dishevelled young man with his quaint cockney accent being good-naturedly heckled by the exquisite elegant old lady . . . Home at 2.30.

---

1 All that is lacking for this assertion is any evidence.

Rab says that Winston looked surly at lunch at the Spanish Embassy and growled at him.

THURSDAY 26TH NOVEMBER

The world is confused, bewildered by the African developments – Dakar ours since several days!! Russians advancing . . . etc. Lunched at the Ritz with Circe Londonderry who was in uniform (Charlie Londonderry is in a nursing home having been operated on for a hernia), Lady Hindlip[1] and the Duke of Alba . . . . Alba told me about his luncheon party yesterday for the Prime Minister, to which he had invited '*mes amis des mauvais jours*'[2] meaning Rab and Croft,[3] who had been helpful over Franco. The PM, talking of India, had said chuckling, 'Since the English occupation of India the native population has increased by a hundred million; since the American War of Independence, the Red Indian population has declined by about a hundred million!' What a wonderful riposte to the American critics of our policy. Alba is an ardent Anglophile; somehow I think that he fears an immediate German occupation of Spain.

Returned *à pied*[4] to the House of Commons, walking part of the way with Simon Harcourt-Smith to whom I am now reconciled. He behaved badly, having cut me publicly for over a year after I had refused to lend him a largeish sum of money. Then I ran into Alec Cadogan, ever correct and charming. At the House I fell asleep in the library where I have often slept alongside the greatest men in England and was awakened by Leslie Hore-Belisha, who pinched my bottom. Startled, I came to, and we went back to his house to gather for tea. He is a stimulating companion certainly, and he offered me eternal friendship and a deep devotion; neither do I want really. When I got back to Belgrave Square Alan Lennox-Boyd was waiting for me; he has become bronzed and beautiful, but is becoming a bit of a bore with his nautical tales. However a glow of warmth came over me. We chatted for a brief time until he buzzed off – he is always buzzing off.

FRIDAY 27TH NOVEMBER

An airgraph letter came this morning from Prince Paul . . . . it made my heart ache, it was so pathetic, remote and resigned. Poor dear boy . . . as I was reading it Princess Olga telephoned from Coppins and I was able to read it out to her. She has heard nothing recently and was worried.

---

1 Hansina Elfrida Cecilia Karr-Harris (1910–88) married in 1939 as his second wife Charles Samuel Victor Allsopp (1906–66), who succeeded his father as 4th Baron Hindlip in 1931.
2 'My friends in bad times'.
3 Formerly Sir Henry Page Croft, since 1940 1st Baron Croft. See entry for 22 June 1939 and footnote.
4 On foot.

MONDAY 30TH NOVEMBER

Laura Corrigan . . . . told me too much: how Maureen Dufferin, from a sense of duty, motored to lunch with Honor, and was accompanied by Bob Coe.[1] They found the Woodmans <u>both drunk</u>. Laura also told me more about Honor's outrageous behaviour, of which I was aware, in Rome; how after a party at the Palazzo Colonna given for us, she went to [illegible]'s room in the Hotel Excelsior and threw herself at him. She slept with him for three nights!! Charming. Count Ciano[2] repeated this story all over Rome; and both Mollie Buccleuch and Mary Marlborough who knew it told Laura at the time. Spring – Easter of 1938.[3] I am becoming increasingly embittered against my wife; in fact I am beginning to hate her.

TUESDAY 1ST DECEMBER

To the House and then returned and gave a little luncheon party for Mrs Corrigan. Came: Princess Olga, lovely and gayer than I have so far seen her; the Duchess of Marlborough and Sutherland (since she adores dukes!); Maisie Pavlovsky; Alfred Beit and Alan, who told Princess Olga that in his view Honor ought to be horsewhipped! She was startled. The party was an immense success and they all stayed, plus Emerald who dropped in after coffee, until nearly five o'clock.

Dined with Leslie Hore-Belisha; a historic four, the ladies being old Princesse de Polignac and Laura Corrigan. The conversation was fantastic and should have been recorded. Ate and drank too much! Came home at 11.30. Rab was still out; he was dining with the Chief Whip; plotting no doubt!!

The Beveridge Report[4] has been made public; it will revolutionise life in England. At first glance I am in favour of it.

WEDNESDAY 2ND DECEMBER

Woke feeling dejected and cold. Walked to the House, and later attended a meeting of the 1922 Committee, which was addressed by Sir William Beveridge.

---

1 Robert Douglas Coe (1902–85) was an American diplomat who served at the embassy in London from 1941 to 1948. He was US Ambassador to Denmark from 1953 to 1957.
2 Mussolini's son-in-law.
3 There are no diaries extant for this period: Channon's awareness of and unhappiness about his wife's behaviour in Rome may explain why.
4 William Henry Beveridge (1879–1963) was Liberal MP for Berwick-on-Tweed from 1944 to 1945. He had been a highly regarded career civil servant and permanent secretary at the Ministry of Food in 1918–19; he left to become Director of the London School of Economics, a post he held until 1937. From 1937 to 1945 he was Master of University College, Oxford. His report *Social Insurance and Allied Services* was published in 1942, and became the template for the post-war welfare state. He was knighted in 1919 and raised to the peerage as 1st Baron Beveridge in 1946.

He is a pleasant, earnest, professional little man, obviously capable of immense work: he explained the Report, which surprisingly enough irritates the Socialists more than it does us. I think that it should be adopted. Anthony Eden spoke in the House; vapid and weak, he was. He should never be allowed to express himself in writing.

My butler Lambert is to be called up on January 16th. Six weeks, I have, in which to find a substitute; or shall I shut the house?

Rab came in about six and I saw at once that he was disgruntled and unhappy; I gave him a drink, thawed him and then gave him a bath; in the water he confessed that he was restless, disappointed about India; and that even the appointment of another Viceroy would end his tension and be a relief: Delhi is his heart's goal, he said; and had only Neville Chamberlain remained PM he would have given it to Rab, whom he particularly liked and favoured. In all our association Rab has never been so gentle and confiding. Lady Butler, his most gracious old mother, dined, as did Peter Loxley and we had a gay evening. Rab laughed again and again; he is always less constrained when Sydney is away.

Peter Loxley somewhat slyly suggested that I should keep a diary; it would be the document of the age; I brushed aside his remark and laughingly said that I did 'sometimes'.

THURSDAY 3RD DECEMBER

Woke refreshed. My dog is ageing and I mind very much. His gaiety is gone.

The lobby hummed with plots! That eunuch[1] Harry Crookshank is alleged to be forming a 'cabal' against the Prime Minister, is supposed to have presented him with an ultimatum saying that unless he is made the head of a separate department – a ministry of his own – that he would resign. He has, however, already twice been offered a peerage and job (West Africa) which he turned down. He has a villainous character and is always <u>treacherous</u>. I fear that Harold Balfour encourages him and has ever been entangled in this plot which will probably fail ...

Alan rushed in, having come up from Ramsgate .... Alan seemed downcast and *désoeuvré* and dreadfully enamoured of [blank], who is unworthy of him. He gave me the impression of being rather mad. He had missed 'the three-liner' at the House. I immediately rang the Spanish Embassy where I was due to dine, with the design of getting him invited, too. But the footman told me that it was a party of twelve; so I had to let it drop; and Alan, after a tray snack here, sadly returned to Brighton. Patsy is at Elveden.

---

1 Rather a cruel remark; Crookshank had been castrated by a war wound sustained on the Western Front.

Emerald picked me up and we went across the Square to Alba's. Pleasant party, Circe Londonderry, whose birthday it is; Lady Pembroke; the Chatfields;[1] Duff; others. Just the twelve . . . . over the port I talked to Lord Chatfield and I did good spadework for Prince Paul by reminding him of a confidential conversation held here in my house in 1939 when Paul had asked Chatfield (they remained closeted for two hours) for certain guarantees and armaments, guns, aeroplanes and tanks! Chatfield admitted all this, and I then asked him if any of these requests had ever been acceded to; and he said 'no', categorically. The English government had let Yugoslavia down badly; and he understood poor Paul's dilemma. It was the old story: we simply didn't have the stuff to give him. I then asked Chatfield to make a note of that long-ago but so important conversation to leave with his papers, as such a memo would go a long way to clear the Regent. He promised to do so. He is well-disposed, deaf and sensible. The party broke up, as wartime dinners often do, at 10.15 and I walked home accompanied by Duff Cooper. At home we found Rab working; he had been to the brilliant revival of *The Importance of Being Earnest*[2] and quite, but only quite, liked it. He had always thought it written by Sheridan. Duff was a touch tipsy and for two hours talked irritating nonsense. Said that the Baldwin and Chamberlain governments had let down the country; that ministers had never warned the people etc. Gently I pointed out that he himself was Secretary for War under Baldwin and First Lord under Chamberlain. Surely it was up to him, if he felt so strongly, to give a lead? . . . He told a damning tale about Harry Crookshank who, he said, rang him up on the morning after his 'Munich' resignation and congratulated him on the line he had taken, and intimated that he would shortly be taking the same course. He did nothing of the kind, remained in the government and has been there ever since – being malicious and disloyal to all concerned. Duff says that Crookshank has hardly ever spoken to him since! Crookshank is the Iago of every government! Duff drank too much and stayed too late and too long. Rab was bored and depressed by his defeatism, and his attacks against the 'Municheers'.

FRIDAY 4TH DECEMBER   *BEDFORD HOTEL, BRIGHTON*

Lunched with Ben Kittredge at Buck's: he is a charming, loyal fellow. Then I came here accompanied by Maimie Pavlovsky: Vsevolod arrived earlier. Alan met us. The hotel is deliciously old-fashioned and the damp salt air uninvigorating. We sent a note to Lord Alfred Douglas inviting him to dine and afterwards fetched him. He is frail but looks young and has vestiges still (he is 72) of charm and even good looks; we took him to Sweetings and had a most excellent dinner of oysters

---

1 For Lord Chatfield, see entry for 29 January 1939 and footnote. Lady Chatfield was Lillian
   Emma Matthews (1888–1977), whom he married in 1909.
2 By Oscar Wilde; and this was the production in which Dame Edith Evans began her
   legendary interpretation of the role of Lady Bracknell.

and burgundy etc. He talked of Wilde; told us how old Lord Queensberry, his horrible father, had attended the first night of *The Importance of Being Earnest* and had arrived with a bouquet of cabbages for the author! The incident caused a sensation at the time; he, 'Bosie', however was not present as Wilde had left him at Algiers to return for the opening performance.

Adorable Alan is madder than ever; he, and the Russias [Vsevolods], drink too much.

Harold Balfour is an ambitious angel but a colossal bore, since he thinks only of the House of Commons. A one-track mind. The newspapers hint that [Archie] Sinclair will go to Delhi and that Harold may succeed him.

There is no doubt a tremendous 'Chips' wave on: people may think that I have been harshly treated but it is pleasant to feel the winds of the world's favour fanning one once more . . . . later went to see Pam Churchill in her flat at 49 Grosvenor Square. Averell Harriman and Max Beaverbrook both rang up whilst I was there; as she talked on the telephone I played with the infant Winston, aged 2½. He is the most bumptious little boy I have ever seen; rushes about; he talks and is already most Churchillian. Pam pointed to a photograph of President Roosevelt which he had sent to her and asked 'Winston, who is that?' 'Grandpapa', the child retorted. He looks like the PM; but has Randolph's eyes and expression. Pam confided in me that Randolph is unbalanced and horrible. I am very sorry for her; but she is happy enough. She attracts me very much.

Alan returned from Elveden at 9.30 having driven all that long way in the blackout; he had been there only for an hour to celebrate Simon's 3rd birthday; and the visit, I regret, depressed him. Patsy is so boring, so lethargic and totally uninteresting and worse, slovenly. He found the Iveaghs depressed. We had a cosy supper together until Harold interrupted us. He is very English in one way: he never sees when he is not wanted.

I listened to Smuts's broadcast and I sat on the sofa where he had been for nearly three hours a fortnight ago. It was almost an uncanny sensation.

MONDAY 7TH DECEMBER

Had some people to dine; it was not my most successful party. Lady Willingdon, who arrived with viceregal punctuality at eight o'clock . . . . Emerald on the other hand was forty-five minutes late, as she so irritatingly and invariably is! She came with Lady George Cholmondeley, and brought Peter Derwent[1] who is

---

1 George Harcourt 'Peter' Vanden-Bempde-Johnstone (1899–1949) succeeded his uncle as 3rd Baron Derwent in 1929. He was a career diplomat and also a poet. He served in the RAF from 1942 to 1944.

now a private in the RAF. I regret that His Lordship was old-fashioned drunk, or, to say the least, in wine, and *vin triste*[1] at that. I found him maddening, as I have always done for twenty years. Dinner was not gay; he was a pool of silence; and complained that my wine was corked; Lady Willingdon whispered that he was either deaf or drunk, and perhaps both! Emerald with mischief in her old eyes and her wrinkled fine face smiling roguishly, declared that no man is ever faithful to his wife for more than three years 'and that', she added, 'is a biological fact'. 'You can never have known my Freeman!' Lady Willingdon retorted. 'Very well, and everything he did in India,' was Emerald's rejoinder. After dinner things went better; both Harold and Rab joined us. Derwent was rude to Harold, and three times disappeared into 'the loo' to be sick: eventually he left . . . . Then we all abused him. The others left at 12.45 a.m.

Linlithgow[2] has been definitely prolonged, or rather extended, until October 1943. The viceregal plum has been hawked all over London; first the Cranbornes refused, then the Devonshires, and lastly the Sinclairs. That I know as a fact. Nobody can be found and I think Rab may be offered it later on. I pray so.

TUESDAY 8TH DECEMBER

Woke, society-surfeited and determined never to give another dinner party. Derwent telephoned me at 8.30 most apologetically and I relented and forgave his *farouche*[3] behaviour . . . Walked to the House, where I lunched with Robin Castlereagh and he told me at some length of the famous Sutton weekend in June or July of 1936, when the Sutherlands entertained King Edward VIII and the Simpsons. Mrs Simpson had been very royal, pleasant and dignified, and had even got on well with Lord Halifax!! who was secretly apprehensive and constantly went to church! This was the high-water mark of Mrs Simpson's power – Ernest Simpson had bored the King by talking about the prayer book, a conversation which Castlereagh at the time suspected had been engineered by Mrs Simpson to impress Halifax. *Peut-être* . . .

I heard this morning at the House that Harold Balfour is to be made a peer in the honours list;[4] I rushed to his room and rang him on the private line to report; he was intrigued . . . . He had not heard the rumour.

A good letter, no 36, came from Major Coats; I can never resist his witchery. And a most reassuring letter came from Nannie enclosing one from my beloved boy. *Tout va bien*[5] there – thank God.

A Xmas present, too, from Fritzi, of welcome handkerchiefs.

1 A sad drunk.
2 The Viceroy of India.
3 Wild, savage.
4 Balfour was ennobled, but not until 1945.
5 All's going well.

WEDNESDAY 9TH DECEMBER

Over-much champagne last night made me sleep soundly and I awoke refreshed. Drove to the House, and rushed to 49 Grosvenor Square to pick up Pam Churchill, who looked like a Hellen.[1] We shopped together and at Cook's I bought her a tiny table for £9.0.0. as a Xmas present. We went back to her attic flat, where I washed and played with baby Winston, who is the most determined brat I have ever seen, before I went to the Brazilian Embassy to lunch. A party of twenty-four – mostly bores, but I talked to Lord Clarendon,[2] the Lord Chamberlain, and liked him .... Overate and came back to No. 5 where I fell into a coma for an hour and ruminated .... I have heard nothing more of Harold's peerage. Then went to the Dorchester to a Free Frog concert; as a member of the Committee I helped to receive the Queen. She came in, dressed in black velvet and smelling of roses. She looked well and slightly flushed, and made the circle. She chatted with one or two people for a moment; but when she came near me, she crossed over very markedly and said 'How are you, Chips? I haven't seen you for ages.' We talked a little; and she asked me if I had seen Princess Olga etc. We talked for about five minutes to everybody's surprise, I thought; and I felt the warmth of her famous charm again and was almost *attendri* towards her. To my left General de Gaulle, his wife, and General Catroux were waiting. Catroux wears his five rows [of] decorations, de Gaulle none at all. He is most maddening, mad, conceited and inflated ... we all followed the Queen into the concert room; she sat between generals de Gaulle and Catroux – the programme was excellent and overlong; as she left she again smiled particularly at me ... soon everybody was talking of it! Charles Peake and Lady Dashwood rushed to me!!! Am I to be restored to royal favour there? ... Emerald had lunched with Winston, who was charming to her and told her how he had hated 'sacking' David Margesson. What hypocrisy! Randolph did it.

Princess Olga and the Duchess of Kent rang up proposing themselves to luncheon on Saturday. I must arrange something.

I fear that the African news is none too good, that is from Tunisia. And I have an uneasy apprehensive feeling that the Germans may even attempt an invasion of this island.

Rab, half-naked, walked into my bedroom this morning and I communicated with him on turning 40: it is his birthday. He asked how old I was, and I retorted '34.' 'You look less!' he replied. He said that my coughing kept him awake; it is my damnable catarrhal cigarette cough.

---

1 Thus in MS. He presumably means 'like a Greek goddess', or classical beauty.
2 George Herbert Hyde Villiers (1877–1955) was Lord Hyde by courtesy until 1914, when he succeeded his father as 6th Earl of Clarendon. From 1931 to 1937 he was Governor-General of South Africa and from 1938 to 1952 Lord Chamberlain.

THURSDAY 10TH DECEMBER

[The Commons] went into secret session. As we waited for the strangers to be cleared, I counted thirty-seven peers in the gallery. Winston was cheered and he held the House enthralled for an hour as he described in dramatic detail the whole story of the African expedition and General Eisenhower's sudden decision to accept Admiral Darlan's co-operation.[1] Evidently Winston, *au fond* a conservative, was enjoying himself and relished the unexpected turn of events ... He told much which surprised the House, but which was no news to me; how the French hated de Gaulle and how the Americans refused to have anything to do with the Free French movement, etc. And how Darlan's sudden help saved time, lives and even perhaps the success of the whole expedition ... He was in the highest fettle and never have I admired him so much; Pétain, he pronounced Petaigne, and described him as 'an antique defeatist'; etc. etc. The House was soon mollified and cheered him lustily; but a few left-wingers were irritated ... I regard Darlan's assistance as a step in the right direction: right in both senses of the word; but the lefties are furious, and fifty are de Gaullistes who will not collaborate. I slept for a little; and no wonder for both Lady Cunard and Walter Buccleuch rang me in the night and kept me gossiping for an hour on the telephone. Walter is so good and kind and dull and misunderstood and underrated.

Before dinner I gave Rab his bath. He had an immense boil or carbuncle on his neck and I found myself wanting to squeeze it and watch the pus jump out ... a strange urge common, I believe, to all of us ...

FRIDAY 11TH DECEMBER

Honor sent me an untidy book as a Christmas present; she is always careless and tactless ... I had sent her a handsome silver bell.

Channon goes with Lady Willingdon to see The Importance of Being Earnest.

The crowded audience often laughed at all the wrong jokes. It was amazing. Some of the subtlest repartees escaped them. Oh! democracy, what dullness is yours! Last time I saw this play was in December 1940 when I took Peter, Emerald and Georgia [Sitwell] etc. for one of his many Melba farewells[2] ... The play made me nostalgic. Francis Queensberry tonight was in a box! He lives well, yet poor 'Bosie' (Lord Alfred Douglas) writes despairingly to Alan begging for some money, since Francis now refuses to help him over his flat and the poor old man is threatened with eviction. It is a ghastly drama ... I brought back the ladies .... to

---

1 Seeing the way the wind was blowing after El Alamein and the German occupation of Vichy France, Darlan had decided to support the Allies.

2 Because there were various false alarms about Coats being sent abroad. Like Dame Nellie Melba, he 'retired' several times.

supper (I had gone around to John Gielgud's[1] dressing room and invited him but he was already engaged).

Harold reports that his luncheon at No. 11 Downing Street was uneventful. I was discussed! Afterwards Winston led him into a corner and asked whether he was really dissatisfied or disgruntled. Harold replied that 'there was a danger of going stale after four years in the same department'! Winston is gay this week: Emerald lunched with him on Wednesday; Mrs Keppel and old Lloyd George yesterday I believe; and today Harold, Geoffrey Lloyd, Pam and others including old Coalbox![2]

I am having domestic difficulties with my staff, as the Ministry of Labour wish to call up both my butler and the cook. I mustn't grumble, as I have had three years and three months of comfort, even of luxury, whilst everyone else has 'pigged it'.

A little luncheon party, which was *réussi*: the Duchess of Kent, Princess Olga, Alice Harding, and Nicholas Lawford. Cranborne was coming but he 'chucked' and I rang up Garrett Moore and got him at the last moment. Princess Olga looked stately, indeed magnificent in black and pearls, and wore violets. The Duchess had a small black mourning veil falling from an arch-hat and looked extremely lovely. And she is 36 tomorrow . . . . They all left late . . . Nicholas and I walked to the RAC where we had a 'Turker' together. It was there that I read that Doris Castlerosse had died. She committed suicide by taking an overdose on Wednesday night; but she survived unconscious for two days, after being rushed to hospital. Her death is no grief to me, indeed I hated her and she was my inveterate enemy ever since I prevented her marrying Arthur Elveden. Nevertheless I am sorry for her, for she loved life, was gay, and once glamorous and must have suffered greatly before taking the decision to die. She made the cardinal mistake of backing a world to which she did not belong, and which she always outraged. It ended by hating and finally killing her. The World must always win. In other days she would have been a successful *courtisane*, a sort of Harriette Wilson;[3] but she was ambitious and wanted to be a social figure. Curiously enough it was her wicked tongue and treacherous nature more than her immoral life which brought about her end. She ruined men, but usually, I must say, rich ones; fastened onto them; and latterly she took to rich ladies. She was not without gaiety or charm or beauty or chic. She stayed with us – against my wishes – at Wasserleonburg[4] and made herself agreeable enough.

---

1 Arthur John Gielgud (1904–2000) was one of the leading actors of the English stage, radio and film of the twentieth century.*
2 Lady Colefax.
3 Prostitute to the aristocracy in Regency times.
4 A castle in Austria.

She was about 46, I suppose;[1] and her whole life has been a procession of lovers, blackmail, debts and a certain crude bonhomie. She recently returned from the USA, and was coldly received by everybody, and this gave her a sense of social frustration and she ended by killing herself from boredom and poverty. Harold says that when the subject was mentioned at lunch on Friday at the Dixième Bureau that the PM looked quite pained and then changed the subject. He was always rather fond of Doris[2] . . . Castlerosse, now Kenmare,[3] was sent for and rushed to the hospital. He, too, is alleged to be upset; he always loved her.

Dined at the Dorchester with Emerald, Juliet Duff and Hore-Belisha, and Diana Cooper who had just arrived from Scotland. Duff in a violent, vehement, tipsy mood joined us later; he attacked everybody and everything, particularly Mr Chamberlain – he still harps on that – and finally I quietly asked him how long he had served under him. Duff, rather nettled, went red in the face. He is so difficult, drunken and opinionated . . . Eventually I left, but not before registering boredom, and walked Juliet home in the rain. Here I picked up Alan who was gossiping with Harold. Alan and I dropped her and later gossiped. Harold is jealous of our friendship and will never allow me to be alone with Alan; he never seems to know when to withdraw. A very English trait.

Yes, Doris killed herself. The world won and it was her malice rather than her morals which defeated her.

SUNDAY 13TH DECEMBER

I was told more about Lady Castlerosse's suicide. It seems that she was more amazed and humiliated by the coldness of her reception on her recent return to England. Lately Eleanor Smith, who has a vitriolic and nimble pen, wrote a lampoon called 'Lady Rat' attacking her. Four different people were kind enough to send Doris copies anonymously of this attack and she developed persecution mania and insomnia, which led to her ultimate suicide. A sad story. These cruel people are her murderers!

More roistering with my big Alan.

MONDAY 14TH DECEMBER

Slept badly, as I was awakened by Emerald telephoning me at 2.30 a.m. She had entertained Duff and Diana, Osbert Sitwell, Olive Baillie, Geoffrey Lloyd and Nicholas Lawford: they had talked 'exclusively of Isaac Newton and Chips'! and

---

1 She was 42.
2 Persistent but strongly denied rumours have had it that they had an affair. Lady Castlerosse's family equally strongly believed them to be true.
3 Viscount Castlerosse, who had divorced his wife in 1938, had succeeded to the earldom of Kenmare in 1941.

had telephoned all over London trying to find me that I might join them! Emerald repeated Leslie Hore-Belisha's remark that 'anybody who doesn't like Chips must be mad'. The world has never been so kind as of late . . . . Emerald said that she liked Nicholas Lawford 'even more than Laura Corrigan likes Pétain'!

Rose lazily, met Diana and we went shopping together. I wondered whether we would meet my harlot Honor, who is up for the night. It would have been more politic to have lunched with Alan and Patsy, who invited me; but she, a sweet apple really, bores me. She is having some sort of intellectual flirtation with Richard Temple and I consider the association unfortunate . . . however Alan is unconcerned and ignores my warnings. She dined again with this semi-adventurer last night.

I lunched alone, after a morning in Diana's enthralling, inebriating company; wrote and slept; tea with Lady Cunard and finally, *malgré moi*,[1] I dined with Barbie Wallace. She is intelligent, but has been bitten by that insidious bug, Eden-itis; it is an instinct for suicide which one finds in the more intellectual social elements of high society: it is *fin-de-race*, a desire for suicide, the last *volupté* after they had had everything else. Otherwise she is an extremely sensible woman. Her youngest boy Billy[2] was there; he is long, lovely, and languorous with lapis eyes and a lackadaisical manner.

TUESDAY 15TH DECEMBER

I think that Shakes Morrison will be moved to the new Ministry of Planning, and that Crookshank will succeed him. Harold Macmillan will become FST.[3] Dr Summerskill[4] electrified the House of Commons with a fiery speech about syphilis!

I am advising old Baroness de Stoeckl to write her memoirs![5]

In the evening I gave an extempore little dinner party for Jay Llewellin who leaves so soon to become Minister of Supply Resident in Washington; it was a highly successful function. Jay; Harold; Alan, up from Newhaven for the occasion; Peter Loxley, ever charming . . . . We drank much, gossiped more, and talked high politics . . . . Jay and Alan remained on for a Hogarthian revel until 2.30 a.m. I have rarely enjoyed myself more.

WEDNESDAY 16TH DECEMBER

Woke, to be massaged at seven, in an almost delirious state of high spirits and excitement which sometimes follows an orgy. Walked to the House . . . . Questions

---

1 In spite of myself.
2 William Euan 'Billy' Wallace (1927–77). His name was for a time connected with Princess Margaret's.
3 Financial Secretary to the Treasury.
4 The Labour MP for Fulham West; see Vol. I, entry for 2 April 1938.
5 Agnes Barron; see entry for 6 December 1940 and footnote. She did write them, and other books.

began by Cunningham-Reid asking why Princess Olga had been allowed to leave England? Anthony retorted that she was still here and that arch four-letter fellow looked abashed; Anthony went on to snub him by saying the Princess Olga had come here with the full approval of HMG . . . . I have heard that Paul's condition is rapidly deteriorating; the government of Kenya have sent a cable advising her immediate return. What can I do? I feel and fear that he may die, will simply wither away . . . Oliver Stanley has conveyed the tragic news to the Duchess of Kent, who wisely decided to keep the information from her sister, so as not to spoil and poison their few remaining days together. *En route* for Kenya, Lelia Ralli must break it to her. Princess Olga is powerless to hasten her departure since it depends on the Air Ministry. I slept in the library, lunched alone, and came home.

Alan reports that Jay Llewellin was suddenly hostile to him as they walked home together in the blackout.

THURSDAY 17TH DECEMBER

How a mercurial and extraordinary assembly is the august Mother of Parliaments.[1] Yesterday one despaired of democracy, it behaved so querulously; today it was sublime. Anthony read out a statement in regard to the extermination of Jews in East Europe; whereupon Jimmie de Rothschild[2] rose and with immense dignity, and his voice vibrating with emotion, spoke for five minutes in moving terms on the plight of these peoples. There were tears in his eyes and I feared that he might break down; the House caught the spirit and was deeply moved. Somebody suggested that we stand to pay our respects to those suffering peoples; and the House as a whole rose and stood for a few frozen seconds in silence. My back tingled – it was a fine moment . . . .

I found both Rab and Jay Llewellin, who had come to say 'goodbye'; he [Llewellin] leaves for America tomorrow. He brought me a brace of brandy bottles, a most welcome present; and was charming and affectionate, kind and gentle. I shall almost miss him now.

Looked in at Mrs Keppel's cocktail party at the Ritz. Pre-war. Ambassadors, fifty people. I sat with Madame Cárcano, who is feline, lovely and perhaps a bit vulpine; her observations are shrewd and penetrating. Duff arrived late and came up to Bettine Abingdon[3] and me and remarked: 'May I join beauty and

---

1 See footnote for 1 April 1941.
2 James Armand Edmond de Rothschild (1878–1957) was Liberal MP for the Isle of Ely from 1929 to 1945. He was a junior minister in the Ministry of Supply from 1940 to 1945, and bequeathed Waddesdon Manor to the National Trust.
3 Elizabeth Valetta 'Bettine' Montagu-Stuart-Wortley (1896–1978) married in 1928 Montagu Henry Edmund Cecil Towneley-Bertie (1887–1963), 8th Earl of Abingdon.

fashion?' And I had what amounts to a reconciliation with Evan Tredegar[1] who was *amiabilité* itself . . . . The world is so kind to me now; I bask in its smiles. How long will it, can it, last? And I now don't really care!

FRIDAY 18TH DECEMBER

My windows are being replaced and they are welcome after two years of blackness.

Shopped, met Diana and John Julius Cooper at Buck's and gave them drinks. John Julius is already improved by Eton. I gave him £1 . . . . Lunched with Emerald, Georgia Sitwell, Leslie Hore-Belisha and Poppy Thursby. Emerald remarked that she was not depressed by the Crucifixion, she had long got used to it. She twitted me, suggested that I become the Greville or Creevey[2] of the age and slyly hinted that I was both. I denied it. Leslie Hore-Belisha and I walked in the drizzling rain to Claridge's to call on Laura Corrigan, who had sprained her ankle. Circe Londonderry was there.

The war news is better; Rommel's army seems to have been outflanked, and part of it cut off.

Cárcano told me yesterday that old Pétain had given him a photograph which proves his senility, for he has inscribed: '*Pour M. Cárcano, qui est un seducteur*'[3] on it, and signed it Philippe Pétain. Cárcano is much teased by his family about it.

Belisha tells me that the only man who hates me is James Stuart. It is a pity that he should be Chief Whip! I don't understand why. Leslie has acted upon my suggestion; on Monday he gave dinner to Rab alone; on Tuesday Anthony Eden was his guest; last night he 'entertained' James Stuart.

I walked home, somewhat apprehensive as there is so much violence and robbery about.

SUNDAY 20TH DECEMBER   *PYRFORD*

Drove here in balmy warm weather and spent the day with my in-laws. They dread any action, any honourable action[4] and still delude themselves that all will end well. I showed my teeth over Paul . . . Lady Iveagh reminiscing about old country-house customs thinks that those days are over forever. She said that the

---

1 Evan Frederic Morgan (1893–1949) succeeded his father as 2nd Viscount Tredegar in 1934. He was a poet, and also an inspiration for Ivor Lombard, a character in Aldous Huxley's first novel, *Crome Yellow* (1921). He developed his own menagerie and was an occultist. Although homosexual he was twice married, first to Lois Sturt (1900–37) (qv), whom he married in 1928 but from whom he separated in 1936.

2 Charles Greville (1794–1865) and Thomas Creevey (1768–1838), a Whig politician, were noted political diarists.

3 'For Mr Cárcano, who is a seducer'.

4 That is, divorce proceedings between Channon and Lady Honor.

last time the King and Queen stayed with her at Elveden they brought a suite of twenty-two, including a page, a postman, dressers, etc. And they all stayed a week.

MONDAY 21ST DECEMBER

A day of Christmas shopping, presents, telephoning, and a headache. The Duchess of Kent has sent me a magnificent silver box for cigarettes which belonged to the Duke, and is in 'affectionate remembrance of my husband'. A touching and handsome memento.

War seems [to be] flaring up in India: Burma is being invaded; and Calcutta has had an air raid. I trust that the Major [Coats] will be safe.

TUESDAY 22ND DECEMBER

The Duchess of Kent, looking radiantly lovely and even gay, came to tea bringing Princess Olga. It was by way of being a farewell; they had been told that Princess Olga and Lelia must be ready to leave tonight! It is all a bungled mystery: they are travelling under Dutch names in the Queen of Holland's private plane. She was to have accompanied them as far as Bathurst but her doctors forbid her to fly high because of her ageing Orange heart, and so she is not going. Even the pilots are not to know whom they are to fly. I at once rang up Harold, who made an investigation and called me back to say that there was no question now of Princess Olga leaving before Xmas. I am so very glad ... They stayed for an hour and we were joined by old Baroness Stoeckl and Lelia Ralli, who brought me a Capo di Monte statuette – Ganymede and the Eagle ... This long protracted tea party prevented me from accompanying Emerald to the National Gallery, where Kenneth Clark had been waiting to receive us and show us the French pictures ... (Emerald has hinted that she may leave me one of George Moore's famous Monets!)

Rab, as he dressed this morning, was pagan in manner, indeed. He can be very charming and boyish, the President of the Board of Education, particularly when he is alone! He dines this evening with Kenneth Clark.

And meanwhile as Princess Olga is further delayed my poor Regent languishes in Kenya ...

I have had several sumptuous Xmas presents including six fresh eggs from the Red Cross at Kelvedon!

How transitory is human attraction: when Alan Lennox-Boyd left me this afternoon a wave of tenderness for him came over me and I could not bear to be parted from him even for a few long hours; yet when Gage rang up begging me either to dine with him or give him dinner (preferably the latter, I am sure!) I refused although I was doing nothing. Yet thirteen years ago he was my whole life and I loved him deeply for three or four years. Now he is a comic and an old bore. Alan came back at ten and we talked for an hour until he left me to call on Godfrey Winn, who has returned for a time – he is a sailor now. Over the telephone he confided in me most indiscreet things about poor J. J. Llewellin! I was shocked but fascinated.

THURSDAY 24TH DECEMBER

Alan breezed up from Newhaven; he is a most exhilarating, and exhausting companion. We lunched in with Raymond Mortimer, whose brilliant little book *Channel Packet*[1] is having a deserved success; it is slightly spoilt by his splenetic political theories; he is forever jibing at the class he most admires and cultivates – high society. However with his warm generous charm, his piercing intelligence, he is a perfect companion. Alan and I had a Turkish bath. I had to listen to three hours' conversation about Adrian Liddell Hart.

How nervous and complicated are the English. Harold dashed in before dinner, too late to change; he was in a fiendish temper and had had a row with Archie Sinclair . . . . Harold says (although I doubt it) that he has been offered FST [Financial Secretary to the Treasury], the usual stepping stone to Cabinet rank. I don't think that he is sufficiently equipped mentally to take on any government job except in a Service Department. He is ideal where he is . . . he Alan and I picked up old Emerald at the Dorchester and escorted her to Claridge's where we dined, a cosy Christmas party, with Laura Corrigan, who had taken endless trouble to organise a party. Alice Harding came. There were presents for all, holly, champagne, sherry, Christmas puddings and every other rarity . . . what would have been an amusing evening was somewhat spoilt by Emerald's absurdly plaintive conversation that she lacked sufficient food, which is <u>nonsense</u>. Alan, fresh from the dangers of the sea, took offence and became nervous . . . Later, he and I went to Westminster Abbey for midnight Mass, which was impressive . . . the dark abbey crowded with soldiers, many of them American and Canadian, praying in the flickering candlelight. Then Alan and I walked about in the icy moonlight. London was never so romantic. We slept together here but his snores disturbed me.

FRIDAY 25TH DECEMBER   *THE GARDENER'S COTTAGE, ELVEDEN*

My tiny car, crowded with parcels, was ready at ten, and Alan and I started forth for Elveden via Henlow. We were delayed by a thick fog. Mrs Lennox-Boyd and her other sons, rather zany both (Francis and George) received us warmly and gave

1 About fishing in Scottish lochs; published in 1942.

us presents and chocolate. Then we came on here and lunched at the Old Rectory with the Iveaghs, Elizabeth Elveden and her mundane petite mother, Freda, Lady Listowel.[1] Patsy, very pregnant, was more lethargic than ever . . . . The Iveaghs gave me a *seicento* tazza. The Elveden children made me nostalgic for my own lad so far away in America. I am profoundly unhappy and lonely, really. My life is a mess . . . The Iveaghs are gentle, affectionate, but self-contained and fundamentally indifferent to everything except themselves – only little Simon Lennox-Boyd, a most independent, red-headed child of 3, seems to have caught their affections. The more beautiful, gentle, engaging, aristocratic Elveden children leave them fairly cold.

Some American officers, shy and hideous, came for cocktails. There are 500 of them living at Elveden. They are untidy, ignorant and unattractive, but their friendliness equals their slovenliness.

SUNDAY 27TH DECEMBER

Drove to London with Alan and later quarrelled with him. Dear selfish boy!

I am despairing, unhappy and wretched . . . .

What will 1943 bring to me? Misery, money and disillusion!!!

MONDAY 28TH DECEMBER

A quiet day of catching up, and regretting my tiff with Alan last night. After lunching with Mrs Corrigan and asking at Hapney's whether I could exchange the unbelievably hideous Christmas present which Vsevolod of Russia had bought for me there, I called at 8b Hobart Place and found my vicious Sinbad of a brother-in-law [Lennox-Boyd] in. He was all charm and smiles and affection and we parted once more reconciled.

Dined in: I had collected cronies during the course of the day: Lady Cunard, exquisite and scintillating; Mrs Corrigan who has become a terrific character; the Coopers, Duff and Diana; Nicholas Lawford; Aleco Matsas; Harold Balfour, handsome in blue velvet which I gave him a year ago; and dear Alan. An uproariously gay and successful dinner party due probably to the fact that there was much to drink (white wine; cocktails; port and brandy) and little to eat: oysters; tomato soup; fish; Xmas puddings and walnuts!! Everyone was lively and gay. The Coopers were tiresome, in their most narrow pro-Semitic, anti-Chamberlain, anti-Municher's mood; but I refused, although twice tempted, to be drawn into a row. The whole evening was quite exceptionally *réussi* and both Diana Cooper and Emerald telephoned on their return to

---

1 Freda Vanden-Bempde-Johnstone (1885–1968) married in 1904 Richard Granville Hare (1866–1931), by courtesy Viscount Ennismore until 1924, when he succeeded his father as 4th Earl of Listowel.

thank me. 'Ripping!' Diana said it was. I was quite sorry that I refused to let Lady Willingdon come!

TUESDAY 29TH DECEMBER

Photographs came of my son in America. He looks thoughtful and intelligent; yet I don't really like them and fear his clothes are too horrible.

Every old lady in London rang me up proposing parties . . . I am quite worn out by the Yuletide exertions and festivities: and I am annoyed to hear nothing from Peter. Miss Wavell has sent me *War and Peace*, the three volumes belonging to General Wavell.

Alan is certainly losing his brilliant mind; it is enflamed, diseased, and all day and tonight he behaved in a wild indiscreet manner which will eventually, unless he controls his lusts, lead to his early political and social destruction. *C'est la maladie du siècle.*[1]

Lunched alone, worked and at five o'clock went to have tea at the Dorchester with Emerald as I much wanted to see Archie Clark Kerr,[2] our debonair Ambassador in Moscow. We fell into each other's arms, yet I found him greatly altered after six years. His mouth has sunk and he looks leathery, shabby and strange and has a queer twisted smile.

The next line has been run through in pencil, and then swirled through in blue biro by Coats deliberately to be made illegible.

Emerald twitted him about his alleged amour with Madame Chiang Kai-shek,[3] which he didn't deny. As we were talking Pamela Berry dropped in; her great wide onyx eyes are more luminous than ever and her tongue as sharp and as wild . . . she immediately embarked upon a picturesque account of a recent visit she had made to see Honor! She had persuaded Sheila Birkenhead to go with her from nearby Hackwood. Honor, whom they both dislike and had not seen for <u>three</u> years, was nervous and ill at ease, and somewhat intoxicated. She tactlessly introduced Pam to Mr Woodman saying 'You both have gypsy blood'! It was an unpleasant visit and undertaken solely from motives of blatant curiosity.

1   It's the illness of the times.
2   Archibald Clark Kerr (1882–1951) was British Ambassador to Peking from 1938 to 1942, to Moscow from 1942 to 1946 and to Washington from 1946 to 1948. He was knighted in 1935 and raised to the peerage as 1st Baron Inverchapel in 1946. He had a baroque private life, though apparently centred upon younger women, which may explain Coats's subsequent deletions. He is celebrated for a letter he wrote to Lord Pembroke from Russia in 1943 telling him that 'God has given me a new Turkish colleague whose card tells me that he is called Mustapha Kunt. We all feel like that, Reggie, now and then, especially when Spring is upon us, but few of us would care to put it on our cards. It takes a Turk to do that.'
3   Soong Mei-ling; see entry for 10 February 1942 and footnote.

When she left us, we went on to Lady Londonderry's cocktail party at the Ritz, Emerald, Archie and I all sharing a taxi. There were thirty people, Mrs Keppel, Eileen Sutherland looking well but too, too thin, Hughie Northumberland and others . . . Archie CK and I drove away together and I felt a wave of sympathy come over us, yet we said nothing very confidential or extraordinary, yet such is human understanding that we were in tune. He is still fascinating although hideous . . . Dined with Lady Cunard and it was much the same get-up, only not so gay or amusing, as last night: Coopers both; Nicholas Lawford; Aleco Matsos; Emerald; Laura Corrigan; I and the two Londonderrys. They are disillusioned and sad but not embittered. Everybody except me attacked the royalties, said what bores they all were etc. Charlie Londonderry told us how he had once escorted (he was an ensign in the Guards at the time) Queen Victoria to the private side entrance of Buckingham Palace, and she had smilingly thanked him and then dropped him a very faint curtsey. A bundle in black bowed to him! He has always remembered it. Everybody agreed that Violet Trefusis is <u>not</u> the daughter of Edward VII but of Lord Grimthorpe.[1] Much royal reminiscing; both Duff and Emerald erudite. She has always had amazing bits of stray esoteric information up her sleeve and startles one by the quaint, provocative way with which she produces them.

Alan sent me a note during dinner, but refused to join us. I walked home with Nicholas Lawford in the cold moonlight.

WEDNESDAY 30TH DECEMBER

Alan fetched me, as did Diana Cooper who told me that Nevile Henderson had died at the Dorchester during the night. He was a misunderstood man; gentle without being anything approaching a gentleman, he had nonetheless insinuating manners and good looks. Indeed he was a great lover and abroad always considered *un grand seigneur* which he decidedly was not. He dressed with care and even elegance, and was somewhat trivial, although conservative in outlook. The Foreign Office always hated him, and he it, for he was determined to prevent war if possible. Göring was his intimate friend, and he was much flattered and feted by the Nazi leaders. I first met him at Bled where he was a successful, much liked, and even adored Minister. The late King Alexander was devoted to him and left him a cigarette case and the use of a shooting box. He practically determined Yugoslavia's foreign policy during the years he was accredited there. These were the days when he was *amant en titre*[2] of Kitty de Rothschild.[3] Later there were others. He was most kind to us when we were in Berlin in 1937 on that

---

1 Ernest William Beckett-Denison (1856–1917) was a banker and Conservative MP for Whitby from 1885 to 1905; he fought in the Second Boer War. He succeeded his father as 2nd Baron Grimthorpe in 1905, and had had an affair with Mrs Keppel.
2 Lover.
3 See entry for 20 June 1940 and footnote.

foolish expedition when I took Honor away from her Hungarian lover, Pálffy.[1] After the war broke out I introduced Henderson to my mother-in-law, and together they ran and organised a Refugee Fund for English refugees. The idea of helping their own compatriots was a startling one for England, as hitherto all money and charity had gone to Czechs and Poles. It was a success.

Alan and I gave luncheon to Gerard Herlihy, my tame Reuters' correspondent. He is lame and an Irish Catholic and a most able lobby journalist who has recently left Reuters and gone into the *Sketch*. But he bores me to frenzy, as do all non-social people: I can barely talk to them at all . . . walked home. It is very cold. Later I joined Lady Willingdon and we went to a film (boring and a 'time-waster') and had dinner at the Allies Club in the Rothschilds' old house in Piccadilly. Excellent food, and many soldiers of all nationalities – but a somewhat sordid atmosphere . . . . On my return Princess Olga rang me up to say 'goodbye': she said I was her greatest friend; the first person she rang and called upon when she arrived; and the last she said she would speak to before she left. We both cried and had a moving, lachrymose conversation.

---

1 Coats has scored through this heavily in the MS, but it is still legible. Franz von Erdödi-Pálffy was a Hungarian nobleman; see Vol. I, entry for 20 August 1937 and footnote.

1943

My New Year has dawned and I have not made any foolish resolutions. I only know that I am older and less attractive and that people go about saying that I am [the] HORACE WALPOLE of the age. Is that a compliment or not? I slept late, went over my accounts and realised that I have spent much too much money. There it is. I have heard nothing from Peter.

Lunched with Laura Corrigan at Claridge's, what she calls a *rawling* lunch: Eileen Sutherland, thin almost as Kitty Brownlow was – it is alarming; Hughie Northumberland, copper-y and enchanting; the two Londonderrys, Alexis [Aleco] Matsas, the young very social Greek; Margaret Stewart[1] who has resumed her maiden name after her disastrous matrimonial adventures; Robin Castlereagh, Laura and I. Excellent food and friendly atmosphere. Charlie Londonderry attacked Mme du Barry[2] until Emerald Cunard twitted him with being too anti-French. In the afternoon, I drove Laura in my little car through the City to show her the acres of destruction. She was impressed. That sad area has been tidied up and looks bare and bleak but not as ghastly as it did when rubble and debris lay about ...

Dined with Emerald, Diana Cooper, Archie Clark Kerr, Francis Queensberry; Nicholas Lawford; and Pam Berry[3] who talked to me about Honor at some length. She is unshakable and wild in her remarks; but she reports unfavourably of the set-up at Shalden; says that Woodman is terrible, a drunken bounder etc. I asked her why the Camroses had opposed her husband's marriage to Honor before either she, Pam, or I appeared on the scene. She said it was because Lady Camrose had thought her uncouth, dirty, rude, unattractive and mad. The whole Berry tribe had hated her. Later when she married me, and became for a time, a great London hostess, they regretted their attitude as they saw her blossom; now, of course, they crow, even more ... I had some private conversation with Archie Kerr. He doesn't like Russia; wants to be appointed to Washington; adores Chungking. He is, however, pro-Bolshie, has become seriously infected with that

---

1 Margaret Frances Anne Vane-Tempest-Stewart (1910–66), from 1915 Lady Margaret by courtesy, was the second daughter of 7th Marquess of Londonderry (qv) and former wife of (Frederick) Alan Irving Muntz (1899–1985), an aeronautical engineer.
2 Louis XV's mistress.
3 Lady Pamela Berry, wife of Michael Berry and daughter-in-law of Lord Camrose, not Mary Pamela Berry, daughter of Lord Kemsley (qqv).

bug. Immensely aged, unattractive, and his charm almost – but not quite – gone. Queensberry was in high spirits and prodded by Emerald, quoted Shakespeare's sonnets. He knows them all by heart; then he quoted Alfred Douglas's poems, and was genuinely enchanting. He is an eighteenth-century character, with his gambling, drinking and rather quaint cockney voice which contrasts dramatically with his love of poetry and his sadness.

I watched with interest the yankee Stuart Preston[1] arrive in sergeant's khaki, is a poet and has considerable cultivation which impressed us all. He is immensely impressed by all of us, more particularly me. I walked to Hyde Park Corner arm in arm with Nicholas Lawford, whose life I have so altered. At Hyde Park Corner, we separated in the cold and I imagine well even now he, too, is writing up his day for I suspect that he keeps a diary. He is so charming, so prematurely aged, and without being a misanthrope, so utterly disillusioned and completely sad.

The honours list is exciting. Miles Lampson becomes a peer (I suggested this to Anthony and others nearly two years ago) and Wavell is a field marshal (that too I suggested to [Leo] Amery and to Harvie-Watt over a year ago). I am so glad. More income for Wavell and Victor Miles[2] becomes an Honourable.

SATURDAY 2ND JANUARY   KELVEDON

I wanted today to be alone and came here to sleep, read and write. It is icy, but the place is ever lovely. And I was thrilled to see spots of green on my pavilion roof – at long last. Shall I live to see it all green? There are fifty-two patients [in the Red Cross hospital] and they bother me not at all.

I wrote to Lampson and Wavell – it is most exciting, their honours.

SUNDAY 3RD JANUARY

Spent the sunny but cold morning at Kelvedon shooting and writing. That more than mad Alan travelled up from Falmouth last night and left by an 8.20 train for Elveden this morning. He is crazy, and reckless to the point of folly. I am disturbed about him and prophesy that their marriage will ultimately crack and crash. His charm outweighs his selfishness and his loveable qualities his infuriating ones.

Drove up 'to town', as the middle classes say, and dined in. Emerald, wittier and more glowing than ever, came accompanied by Master Stuart Preston.

---

1 Stuart Duncan Preston (1915–2005) was for over twenty-five years art critic of the *New York Times*; a sergeant in the US Army based in London, he was taken up by Lady Cunard. Among his friends were Harold Nicolson, Evelyn Waugh, the Duff Coopers, Nancy Mitford and Sibyl Colefax. He was universally known as 'Sarge'. King George VI allegedly said: 'Every day I meet brigadiers and generals. Why can't I meet this sergeant everyone is talking about?'
2 Victor Miles George Aldous Lampson (b.1941) in 1996 succeeded his elder half-brother as 3rd Baron Killearn.

Nicholas Lawford dined and stayed the night; and we were all joined by Alan up from Elveden – after one of his mad lightning journeys – and Harold.

MONDAY 4TH JANUARY

I feel weak and tired after a late night: Emerald exhausts as she exhilarates, and always stays too late ...

Everybody, Emerald included, invited me to dine; but I was world-weary and eschewed it. Had a Turkish bath at the RAC, which is one place where I am really happy and in peace. Alone with one's thoughts and one's sweating body one finds content. Later Alan bullied me into dining with him .... Walked in the very complete blackout to the Carlton, twice tripped against the wet pavement kerb and bumped my head into a Belisha beacon. The Carlton was warm but the food was unsatisfying. Patsy and Alan brought old Howard Whitbread[1] who is well over 80; he is a bucolic *grand seigneur* and talked of Bedfordshire, the House of Commons and had once gone up from Eton to hear Disraeli speak on some great occasion. The ageing Prime Minister had stopped, paused, taken out a coloured bandana from his pocket, blown his nose – which was apparently a signal for his supporters to cheer, which they did with considerable gusto, replaced the handkerchief and continued his oratory – that was all very long ago.

Alan followed and remained the night. I slept with him until his snores drove me to my own bed about 6 a.m.

TUESDAY 5TH JANUARY

Stuart Preston, the cleverest young American I have ever met, comes to call in the early morning. He breezed in today, looking dishevelled. He is a sergeant in the American Army and he described his evening with Emerald. It was history, he said. Peter Quennell and Cyril Connolly and Emerald had discussed literature for some hours – Henry James, and Henry Channon!! Connolly said that I was or rather could have been a great writer! The soirée lasted until 2 a.m.

Top-hatted, I walked to St Margaret's to attend Nevile Henderson's memorial service. It was sparsely attended, but the King was represented. I sat next to Percy Loraine. A cold service in a half-empty church is depressing indeed. Went on to lunch with Laura at Claridge's in her private suite. She was 'rattled', governess-y and irritated by constant messages which arrived from Mary Marlborough who was delayed and finally failed to come. Excellent food, and passable conversation.

Alan and I again had a Turkish bath. I am ageing and get easily fatigued. I went by bus, a unique experience for me, to dine with Mamie and Vesevolod.

---

1 Samuel Howard Whitbread (1858–1944) was Liberal MP for Luton from 1892 to 1895 and for Huntingdon from 1906 to 1910.

Vesevolod told me at dinner that he had lunched with the King of Greece who was crumpled with laughter when V told him that he had sent me seventeen postcards of Queen Mignonne of Yugoslavia – 'the old cow!' as King Timon calls his highly unattractive ex-sister-in-law and fellow Sovereign.

I have some reason to believe that I am becoming gradually impotent; yet no longer ago than last September was dangerously lustily virile – or am I imagining a phase which does not exist?

WEDNESDAY 6TH JANUARY

Day began badly with a long firm letter from Helen Hull[1] in which she tells me that she insists on dismissing the Nannie and hints that Paul should return to me. I have long thought so. Then Emerald rang and made mischief, quoted Edith Kemsley as saying that whilst she herself liked me very nicely, that Gomer was suspicious that I poked fun at them. All untrue. Diana Cooper then 'chucked' me for dinner, which made me too many men. Later Alan on finding Stuart here insisted that I invite him. Laura Corrigan was nettled at a late invitation and refused to come ... all is gone awry – and nothing from India[2] although it is now three weeks since word of any mail has come. The Duchess of Kent rang me at 9 a.m. and I told her that Princess Olga and Lilia [Ralli] were at Bathurst.[3] She asked me to go down to Coppins tonight, but it is too late. I also refused to lunch with Leslie Hore-Belisha and Emerald: one must sometimes be alone otherwise the days would be too long!

Whenever I entertain, which is too often, the party is usually built upon the individual who has caught my interest: tonight, it was Archie Clark Kerr, a very charming, complicated, dissipated Ambassador to Russia. He is young still, but his looks are gone; nevertheless, his frivolous, even somewhat Bloomsbury clothes lend him youth ... I collected the Duchess of Sutherland, who whilst now too thin, and even a touch haggard, has got back her looks; Helen Fitzgerald, Harold [Balfour], who was late having been detained by Archie Sinclair and the Air Ministry. Pamela Churchill appetising and provocative in a black dress with a tiny floral arrangement on her reddish head; Alan; Peter Thursby and Stuart Preston .... Almost at the last moment Emerald Cunard rang up to say that she preferred dining with me to going to Sir John and Lady Anderson's and that she could 'chuck' them in case.

---

1 Helen Huntington Hull (1893–1976) had married William Vincent Astor (qv) in 1914 but they were divorced in 1941. Channon's son Paul, by this point 7 years old, had been evacuated to her care in the summer of 1940, after the fall of France. She was a prominent socialite and political hostess in New York, a patron of the arts, prominent Republican and discreet lesbian.

2 From Coats.

3 On their journey back to Princess Olga and Prince Paul's exile in Kenya.

It was a wretched night but they all arrived in due course and we dined in the Blue Room with the candles. Dinner was successful but Archie behaved oddly: he concentrated on Pam Churchill and talked to her until the coffee came, without addressing a word to the Duchess – and yet he is alleged to adore the duchesses! After dinner he remained behind with the Sergeant [Preston] and Peter Thursby, both extremely good-looking, and only emerged at the end of an hour after drinking much brandy and my best and rare port. Meanwhile, Alan has left for Falmouth by the night train; Pam had rung up Lord Beaverbrook and gone around to see him and Diana Cooper had arrived. All left by 1 a.m. and taxis were easily procured.

THURSDAY 7TH JANUARY

The Duchess of Kent and Lady Kemsley (who was most amiable so Emerald is wrong) rang me up and invited me for the weekend. I may go for a little to both.

The eight o'clock wireless announced that Archie Kerr had arrived in America. As he left here only at 1 a.m., it is unlikely even in these days!!

FRIDAY 8TH JANUARY   *COPPINS*

Slept for ten hours and woke refreshed, Rab and Harold B. attended my lazy levee . . . Stuart Preston looked in and we walked in the Park before I lunched at the Argentine Embassy where an immense party had congregated, [having] been selected in Anthony Eden's honour . . . . A very pre-war function with four kinds of wine which made me so sleepy that I came home and had a siesta before coming here . . . picked up Alice Harding and we drove down arriving just before the blackout. The Duchess looked tired, and her yellow-amber eyes seemed shrunken; she was playing with little Edward who is a lively loveable but independent child. We talked until it was time to dress . . . and arrived *à trois*, later we were joined by Alik Poklewski. He and his wife rarely leave the Duchess alone for an hour; indeed their Argus *accaparant*[1] tactics are odious and irritating. The Duchess, refreshed by her bath, looked as lovely as ever. We talked of the Duke and played backgammon – went up to bed about 12.30. Alice Harding, however and I continued to gossip and she sympathised with me on my 'honourable' troubles and thinks my wife odd, rude and mad.

Anthony looked old and most unprepossessing at luncheon and scarcely addressed a remark to his two neighbours, Mrs Vincent Massey[2] and Lady Camrose, who both obviously bored him. Will this pretty governess really ever become Prime Minister of England? I pray not.

---

1 An argus is a watchful guardian. *Accaparant* is French for demanding attention or monopolising another's time.
2 Wife of the Canadian High Commissioner; see entry for 12 October 1942 and footnote.

SATURDAY 9TH JANUARY

Slept moderately and revelled in a luxurious royal egg breakfast. Little Edward came to my room and played with me; he is a restless child, with a pretty pouting mouth. He asked me if I was a friend of 'Pappa's'! and led me to the tiny nursery and I watched him for a time. He seems to adore his mother, who brought me Michael to see. He is a dream peach-like infant, always smiling and placid and apparently less nervous than the others. Alexandra had a cold and did not appear.

The Duchess opened a huge box and offered me immense photographs of the Duke and herself; I chose two. At eleven Alice and I left and drove back, passing the [Guinness] brewery at Park Royal. I idled all the afternoon.

Stuart Preston picked me up, we fetched Emerald and went to dine with Alice Harding in her tiny garage-cottage . . . . Michael [Duff] imitated Lady Desborough[1] with devilish accuracy; and later did Queen Mary at an *antiquaire* most amusingly. It was a cold night – there was the usual taxi difficulty. Home only at 1 a.m., numb with cold and tired and exhausted, but increasingly intrigued by Stuart Preston whose charm is immense.

SUNDAY 10TH JANUARY

Slept for eleven hours. Harold [Balfour] then told me that Jock Butler,[2] Rab's brother, was killed yesterday near Cambridge on what was almost his first operational flight. He was 29, mild-mannered youth who looked like a portrait by Piero della Francesca;[3] and he lacked Rab's brain and slyer qualities. But he was amiable and not too jealous of his brilliant, ambitious, rich and successful brother. He was recently married to a girl from the Isle of Man. Rab, himself, telephoned to me from Cambridge later; and I offered to join him, to help, but there seems so little we can do. I wonder how moved he will be?

. . . . Alan [Lennox-Boyd], in a highly nervous and emotional state, arrived from Falmouth about six. He is observed by Stuart Preston and is becoming rapidly involved in a romantic friendship with him. We dined *à deux* at Scott's, the famous oyster restaurant in Piccadilly where I have had so many romantic meals – this time, alas, there were no oysters. We talked indiscreetly until I became aware that a man with a pronounced MI5 face at the next table was listening to our conversation.

1　See entry for 6 July 1939 and footnote.

2　John Perceval Butler (1914–43) was a pilot officer in the RAF and was killed in a crash near Oakham. He married, in 1936, Hermione Riggall (1916–2006). He was in fact still 28.

3　Piero della Francesca (1415–92), *né* di Benedetto, was a painter of the early Italian Renaissance.

MONDAY 11TH JANUARY

Woke in a highly nervous state and snapped at Harold and Alan – am I never allowed to be alone?

The newspapers say that Richard Wood,[1] the Halifaxes' youngest and favourite son, has been severely wounded in Algeria or somewhere, and has had both legs amputated. Those three wonderful Wood boys: one dead, another crippled, there is only Charles left.

I dined with Emerald and the Duchess, Duff and Diana; Pamela Churchill; Ann O'Neill; Esmond Rothermere; Leslie Hore-Belisha. A very pleasant evening which ended in my winning £15 at bridge. Duff was gentle and amiable and much impressed by John Julius's excellent report at Eton. I went in to see the little lad who was quietly and happily reading. The boy is an angel – Leslie Hore-Belisha walked me home in the cold blackout; he has recently returned from his monastery!

I have almost decided to bring Paul back and to put him at Ludgrove School in the autumn. Alan rang me twice during dinner and Duff remarked: 'Can I never get through a meal without Alan telephoning to Chips!?'

TUESDAY 12TH JANUARY

The Duchess of Kent came to luncheon accompanied by Mary Herbert: they were both dressed as WRNS and with their tricorn hats reminded me of French ladies *à la chasse*[2] .... I collected only Gaston Palewski, the ubiquitous, garrulous chef de cabinet of General de Gaulle, to meet them; everyone else seemed to be lunching out and I didn't try very hard. It was a successful little luncheon and they stayed on until after three o'clock, and they went on to open a canteen or other ...

Harold B[alfour] tells me that he saw Paul Latham,[3] who was courageous, cheerful and well; he said that he had twice tried to commit suicide for the sake of [his son] Richard and his own friends; he had failed; and, as the scandal is out, it would be cowardly of him to attempt to do so and Harold is sorry for him (Harold, who was once Patsy's[4] lover and the father of her 'removed' twins).

1 See entry for 14 September 1941 and footnote. Charles Wood (qv) was the heir to the Halifax peerage; the other son, Peter, had been killed in action the previous October (see entry for 3 November 1942 and footnote).
2 Out hunting.
3 Recently released after serving a sentence for indecent conduct.
4 This refers to Lady Patricia Latham (qv) and not to Channon's sister-in-law, Lady Patricia 'Patsy' Lennox-Boyd. The only inference one can draw is that Balfour had fathered twins on her, who were aborted.

WEDNESDAY 13TH JANUARY

Slept fitfully and awoke bored with society and life. Stuart [Preston] called early and remained with me too long. Frantic telephoning to console Alan.[1] Emerald Cunard querulous on the telephone because, suddenly, surfeited with society. I have refused to dine with her again for ages to come . . . . Lunched alone on a tray.

Dined in alone with Rab. We were in pyjamas and dressing gown and it was cosy and intimate. He is shocked by his brother's death; yet he reacted coldly; remarked that the tragedy would help him in the constituency and the village . . . . He had to make all the arrangements and he looked worn out. I was sorry for him; and felt words of affection flow out to him to which I doubt he fully responded. I went early to bed . . . . Rab sat up working and answering many letters of condolence. Nothing came from Winston or Anthony Eden and Rab was obviously hurt by their neglect.

Before dinner, I went around to have a drink with Pam Churchill; played with Winston who is an astonishing child. He talks, is determined; and poured me out a cocktail and handed me a cigarette – although he is only about 2½. He called me 'Jock' – a confusion with Jock Whitney[2] who is Pam's present admirer.

There is a congressional enquiry about a diamond-spray brooch which Pam bought on Beaverbrook's behalf and which he sent in the bag to Washington as a wedding present to Mrs Harry Hopkins.[3] The isolationists are using this tale, and similar ones, as a club to hack [at] the Roosevelt White House clique. Max tells everybody that he only sent a prayer book! But Pam, of course, knows the true story.

There is a feeling of unrest and unease that the Tunisian campaign is not going as well as was expected. The Americans are being blamed for the delay, but I suspect that Winston's super-secret mission to Morocco (nobody knows yet) will solve the difficulties. He leaves this afternoon, or has already left.

THURSDAY 14TH JANUARY

The telephone has not stopped ringing since 7.45. I am nearly demented. Lady Grigg rang me from the War Office to say that Richard Wood has lost only his feet – not his legs, but is still dangerously ill. I communicated this latest news to my mother- in-law at Pyrford.

The Duchess of Kent rang me up to say that a quick telegram has come from Princess Olga that she and Lilia Ralli have arrived safely back in Kenya; and that

---

1 What had had happened to Lennox-Boyd that should have required him to be consoled is unclear, but presumably it concerned his relationship with Preston (qv).
2 See entry for 18 November 1942 and footnote.
3 Hopkins, who had been widowed in 1937, had recently remarried, to Louise Gill Macy (1906–63).

my poor Paul's condition is heartbreaking – 'low morally and physically'. I somehow sense that he is going to die and soon. I had a most astonishing conversation with Rab apropos the Duke of Kent.

FRIDAY 15TH JANUARY

The afternoon was nostalgic and a bore that Lambert, my faithful butler, who has been with me since October 1939, goes tomorrow to a training centre. He has been a faithful Jeeves, a most admirable Crichton.[1] We went through cupboards and listed the plate etc. – how many – perhaps too many possessions – I have. Treherne, the new butler, seems well mannered, smiling but slow and dazed. It is little wonder for my household is a curious one but it has played its part in history, moulded lives, given birth to friendships and romance, political cabals and intrigues.

SATURDAY 16TH JANUARY

Got up early, and found Alan already arrived by the night train from Falmouth; but it is not me, but Stuart Preston, whom he has come on this journey to see. I left him and drove to Southend arriving at eleven punctually. It is cold. I had a mass of appointments, received deputations and was generally busy and active. Every hour or so, Alan rang up to announce a change of plan, he had hoped to bring Stuart down here for the night for a honeymoon. I suppose Alan was angered by finding Honor ensconced at Hobart Place, where the little house was in a turmoil; she had scattered her things about untidily, caused confusions, upset servants and been rude to the secretary and so he decided to sleep at Belgrave Square by way of pretext and also, I imagine, to see Stuart more easily. I worked until 7 p.m. and then fell into my bed, dinner-less and exhausted.

SUNDAY 17TH JANUARY

Slept ten hours and had a lovely breakfast and pored over the newspapers. We raided Berlin last night and can now expect a return visit. Much difficulty in starting the car because of the cold, but finally I got off, to drive to Brentwood where I met the lovers,[2] who seem in a swoon of love! I have never known anything like it. I drove them to Kelvedon, where we had an excellent lunch – they disappeared into a locked room – and emerged two hours later. Alan and I then went for a walk. He is annoyed with Patsy for deceiving him about Honor's visit;

---

1 An allusion to J. M. Barrie's 1902 play *The Admirable Crichton* about an ultra-resourceful butler who proves he is a far better man than his employers.

2 Lennox-Boyd and Preston.

and he thinks that the position at Shalden is now deteriorating and that Honor is fed up! And bored and may leave him. I doubt it – yet!

We drove back to London arriving as the blackout fell . . . . Alan and I dined with Laura Corrigan in her suite at Claridge's – turtle soup, oysters mornay, partridge and meringues, a succulent too-rich meal. I ran into Prince Bertil of Sweden in the foyer and took him up to see Laura . . . . as we were drinking sherry the sirens sounded and I thought of poor Emerald and wondered if she would be frightened. Laura was quite calm. There was considerable noise; but the all-clear sounded before ten. Alan and I walked back to Belgrave Square together and found Stuart Preston awaiting us. He is an enchanting Pierrot and seems dazed by his fantastic social and sexual successes. He and Alan slept in the Napoleon bed tonight – last night they shared my small ones here. Am I . . . . running a brothel?

TUESDAY 19TH JANUARY

Tempests in teapots. Walked to the H of C with Stuart Preston, who comes to see me every morning and uses No. 5 as a club. He is more and more enchanting . . . the House was crowded . . . . Oliver Lyttelton made an important announcement but handled the House clumsily. Anthony Eden with a plethora of platitudes congratulated Lloyd George on his 80th birthday. The old man, who was cheered when he had arrived . . . . in faltering and banal terms he expressed his thanks. What a horrible wicked old man really; however today his bearable appearance, his long white locks and enfeebled voice lent him dignity. One should always be old in England. The House then went into secret session for the simple statement which Anthony made that Winston was conferring with President Roosevelt!! Quite a few indignant and foolish MPs made exhibitions of themselves, betraying their ignorance! It then seemed to occur to them that Winston was not in Washington but on a battleship in the southern Atlantic with the President!![1]

WEDNESDAY 20TH JANUARY

There was a raid about luncheon time but I didn't know until this evening how serious it had been. The House went into secret session and Bevin explained the Manpower position[2] in generous detail . . . .

Much telephoning with Alan and Stuart and messages. I am worn out by this too-exalted romance.

When I dined with Pam Churchill at 49 Belgrave Square in her 'attic' flat, she was in an emotional state, having just returned from Deptford where she had been on duty. It had been horrible – about forty children killed, more buried beneath

---

1 On the subject of ignorance, Churchill and Roosevelt were in fact at Casablanca, agreeing on the war aim of unconditional surrender for the Germans.
2 Describing the availability of labour to essential war industries.

the rubble: wailing mothers, slow relief services etc. An appalling tragedy. The school was hit about one o'clock and also a pub.[1] Poor Pam, prettier than ever, was much moved by the horrors.

I found both Rab and Harold still awake on my return and I told them of the horrors of the Deptford and Lewisham raids. Harold ordered an immediate investigation by the Air Ministry.

THURSDAY 21ST JANUARY

I was in a frenzy all the morning because the new butler is so hopeless and the Duchess of Kent had proposed herself to lunch. However I collected a party consisting of the Argentine Ambassador, Emerald, Mary and Sidney Herbert .... Cecil Beaton and Alice Harding who was indecently late, as usual. The Duchess looked lovely in black and wearing many pearls. It was her first social party since the Duke was killed. It went well and the food was excellent! All went well. Emerald was amazing and the Ambassador was charming. And I was able to present Stuart Preston when the Duchess arrived early. He was enchanted ...

I went back to the House of Commons and then fetched Laura Corrigan and took her to Lady Kemsley's cocktail party which was crowded. Laura held forth about Pétain to Beatrice Eden who is so dumb that she has probably never heard of him!! I came home, exhausted by too much society – how sterile it is – and fell into my bed.

FRIDAY 22ND JANUARY

London is humming with my royal luncheon party. I worked this morning and then rang up Paul Latham who answered the telephone, was friendly and pathetic; he invited me to lunch with him and we met at a strange Czechoslovakian café. He is thinner, sadder, improved and we discussed his imprisonment, his love for Richard, his boy; and his flagrantly mercenary and heartless wife, who is bringing a petty and scandalous divorce case against him next week. I cheered him as best I could; he thanked me with tears in his eyes; said that his small mews flat where he is living again has already been robbed – I gathered that he has already relapsed into bad company again. He described his life at Maidstone Gaol as being better really than Eton; more comfortable, better food, and, at least he was not even beaten. Touching. I was sad to leave him as I had never liked him so much ... picked up Emerald at Pam Churchill's. Pam told me how horribly Randolph had treated her; how rough and cruel and inconsiderate he had always been. Emerald and I walked, or rather pirouetted to Christie's: we wandered about Derby House once

---

1 Sandhurst Road School in Catford took a direct hit from a single bomb at 12.30 p.m. that day. It killed thirty-two children immediately and fatally injured six others. Six members of staff also died.

the scene of such grandeur and gaiety; and came on her charmed possessions. Many had been blitzed. She was querulous and inconsequent, remarked that she couldn't possibly place a value on her things as George Moore never kept bills! Eventually she gave me six George II gilt armchairs, damaged but grandiose, and a pair of heavy Chinese Chippendale tall gilt mirrors for which she had paid £300. I shall have them removed to No. 5, store them until after the war, and then repair them. They will do well at Kelvedon.

Adrian and Olive Baillie and Harold dined with me here. She is a granite woman, gentle but determined and, in her quiet way, a great seductress.

Stuart Preston, who has taken the social stronghold of London by storm, looked in later; and we all went on to see Emerald who was entertaining and there I found the Sitwells, Moores, Laura, Coopers and others. Sachie Sitwell asked to be presented to the Sergeant [Preston]: 'I haven't met him yet; that is what comes of living in the country,' he said. The poor Sergeant looked embarrassed and shy and altogether enchanting – which he is. Later he and I and Leslie Hore-Belisha walked home in the moonlight together. Passing the fountain outside Londonderry House, we observed a young airman staggering and dancing and falling to the ground. He was v drunk indeed but resisted our attempts to help him. We parted near Hyde Park Corner and then Leslie calling to me, I caught him up again. Arm in arm we walked along Grosvenor Place (or Guinness Place; as it was once called), and he confided to me that the Conservative Party leaders, i.e. Tommy Dugdale, James Stuart and Harvie-Watt, Harold Mitchell[1] had all made recent and repeated overtures to him. He had dined with them all separately on several occasions recently. He suspects that they are 'sounding' him. Will I, he asked, eventually lead the Tory Party? . . . He then went on to say that he thinks that I, Chips, have started this Belisha wave with our constant praise of him etc. He is partly right . . . then changing the subject, he observed that the fashionable craze for Stuart Preston and his fantastic social success [here several words are heavily scrubbed out and illegible] is an instance of 'mass hysteria' like 'Hitler-worship in Germany'! I really like the Sergeant because he reminds me of myself in my youth.

Pam Churchill told me today that she had spent all day again yesterday working and helping at Deptford. There are now over forty-five dead children.[2] Yesterday a live monkey was also rescued; its survival struck a comic note amidst all the horror and wretchedness. Weeping mothers laughed and the poor animal was revived with hot brandy and rushed in a special WVS car to the Zoo Hospital. The English, indeed are mad.

---

1 Harold Paton Mitchell (1900–83) was Conservative MP for Brentford and Chiswick from 1931 to 1945. He was a Vice Chairman of the Conservative Party, and was created 1st Bt in 1945.

2 This was not so. The total dead at the school, adults and children, was forty-four.

Saturday 23rd January

A wasted – or perhaps not – day? The Sergeant made me his usual early morning call; he is awaiting Alan's frenzied arrival from Falmouth. What *frénésie*! I lunched with Lady Willingdon alone at the Sportsman's Club and as I waited for her I heard the official announcement over the BBC that Tripoli, capital of Libya, had fallen into our hands. The Italian Empire no longer exists . . . Lady W and I lunched alone and then hearing that poor Laura Corrigan was alone and perhaps lonely, I rang her up. We fetched her, took her to a film – *Random Harvest*[1] (there were nostalgic bits in it which reminded me of Honor and my once cold, old not sufficiently bold self). Then to tea at the Overseas League Club – just the three. Lady Willingdon showed us over the vast premises, whilst Laura reminisced about balls there in the Rutland days and of the Prince of Wales talking to Jimmie Corrigan![2] Lady W whispered to me that a cheque would be welcome and when later I drove Laura home I hinted. Later she rang me, getting me out of the bath, to ask if she had understood correctly and I said that she had. A quarter of an hour passed, then Lady Willingdon rang up in a state of tremendous excitement to say that she had been given £500 – (Laura had said that she would send the money immediately). What a kind and generous and spontaneous gesture. But the overseas people, sailors and soldiers, owe it [Mrs Corrigan's largesse] to me; so perhaps my dull afternoon was not wasted.

The Sergeant says that, on his way back last evening, he found that a young soldier outside Londonderry House had completely divested himself of his clothing and was sitting in the cold fountain.

Sunday 24th January

I am wishing that I had gone down to Kelvedon for a whiff of country air and a change of atmosphere. I began the day badly having slept fitfully listening to the cooing of the impassioned lovers in the next room and by snapping at Harold . . . . Now I regret having done so; and indeed, have regretted it all day.

Then I had a revulsion of feeling and fled to RAC Club where I had a Turkish bath and slept blissfully for three hours. Still I feel tired and exhausted and angry – and worse, rather impotent! Alan and the Sergeant were waiting for me on my return and we soon made up our 'tiff' with Harold.

Monday 25th January

Woke somewhat refreshed but still surfeited by society and appalled by the sterility of it and of human companionship generally. Alan breezed in; he had

---

1 Starring Ronald Colman and Greer Garson, a 1942 film based on the novel of the same name published the previous year and written by James Hilton, about the life and loves of a shellshocked Great War soldier.

2 James William Corrigan, her late husband.

been to see a doctor who had assured him that his impotence was of a temporary nature and due to an inhibition. Perhaps mine is likewise? The Sergeant and he had a rapturous hour together and then he drove Alan to the station. And I am here, never alone! I have employed yet another manservant and have now a better footman, oddman and valet in my wartime depleted household!

I had a brilliant letter from Peter on January 15th (no. 34) but nothing at all has come since. I fear he is tiring of our axis, yet hates for various reasons to break it off.

Alan travelled all day to Plymouth and telephoned to say that he had arrived safely; he is my most devoted (and always somehow, *épaté*[1] adherent). I love him and miss him yet he both exhausts and exasperates me at times. The Sergeant rushed off to have tea with Lady Crewe and to dine with Pope-Hennessy. I dined in and alone with Rab. Rab and I discussed old days, the political set-up, the possible rebirth of the Conservative Party and his own chances of both the Premiership and the viceregal throne. He was delightful. Now he has gone to bed . . . and I remember how we both agreed that it was David Margesson's temporary loss of grip, due to an unfortunate occurrence when he was nearly suffocated by being locked in a cupboard at Lavington at a weekend party and of his matrimonial differences, which led eventually to the eclipse of the Tory Party etc. etc. . . . . Rab loathes Winston. But who does he really fundamentally care for? He is a coldish fish at heart; but I am devoted to him.

TUESDAY 26TH JANUARY

To the House, where there was little happening but there were rumours of terrific events and announcements – in other words, the public and the press are vaguely aware of the Winston–Roosevelt meeting, or at least, of something happening. Lunched with Robert Cary, who is a typical parliamentary hack, trying, kindly, interested in everything and knowing a lot about unimportant matters. I gather that Winston is due back tomorrow.

Anthony Eden gushed at me, showed me his rabbity teeth and called me, 'Chips, darling!' He has done this before, the velvety hound.

The Butlers, Sydney and Rab, dined in; I went to Claridge's to dine with Laura Corrigan in her luxurious suite. There I found Cárcano, the dark, sleek, friendly, Argentine Ambassador; Audrey Pleydell-Bouverie[2] *en grande beauté*[3] with her husband, Peter, whom I have not seen since the war – nor presumably has she, since they rarely meet and nobody knows why they married; the Marlboroughs; Harold Balfour; Helen Fitzgerald and Lady Crewe. Much wine,

---

1 Amazed, or astonished.
2 See entry for 3 June 1940 and footnote.
3 At the height of beauty.

high spirits made us hilarious and after dinner Laura introduced a dice game. We shook dice and eventually after much amusement over Laura's quaint French, Harold opened a bottle of Napoleon brandy. The Ambassador drove us all home in his diplomatic car. I have rarely enjoyed myself more. Peggy Crewe, gay and witty and friendly, Audrey, most affectionate and I felt the warmth of the world's favour.

Tomorrow there will be an announcement about Winston's movements and his trip to Casablanca.

WEDNESDAY 27TH JANUARY

Newspapers splash the story of the modern Tilsit to an astonished world, for the secret of the Casablanca meeting was well kept. Winston is going to make a triumphant entry into Tripoli and perhaps go on to Cairo.

House crowded and rather restless. Lunched there, but alone; and later attended the 1922 Committee which Anthony Eden addressed in the highest possible manner. A clear trite little speech telling us absolutely nothing; it did not impress and he had a chilly reception; I noticed however that he referred to himself as a Tory minister – which he isn't.

He was saved from embarrassing questions by the bell announcing, 'Who goes home?' Most ministers thought it a division.

The frantic friendship between Stuart Preston and Alan goes on unabated; it has become a bore. Frantic telephone messages, telegrams, presents all day. And Alan rings me up in despair that his growing, indeed, overwhelming passion, is not reciprocated.

THURSDAY 28TH JANUARY

I had worried, but needlessly, about my little dinner party tonight and although I took no trouble, the food was delicious and well served and the evening an exhilarating success. Mrs Brittain-Jones, the King of Greece's dark *maîtresse en titre* (and perhaps morganatic wife?) was unable to come because of a chill; and so my guests consisted only of the King of Greece, who looked thin and tired but was in the gayest of spirits throughout the evening; Lady Brabourne, who is a lovely good-looking fresh widow; Maimie and Vesevolod; the old Belgian Ambassador, who as he ages looks more and more like my sheepdog; Emerald Cunard and Rab, who was silent, taciturn, almost sullen all evening. Emerald scintillated with her sense and held us enthralled with her witty raillery and gossipy mischief. About 10.30 Archie Kerr, accompanied by Stuart Preston, arrived from Lady Colefax's dinner party. We talked until 1 a.m. when Rab, pale and exhausted, escorted Doreen Brabourne home, and the King left with the gay Russians. Stuart Preston stayed the night here.

Emerald tells me that Duff Cooper, who is in the gentlest of moods, remarked to her that all his life he has tried to make people like him and always failed. He cited me as an example; praised me and added that he knew I only tolerated him because of Diana. This is, of course, true; but I like him better of late.

SATURDAY 30TH JANUARY

Stuart Preston and I walked in the rain to the coiffeur's.[1] Later Lady Willingdon fetched me and we drove to Coppins to lunch with the Duchess of Kent, who was looking immensely lovely and rested. Delicious food: she was her usual affectionate self. The older children were away but Michael was brought down. He has his father's pretty pout and honey hair.

Göring made an extraordinary speech in Berlin today; and twice our planes in small numbers raided the German capital.[2] I dined with Emerald: a boring evening and I was in poor spirits: Juliet Duff, Diana, Rex Whistler and Evelyn Waugh – to whom I foolishly lent £8. Some went on to a party given by Violet Cripps[3] but I refused and walked home in the rain. The weather is fortunately too wet for a retaliation raid from Berlin.

It is ten years ago today that the Nazi Party took over the reins of government in Germany.

SUNDAY 31ST JANUARY

Woke up late, after reading Henry James's *Ambassadors*[4] half the night. Lunched with Laura Corrigan at Claridge's . . . . Then I came back and slept for three hours. I must be ageing, but the result was satisfactory for I was in good form the whole of a fascinating evening; Archie C. Kerr – surely the quaintest Ambassador of all time; Duff and Diana, Olive Baillie, Emerald and I drove to the Queensberry Club, a mammoth place organised and run for the forces by Francis Queensberry. It was packed with silent dashing soldiers and sorts of the WAAF and ATS.[5] Duff introduced Archie in an able, amiable speech and 'The Excellent

---

1 Hairdresser.
2 It was the tenth anniversary of the Nazis' rise to power. Göring was due to address one of the commemorative rallies held that day but his speech was delayed, humiliatingly for him as head of the Luftwaffe, by the first daylight raid on Berlin, by Mosquitoes. When he eventually spoke, in a gloomy address, he said that it was the duty of every one of Germany's 80 million men, women and children to die if Hitler ordered it.
3 Violet Mary Nelson (1891–1983). Having divorced the 2nd Duke of Westminster in 1926 she married, in 1927, Frederick Heyworth Cripps (1885–1977), who in 1977 briefly succeeded his brother as 3rd Baron Parmoor.
4 Published in 1903, the story of an American's visit to Europe to bring back his widowed fiancée's errant son.
5 Women's Auxiliary Air Force and the Auxiliary Territorial Service.

Archie' addressed the khaki-ed mob and answered questions about Russia for forty-five minutes. He was not good, not at all, and he involuntarily made Red propaganda and evaded, as he was obliged to do, embarrassing points. However, he was well received. We then went on to Grosvenor House where the dashing, generous eighteenth-century Marquis [Lord Queensberry] entertained some twenty people to dinner in a private room; there were six magnums of grand champagne, and much gaiety .... There was a very boring singer shouting *Tosca* and people did imitations. Emerald was both bored and horrified. Archie K. and I took her home, luckily finding a taxi, about 1 a.m.

I hear that the PM is in Turkey somewhere but his whereabouts are a 'profound' mystery and secret [known] however only to us, the inner few.

Rab has been on my mind; he is not advancing, he is much on contracting. I have seen so many do this, notably, Shakes [Morrison], once the hope of enlightened Tory England, now an amiable white-head boy taken seriously by nobody and fobbed off with the new Ministry of Towns and Planning. Rab has such obvious defects: he is [illegible], mean, lacking in imagination, bourgeois to the extreme, and so simple in his way of life as to be almost irritating. Yet he has great gifts: shrewdness, calm judgement, and ambition. But he is *au fond* a civil servant. I have hinted much of this to him and he was depressed thereby.

MONDAY 1ST FEBRUARY

Seven years ago today – it was a Sunday,[1] I think – I left Honor and my baby boy at Pyrford and came up to London to spend the day and time with the Regent. He was staying at No. 3 with the Duke of Kent, and although he had gone for the weekend to Coppins he came up to London to see me. We spent the day and evening together. I remember it vividly because it was my first night that I slept in this house; only my room was ready; my servants were busy unpacking; there were crates and un-hung curtains and general confusion. What a seven years! The House has played a considerable role in politics and society and since the war has been, if it was not already so before, the centre of London ... no true character of the times could fail to record the glories and its influence; its splendours and its fêtes ...

A dull-ish day, really. I did so little. Letters and accounts etc. I woke cross and snapped at everybody and rebuked the awkward servants ... Dined with Alice Harding, picking up John Schiff[2] and driving him there in the wet and blackout, a gay-ish party: Emerald, impossible 'as ever' .... Stuart Preston was needless to say also there, laughing hysterically all the time with sheer ecstasy; and Colonel Gaston Palewski full of his journey to Casablanca and his conferences either with

---

1 It was a Saturday.
2 John Mortimer Schiff (1904–87) was an American banker and philanthropist. He was one of his country's leading breeders of thoroughbred horses, and also President of the Boy Scouts of America.

Churchill or Roosevelt. He and de Gaulle dined one evening at Gibraltar and lunched on the following day at the Mansion House with the Lord Mayor. He is frantically French, this Polish Frog . . . luscious food and wine. I drove them all, seven in all home in my tiny car and we could scarcely see in the dark. Emerald was terrified. It was dark, wet and slippery. Both Rab and Harold were asleep when I came in: it was 2 a.m. The seductive Sergeant slept in the Nursery. The news of the Turkish meeting will come out tomorrow.

Alan has given Stuart Preston a Fabergé cigarette case, half-flaunted, half-concealed all evening.

TUESDAY 2ND FEBRUARY

I am entering on the eighth year of residence at the Schloss Chips.

A most quiet day, as I was suddenly surfeited with food, people and drink . . . Walked to the House of Commons which was excessively dull. The Honourable Members seemed unimpressed by Winston's dramatic visit to Turkey – does it forebode another disastrous Greek campaign? He is now, or was, at Cyprus. The newspapers announce that Randolph accompanied him. Why should he? It is monstrous nepotism. Rab thinks that Randolph will cause us much trouble in the future. I don't; for I am convinced that his star will set directly the Churchillian regime ends . . . he is a worthless cad.

I had to be alone today; I was *à bout de mes forces.*[1] But the gay escaping Sergeant dashed in and out a few times; and Natasha Bagration came to see me. Dined alone and am alone now sitting at my lacquer writing table and it is only 9.54. Soon I shall be asleep.

My financial prospects seem to be improved due to my careful handling and care and resolution against foolish extravagance.

Harold B and Rab are dining out, where I didn't ask, and don't care a fig. Alan rang me this morning feverishly from Falmouth; he is in despair and in a temper of love and enraged with the Sergeant Preston who failed to ring up last night. What can we do to assuage so terrible a passion?

All day I have thought of my son and I itch for his company, his love and his return. And this morning, too, came a crazy, demented, wildly foolish pamphlet printed in red type about some Chinaman – this is my mad mother's Christmas card. She ought really to have been locked up ages ago. Only my intervention saved her.

WEDNESDAY 3RD FEBRUARY

I worked, then walked languidly towards the House, meeting Stuart Preston by arrangement in the Green Park on the way. He is charming, gentle, delightful but

---

1 At the limit of my powers.

inconsequent for he treats Alan shabbily . . . lunched at the House, attended the 1922 Committee which was addressed by Brendan Bracken. This hard-hearted, garrulous, red-headed gargoyle is a fraud *au fond*; he is an indifferent minister for he promises all and does little – is inoperative and prejudiced – he made a clear bid for popularity with the old-fashioned Tories today. Before luncheon I looked in on Nicholas Lawford who has his own room behind the Prince's Chamber; as he sat on desks gossiping about Emerald (who tries to throw us together and is both fascinated and mischievous about our friendship), Anthony Eden walked in and caught us. He was affectionate and friendly and after twice calling me 'darling' – a strange habit – he offered to give me a lift anywhere in his car; but I unimaginatively declined and stayed on.

Dined with Mrs Keppel at the Ritz; I was late and bold . . . . They all abused Laura Corrigan little appreciating her great work. Walked home in the dark, which, owing to the increase of hooliganism, is a dangerous thing to do.

Emerald telephoned to me at 1.30 a.m. and insisted on chatting for over an hour. Twice, I fell asleep, yet she continued . . . about Henry James . . . . And then about her dinner with Kenneth Clark where both Oliver Lyttelton and Rob Hudson had violently abused poor Hore-Belisha. They said that he would never 'come back politically'! How wrong they are.[1]

Winston is back in Cairo, remarkably.

THURSDAY 4TH FEBRUARY

Liverish, and bored with the sterility of social life . . . went to the House *à pied* but was delayed by chatting in the Park with Sidney Herbert, and thus missed a question which I had put down to old Ernest Bevin. All day at the House, and was interested to see Jim Wedderburn who returned last night from China with parcels and letters – unless he had lost them – for me. Anthony Eden paid a tribute to the Mission which is alleged to have been a success (my agents tell me it was a failure, particularly in India) . . . Tea with Emerald Cunard, wittier and more exquisite than ever as she cajoled Clarissa Churchill and her devoted dark swain James Pope-Hennessy, Belisha and others. I ate a whole jar of nuts and a box of chocolates and consequently felt heavy and cross and was disagreeable all evening. We dined in: Rab and Sydney Butler; [Lord] Gage; Julian Amery and Jim Wedderburn who made the most glamorous expedition since that of Marco Polo seem dull and pedestrian. He was also rather rude to me! He can be guaranteed to wreck any dinner party with his sullen rudeness and awkward remarks! He has, however, he said, brought me presents from China as well as letters and parcels from Peter in Delhi. He didn't like Peter; said that he was unpopular; and he couldn't even remember the names of the viceregal staff, in fact he was

---

1 How right they were.

intolerant and intolerable! Sergeant Preston looked in later after dining with the old Princesse de Polignac. I was horrible to him and hurt him; probably because he has been so dilatory and slack in his relations with Alan, who complains so bitterly on the telephone of Stuart's casual coldness. I was cold to the Sergeant as only I can be – biting, civil and aloof, but unfriendly and he must have sensed the drop in temperature. I refused to let him sleep here – why should he? And I was glad when Jim left. Nevertheless in spite of these disasters, the Butlers judged the evening a success and I noticed that Rab enjoyed it. I feared it was flat and a failure. I wish I didn't have these black moods – I had a long talk with Ronnie Tree for the first time in many years. He was fawning and surprised.

FRIDAY 5TH FEBRUARY

Alan rang me up to complain again and moan over the Sergeant's indifference!! My mornings are a muddled mess; people in my bedroom – I am not even allowed to dress alone or in peace; three telephones ringing all at once . . . I received a deputation from Southend's Insurance Employees who are opposed to the adoption of the Beveridge Report. Portia Stanley, Helen Fitzgerald and Harold B lunched. Gay and a relief from last night. Jim Wedderburn looked in, vaguer than ever. Mrs Neville Chamberlain rang up and asked me to dine next week.

I walked in the wet to the Ritz about 8.30. London looked lovely, dark lapis blue, dipping to the great searchlight [that] like a mannerist rainbow in the Green Park played on the buildings – [it] lit up Spencer House beautifully – as it revolved, searching the sky for hostile craft. Dined with Mrs Keppel . . . . [she] is still fascinating and witty. James Stuart was with his wife at a nearby table, colder than charity. Perhaps he will not survive, politically, as he is opposed to Winston; secretly works against him.

I have not seen the Sergeant all day, nor communicated with him; I now deplore my rudeness which was really only 'liver'. Alan rang me frantically four times from Falmouth; I fear he is foolish with love, infatuated, crazed and capable of wild measures. It must be an illness; my one half-fear that Alan is seriously mad and will thus never reach the political heights.

Much talk at dinner about the growing hooliganism in Mayfair and of the danger of the streets. I was almost frightened when I walked back; and actually I was accosted by two Canadian soldiers asking for a match, whether they would have assaulted and robbed me, I don't know. It was an ugly night.

SATURDAY 6TH FEBRUARY   *KELVEDON*

The Sergeant looked in; he appeared battered and washed out. He had dined with Clemmie Churchill, Venetia Montagu and their girls and danced at the 400 Club until dawn. He doesn't reciprocate Alan's tremendous passion, and although not averse to accepting the rich presents – a Fabergé cigarette case, a gold watch etc. – would like to end it. His imagination doesn't stretch to its great potentialities. I tried to reason with him unsuccessfully. And then I came here, where I am always shocked and surprised by the charm and beauty of the place.

Lady Petre[1] rang up and asked me over to Ingatestone[2] where I have never been.

I read *King Lear*, my favourite Shakespearean play, and now, it is 10.20, I am going to bed. Already the house, although it shelters sixty-two soldiers and about forty women, is shrouded in silence. Only I am still up. Overhead is the purring of distant aeroplanes which sound sinister and hostile.

SUNDAY 7TH FEBRUARY

Slept long and deeply. It is very cold and clear and beautiful out. About eleven I drove to Ingatestone to call on the Petres. The new, young, not altogether 'quite quite' Lady Petre received me; she is pretty, young, intelligent and alert. And better-bred than I expected. We were immediately on confidential terms and I foresee a friendship if I can make the necessary effort. They are living in what was the gardener's cottage as Wanstead School occupy the Hall – a fourteenth-century affair of charm and dark beauty. In her husband's salad days, it was the scene of licentious living. Lady Petre gave me a drink and showed me her small son[3] sleeping in the sun; he is only a few months old and is down for Eton where Paul is to go. After a time, she fetched her husband – 'Joe' – from an outhouse where he was peeling potatoes. He enjoyed it and I immediately liked him; it is a vicious, aware aristocratic face; he is 29[4] and looks more . . . . I doubt whether they love each other: it is a marriage of reason and commerce, I think. I intend to be friends with them.

Alan rang up again from Falmouth; he is going to break with the Sergeant – or so he says. I doubt it; yet three months ago he was so desperately enamoured of Adrian Liddell Hart. His passions are unhappily never requited. Why is Essex always so cold? I shan't be at Kelvedon in the winter – ever – but shut the house from November until May.

MONDAY 8TH FEBRUARY

Returned to London refreshed and rejuvenated after two days' abstinence from alcohol and freedom from telephone complications. Worked, arranged my big

1 Marguerite Eileen Hamilton (1916–2003), married in 1941 Joseph William Lionel Petre (1914–89), who in 1915 succeeded his father as 17th Baron Petre.
2 The Petres' Essex seat, a short drive from Kelvedon.
3 John Patrick Lionel Petre (b.1942) succeeded his father as 18th Baron Petre in 1989.
4 Inevitably, given Channon's grasp of these things, he was still 28.

week ahead of me. Stuart Preston lunched: he is unwell and looked pale and was *piano*.

Laura Corrigan is giving two dinner parties this week: tonight's she described as 'important' whilst Wednesday's is to be 'chic'. I went with Leslie Hore-Belisha who is becomingly increasingly social, idle and gentle, to have a cocktail with Ghislaine Dresselhuys in her tiny flat at the fashionable 55 Park Lane where the rich and the aristocratic have taken refuge in mild squalor. Emerald was brilliantly funny. Rushed into my clothes but Lady Willingdon arrived before I was ready and made a viceregal scene. Dinner chez Mme Corrigan was amusing . . . . champagne and good food. Food, its absence, its ramifications have taken the conversational place of the weather now in England.

Bed by twelve o'clock. Harold Balfour was working when I came in, but the brace of Butlers had gone to bed after dining with Doreen Brabourne.

TUESDAY 9TH FEBRUARY

The controversial Catering Bill[1] was debated acrimoniously in the Commons. [Ernest] Bevin wishes to become a dictator. At the end of a long debate it was carried, but 116 Conservatives voted against the government to the surprise of the inefficient, ineffectual whips who are hilariously ill-informed. James Stuart truly must be able to handle a crisis; as Chief Whip he is alleged to be tactful with Winston, and is adequate when all goes well . . . I wish he would be replaced. Never before have I dropped into the Opposition's lobby; it was a tonic to vote against the government. One feels brave – and perhaps foolish. I shall often do so now as I really owe this set-up little loyalty. They have done next to nothing for me.

Actually Lady Astor's most tiresome manner, her constant interruptions and jeering did much to rally the Opposition. She always damages any cause which she espouses. The division bell rang as Jim[2] was finishing and half a hundred excited MPs rushed to the Chamber to vote twice against the govt. Great excitement! It is the first time that the coalition govt has been seriously challenged. Beaverbrook, who is always wrong, prophesies that this is the beginning of the duel!! Governments always are doomed and fall eventually on unimportant matters, which bring things to a head. The PM, however, is at the very summit of his popularity and was given a sharp, short but very rousing reception today on his reappearance. He looked well and bronzed. He never gets the enthusiastic welcome that Mr Chamberlain received so often. There is still a slumbering resentment against Winston and he is not popular in the House except amongst his band of followers.

1 A bill to sanction collective bargaining in the catering trades.
2 The Member winding up was actually Malcolm McCorquodale (qv).

Victor Cazalet has returned by bomber from America: he stayed for some weeks with the Halifaxes and tried to soothe their grief. He also reported well of my child, Paul, whom he had been to see. And I had a long night-letter from Geoffrey Lloyd who had been to New York where he gave Paul and Nannie lunch; he cables that the child is happy and in terrific spirits. I can never forget this act of extreme kindness. The bourgeois Birmingham boy can be gentleness itself and I love him deeply. Few others would have taken so much trouble.

Alan rang up four or five times about Stuart Preston; he is wildly, crazily infatuated with him. Indeed all London seems to have quite lost its head over him. The young Pierrot, the gay intellectual Ganymede is amused but unimpressed.

Just before lunch as I was walking in the corridor of the House, nr the Smoking Room, I ran into the Prime Minister who was approaching me. He grunted at poor Harvie-Watt – who looks more than ever like a manse clergyman – and I overheard him say to Harvie: 'If you do, I shall be very angry with you!' Harvie-Watt smiled. Winston then saw me, grinned, made his famous little low bow and murmured: 'How are you?' 'Welcome back, sir!' was my weak rejoinder. 'Thanks!' he said, and the pair passed on. Winston looked tanned by the sun.

WEDNESDAY 10TH FEBRUARY

Stuart Preston, still looking ill, followed me and I walked to the House of Commons, which presented a chastened appearance as it always does when it has behaved badly . . . Went with Bill Astor to the Ritz. Emerald and Alice Harding completed the party. Then it came on to rain; I was unable to find Emerald a taxi, and the afternoon was ruined and wasted waiting on her. She is possessive and unreasonable but her charm eclipses everybody's and her fantastic mind is ever a delight. At length we went to find Stuart Preston, who collapsed yesterday; and found him ill and abandoned in an American ward at 9 North Audley Street. No doctor had been to him; after some trouble I persuaded the American medical authorities to let me take him away; and I have established him at Belgrave Square. I fear that he has flu, and possibly jaundice. A shadow has fallen on fashionable London . . . I went in my little car to the Dorchester at eight o'clock and there fetched Emerald, Duff and Diana and we drove to Claridge's to drink with Laura Corrigan . . . . my entrée at Laura's was well timed for Ronnie and Nancy Tree, who so bore me, had already arrived. I was between her and Emerald and she, Nancy Tree, absurdly dressed in a rich red Van Dyck-ish velvet dress, was evidently determined to be agreeable. I was likewise and we got on splendidly; chaff, talk of Trollope (of whom she has just heard), Ditchley, etc. And I admit that I found her fascinating . . . . I was in a distinguished 'mood' and behaved amiably. One more vendetta perhaps closed? I drove the Coopers etc. back in the blackout and Duff was gentle and really quite nice, as he can be at times.

Alan rang five different times from Torquay; I was goaded almost to madness and boredom.

THURSDAY 11TH FEBRUARY

A rich day . . . . The House was packed; every ambassador, and every Peer that could squeeze himself in was already in the Gallery. The PM, accompanied by Harvie-Watt, Mrs Churchill and Diana Sandys[1] arrived punctually and there was a restless stir in the crowded Chamber. He was called, rose, smiled and acknowledged the applause which greeted him, and then proceeded to speak, mildly dramatically and fully for one hour fourteen minutes. There was only one aside, a very few jokes. He seemed to be in a hurry (it is known that he dislikes continuing into the luncheon hour as he is disturbed by members leaving the Chamber). I listened with interest, sitting on the steps of the throne. Now and then, I glanced about me, and looked up at the Speaker's Gallery where I saw Mrs Churchill, Ava Anderson, Mrs Neville Chamberlain – chic in black and pearls – Mme Maisky,[2] Diana Sandys and Mrs FitzRoy.[3] About one o'clock, I saw Laura Corrigan get up and leave the gallery; she rushed away to lunch with Geordie Sutherland. The PM finished punctually at 1.15 and there was the usual exodus from the Chamber. I found Loelia Westminster who, under an immense hat, was waiting for me. In the Great Hall I came on Jim Wedderburn who ushered me into the Members' Cloakroom where he opened a box and handed me a silver filigree fish of great ugliness ([the] sort of *bibelot* a rich continental exhibits to one); poor well-meaning blustering Jim had bought it in Chungking and brought it all this way back to me as a souvenir of his famous trek. I could scarcely hide my impatience for Peter's parcel, which consisted of six handsome silk handkerchiefs, a fat, but discreet letter, and a lovely silver cigarette case with an emerald push-opener. He had had it made in Delhi; this is my Xmas present!! I was much touched and pleased by his painstaking trouble and impressed, as usual, by his taste . . .

Loelia and I went on to luncheon at Cecil Beaton's, where we found old Princesse de Polignac who grunted an attack on Lord Derwent's ill manners . . . . Palewski, who made eternal boring pro-Frog propaganda for de Gaulle . . . . I was amusing but bored. Home, inspected the Sergeant who is really ill, and a brief respite, which was too soon broken by the arrival of Lady Cunard who remained for an hour – she is so brilliant and divine but can be very boring, too! To rid myself of her (I wanted to write these hectic lines) I took her to the Egyptian Embassy to a huge reception. It was crowded with nobodies and nonentities and we soon left.

1 Churchill's daughter.
2 Wife of the Russian ambassador (qv).
3 Wife of the Speaker (qv).

FRIDAY 12TH FEBRUARY

Busy morning: the Sergeant is still ill and is threatened with mild jaundice.

Alan arrived from Falmouth in an ardent mood and had a rapturous reunion with the Sergeant. Sailors don't care! However, I tore him away from Preston's charms for an hour and walked him to Maimie Pavlovsky's where we had a cocktail. We found the King of Greece and others there; King Peter of Yugoslavia – that excessively silly brainless booby – was expected, too; but he had not arrived before Alan and I left. I hear that this boy drinks much too much and is seen tearing about with second-rate people including chorus girls.

Dined with Emerald .... The room was too hot; the food too rich; conversation languished and everybody was bored . . . [once home] I heard Alan and Harold arguing in the morning room. So I stole quietly and I hoped secretly to bed. Alan, however, woke me and poured out his troubles – troubles over the Sergeant.

A nice letter came again from Archie Kerr from Scotland where, very bored, he was still awaiting the plane which is to 'hop' him over Germany to Russia, a most hazardous and uncomfortable flight.

SATURDAY 13TH FEBRUARY

I wish that I had gone to Kelvedon or indeed anywhere, as the weather is balmy [as] about May-time. Crocuses are out and birds sing in the warm sunlight. Instead I frittered the day again waiting upon Alan, who is more infatuated than ever. He borrowed my car and drove to Pyrford to lunch to see Patsy. I had a long Turkish bath, which somewhat restored my spirits and soothed my irritations, which comes of too rich a regime on a surfeit of society. Dined at the Dorchester with Emerald, giving David Margesson a cocktail in the crowded bar below where Cyril Connolly joined us. We were a merry quartet, if an incongruous one; and I saw that I had been invited as a bridge between the politicians and the men of letters. The evening was enjoyable as last night had been dull. Alan picked me up and we walked back, avoiding dear Harold who will never leave us alone together. Alan then suggested an elaborate entertainment to which I only half-agreed.

SUNDAY 14TH FEBRUARY

It is two years today, on the feast of St Valentine, that Peter drove me in his little car from the Cairene Embassy to Heliopolis and I climbed so sadly into the great plane and was soon *en route* for England . . . We arrived at Khartoum, were met by the Governor and stayed comfortably at Kitchener's vast barrack of a palace . . . Bob Menzies[1] and I. How much have I aged, I wonder, since then? Little has changed in my life since then except that my hairs are greying over the temples, and that distresses me deeply.

1 See entry for 5 February 1941 and footnote.

I was cross, *ennervé* and liverish all day; lunched at home with Alan, later drove him to Paddington (he returned to Torquay) and walked back from there with my blond white dog who was an object of much attention and admiration in the Park. People were sitting in the sun, others rowed the Serpentine. It is a false summer.

TUESDAY 16TH FEBRUARY

Walked to the House where I find much excitement over a speech made last night by Harold Balfour at Oxford. Arthur Greenwood opened the much-heralded debate on the Beveridge Report. The House was crowded and I saw little Beveridge himself. He is an alert, excitable, determined little sexagenarian. John Anderson replied for the govt with what I thought the best, most balanced speech of his career. One listened without boredom; indeed he seemed to have thrown off his usual tedious manner. I left about 4.30 and rushed to No. 5 to receive the Duchess of Kent and give her tea. I had collected a few of her fast friends, Natasha Bagration . . . . Maimie and Vesevolod and others . . . Sydney Butler walked in unexpectedly but was welcomed. The Duchess stayed for an hour and a half and looked lovely in black and many pearls. She seemed less tired, and her lovely face was lit up with its former smile. Needless to say, Zoia Poklewska and her old mother Baroness Stoeckl came to fetch the Duchess. They never leave her for a second . . . . I love them, approve of them and realise how indispensable they have been to the Duchess in her grief; but they are too possessive altogether and, being Poles instead of English, will eventually cause her to be criticised . . . but I am utterly powerless to help.

Later I took Sydney and Rab (they were reluctant, even shy about accepting) to dine with Emerald at the Dorchester. She was gay, pretty, provocative, appetising, knowledgeable and altogether at her very best . . . the others were Diana Cooper, Eddie and Moucher Devonshire and old funny Chester Beatty.[1] A brilliant party and highly successful evening; but I was soon aware that there was an undercurrent of tragedy as Diana whispered to me that a cable had come to Emerald last evening from Courtlandt Palmer[2] in New York saying that Thomas Beecham had just married his adventuress, Miss Humby.[3] Emerald had reeled on receiving it, but was brave now and was what Diana called doing a 'Marie Antoinette'. She has always threatened to commit suicide if old Beecham

---

1 Alfred Chester Beatty (1875–1968) was an American plutocrat who made his money from copper mines. He became a naturalised Briton in 1933 – the same year as Channon – and was knighted in 1954. He was also renowned as an art collector and philanthropist.

2 Courtlandt Palmer (1871–1951) was an American composer in the romantic style. His music was much played in America in his lifetime but is neglected now.

3 See entry for 16 November 1942 and footnote.

deserted her. She has loved this musical scallywag for thirty-nine years. I was desperately sorry for her tonight and loved her deeply. The others were unaware of the drama – and we sat in the candlelight listening to Emerald's – and Eddie Devonshire's – remarkable conversation, first about literature and then cockfighting! The Butlers were impressed, dazed and capitulated completely, admitting her charm and high conversational powers.

A big day, which began well with a long letter from my Major [Coats] who confesses to a lapse with a general at Chungking. I trapped Jim Wedderburn, whom I met in the Smoking Room, into telling me the man's name. It is Grimsdale[1] and he is nearly 50. The tale made me a little wretched.

WEDNESDAY 17TH FEBRUARY

Rab, Harold and the Sergeant attended my levee this morning and helped me to dress. Walked to the House and deliberately fell into conversation with Lawson,[2] the Socialist MP who has just returned from China. He was soon talking about Grimsdale but told me little; but I gather that my rival is 50-ish and not too prepossessing . . .

The boring Beveridge debate continued and tempers are rising; the Socialists threaten to vote against the coalition govt en bloc, thus embarrassing their own leaders and ministers, more particularly Bevin who has announced that he will resign if his party repudiate him by ignoring his advice. Of course he will do nothing of the kind.

I hear that Winston is really quite ill; he attended a Cabinet swathed in a shawl; apparently he caught cold on his return; for the dramatic daily changes of climate and temperature were too much for him. He is an impatient patient, strong but not fit, and a lifetime spent drinking brandy is not conducive to a speedy recovery for pneumonia which he probably has. Some people thought that his illness was a political manoeuvre as he doesn't wish to intervene in the Beveridge debate. It is, however, genuine enough. Instead of him we had Kingsley Wood, who wound up the second day's debate; it was neither a skilful nor convincing speech and he had a rough ride. It is possible that the Report is an imaginative Liberal document, a charter of freedom: I don't know. In my case, the country should not be rushed into it without careful consideration.

1 Gordon Edward Grimsdale (1893–1950) was at this point a major general in the Army. He was British Military Attaché to Chungking and headed the British mission there from 1942 to 1945. He had been a senior officer in military intelligence in the Far East.

2 John James Lawson (1881–1965) started work in a colliery at the age of 12 and became a leading trades unionist. He was Labour MP for Chester-le-Street from 1919 to 1949 and Secretary of State for War from 1945 to 1946. He was raised to the peerage as 1st Baron Lawson in 1950.

Dined with Laura at Claridge's: the Argentine Ambassador, both Sutherlands (poor Eileen looks literally dying and fading away); Walter Buccleuch; Emerald; Bridget Parsons;[1] and Londonderrys, Teenie [Victor] Cazalet .... Cárcano drove Emerald and me home, and then sat with me at No. 5 for an hour discussing the neutrality of his country. He is ashamed of it. I am utterly worn out and long for a quiet evening or day alone; am nervous, almost bankrupt. The Sergeant .... has been removed to St George's Hospital. I am sorry but he is one less item on my too-full agenda.

The Butlers dined alone; nobody invites them. Emerald is becoming a problem; she is mildly inconsequent; inconsiderate, unpunctual – and she irritates everyone. Her relations with Nicholas Lawford are of a sentimental, emotional nature; they are mutually devoted and attracted – and she is thirty-nine years older than he.

My household arrangements are chaotic. No news from the in-laws. They are ageing or perhaps fed up with me. Patsy is at Torquay with Alan, whose passion for Mr Sergeant Preston seems to increase daily. He telephones to me – frantically, hysterically several times a day for news of the [illegible] man. He and the Lawford–Cunard axis are the romances of the moment; both astonishing but only one is silly.

THURSDAY 18TH FEBRUARY

Beveridge Day. I spent most of it in the House and watched the revolt grow. The whips are ill-informed, insensitive to opinion, rumour; and the much-abused Margesson is now missed . . . Herbert Morrison wound up for the govt in a balanced, clever, eloquent speech which revealed his increasing conservatism – was it a bid for the future leadership of a coalition government? The crowded House listened with interest and even the more truculent Socialists, whilst later prepared to vote against their leaders, were too cowardly to barrack Morrison .... his performance was superior to either John Anderson's or Kingsley's words. Nevertheless, 119 votes were recorded against the government in a three-line whip. Practically the whole rank and file of the Labour movement threw over their leaders.[2] There were ironical cheers when the result was announced, and someone remarked that there were only three more votes than had voted against the recent Catering Bill. That reduced the result to an absurdity. Coming into the lobby I saw old Beveridge and his recent bride;[3] they were surrounded by

---

1 See entry for 20 October 1942 and footnote.
2 The rebels' main gripe was no commitment by the government to implement the recommendations of the report as soon as possible, but to wait until the war was over.
3 Beveridge had married Jessy Janet Mair (*née* Philip) (1876–1959) the previous year.

sympathetic Socialists and I thought that the old man was in tears. It was a relief to get away.

Rab, his sister Mrs Portal, and Walter Buccleuch dined with me at No. 5 . . . . Walter Buccleuch, after he had drunk a glass of burgundy, had then to launch a slightly defeatist conversation! But Rab refused to be drawn. Walter is so patriotic, but misled and fundamentally stupid. He deplores the war. I shall always be fond of Walter; he is loyal, rude, Scotch and charming. Geordie Sutherland and Hughie Northumberland also wanted to dine but I hadn't ordered enough food. And I really couldn't entertain three dukes at one sitting – it would be too much like Mrs Corrigan!

SATURDAY 20TH FEBRUARY

A horrible day, cold and complicated. Had a Turkish bath which somewhat soothed my world-weariness. At nine o'clock I fetched Emerald at the Dorchester and escorted her to Ti Cholmondeley where we dined; we were late of course and coldly received. The others were Billy McCann,[1] Osbert Sitwell and his long Ganymede of seventeen years' standing, David Horner, a faded blond who writes dim books about France. Emerald instantly disliked Horner and was rude to him, and later she attacked everybody, abused Queen Mary, Mrs Greville and others. Osbert, to retaliate, criticised the Kenneth Clarks with venom and malice. The tiny room was hot; the atmosphere stifling, and the conversation so acid that I could do nothing and was in despair. Before twelve we left, and the most disastrous dinner party that I have ever attended ended. Emerald, angry, without saying 'goodbye', fled and we were all aghast and anxious for her. Billy McCann confided to me that she had been unpleasant and untactful last evening and had accursed all London. Strange vices and sins. He was *agacé* with her . . . as we were all. Osbert and Horner walked home with me. London was cold but very beautiful. Ti Cholmondeley and Osbert have now telephoned and we all agreed that beloved Emerald had been intolerable. I think that she may have had bad news; probably a cable confirming Thomas Beecham's marriage to Miss Humby. Bad temper combined with bad food can wreck an evening.

SUNDAY 21ST FEBRUARY

Unable to sleep last night, worrying about poor Emerald. I rang her up at 1 a.m. We talked for over two hours and my heart melted for her: we discussed not only Beecham but her crazy daughter, Nancy, too; and I realise that Emerald's unpleasantness and nonsense are due to her fundamental unhappiness – but I couldn't sleep again and woke this morning wretched and white after a *nuit blanche*.

1 See entry for 6 June 1942 and footnote.

Drove Laura Corrigan to Kelvedon where we spent the day: she gave cigarettes to the sixty soldiers and we went over the house, which is beginning now to look shabby and dirty.

Dined at the Belgian Embassy and was extremely funny in French; I enjoyed this continental party of eight men. Good food, wines and bridge . . . . on my return to No. 5 found Alan awaiting me. He had come up from Torquay to see the Sergeant tomorrow. He kept me up too late, as he always does. He is the most exhausting companion I know.

There was a huge pro-Soviet rally and meeting which was addressed by Anthony Eden at the Albert Hall today. Half the fashionables of London crowded to it – always a sign, in other countries except in England, of an imminent revolution.

MONDAY 22ND FEBRUARY

A too-full week began badly. I woke worn out *ennervé*; luckily, Emerald put me off for luncheon as the Sitwells refused to meet Cecil Beaton with whom they have some foolish feud and the party was cancelled.[1] However, Georgia Sitwell dined with me and flirted with both McCann and Harold Balfour; Laura Corrigan and Nicholas Lawford also dined. A quiet evening, uneventful except for one injudicious attack which I launched against Loelia Westminster, whom I am beginning to hate. To my surprise Georgia S, who is her greatest friend, far from resenting my remarks, agreed with all that I said.

Alan spent a mad morning buying rich presents for the Sergeant; then he took them to St George's Hospital, gave them to the patient and sat with him for an hour. Later, he returned to Torquay – taking his mother.

The Prime Minister is no better, and people are reminded that he is, after all, mortal. I think that he will recover this time but pneumonia will leave its traces on his huge physique. Telegrams pour into No. 10 all day; for although his popularity has declined, he is still much liked by almost everybody except me! The Speaker[2] is also very ill and has been given oxygen. I don't think that he will be Speaker now for long; soon after he recovers he will be given a viscountcy and retire.

WEDNESDAY 24TH FEBRUARY

Slept blissfully but woke cross and snapped at Diana over the telephone! The newspapers announce Thomas Beecham's marriage, so now Emerald will be unable to keep her secret and must face the world. I am sorry for her; but as he is neither her husband nor her lover, she must make the best of his desertion

---

1 The feud started in 1941 when the Sitwells objected to some remarks in Beaton's collection of his pre-war writings, *Time Exposure*.
2 Edward FitzRoy.

after thirty-nine years of devotion. All day at the House which was uneventful. Harvie-Watt told me that the PM is better, and that his temp. is now normal.

Dined with Emerald, a cosy but boring evening: Diana; Harold; Helen Fitzgerald; Leslie Hore-Belisha, Violet Trefusis; Peter Quennell. Emerald sparkled from a levee, then prodded Leslie into reciting Ronsard[1] which he did in his perfect classical French. At the end of dinner Emerald led me to her bedroom and together we telephoned to the Foreign Office and asked for Nicholas Lawford who was on fire-watching duty. I left her . . . . and she talked to him for an hour. It is [a] rapturous romance which delights us all. When Emerald returned to her drawing room she found that her guests had left; but I had a few words with her – tender exchanges about Nicholas and she showed me a really handsome Fabergé cigarette case which she has got for him through Chester Beatty. Ninety pounds. This is my doing; he ought to be serenaded but he is such an impersonal, reserved fellow that in hiding his shyness he often becomes cold, almost rude. It is an extraordinary love affair. I walked home alone half-thinking that I should be garrotted – Mayfair is now highly dangerous.

THURSDAY 25TH FEBRUARY

A very full day, a frantic morning arranging my house for the inglorious gala[2] and then I drove to the Brewery at Park Royal where we had our semi-annual meeting . . . .

Drove back to Belgrave Square where I found chaos: champagne being unpacked, furniture being moved, waiters changing, and I was soon joined by the bride and bridegroom, Lord and Lady Dudley themselves! He is 49 and she about 27. They had been married at a Registry Office, then had some form of religious service, a luncheon and came on to me. She was simply dressed in brown velvet and Eric was in a lounge suiting. After an attachment that has lasted seven years, matrimony can hold few secrets for them!! She seems the more in love of the two! . . . . they soon left me and I had an hour in which to tidy the house, dress and rest. I told them, too, how Daisy Fellowes had telephoned to me to ask when the party was! I did not suspect that she was gatecrashing; for whilst she is capable of any criminal actions, I did not think she would commit so common a one as forcing herself unwanted and uninvited to a party! About 5.30 the Dudleys . . . . arrived. The house was a dream of candlelit beauty and the blue dining room shimmered. I had put the glass table at one end in the bow window. Within a few minutes, on the dot of 5.30 Herbert Morrison walked in escorted by three Home Office henchmen. Socialists never know how to behave and he arrived at the very moment of 5.30

1 Pierre de Ronsard (1524–85) was the leading French poet of his era.
2 Channon had agreed to lend his house to Eric Ward, 3rd Earl of Dudley (qv) for the reception after his marriage to Frances Laura Long (*née* Charteris) (1915–90), former wife of the 2nd Viscount Long. They were divorced in 1954.

when he was invited. He was immediately surrounded by fashionable ladies and seemed to enjoy their company. Within an hour all London was there (the butler, Treherne, afterwards told me that 325 people had come). Half the government .... and there was a sprinkling of ambassadors – the Brazilian mistook Shakes [Morrison] for Herbert Morrison who by now was talking to duchesses. I led up Kakoo Rutland and Mollie Buccleuch to him and his one eye[1] roved at them with approval. Champagne and cocktails flowed and I was in a benign, gracious mood and charming to everybody, even to Moggie Gage[2] and the two Trees! Poor Eileen Sutherland (I wonder whether she has typhoid) sat neglected in a corner! I have not heard so much chatter nor seen so much champagne, certainly not since the war!! Everybody was enchanted to see everyone else; and the party had really immense *Stimmung*! Unexpected people like Averell Harriman and Dickie Mountbatten came late. There was an atmosphere of gaiety, youth and distinguished grandeur about the reception which intoxicated everybody ....

The bride and bridegroom, after thanking me profusely, left for Claridge's about 8.30 .... I was sorry when it was over. Soon after nine Laura Corrigan returned and picked me up. We drove to the Dorchester where we dined with Francis Queensberry in a private room he had suggested – two tables; rich food; magnums of champagne, and so the party went on! A curious collection of people .... Leslie Belisha was again induced to quote Ronsard; and our host recited the sonnets with his particular charm, a mixture of cockney and eloquence. His baby face (he is about 50) becomes distorted and vehement. He is a remarkable creature. Duff Cooper unkindly prodded Laura to recite, too, but she refused. Recitations are now the mode.

Home about 1 a.m. after a too-rich day. Receiving 325 people in my house, long and so often the scene of brilliant gatherings, was a strain – but a happy one. It was unkind of me to tell Emerald that Laura Corrigan in her earliest youth wanted to be a poetess and did, indeed, write under the pseudonym of 'The Duchess of Feswick' – now that story will do the rounds of this feverish, frenzied, fascinating London.

SATURDAY 27TH FEBRUARY

Feeling dormant and spent after the varied and anxious activities of the past few days. Lunched with Alan; we had Turkish baths together and I recovered a bit. He and I dined with Emerald Cunard at the Dorchester to celebrate Nicholas Lawford's 32nd birthday. Emerald had taken immense pains with her appearance and the preparations ... the room was candlelit, the food delicious, the wines good. She was dressed as for Derby House in a [illegible] black dress, wore a mantilla

---

1 Morrison had lost the sight of an eye in childhood because of an infection.
2 Imogen Grenfell, Viscountess Gage.*

and black and many jewels which enlivened her looks. So did Diana Cooper who was radiantly lovely. It was a *bataille des bijoux*!![1] Nicholas, who until recently had led an obscure and quiet life, was impressed and touched. Emerald gave him a Fabergé cigarette case; I gave him Edwardian links of hammered gold with tiny diamonds in them; Alan brought champagne; Laura Corrigan sent him a bottle of whisky. Conversation was peculiarly brilliant and Emerald told us anecdotes of Lord Curzon and told us how jealous he had been of me when Grace Curzon was in love with me – at the time when we went to Paris together (and I repulsed her advances, and went out to dine with the duchesse de Brissac, my old love, instead!) This must have been in 1924, I think. After a hyper-successful evening (I am a collector of evenings), Alan, Nicholas and I walked home together, blowing kisses to St George's Hospital where 'the Sergeant' still lies. Alan spent most of the day buying him rich presents and food.

SUNDAY 28TH FEBRUARY

Alan and I slept late together, and after a visit to Sergeant Preston, walked to Claridge's to lunch with Laura C. He then drove to Bedfordshire to see his mother and brother, George, that semi-lunatic has got himself engaged to Lady Brigid Honor King,[2] a spinster of 42.[3] I doubt whether the marriage will come off! There is also the Lord Lieutenant of Bedfordshire on the tapis as Lord Luke[4] has just died. Alan is angling for it; but I think it will go to Simon Whitbread,[5] or possibly even to Harold Wernher[6] whom I suggested as an alternative. Alan ought to have it, but he is so young and poor; dull, ever-pregnant Patsy would be utterly hopeless . . .

Ghislaine Dresselhuys rang me up and in a somewhat mysterious voice asked me to go and see her; I did. We discussed marriage and for a moment I wondered whether she was going to propose to me! Then I realised that it was only as an old man, a sort of father confessor, that she wished to consult that I had been invited to call! She is hesitating between dark, garrulous, short-sighted,

---

1 Battle of the jewels.

2 Brigid Honor King-Tenison (1902–91), Lady Brigid by courtesy, was daughter of the 9th Earl of Kingston. George Lennox-Boyd was killed the following November and they never married.

3 She was 40.

4 George Lawson Johnston (1873–1943), whose fortune was based on Bovril, had been Lord Lieutenant of Bedfordshire since 1936. He was raised to the peerage as 1st Baron Luke in 1929.

5 Simon Whitbread (1904–85), son of Samuel Whitbread (qv). Neither he nor Wernher (*vide infra*), nor Lennox-Boyd received the post.

6 Harold Wernher (1893–1973), from 1948 3rd Bt.*

bespectacled John, Viscount Vaughan[1] and young dashing Denis Alexander[2] – who ought one day to become Lord Caledon. I advised her to wait and marry neither. She loves Alexander but wants to marry Vaughan. I gather that the Kemsleys want her to marry fairly soon and 'settle down': she has been given a fortnight by all concerned in which to make up her mind.

I fetched Duff and Diana and drove them to Welbeck House where we dined with Guy Strutt[3] on disgusting food, i.e. rabbit and carrots! Boring evening until Alan fetched me and I drove him to Paddington. I have almost always had a man in my life and now it is Alan and he suits me as well, if not better, than any other.

Poppy Thursby tells me that Moggie Gage and Mrs Tree both like me so much!! That is unexpected. Feuds of twenty years' standing.

Monday 1st March

My finances are increasingly worrying; I am now almost 'poor'; that is due to taxation. I must economise and do not really mind it.

Felt very well today; as if endless energy has been released. I caught up with many letters and attended to my Southend chores . . . . I met Mrs Churchill in S. Audley Street, looking eager and foolish without a hat. She affects little bows or handkerchiefs as head-dresses! Does she think it Russian or what? At six o'clock I called on Evan Tredegar in his Albany Chambers, E5. I was cold and aloof as I don't want him in my life. I agreed, however, to signing a contract whereby I am to give 'Bosie' – Lord Alfred Douglas – an annual income of £25. I don't think he will long live to enjoy it.[4]

Emerald tried to bully me into dining with her, as did Rab and Sydney, but I refused and went early to bed . . . Emerald, however, disturbed my dreams, by telephoning late . . . . The *volupté* of having an early evening by one's self is a deep luxury. I am now alone in the deserted morning room writing at my lacquer desk and shall soon go to bed.

The Speaker is dying – we can count him out.

Tuesday 2nd March

To the House where I stayed half the day. Actually it rose at one o'clock, owing to the inefficiency of the whips who are inept. Everybody regrets Margesson . . .

We raided Berlin in large numbers last night, so presumably we shall have a return visit tonight.

1   John David Malet Vaughan (1918–2014), Viscount Vaughan by courtesy until he succeeded his father as 8th Earl of Lisburne in 1963. He did not marry Miss Dresselhuys.
2   Denis James Alexander (1920–80) succeeded his uncle as 6th Earl of Caledon in 1968. He married Miss Dresselhuys in April 1943 but they were divorced in 1948.
3   Guy Robert Strutt (1921–2007), son of the 4th Baron Rayleigh.
4   He died in March 1945.

I went to see Ghislaine Dresselhuys again at 55 Park Lane and this time, after listening to her girlish confidences, advised her to accept young Alexander at once.

WEDNESDAY 3RD MARCH

Walked to the House, went out to lunch .... On my return I met the Train-Bearer[1] in the lobby who told me that the Speaker had died at two o'clock. It was then 2.20. I rushed to the Chamber which happened to be crowded, as it was the Naval Estimates. Brabner[2] was speaking when the second clerk, Metcalfe, rose to announce that Mr Speaker had just died. The mace had been removed a moment before. The House gasped, and rose in tribute. Anthony Eden moved that we adjourn until Tuesday. We are in a curious position from a parliamentary point of view; precedents and procedure have been hurriedly looked up! No Speaker had died in harness, as it were, since 1789! What a parliament – three kings; a world war; four prime ministers; an abdication; the Chamber destroyed – and it is not yet over. The lobbies buzzed with excitement, regret and speculation as to who will succeed to the now empty Chair. I think it will be Douglas Clifton Brown,[3] although there are rumours that Shakes Morrison, Ernest Brown and Gwilym Lloyd George are all possible candidates. I walked home and went to bed for an hour where I slept like a little child. Refreshed and handsome once more, I walked with Sydney Butler, whom I like more and more, to Doreen Brabourne's house where she was entertaining twenty selected people for 'sherry'. Gay party of friends, Jock McEwen whom I like more and more, and many others including Mrs Keppel, now recovered.

Everybody invited me to dine, but as Ben Kittredge invited me first, I have to go to him. It was at the Dorchester. Trouble taken; a private suite; but the party flopped as the sirens rang at 8.30 and Vesevolod had to rush away as he is an ARP warden. Maimie Pavlovsky, a dutiful and affectionate wife, was worried about him and soon followed. Their departure broke up the party. I was next to Princess Aspasia of Greece,[4] and feeling well and angry I talked to her very openly about Queen Mignonne of Yugoslavia, and her activities etc. I pointed out that what little chance King Peter had of returning to this throne had been ruined by the plots and tactlessness of his fat intriguing disagreeable mother. Princess Aspasia, who had looked forward to being the mother of a reigning queen,[5] was

---

1 The functionary who walks behind the Speaker in his daily procession to the House of Commons carrying the long train of his robes.
2 Rupert Brabner, Conservative MP for Hythe. See entry for 8 May 1940 and footnote.
3 Douglas Clifton Brown (1879–1958) was Conservative MP for Hexham from 1918 to 1923 and from 1923 to 1951. He was Deputy Speaker from 1938 to 1943 and Speaker from 1943 to 1951, when he was raised to the peerage as 1st Viscount Ruffside.
4 See entry for 6 October 1941 and footnote.
5 Her daughter, Princess Alexandra of Greece and Denmark, did become Queen of Yugoslavia, albeit for only twenty months or so until the monarchy was ousted in November 1945.

considerably shaken; she admitted to me that she hated Queen Mignonne who tried to dominate the young couple and was generally malevolent. I did as much mischief and damage as I could; and perhaps more. I am determined that they will never return to their throne; for they have behaved too badly and ungratefully to Paul and Princess Olga ... I left the party, since the 'all-clear' had sounded and walked to Pam Churchill's where I had been able to dine. There I found Harold Balfour, who had carried the sleeping little Winston to a shelter and later fetched him up again; Averell Harriman; Barbie Wallace .... and others ... the raid, mild as it was, had slightly upset Pam because of her child. Brendan Bracken was in an anecdotal mood but he looks white and ill. It is now 12.30: I have rung up a few people I know, and various unknowns and now shall go to bed.

Lovely levee of naked ministers shaving in my bedroom. But Alan now has alas returned to Brixham. Already I miss him.

THURSDAY 4TH MARCH

A party-free day since the H of C is not sitting because of the Speaker's death. Rab, Harold and Sydney all sat on my bed and we discussed the succession. I enjoy my morning ministerial levee but I like it when they are all away, too!

Called on the Sergeant Preston; and Loelia Westminster has arrived here to stay. My house is full. Everyone I have seen is in excellent spirits, exhilarated, no doubt, by last night's raids. The second one was at about five o'clock this morning; I was only half-conscious of it and dozed through it. There was some gunfire. Hardly anybody knows that 171 people were killed at Bethnal Green.[1] But not by bombs! An accident causing a stampede in a shelter and these many people were all crushed or suffocated. An appalling disaster.

I have lunched alone, which is always the supreme *volupté*. Later I walked Bundi to the Dorchester, called on Emerald .... We went to Lady Kemsley's cocktail party and met a shy foolish-looking individual, a Capt Grenfell,[2] who wrote the controversial *Sea Power* two years ago. Emerald and I chatted and [discussed] her love affair with Nicholas, and then I came home to find a pile of telephone messages ....

The 1922 Committee met this morning and decided that Colonel Douglas Clifton Brown, the present Deputy Speaker, should be elected Speaker. So he is,

---

1 The final death toll was 173. The recently opened Central Line extension station at Bethnal Green in east London was being used as a deep shelter during air raids. On the way down to the platforms on the evening of 3 March a woman tripped over and others fell on top of her, and many were crushed or asphyxiated to death. It is believed to be the largest single loss of civilian lives during the war.

2 Russell Grenfell (1892–1954) was a recently retired captain in the Royal Navy when he published his highly influential book *Sea Power in the Next War* in 1938 (not, as Channon says, two years ago). He became naval correspondent of the *Daily Telegraph*.

or rather was, as good as elected. But I now hear that Winston showed his hand late last night, and more strongly this afternoon, and has decreed that it should be Gwilym Lloyd George. There is much to be said for that. Is Winston sincere in making this gesture to old 'LG', whom he fears and mistrusts but likes? Or does he only want the old rogue to get to hear that he has sponsored Gwilym's candidature? Nobody knows now what will happen ... I repeated all this to David Margesson at dinner ...

FRIDAY 5TH MARCH

Slept ill although there was no raid. The newspapers announce the disaster at Bethnal Green. The enemy propaganda will make much of it; but I fear it had to be released .... All my information re the Speakership, the Prime Minister's intervention and wishes is confirmed. We may have some excitement when the House meets on Tuesday. Gwilym Lloyd George's chances are growing.

I took Lady Willingdon to the film premiere of *Desert Victory*,[1] a magnificent portrayal of the 8th Army's triumphs: it is inspiring, horrible, exciting. I suppose it must be true that death is the greatest of aphrodisiacs ... we sat with Alan Brooke, the CIGS, and other grand red tabs. The distinguished military audience looked like GHQ. We went on to dine with Emerald, an extraordinary evening, over-extroverted .... Food was adequate, and conversation agreeable. Towards the end of the meal Emerald began to bait poor Bee Willingdon who, whilst she reigned for years over all of 250,000,000 people,[2] was unable to bear up to Emerald's brilliant barrage of banter. I was sorry for her as our hostess bristled her. Emerald wins every round of what was a witty and almost uncomfortable duel. Whatever Bee Willingdon said, Emerald repeated *sotto voce* verbatim with much-ironical emphasis. I was bored and induced 'Michael-Angelo' Cárcano to drive me home about midnight. Lady Willingdon, who is called at six-thirty every morning of her life and always has been, left early. Emerald was plagued, petulant, provocative and unexpected ...

SATURDAY 6TH MARCH

Tomorrow I shall be 46!

Presents have begun to arrive: a silver coffee pot .... from Laura; cigarettes from Harold; a wallet from Honor – days ago, it came; linen from Alan and Patsy etc.

I hear that the Baillies are at last going to divorce so that she can marry Geoffrey Lloyd. He spent two hours with me yesterday and never mentioned it! As I write I watched Lady Willingdon ring my door bell and leave a letter – at

---

1 A Ministry of Information propaganda film about El Alamein and the related campaign, directed by Roy Boulting.
2 Lady Willingdon had been Vicereine of India.

this house where the great philanthropist Lord Shaftesbury died in 1886.[1] Called on the Sergeant, still incarcerated at St George's Hospital; he has begun to irritate me. A bourgeois at heart and unappreciative of Alan's too-lavish devotion.

Emerald Cunard has sent me ten exquisite little Meissen pots with tops. Good Dresden. They are a welcome but unnecessary birthday present . . . .

I have suggested to everybody that either Mrs FitzRoy, the widow, or otherwise the son, of the late Speaker should be at least offered the viscountcy that would have been his had he survived another month. People seem to be against raising another family to the peerage.

Dined at the Bagatelle, a fashionable restaurant crowded with young officers dancing with their girls!! Laura, Daphne Weymouth, Dmitri of Russia[2] and I. Daphne and I had a two hours' conversation, intimate and absorbing. She reiterated what I already know: that she only loves Henry Weymouth really: that her passionate affair, which still goes on with Robert Cecil,[3] means little to her, although much to him. Betty Cranborne now cuts her, but Bobbety is well disposed towards her! The old Salisburys take a lenient view.

SUNDAY 7TH MARCH

My 46th birthday and I feel younger, more skittish and better-looking than I have done in years. Are these then the symptoms of old age? All day messages and telegrams poured in. Leslie Belisha, the Argentine Ambassadress, and Loelia Westminster telephoned from the country to wish me a happy birthday; so did Peggy Crewe and others. Cables came, including one from my mother – but the day died without a word from Peter.

I had a Turkish bath, and a rest – and in the evening celebrated by giving a 'young' dinner party: Emerald, Laura, Eleanor Smith, Maimie and Vsevolod; Billy McCann; Nicholas Lawford; Harold Balfour; Daphne Weymouth; Bill Astor . . . . The dining room looked very lovely with the Meissen; the food was excellent; the drink flowed; so did the conversation. All was quite pre-war, the cables and the clothes and the splendour. About midnight the party began to break up and before one o'clock everybody had left. All were a touch tipsy. Harold and Daphne Weymouth had never met before and it was an immediate 'click'; seemed like a *coup de foudre*[4] . . . I went to bed . . . . I heard the sirens sound and for a few minutes there was gunfire. Then I fell asleep.

Happy day. I was born on a Sunday too.

1 Why he should link these two things is unclear, unless he was comparing Lady Willingdon's philanthropic career with Shaftesbury's. In any case, he died in Folkestone in 1885.
2 Prince Dmitri Alexandrovich of Russia (1901–80) was a nephew of Tsar Nicholas II. He spent his exile in France, America and then Britain.
3 Qv: son of Lord Cranborne.
4 Literally, a clap of thunder; idiomatically, an immediate attraction.

MONDAY 8TH MARCH

A beautiful day but I feel weak from too much the night before.

Here I sit dressed like a crow, waiting to go the Speaker's funeral. I want terribly to be alone for a week, by the sea, somewhere by the sea.

A crazy but affectionate cable last night from my poor demented mother. Still she remembered, which is much.

Lady Willingdon, aristocratic but easy, blustering but simple, came to luncheon with me: I gave her the *beaux restes* of last evening's banquet. She drove me to St Margaret's and *en route* I told her the story of Arthur Hope's[1] financial peccadilloes; of how he swindled me and others out of large sums of money. Such is the Governor of Madras!! The church was already crowded when I arrived at 2.10! The great jostled one another ... never have I seen such chaos in a church! The attendants of the House of Commons did the ushering, which was a suitable gesture, but they could not be expected to recognise ambassadors .... There was Nicholas Lawford to do that; he had been borrowed from the Foreign Office for that purpose and he did his best ... but I saw four angry emissaries standing by a pillar and members of the War Cabinet, some of them, were shown into pews usually allocated to servants at fashionable weddings. Anthony Eden, looking old, the Maiskys, Herbert Morrison and others slotted in – but the Lord Chamberlain, Lord Clarendon,[2] sat near me.

At 2.30 the Chaplain read out a foolish notice about air raids and the coffin, covered with a Union Jack, was carried up the aisle .... The service was very dull, flat and frightful. Two hymns from the Revised Prayer Book, which the House of Commons had rejected, were sung. And both the ghastly archbishops took part in the service: the fat foolish Canterbury[3] whose voice is so unimpressive (he is universally detested) and Lord Lang, the horrible old intriguer: he is old now and his once mellifluous voice was almost inaudible: one saw his bald head and wicked little beady eyes. How I hate him – these villains ruined the service. The last post sounded flat ... and even the mourners' procession was muddled, for Harvie-Watt came out ahead of Lord Fortescue[4] who was representing the King. Unimpressed, I walked away with Victor Raikes who agreed that the C[hurch] of England must do better than that to survive. A tepid, mismanaged ceremony if ever there was one. I went to the hairdresser's and walked home, felt ill. My temp

---

1 See entry for 4 January 1940 and footnote.
2 See entry for 9 December 1942 and footnote.
3 William Temple.
4 Hugh William Fortescue (1888–1958) was by courtesy Viscount Ebrington from 1905 until 1932, when he succeeded his father as 5th Earl Fortescue. He was a government whip in the Lords from 1937 and Conservative Chief Whip from 1945 to 1957. He became a Knight of the Garter in 1951.

was 100; but I sat with Rab for an hour who agreed with me that the service had been devastating and disappointing. Now, having had a solitary tray and three glasses of port, I am going to bed.

I met Mrs Keppel in St James's Street and walked with her to Partridge's shop. An urchin pointed at her and I heard him say 'Look at her blue hair.' Mrs K is very intimate with the PM and pretends to be more so. She says that she rebuked him for his two major mistakes, moving Wavell and appointing Temple as Archbishop. She is right. She also added that I was much the most popular man in London society now that I was a bachelor again! I hope she is right this time, too.

TUESDAY 9TH MARCH

I woke at about eight and found Alan, dark and handsome, standing over me . . . He lay on my bed for an hour and breakfasted; then we went to see Stuart Preston, still immured at St George's Hospital; and walked to the House to watch the election of the new Speaker. It was crowded; Sir Gilbert Campion,[1] as Chief Clerk, pointed to people whom he wished to call and I sat in the Distinguished Strangers' Gallery . . . George Lambert[2] in a boring speech proposed Clifton Brown, Tinker[3] seconded him . . . . Cunningham-Reid intervened to protest against parliamentary procedure and talked such obvious nonsense that he bored and angered the House which, however, listened patiently . . . . At last the proceedings ended by Clifton Brown speaking well and modestly; he sat on the corner seat in the third row immediately behind the PPSs. His proposer and seconder went to conduct him to the Chair and, in traditional style, he made signs of protest and reluctance to accept the high honour conferred upon him. Then he went to the Chair, thanked the House, and the Serjeant[-at-Arms][4] (a most charming man always) advanced and placed the mace once more on the Clerks' table. The new Speaker-Elect, still dressed in morning clothes, then called his elder brother, General Clifton Brown,[5] who paid him a graceful tribute. Actually they are alleged to loathe each other, and years ago there was a very shabby story which scarcely

1 See entry for 18 January 1940 and footnote.
2 Liberal MP for South Molton.
3 John Joseph Tinker (1875–1957) was Labour MP for Leigh from 1923 to 1945.
4 Charles Alfred Howard (1878–1958) was a professional soldier who fought in the Second Boer War and the Great War, in which he won the DSO and Bar and reached the rank of lieutenant colonel. He was Serjeant-at-Arms of the House of Commons from 1935 to 1956 and was knighted in 1944.
5 Howard Clifton Brown (1868–1946) was Conservative MP for Newbury from 1922 to 1923 and from 1924 to 1945. From 1889 to the end of the Great War he had been a professional soldier, retiring in the rank of brigadier general.

reflects credit on the new First Commoner in the Kingdom. Henry Page Croft,[1] as he then was, wrote General Clifton Brown a private letter re some political issue on which the brothers happened to differ; the letter hinted that no matter what the Commons did on this particular matter, it could always be arranged to throw it out in the House of Lords. Croft's careless secretary inadvertently addressed the letter to Colonel Clifton Brown, who on opening it must have realised that it was not for him. He promptly sent it to *The Times* which printed it. The fates of the Tories would reveal the whole story . . . Alan told it to me in detail. The new Speaker, Clifton Brown, then adjourned the House until three o'clock. Apart from the tale I have transcribed so sketchily, I have nothing against the new Speaker. He is well liked; has good manners, is simple and straightforward; is audible (perhaps a disadvantage as a Speaker) a good House of Commons man. He is only 63 and now goes practically into purdah for the remainder of his days. No more intimacy; no more Smoking Room colloquies.

Alan and I walked to the Ritz where I lunched with Emerald . . . . and I walked back to Westminster to watch the installation of the Speaker, and as we drew up to the doors, the sirens sounded. There was no gunfire. I went into the Chamber. Clifton Brown was in Court dress and wearing a short clerk's wig. At that moment Black Rod knocked, entered, bowed several times and summoned us to the Lords. We marched in solemn procession through the Princes' Gallery, but the little Robing Room, the present abode of the Lords,[2] was too small to admit many of us. I stayed outside with Emerald and, joined by Max Beaverbrook, we heard part of the very short proceedings. Emerald was soon surrounded by peers of the realm . . . The procession returned and somewhere *en route* Clifton Brown must have changed his wig, for when I reached the Chamber he was already be-gowned and be-wigged in full Speaker's paraphernalia. There were a few perfunctory remarks from Anthony Eden, the Speaker then rose and declared the House adjourned. He walked out with dignity, preceded by the train-bearer, followed by the secretary, and I heard him turn to the attendants and Serjeant[-at-Arms] and say – as if he had done it all his life – 'Usual time tomorrow'!

All this traditional quaint rather Alice in Wonderland ceremony continued whilst a severe air raid was in progress . . . . I walked home, where Alan soon joined me for tea. I refused to accompany him and the immensely pregnant Patsy to the play, and planned a quiet evening. However, half London has telephoned . . . Harold Balfour is out (he was immensely struck and taken with Daphne Weymouth whom he had never met until my birthday party on Sunday. Yesterday he gave her lunch.) And Rab, after dining here off and on for three years returned today to live at 3 Smith Square, his attractive little house which was badly blitzed.

1 See entry for 22 June 1939 and footnote.
2 The Commons were sitting in the Lords' Chamber following the bombing of their House in 1941.

I shall miss him after a time, for I am devoted to him (and deplore his Scotch meanness, his only unattractive trait); but for a little it is pleasant to have my lovely house to myself. I am enjoying the calm and peace of a pyjama evening.

WEDNESDAY 10TH MARCH

This morning I woke feeling ill; indeed I was sick three times during the night and have diarrhoea as well . . . . I stayed in bed nearly all day, taking my temperature too often. About three I got up, walked to the Commons, tried to get some books which Somerset de Chair wanted (he has jaundice) and then went to the Andersons' for tea. She was intriguing, insinuating, interesting as ever . . . . Dined at 3 Lees Place with Lord and Lady Kenmare,[1] a tiny house. Indifferent food but pink champagne. The Kenmares – the newly married couple (I am told that somebody telephoned him on his marriage 'from the frying pan into the furnace'!);[2] Lady Kenmare's extraordinary-looking daughter, Miss Cavendish;[3] Emerald; Daisy Fellowes; the Argentine Ambassador we now meet at every lighted-candle; Gaston Palewski, who tells me that the Fighting French have almost unbelievable rows amongst themselves and really hate one another more than they hate the Germans . . . . ! Early to bed, and Daisy Fellowes, who has lost every vestige of beauty, tells me that she so shocked Stephen Spender[4] by her *outré* conversation the other evening that he left her house.

THURSDAY 11TH MARCH

I had invited Mrs Neville Chamberlain to tea. Laura Corrigan, Lady Willingdon, the two Iveaghs and others came. A successful little party. There was one incident; when Jim Wedderburn arrived both Lord and Lady Iveagh rose and crossed the room, almost but not quite cutting him! They are still smouldering about his visit to Honor last summer and showed their resentment clearly enough. Both Iveaghs were affectionate and delightful. When they left Laura and I went on to Peggy Crewe's cocktail party for Jock Colville, her stepson. He has been in W. Africa and looks improved, bronzed and well – and rather ——[5] which I always suspected. I

---

1 Lord Kenmare was until 1941 Lord Castlerosse. She was Enid Lindeman (1892–1973), heir to an Australian wine fortune, and this was her fourth marriage.

2 Lady Kenmare had been Viscountess Furness until her marriage.

3 Patricia Enid Cavendish (1925–2019), Lady Kenmare's daughter from her marriage to Brigadier General Frederick Cavendish.

4 Stephen Harold Spender (1909–95) was a novelist, essayist and poet and a protégé of T. S. Eliot (qv). He was a communist and outspoken anti-fascist, and a co-founder with Cyril Connolly (qv) of *Horizon*, the literary magazine. He was knighted in 1983.

5 Channon has written a long dash in the MS; he usually does this if alluding to what he suspects is someone's homosexuality. Colville, who later married and had three children, had no reputation for this.

was glad to see him for he recalled the happy Chamberlain days. Like me, he was devoted to Neville.

Natasha Bagration has seen a Free Frog .... recently arrived from Kenya where he saw Princess Olga and Prince Paul. My poor friend is, it appears, dying: he no longer gets up, he neither washes nor eats, nor sleeps . . . and gabbles incoherently of the past and of me. Much of all this I repeated to Oliver Stanley in the House. He is doing all that he can to help and to expedite the move to South Africa as the Cape, being more civilised and salubrious, ought to be of some benefit to Paul – but will it come too late? I fear that he will die, and I know that I, and perhaps only I, could save him; and I will not be allowed to go. It is heartbreaking. Oliver Stanley has been loyal and helpful and straight about the whole affair; he is more red-blooded about it than Bobbety Cranborne.

Anthony Eden left today by plane for the USA – a secret still. What good can that doll do there? What is more secret is that the King of Greece leaves on Sunday for the Middle East by plane, and I hear the King of England is also going on a trip. Is this true? To the Middle East; perhaps to the USA?

Colin Davidson[1] has been killed in W. Africa. This lengthy, evil-tongued Cyclops who has long been my friend – since 1919 – will be much missed by a circle of friends and by Rachel, his wife who worshipped him. He hadn't a pleasant character, was on the make; but was charming. He stayed for too long with us at St Martin in 1935,[2] that fatal summer which, owing perhaps to our lives, wrecked my marriage. He pounced on Honor, on me, on others; and made himself thoroughly objectionable. I regretted my kindness to him afterwards. It was during those weeks that I suggested to him that he marry Rachel Howard, one of the lightest and most charming of women. The marriage had been a great success and they had two children. Colin was good-looking in a distinguished Keppel[3] way; but he was far from handsome and tried to marry every heiress for years, although his tastes were strongly otherwise . . . and his tactics were too obvious and clumsy. I disliked him as one only can dislike v old friends; but he was a cad, although a Catholic; he borrowed money from women and then abused them in public. And although he had a superficial social charm, he was stunted intellectually.

SATURDAY 13TH MARCH   *SWIFTS PARK, CRANBROOK, KENT*

The Duchess of Kent rang up; she wants me to go to Kenya. How can I? Yet I know that only I can save my poor failing, frenzied friend . . . I walked via the India

---

1 Colin Keppel Davidson (1895–1943), son of Colonel Leslie Davidson and Lady Theodora Keppel. He rose to the rank of lieutenant colonel. His widow was the former Lady Rachel Howard. He had in fact been killed in Tunisia.
2 See entry for 9 July 1942 and footnote. Channon has confused 1933, when they probably were in St Martin, and 1935, when the diaries suggest they definitely were not.
3 The family of his mother.

Office whereby I deposited a letter for Peter, to Claridge's and lunched with Laura Corrigan. Then we drove here; nobody asked any questions. This small, compact, cosy comfortable house makes me long to live even more at Kelvedon. A quasi-rural life must be my destiny. The library-cum-sitting room is particularly pleasant.

Victor Cazalet, my host, and a friend for twenty-five years, has no social sense; he has collected a most curious collection of people: Mrs Corrigan; me; Lady Peel (that is 'Beatrice Lillie');[1] André Roy;[2] a young Free Frenchman, effeminate, sad, good-mannered and aristocratic – he has another name, but what it is I don't know . . . . I went immediately to my room and slept until dinner.

Gay evening and unexpectedly the ill-assorted party got on together extremely well. Rich food: duck and champagne, and the house is banked with flowers, azaleas and outrageously rare orchids and early fruit-blossom.

After luncheon, before coming to the country, I took leave of the King of Greece. He goes to Chequers today and then on to Cairo. He told me something of his troubles in the Middle East and I warned him against Rex Leeper, the new Ambassador.[3] But he was already aware of this dangerous man's activities . . .

SUNDAY 14TH MARCH

A dull day, overeating, oversleeping and overtalking. I felt ill. Pork for lunch is too much. Later we went to the farm, the others collected eggs – I could not as I am still so terrified of chickens – and we watched a lamb being born. The fields were spotted by these tiny creatures; and the *accouchement*[4] took place before us. The little thing came out yellow and red and the ewe immediately began to lick it all over. It was some time before it could stand on its legs.

Alan, 'The Sergeant', Leslie Hore-Belisha all rang me up to talk and say, 'goodnight'. I feel desperately heavy, old and ill.

MONDAY 15TH MARCH

The Ides of March! I drove Laura and the Free young Frog [Roy] to London. He behaved with more tact than we did since both Laura and I attacked the ghastly de Gaulle who is his Chief. Roy says he symbolises all France! . . . There was a

---

1 Beatrice Gladys Lillie (1894–1989) was a Canadian actress, comedian and singer who often played in revues written by Noël Coward, and spent much of the Second World War entertaining the troops. She married, in 1920, Sir Robert Peel, 5th Bt; they separated before his death in 1934.

2 André Roy was the *nom de guerre* of Roy André Desplats-Pilter (1904–45), a liaison officer at Free French headquarters in London since 1940, whose principal liaison work to begin with was to have an affair with Nancy Mitford (qv).

3 See entry for 21 November 1938 and footnote. Leeper had just been appointed British Ambassador to the Greek government-in-exile in Cairo.

4 Birth.

fog and we were delayed, and only reached London at 12.30. I found the Sergeant sitting here using my home as a club. I was cold and tried to get rid of him as I had so much to do. He is getting spoilt, takes too much for granted, I fear. I did some frantic telephoning as I remembered that I had both a luncheon and dinner party. I quickly collected Eileen Sutherland and Rab to meet the Duchess of Kent, who arrived punctually for lunch and in uniform.

We talked of poor Paul; she is distraught about him and says that she would like to shake him: she is right. His predicament and despair are exaggerated, really. Eileen Sutherland seems somewhat recovered, but she is still too thin, emaciated and pathetic. After the others left we had a long talk about the Windsors, and she described the now famous Balmoral party given by Edward VIII. How he snubbed and ignored both the royal duchesses, i.e. Marina and Elizabeth;[1] how Mrs Simpson acted as semi-hostess etc. A curious collection of guests, Marlboroughs, Sutherlands, Buccleuchs, a Mr and Mrs Rogers,[2] Kents etc. Eileen too has heard the prevailing gossip that the Windsors are not getting on .... Is it true?

I was tired and inoperative; nevertheless both my little luncheon party and my dinner had *Stimmung*; Emerald, Laura Corrigan and the Foreign Office consisting of Jim Thomas, dark, false, Welsh and debonair; dear Peter Loxley who brought me a bottle of sherry from Gibraltar and a bag of nuts; and Sir Robert Bruce Lockhart[3] dined. Food appalling; oysters ordered from Buck's unopened, but the odd-man conceived the idea of taking them to the Belgian Embassy, where they were opened and returned. Much drink and conversation flowed. Violent attacks on Leslie Hore-Belisha and General de Gaulle. Emerald announced to everybody's amused astonishment that Duff was the head of the Secret Service, and that he ought to succeed Winston!! Lockhart, more than partly inebriated,[4] criticised Anthony Eden to my secret delight ... All stayed too late. 12.30! Jim T – stayed on and was affectionate and disarming – but I trust him not.

Alan is more lovesick than ever.

TUESDAY 16TH MARCH

Woke weak and weary ... and did nothing most of the day, not even walking to the House. I am worried about the two Pauls, my own and the ex-Regent

---

1 Subsequently the Queen Consort.
2 Herman Livingston Rogers (1891–1957) married in 1920 Katherine Moore (1894–1949), who was an old friend of Wallis Simpson.
3 Robert Hamilton Bruce Lockhart (1887–1970) was Director-General of the Political Warfare Executive. He had started a conventional diplomatic career in 1912 by working first as Vice Consul and then as Consul-General in Moscow, and then heading the unofficial British mission to Bolshevik Russia in 1917–18. During this posting he worked as a secret agent and was sentenced to death *in absentia*. He worked as a banker and journalist between the wars. He was knighted in 1943.
4 Lockhart's diaries revealed that he had struggled throughout his life with alcoholism.

languishing at his Kenyan Longwood. I have almost decided to bring back my son and have him to live here. I shan't take steps until April.

Still nothing from Peter in India – a long silence which suggests either neglect and cooling, or that he is at the Burmese front. I am also annoyed at my mother, who owes me huge sums of money and I have had almost nothing from my father's assignment since March 1933.

My digestion is weak, my heart engorged and my brain idle and stultified. All day I rested, read and recovered; and in the late afternoon walked to Victoria Square, where I once lived with Gage, to the Goring Hotel to have tea with Mrs Neville Chamberlain. A motley party of the middle-aged! I advised her to buy 22 Victoria Square, which I really want for myself. Long talk with Lady Maugham,[1] the wife of the ex-Lord Chancellor, and found her pleasant. She told me quaint tales of Lady Cory[2] who lives in Belgrave Square; apparently, that rich vulgarian wants to leave her fabulous jewels to the Canadian govt. She once owned an embroidered portrait of Hitler, which she bought years ago; it had been woven with human hair and was extraordinary and unique. Lady Maugham asked her recently what had become of it and was told that she had burnt it on the outbreak of war.

WEDNESDAY 17TH MARCH

The death of Cardinal Hinsley was announced on the wireless. This aged and distinguished prelate has been several times to Belgrave Square to luncheon.[3] He was old, smiling, gentle and had the suavity and dignity of a Roman prelate yet in his voice there were traces of a North Riding burr; and he remained a Yorkshireman to the end. He was violent in his denunciation of the Nazis; and his death is a blow to the Allied cause.

Walked to the House . . . . I crept to the library and read a long letter from Peter giving a dull account of his Delhi days. The only flat letter I have ever had from him and it depressed and chilled me. Later in the day came another, written ten days before, in which he describes his recent secret expedition to Burma; it was a warm and brilliant letter and I feel better about my friendship. And I thought over other things; the two big romances of the moment, i.e. Alan and Stuart Preston who are sharing a double bed at the Imperial Hotel in Torquay; and Emerald and Nicholas's moonlight rococo love affair.

Fetched Joyce Brittain-Jones at her tiny house in Montpelier Walk and we drove to the Dorchester where we collected Emerald and then we dined *à quatre* with Leslie Hore-Belisha. His small house is compact and comfortable and the

---

1 See entry for 22 March 1939 and footnote.
2 Wife of Lieutenant General George Norton Cory (1874–1968), an American-born Canadian who served in the British Army and, having retired in 1931, was recalled in 1940 as a senior liaison officer to Allied contingents.
3 See entry for 7 November 1941 and footnote.

food and monastic wine quite excellent. Emerald was entrancing but I feared that Joyce was unimpressed. Later we were joined by Gaston Palewski who certainly had vine leaves in his hair, for he told doubtful tales which revolted Lady Cunard. I was forced to drop them all; and my car would hardly go. When we *déposéd*[1] Joyce, Palewski insisted on going in with her! I foresaw trouble as he was exhilarated by wine and she was alone. For a woman of nearly 40[2] who has long been the mistress of a monarch she should have known better![3]

Rab recorded a distinct success in a subtle speech to the newly constituted 1922 Committee this afternoon; and I admired his cool intellectual handling of his critical audience. No man has ever been so cold, so mechanical; he is fond of nobody; yet dislikes nobody. Thus he will get on; but fear he misses much: there has never been a woman in his life (his relations with his wife Sydney are of affectionate tolerance, yet she adores him) and certainly no man. No Peter; no Paul; no Alan has disturbed his donnish equanimity.

Ghislaine Dresselhuys's engagement to young [Denis] Alexander is announced and she rang me up to say that she had followed my advice and told him that he owes it all to me. So many marriages, tacit, illicit, legal and illegal, I have made!

THURSDAY 18TH MARCH

I lunched alone at the House, rested, thought about the speech I must make at Southend on Saturday. Later I went with Peggy Crewe, most amiable and attractive, Osbert Sitwell with whom I am being increasingly *lié*,[4] Joyce Brittain-Jones .... and Audrey Bouverie, whose party it was, to a magnificent Menuhin[5] concert at the Albert Hall. That young violinist reminded me, and I cannot think why, of Hitler! A crowded and fashionable audience: Edwina Mountbatten and her v royal-looking daughter,[6] Lady Cholmondeley and hers;[7] Zia Wernher and hers.[8] What would have been the fashionable debutantes had there been a season. I left the cosy party given jointly by Francis Queensberry and Emerald in honour of Eddy Devonshire who had spoken before at the Queensberry Club. There were no taxis and I had to walk from the Albert Hall and arrived at only 9.30: I was one of the first. Invigorated by the quick 'hike' I felt well

---

1 *Déposer* is the French for 'drop off'.
2 Having been born in 1902, she was at least 40 already.
3 Palewski had a reputation for the ladies, and was known as *l'Embrassadeur*.
4 Literally, linked; he means 'associated'.
5 Yehudi Menuhin (1916–99) was a child prodigy violinist and one of the most famous musicians of the twentieth century. Born in New York, he later became a naturalised Briton and was made a member of the Order of Merit in 1987 and raised to the peerage as Baron Menuhin (life peer) in 1993.
6 Patricia Mountbatten.*
7 Aline Caroline Cholmondeley (1916–2015), Lady Aline by courtesy, was the daughter of the 5th Marquess of Cholmondeley and Lady Cholmondeley, formerly Sybil Sassoon (qqv).
8 Lady Zia had two daughters; it is unclear to which one Channon is referring.

and was witty and gay. I was next to Virginia Cowles who was friendly. She is just back from Algiers where she saw Seymour Berry whom she still loves. His hold over women since I first launched him in London society has been extraordinary. It must partly be because of his beautiful, graceful figure. He is much in my thoughts just now. Daphne Weymouth was opposite and when she left at 11.30 I half-smiled since I knew that she was going to meet Harold B at a flat in Jermyn Street. Their friendship, which began on my birthday flourishes . . . I drove Eileen Sutherland back to Claridge's where she is living. There is some improvement in her health and appearance. Another gay evening when I talked and drank too much . . . .

I have heard nothing more of the royal trip. Perhaps yesterday's tea party was part of the camouflage? I don't really know; but Winston has so eclipsed the monarchy that the King would be well advised to do something to show himself, to take some action, but I fear that Alec Hardinge, that boring bigot, that narrow-minded rat, would always influence him against any imaginative line. Eileen Sutherland, who quite likes Hardinge, thinks he is a disaster in his present post! She tells me that both the K and the Q listen very much to Arthur Penn, who is worse – a dreadful snob, old maid and mischief-maker. I call him Poison Penn and refuse to speak to him.

Joyce Brittain-Jones tells me that she had a tempestuous half-hour with Gaston Palewski last evening after we left them. I foresaw it. He was half-drunk and altogether amorous and he made appalling advances to her. At one moment, she acted Desdemona to his Othello; and it was with difficulty that she got rid of him. It was only by threatening to call non-existent imaginary servants to her rescue that he finally left.

FRIDAY 19TH MARCH   *PALACE HOTEL, SOUTHEND*

The news of Paul is increasingly distressing. The Duchess of Kent and I have had several telephone conversations this week on the subject and both agree that while he has been shabbily treated, he should, nevertheless, pull himself together – as I have done. He is being weak, selfish, hysterical and unmanly and history will take a poor view of him, at least of his attitude at his Kenyan Longwood.

Lunched with Helen Fitzgerald . . . . Harold B, a wing commander and Laura Corrigan at Claridge's. Bored. Then I drove here to be alone, to be away from the telephone and to rest my stomach, nerves and brain. Already I feel better, and am reading the Lieven–Palmerston correspondences[1] and shall soon go supper-less to bed.

---

1 The *Lieven–Palmerston Correspondence 1828–1856*, translated and edited by Lord Sudley, had just been published. The letters were between Princess Lieven, wife of a Russian ambassador to London, and Lord Palmerston, Prime Minister from 1855 to 1858, and from 1859 to 1865.

SATURDAY 20TH MARCH

Slept magnificently and woke much refreshed and wrote out a speech which I afterwards delivered to about a hundred people, the well-attended annual meeting of our association. I was much complimented.

The Germans are advancing in Russia. The war has flared up again in North Africa. I am alone, always alone: and how I love it! I have read and reread avidly the Lieven–Palmerston correspondence. In the parent-game which appropriately enough we used to play at Panshanger,[1] I am sure that I should be allotted Princess Lieven as my female progenitor. I am very like her and how I hate Palmerston, as she did. He reminds me of Anthony Eden – and can one say worse of anyone?

SUNDAY 21ST MARCH

It is icy, a belated winter has now set in. I am still tired, but beginning to be bored, a symptom of recovery. I almost wish that I was dining out in London this evening. I have been alone all day, except for giving audiences to constituents . . . . The first instalment of Duff Cooper's *King David* appeared in the *Sunday Times*.[2] Quite unreadable; he is a dull writer and a fraud and a bore, although a well-read one.

Hitler made a short but unimportant speech to the German people today; although his armies are once more advancing into Russia he must regret the adventure.

The Prime Minister's recent broadcast, to which I listened with rapt interest, will be a landmark in England's political history and development.[3]

MONDAY 22ND MARCH

Arrived back by car about seven after a day of interviewing constituents – their problems, cares and domestic tragedies are often Babylonian . . . Here at home I find a plethora of notes and messages. I went to dine with Emerald at what she called a *haute bohème*[4] dinner party, so it was: Stephen Spender, the poet, was in an auxiliary-fireman uniform and his wild hair, yet a gentle expression and an extremely weak handshake – always a tell tale – made me whisper to Eddie Sackville-West, 'How is that pansy Rodin?' . . . . Then I went to Diana C's room and sat on her bed for an hour, as she has flu, and then came home exhausted.

---

1 A house in Hertfordshire inherited by Lady Desborough (qv) in 1905. It was demolished in 1954.

2 The book was a biography of the biblical King.

3 In it, Churchill set out his vision of how post-war Europe should develop.

4 High bohemian.

TUESDAY 23RD MARCH

I am tired out by one London evening! . . . Dressed in a morning coat and carrying my top hat, I went to Westminster Cathedral before eleven. It was already crowded almost to suffocation for the Requiem in honour of His Eminence.[1] I joined Rab and Harry Crookshank and we were led to the second pew, almost under the coffin. General de Gaulle made an idiotic entrance – *entrée du souverain*[2] – and sat immediately in front of me. Sikorski,[3] who had a grander place, was simpler in his manner. The *corps diplomatique* sat to my left. There must have been a 1,000 or more priests, monks, prelates and bishops all wearing their grandest surplices and most glittering vestments. Soon the endless ceremony began; the intoning, the candles, the singing were all impressive . . . and I watched for a long time transfixed. In the procession I saw my friend the Abbot of Buckfast.[4] At one moment I was aware of a different smell from the heavy incense and of a slight rustling and looking up I saw it was the very seductive Argentine Ambassadress, Madame Cárcano, arriving late, and exuding through her sables an aroma of Chanel! . . . The interminable service continued; but my bladder began to disturb me and, after an hour, began to be painful. Soon I could think of nothing else, and the Lorca[5] scene became blurred; I wondered would I hold out? It was impossible to escape except by tripping over General de Gaulle and almost entering the conclave of officiating purple-robed priests . . . and I envied and admired Mme Monteiro,[6] the Portuguese Ambassadress, whom I saw get up, leave – for an obvious purpose – and soon return. Why must all Roman Catholic functions be so interminable? By midday I was in pain, by one o'clock I was almost fainting. Meanwhile two men had collapsed. At last it was over, the clergy processed out: it was like a Bellini[7] procession. I held my breath and finally bolted to the Army and Navy Stores where I found a lavatory . . . then the tension passed, my mind

1 The late Cardinal Hinsley.
2 Like the entrance of the King.
3 Władysław Eugeniusz Sikorski (1881–1943), the Prime Minister of the Polish government-in-exile from September 1939 until his death in July 1943; he had earlier been Prime Minister of Poland from 1922 to 1923. He was also a general in the Polish Army and Commander-in-Chief of their armed forces. His death, in a plane crash, remains the subject of many conspiracy theories.
4 Hermann Bruno Fehrenbacher. See entry for 18 August 1942 and footnote.
5 He apparently alludes to Federico del Sagrado Corazón de Jesús García Lorca (1898–1936), a Spanish poet, playwright and theatre director, who brought the surreal and symbolism heavily into his work.
6 For the ambassadress, see entry for 28 November 1938 and footnote. Her husband, Armindo Monteiro, was Portuguese Ambassador to London until mid-1943, when his government, deeming him too pro-British, replaced him with the Duke of Palmela, thought to be more 'neutral'.
7 The family of fifteenth-century Venetian painters.

went back to the beauty and splendour of the impressive service. I went on to the H of C.

Dined, Harold, Helen Fitzgerald and I with Violet Cripps in a tiny mews flat – in Mount Row. Violet cooked an excellent meal and we had champagne and gay conversation. Too late to go on to Emerald, who had Oliver Lyttelton, Rob Hudson and others dining.

Poor Phyllis de Janzé died on Monday last; or rather she burst: she had dropsy or water in her heart; and swelled up. Her body was covered with scars where she had burst . . . and she had suffered horribly for months. Hubert Duggan, my erstwhile Ganymede and her devoted but not always particularly faithful lover since 1934, is prostrated with grief and has collapsed. He is in bed at 18 Chapel Street; long their *nid d'amour*, she has left it to him.

WEDNESDAY 24TH MARCH

The American Sergeant, Stuart Preston, has returned to Torquay for his visit to Alan; he walked with me to the H of Commons. I find him spoilt and intolerable; he abused Alan for his manner and manners, even his lavish generosity which has been the means of providing him with a series of expensive presents. The boy is a bore, although his charm is great. I have never liked the Irish! Now I propose to drop him abruptly . . . at the House I thought that Winston looked old; but he is alleged to be more benign. I fled to Claridge's, attended a meeting of the 'Wings Club' chez Laura Corrigan, and lunched with her afterwards: the Belgian and Argentine ambassadresses, Mary Marlborough, 'Baba' Metcalfe and others. Just the twelve, too-rich food. I came home to recover but was not long allowed to rest for the Sergeant 'popped in'; I really cannot stand his ever-thereness and do not want a 'familiar' about. However, we walked to the Dorchester together and I picked up Sydney Butler and squired her to the French Concert, and having successfully shed the Sergeant, returned home and changed and went out to dine with Laura. It was Corrigan day. A big party: I was between the Argentine Ambassadress and Helen Fitzgerald. Turtle soup; salmon; poussins and pot-de-crême. After dinner we again played that ridiculous dice-game and I won a bottle of valuable Napoleon brandy: everybody said it was because Mary Marlborough kept the score that I won! The recently wedded and bedded Dudleys were there and both seemed irritable and cross – perhaps a case of 'post-copulates'? She was wearing the Dudley pearls, ropes and ropes of them, all only moderate in size, and an emerald shamrock brooch given to Eric's mother when Lady Dudley[1] was Vicereine of Ireland. Poor Harold was entranced as being in love with both Daphne Weymouth and Helen Fitzgerald, he had to avoid them both . . . . An

---

1 Rachel Anne Gurney (1868–1920) married in 1891 William Humble Ward (1867–1932), from 1885 2nd Earl of Dudley. He was Lord Lieutenant of Ireland from 1902 to 1905.

aerograph came from Kenya from Lilia Ralli in which she says that Paul is more ill than ever.

Deaths so far this year have been varied: the Speaker; Colin Davidson; the Cardinal; now Phyllis de Janzé, a mixed bag. In a way she was the Harriet Wilson of her time; she was a cocotte, slept with hundreds of men (at least until she met Hubert), took money from them etc.; yet she remained a lady .... She was well read, had 'house sense', could conduct a conversation skilfully, and with her green Egyptian eyes and ever-dyed hair, she looked extraordinary. She was long Old Wimborne's[1] mistress. I shan't miss her as we have been enemies of recent years; for she feared my once all-dominating influence over Hubert; when I withdrew it he went to pieces and became ambitionless, inoperative, just a .... womaniser.

THURSDAY 25TH MARCH

Old [George] Capel Cure is dead at the age of 90. He lived until the war at [blank; Blake Hall] and occasionally came to Kelvedon. His MP, Winston Churchill, he always described as an insolent young puppy! Everybody is a-dying.

Evidently I overreached myself gastronomically yesterday as today I felt congested, cross and conceited. I must beware of my liver and the perils it leads me to. Last week I was angry with Loelia Westminster; this morning the unfortunate Sergeant was the victim. I snapped at him when he came to pay his tactlessly early call at 10.05 a.m.; and sad he fled and later reported my bad temper to Emerald who rebuked me telephonically. He is, I am convinced, a 'sponger'. I walked to the House alone – the *volupté* of half an hour to oneself is deep, rare and unrivalled. It was the Catering Bill again. I voted against the govt, listened to much of the long debate and eventually walked home – still dark and angry ...

Emerald, [Nicholas] Lawford and I dined here and we were joined by Harold Balfour, and Rex Whistler who has arrived to stay here for a week. He is a gentle fawn, intelligent and good company (but I have never liked or loved him really) and in his mild way no one is so malicious. Duff, he detests. Emerald was sad and depressed but endearing. The food was delectable.

FRIDAY 26TH MARCH

I am slightly recovering ... and was well enough to attend the lobby lunch at the Savoy. The guest of honour was Herbert Morrison. To my surprise I was next to John Anderson at the top table. Attlee was one off me to the right; and [A. V.]

---

1 Ivor Churchill Guest (1873–1939) was the son of 1st Baron Wimborne and succeeded to the barony in 1914. Lord Lieutenant of Ireland from 1915 to 1918, he resigned after the Easter Rising, in which he had declared martial law, but was quickly reappointed. He married, in 1902, Alice Grosvenor (1880–1948), daughter of 2nd Baron Ebury and later the mistress of the composer William Walton.

Alexander to the left. My near neighbour was a Police Commissioner who told me astonishing stories about the sexual and criminal life of London. Anderson and I gossiped politically . . . . slyly I undermined Arthur Hope and told him the tale of the 'dud' cheque and other particulars of his fraudulent career. Anderson who is rigid, honest, and correct, was much shocked. The proceedings were endless and I gazed about me; half the govt was present but they sat at round tables. I was the only MP who is not in the Cabinet who was at the top table. I am sure that there will be comment as already busybodies are asking why I should have had so grand a place at the Cardinal's Requiem. Rab was carelessly dressed – he is never sleek; only the ex-chief whips and the present one were well groomed. At last, the Chairman . . . . rose, spoke well enough but not too long: it was 'midnight oil' and then he was followed by Herbert Morrison, who beguiled us amusingly but often with doubtful taste for forty-five minutes. He has rich humour, a caustic wit and much conceit: these are indispensable ingredients for an excellent speech. And so perhaps it was. He only said one important thing, that he would live or commit suicide with the Socialist Party; if once again it was determined to commit suicide. Probably he wished to quash a growing report that he was prepared to follow Churchill and head a coalition govt. Morrison is really rather an old Tory himself . . . My mind wandered and I thought of other lobby lunches: last year it was Winston, in 1940 it was also Winston who as First Lord was the guest of honour, and Neville Chamberlain had sat silent, a little sad and a touch neglected . . . those city lunches are always great occasions, in govt a parliamentary institution of importance.

After a Turkish bath at the RAC, I felt better, walked home and found that Harold B had got off at last. He left for Gibraltar this afternoon and will be in Cairo probably by Monday.

WEDNESDAY 31ST MARCH

To everyone's surprise there was not a raid either on Monday or last night. Has the German bombing force lost its sting and powers, or are they cooking up something more devastating?

All day, mostly, at the H of Commons, the Catering Bill again . . . . I walked home, having mislaid – and how can we lose anything so huge – my brother-in-law. Alan adores me; I am his love, his life, his all. But he is infatuated to an alarming extent with Stuart Preston, 'The Immortal Sergeant', and talks of nothing else . . .

I gave a dinner party of 'Waifs and Strays' and it was remarkably successful; *d'abord* my house looked rich and civilised, as it was a bank of blooms brought up from Kelvedon . . . . Later we were joined by Alan and Geoffrey Lloyd who had dined together, and by Emerald and Venetia Montagu, who had dined with Hamilton Kerr and were quite funny about it. I like him well enough but cannot understand why Emerald should suddenly take him up as he is both a bore and *à côté*. The party broke up reluctantly about one o'clock. I didn't invite Stuart Preston as I am bored with him and the situation which has developed between him and Alan L-B. I fear I have offended the poor boy. At any rate he is a 'sponger'; he came to No. 5 several times today for a bath, to meet Alan and write letters. And that is a bore. Alan stayed on very late, put me to bed, and eventually fell asleep on my bed, snoring very much . . .

Nicholas Lawford is staying at No. 5, and Rex Whistler has been here for a week: he is dreary, vague and malicious; yet he has considerable charm and his genius is undisputed. Somehow I cannot get fond of him. He is recklessly inconsiderate but unintentionally so; and he leaves a wake behind him of forgotten assignations and broken engagements.

How I should like to be able to keep both Belgrave Square and Kelvedon after the war but I fear that would be impossible. Nobody now has two such grand houses.

There is romance in the atmosphere . . . . Emerald is obsessed of [*sic*] – and indeed in love with – Nicholas Lawford. Alan and the Sergeant quarrelled and became reconciled. But there is nobody for me. It is all my luck and strange. Perhaps Emerald is right when she says that I am in love with the Duchess of Kent. Her beauty and elegance yesterday was striking. I have never seen her look so 'well', certainly not so since the Duke died.

THURSDAY 1ST APRIL

I had rather a headache on awaking as Alan only left my bed at 4 a.m. He talks of nothing but Sergeant Preston and is becoming a tremendous bore . . . Alan, George Gage and I lunched with Emerald at the Ritz, a pointless little function. To my amazement Virginia Cowles was nearby with Arthur Penn . . . . Alan and I rushed away, shopped; he bought lavish presents for Preston, and offered me gold snuffboxes, clocks and grand presents which I didn't accept – no doubt foolishly. Then we had a quick Turkish bath together, picked up Patsy, his pregnant wife, and went with Laura Corrigan to hear Tauber[1] in *Old Chelsea*.[2] Dined richly afterwards with her at Claridge's; Alan came home with me, their new child is due on May 6th. Patsy reports that her mother[3] is far from well; is grey and dejected.

FRIDAY 2ND APRIL

Another late night with that huge spreading Alan snoring in my bed – several times I woke thinking it was the long-delayed retaliation raid against Berlin. The Germans must be much weakened not to attempt revenge.

---

1 Richard Tauber (1891–1948) was an Austrian opera singer and actor. He had sought exile in Britain when the Nazis annexed Austria in 1938.
2 An English operetta composed by Tauber, with words by Fred S. Tysh.
3 Lady Iveagh.

SATURDAY 3RD APRIL

Alan rang me three times on the telephone from Henlow to chatter about Stuart Preston. He is being intolerable really.

Kelvedon is lively and vernal, and it is a joy to be once more alone for a time. Before I left [London], I induced Rex Whistler, who is staying with me, to make a drawing of my beloved Bundi; he did a charming sketch in twelve minutes. It is an exquisite fantasy. He wanted to accompany me here but I refused, as I must be alone.

SUNDAY 4TH APRIL

A glorious lyrical day; I got up fairly early – double summer-time began this morning – and worked in the Kelvedon garden, picked baskets full of daffodils etc., sweated and bathed and dressed afterwards. Then reluctantly returned to London where I found Rex Whistler still staying. He left late . . . I rushed off to lunch with Laura Corrigan where I found Emerald, who irritated me with her scandalous *potins* re the Harding *ménage*; Ti Cholmondeley; Daphne Weymouth, who had not been to bed at all, but had gone out all night to nightclubs with Billy Hartington, Andrew Cavendish[1] and Elizabeth Leveson-Gower[2] . . . We went driving in state to the Albert Hall to hear Menuhin play. A lovely day . . . Walked, and dined in and alone.

MONDAY 5TH APRIL

I am writing to Helen Hull to send me back my child – life is slipping by and I want and ache for him.

Alan L-B is on the verge of a breakdown and I am alarmed about him; he is mad, half-hysterical and quite frenzied with love.

Later I met Alan who [still] seemed crazed with excitement and love. He had been chucked by Stuart Preston; they had met earlier in the day . . . . quarrelled and under the arcade of the Ritz agreed to part. Alan is now desperate.

Julian Amery looked in late and engaged Emerald in an exhilarating intellectual conversation. Each was seduced.

1 Andrew Robert Buxton Cavendish (1920–2004), Lord Andrew Cavendish by courtesy, was the second son of the 10th Duke of Devonshire. When his elder brother Lord Hartington (qv) was killed in 1944 he assumed his courtesy title and succeeded their father as 11th Duke of Devonshire in 1950. He married, in 1941, Deborah Mitford (1920–2014). He served as a junior minister for Commonwealth Relations from 1960 to 1964, appointed by his uncle, Harold Macmillan (qv).
2 See entry for 1 May 1939 and footnote.

Doreen Brabourne tells me that her eldest boy[1] is missing. I had a confidential conversation with Alice Harding who tells me that she still loves her husband, and will not divorce him, although the tale of his attachment to a man, whom he loves, is alas true.

TUESDAY 6TH APRIL

The new financial year opens today: my balmy days are past. I must economise and be careful.

Dressed superbly, I picked up Angier Duke[2] and we lunched with the Fitzgeralds at Claridge's: Pam Churchill, lovely, soft, amusingly seductive, the Cárcanos . . . later shopped with the Cárcanos and came home for a brief moment. Alan and I escorted Mrs Corrigan to the Guards Chapel where we attended Ghislaine Dresselhuys' wedding (for which I am largely responsible) to Denis Alexander, who looked slim and a child. She was a radiant baroque beauty under her tiara of diamonds. (I had met the bridegroom lunching at Claridge's and when I asked him what he proposed doing until the ceremony, he answered that he would probably be going to a film). The Guards Chapel, so reminiscent of Ravenna, was crowded with the Corps! Every ambassador, every Berry . . . Neville Berry[3] was best man. Loelia Westminster was in the pew ahead of ours and seemed cold. We went on *en masse* to the Belgian Embassy, which old Cartier[4] had lent to Lady Kemsley for the reception; it was crowded. Ghislaine kissed me, there was champagne and Mrs Keppel, who had imbibed a lot, whispered to me: 'The De Beers people must be very pleased by Ghislaine's headdress.' Neville Berry proposed her health; there were many references to General Alexander and the 8th Army, which pleased the Kemsleys and perhaps soothed them for their disappointment over Dresselhuys not marrying a duke. Her mother worships her; and Gomer Kemsley is fond of her, and has settled money on her. I doubt somehow if the marriage will be a success. (I sent an antique Dutch silver box in the shape of a book. From the Lennox-Boyds a silver Cartier cigarette box.) Edith Kemsley wore an absurdly huge hat which caused a titter.

---

1 Norton Cecil Michael Knatchbull (1922–43) succeeded his father as 6th Baron Brabourne in 1939. He had been captured by the Germans in Italy. He escaped while being transported to a prisoner-of-war camp later in the summer of 1943 but was recaptured by the SS and together with a brother Grenadier Guards officer, Arnold Guy Vivian (1915–43), was executed by them on 15 September. The officer responsible was later tried for war crimes and executed.

2 Angier Biddle Duke (1915–95) was from a prominent American family of wealthy industrialists and philanthropists. He fought in the United States Army Air Force and in 1949 joined the US Diplomatic Service. He later held several ambassadorships and served as Chief of Protocol of the United States under presidents Kennedy and Johnson.

3 William Neville Berry (1914–98), third of the six sons of the 1st Viscount Kemsley (qv).

4 The Ambassador (qv).

The evening was a disaster; I had felt ill all day and arranged to dine in and alone, refusing Emerald's blandishments to attend the first night of the ballet; weakly I capitulated after several messages, when Diana Cooper came to the Embassy to fetch me. She is staying with me at No. 5, and I couldn't refuse. She looked astonishingly lovely; and we sallied forth together and joined Emerald's huge ballet party: Hudsons, Butlers, and many many more, including Buck De La Warr, who is having an affair with Mrs Hannah Hudson[1] (Rob's dark and eager Baltimore wife). The ballet *Quest*[2] was a huge success and rapturously received; old Alice Wimborne, becomingly dressed in uniform, sat proudly with William Walton, the composer. But the honour went to Freddie Ashton, whom I had always tried to avoid, and considered a bore. He had a tremendous reception and made a speech. It was only after the performance was over did I discover that the subsequent supper party, to which everybody was going, was to be given by Kenneth and Lady Clark at the Savoy. Weakly, reluctantly, protesting I allowed Diana to lead me there; but I was in a disagreeable, liverish mood and when I ran into Kenneth in 'the Gents' and he failed to say 'good evening' (his bad manners are proverbial) I saw red. I bolted from the hotel, and passing Emerald and Diana announced that I would not attend the supper party which was due to begin in the Pinafore Room. Both tried to persuade me to remain; I said I wasn't invited (it turned out that I was but I was unaware of this) and emerging into the cold, I walked home, angry, frustrated, exhausted. Frantic telephone messages later failed to budge me, and I went to bed, after a heart-to-hearter with Nicholas Lawford...

WEDNESDAY 7TH APRIL

London is in ferment today; my snubbing Kenneth Clark has caused a sensation and succeeded in spoiling their supper party. Apparently she [Lady Clark] followed me on to the Strand to catch me, and didn't. Kenneth was contrite.

A dreadful day. Loelia Westminster rang me up in tears, said she had been everywhere accused of being malicious etc., and she pledged her deep devotion to me.[3] I believe her. She is tactless, a gaffeur, and awkward but well-intentioned. I broke to her the news of 'Flash' Kellett's[4] death; he was killed in North Africa. A gay, dashing, vulpine-looking horseman, he was a colourful figure in the Commons where he succeeded Arthur Hope in the Aston Division of

---

1 Hannah Randolph (1891–1969) married in 1918 Robert Spear Hudson (qv).
2 Walton's ballet *The Quest*, of which this was the first performance, was based on *The Faerie Queene* by Edmund Spenser.
3 One presumes this was an accusation about her conduct to society in general rather than to Channon in particular.
4 Edward Orlando Kellett (1902–43) had been a professional soldier before becoming Conservative MP for Birmingham Aston in 1939. He reached the rank of colonel and was killed in action in Tunisia. He was a noted big-game hunter.

Birmingham; but he early rejoined the Army and went to the Middle East where I several times saw him. He adored dukes and horses and duchesses . . . I sent a note to Julian Amery suggesting that he stand for Aston.

Alan and I walked to the House where we arrived just in time to hear Winston announce the recent victories in Tunisia; the fighting is in the neighbourhood of Sfax,[1] El Djein etc.

We lunched with Emerald, Diana Cooper, and Francis Queensberry at the Ritz – My 'chucking' the Clarks was the sole subject of conversation and I was consoled they have sent me many messages and apologies; but I have no quarrel with them; they behaved naturally enough, and were unaware of my presence at the play.

Diana Cooper returned to Bognor. I dined with Laura Corrigan, the Duke of Alba, Eileen Sutherland, Charlie Londonderry and Violet Cripps. An amusing evening. Alba is full of the ball he is to give in Seville at the end of the month. Soon after the others had left, Alan joined us at Claridge's; I saw that he was excited and flushed. He had been dining with Stuart Preston at La Belle Meunière but the attempt at reconciliation had failed. However he was pleased with himself. An hour later when we began to walk home together, he suddenly reeled and I saw that he was old-fashioned Bullingdon drunk.[2] The impact of fresh air was too much for him; he sang, shouted, lay in the street – Mount Street. It took exactly two hours to pilot him home here; once he broke away from me and escaped into the Park; twice he was nearly run over and I feared any policeman would arrest him. 'Member of Parliament arrested for drunkenness!' It was a Hogarthian progress and it is now 2.30 a.m. Nicholas Lawford and I put Alan to bed in the Nursery, after I had slipped five aspirins down his throat. What an evening.

THURSDAY 8TH APRIL

Alan woke me at 6.30 and crawled back to his home at Hobart Place where Patsy was awake and desperately awaiting him . . . Went to the House of Commons which I left, taking Julian Amery with me (he was thrilled) and we lunched with Alice Harding at Regent's [Hanover] Lodge. The Duchess of Kent looked lovely but fatigued; Cecil Beaton and the obese *ménage* Poklewski completed the party. Gay banter which amused the sorrowful Duchess . . .

Alan, still half-hysterical, and headed for a nervous breakdown, follows me about moaning about his lost Sergeant.

FRIDAY 9TH APRIL

A dull day, except for an unfortunate fortuitous meeting between Alan and the Sergeant here; Alan was rapturous, the Sergeant cold; but they walked off together.

---

1 Where Kellett (*vide supra*) was killed, and is buried.
2 A reference to the dissolute Oxford dining club (qv).

He came back in half an hour's time and collapsed, even foamed at the mouth. That brilliant creature is going surely mad. I sent for Dr Law and asked his advice and confided in him my fears. We have agreed to send Alan to a nursing home for a month on the pretext of having his tonsils out: the rest will quieten him. Meanwhile Dr Law gave me some soothing pills for him.

Laura Corrigan and I dined with Vsevolod and Maimie of Russia. Pleasant cosy evening interrupted by the hysterical arrival of Alan. We drove him to Paddington where he caught the 11.30 train for Torquay on a quite trivial and futile journey which will not end in a lovers' meeting.

Stuart Preston has behaved very shabbily indeed.

MONDAY 12TH APRIL

Kingsley Wood's Budget was a tame affair; the House was bored and *philosophère*[1] and not overcrowded. The most uninteresting Budget of my career.

Alan is worse; I fear that he will kill himself. He is behaving just as poor Edward Marjoribanks[2] did.

TUESDAY 13TH APRIL

Big news. I hear that Wavell may come here next week; and it is almost certain that Peter will come with him and also, permission has been granted to Paul and Olga by the govt and Smuts for them to go to live in S. Africa. Both items are [blacked out] in their consequences: I can think of nothing else.

I spent the lovely long day at Kelvedon where it was hot and perfect. After gathering masses of flowers, which I distributed on my return, I came back to London. A reception at Lady Crewe's; all London, poets and celebrities and friends. I had a light dust-up with Lady Colefax whom I snubbed.

WEDNESDAY 14TH APRIL

The Wavell party is due on the 20th, next Tuesday . . . . probably Peter will be with them. I could not sleep last night for sheer excitement and nerves.

The almost impossible has been accomplished. I have got Alan into a nursing home at 31 Queen's Gate. He has telephoned to me from there; at 6.30 his tonsils are to be removed!

I feel ill and nervous and overwrought: Alan has worn me out.

Alan was successfully operated upon for his tonsils and adenoids. Patsy rang me at 8 p.m. to say that all was well. He will be confined for a fortnight.

---

1 There is no such word in French: presumably he means 'philosophical'.
2 Channon's Oxford friend who committed suicide. See entry for 1 November 1938 and footnote.

The Spanish Ambassador rang me to ask if I could give him my golf balls. *Nous en sommes là!*[1]

THURSDAY 15TH APRIL

Lunched with the Duke of Alba at the Spanish Embassy; that palatial house at 24 Belgrave Square which I was largely responsible for its being an Embassy when I induced Merry del Val[2] to buy it, still has a spacious atmosphere .... Alba told me that he had sent the golf balls I gave him recently to his King; i.e. the Count of Barcelona, now living at Lausanne ...

Dined with Laura Corrigan .... I walked back to Buckingham Palace with Ulick Alexander,[3] who confided to me his serious misgivings about 'the Black Rat';[4] he begged me to get the govt to have him removed as he is ruining the monarchy and always gives the King foolish and misguided advice. I told him what I thought; and added that the King should go to Australia and New Zealand now, passing by Tunisia. Ulick promised to pass on the tip. He likes Alec Hardinge but insists that he is a disaster, a national calamity. Mr Chamberlain had advised his removal several times, it is a pity that he didn't insist. Winston is against Hardinge too or at least was; but he has been influenced by Anthony Eden, who plots with him. Eden is ready to keep him where he is.

Alan is suffering; he cannot speak and he seems madder than ever.

FRIDAY 16TH APRIL

A cable came from P announcing the stupendous news. He arrives here on Tuesday next. I am anxious with anticipation.

SATURDAY 17TH APRIL   *LEEDS CASTLE*

Today I behaved badly for I awoke weary, and could neither face Southend nor the intense tedium of writing a speech and so I 'chucked' an engagement to address Sea Cadets! Actually it was urgent that I look after Alan, who seems more mad than ever; I sat with him for a time and feared for his reason. And then I .... drove to Leeds in my car, picnicking in the intense heat on the way .... it was a lyrical day, the heat, the gauze-like mist rising from the fruit blossoms, the spinach-green fields ... all were intoxicating.

My thoughts are only with Wavell and Peter ... when will they arrive?

---

1 There we are!
2 Alfonso Merry del Val y Zulueta (1864–1943), Spanish Ambassador to Great Britain from 1913 to 1931.
3 See entry for 28 August 1942 and footnote.
4 Alec Hardinge.

SUNDAY 18TH APRIL

The hottest day I have ever known in England; I lay naked until 7.30 p.m. wearing only slacks for luncheon. An unforgettable lunch hour; I am quite bronzed and I revelled in plovers' eggs and champagne.

MONDAY 19TH APRIL

Drove Adrian Baillie up to London; the rest of the house party are suffering from sunburn and stroke . . . . Diana Cooper has arrived to stay here. After visiting Alan, whose condition is really alarming (his voice is hoarse; his throat pains him and he moans and raves about Stuart Preston), I fetched her at the Dorchester. She was sitting on Emerald's bed; she, great lady and pale-blue stocking, was resting and looked not unlike Boucher's portrait of Mme de Pompadour. Coyly, charmingly, she showed us Nicholas Lawford's letters which she had in bed with her. 'They will hatch!' I warned her.

Adele Cavendish,[1] tiresome, treacherous, lying and common, came to dine as did Natasha Bagration whose birthday it is. I gave her a Fabergé elephant and a bottle of whisky. Others were Jock Colville, now in the RAF, a chum of my Chamberlain days, and Adrian Baillie . . . . I was bored by my party and wished that I had been free to dine with Emerald, who had D'Arcy Osborne,[2] our Ambassador to the Vatican. He has recently returned from Rome, and predicts that Italy will drop out of the war by Christmas. Diana came in very late.

TUESDAY 20TH APRIL

A day of disappointment: I woke nervous and ill and even dreaded P's arrival, as I so want to be well and gay for him. As it was I couldn't cope . . . I went out, telephoned to Belgrave Square a dozen times for news, driving my servants demented. It was not until three o'clock that I heard that the great party is not now due until Thursday; by then I had recovered and was disappointed.

Lunched with 'Coalbox'[3] who was out to be agreeable, and had collected a nice party to placate me . . . . I admired Sibyl's energy and social genius . . . We all went to the House of Lords to hear Max Beaverbrook make a fool of himself with his ill-timed motion about a Second Front, but he had unexpectedly withdrawn

1 Adele Astaire (née Austerlitz) (1896–1981), sister of the dancer and actor Fred Astaire, married in 1932 Charles Arthur Francis Cavendish (1905–44), son of the 9th Duke of Devonshire.

2 Francis D'Arcy Godolphin Osborne (1884–1964) joined the Diplomatic Service in 1919. He was appointed Envoy Extraordinary and Minister Plenipotentiary to the Holy See in 1936, serving until 1947. After Italy entered the war he was effectively confined within the Vatican, where he ran a highly efficient escape organisation, helping almost 4,000 Jews and Allied servicemen to evade the Nazis. This was his only trip home during the war, and during it he was knighted. In 1963 he succeeded his second cousin, once removed, as the 12th and last Duke of Leeds.

3 Lady Sibyl Colefax.

it (he'd been got at evidently, by Winston.) There I met my father-in-law, and walked with him across the Park and we discussed Alan and his eccentricities. The Iveaghs are evidently worried . . .

I am spending the later afternoon and evening alone, arranging Peter's room and preparing myself, my inadequate staff and my house for his long- and eagerly awaited arrival.

Rab came to see me, looking unusually untidy and unkempt. His clothes are terrible; and he must have noticed the difference between our appearances for he remarked that I 'looked most distinguished'!

WEDNESDAY 21ST APRIL

The Duchess of Kent rang me twice to break the bad news that Prince Paul is now suffering from 'malignant malaria' which means that he will die. I can see no other solution and I am half broken-hearted.

Had a cocktail with Maimie and Vsevolod and Prince Bernhard of the Netherlands[1] who is breezy, bronzed, debonair and democratic. He is having an affair with Lady Orr-Lewis[2] who was with him, a pretty woman, chic and common. Evelyn Waugh fell asleep as we talked.

Now I am all alone for the last time – tomorrow *Le retour du héros*[3] – The Merry Major will be here. And when he leaves, shall I make friends with Prince Bernhard?

The guns opened heavy fire last night; people are beginning, too, to complain that airplanes keep them awake which is not unfunny.

Now I shall shut this diary for a feverish, and I dare to hope, frantically happy fortnight.[4]

THURSDAY 22ND APRIL

After an unsatisfactory semi-sleepless night (during which I was twice sick for excitement and news), I woke worn out and white . . . About 9.30, as I was dressing a message came from Elstree aerodrome that they had arrived and would soon be at No. 5. In a frenzied forty minutes I fussed and dressed and then went to the morning room. From the window, I saw a taxi and in it Major Coats. We fell into each other's arms rapturously. He is thinner, handsomer, gentler, yet little, seductive, simple, subtle, wise and sweet . . . He is going to stay here and the Field Marshal will join us, if we wish him to, later. (I am not sure that I do,

---

1 See entry for 3 March 1942 and footnote.
2 Doris Blanche Lee (1898–1960), married in 1929 John Duncan Orr-Lewis (1898–1980), who succeeded his father as 2nd Bt in 1921.
3 The hero's return.
4 Which he did not.

honour though it would be.) P and I gossiped until nearly luncheon time when I led him to his mother's Pont Street flat and deposited him there. I insisted on this. Bill Astor and I lunched at the Argentine Embassy and I persuaded them to give a dinner party on Wednesday next (for Peter, although neither they nor he know it). P had left Delhi on Sunday, slept at Baria, arrived at Cairo on Monday, stayed there with the Lampsons; on Tuesday it was Tunisia and dinner with Eisenhower;[1] Wednesday yesterday they crossed to Gibraltar, lunched with Mason-MacFarlane,[2] the Governor and took off about 9 p.m. and after a hazardous trip reached England and Elstree this morning at 9.30. They may stay a fortnight!!

He lunched with his mother and then P came in at three, and worn out by excitement, Eisenhower and emotions, as well as lack of sleep, collapsed for an hour. I left him in peace as I played with and counted the many presents he brought me! At 4.30 he came down and we welcomed the Duchess of Kent at the door, she was accompanied by Natasha Bagration. Mollie Buccleuch, Bill Astor, Rab Butler and Laura Corrigan, also came for tea. Laura whispered that it was very elegant! She took immediately to Peter.

P dined with his mother in her flat and later fetched me at Emerald's. Later we dined at E's . . . . Emerald and Nicholas had had a lovers' quarrel and she was petulant, unpleasant and frankly cross. Lady Kitty [Lambton][3] told her that she [Lady Cunard] had for half a century danced a cancan on all our altars – a scathing, damning and half-true jibe. Peter lightened the atmosphere by his arrival. Emerald dubbed him Prince Florizel.[4]

Friday 23rd April

We got up early; I was nervous, yet happy enough and not disappointed, indeed, was ecstatic . . . P went to the War Office . . . . P said that the Field Marshal much wanted to see me and would look in about six. Frantically, in spite of it being Good Friday and everyone away, I tried to arrange a cocktail party and finally collected some twenty people but it was rather a 'mixed bag'. Promptly Wavell arrived,

---

1 See entry for 18 November 1942 and footnote.
2 Frank Noel Mason-MacFarlane (1889–1953) had fought with distinction in the Great War, winning the Military Cross with two bars. Before the Second World War he was British Military Attaché in Berlin, during which time he advocated that the government should have Hitler assassinated. He was Director of Intelligence to the British Expeditionary Force in 1939–40 and served as Governor of Gibraltar from 1942 to 1944. He was elected Labour MP for Paddington North in 1945, but retired the following year because of ill health. He was knighted in 1943 and retired from the Army in the rank of lieutenant general.
3 Katherine de Vere Beauclerk (1877–1958), Lady Katherine by courtesy, daughter of the 10th Duke of St Albans, married in 1921 as her second husband Major General Sir William Lambton (1863–1936).
4 In Shakespeare's *The Winter's Tale*, son of the King of Bohemia.

greyer, deafer, gentler and shyer than ever. He doesn't focus well and misses doors and tables sometimes . . . the greatest general of our day walked in simply and sat down and I led up various people including the old Belgian Ambassador, the Cárcanos (our fashionable Argentines) etc. He drank three cocktails, stayed for nearly three hours and was charming but seemed 'terrified' of the famous, chic, seductive, fashionable Mme Cárcano and avoided her!

P and I walked nostalgically to the Belle Meunière where we dined *à deux* . . . *enfin seule.*[1]

SATURDAY 24TH APRIL   *FARNHAM PARK*

The Field Marshal himself came to see me at 9.30 – I was not dressed!

P and I up with the lark; he dashed to see his mother whilst I organised. Then with the car loaded with presents and luggage we embarked on our *villégiature,*[2] driving first to Sutton where we lunched with the Sutherlands. Eileen was ill and looked it; Geordie, ageing slightly, too seemed '*piano*'. Sutton always a cheerless house seemed bleak.

Tea at Send Grove with Loelia Westminster, who was affectionate and charming, and probably pleased by our reconciliation. To her I presented an expensive bottle of Napoleon brandy. (I gave its twin to the Kemsleys later.) She was alone . . . then followed a lovely sunlit drive to Farnham via Eton where we stopped. Peter noticed that the room where the block was kept and where he was whipped at the age of 17, had been destroyed by bombs. 'That will teach them!' he laughed. He was a fascinating companion, all day. Here at Farnham, where I brought him, we found Emerald Cunard; that dear old sheepdog and gentleman, the Belgian Ambassador; Sir Ronald Graham,[3] an erstwhile envoy to Rome (he has immensely aged and now has sunk into deep dignified somnolence); Denis and Ghislaine Alexander, the very newly married couple . . . . Good food: luxury and pleasant evening.

A great success, our tour, so far. Emerald told fabulous tales about Lord Curzon.

EASTER SUNDAY, 25TH APRIL

P gave me a magnificent pair of sapphire and star-sapphire links, quite the handsomest and lovely [*sic*] I have ever had or seen (a little like a ruby set I saw years ago in Bulgari's shop in Rome). I gave him a gold snuffbox. In the morning, we went for a long walk to Stoke Poges and we talked of Winston and his uncontrollable unfortunate disapproval, indeed jealous dislike of Wavell. Then on

1 Alone at last.
2 Holiday.
3 See entry for 5 August 1939 and footnote.

to Coppins where we had drinks with the Duchess and Natasha and the Duchess of Kent was in better spirits and v sweet and charmingly beautiful . . .

MONDAY 26TH APRIL   *5 BELGRAVE SQUARE*

Peter woke me and was wonderfully affectionate and altogether divine. We gossiped . . . have never had so fascinating a companion.

I heard the bombshell that Russia has broken off diplomatic relations with Poland. This is a catastrophic development in the war: The Russians have obviously massacred 8,000 Polish officers[1] and are trying to get out of it; yet for the Polish government to raise the issue now was tactless and unfortunate. All my sympathies, naturally, are with the Poles.

I am involved in an unpleasant 'plotting' and I blame the King of Greece and I shall never see or trust him again. He is an old friend but always a gossip and a German at heart and I am beginning to hate him. About a month ago I met him at Claridge's, just as he was leaving for Cairo, and he stopped me, was affectionate etc. and then said that he had heard that Rex Leeper, who has been nominated our Ambassador to Greece, is an extreme left-winger, anti-royalist etc. He asked me if that was the case; and I answered him truthfully that I thought it was – at least I had always heard so! It seems that he repeated these remarks of mine and they have reached the Foreign Office; for I have had an angry letter from Jim Thomas about the matter. I replied to his accusation that Leeper was constantly discussed but that Leeper's name has never been mentioned at No. 5. I foresee trouble. 'Put not your faith in princes, at least not in Greek ones.' He is a blundering, tactless Hun.

TUESDAY 27TH APRIL

Everybody deplores the Polish–Russian break; but I think it is just as well that the Russians have revealed their real brutality.

WEDNESDAY 28TH APRIL

The Field Marshal proposed himself to luncheon and I hurriedly collected not only the food but the guests and we had a distinguished little party: Lady Wilson[2]

---

1 He refers to the massacre at Katyn in Poland in April 1940 of 22,000 Polish officers, NCOs and professional men on Stalin's direct orders. The Germans discovered the mass graves in the winter of 1942–3 and announced the details, on Goebbels's orders, in April. General Sikorski, on behalf of the government-in-exile, demanded an inquiry by the Red Cross. The Soviets, determined to lie about their culpability (as they did for decades to come), accused Sikorski of collaborating with the Nazis and broke off diplomatic relations.
2 Hester Wykeham (1890–1979) married Henry Maitland Wilson (qv) in 1914.

(with General Sir 'Jumbo'); self; Lady Willingdon; the Field Marshal; Diana Cooper; Rab; Virginia Cowles; Peter. A great success.

Lady Willingdon was abrupt and direct and almost comically pleased to meet Wavell, whom she had never before seen. Diana made him talk, and he was quite fascinated by Virginia Cowles. As he left, he rather shyly and affectionately asked me if he could have a cocktail party here in the afternoon as he had so many people to see. Nearly thirty people came! . . . . Peter was out and for three hours I looked after the FM presenting various people to him. He hardly spoke to Duff, ignored the Kemsleys . . . . The party went on until 8.30, when Wavell left to dine with Winston at No. 10. P and I changed frantically; since we were already so late, and then escorting Diana, who looked a vision, we walked across to the Argentine Embassy where we found a pre-war dinner party of about twenty! . . . . An exhilarating evening with much champagne. Loelia Westminster, the Dudleys and Coopers came home with us and sat and bored Peter and me for over an hour.

THURSDAY 29TH APRIL

Peter gets up early and rushes to the War Office to be on duty with the Field Marshal, whom he adores, shadows, and never leaves . . . Today he took him to be photographed at Harleys[1] . . .

Alan came up to see me; but I fear I was unkind as I can only think of Wavell and of Peter . . . However we had a brief visit, and he returned to Henlow. He is still far from well.

Sidney Herbert dropped in to see Peter, as did Mrs Coats. Diana still here and we all had drinks together; and I could not resist telling them how Emerald and I walked home for luncheon and passed the Foreign Office and how Emerald stared up at the windows lovingly in the hopes of a glimpse of Nicholas. She is still idiotically in love.

FRIDAY 30TH APRIL

My life is a long whirl of excitements and engagements . . . last evening I rested a bit until Peter danced in, gay, pretty, tossing his fair head, and looking like an amber and golden statue . . . we talked v v late and the dawn found us still together.

This morning, there was more viceregal gossip but no decision seems to have been reached . . . . Rab rang me several times, half-excitedly, half-hoping, half-dreading that the report[2] was true and had I heard any more?

I lunched with the Amerys at Eaton Square. She was away, but Leo and Peter had a confidential chat, as I had arranged whilst I gossiped with Julian. We found

---

1 Presumably a photographic studio.
2 A rumour had gone round Whitehall the previous day that Butler was about to become Viceroy.

out nothing however about the Delhi appointment . . . at four o'clock the Field Marshal . . . . came here to see me . . . . I then found myself alone with the FM and we gossiped – mostly about Peter – for half an hour. He was playful about Winston, and I knew at once that he really doesn't like him.

Diana Cooper, rapturously lovely and gently affectionate and altogether perfect (they are v alike, she and Peter and have the same skin . . . .) has left for Bognor but the Field Marshal has now proposed himself and wants to stay here.

Saturday 1st May

Peter lunched with his mother, and packed the General off to Norfolk where he has gone to spend the weekend . . . . P gave a little party which I interrupted for a bit. He lives in a worldly whirl which is scarcely his fault, since Wavell is both possessive and dependent and is, indeed, a career. He adores Peter, he trusts him completely, relies on his judgement; and sometimes I think my Ganymede *is* Wavell from time to time. The Field Marshal looks up at him so affectionately from time to time as if seeking his approval. There is much human understanding in this curiously secretive relationship.

P and I dined with Emerald where we met Sachie and Georgia Sitwell; Clarissa Churchill; D'Arcy Osborne who is home on leave after his three years' incarceration at the Vatican, where he is our resident Minister. He has aged; says that life there is distressingly dull; there is little to eat; no society; he dines alone every night and occasionally borrows a book from a colleague. Almost a prisoner's life.

Sunday 2nd May

Peter and I drove to Kelvedon in his ex-car. I had prayed for a sunlit day but it was overcast and grey and he said he was glad as it was more English. Could man be more tactful? More gracious? We lunched and wandered about amongst the trees and gardens of what may be our future home; and then we picked masses of flowers, huge baskets of them and returned to London. We were so happy together; and when we passed a suburban villa he remarked that we should be equally happy there. Kelvedon did look a dream . . .

Monday 3rd May

What I had half-hoped for, or rather dreaded has come to pass! The Field Marshal has arrived to stay; he wanted to come last week but P and I feared that he would disturb the *Gemütlichkeit* and I didn't encourage the idea. However, the luggage came this morning and I put him in the big room which had been Peter's. P has now moved into mine which we shall share . . . . My household is in confusion and the depleted and inadequate staff quite demented.

I took Wavell and Peter to luncheon at the Belgian Embassy where we found a large and distinguished party including Winant,[1] whose fascinating appearance impressed Peter . . . . Later I drove my Field Marshal to the Dorchester to call on the Kemsleys, as Gomer K. wanted a quiet talk with him. I left them together for half an hour, as I played ADC waiting in the corridor. The meeting was a success (Wavell had never heard of the Kemsleys until I introduced them to him ten days ago). We then drove grandly in the impressive car to call on Virginia Cowles, who received us so rapturously: I again left him to her charms for twenty minutes. She was entranced as are all people who are able to thaw him. He is easy, amiable, even affable and affectionate to those he likes! – but he has lapses or rather long periods of brooding stubborn silence. Luckily he is easy with me, I adore him. This evening I heard him swearing in his room because he had mislaid something! He came down to dinner in a shabby tweed; and said it was a relief to be out of uniform.

He described his long interview with Queen Wilhelmina this afternoon, and showed us the immense Grand Order of Orange, or whatever the decoration is called, which she gave him. The ribbon is yellow; the stars are of steel and it makes a good show. She has no S[ex]A[ppeal], he remarked drily. Peter laughed and described their tea *à trois*, as he tossed his head so engagingly. After dinner . . . . [Peter] was worn out; overwrought, and even a touch querulous, and I gather, he is disappointed about his plans as the party (including Winston?) go to America on Wednesday, but poor Peter is to be left adrift in New York whilst the grands proceed to Washington. I am in a haze of affection; and I hinted, however, to the General, that he might bring Paul back to me in his seaplane, or is it battleship? He may do so.

TUESDAY 4TH MAY

A ghastly day: the climax. Peter and I shared a small bed, but slept easily, got up early as the FM was to be called at seven. I heard him moving about in the next room. All morning was a frenzy of telephoning, last-minute shopping, engagements, forgotten commissions etc. P lunched with his mother alone; I was obliged to refuse the FM's invitations to lunch as I was engaged with Alec Cadogan, who entertained at the Savoy . . . . I was glib, both hysterically happy and miserable: only a few more amber hours remain.

About six o'clock my cocktail party for the FM began. It was crowded, fashionable and distinguished . . . . About forty-five came. The FM said he had never met so many interesting and distinguished people . . . and he seemed to

1 The American Ambassador: see entry for 30 March 1941 and footnote.

enjoy himself throughout as he was easy and affable to all . . . and he made an immense impression as he invariably does. A few cocktails loosen his tongue. I was miserable when they once had finally left yet tried to be gay. P had recovered his spirits; and spent frantic hours with the luggage, his and the FM's . . . By eight o'clock they had all left. And P and I drove to Pratt's Club to dine, where unfortunately Esmond Rothermere joined us and bored us. Still it was a contact for Peter and I selfishly allowed it to continue. The FM and his sisters[1] dined in the blue dining room *à trois*. We rejoined them about ten and he playfully showed us his [Field Marshal's] baton, a gold and red plush affair built by Spink's. The King gave it to him this afternoon during a long audience at Buckingham Palace.

At 10.30 P drove him to the secret station by Holland House and saw him off – in half an hour they had returned as the train was delayed for an hour. In the interval P rushed to 8 Pont Street to take leave of his adoring, proud and half heartbroken mother. How she worships him! Once more they started off, again the General half-hugged me and murmured affectionate words of gratitude for my hospitality and kindness (I almost cried!) and again he kissed his sisters, 'goodbye' and they left. I am now waiting Peter's return for the second time.

I almost forgot to record that I am an uncle for the sixth time. Patsy Lennox-Boyd produced her third son[2] this morning at the Dorchester at 6.25 a.m. She was quite alone, except for her gynaecologist. It was all easy and effortless. Childbirth can be simple.

In the midst of the cocktail party a tiny parcel came. It was from Mrs Ronnie Greville's executors and was a small bloodstone round box; inside were two pills which poor Maggie never took. Whilst a small and simple memento, I am nevertheless enchanted to have it.

WEDNESDAY 5TH MAY

I had not long to wait last night as P soon returned; exhausted with excitements and emotions but we were soon asleep. It was about 12.45 a.m. At ten to four this morning we were called, and a horrible hour followed whilst he dressed, cried and was twice sick. Then I went down to the front door; it was still dark; and we embraced sadly and gently; he got into the waiting car; and was whisked away. I looked at the clock; it was 4.50 a.m. When if ever shall I see him again? In a way I love him more than ever; yet a stillness, a certain calm has come into our relations;

---

1 Florence Anne Paxton Wavell (1882–1968) and Lillian Mary Wavell (1884–1974) had come up from the country to visit their brother.

2 Mark Alexander Lennox-Boyd (b.1943). He was Conservative MP for Morecambe from 1979 to 1997. He served as a whip from 1984 to 1988, as parliamentary private secretary to the Prime Minister, Mrs Thatcher, from 1988 to 1990, and as a Foreign Office minister from 1990 to 1994. He was knighted in 1994.

there is less frenzy and violence . . . I went back to sleep, taking three aspirins.
Woke at 9 a.m. and found myself alone; felt capitulated. In my tray was a long
letter from P written in India, announcing his imminent arrival, and he talked of
all we would do – and now have done. It is over. They – Peter and the FM – are on
their way to America. The newspapers report that General Andrews,[1] and General
Barth[2] were killed on Monday in Iceland. On Friday afternoon they were both
here in this house for a secret conference with Wavell. The week before Barth had
looked in for cocktails. It seems endlessly tragic.

Worn-out, exhausted, I wandered to the House of Commons, met Alan,
made up my row with Jim Thomas,[3] and then went with Alan to the Dorchester
to see Patsy and the new baby, born yesterday. We went up in the lift with Lord
and Lady Iveagh! The baby is prettier than the last one, 'Topher', was at his birth.
He looked Levantine. Patsy was sitting up, smiling and gay and seeming quite
unconcerned. Her phlegm and calm are immense.

Had a Turkish bath; slept a sound hour; dined with Emerald . . . . Bored and
spent, I was glad of an offer of a lift from old Cartier and I am now home. It is
10.50. The house is silent, deserted, but there is an amber ambience: an aroma of
Peter everywhere; I whiff it and it stabs . . . What witchery is his? . . .

THURSDAY 6TH MAY

Although anguished, life must flow on . . . . I slept until ten; walked to the H of
C. Winston was conspicuously absent. Of course he has gone with Wavell and P. I
was *distrait*, couldn't attend to what I heard . . . thought only of my travelling tired
Pierrot.

Dined in and alone: Alan rang from Brixham and pleaded with me to join
him at Torquay next week. As I need a rest, I have decided to go on Monday after
a weekend at Leeds [Castle]. I shan't take the diary,[4] and shall have a complete, I
hope, rest.

FRIDAY 7TH MAY

More messages from the Marshal and the Major! I slept eleven hours and have
now almost recovered my equilibrium.

---

1 Frank Maxwell Andrews (1884–1943) was a lieutenant general in the United States Army who
   had recently replaced Eisenhower (qv) as Commander of all US troops in Europe. He was
   killed with thirteen others when his Liberator aborted a landing on an inspection tour of
   Iceland and flew into a mountainside; only the rear-gunner survived.
2 Charles H. Barth (1903–43) was a US Army brigadier general who died when accompanying
   Lt Gen. Andrews (*vide supra*) on his Iceland mission.
3 See entry for 26 April 1943.
4 Not for the first time, he changes his mind.

The African war draws to a close; we shall be in Tunis and Bizerta by tomorrow. The Axis rout has been complete.

Most of the sad and silent day was spent in fagging for Peter, and thinking of all that was left unsaid, undone . . . I feel flat, divorced, amputated. Most gushing and grateful letters have come from the two Miss Wavells, whom I like.

Went to see Patsy and the newborn, Mark Alexander, a sweet baby and the prettiest of Patsy's many boys. She looked quite beautiful and was calm and charming, although she admitted to being offended with Honor who has characteristically ignored the arrival of the last infant.

At about six o'clock, a ghastly wartime hour, I joined Laura Corrigan's party consisting of the two Cárcano girls; Angier Duke; Sarah Churchill . . . . Sheila Milbanke; Billy McCann . . . . and Ben Kittredge. After cocktails we went to see Noël Coward in a ghastly, cheap, boring, suburban play called *This Happy Breed*.[1] He acted well . . . I sat out the second act with Angier Duke, making arrangements for P to stay in Washington with his wife. Then dinner and bed. Sarah Churchill is a fascinating girl of considerable character; she is far superior to both her parents.

I am still tired and think only of the past feverish, frenzied fortnight and cannot concentrate, even on the African victories!

The ship . . . . sailed on Wednesday night for Scotland; it cannot reach Chesapeake Bay before Monday evening; and more probably it will be Tuesday before they dock and the world knows . . . I pray for its safety.

SATURDAY 8TH MAY   *LEEDS CASTLE*

Still no news, except that the vessel with its important (and to me, vital) cargo was very crowded. There is also talk of Duff Cooper . . . . going to India.

I drove here with Nicholas Lawford, whom I invited in lieu of Peter. It is icy and grey and cold . . . . ! The party consists of Adrian and Lady Baillie, my hosts; her father, old Lord Queenborough; his two half-sisters, Audrey[2] and Enid Paget;[3] Emerald Cunard is staying – gay in the country and rather too much given to unkind sparring with Lady Willingdon who doesn't stand up to it well; Geoffrey Lloyd; and Leslie Belisha. I am bored but rested. Emerald, more madly ensorcelled by Nicholas than ever, sends him notes across the castle every few hours.

---

1 Coward had written the play in 1939 and its dress rehearsal was the night before Germany invaded Poland; it had to wait until 1942 for a performance. It is the story of a lower-middle-class family between the wars, and their interaction with the great events of the times. Despite Channon's dismissal of it, it was widely acclaimed and made into a hugely successful film in 1944, directed by David Lean, with Robert Newton as the paterfamilias (a role played on stage by Coward) and also starring Celia Johnson (qv), Stanley Holloway and John Mills.
2 Audrey Elizabeth Paget (1922–91) became an aviatrix.
3 Enid Louise Paget (b.1923).

We are in Bizerta and Tunis. Harold Balfour, after some delay, arrived back at B Square this morning. He rang me here and gave me the news! He actually watched the battle for Bizerta and slept Thursday night with General Montgomery; spent Friday, yesterday at Gibraltar, and flew here in the evening. Bad weather over Finisterre. Arrived about 2 p.m., he brought me oranges and silk socks.

SUNDAY 9TH MAY

A cold tempest rages and I shaved and was bored; spent most of the day with Geoffrey Lloyd. Old Lord Hardinge[1] came to lunch, he was on sticks, Lord Queenborough, aged 82, who is about six months[2] his junior, remarked to me, 'Poor Charlie Hardinge! He looks an old crock, doesn't he?' Queenborough is an octogenarian of immense vigour, having produced three daughters by his second wife when he was over 60! Much banter here and Lady Willingdon, who had been rather cruelly chaffed by Emerald, reasserted herself with the announcement that Flaubert[3] had been in love with her when she was 17! We gasped and wondered, is she then the original of Salammbô?

The number of prisoners is growing; the conquest of Tunisia is all but over. It has been a tremendous victory.

MONDAY 10TH MAY   *IMPERIAL HOTEL, TORQUAY*

I drove Lady Willingdon up to London and Enid Paget too. Bee Willingdon, I really think that great proconsular ex-Empress definitely wants to marry me. Her son, Niggs, she confided to me, is to embark upon his third matrimonial venture shortly. She is depressed about [it].

It is grey, windy and cold; and my thoughts are with P tossing still at sea . . . I signed my letters, repacked and caught the 1.30 train for Torquay . . . . five-hour easy journey. Alan, wearing a black sou'wester, met me and drove me here, where we have the same small suite which he shared so happily with Stuart Preston recently before their dramatic and somewhat mysterious rupture. Alan's jaws are still enflamed, but he is improving hourly and is already half-cured! We dined cosily together *à deux* in the most comfortable pre-war hotel, which is crowded with

---

1 Charles Hardinge (1858–1944) joined the Diplomatic Service in 1880. He enjoyed the patronage of King Edward VII, and was Permanent Under-Secretary at the Foreign Office by 1906, having been Ambassador to Russia for the preceding two years. He served as Viceroy of India from 1910 to 1916, before returning to run the Foreign Office until 1920, and spending the last three years of his diplomatic career as Ambassador to France. Heaped with honours, he received the first of his six separate orders of knighthood in 1904, and was raised to the peerage as 1st Baron Hardinge of Penshurst in 1910. He became a Knight of the Garter in 1916. His son and heir, Sir Alexander Hardinge (qv), was Channon's *bête noire*.
2 Actually, three years.
3 Gustave Flaubert (1821–81), eminent French novelist. As Lady Willingdon was only 5 years old when Flaubert died, this can hardly be true.

escapists, tennis and ping-pong playing lesbians and cocktail-drinking colonels who have never seen a blitz. The standard of food and service is decidedly pre-war.

TUESDAY 11TH MAY

A wretched day . . . . I wrote; I slept; Alan and I philandered, and later we drove to Brixham to see Alan's boat which is on the grid undergoing repairs. Brixham, which in any case looks Belgian, is untidy, wet and grey and curiously crowded with Belgian craft and Belgian refugees; the untidy streets are crowded with dark, dirty, grubby children chatting in Flemish.

I slept with Alan last night in a small-ish bed. He is too big for that and he snores; yet I like his companionship.

No news yet of the arrival. Nicholas Lawford rang up to say that they are arriving tonight in Washington.

WEDNESDAY 12TH MAY

A gale howled all night. I slept with A again; and on the eight o'clock news we heard of the arrival of the great ship. I immediately from my sleepy, shared bed sent off a mass of cables about Peter – to Nannie, Jay Llewellin, Peter himself, Mrs Angier Duke,[1] Serge Obolensky and Mrs Vanderbilt . . .

Alan is in decidedly better spirits; and although he talks of Stuart Preston *ad nauseam*, he is recovering. We compared our trials. There is the lesson.[2]

THURSDAY 13TH MAY

A lovely, luscious Devon day – all blue and white. We drove to Brixham, but not until P's cable that he had arrived in New York and was staying with Mrs Otto Kahn[3] was repeated to me.

Alan and I lunched with the monks at Buckfast; but the beloved Abbot was away; instead we were received by the Father Prior, a quite undistinguished little friendly fellow. Old Father Milletus[4] was affectionate and welcoming and in good health. Alan was immensely impressed by the incense, the ritual and the male life. Good lunch; the reader read out a passage from the life of George V in which Mrs Keppel was mentioned. Alan and I exchanged winks. Later we lingered over liqueurs in the Abbot's sitting room and then drove reluctantly away. I should be

1 Formerly Margaret Screven (1903–64), the wife of his new friend.
2 Presumably about their intimate involvements with other men.
3 Adelaide Wolff (1875–1949), married Otto Hermann Kahn (1867–1934), financier and philanthropist, in 1896.
4 See entries for 21 and 25 August 1942.

happy enough in the peace and calm of Buckfast but Alan, attracted as he is by dogma and ritual and a male life, would be driven dotty . . .

Called at Powderham where we found a bevy of females sitting on the lawn. Lady Devon,[1] who is a brunette of charm and obviously highly sexed, advanced and kissed Alan. She is his cousin; she was surrounded by children of all ages . . . . After this gay visit and we [had seen] over the grey castle, we went back to Torquay, stopping at the Cary Arms Hotel at Babbacombe: it is a tiny attractive port nestling in an almost secret cove by the blue sea. A steep road runs down to it; and it was there that Alan had been rapturously but so briefly blissful with his treacherous Stuart Preston who has so recklessly blighted his existence.

Alan and I dined nostalgically in this most luxurious pre-war hotel; he begged me to stay on but I refused, and he drove me to Newton Abbot where I caught a train at 12.35 a.m. for London, and exerting my rights as an MP easily obtained a wagon-lit. I have enjoyed the brief stay here at Torquay, being with, and staying with Alan, all day and all night. I love him dearly.

The war in Tunisia is over. There is not a German or Italian at large; but my heart is not there; it is in New York and I am wondering what Peter is doing, and whether he is happy, and has yet seen my son? It had always been my dream to take P to New York; and now that, too, is denied to me. Soon there will be few places left to go to together.

FRIDAY 14TH MAY

Back in London, after a comfortable journey. Breakfasted with Harold B, who was rhapsodic about his great astronomical trek to S. Africa and back. The tour was a complete triumph; and he was able to help Paul and Princess Olga, whom he met in Nairobi. He also sent for Alexander[2] in South Africa and warned and begged the lad to be careful and to pass his examinations. He is staying in Pretoria.

We raided Germany heavily last night, whilst Chelmsford was badly battered here.[3]

By going to Torquay, I have missed a spate of dinner parties which is a blessing. I am turning against them.

Evening alone. My intuition is failing me for I am unable to decide whether I think the travellers will return. I am praying so.

1 Sybil Venetia Taylor (1907–2001) married in 1939 as her second husband Charles Christopher Courtenay, who in 1935 succeeded his father as 17th Earl of Devon.
2 Son of the ex-Regent and Princess Olga.
3 Chelmsford had a large Marconi factory and also a ball-bearing factory, close to residential areas. In the 13 May raid fifty people were killed and 1,000 made homeless.

SATURDAY 15TH MAY

Channon had offered the 10th Duke and Duchess of Marlborough his house as the venue for the reception after their daughter Sarah's[1] wedding.

Early my home was in a turmoil; furniture was being moved; the servants were noisy and excited; parcels came and telegrams poured in; the telephone never stopped. About eleven the Marlboroughs accompanied by Blandford[2] (a very handsome, good-looking, English-looking boy of about 17) and his youngest sister[3] called and we put the final finishing touches to the appearance of the house. Then they left; I hid a few valuable *bibelots*, lunched and dressed and awaited guests, having decided not to go to the wedding itself at St Margaret's; Sarah, looking like a blue lupin, and magnificently dressed, arrived with her smiling determined-looking sailor husband (who I suspect of having a character of granite) at about 3.10. The Marlboroughs, the pages, Charles Churchill[4] (Mary's wartime baby which she adores), and Winston Churchill, the PM's most determined infant grandson, were with them. They were all photographed on the steps of No. 5 – and the bombed house made an appropriate setting. Baby Winston is 2½, and already frighteningly like the Prime Minister. He posed with a swaying arrogance, put a whistle in his mouth and the crowd on the pavement roared with laughter . . . after his brief pause on my threshold, I escorted Sarah up to the Empire bedroom where photographers had established themselves, and then I went down and helped Mary and Bert[5] to receive the guests who were already arriving. Mrs Winston Churchill was one of the first; fashionably dressed, fussy, smiling and tiresome (I don't really like her, as I formerly did). She then made an almost regal *entrée* and was soon surrounded by social sycophants. Perhaps 200 others appeared, the majority were young; and there were many Americans amongst them, sly and unbending. Cider cup was passed by the many too many waiters, and iced coffee and cake! Later a limited amount of champagne was produced.

Russell is quite an unknown American; but his lovely wife who has an independence of mind and spirit as well as vitality and great beauty, adores him. I hope that they will be happy. I have never known a woman more in love; and I was

---

1 Lady Sarah Spencer-Churchill; see entry for 11 July 1939. She married Edward Fariman Russell (1914–2001), an American newspaper publisher who had come to Britain and joined the Royal Naval Volunteer Reserve before America entered the war. They divorced in 1966.
2 John George Vanderbilt Henry Spencer-Churchill (1926–2014) was Earl of Sunderland by courtesy until 1934, then Marquess of Blandford by courtesy until 1972, when he succeeded his father as 11th Duke of Marlborough. He was first cousin, twice removed, of Winston Churchill.
3 Rosemary Mildred Spencer-Churchill (b.1929), Lady Rosemary by courtesy.
4 Lord Charles Spencer-Churchill (1940–2016).
5 The Duke and Duchess of Marlborough.

saddened, for when one is infatuated oneself, other people's happiness makes one nostalgic ... Mrs Churchill told me that the ship (it was the *Queen Mary*) was a day late, but she hadn't heard whether they had had good weather (I thought of poor P, who is a bad sailor) ... I remarked politely that I hoped that the PM had had some rest ... I talked with others; the Argentine Ambassador, to my surprise, kissed me on both cheeks – why? .... Sarah, still in her wedding raiment, and accompanied by her husband .... drove to the Dorchester to see some American sailors, and then returned. By about six the party was breaking up as people were rushing to the country for the fine weekend. I saw Mrs Churchill to her car, and she became effusive, but called me 'Mr Channon' instead of 'Chips'. However, she waved 'goodbye'. Pam Churchill was her usual enchanting self, exuding sexual attraction.

At last they all left: I was warmly embraced by the bride, and by Mary Marlborough and thanked a thousand times for lending the house etc. .... I noticed just as the car was driving away that Russell pressed a parcel into his mother-in-law's hand, and then kissed her. She showed it to me: it was a gold inscribed cigarette case and she was touched. Perhaps it was the end of a long battle which he has won, and the Marlboroughs were determined to prevent the marriage – and they failed. I don't really see why it shouldn't be a success. The couple drove off to stay at Barbie Wallace's house on the Lavington estate.

I sat for a few minutes in my chaotic house, read my letters, changed into country clothes, and then drove here [Send Grove], stopping off at Pyrford to call upon the Iveaghs. They were not there, but at Elveden. However, I saw Brigid who looked fat and hideous. She is recovering from German measles and I gave her two of Harold Balfour's oranges. I hope she doesn't give me German measles in exchange. She tells me that Hugh Euston is arriving at Pyrford tomorrow to spend the day with her. How I wish that she would marry him; but she has refused him so often and now I believe that he is reserved for a higher destiny – the very throne itself!

Here I found only Loelia Westminster, my hostess; and Lord and Lady Durham,[1] whom I have always much liked.

TUESDAY 18TH MAY

Last night was the most disturbed that I recall since the big Blitz on Britain.[2] I was asleep before eleven but was soon awakened by the sirens and booming, shelling, firing – and perhaps bombs? – followed. Then an 'all-clear'! Then again another alert – I was only half-conscious of what was happening and do not remember

---

1 John Frederick Lambton (1884–1970) succeeded his father as 5th Earl of Durham in 1929.
  He married in 1931, as his second wife, Hermione Bullough (1906–90).
2 This was a far less significant raid than Channon perceived.

the third raid. However, I woke exhausted this morning. No interesting letter ... I walked to the H of C, where we were soon in secret session as it had been found necessary to alter the time of the thanksgiving service tomorrow at St Paul's[1] as the secret had leaked out. It is now to take place at 6 p.m. Anthony Eden made the announcement.

From all accounts Winston and Wavell are not getting on well together. I foresaw as much. Winston remarked to someone before he left that 'Wavell spends too much time in the air. Will fly anywhere and preferably to a banquet than to a battle!' What a monstrous and untrue comment. I hate him; but we cannot do without him.

Much chaff about Lady Leconfield,[2] whose strange antics are the light relief of the war. She undresses on every possible occasion and is said to have walked naked down the Grand Staircase of Claridge's recently. Lady Willingdon told me in confidence that Lady L has three times stripped in her house lately. Walking in Davies Street I was pursued by Grace Curzon, who looked as elegant, chic and lovely as ever. She pleaded with me to take Hubert back; he is dying; must rest completely for two years as his heart has given out. She seemed so sad and we talked of old days ... she remarked (and I was shaken) that she had never loved Lord Curzon (George!), even disliked him but had married him for the sake of her boys, and just when they were old enough to need his advice and power he died! This is, of course, untrue. She married him solely for his great social position which she shared and revelled in. She has always been a devoted, kind and affectionate but wildly foolish and selfish mother. I promised to do what I could with Hubert, but I shan't; for it is almost impossible to revive dead friendships of that nature. I don't even like him now; and he infuriates me. It is partly, I suppose, because I treated him somewhat shabbily; and we can never forgive people one [*sic*] has let down!

I feel so old and tired – why? The Wavell visit took a lot out of me in many ways. Soon they will be back again. I am convinced of it now.

WEDNESDAY 19TH MAY

A cable from P announces that he has flu in New York, and is presumably staying with Mrs Otto Kahn. He was overtired, overwrought; and I sometimes wonder whether he has a weak chest, or lungs; he has many of the qualities of the tubercular. I answered at once; and then walked to the House of Commons where a rather unreal debate soon took place on the sad subject of refugees.

---

1 To mark the victory in North Africa.
2 Beatrice Violet Rawson (1892–1956), married the 3rd Baron Leconfield (1872–1952) in 1911. She was the mother-in-law of Victor Warrender, 1st Baron Bruntisfield (qv).

A walk and talk with Nicholas Lawford who betrayed a rigidity, a frigidity of which I have long suspected! He has broken off relations with Emerald and wants never to see her again. She has killed the affair with too much telephoning, etc. He seemed quite firm and determined and I sympathised with him.

At six o'clock the great *Te Deum* to celebrate our victories in Africa was held in St Paul's Cathedral. Owing to a ridiculous tale the time had to be altered from noon. It seems that Charlie Londonderry's butler opened his whip[1] at Mount Stewart and telegraphed to him in London; the Irish censorship stopped the telegram and informed the Authorities. The great church, crowded with all the notabilities of England, might have proved too tempting a target for the Luftwaffe and it was decided to alter the time. Even so, there was some uneasiness all day that the Germans might get to know and bomb us. Nothing of the sort happened. Instead we had an impressive, effortless English simple service though it had been hurriedly organised. I took Laura Corrigan as my guest, and she was enchanted. We arrived at 4.30 and already the church was half full with peers, MPs and service people. Nobody was elegantly dressed. We watched the late arrivals; Socialist ministers looking self-conscious and awkward in their tailcoats – as they always do. Attlee appeared with Mrs Churchill; the Butlers, others – half the government. And then the choir, including the Archbishop of Canterbury, magnificent in full regalia of white satin and gold, went to the grand entrance to receive the royalties. After a pause, the procession returned, solemn, stately and dignified. The King and Queen looked small and unimportant (though she was gracious in grey and smiled, and leaned back, a new walk she has recently acquired). Immediately behind them came the two princesses [Elizabeth and Margaret] dressed alike in blue which made them seem like little girls; then the kings of Norway and Yugoslavia, an ill-assorted brace of monarchs, one so immense and the other so small and insignificant; then Princess Marina in fashionable black and pearls and looking rich and resplendent, and as ever, quite the cynosure of all admiring eyes, she walked with Crown Prince Olaf of Norway .... and finally the Mountbattens – do they go in the procession now? Both were in uniform.

The service was short, impressive, and the *Te Deum* superbly sung by the choir. I looked up to the painted cupola and thought .... of the grandeur of England, and was moved ... the proceedings lasted about forty-five minutes and then the procession filed out much as they had come in. They were followed out by the ambassadors and by tall ... de Gaulle etc. The big rectangular doorway had been opened and the sunlight flooded the church and the bells began intoning. The Bells of Victory. There were rumours that Montgomery was somewhere in the church. Laura and I headed our way out, talking to various people .... I was struck by how plain and unattractive the princesses looked and how shy and stiff

---

1 The letter from the Whips' Office in the House of Lords requesting his attendance.

they seemed. Shocking. I trust that Hugh Euston[1] will be a salutary influence. The portico was bathed in hot rich sunlight; the bells kept chiming; there was the usual pause as people awaited their cars; there was the usual polite gaping crowd.

Dined with Emerald and when I arrived my heart sank. Never has a party been so ill-assorted – or more successful. Emerald . . . . Lady Camrose, Alec Hardinge; Sydney Butler; me, Professor Joad; Bridget Paget; Rab; Lady Crewe; Lord Camrose. Only Emerald's puckish brain could have collected such an assembly – Bridget Paget was drunk, as she always is, poor unhappy demented sad woman, and prattled about the Portlands. Alec Hardinge, the 'famous Black Rat', was in an amiable mood, and smiled quite pleasantly. He was agreeable to me. Professor Joad, I immediately liked; and feeling well and frivolous and foolish, I at once dominated the dinner, rather to Rab's surprise. Soon Joad and I were exchanging jokes and addresses, and we turned the conversation into happiness. Everybody except Joad and me admitted to being miserable, which is far from true.

THURSDAY 20TH MAY

Again a most noisy night; one awakes cross and nervous after a semi-sleepless night.

The newspapers give a vivid account of Winston's speech to Congress, and reports that the Windsors were cheered on their arrival and departure.[2] Never before have they had an ovation in the USA. It is Winston's doing, and his attentions to them that have obviously affected American opinion. People here are a touch annoyed. I think it is excellent.

James Gunn is now paid in full the £750 he asked for my portrait. I sent him the balance (£200) yesterday.

FRIDAY 21ST MAY

Lunched with Laura Corrigan, a large, fashionable party. As Bill Mabane, the Under-Secretary for Food, was making his debut there, I rang her up and warned her to make the food simple. She did.

Later, I dropped in at a Dutch cocktail party . . . . I had expected to find the *corps diplomatique*; instead every pansy in London was there and I was annoyed and bored . . . . Vsevolod of Russia, who was bored and angry, led me away just as I was enjoying myself, and we went back to his house to see Maimie who

---

1 Euston, heir to the Grafton dukedom, was spoken of as a potential husband for either of the princesses.
2 According to Michael Bloch, in his book *The Duke of Windsor's War* (1982), the Windsors received more applause than Churchill when they appeared in one of the galleries; and Churchill appeared disconcerted by this.

is in bed with bronchitis. Evelyn Waugh, in grey flannels and his shirtsleeves, was sitting on her bed. Evelyn, whom we call 'Mr Woo', is a bore, and certainly common, still he is a brilliant impressionistic writer, I suppose – or fear. He is a great drinker and a fervent Catholic; and he has had a devastating influence on Hubert Duggan whom I have now washed out as dead, or as good as dead.

SATURDAY 22ND MAY

A ghastly day. I drove to Kelvedon, called to P etc. At three o'clock a telephone message came from Kavanagh, my temporary, and slightly sinister valet, to say that Belgrave Square was in flames! Bessie, the housekeeper, had discovered the fire about two. The Fire Brigade were fighting it etc. Feeling sick at heart, I jumped into my car and rushed to London, ignoring traffic lights and speed restrictions, not knowing whether I should find my lovely, famous and now historic house in flames . . . Outside were the fire engines, smoke poured through the windows and an appalling scene of devastation greeted me! Dropping chunks of wood, spluttering embers, dripping water, rushing men and the smell of burning everywhere. The servants looked terrified and panic-stricken; the dome over the hall was destroyed and the staircase was bared to the heavens! I could have cried from exasperation and hopeless helplessness. Shall I have to leave the house: move to the Ritz, and what of Peter and his possible return? Is this the judgement of the gods? There are two theories as to how the fire started; either a bit of hot shrapnel got embedded into the woodwork last night and has been smouldering ever since; or else the cook, who smokes, went up onto the roof this morning, as I'm told she did, and dropped a cigarette. I don't know; the latter explanation is the most plausible, although the barrage last night was heavy and at 3 a.m. I feared that the house was hit . . . When I left for Kelvedon this morning at 11.30 all was well. Bessie, the housekeeper (my adoring and devoted ally) was in her room at 12.30 when she heard the gong announcing the servants' dinner. She went down. Soon after two she found the house ablaze . . .

My stair-carpet is ruined; various articles of furniture are damaged. And I am reminded of a similar fire in my flat (then 43 Gloucester Place) just ten years ago this month when Freddie Birkenhead threw a lighted cigarette into a waste-paper basket and the place was burnt out. He narrowly escaped being burnt to death.

Unhappy and dejected I went to dine with Vsevolod and Maimie who were very sweet to me.

SUNDAY 23RD MAY

I left Belgrave Square early for Pyrford where I stayed until 10 p.m., thus allowing the servants the whole day in which to try and tidy the house. They did. The Iveaghs were most friendly and affectionate; as was Brigid (who is fast losing her looks.) Fritzi of Prussia was staying there; he looks hale and distinguished and seems happy in his curious life. He has been transferred to Wantage . . . . all day he does agricultural work and dines with the family, whom he likes. He is much happier there than with the Mounsey-Heyshams near Carlisle.

MONDAY 24TH MAY

The servants worked like Trojans and the house was improved. Stains are disappearing and there is a semblance of order.

TUESDAY 25TH MAY

The house still smells of smoke, and filth abounds . . . but there is an obvious improvement and a sense of order. I had prayed for more money but I didn't expect it from an insurance company.

Dined with Helen Fitzgerald, Angier Duke, Violet Cripps and we were joined by Mary Marlborough. Before we went to *Present Laughter*,[1] Noël Coward's fashionable comedy; it is excessively boring and dull. The oldest Emerald and Mrs Vanderbilt jokes, and even some of mine. Laura C was there with Diana, Eddie Devonshire and Jock McEwen. I was bored.

A most mysterious cable has come from Peter – who is really ill – does he mean that the Field Marshal, whom I believed [to be] in New York, is returning and to me? I trust so. This ghastly illness of Peter's torments me – and meanwhile I am rapidly losing weight. I weigh now just over 10 st. Before the war I was 13. Is it rationing, love or anxiety, or a mixture of all three?

THURSDAY 27TH MAY

I very nearly went to Kelvedon for the day, and finally decided to go to the H of Commons for a bit on my way. There I found Nicholas Lawford who confided to me that he had read a govt cable that P is very ill indeed. I was distraught . . . and then at 12.30, I was given a message from the Air Ministry that the Field Marshal was in England and would arrive at Belgrave Square in the hope of staying with me sometime this afternoon. I was in a fever and hurriedly rushed home to make final arrangements. What a mercy that I didn't go to Kelvedon as I had planned.

I hurriedly tidied up the house, telephoned frantically and by 4 p.m., when he was due, I was waiting for him, flanked by Diana Cooper and Phyllis Shearer (a great friend of his; a second-rate little woman, but pretty and pleasant and provocative).[2] His temporary ADC, one Captain McKennell, arrived first with

---

1 Like *This Happy Breed* (*vide supra*), *Present Laughter* was written in 1939 but not produced until 1942; it is one of Coward's best-known comedies.
2 I have been unable to find any further information about her.

the luggage and announced that the FM had gone straight to the War Office but would soon be with us. And he was. Soon he walked in, smiled in his gentle humorous way and said, 'Hello Chips!' greeted Diana and bewailed Peter's illness and absence . . . . As the FM dressed into blue mufti, I sat with him, and he showed me a ghastly letter in which the Head Doctor [some words are crossed out] in New York says that P was acutely but not dangerously ill with a temp of 104. I am in despair about it . . .

Later, at eight o'clock we sallied forth to dine at Pratt's Club, where I had invited the Duke of Devonshire and Lord Rosebery to dine with us. Eddie didn't come but Harry Rosebery was already waiting. They [Wavell and Rosebery] are v old friends but Harry, who is one year the older, seems much younger – probably because he has devoted his life to pleasure. They were enraptured to see each other, and talked of the last war . . . . Gradually, the other members sitting at the round table joined in and the subject turned not unnaturally to India and the much-debated question of the future Viceroy. The FM expressed no opinion but listened. He was in blue mufti. At the end of the table sat a KC named Beyfus,[1] who suddenly intervened with 'Why not send old Wavell?' An amused shudder went around the table; I tried to save the situation and pointing to the FM I suggested to Beyfus that he ask him direct. The poor man blushed deeply, swallowed his port and bolted. We sat for a bit . . . . then at length, the FM and I walked home via St James's Park.

Friday 28th May

The FM went off at 9.30 to the War Office; and I was left to cope with his correspondence, messages and to make engagements. He has none. Luckily, I caught Duff Cooper who said that he would be enchanted to see him, and to give him lunch. Then I hinted discreetly on the telephone to the Amerys that they invite him to dine – who did so actually. The Sec of State for India was actually unaware that he had arrived! This meant changing their plans, as they had intended to go to Bailiffscourt;[2] however they were enchanted and agreed. A quarter of an hour later, McKennell, the frightened, frenzied ADC, rang me to say that the FM was sorry that he couldn't dine with me but he had to go to the Amerys'!! This was the time it took for my plot to materialise. I had most of the morning to myself and then walked to 11 Downing Street, where the FM was closeted with Attlee, there I picked him up and we drove to Buck's Club where Duff Cooper had engaged a private room and arranged matters *en prince*.[3] However, I led the FM through the public room and introduced Esmond Rothermere, Freddie

---

1 Gilbert Hugh Beyfus (1885–1960) tried several times, unsuccessfully, to become a Liberal and then a Conservative MP. He spent much of the Great War in a prisoner-of-war camp. His legal practice concentrated on defamation and the gaming laws.

2 Lord Moyne's estate in Sussex, near Arundel.

3 In princely fashion.

Birkenhead, and Christopher Chancellor[1] to him – and others. Quite an *entrée*!
Duff had collected Shakes Morrison, and an American called John Cowles,[2] who
is Wilkie's right-hand man. The food was delicious and the conversation super:
whenever it flagged I did a Peter – that is I gave Wavell a prod or a lead; and all
was well. I told Duff how much he had enjoyed *David*,[3] which pleased him, and
the conversation continued for twenty minutes on that theme. The FM quoted
the Bible, Kipling and Shakespeare; for he has the most prodigious memory.
Morrison capped him; the American was left impressed and breathless . . . Later
FM and I shopped, bought many books and then I left him for a little. He said he
would be in by 6.30. I walked home where I found a message that he was already
on his way to Belgrave Square. It was only five o'clock. I telephoned frantically and
collected Virginia Cowles, Lady Cunard, Angier Duke, Sidney Herbert and one or
two others . . . . then I took him up to the Napoleonic bedroom which has seen so
much love and life these seven years, and chatted to the great man as he changed. I
am now not in the least frightened of him; he is easy, simple, gentle and quite easy
to lead and manage; agrees to anything. Peter's job, whilst it is always exhausting
to subordinate one's personality to another's, is simpler than I thought; but it must
be wearying always to keep him amused . . . I walked him to the Amerys in Eaton
Square, and having refused to dine with them, I returned and fell into my bed . . .

SATURDAY 29TH MAY   *NORTHWICK PARK, BLOCKLEY,*
                                          GLOUCESTERSHIRE

The FM came in about 10.30 last night; half-awake, I heard him call out 'Chips!'
but I took no notice and turned over . . . he was up early this morning and came
into my room in his dark blue silk dressing gown which Peter had given him,
and we talked and tried to make plans . . . at last I got rid of him, completed
my dressing; gave orders and packed. The FM and I left London. We were off
together in his car at 9.50. He had wanted to leave by nine, not by ten! Of course
the roads were deserted and we drove fervently; occasionally the FM tapped the
window and ordered the driver to stop and give lifts to soldiers. It was amusing to
watch their manner change when they twigged that it was Field Marshal Wavell
inside. We talked the whole way; and I gather that he is annoyed, for indeed he
said so, with Winston who wrote him rude pontifical notes on the ship, and in
Washington. They didn't get on well this time; he saw little of him intimately in

---

1 Christopher John Howard Chancellor (1904–89) worked for Reuters from 1930 to 1959,
   being its General Manager from 1944. He was knighted in 1951.
2 John Cowles (1898–1983) was an American newspaper and magazine publisher with titles
   in the Midwest, and also a substantial comic book empire. He was a substantial financial
   supporter of Wendell Wilkie (see entry for 30 October 1940 and footnote).
3 His biography of King David.

Washington; but one day lunching with him and the Pres[ident] and one other
(the CIGS, I think) at the White House, Winston openly attacked him in front
of the President who gently took Wavell's part. The FM had been very annoyed;
and I wonder whether the rift between them is not serious and undermining?

We rushed through Oxford, and as we approached Woodstock, I asked him
if he had ever seen Blenheim: 'Only from the air,' he replied. So we called at the
Palace. The magnificent facade is spoilt now by a dozen huts and military mess,
and the Marlboroughs are living in the private rooms on the left; they were out
when I went in but at length I found them and Mary [the Duchess] and Blandford
rushed to meet the Field Marshal and graciously received him and showed him
about – we wandered in the formal gardens, saw the great imposing terraces
which Blandford's father, old 'Sunny' Marlborough constructed during his dying
years, and died broke in consequence. The FM was interested. The baby Lord
Charles lay sleeping in a pram, but woke and blinked prettily at the FM. We left
the Marlboroughs, sadly, and we drove out by the far gates and the monuments;
and here I was immensely struck by the FM's quickness in reading a map and
knowing his whereabouts. The old campaigner coming out. We arrived here
at 1.10 and were greeted by Captain George Churchill[1] our host. He is the FM's
oldest and perhaps closest friend, and has been for nearly forty years. He is an old
maid of a man, aged 66 or 67; pleasant, house-bound, must have been handsome
at the time of Queen Victoria's jubilee. The house, however, is fascinating, it is
built of the yellow Cotswold stone and has been several times added to. It was the
seat of the Lords Northwick, a Dutch merchant family which settled in England in
the time of Charles II. The second Lord was immensely rich and spent most of his
ninety-four years of life collecting pictures and other treasures. He had luck, flair
and great taste. In 1832 he added a vast picture gallery which spoils the symmetry
of the house: but the contents are truly magnificent. Almost every painter,
except the moderns, are represented – Leonardos, Saverys,[2] Holbeins, Kuyps,[3]
Sir Joshuas [Reynolds] etc. The last and 3rd Lord Northwick left the place and
collection to his widow who at her death left it to George Churchill, then a young
man; he was her grandson – not his – by a previous marriage. The Northwick
family had become extinct in the male line. Churchill's whole life is his house and
his collection, and one could say that it has either ruined or made him.

There are three young airmen, two Canadians, and one Australian, staying
here. We all lunched together in the small dining room and then our host showed
me the pictures. The *Madonna of the Cherries* perhaps by Leonardo da Vinci, is

---

1 Edward George Spencer-Churchill (1876–1964) was a captain in the Grenadier Guards, and
   fought in the Second Boer War and the Great War. He had inherited the estate in 1912 from
   his maternal grandmother, the widow of the 3rd Baron Northwick.
2 A family of Flemish painters of the late sixteenth and early seventeenth centuries.
3 Usually spelt Cuyp, another family of Flemish painters from the Dutch Golden Age.

the FM's favourite. A fascinating canvas. The FM and I have adjoining rooms
.... 'I usually have this suite with Queenie [Lady Wavell]!' he laughed, 'Now it
is you, Chips!' and again he smiled that sure but slow smile which so captivates
me. His room (usually 'Queenie's'!) is large, mine is small; and the house whilst
rich in atmosphere and overladen with priceless and rare possessions, is stark
and uncomfortable. No *luxe*, no comfort. After only a moderate luncheon I hoped
to sleep, but the FM came to my room and suggested a walk. I couldn't refuse.
The walk developed into a 'hike', we must have tramped six miles, passing a brick
kiln where we were stopped by a Home Guard! The FM modestly refrained from
saying who he was. Then after a long detour up a country road, we arrived back in
time for tea in the long gallery .... Then another walk *à trois* and we photographed
the swans ... from seven to eight I telephoned frantically as messages poured in.
The Army Council wanted the FM to lunch and dine on Monday etc....

After dinner more picture conversation – could I inherit all these treasures
if I made 'a thing' of Captain Churchill, became his 'stooge', and came here every
weekend: or is it too late? ... I am tempted.

SUNDAY 30TH MAY

Slept well and breakfasted on eggs, coffee and strawberries with the FM. Then
another hike, as we skilfully avoided going to church. The Wavell family have often
stayed here and the Visitors' Book is full of their signatures. Crawford Greene,[1] a
rather unattractive MP for Worcester, Lord and Lady Dulverton[2] and others to
luncheon. The FM very bored – I know now when he is, because his face goes grey
and he doesn't speak. Long lapses of silence! He whispered to me, 'Let's get off
soon!' I quickly ordered the car, and after he had signed half a dozen autographs,
we departed. I was almost sorry to leave my gentle host and his hospitable house
so crowded with loveliness. At Oxford we stopped to call on an old general, Sir
Something Swinton,[3] who is about 76. The old man was delighted and his wife[4] and

1 William Pomeroy Crawford Greene (1884–1959) was born in Australia. He was
   Conservative MP for Worcester from 1923 to 1945.
2 Gilbert Alan Hamilton Wills (1880–1956) was a tobacco baron; the family company that
   bore his name became part of Imperial Tobacco, of which Wills was President. He was
   Conservative MP for Taunton from 1912 to 1918, and for Weston-super-Mare from 1918 to
   1922. He succeeded his father as 2nd Bt in 1909 and was raised to the peerage as 1st Baron
   Dulverton in 1929. He married, in 1914, Victoria May Chichester (1887–1968).
3 Ernest Dunlop Swinton (1868–1951) won the DSO in the Second Boer War and helped
   develop, and name, the tank during the Great War. He became the government's official war
   correspondent on the Western Front. He retired in 1919 in the rank of major general and then
   became Chichele Professor of Military History at Oxford University and a fellow of All Souls.
   He was knighted in 1923. Channon is even more confused than usual about his actual age.
4 Grace Louise Clayton (1869–1952) married Ernest Swinton (*vide supra*) in 1897.

Sir Harold Percival[1] (the Steward of Christ Church) joined us and gave us tea in the v 'North of Oxford' front parlour of their little house. She was drab, but Swinton, now nearing 75, is a dear and is an old bird. Unaware of my Guinness connection he told us later of old Lord Iveagh and [Christopher] Bland and of the Elveden picture collection which, of course, quite eclipses the Northwick one ... We then came back to London; the FM disparaged Mr Chamberlain, said slightly charming things of him and remarked that we had 'made a mistake to give up Czechoslovakia without a fight for it'! It is the old Munich schism which so divides people and in Wavell's case I at once detected the nefarious Cranborne influence ... I was piqued. We both dozed for a bit and awoke reconstituted as the fast car raced towards the capital. Wavell is the gentlest, the 'good-est' of men; he is almost, but luckily not quite, a saint. He is kindly, affectionate, yet shy and detached and is often dreamy and vague and withal the soldier of all time ... at Belgrave Square we found a staff officer awaiting us with papers and we made various arrangements ... and then I came upstairs and tried to remember all he had told me during the past two days of his disagreements with Winston (he fundamentally both hates and admires him). He and the PM had two tiffs on the trip out; Winston is always expecting miracles (rabbits) to come out of an empty hat. Lately he has been angry and disappointed by the Burmese campaign, which has not exactly been a triumph – but it has kept the Japs occupied and anxious for many months at small expense to us. Unreasonable genius, is this Winston! I feel in my bones that the PM will either move or *dégommé* him – when he dares.

The FM changed from his blue flannel suiting back into uniform, and we drove to the Dorchester to dine with Lady Cunard. I had proposed ourselves and was rather apprehensive lest the party was singularly ill-chosen. So it was. A scratch Sunday collection of boys and girls: Bridget Parsons,[2] Enid Paget, Jim Lees-Milne,[3] James Pope-Hennessy! Hardly the set-up for the Field Marshal. However he was in v high spirits and treated like royalty, soon he dominated the chill dinner and it became hilarious. We were joined by Francis Queensberry and before long the FM was quoting Shakespeare sonnets, Keats, Kipling, the Bible – it was a duet between him and Queensberry – the FM's love of reciting, which moved us all. We were interrupted by General Nye,[4] the Vice CIGS, telephoning,

1 Harold Franz Passawer Percival (1876–1944) was a professional soldier until after the Great War (in which he served as Deputy Director of the War Office from 1917 to 1918) and was Steward of Christ Church, Oxford, from 1928 until his death. He was knighted in 1921.
2 See entry for 20 October 1942 and footnote.
3 See entry for 12 November 1942 and footnote.
4 Archibald Edward Nye (1895–1967) had intended to be a schoolmaster but joined the Army at the outbreak of the Great War as a private soldier. He was commissioned in 1915 and won the Military Cross shortly before the Armistice. He remained in the Army and had a successful career as a staff officer, becoming Sir Alan Brooke's (qv) deputy in 1941 and holding that position until the end of the war. He retired in the rank of lieutenant general in 1946 and served as Governor of Madras until 1948. He was knighted in 1944.

and he broke the charm; but it was time, for I had to escort him to King's Cross, where he was to board the special train to take him to a hush exercise in the North. I piloted him to the train where we were received by General Paget[1] C-in-C, Home Forces, taken aboard, given drinks in the luxurious saloon. They buzzed me to come along; but I had no luggage. I crept to the FM's bedroom and I placed *The Land of the Great Image*[2] there and finally left, driving home in his grand car.

MONDAY 31ST MAY

The FM returned about 5.30 p.m., bronzed, gay, debonair and affectionate . . . . We chatted as he wrote letters – I fagged for him generally – and later we had baths and dressed . . . . I went on to Claridge's where there was a gala dinner party given by the Portuguese Ambassador, the Duke of Palmela,[3] an alert, young-ish-looking man (the hopes of a future Portugal, I am told) and his intelligent, domineering, able, and slightly moustachioed wife. Big party of Kemsleys, Duff [Cooper], etc., Winant, looking vague and dreamy (he sat on a sofa with Emerald for an hour after dinner) . . . .

Home late. The FM already in bed and I crept up quietly.

TUESDAY 1ST JUNE

Lunched at 'The Senior' with my FM, and Rupert Hart-Davis,[4] a nephew of Duff's: he is a publisher and a captain. General Montgomery was at the next table and we joined him for a little. He was in battledress, which is a tiresome pose, since he is staying inconsistently in a grand suite at Claridge's.

I had a large cocktail party for the FM, and later took him to dine at the Dorchester . . . . I had a tray and am now falling into bed. Harold Balfour in pyjamas dined with me. I must turn him out when P returns as there are insufficient servants to look after us all. This is a lie – he would spoil the atmosphere.

1 Bernard Charles Tolver Paget (1887–1961) joined the Army in 1907 and won the Military Cross and the DSO in the Great War. He was a successful staff officer between the wars, serving as Commandant of the Staff College at Camberley from 1938 to 1939. He was General Officer Commanding Home Forces from 1941 to 1944, when he became Commander-in-Chief, Middle East. He was knighted in 1941 and retired in the rank of general.
2 A work of historical fiction by Maurice Collis, published in 1942, about a Portuguese friar in Goa in the seventeenth century.
3 Dom Domingos Maria do Espirito Santo José Francisco de Paula de Sousa Holstein-Beck (1897–1969) had just taken over as Ambassador. His wife was the former Maria do Carmo Pinheiro de Melo (1901–86), daughter of Count de Arnoso.
4 Rupert Charles Hart-Davis (1907–99) founded his own publishing company and wrote a biography of the novelist Hugh Walpole (qv). His monument is the *Lyttelton/Hart-Davis Letters*, six volumes of correspondence between him and his former housemaster at Eton, George Lyttelton. He served in the Coldstream Guards during the war but never saw action, being stationed in or near London. He was knighted in 1967.

THURSDAY 3RD JUNE

I walked to the War Office . . . . and as I waited in the vestibule and chatted with Lady Grigg, General Paget, 'Dickie' Mountbatten and others with [i.e., accompanying] Wavell came down. We then drove to Kemsley House to lunch with His Lordship of that name; I had arranged it . . . . Good conversation. Reitz[1] told an amusing tale: the Turkish Ambassador in Russia is Mustapha Kunt! Because of his unfortunate name he could not be appointed to London! Then a Jewish tale: I know at Dunkirk time, the King had consulted the Chief Rabbi; they had chatted and the Rabbi whilst assuring the monarch that all would be well added, 'All the same sir, I should put some of the colonies in your wife's name!' Much laughter. After luncheon the FM and I drove for a bit about the City and I pointed out the devastation.

At five o'clock the FM left for High Wycombe to spend the night with Air Marshal Harris[2] and the Bomber Command. I refused.

SATURDAY 5TH JUNE   *KELVEDON*

I came here alone to rest – worn out. I thought much of Wavell; 'In War, was never lion raged more fierce, In peace, was never gentle lamb more mild.'[3]

SUNDAY 6TH JUNE

I came up to London after tea and received the FM . . . . I collected a small dinner party of Lord and Lady Londonderry, Lady Willingdon, Harold Balfour . . . . to dine to meet him. A great success – he likes society with a capital S, though he has had little of it before; I am civilising him and making him popular. Yet I fear this good, gentle, affectionate warrior is unhappy. He fears that he may be for the high

---

1 Deneys Reitz (1882–1944) was a South African who fought against Britain in the Second Boer War. He was later a politician and lawyer and wrote three acclaimed volumes of autobiography. From 1943 until his death he was his country's High Commissioner to London.

2 Arthur Travers Harris (1892–1984) emigrated to Rhodesia at the age of 17 but returned to enlist in the Great War. He was commissioned into the Royal Flying Corps in 1915. He stayed in what had become the RAF after the war rather than return to Rhodesia, and by the outbreak of the Second World War was an air vice marshal. He firmly believed in strategic bombing and became Commander-in-Chief of Bomber Command in 1942, when he was knighted. His approach reflected his belief that Germany could be bombed into surrendering. He became marshal of the Royal Air Force in 1946 but refused a peerage because no separate campaign honour had been awarded to those who served under him, such was the disquiet the Attlee government felt about area bombing, and the 1945 raid on Dresden especially, when 25,000 people died. Churchill persuaded him to accept a baronetcy in 1953.

3 From Shakespeare's *Richard II*, Act II, Scene I.

jump – that Winston will sack him. I don't think he will dare to do it. More likely he will be Viceroy.

MONDAY 7TH JUNE

An unbelievably beautiful day. Journey's end . . . The Duchess of Kent had proposed herself to luncheon and came, accompanied by Zoia and Alik Poklewski. The FM was shy and sleek and sweet but although he much admired the Duchess he was ill at ease. Isn't it extraordinary how the great such as he, hero of the World War, are timid with royalty, particularly dazzling royalty. She kicked me twice under the table, whispered, 'He isn't easy' . . . However the party was a success. But I kept hoping, watching for Peter who was due to return. And at three o'clock, lovely lithe, coral and delphinium-looking, he did step out of a taxi. I was overwhelmed with emotion and delight. After the others left, we had a terrific hour together and both broke down with emotion and passion. He has been so ill, yet looks as beautiful as the dawn . . . but he is weak.

Masses of people dropped in for cocktails: Peter was *ébloui*.[1] And I had invited Arthur Longmore[2] and Oliver Lyttelton to dine to meet the Field Marshal. Instead I took Peter out to Scott's; where we used to go so often in 1939 in the first flush of our feverish friendship . . . it was a nostalgic unforgettable evening!! He was sweet, better, fascinating . . . Can any friendship have ever been so deep, so intense, so understanding, so passionate? . . . only I would desert Wavell, Longmore and Lyttelton to dine with Peter. And I did. The other three dined in without us.

Happiness sublime.

TUESDAY 8TH JUNE

P saw my little boy; brought me snapshots of him. He adores Paul and says he is a fascinating little fellow. Bless him.

Today Winston addressed the Commons; and I had taken the precaution of obtaining seats for the FM (and for Peter). They went out early, but joined me at the H of C at 11.30 and I escorted them into the crowded Commons . . . . The PM was less discursive and amusing than usual. He looked bored. And so, I fear, did the FM, to whom he paid no tribute, although other generals were mentioned. I hear that WC cannot make up his mind about Wavell; he vacillates between possessive admiration of him and ridiculing and belittling him . . . when he sat down, I went to fetch the FM and escorted him, followed by P, to the lobby where he had an ovation. I saw Lloyd George approach, his white mane falling on his

---

1 Dazzled.
2 See entry for 3 January 1941 and footnote.

bright blue suit, and I went up to him and led him to Wavell and introduced them. It was a great moment.

I took the FM to dine with Emerald to meet Prof Joad – not a v successful evening as one guest (female, I regret to report) was very much the worse for drink and behaved in a Hogarthian manner. She raved, ranted and was coquettish, threw spoons at David Margesson and told incoherent tales of elephants and earwax. We were all embarrassed except the FM, who seemed oblivious (later he remarked that he was sorry for her as she must be desperately unhappy to make such an exhibition of herself!). She has recently taken to cocktails – it is fatigue, *tedium vitae* and *tedium bellae*.[1] FM and I walked home together.

P was charming, but easily tired and he is obliged to rest for several hours every day. He was more ill in New York than he realised . . . .

WEDNESDAY 9TH JUNE

P and I lunched together and later dined alone *à deux*. The FM dined with Joan Bright,[2] who is a remarkable girl, able, energetic and keen. She is <u>not</u> quite a lady and she holds down an important job in the War Cabinet as secretary to 'Pug' Ismay – Sir Hastings Ismay.[3]

Lady Astor came up to me in the lobby today and confided in me that Wavell is 'for the high jump'. A Cabinet minister, so she told me, had remarked after seeing her talking with the FM yesterday, 'So you are burying your dead!' She thinks that Winston is determined to get rid of him. I told P, who was much depressed – he is easily led and has little real insight into London, its lobbies and salons, for all his cleverness in dealing with people. Human relationships are his thing.

I attended a memorial service for old Merry del Val,[4] who died recently in Spain. He was a *grand seigneur*, a handsome hidalgo who loved England and for many years he was kindly and courteous to me; but I never have liked Spaniards: there is something cruel in them. He was the best of them and an excellent Ambassador; in recent years he turned against England somewhat, as he thought that we behaved stupidly over the Civil War, which, indeed, we did.

---

1 Channon's Latin leaves something to be desired, but what he means is 'tired of life' and 'tired of war'.
2 Penelope Joan McKerrow Bright (1910–2008) was once a girlfriend of Ian Fleming and is thought to be the prototype for Miss Moneypenny in the James Bond novels. She was born to a British family in Argentina and through a friend was recruited to the War Office in 1939, and was given a succession of highly sensitive and secret jobs, one of which was to be the assistant to Ismay (qv), and another of which was to run the Secret Intelligence Centre.
3 See entry for 12 January 1940 and footnote.
4 See entry for 15 April 1943 and footnote.

THURSDAY 10TH JUNE

P has been making a little quiet investigation and learns that it is on the *tapis*[1] to make Wavell Governor-General of Australia. *Dégommé* indeed! I doubt whether this will happen, and think that it will be Delhi, as Winston would not dare to shelve him so brusquely. P's informant is Miss Joan Bright, a metallic, brilliant girl employed at the War Cabinet Offices . . . . I suspect that she is an intriguer. She flirts with all the brigadiers and 'Pug' Ismay is alleged to be infatuated with her.

Lord Iveagh sent me a cheque for £500 this morning, a welcome contribution to my larder. He says that it is for 'political expenses'!

P and I had drinks with the Amerys – sherry in their gloomy but highly friendly house in Eaton Square. He [Wavell] dined with old friends, 'chucking' the Londonderrys to do so; and later he went to the first night of *Colonel Blimp*.[2] It was a huge gala attended by all London. The FM went in mufti, wearing one of my suits. (It is extraordinary how well my clothes fit him!) There was a rumour in the crowded theatre that he was there, but being in civilian clothes he was not recognised. Indeed I saw him wander away with the Londonderrys unrecognised by the crowds who were waiting for him. I went with Laura Corrigan who had Eddie Devonshire – her latest ducal conquest – Barbie Wallace and Bill Mabane. We sat quite near the Churchillian party and Winston looked fat and smiling as he sat surrounded by the Edens and Oliver Lyttelton and his own family. He had a very enthusiastic reception from the cheering crowd. The film was intolerably long and I was bored to death. Later we returned to Claridge's where I dined with Laura. P was below with his mother and we were able to exchange a few brief words.

The FM is an angel, but he is an exhausting one and he seems to fill the house here. He is called at 7.15 but does not come down until nine o'clock. But all the time I am aware of his presence and so is P. It is a bit of a strain. The FM is oblivious of the tender attentions lavished upon him; although he is occasionally affectionate, and always gentle and good-natured. But he is stingy and never pays for anything. He is still unused to money. This afternoon he gave a tea party to some of his old ladies – 'funnies' they are.

The plot to oust Alec Hardinge is thickening and I shouldn't be surprised if we won. But for the K[ing] and Q[ueen] it is rather like sacking a devoted and cross governess of whom one has long since tired.

---

1 Carpet.
2 *The Life and Death of Colonel Blimp* was one in a sequence of celebrated films made during the war by Michael Powell and Emeric Pressburger. Thinking it mocked the officer class, Churchill considered having it banned while it was in production; luckily, he thought better of it.

The FM comes to my room as he dresses, and again in the evening when he goes to bed. He likes conversation at all hours. I am worn out by it all. The routine is much the same: P sleeps in the tiny upstairs bedroom overlooking the square, and either breakfasts alone or has his morning tray *chez moi*; the FM sleeps in the big Empire bedroom, breakfasts alone – and through the communicating bathroom door I often hear him muttering to himself, quoting poetry etc. At about eight o'clock we all assemble below in the morning room,[1] make plans for the day; take decisions; the FM dictates a few notes to Miss Sneath,[2] and then at about 9.30 he, accompanied by Peter, leaves for the War Office. I then rush to the telephone to warn McKennell, his temporary [ADC], that they are *en route*. It is all clockwork.

Friday 11th June

There is no news yet as to when they are returning to India. P is depressed, fears that the FM is in for the high jump, possibly retirement, or more likely Australia. The darling Merry Major thinks that he may be only a lieutenant next week. I think that they will go to Delhi; and indeed my agents so inform me.

Channon and Coats spend an idle weekend at Kelvedon while Wavell visits friends in the country.

Tuesday 15th June

A big day. P and I drove up, the car laden with flowers that we had picked. I dropped him at his doctor's and came home. When I arrived at about eleven, the FM had already gone to the War Office but he rang up that he wanted to see me, and would soon return. He did in high spirits. (Meanwhile I heard from my rather sinister prying servant Kavanagh that the FM had arrived last evening about seven and had gone to dine at No. 10.) I felt that there was something afoot: McKennell reported to me that the FM was jolly and in high spirits. I soon saw that he was. He paced the morning room, almost distractedly, and then confided in me the following tale which nobody, he added, knows. He received a summons at Little Somborne[3] to come up to London last night to dine at No. 10. His first impulse had been to refuse as he thought it inconsiderate of Winston to ignore him all this time and then so suddenly want to see him on a Bank Holiday. However, he came, and at No. 10 he found himself alone with the PM who was in a rollicking mood. Almost at once he offered him the Viceroyalty [of India] and Wavell admits that he was dumbfounded . . . he had never taken my hints and jokes on the subject seriously. Of course he accepted, provided

---

1 A swift contradiction of the note in the same entry, saying that Wavell did not come down from his bedroom until nine o'clock.
2 Channon's secretary.
3 In Hampshire, where Wavell had spent the weekend.

that Lady Wavell agreed, and an urgent cable was written out and dispatched to her![1] I congratulated him and begged him to tell Peter which at first he refused to do, as then he must tell the others on his staff. P, I pleaded, was in a special relationship. He left me after inviting me to lunch with him at the Athenaeum. P then came back and I told him. He was stunned, surprised and overjoyed. Afterwards, I then walked to the Athenaeum, found the Field Marshal waiting for me and we lunched *à deux* discussing the appointment. At one point he shut me up somewhat brusquely I thought – but explained that he thought people at the adjoining table were listening. Only I knew the secret. P picked us up at 2.20 and we went shopping, we three, in the guard car, all the afternoon . . . . I was tired and disgruntled and over *émotionné* by the dazzling appointment at which I rejoice but rather deplore – for he is really not up to it. He is deaf and a bit too bourgeois in many ways; still for me it is a triumph and it will please P.

Many people, too many, dropped in for drinks. About thirty come every day and now my gin is gone.

I had a long talk with the FM and begged him not only to accept the offer but to rejoice in it. Delhi and viceregal trappings rather than Cheltenham and the simple life. It is not given to every soldier to have so brilliant a retirement.

WEDNESDAY 16TH JUNE

The secret is still inviolate; but rumours are flying about. Some suggest Anthony Eden; others Oliver Lyttelton. Only P and I know the truth. Nothing can be announced until Lady Wavell replies and the King returns from his successful but too long delayed African tour.

The FM is enchanting and enchanted with me and with life. No wonder, for he has eclipsed his model and hero, Lord Allenby. His battles and victories have been greater and he is to be a Viceroy, whilst Allenby was only High Commissioner in Egypt. P says that I am the FM's best and perhaps only friend: I must say that his own are a dreary, mummified lot – a drab collection of 'dug-ups' who have not kept pace with life. 'Archie' likes life and youth.

This afternoon I took the FM out shopping, and then we went to the Turkish bath at the RAC and shared a cubicle. We slept together for half an hour. Usually the FM wears my clothes, shirt, suit etc. But tonight I forced him into uniform.

Nobody yet knows the secret and nothing has come from Lady Wavell. P is getting anxious, but is sure that she will agree.

FRIDAY 18TH JUNE

A cable was on my breakfast tray announcing that my mother died yesterday in St Luke's Hospital, Chicago where in the days of long ago (1927, I think!) I

---

1 She had not accompanied her husband to London and was still in Cairo.

had my tonsils out. I know no more. I have had no regrets, little remorse, still less sadness – yet. Her death is a release to her and me, and everybody. For years and years she has been a problem for she was more than half-mad, even eccentric, always unattractive and supremely selfish. I think she was, as doctors, psychiatrists as long ago as 1923 declared, a paranoiac and even dangerous, but always untidy, careless, suspicious, strange, depressed, lonely, she led a ghastly life and should have died thirty years ago. Of course, it is a shock.

Old Stephen Gaselee died, too. He was an absurd yet somehow distinguished figure and long the librarian of the Foreign Office, he will be missed. He died a gastronomic death since all his life he ate and drank too much.

Wavell is to be a viscount – but of what? I suggested 'of the Western Desert'; P wants 'of Kerin'![1] It is agreed that he will keep the name of Wavell.[2]

I was supposed to be lunching with Lady Willingdon but I hadn't quite the heart for a large luncheon party and so privately arranged on the telephone for the FM to go in my place! Indeed he thought – although he had never been invited – that he was the guest of honour . . . . I 'chucked' Emerald's dinner party, preferring to be alone on the first evening of my mourning; however I escorted FM there and deposited him with her in her Dorchester suite. And I walked home alone – motherless, an orphan[3] *enfin* – through the Park.

SATURDAY 19TH JUNE   *HIMLEY HALL, DUDLEY*

I decided to come here in spite of my own mother's death since I can do nothing at this distance. Indeed I know of no details . . . The FM, P and I lunched and left at two o'clock in his [Wavell's] fast car. We chatted all the way; he, very gay; P, as ever subdued in his presence. We stopped at Northwick to have tea with George Churchill and to see *The Madonna of the Cherries*; the pseudo Leonardo about which the FM has written so lovely a poem. (He gave me the MS.) I think that he hopes old Churchill will leave it to him. *En route* for Northwick . . . . we lost the way. FM very irritable and ticked off poor Peter unmercifully. P behaved beautifully but I was furious. Here we found the Argentine Ambassador, the chic Mme Cárcano, the two girls . . . . and one or two others. The house is comfortable, even luxurious but it is half-shut up. P and I share a room – the rapture of that. A huge dark bed, and an adjoining cot are our accommodation.

I was somewhat shocked by the FM's sharpness to P because he cannot read a road map. I have long known that. Later the FM made amends and was affectionate. I suggested inviting the Baldwins over, and he would have been interested, but Laura Dudley[4] would not hear of it. She has immensely improved,

---

1 Referring to Wavell's 1941 victory in the Battle of Keren [*sic*] in Eritrea.
2 He became Viscount Wavell of Cyrenaica and of Winchester, in the county of Hampshire.
3 He had of course been orphaned when his father died; the death of his mother rendered him a double orphan.
4 *Née* Charteris; see entry for 25 February 1943 and footnote.

and is even beautiful now, and chic and covered with jewels; more she has the glow of someone who is much loved . . . .

The viceregal appointment is public; it was announced this morning and every newspaper is full of it. Eric Dudley is enchanted to be entertaining him.

SUNDAY 20TH JUNE

P and I spent practically the entire day together; we slept and bathed and breakfasted together, and came down late dressed more or less in each other's clothes. The others, this morning, went out riding (neither P nor I can abide a horse) and the FM was delighted – should I say the Viceroy-designate – to have exercise. He rode with Laura Dudley and the Argentine Ambassador. Curiously enough he fell, took what might have been a nasty toss – at exactly twelve o'clock noon, the very moment when he ceased to be Commander-in-Chief in India. He joked about it later: he isn't really hurt. What he minds more, he said, was that his pay stops from noon today (except his Field Marshal emoluments) until he assumes the Viceroyalty on October 18th – the bliss of having Peter – and him, too – for four more months is indescribable.

Rich lunch; the others played golf; P and I went to our room, slept and later went for a long walk together in Himley Park in the afternoon . . . . I thought of my old mother being buried today at four o'clock in the little La Belle Cemetery at Oconomowoc, Wisconsin where she was born. The wheel for her has turned full circle. Shall I inherit anything?

Backgammon and schnapps and now to bed. The new Viceroy is having the time of his life, and this gay bachelor existence suits him.

MONDAY 21ST JUNE

The Field Marshal, Peter and I all in the highest spirits drove back to London arriving just before two o'clock. The roads were deserted; it is high summer.

Another intoxicating day, but it is a slight strain having the FM in the house as he is *un peu sur le dos*,[1] and one never knows when he might walk in. P sleeps in the smallest room on the third floor, whilst the FM and I have the conjugal suite below and I am always hearing him splutter and mutter and blow his nose. He is noisy and heavy in his movements; but he is an angel and a v great man.

TUESDAY 22ND JUNE

The FM now wears my clothes since he is out of uniform and has no civilian suits. He wore my black suit today and looked well: I lend him everything, shirts, socks and studs.

---

1 A little on my back.

Tonight was the Kemsleys' vast banquet in honour of Wavell. Though it was hurriedly arranged, it was a huge success. I had to break it to the FM that it would be a large important affair and that he must dress. As he had no clothes I lent him an old dinner jacket and I dressed him, putting on his links and pearls (mine) etc. The FM had to be primed that he must make a speech. He has hardly ever done so before. We arrived punctually *à trois* and were received by the Kemsleys in a private room. They had collected half the government and most of London: the Amerys, the Spanish and Belgian ambassadors, the fat foolish Archbishop and Mrs Temple; Brendan Bracken; the Greenwoods;[1] and many, many more. Wavell sat on Lady Kemsley's right facing Lord Kemsley. The table was a vast empty square and P and I were able to wave to each other and exchange *oeillades*[2] and jokes. The tremendous and distinguished gathering was a success and gay. After dinner, Kemsley spoke, proposing the health of the great guest and my poor FM rose shyly to his feet and began his speech by saying that two very unexpected things had happened to him: he had become Viceroy of India 'and he was entirely dressed by Chips'! Everybody laughed, although I felt a touch foolish and uncomfortable since everyone glanced at me. The Trees[3] were obviously enraged. I felt a pang of anxiety and hurt since I know that he hates speaking and must have been shy and ill at ease. However he acquitted himself better than I should ever have thought probable; as it was obvious that he made an excellent impression. P was very charming and turned the full battery of his colossal charm on to everyone whom he talked to; and they were dozens.

We walked home *à trois* and I felt somehow that perhaps tonight was the high-water mark of the Wavell visit, at least as it concerns me: the banquet was a stupendous send-off for the Viceroy-designate; he was charmed and charming. P was *exalté*;[4] and I was blissful, P was blissful ... the dinner will perhaps rank with the farewell one for Lord Curzon attended by all the Souls.[5]

The world's press is favourable to the 'surprise' appointment; indeed it has had an excellent reception in all quarters. London society blames – or gives me the credit for it. I have had several letters of congratulations!

WEDNESDAY 23RD JUNE

The FM went out early, after our little morning conference *à trois* in the morning room. He was wearing my recent brown suit and looked and seemed skittish.

P and I lunched alone at the Travellers Club; the food was atrocious and P complained. He likes *la bonne chère*.[6] Later P organised a cocktail party; mostly

---

1 Arthur Greenwood (qv) and his wife Catherine Ainsworth Brown (1881–1961).
2 Winks.
3 Ronald and Nancy Tree (qqv).
4 Exultant.
5 In 1898, as Curzon left for his Viceroyalty.
6 Good food.

of his own friends: it was not the usual success, or, at least, so I thought as many of the people were unsuitable for the Viceroy, being young and unimportant. I hoped that he would not come in, but he did and seemed to enjoy it. About forty people came, including Sydney Butler who arrived unexpectedly. She chatted with Wavell and whispered afterwards to me that he was 'too old for the job': he was tired and seemed deafer than usual, and he had a fit of his curious detachment when he does not attend to what is being said; when he seems not to focus.

He, P and I went to dine with Emerald in her Dorchester suite: Alice Harding, Stuart Preston – the now slightly *démodé* Sergeant who once caused such a social stir a few months ago; Lord Berners; Duchess of Westminster; Venetia Montagu and Lady Islington[1] who gave us amusing imitations of Lady Oxford. We came home together. P and I had a long talk; and we were both a touch tipsy and possibly tired and irritable. He told me that there was mischief afloat; it seems that Joan Bright, who always repeats everything, and is not a lady and is unaccustomed to the *haut monde*, rang up P and saw him; she had heard from a War Cabinet source that Wavell was being much criticised for going so much *dans le grand monde*[2] as he was now Viceroy, and I gather that I, too, was abused for my kindness and hospitality. Such is the jealousy of this world. I have bled for him, I have surrounded him with tender attentions; made his London life – and so people gossip. P, who is not quite as clever about society as he imagines (he is always brilliant and tactful with individuals), was upset yet sweet. His own intimates are all appalling and 'second-raters' and I mean to wean him away from them. I wheedled it from him that the man who had made mischief was 'Pug' Ismay . . . . one of Winston's favourites and buddies. He is a good soldier, was a definite success in India as Military Secretary to the Willingdons, but is scarcely a social figure and knows nobody except the Butlers. I have always found him tiresome and hostile . . . I went to bed annoyed and disgusted with the world, and a touch disillusioned by P's manner . . . but he is a golden angel; only sometimes his nerves get frayed.

Thursday 24th June

I did not sleep; too much tobacco, wine and society and surfeit and I felt cross with everybody. Indeed I did not get up, so the Field Marshal came up to my room and was affectionate and asked if he could do anything for me: P was still depressed. They went off to the India Office, which is now their seat of work. I to the Commons, where the atmosphere was excellent. Later I fished up the

---

1 Anne Beauclerk Dundas (1869–1958), married in 1896 John Poynder Dickson-Poynder, 6th Bt (1866–1936). He was raised to the peerage as Baron Islington* on assuming the Governor-Generalship of New Zealand in 1910.
2 In high society.

Field Marshal and Peter and we went to Oscar Solbert's[1] cocktail party which had been arranged in Wavell's honour. Many American officers were present; drinks flowed there and unheard-of things to eat like nuts and fruit. The Greek princesses were friendly; indeed I felt that they went out of their way to be so. So was the King of Yugoslavia, and we talked of his boyhood days at Bled. I told him that nothing would ever shake my love, loyalty and affection for his 'Uncle' Paul. He did not reply to that, but we chatted of other things. Olaf of Norway was plump and dull.

Bill Astor attacked me in the H of C about Wavell: I think he is madly jealous. I told him that he was a 'scold' like his mother; but we parted friends.

FRIDAY 25TH JUNE

Rab came to see me just after the others left; I pumped him and he inferred[2] that I was generally believed to have 'rigged' the Viceroyalty. He hadn't heard a word of criticism and even Ismay had been pleasant about the whole episode. Yet I wonder whether those horribly mischievous Cranbornes are not behind this little cloud – why can people so upset one?

SATURDAY 26TH JUNE

Today is P's 33rd birthday. He went out early to see his mother whilst Cecil Beaton photographed the Field Marshal in every room of the house and in every position. I was rather against this performance as it slightly cheapens him, but P was determined. The FM lunched at his club and drove down [with] Joan Bright to stay at Much Hadham with the Normans.[3] He won't like that much: a dull, cold, uncomfortable house but since he is flirting with Joan Bright I expect he will be happy. Mary Herbert, however, reigns in his heart and I hear that Lady Wavell hates her. They are both expected back next week.

P and I lunched à deux and I had a cake with one candle for him; and I gave him a handsome Fabergé cigarette case which he coveted. (It cost me £176 about a year ago, and is worth much more now.) He lost a stud we were playing with and the morning room was literally ransacked in vain. About teatime we left for Leeds [Castle], taking Enid Paget with us. P never addressed a word to her: he is bored by girls. I came to Leeds for the weekend where we found Geoffrey Lloyd, Kay

---

1 Oscar Nathaniel Solbert (1885–1958) was a Swede whose family emigrated to the United States when he was a child. He became a professional soldier and served as Military Attaché to the United Kingdom from 1919 to 1924. He retired and worked for Kodak between the wars, returning to uniform in 1942 and, based in London, became Chief of Special Services in Europe. He retired in the rank of brigadier general. It was he who advised the Duke of Windsor to go to see Hitler.
2 Thus in MS. He means 'implied'.
3 See entry for 27 January 1940 and footnote.

Norton and four faceless RAF sergeants. They looked ghoulish but we all took immense pains to be kind to them and drove them into Maidstone ... they came to the castle in shifts to recuperate; Olive Baillie is brilliant with them.

On our arrival we found that we had been put in opposite wings of the castle and I bribed the butler, an old ally, to move us into adjoining rooms. We are now installed in the yellow suite and are isolated, together and happy. I am glad that the FM did not come.

MONDAY 28TH JUNE

P went out early; and the FM returned at luncheon time and went out soon again. P and I lunched with Laura Corrigan .... Afterwards we joined the FM and went shopping with him, taking him to Lesley and Roberts where we selected about a dozen suits; and then I took him to my shirtmaker, Herman, where we spent a small fortune. He possesses no clothes whatever and wears all mine; however he has been given practically unlimited coupons and I have managed to scrounge quite a few for my own use.

I feel rather guilty about Harold Balfour, having 'turned him out'[1] – and, although I love him, he bores me dreadfully and I don't want him back. He not unusually blames and dislikes Peter. I left him at Pratt's and walked to the Mirabelle restaurant to meet P. We returned to Pratt's, where we found the Sergeant; i.e. Stuart Preston dining with Harold Nicolson. That also is a great collage. We left them, walked home, and found the FM rather *affairé* trying to answer hundreds of letters of congratulations. He was in his dressing gown. P and I exchanged a few words with him and then left him to work.

TUESDAY 29TH JUNE

I heard doors banging in the wee hours, and I think that the FM must have fallen asleep in the morning room and awakened hours later. He is inclined to do that sometimes. I didn't sleep v well and the Duchess of Kent rang me early to say that she had had a cable at last to say that Paul and Princess Olga had arrived at J'burg on the 25th and were staying at the Langham Hotel. It is a relief to her and to me to know that they are safe, and presumably happy.

P and I lunched at Buck's and later met the FM and took him out shopping; later I had a Turkish bath at the RAC with Alan; he is jealous of P, and of my infatuated absorption in him and Wavell. I felt guilty; Alan is the most loving and loyal lad alive. P went to dine with Laura [Corrigan]; I escorted the FM to the Dorchester where we dined with the Camroses .... A successful evening but I fear he was bored. Yet it was important for him to go: he owes this link, like so

---

1 To make room for Wavell and Coats at 5 Belgrave Square.

many others, to me. In spite of his boredom during the earlier part of dinner, he cheered up after champagne and became almost hilarious. He was wearing my black suit after having worn my brown one all day. I failed, although I tried, to get him into a dinner jacket. He walked back. P came in with Bill Astor and I thought them both drunk.

WEDNESDAY 30TH JUNE

I had rather a feline epistle from Jac[queline] Lampson – or rather Killearn.[1] She is upset and disappointed and enraged by Wavell's appointment, which she blames entirely on my machinations. I had been working for them originally. She is furious. The FM was to have come [to lunch] but was summoned to the Guildhall where Winston was given the freedom of the City. I gather it was an impressive ceremony. The FM wore my light grey suit and it was commented on by the newspapers.

I think occasionally of my mother and wonder what will happen to her estate: so far no will has been found so I suppose she must have destroyed it. Am I her heir? She was so unbalanced that she is quite capable of any mad action.

P and I, after some discussion, decided that the Dorchester is the most suitable place for the Wavells to stay at; and I have selected a suite and reserved it. Lady Wavell is expected soon.

THURSDAY 1ST JULY

I lunched at the Spanish Embassy . . . . Brendan Bracken announced before everybody at the Embassy lunch that I had been the first to say that Wavell should be Viceroy: 'We've done everything you wanted, Chips!' he added, 'made him a field marshal, a viceroy and now a viscount – in spite of Alec Hardinge.' He then went on to explain that Alec Hardinge had tried very hard to fob off Wavell with a barony and had even written a memo to the King on the subject which infuriated Winston. BB hinted that this small act might prove his undoing, as such acts often do in the end.

There is a second entry under the same date.

THURSDAY 1ST JULY

The Field Marshal – now my Lord Wavell of the Middle East – a viscount and a viceroy – came in late last night. I heard the front door slam about 12.30 a.m. He tells me that he enjoyed his dinner chez les Cholmondeleys, which I had engineered.

1 Following her husband's recent elevation to the peerage.

Present: Desmond MacCarthy;[1] Ronald Storrs[2] and Siegfried Sassoon[3] and his hosts. He came to my bedroom in his rather middle-class silk dressing gown at 9.10. (I was half-naked and toying with my coffee and strawberries.) He and Peter went off to the India Office at ten. I walked to the H of C . . . . no news. The PM answered Questions and was particularly gay and amiable; indeed he was boisterous and his charm captivated the House. I talked with Nicholas Lawford for a bit – he is still adamant and cruel about Emerald – and parted from him with some distaste in my mouth.

Lunched at the Spanish Embassy: the Belgian Ambassador; Lord Lytton;[4] Rab; Brendan Bracken; [Ivone] Kirkpatrick;[5] Lord Kemsley; Malcolm Robertson.[6] Good food and brilliant conversation.

Brendan drank much brandy . . . . Walked away with Rab who came home with me. Now I am alone.

P rang up; rather petulant as he is when tired . . . Later he came in, gay, insouciant, adorable . . . . Has there ever been so marvellous a male, so fascinating a friend, so superbly perfect? We helped the FM to entertain a collection of Walpole-ian old ladies to tea. Dull dames of no interest. Then I watched P have his bath. An unreal spectacle – Venus rising from the sea . . . . I dined in alone with Field Marshal the Viscount Wavell – of what? Kerin [sic]? Middle East? P is going to a Colefax party to which I am uninvited. I half hope that he will not go. The FM easy and confidential at dinner. Lobster, mixed grill and raspberries.

The Duchess of Kent rang up and proposed herself to luncheon tomorrow.

For some unexplained reason I have twice done today's diary . . . . This is the better entry.

---

1 Charles Otto Desmond MacCarthy (1877–1952) was for many years drama critic and literary editor of the *New Statesman*, and a member of the Bloomsbury group. He later worked for the *Sunday Times* and edited *Life and Letters*. He was knighted in 1951.
2 Sir Ronald Henry Amherst Storrs (1881–1955) had been Governor of Jerusalem, of Cyprus, and of Northern Rhodesia. See Vol. I, entry for 27 June 1923 and footnote.
3 Siegfried Sassoon (1886–1967) fought with distinction in the Great War, winning the Military Cross, but when suffering from shell-shock caused a national uproar in 1917 when protesting about the way the war was being fought. He began publishing volumes of verse during the war, but became celebrated after it for his semi-autobiographical *Memoirs of a Fox-Hunting Man* and *Memoirs of an Infantry Officer*, among other prose works and more verse.
4 2nd Earl of Lytton; see entry for 16 July 1942 and footnote.
5 Of the Foreign Office; see entry for 3 April 1939 and footnote.
6 Malcolm Arnold Robertson (1877–1951) joined the Foreign Office in 1898 and was Ambassador to Argentina from 1927 to 1929, having been Envoy Extraordinary and Minister Plenipotentiary since 1925. From 1940 to 1945 he was Conservative MP for Mitcham. He was knighted in 1924.

FRIDAY 2ND JULY

The Duchess of Kent; Angier Duke – the most popular and fashionable of all the Americans in London, and launched by me; Lady Willingdon, P and I and Alice Harding to luncheon here. The FM I didn't invite. I am rather worn out by so big a dose of society and constant companionship. All my life I have been occasionally alone for an odd day or evening or more. Now I scarcely have an hour and my batteries are running down. I look like a skeleton and am fast losing weight; but I feel well and am vigorous.[1]

Eleanor Smith and the [Duff] Coopers called whilst I hoped to rest. I had refused to accompany P and his mother to the play in the evening and ordered a snack meal for Peter and his mother and me in; at the last moment the Field Marshal, who had sat talking to Joan Bright for an hour, suggested dining in too. The larder was ransacked and strained but we managed the lot; but Peter was furious to find his chief here and said that the evening had been ruined etc. He is slightly fed up with Wavell at the moment; he is a strain, and P is never at his best with him; his great gaiety evaporates and he is always watching him and wondering whether he is happy and saying and doing the right thing.

Later we heard that the Duchess of Kent had had a motor accident on her way back to Coppins after lunching with us. I rang up and was told she was well and unharmed so I did not disturb her.

P very petulant with the FM. P is moody; he is a complete woman in mind, and is subject like them to inexplicable reactions and passing fancies.

I have high hopes that Alec Hardinge will soon be *dégommé*. It is time.

MONDAY 5TH JULY

P went out early and after doing my letters I walked to the Ritz to meet him; I was early – and who is not early for an assignation with P? – and joined Bert Marlborough for a cocktail, and then I walked along the lobby and glanced at the tape. In the lobby of the Ritz, I read the horrifying news which had only just come through that a plane had crashed at Gibraltar and that General Sikorski, the leader and hero of Poland, had been killed. I thought at once of Victor Cazalet, and wondered whether he had been with him; and then of Lady Wavell [who] also is supposed to be *en route*. A moment or two later the tape ticked out the words that 'Colonel Cazalet, MP for Chippenham was among the victims.' I felt slightly sick and cold and numb; for he was one of my very oldest friends, a loyal and loving lad. Everything blurred for a bit . . . . Then I went out into Albemarle Street to meet Peter and sadly, (for he liked 'Teenie' Cazalet, too) we went to the 400 Club where we lunched *à deux*. P and I had people in for cocktails and dined later together at the Ritz for a change. The FM dined alone and early at his club and

---

1 Rhodes James wrongly attributes part of this entry to 30 June. It is thus in the MS.

came in to write letters; his correspondence is colossal but P and I think that he revels in it. He was still writing when we came in.

What an appalling year: the death toll grows. Soon all my contemporaries will be gone, Victor is a great loss; he was a clumsy *animateur*;[1] devoid of subtlety, and unconscious of sex, though he had the hardness of the Christian Scientist yet he combined it with the kindest heart imaginable: no service was too trivial or too great for him to perform for a friend. He made of friendships a cult, and although he much preferred them to be high-born, rich and famous (he was an open, colossal snob) he was nevertheless equally painstaking with others, and the downtrodden. His lobbies were Poles and Jews and his phobia was Russia. He did not live altogether in vain, for he frustrated Anthony Eden in his attempts to cede the Baltic States to the Soviet Union. Eden, who was an old friend, never forgave him. Now he is near to admitting that 'Teenie' was perhaps right. For more than twenty years I have watched Victor's frustrated career; he spent those long years entertaining and ingratiating himself to the Great but he got nowhere; for everything he did was slightly second-rate – except his game-playing. His taste was deplorable, his houses always common and ghastly. He had good looks after a fashion and only latterly was he beginning to look bald, but actually his appearance hadn't much changed since the Versailles days of 1918 when he was ADC to the Allied Council there – a sort of job that my P is doing in Cairo. Teenie, as he was always called by his friends, was the least common and the most outstanding of his family.

Teenie was a famous character in London society and known the world over. Too many people accepted his hospitality and abused him afterwards; indeed people were malicious about him who were never unkind about anyone else; for he aroused fury and contempt in some – usually men. Harold Nicolson, who hated him, once remarked to me 'the nearest Teenie ever got to sex, was once when he got an erection thinking about a young duke at Eton'! Women were ever his allies; they didn't bore him, as they bore me; and his manner to them was very great; especially to old ones. Since the war it was as if he had a prescience that he would not live, for he spent his love being kind to his old friends and doing them great services. He was intimate with Baldwin; had been with Lloyd George; in later years his passion, which was reciprocated, was Edward Halifax. Indeed at one time Teenie was known as 'The Pompadour of the Foreign Office'; they were inseparable. Nobody knew or loved Victor more than I did: ever since 1917 or 1918 I have known him intimately, slept with him even, spent hours in his company – yet he was fundamentally too selfish to be the perfect companion. About two years ago I decided that he should marry Irene Ravensdale[2] and soon got them

---

1 Host.
2 See entry for 3 April 1942 and footnote.

en situation.[1] He proposed to her over and over again, but insisted that it should be *un mariage blanc*[2] and she refused him. His horror of alcohol and anything whatever to do with the sexual acts was certainly abnormal. What, now, will happen to Great Swifts [Swifts Park], that highly comfortable uninspired house in Kent which he liked so much?

TUESDAY 6TH JULY

A horrible day! After the FM and P went to the India Office, and I had attended to their various little arrangements, I went to fetch something from his [Wavell's] bedroom and there I saw a letter from his sister about me! She is an old hell-cat, is Miss Nancy![3] She told him that Bobbety Cranborne had told her how much he disapproved of our great friendship, and that he knew I had been most kind and that the FM and I were devoted to each other, he nevertheless thought as Wavell was now Viceroy he should see only older governmental people. I am furious and indignant, but my hands are tied since I cannot reveal that I have read someone else's letter. I don't suppose that the FM would take it at all seriously. Cranborne I have always loathed: her more. She[4] is the worst of the two; a wicked, envious, spiteful, half-mad woman, she is hated by everybody and all her life she has been horrible to him. Still he was helpful about moving Paul. I have always snubbed and ignored that little group and it is a compliment that they resent it!

The FM, P came into lunch with me and Diana [Cooper]: all seemed serene and I felt less anxious and *ennervé*: yet this little *potin* is disagreeable. Why cannot people let others alone? And not interfere with their happiness? There are some people who must always tamper with other people's happiness. Lady Astor is the supreme example, but I am told that she is 'nice' over this. Luncheon was a success.

The PM paid a suitable tribute to both Sikorski and to Victor Cazalet in the House. Incidentally there was also another MP in the plane, a good-looking but unexciting man, Lt Colonel Whiteley,[5] who sits for Buckingham. Nobody mentions him; and although married with children who may have loved him, it is the [illegible] Cazalet who gets all the publicity.

The FM came in before dinner and I had a word with him; said that I had heard of the Cranbornes' jealousy and malice. (I didn't add that they had already always patronised the Wavells, who were the poor man at the great man's gates!)

1 In a position for him to do so.
2 With no sexual relations.
3 Florence Anne Paxton 'Nancy' Wavell (1882–1968) was Wavell's elder sister. How she came to be friends with Lord Cranborne is unclear: possibly through her brother.
4 Lady Cranborne.
5 John Percival Whiteley (1898–1943) was a professional soldier who had retired before the war but returned to service in 1939. He was evacuated at Dunkirk and was working with the Poles as a liaison officer when killed. He was Conservative MP for Buckingham from 1937 to 1943 and was in fact a brigadier at his death.

The FM was charming; said he had long known about it and laughed. I suspect Ismay has made trouble; and also a stupid interview appeared in the *Express*. It had nothing to do with me but I was quoted. Too wicked.

We are all a bit anxious about Lady Wavell: where can she be? No message has come from her for a long time and the FM was obviously shaken by Teenie's death, as she might so easily have been in the same Liberator.

WEDNESDAY 7TH JULY

I was all day at the H of Commons. The PM sat for some time in the Smoking Room with Shakes Morrison, whom he is alleged to like, but has treated somewhat shabbily. The PM looked like an old bull and stared at everybody including me. I am still angry with the Cranbornes. At four o'clock I met P in St James's Park and we spent an hour on a park bench talking – it is four years today since the big Blenheim ball where we first began our tremendous axis. To commemorate the anniversary I gave him a diamond and onyx parure complete of eleven pieces. It is a very grand affair, a Cartier set which I picked up second-hand! It is the first of three anniversaries which we have spent together. Sitting in the Park he gave me an exquisite Russian egg with a motto inscribed in it which refers to one of our innumerable private jokes.

Then we parted and I went to cocktails to Lady D'Abernon.[1] She has a new flat in Westminster Gardens, in the hideous building where the Churchills used to live: she has succeeded in making it attractive with some of her fine French things, books and *bibelots*. Lady D'A looked magnificent and yet she must be nearly 90.[2] There is scarcely a line on her face . . . . At the party was Mrs Churchill, and her daughter, the much-publicised Mary, who, people say, is taking Randolph's place in her father's affections. I talked with Mrs C – who is very 'airy' now; Alec Hardinge was there and friendly enough too. His outward manners are always perfect and I was polite to him for I hear that the 'Black Rat' is going, is almost gone; the King has almost decided to take the great step and dismiss him. Twice Mr Chamberlain tried to dislodge him, but he was always weak about getting rid of people, particularly his enemies. Winston has never liked or trusted him because of his sinister role over the abdication, but he has tolerated his presence to please Anthony Eden who is his 'alter ego' and a dangerous combination it is. I could see from his manner and that of others that my friendship with Wavell has caused an immense stir. The Amerys and most say that I have improved him beyond all measure and made him Viceroy; most of London is loud in my praises; but there is an anti-group, too, of my enemies

1 Helen Venetia Duncombe (1866–1954) married in 1890 Edgar Vincent (1857–1941), from 1914 1st Baron D'Abernon. She was one of the most famous hostesses and beauties of her generation.
2 She was 77.

and who are jealous. This is natural and I cannot really blame the Cranbornes whom I have always attacked, ridiculed and insulted. Bobbety Cranborne, too, is pro-Honor, and did his best to break up my marriage. Now he would break up my friendship with Wavell.

THURSDAY 8TH JULY

Didn't sleep. P had breakfast on my bed. They were both out early; and both are secretly perturbed about Lady Wavell, who with her daughters, has disappeared somewhere in the Middle East. I was exhausted, and spent the day at the H of C, where I lunched and slept.

I took the FM to dine with the Londonderrys who had taken a private room at the Ritz. Rather *manqué*: too much family . . . . We left early together and walked home down crowded Piccadilly. Rather an emotional walk. When we described the grand dinner party to P he remarked, '*C'est magnifique, mais ce n'est pas la guerre!*'[1] which made the FM laugh. He tells me that he has practically decided to call himself Viscount Wavell of the Western Desert; but would that be allowed by the pernickety College of Heralds?

Can Lady Wavell have eloped with a Pasha?

FRIDAY 9TH JULY

I lunched with 'Coalbox' [Lady Colefax]; Emerald; Duff; Oliver Lyttelton; Loelia Westminster; the great inseparables, Esmond Rothermere and Ann O'Neill; Ronald Storrs; Barrington-Ward,[2] the amazed editor of *The Times*. Conversation was the most brilliant I have ever heard, and led by Emerald, a volley of wit and indecency which continued until 3.30. I went away weary and exhausted. In the course of it, Emerald remarked to me, 'Your Field Marshal is riddled with idealism.'

Old Sir George Sitwell[3] died in Switzerland yesterday; a horrible, crafty cruel man, he was 83; all his life he has treated his children shabbily, and he made the life of his poor wife, Lady Ida, a torment. Everybody hated him: he was a full-Renaissance character, and with his red pointed beard looked like a Borgia. He came twice to Belgrave Square to see me, and I went on two occasions to his vast gloomy fortress-palace-castle, Montegufoni, near Florence . . . He looked, and probably was, a sadist, and had long, tapering, very white fingers and hands.

1　'It's magnificent, but it isn't war.' The line was supposedly uttered by the French Field Marshal, Bosquet, when witnessing the Charge of the Light Brigade.

2　Robert McGowan Barrington-Ward (1891–1948) edited *The Times* from 1941 until his death. He fought with great distinction in the Great War, winning the Military Cross and the DSO, and had planned to be a barrister before being offered a job on *The Observer*. He joined *The Times* in 1927 and, drawing on his own experiences in the Great War, firmly supported the paper's pro-appeasement line.

3　For both Sir George and Lady Ida, see entry for 26 July 1939 and footnotes.

He had an easy smile and was good-mannered with strangers but persecuted his wife with utmost cruelty. When he allowed her to go to prison for some offence of forging his name, she remarked that her detention was the happiest two years of her life. She was at Montegufoni a nervous, dark, wiry, unhappy, woman obviously terrified of him. What can their home life have been? Yet they produced three brilliant and very unusual children; and they were both devoted to their little grandson, Reresby . . . it so happened that Georgia and Sachie were dining with P and me tonight and rang up about it: I said that I, too, was in mourning . . . . they should come and dine anyway and they did – but before that there was a complication. Miss Wavell,[1] the parochial busybody, rushed up to London, and saw the Field Marshal at the Sportsman's Club. What she told him I don't know, but he came up to my room much upset and shaky, though kind to me: he wanted to find Peter. P soon came in and as I was in my bath I half-overheard their conversation. Miss Wavell had made more mischief, criticised her brother's way of life etc. She also was malicious about Peter.

I had a word with him hurriedly before dinner and he assured me that all was well; but I knew he was lying. The FM dined out and our little party proceeded . . . . About eleven the FM came in, and joined us. Later he told me that as Lady Wavell was arriving on Tuesday he was moving into the Dorchester and would spend the weekend with his old friend, Sir Arthur Smith[2] who has the London command. He was v sweet as ever, and I shall always be devoted to him. I went to bed.

Saturday 10th July

We heard of the invasion of Sicily[3] which began this morning. I hid in the Turkish bath: P took his mother to a play. I walked around to the Dorchester and there Mr Ronus[4] startled me by telling me that Peter was moving in there on Monday. Disillusioned, angry, fuming and half-broken-hearted I went home and lay down. For an hour I debated with myself whether after what seemed an act of to me treachery on P's part, I would not break with him; or did he intend to keep an axis going – but at a distance. Then I sent for him and told him what I had discovered.

---

1 It is not clear which of his sisters this was: given Channon's earlier remarks about Nancy Wavell, probably she.

2 Arthur Francis Smith (1890–1977) joined the Army in 1910. He was Chief of Staff at Middle East Command from 1938 to 1942, when he became General Officer Commanding London District. He later had the Iraq command and was the last Chief of the General Staff of the Indian Army before independence.

3 Operation Husky, launched on the night of 9/10 July using partly British and Commonwealth troops who had triumphed in North Africa, but also Americans under the command of General Patton, recaptured Sicily from the Axis within six weeks. It brought down Mussolini and forced the increasingly overstretched Germans to intervene in Italy.

4 George Albert Ronus (1888–1970), a Swiss, was Managing Director of the Dorchester Hotel from 1939 until his death.

He wept; said he had taken a room there at the FM's request as he wanted him to be with him; he had intended telling me tomorrow after a happy weekend together. He seemed guiltless and upset. I was firm and refused to let him go: if he must choose between the FM and me, he had better choose me. He said there was no such proposition – in any case it would be me; but the situation didn't arise; he would only stay a few days there . . . . and then return. However, since I seemed to mind, he would refuse to go . . . and would tell the FM so. I had taken tickets for Turgenev's play, *A Month in the Country*;[1] but felt too emotionally upset to go; however P persuaded me, and we went together. He was sweetness itself and I cursed myself for doubting his love and loyalty. But the play got on my nerves – I was still too disturbed – and we left, dined *à deux*, and had a reconciliation.

SUNDAY 11TH JULY   FARNHAM PARK

. . . . When I said, 'Isn't it wonderful about Sicily?' Laura [Corrigan] had answered, 'Sicily who?'

Here at the Kemsleys I find a pleasant party: the change of scene is a relief. The Belgian Ambassador; Mrs Neville Chamberlain, stranger and more fey than ever; Doreen Brabourne . . . . and others. I am eating like a pig for the first time. The food is delicious and I feel well. Spent the evening talking with Mrs Chamberlain, ever an ally.

MONDAY 12TH JULY

Got up early after a peaceful night. The *soulagement*[2] of sleep after sorrow is ever a miracle.

Kavanagh, the rather sinister valet, whom I took from Lord Petre, left my service today to join the RAF. I had tried to get a deferment for him; but I am immensely relieved by his departure.

I had a drink with Robin Castlereagh at the Turf Club; he is so charming, and shrewd and intelligent yet he is uninterested in life, and consequently so bored that in his idleness gives way to a natural inclination towards drink and has fits of alarming drunkenness when he writes outrageous letters to his parents. I am sorry for him since he knows he is not a fool which makes matters worse . . . . Before we had lunch we walked to St Margaret's together and attended the memorial service held jointly by the Whiteley and Cazalet families. It was over-crammed and people stood up everywhere. The unknown Whiteleys must have been surprised by so distinguished and fashionable an attendance! There

---

1 A play written in 1848–50 but not staged until 1872, by Ivan Sergeyevich Turgenev (1818–83), Russian novelist, playwright and poet. It is about marital problems in an aristocratic Russian household.
2 Relaxation or relief.

was a woman lunatic near the choir who made a mild disturbance. All London was there.

P and I had tea alone with Lady Willingdon who gave him advice about India. She is a most staunch ally and stalwart friend. We then parted from here and later dined *à deux*. He has moved into the big room next to mine which is a joy and worth everything. He said that the FM had been charming about me and of course agreed that P should stay on with me: he had only thought that by 'foisting'!!! his ADC on me, he was abusing my hospitality for a further period. Oh: the blindness of great men. So that teapot tempest has blown over although I am not sure it has not left scars . . . rather luckily we did not dine in pyjamas, as we intended, for as we were talking about 9.30 the FM dropped in and remained chatting amicably with us for nearly two hours! P says that the FM is 'in love' with me; and that I am better with him than anyone he has ever known. He moved to the Dorchester today. He was very sweet. Never again will I distrust either P's love or his devotion: to think that we might have quarrelled over a misunderstanding!

There is further delay over Lady Wavell's arrival. She was due tonight.

WEDNESDAY 14TH JULY

A troubled night; for we had hardly settled down when the India Office rang to say that Lady Wavell would arrive at 2.30 a.m. . . . . . poor Peter spent three hours telephoning the War Office, the Dorchester, the Field Marshal and the various departments of the Air Ministry as conflicting messages poured in. She should have arrived yesterday but her plane had had to turn back . . . . because of bad weather. P was distraught and as he had to telephone all night and to get up, I came back to my own bed . . . . To add to the confusion there was an air raid, not violent but somewhat noisy. I thought as I lay alone (and there is nothing that I hate quite so much) of another night just ten years ago to the hour, it was the night before I was married . . . and now.

P went to the Dorchester to arrange the rooms and meet Lady Wavell who arrived early and exhausted; she was accompanied by Felicity,[1] whom Napier Alington always called Ferocity.

I lunched at the Savoy, the annual banquet given in secret by the 1922 Committee in honour of the PM. He arrived late, had a poor reception, made a boring humourless uninformative speech and went away.

THURSDAY 15TH JULY

P came to my room at 1.45 a.m. in the highest spirits; he had dined and wined Felicity Wavell and escorted her to the . . . . fête for the French Grenouilles but

1 Her daughter. See entry for 18 August 1941 and footnote.

really an excuse for a ball. It was crowded, gay and enjoyable and second-rate and Felicity had been thrilled to meet Noël Coward etc. P was in tremendous form. All his little clouds have seemingly lifted. He is to be Comptroller to the Viceroy and everybody now knows it. This means an income of about £1,200 per annum and many 'perks', including two houses, one at Delhi and the other at Simla. He proposes to lend them both to Lady Wavell for her war work and in exchange will take a suite in the Palace and thus keep his intimate contact with them and save money: all an excellent arrangement.

I lunched with Alfred Beit[1] at the House of Commons after nearly an hour's flirtatious conversation with Lady Wavell on the telephone. P and I went to dine with Cecil Beaton in his little house full of Victoriana and roses and plush – and we were in uproarious spirits . . . . Very gay evening and I was in Himalayan spirits: it is a relief, I think, to know that the Wavell family are here and safely cared for at the Dorchester.

FRIDAY 16TH JULY

There is a story put about by P. J. Grigg, the War Minister, that a black cat walked between him and Sikorski as they were shaking hands after parting at Gibraltar. Sikorski made a joke about it. Less than five minutes later his plane crashed before Grigg's eyes.

SATURDAY 17TH JULY   *BEDFORD HOTEL, BRIGHTON*

Glorious news awoke me on this gloriously lovely day – Alec Hardinge has resigned for reasons of health! The monarchy is saved and peace reigns in Buckingham Palace, which in time will be reconciled to London. For four years I have worked hard to bring about his downfall and I must say his tactlessness and many enemies were of great assistance. It is also a defeat for the Eden clique. The Black Rat gone! But why not before?[2]

Diana [Cooper], Venetia [Montagu], Juliet Duff all looked in during the morning and we shook cocktails to celebrate. There is a jubilation throughout fashionable London. There will be immense repercussions!! The Rutland boys are having a ball tonight at the Dorchester given for them by their mother, Kakoo. As I am in mourning, we decided not to go, [but] came here to Brighton instead. We have a back bedroom and bath; and a sitting room horribly furnished . . . .

---

1 See entry for 21 December 1938 and footnote.
2 The answer is that until the end of June Hardinge's successor, 'Tommy' Lascelles, claimed not to have been willing to assist Hardinge to the exit. But at last Lascelles himself had had enough of Hardinge's charmlessness and discourtesy, and believed him destructive to the interests of the royal family; he himself threatened to resign, which forced Hardinge out.

Everybody says that I am dying. I weigh under ten stone – a loss of nearly three since the war [began].

SUNDAY 18TH JULY

All day at Brighton in the warm sunshine . . . . We gave 'Bosie', Lord Alfred Douglas, lunch at Sweetings – he is ageing but still gay and young in manner; he now boasts of his relations with Wilde and was fascinating about him and them. He is rather litigious and fights everybody. I don't know quite how he lives: it is true that Alan and I help him financially but not on a large scale.

After a Sweetings snack, P and I came up to London by the evening hour – almost glad to be back in the comfort of Belgrave Square. Wartime hotels are horrid.

MONDAY 19TH JULY

Alan has arrived: he is angry and jealous of P and resents his presence and my desertion to him. I lunched with him and had tea with him and my in-laws, Patsy and the three boy babes, all in Hobart Place. They are a noisy trio yet I long for them. Poor Patsy looks worn out. Lady Iveagh said that I must look after myself, and that she is worried about my health. I promised her to do so, and also to try and get Hugh Euston appointed as ADC to Wavell. He has long wanted to marry Brigid and her mother is tired of the situation; he would have succeeded had it not been for Honor's malign influence; she has always poisoned Brigid against him on the grounds that he is a future duke and delicate. But not everybody wants lusty grooms as bedfellows.

Today would be my mother's 74th birthday, since she was born at Oconomowoc, Wisconsin on July 19th, 1869. I have had no news of her estate or dispositions. I walked to the Dorchester, meeting Doreen Brabourne in the street; she is overjoyed about the fall of Alec Hardinge whom she likes, but deplored as a fatal influence. She dislikes the Queen, who gossips about her ladies-in-waiting; one to the other, nobody trusts her; she was in league with the Black Rat and yet intrigued against him.

Joining Lady Wavell, Felicity, Peter and Guy McLaren[1] we went to the Gate Revue – *Light and Shade*.[2] Coming out the large military car was recognised and a crowd collected. Several girls rushed up and asked me if I was the Field Marshal. I was flattered – but do I look so old? We dined at the Dorchester and he soon joined us. He had dined at the Ritz with Bill Astor and a party of MPs and had

1 Guy Lewis Ian McLaren (1915–78) fought in the Coldstream Guards during the war.
2 A revue by Herbert Farjeon, which had opened at the Gate in 1942; the Gate itself had been in Villiers Street but was destroyed in an air raid in 1941: its revues kept its brand name but took place in other theatres.

been v bored, he said. He, too, was glad about Alec Hardinge's fall and I told him how the Rat had tried to block his viscountcy. His one eye flashed with anger. Some people think that Tommy Lascelles[1] will not be a good appointment *que au Palais tous les rats sont gris*.[2] Most people think that anything is better than Hardinge. At least Lascelles has moved about in the world and might look – yet isn't really – hard-nosed.

Lady Wavell was enchanting. She is voluminous, untidy, badly arranged but has a gay, girlish giggle and a seductive smile. She quite rules her Archie.

WEDNESDAY 21ST JULY

Slept beautifully and feel almost myself again. The FM and Lady Wavell, he wearing my black striped suit, lunched at Buckingham Palace . . . . P and I later shopped and I dropped him for a little and rejoined him at the Dorchester . . . . On my way there the royal car flashed by me at Hyde Park Corner and as I lifted my hat, the Queen saw me and waved – and Hardinge has been only removed a few days!

I dined at the Spanish Embassy and was bored. A luxurious tedious evening which broke up luckily early. I was between Mrs Oswald Birley,[3] who is indeed a dark and glamorous beauty, and Mairi Bury;[4] others were Derek Bury,[5] the Hudsons and mad sultry old Alice Wimborne, whom I had not seen really since the War [began]. Three years of content 'fucking' from Willie Walton, the composer, has done her good; she was amiable and in good looks and well-dressed. It was up to her to leave, but as she settled down for an all-night sitting, I got up and so broke up the party. I wanted to get home to P, and in any case Alba likes going to bed early. P was waiting up in the highest spirits and gaiety.

THURSDAY 22ND JULY

Today is my mother-in-law's birthday: I think she is 61, one year younger than Halifax.[6] It is also little Christopher's 2nd birthday, and the second anniversary of the day I left the Foreign Office. For two long years I have been a freelancer and doing little.

---

1 See entry for 1 August 1940 and footnote.
2 At the Palace all the rats are grey.
3 Rhoda Vava Mary Lecky Pike (1900–81), married in 1921 Oswald Hornby Joseph Birley (1880–1952), a leading portrait painter much patronised by the royal family. He was knighted in 1949.
4 Formerly Lady Mairi Stewart; see entries for 20 June 1939 and 9 May 1942 and footnotes.
5 Derek William Charles Keppel (1911–68), by courtesy Viscount Bury from 1942, when his father succeeded as 9th Earl of Albemarle.
6 She was 62, three months younger than Halifax, her brother-in-law.

Fish[1] died in Lisbon. He was formerly American Minister in Cairo. An old, grey little man without charm he occasioned the *mot*, 'When Chips came to Cairo Fish left,' for he was immediately transferred.

The Field Marshal's guard car came to fetch me at No. 5, drove me to the Dorchester . . . . I lent the FM my golf clubs – grand ones given me by Harrison Williams[2] in Palm Beach in 1934 and rarely, if ever, used since . . . Then we drove in semi-state, I as the cox to Lord North Street to dine with Sibyl [Colefax] at a dinner which I arranged. Lady Wavell didn't want to go, but she quite enjoyed it. Coalbox was enthralled and had taken some trouble. Party consisted of herself, me, Felicity Wavell, the Viceroy and Vicereine to be, the Duchess of Devonshire, Oliver Lyttelton, Stephen Spender, T. S. Eliot,[3] the poet, and Harold Nicolson etc. I was next to Moucher Devonshire who was delightful as ever . . . The FM concentrated on Stephen Spender, who with his long hair and height has great good looks, of a fine kind, and – rather to my annoyance – ignored Eliot whom he had asked to meet, and who came to London especially.

SUNDAY 25TH JULY

I slept for fourteen hours, telephoned, rested, recovered, recuperated and missed P. I feel 14. I dressed in the afternoon and went to see Ti Cholmondeley. I came home and found the Field Marshal awaiting me. He stayed for two hours and I saw him shake cocktails. His family, I fear, bore him. He was gay, garrulous, and told me tales of his youth and his relations. I refused to dine with him as I had arranged to go to Emerald's; she complains that I neglect her . . . . Gay little party in a low key. I left early and ran into Sir Lancelot Oliphant[4] in the corridor [of the Dorchester], who told me the astonishing news that Mussolini had resigned and

1 Bert Fish (1875–1943) was an American judge who directed the finances of the Democratic Party during Roosevelt's 1932 campaign, for which his reward was to become American Ambassador to Cairo in 1933; and, while still resident in Cairo became America's first Ambassador to Saudi Arabia, in 1939. He was moved to Lisbon as the Ambassador to Portugal in February 1941, shortly after Channon's departure from Egypt.
2 Harrison Charles Williams (1878–1953) was a wealthy American businessman. He hosted the Prince of Wales when the Prince visited the United States in the years before becoming King.
3 Thomas Stearns Eliot (1888–1965) was American by birth but moved to England in 1914 and took British citizenship in 1927. He made a reputation as one of the greatest poets of the twentieth century, winning early acclaim for 'The Love Song of J. Alfred Prufrock' in 1915 and *The Waste Land* in 1922. He had just published *The Four Quartets*. He won the Nobel Prize in Literature in 1948 and joined the Order of Merit the same year.
4 Lancelot Oliphant (1881–1965) entered the Foreign Office in 1903. He was Ambassador to Belgium from 1939 and was captured and interned by the invading Germans in 1940 until September 1941, when he returned to London and resumed ambassadorial duties towards the Belgian and Luxembourgeois governments-in-exile. He was knighted in 1931 and retired in 1944.

that Fascism in Italy has been overthrown. Could it be true? Is it the end of the war? I rushed back to Emerald's party, but nobody would believe me – I said I had secret agents – Gladwyn Jebb,[1] who after all is an important FO official, rang up the Foreign Office and the Resident Clerk confirmed the news. Everyone was stunned. I fled and rang up Wavell but could get no reply . . . . Dazed and jubilant I walked home – Alan came in and was exceedingly grumpy and disappointed about something, a private plan which had gone wrong, so much so that he forgot Mussolini.

The war must be more than half over when the satellite energy runs out – this must mean that very soon.

1 See entry for 20 July 1939 and footnote.

Index

Picture Acknowledgements

Images of 5 Belgrave Square © Alfred E. Henson/Country Life Picture Library. Neville Chamberlain's Flight to Munich by British Pathé/Mary Evans. Sir Nevile Henderson, British Ambassador to Germany, boarding airplane at Heston Aerodrome by Glasshouse Images/Alamy Stock Photo. Sir Samuel Hoare by Mary Evans/Grenville Collins Postcard Collection. Rab Butler at the Foreign Office by Reuben Saidman/Popperfoto via Getty Images. Winston Churchill and Anthony Eden, 1939, by Fremantle/Alamy Stock Photo. Duff Cooper and Diana Cooper, 1938, by Sueddeutsche Zeitung Photo/Alamy Stock Photo. Churchill becomes Prime Minister © John Frost Newspapers/Mary Evans Picture Library. Earl and Countess of Iveagh © National Portrait Gallery, London. Harold Harington Balfour, 1st Baron Balfour of Inchrye © National Portrait Gallery, London. Sir John Simon by Central Press/Getty Images. Miles Wedderburn Lampson, 1st Baron Killearn © National Portrait Gallery, London. Sunday Pictorial Dismissal of war minister Isaac Hore-Belisha by John Frost Newspapers/Alamy Stock Photo. Lord Beaverbrook by Topical Press Agency/Getty Images. Damage to the House of Commons, December 1940, by Trinity Mirror/Mirrorpix/Alamy Stock Photo. Sir Osbert Sitwell © National Portrait Gallery, London. Rex Whistler © National Portrait Gallery, London. Sir Thomas Beecham by Popperfoto via Getty Images. Lord Alfred Bruce Douglas © National Portrait Gallery, London. Prince Paul of Yugoslavia and Adolf Hitler by Imagno/Getty Images. Prince Philip of Greece at Gordonstoun by PA Images/Alamy Stock Photo. King George II of Greece via Wikimedia Commons. Prince George, Duke of Kent by Elliott & Fry/Hulton Archive/Getty Images. Princess Marina, Duchess of Kent by James Jarche/Popperfoto via Getty Images. Captain Lord Louis Mountbatten, 1942 © Hulton-Deutsch Collection/CORBIS/Corbis via Getty Images. General Jan Smuts of the Union of South Africa via Wikimedia Commons. General de Gaulle via Wikimedia Commons. Australian Prime Minister Robert Menzies, Declaration of War Broadcast, September 1939, via Wikimedia Commons. The Marchioness of Londonderry © Illustrated London News Ltd/Mary Evans. Loelia, Duchess of Westminster © Yevonde Portrait Archive/ILN/Mary Evans Picture Library. Horse racing at Royal Ascot by PA Images/Alamy Stock Photo. Edward William Spencer Cavendish, 10th Duke of Devonshire via Wikimedia Commons. Chips Channon © Cecil Beaton Studio Archive. All other images © Trustees of the literary estate of Henry 'Chips' Channon. Every effort has been made to trace copyright holders and to obtain their permission. The publisher apologises for any omissions and, if notified, will make suitable acknowledgment in future reprints or editions of the book.